The Oxford Guide to Literature in English Translation

Advisory Board

Mona Baker   Stuart Gillespie   André Lefevere   Anthony Pym
Douglas Robinson   Daniel Weissbort   Janice Wickeri

The Oxford Guide to Literature in English Translation

Edited by
Peter France

OXFORD
UNIVERSITY PRESS

OXFORD
UNIVERSITY PRESS

Great Clarendon Street, Oxford OX2 6DP
Oxford University Press is a department of the University of Oxford.
It furthers the University's objective of excellence in research, scholarship,
and education by publishing worldwide in

Oxford New York

Athens Auckland Bangkok Bogotá Buenos Aires Calcutta
Cape Town Chennai Dar es Salaam Delhi Florence Hong Kong Istanbul
Karachi Kuala Lumpur Madrid Melbourne Mexico City Mumbai
Nairobi Paris São Paulo Singapore Taipei Tokyo Toronto Warsaw

and associated companies in Berlin Ibadan

Oxford is a registered trade mark of Oxford University Press
in the UK and certain other countries

Published in the United States
by Oxford University Press Inc., New York

Introduction © Peter France 2000
Text © Oxford University Press 2000

The moral rights of the author have been asserted
Database right Oxford University Press (maker)

First published 2000

British Library Cataloguing in Publication Data

Data available

Library of Congress Cataloging in Publication Data
The Oxford guide to literature in English translation / edited by
Peter France.
Includes bibliographical references and index.
1. Literature—Translations into English—History and criticism.
2. Language and languages—Translating into English—History.
I. France, Peter, 1935–   .
PR131.094 2000
820.9—dc21

ISBN 0–19–818359–3

1 3 5 7 9 10 8 6 4 2

Typeset by Jayvee, Trivandrum, India
Printed in Great Britain
on acid-free paper by
T. J. International Ltd.,
Padstow, Cornwall

Contents

Part II Translated Literature

Contents

Advice to Readers

Contents

In Part II a list of the contents of each section is given at the head of the section. Entries within each section are generally arranged either in roughly chronological order (if the section concerns a single literature) or alphabetically (if there are number of literatures involved), or by a combination of the two.

Dates

Birth and death dates of original authors are not generally given if the period of their activity is clear from the context. Birth and death dates are usually given (where known) for translators born before 1870, with the exception of well-known writers such as Dryden or Shelley. Approximate and uncertain dates are given as *c*.1528 or ?1528; *c*.1528–1569 means that the birth date only is approximate, whereas *c*.1528–*c*.1569 means that both dates are approximate. 1520/5 means 'at some time between 1520 and 1525'.

In the body of the text, the dates given for originals are normally those of first publication, or, for plays, first production, but for works where publication happened long after the event, dates of composition are given. Dates of translations, if not given in the text, will be found in the bibliographies at the end of entries.

References

In Part I, references are made parenthetically, using the 'Harvard' system, to the general bibliography placed at the end of Part I. In Part II, a modified version of this system refers to the bibliographies at the end of each entry.

Cross-references are made to entries, or subsections of entries: thus '[I.a.5.iii]' refers to the third subsection ('Challenging Grammatical Gender') in the entry [I.a.5] on 'Translation and Gender'. Running heads help to locate entries.

Titles

When a work is first mentioned, the original is usually given in italic, followed in brackets by the date of first publication and a translation of the title where this is not obvious from the context. Titles, proper names, and quotations have where necessary been transliterated according to a standard system; for Chinese names two different transliterations are given [see II.f.1].

Bibliographies

In addition to the authorities cited in the References for Part I, a brief list of general reading is given in Further Reading, p. xiii.

The bibliographies in Part II are arranged differently according to the nature of the subject. Broadly speaking, there are two main types. For works with a long translation history, translations are arranged chronologically within each section of the bibliography; otherwise, translations are arranged alphabetically by translator's surname within each section. All bibliographies are selective, both in the translations listed and in the authorities cited. Information concerning reprints, availability in current series, etc. is given in square brackets. Where a book was published in more than one place (e.g. London and New York), in some cases only one place of publication is noted. In the case of anthologies, the abbreviation 'ed.' or 'eds.' indicate that the individuals named acted as editors rather than as translators (although they may have translated some parts of the anthology).

Index

The index covers both Parts and includes names of authors and translators and titles of anonymous works. It does not include names and titles which figure only in the bibliographies.

Translators' Names

In each entry, when a translator into English is first mentioned, his or her surname is given in bold type.

Recent Publications

The cut-off date for most entries is 1996; publications from 1997 to 1999 are covered less systematically. References to 'this century' are of course to the 20th c.

Further Reading

The following is a select list of general works and similar material relating to the subject of the *Guide*.

Encyclopedias and Bibliographies

BAKER, M., ed., *Routledge Encyclopedia of Translation Studies*, London / New York, 1998.

CLASSE, O., ed., *Encyclopedia of Literary Translation*, London, 1999.

FRANK, A. P. et al., eds., *Übersetzung * Translation * Traduction (An International Encyclopedia of Translation Studies)*, Berlin / New York, forthcoming.

PARKS, G. B., and TEMPLE, R. Z., *The Literatures of the World in English Translation: A Bibliography*, 3 vols., New York, 1968–70.

UNESCO, *Index Translationum: Répertoire international des traductions*, Paris, 1932– .

Readers in Translation Theory

LEFEVERE, A., ed., *Translation / History / Culture: A Sourcebook*, London / New York, 1992.

ROBINSON, D., ed., *Western Translation Theory from Herodotus to Nietzsche*, Manchester, 1997.

SCHULTE, R., and BIGUENET, J., eds., *Theories of Translation: An Anthology of Essays from Dryden to Derrida*, Chicago, 1992.

VENUTI, L., ed., *The Translation Studies Reader*, London / New York, 2000.

General or Introductory Works on Translation Theory and History

BASSNETT, S., *Translation Studies*, London / New York, 2nd edn., 1991; 1st edn. 1980.

DELISLE, J., and WOODSWORTH, J., eds., *Translators through History*, Amsterdam, 1995.

GADDIS ROSE, M., *Translation and Literary Criticism*, Manchester, 1997.

GENTZLER, E., *Contemporary Translation Theories*, London / New York, 1993.

KELLY, L. G., *The True Interpreter: A History of Translation Theory and Practice in the West*, Oxford, 1979.

STEINER, G., *After Babel: Aspects of Language and Translation*, Oxford, 1975; 2nd edn. 1992.

See also References for Part I, in particular Barnstone, Benjamin, Berman, Brower, Catford, Cohen, Hermans, Holmes, Lefevere, Newark, Nida, Robinson, Toury, Venuti.

General Anthologies

CAWS, M. A., and PRENDERGAST, C., eds., *The HarperCollins World Reader*, single-volume edn., New York, 1994.

FADIMAN, C., WASHBURN, K., and MAJOR, J. S., eds., *World Poetry: An Anthology of Verse from Antiquity to our Time*, New York, 1998.

STEINER, G., ed., *The Penguin Book of Modern Verse Translation*, Harmondsworth, 1966.

TOMLINSON, C., *The Oxford Book Of Verse in English Translation*, Oxford/New York, 1980.

VAN DOREN, M., ed., *An Anthology of World Poetry*, New York, 1928.

Journals

Target, Amsterdam/Philadelphia, 1989– .

Translation and Literature, Edinburgh, 1992– .

The Translator, Manchester, 1995– .

TTR, Montreal, 1988– .

Contributors

Contributors' names are here listed alphabetically by surname. When seeking to identify them from their initials, the reader is advised to look under the last initial (or second-last, if they are hyphenated or joined by an apostrophe).

GA   Gunilla Anderman, Centre for Translation Studies, Department of Linguistic and International Studies, University of Surrey, UK

KA   Katherine Arens, Department of Germanic Studies, University of Texas at Austin, USA

MB   Mona Baker, Centre for Translation Studies, UMIST (University of Manchester Institute of Science and Technology), UK

HGB   Heloisa Gonçalves Barbosa, Faculdade de Letras, Universidade Federal do Rio de Janeiro, Brazil

SB   Susan Bassnett, Centre for British and Comparative Cultural Studies, University of Warwick, UK

PCB   Paul Bishop, Department of German, University of Glasgow, UK

JB-B   Jean Boase-Beier, School of Language, Linguistics, and Translation Studies, University of East Anglia, Norwich, UK

WB   Warren Boutcher, School of English and Drama, Queen Mary and Westfield College, University of London, UK

ADPB   A. D. P. Briggs, Department of Russian, University of Birmingham, UK

JLB   John L. Brockington, Department of Sanskrit, School of Asian Studies, University of Edinburgh, UK

GB   Glyn Burgess, Department of French, University of Liverpool, UK

PB   Peter Bush, British Centre for Literary Translation, University of East Anglia, Norwich, UK

DC   David Callahan, Departamento de Línguas e Culturas, Universidade de Aveiro, Portugal

TC   Thomas Clancy, Department of Celtic, University of Glasgow, UK

VC   Virginia Cox, Christ's College, Cambridge, UK

RC   Robert Cummings, Department of English Literature, University of Glasgow, UK

ACz   Adam Czerniawski, poet and translator, UK

SMD   Stephanie Dalley, Oriental Institute, University of Oxford, UK

DD   Dennis Deletant, School of Slavonic and East European Studies, University of London, UK

HMD   Helen Dennis, Department of English and Comparative Literary Studies, University of Warwick, UK

AD   Alan Deyermond, Department of Hispanic Studies, Queen Mary and Westfield College, University of London, UK

ME   Michael Edwards, School of English and Drama, Queen Mary and Westfield College, University of London, UK

RE   Roger Ellis, School of English, Communication and Philosophy, Cardiff University, UK

MF   Michael Falchikov, School of European Languages and Cultures, University of Edinburgh, UK

BF   Bill Findlay, Department of Drama, Queen Margaret University College, Edinburgh, UK

RF   Ruth Finnegan, Faculty of Social Sciences, The Open University, Milton Keynes, UK

PF   Peter France, School of European Languages and Cultures, University of Edinburgh, UK

RTF   Richard France, formerly Wycliffe Hall, Oxford, UK

GF   Graham Furniss, Department of African Languages and Cultures, School of Oriental and African Studies, University of London, UK

JMG   Janet Garton, School of Language, Linguistics, and Translation Studies, University of East Anglia, Norwich, UK

VG   Van Gessel, Department of Asian and Near Eastern Languages, Brigham Young University, Utah, USA

SG   Stuart Gillespie, Department of English Literature, University of Glasgow, UK

WG   William Gillies, Department of Celtic, University of Edinburgh, UK

JG   Jeffrey Grossman, Department of Germanic Languages and Literatures, University of Virginia, Charlottesville, USA

TJH   Terry Hale, Performance Translation Centre, University of Hull, UK

SH   Stephen Halliwell, Department of Greek, University of St Andrews, UK

MH   Mike Harland, Department of Hispanic Studies, University of Glasgow, UK

ECH   Celia Hawkesworth, School of Slavonic and East European Studies, University of London, UK

TH   Theo Hermans, Department of Dutch, University College London, UK

CH   Clive Holes, Oriental Institute, University of Oxford, UK

MJH   Michael Holman, formerly Department of Russian and Slavonic Studies, University of Leeds, UK

DH   David Hopkins, Department of English, University of Bristol, UK

EH   Eva Hung, Research Centre for Translation, Chinese University of Hong Kong

PLH   Peter Hunt, School of English, Communication and Philosophy, University of Wales, Cardiff, UK

GH   George Hyde, Department of English, Kyoto Women's University, Japan

BWI   Barry Ife, Department of Spanish and Spanish-American Studies, King's College, University of London, UK

LI   Louis Iribarne, formerly Department of Slavic Languages and Literatures, University of Toronto, Canada

RI   Robert Irwin, UK

DLJ   David Lyle Jeffrey, Department of English, University of Ottawa, Canada

LJ   Laurie Johnson, Department of Germanic and Slavic Languages, Vanderbilt University, Tennessee, USA

DJ   David Johnston, Department of Hispanic Studies, Queen's University of Belfast, UK

CK   Catriona Kelly, New College, Oxford, UK

RK   Robin Kirkpatrick, Faculty of Medieval and Modern Languages, University of Cambridge, UK

AK   Alet Kruger, Department of Linguistics (Translation Studies), University of South Africa

KK   Keneva Kunz, *Scriptorium*, Reykjavik, Iceland

NdeL   Nicholas de Lange, Reader in Hebrew and Jewish Studies, University of Cambridge, UK

CMGL   Caoimhín Mac Giolla Léith, Department of Modern Irish, University College, Dublin, Ireland

FL	Franklin Lewis, Department of Middle Eastern Studies, Emory University, Georgia, USA	ADBP	Adrian Poole, Trinity College, Cambridge, UK
KL	Karl Leydecker, Department of German, University of Stirling, UK	ADP	Anthony Pym, Departament de Filologia Anglogermànica, Universitat Rovira i Virgili, Tarragona, Spain
JL	Jennifer Lorch, formerly Department of Italian, University of Warwick, UK	PDR	Donald Rayfield, Department of Russian, Queen Mary and Westfield College, University of London, UK
JM	John McRae, Department of English Studies, University of Nottingham, UK	BR	Barbara Reynolds, formerly Department of Italian, Universities of Cambridge and Nottingham, UK
KM	Kirsten Malmkjær, Centre for Research in Translation, Middlesex University, UK	MR	Matthew Reynolds, St Anne's College, Oxford, UK
RHM	Ronald Martin, formerly School of Classics, University of Leeds, UK	DBR	David Ricks, Department of Byzantine and Modern Greek Studies, King's College, University of London, UK
TM	Tom Mason, Department of English, University of Bristol, UK		
MM	Michael Mitchell, formerly Department of German, University of Stirling, UK	JTR	Thomas Rimer, Department of East Asian Languages and Literatures, University of Pittsburgh, USA
BOM	Brian Murdoch, Department of German, University of Stirling, UK	DR	Douglas Robinson, Department of English, University of Mississippi, USA
JN	James Naughton, St Edmund Hall, University of Oxford, UK		
VN	Vrej Nersessian, British Library, London, UK	MGR	Marilyn Gaddis Rose, Center for Research in Translation, State University of New York at Binghamton, USA
AN	Andrew J. Newman, Department of Islamic and Middle Eastern Studies, University of Edinburgh, UK		
CN	Carl Niekerk, Department of German, University of Illinois at Urbana–Champaign, USA	FR	Felicity Rosslyn, Department of English, University of Leicester, UK
HO'D	Heather O'Donoghue, Faculty of English, University of Oxford, UK	MS-C	Myriam Salama-Carr, School of Languages, University of Salford, UK
JO	Jeff Opland, School of Oriental and African Studies, University of London, UK	HS	Hiroaki Sato, author and translator, New York, USA
SP	Saliha Paker, Department of Translation and Interpreting, Bogazici University, Istanbul, Turkey	AMS	Angela Scholar, London, UK
		JS	Jan Schwarz, Department of German, University of Illinois at Urbana–Champaign, USA
KAP	K. Ayyappa Paniker, formerly Department of English, University of Kerala, India	MAS	Martha Ann Selby, Department of Asian Studies, University of Texas at Austin, USA
DEP	David Pollard, Department of Chinese, Translation and Linguistics, City University of Hong Kong	OS	Oleksa Semenchenko, School of Modern Languages and Cultures, University of Leeds, UK
		ARS	Alison Sharrock, Department of Classics, University of Keele, UK

Contributors

SS   Sherry Simon, Département d'Études Françaises, Université Concordia, Montreal, Canada

AS   An Sonjae (Brother Anthony), Department of English, Seo-Gang University, Seoul, Korea

RS   Robin Sowerby, Department of English Studies, University of Stirling, UK

PGS   Paul Starkey, Centre for Middle Eastern and Islamic Studies, University of Durham, UK

RJS   Richard Stoneman, Department of Classics, University of Exeter, UK

MS   Michael Syrotinski, Department of French, University of Aberdeen, UK

GS   George Szirtes, poet and translator, UK

AT   Arthur Terry, Department of Literature, University of Essex, Colchester, UK

MWT   M. Wynn Thomas, Department of English, University of Wales, Swansea, UK

FMT   Farouk Topan, Department of the Languages and Cultures of Africa, School of Oriental and African Studies, University of London, UK

HT   Harish Trivedi, Department of English, University of Delhi, India

BV   Börje Vähämäki, Finnish Studies Program, University of Toronto, Canada

LV   Lawrence Venuti, Department of English, Temple University, Philadelphia, USA

AV   Anthony Vivis, writer and translator, UK

PV   Paul Volsik, Université de Paris VII, France

DW   Daniel Weissbort, Department of Comparative Literature, University of Iowa, USA

RW   Robert Welch, Coleraine Centre for Irish Literature and Bibliography, University of Ulster, UK

JKW   Janice Wickeri, editor, *Chinese Theological Review*

JWW   Judith Weisz Woodsworth, Department of Modern Languages, Mount Saint Vincent University, Halifax, Canada

YW   Yenna Wu, Department of Comparative Literature and Foreign Languages, University of California, Riverside, California, USA

JZ   Jan Ziolkowski, Department of Comparative Literature, Harvard University, USA

Introduction

Pushkin, according to Vladimir Nabokov in the Foreword to his translation of *Eugene Onegin*, 'likened translators to horses changed at the posthouses of civilization'. Translation has been a crucial process in world culture over the last two or three millennia, and is perhaps more so today than ever, in an age of global communications where Goethe's ideal of world literature (*Weltliteratur*) seems closer to becoming a reality. Since 1932 the *Index translationum*, now run by UNESCO, has provided an annual register of translations throughout the world; even in its necessarily incomplete form, this gives an impressive idea of the way writing is crossing national frontiers in all directions.

The rise of English as a world language [see I.b.4–5] has affected this traffic of words substantially, and not necessarily for the good. The English-speaking countries, secure or complacent in their linguistic dominance, today translate proportionally far less than their neighbours, and their literary culture is the poorer for it. Even so, this culture, using the expression in its broad sense, has been in large measure shaped by translated texts, from the Bible to Freud, from Ovid to Dostoevsky. Yet in the history of English literature, the post-horses have generally had to make do with a small corner of the stable.

Due obeissance is made, of course, to the Authorized Version of the Bible, as to some of the classic Elizabethan translations: North's Plutarch, Florio's Montaigne are recognized not only as influences on Shakespeare but as major works in their own right. The same is true of a few poetic translations: Dryden's Virgil, Pope's Homer, Fitzgerald's Omar Khayyam, and in the 20th c. the work of Ezra Pound, Charles Tomlinson, or Edwin Morgan. But one would look in vain for serious discussion of Constance Garnett's Turgenev and Dostoevsky in histories of 20th-c. English literature, and few anthologies of English poetry make much room for translation.

Worse still, much translation has traditionally been done anonymously. To use the expression recently popularized by Lawrence Venuti (*The Translator's Invisibility*, 1995), the translator in such cases remains invisible. This was quite normal practice in the 17th and 18th c., as was a cavalier attitude to previous translations which might be recycled or revised with or without acknowledgement (as in the case of Tobias Smollett). Things have not changed radically since then. Unattributed translation was common at least until the early 20th c. (e.g. Vizetelly's Zola translations [II.g.9.vi]), and even today the translator's name is frequently hidden away in some inconspicuous place and ignored by advertisers or reviewers, who act as if the book came immediately from the original author. Nor has the unacknowledged recycling and reprinting of old material disappeared; inexpensive reprint series habitually reissue 100-year-old translations on which copyright has lapsed, without giving any indication of their provenance. *Caveat emptor*: buyers of translated literature need to be on their guard.

The silence surrounding translation has been more often breached in recent years. For one thing, new views of writing cast doubt on the clear hierarchical distinction, a distinction sometimes expressed in gender terms [see I.a.5.ii], between the so-called original (primary, 'male') and the translation (secondary, 'female'). At the same time, there has been a growth of interest in the actual phenomenon of translation and the problems it poses. This flourishing of the new discipline of 'Translation Studies' [see I.a.1.iii] has brought with it the desire to do greater justice to the place of translation within our culture, to encourage awareness of what goes on in translation, to make translation and the translator more *visible*.

The present *Guide* is intended to play a part in this movement. It is not addressed primarily to the Translation Studies community, but to ordinary readers and students of literature, who inevitably turn to translation from time to time, whether for business or for pleasure. All too often such readers (and they include students of English and Comparative Literature) act as if in reading a translation they were reading—perhaps with some loss of intensity—the original. (In the same way, it is not unknown for philosophers to discuss the ideas of Descartes or Kant as if they had written in English.) But translations are not, nor should they be, transparent windows onto an 'original', and the aim of this volume is to suggest to readers that translation involves transformation, and that this transformation is worthy of our attention.

In order to do so, we address the following questions, among others:

What has or has not been translated into English from the literature of the world?
How has translation shaped for English speakers a 'canon' of world literature?
How have translators seen their task, and in what social context have they worked?
Under what guise have the greater and lesser works of world literature been transported into English?
What is the nature and quality of the different translations currently available to readers?

The contributors to the *Guide* are specialists in their various fields, but their answers to these questions are often incomplete and tentative. Incomplete, because we have aimed to cover an immense field highly selectively so as to produce a single volume which is accessible to the general reader. Tentative, because there is not at present, for many of the subjects discussed here, the exhaustive bibliographical database needed for a complete account of literary translation in English. It is to be hoped that this will one day exist; meanwhile, we hope to demonstrate the magnitude and interest of the field, while offering, as the title implies, some guidance within it. Other important reference works in this area are listed in the Further Reading section.

The *Guide* is divided into two interrelated Parts. Part I offers an overview of some of the contexts within which the subsequent discussions of particular translations need to be set. It opens with discussions of some of the major theoretical or methodological questions raised by translation. Then comes a series of contributions, some of them polemical, to the general history of translation in Britain since the Middle Ages, and in modern North America. And finally, the problems raised for the translator by specific text types such as poetry or drama are the subject of separate essays.

The word 'literature' in the title is, of course, a problematic word in the year 2000. It is understood here in a fairly broad sense, including not only fiction, poetry, and drama, but a variety of discursive writing, including some of the classics of philosophy, and a fairly large number of texts (including religious writings) whose original function was not what we normally understand by literary today. Gideon Toury, in his *Descriptive Translation Studies and Beyond* (1995), makes an important distinction between the 'translation of literary texts' and 'literary translation'. A text considered as 'literary' in the original may be given a 'non-literary' (i.e. informational) translation, whereas all kinds of text may through translation become a part of the literature of the target culture. On the whole the translations discussed here are those designed to be read as literature, but there are many exceptions.

Part II, the main body of the *Guide*, is devoted to critical descriptions of the translation into English of writing from all over the world. The greatest space is given to works which have had the greatest and most lasting impact on English-speaking culture since the Middle Ages. (For the most part these are classics of high culture, although Terry Hale [I.b.4] reminds us of the great importance of translation for popular culture in the 19th c.) In addition to the Bible, this means above all the ancient literatures of Greece and Rome and the medieval and modern literatures of Europe, but also the major literatures of Asia and the Middle East. At the same time, it seemed essential to make room for writing in such languages as Turkish or Armenian, Swahili or Korean, which, although translated, has remained relatively little known to English-speaking readers. There are thousands of languages in the world, of course, and many gaps in the *Guide*, since we have not aimed to provide a complete account of translation into English.

By the same token, the treatment of the areas which are covered is deliberately selective. This concerns both the choice of writers and works and the listing and discussion of translations of any given works. This is not an encyclopedia. For this reason, rather than giving separate entries for individual works (with a few notable exceptions), we have grouped works under writers (e.g. Pushkin, Virgil) or, more frequently, under some broader heading such as 'Nineteenth-Century French Fiction' or 'Chinese Poetry'. In some cases, indeed, one single entry surveys the whole literature of a language (e.g. Romanian, Georgian) or even of a group of languages (e.g. the languages of West Africa).

The broader the field, the more essential it became for contributors to concentrate on important works and translations. As one might expect, almost every contributor would have liked more space, but most came to agree, if reluctantly, that worthwhile things can be said in the limited compass demanded by a manageable single-volume work.

The entries in Part II differ quite markedly in the way their subjects are treated. The nature of the topics was very diverse, and contributors had considerable freedom to determine the best style of approach. In some cases, where the material is not well known to most English-speaking readers, a good deal of the entry may be devoted to recording what currently exists in translation (often works will have been translated once only), and how this relates to the literary canon in the original language. Elsewhere, where we are dealing with much-translated writers such as Homer or Montaigne, the stress is more on the translation history of the work, together with a comparative analysis of different translations.

Where translations are compared, there has been no attempt to impose neutral description rather than critical evaluation. Nor is there any party line here. Contributors have been discouraged from grinding their own axes too loudly, but have felt free to offer judgements. This is a guide, after all, and anyone offering guidance will be concerned not only with the *nature* of existing translations but with what is perceived as the *success* or *failure* with which different (often equally valid) translation projects have been executed. Criteria for evaluation are discussed below [I.a.1]; but even when judgements are couched in apparently objective language, no critical evaluation can pretend to universal validity.

It remains to thank those who have helped with the making of this book. My first debt of gratitude goes to the members of the editorial advisory board, Mona Baker, Stuart Gillespie, the late André Lefevere, Anthony Pym, Douglas Robinson, Daniel Weissbort, and Janice Wickeri, who advised me on the contents and shape of the volume, helped me find contributors, and then read and commented on the entries as they came in. It is a source of great sadness that André Lefevere, an outstanding translation scholar and a good friend, who had committed himself to the project with enthusiasm and was to have written a substantial group of entries, died tragically and unexpectedly while still at the height of his powers.

Friends and colleagues who were not members of the editorial board gave help and encouragement in a variety of ways, especially when it came to the difficult task of finding the right contributors. Willie Gillies advised on the Celtic section, and Tom Rider masterminded the Japanese entries with exemplary efficiency; Arthur Terry was full of encouragement and helpful ideas, especially for the Hispanic section. Many others, some of them not in the end contributors, made excellent suggestions, and I am grateful to them all.

All along the way, my wife, Siân Reynolds, herself a notable translator, gave me good advice and cheerful encouragement. I have also benefited once again from the professional and editorial support of an Oxford University Press editorial team. My thanks go to Andrew Lockett, Jason Freeman, and Sophie Goldsworthy, who in turn took responsibility for managing the project, to Sarah Barrett, for her patient and meticulous work as copy-editor, and in particular—as formerly—to Frances Whistler, whose enthusiasm, good humour, eye for detail, and critical sense have been invaluable.

But above all I must thank those who actually shouldered the job of writing, a difficult job not only because of the knowledge called for, but because of editorial pressure to be concise. They responded patiently, usually positively, to suggestions for change, even Procrustean cuts, to requests for further information, and in some cases to anguished reminders about deadlines. This enterprise has brought together over 100 people from different countries and from many different specialities, some quite remote from my own, and I can only be thankful for the way in which all the entries came together more or less in time. I feel that I have learnt a huge amount from editing this book, and I hope readers will feel the same.

Peter France
Edinburgh, 1999

Part I

Theory and History

a. Theoretical Issues

1. Translation Studies and Translation Criticism 2. Norms of Translation 3. The Limits of Translation
4. Linguistic Perspectives on Translation 5. Gender in Translation 6. Varieties of English

1. TRANSLATION STUDIES AND TRANSLATION CRITICISM
Peter France

i. What Is a Good Translation? One of Rudyard
Kipling's last stories, 'Proofs of Holy Writ', is a conversation piece between Ben Jonson and William
Shakespeare set in a Stratford orchard about 1611.
'Will' has received from Oxford some proofs of
the 'one Bible, which the church shall be bound to'
[see II.c.i.vi], with a request for professional help
with the translation. We see him working on some
verses from Isaiah 60 ('Arise, shine, for thy light is
come . . .'), comparing the existing versions in the
Coverdale, Douai, and Geneva Bibles and feeling
his way to something better:

Presently he took back the proof, chose him another apple
and grunted. 'Umm-umm! "Thy sun shall never go
down." No! Flat as a split viol. *"Non erit tibi amplius Sol—"*
That *amplius* must give tongue. Ah! . . . "Thy sun shall
not—shall not—shall no more be thy light by day" . . . A
fair entry. "Nor"?—No! Not on the heels of "day".
"Neither" it must be—"Neither the Moon"—but here's
splendor and the ramshorns again. (Therefore—*ai-ai!*)
"Neither for brightness shall the Moon." (Pest! It is the
Lord who is taking the Moon's place over Israel. It must be
"thy Moon".) "Neither for brightness shall thy Moon
light—give—make—give light unto thee." Ah! . . . Listen
here! . . . *"The Sun shall no more be thy light by day: neither for
brightness shall the Moon give light unto thee".*'

It is a fantasy of course. No doubt it draws on
Kipling's memories of composition (if not translation), and it echoes what many translators say
about the instinctive, tentative way they work,
with voice and ear playing a crucial role. But it is
also, in its light-hearted way, a piece of translation
criticism. Like much translation criticism, it proceeds largely by comparing different versions.

Indeed, it may imply a stylistic critique of the King
James Bible, since the version proposed by Will dif-
fers in one or two ways from the established text
('Rise, shine' is preferred to 'Arise, shine').

Perhaps Kipling is cheating, taking as his point of
arrival a translation which has acquired sacred
status in the English-speaking world and putting
the comments into the mouth of the author of our
other 'holy writ'. There is a kind of terrorism at
work here. But what are the criteria by which translations are praised or condemned in this imaginary
'translation workshop'? Like many evaluations of
translation, the judgements here are personal,
metaphorical, and hard to argue with. Occasionally
there is a reference to the source text (and even then
not the 'real' source, the Hebrew, but to the Latin
Vulgate), but above all the criteria concern the
beauty or power of the target text. 'Flat as a split
viol' is bad; what is wanted is a translation that 'gives
tongue'. There is a kind of universalizing, absolute
notion of good writing at work here, and one that
remains powerful in spite of all one's awareness of
the relative nature of taste judgements. A text
works or it doesn't. If you feel its power, so much
the better for you; if you don't, so much the worse.

The language of the discipline of Translation
Studies is very different from this. Theorists and
scholars have a far more complex agenda than
deciding between the good and the bad; they are
concerned, for instance, to tease out the different
possibilities open to the translator, and the way
these change according to the historical, social, and
cultural context. Sometimes they seek scientific
neutrality in their descriptions of translation
behaviour, but often the theoretical or scholarly

apparatus leads to, or derives from, a particular and partisan view of what makes a good translation. Nor is this to be regretted. It is no doubt desirable to avoid confusing criticism and scholarship, but the need for evaluative criticism is a fundamental one in any society. This opening article, touching briefly on concerns addressed more fully in the essays that follow, will explore the relation between translation theory, the new discipline of Translation Studies, and the time-honoured practice of translation criticism.

ii. Theories of Translation Translation Studies is a recent arrival on the scene, but as Douglas Robinson shows [I.a.3], there has been translation theory as long as there has been translation; selections from major translation theorists from Cicero onwards are available in English translation in a number of books (e.g. Lefevere 1992b; Schulte and Biguenet 1992; Robinson 1997). The relation between translation theory and translation might seem similar to that between poetics and literature, but there is one special feature of translation theory: until quite recently, with few exceptions, it was the work of *practitioners*, some of them eminent ones. Many of the most famous texts are not so much academic treatises as short personal statements, often conceived as prefaces to translations made by the author: for instance, John Dryden's preface to Ovid's *Epistles*, Friedrich Schleiermacher's essay 'On the Different Methods of Translation', or Walter Benjamin's 'The Task of the Translator'.

It is hardly surprising, then, that such theoretical texts are often strongly normative, indeed that translation theory is often translation ideology (see Toury 1995: 62). The theorist will defend the translator's method, implicitly or explicitly condemning other methods. Thus Dryden, while apparently setting up three possible models of translation—metaphrase, paraphrase, and imitation [see I.a.3.iii] —clearly does so in such a way that the two extremes of pedantic literalism and licentious imitation cancel each other out; the tripartite presentation serves to recommend the middle course, which corresponds to the fluency so influential at the time [see I.b.3]. Schleiermacher, who has been rediscovered and much exploited by 20th-c. translation theorists, operates differently. He sets up a series of dichotomies, which tend to channel the reader to choose one method—'taking the reader to the author'—not only as the best practice but as the only 'true' form of translation, at least for great literary or philosophical texts [see I.a.3.iii].

It is perhaps worth considering more closely in

this respect some influential 20th-c. theorists, all of them practising literary translators. Walter Benjamin's 'The Task of the Translator' was originally published as the preface to his 1923 German translation of Baudelaire's 'Tableaux parisiens'. This difficult text has acquired talismanic status in recent discussions of translation, its message being relayed and developed, for instance, by George Steiner (1975) and by Jacques Derrida (1985). Much of Benjamin's appeal lies in the exalting vision he offers of translation as the necessary continuation (*Fortleben*) of the original rather than a secondary, subservient activity. (Some of the headiest modern statements, for instance those of Jorge Luís Borges or the remarkable *Le Ton beau de Marot* (1997) of Douglas R. Hofstadter, have tended to liberate the translator from the stigma of coming after, at best a faithful servant.)

Benjamin's conception of the nature of translation carries clear implications for evaluation. At the beginning of his essay we are told that the 'hallmark of bad translations' is that they are concerned to transmit information, to serve the reader by conveying the sense of the original. The 'genuine' translation is different, less concerned with sense than with language and form: 'A real translation [such as Hölderlin's Sophocles] is transparent; it does not cover the original, does not block its light, but allows the pure language, as though reinforced by its own medium, to shine upon the original all the more fully. This may be achieved, above all, by a literal rendering of the syntax . . .' (Benjamin 1968: 79). One is struck again by the move whereby the preferred translation practice, here a kind of 'foreignizing' literalism (to use the term popularized by Venuti, 1995a), is declared to be 'real' translation, with the implication that a meaning-centred translation is not just bad, but not translation at all.

A similar point of view is found in the more fully developed 'poetics of translation' of the French scholar Henri Meschonnic, also a translator. In his 'Poétique de la traduction' (Meschonnic 1973: 305–454), linked again to the author's practice (in this case Bible translation), Meschonnic advocates what he calls 'décentrement'. Akin to Venuti's 'foreignization', this manifests the distance between original and translation; it is is opposed to the common practice of 'annexion' (domestication) which creates the illusion of a text originally, 'naturally' written in the target language. The effect of this argument is again to enhance the dignity of translation—the price to pay being that 'bad' translations must be exposed and denounced. Meschonnic's theses on translation lead directly to an assault on translations which he deplores, translations which fail to produce a literary text worthy of the original (his particular example being a French translation of Paul Celan which he denounces as 'a massacre of the poetry of Celan and of poetry in general' (p. 369, my translation), because it has annexed the German poet to the norms of modern French poetry.

Another of Meschonnic's targets is the American Eugene Nida. In a number of publications, basing himself partly on his experience as a Protestant Bible translator, Nida set out what he called in his most important book a 'science of translating', which was very influential in the 1960s and 1970s. This science, drawing on a number of theories in linguistics, notably those of Chomsky, is presented as being descriptive and objective. In fact, the 'scientific' manner conceals an agenda as marked as that of Meschonnic, but opposed to it. Nida allows for the possibility, in different situations, of translations of different kinds—which he divides broadly into two camps, that of 'formal equivalence' and that of 'dynamic equivalence'. His preference, however, is evidently for the latter; his notion of a good translation gives paramount importance to the communication of meaning. His 'three fundamental criteria . . . basic to the evaluation of all translating' are as follows: (1) general efficiency of the communication process, (2) comprehension of intent, and (3) equivalence of response (Nida 1964: 182). In saying this, Nida feels that he is expressing the common view among translators, but his argument has been far from commanding general assent among those concerned with literary translation.

The question of Bible translation [II.c.1]—as of sacred texts in general [I.c.3]—is a major area for theoretical debate between practitioners. Another is the translation of poetry. The difference between Meschonnic and Nida is echoed, though by no means replicated, by the disagreements between those who champion formal mimesis and those who see the task of the translator of poetry as being to work outwards from the original impulse towards a new poem. To these could be added the unusual and extreme position adopted by Vladimir Nabokov (1955), who condemns all attempts to make a new poem and—precisely contrary to Benjamin—sees the translator's task as being (with the aid of extensive footnotes) 'to reproduce with absolute exactitude the whole text, and nothing but the text'.

As Daniel Weissbort reminds us [I.c.1], these dichotomies are often less absolute in practice than they at first seem, but they do produce very different criteria for the judgement of poetry translations. Such debates are by no means peculiar to the

English-speaking world. Joseph Brodsky's belief that 'meters in verse are kinds of spiritual magnitudes for which nothing can be substituted', and that therefore 'a translator should begin his work with a search for at least a metrical equivalent to the original form', led him to damn the Mandelstam translations of Clarence **Brown** and W. S. **Merwin** [II.p.7.iii] in the columns of the *New York Review of Books* (Brodsky 1974). This very 'Russian' position was later rejected in an article in *World Literature Today* (1979) by the French poet-translator Yves Bonnefoy, whose theory of poetic translation also corresponds, unsurprisingly, to his own practice. His argument is that the task of the poetic translator is to relive the act which produced the original poem and to discover in a new language the 'original intention and intuition . . . stripped of that fixed form which is only its footprint' (Bonnefoy 1990: 152, my translation). Bonnefoy is less inclined than Brodsky to criticize what he sees as bad translations, but again the theoretical discussion produces criteria by which translations might be evaluated.

One could cite many other influential theoretical statements made in prefaces and short essays by practitioners, all of them tending to build universal norms on the basis of their own preferred practice. If in the 18th c. fluent domestication was the norm [see I.b.3], it would seem that the pendulum has since then swung the other way, at least as far as translation theory is concerned. By the end of the 20th c. it had become normal to advocate 'taking the reader to the author', as Schleiermacher put it [see I.a.3.iii]; on this view translation ideally opens a window on to something different, enriching the language and culture with foreign elements. But that is no doubt not the end of the story.

It would be an exaggeration to say there is nothing new under the sun, that theorists are all the time rephrasing old dilemmas ('faithfulness' against 'beauty', the literary against the literal, sense-for-sense against word-for-word). Even so, although the debate anchors itself to new philosophical or political foundations, the reader may sometimes feel sympathy with George Steiner when he writes: 'Over two thousand years of argument and precept, the beliefs and disagreements voiced about the nature of translation have been almost the same. Identical theses, familiar moves and refutations in debate recur, nearly without exception, from Cicero and Quintilian to the present-day' (1975: 239).

Steiner himself, writing at the beginning of the development of Translation Studies (about which he remains sceptical), offered in *After Babel* a wide-ranging and ambitious discussion of a whole range of questions involving the philosophy of language and translation. It is, like many of the major writings on translation of the last quarter of the 20th c., written from the point of view of the observer rather than the practitioner, and is not concerned to advocate any particular method of translation. Nevertheless, it too is prescriptive in that it sketches an *ideal* of translation (not unlike that of Benjamin and his followers), in which the translation meets the original as an equal. *After Babel* contains illuminating analyses of particular translations (e.g. those of Gerard Manley Hopkins by Pierre Leyris), in which Steiner, practising a 'critique des beautés', tries to show what literary translation should aim to be.

iii. **Descriptive Translation Studies** While it is natural for translators to make theories in order to defend their own practice, and equally natural for teachers of translation to offer criteria by which it may be produced or evaluated, it is not inevitable that discussions of the subject should be prescriptive. Translation Studies can aim to be a (human) 'science' (like linguistics or sociology) that studies behaviour, rather than an 'art' (like rhetoric) that imparts a skill. Indeed, one of the most striking features in the development of the discipline has been the search for scientific status. We have seen, for instance, that Nida presents his distinctly normative theory of translation as a descriptive account. Others have gone further in their search for neutral objectivity.

The modern term 'Translation Studies', which was launched by James S Holmes in 1972 (Holmes 1988), covers many different approaches to the subject. Within this broad field it has become customary to make a distinction between 'linguistic' approaches and those grouped under the broad heading 'cultural'. As Mona Baker points out, however [I.a.4], these are by no means mutually exclusive.

Those studying translation from the standpoint of applied linguistics—and particularly those with an interest in translator training or in machine translation—understandably tend at times to be prescriptive in their approach. Like the traditional language teacher, but with a greater theoretical sophistication, they may aim to determine the kind of 'equivalence' that makes a 'good' translation. J. C. Catford, for instance, defines the main concern of translation theory as being 'to determine appropriate translation methods' (quoted in Toury 1995: 17).

However, it is just as possible, and has become increasingly normal, for linguistically trained students of translation to describe or analyse what actually goes on in translation without seeking to adjudicate between performances. And in so far as this is done in reference to the social, political, and cultural context which surrounds and in part determines the act of translation, the investigator will find him- or herself asking questions very like those of the 'cultural' specialist.

The most single-minded attempt to create a non-normative type of translation study has perhaps been that associated with so-called 'descriptive translation studies'. In his *Descriptive Translation Studies and Beyond* (Toury 1995), Gideon Toury, a leading representative of this school, takes issue with the statement by Catford quoted above. In Toury's view, while 'applied' translation studies (including translator training and translation criticism) quite properly concern themselves with what should be, the empirical student will confine him- or herself to describing and analysing what is. Translation Studies are not primarily concerned with teaching us how to translate, any more than linguistics is primarily concerned with teaching us how to speak.

Toury's particular emphasis is on describing translations as 'facts' within the receiving ('target') culture. He asks how they relate to other kinds of writing, what social and political pressures determine their production, and so on. This does not exclude consideration of the relation between the source text and the translation (which was virtually the only concern of most earlier translation theorists); Toury examines how different pressures within the target culture affect the 'manipulation' of the source text (to use a term given wide currency by Theo Hermans (1985)), but characteristically this analysis is non-judgemental. For instance, the different Hebrew versions by Abraham Shlonsky of Hamlet's 'To be or not to be' are compared, but simply with a view to showing the process of adjustment to the norms of Israeli culture (Toury 1995: 193–205).

Norms are at the centre of of this type of inquiry. In the present volume, Theo Hermans [I.a.3] discusses how these are created and maintained, and the pressure they exercise on the practising translator. Norms, which affect the evaluation as well as the production of translations, may concern many different issues, for instance:

a) What is to be translated (what type of texts? complete texts or extracts?, etc.)?
b) How is a translation to be designated, if at all?
c) What stress is to be given to adequacy to the source text, and what to acceptability within the target culture? (See below.)

These norms are complex and subject to change, as the historical section of Part I of this *Guide* shows very clearly [I.b.1–5]; they can easily be flouted for particular purposes, but their existence and importance are undeniable.

The essential thing about Toury's approach is that such norms are not simply adopted by the theorist (as is often the case with Nida), but are studied in as neutral a manner as possible—a position poles apart from the committed criticism of a Brodsky or a Meschonnic. There is certainly a good argument for separating 'science' from 'criticism', as Roland Barthes advised in the heyday of structuralism (Barthes 1966). This is more easily said than done, however, especially in history and the human sciences. Here, depending on the context, a descriptive statement can easily carry a positive, or more frequently a negative, connotation. As Sartre put it in *What Is Literature?* (1948), to name something is to create a new awareness, often a critical awareness. When Marx analyses the 'German ideology', the effect is far from neutral. Similarly, when students of the social and political factors conditioning translation describe the links between given types of translation practice and, say, patriarchal gender relationships [see I.a.5] or colonial power (Niranjana 1992), they tend to suggest negative judgements on actual translations, or to propose alternative, more acceptable forms of translation.

Description may be far from neutral, then, and even those who aim for objectivity as scientific observers may well engage elsewhere in activities (translation, teaching, criticism) in which evaluation has an essential role to play. Such was the case, for instance, with André Lefevere, in some ways a follower or ally of the 'descriptive' school, who never felt inhibited about making personal taste judgements. Toury recognizes that the scholar may also be a critic; more than this, he suggests that the findings of descriptive science can inform and improve critical practice (Toury 1995: 17–19). This is the case if only because the critic with the broad vision offered by descriptive translation studies will be less inclined to make hasty judgements on the strength of locally prevalent norms. Recognizing that such norms are the product of a complex and changing social and cultural environment, he or she should be more open to different practices. The problem, of course, will lie in reconciling this openness with the continuing need to assess translations.

For evaluation is inescapable. Given the mass of material confronting any member of society, some sort of critical sifting is necessary. We may be aware that norms are not absolute, but in cultural life they are both inevitable and desirable, and it is precisely evaluative criticism which in large part maintains and modifies them. Furthermore, it is hard to disagree with Antoine Berman—a critic of Toury's neutral stance—when he champions the cause of responsible translation criticism. Discussing (and to a certain extent regretting) Henri Meschonnic's severe negative judgements, Berman, whose *Pour une critique des traductions* (1995) is perhaps the most serious treatment of translation criticism, writes that without proper criticism translators will work—as they have long worked—with the impunity and irresponsibility that are born of 'invisibility'. Without criticism, they can get away with murder; with criticism, even hostile criticism, their work is given the recognition it deserves.

iv. Translation Criticism and Its Criteria What, then, are the criteria generally invoked by those who offer evaluations of translation, for instance in the present volume? Outside the specialized fields of Translation Studies, translator training, and the like, there are two widespread types of criticism, usually practised without a great deal of theoretical awareness: that of the language teacher (who may also be a teacher of foreign literature) and that of the journalist-critic.

Almost all foreign language learning involves some element of translation, even if this is less prominent now than it once was. The teacher will propose a foreign text (often literary in nature) for translation, frequently offering a model version against which to judge the efforts of students. Judgements are in large part negative and local, noting errors in comprehension or failures to find adequate equivalents for particular expressions in the target language. The basic criterion here is one of *adequacy* to the source text.

Against this, the journalist-critic, faced with a literary translation, will in many cases not comment on the translation at all, acting as if it gave unmediated access to the original. If the translation is noticed, the critic may compare it favourably or unfavourably with the original, but the dominant tendency is to judge it on its naturalness, fluency, elegance, and so on—is it well written? Venuti gives some characteristic examples, such as: 'the style is elegant, the prose lovely, and the translation excellent' (Venuti 1995a: 2). Here the translation is judged according to the norms currently operating within the target culture—which may favour copiousness or brevity, plainness or decoration, and so on. It is assumed that the translator's task is, as John Denham famously put it, to make the foreign author speak English 'not only as a man of this

Nation, but as a man of this age' (Denham 1656: A3ʳ). The criterion here is one of *acceptability* to the target culture.

Adequacy and acceptability, the terms used by Toury (1995: 56–7), correspond, of course, in many ways to the familiar fidelity and beauty. It is, however, worth looking at the implications of both in a little more detail, since the concepts are perhaps less straightforward than first appears.

The basic level of adequacy involves questions of understanding and misunderstanding. These might seem simple and entirely non-ideological—it is just a matter of getting it right or wrong. To translate the French word 'pétrole' (oil) as 'petrol' might lose you your job if you are a professional translator in a company. But one must ask how well this simple model applies to literary translation.

The practice of translation critics would suggest that the 'pedantic' language-teaching model remains important for judging the translation of imaginative literature, let alone science or philosophy. While there can be endless debate about meaning, there is, arguably, an implicit pact between translator and reader that the basic elements of signification in a text will be rendered with a reasonable degree of accuracy. We have seen how Nabokov urges the translator to sacrifice *everything* to the exact contextual meaning of the original—any other way, he suggests, would be a dereliction of duty. This is an extreme position; what is more, adequacy may mean other things besides lexical equivalence. Nevertheless, other things being equal (if they ever are!), most readers of translation would probably agree with the type of criticism launched by Timothy Buck against the inaccuracies in the **Lowe-Porter** translations of Thomas Mann [see II.h.11.v]. The question is: how much importance should be attached to failings of this kind, which are generally the result of ignorance or negligence rather than deliberate policy? Certainly it would be excessive to make this kind of accuracy the principal criterion for assessing the value of a literary translation.

Beyond this basic level, adequacy means rather doing justice to the values and/or the formal qualities of the original. This is often presented in ethical terms, as a respect for, or openness to, the Other, a refusal of the lazy or self-indulgent tendency of translators to make everything over in their own image. Sometimes this is taken to imply the self-effacement of the translator, who becomes the humble servant of the original, nothing more. But Berman insists, quoting a French translator of Yeats, Jean-Yves Masson, that on the contrary respect for the other implies *dialogue*:

If the translation *respects* the original, it can, and even *must*, enter into dialogue with it, face up to it, stand up to it. The dimension of respect does not entail the annihilation of the person who respects his own respect. The translated is first of all an offering to the original text. (Berman 1995: 92; my translation)

Interestingly, this notion of dialogue leads Berman to resist the 'exaggerated literalism' of certain contemporary translators. For of course one manifestation of respect for the other is the type of translation which attempts to preserve as much as possible of the syntax, prosody, or even lexis of the source text. The criterion here is primarily aesthetic rather than ethical, perhaps, although the two often coalesce, as in the case of Brodsky, for whom the translation of metre by free verse is, if not sacrilege, at least deception of the reader (Brodsky 1974).

What emerges from this discussion is that such words as 'literalism' are very hard to pin down. The term can be applied to what is imprecisely called 'word-for-word translation', in which each lexical item in the original is rendered (as far as possible) by an equivalent one in the translation. Necessary in some technical translation, and sometimes demanded in the translation of sacred texts [I.c.3], this will normally offend against the other type of literalism, which consists in respect for the 'letter' of the original—not the semantic content, but such formal elements as sound, metre, rhythm, and syntax. If, as Meschonnic believes, all of these are essential elements in the original, then an 'adequate' translation will approximate to them as nearly as possible. It remains an open question whether this approximation is best achieved by actual imitation (rendering hexameter by hexameter, alliteration by alliteration, nominal construction by nominal construction) or by seeking in the target language other ways of producing the same literary effects.

It seems almost inevitable, given the difference between languages—even languages as close as German and English—that attempts to replicate the specific features of the original will strike most readers as odd, if not actually unacceptable. The strangeness may come from the foreignness of the world view embodied in the original, e.g. the Arabic *Muʻallaqāt* [II.b.3], but it is even more likely to result from the attempt to calque grammatical, prosodic, or other formal features of the original—for instance, the labyrinthine sentences of Proust [II.g.13]. It is a moderate form of this strangeness which is often condemned as 'translationese' (writing suspended somewhere between the source and target language). In such cases, the critic may well suspect that it is less the fruit of design than of incompetence—failure to realize the conditions of normal transfer between languages.

Where the effect of estrangement is more pronounced, it will generally be evident that this is due to a deliberate choice on the translator's part: to confront the reader with a new and alien world. Such was, in France, the 1964 translation of the *Aeneid* by Pierre Klossowski; here Virgil, far from appearing with all the familiarity bred of long assimilation, emerged in all his potential foreignness. The translation is not literal in the sense of word-for-word, but offers in French a syntax—in particular a word order—that casts the well-educated reader's mind back to the original Latin (see Cox 1997). French readers were very divided by this foreignizing type of adequacy, as English speakers have been by **Fox**'s Buberian translation of the Pentateuch [II.c.1.xi] or Ezra **Pound**'s versions of Italian, Anglo-Saxon, or Provençal poetry [II.m.4.v; II.o.1; II.g.2]. Generally speaking, however, such translations correspond more easily to the current norms for poetry translation, with its relatively small and receptive readership, than to prose fiction or drama, where the target culture imposes its own patterns more powerfully.

It is worth noting that the advocacy of foreignizing translation is not necessarily motivated wholly, or even in part, by the respect for the original of which Berman speaks. Its value may be seen to lie rather in the challenge it issues to the dominant norms of the target culture. A translation that disturbs, like Klossowski's *Aeneid* or Paul **Blackburn**'s troubadour lyrics [II.g.2.iii] may be praised today less because it 'takes the reader to the text' (as Schleiermacher put it) than because in breaking the illusion of naturalness and advertising the fact that it is indeed a translation, it contributes to a modernist (or as we now say, postmodernist) subversion of the dominant culture. In Lawrence Venuti's eloquent presentation (Venuti 1995a), the attack on 'fluency' is seen as a quasi-political act of resistance.

As this suggests, acceptability (or, more negatively, domestication) has had a poor press recently, but it has long been, and still remains, an essential criterion for judging the success of a translation. It would be wrong to oversimplify this notion. At its most limited, in talking for instance of 20th-c. Britain, it might be construed as conformity to a model of 'good writing' which is simply taken for granted—as we saw in Kipling. For many British readers, such a model was provided by such works as Fowler's *Modern English Usage* or *The King's English*,

with their declared preference for the familiar over the far-fetched, the concrete over the abstract, the single word over the circumlocution, the short word over the long, the Saxon word over the Romance (Fowler 1931: 11). If one accepted a given stylistic doctrine as possessing general validity—as perhaps some of the translation theorists of 18th-c. Britain did [I.b.3]—then translations could all be judged by their conformity to conservative literary taste.

The real picture is more complex. A literary culture as large and varied as that of the English-language world knows many different types of acceptability. What goes down well in London may do less well in Glasgow, Los Angeles, or Lagos [see I.a.6.i]. A translation may be aimed at a particular subculture and therefore couched in a specific variety of the language. In particular, for literary texts, *generic* distinctions are important. At one end of the scale, books for children or young people [I.c.4] are normally translated fairly freely, and in such a way as to mask their foreignness; often enough the translator's identity or even the fact of translation goes undeclared (when I first read Jules Verne, I had no idea he was French). At the other end, as we have seen, poetry translation (particularly when the original is printed alongside the translation) often foregrounds the element of translation, and notions of acceptability here will be more elastic than for prose fiction.

The critique of domestication, which was broadly philosophical in Schleiermacher or Benjamin, acquired a more political dimension in the late 20th c., as translations began to be criticized for their complicity with an oppressive order. Among critical treatments of colonial translation one could cite, among others, Eric Cheyfitz's *The Poetics of Imperialism: Translation and Colonization from 'The Tempest' to Tarzan* (1991) and Tejaswini Niranjana's *Siting Translation: History, Post-Structuralism, and the Colonial Context* (1992). Written from different perspectives, these two books both argue that translators have been parties to the appropriation of the cultures of the vanquished, be they the native peoples of America or the ancient civilizations of the Indian subcontinent. Cheyfitz, for instance, writes: 'From its beginnings the imperialist mission is, in short, one of translation: the translation of the "other" into the terms of empire' (p. 112). 'Translation' is obviously used in a very broad sense here, so that 'colonization is translation' (p. 117). Such an ideological critique would seem to imply a more general condemnation of the assimilationist translation practices which the criterion of acceptability tends to valorize. It is less clear what could be put in their place, except perhaps to give up translating altogether, since translation, however respectful of the original, is always also appropriation.

Clearly, in such political judgements, it all depends on who is translating whom. A domesticating policy may be condemned when practised by colonizers, but a similarly target-oriented policy may, from a similar political standpoint, be advocated as an act of resistance by less powerful cultures, when they appropriate for their own use the culture of the powerful. Such, roughly speaking, is the notion of 'cannibalism' advocated by certain South American translators, and related in its turn to Derridean notions of translation as transformation (see Gentzler 1993: 192–3).

It would be too crude, however, to line up such inventive theoretical explorations on either side of a simple adequacy/acceptability divide. The critique of colonialist assimilation is a different thing from the notion of respect for the other, and the advocates of a strong, 'cannibalistic' translation practice are not saying the same thing as the 18th-c. champions of fluency. The issues raised here go beyond the search for criteria for the evaluation of translations; they hint rather at the possibility of positive 'rewriting' practices in which neither fluency nor accuracy are any longer the writer's or reader's real concern.

Meanwhile, in the day-to-day process of evaluating the thousands of translations that are published, critics will continue to negotiate between rival claims. Their judgements will necessarily depend on the situation in which the evaluation takes place. The development of Translation Studies has at least taught us to ask, not simply: 'Is this a good/bad translation?', but rather: 'What is the purpose of this translation? Who is it aimed at? How well does it achieve its purpose?' It is within such a framework that translation critics should continue to assess translations in terms of both adequacy and acceptability. Ideally, they will do so with the subtlety and rigour of Antoine Berman (1995) in his book-length discussion of the French translations of a single poem by John Donne.

2. NORMS OF TRANSLATION
Theo Hermans

i. The Concept of Translation Norms It is reasonable to assume that there is a concept called 'translation' and a form of behaviour called 'translating' with which we feel we are entirely familiar in our own contemporary language and culture. Because 'translation' and 'translating' have a public, socially recognized meaning, they refer to certain actions and exclude others. Someone who wants his or her actions to be recognized by others as 'translating' has to take into account the current usage of the term. This is what entitles us to expect of translators that, as they go about their task, they select certain appropriate options from among a range of permissible options. The set of permissible or legitimate options constitutes what we refer to as 'translation'.

The meaning of the term, or of that term or cluster of terms in another language which, rightly or wrongly, we translate as the English term 'translation', is codified in dictionaries. There are also professional activities called 'translation', we have organizations representing translators, institutes for translator training, and so on. In other words, in our own cultural environment at the present moment, as in other contemporary cultures and in past cultures, we encounter terms which—again, rightly or wrongly—we interpret as denoting the concept and the activity that we recognize for ourselves as constituting 'translation'. There is a peculiar complication built into the idea of 'translating translation', whether between languages or within one language (either way we perform the very operation we are talking about), but let us leave that aside here. For the present purposes we need to bear in mind that when we use the term 'translation' or its counterpart in another language we appeal to a recognizable and circumscribed category, both a known concept and a socially acknowledged practice.

The category called 'translation' consists of the production of utterances which are recognized as communications of a certain kind, and of statements about translation. The two are held together by the fact that whenever we come across an instance of 'translation' (a translated text, an occurrence of the term 'translation', a statement about it), we activate certain expectations, which we assume others in our community will share. The expectations may subsequently be fulfilled or disappointed. If they are disappointed we tend (not necessarily, and not always, but mostly) to respond by branding the offending occurrence as an error, a transgression. In so doing we reaffirm the boundaries of the existing concept of translation and the permissible practices and statements within its sphere. The implication is that our concept of translation is circumscribed not only by cognitive expectations but also, even primarily, by normative expectations, or norms. Since norms are relevant for the reception and consumption as well as for the production of translations, and involve selection and control mechanisms at various levels, it is worth exploring the concept further.

Let us remember that, as regards translation, norms are relevant to the entire transfer operation, not just the actual process of translating. This latter process is necessarily preceded by a number of other decisions, including the decision to translate rather than do something else with a given source text. Translation merely constitutes one among a number of possible modes of the intercultural movement of texts. Other modes include, for example, importing or exporting texts in untranslated form, although it should be noted that deploying materially the same text in a different linguistic and cultural environment inevitably lends that text a different 'load', for it is bound to be perceived differently. Summary, paraphrase, adaptation, gloss, critical commentary, and other forms of what André Lefevere broadly called 'rewriting' (Lefevere 1992a) constitute a further set of alternative modes, as do transformations into other semiotic media, and so on.

The initial choice of one or other mode of transfer will probably be made by whoever is the prime mover instigating the process. This may be an agent in the source culture or, more usually, in the target culture. The choice may be delegated, and it may turn out to be impracticable. It may be modified by the initiator's or the translator's assessment of what is socially, politically, culturally, and/or ideologically feasible, i.e. what is likely to be tolerated, permitted, encouraged, or demanded by those who control or are otherwise in a position to influence the means of production and distribution and the relevant institutions and channels in economic, social, ideological, and artistic terms. They include publishers, patrons and censors, government agencies, fund-giving bodies, pressure groups, critics, reviewers, and indeed the book-buying public. In principle, the calculations informing the decisions may be purely a matter of loss and gain. Whenever choices have to be made in the context of preexisting cultural practices, however, norms are likely to play a part.

The basic assumption in the discussion of translation norms is that translation, like any other use of language, is a matter of communication. As such it constitutes a form of social behaviour requiring a degree of interaction and co-operation among those concerned. For communication to take place, the participants need to coordinate their actions to a certain extent, not only on the level of immediate interpersonal contact, but also across time and space if the situation requires it. Norms, like conventions, arise as answers to coordination problems of this kind. The classic definition of convention (Lewis 1969) hinges on this point. Conventions, as David Lewis defines them, imply the expectation, shared by all, that in a given situation one member of the group is more likely to do one thing than another. Conventions have a socially regulatory function. They restrict the number of practically available options in recurrent situations of a given type by offering the individual a particular option as the one known to be preferred by everyone else.

The difference between a norm and a convention lies in the modality of the expectation. Norms tell individual members of a community not just how everyone else reckons they are probably going to behave in a given situation, but how they *ought* to behave. Norms imply that there is, among the range of options that present themselves, a particular course of action which is generally accepted as 'proper' or 'correct' or 'appropriate'. That course of action, it is agreed, *should* therefore be adopted by all who find themselves in that type of situation. Each time a norm is observed, its validity is confirmed and reinforced.

Norms can and will be broken. Which norms are observed or broken by whom, where and when, depends on such things as the nature and strength of the norm, the kind of sanction that might apply, and the individual's status in a given community. In the 1960s, Louis and Celia **Zukofsky** rendered Latin poetry into English (Catullus 1969), radically privileging the sound of the words over their lexical meaning. Even with onomatopoeic lines this was a daring option, as Catullus' 'multis raucisonos efflabant cornua bombos | barbarique horribili stridebat tibia cantu', rendered in the Loeb edition as 'many blew horns with harsh-sounding drone, and the barbarian pipe shrilled with deadful din', became in the Zukofskys' hands 'mules there raucous sound nose a flybynight horn how pompous | barbaris horrible lilling strident but tibia cant too'. It is relevant to know, however, that this was done in a literary context, that even there it was interpreted as a provocative challenge to prevailing norms, that already at this time Louis Zukofsky was widely recognized as a prominent poet in his own right, etc. The young graduate who approaches, say, Penguin or Viking or Harvill with the aim of making a career as a translator of contemporary Italian fiction into English would be ill-advised to follow the Zukovskys' example. This is not because the 'phonemic' mode of translation à la Zukofsky cannot be applied to, say, contemporary Italian fiction, but because commercial publishers of fiction in translation, and with them presumably most critics and readers, are unlikely to accept such a defiantly unconventional mode. In the same way explicitly gendered translations [I.a.5.iv], for example, may be acceptable to some publishers and audiences but not to others.

Norms can be strong or weak, limited or extensive in scope, more or less enduring over time. They can take the form of obligations or prohibitions, and exert different degrees of pressure on the choices individuals make. Because in an irreversible temporal sequence no two situations are ever exactly the same, each instance of compliance or non-compliance with a norm changes the norm, however slightly. Expectations may be fulfilled or disappointed in given instances; either way the experience will lead to an adjustment of the norm, which becomes stronger or weaker as a result. Being cultural entities, norms are subject to change.

ii. Norms and Social Control Since norms are not innate, they need to be acquired. They are inculcated as part of a process of socialization. Just as learning to speak means learning to speak 'properly', in accordance with the linguistic conventions and norms of the relevant community, so learning to translate means learning to operate with and within the norms of translation. This means anticipating, accommodating, calculating and negotiating the expectations of others concerning the social category called translation. In the same way readers learn what they can and cannot expect when they pick up a book labelled 'translation'. On both sides of the equation, in fact on all sides, since the production and consumption of translation involve more than just two parties, certain expectations are activated, certain bonds entered into. They may be clearly stated and understood by all concerned, or remain fluid and unspoken. The question of who controls whom in this respect depends on power and position. Norms are not independent of local conditions, and of the power relations between and within communities, whether these relations are material (economic, legal, financial) or what Pierre Bourdieu calls 'symbolic', i.e. relations that have to do with status and legitimacy, and with who confers legitimacy (Bourdieu 1991; 1993).

In large, complex, and differentiated societies, a vast multiplicity of different, overlapping, and often conflicting norms coexist. The translator's work is inevitably entangled in several of these networks at once, if only because translation always caters for other domains. The product of the translator's labour is never a 'translation *per se*': it is a translated computer manual, a translated novel, a translated medical record, etc. In each case the translator enters an existing network of discourses and social relations. His or her translation discourse occupies a place in, or at least in relation to, that network. It is part of the ambivalence of the translated text that it is expected to comply both with the 'translational' *and* with the textual norms regarded as pertinent by a given community in a given domain. If the translation does this, because the translator has made the requisite choices, it will be deemed a 'legitimate', 'proper', or 'good' translation.

Learning to translate correctly, then, means the acquisition of the competence, the skill, required to select and apply those norms that will help to produce legitimate translations, i.e. translations socially recognized as legitimate within a certain community and its concept of translation. Just as one of the main functions of the educational system as a whole is that of transmitting the requisite social skills, expectations, and attitudes, continually reproducing and reaffirming the community's dominant values and models in the process, so, in the field of translation, one of the roles of the translator training institute consists precisely in continually reproducing within itself the social category called 'translation'. This does not prevent different groups or sub-groups from propagating alternative translation modes. In the contemporary world, for example, feminist and postcolonial agendas explicitly challenge the dominant forms of linguistic expression and of translation. The 'libertine' translators of 17th-c. England [see I.b.3] rejected the prevailing emphasis on literalism where the translation of literature was concerned—and realized that the strict 'grammarians' might be unwilling to label these much freer products 'translations' (T. R. Steiner 1975).

A point to stress is that norms are social as well as psychological realities: they involve not just individuals, groups, and communities but also power relations. Norms operate in a complex and dynamic social context, which may be a cultural domain, such as the domain of literature. We can think of this context in terms of a 'system' in the sense of systems theory (Toury 1995) or in terms of a 'field of cultural production' in Pierre Bourdieu's sense, or indeed in other terms. What is important is that norms are deeply implicated in the social and cultural life of a community. They involve different and often competing positions and possibilities, they point up various interests and stakes being pursued, defended, coveted, and claimed—and the desires and strategies of both individuals and collectives to further their own ends.

It is also the stratified social context, and the hierarchy of the power relations in it, which explains the greater prominence as well as the greater binding force of some norms as opposed to others. The institutions or agents who exercise normative control tend to occupy positions of power and dominance in the particular field where the norms apply, or indeed in higher-level fields, i.e. fields closer to the overarching centres of power in a community. Generally speaking, the possibility of effectively subverting dominant norms arises either in conditions of weak normative control, when the transgressor is relatively immune to sanctions (e.g. Louis Zukofsky), or in conditions of strong normative control, when a transgressor is prepared to accept sanctions and serve as a visible role model for other potential transgressors to challenge the powers that be. In the early 16th c. William **Tyndale** defied the authorities by translating the Bible into English without their permission and without adhering to their preferred interpretation—but he had to flee England to complete his project; even so he was eventually captured, tortured, and executed [see II.c.1.v].

In themselves, norms are neither true nor false. They do not represent assertions about existing states of affairs. Rather, they stipulate what 'ought' to happen, how things 'should' be. The content of a norm is a notion of what is 'proper' or 'correct'. This is an intersubjective notion, a conceptualization of patterns of behaviour regarded as correct, or at least as legitimate, and therefore valued positively. What is 'correct' is established within the community, and within the community's power structures and ideology, and mediated to its members. The directive force of norms, their executive arm, serves among other things to delimit and secure these notions of correctness. The notion of what constitutes 'correct' behaviour, 'correct' linguistic usage, or 'correct' translation is therefore a social and cultural construct.

Notions of correctness are abstract entities, values, which, in order to become socially or culturally operative, have to be fixed both subjectively and intersubjectively, so that personal and collective attitudes can be attuned to them. In practice, they often appear in the more schematic but mentally manageable form of models, understood here as patterns (e.g. the elements and precepts of a poetics) derived from more abstract prototypical values and instances, or as specific products (e.g. individual texts) recognized as embodying those values.

The canonized models are likely to be the models adopted and promoted, or even imposed, by the dominant groups in a given community.

In the case of translating, the models being referred to are textual, discursive entities. They cover the substance of what is normally called a 'poetics' (i.e. a 'poetics of translation'), a set of principles and practical rules, together with a set of examples of good practice. Particular groups or subgroups may adopt a certain configuration of translation models and prototypes in opposition to other groups, to compete with them and because there are certain material and symbolic stakes to be defended or claimed. As individuals weave their way through and around these configurations, they take up positions and build alliances, so as to achieve their own aims and ambitions as well as those of the groups with which they have aligned themselves. The way in which the young Ezra **Pound** used a decidedly novel and controversial form of translation to help, as he put it, 'break the mould' of Victorian and Edwardian poetry, is a good example [see II.g.2; II.m.4]. Pound's early translations also served as effective models in the effort to establish the modernist poetic of a new generation. At first, however, Pound's translations, like his other poems, were published only in little magazines and by small, marginal publishers.

The marked intertextuality which results from these strategies has a social relevance. In translating run-of-the-mill detective novels or popular romances, for example, the choice of a particular textual model may well mark the translation as 'literary', but it may also spell the end of a lucrative contract, as the publisher may not look favourably on the use of a 'high' literary register for books intended merely for entertainment. At the same time, the textual models relevant to translation will rarely be those of the receptor or target culture only. The specificity of translation stems from the fact that it refers, expressly or tacitly, to a preexisting discourse in another language which it claims to represent and to re-enunciate. This complicates the intertextual nature of the target text. It has to find a place among other texts in the target culture environment, while simultaneously it points back towards the source text about which and for which it speaks. This complication also highlights the hybridity of translated texts. They are written in the target language, but the cultural and textual 'otherness' of the source is unlikely to be wiped out altogether in translation. Translated texts invariably signal to textual models of at least two cultures at once.

iii. Norms and Translation History

There is another aspect to this issue. As we know, texts require a frame of reference shared between source and receiver to be able to function as vehicles for communication. The various forms of linguistic, temporal, and geographical displacement brought about by translation also dislocate this shared cognitive frame. Of course, we recognize that in translating, in repackaging and recasting a source text for a new recipient in a different cultural environment, a degree of alteration and adjustment, and hence a degree of manipulation, will take place. It is not only the fact itself of the dislocation that is of interest. At least as interesting is its social and historical conditioning, the particular ways in which translation, as different communities have construed it at different times and in different places, remodels its primary material. In looking at a translation, the interesting question is not really whether the source text has been transmitted more or less intact. It never has, for obvious reasons: languages and cultures are not symmetrical or isomorphic, and the flow of time is irreversible. What is of interest in translation is the nature and selectivity of the changes that have come about in the process, and the factors inducing certain changes rather than others. Aristophanes' *Lysistrata* is a play about women going on a sex strike to force their men to end a war [II.i.6]. A desire to uphold prevailing standards of decency led translators to render an explicit mention of the penis (l. 1119) as 'nose' (**Hickie**, 1902), 'leg' (**Way**, 1934), 'life-lines' (**Dickinson**, 1970) or 'anything else' (**Fitts**, 1954), just as several translators simply omitted the reference to the leather dildo in line 109. In 1837 C. A. **Wheelwright**'s translation omitted both the women's oath and the play's final 400 lines depicting their triumph, while L. **Housman**'s version, published by The Women's Press in 1911, featured a rousing passage championing the women's cause but not found in Aristophanes' Greek. Here the motives were undoubtedly ideological. The 1938 translation by Gilbert **Seldes**, which was meant for the theatre, leaves out the choruses but adds other scenes to facilitate the stage performance (Lefevere 1992a).

In translating, i.e. in rewriting, recasting, appropriating, and relocating a given source text, the translator attunes the resulting entity to a new communicative situation. Just how much and what kind of recasting and appropriation is required, permitted, or acceptable will depend on prevailing concepts and norms of translation in the host culture, and on who has the power to impose and enforce them. To the extent that translation is construed as a re-enunciation of a pre-existing text, the practice of translation inevitably results in tensions within the translated text itself. The idea of hybridity suggested above extends to the fact that translated texts have a hybrid discursive subject (whose voice do we listen to when Boris Yeltsin speaks through an interpreter?). At the same time, translations cannot help being enmeshed in the discursive forms of the recipient culture, including the whole array of modes which a culture may have developed to represent anterior and differently coded discourses. Translation—like adaptation, pastiche, parody, commentary, sequel, remake, plagiarism, etc.—constitutes one mode of textual recycling among others.

The specific and always historically determinate way in which a cultural community construes translation, therefore, also determines the way in which translation, as a cultural product, refers to its source text, the kind of image of the original which the translation projects or holds up. In other words, the 'other' to which a translated text refers is never simply the source text, even though that is the claim which translations commonly make. It is at best an image of it. Because the image is always slanted, coloured, preformed, overdetermined, but never innocent, we can say that translation constructs or produces or, as Tejaswini Niranjana (1992: 81) has it, 'invents' its original. Translation is of interest because it provides first-hand evidence of how cultures manufacture seemingly transparent but in fact heavily selective and loaded representations of other cultures.

As a rule, though, translations are made in response to or in anticipation of real or perceived demands and needs of the recipient culture. If this is the case, then the selection of texts to be translated, the mode that is chosen to (re)present the source text, the manner in which translation generally is circumscribed and regulated at a particular historical moment, and the way in which individual translations are received, all this tells us a great deal about the cultural community that engages in translation. What exactly does it tell us? We could say that translation, through its selectivity, normativity, and overdetermination, presents a privileged index of cultural self-reference, or self-definition. In reflecting about itself, a culture, or a section of it, tends to define its identity in terms of 'self' and 'other'. It describes its distinctiveness in relation to that which it perceives as different, that which lies outside the boundary of its own sphere of operation. Translation offers a window on cultural self-reference in that it involves not only the selection and importation of cultural goods from the outside world but at the same time, in the same breath, as it were, their transformation into terms which the recipient culture recognizes, to some extent at least, as its own. As was indicated above, the transformation is not random, transparent, or innocent. Translation may be described as 'regulated transformation' (the term is Derrida's (1985), although Derrida neglected to indicate who does the regulating), but it is important to realize that the rules according to which the regulated transformation takes place are themselves historical, cultural, ideological products. The transformation always serves a purpose, and therefore an interest. That is probably why different cultural groups are so keen to control and regulate it. Concepts of translation, and hence the practical norms of translation, arise as part of cultural constellations which involve power relations within and between communities.

The history of translation leaves in its wake a large number of dual texts, foreign writings, and their 'regulated transformations', together with countless retranslations and reworkings of existing translations. It provides us with a uniquely accessible series of selective, cultural constructions of the 'other', and therefore with a mass of privileged material to observe the workings of cultural self-definition. It hardly needs adding that, seen from this perspective, resistance or indifference to translation, even the absence of translation, will be as informative as the enthusiastic pursuit of this or that particular type of translation—and it is important to remember that when translation occurs it is always a particular type of translation.

For anyone with a more than casual interest in translation, the issue of who or what regulates translation, and to what end, offers a full research programme. The questions that will be asked are bound to lead into much broader issues. They are likely to include some or all of the following. When and why does a given community feel the need or perceive an opportunity to import texts from beyond a language barrier, and to do so by means of translation? What are the prevailing ideas about cultural import, translation, and translatability? What texts appear to be available for importation and translation, and why are certain texts more available than others? What is selected for translation from the range of available texts, and who makes the relevant decisions, on what grounds? Who produces the translations, under what conditions, for whom, with what effect or impact? What form do the translations take, i.e. what choices have been made in relation to existing expectations and practices in the same discursive field and in comparable fields? How is translation taught and learnt, and who speaks about translation, in what terms and with what authority or legitimacy? [see also I.b.5.iv].

3. THE LIMITS OF TRANSLATION
Douglas Robinson

i. The Question of Limits Any attempt to define what translation *is* must at some point address the negative issue of what translation is *not*—which is to say, the limits of translation. At what point does translation shade into something else? Whatever is left inside these limits will be, by definition, the essence of translation.

The limits of translation are also used, correlatively, to define not translation itself but translatability. Translation is possible with certain types of texts, or with certain types of word and phrase, impossible with others. As the translator approaches the limits of translatability, the job becomes more and more difficult, until at last s/he must give up entirely, declaring a certain passage or idea or entire text untranslatable.

The correlation between these two conceptions of the limits of translation lies in the fact that the more broadly the definitional limits of translation are set, the broader the range of textual phenomena that will be considered translatable. If 'translation' is defined narrowly as the exact rendition of *everything* in the source text, including meaning, syntax, and mood, then translation itself becomes impossible; every text lies beyond the 'limits of translation'. If it is defined broadly as a text that stands in some significant relation to a source text, including very free imitations, then translation becomes ubiquitous; virtually everything can be read as a translation, and the limits of translation are potentially infinite. In between these two extremes, the battles over the limits of translation have traditionally been fought.

ii. Theory: From Rome to the Renaissance Historically, fairly narrow limits have been set to translation. For ancient Rome, translation was strict, slavish literalism; any liberties the rewriter might be inclined to take with the source text were by definition beyond the limits of translation. Thus in his *Ars poetica* (*c*.20 CE, The Art of Poetry), Horace encourages the writer *not* to be like the 'faithful translator', who sticks too closely to the original; writers who seek a reputation for original creation must recast traditional materials (source texts) in new ways. 'Nor trouble', he writes, in E. C. **Wickham**'s translation, 'to render word for word with the faithfulness of a translator' (Robinson 1997: 15).

This association of translation with strict literalism, and thus of any kind of interpretive or other semantic 'freedom' with non-translation, carries on well into the Middle Ages and beyond. (Indeed, it survives into the present, in the assumption many non-translators harbour that all translation is by definition word-for-word.) In his commentary on Porphyry's *Eisagoge* (*c*.510 CE), Boethius alludes to Horace's *fidus interpres* (faithful translator / interpreter) slyly in defence of literal translation: 'I fear that I shall commit the fault of the faithful interpreter when I render each word by a word corresponding to it' (Robinson 1997: 35). Three centuries later John Scotus Erigena makes the same allusion in the prologue to his translation of Pseudo-Dionysius the Areopagite's *De caelesti hierarchia* (mid-9th c., Of the Celestial Hierarchy): 'If someone should find the text of the aforesaid translation obscure or impenetrable, let him consider me the *translator* of this work, not its expositor. Indeed I fear that I have incurred the blame of the faithful translator' (Robinson 1997: 37). The limits of translation are firmly fixed, for these writers, at literalism; even if they are faulted for not exceeding those limits, they will stay inside them lest they become something other than translators, such as expositors or commentators. As Glyn Norton shows at some length (Norton 1984: 57–110), Horace's lines about not emulating the faithful (literal) translator were read and misread in a wide variety of ways in the French Renaissance, many of them still in support of the ancient notion that only literal translation is *truly* translation.

Beginning early on, however—indeed, three decades before Horace—this narrow delimitation of translation was persuasively opposed by a position that would eventually expand those limits to include sense-for-sense translation. The first writer to make this argument was Cicero, who described his own creative use of translation to expand his oratorical skills. In *De oratore* (55 BCE, On the Orator), he has his dialogical persona Lucius Crassus describe his experiments in self-training: he first tried paraphrasing Latin authors in Latin, hoping to learn what they knew and then improve on it, but found that this was leading him into bad habits,

and so tried what we would nowadays call sight-translation instead:

Afterwards I resolved . . . to translate freely Greek speeches of the most eminent orators. The result of reading these was that, in rendering into Latin what I had read in Greek, I not only found myself using the best words, and yet quite familiar ones, but also coining by analogy [*exprimerem imitando*] certain words such as would be new to our people, provided only they were appropriate. (Robinson 1997: 7)

In *De optimo genere oratorum* (46 BCE, The Best Kind of Orator), too, describing a similar exercise with the orations of Aeschines and Demosthenes, he outlines the specific innovation that would eventually, in Jerome's letter to Pammachius (395 CE), become sense-for-sense translation: 'And I did not translate them as an interpreter, but as an orator, keeping the same ideas and the forms, or as one might say, the "figures" of thought, but in language which conforms to our usage' (Robinson 1997: 9). Here the *interpres* or translator / interpreter is still associated narrowly with literalism; but the act of translation, or what Cicero here calls *conversio*, is given two competing forms, *conversio ut interpres* (translating as a translator) and *conversio ut orator* (translating as an orator, conveying the same ideas but with an eye to persuading a different audience in the target culture).

This expansion of the limits of translation to include the assimilation of a text to the cultural expectations and linguistic norms of a target audience found followers in such Roman writers as Pliny the Younger (the letter to Fuscus Salinator around 85 CE), Quintilian in the *Institutiones oratoriae* (*c*.95 CE, Institutes of Oratory), and Aulus Gellius in the *Noctes atticae* (*c*.100 CE, Attic Nights; all anthologized in Robinson 1997); but it was not until the end of the 4th c. CE, with the highly influential writings of Augustine and Jerome, that this approach received its hegemonic formulation. Jerome especially, in the letter to Pammachius, defended what he called, analogically with Horace's term 'word-for-word', 'sense-for-sense' translation: 'Now I not only admit but freely announce that in translating from the Greek—except of course in the case of Holy Scripture, where even the syntax contains a mystery—I render, not word for word, but sense for sense' (25). Since the entire letter is an attack on word-for-word translation in Bible translation, this 'exception' rings somewhat false: Jerome is arguing that, since the Septuagint [see II.c.1.ii] Seventy and the Evangelists translated sense for sense, he should be allowed to as well. Indeed, his early remarks in the letter articulate a strong sense of the transition he is encouraging from an older, narrower conception of the literalist limits of translation to the broader limits of sense-for-sense translation:

But do they [Terence, Plautus, Caecilius] ever stick to the literal words? or instead, do they attempt to preserve the beauty and elegance of their originals? What is called fidelity in 'interpretation' the learned designate as pestilent minuteness. Twenty years ago, my teachers favored such minuteness; and even then I remember being the victim of a mistaken notion of translation similar to the one which attacks me today. (Robinson 1997: 26)

Depending on whether one takes a 'free' translation to be a bad translation or no translation at all, then, this hierarchy could be represented either as in Fig. 1 (if free translation is bad translation):

Fig. 1

or as in Fig. 2 (if 'free' translation is no translation):

Fig. 2

iii. Theory: Dryden to the Present This debate between word-for-word and sense-for-sense translation, or what we might call the 'narrow' (or 'minute') and 'expanded' conceptions, has by and large marked off the 'limits of the limits' of translation in the West—the territory within which it is acceptable to discuss what translation is and what it is not. The sense-for-sense / word-for-word debate continues to rage even in our own day, often with slightly shifted terms, as when Eugene A. Nida calls word-for-word translation 'formal equivalence' and sense-for-sense translation 'dynamic equivalence' (Nida and Taber 1969) or Peter Newmark (1981) calls the two 'semantic' and 'communicative' equivalence respectively.

Another influential set of terms for these categories are those borrowed by John Dryden from the rhetorical tradition in his 1680 preface to his collection of contemporary translations of Ovid's *Epistles* (see Robinson 1997: 172–3): *metaphrase* and *paraphrase*, originally derived by Quintilian from Philo

Judaeus and used throughout the Renaissance and after to mean the imitative rewording of classic texts one word or one sentence at a time, respectively; and *imitation*, originally a Latin coinage popularized by Cicero in the *De oratore* passage quoted above (*exprimerem imitando*, lit. 'expressed imitatively', or coined by analogy) to mean a freer rewording of classic texts in one's own style. For Dryden metaphrase becomes literalism, 'turning an author word by word, and line by line, from one language into another', and paraphrase becomes sense-for-sense translation, 'translation with latitude, where the author is kept in view by the translator, so as never to be lost, but his words are not so strictly followed as his sense; and that too is admitted to be amplified, but not altered'. Even though he considers metaphrase and imitation 'the two extremes which ought to be avoided', and paraphrase the 'mean betwixt them', metaphrase for Dryden, as for the entire theoretical tradition he is here rewording, is still translation, while imitation becomes something else altogether and thus moves beyond the limits of translation: 'where the translator (*if now he has not lost that name*) assumes the liberty, not only to vary from the words and sense, but to forsake them both as he sees occasion; and taking only some general hints from the original, to run division on the groundwork, as he pleases' (emphasis added). As Dryden later remarks, 'imitation of an author is the most advantageous way for a translator to show himself, but the greatest wrong which can be done to the memory and reputation of the dead'.

Imitation, then, like 'free' translation, has become a popular term for translations determined by some to lie beyond the limits of translation. Others include version, variation, adaptation, and the German *Umdichtung* ('repoeming', poetic re-creation). In general, whenever the structural or semantic correspondences between a source text and a target text are taken to be too loose to allow the result to be given the term 'translation', another term is employed to make it clear that a given work is *not* a translation: that it lies beyond the limits of translation. This ensures a certain level of definitional purity: such theorists are relieved of the awkward necessity of referring to certain 'translations' as '*not*-translations'. If for example a purist argues that translation means translating meaning, and someone offers as a counterexample Celia and Louis **Zukofsky**'s translation of Catullus [see I.a.2.i], which renders the sound of syllables rather than meanings, the purist can then respond: 'But then that is not a *translation*; it is an *imitation*, or an *adaptation*, or a *traducson*'.

Over the past two and a half centuries, however, various translation theorists have increasingly been expanding the traditional limits on the discussion of the limits of translation, especially in sociological directions. The theoretical transition this has entailed is perhaps clearest in the famous 1813 lecture by Friedrich Schleiermacher, 'Über die verschiedenen Methoden des Übersetzens' (On the Different Methods of Translating), in which he draws on the entire history of earlier terms for translating in order to declare most of them beyond the limits of *true* translation. His first dualism is between 'translation proper' (of scholarship and art) and 'interpretation' (which he redefines to mean something like object-oriented technical translation and declares beyond the pale). His second, an expansion of 'translation proper', is between Dryden's terms 'paraphrase' and 'imitation'. Schleiermacher sees the former as more common in scholarship, the latter in the fine arts, but takes both to deviate from 'translation in the stricter sense' and thus rules them beyond the limits of 'true' translation: 'they are only here to mark off the boundaries of our true investigation' (Robinson 1997: 229). His third and final dualism, then, moves from formal considerations to more sociological ones. Here he distinguishes between 'taking the author to the reader', making the foreign text easily accessible to the target reader (what modern foreignists call 'assimilative' translation), which once again Schleiermacher rules beyond the limits of true translation; and 'taking the reader to the author', inducting the reader into the difficult realm of the foreign (foreignism proper), which for Schleiermacher, as for élitist theorists for almost two millennia before him and two centuries after him, is the only true form of translation (for a critique of this dualism, see Pym 1995).

Traditional as this approach is in its broadest outlines, it is also—in pronouncements on translation from German pre-romantics such as Herder in the mid-18th c., through German romantics like the Schlegel brothers, Goethe, Schleiermacher, and Humboldt around the turn of the 19th c. (anthologized in Robinson 1997), to post-romantics like Walter Benjamin, Antoine Berman, and Lawrence Venuti in the 20th c. (Benjamin 1968; Berman 1992; Venuti 1995a)—strikingly novel. For these writers the crucial point is not what segment the translator selects for translation—the word, the phrase, the sentence—but the sociocultural tensions the target reader feels, or is intended to feel, between his or her native culture and that of the foreign text. Foreignism, the insistence upon retaining in the translation some feel of the foreign original, remains

technically a moderate form of literalism; but rhetorically, ethically, pedagogically, politically, it becomes something quite different, concerned less with protecting the sanctity of a worshipped text, as literalism often has been, and more with opening the target culture up to the transformative influence of the foreign. For the foreignists, the limits of translation are social and political: whatever inserts the foreign into the native in beneficially transformative ways is good translation; whatever gives the target culture more of the same, more of what readers are already accustomed to seeing, is bad translation, verging on no translation at all— 'turn[s] translation away from its pure aim' (Berman 1992: 5)—and thus, as for Schleiermacher, lies beyond the limits of translation.

Another project aimed at rethinking the limits of translation is that undertaken by what has been called the 'manipulation' school of translation studies (see e.g. Hermans 1985: Lefevere 1992a). Here translation is grouped together with other forms of textual manipulation or 'rewriting', such as criticizing, editing, anthologizing, writing histories in order both to explore its commonalities with those other forms and to distinguish them from them. When translating is contrasted with criticizing, for example, we approach the limits of translation as the translator is perceived as 'adding' his or her 'own words' to the original text; this, obviously, is a useful way of reframing the literal/free debate as conducted by Horace, Boethius, Erigena, and others.

As Rita Copeland has shown, many medieval translators glossed freely, added their own or other writers' comments to their translations; this was accepted in the rhetorical tradition that was first articulated for translation theory by Cicero as *conversio ut orator*, while being shunned by the grammatical tradition to which Boethius and Erigena adhered, and which Cicero called *conversio ut interpres* (Copeland 1991). This clash has traditionally been conceived in terms of segmentation, the length of the textual unit—word, phrase, sentence, text—that the translator selects for translation before moving on to the next; the manipulation school would reframe it in terms of voice, specifically of the perceived ownership of voice. The socially controlled limits of translation in this case are reached when the translator is perceived as speaking in a voice that is not the original author's, or using words that the author did not write and could not have written.

Contrasting the translator with the editor brings an entirely different perspective to the definition of the limits of translation. The editor, like the translator, is expected to provide (in the 'text') only the words of the original text; commentary is relegated to a separate portion of the text, introductory or annotational matter that is not normally considered the 'text'. The critical practice of distinguishing 'authentic' text from interpolations, corruptions, addenda, etc., is equally controversial in both editing and translating—and, perhaps, equally important. The most obvious difference between editing and translating is that the former is typically performed in the same language as the original text, the latter in a different one; hence one might say that the translator of, say, Old English texts begins to approach the limits of translation as s/he moves toward the modern era. Does one translate or edit Chaucer? By the time we get to Shakespeare, we are clearly editing—even though the modernizations often involved in that editing process are not radically different from those involved in editing/translating Chaucer, or even *Beowulf* [II.0.1].

iv. **Against Dualism** Above all, modern translation theory tends to insist that the limits of translation are never stable. They are defined pragmatically, in large-scale social and political contexts, and shift as those contexts shift. The limits of translation will be placed at different points depending on what scale one is employing, who is employing it, under what constraints, for what audience, to what purpose. In this theoretical framework it is impossible to determine the limits of translation in any stable or universal way, because those limits depend so utterly on contextual and perspectival factors like who, when, how, or why.

The pragmatically shifting location of the limits of translation as they are conceived in contemporary theory might be illustrated with a tool developed by fuzzy logicians: the *sorites* series, which moves by gradations across the grey area between bivalent poles. Let us illustrate this by taking as our source language text a Spanish sentence that contains a generally recognized limits-of-translation problem—a food that exists only in Mexico, *mole*, a chocolate-base curry—and building a *sorites* series of English translations of it, changing a single word in each sentence:

S   A mí me no gustan moles.

E1   For me, me not please moles.
E2   Me, me not please moles.
E3   Me, I not like moles.
E4   Me, I don't like moles.
E5   Me, I don't like mole.
E6   Me, I don't like mole dishes.

E7   Me, I don't like *mole* dishes.
E8   I don't like *mole* dishes.
E9   I personally don't like *mole* dishes.
E10   I personally don't like curry dishes.
E11   I personally don't like Mexican curry dishes.
E12   I personally don't like Mexican chocolate curry dishes.
E13   I personally don't like Mexican chocolate candy dishes.

In order to define or 'place' the limits of translation (the absolute borderline between 'translation' and 'non-translation') in any kind of fixed or essentializing way—the central project of traditional translation theory—we must select a single gap in the *sorites* series and draw the dividing line there: say, between E9 and E10, or perhaps between E12 and E13. E13 clearly gets *mole* wrong; *mole* has nothing to do with candy. Therefore, one might argue, E12 reaches the limits of translation; E13 and any further attempt in that direction (E13 + *n*) would lie beyond the limits of translation. The most interesting fuzzy area, in fact, is E10–12, where none of the English paraphrases is either clearly right or clearly wrong. There is at once significant overlap and significant divergence between their respective semantic fields and that of *mole* in the original. Here the limits of translation are considerably harder to draw, and hence also more interesting for a more definitionally open-minded approach to the field.

The shifting definitional territories claimed by traditional theories might also be mapped onto this series. If we are determined to mark off a limit or border between word-for-word and sense-for-sense translations, for example, we might seek to identify single translations as the 'true core' of each—say, E1 as literal and E9 as sense for sense—or, more loosely, to identify a certain *range* as literal and another as sense-for-sense, for example, E1–3 and E4–12, respectively. Or we could follow Lawrence Venuti (1995a) and distinguish between foreignizing translations (E3–7? E4–9?) and domesticating translations (E6/8/9–12?), or identify a single translation as the ideal foreignized form (E4? E5?).

What the hypothetical traditional translation theorist is doing here is chunking the problematic *sorites* series into discrete binary categories by highlighting specific steps as 'obvious' or 'natural' limits and repressing all the variations that surround them, so that it seems as if s/he has 'found'—not just invented or imposed—the organic split between binary poles. Identifying E4 as the ideal 'foreignizing' translation and E11 as the ideal 'domesticating' translation, for example, the foreignist theorist can then proceed to build an entire bivalent model for the limits of translation (and, beyond that, for the assessment of translation 'quality' within those limits—by which euphemism s / he may be pleased to mean the ways in which actual translations can be forced artificially into the terms of his or her bivalent logic, and so judged or evaluated).

The problem with this older dualizing and essentializing approach to the limits of translation is not only that the binary logic imposed on any given translation task (or, *a fortiori*, 'all translation', 'true translation', 'translation proper', 'translation in itself') is inevitably arbitrary. It is also that the *sorites* series itself, the series of numbered steps, is arbitrary as well. The shift from E6 to E7 above, which adds italics to *mole* to indicate that it is a foreign word and thus probably not the burrowing rodent, is small enough and subtle enough to remind us that there are infinite gradations between alternatives that this one-word-at-a-time method represses. Minute shifts in stress and tonalization and other prosodic features could turn this list of thirteen alternatives into hundreds, thousands, millions. Chaos theory calls these proliferating differentials 'fractals'. As the fuzzy logician Bart Kosko puts it, 'Precision up, information up. Information up, fuzz up' (Kosko 1994: 37). The closer and more carefully one looks, the fuzzier things get. The gradations between artificial poles like 'sense for sense' and 'word for word', or 'domesticating' and 'foreignizing', or even 'translation' and 'non-translation', are not only potentially but actually infinite. It is

only by refusing to look closely and by wilfully ignoring this reeling complexity—and convincing the reader to do the same—that the scholar can go on pretending to refer his or her reductive binary categories and the 'limits' between them to reality. With the conspicuous exception of the foreignist school, recent translation theorists have been less and less interested in ignoring that complexity. They are as a result increasingly willing to sacrifice definitional purity to a more chaotic, and thus also, they claim, more realistic understanding of translation as theoretically limitless and 'limited' only practically, in specific pragmatic situations and for specific pragmatic and often polemical purposes.

One of the most monumental treatises on translation to appear in the past few decades, however, George Steiner's *After Babel*, argues that there are some 'natural' or 'intrinsically human' limits to translation. Drawing on the work of Edward Sapir and Benjamin Lee Whorf, and harking back to the work of Wilhelm von Humboldt and other German romantic thinkers, Steiner explores the limits imposed on translation by the expressive traditions of different languages, and ultimately by the expressive repertoires developed by humans everywhere (G. Steiner 1975). Our inability to translate foreign ideas for which our native tongue possesses no equivalent is only a special case of our more general human inability to express the ineffable in words. If this is the case, then the translation of religious and mystical texts, and of the more vatic forms of lyric poetry, might be a place to look for more 'permanent' or stable, perhaps even universal, translation limits.

4. LINGUISTIC PERSPECTIVES ON TRANSLATION
Mona Baker

i. **Introduction** Any discussion of translation or translated literature inevitably draws on some set of assumptions concerning the way language is structured, the way this structure is manipulated to create special effects, and the processes by which language use comes to reflect and influence social attitudes and cultural values. Detailed attention to the linguistic make-up of a literary text and its translation is particularly evident in certain types of study, such as those which concern themselves with questions of gender: as Sherry Simon explains [I.a.5.iii], works by feminist authors such as Louky Bersianik directly address the role that language plays in constructing certain cultural values. But practically all scholars who have concerned themselves with the study of translation, particularly lit-

erary translation, have had to address linguistic issues at some stage, with greater or lesser degrees of sophistication.

Linguistics, the academic discipline which concerns itself with the study of language at large, has traditionally been seen to provide a set of tools which enable us to produce more, and more sophisticated, descriptions of the language of translation. In recent years, however, the value of linguistic descriptions of translation has been questioned within the emerging discipline of Translation Studies. Indeed, much of the current literature on translation assumes that there exists a clear-cut divide between two broad orientations in the study of translation: one informed by linguistics and generally referred to as 'linguistically oriented', and one largely based on a mixture of cultural studies and literary theory, generally known as the 'cultural' approach, and sometimes presented as having initiated a 'cultural turn' in the study of translation (Baker 1996a; Venuti 1996; Lefevere and Bassnett 1990). But there is a great deal more diversity and overlap in scholarly work on translation than is often acknowledged. More importantly, it would seem that the most illuminating descriptions of translated literature defy being subsumed under any labels and draw freely on a wide variety of research tools, including those of both linguistics and cultural studies.

A good example comes from recent work by Keith Harvey on translations of the camp style associated with homosexual characters in French and Anglo-American postwar fiction (Harvey 1998). Harvey, a linguist by training, offers a detailed linguistic analysis of the features of camp in both languages, including the inversion of gender-specific terms ('girl talk'), renaming, the use of empty adjectives such as *adorable*, the use of French in English dialogue, and formal expressions of ambivalent solidarity. Ambivalent solidarity (or what Quentin Crisp calls 'stylized cattiness') is expressed through alternating moves of support and attack, or feigned support accompanied by innuendoes relating, for example, to another gay man's sexual prowess. Harvey supplements this formal description by a detailed study of other factors which influence translation choices, such as the existence and visibility of gay subcultural codes and the existence or absence of an established gay literature in the target culture, negative or positive evaluations of camp within each culture, the sexual identity of the translator, and the translator's identification with a gay subcultural group. In other words, recent studies of translation incorporate in their descriptions formal linguistic analysis, analysis of the cultural setting of translation, publishing strategies, autobiographical detail, and much else.

ii. **Historical Overview: Early Approaches** Linguistics and translation have long had what Peter Fawcett (1997a) aptly calls a 'love–hate relationship'. At one time, Translation Studies was widely thought of as a branch of applied linguistics, and its status as such was rarely questioned. Today, it is increasingly being recognized as an independent discipline and there is some question as to how much it should draw on linguistics. Some writers argue that the study of translation must break away from its traditional association with linguistics and develop more culturally and historically oriented models of research. Others insist that detailed linguistic descriptions must provide the starting-point for examining any work in translation. A brief summary of the history of this troubled relationship between linguistics and Translation Studies may help us understand the reasons for the current resistance to linguistic models and perhaps place the contribution of linguistic approaches in a more realistic perspective.

During the 1950s, 1960s, and 1970s, when Translation Studies was still struggling to establish a place for itself in the academy, linguistics had already come to be recognized as a fully fledged 'scientific' discipline, and had developed an impressive range of research methods and tools of analysis. Given that language is the raw material of translation and that Translation Studies needed a role model to follow in order to establish itself in the academy, linguistics naturally became the main source of theoretical and pedagogical insights. Initially, partly because linguistics itself was less sophisticated in its approach to language at the time, linguistic studies of translation were often extremely simplistic in their approach to meaning and highly prescriptive in their pronouncements on translation. There were far fewer descriptive studies than there are now. The thrust of much linguistically oriented work was that clear guidelines had to be developed to ensure that translators had a set of ready-made, reliable solutions for linguistic difficulties. These difficulties were perceived as essentially formal in nature: lack of equivalence at word level, culture-specific items, difficult syntax, non-matching of grammatical categories such as gender, and so on. And often translation was firmly believed to be a branch of applied linguistics rather than a separate, albeit emerging, discipline in its own right. This view of the study of translation is still held by some linguistically oriented scholars such as Roger Bell (1991: p. xvi), who attempts to develop 'an intellectually satisfying and practically applicable theory of translation within a broadly defined applied linguistics'. But translation scholars associated with the linguistics paradigm today are among the most active in promoting Translation Studies as an independent discipline. The vast majority simply see linguistics as a major (but not the only) source of insights and research tools in the discipline.

Initially, then, much of what went on under the banner of linguistics in Translation Studies proceeded along the following lines: here is a source text in language A; how can it best be translated into language B given what we know about the characteristics of languages A and B? A classic example of this approach is Vinay and Darbelnet's *Stylistique comparée du français et de l'anglais: méthode de traduction* (1958). Some studies attempted to formalize in more general terms the various ways in which translators should proceed to transfer the units of a source text into another language in order to produce an accurate target text. This is typical of the work of Bible translators in general, especially Eugene Nida [see II.c.1.xi].

A third type of study is exemplified by J. C. Catford's *A Linguistic Theory of Translation* (1965). Unlike Bible translators, Catford was more interested in what *can* be done in translation, given what we know about the way language works in general. In other words, he was interested in exploring the potential that language as such offers the translator. One of the interesting types of translation he proposed was phonological translation. This is an idealized category, based on the idea that a translator might want to give absolute priority to the phonological level, so that the choice of vocabulary and syntax is dependent on the criterion of sound alone. But it can be seen to apply to a large extent in highly experimental work such as the Zukofskys' translation of Catullus (*O rem ridiculum, Cato, et iocosam*, 'O ram ridicule home, Cato, the jokes some') [see I.a.2.i]. Other examples include humorous collections such as the *Mots d'heures: gousses, rames, The d'Antin Manuscript*, and *N'heures souris rames: the Coucy Castle Manuscript*, by the pseudonymous Luis d'Antin Van Rooten. The Humpty Dumpty rhyme, for example, is rendered in *The d'Antin Manuscript* as 'Un petit d'un petit | S'étonne aux Halles | Un petit d'un petit | Ah! degrés te fallent . . .'. This suggests that exploring the potential of language as such need not be totally irrelevant, though today this line of research is not generally favoured in linguistically oriented studies. There is far more interest now in investigating actual translational behaviour.

Generally speaking, however, the literature on translation during this early period was by and large pedagogical in orientation. The approach to meaning and to what translators actually have to do was essentially simplistic and divorced from context.

iii. Historical Overview: Since 1980 During the 1980s and 1990s, a new generation of translation scholars with training in linguistics began to carry out more sophisticated descriptive studies. These focused more on exploring what actually happens in translation than on exploring what should happen or what can potentially happen. The starting-point for much of this work was the idea that meaning is diffuse, in the sense that it is not located in the word or grammatical category but is signalled by a variety of means which cross the traditional boundaries of word, phrase, clause, sentence, and even text. It is also unstable, in that it is only realized in text, and a 'dictionary' meaning may even be negated within a specific textual environment. Moreover, meaning is now understood to be culturally constructed and all language use is seen as mediated (culturally, ideologically, cognitively). Language, both generally and in translation, has come to be seen as intimately linked to the social and cultural context in which it is produced.

There are various practical implications of this current view of meaning and language. The first is that linguistics and (eventually) linguistically oriented studies of translation began to widen their scope of analysis: they gradually moved outwards from the word to the sentence, to structures above the sentence, to the text as a unit of analysis, and finally to the text as a cultural artefact embodying the values that a given culture attaches to certain practices and concepts. Second, having accepted that all language use is mediated, linguistic studies began to put more emphasis on the role of ideology in translation, both in terms of the conflict between source and target ideologies or world views and in terms of the translator's and other participants' own ideology and personal stakes in the communication. Ideology here is not understood in the political sense but rather as a 'point of view' which derives from 'the taken-for-granted assumptions, beliefs and value-systems which are shared collectively by social groups' (Simpson 1993: 5). Language is assumed to 'of necessity *reflect* . . . and . . . *construct* ideology' (p. 6).

In recent years, a number of linguistically oriented studies have foregrounded the issue of ideology in translation. For example, Williams (1992: 75) has argued that 'considerations of ideology and point of view are of relevance to the translator—not to mention the literary critic and even perhaps the writer'. His position is compatible in some respects with recent calls for privileging 'weaker' cultures in translation. He argues against carrying over certain English generic formats and stylistic features in Arabic translation because this practice is 'not totally beneficial to the continuing individuality of the various Arabic cultures' (p. 91). In particular, the use of the passive to report scientific experiments, which implies the validity of the experiment regardless of the experimenter, clashes with 'the established high visibility of the writer and the reader in Arabic written texts'.

Ian Mason (1994) analyses a text and its translation which appeared in a bilingual format in the

UNESCO Courier (Tiene la Historia un Destino?/ History or Destiny?). He demonstrates that the source and target texts express two very different world views and ideologies. The source text concedes that the Spanish conquistadors were the official chroniclers of Mexican history, but states that there were also indigenous voices that remain under-represented; these voices have preserved the 'memory' of the peoples of Mexico. The discourse is one of a nation striving to forge its own destiny by actively searching for its past and recording it. In the target text, the role of memory is downplayed and 'the active search for the past and the task of recording it turn into a passive "view" of the past and a "desire" to interpret it' (Mason 1994: 29).

This study is typical of linguistically informed research in two respects. First, although the focus is very much on ideology, Mason suggests that 'there is no need to attribute the divergent discourse of the target text to any deliberate intention of the translator' because mediation 'may largely be an unconscious process' (p. 33). In other words, unlike some of the work done on translation from a cultural studies perspective (e.g. Niranjana 1992), there is no attempt here to promote a view of deliberate, conscious manipulation on the part of the translator. A similar view of ideology is expressed in a study by Peter Fawcett of Stuart Gilbert's translation of André Malraux's *La Voie royale*, where he explicitly refers to racist elements in the translation. In his conclusion, however, he states that he 'should have been saying not that Gilbert was a racist, but that he was living and writing in times when the pressure of the dominant discourse made such language almost inescapable, since it was part of the wallpaper, so to speak' (Fawcett 1997b: 264).

Second, the linguistic analysis offered to support the statement that there is an ideological mismatch between source and target texts in Mason's study is far more detailed and more varied than the analysis we find in the work of scholars associated with the cultural paradigm. Mason supports his claims with analyses at a variety of levels. Lexically, he points out many differences in the choice of vocabulary (*sabios* becomes 'diviners', *testimonios* becomes 'written records', and so on). He also analyses the divergent structures of the two texts in some detail, particularly with reference to the flow of information or the linear arrangement of elements in a clause. In this kind of analysis, the clause is treated as a message rather than as a string of grammatical and lexical items. As a message, it consists of two elements: the *theme*, what the clause is about, comes first and provides a point of orientation. The *rheme* is what the speaker or writer says

about the theme, and provides new information. Mason shows how the source text places 'effort'/ 'memory'/'destiny' in theme position, providing a point of orientation at the beginning of sentences. The target text, by contrast, puts humans in theme position and places in rheme position (where new information is usually placed) verbs that do not portray these humans in a proactive role: for example 'met with mixed fortunes', 'succeeded one another'. Cumulatively, the effect is one of portraying a view of destiny as passive observation rather than personal commitment.

Such detailed analyses at a variety of levels are noticeably different from the discussions found in works such as Venuti (1995a) or Venuti (1996). Apart from analysing poetic devices such as metre, rhyme, alliteration, and so on, Venuti draws on categories which a linguistically oriented researcher would consider too broad and too restricted to the traditional levels of vocabulary and syntax: archaisms, dialect, regional choice, syntactic inversions. A linguistically oriented scholar would typically want to provide analyses which offer finer distinctions at the levels of lexis and syntax and which also incorporate other levels of description, such as information flow, cohesion, linguistic mechanisms of expressing politeness, norms of turn-taking in conversation, and so on.

The 1990s, then, have witnessed a growing interest in the role of ideology and power-play in shaping translational behaviour, with most studies adopting a descriptive, theoretical approach to the data. This contrasts with the earlier simplistic treatment of culture as a question of cultural artefacts, for instance in much of the work by Peter Newmark and Eugene Nida, and essentially as a problem that had to be solved at the applied level. It also means that the emphasis on the translator's obligation to be totally neutral, which was traditionally taken for granted as part of a strict code of ethics that governed all translation work, has now begun to give way to a realistic view of translators and interpreters as real personae in any communicative act. Descriptive studies in sensitive areas such as face-to-face interpreting in particular have shown quite clearly that interpreters are not totally neutral, even when they believe they should be. These studies are largely informed by research in sociolinguistics and the ethnography of speaking, in particular the work of Erving Goffman and Dell Hymes (see e.g. Wadensjö 1992; Berk-Seligson 1988; 1990; Roy 1993).

One area that throws doubt on assumptions of a clear-cut divide between linguistically and culturally oriented studies is signed language interpreting and translation. Scholars working in this field have always, and by necessity, had to draw very heavily on linguistics *and* to consider questions of culture and ideology. The deaf community has suffered as a minority from marginalization worldwide, and part of its struggle to affirm its identity has involved demonstrating that signed languages do not consist of arbitrary gestures but are languages in the full sense of the word. For example, a bid was recently made to secure recognition of British Sign Language as one of the many source languages for which funding might be sought from the Translation Committee of the Arts Council of England: this is the committee that allocates subsidies to allow publishers to bring out in English translation literary works which would not otherwise be commercially viable. The argument was essentially for the right of the deaf community in Britain to be recognized as a distinct cultural group by the institutions of the dominant, hearing culture. Winning this argument would secure access to public funds in order to support translations of signed language poetry into English. But this argument had to be fought on linguistic grounds. The Committee required proof that BSL *is* a language before it would officially recognize it as a source language for translation. Thus we see that issues of language are inextricably linked with issues of culture and of ideology in this type of translation. There is no question here of choosing between approaches, of prioritizing a specific approach, indeed not even of positing a distinction between approaches to start with. The kind of close attention to linguistic detail that we find in the work of writers such as Mason becomes a prerequisite to any successful promotion of a cultural agenda.

iv. The Use of Corpora in Studying Translation

Another area of research which emerged in the 1990s involves using computerized corpora to study the language of translation as such. This work is informed by a specific area of linguistics known as corpus linguistics. Corpus linguistics relies on the large-scale analysis of a very large body of authentic running text to capture regularities in language use. The texts are held in machine-readable form and are thus amenable to automatic or semi-automatic analysis. Within linguistics, this methodology has revolutionized lexicographic practices and methods of language teaching. In spite of its initial focus on regularities, it is highly relevant to the study of literary texts in general, and hence of literary translation. John Sinclair, one of the leading scholars in corpus linguistics, explains that the initial focus on repeated events 'does not mean that

unique, one-off events are necessarily ignored, but rather that they cannot be evaluated in the absence of an interpretative framework provided by the repeated events' (Sinclair 1996: 81). The creativity we associate with literary texts in particular can only be explained against the backdrop of typical language patterning.

Here is an example. Bill Louw (1993) describes a phenomenon of linguistic patterning now known as 'semantic prosody'. A semantic prosody is a consistent aura of meaning which a lexical item acquires through its repeated association with other items in the language; it often expresses attitudinal meaning. Louw uses this notion to explain a feature in the poem 'Days' by Philip Larkin, which starts 'What are days for? | Days are where we live'. 'Days are where we live' should communicate happy associations, and yet it is 'a line which leaves the reader with inexplicable feelings of melancholia', and foreshadows the theme of death which emerges in the second half of the poem (p. 162). By looking at the occurrences of *days* in a corpus of 37 million words, Louw is able to demonstrate that *days* has a very strong association with items such as *gone, over*, and *good*. Our experience of the language, our regular exposure to this type of patterning, makes us subliminally associate *days* not with where we are now but with where we were, where we *have lived* and where we perhaps are unable to return.

A number of translation scholars are currently engaged in building a corpus of translational English, with a view to identifying features which distinguish the language of translation from that of ordinary language users (Baker 1996b; Laviosa 1997). It has been argued (Baker 1996b) that translation is subject to a set of constraints which inevitably leave traces in the language that translators produce: the fact that a translated text is constrained by a fully articulated text in another language, for instance, would seem to be a major and unique constraint. Moreover, a variety of claims have been made about the language of translation in recent years. These claims need to be tested by analysing a large body of translated texts, including fiction, a category which is well represented in the Translational English Corpus (Laviosa 1997). For example, Anthony Pym suggests in this volume [I.b.5.iv] that 'translations into English have tended to be in a language that is less specific, more international, than most works originally written in English'. Researchers engaged in corpus-based analysis of translated text want to examine claims of this type closely: they want to identify the actual features which make the language of translation less specific.

The idea that the language of translation is distinct from ordinary language has been debated in the literature for some time. With the exception of corpus-based work, however, no attempt has been made to investigate this issue on a large scale. One of the earliest references to this issue can be found in Frawley (1984). William Frawley suggested that the confrontation of source text and target language during the process of translation results in creating what he called a 'third code'. In other words, the code (or language) that evolves during translation and in which the target text is expressed is unique. It is a kind of compromise between the norms or patterns of the source language and those of the target language. A concrete example of this phenomenon can be found in Bernard **Dulsey**'s English translation of an Ecuadorian novel (*Huasipungo*) by Jorge Icaza. The word *pes*, which is a derivative of the Spanish *pues*, is borrowed directly in the translation. *Pes* means something like *well* or *then* and can simply be used as a filler. The pattern of borrowing in this particular translation illustrates how the third code works in practice. In addition to the positions in which it would normally occur in the Ecuadorian dialect, *pes* also occurs in the English translation in positions where it would not occur in its original code. So we have two patterns. The first is straight borrowing, as in 'Dónde estáis, *pes*?' | 'Where are you, *pes*?'. Here *pes* occurs at the end of the clause, where it would normally occur in the Ecuadorian dialect and where *pues* would occur in Spanish. The second pattern, which occurs in the same translation, follows the norms of *Well* in English, as in 'Dos o tres veces he sido capataz, *pes*' | '*Pes*, I have been a foreman a few times'. In effect, this second patterning tries to accommodate the lexis of the source text and the syntax of the target language. In both cases we end up with a 'third code' in Frawley's terms: a pattern where either the borrowed word would not occur in its original environment or the equivalent of the borrowed word would not occur in the target environment.

The notion of the third code provides a useful starting-point for explaining some of the concerns of translation scholars who are attempting to apply the techniques of corpus linguistics to investigating the language of translation. It is useful because Frawley approaches what he sees as different in the language of translation from a descriptive and theoretically sophisticated angle. There is no question here of talking about 'translationese', with all the pejorative connotations of this term. Translation results in the creation of a third code because it is a unique form of communication, not because it is a faulty, deviant or sub-standard form of communication.

Scholars working in the area of corpus-based studies are interested in investigating the notion of the third code more closely. First, they stress that the co-presence of codes is not the only constraint that operates in translation: other constraints exist and contribute to the distinctive patterning of translated text. Moreover, the nature of this co-presence of codes itself needs to be clarified. This is because the mere presence of two codes in the same event is not sufficient to distinguish translation from things like the speech and writing of second language learners, where it is also recognized that the learner or speaker is consciously operating with two codes. Second, scholars working in this area also wish to develop a methodology for investigating the distinctiveness of translational language. Having access to a vast amount of translated text in machine-readable form, and a suite of software tools to process it with, is only a starting-point. One has to develop a method for approaching the data: knowing what to look for and how to look for it. And third, scholars ultimately want to be able to provide a detailed description of the language of translation and to offer some hypotheses about the motivation behind certain types of patterning.

For example, let us assume that we do find, as is often claimed, that there is a tendency towards normalization in translated English. That is, translators into English tend to be more conservative in their use of language, drawing heavily on core patterns of English and largely avoiding highly marked patterns. There is in fact some evidence for this tendency in the Translational English Corpus, but the corpus is currently too small to substantiate strong claims: it is approximately five million words, which is very small by the standards of corpus linguistics. But one interesting feature is that there is a striking homogeneity among the translated texts compared to texts originally written in English, in the same domain. That is, whatever area of patterning we look at, the translated texts seem to behave more like each other, while the original texts are more individual in their make-up.

One possible explanation for this phenomenon, if it were to prove widely representative of translated text, is that translators subconsciously respond to what they perceive to be the textual and social status of translation. They know that translations are not received in the same way as original texts. Readers and reviewers have different expectations concerning what constitutes a good translation and what constitutes a good original work of literature. The reception of *Ulysses* would almost certainly have been different if it had been presented to the literary community as a translation from another language. Subconsciously, then, translators may monitor their linguistic output in order to conform to the expectations of readers and reviewers. So they end up drawing on the 'safer', more typical patterns of the language.

Pym [I.b.5.iv] offers another possible motivation for the kind of patterning we are beginning to identify even in translated English fiction. Translations into English have tended to use a less specific, more international form of the language because of the status of English on the world market and because 'translators and publishers set about to address many regions at once'. This might explain certain types of patterning that have been observed in the Translational English Corpus. For instance, the most frequent words in English are significantly more frequent in translational English, and this applies to both newspaper texts and translated novels and short stories. Also, both type / token ratio and lexical density are consistently lower in translational English. Type / token ratio is a measure of the variety of vocabulary used in a text or corpus: the higher the ratio the more varied the vocabulary used, the lower it is the more restricted a text or corpus in terms of the number of different words that occur in it. Lexical density is a measure of the redundancy built into a text: it concerns the ratio of lexical or content words vs. grammatical items. The higher the ratio of lexical items such as 'love'

or 'peace' and the lower the ratio of grammatical items such as 'the' and 'in', the more dense the text. Conversely, the higher the ratio of grammatical items the more redundancy is built in and the easier it is to process a text.

This may all sound too technical for the non-linguistically trained reader interested in understanding how the language of translation functions and how it differs from ordinary language. As in all specialized fields, the analysis is inevitably too focused on very specific phenomena, and draws on specialized terminology. In due course, the results of such analyses can be expressed in less technical language for the layperson. In the first instance, however, linguistically oriented scholars would argue that the analyses themselves have to be undertaken in order to support or refute the claims made about translational language from a more informed position.

Linguistically oriented work thus continues to demonstrate the relevance of linguistic insights to the study of translation. It has gained considerably in sophistication in recent years, by widening its scope of analysis and by increasingly paying attention to cultural and human factors. More importantly, recent studies of translated literature in particular (e.g. Harvey 1998) explicitly draw their insights from a wide range of sources: from cultural studies to formal logic and from literary theory to functional linguistics. This suggests that the time has perhaps come to abandon some of our unproductive assumptions about clear-cut divisions in the discipline.

5. GENDER IN TRANSLATION
Sherry Simon

Contemporary feminist theory has stimulated interest in issues which are vital to the understanding of translation practices. It is hardly a coincidence that the period (1970s and 1980s) which saw the development of feminist and then gender studies also witnessed a remarkable growth in translation studies. The entry of gender into translation theory owes much to the increased importance given within a wide range of disciplines to subjectivity and ideology in language.

There are at least four important, but quite different, areas of concern through which gender issues have become relevant to translation studies: (1) investigation of the historical and contemporary role of women as translators; (2) critique of the language traditionally used to describe translation and especially the metaphorics of translation which

feminize the translator in relation to the author; (3) analysis of the particular technical difficulties and ideological questions involved in translating gendered language; (4) promotion of *feminist translation* as a set of principles guiding translation practice.

Translation and feminist studies have several common concerns, in particular the distrust of hierarchical, gendered roles, and the deep suspicion of rules defining fidelity (who decides what being faithful means?). Both feminism and translation studies question the way 'secondariness' comes to be defined and canonized as 'inferiority' (why is the translation almost always 'inferior' to the original?). Translation studies also explore critically the ways in which gender differences are expressed in language and transferred from one language to another.

i. The 'Translatress' Despite its historical status as a weak and degraded version of authorship, translation has at times emerged as a strong form of expression for women—permitting them access to the world of letters, allowing them to contribute to the intellectual and political life of their times and to engage in stimulating writing relationships. Translation was a particularly important writing activity for women during the Middle Ages and the Renaissance, when they were otherwise excluded from public writing careers. During this long period, translation was one of the few writing activities that were socially approved for women. Of the five women whose names we know who wrote in Middle English [see I.b.1]—Julian of Norwich, Margery Kempe, Juliana Berners, Eleanor Hull, and Margaret Beaufort—three were principally known as translators (Barratt 1992: 13).

We must recall that to publish or to appear in print was considered aggressive behaviour for females during this period in European culture. Authorship was seen as a distinctly male activity and the female writer, exposing herself to the public eye, was vulnerable to accusations of presumption (Krontiris 1992: 17–18). Translation offered an opportunity for women to become involved in literary culture in a way that did not openly challenge social or literary power arrangements. Women could become involved in the production and circulation of texts without being perceived to have overstepped the bounds of propriety.

Paradoxically, religion (which reinforced the subservience of women) emerges as an area through which some women were able to contribute to the cultural activities of their age (Krontiris 1992: 10). In England, for example, during the Reformation, women were strongly discouraged from writing, but they were encouraged to translate religious texts. And so the great majority of existing texts and translations by English women of the period are on religious subjects.

Even the learned women at the very centre of cultural life of England published only translations: this is notably the case for the revered patroness of letters, Mary **Sidney**, Countess of Pembroke (c.1555–1621), sister of Philip Sidney. It is evident that Mary Sidney's translation work was very much involved with the cultural and political conflicts of her age, though the very fact that she confined herself to translation was perceived favourably. The example of Mary Sidney was used as a weapon to silence her goddaughter, Mary Wroth, who had the ambition of being a writer and publishing the first known full-length work of fiction by a woman. Wroth was admonished to imitate her 'vertuous

and learned Aunt, who translated so many godly books' rather than create 'lascivious tales and amorous toyes' (Hannay 1990: 208–9). Translation, not creation, was the province of a learned woman.

Margaret **Tyler** is an exceptional figure of this period. She is best known for her translation of a Spanish romance entitled *A Mirrour of Princely Deeds and Knighthood* (1578) by Diego Ortúñez de Calahorra. Tyler's work seems to have introduced this genre into England; its immense influence created the fashion for Spanish romances of chivalry in England, and it was followed by many similar works in English. But it is the vigorous preface which accompanies this translation which especially defines Tyler's importance for our topic. She defended the right of women to read and translate works which are not restricted to the area of 'divinitie', and in particular to take on the daring deeds of chivalry and romance. She also encouraged women to take up the pen. This preface has been compared to a feminist manifesto and called a 'landmark in feminist literary history' on account of its being 'both the boldest criticism of patriarchal ideology by a woman writer up to that time and one of the very few female-authored documents before the eighteenth century to deal with the problems of the literary woman whose imaginative voice is inhibited by patriarchal divisions of genre and gender' (Krontiris 1992: 45).

During the Renaissance, then, in England as well as in the rest of Europe, translation had capital importance for women, as it was one of the only modes of intellectual activity which allowed them to escape the interdiction against public expression. While some commentators assume that this work had little impact, lamenting the fact that women were 'only translators', others have seen in translation a real contribution to the spiritual life of the times and a site from which dominant norms could be challenged and resisted. A comprehensive understanding of women's writing activities during this period will only be possible when the work initiated by literary historians like Hannay and Krontiris is pursued in greater depth.

Aphra **Behn**, Germaine de Staël, Margaret **Fuller**, Eleanor **Marx-Aveling**, Lady **Gregory**, Constance **Garnett**, Jean Starr **Untermeyer**, Willa **Muir**, and Helen **Lowe-Porter** are just a few of the women translators who, beginning particularly in the 18th c., played prominent social and political roles through their activities of literary mediation. The fact that all these women combined their interest in translation with progressive social causes is more than coincidental; they understood that the transmission of significant literary texts was an essential, not an accessory, cultural task. The translation of key texts is an important aspect of any movement of ideas. This is evident for first-wave feminism and for the causes to which it was allied, especially the anti-slavery movement in the 18th and 19th c.

Aphra Behn (1640–89) is the best known and most prolific of early women writers; she was the first professional woman writer (Spender 1992: 39) and in her own time a celebrated woman of letters [see I.b.3.iii]. That she was an active translator is not entirely surprising, as translation was recognized as a primary creative activity for Restoration writers. Perhaps the most surprising element of Aphra Behn's translations was that she translated from Latin (though possibly indirectly, from pre-existing cribs) as well as from French. This was highly unusual, for women of Behn's time were rarely taught the classical languages—if they were taught to read at all. That Aphra Behn translated Ovid's *Epistle of Oenone to Paris* is therefore of unusual significance. And that the poem was chosen by Dryden, or the publisher Jacob Tonson, for inclusion in *Ovid's Epistles, Translated by Several Hands* (1680) was a clear indication of the prestige of this work [see II.b.5.ii].

Perhaps the two most important works Behn translated are by the moralist La Rochefoucauld and the philosopher Fontenelle. Her rendering of 400 maxims by La Rochefoucauld, entitled *Seneca Unmasqued; or, Moral Reflections* was appended to the *Miscellany* of 1685. Particularly noteworthy as a contribution to reflection on translation in the 18th c. is Behn's preface to her translation of Fontenelle's *A Discovery of New Worlds* (1688), in which she explores some of the general structural and rhetorical problems of equivalence between English and French. Some of her comments are inaccurate, but they point to her interest in a scholarly grounding for translation.

Cultural historians have yet to bring to light the full networks of writers and translators who ensured the transmission of feminist and other emancipatory texts across national frontiers during the 18th and 19th c. Various international organizations of anti-slavery associations existed, and translation was considered a task important to them (Kadish and Massardier-Kenney 1994: 37). Other elements of the traffic in political writings beginning in the late 18th c. centre on Mary **Wollstonecraft** (1759–97). She herself translated a book by Jacques Necker, *On the Importance of Religious Opinions* (1788), as well as Madame de Cambon's *Young Grandison* (1790). Wollstonecraft's own *Vindication of the Rights of Women* (1792) was of course widely

translated (the 1832 translation into German by Henriette Herz helped pave the way for the women's movement in Germany).

As influential cultural mediators of the 19th c., Madame de Staël, Margaret Fuller, and Eleanor Marx-Aveling used translation in the service of explicitly political causes. Madame de Staël (1766–1817) did not herself publish translations (although she translated extensively within her own work), but her fiction and theoretical writings initiated a new translational sensibility in European letters. As a militant cosmopolitan, de Staël forced her audience to become aware of the interdependence of national traditions. She articulated the interconnections between literature and society across national boundaries, insisting on exchange as a decisive element of creativity and intellectual vigour.

Resemblances between the career of Madame de Staël and that of Margaret Fuller are not hard to find. Margaret Fuller (1810–50) was known during her lifetime as the 'Yankee Corinna' (Durning 1969: 19), in reference to the heroine of de Staël's novel about Italy, as well as to Fuller's support for internationalist libertarian causes. She consciously patterned her life after that of Madame de Staël, setting up a 'Conversation' group in Boston which was to be a replica of de Staël's salon. And Fuller's activities as a promoter of literary cosmopolitism, her support of Italian nationalism, and her devotion to German literature make her an exemplary follower of de Staël.

Eleanor Marx-Aveling (1855–98) is not best known as a literary figure. The daughter of Karl Marx [II.h.8], she is most widely known as a social activist; but she was in fact heavily involved in the world of letters, and did a substantial amount of translation work, from French and from Norwegian—which she learnt in order to read and translate Ibsen (Kapp 1972: 99). Her most influential translation was Flaubert's *Madame Bovary*; her somewhat literal translation was for a long time used as the standard version. Marx's main motivation in translating the work was to challenge conventional standards of morality. Her translations were politically motivated, as were those of Lady Augusta Gregory (1852–1932), who was a central figure associated with the Gaelic Revival and Irish Literary Theatre (later the Abbey) in the early 20th c. She was a poet and prolific playwright. Her translations from Irish into Kiltartan Anglo-Irish dialect were aimed at transferring into English the power and energy of Irish folklore (Kohfeldt 1985).

The one translator's name that many readers during the first part of the 20th c. would have been likely to know is that of Constance Garnett (1862–1946), translator of some 60 volumes of writing by Russia's most notable modern writers [see II.p.3–6]. It has become a cliché to observe that the English-speaking world has, in reading Turgenev, Tolstoy, Dostoevsky, and Chekhov, been listening principally to the voice of Constance Garnett. The breadth and impact of Garnett's translation work, and her personal celebrity as a translator, makes her an extraordinary figure in 20th-c. literature. Part of her success lay in the extraordinary appeal of the newly discovered Russian writers for the English-speaking public, but the sheer number of her translations was also a crucial factor.

Few translators have left chronicles of their experiences as translators. The account which Jean Starr Untermeyer provides of her translating relationship with Hermann Broch is, for this reason in particular, of exceptional interest. Her memoirs, *Private Collection* (1965), provide a remarkable perspective on the dynamics of her work with the exiled author Hermann Broch, a relationship whose tensions were exacerbated by the historical moment (the years of the Second World War), by the immensity of the task (a huge modernist tome, *The Death of Virgil*, constantly rewritten and revised), and by the personalities of the protagonists. Untermeyer began working on the translation in 1940, before the German work was published. The moments of intimacy and frustration which developed between author and translator were not extraneous to the translation process but seemed rather to be a necessary component of it. Untermeyer received the highest praise for her translation.

Willa Muir was an early feminist, first by temperament and then by political conviction. *Women: An Inquiry* was published by the Hogarth Press in 1925. As translators, Willa and her husband, the poet Edwin Muir, are best known for their English versions of six books by Franz Kafka [II.h.11.iv]. The Muirs translated *The Sleepwalkers*, by Hermann Broch, and Willa herself another novel of Broch's, *The Unknown Quantity*.

The long literary relationship between Thomas Mann [II.h.11.v] and his translator, Helen Tracy Lowe-Porter, is chronicled in John Thirlwall's *In Another Language* (1966). Cut off totally from his German reading public during the war, Mann was dependent upon his American readers not only for critical esteem but also for his revenue. The pressure he put on his translator was evident: she could make or break the reception of Mann's writing. Despite this tension, relations between Mann and Lowe-Porter remained largely courteous and friendly, and took the form of a voluminous correspondence.

A more contemporary account of a translating relationship is that of Suzanne Jill **Levine**'s 'closelaborations' with Guillermo Cabrera Infante over his novel *Tres tristes tigres* (1967, Three Trapped Tigers). The wealth of Levine's examples of her work of 'transcreation', the extent of the literary knowledge and imagination which inform her practice, the strong sense of the cultural inequalities which feed translation, these define a superbly self-conscious (and self-confident) practice of translation.

Beyond their anecdotal interest, and their value as chronicles of the translation process, these accounts show in what ways gender difference acts—in sometimes productive, sometimes negative ways—on the activity of language transfer. They also show that the activities of translators, women or men, can never be understood in isolation, but must always be examined in relation to a social, political, intellectual, or aesthetic framework. Like other acts of writing and communication, translation belongs to a world of roles, values, and ideas; it is in itself an intensely *relational* act, one which establishes new connections between text and culture, author and reader.

ii. The Metaphorics of Translation: The Career of 'Les Belles Infidèles'

Because they are necessarily 'defective', all translations are 'reputed females'. With this analogy, John **Florio**, in the 1603 preface to his translation of Montaigne [II.g.5.ii], summarizes the tradition of double inferiority which has relegated both translators and women to the lower rungs in their respective hierarchies. Translators are handmaidens to authors, women inferior to men. This historical association finds contemporary resonance in the recognition that the translator still occupies a '(culturally speaking) female position' (Jouve 1991: 47), but one which today is being reinterpreted and radically challenged.

Whether affirmed or denounced, the femininity of translation is a historical trope which runs through centuries of Western culture. The authority of the original over the reproduction is linked with imagery of masculine and feminine; the original is considered the strong generative male, the translation the weaker and derivative female. We are not surprised to learn that the language used to describe translating draws liberally from the vocabulary of sexism, drawing on images of dominance and inferiority, fidelity and libertinage.

John Florio's reference to translations as 'female' has spawned a rich progeny. In numerous prefaces and critical texts, including work as recent as George Steiner's *After Babel* (1975), the relation between author and translator, original and translation, is frequently sexualized. Lori Chamberlain suggests that the use of hierarchical terms in metaphor aims to smooth over the conflictual relationship between original and translation and resolve anxiety over ownership of meaning disturbed by the bastardized products of interlinguistic transfer (Chamberlain 1992: 66).

The extraordinarily long career of the term 'les belles infidèles' is a particularly pertinent example. Introduced by the French critic Gilles Ménage (1613–92), the adage declares that, like women, translations must be either beautiful or faithful. Its success is due in some measure to the way it positions fidelity as the opposite of beauty, ethics as the opposite of elegance, the drudgery of moral obligation as incompatible with stylistic (or marital) felicity. It is certainly not fortuitous that the expression was coined at a time when translations were considered as the principal means by which French was to be legitimated as a national language. The strategy used by Nicolas Perrot d'Ablancourt and his school of translators in their 'belles infidèles' was in fact a blatant policy of infidelity. He and his fellow-translators, many of them members of the Académie Française, sought to enhance the prestige of French literature by providing translations of the Ancients, yet they wished at the same time to consolidate the norms of elegance of a nascent prose style (Zuber 1995).

The conflict between beauty and fidelity, between letter and spirit, reaches far back into the memory of western culture. The terms which we use to divide production from reproduction include some of the most fundamental concepts of our philosophical vocabulary. Derrida has shown how these recurrent oppositions stem from a complicity between gender conceptions and writing, mimesis and fidelity (Graham 1985). The conventional view of translation supposes an active original and a passive translation, creation followed by a passive act of transmission. But what if writing and translation are understood as interdependent, each bound to the other in the recognition that representation is always an active process, that the original is also at a distance from its originating intention, that there is never a total presence of the speaking subject in discourse? This reconceptualization of translation makes the familiar gendered and hierarchical language inappropriate and unproductive for understanding translation.

Feminist translation thus reopens the dilemma of fidelity, asking in new ways a question which runs throughout the history of translation in the western world. To whom and to what is the translation to declare its fidelity? Participating in a sensibility which is suspicious of any foundational truths, which sees both the 'meaning' of the original and the 'message' intended for the reader as uncertain, as being constantly subject to interpretation and distortion, feminist translation understands fidelity as a movement synchronous with the writing project—a project in which both writer and translator participate.

iii. Challenging Grammatical Gender Feminist critique of language began with a campaign against sexist terms. Over the years, however, the critique of sexism in language has moved from a largely corrective and action-orientated attention to vocabulary (seen in the work of Louky Bersianik or Mary Daly) to a broader examination of the symbolic power of the feminine in language. Attention has shifted from critical analysis of a single linguistic code to the conceptual terms regulating the intervention of individual and collective subjects within speech and writing.

The term 'gender' is derived from a term meaning 'class' or 'kind', which referred to the division of Greek nouns into masculine, feminine, and neuter. Grammatical gender means that nouns are placed in classes not according to their meaning but according to their form. This form determines the way the word will behave grammatically when it comes to the agreement of adjectives, articles, and pronouns. These are formal properties and have nothing to do with meaning. Latin and Greek had three genders (as does modern German); there are also languages with two (French) and languages which have a much larger set (Bantu languages). English has 'natural' gender rather than grammatical gender. This means that gender is attributed not by form but by meaning.

Gender is not normally considered a 'significant' element of language for translation. Because grammatical categories belong to the structural obligations of a language, they are, like the other elements which constitute the mechanics of a language, meaningless. Roman Jakobson shows, however, that grammatical gender can be invested with meaning in certain cases, as when language is turned away from its instrumental or communicative functions and used in poetry and mythology. Grammatical gender then takes on symbolic meaning, as when the poet wishes to emphasize the mythological origins and gendered identities of the terms for the days of the week, the terms for night and day, or sin and death (Jakobson, in Brower 1959).

That gender differences in language exercise a powerful imaginary role, even in English which has only 'natural' and not 'grammatical' gender, is clear in the 'thought experiment' reported by Deborah Cameron, in which participants, presented with pairs of words like *knife/fork, Ford/Chevrolet, salt/pepper, vanilla/chocolate* agreed to identify one element as masculine, the other feminine. There was in fact a wide consensus among participants in giving masculine gender to the first item of any pair, feminine to the second. This phenomenon is called 'metaphorical gender' (Cameron 1992: 82). The experiment shows how pervasive is the gendering of the relationship between strong/weak, active/passive.

These considerations emphasize that, despite the absence of a strict version of grammatical gender, gender distinctions continue to operate massively through the English language. Indeed, they mark the work of grammarians who present the masculine as a 'unmarked' form, the simple form of the word, a form which can be used generically, and with relative neutrality of meaning. And examples from common usage show that even when an English pronoun is theoretically neutral, it can carry an implicit gender charge. Formulations like 'members of Parliament and their wives', or 'the Greenlanders often swap wives' (Scott 1984: 13) show that the apparent gender neutrality of English is constantly belied by the identification of the species (mankind) with the male.

In these cases, grammatical gender must be taken into consideration for translation. While grammarians have insisted on gender marking in language as purely conventional, feminist theoreticians follow Jakobson in re-investing gender markers with meaning. The meaning which they wish to make manifest is both poetic and, especially, ideological. They wish to show in what ways gender differences serve as the unquestioned foundations of our cultural life.

These considerations form the basis for Howard **Scott**'s feminist translation of the novel *L'Eugélionne* (1976) by Louky Bersianik (Scott 1984). A major part of the book deals with how language, in this case the French language, plays a role in the oppression of women. Two aspects of language are especially emphasized: naming strategies and grammatical gender-marking. Both involve dilemmas for translation, because they use language-specific devices to foreground these grammatical features of French-language usage. Scott explains that his role as a translator of the book was not to provide an erudite *explanation* of sexism in the French language for the English-speaking reader, but to provide an equivalent political message. How is this to be done? The grammatical conse-

quence of accepting the masculine as the norm is the humiliating fact that the verb which agreed with a phrase such as 'Three hundred women and one (male) cat' would have to be in the masculine ('Trois cents femmes et un chat sont *allés . . .*'), according to the rule that any masculine element in a noun phrase (however minimal!) will dictate the grammatical agreement of the predicate. While the French women in Bersianik's novel picket the Académie Française asking for a change to put an end to the humiliating and illogical superiority of the masculine, Scott's English-speaking picketers address themselves to the 'Guardians of Grammar', and ask why it is logical to say 'Everyone please take off his boots', when there are 300 woman and one man in the room. They propose that permission be granted for the use of the indefinite 'their', even for use in the singular. This would allow the request to be rephrased as 'Everyone please take off their boots'. Would this not be a more just and logical formulation? They ask further, 'Why does a MASTER wield authority, while a MISTRESS waits patiently for her lover and master to come to her?', 'Why are CHEFS male, while most of the COOKS on this planet are women?', and so on. Howard Scott shows, then, that the persistence of 'natural' gender in English makes many of Bersianik's critiques equally pertinent in that language.

Scott's emphasis on the persistence of gender-marking in English is echoed by Susanne **de Lotbinière-Harwood**'s insistence that 'We need to *resex* language' (de Lotbinière-Harwood 1991: 117). French texts by Bersianik and Michèle Causse have given de Lotbinière-Harwood the opportunity to develop a translation practice which 'aims to make the feminine visible in language so that women are seen and heard in the world' and thus give the lie to the apparent neutrality of English. English, too, is a ' "he/man" language, that is, it too uses the masculine pronoun "he" and generic "man" as universal signifiers'. When Louky Bersianik asks 'Quel est le féminin de garçon? C'est garce!' ('What is the feminine of boy? It's slut!', *garce* not really being the feminine form of *garçon* but a derogatory term meaning 'slut' or 'whore'), de Lotbinière-Harwood translates: 'What's the feminine of dog? It's bitch'.

And in her translations of Nicole Brossard's *Le Désert mauve* (1987, Mauve Desert), de Lotbinière-Harwood seeks out every expression of gender-marking, spelling 'author' as 'auther', as a way of rendering the feminized *auteure* pioneered and widely used by Quebec feminists; and rendering the *amante*, lesbian lover, by 'shelove' (Simon 1995: 123).

iv. Feminist Translation? Where the feminist project of translation finds its most felicitous applications is in regard to texts which themselves constitute innovative writing practices. This is the case particularly of the language-centred texts of French feminist writers like Hélène Cixous, and of Nicole Brossard, France Théoret, Madeleine Gagnon, and Louky Bersianik in Quebec [see II.g.16.i].

Luise von Flotow's useful discussion of feminist translation emphasizes the fact that the cultural and social context of feminism has had much to do with the vigour and boldness of translation by women in Quebec and English Canada. Von Flotow names and describes three practices of feminist translation: supplementing, prefacing and footnoting, and 'hijacking' (von Flotow 1991). 'Hijacking' touches on the more controversial and problematic aspects of feminist translation. Von Flotow refers to the appropriation of a text whose intentions are not necessarily feminist by the feminist translator. Her example is the feminizing translation of Lise Gauvin's *Lettres d'une autre* (1987, Letters from Another) by Susanne de Lotbinière-Harwood. The author used the generic masculine in her text; the translator 'corrects' the language, avoiding male generic terms where they appear in French and using *Québecois-e-s* where the original was happy with *Québecois* in all cases. While it is known that the author has feminist sympathies and worked in collaboration with the translator, Harwood explains in her preface: 'My translation practice is a political activity aimed at making language speak for women. So my signature on a translation means: this translation has used every translation strategy to make the feminine visible in language'.

What is remarkable about this explanation is that the signature of the translator is given authority equivalent to that of authorship. De Lotbinière-Harwood's autobiographical style of writing reinstates the authority of the personal register for the translator, giving content and positionality to the translator's 'I'. But this example also illustrates the potential conflicts of such renewed authority. Is this 'I' to be allowed to become a rival of the author? While we know, in this particular case, that the author seems to have been willing to abdicate her textual authority in favour of the translator's more radical stance towards language, one could wonder what the consequences of such a gesture might be in other circumstances. What would be the result of a translation which blatantly redirected the intention of the original text, consciously contravening its intentions?

Such a move would not be consistent with the dynamics of feminist translation, where there is deliberate collusion and cooperation between text, author, and translator. Author and translator are operating in a frame of contemporaneity, their work engaging in a dialogue of reciprocal influence. Feminist translation implies extending and developing the intention of the original text. That is why the most successful examples of such practices are to be found in an appropriate match between text and translating project.

One of the most important contemporary feminist writers to investigate these processes of meaning-creation is Nicole Brossard, a Quebec feminist writer who has achieved an international reputation. Her writing is important here because of its powerful avant-garde techniques, which have engaged the theory and practice of feminist translators, notably Barbara **Godard**. Godard emphasizes the 'transferential process' of translation, the reading subject becoming the writing subject. Like the author, the translator uses disjunctive strategies, breaking with a unified language (Godard 1995). For example, Brossard uses English words in her French text in order to disrupt the code and to enhance the power of certain terms. Godard indicates the passages which Brossard wrote in English in bold face. Elsewhere, she introduces French into her own text, this time without italics or bolding, in order to reproduce Brossard's strategy.

The interventionism of the translator is by no means gratuitous, but solicited and oriented by the text itself. Godard's translation follows the mode of meaning generated by Brossard rather than the strictly surface phenomena which result. These strategies include using graphic modes of representation—in *These Our Mothers* (Brossard 1983), particularly, where this title is represented with a giant 'S', the rest of the words agglutinating around it. In the text, a single French word can be translated by two variants, which are put one on top of the other, for example *défaite* being given as 'defeat' and 'de facto'; *mère* is occasionally rendered 'm ther'. 'Pour écrire, rêver est un accessoire' becomes 'Dreaming is an accessory to writ(h)ing'. 'Chaque fois que l'espace me manque à l'horizon, la bouche s'entrouvre, la langue trouve l'ouverture' becomes 'Each time I lack space on the her/i/zon, my mouth opens, the tongue finds an opening, (her eye zone)' 'La mère recouvrant la mer comme une parfaite synthèse', becomes '(Mère) She covering (mer) sea like a perfect synthesis'. Only very occasionally does Godard use footnotes, as in an explanation of the French word *élan*, referring both to a burst of feeling and to a moose, the second meaning being important in Brossard's reference to hunting. There is no sense here of the translator's note disturbing the tranquil transparency of the page: Brossard herself uses many kinds of graphic device to complicate the visual aspect of the page.

In this way, the project of the feminist translator accords with the impulse of the text, questioning the most basic relationship of word to object, word to emotion, word to word. Brossard's writing places transformation at the very centre of its complex attention to the mechanisms of representation. It puts into play a dynamic of multiplicity and mimicry which makes linear and transparent meaning impossible. This conflation of writing with translation and transformation is clearly at odds with a long-dominant theory of translation as equivalence of fixed meanings. Feminist writing and translation practice come together in framing all writing as rewriting, all writing as involving a rhetoricity in which subjectivity is at work.

Feminist translation principles are also involved in other areas of cultural transmission. Two examples can be highlighted here: the first is the transatlantic displacement of the writings of the French feminists, Luce Irigaray, Julia Kristeva, and Hélène Cixous into the Anglo-American intellectual world beginning in the the early 1970s and continuing to the present [see II.g.13]. This exchange brings to light the network of tensions which are so characteristic of our current intellectual context— the conflicting pulls of internationalist feminist solidarity and the reconfirmation of national affiliations (Freiwald 1991). The 'taming' of French feminist theory in the Anglo-American context involved a merging of philosophical systems, on the one hand the speculative Continental tradition and on the other the more empirical Anglo-American tradition. This process of accommodation was facilitated by various levels and procedures of mediation: commentary, interpretation, and translation.

But the transatlantic passage of French feminist thought also brought about significant effects of distortion and appropriation. These effects inevitably accompany any important movements of ideas; they result from the diversity of interests and desires which command the exchange, and from the reformulation and renewals demanded of the target language. The distorting effects of the exchange are perhaps best witnessed in the reception given to the work of Hélène Cixous, whose work was until recently interpreted on the basis of a very narrow sampling (Penrod 1993).

The second area is contemporary feminist Biblical translation [see II.c.1.xiii]. What is particularly striking about the feminist intervention in this area is that it does not consider itself, and is not often considered to be, an aberration in an otherwise seamless tradition. Rather, it appears as yet another social and ideological stance from which translation can be undertaken—the new face in a long line of such competing figures going back to the Septuagint [see II.c.1.ii]. The debates over feminist and inclusive-language interpretations of the Bible enhance our understanding of translation as a substantial interpretive move, at the same time as they draw attention to the conflictual implications of gendered language (Bird 1988; Simon 1996: 111–33). While there are strong and powerful voices calling for inclusive-language versions of the Bible (versions which neutralize gendered language), there are equally insistent voices—among feminists—calling for versions which remain attentive to the highly patriarchal language of the originals. On the one hand, there is a drive to express the libertarian potential of the Bible; on the other, an emphasis on the historical and cultural roots of the text. As is often the case with the Bible, the interaction between philology and exegesis, meaning and dogma, becomes particularly intense. The long history of the Bible magnifies the import of translation issues, showing them to be ideologically saturated. In contrast to most other areas of cultural transmission, where translation is so often treated as a mechanical act, Biblical scholarship has always recognized that translation carries with it both the dangers and the promises of interpretation.

In both the transportation of French feminism and new projects of Bible translation there is a particularly revealing imbrication of gender and language issues. Consciously feminist principles are invoked in the choice and manner of the texts translated. These connections allow us to see how translation frames and directs ongoing processes of intellectual transmission. The links of mediation are not automatic; they are not imposed or organized by some dispassionate cultural authority. Rather, translators are involved in the materials through which they work; they are fully engaged in the process of transfer.

What feminist theory highlights is this renewed sense of *agency* in translation. There is emphasis on the speaking voice of the translator and her active role in the translation process, and a willing recognition that translators are interventionist. This does not mean that the translator is 'free' to do whatever she wants, but that her work is shaped and focused by its final aims. This recognition provides an essential critical perspective on translations as products of the ideological tensions of their times. It allows us to make cultural sense of the 'difference' between original and translation.

6. VARIETIES OF ENGLISH
John McRae and Bill Findlay

i. Which English? Self-translation and New Englishes In the post-colonial world a new problem emerges—how much can local varieties of English be used as the language of literary creation—and by the same token, of literary translation? For a writer like the Kenyan Ngũgĩ wa Thiong'o, for example, a return to his own language, Gikuyu, was a necessary part of his development as a writer in the 1970s and 1980s: his novels and plays were then self-translated into standard English rather than being written directly in English. His 1986 essay *Decolonising the Mind: The Politics of Language in African Literature* is a significant exploration of the issues, and implicitly of their importance to the translator.

Self-translation poses the basic question, which English is to be chosen? Samuel Beckett [II.g.14] largely used his own translations, writing first in French in order to achieve greater 'purity' of language. For the postcolonial writer and for any translator of postcolonial writing the problem opens up a new range of questions: purity is much less the issue now; variety and richness of linguistic resources are what the translators want to experiment with.

The first possibility is that of translating into a distinct and recognizable 'new English', a variety of English which tries to echo the local flavour of the English used in the area. However, in translating his 1982 novel *Devil on the Cross* from Gikuyu, Ngũgĩ opted for a more neutral, widely acceptable English rather than any local variety. It is in poetry that the more vivid use of local varieties has begun to be found: in the writings of recent poets of Caribbean origin such as John Agard or Benjamin Zephaniah, who very consciously are engaged in 'breaking Englishes' rather than writing 'broken English' or standard English. Where 'broken English' is considered an inferior form of standard English, poets such as these consider 'breaking Englishes' a creative experiment with the rendering of an English which is between standard English and a local language or dialect.

The novelist Timothy Mo in *Brownout on Breadfruit Boulevard* (1995) rendered the Pilipino language and the fragmented English of the Philippines in a manner which was widely misread by British critics: since the new Englishes are not properly codified, much of the writing has to be based on the sounds of the language rather than on any recognizable word formation or grammatical patterns. There are no established ground rules for the rendition of most local Englishes, and throughout history attempts to render them have been the subject of controversy. As the following quotation shows, there is a fine line between 'bad' translation and vivid rendering of a locally based 'English': 'Hi! Hows my kind friend today forever? If you the one to asking regarding me from my side just the same OK' (p. 14).

The process of fashioning new mixes of languages can be traced back more than a century. In the Caribbean, for example, *Tom Cringle's Log* (1829) by Michael Scott was the first novel to record the colonial non-standard English of both whites and blacks. Henry G. Murray began to blend Creole and standard English in *Tom Kittle's Wake* (1877), a 'dramatic monologue' where dialogue and inner monologue are in Creole and the narrative in standard English. This code-switching and playing with registers becomes a feature of the exploration of new Englishes worldwide. Such new directions in creative writing have considerable implications for translation, and translation has not always kept pace with innovative linguistic experiments, despite their long-standing presence in such writing.

New Englishes are not the same as a bland World English or International English; rather, they are vivid local varieties which can combine anything from pidgin or Creole to Shakespeare and the Authorized Version, to American and other geographical influences. A multilingual society such as that of South Africa has inevitable produced a great deal of writing which mixes languages, such as W. C. Scully's *Kafir Stories* (1895), which included many Xhosa words and phrases, as well as oral narrative styles.

Since *Sozaboy: A Novel in Rotten English* (1985) by the Nigerian Ken Saro-Wiwa, there has been an expanding awareness of the rejection of 'standard' English and the self-conscious creative use of 'rotten' English in African writing. The novel uses a wide range of registers of pidgin, broken, and semi-literate English to explore the language and ways of people who are neither part of the élite nor of the bourgeoisie, nor even stereotypical workers or peasants. His exploration of new ways of rendering local Englishes relates closely to the affirmation of local African languages expounded by Ngũgĩ and others, but is more of a challenge to what English is and what it represents than a return to local linguistic and cultural roots.

The philosophical background is also important here. Indian writing in English from Raja Rao to R. K. Narayan investigates Indo-Aryan rather than Judaeo-Christian influences. A good example of this is found also in Malaysian writing: the major novel by Shahnon Ahmad, *Ranjau Sepanjang Jalan* (1986, tr. 1989), is a peasant novel in a clearly Muslim tradition. The title literally translates as 'Traps along the Way', and the language of the novel is strongly influenced by the local Kedah dialect. The recognized translation, by Adibah **Amin**, however, uses no dialect forms and even takes a Christian reference for its title: *No Harvest but a Thorn*. Where the original title suggests a path and destiny, in keeping with Islamic concepts, the translation superimposes Christian preconceptions and imagery on the simple tale of poverty and suffering. In the translation several words are retained in Bahasa Melayu to keep 'local colour', but the language of the translation is standard educated English.

Interestingly, one of the major novels in English from Zimbabwe uses the same Biblical reference: *Harvest of Thorns* (1989), by Shimmer Chinodya. This family/nation saga has no link at all to the country's Shona or Ndebele linguistic background, but reflects rather the missionary influence on language and education during the period of colonial occupation in Rhodesia. These two examples show how translator and author adopt a frame of reference to meet reader expectations. With the assertiveness of new Englishes such as Caribbean English (and indeed Scottish English) the necessity of this kind of adaptation is lessening.

A more recent literary work from Malaysia shows a more adventurous exploration of the possibilities of translation. Ramli Ibrahim's trilogy of one-act plays, *In the Name of Love* (1993), invents a new kind of Malaysian English. The self-translation uses the kind of interjections and locally based terminology which are so often kept in order to retain local flavour, but the text reads with Malaysian rhythms, cadences, and inflections. It is perhaps significant that this step forward in translation technique should happen in drama: the playwright/translator also happens to be a frequent performer of his own work, and thus closer to the needs of the speaker of the text.

This sentence from the English version of *Mak Su*, the first part of *In the Name of Love*, brings together some of these features: 'Now, if you warned me you're coming today, I'd prepare you *tupat sotong*. But you appear just suddenly like this—like a *malaikat*! Where got time to do it?' Here the grammatical tenses are fractured, the rhythms clearly not standard English, and two Malay terms are kept in the original and glossed in footnotes in the published text (they would translate as 'stuffed cuttlefish' and 'angel' respectively); the use of the indefinite article is an interesting feature of this kind of mix of languages in translation.

The phenomenon of glossing words which the reader may not be able to identify is universal: the Pacific novels of Albert Wendt contain many Samoan words, just as Hugh MacDiarmid's Scots poetry required glossing, and Ramli Ibrahim provides a gloss of 'near-equivalents' in the published version of his text. What is interesting is how glossing is felt less and less necessary as new Englishes achieve greater readership acceptance.

In Indian writing, Nissim Ezekiel's *Poems in Very Indian English* (1976) parody character types through their speech patterns (the use of the present continuous tense, for instance), making rather controversial (and, it might be said, dated) use of various Indian Englishes for comic purposes. This comic play on language and voices is a universal phenomenon, part of the emergence of recognizable local, often dialect, language—it can be seen in Tom Leonard's use of Glasgow Scots, in Benjamin Zephaniah's generalized 'African' in 'As a African', and on to the mix of Malay, English and other influences in the writings of the Malaysian poet Cecil Rajendran, or the creolized poetry of Mauritius or Papua New Guinea.

The main issue is not simply one of language system (English as an International Language) and its varieties (the new Englishes) but rather the question of the social, cultural, and ideological positions in which people use language (Pennycook 1994: 31). How language represents the world, where postcolonial writing abrogates the privileged centrality of 'English', will be a fascinating development as more and more cultures find their own means of expression in some kind of English, rather than playing the standard-English game or being caught in some kind of translation trap.

The playwright Mahesh Dattani, born in Gujarat, domiciled in Karnataka where the main language is Kannada, writes in English; although he speaks all three languages, English is 'my native language'—it is educated Indian English, but recognizably the English of southern India rather than of Mumbai or Delhi. And the playwright refuses to 'translate' this English into a bland, neutral, universally recognizable Indian English.

Local Englishes are currently self-assertive expressions of local identity. From West Africa to the South Pacific, from immigrant England to the islands of the Caribbean, there are more and more Englishes flourishing, both as spoken and as written language. They have been too little exploited for translation. In future they are likely to be ever more valid options for creative writing and for translation.   JM

ii. Translations into Scots Like its literary tradition, Scotland's literary translation heritage is multilingual, with work in Gaelic, Latin, Scots, and English. The substantial body of translations into English ranges from Sir Thomas **Urquhart**'s translation of Rabelais's *Gargantua* and *Pantagruel* in the 17th c. [II.g.5.i] through to Alastair **Reid**'s of the poetry of Jorge Luís Borges and Pablo Neruda today. But translations into Scots have a longer history, reflecting the linguistic history of Scotland.

Scots and English share a common ancestry as dialects of Old English. In the Middle Ages the differences between them grew more marked with the establishment of England and Scotland as independent kingdoms. From the mid-15th to the 16th c. Scots became an all-purpose national language, as distinct from English as Dutch from German. But it was to suffer three setbacks: it lost spiritual prestige through the importation of an English translation of the Bible for public worship following the Reformation; it lost social prestige and patronage through the Union of the Crowns in 1603 when the King of Scots, James VI, removed his court to London; and it lost political prestige with the Union of the Parliaments of England and Scotland in 1707. The sum effect was that Scots ceded its official status to English, thereby losing its prose register, fragmenting into its various spoken dialects, and through time becoming identified with the speech of the humbler classes. Dilution and a degree of conflation with English have subsequently occurred and have contributed to misperceptions of Scots today as but a dialect of English.

Whilst Scots has a sustained literary history stretching back to about 1300, literary translation has been practised more fitfully. Two periods are of most significance: the 16th and 20th c. The 16th c. saw Scots secure as a national language, spoken from palace to plough, with demotic to courtly and literary registers, and with a literature boasting poets of the stature of William Dunbar, Robert Henryson, and Sir David Lindsay. The maturity of the language is evident in the translation of Virgil's *Aeneid* published in 1513 by the poet Gavin **Douglas** (*c.*1474–1522) [see II.n.2.i]. Douglas unequivocally asserts in a prologue that his translation is 'Writtin in the langage of Scottis natioun'. Notwithstanding

his linguistic patriotism, he is open to borrowing eclectically if it serves Virgil:

Sum bastard Latyn, French or Inglys oys   [*use*]
Quhar scant was Scottis—I had nane other choys.
Nocht for our tong is in the selwyn skant   [*in itself*]
Bot for that I the fowth of language want   [*abundance*]

(Douglas 1957–64: ii. 6)

Douglas sets out a new approach to translation in the Prologues, Conclusion, Direction, and Exclamation offered in his *Aeneid*. He vigorously denounces the older, medieval tradition as represented by the English translator William Caxton in his *Eneydos* (*c.*1490), and emphasizes a translator's duty to respect the integrity of a source text: 'Rycht so am I to Virgillis text ybund, | ... And thus I am constrenyt als neir I may | To hald hys vers and go nane other way' (Douglas 1957–64: ii. 11). His translation will differ from predecessors whom he accuses of 'perverting' Virgil through adaptation, abridgement, omissions, insertion of non-Virgilian material, and a cavalier disregard for the letter of the original. No earlier translator in Britain discussed the theory of translation in such detail, which adds to the significance of Douglas's *Aeneid* as the first translation from the original of a major classical poem into either English or Scots. But the work's greater celebrity stems from the quality of Douglas's translation, making it still the most renowned of Scots literary translations in the English-speaking world (Ezra Pound judged it better than Virgil even).

The 16th c. saw other Scots translations, such as John **Bellenden**'s versions of Latin prose works by Livy (*History of Rome*, 1532) and Hector Boece (*Historie and Croniklis of Scotland*, 1533—commissioned by King James V); Murdoch **Nisbet**'s of the entire New Testament and parts of the Old (*c.*1520); and John **Burel**'s of a Latin *comoedia*, *Pamphilus de Amore* (*Pamphilus Speakand of Lufe*, 1590/91). More important as literary translations were the efforts of the 'Castalian Band' of court poets brought together in the last two decades of the century by the poet-king **James VI** (1566–1625). Taking as his model what the Pléiade poets had achieved for French in the 1550s and 1560s, James encouraged the writing *and translation* of poetry as a means of advancing the literary status of Scots. The King himself translated Salluste du Bartas's *Uranie* (Du Bartas reciprocated with a version of James's *Lepanto*), and commanded Thomas **Hudson** to translate Du Bartas's *La Judith*, correcting it with his own hand when completed. He also encouraged John **Stewart** of Baldynneis (*c.*1545–*c.*1605) to translate Ariosto's *Orlando Furioso*, William **Fowler** (1560–1612) to translate Petrarch's

Trionfi and Machiavelli's *Prince* (unpublished at the time), and other members of his poet band to produce versions of Ronsard and poets of the Pléiade.

James published in 1585 *Ane Schort Treatise, Conteining some Reulis and Cautelis to be Observit and Eschewit in Scottis Poesie.* Those *Reulis and Cautelis* (rules and cautions) provided a manifesto for his Castalian Band. James emphasized invention over imitation, and cautioned against the dangers of translation, where 'ye are bound, as to a staik, to follow that buikis phrasis, quhilk ye translate' (James VI 1955: 79). In contrast with Gavin Douglas's attention to fidelity, James advocated a freer approach so that the poetic virtue of one's 'awin inventioun' would not be stifled. Yet James's advocacy of invention in translation was not at the expense of scholarship, for he encouraged comprehensive knowledge of the work to be translated, including searching out and reading earlier and contemporary translations in other languages.

With King James's accession to the English throne in 1603 and the departure of the Scottish court to London, his Castalian Band of poets dispersed. The Scots literary tradition flowed on nonetheless, reaching high points in the poetry of Ramsay, Fergusson, and Burns in the 18th c., and in the novels of Scott, Galt, Hogg, and Stevenson in the 19th. But translations into Scots were scant: some classical Latin verse in the 18th c., and parts of the Bible in the late-19th c.

The catalyst for the 20th-c. revival of literary translations into Scots was the 'Scottish Renaissance' movement which emerged in the 1920s. The moving force was the poet and nationalist C. M. Grieve, who wrote under the name Hugh **MacDiarmid**. MacDiarmid argued for the revitalization of Scots as a literary language, and in his own work he developed a 'synthetic Scots' medium which borrowed from reference works, dictionaries, and earlier literature. It was an approach which looked back to the Golden Age of Scots in the 15th and 16th c. and forward to a hoped-for new age of political and literary independence. In this context, translating into Scots was an act of cultural politics: it was to be a contribution to developing the language's range, to demonstrating the creative potentialities which still resided in it as a literary medium, and to asserting its distinctiveness from English. MacDiarmid himself translated or adapted poetry from Russian, French, and German, and his lead was followed by a number of other poets.

The effects of MacDiarmid's Scottish Renaissance philosophies and achievements continue to ripple through Scotland's literary culture, and for the past 70 years there has been a sustained output of translations into Scots (France and Glen 1989). Poetry has been translated from most of the European languages and some of the Asian languages, with work from Russian, Italian, French, and the classical languages predominating. Translations of collections of poetry by single authors that have attracted particular praise are Robert **Garioch**'s of Giuseppe Belli (Garioch 1980), Edwin **Morgan**'s of Vladimir Mayakovsky (Morgan 1972 [see II.p.7.iii]), and William **Neill**'s of Homer (Neill 1992). Sir Alexander **Gray**'s translations of European balladry and folk-song have also been acclaimed (Gray 1932; 1949; 1954).

No one theory of verse translation has prevailed, but most postwar translators have tended to follow the Scottish Renaissance example in employing a 'synthetic' Scots. That said, demotic Scots does sometimes feature, as in Garioch's translations of Belli's sonnets; and it can be harnessed to an experimental approach which at the same time draws on a literary Scots, as in Morgan's matching of Mayakovsky's modernist exuberance.

Whilst there is now a substantial corpus of poetry translated into Scots this century, much less prose has been translated. This deficiency reflects the historic loss of a prose register and the lack of a settled grammar and orthography. However, one outstanding prose translation has been produced: William Laughton **Lorimer**'s *The New Testament in Scots* (1983) [see II.c.1.viii]. This translation—an unexpected publishing success—can be seen as a late fruit of the Scottish Renaissance, for Lorimer was of the same generation as MacDiarmid and shared some of the same motives in wishing to see Scots revitalized. A professor of Greek at St Andrews University, he concluded from his research that the New Testament was written by many hands, and his Scots accordingly eschews uniformity in favour of stylistic variety. A Scots prose translation-in-progress which, to judge by instalments already published, may rival Lorimer's in importance is Brian **Holton**'s of the Chinese medieval novel *Shuihu zhuan* (*The Water Margin*) [see II.f.4.ii].

A significant development dating from the 1940s has been the translation of drama into Scots. Robert **Kemp**'s translations of Molière's *L'École des Femmes* (*Let Wives Tak Tent*, 1948) and *L'Avare* (*The Laird o' Grippy*, 1954) led the way [see II.g.6.v]. There have since been translations by different hands of a number of other plays by Molière, making him the most translated dramatist. Other classical playwrights whose work has been translated include Aristophanes, Aeschylus, Goldoni, Kleist, Gogol, Gorky, Racine, Beaumarchais, Ibsen, Rostand, and

Hauptmann. The translation of contemporary plays into Scots only commenced in the 1980s, since when a number of plays by Dario Fo [II.m.9] and Michel Tremblay [II.g.16.i] have been translated, as well as single plays by Enzo Cormann, Michel Vinaver, Ludmilla Petrushevskaya, and Daniel Danis. Scots translations have today become an established feature of the Scottish theatre scene.

The translations of classic plays have tended to draw on a literary or 'traditional' Scots, albeit with a spoken base; though in some recent cases—Liz **Lochhead**'s *Tartuffe* (1985) and Edwin Morgan's *Cyrano de Bergerac* (1992)—this has been blended with a demotic Scots and other registers to create an individualistic 'theatrical Scots'. In contrast, contemporary plays have in the main been rendered into an urban demotic Scots. The corpus of classic and contemporary plays translated demonstrates the rich linguistic resource available to the Scottish translator, ranging from standard English to varieties of Scots.

The question why translators of poetry, prose, and plays should continue to use Scots today invites many answers. An important one is the flexibility of choice afforded by a Scots-and-English resource.

Another is the sense that translators have of working within a literary and linguistic tradition which retains a 'national' dimension and which is hospitable to published and performed Scots (as demonstrated by public interest); translation is thus a means of adding to and advancing that tradition. Translators may also be motivated by a belief that for certain work, Scots, or Scots and English in combination or contrast, is more effective than a standard English medium in rendering the letter and/or spirit of a source work. For the translator of poetry this might be bound up in part with the phonaesthetic qualities of Scots, and/or the enlarged choice of vocabulary and rhymes that Scots and English afford; and for the translator of prose and drama it can be influenced by considerations of linguistic equivalency in matching a dialect or non-standard source medium, or by the opportunities that Scots affords for stylistic variety and register shifts. Whatever the reasons influencing a translator, the sum effect is that the period since the Second World War has, in terms of quantity and variety of literary genres translated, been the richest in Scotland's literary history for translations into Scots.

b. Historical Development

1. The Middle Ages   2. The Renaissance   3. Neoclassicism and Enlightenment
4. Romanticism and the Victorian Age   5. Late Victorian to the Present
6. Translation in North America

1. THE MIDDLE AGES
Roger Ellis

i. Problems of Definition For the purposes of this chapter, we can reckon that translation in England begins with Pope Gregory's mission to England in 597 of St Augustine of Canterbury, accompanied by Frankish interpreters, to convert the pagan English. Where the Middle Ages shades into the Renaissance is much more difficult to decide.

William **Caxton** (c.1422–1491), who began his illustrious publishing career with his own translation of a French version of the Troy story, provides the cut-off point for this exercise in 1490, with his last published translation. This is his *Eneydos*, a translation of Virgil's *Aeneid* based on an intermediate French version. Admittedly, claims could also be advanced for the inclusion of other writers: John **Skelton** (c.1460–1529), whom Caxton cited in the prologue to the *Eneydos*, and who (c.1488) produced a translation of the *Bibliotheca Historica of Diodorus Siculus* from the Latin version of the Italian humanist Poggio Bracciolini; still later, Gavin **Douglas** (c.1474–1522) (see below).

The other terms of the discussion, 'English', 'literature', and 'translation', are also problematic. In the Middle Ages, literary culture was an amalgam of English and Latin cultures. In addition, the three centuries after the Norman Conquest witness a thriving Anglo-Norman culture. This mix of cultures, observable, for example, in bi- and trilingual texts and macaronic verse, presents students of translation with a considerable challenge.

To take a single example, the celebrated account by **Bede** (673–735), in his *Historia Ecclesiastica* (Ecclesiastical History of the English People; Colgrave and Mynors 1969), of the miraculous 'translation' of the illiterate Anglo-Saxon poet **Cædmon** (before 680) into a composer of religious poetry, includes a version, in Latin prose, of the first such song Cædmon was inspired to utter (*Historia*, iv. 24). An Anglo-Saxon version of Bede provides a version of the song in Anglo-Saxon alliterative verse. Scholars have generally assumed that the Anglo-Saxon version is the original and the Latin a translation from it, since translation from the vernacular into Latin is common throughout the medieval period and after—a reflection of the greater prestige enjoyed by Latin and the wider circulation its use made possible. But recently an alternative and easier reading has been proposed: that the version we think of as Cæmon's original is in fact a translation from Bede's Latin version (Frantzen 1990: 146). Rather than talk of an original and a translated text, it seems we must talk of two different versions of the one text.

The situation is yet more complicated when we have versions in Middle English, Latin, and Anglo-Norman to reckon with: texts like the anonymous *Ancrene Wisse* (Guide for Anchoresses) (early 13th c.) and St Edmund of Abingdon's *Speculum Ecclesiae* (Mirror of the Church) (c.1230) survive in English, French, and Latin versions; *Mandeville's Travels* (mid-14th c.) survives similarly in English and French versions. The precise relationship of these versions to each other has in the past caused considerable debate: what Barratt (1984: 418) has called 'the symbiotic relationship that should exist between Middle English, French and Latin studies' applies with equal force to the study of medieval translation.

An entry, then, devoted to the study of translations into English in the Middle Ages risks partiality if it does not at least remind readers of the complex linguistic situation in which such translations occurred. Consider, for example, the case of Bishop Robert **Grosseteste** (*c*.1170–1253), who produced important Latin translations of Greek texts: translations which, as his contemporary Roger Bacon noted, improved considerably upon existing versions. Grosseteste was also cited as one of two native authorities on translation by the Wycliffites (Hudson 1988: s.v. Grosseteste). Yet Grosseteste's only claim, otherwise, to a place in a volume restricted, like this one, to the study of 'literature in English' would be that he directed the clergy of his diocese to use the vernacular to instruct the laity, and wrote a religious allegory in French, the *Château d'amour* (Castle of Love), later translated into Middle English.

Major problems of definition remain even with a text like the *Boece* (?1380) of Geoffrey **Chaucer** (*c*.1343–1400). Here we can have no doubts about the closeness of the translation to its ultimate original, the *Consolatio Philosophiae* (Consolation of Philosophy) of Boethius [II.n.12]. But that awareness merely triggers another, more fundamental question: of finding an understanding of the term 'translation' adequate to the study of medieval texts, most of which, one way or another, can be described as translations. The *Consolatio*, for example, reached Chaucer with a whole variety of added interpretative aids, in the form of interlinear and marginal glosses and more extensive commentary, and of a French translation by Jean de Meun, all of which Chaucer used to supplement his original.

Moreover, prior to the advent of print culture, translators regularly worked with copies at one or more removes from their originals. Consequently, translators might find themselves forced to act as textual critics of those originals even as they attempted to translate them. Thus, for example, Caxton claims to have produced his translation (?1481) of the *Legenda Aurea* (Golden Legend) of James of Varaggio from three versions of the text, in Latin, French, and English. Similarly, the anonymous *Myroure of Oure Ladye* (1435–57, translated for the Syon nuns from the Office produced for her Order by St Bridget of Sweden, recognizes several variants for one of the antiphons, and produces translations of each so that, whatever version the sister has in her Latin copy, she will be able to make sense of it (Blunt 1873: 272). But few translators were as well

placed to make sense of the complex textual traditions of the works they were translating.

It follows that the original needs to be seen as the point of departure for a translation rather than as a standard against which the translation can be measured. And since translators worked in a culture where respect for authoritative texts accompanied wholesale scribal reinterpretation and reappropriation of those same texts, as the work of Copeland (1991) has demonstrated, they were themselves usually acting not as scribes but almost as authors in their own right.

Scribe and author: these are the two ends of a spectrum of practice outlined by St Bonaventura in 1250–2—the middle terms are compiler and commentator—onto which translators' practices can be usefully mapped. It follows, therefore, that our understanding of the term 'translation' has to be flexible enough to include interlinear glosses as one end of a spectrum that shades at the other into original composition.

The Psalter (*c*.1340) of Richard **Rolle** (*c*.1300–1349), a text which was still being read a century and more after its composition [see II.c.1.iv], provides excellent exemplification of these points. In his preface Rolle declares that the translation exists as a crib for the Vulgate Latin, and he gives the Vulgate a position of honour, verse by verse, before the translation. He also carefully distinguishes the translation proper from the extensive commentary which follows. Rolle is like many later Biblical translators in his respect for the original. But the sheer scale of his commentary threatens to disrupt this neat hierarchical patterning of original, translation, and commentary. In any case, the commentary, though based on the standard Latin commentary of Peter Lombard, systematically modifies Lombard's material. Medieval translation's obsession with questions of its own origin, and professed dependence on that origin, are therefore intensely paradoxical, a partial reflection of the central role played by religious institutions in the production, as well as the licensing, of translations.

Secular authority is less evident as a force to be reckoned with, though instances do occur of the commissioning and translation of work by members of the nobility. At the end of the 14th c., for example, Lord Berkeley commissioned translations by **John of Trevisa** (*c*.1342–1402) and John **Walton** (*fl.* 1408–10); in the 15th c. Humphrey Duke of Gloucester, 'the only patron of English letters in the Middle Ages who can bear comparison with the great continental patrons' (Pearsall 1977: 194), commissioned numerous translations. Caxton regularly dedicated his translations to the nobility, and published translations by them (Earl **Rivers**; the Earl of **Worcester**), acknowledging their importance as the source of funds and publicity for his own translation projects.

The third member of our trio, 'literature', is less problematical, because there is a general consensus, at least among medievalists, that the Middle Ages had a much more all-embracing view of literature than we do.

ii. Old English Another date, 1066, the year of the Norman Conquest, serves to subdivide the material in this chapter, though it enjoys no more absolute status than dates earlier offered. After the Conquest, knowledge of Old English survived at a number of monastic centres into the 12th c.—for example at Peterborough, whose copy of the Anglo-Saxon Chronicle switches decisively from Old to Middle English for the last years (1132–54)—but declined dramatically after the 13th c.

Two forces shape developments in translation in the Old English period. The first was a drive to make more widely available the riches of Latin, particularly Christian, learning: the second, the negative of the former's positive, the Viking invasions from the late 8th c. onwards.

At first the Church's missionary instincts were the main motive force. Thus Bede, who himself produced translations of basic religious texts like the Apostles' Creed and the Lord's Prayer, writes how Cædmon produced poetic versions of Biblical narratives translated for him from Latin (*Historia*, IV. xxiv). Neither Bede's nor Cædmon's translations—the latter, strictly, intralingual translations—appear to have survived, though until this century Cædmon was credited with the authorship of many surviving Old English Biblical paraphrases in verse, one of which, *Genesis*, includes a fine passage, now called *Genesis B*, translated from an Old Saxon poem. Bede's translations may have had a fairly restricted scope: the laity were to have (only?) what they needed to enable them to comprehend the liturgy and the elements of their faith.

In the aftermath of the Benedictine reforms of the 10th c. and of the Viking invasions, similar aims seem to have inspired the much more extensive translation activity of **Ælfric** (*c*.955–*c*.1010), a monk at Cerne Abbas from 989 and abbot of Eynsham from 1005. During his time at Cerne Abbas, Ælfric also produced numerous translations of books of the Old Testament and freely adapted saints' lives, in what has been called 'the first comprehensive and systematic treatment of biblical, liturgical and . . . devotional topics to be issued in the English language' (Remley 1996: 88). Other Biblical translations produced during the Old English period include versions of the Psalter and the Gospels.

Ælfric's audience was an unlearned one, and his work is driven by the need to guard against the misinterpretations which might all too easily follow his readers' free access to the Bible in translation. This ambivalence towards translation—desirable in principle, needing careful control in practice—will resurface later in the Middle Ages, as we shall see, and may indeed be one of its defining characteristics.

No such ambivalence characterizes the other principal translation project of the Old English period, instigated 100 years before Ælfric by King **Alfred** (reigned 971–99). It is probably significant, of course, that it was a royal initiative which assembled 'a pleiad of English and foreign scholars', two English, one Saxon, and one Frankish, so as to make more widely available 'those books most necessary for men to know' (Swanton 1993: p. xvii). Such royal initiatives, always part of a programme to define, enhance, or preserve a sense of nationhood, certainly occur abroad (Alfonso X of Castile, Charles V of France); Alfred's is the only such initiative in England until at least the 16th c.

Alfred aimed to fortify his people against the disruptions caused by the Viking invasions of the previous century, and to restore the learning of the times of Bede and his contemporaries, as his preface to his translation of the *Cura Pastoralis* (Pastoral Care) of Pope Gregory makes clear. Undertaken 'amidst other various and manifold cares of this kingdom', it was followed up by translations of Boethius [II.n.12] (parts of it later reworked), of Orosius, of some of the Psalms, and of the *Soliloquies* of St Augustine.

Ælfric, and after him William of Malmesbury, thought that Alfred also translated Bede's *Historia*, though this translation is now thought, like that of the *Dialogues* of St Gregory, to be the work of one of Alfred's translation team. The achievement of Alfred and his team was considerable; later translators, like **Marie de France**, John of Trevisa, and the author(s) of the Wycliffite Bible, all cite Alfred as an authority.

The translations noted in previous paragraphs were mostly in prose. For much of the Old English period there was also a lively tradition of translation in verse, principally of religious texts, for a monastic and learned readership. One writer, **Cynewulf** (?first half of the 9th c.), has named himself in four poems, three of them translations: *Elene* and *Juliana*, examples of hagiographic literature, and *Ascension*, a homily by St Gregory. Otherwise, the verse translations are anonymous.

Space permits mention of only a few titles of other translated works in the period: *The Phoenix*, a metrical version of the allegorical *De Ave Phoenice* of Lactantius, 'perhaps the most graceful . . . of all the Old English religious poems' (Greenfield 1966: 183); a prose version of the Greek-Latin romance *Apollonius of Tyre*, the sole surviving witness to 'the existence of an Old English romance genre' (Swanton 1993: p. ix), preserved in a manuscript which also contains a rendering into poetry of a Latin poem on the day of Doom by Bede; and riddles in the Exeter Book translated from the *Aenigmata* of Aldhelm (*c*.639–709), a near-contemporary of Bede.

iii. Early Middle English The Middle English period covers the four centuries between the Norman Conquest and Caxton's printing press, but it can be conveniently divided at 1349, the year of the Black Death, into early and late Middle English. Prior to that date, literary culture was trilingual. By comparison with the languages used for learning (Latin) and polite culture (Anglo-Norman), English was initially marginalized as a literary medium both geographically—though it held its own in the west of the country—and socially.

Thus, in a note added to his *Polychronicon*, John of Trevisa notes how 'oplondysch men' (upland, uncultivated men) did their best to be thought better of by learning French; the *Holkham Bible Picture Book* (*c*.1326) uses French for all speeches except at the Nativity, when it additionally allows the shepherds, like their counterparts in the cycle plays, to copy the angels in mangled English. Admittedly, the picture was changing by then: witness the late 13th-c. romance *Of Arthour and Merlin*, produced, according to its prologue, for the 'mani noble . . . that no Freynsche couthe seye' (who know no French).

Such considerations may help to explain the relative paucity of original English material as well as of material translated into English in the 200 years after the Norman Conquest. For example, in about 1200 a Worcestershire priest, **Laȝamon**, produced a version in English of the *Historia Regum Britanniae* (*c*.1135, History of the Kings of Britain) by Geoffrey of Monmouth. Laȝamon worked from an intermediate Anglo-Norman version of Geoffrey's text by the Jerseyman Wace, the *Brut* (1155), and he transformed Wace's couplets and courtly narrative into a semi-Old English, semi-heroic poem.

This recourse to earlier traditions, understandable as a way of preserving a sense of Englishness in the face of French domination, effectively sidelined itself: Geoffrey's Latin original survives in 190 manuscripts, Wace's translation in 26, Laȝamon's *Brut*

in two (Pearsall 1977: 109). The dominance of French culture can also be seen in another translation from about the same time and place, which also, like Laȝamon, draws explicitly on Old English traditions, in this case, the prose of Ælfric: a Middle English translation from Latin of the life of St Margaret, preserved in only two manuscripts. *Six* versions of the life were produced in Anglo-Norman before 1300.

The English St Margaret belongs to a group of texts, the so-called Katherine Group, all but one translated from Latin works and all similarly marked by a 'fondness for native, not to say archaic' expression (Bennett 1986: 290). These are linked to the earlier-noted *Ancrene Wisse*, written for three gently-born sisters who had embraced the anchoritic life. *Ancrene Wisse* was still being copied in the 16th c., but the other texts in the group had a much more restricted circulation. For all that, there is nothing insular in the outlook of these writers.

In this respect comparison is instructive with another major group of translations in the 13th and 14th c., the mostly anonymous Middle English romances. For all that so few copies survive of them, these were pretty certainly popular works. They were often translated from French originals, though less often in the 14th c. than in the 13th. Two of the *Lais* of Marie de France were independently translated (*Sir Launfal, Lai le Freine*); Chrétien de Troyes's *Yvain* was the source of the anonymous *Ywain and Gawain*.

A consistent pattern of changes emerges in these translated romances, a reflection in part of the increasingly bourgeois audience for whom they were being produced. The plot is stripped to essentials (Bennett 1986, on *Floris and Blauncheflour*); there is less 'delicacy and subtlety of sentiment' (Pearsall 1977: 144); and the ironies and humour of the original are broadened (Field 1989, of *Ipomedon A*, a translation of Hue de Roteland's *Ipomedon*).

iv. Chaucer and His Contemporaries We may never know exactly how and when English took over from French as the dominant literary medium of the later Middle Ages. In his *Polychronicon* John of Trevisa explained the change in terms of the catastrophic effects of the Black Death on grammar school education, but even before then French had been in decline. Translations and original writing in French continued into the late 14th c., notably with the *Mirouer de l'Homme* (*c*.1374–80, Mirror of Man) by Chaucer's illustrious contemporary John **Gower** (*c*.1330–1408). And Gower's major English work, the *Confessio Amantis* (Lover's Confession), included many stories translated from the classics, and could thus almost count as a translation.

Nevertheless, it was Chaucer's decision to write only in English which would prove critically important for future developments of English literary culture. Hence, in the prologue to his *Treatise on the Astrolabe* (1391), Chaucer's comment on Richard II as 'lord of this langage'. Within 100 years Caxton would be printing an English–French phrase book (*c*.1480), the English elements translated from the Flemish half of a similar book.

Chaucer was acknowledged from the beginning as a translator of note. His first major translation, part of the courtly romance-cum-encyclopedia *Le Roman de la rose* (The Romance of the Rose) by Guillaume de Lorris and Jean de Meun [II.g.3], may have earned him the honorific 'grant translateur' from his French contemporary Eustache Deschamps, though possibly Deschamps was thinking of him 'as a poet of Troy' (Patterson 1991: 103), hence as author of *The House of Fame* and *Troilus and Criseyde* (*c*.1386), the latter a version of Boccaccio's *Il Filostrato* (The Man Prostrated by Love), with much original writing added and other material translated from the very differently oriented *Consolatio* of Boethius [II.n.12].

To these titles we ought to add *The Legend of Good Women*, a series of narratives based on writings of Ovid and Virgil; *Melibee*, a translation from an intermediate French version by Renaud de Louens of a treatise by Albertano of Brescia, the *Liber Consolationis et Consilii* (Book of Consolation and Counsel); *The Clerk's Tale*, a version of Petrarch's retelling of the last story in Boccaccio's *Decameron* [II.m.3], again supplemented by an intermediate French version; and the *The Man of Law's Tale*, translated from an episode in the Anglo-Norman chronicle of Nicholas Trevet.

No less striking than the wide range of subjects attempted—courtly romance, moral allegory, scientific handbook, classical literature—is the range of practices followed, which produce close translations (*Roman, Boece, Melibee*) as well as translations which critically rework their originals (*Troilus, Clerk's Tale*).

Chaucer's example directly inspired several translators in the last years of the 14th c. and first decades of the 15th. Thus his *Boece* was used to supplement its Boethian original for a verse version of the *Consolatio* (1410) by John Walton, who may also have produced a version of the *De Re Militari* (On Military Strategy) of Vegetius.

Other major translation projects were also undertaken at this same time, in a ferment of activity. John of Trevisa produced translations of several huge works, notably (1398) Bartholomew the Englishman's *De Proprietatibus Rerum* (On the Properties of Things), Ranulph Higden's world history, the *Polychronicon* (1387), and a manual of medieval statecraft, the *De Regimine Principum* (On the Rule of Princes), by Aegidius Romanus. At much the same time an anonymous writer was producing a version of that storehouse of medieval travel lore and natural history, *Mandeville's Travels*.

An anonymous cleric was also producing for a noble lady a radically reworked version of the German Dominican Henry Suso's *Horologium Sapientiae* (Hourglass of Wisdom, translated as *The Seven Poyntes of Trewe Wisdom*), and the anonymous author of *The Cloud of Unknowing* was tackling the summits of that Everest of apophatic theology, the pseudo-Dionysian *Mystical Theology* (in translation, *Hid Divinity*), and also, possibly, the lower slopes of Richard of St Victor's *Benjamin Minor*. Many of these translations were reissued in printed versions, the Mandeville as late as 1725. Others were cannibalized: the *Seven Poyntes*, for example, in Nicholas Love's *Mirrour* (see below) and a 15th-c. morality play, *Wisdom*.

Several translations of the same texts were produced or projected. In addition to examples listed above, we may note several versions of Mandeville, and a version of Aegidius Romanus which Thomas **Hoccleve** (*c*.1367–1426) incorporated in his *Regement of Princes* (1411–12). Similarly, Hoccleve planned, but did not execute, a version of Vegetius for the Duke of Gloucester.

Translation is also characterized in this period by an aggressive self-confidence about the adequacy of the English language for the translation of texts from other languages. If we except remarks by King Alfred in the preface to his *Pastoral Care*, hardly anyone in England before Chaucer had defended translation by stressing the virtues of linguistic relativity. Chaucer does, in his prologues to Book II of *Troilus* and the *Astrolabe*. Trevisa similarly provided his *Polychronicon* with two prologues, the first a spirited defence of vernacular translation, the second a description of some of his distinctive practices. Such material appears regularly throughout the 15th c. as part of a translator's self-definition, the defence of vernacularity most tellingly and, for its author unfortunately, in the writings of Bishop Reginald Pecock (*c*.1395–*c*.1460).

I say 'unfortunately' because Pecock was to lose his bishopric as a result of another translation project greater than any thus far noted which, by virtue of its perceived threat to religious and secular authority, had led to a massive crackdown on unauthorized Biblical translations and a general retrenchment in the field of translation: the Wycliffite Bible (c.1385–97).

v. The Wycliffite Bible A collaborative venture by anonymous translators—Caxton later ascribed it to Trevisa—this Bible [see I.c.3.iv; II.c.1.iv] survives in a huge number of manuscripts, and in at least two versions. The earlier is much more literal; the later is more attentive to the rhythms of English syntax, and is accompanied by a prologue, Chapter 15 of which explains the methods of the translators and offers a strong defence of translation in general (Hudson 1978). The achievement of the translators becomes the more impressive when we consider how little precedent there was for such a version. The translation was part of a collaborative, and genuinely radical, project of book publication, distribution, and ownership which was well under way by 1388 (see Hanna 1996, who also comments on Chaucer, Trevisa, Walton, and Pecock).

The process by which ecclesiastical authority became alarmed enough by the threat posed by the Wycliffites for Archbishop Arundel to issue a total ban on unauthorized Bible translations between 1407 and 1409 has been documented by Hudson, and Watson (1995) has shown the regrettable consequences of the ban for the development of what he calls a 'vernacular theology'. In the secular sphere, too, the usurpation of the throne by Henry IV in 1400, and the need of the Lancastrians to legitimize their dynasty, would also have definite, if less easily quantifiable, effects on the production of translations in the first half of the 15th c.

Not the least of the ironies of the clampdown was its attempt to put into reverse a process which the Church itself had initiated in the Fourth Lateran Council (1215), to counter the spread of another heretical movement, the Cathars, by providing sufficient religious education to enable the laity to meet the heretics on their own ground.

One consequence of the ban was the copying by the Wycliffites not only of their own texts but also of orthodox texts like the Rolle Psalter with heretical material interpolated silently. In the obverse of this textual contamination, a translator, whom we know only by his initials (**MN**), actively drew attention to his interventions in his translation of *Le Mirouer des simples âmes* (The Mirror of Simple Souls), a work burned in Paris in 1310 along with its author, Marguerite Porete. The translator produced not one but two versions of the work. In the second, aware of the possibility of misinterpretation, he took pains to demonstrate—an open question even today—the orthodoxy of Marguerite's text.

A more immediate consequence of the ban was Arundel's licensing in 1410 of the *Mirrour of the Blessed Lyf of Jesu Christ* by Nicholas **Love** (d. 1424), a translation of the influential pseudo-Bonaventuran *Meditationes Vitae Christi* (Meditations of the Life of Christ). This work survives in numerous copies, and was prized by Sir Thomas More. It has many attractive features, for example Love's awareness of operating within a tradition of English writing, and his care, like MN, to distinguish his own additions to the text from the words of the original.

But its real significance lies in its return to an older, safer form of Bible paraphrase and Biblically inspired meditation, as also in its attack on Wycliffite teaching about the Eucharist. Echoes of Ælfric may be heard in Love's declaration in his prologue that he is providing his lay readers with 'milk of lyghte [easy] doctrine and not with sadde [serious] mete of grete clergie [learning]'.

If Love represents one response to the Wycliffite challenge throughout the 15th c., Pecock surely represents the other, with his defence of the vernacular as a way of taking the argument to the enemy. Sadly, his commitment to the vernacular contributed to his own condemnation in 1457 as a heretic.

vi. The Fifteenth Century Retreat into safer waters can be readily seen in the immediate aftermath of the unsuccessful Wycliffite uprising of 1414. In 1415 Hoccleve wrote to the heretic Sir John Oldcastle, to recommend a diet of reading matter appropriate to his knightly station and duties: not the Bible, though Old Testament books 'pertinent to chiualrie' could be consulted, but Vegetius (see above), the romance of Lancelot (fodder for the ladies, according to Chaucer's *Nun's Priest's Tale*) and the sieges of Thebes and Troy.

Lancelot comes into his own later in the century, in the *Morte Darthur* (1470) of Sir Thomas **Malory** (?1416–1471), a work which conflates French and Middle English sources and represents the full flowering in late Middle English of the seeds first sown over 300 years earlier by Geoffrey of Monmouth. As for the Thebes and Troy stories, both were translated early in the century by the indefatigable translator and first-generation Chaucerian John **Lydgate** (c.1370–c.1450).

Similarly, Caxton's first translation and first published work was, as earlier noted, a prose version of the Troy story offered in spite of the existence of Lydgate's verse version because Lydgate 'translated after some other auctor than this is'—Caxton was translating from the French of Raoul le Fevre; Lydgate had translated from the Latin of Guido delle Colonne—and because some people might prefer to read the story in prose.

To a limited extent it is possible to claim that translation in the 15th c. broke new ground. Thus Osbern **Bokenham** (1392–c.1447) provides for his *Legendys of Hooly Wummen* (1447), saints' lives mainly translated from the *Legenda Aurea*, an up-to-date prologue explaining original and translated works by way of Aristotelian frames of reference. Or consider Bokenham's contemporary and co-religionist John **Capgrave** (1393–1464), an Austin friar who seems to have 'run a "publishing house" for his own works from his headquarters in Lynn' (Pearsall 1977: 252). Capgrave provides his longest translation, a *Life of St Katherine*, with a fictional pedigree including translation from Greek to Latin and thence to an anonymous West Country version.

Capgrave's example can show that, overall, a greater professionalism characterises literary production in the 15th c. Hence the commercial London scriptorium (c.1420–50) of John **Shirley** (c.1366–1456), who published translations and produced several himself. This growing professionalism paves the way for Caxton's press.

Nevertheless, translation in the 15th c. was largely driven by reaction to the explosive events at the turn of the century, both positive, in the figures of Chaucer and other translators, and negative, in the figure of Archbishop Arundel. Two very different examples will make the point.

First the positive: Chaucer's *ABC to the Virgin*, a translation of a tiny part of the *Pelerinage de vie humaine* of Guillaume de Degulleville, was borrowed for two versions of the whole work made in 1425–8, the first an anonymous prose version, the second a verse version by Lydgate.

Then the negative: the translator of the Brigittine *Myroure of oure Ladye* had to secure episcopal permission for the translation of Bible verses in the

work. He did not translate the Psalm verses, because he knew the sisters had access to copies of Rolle's Psalter, which by virtue of its antiquity had escaped the ban.

Caxton's enormous output also provides clear evidence of this characterization of translation in the 15th c. as a reaction to events at the beginning of the century. The classics of the previous century figure prominently among Caxton's publications: Gower's *Confessio*; Chaucer's *Boece* and *Canterbury Tales*, the latter speedily reissued in a revised edition; a modernized edition of Trevisa's Higden. A Chaucer revised, a Trevisa modernized: this could almost be an epitome of the period. Caxton may also have printed a modernized version of those parts of the *Morte Darthur* which Malory had taken from a late 14th-c. alliterative romance, though possibly (Lacy 1986: s.v. Malory) Malory himself revised the text. Caxton also projected, but did not complete, a modernized version of a text 'wryton in Olde Englysshe'.

Translation in the 15th c., then, is like the prolonged aftershock of developments at the end of the 14th. The 'premature Reformation' (Hudson 1988) to which those developments contributed—and, one might add, the premature Renaissance—had to wait till the next century for their full flowering in England. And even then the effects of those earlier developments were still being felt. Around 1520, Murdoch **Nisbet** produced a Scots translation of the Wycliffite New Testament. A few years earlier Gavin Douglas had made a major translation of the *Aeneid* [see II.n.3.i], based, he tells us, on Virgil's Latin, and not, like Caxton's, on an intermediate French version, since Caxton is no closer to Virgil than 'the devill [to] Sanct Austyne' (Douglas 1957–64: ii. 11). Yet he too had to reckon, if not grapple, with the long shadows cast by Chaucer, and he sometimes makes his hero sound like the hero of a medieval romance.

2. THE RENAISSANCE
Warren Boutcher

i. **Introduction** 'A study of Elizabethan translations is a study of the means by which the Renaissance came to England' (Matthiessen 1931: 1). In an Italian or French literary context, the term 'Renaissance' would refer to a rediscovery of classical and Biblical letters in the ancient languages of Greek and Latin. The principal result would be new texts and editions in those languages, accompanied by new commentaries. In 16th-c. England virtually no classical and Biblical learning of this primary kind

was produced. For the majority of educated people, ancient letters were rediscovered by means of a comparative process of ongoing translations between Latin and a group of European vernaculars including English (Boutcher 1996).

In the last 50 years, however, critical discussion of this process has been marginal to English Renaissance studies. Critics of the era of modernism, a movement itself centred in creative polyglot translation, were the last fully to appreciate its importance. In the postwar period, most Tudor and early Stuart translations have returned to something like the obscurity they suffered before late Victorian editors republished them for the first time in centuries.

The problem may be that if we read these works as 'translations' in the modern sense they will inevitably disappoint, because good modern translations will almost always be found to be more faithful, more fluent, more sensitive to literary texture. What, though, if we read Renaissance translations as 'original' works by authors who happen to be translating? Such a reading may be warranted; the conditions for translation practice in this period were radically different from modern ones. Renaissance translators read and anatomized texts from the point of view of their training in rhetoric, a form of literary sensitivity very different in emphasis from that of 20th-c. translators, if only because it is less mindful of the hard-and-fast distinction between original and translated texts.

How, then, should we approach anew the legacy of editorial and critical work on English Renaissance translation left to us by the Victorians and the modernists, but largely ignored in the postwar period? One approach would simply be to revive critical appreciation of the canon of literary, mostly Elizabethan and Jacobean translations (c.1570–c.1620) put in place by the Victorians, and enthusiastically reassessed in the era of T. S. Eliot (Eliot 1960: 33–6). This canon, published in the 'Tudor Translations' series, provided a home-grown version of the classical, linguistic, and intellectual background needed for serious exposition of the literature of Shakespeare and his contemporaries. The Victorians saw these rediscovered translations as adventurous, pioneering works. They were thought to represent early progress towards the later literary supremacy of English as the medium of world literature and world empire (Whibley 1909).

This chapter will take a different approach. The aim is certainly not to displace the prewar period's critical sense of the literary ebullience and vigour of the work of Elizabethan and Jacobean translators such as Thomas **Hoby** (1530–66), Thomas **North** (c.1535–c.1601), John **Florio** (c.1553–1625), George **Chapman** (c.1559–1634), Philemon **Holland** (1552–1637), Thomas **Shelton** (*fl.* 1612), Christopher **Marlowe** (1564–93), John **Harington** (1560–1612), and Josuah **Sylvester** (1563–1618). T. S. Eliot was surely right when he found more felicity in their works than in the translations of any period into any language (Eliot 1932: 104). The aim is rather to offer a wider historical and cultural focus, to consider the

changing conditions of translation across the period as a whole, and to introduce a sense of how the preceding (1500–70) and subsequent (1620–50) phases might fit into a more general picture of this crucial epoch in the history of translation into English. The preceding phase, in particular, established a new set of conditions for translation which we need to understand in order fully to appreciate the nature of later translators' achievements.

ii. Literary Pedagogy and Oratorical Theories of Translation The late Victorian literary historian Henry Morley, the first editor of John Florio's translation of Montaigne's *Essayes* (1603) [II.g.5.ii] in over 250 years, described his work as a search in the work of all the great English writers of the past for what he called 'the one Mind in them all'. Foreign literatures had to be invoked as the sources of literary-historical change and progress, but in a manner that did not threaten the homespun integrity of this 'Mind'. The image of a great river naturally presented itself, a river into which foreign tributaries flowed and became lost in a single English current (Morley 1887–95: i. 2–4). According to this view, Florio was participating in the rise and 'triumph' of the English vernacular and making it possible for Montaigne to 'influence' Shakespeare.

Florio, though, was an exiled Italian, and his trade at the time of the translation was private tuition in French and Italian for noblewomen and a few English humanists and gentlemen (Yates 1934). His aim was a triumphant role for the vernaculars in general in the ceaseless process of to-and-fro between languages that constituted European polyglot learning. He imagined that his translation would serve his lady pupils 'to repeat in true English what you reade in fine French', as well as to tell 'thousands' of more vulgar readers things they could only otherwise be taught 'in an other language' (Florio 1910: i. 1). The goal was not to supplant French, but to dignify English in its role as the local means of learning international languages and the encyclopaedia of knowledge that came with them.

The fantasy for some translators was that one day the tables would be turned and Latin or Italian would be considered just stiff or lame aids for learning English (Davis 1955: 222). But the concept of an organically grown literary English expressive of an independent national character did not exist in this period; the understood context for the 'rise' of an authoritative English was always the comparative European one. One learned to write good English, to think sharp English thoughts, even to act effectively in English circumstances, by lively translation from Latin or Italian books.

For in the 16th c. new ideas about translation flowed from new ideas about literary pedagogy. In particular, they flowed from the ideas of the humanists about the teaching in tandem of Greek and Latin as literary rather than philosophical or technical languages. The choicest Roman authors (for Latin was the central subject) such as Virgil and Cicero were taught as brilliant imitators and translators of the best of Greek authors—Homer and Demosthenes. The goal of such pedagogy was the education of the 'orator'. The orator is the noble speaker in the Roman forum who marshals ('invention' and 'judgement') all his polymathic learning ('philosophy'), with vivid style ('rhetoric') and argumentative force ('logic' or 'dialectic'), to move and persuade his audience to his point of view on an urgent and widely resonant issue, in a way suitable to the place and occasion ('decorum').

It followed, for influential French humanist theorists of translation such as Jacques Peletier du Mans and Étienne Dolet, that the ideal form of translation was 'oratorical' translation, to be judged in the same terms as any other oratorical composition. As the Tudor humanist and translator Nicholas **Grimalde** (c.1519–1562) puts it in the prefatory material to his version of *Marcus Tullius Ciceroes Thre Bokes of Duties* (1556): 'Howbeit loke, what rule the Rhetorician gives in precept, to be observed of an Oratour, in telling of his tale . . . the same rule should be used in examining, & judging of translation.' The question to be asked is thus: what point is the *translator* making by using the rhetorical resources at his disposal in the source text?

A practical example will show how this approach to translation flowed from a new approach to the teaching of literary language. William Kempe, an Eton schoolboy in the 1570s, explains in 1588 how a textbook of Cicero's *Epistles* should be used in the third form of a grammar school. After the boy has studied, say, the short Latin text of a letter from Cicero to his absent wife, expressing worry about the arrival of messengers and about her health, he shall be set an exercise. The schoolmaster gives the boy 'an Epistle in English of the like sentence'—not, now, from Cicero to his wife, but from Peter Cole to John and Charles his sons, expressing worry at their lack of letters and care for their learning. The boy then has to translate this English variation on the Latin original back into Latin, imitating Ciceronian style as closely as possible (Baldwin 1944: ii. 253–4).

Here, translation is the core exercise in general grammatical and rhetorical learning in the forces or 'virtues' of words and ideas as they have been handled by the best authors: in this case, the virtues of literary Latin and of thought for a dependant's wellbeing, as handled by the best Roman orator. Since it is the forces rather than the authors that are the primary object of study, fidelity to the author's literary creation takes the form of fidelity to his particular handling of this common stock of words and ideas. It is only by imagining the author on the model of the good father or husband, the wise legislator or the Holy Ghost, that the resulting variety of reconceived topoi are reduced in the pedagogical and analytical process to a single design of the common good ('commonweal') or Christian salvation. Such reduction is implicit in the 'sentence' chosen by the teacher in this case: the pupil is to learn good Latin along with the piety of paternal solicitude.

The next step is to understand how this method focused exclusively on the learning of good Latin, not good English, informs literary translation from Latin and other languages into English. The answer is: by analogy. In Kempe's account, the pupil learns to compose Latin as Cicero might have done in an English situation, a situation analogous to one in which he did compose. In the process he stretches and illustrates his capacities in Latin.

Translation whose final goal is an English not a Latin text, then, is the process whereby the pupil learns to compose *English* as Cicero might have done in an English situation analogous to one in which he did compose. In the process he stretches and illustrates the capacities of English. The enthusiastic translator will call upon as many different resources as possible to reanimate and revisualize the sense of what he would have called his 'copy', the model whose forms he is to repeat and elaborate. Many of these will be domestic: from the existing idiomatic and aural resources of English (proverbs, onomatopoeia, alliteration), to regional voices such as the West Country accent used by Arthur **Golding** (c.1536–1606) in his translation of Ovid's *Metamorphoses* [II.n.6.iii], to the figures of late medieval allegory and English equivalents in religion and custom and social situation (Lyne 1996).

Where these resources fail, however, the translator will with caution propose a borrowing of the form of the foreign word, idiom, or figure as a necessary addition to the stock of English literary words and figures. In this spirit Florio proposes the naturalization of the following French locutions, accompanied by familiar English synonyms in the translation itself: 'entraine, conscientious, endeare, tarnish, comporte, efface, facilitate, ammusing, debauching, regret, effort, emotion' (Florio 1910: i. 11). Familiar now, these words looked strange and 'uncouth' then. The overall outcome is very different from the resolution of local and personal allusions into generic language that is the hallmark of a fluent modern translation. It is more like doing an 'impression' of Cicero as an eloquent Tudor English gentleman.

Once again, the theoretical terms needed to describe the virtues of the translator's active re-creation of the elements of the common literary stock are those of general rhetorical theory: specifically, the Greek terms *energeia* and *enargeia*, translated into Latin by such terms as *actus*, *evidentia*, and *efficacia* (Norton 1984). They occur in English vernacular poetic theory: Philip Sidney uses *energeia* ('forciblenes') to denote that quality of a compilation of the rhetoric of love which makes it seem animated by the passions of a real situation (Smith 1904: i. 201). George Puttenham uses the two terms to denote the techniques (*enargeia*) for heightening the artificial impact of the aural and visual aspects of language, and the techniques (*energeia*) for making the overall sense more vivid and forceful to the intellect—'efficacie by sence' (Smith 1904: ii. 148). When George Chapman justifies his selection of Homer's description of *Achilles Shield* (1598) as a passage worthy of issue in English in its own volume, he does so by implicitly using such terms: 'all things [are] here described by our divinist Poet as if they consisted not of hard and solid mettals, but of a truely living and moving soule' (Smith 1904: ii. 298).

However, the full-blown theory of Christian oratorical translation, dependent chiefly on Cicero and St Jerome [see I.a.3.ii], is not laid out in explicit detail in any vernacular English text or translation preface published in this period, though parts of it occur piecemeal, as we have seen in Grimalde, and as could be exemplified from the version of *Three Orations of Demosthenes* (1570) by Thomas **Wilson** (c.1525–1581) and George Chapman's *Seaven Bokes of the Iliades of Homere* (1598). A substantial theoretical treatise on Christian oratorical translation was in fact published in the 16th c. by an Englishman, Laurence Humphrey, but it was written in Latin, published in Basle, and never translated into English!

The title of this work, published in 1559, can be translated as *The Interpretation of Languages, Or, On the Method of Translating and Explicating Sacred and Profane Authors, in Three Books*. Humphrey's work offers no modern-style concept of literary translation as a distinct process applied to a distinct category of secular texts including prose fiction, drama,

and poetry, the goal of which is to balance idiomatic smoothness with fidelity to authorial style and intention. *Literary* translation into English is judged in relation to the general European transmission of the schemes and skills of classical *learning*. It follows from this that a proper literary translation is not really distinct from other forms of imitative literature that transmit and apply the schemes of learning—it is just a special case, a work rewriting one particular original, rather than drawing more eclectically on a number (Trousdale 1976). It is, in many ways, a much more difficult act to pull off, for the translator cannot hide his or her traces and is always more open to the charge of slavishness, or lack of inventiveness, in the composition. For this reason, some commentators—including one royal translator, King **James VI** of Scotland [I.a.6.ii]—advised against it (Smith 1904: i. 221).

Furthermore, Humphrey's treatise makes it clear that the learning in question is not just learning in languages. For translation is the exercise at the core of a wide programme of applied learning in a variety of adjacent subjects. This programme is usually referred to now as humanism, and its teachers as humanists. In England, the subjects in question include Latin and the chief modern languages, poetry, rhetoric and logic, moral philosophy, history, and even take in areas of medical, natural, and astronomical science, as well as law and the customs of nations. One can learn anything by means of a translation. Scientific and mathematical translations such as that by Henry **Billingsley** (d. 1606) of Euclid's *The Elements of Geometrie* (1570) are as representative of 'Tudor translations' as those selected by the Victorians.

Philip Sidney defends poetry as the key to 'all humane learning', to 'all knowledge, Logick, Rethorick, Philosophy, naturall and morall' (Smith 1904: i. 180, 206). If one is looking for vivid actualizations of the meaning of piety, one can go on the one hand to 'the poeticall part of the scripture' (*Psalms*, *Proverbs*, *Ecclesiastes*, and the *Song of Songs*). The completion by Mary **Sidney** (c.1555–1621) [I.a.5.i] of Philip's own unpublished manuscript translation of the *Psalms* is one of the greatest of the period.

Philip Sidney offers another major literary source for piety, however: Virgil's *Aeneid*, Books II and IV, exactly the *Certain Bokes of Virgiles Æneis* (1557) translated by Henry Howard, Earl of **Surrey** (c.1517–1547), the greatest of the pre-Elizabethan poetic translators along with Thomas **Wyatt** (1503–42). In these two books one can see and hear how Aeneas 'governeth himselfe in the ruine of his Country; in the preserving his old Father, and carrying away his religious ceremonies; in obeying the Gods commandement to leave *Dido . . .* etc' (Smith 1904; i. 179–80). Such an understanding of Virgil's text is often dismissed by modern commentators as unpoetic, reductive, or moralistic. But T. S. Eliot and Ezra Pound saw that compared with the ethos of later, post-1650 neoclassicism—which 'put the classics into silk stockings'—the Tudors and early Stuarts had a 'living' relationship to these ancient and foreign texts, a sense that they were as ready to hand as Biblical texts for immediate application to actual problems and experience (Pound 1973: 356; Eliot 1960: 35). In far-fetched books, compellingly present emotions and situations were being discovered. The central means of discovery was adaptive translation, or 'attentive translation', as Sidney calls it.

The paragon of English Renaissance man, Hamlet the Dane, makes discoveries by these means in Act II Scene ii of Shakespeare's play. From the Player's repertory, the Prince wants to hear again the section of the 'passionate speech' of 'Aeneas tale to Dido' evoking in vivid detail the slaughter of Priam. The speech is an oratorical set piece, an adaptive translation or 'imitation' made on a basic pattern provided by Virgil. From a Renaissance rhetorical viewpoint, the exemplary significance of this book as a whole is that Virgil—in the persona of Aeneas—succeeded in putting the fall of Troy before our eyes. The more particular pattern is the passionate action that can be caused by witnessing 'a dear father murder'd'.

The purpose of Hamlet's impromptu commission to the Player to perform this particular vernacular imitation is to enable him to visualize and apprehend more strongly what has happened to his father, and what his and his other courtiers' reactions should be. The expectation is that it should provide a pattern for the furthering of his purpose: it does so in that he commissions a performance of another translated and adapted melodrama—the image of a murder done in Vienna 'written in very choice Italian'—in order to flush out the guilty passions of Claudius. Just like a Renaissance translator, Hamlet adds a passage pointing up the topical relevance of the play for its audience on this occasion.

Tudor and early Stuart translations are, like particular stage productions, original and unique performances of texts. At the textual level, we have first to see, hear, and apprehend the visual, verbal, and intellectual patterns the translators saw in their model. There then follows the task of understanding how they sought equivalent English patterns and borrowed strange ones in the making of their own version. Beyond this lies the task of recovery of the personal questions and strategic purposes animating their translations. These may resolve to a single pattern, as they do in Hamlet's case, or they may yield multiple patterns of applied interest, or they may prove to have originated in a single application of a single text but to have diversified as more and more of the text was translated.

Indeed, the appearance of a whole work in translation may originate and develop in precisely this way: Christopher **Watson** (1545–81) notices shining allusions to Polybius' *History* in an English oration from Edward Hall's *Chronicles* and decides to translate the first book as *The Hystories of the Most Famous and Worthy Cronographer Polybius* (1568), though a translation of the whole work never appears; George **Sandys** (1578–1644) [II.n.6.iii] translates verses from Ovid's *Metamorphoses* as he needs them to embroider his travel narrative, then issues a small publication of five complete books, then by royal patent a larger publication of the whole poem (1632) entitled *Ovid's Metamorphosis Englished, Mythologiz'd and Represented in Figures* (Davis 1955: 199–204).

iii. Social and Cultural Conditions We have, then, an alternative context for translation into English during this period: not the triumph of English but the rise from the late 15th c. of a new continental European trade in Graeco-Latin, Latin, French, Spanish, Italian, and 'Dutch' (meaning both High and Low German) books; as well as, side by side with this trade, new forms of polyglot literary training and new understandings of the European literary past, *into which* translators, tutors and writers like Laurence Humphrey would attempt to insert a newly 'illustrated' or more widely and demandingly used English vernacular (Loewenstein 1996).

In the new, 16th-c. western and northern European market of ideas, England is the biggest net importer, open to the widest range of foreign products (Higman 1993). Access to this new world of the continental printed book brings with it the overwhelming sense of marginalization, of alienation from a vast body of European textual learning organized and presented from the point of view of others' needs and others' pride. Energy goes not into competitive English-based reproductions of the Greek and Latin texts, but into free vernacular naturalization of the foreign products. Even in the case of translation of the classics into English, however, translators were conscious of belatedly and somewhat basely emulating the sumptuous Italian, French, and Spanish translations of Greek and Latin works already arriving in gentlemen's libraries via the import market (Bolgar 1954; Nørgaard 1958).

What difference does this make to the practice of translation? It is the difference between translating into and out of two very different kinds of literary mainstream. Modern translators are conscious that English has become the world's lingua franca, in the way that Latin once was, and that it is the vehicle of a great and independent body of classical English and modern, Anglophone, 'world' (American, Irish, Canadian, Indian etc.) literature. They are for the most part translating for people who will never see or read a copy of the 'original' book, who will take the translation for the original. The translator must be invisible.

In retrospect, it is possible to trace the distant origins of this situation in the unofficial list of translated and indigenous works in English which unlearned gentlemen and courtly ladies could consume by the 1590s. It is more important to note, however, that translators in this period actually worked in cultural conditions almost diametrically opposite to modern ones. For virtually nobody outside the British Isles ever dreamt of needing to learn English. Tudor and early Stuart translators were translating into a literary language that from a courtly perspective was still a local pedagogical means of learning a *run* of authoritative international languages. Prestigious continental books of general or classical authority were being accommodated to particular 'local' circumstances in England, in—as we shall see—an atmosphere of potential ideological controversy.

It is not surprising, then, that translators will often check several copies of their text in two or more of these languages, neither necessarily privileging the language of 'original' composition nor imagining their own version to be a definitive work which will in some sense substitute for that original. This was true even of the translators of the King James Bible [II.c.1.vi], who, according to John Selden, regularly checked their text against new French, Spanish, and Italian versions on the market (Hammond 1993: 33).

For the consumer, a translation was a cheap and reader-friendly way of importing a book and hiring an expert commentator to explain its meaning and relevance. Indeed, it is likely that many translations were issued to cash in on demand for particular European editions of prestigious texts (Norbrook 1994: 54). Especially early in the period, the importing of continental books and the employment of foreign humanists was an expensive business. Each precious imported book could have a unique life-history as an 'offering' or an acquisition made in particular circumstances, and might be personalized with a binding appropriate to the recipient, annotations added in manuscript, and even a new status as a family heirloom. Likewise, most cultivated aristocratic households of the first rank employed foreign scholars as family servants. This context of élite reception of the imported book and the foreign scholar is carried over into the marketing of translations. They are presented in printed dedications to particular patrons, and in prefaces to the general reader, as naturalized or captured strangers needing welcome, rehousing, and protection.

Another crucial difference between the conditions of Renaissance and of modern translation is the very strong tradition of offered or commissioned manuscript translations dedicated to particular patrons on particular occasions such as New Year, or the birth or death of a relative. The offering could also be made, of course, to oneself, a literary exercise performed as part of one's secular and religious meditations in particular circumstances. Translating the psalms, in particular, was a way of conducting a self-examination and was perhaps the most common form of literary translation (Zim 1987).

As occasional pieces, these translations were usually pointed towards an urgent issue of the moment in the household of the dedicatee. This could range from the question of the correct ethos for the early education of a gentleman's precious new-born son to the provision of 'remedies' for particular medical or psychological problems—such as those caused by incarceration in the Tower of London, or—in the royal household—a pressing issue in foreign policy.

This variety of places, occasions, and purposes corresponded to the variety of social positions and roles one finds translators filling. Anybody with an education might translate in a multiplicity of personal and career circumstances, for it was considered a suitable sign of one's intellectual preparedness for services of all kinds. The nearest one gets to a 'professional' translator is a schoolmaster such as Philemon Holland, or hack scholar-translators employed by printer-booksellers to turn out English copies of foreign books they have imported personally and entered under the period's version of 'copyright' as their property. Except in these latter circumstances, we are a long way from the 'invisible translator' of this century: John Harington and Philemon Holland are actually engraved on the title-pages of their translations of, respectively, Ariosto's *Orlando Furioso in English Heroical Verse* (1591) [II.m.6.i] and Xenophon's *Cyropaedia* (1632) [II.i.10.iii]—the former with his dog!

It was, then, the point the translator wished to make, or the meditation he or she wished to offer regarding a particular issue on a given occasion, from a particular place, by *means* of a translation, which prevailed over any desire to offer a textually accurate version of a noted author's work. When the depressed Queen Katherine of Aragon commissioned Thomas Wyatt to translate Petrarch's book on the remedy for ill fortune, he told her that *Plutarckes Boke of the Quyete of Mynde* (1528) would do just as well for her purpose, and gave her that instead. In the 1590s, some of the private meditations of Queen **Elizabeth I** on the state of her personal and political rule took the form of translations of Boethius's *Consolation of Philosophy*, Plutarch's essay *On Curiosity*, and Horace's *On the Art of Poetry*. They were private only in that they were not published—a copy is found in the State Papers (Sharpe 1994: 120–3).

English Renaissance translation is fundamentally, to be sure, a receptive process, but the reception is active and explicit. The translator ostentatiously receives, socializes, and re-employs a highly resourceful but potentially suspect representative of classical or continental culture in new English circumstances. There is a sense that special arrangements have to be made at every point to relocate the book in England, and to guarantee that its contents are worthwhile, harmless and, above all, useful and vivid for English readers. The whole book is thoroughly 'Englished' by a kind of multimedia transformation, a transformation which often includes the addition of aids such as maps, engraved illustrations and commentaries.

We shall see, however, that the nature of the representatives chosen, and of the special arrangements made, are by the end of the 16th c. less likely to be a straightforward expression of establishment pedagogy than in the preceding period. An engraving adapted from an Italian edition of Ariosto for John Harington's English edition is changed to allow us to 'see' in greater depth the events described in the text (Rich 1940: 56–7). Inside houses whose walls have been cut away, the English engravings show us the Italian debauchery in more graphic detail—so that the Protestant reader can, of course, more profoundly disapprove!

iv. 1500–1570 A claim could be made for the translation by Alexander **Barclay** (*c.*1475–1552) of Sebastian Brant's *Shyp of Folys of the Worlde* (1509) [II.h.2.i] as the first of the significantly humanist-influenced Tudor translations to be published. Performed by a secular preacher and educationalist, it showed both the clear influence of humanist grammar school teaching methods—including the local-ization and domestication of allusions and references to Devon and England—and the impact of the growing trade in imported continental books on the environment of translation (Orme 1989: 259–70). Contemporary with Barclay—who was Scottish by origin—is the efflorescence of humanist translation in Renaissance Scotland, beginning with the *Eneados* of Gavin **Douglas** (*c.*1474–1522) [I.a.6.ii; II.n.3.i].

If the King James Bible is the most important translation in English history, then the most important translator is the radical secular preacher William **Tyndale** (1494–1536) [II.c.1.v], whose labours first opened the way for its production. John Foxe includes the story of Tyndale's early work in his vast and polemical collection of the *Acts and Monuments* of the Reformed English Church (1563). In this account, Tyndale transfers from Oxford to Cambridge, then returns to his native county as a tutor in the household of Sir John and Lady Anne Walsh of Little Sodbury in Gloucestershire. At Walsh's table Foxe falls into dispute with sundry learned doctors of the Roman Catholic Church (the date is the early 1520s). Lady Anne asks why they should believe him above 'great, learned and beneficed men'? Tyndale's deferred reply is a translation—almost certainly in manuscript—of an imported Latin book present in the household, Erasmus's manual of pious learning for the Christian soldier, *Enchiridion militis Christiani*.

The immediate effect of this gift is that 'those great prelates were no more so often called to the house'. The readings of the secular preacher have literally displaced the obscure doctrines of the prelate, and the household is reformed. This story about a translation is thus moulded by Reformation ideology. The translation is later (probably) published in printed form, with government sponsorship, to the benefit of the whole commonwealth (Devereux 1983).

But, the story goes on, Tyndale's readings proved too controversial for Gloucestershire ecclesiastical society, and he flees to London. There he seeks service as a translator of the Greek New Testament with the Bishop of London by offering a translation from the Greek of Isocrates. Refused, he understands finally that there is place for his work neither in the Bishop's house, nor in the whole of England. He continues his activities from Antwerp, and is eventually arrested by the Imperial authorities and executed for heresy (Daniell 1994: 61–90).

The case of Tyndale and the official unacceptability of his independently produced Bible translations—contraband translations which, in the event, were incorporated into the official English Bible—

51

alerts us to the nature of the ideological context of translation in this period. The ideological policy of the English monarchical, ecclesiastical, and patriarchal state during and after the Reformation was to maintain political and institutional control over individual and group reading. Reading, here, encompasses interpretations and translations of the texts of Scripture, the law, and classical antiquity (in that order of importance). The premiss of *Leviathan* (1651), by philosopher and translator Thomas **Hobbes**, is that loss of such control on the part of the Protestant monarchical establishment precipitated the civil war.

This ideology extended to the issue of the kind of reading and translation that could appropriately be undertaken by women, and in what circumstances. Supervised by their husbands and brothers, they were supposed to translate religious works only (Hannay 1985). In practice, they were confined neither to devotional purposes in such translations, nor completely to religious literature [see I.a.5.i].

Thus *all* directed reading and translation was supposed to redound to the good of the commonwealth. In the case of the English Bible, textual minutiae could prove of immense ideological significance. The annotations and directions for reading accompanying the Tyndale-inspired Matthew Bible of 1537 (printed at Paris) soon proved too controversial for the royal and ecclesiastical establishment, and the job of revision was given to Miles **Coverdale** (1488–1568), eventually responsible for the Great Bible of 1539–41 [II.c.1.v]. He removed the overly Protestant notes, but he left in the margins the signs in the form of hands which 'pointed' to key passages. According to Foxe, even this was still too ideologically sensitive for the clergy (Pollard 1911: 16–17, 229, 237, 245).

In this light, the King James Bible can be seen as the result of an attempt to remove the signs of the process of independent, controversial reading (which started with Tyndale) from what becomes, relatively, a *neutral* text: the prototype, perhaps, for the fluent modern translation? Until at least 1640, the King James Bible coexisted uncomfortably with a more controversially pointed text—the Geneva Bible (Hill 1993).

The era of struggle between 1525, the year of Tyndale's first New Testament and of the beginnings of Reformation controversy in England, and 1570, the year of the settlement of England's independent Protestant regime and of Thomas Wilson's Demosthenes, saw sustained court and governmental interest in the publication of religious and secular translations conducive to the

emergent Protestant establishment's version of civility and piety. This interest centred on Englished versions of the continental publications of Erasmus (McConica 1965). Thereafter, the interests at work are more various, and the image of the good commonwealth man produced on the pattern of classical soldiers and orators such as Virgil's Aeneas and Lucan's Pompey, or of politic continental gentlemen such as Montaigne and Machiavelli (Raab 1964), becomes openly contentious.

Thus from c.1525 to c.1570—allowing for the Roman Catholic hiatus under Mary (1553–8), which saw no drop in translation activity—it is Christian humanist pedagogy, as initially inspired by Erasmus, which contains within a single framework the goals of religious and secular translation, and seeks to identify both with a Protestant establishment ethos.

The condition, then, for the greater freedom admired by the Victorians in the translations of the period that immediately followed was the relative confinement of humanistic translation during this earlier period: confinement to the circles and servants of Privy Councillors, courtiers, political figures prominent in the establishment and local government, and scholars of key Oxbridge colleges such as St John's Cambridge, and Magdalen Hall, Oxford; confinement in vernacular translation to the canons and theory of Ciceronian humanist translation; confinement in source material to classical poetry, classical history, stoic philosophy, and modern court humanism (Desiderius Erasmus, Baldassare Castiglione, Antonio de Guevara); confinement, in ethical terms, to the commonweal ethos of the 'independent' stoic and the 'honest' courtier, to Erasmian piety and a political morality offering schematic and Plutarchan lessons applicable to contemporary affairs; confinement, as 'textbooks' and manuals, to the scope of petty and grammar school teaching and parish sermons.

v. 1570–1620 After 1570 there is an explosion of local, informal cultures of learning outside the establishment links connecting grammar schools, Oxbridge colleges, Inns of Court and the corridors of power. The pious single-mindedness of the counsels offered in readings and translations and the close relationship between translation and establishment schooling are both dissolved. Multiple possible reading paths through texts are now entertained in private and local academies of scholars, gentlemen, and nobles. When single-minded literary translation of whole works returns in the early Caroline period, it is secularized and brought closer to philological scholarship, in a recognizably neo-classical fashion. The way is led self-consciously by Ben **Jonson**, who in his conversations with the Scottish poet and translator William **Drummond** (1585–1649) scorned most Elizabethan and Jacobean translations, and who set a new benchmark with his translation of Horace's *Art of Poetry* (1640).

Even within establishment circles the Erasmian ethos is out of fashion by 1570, as it is in learned Europe generally, and the question of the ideological control of the English Bible takes centre stage alone, segregated from the question of morally and politically correct forms of classical literary training. It is this which Thomas Nashe—perhaps with tongue in cheek—is lamenting in 1589, when he recalls the glory days of the earlier Tudor translation of learning, centred at his own college, St John's, Cambridge (Smith 1904: I. 312–15). Literary history was to reverse his judgement. In what came to be considered by the Victorians the post-1570 golden age of translation, the gradual unyoking of literary from Biblical and legal exegesis (which remained, nevertheless, parallel pursuits) actually freed the former, relatively speaking, from its obligations of plain-speaking fidelity to the classical 'author' (modelled on the Holy Ghost) and to the royal establishment's Christian commonwealth values.

In other words, there was no linear progress towards the fluent modern translation of the classic, respectful both of the author's intentions and of normal or neutral domestic values. For an interim, translation was freer, and the justifications for such freedom became more eclectic, as when the leading university intellectual John Case justified Richard Haydocke's wholesale appropriation (1598) of Giovanni Lomazzo's *Tracte Containing the Artes of Curious Paintinge, Carvinge and Buildinge* to his own purposes by drawing on a whole variety of arguments and images. Singularity of purpose and close fidelity are rare: the canon of encyclopedic texts held to teach everything—from the commonplaces of human passion to the topography of the Near East—exploded well beyond Virgil's *Aeneid* II and IV and the *Psalms*. Unorthodox texts that had never appeared on a school or university curriculum found their English translators: Christopher Marlowe's clandestinely printed version of *Ovid's Elegies: Three Bookes* [II.n.6.ii] is in debt to school translation only for its method, not for its general ethos and ideology (Jacobsen 1958).

The typical literary translation in this period was the copiously varied and multiply applied translation of the encyclopedic poet, novelist, historian, or philosopher: North's 1579 version of Plutarch's *Lives of the Noble Grecians and Romanes*, Florio's Montaigne, Chapman's Homer, Holland's version of Livy's *Romane Historie* (1600), Harington's Ariosto, Sylvester's translation of the *Devine weekes and workes* of Guillaume de Salluste du Bartas (1605), Sandys's Ovid, the translation by Shelton of Cervantes' *History of Don-Quixote* (1612, 1620), Caesar's *Commentaries* (1600) by Clement **Edmondes** (c.1564–1622), *Seneca His Tenne Tragedies* (1581) including work by Jasper **Heywood** (1535–98), and the *Workes of L. A. Seneca both Morrall and Natural* (1614) by Thomas **Lodge** (c.1558–1625) [for all of these translations, see the relevant entries in Part II]. What gives such literarily miscellaneous works coherence is the particular culture of varied commentary and applied learning they represent. They are faithful to the multiplicity of possible applications that gentlemen, yeomen, and merchant readers might make on the basis of what was called the 'groundwork' of the original copy (Davis 1955: 217).

This multiplicity is typically manifested not only in the greater freedoms taken with the copy text itself, in the interpolations made, the typographical pointers added, but in the elaborate prefatory materials and commentaries with which the main text is accompanied. In the commentaries added to each book of Harington's Ariosto or Sandys's Ovid we see examples of the multiple discursive paths that can be taken through and beyond the poet's groundwork by the translators and their friends, relatives, and patrons.

John Florio [II.g.5.ii] does not for a moment permit his readers the illusion that they are reading Montaigne—if for no other reason than that they might simultaneously be doing so in French!—and he will disappoint if compared with later translators who do. Florio offers, rather, his own and his scholarly friends' re-creation of Montaigne as a noble Elizabethan commentator speaking privately and frankly to a friend—perhaps a reincarnation of Philip Sidney conversing with his relatives, close associates, and foreign humanist friends.

Furthermore, unlike the scholarly English humanist exiles who read Demosthenes at Padua with establishment figure and translator Sir John **Cheke** (1514–57) while England was in Roman Catholic hands (the background to Thomas Wilson's translation of the Greek orator), Florio and his friends are not so single-mindedly in pursuit of an Edwardian definition of faithful oratorical style, the common good, and national salvation. If the French has a single authorial design (a moot point), it is lost in the English, even though a

multiplicity of perceived patterns recur in Elizabethan forms in the normal manner.

With such loss there is gain, however. For the re-
creation is directed in the first instance at a group
of noble families who own multiple copies of the
French *Essais* and for whom the translators teach
and study; and ultimately it is the common culture,
the shared sense of a particular political moment in
England potentially uniting this group, which
makes the English version an original work. In this
general respect there is of course continuity with
the Paduan context of Wilson's Demosthenes:
what has gone is the pious single-mindedness of the
readings and the close relationship to orthodox
schooling. Secular translation is released from ideological confinement, and becomes the principal
literary means of heterodox comment on contemporary morality and politics.

vi. 1620–1650 By the end of the Jacobean era it is
thus not surprising to find translations both reflecting and producing the increasing ideological het-
erodoxy of English society. In the late 1620s two
celebrated classical translations were dedicated to
members of the household of William Cavendish,
second Earl of Devonshire. Both the complete version of Lucan's *Pharsalia* (1627) by Thomas **May**
(1595–1650) [II.n.8.i] and Thomas Hobbes's
complete rendering of Thucydides' *Eight Bookes
of the Peloponnesian Warre* (1629) [II.i.10.ii] self-
consciously rise above schoolroom pedagogy and
courtroom rhetoric into a sphere of aristocratic
humanist learning and noble counsel.

Thomas May's long-standing relationship to
Lucan was far from single-minded. The 1627 version of the translation, however, idealizes Pompey
as a republican leader and regrets Rome's drift into
empire. May's dedications to the individual books
situate the work amongst a politically independent
and hawkish nobility tending towards parliamentary opposition to royal policies (Norbrook 1994:
57–66).

Hobbes's Thucydides was perhaps the greatest
English humanist translation from classical history.
He went back directly to the most philologically
authoritative Greek text, consulted other continental translations and commentaries, and consistently
interpreted the work as the supreme classical
instance of rhetorical historiography. His own
paratextual apparatus—including a 'Life' of Thucydides and an original engraved map—eschewed the
tendency towards digressive and copious readings.
Instead, in the title-page engraving, in his annotations and marginal notes, he focused the text on a

single purpose. Thucydides had demonstrated the
ineptitude of democracy and the wisdom of single
rule: Hobbes made him speak to the English, advis-
ing them to avoid the advice of the popular pleaders
in the English parliament (Skinner 1996: 229–49,
286–7).

Both of these classical translations are listed
under 'History' in bookseller William London's
1657 catalogue of the most 'vendible' books available for purchase by his clientele, the northern
provincial élite. In this catalogue, Erasmus is still in
print, but his works are now firmly confined to the
category of books for academic and school learning
in the Hebrew, Greek, and Latin languages. The
general guides to the world of learning and reading
for the gentleman are now the new philosophers:
Francis Bacon, the englished Montaigne, and various other essayists. Learning is cleanly divided into
divine and humane study, given roughly equal
weight in the catalogue as a whole.

Segregated, then, from Biblical commentary and
translation, humane study is divided into categories
that are recognizable to modern readers. These
include one which resembles English literature as
we know it. In fact, under the single heading of
'romances, plays and poems', alongside 'original'
works by Elizabethan, Jacobean, and Caroline
authors, can be found works that begin to look like
an unofficial canon of secular, philologically more
authoritative literary translations: Ben Jonson's
Horace, Shelton's Cervantes, Chapman's Homer,
Musaeus' *Hero and Leander* translated by Sir Robert
Stapleton (d. 1669), the partial version of *Aeneid* II
by Sir John **Denham** (1615–69), the first complete
Virgil in English (1649) by John **Ogilby** (1600–76).
Here is a list of world classics in English much
more respectable than the one available in the early
1590s.

This category, then, though very low in William
London's puritan and utilitarian set of priorities, is
most significant for our purposes. At the beginning
of the period, one could not talk of English literature and literary translation of foreign *œuvres* into
English in anything like the modern sense. One
had to talk of the local application of European
learning, of imported books with new life-histories,
of the revisualization for English eyes of Priam's
death, Dido's passion, and David's penance. By
1650, however, it appears that space has begun to
clear for talk of both. A decade on, at the Restoration (1660), a whole era has passed. Never again will
the importing, reading, and translating of foreign
books be as visible, as significant, and as controversial a process in English history.

Few English Renaissance translations are currently available in editions accessible to the general reader. The exception is Thomas Hoby's translation of Castiglione's *Book of the Courtier* (1561), published by Everyman. Many can be consulted in rare scholarly editions, including the two out-of-print series (1892–1909, 1924–7) of 'Tudor Translations'. The best guide to primary and secondary bibliography is still *The New Cambridge Bibliography of English Literature*, vol. i: *600–1600*, ed. George Watson (1974). Other useful general studies include Conley (1927), Devereux (1983), Ebel (1967; 1969), Hannay (1985), Jones (1953), Lathrop (1967), Matthiessen (1931), Zim (1987), and chapters in Bennett (1965; 1969; 1970).

3. NEOCLASSICISM AND ENLIGHTENMENT
Lawrence Venuti

i. Introduction This period witnessed the decisive emergence of *fluency* as the most prevalent strategy for rendering foreign poetry and prose, both ancient and modern. Translators aimed for a stylistic refinement that usually involved a significant rewriting of the foreign text, but that at the same time worked to mask this rewriting. They achieved an extraordinary readability, an ease and transparency that produced the illusion of original composition. And their achievement is all the more remarkable because this illusion was secured not only in plain prose, but in a most artificial poetic form: the heroic couplet.

Which is to say that the overriding project in translation at this time was to make the foreign recognizably, even splendidly English. Translators enacted a subtle inscription of the foreign text with distinctively English literary canons, making it serve distinctively English cultural and political agendas. Translation strategies were rarely wedded to a programme for preserving the foreignness of the foreign text. On the contrary, they were guided primarily by domestic values that were assuming cultural dominance or had already attained it during the 17th and 18th c.—often with help from striking English versions of foreign literatures.

Thus translation contributed greatly to the development of the major literary forms in the period. Satire, the novel, and drama were all cross-fertilized by select translations of European writing, classical and contemporary. While translation fed and moulded British literary traditions, it also nurtured the careers of writers, establishing personal reputations and constructing new concepts of authorship as the patronage system was complicated by the expansion of the literary market-place. Translations addressed and created diverse readerships, including aristocratic and bourgeois élites as well as a more heterogeneous mass audience, cutting across social divisions and political factions.

ii. The Establishment of Fluency Sir John **Denham** (1615–69) powerfully demonstrated the translation practices that later came to assume such importance. *The Destruction of Troy* (1656), a partial version of Virgil's *Aeneid* II [see II.n.3.i] that exists in different drafts made some twenty years apart, reveals Denham moving toward greater fluency in the couplet, maintaining formal continuity through syntax and rhyme. He also used current standard English with minimal Latinate and archaic forms, treating the Latin text freely enough to address an English cultural and political situation. As Denham's preface makes clear, this translation method sought a naturalization that was inherently anachronistic. 'If Virgil must needs speak English', he wrote in a much quoted formulation, 'it were fit he should speak not only as a man of this Nation, but as a man of this age' (Denham 1656: A3ʳ).

Denham's Virgil was partly a nationalistic gesture, an effort to champion an *English* version against what the translator called 'that Fools-Coat wherein the French and Italian have of late presented him', burlesques like Paul Scarron's *Virgile travesti*. Yet the domestic constituency that Denham addressed was not so much an English-speaking nation as a specific class, the staunchly royalist segment of the Caroline aristocracy displaced during the Interregnum. In *The Destruction of Troy*, the architectural features of Priam's palace bear a strong resemblance to Whitehall, and the excerpt ends at Priam's decapitation, eerily evoking the execution of Charles I.

The freedom required by fluency was not particularly new or peculiar to English translating at the time. It was a neoclassical aesthetic that slowly emerged in England during the 16th and 17th c. and currently prevailed in France, where Denham and such other poet-translators as Abraham **Cowley** (1618–67) lived in exile with the Caroline court. Behind their versions of classical literature lay two important determinants: Horace's famous recommendation to translate sense instead of word for word [see I.a.3.ii] and the naturalizing strategies of contemporary French translators. Nicolas Perrot d'Ablancourt revised Tacitus's elliptical prose by inserting explanations and deleting digressions 'to avoid offending the delicacy of our language and the correctness of reason' (D'Ablancourt 1640: n.p., my translation).

English translators at this early stage were less likely to justify their domesticating revisions by citing universal norms of rationality, preferring instead to adopt a more nonchalant individualism. Cowley described his 'libertine way of rendering foreign Authors' as purely a matter of personal taste: 'I have taken, left out, and added what I please' (Cowley 1656: Aaa2^{r-v}). What pleased him was initially idiosyncratic and affiliated with courtly circles, not only his choice of Pindar— rarely translated in the 17th c.—but his strategy of free adaptation. Yet Cowley's *Pindarique Odes* (1656) came to rank among the most widely circulated of translations, appearing in the twelve editions of his works published between 1668 and 1721 [see II.i.7.ii].

Translators repeatedly tried to distinguish between translation, imitation, and adaptation [see I.a.3]. But their distinctions were often blurred in the movement between theory and practice. Cowley's method was both notorious and exemplary, criticized for its excessive freedoms yet inspiring a veritable trend for paraphrastic renderings.

Horace and Juvenal were frequently subjected to bold updatings. John **Oldham** (1653–83), much admired by leading poets and translators, turned the Roman satirists against the 'fops', 'Court-Parasites', and 'hect'ring Blades' on the English scene (Oldham 1987: 113, 181, 250). In 1690, John **Glanvill** (1664–1735), a wealthy barrister who dabbled in translation from Latin and French, imitated selected Horatian odes 'with Relation to His Majesty, and the Times', celebrating William III's recent accession. At the height of his poetic career, Alexander **Pope** (1688–1744) produced his witty *Imitations of Horace* (1733–8) [II.n.7.ii], in which translating served the ends of political satire. And the first poem that Samuel **Johnson** (1709–84) published over his signature was his 1749 Juvenalian imitation, *The Vanity of Human Wishes* [II.n.7.iv].

Johnson's *Dictionary of the English Language* (1755) defines 'imitation' as 'a method of translating looser than paraphrase, in which modern examples and illustrations are used for ancient, or domestick for foreign'. Most translations in the 17th and 18th c. in fact contain imitation and paraphrase to varying degrees, but some pursue these strategies throughout and advertise them in titles. The general freedom of the translating indicates that the audience included two large segments: educated readers who were familiar with the foreign texts as well as versions in other modern languages and who were therefore capable of appreciating the ingenuity of a translator's domesticating choices; and readers who lacked training in languages and literatures and who therefore appreciated the translations as English-language poems.

In the early modern period, translation theory continued to be governed by the disciplinary division between grammar and rhetoric that shaped Western definitions of translation from antiquity to the Middle Ages. Translators avoided a grammatical emphasis because it meant close adherence to the foreign text, a reduction of translation to a matter of linguistic correctness. They were much more interested in rhetorical effect and so they focused on cultivating a literary form in English, conceiving of translation as the persuasive conveyor of cultural and political values. A translation of a poem must be compellingly poetic according to domestic literary standards. The translator adds 'a new spirit', wrote Denham, 'which gives life and energy to the words', endowing the translation with seeming originality by enabling it to work on its own terms (Denham 1656: A3^r).

English translators were thus theorizing the aesthetic autonomy of the translated text. Yet they also made clear that their theories served certain social interests. During the Interregnum, a feudal class hierarchy was repeatedly imposed on the two competing translation methods, a literary compensation for the displacement suffered by the Caroline aristocracy. Grammatical literalism, associated with schoolteachers and foreign language manuals, was described as 'vulgar', 'slavish', and 'servile', whereas a rhetorically oriented freedom was judged 'noble'.

iii. Dryden, Pope, and Financial Success After the Restoration, when a new generation of royalist translators took up the antithesis of freedom and literalism, it was redefined to register the altered political situation. In the preface to his translation anthology, *Ovid's Epistles* (1680) [II.n.6.ii] John **Dryden** first formulated his extremely influential concept of 'Paraphrase, or Translation with Latitude', as a means of moderating between two factional extremes: on one hand, the libertine 'Imitation' favoured by predecessors like Cowley, now seen as too cavalier with canonical texts; on the other hand, the word-for-word 'metaphrase', now not simply linked to 'pedantical' grammarians but to 'Superstition, blind and zealous', suggesting the fanaticism of the radical Protestant sects that proliferated during the Civil Wars (Dryden 1956: 182).

Dryden's practices were actually far less conservative than such theoretical pronouncements would imply. In his expansions and compressions of foreign texts, he refined the heroic couplet, making it more pointed and balanced than Denham's; he introduced prosodic innovations to improve fluency, such as triplets, where rhyme and syntax propelled the verse and underscored the meaning; and he constructed a more artificial diction, latinate and periphrastic. 'Poetry requires Ornament,' he wrote in the 'Dedication of the Æneis' (1697), 'and that is not to be had from our old Teuton Monosyllables' (Dryden 1958: 1059). Dryden's Aeneid resorted to such poeticisms as 'briny waters' and 'crystal streams', 'finny coursers' for Neptune's horses and 'woolly care' for Polyphemus' sheep. He also borrowed freely from previous English translations of Virgil, repeating rhymes, phrases, and entire lines. And he subtly quoted from canonical figures in English literary history, notably Spenser and Milton.

Dryden both consolidated an emerging tradition of English literary translating and invested it with considerable authority. That a poet of his stature should have a consuming interest in translation shows not only that he held it in high esteem but that it proved instrumental in defining literary authorship. Over two-thirds of his non-dramatic poetry consists of translations.

Most of these projects were devised after 1688, when the fall of the Stuart monarchy deprived Dryden of his long-held posts as Poet Laureate and Royal Historiographer. Lacking the patronage that had enabled him to devote his poetry to public issues, he turned to translating as an oblique way of articulating political and theological positions. He chose foreign texts that lent themselves to this indirect sort of social engagement: satires by Juvenal and Persius, epics by Virgil and Ovid, tales by Chaucer, history by Tacitus. And from the enterprising publisher Jacob Tonson Dryden received contractual terms that allowed him to profit handsomely from the subscriptions to his translations. His complete version of Virgil [II.n.3.i] netted him more than £1000.

Dryden exercised a decisive influence on Pope, whose versions of Homer's Iliad and Odyssey [II.i.2.ii] are the most accomplished examples of literary translation during this period. Pope too believed that the translation of poetry should not be blandly accurate but richly poetic, emulating the aesthetic merits of the foreign text yet competing with them in the development of domestic literary effects. 'Diction and Versification only are [the translator's] proper Province', he argued, 'since these must be his own' (Pope 1967: 19).

For Homer, Pope crafted a lofty poetical language, a 'Mixture of some Græcisms and old Words after the manner of Milton', and cast it in couplets distinguished by their symmetry and metrical facility, designed to mimic the 'spreading and sonorous Fluency' of Homer's Ionian dialect (pp. 17, 11). More often than not these effects required Pope to revise the Greek text. He replaced repetitive Homeric epithets with elegant variations. He avoided what he called 'little or ridiculous' literalisms (his example was rendering εινοσιφυλλοζ as 'leaf-shaking') for more 'majestic' periphrases ('The lofty Mountain shakes his waving Woods'). And he omitted physical references that he found offensive to an English sense of moral propriety.

These revisions aimed for an epic poetry that was suitably elevated and eminently readable. Their overall impact, however, was to domesticate Homer in a peculiarly English way, assimilating Zeus to Milton's God, for example, and transforming the brutal, somewhat childish heroes into English gentlemen possessing a masculine dignity. In Pope, the weeping that overcomes Achilles when he surrenders his mistress Briseis is described as manly 'Tears of Anger and Disdain', an addition to the Greek text designed to draw a contrast with her femininely 'soft Sorrows'. Pope's translating went beyond such tacit inscriptions of English values because he produced an annotated edition. He rarely ignored the opportunity to justify significant departures by citing Homeric commentators, past and present.

This sort of translation was inevitably faulted for inaccuracy by contemporaries who preferred a more scholarly precision, like the classicist Richard Bentley. Yet most readers, whether or not they knew classical languages, were enthralled by the sheer poetic force of Pope's writing. Samuel Johnson, in his Life of Pope (1779), shrewdly observed that the poet translated Homer 'for his own age and his own nation' and therefore 'knew that it was necessary to colour the images and point the sentiments of his author' (Johnson 1905: 240). Pope believed Homer's most characteristic feature to be his unparalleled 'Invention', an imagination fertile enough to rival 'Nature', so that after him authorship can only take the form of 'Contraction or Regulation', a discreet pruning of his genius in conformity to a neoclassical aesthetic (Pope 1967: 16–17, 3). For an ambitious poet like Pope, translating Homer was a strategic choice, an appropriation of the 'wild' Greek text to display the refinement of his literary talents and build an élite readership of equally refined tastes.

Pope was enormously successful in achieving these results. His fluent couplets and decorous diction set the standard for verse translations of classical poetry. And the subscription lists indicate that his audience crossed class and party lines, including aristocrats and bourgeois, landowners and lawyers, scholars and merchants, Tories and Whigs. Moreover, instead of selling his copyright in the translations, Pope licensed it to the publisher Bernard Lintot in unprecedented contracts that allowed the poet to control the printing process and maximize his profits. His income for the *Iliad* alone amounted to £5000, more than twice the publisher's return. For the *Odyssey* the favourable arrangements led Pope to hire collaborators sympathetic to his overall design, including the Greek scholar William **Broome** (1689–1745), who received £570 for translating several books that maintained the same smoothness of versification throughout.

Pope's commercial success was partly made possible by contemporary developments in copyright law. In 1710 the Act for the Encouragement of Learning established authors as the original holders of the right to reproduce their works, permitting them to bargain with printers and booksellers and multiplying the numbers of professionals who turned to writing for their livelihood. From the translator's point of view, the most remarkable fact about early modern copyright law is that it extended the concept of authorship to encompass translation as well as original composition.

A translation was seen as an independent creation that did not infringe the copyright of the foreign author who produced the underlying work. This line of thinking was aired in *Burnett* v. *Chetwood* (1720), where the justice asserted that 'a translation might not be the same with the reprinting of the original, on account that the translator has bestowed his care and pains upon it'. The translator's ownership of the translation resided in the expenditure of labour, a view that reflected John Locke's individualistic theory of private property. By investing the translator with bargaining power, copyright law provided professional writers with an important incentive to develop translation projects.

Yet even before the Act of 1710, translating was a course taken by many men and women who used their writing to support themselves and their families. After a prolific career as a dramatist and novelist, Aphra **Behn** (1640–89) wrote a series of book-length translations from French, both prose and poetry [see I.a.5.i]. Her debut as a translator occurred in 1680, when she contributed to Dryden's Ovidian anthology. She made the self-effacing gesture typical of Restoration literary women by having him announce in the preface that she was ignorant of Latin. Yet Dryden's brief, flattering remarks attest to the fact that Behn had aggressively entered a translating tradition formerly dominated by men: he singled out her translation as the only one in the book to adopt 'Mr. Cowleys way of imitation' (Dryden 1956: 186).

For the most part, Behn's translations were characteristic of prevailing English practices. They reveal a tendency towards paraphrase to secure easy readability, amplifying for the sake of clarity or literary effect. In introducing *A Discovery of New Worlds* (1688), her popular version of Fontenelle's *Entretiens sur la pluralité des mondes*, she mentioned that while she 'kept as near his Words as was possible', she 'was necessitated to add a little in some places, otherwise the Book could not have been understood' (Behn 1993: 76). Her translations also reveal an anglicizing tendency that occasionally involves topical allusion. In the reflections on death that conclude *Seneca Unmasqued* (1685), her partial version of La Rochefoucauld's maxims, she inserted several references to recent criminal executions in England.

Behn differed from many of her contemporaries in using translation to question and revise gender stereotypes. This is evident in her choice of foreign texts, which emphasized writers of her own time and included philosophy and science as well as literature. She was attracted to Fontenelle's dialogues on the Copernican cosmology partly because one of the interlocutors is a marquise, and women, as Behn asserted of herself, were 'not supposed to be well versed in the Terms of Philosophy' (Behn 1993: 72). Behn saw translation as a remedy for the limited education given to women in the period. It was also a form of writing where she could suggest that gender is not biologically determined, but culturally constructed, shaped by generic convention and audience expectation. In her 1684 version of Tallemant's *Le Voyage de l'Isle d'Amour* (1675, Voyage to the Island of Love), she assumed the persona of a male lover and introduced a sensuality so exaggerated as to force a self-consciousness upon the reader.

iv. Eighteenth-Century Novels and Plays Translations provided a potent impetus for the growth of the novel during the late 17th and 18th c. Of the epistolary fictions published between 1660 and 1740, approximately one-third were translations, mostly from French, some 150 publications (Day 1966: 29). In 1678 Sir Roger **L'Estrange** (1616–1704), a royalist pamphleteer for whom translation was an important source of income, rendered Guilleragues's *Lettres portugaises* (1669) as *Five Love Letters from a Nun to* *a Chevalier* and thereby started a craze for *chroniques scandaleuses*, narratives of passion that frequently represented aristocratic promiscuity in thinly disguised accounts of actual affairs. L'Estrange successfully evoked the rarefied female sensibility represented in the French text, yet his handling was rather free, resulting in an engaging style that often dipped into a racy colloquial register. In a characteristic rendering, he turned 'Et pourquoi avez-vous été si acharné à me rendre malheureuse?' into 'And why so bloudily bent to make me Unhappy?' (L'Estrange 1678: 12). L'Estrange's translation, running to ten editions by 1716, was not just widely read, but imitated for decades by novelists and translators alike.

The 1720s in particular saw a sudden increase in scandal fiction largely driven by the indefatigable Eliza **Haywood** (?1693–1756). After abandoning her husband, she supported herself and her children by writing novels and seven translations. In the preface to her translation of Boursault's *Lettres nouvelles* (1697) as *Letters from a Lady of Quality to a Chevalier*, Haywood described her method as paraphrase, although clearly adjusted to the demands of sensational storytelling. She referred to editing the French text 'where I thought so doing would render the whole more entertaining' and claimed 'not to exceed the Meaning, wherever I have heighten'd the Expression' (Haywood 1721: pp. iv–v). In 1724 she translated Madame de Gomez's *Les Journées amusantes* (1721) as *La Belle Assemblée; or, The Adventures of Six Days*; here the erotic intrigues explored the theme of persecuted virtue that recurred so often in Haywood's own fiction. Her novels and translations appealed to the prurient fantasies of the varied readership who sustained her long career.

Don Quixote exerted a tremendous influence on English literature, judging by the countless references and imitations as well as the sheer outpouring of translations [see II.k.5.i]. Between 1650 and 1755, approximately 40 partial or complete versions appeared. They represent an interesting case study in the domestic canonization of a foreign text, since their strategies varied with the changing assessments of Cervantes' novel.

The allusions to it in Samuel Butler's popular mock epic, *Hudibras*, no doubt piqued the interest of English readers, but the broadness of Butler's satire also encouraged travesties of the Spanish text. In 1687 Milton's nephew, John **Phillips** (1631–1702), a translator who also wrote burlesque poetry, published a comical version peppered with Billingsgate, thieves' cant, and English place-names. In 1711 Edward **Ward** (1667–1731), a tavern-keeper who wrote spy novels and travel narratives, published a partial adaptation in 39 cantos of Hudibrastic verse. Peter **Motteux** (1660–1718) argued that the farcical approach should be avoided, yet a less extreme form of it can be glimpsed in the lively colloquial paraphrase he began publishing in 1700, the most frequently reprinted version during the 18th c. As Cervantes gradually came to be judged a satiric novelist of great historical consequence, an innovator who contributed to the demise of aristocracy, farce gave way to more respectful treatments that followed strict canons of accuracy. 1742 saw the appearance of a close version by Charles **Jarvis** (1678–1739), the first to be printed with annotations.

The canonical status that *Don Quixote* enjoyed in the period motivated translations by ensuring their profitability. Publishers scrambled to print fine illustrated editions that exploited previous English versions. In 1700 Captain John **Stevens** (d. 1726) 'corrected' John Shelton's 1612 translation. In 1749 Tobias **Smollett** (1721–71), whose own novels were deeply influenced by *Don Quixote*, accepted a commission for a translation even though he knew little Spanish. What Smollett actually published, six years later, was a spirited revision of Jarvis's version, made with the help of collaborators, in which entire passages and notes are copied almost verbatim. This recycling, fairly normal for the time, went unacknowledged in Smollett's preface, where he instead described his translation method, in terms typical of the period, as an endeavour 'to retain the spirit and ideas, without servilely adhering to the literal expression' (Smollett 1755: p. xxi).

Translations also had a significant impact on English drama by initiating or sustaining trends and by bringing the latest international hits to London, Dublin, and provincial theatres. Katherine **Philips** (1631–64), a merchant's daughter whose literary talents gained her entrée into aristocratic circles, helped to create the Restoration vogue for heroic tragedies with *Pompey*, her couplet version of Corneille's *La Mort de Pompée* (1644) staged to much acclaim in 1663 [see II.g.6.iii]. Philips's *Letters from Orinda to Poliarchus*, her correspondence with Sir Charles Cotterell, the King's Master of Ceremonies, documented the production and reception of her translation project. She was initially encouraged by Roger Boyle, Earl of Orrery, who examined her drafts. And she was disappointed when several court poets, led by Edmund **Waller** (1606–87), wrote a competing version that overshadowed her success.

In an assertion of authorship that belied her otherwise submissive self-presentation, Philips questioned 'the Liberty [that her competitors] have taken in adding, omitting and altering the Original as they please themselves', and she implicitly aligned her work with Denham's method (Philips 1729: 166). 'The Rule that I understood of Translations', she asserted, 'was to write to Corneille's Sense, as it is to be suppos'd Corneille would have done, if he had been an Englishman, not confin'd to his Lines, nor his Numbers, (unless we can do it happily) but always to his Meaning' (p. 83). It was in fact Denham who completed Philips's version of Corneille's *Horace*, left unfinished at her untimely death from smallpox.

In 1765 George **Colman** the Elder (1732–94), whose own plays anticipated the rise of sentimental comedy, published a blank verse translation of Terence that was well received. Yet classical sources were not as influential in the 18th c. as the contemporary European theatre. The playwright and novelist Elizabeth **Griffith** (?1720–93) was very successful with her translations and adaptations of French and Italian plays. A professional whose writing supported her husband and two children, she shrewdly elicited commissions from the theatre manager David Garrick, who staged her work at the Drury Lane. In 1769 *The School for Rakes*, Griffith's adaptation of Beaumarchais's *Eugénie* (1767), ran for nine nights and appeared in three editions, earning her in the range of £600.

Griffith's choice of foreign texts as well as her translating strategies spoke to audiences taken with the contemporary literature of sensibility. She appreciated *Eugénie* because it was inspired partly by Samuel Richardson's *Clarissa* and had an English setting and characters. But she felt compelled to eradicate Beaumarchais's reliance on 'Spanish manners', evidently recognizing that he imitated a Spanish dramatic form, the comic *entremés* (Griffith 1769: 3). And she strengthened the moral themes by adding and revising characters, endowing the rakish Lord Eustace, for example, with 'compunctions'.

After retiring from a 10-year career as an actress, Elizabeth **Inchbald** (1753–1821) became a highly successful writer of novels, comedies, and adaptations of French and German plays. Her most famous adaptation was *Lovers' Vows* (1798), based on Kotzebue's Rousseauesque melodrama, *Das Kind der Liebe* (1791, The Love Child). Inchbald's frank preface made clear that, 'wholly unacquainted with the German language', she worked from a 'literal' version to fashion what she felt was an eminently stageworthy text, determining from the outset that 'in no one instance, I would suffer my respect for Kotzebue to interfere with my profound respect for the judgment of a British audience' (Inchbald 1798: p. ii).

The British audience that Inchbald addressed, however, was undergoing a conservative reaction against the ideas and events of the French Revolution. Her strategy was to tone down Kotzebue's liberalism. She was particularly concerned about the subversiveness of the character Amelia, whom she described as 'indelicately blunt' in 'the forward and unequivocal manner in which she announces her affection to her lover', disregarding class status and defying parental authority (1798: p. iii). To elicit the audience's sympathy, Inchbald drew on 'manners adapted to the English rather than the German taste', and replaced Amelia's original 'coarse abruptness' with 'whimsical insinuations'.

Yet Inchbald nonetheless retained the titillating sense of impropriety that the play evoked in the largely middle-class spectators who made it popular. Stagings in London and elsewhere were frequent, and roughly 10 editions of the text appeared within a year. Kotzebue's plays 'create Jacobinical feelings, almost irresistibly', wrote the poet Robert Southey in 1799, when his own revolutionary fervour had subsided into an acquiescent conservatism. Inchbald's adaptation was chosen for the private theatrical in Jane Austen's *Mansfield Park* precisely because it championed extreme social values that the novelist found deserving of critical scrutiny.

The most controversial translations of the period were written by James **Macpherson** (1736–96), a Scottish poet who was inspired by his research into ancient Gaelic poetry [see II.d.4.ii]. The works in question were a collection of *Fragments* (1760) and two epics, *Fingal* (1762) and *Temora* (1763), which he attributed to the third-century 'Highland Bard' Ossian. Because Macpherson failed to produce his Gaelic originals, the authenticity of his translations was questioned in public debate that lasted long after his death.

Macpherson's project was rooted in Scottish nationalism. He intended to reform the canon of medieval British literature by challenging 'the prejudices of the present age against the ancient inhabitants of Britain, who are thought to have been incapable of the generous sentiments to be met with in the poems of Ossian' (Macpherson 1762: A5ʳ). In order to invest Gaelic poetry with authority, he needed his English text to pass as a translation of authentic originals. And although he apologized for writing an 'extremely literal' version, departing from prevailing practices, he actually translated with a freedom typical of Pope or Johnson, and allied Gaelic poetry with canonical literary works in English (Macpherson 1760: p. vi). The syntactical inversions he used to mimic the

Gaelic originals were drawn from the King James Bible, Milton, and Pope's Homer. Macpherson practised translation as cultural preservation and transmission, creating an Ossianic role for the translator as a bard singing the glory of Celtic warriors. But he was undoubtedly developing a new poetic discourse that transformed British cultural traditions, a primitivism that was much admired and imitated by poets throughout Europe.

v. Techniques of Fluency The goal of fluency, of immediate intelligibility and easy readability, dominated translation during the 17th and 18th c., and it was achieved by a variety of actual practices. The most pronounced tendency was toward explicitness, a clear lexicon and linear syntax, and this led to editing foreign texts, deleting and inserting passages, adding annotations. Philip **Francis** (?1708–1773), whose poetic versions of Horace in the 1740s [II.n.5] were recognized as both accurate and lyrical, sometimes 'ventured to change the Expression, as it could not be understood by an English Reader', replacing the subtle phrasing of the Latin texts with the plainest English terms. In *Odes* II. v., for instance, Francis rendered the 'ambiguoque vultu' of the captivatingly androgynous Gyges as 'his boyish, girlish face' (Francis 1743: 202–3).

Because the explicitness was directed to English-language audiences, the translating simultaneously assimilated the foreign texts to English literary values, making them fit for English consumption. Foremost among the privileged forms and themes was the heroic couplet. Although the fashion for the couplet did not last long on the tragic stage, only a couple of decades after the Restoration, in poetry it was so strong as to cross generic distinctions, appearing in translations of epics, satires, and philosophical treatises. The translation that most vied in popularity with Dryden's Virgil and Pope's Homer was the 1682 couplet version of Lucretius' *De Rerum Natura* by Thomas **Creech** (1659–1700) [see II.n.2]. In 1718 Joseph **Trapp** (1679–1747) challenged the fashion with a version of the *Aeneid* in Miltonic blank verse. But although his subscribers included such leading figures as Addison, Arbuthnot, and Swift, he failed to make an impact. In 1739 the anonymous author of *Letters Concerning Poetical Translations* ranked the couplet version of Christopher **Pitt** (1699–1748) over Trapp's, arguing that 'the rhym'd Verses have not only more Harmony and Conciseness, but likewise . . . they express Virgil's Sense more fully and more perspicuously than the blank Verse' (p. 62).

The dominance of the couplet produced at least one translation curiosity. In 1663 James **Wright** (1643–1713) published a collection of Martial and other poets entitled *Sales Epigrammatum*, in which he reduced entire unrhymed Latin poems to single couplets since, he believed, 'in Epigrams of six, eight, or ten verses, the Salt, the Conceipt of all is referred to a Distick in the end' (Wright 1663: A4).

The domesticating tendencies also included the imposition of a rigidly hierarchical decorum, in which dialects and discourses were assigned to specific literary genres or deemed appropriate for canonical foreign texts. Standard current usage dotted with archaism was reserved for most poetry translations, whereas prose was more likely to contain colloquialisms. In Wright's theoretical dialogues, *Country Conversations* (1694), an interlocutor complained not only that the colloquial coinage 'Mob' (from 'mobile') was too recent to be used in rendering a Horatian ode, but that it was 'a kind of Burlesque word, and unsuitable to the Dignity of *Horace*' (p. 42).

The Stuart Restoration seemed to encourage free adaptations in the shape of salty burlesques, such as *Scarronides; or, Virgile Travesti* (1664), wherein the poet Charles **Cotton** (1630–87) opened his homage to the French parodist with the lines, '*I Sing the man*, (read it who list, | A *Trojan*, true, as ever pist)'. As the period unfolded and a characteristically bourgeois set of values came to dominate English culture, burlesque adaptations like Cotton's Scarron or Phillips's *Don Quixote* grew rare, and the adherence to decorum occasionally became so strict as to result in sheer bowdlerization. Creech's Lucretius left out the risqué passages. Samuel **Dunster** (1675–1754), a clergyman whose prose version of Horace was reprinted several times, acknowledged that 'I have castrated our Poet, in translating nothing that bordered on Obscenity, or that was contrary to the Rules of Decency and good manners' (Dunster 1712: A6^r).

The domestication was most violent in the marked tendency toward topicality. Translators chose foreign texts whose themes might be bent into commentaries on contemporary social situations. And to support such anachronistic applications they resorted to textual apparatus, prefaces, or annotations that invited the reader to create historical allegories. In many cases, translations were simply filled with allusions to British figures, events, and places.

Aesop's fables [II.i.11.iv] were submitted to a series of propagandistic adaptations whose ideological standpoints changed with each new crisis faced by the British monarchy (Patterson 1991). In 1651 John **Ogilby** (1600–76) published a paraphrase of selected fables that referred to specific events before and during the Civil Wars, using the Aesopian form to analyse the causes of the royalist downfall and the defects of the parliamentary opposition. In 1692 L'Estrange published his mammoth folio collection of fables, each followed by lessons that reflected on the reversals suffered by the Stuart monarchy from a Jacobite point of view. And in 1722 Samuel **Croxall** (d. 1752) issued a children's version that not only became the most frequently reprinted in the 18th c. (18 editions), but explicitly criticized L'Estrange's tendentiousness while favouring the Whiggish supporters of the Hanoverian succession.

vi. Resistance to Domestication Although fluent domestication constituted a veritable discursive regime in English translation, alternative theories and practices did in fact exist, and their reception ranged from harsh criticism to utter neglect. These alternatives aimed to proclaim, not to elide, the linguistic and cultural differences of the foreign text by experimenting with translation discourses and by choosing to translate literatures that were marginalized by dominant domestic values. In 1712 John **Ozell** (d. 1743), the author of some 30 workmanlike translations from French and Spanish, unwittingly challenged Pope's Homer (Pope's *Proposals* appeared the next year) by rendering a very different French translation of the *Iliad*, the scholarly prose version by the noted classicist Anne Dacier. As a result, Pope satirized Ozell in the *Dunciad*, to which Ozell responded with a self-congratulatory advertisement in the *Weekly Medley*, which in turn drew a more biting attack from the poet.

A more significant challenge to Pope's canonical status was the 1791 version of Homer written by the poet William **Cowper**. Cowper deliberately devised a project that competed with Pope's at every level. He collected 498 subscriptions in emulation of his predecessor's 600; knowing that Pope's Homer made a fortune, he was disappointed to be offered £1000 for his work. Most importantly, Cowper opposed Pope's use of the heroic couplet and elegant diction because it led to inaccuracies that he felt were inappropriately domesticating. In an anonymous letter to the *Gentleman's Magazine*, Cowper had attacked Pope's translation, complaining that 'instead of Homer in the graceful habit of his age and nation, we have Homer in a straight waistcoat' (Cowper 1785: 611).

What Cowper offered, however, was a closer version that substituted one form of domestication for another. He used irregular blank verse and syntactical inversions to imitate the Greek text, its simplicity and sublimity, but these choices were in fact

inspired by Milton. Nonetheless, Cowper's translation discourse was sufficiently defamiliarizing to provoke unfavourable reactions, even from associates. Henry Fuseli, who revised the poet's work, later published an anonymous review that criticized the 'intemperate use of inversion, ungraceful in itself [and] contrary to the idiom of his language' (Fuseli 1793: 3).

A translator who had better success in opposing the dominant tendencies of the period was Dr John **Nott** (1751–1825). A physician who occasionally ministered to aristocratic travellers on the Continent, Nott published a number of translations that drew impressively on literary traditions in classical, European, and Eastern languages. He reformed the canon of foreign literatures in English by developing translation projects that focused on the love lyric instead of epic or satire, the most widely translated genres. All his translations were at once poetic and scholarly. He produced versions of Johannes Secundus Nicolaius (1775), Petrarch (1777), Hâfez (1787), and Bonefonius (1797), as well as the first book-length collections of Propertius and Catullus [II.n.4].

Nott's careful scholarship prevented him from acceding to the physical squeamishness of English literary decorum. He rejected the 'fastidious regard to delicacy' that required the deletion of the explicit sexual references in Catullus's poems because he felt that 'history should not be falsified' (Nott 1795: I. x–xi). His renderings of the Latin words for anal and oral intercourse were not exactly pornographic (e.g. he used 'pathics' for 'pedicabo'), but they were obscene enough to provoke a moral panic among reviewers, who renewed the attack decades later when expressing their preference for George **Lamb**'s bowdlerized Catullus (1821). Nott saw his translating as cultural restoration, a historical labour of bringing into English foreign works that remained unappreciated because they ran against the grain of contemporary English values.

vii. Theories of Translation During the 17th and 18th c., translation was normally theorized in prefaces of varying length which often included commentary on the foreign text. Occasionally the theorizing occurred in verse (heroic couplets, of course), whether in the form of commendatory poems attached to translations or extended treatments like the famous *Essay on Translated Verse* (1684) by the Earl of **Roscommon** (?1635–1685) and *Translation: A Poem* (1753) by Thomas **Francklin** (1721–84). Although almost a century elapsed between the publication of these two verse essays, they document the overwhelming consensus in

English translation theory. Francklin, reiterating concepts that became commonplaces after Roscommon's statement, satirized as 'servile mimics' translators who lack the poetic invention whereby Pope 'made immortal Homer all our own' (Francklin 1753: 3, 10). In a book-length introduction to his immensely popular version of *The Four Gospels* (1789), George **Campbell** (1719–96) linked fluency to the Biblical canon while providing a theological rationale for the traditional criticism of literal translation. 'A slavish attachment to the letter', he wrote, 'is originally the offspring of the superstition, not of the Church, but of the synagogue' (Campbell 1789: i. 456).

Free, fluent translation was valued so highly that it created a distinctive critical lexicon in the periodicals, even when they became politically contentious during the reign of George III. Devoting their attention more to style than to accuracy, reviewers habitually described acceptable translations as 'clear', 'elegant', 'natural', 'perspicuous', 'smooth', 'unconstrained'.

The first systematic treatise in English appeared at the end of 18th c., the compendious *Essay on the Principles of Translation* (1791, 1797, 1813) by Alexander **Tytler** (1747–1813). A Scottish lord associated with the 'common sense' school of philosophers, Tytler consolidated the dominant trends in theory and practice, offering a fascinating source of commentary on many translations into English and other languages. He advocated free translation that possessed the 'ease of original composition' because he found transparent discourse consistent with Enlightenment humanism, the assumption of an essential human nature characterized by universal reason. Yet Tytler's concept of aesthetic judgment was also liberal, resting on the 'freedom' of 'individual taste', which meant ultimately that he privileged the élite literary values that had shaped English translation since Denham. Tytler praised the 1793 version of Tacitus [II.n.10.iv] by Arthur **Murphy** (1727–1805) precisely because Murphy's elegantly turned sentences smoothed out the elliptical brevity of the Latin text.

For Tytler, good translation was not only fluent but respectful of English literary decorum. He urged the translator to 'prevent that ease from degenerating into licentiousness' by refusing to render classical literature into popular dialects and discourses, 'the style of the Evening Post' or 'the low cant of the streets' (Tytler 1978: 119, 220). And he heartily applauded Pope's expurgation of Homer, who, Tytler agreed, tended 'to offend, by introducing low images and puerile allusions' (p. 79).

viii. Conclusion In the 17th and 18th c. fundamental changes occurred in English translation theories and practices, in the translator's cultural status, and in the uses to which translations were put by writers, readers, and publishers. As with other moments in the English translation tradition, dominant social trends influenced the selection and reception of foreign literatures. Canons of translation accuracy were thoroughly domesticating, consistent with the cultural values of British social élites, whether the aristocracy or the middle classes. In the domestic canons of foreign literatures, classical poetry remained central, although a heterogeneous mass audience supported the translation of modern works, both narrative and dramatic. There was also an enormous French influence on English literary genres and traditions, including translation theory and practice.

Poets and translators absorbed French theory through the prefaces and translations of authors like d'Ablancourt. By 1760, when the first French treatise appeared in English, Charles Batteux's *Principles of Translation*, the ideas were indistinguishable from those that already prevailed in contemporary English translation. Batteux incorporated the basic assumptions of Enlightenment humanism ('Men are naturally the same in all places, and in all times') while recommending translation strategies that revise recalcitrant linguistic and cultural differences in domestic terms (Batteux 1760: 24). 'We must entirely give up the expression in the text translated', wrote Batteux, 'when the sense requires it for perspicuity, the sentiment for vivacity, or the harmony for delight' (p. 56).

English translation in this period was theorized and practised, essentially, as an appropriation of foreign literatures to serve domestic cultural and political agendas. 'I Trade both with the Living and the Dead, for the enrichment of our Native Language,' asserted Dryden, referring as well to his own profitable use of translation to build his literary career and to earn his livelihood (Dryden 1956: 1059). And indeed during the 18th c. commerce came to motivate certain translation projects that were imperialistic in the strict sense, not merely literary, but brutally economic. Sir William **Jones** (1746–94), the renowned Orientalist scholar who presided over the Asiatic Society and acted as an administrator of the East India Company, translated the *Institutes of Hindu Law* [II.l.2.i] to increase the effectiveness of the British colonial presence, constructing a transparent representation of the 'Hindus' as unreliable interpreters of their native culture. Jones hoped that his translation would be imposed as 'the standard of justice' to 'many millions of *Hindu* subjects, whose well-directed industry would add largely to the wealth of *Britain*' (Jones 1970: 813, 927) [see II.k.1–2].

Yet here too dissenters took other paths. The multi-talented Nott once undertook a three-year stint as surgeon on a vessel of the East India Company. He translated the Persian poet Hâfez

[II.q.2.ii], however, to question the English veneration of classical antiquity and to rectify the unwarranted neglect shown in imperial Britain toward 'the language of the conquered' (Nott 1787: p. vii).

By the end of the 18th c., the theories and practices of English-language translation were thus riddled with the contradictory values and ideologies that characterized modernity.

The starting-point for research in English translation during this period consists of two bibliographies: F. Bowers's *New Cambridge Bibliography of English Literature*, ii (Cambridge, 1940) and S. Gillespie's 'Checklist of Restoration English Translations and Adaptations of Classical Greek and Latin Poetry, 1660–1700', *Translation and Literature*, 1 (1991), pp. 52–67. The views presented in this historical survey are developed at greater length in Lawrence Venuti, *The Translator's Invisibility: A History of Translation* (London / New York, 1995).

4. ROMANTICISM AND THE VICTORIAN AGE
Terry Hale

i. Introduction The present-day status of English as a world language is commonly seen as having two specific causes: the expansion of British colonial power during the 19th c. and the emergence of the USA as the leading economic power during the 20th c. It was not until after World War I, however, that English began to challenge French as the dominant language of social, diplomatic, commercial, and intellectual interaction on the European and international levels. At the beginning of the 19th c., the situation of English was largely that of what would nowadays be called 'a less frequently spoken language'.

The marginal status of English during much of the period is exemplified by the fact that the relatively limited amount of translation of English prose and poetry into languages such as Spanish, Portuguese, Russian, and Italian frequently occurred via French as a relay language. This, for example, seems to have been the fate of M. G. Lewis's *The Monk* (1796), one of the most successful examples of the Gothic vogue at the end of the 18th c., when it was translated into Spanish in 1821. Even as late as the mid-19th c. it was common for a Spanish translation of an English classic such as Defoe's *Robinson Crusoe* to be advertised as based on the latest French edition. Given the considerable degree of ideological manipulation that could occur when literary texts were translated from English into French, it is more than likely that these subsequent translations reveal a further level of cultural interference.

Even more significant, however, is the fact that so little translation from English into European languages other than French occurred during the 19th c., though there were exceptions to this rule

(the novels of Sir Walter Scott, for example, enjoyed widespread popularity). To take the case of Spanish again, translations of French novels outnumbered translations of English novels by more than ten to one during the period 1800–50. This is clearly demonstrated by a survey of the bibliography produced by J. Fernandez Montesinos (1973) of Spanish language translations published during that period. Today, of course, this situation has been largely reversed [see I.b.5.vii].

French cultural hegemony was by no means limited to the Iberian peninsula, however: it was keenly felt in Britain and the USA. With regard to Britain, French hegemony asserted itself in three ways: first, in the pre-eminence of French theatre on the London stage throughout the 19th c.; secondly, by means of the sheer volume of translations of French prose works, not only narrative fiction but also historical studies and memoirs; thirdly, in the creation of a not insubstantial critical literature, mainly of a journalistic nature, seeking to classify and evaluate this vast output of translated works. These phenomena are clearly linked to the rise of mass culture during the 19th c. With episodic exceptions (such as Russian literature in the 1870s), literatures other than French fared less well, at least in the popular market-place. Serious discussion of the translation process itself, and the criteria by which translation should be evaluated, tended to remain a high cultural activity, however, frequently linked with the translation of the Greek and Latin classics. One of the most important controversies of the period, that between Francis Newman and Matthew Arnold, centred on the correct manner of translating Homer into English.

The following entry will examine each of these four phenomena: stage translation, translation of narrative prose, attempts to exercise control, and translation in relation to high culture. In general, the history of translation in Britain throughout the period is closely linked with attempts by cultural intermediaries such as theatre proprietors, publishers, journalists, academics, translators, and playwrights to contain, manage, or exploit French cultural hegemony in relation to the domestic market-place. Today, at the end of the 20th c., Britain and the USA demonstrate strong resistance to translation (exemplified by extremely low translation rates in both countries) while British and American authors tend to dominate bestseller lists world-wide [but see I.b.5.vii]. Throughout the period 1770–1900 the very opposite held true. In order to understand the practice of translation in Britain from the late 18th c. through to the end of the 19th c., it is essential to bear constantly in mind that translation occurred in an entirely different cultural context from the one we know today.

ii. Stage Translation We shall begin by examining the situation with regard to the theatre, not only because the subject has been largely neglected by translation theorists, perhaps because of the low prestige accorded to many of the cultural artefacts of the 19th-c. British stage, but also because, arguably, the theatre was subject to a more powerful dynamic of cultural adaptation and change than the novel. Indeed, it is possible that developments in the 19th-c. theatre anticipate by some years similar developments in prose fiction.

The extent to which translation was integrated in British culture in the 19th c. is clearly evidenced by the theatre. Allardyce Nicoll suggests that as many as half the plays performed in English in the period between 1800 and 1850 either were suggested by Parisian models or were simply adaptations by English authors (Nicoll 1955; Rahill 1967: 115–16). It is likely that a similar proportion of plays in the second half of the century had the same origins. However, it should be said from the outset that the distinction between translation, adaptation, and a new or original play was by no means a simple one. Writing in the early 1870s, the British playwright Tom **Taylor** (1817–80), for example, considered it quite legitimate for a play to be described as a 'new' one if it considerably altered its source (Tolles 1940: 116). Writing about the same time (also in response to the controversy launched by 'Q', pen-name of Thomas Purnell, dramatic critic of *The Athenaeum*), James Robinson **Planché**

(1795–1880), would seem to concur that the inventiveness or originality of the translator or adapter is the central issue. His defence of a practice which by present-day standards would be termed plagiarism is a curious one:

The crime [reliance on French sources], if it be one, carries its own punishment along with it—a poor bald, literal translation fails, and a clever, spirited one, succeeds . . . The mere literal translator, whatever may be the merit of his work, cannot . . . lay claim to its *invention* . . . There is much more art required to make a play actable than a book readable, and in cases of adaptation or reconstruction, where only the plot or a portion of it has been taken, and the dialogue wholly or the greater part of it re-written—why is the dramatist, however humble, to be denied the privilege so kindly accorded by 'Q' to Shakespeare, Molière, and Boucicault? (Planché 1872: i. 246–7).

In other words, the commercial success of a play is so dependent on the skill of the translator that a proprietary interest in the work is created.

Both Taylor and Planché were capable of taking great pains to alter the originals to suit the taste of their English audience. Indeed, the degree of liberty with which they treated their source texts was largely out of keeping with the 19th-c. reaction as far as prose was concerned against such 17th- and 18th-c. strategies as paraphrase and imitation [I.b.3]. Unfortunately, little systematic attempt has yet been made to analyse the ideological manipulation to which such texts were subject. Although a number of those involved in translating or adapting French plays for the London stage wrote memoirs of their professional careers, it is significant to note that they rarely if ever discuss the specific practices which informed their work. Such is the case, for example, with Planché, whose autobiographical *Recollections and Reflections* (1872) is otherwise uniquely informative about the 19th-c. theatre. That translation was central to his work for the theatre is in no doubt. Indeed, it was his translation from the French of Carmouche, Jouffroy, and Nodier of *The Vampire* (1820) for the Lyceum which brought him to public attention. From 1818 onwards he visited Paris regularly, scouting for scripts with which to return home. In fact, Planché seems to have seen his work as theatrical intermediary (i.e. being familiar with developments abroad, finding suitable material, and persuading the managers of the various London theatres with which he was associated to mount productions) as of equal importance to his work as a translator in the narrow sense. It would seem that the successful translator for the theatre in the 19th c. was a man (rarely, if ever, a woman) with a considerable network of contacts and a shrewd eye for the commercial possibilities of foreign material.

Obviously, one factor strongly influencing the use of French material was the absence of international copyright legislation: French authors received no remuneration for works performed in Britain. However, a number of other factors, both institutional and cultural, can be advanced to account for the phenomenon. An article published in *Belgravia* in 1867, for example, attributes 'the commonness of translations and the scarcity of original dramatic writing' to a number of institutional factors (Hitchman 1867: 60). First, it is claimed that the cost of mounting plays, especially those requiring the sort of elaborate scenery that audiences had come to expect, increased substantially during the 19th c. In order to compensate for the expense and labour that a new production entailed, it is implied that managers preferred plays which had already been tried and tested abroad and so had a greater likelihood of enjoying a long run. Indeed, managers had come to view 'native talent' with some mistrust (though it is further suggested that the judgement of managers and critics in this respect was frequently questionable). Secondly, it is claimed that the 'sums paid even for good dramatic work [in Britain] are notoriously inadequate; so much so, in fact, that . . . there is not a single instance of any dramatic author in this country living by the profits of his vocation' (Hitchman 1867: 61). This situation—which is strongly contrasted with that prevailing in France, where it is said that successful dramatists receive proper remuneration—is claimed to be responsible for the amateurish quality of many British plays. Thirdly, the number of theatres in London is deemed to be so inadequate as almost to exclude competition. Fourthly, the London theatre is considered to be weakened by the lack of professional training for actors, while many minor parts are said to be considerably diminished as a result of the 'star' system. Finally, the system of criticism—which is characterized as almost openly corrupt—is claimed to be in need of wholesale reform.

Although Hitchman's analysis of the institutional structures which he claims served to discriminate against 'native' plays in favour of those with foreign origins is in some respects a convincing one, it is likely that the dominance of French theatre on the British stage at this time was as much a matter of the appeal of fresh dramatic forms combined with a more populist ideology. Rowell notes that the population of London trebled between 1811 and 1851 (Rowell 1956: 1). It was on the ranks of this swelling urban proletariat that the London theatre and the provincial theatre alike would henceforth depend for their livelihood. Equally significantly, British playwrights (perhaps for the institutional reasons noted above) were slow to master the dramaturgy of such new forms as the melodrama.

The term *mélodrame* was coined by Rousseau to describe his 'scène lyrique', *Pygmalion* (1770), in which a dramatic monologue is interspersed with music and pantomime. By early in the 19th c., the term had come to designate a theatrical mode in which crude representations of virtue and vice directly confront each other. In Guilbert de Pixerécourt's *Coelina; ou L'enfant du mystère* (1800), for example, the virtuous heroine, a rich orphan, is persecuted by her villainous uncle, who wishes to marry her to his son. In recent years the cultural significance of melodramas of this sort has been the subject of lively debate. One important line of investigation—which seeks to link the semiotics of melodrama with those of the French Revolution of 1789—has been articulated by Peter Brooks (1976) in terms of an audience engaged in a process of moral recognition and relocation. Whatever the truth of this view, it is certainly true that melodrama was well matched to the emotional and cultural expectations of the new audience that the theatre began to attract in Britain in the early 19th c. Pixerécourt's *Coelina* was introduced, without mention of the name of the French author, to an English public by Thomas **Holcroft** as *A Tale of Mystery* in 1802 (the first use—on the title-page—of the term 'melodrama' in English).

Although Pixerécourt was the author of some 120 plays, more than half of which were melodramas, he was by no means the only French playwright whose work found its way on to the English stage. However, although a number of detailed studies on French, British, and American melodrama have been published in recent years, commentators have hitherto neglected to examine the philosophy underlying the translation and adaptation practices involved. Indeed, some commentators seem to assume, at least implicitly, that performances were more or less uniform across cultures. Rowell does suggest, however, that in the light of enduring British anxiety over events in France, Pixerécourt's politics 'were indefensible before an English public; it was only his power to thrill that could be exported, and to extract their sting his settings were turned into a Spain, Italy, or Bohemia of wholly indeterminate period and place' (Rowell 1956: 45–6). More specifically, such changes were no doubt introduced to circumvent the intervention of the Lord Chamberlain's office. John Larpent, the Examiner of Plays from 1778 to 1824, refused a licence, for example, to *The Wanderer*, a drama about the adventures of the Pretender, by the German playwright Kotzebue [see I.b.3.iv], on political grounds. Indeed, it has been claimed that 'politics in any national dress was forbidden territory in the English drama' at this time (Findlater 1967: 56).

Although Pixerécourt died in 1844, in one form or another French theatre continued to dominate the London stage in the mid-century. Situated just off Drury Lane, the Olympic Theatre was one of London's most successful minor theatres in this period. Indeed, during the 1850s and 1860s the theatre's name became synonymous with a particular type of play—termed 'Olympic Drama'—characterized by a cleverly devised narrative, neither over-melodramatic nor overtly literary in nature, with easily identifiable heroes and villains, and clear dramatic possibilities for confrontation and resolution. The rules governing the construction of this sort of play largely derive from the French theatre, particularly the work of Eugène Scribe. When Planché met Scribe in the Garrick Club in 1850, the former was introduced with the remark: 'Encore un qui vous a pillé' (Another one who has plagiarized you). Planché claims he replied: 'Impossible de faire même du nouveau sans piller Mons. Scribe' (Impossible even to do anything new without plagiarizing Monsieur Scribe) (Planché 1872: ii. 148).

Tom Taylor, who worked for the Olympic from 1853 to 1860, is generally considered the best English exponent of the 'well-made play'. The extent to which Taylor had mastered the formula developed by Scribe is exemplified by *Still Waters Run Deep* (1855), which, in the words of his biographer, rapidly established 'a tenacious hold on public favour . . . which few Victorian pieces can equal' (Tolles 1940: 138). The plot is deceptively simple. John Mildmay, a mild-tempered businessman, quietly but efficiently entraps a swindler who has wormed himself into his family's confidence. By so doing, he preserves his wife's reputation, avoids a substantial financial loss, and establishes himself as master in his own home (which has previously been ruled by his wife and his wife's strong-minded aunt). The scope for confrontation between the various characters hardly needs emphasizing. Significantly, Taylor describes *Still Waters Run Deep* as 'an original comedy'. In fact, the plot and much of the dialogue is taken from an earlier novel entitled *Le Gendre* by Charles Bernard. Taylor's work as translator/adapter is a thorough one: the scene of the action is moved to Brompton, the names of the

characters and their manner of speech and behaviour are entirely anglicized; and the sexual innuendoes of the original are neutralized by altering the relationship between the ladies who compete for the swindler's affections from mother and daughter to aunt and niece (Tolles 1940: 136–7). In short, Taylor's strategy is thoroughly to domesticate the French text, so much so that all evidence of its cultural origin is effaced.

iii. Narrative Prose Like the theatre audiences, the 19th-c. British reading public was by no means restricted to the middle and upper classes. Indeed, the history of translation during the period 1770–1900 is closely linked to mass schooling, increased literacy rates, technological innovation in the printing industry, and the commercial development of publishing. Literacy rates in Britain, as evidenced by the minimal ability to sign one's name at marriage—considered by some historians as indicative of at least moderate reading ability—had remained static at around 50 per cent from the 1750s to the 1830s. In contrast, the rate of literacy almost doubled in the course of the following 60 years, attaining 95 per cent by 1900 (Mitch 1992: p. xvi).

And as with the theatre, this new public demanded a literature of its own. One of the first examples of the impact which mass culture would have on fiction is provided by the rise of the Gothic novel. From the point of view of Translation Studies, it is interesting to note that the Gothic was a genre which began with an act of pseudo-translation (Horace Walpole's *Castle of Otranto*, 1764); that a number of the genre's early figures were themselves translators (e.g. Charlotte Smith, who was responsible for a version of Prévost's *Manon Lescaut* in 1786); and that a number of early Gothic novels consisted of extremely free adaptations of French works (e.g. Sophia Lee's *The Recess*, 1783–5, which is clearly based on Prévost's *Cleveland*). Indeed, some commentators have almost gone so far as to suggest that the English Gothic novel, at least in its early form, is little more than a generic mutation occasioned by the translation of the French sentimental adventure story (Foster 1927; Hale 1998). After 1796, writers and translators, particularly M. G. Lewis, also looked to Germany for material. It is also to be noted that there is a clear link between stage adaptations of Gothic novels and the rise of melodrama.

The Gothic novel was mainly disseminated by means of the circulating library. However, the periodical press was another important medium for translated fiction. By 1840, William Hazlitt's *Romancist and Novelist's Library* could boast in a prospectus that in the course of 78 issues, costing no more than two pence each, it had printed more than three-and-a-half million words 'by some of the most eminent British, American and Foreign writers'. Almost a third of the works published were translated. Among the continental writers who vied for space among reprints of English Gothic novels were Marmontel, Bernardin de Saint-Pierre, Mme Cottin (the early 19th-c. author of a number of sentimental bestsellers), Alexandre Dumas, Victor Hugo, Paul de Kock (a popular French author whose works were considered slightly scurrilous by English reviewers), Mme de Duras, Goethe, and Schiller.

It is difficult, however, to detect any particular editorial policy behind such a selection except one intended to balance popular 18th-c. classics (Marmontel, Bernardin de Saint-Pierre) with more contemporary writing (Dumas, Hugo). With regard to the translation strategy employed, however, it is possible to note a closer literal reading than would have been the case 50 years earlier. This, perhaps, is a product of the legacy of the German romantics, mediated by commentators such as Thomas Carlyle [II.h.3; II.h.5], who emphasized the need for a more faithful translation practice. The translation of Hugo's *Notre-Dame de Paris* [II.g.9.iv] published by the Romancist and Novelist's Library, for example, would seem largely to follow that of Frederic **Shoberl** of 1833 (despite assurances that a new translation had been commissioned), a version preferable to that by William **Hazlitt** which had preceded it a short while earlier. In the Shoberl translation the penultimate sentence of the book reads: 'He must have come hither and died in the place.' The Hazlitt translation reads: 'Hence it was inferred that the man must have come thither of himself and died there.' (In Hazlitt's defence it should be said that his translation overall was not as prolix as this example would suggest.) Nonetheless there are exceptions to this rule: in common with earlier translations of Schiller's unfinished *Der Geisterseher* (1800), for example, the anonymous version in the Romancist and Novelist's Library does not fail to complete the story according to its own lights.

Indeed, so central was translation to the periodical press that by the mid-century, in the words of Louis James, 'French fiction formed the backbone of *The London Journal, The London Pioneer,* and *The Family Herald . . .* and appeared liberally elsewhere: not a single issue of *The London Journal* [between 1845 and 1849] was without some French literature in translation' (James 1963: 159). Given that a circulation of 500,000 copies is claimed for *The London Journal* (James 1963: 45), this is to place translation at the centre of British popular culture. Among the most popular French novelists published by *The London Journal* were Eugène Sue and Alexandre Dumas [II.g.9.i]. Indeed, there were long periods during which British fiction was virtually excluded from the periodical. From 1 August 1846 until 29 May 1847, for example, Dumas's *Monte Cristo* was running simultaneously with Sue's *Martin the Foundling; or, Memoirs of a Valet de Chambre.* Moreover, the magazine also serialized (beginning on 5 April 1845 and not concluding until 3 May 1851) Thiers's *History of the Consulate and the Empire of France under Napoleon.* As with the Romancist and Novelist's Library, translations are almost always anonymous, show a tendency to literalness, and frequently exhibit signs of being hurried. In terms of editorial policy, it would seem that *The London Journal* was moderately left-wing, that it sought to fulfil a function not only of entertainment but also of popular education, and that its readership was politically aware. It is also interesting to note that the number of translations published diminished rapidly during the 1850s, though it is difficult to assess whether this was due to the fact that British writers had mastered the craft of serial fiction or to shifts in the political opinion of the readership.

The former hypothesis does not seem an untenable one in the light of the career of G. W. M. **Reynolds** (1814–79), the first editor of *The London Journal.* Reynolds was not only responsible for early translations of various works by Victor Hugo, but also established himself as a major popular novelist in his own right with *The Mysteries of London.* This vast work, the composition of which (including various sequels) spanned some 10 years between 1845 and 1855, is clearly indebted to Sue for its manner of construction. Indeed, it could be argued that the English publication of Sue's *Les Mystères de Paris* in the mid-1840s was one of the major literary events of the mid-century. At one stage it would seem there were at least four different translations, by no means all recorded in the catalogue of the British Library, appearing simultaneously. Contemporary magazines and journals referred to 'mystery-mania'. But the real reason for the success of such works is to be found in the attitude of a newly literate readership towards the descriptions of poverty they contained and manner in which the social responsibility for such conditions is assigned. The link between political agitation in Britain and publishing ventures of this kind is shown by an unpublished letter of 3 December 1850 from George Eliot to her publisher, John Evans. Although Eliot declines to undertake the translation of Sue's *Les Mystères du peuple* (1849–56, The

Mysteries of the People), the original promoter of the project was apparently the political activist Louis Blanc, who had fled to England following the 1848 revolution.

Whatever the impact of authors such as Sue and Reynolds, translations of French mystery and crime fiction dominated the British and American market-place in the final third of the 19th-c. (though fictional detectives would seem to have been a familiar figure on the stage some years earlier). In Britain, the firm of Vizetelly was particularly important, publishing dozens of novels in the 1880s by authors such as Émile Gaboriau, considered by critics as the inventor of the detective novel (as opposed to the short story, which is attributed to Poe), and Fortuné du Boisgobey.

Though Henry Vizetelly only turned to book publishing in 1880, by which time he was already 60 years old, he was an important figure in the history of translation in the 19th c. Coupled with his keen commercial sense (he had earlier founded the *Illustrated London News*, the first periodical to exploit developments in the domain of photography), there is also a clear political agenda behind Vizetelly's activity as a publisher. According to his son, Vizetelly played 'a prominent part in the agitation for the repeal of the taxes on knowledge, such as newspaper stamp and paper duty, being honorary secretary for the removal of the latter impost' (Vizetelly 1904: 247). However, his career as a publisher supports Venuti's contention that domestic values control the translation market (Venuti 1995a: 19). Thus, his initial project was to produce a series of 'cheap translations of works of high repute' (Daudet, Sand, Mérimée, etc.) for which he quickly discovered there was 'little or no demand'. Indeed, he further discovered that 'if French fiction was to be offered to English readers at all, it must at least be sensational', and it was at that time that he launched 'a cheap series of Gaboriau's detective stories, which found a large and immediate market' (Vizetelly 1904: 249).

Commentators nowadays tend to discuss Vizetelly only in relation to one author, Émile Zola [II.g.9.vi], or to his contribution to the overthrow of the triple-decker format for new prose fiction (a format which even such popular novelists as Mrs Braddon found a burden) in favour of the novel in a single volume. Arguably, it is unlikely that Zola would have had the impact he did in Britain if the ground for naturalism had not been prepared earlier by almost a century of sensation fiction, whether in the form of novels or plays. Significantly, one of Zola's most popular titles in English translation, as indicated by the fact that by 1992 at

least seven different translations had been published, was *Thérèse Raquin* (1867). This work, which is essentially that of a murder followed by a joint suicide, is one of the author's most sensational works. The translation of Zola into English also raises a number of issues with regard to political interference in the editorial process which will be discussed in the next section.

iv. Censorship and control In 1891, a character in a short story by Oscar Wilde remarks: 'Why, if it were not for dear Lady Jansen, who sends me all the worst French novels she can find, I don't think I could get through the day' (Wilde 1973: 180–1). Though Wilde's Lady Clementia is being ironic, the moral condemnation to which French literature (whether prose, poetry, or drama), especially in translation, was subjected by cultural commentators, particularly journalists, throughout the 19th c. occasionally had serious consequences. Indeed, the son of Henry Vizetelly attributed his father's death to the persecution he received at the hands of politicians, journalists, and the legal establishment.

In the mid-1830s, the conservative *Quarterly Review* published two articles on the subject of contemporary French literature, the first dealing with the drama and the second with the novel. Priority was given to the drama as 'the most popular walk of literature' and so 'affording the best test of the new taste of the nation' (anon. 1834: 180). However, the theatre of Hugo and Dumas is also said to provide examples which are 'more striking—we may add, more astonishing—than even their poetry and their novels;—both of which, however—and particularly the latter—exhibit the same extravagance, absurdity, and immorality which we shall have to reprobate in their drama' (p. 180). The anonymous writer's apoplectic punctuation is the first indication the reader is given that moral considerations will take precedence over literary considerations. Indeed, the writer's objection to French romantic drama would seem to be entirely moral in nature. Thus, of the ten plays by Hugo and Dumas which are surveyed, it is claimed:

Of the female characters . . . we find that *eight* are *adulteresses*, *five* are *prostitutes* of various ranks, and *six* are victims of *seduction*, of whom two are brought to bed almost on the stage. Four mothers are in love with their own sons, or sons-in-law, and in three instances the crime is complete. Eleven persons are murdered, directly or indirectly, by their *paramours*; and in six of these pieces the prominent male characters are *bastards and foundlings*; and all this accumulation of horrors is congregated in ten plays of two authors, produced within the last three years in the city of Paris. (p. 210)

Nor does the reviewer fail to draw the appropriate political conclusions from such perceived moral failings. The abandonment of rhyme after Hugo's *Hernani* (1830), for example, is claimed to have resulted in the abandonment of 'all regularity—we may almost add—all decency' on the French stage (pp. 191–2). The article, which began by asserting that 'literature had the chief hand in preparing the French Revolution', concludes with the warning: 'In France, we think, it will be very soon discovered, that the Government must control the stage, or the stage will overthrow the Government, and, ultimately, the whole frame of society' (pp. 177, 211).

Translators and adapters for the stage were particularly sensitive to both the moral sensibilities of their audience and their dramaturgical expectations. 'This drama is in no sense a translation, and ought not, I think, in fairness, to be called even an adaptation of Victor Hugo's fine play, *Le Roi s'amuse*', wrote Tom Taylor in his preface to *The Fool's Revenge* (1859).

On looking at Victor Hugo's drama . . . I found so much in it that seemed to me inadmissible on our stage—so much, besides, that was wanting in dramatic motive and cohesion, and—I say it in all humility—so much that was defective in that central secret of stage effect, climax, that I determined to take the situation of the jester and his daughter, and to recast in my own way the incidents in which their story was invested . . . .

One of the many changes that Taylor made in *The Fool's Revenge* was to shift the setting from the French court of Francis I to Renaissance Italy, compress the action, reduce the size of the cast, and altogether avoid the moral issues of the original with regard to the seduction of the heroine by introducing a revenge plot.

More generally, however, English translators and theatre managers throughout the century seem to have avoided mounting the more problematic French plays. The works of Émile Augier, commonly considered to have been a precursor of naturalism, and Alexandre Dumas *fils*, who likewise dealt with themes considered immoral at the time, were routinely ignored. Paradoxically, though *La Dame aux camélias* (1848) was proscribed in any recognizable English stage version, the Lord Chamberlain's office licensed Verdi's operatic version of the play, *La Traviata*, for performance, presumably on the grounds that the audience for opera was less susceptible to being corrupted than a theatre audience. Nor was censorship an issue only in connection with French plays. The first public performance in Britain of Ibsen's *Ghosts*

(1881) [II.o.9]. was not permitted until 1914, some 33 years after it was written (though a controversial private perform-ance, outside the control of the Chamberlain's Office, occurred as early as 1891). The history of dramatic translation in the 19th c. is as much a history of what was not translated as of what was.

The influence of those seeking to limit access to translated works on moral or political grounds was by no means restricted to the theatre, however. The same writer in the *Quarterly Review* in the mid-1830s who attacked the theatre also attacked the novel. Indeed, he claims that though the theatre may be the more pressing evil, the novelists of the modern French school are 'still more immoral than the dramatists' (anon. 1836: 66). In particular, Hugo, Dumas, Balzac, and George Sand are singled out for attention. All four of these authors are accused of being the heirs of Rousseau, and thus guilty by association of inventing 'revolutionary paradoxes on the nature of government and the constitution of society' (p. 66). Underlying criticism of this kind it is impossible not to see British anxieties about French revolutionary upheaval spreading to Britain, anxieties which had been revived by the revolution of July 1830. As such anxieties faded once again, Balzac and Sand would be perceived not as politically problematic writers but only as morally problematic. 'Madame Sand's novels have been, and still are, looked upon by a large class of readers as the most immoral and pernicious ever written,' wrote an anonymous author in the June 1868 issue of *Belgravia* (anon. 1868: 157).

Such moral condemnation seems to have been responsible for retarding the translation of a number of the works of the authors concerned. Two of George Sand's most controversial novels, *Indiana* (1832) and *Mauprat* (1838), for example, seem not to have been translated until more than 50 years after their first publication. In the mid-19th c., her work was nonetheless extremely popular in translation, with as many as 30 different titles being available at one moment, though a detailed study of the strategies employed by her various translators remains to be written. Balzac fared less well. Very few of his works were translated into English before his death in 1850, though a version of *La Peau de chagrin* (1831) was published in Philadelphia as *Luck and Leather* as early as 1843.

By and large, publishers preferred to avoid any legal complications with the authorities. This is exemplified by the circumspection with which an author such as J.-K. Huysmans was treated. Author of *A rebours* (1884, Against Nature), a novel which is now considered to have been a major influence on Wilde's *The Picture of Dorian Gray*, though few would have been familiar with his name outside literary circles, Huysmans's later Catholic novels were generally translated into English within a year or two of their initial publication. However, *A rebours* was not published in translation until 1922. Even then the translation by John **Howard** (Jacob Howard Lewis) was not only heavily bowdlerized but initially only available in the USA. Amongst numerous cuts and alterations, the whole of Chapter 6, in which Des Esseintes (the novel's main protagonist) seeks to corrupt a 16-year-old boy by taking him to a brothel, was omitted.

The consequences of sailing too close to the wind may be seen in the case of Zola's British publisher towards the end of the century. Although the translations of his work published by Vizetelly had had the passages most likely to cause offence excised (e.g. the description of the onset of Catherine's menstruation in *Germinal*, 1886; tr. Albert **Vandam**, 1886), by 1888 a self-appointed group of guardians of public morality led by W. T. Stead, editor of the *Pall Mall Gazette*, had been formed in order to suppress such pernicious writing. After being warmly censured by a poorly attended sitting of the Commons, Vizetelly was charged with obscene libel for publishing translations of *La Terre*, *Pot-Bouille* and *Nana*. Although Vizetelly was fined only £100, his stock was confiscated, effectively putting him out of business. Six months later, he was again on trial for other translations which he had allowed to remain in circulation. Vizetelly was 70 years old, in poor health and close to bankruptcy. The Recorder remarked that there was little point in fining him as he had no money and accordingly sent him to prison for three months (King 1978: 228–54).

The issue of censorship (more commonly in the form of self-censorship) is an important one with regard to translation in the 19th c. Earlier in the century, the circulating libraries (and Mudie's in particular) had exerted moral vigilance over the printed word; later in the century the railway libraries fulfilled a similar function; by the end of the century, control had become a matter of judicial intervention. The consequence of this was not only that the editorial process could be, on occasion, highly intrusive, it also effected editorial policy with regard to what was or was not published. Although the translation of prose works was governed by different translation practices, the written word was potentially as subject to control as the spoken word.

v. High Cultural Practice By the mid-19th c., translation in Britain was typified by two radically different discursive practices. In the domain of theatre translation, texts were dismantled and reassembled according to entirely local criteria of linguistic and cultural appropriacy: plots were commonly subject to substantial alteration; settings could be shifted to entirely new locations (e.g. Tom Taylor's relocation of *Still Waters Run Deep* to Brompton); and dialogue was generally subject to major revision. In the domain of prose fiction, on the other hand, the reader could expect a much lower degree of direct intervention from the translator or publisher unless issues of censorship or self-censorship were involved. In common with 18th-c. practice, passages considered too 'warm' or 'sensuous' were often toned down. Rarely were plot structures or settings subject to manipulation in narrative fiction. Indeed, if anything translations of narrative fiction deliberately maintained a suggestion of cultural difference. The opening chapter of the version of *The Mysteries of Paris* published by Chapman and Hall in 1845, for example, is entitled 'The *Tapis-franc*', even though the term requires footnote explication. The same holds true of the Appleyard edition of the same year. Generally speaking, these two discursive strategies would seem to correspond with Venuti's concepts of domestication and foreignization (Venuti 1995a).

In the domain of high cultural practice, Francis **Newman** (1805–97), the polymath brother of the cardinal, launched a call for a translation strategy for the classics based on a high level of archaicism and the employment of a ballad metre (a form he identified as both antiquated and popular) with the publication of a controversial translation of the *Iliad* [II.i.2] in 1856. Newman's experiment represented an attempt to translate against the grain of dominant literary values, especially those of university scholarship, though it was nonetheless an ill-conceived one. Newman's lexicon may have been astonishing in its historical breadth, but it could also be, on occasion, impenetrable (especially to a non-élite audience). Moreover, Newman's project, looking back as it did to a picture of Homer the balladist exemplified by William Maginn's *Homeric Ballads* (1838), was already out of date. As 19th-c. Britain became more assured, both as an industrial and as a colonial power, it required a Homer endowed with a grandeur to match its own. That vision of grandeur was articulated by Matthew Arnold.

Had not Arnold chosen to engage in a polemic against Newman, it is likely that the latter's translation would have sunk without trace. In his Oxford lectures *On Translating Homer* (1860), he stigmatized Newman's approach as 'ignoble': 'The ballad-style and the ballad-measure are eminently inappropriate to render Homer. Homer's manner and movement are always both noble and powerful: the ballad-manner and movement are often either jaunty and smart, so not noble; or jogtrot and humdrum, so not powerful' (cited in Venuti 1995a: 132). Instead, drawing a parallel between the simplicity and natural intelligibility of the English language (and, implicitly, British culture) and Homer's 'plainness and naturalness of thought', Arnold argued that Homer should be rendered in hexameters and modern English. According to Venuti, a translation strategy as transparent as the one Arnold proposes here conceals a whole raft of domestic values. In this respect, however, the translator merely articulates the conclusions the reader might have drawn from the original text had he or she been able to read it in the original. There is no shortage of evidence to suggest that a political leader such as Gladstone, who had a thorough knowledge of ancient Greek, looked to Homer for guidance in the conduct of the nation's affairs (Jenkyns 1980: 199–203). Much detailed work remains to be done, however, on the mass of translations from Greek and Latin produced during the 19th c. It is possible, for example, that the British middle classes read the classics in order to explore their own political aspirations, seeing in Greek literature a product of Athenian democracy and in the Latin orators a model of republican discourse. In either case, one would expect such translation projects to reveal, whether implicitly or explicitly, submerged values and objectives.

Indeed, the entire relationship between the reception of prestigious translation projects, the aesthetic values of the translation, the underlying editorial judgements, and Victorian political and social life is a subject worthy of close investigation. The easy readability of the 1861 translation by Sir George **Dasent** (1817–96) of the *Njals Saga* [II.n.2] is shown by the fact that it could be reissued as late as 1900 in an edition intended for the general reader:

The present reprint has been prepared in order that this incomparable Saga may become accessible to those readers with whom a good story is the first consideration . . . Some of the best fighting in literature is to be found

between its covers. Sir George Dasent's version . . . is now offered afresh simply as a brave story for men who have been boys and for boys who are going to be men. (Lucas 1900: p. vii)

Likewise it is significant to note that the majority of 19th-c. dramatic adaptations, abridgements, and selections from the *Thousand and One Nights* [II.b.5] are generally linked to tales with urban themes. Nor is it coincidental that the *Nights* depict 'a well-ordered and peaceful world where commerce and business flouish', while in the account of Sinbad's voyages the Victorian concepts of hard work, seriousness, and skill are emphasized (Ali 1981: 119). Victorian commentators were unsympathetic to translations which sought to exploit such works in the interests of alternative or private agendas. Thus, Sir Richard **Burton**'s translation of the *Nights* was condemned for following his own penchant for the erotic and the grotesque. Appropriately, when Burton died he was working on an expanded version of his 1886 translation of *The Perfumed Garden*, a 16th-c. manual of Arab erotology. However, the unpredictability of Victorian popular journalism is such that his widow was roundly condemned when she later admitted to having destroyed the manuscript (Farwell 1988: 399–400).

The relatively few translation theorists who have discussed the 19th c. in any detail have tended to concentrate their attentions on high cultural practice. Such an approach has been eschewed here in favour of one which links the translation process with the commercial environment in which it occurred, whether that of the theatre or of the publishing house. The majority of translation projects were undertaken by poorly paid anonymous writers. In the absence of specialist studies of the strategies adopted by 19th-c. translators, whether with regard to a specific genre such as the melodrama or in relation to individual authors such as Hugo and Dumas, much of the above analysis must remain provisional. We have also sought to examine the process of translation in relation to wider ethical and political debates of the period. The history of translation in the 19th c. is one of a relocation of cultural hegemony from France to Britain. Arguably, the current lack of research on translation in the 19th c. is one of the many consequences of Britain's 20th-c. position as a world language.

5. LATE VICTORIAN TO THE PRESENT
Anthony Pym

i. Translators Literary translation into English has been marked by several major shifts in the course of the 20th c. One of the most prolonged has involved the social location of translators. At the end of the 19th c. translators were likely to be original authors or on the fringes of writerly circles; their work was subject to critical and commercial constraints similar to those of other literary texts; and if translations were discussed at all, it was more often than not on their moral virtues, as values entering English, rather than as potential equivalents to anything foreign.

By the second half of the 20th c., however, the people producing translations could no longer be assumed to issue from the milieux of literary journals, underemployed women, and occasional churchmen. More and more translators are academics or from academic backgrounds; they tend to be intimately concerned with the linguistic qualities of their originals as well as with effects within the target culture; and translations are more frequently discussed and evaluated as translations, in terms of fidelity or openness to their source texts rather than inventiveness or acceptability within their target literature. Indeed, when academics now assert that English translations have 'improved' since the 1920s or 1930s, they quite possibly mean that the diverse social groups of translators have moved closer to the norms of scholarship.

Much else has happened, of course. Yet the numerous change factors may be organized around a roughly chronological progression from Victorian belletrists to late 20th-c. teachers of foreign languages and literatures.

For all the formal innovation that British aestheticism may have developed from exchanges with French post-romanticism, translation became more of an issue with respect to the content-derived problematics of naturalism. In 1888 Zola's novels were withdrawn from the circulating libraries and his British publisher, Vizetelly [see I.b.4.iv], was imprisoned under pressure from the National Vigilance Association. Writers of the order of Edmund Gosse, George Moore, and Arthur Symons petitioned for the publisher's release; conservatives opposed any concession to what Tennyson had generically labelled 'poisoned honey, stolen from France' (in his 'Epilogue to the Queen' of 1873). The terms of debate were fixed for the 1890s: translations from contemporary cultures, along with the general importing of rival foreign values, presented a risk for the moral health and unity of the British nation. For aestheticism, the culture of such translations could thus be allied with the counter-values of decadence and the general *Yellow Book* milieu, remarkably open to European trends, especially French. Opposed to them was a nationalist culture that tended to restrict literary translations to work from the ancient classics, in the spirit of embellishing the *translatio imperii*, the classical transfer of empire to the British. The Arnold–Newman debate over Homer translations [see II.i.2.iii] certainly partook of that frame (Venuti 1995a: 119–40); Arnold won the debate and enjoyed lasting influence. Yet classicist translation as a whole was overtaken by the problematics of foreign cultures that were very much alive.

Translation would nevertheless seem to have been of central concern on neither the aestheticist nor the naturalist side of early modernism. The most obvious reason is that the narrow producing and receiving milieux of the literary journals considered themselves generally able to read in French if not German: Wilde wrote his *Salomé* in French (although he had it translated by Douglas), and Yeats somehow believed he understood Villiers's *Axël* despite only rudimentary French, thanks to a mystique of literary communication that might well have served various literary translators in their self-assured forays into foreign tongues: philological knowledge was rarely a decisive yardstick for measuring the value of a translation. Literary translations within the aestheticist frame could thus become *exercices de style*, presented as formal experimentation or exotic fruits: John **Payne** did not flinch from tackling everything from the *1001 Nights* to Villon and Heine; John **Gray**'s *Silverpoints* (1893) was presented as 'spiritual poems, chiefly done out of several languages', the spirit being clearly of more importance than the languages, and a Richard **Le Gallienne** could openly claim to 'paraphrase' the *Rubáiyát* (1897) and Hâfez's *Divan* (1903) [see II.q.2].

These translators were either authors in their own right or were attached to writerly institutions, mainly manifested in small periodicals, where they operated as cultural intermediaries on more than one level. Since a nationalist critique was likely to consider their work morally suspect because of the very foreignness of their material (or indeed imperialistically laudable because of the same foreignness), there was little sense in ethical debate over the proper degree of fidelity to the letter of that material. The resulting lack of concern for linguistic accuracy left the translators free to move about between foreign languages and indeed between foreign aesthetics: Arthur **Symons** did his naturalist duty translating Zola in 1894, Verhaeren in 1898, published his influential study of European Symbolism in 1899, then moved on to d'Annunzio in 1899–1902 and Baudelaire [II.g.11] in 1905.

The relative openness of early modernism might be seen as extending through to the 1930s of Eliot, Pound, and Joyce, accumulating connections to the legacies of Wilde, Shaw, Yeats, and perhaps Conrad. It is important to note, though, that the names just cited do not include any English-born writer. English-language modernism was an international phenomenon even without translation; London functioned as a literary capital for foreigners and transnational publishers, servicing a growing network rather than a unified national literature. The richness of this network was such that translation remained on the fringes of creative processes, becoming a front-line mode of influence in remarkably few cases (one might nevertheless think of Rilke and Stephen Spender [II.h.14]). In retrospect, there was surprisingly little real debate about the American Ezra Pound's attempts to bring translation into a more central historical position, notably through the poetic practice of *Cathay* [see II.f.2] and his essays of the 1920s.

Progressive improvement in the legal and commercial status of authors might be benchmarked by the founding of the Society of Authors in London in 1883, the Net Book Agreement of 1899, and the Copyright Act of 1911. Writing became a profession from which a sizeable group of people could live. On the fringes of that profession, translators gradually developed as something other than a group of authors seeking inspiration or innovation. Opposite to the Pound of *Cathay* there stood Arthur **Waley**, who from 1918 published his translations from Chinese [see II.f.2] while working as Assistant Keeper at the British Museum. There were relatively few full-time literary translators at this stage: Callahan's study of early 20th-c. British translators from Spanish finds little evidence of translation as a financially necessary full-time activity; he concludes that, in this particular field, 'most translators appear to be young people who want to do almost anything to penetrate the literary world and to make a living from literary activity' (Callahan 1993: 104).

In such a situation, translators remained largely subordinate to the myths of authorship: the Copyright Act of 1911 allowed that translators owned copyright in their work, but only with the permission of the author (see Venuti 1995b). It was in this subordinate space that English letters could then project the role of specialized translators known for their translations rather than any original works: a Constance Garnett for Russian [see II.p.4–6] or a C. K. Scott Moncrieff for French [see II.g.14] would become names allied (reductively) with work from particular languages, although few further names would be known to the wider public. Other translators have tended to be known within specialist circles: Aylmer Maude or Michael Glenny for Russian; and more recently Giovanni Pontiero for Portuguese. Some notoriety might also ensue from events like the 1971 Hochhuth case, where the translator was held responsible for libel by the original author [see II.h.i]. But in general, as Steiner would remark in 1975, 'It is only lately that the translator . . . has begun emerging from a background of indistinct servitude. And even here his visibility is often that of a target: his role in making Dostoevsky or Proust available to us is underlined because it is felt that the work needs redoing' (G. Steiner 1975: 271). Yet this 'need of redoing' is at least a mode of awareness incorporating reference to source texts, a far cry from the debates about suspect foreign values entering a national literary system.

ii. Anthologies and Series In the modernist context, translation was perhaps only of social concern to the extent that it could enable foreign texts to reach mass readerships. This was the factor behind the originally ethical concerns with European naturalism; it remained a factor wherever circulation extended beyond the readerships of literary journals, notably in the field of education. The main instrument of control in this sense was 'representative' anthologization, either in book form or as series.

The pedagogical anthology would typically select 'the best' texts of a foreign literature or period, employing conservative criteria, ignoring contemporary texts, and tending to place control in the hands of editors with respectable social profiles. Such anthologies could also be non-translational, finding their place in the foreign-language classroom: the Gowans and Gray series of '100 Best Poems' in English, French, Spanish, and German were produced in the first decades of the 20th c. and remained in print through to the 1950s. These classroom anthologies were thus quite different in approach and strategy from the early modernist anthologies that collectively raided the past in search of fixed poetic forms and which maintained a direct link with the literary production of the moment. A conservative collection of translations such as Babette Deutsch and Avrahm Yarmolinsky's *Contemporary German Poetry* (1923) [II.h.13.i] could nevertheless present relatively unknown material, paving the way for the more personalized and adventurous efforts of the poet-translators of the 1950s and 1960s.

Alongside the non-translational classroom anthologies, the English series of translations built on the European tradition of pedagogically explained classics, editing foreign texts to suit the purposes of a middle class keen to purchase high culture (see Kahn 1963). The series that are still very much with us today began with the young century: the World's Classics from 1901, Everyman from 1906, Loeb from 1912. Despite the different markets targeted by these series—Loeb was certainly for beginning classics scholars—their original emphasis was generally on translations of the classics or at least of the 'great texts' of the past, in keeping with the bourgeois inheritance of culture and steering clear of any contemporary decadence. The established series were joined by the Penguin Classics in 1946, which began with E. V. Rieu's translation of the *Odyssey*. It should be noted, however, that this key moment in the translational appropriation of the classical canon had a decidedly popular and even oppositional touch: Rieu was trained as an academic but never went into academic life; his translation of the *Odyssey* was offered to Allen Lane at Penguin as a trial and it was Lane's decision, against advice from his editorial staff, to publish it. Lane also decided that Rieu should be in charge, from home, of the new Penguin Classics. The reaction of the academic world was sceptical since there were other more 'learned' translations on the market. Rieu nevertheless found praise for his attempts to address a wider market, and he always insisted on the well-turned phrase in 'plain English'. Indeed, he is said to have asked his translators to read their translations aloud (see, on the history of the Penguin series, Penguin Books 1985; Radice and Reynolds 1987; Hare 1995).

Like the anthologies, the translational classics series sought to include 'safe' translations, privileging prose over verse, seeking readerships on the wide market for which they were designed. Yet, once again like the anthologies, the series have progressively become more adventurous: by 1997 Penguin Classics had accumulated over 800 titles, including a 'Poets in Translation' corner that purports to offer 'the best translations in English, through the centuries, of the major Classical and European poets'.

Despite the traditional elements here—the bland guarantee of 'the best', the restriction to sure values (the sub-series includes Homer, Horace, Martial, Virgil, the Psalms, and Baudelaire)—this venture does make the historical role of translation explicit, according selected translators a creative subjectivity that anthologization had previously denied.

In the absence of reliable statistics, one might claim that, at least since the time of Rieu, academics have increasingly entered the translation profession as anthologizers and editors of one kind or another. Yet this process was undoubtedly slow and subject to major exceptions: Klein (1995: 65) makes the point that the prime movers behind the anthologization of German poetry after 1945 were the poet-translators Edward Davidson, Christopher Middleton, Geoffrey Chase, Patrick Bridgwater, and especially Michael Hamburger [see II.h.13]. These were nevertheless poets of philological virtue, bringing with them significant closeness to their originals and perhaps a correspondingly greater distance between the language used in literary translation and the idiom of original literary creation.

iii. British and American Publishing

In the United Kingdom the increased attention to the detail of foreign texts, even among the most creative literary translators, has allowed fairly staid academic translations into the lists of some of the larger publishers (Oxford, Everyman, Penguin, and to a lesser extent Heinemann), most expressly in bilingual versions or plain-prose translations given beneath the foreign-language text. More adventurous literary translations might then be published by smaller specialized imprints. This is one of the areas where significant differences surface between the British and American scenes: in the United States this same process has tended to be led by the academic presses that developed in opposition to trade publishers, riding on a distinction that is by no means as clear-cut in the United Kingdom (the Oxford and Cambridge 'university' presses are at once academic and trade). Yet this does not mean that there is any over-riding reason to consider British and American translations in terms of two completely different systems.

On both sides of the Atlantic, post-1945 translation came to serve an increasingly common cause, developing remarkably neutral linguistic registers and obviating any general need for retranslation across the British/American divide: there have been few calls for retranslation such as one finds between American and Iberian Spanish or Portuguese. Even when British and American literatures have developed remarkably different idioms, as might be the case in post-1960s poetry, they draw on a common stock of translations, used more as sources of information and background than as instruments of creation.

At the same time, there are differences in attitude across the Atlantic divide. American translators have tended to be the more dynamic and innovative, as might be exemplified in the American Standard Version of 1901 [II.c.1.vii] or the overt proclamations of Ezra Pound, both of which proclaimed the principle of overt retranslation well before the idea entered the Penguin Classics. There would also seem to be a difference in reception norms: few outcries ensue when American translations, with the minor necessary orthographic and lexical changes, are co-published or reprinted in British collections; but when an occasional translation slips the other way and enters a mainstream American market, some vocabulary must be rewritten and a reviewer might remark an 'occasionally disconcerting British accent' (as in Dickstein, in Venuti 1995a: 3). Such notes nevertheless remain in subordinate clauses. In general, one must be surprised at the ease with which the two countries share translations, an ease assisted by the relatively unlocalized language used by translators.

The remarkably common tradition of British and American publishing in the field of translations also owes much to the cultural politics of allies through two world wars and a long Cold War. French literature has maintained pride of place in the shared translation culture, remaining the source from which most linguistic interference is tolerated. The difficulty of restoring the image of Germany after the Second World War was also common to both sides of the Atlantic, although translations from German were certainly carried out both before and after the war: cultural rivalry can be as much a motivation for translation as can literary affinity. Russian literature, listed as the second most translated language in the 1980s, has benefited from a similar logic: American and British publishers favoured dissident and especially exiled writers from eastern Europe throughout the Cold War years, manipulating a distorted image that is still hard to redress and benefiting from the expansion of Slavic Studies since the 1960s. Other international factors bearing on the selection of source texts include rapid translations of Nobel Prize winners and tie-ins with major film releases. More profoundly, phenomena like the boom in Latin American literature in the 1960s and 1970s concerned many literatures as well as English, as translators and critics across Europe latched on to

experimental fiction as an antidote to the dominant realism of the day [see II.k.11].

Beyond these external factors, the number of trans-Atlantic co-publications since 1960 is very much the fruit of the progressive conglomeration of the publishing industry, leading to a situation where publishing in the United Kingdom in the 1990s is dominated by just four major companies. These groups are able to harness the resources of literatures in English and sell to readerships across the globe. British publishers may take over American translations or purchase translation rights directly, normally for the whole of the ex-empire, then perhaps sub-license to an American publisher. Despite complaints that editors in the larger firms do not know foreign languages and take virtually no interest in translations, there is no hard evidence that conglomerization can be causally linked with any overall decline in the number or quality of translations in English, nor that the large publishers are set on killing off cultural diversity: when a large publisher like Collins takes over a small specialized imprint like Harvill, it actively recognizes the value of a list that includes numerous translations, in this case particularly from Russian. The larger publishers who take an active interest in translations do, however, seek the widest possible readership across the globe, entering networks in Asia, eastern Europe, and Africa (Heinemann's African series might actually do much to allow one half of Africa to read the other).

Outside the big networks, there are some 2000 small publishers in Britain. These presses have steadily published more translations than the larger firms, albeit with lesser print runs and with only occasional reprints. This particularly concerns specialized publishers such as Harvill and Verso. The latter, a left-wing London imprint with strong European contacts, maintains translations at about 20 per cent of its output, publishing writers such as Jean Baudrillard, Étienne Balibar, Christa Wolf, and Hans Magnus Enzensberger (see Imrie 1992). Yet this ideological commitment to translation is hampered by the limited weight of such enterprises within the field of English-language publishing: when an intellectual star system raises the translation rights for a title by Deleuze and Guattari to some $20,000, or the rights for Louis Althusser's L'Avenir dure longtemps are sold for some $50,000 in Italy (Imrie 1992: 131), small specialized publishers find it difficult to compete. A prestigious intellectual writer like Jacques Derrida is mostly too expensive to be translated beyond the large American academic publishers. Since market pressures thus mean that the big names are brought out by the larger publishers and more often than not in the United States, small publishers are forced to use their translation policies to sweep up the crumbs or to bet on a rising star. Either way, the smaller publishers, be they trade or academic, can scarcely afford to make translation a centrepiece of their market strategies. Nor can they afford to pay all their translators well.

iv. Translation Norms [see also I.a.2] The international growth of publishing in English provides one reason why the language of translations should have tended to eschew traces of foreign source languages, increasingly conforming to the idea that a translation should not read like a translation. One thus finds countless statements to the effect that 'translations should read as if they were not only written but also thought in English' (so Anthea **Bell**, translator of more than 200 books and co-translator of the superbly re-created English *Asterix* [see I.c.4.iv]). Yet the actual texts rarely show such absolute re-creation, nor the 'dynamic equivalence' sought by Nida (1964) [see II.c.1.xi]. Translations into English have tended to be in a language that is less specific, more international, than most works originally written in English. Translations for children, to cite a prime example, rarely have the flavour of a regional English (although all childhoods are regional), simply because translators and publishers set out to address many regions at once. For similar reasons, the 'committee language' of many modern Bible translations might be lamented as symbolic of a widespread delocalization of translations.

A better description of the dominant base norm could be Gideon Toury's proposed law (1995: 278) that tolerance of foreign traces tends to decrease when translation is carried out into a literature seen as major or prestigious, and that tolerance will thus increase in accordance with the prestige accorded to the source culture. This principle would seem to have some general validity with respect to 20th-c. translations, since it states only that a self-perceived major system such as English literature will have little tolerance of what some call 'translationese' yet greater tolerance with respect to prestigious foreign fields such as French critical theory. It does not say that translations are or should be like non-translations. Yet if this has become a fundamental norm, there are certainly numerous further factors and phenomena that must be accounted for.

At the beginning of the 1960s J. M. Cohen argued that 20th-c. translation was influenced by science teaching, which had placed increased emphasis on accuracy, prose-meaning, and interpretation,

neglecting the 'imitation of form and manner' (Cohen 1962: 35). One would want to add that the influence of science was but part of the growing role of educational institutions, and that this, coupled with the requirements of international publishing, privileged exacting plainness over adventurous literariness as a goal in literary translation.

Beyond such generalizations, the dominant norms have periodically been made visible by notable exceptions. Works like Tony **Harrison**'s versions of *Phèdre* (1975) [II.g.6.iv] and the *Oresteia* (1981) [II.i.3.iii] are anything but anonymous 'scientific' renderings, and translation has certainly remained available as a mode of serious literary creation. Nor can the regime of common neutral speech be condemned as a powerless ubiquitous norm. In the field of Bible translating [II.c.1], for example, the adoption of plain prose in cases like Moffatt's 1928 use of real-life speech broke with the 'timeless' quality of the archaizing Authorized versions, thus showing that fluency can sometimes be foreignizing. Bible translations also give us examples of highly localized language like the Gospels in Scouse, where the problematic comic effect ensues not only from the supposedly unnecessary status of the translation but also from its radical departure from the norms of placeless translational language. Yet this in turn differs from the serious localization of W. L. **Lorimer**'s *New Testament in Scots* or Everett **Fox**'s *The Five Books of Moses*, which followed French experiments in highly literalist translation.

Since the detection of translation norms must often focus on the moments when they are broken or challenged, the work of reviewers and critics provides an important historical key. In keeping with the general base norm described above, translation criticism since 1945 has been analysed by Lawrence Venuti (1995a) as consistent vindication of the norms of 'fluency' or 'transparency to the original', to the cost of the formal work that Cohen had regretted not finding in the 1960s. Yet careful reading of the reviews, even those Venuti uses as examples, shows at least two norms at work.

On the one hand, there are indeed explicit calls to 'natural' or 'fluent' English, marked whenever the translator appears to deviate from this goal by drifting into what has been called 'a recognizable variant of pidgin English known as "translatorese"' (*TLS* 1967: 399). Such calls to fluency may be seen as attempts to defend the English language from outside contamination, implicitly jingoistic in the assumed superiority of non-hybridized English and the corresponding wholesale degrading of all pidgins. On the other hand, reviewers also reflect a kind of visibility that accords prestige to the source culture. Venuti cites cases such as the one already glimpsed above: 'In Stuart Hood's translation, which flows crisply despite its occasionally disconcerting British accent, Mr Celati's keen sense of language is rendered with precision' (Dickstein, in Venuti 1995a: 3). Here the norm of fluency is allied with criticism of a particular target culture. If anything, the source-culture values are recognized as being more prestigious than those of this particular standard English. An even clearer example is cited by Venuti: 'Often wooden, occasionally careless or inaccurate, it shows all the signs of hurried work and inadequate revision. . . . The Spanish original here is ten words shorter and incomparably more elegant' (p. 3). The norms at work here, alongside a concern for fluency, are those of fidelity and precision, once again according prestige more to the source than the target culture.

It is clearly insufficient to characterize these norms in terms of the one simple strategy ('transparency' or 'fluency') which might then be opposed to one alternative strategy (mostly 'foreignizing' or 'literalist' translation). The evidence of the criticism, even without the numerous alternatives taken in actual translating, suggests that strong values have been attached not just to invisibility and its associated protection of standard English, but also to the preservation of accuracy and thus the translator's duty to remain a trustworthy guide to the foreign. Further, the calls to duty, whether expressed in terms of equivalence or fidelity, are embedded both in ideologies of re-creation (i.e. 'doing what the author would have done in the target language') and in insistence on philological accuracy (as in the example above). Complaints about 'invisibility' tend to force this diversity into contradictions: as mentioned, a 'fluent English' translation of the Bible, along with colloquial and dialectical versions, is bound to be visibly translational simply because read against the background of the King James Version. By the same token, when Ronald Knox (1949) seeks 'timeless' rather than contemporary language in Bible translations, this by no means makes him a foreignizing translator. The translator's textual visibility may only work for the brief moment of norm-breaking, quite independently of the nature of the norms involved. All in all, the array of translation practices is far from uniform and is better described in terms of diversity than any specifically English hegemony of 'fluency'.

v. Translation Studies In European terms, English-language academics came to the scholarly study of translation rather late in the day. Apart from interspersed historical pieces, there were relatively few publications before 1990. One should certainly appreciate the role played by Ezra Pound's essays from 1917–18, 1920, and 1929 (Pound 1954; 1973), as well as Hilaire Belloc's comments in 1929–31, not to mention theoretical comments by E. S. Bates (1943), Ronald Knox (1949, 1957), I. A. Richards (1953), Vladimir Nabokov (1955), T. H. Savory (1957), Eugene Nida (1964), J. C. Catford (1965) and the fine collective volume edited by Reuben Brower (1959). Yet none of those names can be strung with others to form anything like a school of thought; these were essentially occasional writings by creative writers, creative translators, literary critics, evangelists, applied linguists, and a zoologist (Savory was a specialist in spiders).

It was not until George Steiner's *After Babel* (1975) that English readers had any broad vision of Translation Studies as a discipline. At that time Professor of Comparative Literature in Geneva, Steiner formulated his view of translation in very European terms, doing much to incorporate Schleiermacher and Benjamin into a broad hermeneutic approach. *After Babel* was very different from the endemic norms and prescriptive linguistics that had characterized many of the previous writings on translation. Its influence has been diffuse and inseparable from general changes in European literary studies. Susan Bassnett's handbook *Translation Studies* (1980) might then be seen as a packaging of historical vision in a format suited to the teaching of theory, promoting awareness of the political role translations play in their relation to the target culture. Through her collaboration with the Belgian American André Lefevere, Bassnett has been able to develop this politicized perspective as a specific flavour within Descriptive Translation Studies, to the point where she and Lefevere could announce, at the beginning of the 1990s, that a 'cultural turn' had taken place, privileging the cultural implications of translation rather than the linguistics of the source text. Yet one might equally posit that the 1980s had seen very little activity in English-language translation studies, allowing undue prominence to linguistically framed textbooks such as Peter Newmark's (1981; 1988). Newmark retained a specific prescriptive input in his privileging of 'semantic' over 'communicative' translation, mostly in the sense of revering 'authoritative' authors (strangely coinciding with the leaders of bourgeois democracies). In this intellectual climate, the 'cultural turn' was perhaps rotating in a vacuum.

In the 1990s English-language Translation

Studies has been marked by extensive internationalism, as the general growth in European translator training has given rise to numerous publications in English. A study of the earlier debates should show there had always been strong investment in transatlantic exchange, as seen in Pound's early challenge to Victorian and Edwardian diction, the Zukofskys' phonetic experiments freely referred to on both sides of the Atlantic, or even British Bible committees looking over their shoulders at the work of their American counterparts. Many recent debates have been initiated in North America yet take root across the English-speaking world. This would certainly seem to be the case in the development of feminist and postcolonial approaches to translation, and more generally with the application of deconstructionist tenets.

Fruits of recent British activity are the journals *Translation and Literature* (from 1993) and the *Translator* (from 1995), as well as a publisher specializing in Translation Studies (St Jerome in Manchester). Yet these publications must find a place within the far wider field of general European Translation Studies (much of it in English), which in turn increasingly depends on the growth in translator training.

vi. Translator Training Translators traditionally learn their craft in non-institutionalized frameworks. For many, translating remains a part-time activity. Yet there have been various moves to enhance the professional status of translators, and specialized university-level training has been increasing since the 1960s.

There are several professional organizations representing translators in the United Kingdom, notably the Institute of Linguists (founded 1910), which organizes exams for centralized accreditation, and the Institute of Translating and Interpreting (founded 1986), which has organized international conferences on literary translation and runs a 'guardian angel' scheme to help beginners enter the profession. The specific concerns of literary translators are more likely to come under the aegis of the Translators Association (founded 1958), which George Astley established as a section of the Society of Authors because, as his widow is reported as saying, 'he saw translators having such a rotten time' (Crampton 1994: 52). On another level, the British Centre for Literary Translation at Norwich, founded by Professor Max Sebald in 1989, is funded by the Arts Council of England and gives residential grants to literary translators.

None of these professional organizations actually runs training programmes for translators, which is increasingly the responsibility of the higher education system. The main foreign languages dealt with in the translation programmes are French, German, and Spanish, with wider ranges available at the universities of Bath (where French is obligatory), Leeds (east European languages, Arabic and Chinese), City University (including Bengali), Heriot-Watt in Edinburgh (with Arabic), and Surrey (European languages). The only programme specifically concerned with literary translation would appear to be the MA at Essex University.

The motor behind this growth is not hard to locate: the globalization of national economies, especially the moves toward European unification, have created new markets for specialists in cross-cultural communication. An important part of this process has been the development of English as the international lingua franca.

vii. Translation and the Internationalization of English The 20th c. has seen the English language develop from its apogee of properly imperialist expansion under Britain to its role as an instrument of cultural expansion by the United States. Yet the language now enjoys confirmed status as the world lingua franca in accordance with criteria of efficiency that go beyond the machinations of any world power: international English depends as little on empire as did medieval Latin on the Romans. More important is the actual extent of internationalization. In the 1990s it was estimated that speakers of English as a first language numbered some 320 million worldwide; English is an official or dominant language in over 60 countries and is 'routinely in evidence' in a further 75 countries (Crystal 1997). Colonialism has left English as the matrix language for some 44 creoles and pidgins across the globe; its standard British and American forms are embedded in a maze of class-based and regional varieties that give the language an enormous internal diversity.

One clear result of this expansion is that the delocalized English of many translations corresponds to an international market. For example, the blandness of the *Good News Bible* (1976) is expressly designed for readers 'who speak English either as their mother tongue or as an acquired language' (1966: p. iv). Another consequence is the use of English as a target language for non-native or bilingual writers: self-translation into English has been used, for various reasons, by writers like the Bengali Rabindranath Tagore [II.l.5.ii], the Franco-Irish Samuel Beckett [II.g.5], the German Hans Magnus Enzensberger, and a string of Gaelic poets [II.d.4].

A slightly different question is the case of African and Caribbean writers who face the choice of writing in a creole or standard English: remarkably, but also understandably, translations of post-colonial literatures by African or Caribbean writers are almost invariably into standard English [see I.a.6.i; II.g.16]. The questions posed with respect to original creation are rarely asked of translation.

Given the rise of international English, perhaps the most surprising aspect is the relatively minor part that translations continue to play in its development. If literary histories traditionally exclude or downplay the role of translations, it is not necessarily due to any taboo on subversive hybridity: it may well be because there have been relatively few translations into 20th-c. English. The language has somehow failed to become a huge storehouse of world literature (the role Schleiermacher envisaged for German in 1813). The statistics are eloquent in this regard: Unesco figures for the period 1948–86 show an average of just 838 translations per year for the United Kingdom (1783 for the United States), well below the numbers for the Soviet Union (4565), West Germany (4442), Spain (3228), France (2112), and indeed all major European countries. In terms of historical development over the same period, some kind of steady growth is confirmed by Unesco and Whitaker's figures, with translations in the United Kingdom rising from about 500 a year around 1950 to about 1100 around 1985. Yet this reflects the general development of the publishing industry more than any pronounced growth in the number of translations, the level of which has hovered around 3 per cent of total book production in both the United Kingdom and the United States. This may be compared with 1989–91 percentages of up to 14 per cent in Germany, 18 per cent in France, and 25 per cent in Italy. In relative terms, the United Kingdom would seem to be the country that translates the least in Europe.

At the same time, English is by far the most translated language in the world, accounting for some 60 per cent of the translations published in Europe, as compared with 14 per cent for French and 10 per cent for German. In some cases this means English-language writers are better known abroad than at home: Edgar Wallace, a prolific but forgotten thriller-writer in Britain, is still widely read in German translation. Other cases include John Dickson Carr, who remains popular in Italy and France, Lawrence Norfolk, who has been more successful in German translation than in English, and A. J. Cronin, who appears to be popular worldwide.

In general, then, other languages translate from English, but English receives relatively few translations from anywhere. The imbalance would appear to be even more pronounced with respect to specifically literary translations: whereas 'literature' was the category with the most translations in France, Italy, Spain, and Germany in the early 1990s, in the United Kingdom it accounted for 19 per cent of translated titles, less than 'social sciences' (31 per cent) and 'science and technology' (29 per cent). The British literary system would appear to be relatively closed to translations.

Yet the above figures need not be direct consequences of any pronounced Anglo-American cultural closure. Translations in English are still numerous enough to have considerable historical weight: for the period 1960–86 the *Index Translationum* lists more than 2.5 times as many translations in Britain and the United States (1,872,050) as in France (688,720) or Italy (577,950). More important, since literature in English is a vast and diverse phenomenon, many of the non-translated English texts read in Britain are in fact from other cultures, effectively fulfilling much of the diversifying role that translations play in less extensive target languages (see Constantin, in Barret-Ducrocq 1992). This might in turn explain why relatively few subsidies are available for translations (some £72,000 in the United Kingdom in 1992): 20th-c. English has proved able to develop robustly from its own internal varieties, so it would appear not to need numerous translations as instruments of protection or stimulation.

To be sure, internal diversity should not be held up as an excuse for cultural complacency. Given the special importance of literature in the dynamics of British cultural identity, one senses that the reluctance to open the literary canon is greater than anything that can be explained in terms of language barriers. Contemporary British culture seems more open in cuisine, music, painting, and architecture, for instance. The result is that, beyond the occasional bestseller, the readers of literature in translation may well form a thin social grouping spread out over a very wide area, closely associated with university training. The restricted nature of that readership does not mean there are few translations to choose from—quite the contrary, the space of the English language is so vast that there are numerous translations—nor that these cultural systems are inward-looking or stagnating—literature in English has a very dynamic diversity, with numerous processes of post-colonial hybridization that require little formal translation. In fact, the real risk of these low translation rates is perhaps that they underwrite a lack of eurocentricism: British culture has had great difficulty trying to develop some sense of belonging to a uniting Europe, and the proportional paucity of translations from other European languages, now outweighed by the wider world of literature in English, is likely to keep that sense from developing into any substantial feeling of European identity. Global publishing in English thus bolsters the sad illusion of a self-sufficient English literature.

6. TRANSLATION IN NORTH AMERICA
Judith Weisz Woodsworth

i. Introduction Since the so-called 'discovery' of America over 500 years ago, translation—in the broad sense of oral and written interlingual communication—has played an important role. Not only did the Europeans come into contact with aboriginal peoples, they interacted and often clashed with one another. The Europeans spoke different languages: English, French, Spanish, Dutch, and Portuguese. As they vied for possession of the new territories and established themselves in different regions of North and South America, the issue of language was fundamental to political, cultural, and social relations among themselves, and with the native cultures. Translation practice and theory reflect the ways in which these associations evolved.

Very early on, English became the dominant language of the United States, and English-speaking settlers took control politically and linguistically. Translation served the interests of English-speaking people, colonizing the natives initially and later helping to assimilate immigrants from non-English countries. While the problematic role of translation in colonization and imperialism in America has been raised and discussed in the scholarly community (Cheyfitz 1991), translation is also seen as an essential element in the construction of the American consciousness, and a contributing factor in the building of national culture and identity.

Canada followed roughly the same path as her neighbour to the south with respect to the colonization of native peoples and suppression of their language and culture. Less concerned with making its mark on the world scene, Canada has been preoccupied with its internal struggle for national unity. The identity of the country has been inextricably bound with the coexistence of two 'founding nations': the English and the French. Their relations, at times cordial but often adversarial, have been expressed in terms of political, religious, cultural, and above all linguistic difference. Under the influence of forces such as mass culture and the Internet, many of the distinctive features of each of the two groups have faded into an essentially all-

American background. Thus, in the latter part of this century, the overriding difference between the two cultures is language.

The literary and academic interest of the two dominant groups in each other has been for the most part to the exclusion of other ethnic communities, which have, however, formed as much a part of the social fabric in Canada as in the USA. From the point of view of translation, and consequently Translation Studies, the English and French appear to have had 'eyes only for each other', until recently at least. This is in sharp contrast to the USA, where cultural exchange has brought the dominant English-language culture into contact with a wide range of other ones.

This entry will deal with the two English-speaking (or primarily English-speaking) nations of North America, leaving Mexico aside, and will examine the parallel and divergent ways in which translation has evolved within the two societies.

ii. Contact between Europeans and Native Peoples Interpreters were crucial to the Europeans who first landed in the New World. They faced not one foreign language but a number of different ones—some as closely related as French, Spanish, and Italian, others as distinct from each other as English and Chinese, all without a written tradition or grammar (Pentland 1993: 5).

It was common practice for the newcomers to abduct one or more Indians, either as trophies of their voyage or as prospective interpreters. On his first voyage to Canada in 1534, Jacques Cartier took two sons of an Iroquois chief back to France, where they were schooled in the French language. When Cartier returned to Canada on his second voyage, he used them as interpreters. The practice of kidnapping Native Americans for use as interpreters occurred elsewhere in North America. The story of Doña Marina (also known as *la Malinche*) is well known. An Indian princess and slave, she was given to Cortés in 1519, and she served the cause of the conquering Spaniards as they made their way through present-day Mexico (Woodsworth 1997).

Indians were still being abducted in the 17th c. By

then, however, new methods of 'recruiting' interpreters were emerging. Samuel de Champlain initiated a system of 'resident interpreters' (Delisle 1977). French adventurers were sent out to live with the Indians, often as adolescents. They learned their languages and customs, and won their trust. Étienne **Brûlé** (c.1592–1633) is a notable example. First sent to live among the Algonquins, he later became known as an interpreter of the Huron language, and even helped write a Huron dictionary. Similar cases were found in the American colonies during the 18th c. Conrad **Weiser** (1696–1760), a Pennsylvanian of German descent, acquired a knowledge of Iroquois languages and customs while living with the Mohawks as a young man. He served as Pennsylvania's official Indian agent and interpreter during the 1740s and 1750s (Hagedorn 1988: 76). Simon **Girty** (1741–1818), an Irish immigrant's son who had been kidnapped as a boy by the Senecas and came to know a number of Indian languages, served the British during the revolutionary war (Venuti 1997).

Sacajawea (c.1790–1812 or 1884) was a Shoshoni Indian woman who accompanied the Lewis and Clark expedition (1804–6) to the Pacific coast. Sold as a slave to the French interpreter and adventurer Toussaint Charbonneau, she became his wife and accompanied him when he signed on with Lewis and Clark in 1805. She helped form the chain of interpreters by which the explorers Meriwether Lewis and William Clark communicated with various Indian nations they met along the way. Officially, Sacajawea was not a guide, but only the Indian wife of the expedition's interpreter. In fact, in the account left by Meriwether Lewis, *The History of the Lewis and Clark Expedition*, she is not even referred to by name, although her possible usefulness is mentioned (quoted in Karttunen 1994: 23). There is no doubt that she performed crucial translation tasks, mediating between the European members of the expedition and the Indians they came across. It is problematic that so critical a cultural intermediary should remain practically nameless in the chronicles and that her work went unrecognized through payment or other means.

As a result of recent interest in American Indian history and the application of ethnohistorical methods, some interesting examples have come to light which concern the history of translation. One such study (Hagedorn 1988) lists over 30 interpreters who served as 'cultural brokers' during Anglo-Iroquois councils over a 30-year period alone (1740–70). Andrew **Montour** (c.1710–72), *métis* son of an Indian interpreter known as Madame Montour and an Oneida war chief named Caron-

dawana, was one such interpreter, working in Pennsylvania and New York. He was exposed from childhood to a variety of Indian cultures and languages. His mother was fluent in French, and knew other European languages. Linguistic proficiency, however, was not the only knowledge needed. Because of the elaborate protocol associated with the treaty conferences, interpreters like Montour 'mediated the exchange of cultures as well as the exchange of words and promises' (Hagedorn 1994: 46). Montour was a prominent Indian officer and interpreter, his services being specifically requested by George Washington during the Seven Years War.

Jerry **Potts** (c.1837–96) was born in the American West to a Scots fur trader who had married a Blackfoot Indian. After his father's death he was 'adopted' by another Scotsman, Andrew Dawson, who educated him and taught him the fur-trading business. During his travels with Dawson, he learnt to speak several Indian languages, including Cree, Sioux, and Crow, in addition to his native Blackfoot. The North West Mounted Police was established by the Canadian government in 1873 to deal with increasing disturbances over whisky peddling, and the threat of American traders invading Canada's newly acquired territories. Jerry Potts was hired as their interpreter and guide at a rate of $90 a month (Fardy 1984: 62), about three times as much as the Mounties themselves.

Potts had all the skills required to be a superior guide, including the linguistic skills to be an interpreter. He has been described as being particularly 'laconic' in his translations. While his translations were perhaps unduly brief and even unfaithful, Potts is credited with acting not only as interpreter but also as mediator. It is said that the Canadian West remained relatively free of violence, compared to the USA, largely because of Pott's role.

Sarah **Winnemucca** (1844–91) was another 'Indian princess' who worked as an interpreter. Unlike Marina and Sacajawea, however, she was educated, literate, and left a written record of her life, *Life among the Piutes: Their Wrongs and Claims*, published in 1883, one of the first books published by a native in the USA. As a teenager, she spent 10 years with white people, which gave her the opportunity to master English and learn some Spanish. She had some schooling, which stood her in good stead for her later work as a lecturer, interpreter, writer, and lobbyist for her people. Sarah's career is striking in that she actually worked as a professional interpreter, with a series of paid jobs. She interpreted for several years for agents with the federal Bureau of Indian Affairs and became an interpreter on the Malheur reservation in Oregon. Sarah taught in school and was one of the few to challenge the assumptions of the boarding-school method, advocating having Indians taught by Indians in their communities, rather than separated from their families (Karttunen 1994: 71).

At the same time as the explorers and adventurers moved across the continent on expeditions of conquest and commerce, various Christian communities began to work the same territory. Many of the missionaries studied native languages and compiled grammars and dictionaries so that they could make their sacred texts accessible to the people they sought to convert. In New France, the Récollets began missionary work with the Indians in 1615 at the invitation of Champlain. In 1625, they were joined by the Jesuits.

John **Eliot** (1604–90), a Cambridge-trained Puritan minister, arrived in the Massachusetts Bay Colony in 1631, just 11 years after the first pilgrims. He collaborated on an English translation of the Psalms known as the *Bay Psalm Book* (1640). After preparing an Indian catechism (1653) with the help of an Indian informant, he translated the New Testament (1661) and then the whole Bible (1663) into Algonquian, the language of the Massachusetts Indians. This was the first Bible to be published in North America.

Silas **Rand** (1810–89), a Baptist minister and missionary who also happened to be a philologist and ethnologist, translated several parts of the Old Testament and the entire New Testament into Micmac, an Algonquian language of Atlantic Canada, which he published in 1875. His anthropological interest in Micmac mythology inspired him to collect legends and preserve the native culture through translation. In 1864, he published *Legends of the Micmacs*, which remains a key to understanding the Micmac oral tradition (Gallant 1990).

iii. Canada: French/English Relations and Bilingualism The relations between the French and English eventually took the form of a contractual union of two so-called 'founding nations', a state in which translation has become institutionalized and fundamental to the very self-definition of its people.

In 1763, British acquisition of Canada was confirmed by the Treaty of Paris. Approximately 60,000 French Canadians now faced a North America that was British from the Gulf of Mexico to Hudson's Bay. During the early years of military rule, the British made use of secretary-translators to translate their edicts and proclamations into French. A decision was made to adopt British criminal law, but retain French civil law. Guy Carleton,

named Governor in 1767, appointed a bilingual jurist to translate the French laws into English and translate official English documents into French. This established, from the beginning of English rule, a tradition of official bilingualism.

After the American Revolution and the influx of Loyalists to Canada, there were increasing difficulties because of the contact of two different religious, legal and social systems. As a partial solution to the problem, the old Province of Quebec was divided into two parts, Upper and Lower Canada, each with its own legislature. In the newly established parliamentary system, laws were enacted in English but French remained as a language of translation.

In the 1830s serious problems arose in Lower Canada, aggravated by an assembly with a majority of French Canadians trying to gain control over an executive council composed mainly of Englishmen. A rebellion broke out in 1837, with a smaller one in Upper Canada around the same time. Sent out in 1838 to inquire into Canada's political problems, Lord Durham recommended that the French people be assimilated through the union of Upper and Lower Canada into a single Canada, with English as the only official language. This was done in 1840, but it provoked strong reactions among the French. An amendment to the Act of Union introduced the following year provided for the translation of laws into French. This was the first bill to deal specifically with translation, the first of many to come that would shape the future of the translation industry.

In 1867 the British North America Act established a Confederation of four provinces, Quebec, Ontario, New Brunswick, and Nova Scotia. English and French were placed on an equal footing in Parliament as well as in federal and Quebec courts. These legal obligations caused the volume of administrative, legal and commercial translation to increase. In 1934, a federal government Translation Bureau was created.

French Canadians sought to protect their language and culture and ensure that they had sufficient opportunity to participate in decision making. In 1963, in response to growing political unrest in Quebec, a Royal Commission on Bilingualism and Biculturalism was set up. Its recommendations led to the Official Languages Act (1969), which made it mandatory for all government documents to be produced in English and French. This legislation, and the promotion of bilingualism by Pierre Trudeau's government, had far-reaching consequences. By its 50th year (1984) the Translation Bureau in Ottawa had grown from 100 translators to over 1000.

In Quebec, however, nationalist sentiment continued. What Quebeckers wanted was a French society, and what they continue to want to this day is a society—and even independent state—that they can govern themselves. The Parti Québécois, first elected in 1976, legislated the Charte de la Langue Française (1977), which made French the only official language in the province of Quebec, although a number of public services continue to be offered in English. The main objective was to achieve *francisation* in business and the public sector. Terminology had to be generated for different sectors of the economy and a massive volume of documentation translated into French. Translation, as well as the subfield of terminology, became a vital occupation in Quebec.

iv. Canada: Translator Training and Translation Studies As a result of the political events outlined above, and legislation enacted in response to those events, translation grew into a veritable industry. Around 6000 individuals make their living as professional translators. The profession is well organized, with professional associations in eight of the Canadian provinces and the North West Territories, with a single national umbrella organization, the Canadian Translators and Interpreters Council (CTIC). Translation is recognized as an accredited profession in some jurisdictions, with a 'reserved title' provided for under the law. Standards are well defined, rates of remuneration uniform and fairly high, and working conditions good.

The growth of a language industry led to a need for adequate training. Professional translation had been taught, albeit not in a very structured way, at the University of Ottawa since 1936, at McGill since 1943 and the University of Montreal since 1951. In 1968, coinciding with the recommendations of the Bilingualism and Biculturalism Commission, the University of Montreal began to offer the first full-time degree programme in translation. Between 1968 and 1984, a new translation programme of one kind or another was launched every year (Delisle 1987: 34).

The Canadian Association of Schools of Translation (CAST) was formed in 1973 to coordinate translator training activities in the country. Over the years, the schools have moved toward a high level of theoretical reflection along with increasing professionalization in response to the demands of the workplace. In recent years, several research-oriented postgraduate programmes have been established, including a new doctorate in Translation Studies at University of Ottawa.

As translation courses proliferated, it became apparent that concepts had to be clarified, pedagogical strategies developed, and textbooks and other teaching materials developed. Jean-Paul Vinay and Jean Darbelnet, Montreal linguists who taught translation in the early years at University of Montreal, laid the groundwork with their well-known *Stylistique comparée du français et de l'anglais* in 1958. This was followed by a wealth of new publications in more specialized aspects of translator training. In the 1960s practising translators produced glossaries, vocabularies, and works on usage. By the 1970s, textbooks began to appear: Robert Dubuc's *Manuel pratique de terminologie* (1978) and Jean Delisle's *L'Analyse du discours comme méthode de traduction* (1980), for example. Gradually the reflection on translation broadened. Works of history appeared, such as Louis Kelly's *The True Interpreter* (1979), Paul Horguelin's *Anthologie de la manière de traduire* (1981), and Jean Delisle's more local works on the history of translation in Canada. The periodical *Meta* was established in 1955, and since then several other magazines and scholarly journals have been launched.

There has been a move in the past 10 years to create a place for translation research in its own right. While the professional associations would occasionally devote special sessions of their regular meetings to pedagogical or theoretical issues, Translation Studies *per se* was marginalized. As a solution, the Canadian Association for Translation Studies (CATS) was launched in 1987. Its aim has been to promote and disseminate research in translation and related fields, which it has accomplished through an annual conference and *TTR*, a journal with a distinctive research orientation and national and international participation.

As translation moved more solidly into the academy, scholars in fields other than linguistics began to examine translation phenomena, bringing a diversity of perspectives to bear on the act of translating: history, semiotics, cultural studies, postcolonial theory, feminism. Translation scholars in Canada have contributed to the construction of a field of inquiry in its own right and the production of a significant body of knowledge (e.g. Brisset 1990; Delisle and Woodsworth 1995; Simon).

v. Literary Translation in Canada The separate status of literary translation in Canada is reflected in the existence of a separate professional association, the Literary Translators' Association of Canada (LTAC), founded in 1975 as a national association distinct from CTIC.

Writing about the status of literary translation, eminent translator Philip Stratford says:

Due to the inexhaustible mountain of work to be done, a strictly pragmatic attitude dominates the profession in this country. Most talented translators ... spend their lives as anonymous, competent, well-paid functionaries; as a corollary, literary translation is looked upon as a marginal activity, slightly frivolous, and economically uninteresting. (Stratford 1977: p. iii)

The facts support this claim. Before 1920, 10 translations of literary works were published in English, two in French; by 1960 there were fewer than 40 additional English titles and 10 French ones, around half of which had been translated and published elsewhere, in England, France, or the United States (Stratford 1977: p. ii).

The first major French-Canadian novel, *Les Anciens Canadiens* (1863) by Philippe-Joseph Aubert de Gaspé, was translated first by Georgiana M. **Pennée** in 1864, then by Sir Charles G. D. **Roberts** (1860–1943), a Canadian writer known for his poetry and animal tales, in 1890. Roberts recognized the 'ethnographic' role of the translator and the importance of translation as a bridge between two literatures (Simon 1994: 53). There were sporadic efforts to translate other works, including the classic *Maria Chapdelaine* by Louis Hémon, which was actually translated twice in one year, 1921, by W. H. **Blake** (1861–1924) and Sir Andrew **Macphail** (1864–1938).

The growth of literary translation since the 1960s can be attributed to two factors: one political, the other institutional. English-speaking intellectuals of the 1960s began to take an interest in Quebec, perhaps out of admiration for its distinct culture, perhaps out of a sense of mission, a wish to bridge the gap between the so-called 'Two Solitudes', to borrow a title from English-Canadian novelist Hugh MacLennan (Woodsworth 1994) [for translation of Quebec writing, see II.g.16].

An interesting phenomenon of this time is that there were far more literary translations into English than vice versa, while in the field of non-literary translation approximately 85 per cent of translation occurred from English to French. In the past 10 years, attitudes have changed: the exchange of literatures through translation has balanced out. Perhaps because of a strengthened sense of nationhood, Quebec writers and translators have been more open to other literatures.

In 1972 the Canada Council introduced a Translation Grants Programme. Because of the very small publishing market in the country (2000 is a large print run), few writers or translators can make a living from their work. For over 20 years the Canada Council has provided individual grants to translators and general grants to publishers. This financial support has enabled Canadian publishing houses to survive, including some smaller ones that have consistently published works in translation. The magazine *Ellipse* has since 1969 published translations of poetry and has brought together a distinguished group of poetry translators. In 1974 the Canada Council established a prize for outstanding translations in French and English; it is now included in the prestigious Governor General's Literary Awards. The Literary Translator's Association has been instrumental in furthering the cause of translators and improving their visibility, through changes to copyright legislation, advice to their members on contracts, and so on.

Canadian literary translators have generated a considerable body of reflection on their work. Several anthologies and collections of conference papers have been published over the years. *Mapping Literature*, for example, edited by Sherry Simon and David Homel (1988), resulted from a conference organized by the Literary Translators' Association, and Sherry Simon's *Culture in Transit* (1995), brings together essays by some of the country's most accomplished French–English translators.

The work of feminist translators, such as Barbara **Godard**, Luise **Von Flotow**, and Susanne **de Lotbinière-Harwood**, is a distinctive feature of literary translation in Canada, because these translators have both promoted and theorized the activities of literary mediation, stimulated creative practices, and opened up innovative theoretical debates through their work on feminist texts (Simon 1995) [see I.a.5].

vi. Canada: Languages other than French and English Discussions of language and translation have primarily focused on English and French. Yet the linguistic landscape of Canada is by no means confined to the two 'official' languages. The preoccupation with the survival of French language and culture in Quebec, and the political urgency in the rest of the country caused by the threat of Quebec separation, have somewhat overshadowed the concerns and activities of other linguistic groups. Canadian translation scholars have rarely turned their attention to translations from other languages.

Watson **Kirkconnell** is an example of this marginalization. A man of phenomenal achievements, Kirkconnell is cited briefly in the *Canadian Encyclopedia* under the rubric 'Ethnic Literature' but is virtually unknown in translation circles. Kirkconnell was a professor of Latin and English and author of dozens of volumes of prose and poetry. To overcome his grief at his wife's untimely death in 1925, he undertook the translation into English of elegiac poems from other languages. The result was *European Elegies*, a collection of 100 poems from approximately 40 languages.

At the time, Kirkconnell was a professor in Winnipeg, a city peopled with 'New Canadians'. For the next 26 years, until he became President of Acadia University in Nova Scotia, he lived in close contact with immigrant groups (Kirkconnell 1967). His most ambitious undertaking was verse translation from Ukrainian [see II.e.11], and he also translated substantial amounts from the Hungarian, Polish, Norwegian, Icelandic, Swedish, and several other languages, including French. The fact that his work came at a time when Canadian biculturalism was being affirmed can perhaps explain the fact that his work has been overlooked.

There is some sign of a change in this regard, with more writing in languages other than the two official ones, and some translations from foreign languages. For example, the 1997 winner of the LTAC Glassco prize was Don **Coles** for his English translation of poems by the Swedish poet Tomas Tranströmer. Canada continues to be a country of immigration, although the provenance of New Canadians has now shifted from Europe to other parts of the globe. Canadian cities are increasingly multicultural and there is a growing need for translators and interpreters, particularly within the court system, for a significant number of languages.

Canada is also entering a new era with respect to aboriginal languages. Some of these languages, such as the Indian language Cree and the Inuit language Inuktitut, have writing systems and a body of literature. In 1984, the Official Languages Act of the North West Territories gave 'official aboriginal status' to seven native languages. With the establishment of the new Canadian territory of Nunavut in 1999, and its transition to self-government, there will be considerable work in translation and interpreting among the Inuit.

vii. The USA: Translation and the Development of a National Culture
In the United States, unlike Canada, there has not been any legal obligation to translate. Nevertheless, translation activities extended beyond the period of contact with native Americans. Translation was an instrument in American internal relations with non-English immigrant groups, and cultural and commercial relations with the rest of the world, and it played a significant role in the affirmation of American identity and the creation of a national literature.

The first book to be printed in Britain's American colonies was the *Bay Psalm Book*, the name commonly applied to *The Whole Booke of Psalmes Faithfully Translated into English Metre* (1640). The translators were Puritan clergymen John Eliot, Richard **Mather**, and Thomas **Weld**. In keeping with their religious values, the translation aimed to be more literal and not necessarily as elegant as the King James Bible [see II.c.1]. The translation strategies employed also had political ramifications in that they reflected the puritans' dissent from the Anglican Church and helped to affirm their autonomy from England (Venuti 1997).

As in other colonial situations, translation contributed to the development of a national culture distinct from that of the mother country. An important example is the anthology edited by writer and philosopher George **Ripley** (1802–80), *Specimens of Foreign Standard Literature*. Co-founder, with Ralph Waldo Emerson and Margaret Fuller, of a Transcendentalist publication, editor of the *Harbinger*, a journal of social reform, popular book reviewer for the *New York Tribune* from 1849 to 1880, Ripley was an influential intellectual figure of his time. His 14-volume anthology included some of his own translations of French philosophers and writers. During the 19th c., more popular genres of European literature—theatre and popular novels, for example—were also translated and well received by mass audiences [see I.b.4].

The poet and critic Ezra **Pound** is also well-known for his translations, for instance *The Seafarer*, from an Anglo-Saxon text [II.o.1], *Cathay* (1915), a sequence of adaptations from the classical Chinese [II.f.2], and *Homage to Sextus Propertius* [II.n.4.iv]. It was never Pound's intention to produce a close or literal translation. Instead, he experimented with a range of techniques, importing foreign forms and texts and using translation to challenge existing literary norms. Often charged with incompetent or inaccurate translation, Pound was nonetheless credited with being one of the most influential verse translators of his time, generating scholarly debate and introducing innovation not only to the American national culture but to the Western tradition in general.

The choice of foreign texts to be translated has been influenced by American foreign relations. Since World War II, the languages most frequently translated into English have been French, German, Russian, Italian, and Spanish. When works of Russian literature have been translated, they have generally been consistent with American anti-Communist or anti-Soviet sentiment: the works of Alexander Solzhenitsyn, for example (Venuti 1997). Latin American literature [II.k.10–11] has enjoyed considerable success in translation in the USA, beginning in the 1950s with translations of Jorge Luís Borges and continuing into the 1960s and 1970s, because of the intrinsic appeal and innovative quality of the texts, as well as the immediacy of pan-American relations.

Non-literary translation and interpreting have thrived in the second half of the 20th c., so crucial are they to the political and economic objectives of American government and business, while literary translation has been regarded by many as a secondary activity, 'mechanical rather than creative' (Gentzler 1993: 8). Book production has increased fourfold in the past 50 years, but the number of translations has remained the same, representing between 2 and 4 per cent of the annual total of books published (Venuti 1995a: 12–13). American publishers have sold translation rights for English-language books, turning many of these into global bestsellers. Anglo-American cultural values have been imposed on a vast foreign audience, while at the same time the culture at home has remained 'aggressively monolingual' (Venuti 1995a: 15). During the 1960s and 1970s, however, literary translation experienced a certain boom. The sale of translated texts reached an unprecedented high, related to a popular interest in 'alternate value systems' (Gentzler 1993: 9). Particularly popular during this time were works of poetry. [On the publishing of translation in the USA, see I.b.5.iii.]

There is some evidence that more recently the American tendency toward 'fluent' translations is being offset by more inventive foreignizing texts, such as a new version of Dostoevsky by Pevear and Volokhonsky [II.p.5]. The Loeb Classical Library [see II.i.1] was taken over from the London firm of Heinemann by Harvard University Press in 1989. Many authors are due to get a facelift. Aristophanes, for example, will be retranslated by Jeffrey **Henderson**, a classics professor at Boston University, who will restore the 'scurrilous tone of the author' [see II.i.6] and reveal the erotic world of Aristophanes' society, long obscured in the prim Loeb edition (*Chronicle of Higher Education*, 1998).

viii. Organization of the Profession and Training in the USA Professional organizations have been slower to emerge in the USA than in Canada. The American Translators Association (ATA) was formed in 1959 (compared with the first association in Canada, the Cercle des Traducteurs des Livres Bleus, 1919). The Translation Committee of PEN was founded in 1959 as well, to protect and support the work of literary translators. It has had a continued concern to ensure that translators are given

full credit for their work, and in 1993 persuaded the Library of Congress to include the names of literary translators in its cataloguing system. In 1978 the American Literary Translators Association (ALTA) was founded. It also organizes an annual conference and publishes a journal, the *Translation Review*.

In 1965 a National Translation Center was established at the University of Texas at Austin, and in 1973 the Translation Center at Columbia University was created. Funding for translation itself has been made available through the National Endowment for the Arts, while grants have been provided for research through the National Endowment for the Humanities. Events such as these, and in particular the creation of structures within academic institutions, have contributed over the past 30 years to the growth of a body of knowledge around translation.

Training in literary translation developed through the 'translation workshop' concept, which originated in 1964 at the University of Iowa and later spread to institutions such as Columbia, Princeton, and Yale. The State University of New York at Binghamton developed a Center for Research in Translation which since 1971 has provided postgraduate training in translation; it has also organized symposia and issued a number of publications, including its occasional papers, *Translation Perspectives*.

ix. Translation Studies in the USA Translation theory is a relatively new field in the United States. Commentary from the 1950s to the 1970s was generally unsystematic. Two anthologies by Brower (1959) and Arrowsmith and Shattuck (1961) are early examples, but the practice of publishing collected essays continues (Schulte and Biguenet 1992). Through a series of interviews with translators, Edwin Honig (1985) provides insight into the process of translation. This is what Gentzler calls the American workshop approach, a 'look into the black box of the human mind as it works and reworks during the activity of translating' (1993: 41).

In reaction to the workshop approach, Joseph Graham attempted to move 'beyond the personal anecdotes and pieces of advice' (Graham 1981: 23) to develop a more scientific or objective understanding of translation. In the 1980s, the arrival in the USA of a number of new theories, primarily French and German and thus imported to their American audiences via translation—psychoanalysis, phenomenology, Marxism, feminism, poststructuralism—had an impact on academic discourse in general, and on the theorization of translation in particular. Joseph Graham's important collection of papers (1985), which originated in a conference in Binghamton, represents poststructuralist styles of thinking.

Through the 1990s translation has become an object of scholarly inquiry in its own right. American theoreticians of translation who have made their mark worldwide include Doug Robinson, author of *The Translator's Turn* (1991) and a number of other publications on translation theory and history; Edwin Gentzler, author of a thorough review of contemporary translation theories (1993); and Lawrence Venuti (1995a), champion of the 'visible' translator, opponent of the kind of 'fluent' translation that typifies much of the work that has been done in the USA. Suzanne Jill Levine, translator of Latin American literature, has produced a book reflecting on her work as a 'subversive' translator (1991), and Tejaswini Niranjana, an Indian who worked at the University of California, approaches translation from a postcolonialist perspective (1992). Translation phenomena have attracted increasing attention in the context of cultural studies, where they help to shed light on relations between institutions, ideologies, and cultural practices.

c. Text Types

1. POETRY
Daniel Weissbort

i. Introduction If more has been written about the translation of poetry than about that of prose, it should be remembered that poetry embraces or once embraced epic and narrative verse, so that discussion cannot be said to have confined itself to a genre of limited diffusion. The translation of poetry, particularly classical poetry, and in particular the *Odyssey* and *Iliad*, engaged the attention of most major translators until comparatively recently. Until the 19th c., it was not unusual for major poets also to translate poetry. In the late 20th c., encouragingly, this seems again to be becoming a norm, witness Ted **Hughes**'s superbly readable translation from Ovid's *Metamorphoses* (*Tales from Ovid*, 1997) [II.n.6.iii].

Prescriptions, of course, abound, although it is hard to relate them to the actual results, since the terms employed are often ambiguous. Robert Frost's quip that in the translation of poetry it is precisely the poetry that gets left out is routinely quoted, since it restates the widely held assumption that what defines poetry is that it *is* untranslatable. The notion that anything less than total or absolute translation must be unacceptable underlies this view and has promoted the establishment of rules of procedure, it being understood that there must always be a single correct way [see I.a.2]. Less absolutist or more realistic attitudes encourage translators to define or describe, rather than simply seek to defend their methods and aims by making normative assertions that underwrite their own approach.

The more flexible attitude to language and to the reciprocities of linguistic inter-traffic characteristic of many translators at this time has permitted individual practitioners to be more self-aware in distinguishing between different methods. Strategic decisions, and therefore choices at the micro-level as well, are now more often based on a summary of the gains or losses entailed in the different approaches. For instance, if the translator is working on a sequence of poems, it is likely that the strategy once adopted will be adhered to throughout. If, however, a number of disparate poems, even by the same poet, is being translated, it is equally likely that decisions, however influenced by individual predilections, will be made anew with each poem. The variability in translations reflects variability in source texts. Some poets or translators of poetry may know or believe they know what they are up to; others may not until afterwards, when they have become plain readers again. Critics, of course, will often discover patterns, influences, of which the writer is unaware. The translator, at once reader, writer and critic, may, as writer or *re*-writer, be inclined to imitate the original author and make room for improvisation.

Paradoxically, this non-normativeness seeks to systematize flexibility or to mirror the creative process itself. At the same time it recognizes the translator's individual creativity as well as his craftsmanship. The stakes being higher, the risks are greater. On the other hand, human fallibility is implicitly acknowledged. Translations may be regarded as non-exclusive parallel texts, functioning both as commentaries on the source text and as texts in their own right.

ii. Sixteenth to Eighteenth Century It is instructive to consider this question historically, although when comparing the practices of one's own time, however indirectly, with those of earlier generations, it is also often hard not to be condescending, in spite of one's esteem for monuments of historical translation such as those mentioned below. A non-defensive or non-judgemental examination of the undeniably great translations of our tradition may therefore be salutary.

Consider, for instance, Alexander **Pope**'s Homer (*Iliad*, 1715–20; *Odyssey*, 1725–26) [II.i.2]. This work is composed in the heroic metre, rhyming iambic pentameter couplets, of which Pope's translation is regarded as the outstanding example. It is arguable that no other formal choice was possible, that for Pope the form was simply a given. Pope's mastery of heroic metre and its enshrinement in his translation of the Homeric poems, the master epics of our civilization, ensured the memorability of his version, its durability, unlike many or most translations of poetry, even of the *Odyssey* or *Iliad*, which have a limited currency.

It has been suggested by George Steiner (1966) among others that the Augustan age was the last time that an epic poem *could* have been rendered with assurance in English. English was felt to be fully equal to the task of representing the most majestic works of the past. And yet, perhaps for this very reason, Pope's work was soon to be criticized. Indeed, it was criticized in his own time as an excellent example of its eminent author's art but as unrepresentative of Homer ('[A] very pretty poem, Mr Pope, but you must not call it Homer', commented Richard Bentley, Master of Trinity). One may infer that the original was deemed somehow to have eluded its distinguished translator; Homer himself was therefore in danger of being lost from sight. Not long after, the poet William **Cowper** produced a significant critique, arguing that the demands of rhyme, so consummately deployed by Pope, precluded exact translation [II.i.2.iii]. As he put it, in his preface to his own translation of the *Iliad* (1791): 'No human ingenuity [i.e. not even Pope's] can be equal to the task of closing every couplet with sounds homotonous, expressing at the same time the full sense, and only the full sense of his original.' To escape the tyranny of the rhyming couplet and facilitate a closer approximation to the sense, he proposed, instead, Miltonic blank verse. Of course, for the classically trained gentleman the translation was to be enjoyed alongside the original as a demonstration of the versatility and expressiveness of English. During the period between the lives of Alexander Pope and Samuel Johnson, what might be called assimilative translation, the approach that sought to make acquisitions for the language and the national culture rather than to sat-isfy an interest in the foreign, was at its most accomplished [see I.b.3], so that the variations recorded here represent not so much contradictions as differences of focus. Cowper's questioning of Pope's method, even if he went no further than to suggest the substitution of Miltonic blank verse for the heroic couplet that was the dominant form at the time, may be read as a challenge to the uninhibited englishing of foreign texts, the notion that a translation should represent what the original author might have written had he been writing in English and in the contemporary period.

One can readily imagine Pope agreeing with Cowper, while maintaining that all a translator could do, after all, was to write as well as he was able. For Pope this meant translating the Greek hexameters into heroic couplets. In his intelligent and scholarly 'Preface to the Iliad of Homer' he insisted, as did John Dryden before him, on a balance between fidelity and freedom: 'It is certain no literal translation can be just to an excellent original in a superior language: but it is a great mistake to imagine . . . that a rash paraphrase can make amends for its general defect . . .' Cowper surely would not have disagreed with this. Pope began unexceptionably enough: 'It is the first grand duty of an interpreter to give his author entire and unmaimed.' But he continued: 'and for the rest, the diction and versification only are his proper province, since these must be his own, but the others he is to take as he finds them.' Form and content were treated as independent of one another, whereas Cowper seemed at least to query this assumption. Yet Pope's elaborate commentary on the text shows him to be remarkably sensitive to form. Only, the idiom he commanded was not a subject for debate. English had, as it were, attained the commanding heights; it was not in a mood to be colonized or infiltrated by foreign importations, even from the Greek and Latin classics. Monumentally accomplished as Pope's work is, the translation remains a celebration of English rather than of Homer's Greek text, although when read in conjunction with the notes (as Nabokov's translation of Pushkin's *Eugene Onegin* (see below) should be read together with his commentaries) a somewhat different impression may result.

A century or more earlier, in the heyday of Renaissance translation, versions arguably had been more permeable, not least because the English language itself was in a less stable state. As Ezra Pound, in his 'Notes on Elizabethan Classicists' (1917), said of Arthur **Golding** (*c.*1536–1605), translator of Ovid's *Metamorphoses* [II.n.6.iii]: '[He] was endeavouring to convey the sense of the original to his readers . . . intent on conveying a meaning, and not on bemusing them with a rumble' (Pound 1954). In Pound's opinion, 'The quality of translations declined in measure as the translators ceased to be absorbed in the subject matter of their original'. While clearly the aim, in Rossetti's words, was 'to endow a fresh nation [the English], as far as possible, with one more possession of beauty' (quoted in Lefevere 1992b), the malleability of the language, irrespective of whether the translator's approach was literalistic or not, made it less resistant to foreignization (to use a currently fashionable term). The translators' absorption in the subject matter of their (mostly) classical originals, even if they aimed at readability and were prepared to move quite far in the direction of what we have now been persuaded to call domestication, permitted the language, as it were, to do its work.

George **Chapman** (c.1559–1634), for instance [see II.i.2], in his verse epistle to the reader, insisted on the need to make Homer speak English according to the genius of the English language, anything less than that being patently absurd. So he accused the literalistic pedants ('great Clerkes') of disloyalty to the language. However, the need to pay strict attention to what the author is actually saying is reaffirmed, Chapman observing that he takes fewer liberties with the sense than previous translators. In the final count, however, it is art that is the key. Only poesie could open poesie, as Sir John **Denham** (see below) put it, so that Chapman also claimed the right to deploy his own talents. And yet the focus on narrative content rather than on fine style allowed 16th- and 17th-c. translators, albeit with elaborate flourishes and the provision of what foreignizers today would regard as anachronistic contemporary detail, to stay quite close to the literal sense, maintaining a measure, a tempo, which might sometimes have lacked stateliness but which was extremely seductive.

There is agreement on the need for the source text, its subject-matter, to be accurately or fully rendered; confidence, however, varies considerably as between a Chapman and a Pope, the former more vociferous in upholding the English language, maybe because he is less sure of it. One might say that Chapman was bolder, took greater risks than Pope, except that this would be to ignore the historical differences. In any case, he was also more emphatic about the transformative magic of art, claiming to be filled with Homer's spirit, as if the text had been dictated to him in English by his mighty predecessor.

The increasing domination by the English language (as such or as a given) of the process of trans-

lation is expressed in Sir John Denham's preface to *The Destruction of Troy* (1656) where the author defines a 'new way' of translating, in this case Virgil:

I conceive it a vulgar error in translating Poets, to affect being *Fidus Interpres* [. . .] [W]hosoever aims at it in Poetry, as he attempts what is not required, so he shall never perform what he attempts, for it is not his business alone to translate Language into Language, but Poesie into Poesie; & Poesie is of so subtile a spirit, that in poring out of one Language into another, it will all evaporate; and if a new spirit be not added in the transfusion, there will remain nothing but a *Caput mortuum*, there being certain Graces and Happinesses peculiar to every Language, which gives life and energy to the words . . .

Denham and other royalist proponents of the so-called 'new way' sought, on their return from France, in effect to exclude the foreign. If the method was perceived as 'new', this was perhaps because the potentiality of the English language appeared to have increased [see I.b.3.ii]. This englishing of the source text culminates in such works as Samuel **Johnson**'s *The Vanity of Human Wishes* (an imitation or modernization of Juvenal's Tenth Satire [II.n.7.iv]). By Cowper's time, the grand edifice is beginning to crumble.

iii. Nineteenth and Twentieth Centuries The Ciceronian precept of sense for sense rather than word for word [see I.a.3.ii] continued unchallenged until the 19th c., when the ideal of lexical accuracy, closeness to the actual wording and even to the syntax of the source text, began to influence some translators of poetry. Translators tried openly to accommodate non-English patterns of speech, or strove for an antique effect when rendering poetry from the remote past. Thus, if on the one hand there was an Edward **FitzGerald** with his naturalizing reconstruction of the *Rubáiyát of Omar Khayyám* (1859) [II.q.2.iv], there was also a Robert **Browning** with his literalistic rendering of Aeschylus' *Agamemnon* (1877) [II.i.3.ii]. In his preface to the latter, Browning spoke of being 'literal at every cost save that of absolute violence to our language'. This version was castigated later by Ezra **Pound**, who himself experimented with a kind of phonic or archetectonic literalism (e.g. 'The Seafarer' [II.o.1]). For Pound, Browning's work was irredeemably Victorian; a Victorian himself, he set out to demolish that tradition.

Richard **Burton** (1821–90), a remarkable linguist as well as an explorer, favoured a literalism that would not domesticate the source texts. While, for instance in his translation of Catullus's *Carmina* (1894), he admitted that there was considerable truth in the Ciceronian prescription, he also observed that '"Consulting modern taste" means really a mere imitation, a recast of the ancient past in modern material . . . Moreover, of these transmogrifications we have already enough and to spare.' He concluded: 'As discovery is mostly my mania. I have hit upon a bastard urging to indulge it, by a presenting to the public of certain classics in the nude Roman poetry . . .' In his Introduction to the *Book of The Thousand Nights and a Night* (1885) [II.b.5], Burton apparently tried to steer a course between lexical literalism and sense-for-sense; he aimed at 'preserving intact, not only the spirit, but even the mécanique, the manner and the matter'. In the 'versical portion', however, he sometimes abandoned the Arabic metres ('which are artificial in the extreme', especially the monorhyme, which easily becomes monotonous in English). That is, Burton, while eager to avail himself of the opportunity to extend the range of English, was reassuringly pragmatic about it.

How to render Greek and Latin poetry was vigorously debated at this time, with closely if somewhat otiosely argued articles in leading journals on the appropriateness of syllabic verse, on the merits or demerits of the hexameter in English, and so forth. Matthew Arnold famously debated such issues with Francis **Newman** (1805–97), the latter having produced in 1861 a would-be popularizing translation of the *Iliad*. Confident as ever of occupying the high ground, Arnold accused Newman of debasing Homer, failing to convey his 'nobleness' (Arnold 1861). In fact, Newman's antiquarian version, with its echoes of Anglo-Saxon poetry and alliterative verse, aiming to communicate the 'strangeness' of the original, was among those Victorian experiments that anticipated later developments.

To spring forward a century and a half, Vladimir **Nabokov**, in his remarks concerning his own translation of Pushkin's novel in verse *Eugene Onegin* (1964), seems almost to be echoing Cowper, though in more challenging and decidedly less apologetic terms, even allowing for differences in historical circumstances: 'The person who desires to turn a literary masterpiece into another language has only one duty to perform, and this is to reproduce with absolute exactitude the whole text, and nothing but the text' (Nabokov 1955). Of course, confusingly enough, Pope too had demanded faithfulness to the text: 'It is the first grand duty of an interpreter to give his author entire and unmaimed', as did Chapman before him: 'and yet as much aborre | More licence from the words than may expresse | Their full compression and make cleare the Author.' Nevertheless, each apparently had something

rather different in mind. Nabokov, for one, emphatically rejected the notion that 'poesie is to be opened with poesie'. For him, such treatment of a text, whatever else it might be, was not translation. He argued instead that no attempt at formal mimesis, at a parallel or equivalent poetry, could produce anything other than a different poem. A poem could not be translated, reproduced, or reassembled in the target language. Nabokov noted, however, that it could be made usefully accessible to the target-language reader through 'copious footnotes, footnotes reaching up like skyscrapers to the top of this or that page so as to leave only the gleam of one textual line between commentary and eternity'. His challenge was clear, or at least sought to clear the air:

I want such footnotes and the absolutely literal sense, with no emasculation and no padding—I want such sense and such notes for all the poetry in other tongues that still languishes in 'poetical' versions, begrimed and beslimed by rhyme.

While Nabokov's actual translation of *Onegin*, as distinct from his commentary on the poem, is generally regarded as something of a linguistic oddity [II.p.2.iii], he has found supporters too, especially among those, often poets themselves, seeking to get on closer terms with a great foreign original than the usual poeticizing version permits. That Nabokov, in a sense, gets too close for comfort is regarded by readers such as these as a bonus. Unquestionably the reader could not receive the foreign text passively, but was required to invest a good deal of hard work in it. What was gained, however, was worth the effort, an interpretation, less completely mediated or digested, even if it was not entirely one's own.

Or perhaps not? Nabokov's lexical literalism itself represents an ideal, arguably as unattainable as any other. Even at the primary level, that of conveying by whatever means 'the absolute literal sense', his demands are unrealistic. At the same time, it is no accident that after expressing total scepticism with regard to the translatability of poetry he should have sought rather to yoke modern textual scholarship at its most formidable (and, in his own case, idiosyncratic) to the business of conveying foreign texts. He seemed to accept what so many had denied: the logical impossibility of importing or smuggling foreign texts across linguistic borders, without alteration.

Among the Nabokovians, for instance, was the American poet, critic and translator Stanley **Burnshaw**, who edited an innovative anthology *The Poem Itself* (1960). For Burnshaw, as for Frost, poetry is 'that which gets lost in translation'. He insisted that 'the only way one could experience the poetry of a language one did not command was by learning to hear and pronounce (if only approximately) the sounds of the originals and "simultaneously" reading literal renditions'. Accordingly, Burnshaw provided readers with 'the poem itself' in the original language, followed by a line-by-line literal prose rendering and informational commentary.

In a sense, Nabokov and Burnshaw can be regarded as heirs of the romantics, with their belief in the sacredness, uniqueness, hence untranslatability (strictly speaking) of languages. Friedrich Schleiermacher [see I.a.3.iii] had affirmed that there were only two ways of translating: 'The translator either (1) disturbs the writer as little as possible and moves the reader in his direction, or (2) disturbs the reader as little as possible and moves the writer in his direction.' The German poet Friedrich Hölderlin (1770–1843), in his translations from the Greek, is commonly regarded as an example of the first kind of translator; Nabokov and Burnshaw, in their own way, are similarly inclined.

It is, of course, fanciful to align William Cowper with Schleiermacher's thinking, and yet not entirely so. In his time, Cowper could envisage only blank verse, the unrhymed iambic pentameter, as an alternative to Pope's rhyming couplets as a solution to the problem of translating Homer. Nabokov was able to conceive of a far more radical solution in relation to *Eugene Onegin*: 'The problem, then, is a choice between rhyme and reason: can a translation while rendering with absolute fidelity the whole text, and nothing but the text, keep the form of the original, its rhythm and its rhyme?' In his view it could not; both rhythm and rhyme had to be abandoned. This amounted to a denial of the possibility of formal translation, whereas for Cowper the game was not yet up; other approaches might still be tried. Nevertheless, taking issue with so illustrious a predecessor as Pope was momentous. Cowper's greater concern for the literal sense suggests that a turning-point was approaching. The professionalism of classical scholarship, the German science of 'antiquity', were to make it harder for poets to impose what might be taken as their own vision on a Homer, Virgil, or Horace.

iv. **Problems of Practice** Nevertheless, distinctions between the various approaches to translation often seem, at the very least, problematical; there appears to be more general agreement than disagreement. It is when one examines the translations themselves that actual differences become more apparent. The locus classicus for English translation theory is in the prefaces to the many translations produced by John **Dryden** or published under his aegis, the most influential being the preface to Ovid's *Epistles* (1680). It is here that Dryden explicitly defines the tripartite division that, until very recently, remained the starting-point for most discussions on the translation of poetry [see I.a.3.iii].

Like so many of his predecessors, Dryden rejected 'metaphrase, or turning an author word by word, or line by line, from one language into another'. He also cautioned against the third, imitation, pragmatically settling for the middle one, 'paraphrase, or translation with latitude' (although, on another occasion, he equated paraphrase evidently with what here was called 'imitation'). This conclusion seemed to be in the spirit of reasonableness, on the one hand avoiding pedantry and on the other eschewing excessive licence. But what Dryden understood by metaphrase was formal as well as lexical literalism, while his notion of paraphrase oscillated between metaphrase and imitation. Dryden's own translations, his major work, the *Aeneid* of 1697, for instance, often took considerable liberties with the text, amplifying or paraphrasing. Nevertheless, his warning against imitation, his example being Abraham **Cowley**'s 'Pindariques' (1656) [II.i.7.ii], which purported to be an 'imitation' of odes by the Greek poet Pindar, is still worth heeding. Somewhat intransigently, Cowley commended his own method, contrasting it with word-for-word translation and not acknowledging, as did Dryden, any middle way. While himself not directly criticizing Cowley, Dryden clearly regarded the latter's approach as risky, if followed by lesser poets than Cowley himself and if applied to less problematical texts than Pindar's Odes. So, where Cowley advanced a theory of poetic translation, Dryden saw only an exceptional case.

The Ovid preface is thus a polemical text, occasioned by the publication of a translation that Dryden feared might set a dangerous precedent. Even if Cowley's Pindariques were impressive, '[y]et he who is inquisitive to know an author's thoughts will be disappointed in his expectation; and 'tis not always that a man will be contented to have a present made him, when he expects the payment of a debt.' An ethical question was raised here, Dryden adding: 'To state it fairly, imitation of an author is the most advantageous way for a translator to show himself but the greatest wrong which can be done to the memory and reputation of the dead.'

Dryden established clear enough parameters for his time and to some extent for ours; it has been possible to adapt his comments to the needs and perceptions of later generations. Of course, he treats form and content as distinct, or rather form as a given, so that content inevitably dominates. Even if Dryden recognized the desirability of 'individuating authors', this having to do precisely with style or manner, the translator *was* free 'to vary the dress', if needs be. Nevertheless, Dryden's concerns about imitation remain relevant, for instance, in respect to the example set by Ezra Pound, whose influence on the translation of poetry has been paramount in the 20th c. but not wholly positive. Pound, reacting to the Victorians, although his own early translations were themselves quite Victorian in their antiquarianism, advocated the kind of licence ('make it new') about which Dryden had expressed doubts. The results were, of course, extraordinarily compelling. Pound had a pedagogical programme, and his translations were integral to it. Imagism, for instance, which sought to dispel vagueness, to clarify and make more concrete, was closely linked to Pound's translations from the Chinese [II.f.2.iii]. With his celebrated 'Seafarer' (1912), a translation from the Anglo-Saxon [II.o.1], Pound introduced into English a new prosody, or rather reintroduced linear, alliterative verse. Here he aimed to convey the *feel* of the Anglo-Saxon text, its physical impact, the semantic content being considerably altered in the process. However, while Pound himself was capable of splendid work in this manner, the same could not always be said of those who succeeded him.

Pound's influence, besides being problematical when viewed in a late 20th-c. perspective, is also rather ambiguous. On the one hand, he appears to emphasize content, especially, of course, with regard to classical narrative poetry (see his remarks concerning Golding and the Elizabethans); on the other, he is plainly intent on approximating the physical or aural effect of the source text. 'The Seafarer' is thus both a copy and a rewrite. Insofar as it is a copy, it presages Pound's later tendency, in the *Cantos*, to incorporate actual foreign texts rather than translations of them. Here we see literalism, as it were, taken to its logical and somewhat absurd extreme.

From Pound's contributions derive many of the tendencies that have manifested themselves in the middle and even late 20th c. A curious example is provided by Louis and Celia **Zukofsky**'s phonomic or homophonic translations of Catullus [I.a.2.i], where the Latin sounds are quite literally imitated. The emphasis placed on sound is substituted for what, more traditionally, is placed on content or sense. While this experiment or exercise might provide a useful corrective, redressing the balance in favour of the acoustics, the results are invariably modernistic (Joycean), since all resources of the language must be simultaneously drawn on for there to be any hope of mimesis. The naïvety of the procedure obliges one to conclude that Zukofsky, hardly a naïve writer, took advantage of it to exercise his linguistic imagination. The theoretical subtext must surely be (yet again) that since translation of poetry is by definition impossible, a specialized form of literalism is all that may be attempted.

At the other end of the scale are the far more conventional 'imitations' of Robert **Lowell**. In the introduction to *Imitations* (1961), his volume of (often) very free paraphrases, Lowell notes:

I have been reckless with literal meaning, and laboured hard to get the tone. Most often this has been *a* tone, for *the* tone is something that will always more or less escape transference to another language and cultural moment. I have tried to write live English and to do what my authors might have done if they were writing their poems now and in America.

Obviously a good deal of wishful rather than rigorous thinking has gone into this statement. It is honest, self-deprecatory, and yet at the same time somewhat bellicose. But like his predecessors, Lowell claims more freedom than he actually takes, since most of the translations could not be described as being 'reckless with literal meaning'. Still, by 'tone' Lowell evidently means *his* tone or repertoire of tones. In an interview with the present writer, Stanley **Kunitz**, the American poet and translator (with Max Hayward) of Anna Akhmatova [II.p.7.iii], observed that '[Lowell] thought it was more important to produce a poem by Lowell. . . . My intention is quite different. I insist on the premise of affection for the original text and loyalty to it, *insofar as it is compatible with the production of a new poem in English*' (Weissbort 1989). In view of the latter part of that statement, the difference between this writer's approach and Lowell's might seem less radical than is supposed, since it can hardly be denied that the 'new poem in English' would in fact be a poem in part authored by Stanley Kunitz. However, the attitudes or temperaments denoted are distinctive enough.

Lowell continues his polemical survey of the options open to and rejected by him, concluding with a helpless but defiant gesture that culminates in an oblique invocation of the muse of poetry:

Strict metrical translators still exist. They seem to live in a pure world untouched by contemporary poetry. Their difficulties are bold and honest, but they are taxidermists, not poets, and their poems are likely to be stuffed birds. A better strategy would seem to be the now fashionable translations into free or irregular verse. Yet this method commonly turns out a sprawl of language, neither faithful nor distinguished, now on stilts, now low, as Dryden would say. . . . I believe that poetic translation—I would call it an imitation—must be expert and inspired, and needs at least as much technique, luck and rightness of hand as an original poem.

While Lowell is content usually to reproduce the form of the original, he also lets go of the source text's physicality, substituting for it another of his own contriving.

Joseph **Brodsky**, winner of the 1987 Nobel Prize for Literature, insisted on mimetic translation of his own work, controlling the process closely and towards the end of his life virtually taking it over [II.p.7.iv]. For Brodsky, mimetic translation entailed the reproduction of both rhyme and metre as well as an approximation of the architectonics of the source text, even at the expense of surface smoothness or of idiomatic English. The lexical mimesis of Nabokov, however, was not for him, since the actuality or presence of the whole linguistic artefact took precedence. Criticized by the French poet Yves Bonnefoy (himself a noted translator of Yeats, among others) for his angry dismissal of the Clarence **Brown**–W. S. **Merwin** translation of Osip Mandelstam [II.p.7.iii] and for his apparently somewhat naïve, literalistic assumption that form was transferable interlingually, Brodsky stubbornly maintained his position, endeavouring to prove his point by himself producing translations that appeared to bring English and Russian prosody closer together. He was prepared to take liberties with the semantics, the content, to the point sometimes of rewriting whole passages. As both author and translator, he was of course at liberty to do this. Still, Brodsky's controversial englishings (and even some of his original English poems) arguably pointed in the direction of foreignization, although Brodsky himself took no part in the internecine struggle between domesticators and foreignizers (see Venuti 1995a). Collectively, these self-translations make a powerful case for greater boldness. If, from this point of view, Nabokov's literalism might be regarded as a retreat from poetic translation, Brodsky's very different literalism is optimistic, even confrontational.

No value judgement is intended, even if the author of this essay, as a translator of Russian poetry himself, admits to a certain bias with regard to Brodsky's much criticized approach. Besides, it is important to note that engagement with the source text in the translation of poetry may be multifarious, the Zukofskys and Lowell representing two extremes. Brodsky, radical though his

approach may appear, is located somewhere in between.

This essay began, perhaps rather sanguinely, by claiming that translators now were less interested in making rules for the correct translation of poetry than in describing what they actually did and hoped to achieve. In recent years, a number of theorists have sought to define the options. By far the most persuasive of these scholars is James S **Holmes**, himself also a poet and translator of poetry (Holmes 1988). Holmes's spectrum of the 'meta-literatures' surrounding a poem is both more lucidly defined and broader than most such schemes. At one end is the critical essay in the language of the poem, and at the other is the poem inspired by a poem. Between these are: the critical essay in another language; the prose translation of a poem; verse translation of a poem (or metapoem); imitation; poem 'about' a poem. The first four types have interpretation of the original as one of their major purposes, but since verse translation functions both as meta-literature (interpretation) and as primary literature (poem in its own right), it relates to the poetic traditions of both source and target languages.

With regard to the vexed question of form, Holmes posits four approaches: mimetic, where the form of the original is kept; analogical, where the translation seeks functionally to parallel the form in the original's poetic tradition; organic or 'content-derivative' form, starting from the semantic material and allowing it to take on its own unique poetic shape; deviant, where the metapoem is cast into a form that is in no way implicit in either the form or the content of the original. One might come up with other types of 'meta-literature' and other 'forms', but the point is that Holmes and others who followed him (e.g. Lefevere 1975) were trying to redefine the particular role of the translator of poetry, to secure for him an honourable place within the creative community, so that he or she was no longer faced with the choice of being either a slave or a troublemaker.

At the present time, as has been intimated, a matter much discussed among translators concerns domestication or naturalization as against foreignization. To return to Holmes's categories, analogical form, which seeks to import the source poem into the native tradition, may be said to domesticate it (e.g. Pope's *Iliad* in heroic couplets, or Robert **Fitzgerald**'s analogical translation of Homer into blank verse); mimetic form, on the other hand, emphasizes the strangeness, the foreignness of the original (e.g. Richmond **Lattimore**'s mimetic translation of Homer into hexameters).

The question of foreignization as against domestication affects translators of poetry in a more fundamental manner than it does those of prose, if only because poetry is read by a small minority now, so that the commercial risks of publishing foreign-looking versions is also less significant. Their readership being so limited, poetry translations can be more precisely targeted, and one supposes that translators may feel more inclined to experiment with the radical or estranging forms of translation that some postcolonial critics, like Venuti, are seeking to promote.

That being said, the particular approach adopted remains a matter for the judgement of individual translators (what readership he or she has in mind; what he or she deems it will accept) and of negotiation. The latter is a complex internal process, having to do, very broadly, with aesthetics and ethics. The translator of poetry, to borrow from Conrad, is a secret sharer.

2. THEATRE AND OPERA
Susan Bassnett

i. The Problem of the Play-Text Translating for the theatre is fraught with problems; although it has flourished as an art, it remains probably the least explored field in Translation Studies and there are very few serious examinations of the complexities of transferring a play across cultures. André Lefevere pointed out that there is practically no theoretical literature on the translation of drama as acted and produced (Lefevere 1992a) and Patrice Pavis noted that questions of translation and performance have 'hardly been taken into consideration' (Pavis 1992: 136). This is probably due in part to the collaborative nature of the theatrical process and in part to the difficulties of defining what a play-text actually is.

The absence of a theory of the play-text has preoccupied drama theorists for decades, just as the problem of the relationship between written text and performance has preoccupied performance analysts. Stanislavsky, for example, devised his theory of a gestural subtext, the physical dimension of the play that an actor could unlock with careful preparation and close study, and others have followed similar lines of inquiry. For, unlike other types of text, the play is written to be spoken and is therefore a kind of blueprint that actors use as the basis of their performance. It has been argued that the play text is incomplete without that physical dimension, that in its written version it awaits realization in performance. Pavis warns that any discussion of the translation of a play text needs to take the performance dimension into account, since the play is not simply a literary text, written to be read, but a text that 'reaches the audience by way of the actors' bodies' (Pavis 1992: 136).

What we have, therefore, is a troubled and troubling notion of the play, for far from being complete in itself, like a novel or a poem, it is arguably only part of the total equation that is the play in performance. The reader of the play may experience a sense of something lacking, a lacuna that can only be filled when the play is made physical. The play as literature is distinct from the play in performance, though the two are intimately connected.

Naturalist theatre saw another shift in the concept of the play, for the task of the writer was now to provide a complete text, with carefully constructed speeches for all performers and with detailed notes to actors and directors in the form of stage directions. Sometimes, these stage directions become narrative, as in this passage from Bernard Shaw's *Great Catherine*:

Superficially Patiomkin is a violent, brutal barbarian, an upstart despot of the most intolerable dangerous type, ugly, lazy and disgusting in his personal habits. Yet ambassadors report him the ablest man in Russia, and the one who can do most with the still abler Empress Catherine II, who is not a Russian but a German, by no means barbarous or intemperate in her personal habits. She not only disputes with Frederick the Great the reputation of being the cleverest monarch in Europe, but may even put in a very plausible claim to be the cleverest and most attractive individual alive.

This kind of passage, a feature of the realist drama of the period, functions more as an aid to the reader of the play on the page than as advice to an actor. André Helbo makes a distinction between four types of stage direction, suggesting that some are meant for the actor, some for the staging, some for the implied spectator and some for the reader (Helbo 1987: 103). What is clear is that there are very different kinds of stage direction, and very different kinds of play, and in consequence some plays are more easily accessible to readers even without the performance dimension.

The case of opera introduces other issues to the question of the relationship between text, performance, and translation. The libretto, (originally 'little book') can serve both as a text to be sung and as a guide to the audience, to enable them to follow a work in performance. Until well into the 20th c., lights in the auditorium allowed the audience to read the libretto during a performance. There followed a movement away from reading, towards a policy of singing the work in translation, but since the 1980s there has been a shift back to audience reading, with the development of the surtitle. New technology means that an electronically transmitted text can be presented on a monitor above the stage, providing a translation of the text being sung in the original language throughout the performance.

The great difference between the translation in the form of a libretto and the translation in the form of surtitles lies in the relationship with the source text. Traditionally, libretti have included both the source and target languages on facing pages. Often very literal, and not always corresponding to the text sung by performers, the libretti nevertheless were complete texts, often line-by-line, word-for-word translations. The surtitles, in contrast, like film subtitles, tend, due to the constraints of space and speed of printing, to be abbreviated versions of the sung text. This means that the surtitle is basically a means of providing the audience with basic information, rather than a translation of the words used in performance. Nevertheless, it is significant that the surtitle continues the practice of reading that held sway for so long with opera-going audiences.

Any theory of translation of theatre and opera texts needs to take into account both the problem of determining exactly what the relationship between written text and performance is, and the problem of huge variations in reading and writing practices. Is the dramatic text literature, as Jiří Veltrusky argues (1977), or is it another kind of text altogether, a hybrid that cannot be considered as a complete entity? Depending on the response to this question, translation practice varies considerably.

Theatre and opera are multi-dimensional arts. Tadeusz Kowzan proposes five semiotic systems that underpin all performance, and may be present together or separately, according to the type of performance being staged. The first of these is the spoken text, for which there may or may not be a written script, the second is bodily expression, the third the actor's physical appearance (height, gestures, features, etc.), the fourth the playing space (size, shape, lighting, props, etc.), and the fifth non-spoken sound, including music (Kowzan 1975). From these five categories, he determines 13 distinct subsections: words, intonation, mime, gesture, movement, make-up, hairstyle, costume, props, decor, lighting, music, and sound effects, which he classifies as either auditive or visual signs. This structuralist breakdown of performance serves as a basic map, and remains a useful tool for understanding the complex interrelationship between sign systems in theatre. For theatre is above all a collaborative process, and the final performance is the result of interaction between different sign systems and different individuals. The spoken text (or written text, if there is one at all) exists as only one element of that collaboration.

The task of the translator, therefore, is to render the single element of written text into another language. This might not seem, on the surface, any different from any other kind of translation practice, but the difficulties arise when we return to the vexed question of determining exactly what a play text is. For if there is some kind of coded gestural text inside the play, which actors, directors, designers and other practitioners can decode and render actual in corporeal terms, then it follows that the translator needs to take this factor into account, for practitioners in the target culture will also want to actualize the play in their own language and physicality.

ii. Speakability A term commonly used by translators of plays is 'speakability', or 'performability'. This is supposed to mean that the text is more accessible to actors, that it has a quality that enables it to be performed more effectively. Claims are often made that a new translation is somehow more 'performable' than an earlier version, or that a playwright such as Racine [II.g.6.iv] or Ibsen [II.o.9] has been rendered more 'speakable'. In his introduction to six plays by Chekhov in English, Robert Corrigan declares:

The first law in translating for the theatre is that everything must be speakable. It is necessary at all times for the translator to hear the actor speaking in his mind's ear. He must be conscious of the gestures of the voice that speak—the rhythm, the cadence, the interval. He must also be conscious of the look, the feel, and the movement of the actor while he is speaking. He must, in short, render what might be called the whole gesture of the scene.

(Chekhov 1962: p. xl)

Corrigan proposes that the translator should always 'stage' the play in his or her own mind, and should be aware of the performance dimension while translating. But there are problems with this argument. First, speakability or performability defies precise definition; it is presented as a quality and yet there are no guidelines for interpreting it or for defining it. Some claims for the 'speakability' of a translation that reads in a stilted manner are blatantly wrong, but in any case 'speakability', if it existed at all, would be bound to be subject to patterns of linguistic change.

Moreover, what Corrigan suggests should be the first law in translating is plainly an impossibility. A translator cannot be actor, director, designer and audience all at the same time. A translator can only be a translator, perhaps with some awareness of the factors involved in performance, even with a fantasy about an eventual performance, but no more than that. The vague concept of 'performability' has been used not so much as a means of enabling a translator to create a better translation, but rather as a means of disguising the difficulties inherent in translating a text that may not be complete in itself. It is also a universalizing concept, that erases the very obvious differences between systems which lie at the heart of good translation practice.

Malcolm Griffiths claims that

Translators for the theatre are enmeshed in a protean activity which requires as much familiarity with theatre practice, cultural contexts and social history as it does with spoken and written languages. (Griffiths 1985)

This is a large statement, but serves to illustrate the futility of relying upon an ill-defined notion of 'speakability' as a criterion for translation. What is being suggested here is that theatre practice in different cultures has its own genealogy and its own traditions; audiences in different cultures have different horizons of expectation. So, for example, all plays produced in contemporary Britain must endeavour to conform to the audience expectation that they will last for roughly two and a half hours' playing time. Obviously there are variations, but this is the accepted norm. This means that a play lasting four or five hours will be exceptional, and performance styles, staging practices, and theatre managements gear themselves around this time constraint.

In Germany, in contrast, there are no such expectations. Performances may last much longer than two and a half hours, without audiences becoming impatient; actors move at a more leisurely pace; stage effects can be more time-consuming. In *nō* theatre [II.f.8.ii], or *kabuki* [II.f.8.iii], or in European-based theatre that draws upon non-European traditions, as does the work of Peter Brook or Ariane Mnouchkine, performance time can be very much longer. However, in the case of a seven- or eight-hour performance, for example, audience behaviour will not be the same as that of an audience sitting in seats for a mere two and a half hours, and there will be more moving around and greater

flexibility in concentration. Similar flexibility operated in British theatres in the 18th and 19th c., when several plays were performed in the same evening, often with short interludes between them.

The point is that audience expectations are by no means universal, and performance styles are geared to accommodate those different expectations. Actors adjust their rhythms in accordance with the conventions and expectations of their own culture and tradition. French classical drama [II.g.6], performed in stylized costumes and delivered in high-pitched voices, was written to accommodate a unique style of playing in vogue at the time. Today, no audience would tolerate it, and the text has to be interpreted by modern actors accordingly. If there is such a thing as a gestural subtext in the plays of Racine and if the lines he wrote had the quality of 'speakability', then both were devised in accordance with a performance style that has ceased to exist. This means that any modern French performance of a Racine tragedy is a form of translation, and any version in any other language is doubly a translation, both interlingual and intersemiotic.

Such a translation is also inevitably *intertemporal*, and the question of time is significant in theatre translation. First, there is the time taken by actual performance, which, as we have seen, can vary across cultures. Then there is the time of the play itself, and also the audience's own time, which is embedded in the wider cultural context where time can have different meanings. Moreover, audience expectations, which are culturally determined, will differ according to context. The plays of Harold Pinter, for example, rely heavily on the use of silences and pauses. This works well in a British context, where sudden silences can signify all kinds of concealed anxieties: embarrassment, anger, dismay, pain, menace, and so forth. Transposed into another culture, where silence may have a completely different set of meanings, the pauses in Pinter's plays can present the actors and the audience with difficulties. In Italian, for example, where verbal delivery in both everyday speech and on the stage tends to be rapid and where silence in a social context is usually a sign that something has gone horribly wrong, Pinter's silences are hard to render adequately. Actors tend either to rush through the plays, or to linger too long over the pauses indicated in the text, thereby sending confused signals to audiences unused to decoding the complexities of British silences. Similarly, in cultures where long silences are an accepted aspect of social interaction, as in the Nordic countries, care has to be taken to stress the significance of Pinter's silences in other ways.

A crucial problem facing the translator is speech rhythm, for the language of play texts varies considerably. Verse drama, which may be considered as a genre in its own right, follows conventional patterns of versification which may or may not be translatable. Blank verse, or iambic pentameter, is the classical English form for verse drama (e.g. the plays of Shakespeare), while the alexandrine is the classical French verse form. Translators of Racine and Corneille, like French translators of Elizabethan dramatists, have often used analogical verse forms, replacing one classical form with another, blank verse by alexandrine and vice versa.

Plays that are not written in verse present different kinds of difficulty for translators, the most important of which is the question of the ageing of the language. It is commonly held that plays require retranslating at regular intervals, usually every 20 years or so. There is no adequate explanation of this assumption, but it does seem that spoken language ages at a faster rate than written language, and since a play is essentially a transcript to be spoken, it follows that the ageing process will be more marked in a play translation than in other types of written text because the source text will contain more time-bound markers. Such markers may include vocabulary, syntax, rhythm, tone, and even changes of register and intonation.

iii. Dialogue and Deixis Theatre analysts struggling to determine the precise nature of the play-text have been concerned to identify units in a play. Stage directions, which vary markedly from culture to culture, may indicate one system of units. A play may be divided into acts which roughly correspond to moments in the narrative. So, for example, the classic five-act formula presents the basis of the story-line in the first act, extends the complications of that story in Act II, reaching a crisis point in Act III, and then starts to unravel the strands in Act IV, leading to a resolution in the final act. The three-act formula of the well-made play similarly uses the first act to introduce various narrative lines, extends or twists them in the second act, and then uses the third act either to bring everything to crisis point or to combine the different lines in a final denouement.

Division into scenes is governed by conventions of a different kind. Scene division may correspond to units of meaning within the plot, or may simply be a way of signalling the entrances and exits of different characters. The two English translations of Ionesco's *La Cantatrice chauve*, for example, employ different methods of scene division. Donald Watson follows the English convention, and his version consists of one extended scene, whilst Donald Allen's translation follows the French convention and breaks the text down into numerous short scenes in accordance with the movement of the characters on and off the stage (Ionesco 1958a; 1958b). The effect on the reader of these two versions is therefore quite different.

In performance, these textual divisions may or may not be used. Actors and directors may follow editorial guidelines, or may change them for their own specific purposes. The production by Jan Kacer in Prague of Alois Bejblik's translation of Shakespeare's *The Tempest* in the 1980s deliberately altered the standard act and scene division to make an important ideological point, bringing the curtain down midway through Act III, sc. ii on Stephano's line, 'Thought is free'. In this way, a subversive anti-authoritarian statement was made through the device of a translated play and an imaginative interpretation of the units of meaning of the text.

The fact that performance units do not necessarily coincide with unit divisions in a written text further complicates the relationship between the written and the performed. Pavis used a series of negatives to describe the relationship between dramatic text and what he calls the *mise-en-scène*:

(i)   the *mise-en-scène* is not a staging of a supposed textual potential.

(ii)   *the mise-en-scène* does not have to be faithful to a dramatic text.

(iii) the *mise-en-scène* does not annihilate or dissolve the dramatic text.

(iv)   different *mises-en-scène* of a common text, particularly those produced at very different moments in history, do not provide readings of the same text.

(v)   the *mise-en-scène* is not a stage representation of the textual referent.

(vi)   the *mise-en-scène* is not a fusion of the two referents of text and stage.

(vii) the *mise-en-scène* is not a performative realization of the text.   (Pavis 1992: 26–8)

In this list of differences, Pavis attempts to illustrate the interdependence of the written and performed versions of the same text, whilst underscoring the differences between them. This returns us to the problem of whether there might be some kind of inherent 'performability' factor within a play text, and if there is, how it might be translated. In the 1980s, theatre analysts turned their attention to the fact that at the heart of dramatic dialogue there lies the notion of the *deixis*, the '*I* addressing a *you here* and *now*' (Elam 1980: 139). This means that a dramatic text can be broken down into a series of deictic units, which give indications of where speech is to be directed. The following example shows how the deictic units in a short scene from Shakespeare's *Richard II*, Act V, sc. i, give clear indications of who is speaking to whom, simply through the pronoun system:

QUEEN. And must we be divided? must we part? [*addressed to Richard, and through him a general plea to all on stage and audience*]

KING RICHARD. Ay, hand from hand, my love, and heart from heart. [*directly to the Queen in reply*]

This can be seen as one deictic unit.

QUEEN. Banish us both, and send the king with me. [*to Northumberland*]

NORTHUMBERLAND. That were some love but little policy. [*in reply to the Queen, but also a general statement*]

This exchange can be seen as a second deictic unit, between two speakers.

QUEEN. Then whither he goes, thither let me go. [*in reply to Northumberland, but also a general statement, this time with a clear Biblical allusion*]

KING RICHARD. So two, together weeping, make one woe. [*in reply to the Queen, but also a general statement to the stage and audience*]

These speeches constitute a third deictic unit, and Richard's speech then continues, marking the opening of a 16-line deictic unit between him and the Queen. The deixis in this scene is a kind of choreographic patterning that actors can follow: we assume that the characters turn towards and away from one another, and in the final 16 lines there is a word-play sequence that involves kissing.

The breaking down of a play-text into deictic units has implications for translation, since the translation unit and the deictic unit may well be usefully combined. However, a comparative analysis of translations shows that this rarely, if ever happens, and most translators appear to follow the same strategy that they would employ when translating narrative, despite the fact that inconsistencies in plotting and characterization are a marked feature of the play-text, because theatrical effect is so often more important that narrative consistency. This fact has bedevilled critics for generations, leading them to query the inconsistencies in the representation of such characters as Richard II or Hamlet, presupposing that the criteria of characterization that apply in prose will also be bound to apply in the theatre.

iv. Version, Adaptation, and Translation The terms 'version' or 'adaptation' are frequently used with reference to translation of texts for theatre,

and this terminology can have different meanings. One use of the terms implies a degree of variation from the source text, so that a 'translation' might be perceived as closer to the original than something described as a 'version' or as an 'adaptation'. But 'adaptation' can also be used to describe the process of dramatizing a novel, for example, and in this sense it is often used as a synonym for 'screenplay' when the source text is not set out in the form of a play. Hence *Sense and Sensibility* or *War and Peace* in the cinema are described as 'adaptations'.

Some critics argue about the use of this terminology, suggesting that a translation is somehow more 'faithful' to the original than a version or an adaptation. This argument is based on the flawed premiss that there *is* such a thing as a 'faithful' translation in the first place, an assumption called into question by Translation Studies. For all translations reflect the translator's interpretation of the source text, so that a translation is basically the product firstly of a single individual's reading and then of his or her second-language rewriting. Translation inevitably involves rewriting and manipulation of the source, as translators and theorists from Dryden to Derrida have pointed out [see I.a.3], and the act of translating always leads to changes.

There is also another, more recent use of the terms 'version' and 'adaptation'. In some countries, particularly in the English-speaking world, it is common to market translations as being made by well-known playwrights, even if these have no access to the source language. Thus Trevor Griffiths has 'translated' Chekhov into English with no knowledge of Russian, Christopher Hampton has 'translated' Ibsen, Howard Brenton has 'translated' Brecht. In these cases, a translation is produced by a writer with knowledge of the source language, and the playwright then takes it over and rewrites it. The problems arise when the term 'translation', which implies knowledge of more than one language, is used to describe the work of English writers, and a way round this ethical and legal difficulty can be found by use of the term 'translation' to describe the text produced by interlingual transfer and 'adaptation' or 'version' to describe the text rewritten in English. Needless to say, professional translators find this practice deeply offensive. Malcolm Griffiths argues that the shifting use of these various terms is not only a matter of etiquette or happenstance, 'but a case of revealing or concealing the nature of the work undertaken to produce the text' (Griffiths 1985: 174). He notes the inconsistency with which native

English playwrights use the terms, as well as their inconsistency in crediting adequately the work of the translator they have utilized.

In opera, translators face a different problem of status. The translation of opera texts has tended to be regarded traditionally as undesirable, as a form of debasement of the original. The libretto or the surtitle offer a way round the problem by providing the audience with a text that allows them access to the meaning of the words being sung, without the need for a translation of those words within the performance. Where a translation is performed, the constraints upon the translator are much greater than is the case with play-texts, and may be compared to the constraints faced by translators who work in dubbing or film subtitling. The musical rhythms dominate the verbal structures, and translators have to reconceive the text entirely.

v. Acculturation in Translation Timberlake Wertenbaker distinguishes between translation and adaptation, arguing that what is interesting about translation is that 'you try to transport an audience into the play, as opposed to trying to fit the play to an audience' (Wertenbaker 1989). She raises here the basic dilemma for all translators: whether to bring the text into the target system or to try and interest target readers sufficiently for them to want to explore the source text in its own context. Theatre translators appear to have employed quite different strategies at different times, but there is a dominant tendency towards the acculturation of the play-text, which some critics have seen as inevitable (Heylen 1993). Sometimes that acculturation involves deliberate changes on the linguistic level, elsewhere it involves more substantial shifts. So Peter Watts's Penguin translation of three plays by Ibsen contains a prefatory note in which he explains that he has dropped the Norwegian system of address by trade (Carpenter Engstrand, Editor Howstad, etc.) because an English audience might find such foreign elements 'outlandish or even irritating' (Ibsen 1964: 18). Instead, he has endeavoured to make the characters speak in the kind of English that would be used by similar characters 'of roughly the same walk of life'. What he is implying here is that he has interpreted the linguistic variations in terms of class, and has recast the Norwegian class system into an English one [see II.0.9].

Edward Bond, on the other hand, in his translation of Frank Wedekind's *Spring Awakening* [II.h.12.ii], is more concerned with changes in language that reflect changes in world-view. Noting that some of the original German descriptive passages sounded artificial, he explains how he has altered the text for English audiences:

If I had kept *all* the original elaboration it would have been unspeakable by contemporary performers. Performers at the turn of the century thought and spoke in paragraphs. For better or worse, contemporary performers think and speak—and their audiences think and listen—in sentences. The architectural construction of paragraphs sounds artificial to us. It has been destroyed by the wisecrack, the retort, the exclamation.   (Wedekind 1980: p. xxxvi)

Bond draws our attention to the way in which language changes, together with audience expectations and performance styles. As a man of the theatre as well as a translator, he is aware of the historical dimension of theatre, and seeks to take that into account in his translating. In their different ways, both Watts and Bond acculturate their source texts into the English system, justifying their methods in different ways but with similar aims in mind. Both are well aware that conventions operating in English-language theatre demand that plays be absorbed into the target culture as painlessly and totally as possible.

Translation of a play involves deliberate choices on the part of theatre managements, funding bodies, actors and directors, and foreign texts are often chosen because of the specific needs of the target system (Aaltonen 1996: 73). Many play translations are undertaken in order to expand a repertoire, because it is felt that there is a good chance of commercial success, or because the play offers a vehicle for an individual actor, rather than for any aesthetic qualities of the source text, or on account of its status in the source system. The great international actresses of the 19th c. such as Adelaide Ristori or, later, Eleonora Duse commissioned translations in order to extend their range as performers and to introduce new work from overseas to revitalize their own country's somewhat stagnant theatre. The impact of French plays upon the Italian theatre was a direct result of translation, as was the mania for Ibsen's drama that swept Europe at the end of the century. A period of intense playwriting activity is generally not one of great theatre translation, but conversely, a period where there is relatively little native theatre being produced tends to be a time of increased translation.

Once the translation is commissioned, there is then the problem of whether it will be accepted by audiences. The history of theatre translation is full of anomalies: in some cases plays transfer well, in other cases they fail to make any impact, and explanations of these variations abound. The case of

Luigi Pirandello [II.m.12] is an interesting example of a playwright whose drama went through a period of great popularity, when his plays were translated into many other languages, and then sank into relative obscurity. Ironically, Pirandello's reputation as a key figure in 20th-c. theatre history is not matched by translations of his plays, many of which remain almost unknown. This is in contrast to the work of playwrights like Ibsen or Strindberg, whose plays have been translated continuously throughout the century and continue to be performed all over the world. One conclusion to draw is that there may be elements in Pirandello's theatre that do not transfer easily across cultural boundaries.

Nicholas Wright, the English translator of the National Theatre production of Pirandello's *Six Characters in Search of an Author* in 1987 attempted to deal with the traditional resistance to Pirandello in English by acculturating elements of the play. In Act I, when the play opens, the actors are rehearsing another play by Pirandello, and the device of the play-within-a-play is thus given an extra twist of Pirandello's special ironic humour, as the actors confess themselves mystified by the obscurity of his work. Wright changed the play-within-a-play, so that the English actors were seen rehearsing a production of *Hamlet*, a device that altered the relationship between reality and the imaginary in very radical ways. Wright felt that it was necessary to make substantial changes because the innovatory impact of the play had lessened since the 1920s, and the idea of the play-within-a-play was no longer striking. Nevertheless, critical opinion was generally unfavourable.

Chekhov [II.p.6], in contrast, is a writer whose work has been frequently translated and who can be said to exist practically as an English playwright in his own right. Michael Frayn has claimed that Chekhov is universal:

The good thing about Chekhov is that you don't need to know a word of Russian to be able to translate his plays, because everyone knows what Chekhov is about, everyone knows by some sort of inner certainty what Chekhov intended and what he was saying and the idea of referring it to some original text is absolutely odious.

(Frayn: 1989)

Elisaveta Fen, on the other hand, asserts (as did Chekhov himself) that his work is inherently, fundamentally Russian and therefore totally culture-bound (Chekhov 1959). And Trevor Griffiths challenges Frayn's argument by pointing out the social implications of his definitions, and suggests that the success of a particular reading of Chekhov, resulting in the invention of an English Chekhov, is due to the way in which the English middle classes interpreted the Russian writer's evocation of a vanishing world (Chekhov 1978: p. v).

Many factors contribute to the tendency towards acculturation of a theatre text. Obviously the expectations of the audience are crucial, as are the theatrical conventions operating in the target culture. Plays tend to be translated when the target system has particular needs that only foreign playwrights can fulfil. In her study of French translations of *Hamlet*, Romy Heylen analyses the ways in which the play was modified to meet the needs of the target audiences. Translation, she maintains is a decision-making process, 'a socio-historical activity of a profoundly transformational nature' (Heylen 1993: 24). She traces the history of French translations of this play from the bowdlerizing version by Jean-François Ducis in the 18th c., through the romantic version by Alexandre Dumas and Paul Meurice to Yves Bonnefoy's multiple versions and Daniel Mesguich's 1977 *Le Hamlet de Shakespeare*, which self-consciously emphasizes the translation processes that the source text has undergone in its transformation into a French text. Similarly, the first Finnish translation of *Macbeth* in 1834, entitled *Ruunlinna* (Crown Castle), set the play in Finland with Finnish characters, and was written in the traditional metre of the Finnish epic poem *Kalevala* (Aaltonen 1996).

At other moments, there may be an active government policy of acculturation. Werner Habicht discusses attitudes to Shakespeare in the Third Reich, and quotes a booksellers' journal from 1940 that claims Shakespeare as a German writer, not only because of racial kinship but also because of the history of German response to Shakespeare's plays and the existence of a long tradition of translations (Habicht 1989: 112).

A recent development in the theatre is the transcultural performance, which draws upon a range of different theatrical systems. It is possible to argue that this kind of theatre, famously developed by such figures as Peter Brook or Pina Bausch, does not have a source text at all, since the foreign text and culture are not taken as points of departure. This is precisely what Erika Fischer-Lichte suggests (Fischer-Lichte *et al.* 1990). In this kind of theatre, the communication of the foreign is not posited as a feature of the performance; rather, the performance seeks to combine different elements in a new whole. Discussing Eugenio Barba's intercultural work with *Faust*, Pavis defines it as a western vision conveyed by eastern traditions that is reworked by a western director, using performers from both east and west, which results in the 'neutralization' of one theatrical and cultural tradition by another. (Pavis 1992: 177)

Although intercultural theatre may be a new development, opera has long had an intercultural dimension, made possible by a more restricted concept of translation. When operas are performed in the source language, singers learn their roles in that language, combining music and sound patterns without necessarily having any conversational or writing ability in the language. It is therefore commonplace to have singers from China, Bulgaria, the United States, or Italy all performing in the same opera, provided there is a common language in which all will sing. The increased internationalization of opera means that this pattern is likely to continue.

3. SACRED TEXTS
Douglas Robinson

i. Problems of Definition Every key term in the seemingly simple and straightforward phrase 'the translation of sacred texts' is historically problematical:

Translation. Can sacred texts be translated? Is a viable translation of a sacred text still a translation, or is it something else, something new? Should sacred texts be translated? How, when, for whom, and with what safeguards or controls?
Sacred. Is a translated sacred text still sacred, or is it a mere 'copy' of the sacred text? What is sacrality, in what does it lodge or reside or inhere, and can it be transported across cultural boundaries? Does it have a stable centre that resists distortion or change when it undergoes such transportation?
Text. What boundaries shall we set up around the textuality of sacred texts? What is a sacred text in an oral or illiterate culture? Even in a literate culture that identifies a single book as its sacred text, what are the limits of that text? Do its liturgical uses count? Do prayers based on it count? Do hymns or chants taken from it count? In the Church of Jesus Christ and Latter-day Saints, the Prophet receives a revelation from God every month, and it is published in the church magazine; is every issue of that magazine a sacred text?

The translation of sacred texts both within individual cultures and over the historical course of whole civilizations might usefully be reduced to a simplified myth or narrative—one that, like all such myths, would only pretend to reflect the reality it represents in the aggregate, not in every minute detail. Significant exceptions to specific claims made here are legion. However, if the myth is taken as an aid to thinking, not as an accurate representational history, it may serve the valuable function of organizing thought about the subject.

ii. Stage 1: Early Unregulated Translation The first stage of the translation of one's own sacred texts historically involves very little control over it.

Such translation is neither required nor forbidden; it is neither an obvious task to undertake nor dangerous enough to ring round with prohibitions. Anyone who needs a translation is free to ask for one, and anyone capable of making one is free to make it; but neither seems to occur with any great regularity. We do not know much about this stage; the early rationalist impulse to control access to sacred texts is also by and large the impulse to organize institutionally and keep clear records of organizational decisions, and this period before such controls is poorly documented and based largely on speculation.

We do have a few very ancient sacred texts that reveal a fairly casual attitude toward translation, such as a bilingual Akkadian/Sumerian sacred text from the 7th c. BCE, a hymn to Sin, the moon god; overt translation of sacred texts seems to have been relatively common in ancient Mesopotamia as well (Barnstone 1993: 146). But we know almost nothing about the social, cultural, and political situations in which these texts were produced, or the purposes to which they were put. Is it true, as we speculate from our own historical situations today, that the religious users of these texts really did not mind that they were translations of older religious texts from other cultures?

It may also be that such an unregulated state never really existed—that it is the product of a nostalgic imagination given to visions of a lost Golden Age of untrammelled freedom, which we must work to regain.

iii. Stage 2: Regulated Translation The second stage (which may in fact be the first, and is certainly the first for which we have adequate evidence) involves the imposition of increasingly strict controls on who translates what, how, and especially for whom, and whether and how and with whom the resulting translations are shared and discussed. Typically this stage has entailed either the forbidding of all translation or the restriction of translation to a small group of insiders or initiates in one or more of the following ways:

(a) the original (untranslated) texts are kept out of the hands of the 'profane' (outsiders), even out of their minds (i.e. the very existence of many sacred texts is kept a secret from them), and thus unavailable for translation;

(b) the texts are written in ciphers, or retained in ancient scripts readable only by a small, specially trained priesthood, and thus protected against discovery by the profane;

(c) they are 'translated' (interpreted) only orally, to specially selected receivers (initiates), by members of the priesthood and only within the ritual space.

There is no scholarly consensus as to why this secrecy was maintained. Some scholars (Kerenyi 1955; Burkert 1987) have argued that there is typically no real need for it, as the religious 'secrets' or 'mysteries' are typically experiences that are by their very nature ineffable. The word 'mystery' comes from the Greek verb *muo* ('to close'); but scholars disagree over whether what was normatively kept closed was the mouth ('don't tell', hence also 'don't translate') or the eyes ('don't see'). If it was the former, the mystery religions were based on secrets that were determinedly kept from outsiders; if the latter, on powerful mystical experiences that took place in the dark, without sight ('don't see'), and were later impossible to articulate.

The most plausible solution to this scholarly debate is that esoteric religion underwent an evolutionary development from a more 'primitive' emphasis on ineffable closed-eyes experience (which may or may not coincide with stage 1) to a more 'modern' emphasis on restricting articulations of that experience to the initiated (stages 2 and 3)—and that in important ways both aspects are present in evolutionary stages as well, in trace form, even after translation is 'freely' permitted. The ancient mysteries, for example, are generally thought to have flourished from about the 6th c. BCE to the 4th c. CE; and while this 1000-year history does show a marked movement from primitive 'open' mysteries, in which everyone could participate without secrecy, but also without telling or writing about them (ancient vegetative rituals, nature worship), to more modern 'closed' mysteries, controlled by a priesthood and regulated for in-group inclusions and out-group exclusions, there are also documented cases of bans on divulging the mysteries to the profane very early on. The emphasis on the ineffability of the mysteries continues until very late.

The translation of a culture's sacred texts is typically regulated in order to maintain group cohesion. If the group's sacred text is the product of direct divine revelation from the gods, interpreted by the group's own priests, and understandable only to the group itself, there is a strong social mandate for the group's existence: the group exists precisely in order to worship the god(s) named in the text, indeed was almost certainly formed (according to myth) in order to provide such worship. Such regulation is different depending on whether the translation process is (a) out of a foreign language into the group's own language (appropriation of alien religious traditions), or (b) out of the group's own language into a language or languages perceived as other, alien, including class dialects and despised vernaculars (dissemination of esoteric religious traditions to outsiders).

Both (a) and (b) have been enormously problematic for religious traditions in this second stage. Overt appropriative translation of foreign sacred texts would seem to suggest, first of all, that the religion so attested is the product of direct divine revelation and not of mere cultural borrowing from others—a perception that seems to relegate the receptor culture to a secondary and imitative status, isolated from the 'true' otherworldly sources of religion.

Translation [of sacred texts] denies itself. Since it popularly signifies unoriginality it is taboo for religious authors—and even more so for gods. Any authentic self-esteeming god or goddess must deny being born of translation. What powers would remain were it known that a century earlier a divinity was working for another civilization? (Barnstone 1993: 144)

Hence, as Barnstone sums up this negated or denied mode of translating sacred texts, 'translation is frequently a historical process for creating originals' (p. 141).

And it may well be that this insistence on denying the translational origins of a religion is closely tied, socially and psychologically, to the need to block the translation of its sacred texts into other languages as well. If religious texts flow freely from culture to culture, they lose the mystical or supernatural power that seems to arise out of claims of direct divine revelation. These claims are typically augmented, as the Russian language theorist V. N. Voloshinov (1973) argues persuasively, by the use of what he calls the 'alien word': the gods spoke to the priests in some alien language, which remains comprehensible only to them. If the texts written in that alien language were translated into the vernacular of the masses, they would lose their power and become commonplace or market-place texts. Such have been the arguments lodged against vernacular translations in a great variety of historical circumstances, from ancient Hellenistic Judaism prior to the translation of the Hebrew Bible into Greek, to the battles over vernacular Bible translation in Europe from the 14th to the 16th c., to similar battles over the vernacular translation of Sanskrit sacred texts in the same period, to numerous contemporary attempts to protect various sacred texts from secularization through translation even today (see Robinson 1996: 171–5).

Secularized and otherwise displaced forms of this mind-set have generated powerful polemics against literary translation in general, especially of poetry, typically in favour of (*a*) the free imitation of foreign classics, (*b*) foreign language learning, and/or (*c*) original creation:

A long and illustrious line of translation theorists has urged the free imitation of foreign classics, beginning with Cicero, Horace, Pliny the Younger, and Aulus Gellius in ancient Rome [see I.a.3.ii] and continuing through a host of Renaissance theorists, most notably Joachim du Bellay in his *Défense et illustration de la langue française* (1549, Defence and Illustration of the French Language); the grammar-translation method based on this tradition has remained in use in foreign-language classrooms well into the 20th c.; and the 'anxiety of influence' literary theories of Harold Bloom seem to belong to the same tradition (Bloom 1975).

Foreign language learning as an alternative to translation has been advocated strenuously by a wide range of writers from Roger Bacon in the *Opus Maius* around 1268 to Arthur Schopenhauer in the *Parerga and Paralipomena* (1851), and continues to be espoused by many professors of modern languages and comparative literature today.

The third alternative to translation, original creation, was first argued persuasively by Dante in *Il Convivio* (1304–7, The Banquet) and became the literary battle-cry of the Renaissance. In this era translation is increasingly perceived as slavish, submissive, and secondary; many writers call for a moratorium on translation from the classical languages so that the European vernaculars can build literary strength on their own terms.

Like esoteric religious leaders, all these thinkers are saying *don't translate*—because translation distorts the meaning of the original or because the original is too powerful, too brilliant, for the untrained eye, and could be dangerous (the masses aren't ready for it yet).

iv. Stage 3: Struggles for Expanded Access The history of religion shows, however, that the masses

eventually demand and get vernacular translations of sacred texts: the Septuagint for the Hellenized Jewish community in intertestamental Alexandria; the Itala and Vulgate for Latin-speaking Christians of the 4th and 5th c.; the Lollard (Wycliffite), Tyndale, Geneva, Coverdale, King James, and Douay–Rheims Bibles for English-speaking Christians from the 14th to the 16th c. [see II.c.1.iv–vi]; and so on. This third stage, a transitional phase from a rigidly enforced ban on vernacular translation (stage 2) to open translation for all and sundry (stage 4), is typically a difficult one, beset with wrangling between stage 2 thinkers who continue to believe that the sacred text is potentially dangerous to unlearned readers, and that vernacular translation will mean the end of civilization as we know it, and stage 4 thinkers who have already come to believe that the text was originally written for the masses and should not be kept from them now.

One mode that is typical of this transitional period is literal translation, which serves the multiple purposes of:

(*a*) reverencing the syntactic and semantic contours of the original language, which is still, either openly or subliminally, worshipped as the language of divine revelation, invested with all the authority and power of the alien word (a stage 2 preoccupation that dies very slowly);

(*b*) making the sacred text available to the masses, and thus nominally satisfying the increasing demand for popular access to esoteric texts long controlled by a small educated and élitist priesthood; and

(*c*) keeping it largely incomprehensible to the masses, who see that it is in their language but cannot make sense of it without comparing the target-language phrasings to the original, which they cannot read.

Literalism often acts as a brake on too-rapid movement from the antitranslational stances of stage 2 to the easy tolerance of stage 4. Whenever influential forces in society begin to feel that the translation of sacred texts is out of control, that too many people are gaining access to the hieratic texts, new canons of literalism are imposed. 'Loose' or 'free' translators are censured, punished, even executed (the most famous case being Étienne Dolet, executed in 1546 after having been found guilty of heresy by the Sorbonne for, among other charges, 'adding' blasphemously to a text attributed to the divine Plato). Some of the most famous texts in the history of translation theory have been written by representatives of a 'loose' or 'free' (stage 4) approach who have run into the brick wall of literalist disapprobation and have tried to explain or argue or scream their way through it: St Jerome's letter to Pammachius (395 CE), Martin Luther's 'Circular Letter on Translation' (1530), and the extensive *œuvre* of Eugene A. Nida, whose theories of dynamic equivalence (Nida 1964) are regarded as orthodoxy by most but are still considered dangerously radical in some conservative Bible translation circles. The tugs and pulls of literal and 'free' translation run both ways in this transitional period: the first Wycliffite Bible was 'safely' literal, while the second took more risks (and incurred greater wrath) by translating more loosely; William Tyndale translated more boldly than any of his followers for the next century, and when King James commissioned the revision of existing translations in the early 17th c., the committee he appointed systematically pushed Tyndale's renditions back toward the relative safety of greater literalism [I.b.2.iv].

As attitudes toward the translation of sacred texts have been secularized over the centuries, this literalism has survived in very powerful forms, usually among various secular priesthoods (especially the professoriate), which use it to protect the authority of the texts they canonize. Various theories and methods of literal or 'foreignizing' translation have proved surprisingly tenacious, from ancient times right up into the present: from Boethius through John Scotus Erigena to a host of medieval and Renaissance thinkers, up to the German Romantics (Johann Gottfried von Herder, the Schlegel brothers, Novalis, Johann Wolfgang von Goethe, Friedrich Schleiermacher, Wilhelm von Humboldt; all excerpted in Robinson, 1997), and on into the 20th-c. post-romantic thought of Martin Heidegger, Walter Benjamin, Antoine Berman, and Lawrence Venuti [see I.a.3.iii]. For the most influential recent representatives of this approach, from Schleiermacher to Berman and Venuti, the aim is no longer to protect the sanctity of the canonized source text by mystifying the target readership. However, many of the ancient attitudes still survive in these 'foreignizing' approaches, notably in their assumption that 'free' or 'loose' (or, as they have been recently renamed, 'assimilative' or 'reductive') methods are ethically pernicious because they are too easy for the target reader, and thus do not sufficiently transform him or her in the image of the quasi-worshipped original text.

v. Stage 4: Open Translation In the fourth stage, which begins in Europe in the late Middle Ages (especially with the Lollards in the late 14th c.) and continues into our own day, the sacrality of sacred texts no longer means that they are dangerous to the unlearned and otherwise unprotected, or that they must therefore be kept from the profane. This attitude is closely associated in the West with emergent exoteric Christianity, a dogmatically central but institutionally peripheral attitude that for many centuries struggled in vain against the dominant esotericism inherited from the mystery religions. It was not until the 14th c. that large groups of increasingly influential Christians began to clamour for true exotericism or complete free access to all sacred texts for all believers. Philosophically this attitude was and remains closely tied to rationalism and the demystification of the mysteries, and socially to the emergent middle classes and their pragmatic impatience with exclusivist, élitist secrets.

But this new openness does not mean absolute freedom. Doctrinal purity remains an important concern in this period, and new methods are devised—especially universal education and literacy—to ensure the proper interpretation of sacred texts by believers given 'free' access to them. Instead of controlling the act of translation, as in stage 2, or the comprehensibility of actual translations, as in stage 3, these stage 4 educators (Martin Luther in the forefront) seek to control the reader's mental preparation for translation, so as to ensure that 'free' interpretations will be as orthodox as possible (Luther, in Robinson 1997: 84–9).

Other, more subtle restrictions also emerge in this period. The exoteric/universalist principles on which the advocacy of open translation is based proclaim the absolute communicability and thus also translatability of every religious truth, to every believer in every culture and language in the world. For this to become possible in practice, the conception of 'sacred text' must be severely restricted to transcendental meaning, or what Noam Chomsky would later call its 'deep structure' (Chomsky 1965)—that part of any text which is supposedly universal and therefore universally translatable. This restriction seems so obvious to us today, deep as we are into the fourth stage, as to be unnoteworthy, indeed almost 'natural'. But consider what is excluded from such a definition: the felt textures of the words in the original language; the various experiences of reading the original words aloud and to oneself, or hearing them read or shouted or sung in worship services; the shape of individual characters and the frequency with which they appear in the text; diacritics, acrostics, illuminated characters, and other decorative features. All of these textual features, which figured so strongly in sacred textual traditions in the second and third stages—

and militated so strongly against translation—must now be excluded as peripheral or even irrelevant to the sacrality of the text.

From a stage 2 or stage 3 perspective, where those features are considered the very essence of textual sacrality (for example in mainstream Judaism and Islam even today—not just in Kabbalistic or Sufi mysticism), this stage 4 exclusion seems wilfully perverse (Dan 1986). How can one so bowdlerize a sacred text just in order to ensure its translatability? Stage 3 Christians feel much the same way about completely demystified Bible translations: when the solemnity of the King James Version is sacrificed to easy accessibility in the Living Bible or Today's English Version, most of the Bible's sacrality is lost in the process. Various new literal renditions, notably the German translation of the Hebrew Bible by Martin Buber and Franz Rosenzweig, have appeared in recent decades in protest against what many believe is an unnaturally denatured conception of sacred text. The Bible is sacred, for stages 2 and 3, not only because it is true, but because it ushers the believer into a sacred *experience* of power and mystery. Stage 4 is not only

willing but eager to banish such experiences from consideration.

Sacred texts have also been translated by non-believers, often for purposes of debunking or other propagandizing. The Koran, for example, was first translated into Latin at the behest of medieval Christian leaders who wanted to be able to combat the Islamic 'heresy' more effectively [II.b.2]. Tejaswini Niranjana shows in *Siting Translation* how the British colonizers translated the sacred texts of India in assimilative ways in order to provide a 'native' mandate for submission to the Crown: if the Indians' 'own' ancient texts as translated by the British seemed to anticipate and justify British rule, resistance would increasingly appear futile (Niranjana 1992). Scholars have frequently translated sacred texts, generally those of ancient or dead religions, in quest of discursive neutrality—with no desire to polemicize for or against the religion itself—but postcolonial scholars of translation in particular have argued strenuously against the notion that translated discourse can ever be neutral or value-free. Translators always, often in very subtle ways, impose their own value systems on their work.

4. CHILDREN'S LITERATURE
Peter Hunt

Anything we create for children—whether writing, illustrating, or translating—reflects . . . our respect or disrespect for childhood.   (Oittinen 1993: 15)

i. Introduction In the field of children's literature, translated texts have had an influence quite disproportionate to their number. It is also clear that most of the original translations of the highly influential folk- and fairy-tales were intended for adults, and only subsequently became, as Tolkien put it, 'relegated to the nursery'. This is also true of many 19th-c. romances, such as Jules Verne's *Vingt mille lieues sous les mers* (1870, Twenty Thousand Leagues under the Seas) which are still published in 'children's' editions. Since 1900, the relatively few children's books which have been translated have had an equally powerful influence; Erich Kästner's *Emil und die Detektive* (1929, Emil and the Detectives), for example, has been seen as the forerunner of million-selling series such as Enid Blyton's 'Famous Five'. However, 20th-c. publishing for children in the UK has been marked by serious xenophobia, despite the growing internationalization of the publishing industry. Currently about 7000 titles are published each year; of these, only a tiny proportion, estimated at less than 2 per cent,

are translations. In contrast, in continental European countries, the figure varies between 30 per cent and 70 per cent (Jobe 1996: 519).

The situation is complicated by the phenomenon of the 'retelling'. The low literary status of children's books, and their intimate integration into popular culture means that stories are commonly reworked to suit the ideologies of an age, or its image of childhood, and it is not always clear how far translation is involved. Thus the most influential children's version of Norse mythology [II.o.2] was a retelling—*The Heroes of Asgard* (1857) by Annie (1825–79) and Eliza **Keary** (well-remembered by the children in Kipling's *Puck of Pook's Hill*)—and perhaps the most influential version of the Greek myths was Charles **Kingsley**'s *The Heroes* (1856) (a book which has been translated *into* Greek!). Even relatively modern classics, such as Arthur **Ransome**'s collection of Russian folk-tales, *Old Peter's Russian Tales* (1916), are the work of a self-declared *rédacteur*, rather than direct translations.

Riitta Oittinen has suggested that 'there is no real methodological difference between translation and adaptation . . . adaptation is part of translation and not a parallel process' (Oittinen 1993: 95). If this is generally true, the unequal power-relationship between adult writer/translator and child reader makes it more true of children's literature. All books for children reflect changing perceptions of what childhood is and should be; indeed, to have translations 'for children', there had to be a recognizable concept of childhood, which scarcely existed until the 18th c. Hence while traditional tales such as William **Caxton**'s *Aesop's Fables* (translated from the French, 1484 [see II.i.11.iv]) were appreciated by the whole society, it was only in the 18th c. that versions appeared which were specifically *for* children. Indeed, it can be argued that most traditional tales—in whatever form, and however commonly associated with children—are not truly part of children's literature at all.

ii. Seventeenth and Eighteenth Centuries The earliest book specifically designed for children was almost certainly *Orbis Sensualium Pictus* (1658, translated by Charles **Hoole** (1610–67) as *A World of Things Obvious to the Senses*, 1659) by the Czech writer John Amos Comenius (Jan Komensky) [II.e.3.i]. This book, which was 'famous throughout Europe as the first pictorial encyclopedia' (Darton 1982: 58) influenced children's book design, and remained in print into the 19th c.

From the late 17th c. to the late 19th c., there was a continuous tension between the fanciful and the didactic in children's literature. In adult literature, the fantastic was a matter of short-lived fashions, but over the years it came to permeate child culture. Ali Baba and Sinbad the Sailor appeared in English in the *Arabian Nights' Entertainments* [II.b.5] from 1706 to 1721 in an anonymous translation of Antoine Galland's *Mille et une nuits* (1704–1717); Aladdin, who featured in pantomime at Covent Garden in 1788, appeared in volumes IX and X. However, the first translation of these tales for children, *The Oriental Moralist or the Beauties of the Arabian Nights Entertainments*, was published as late as *c.*1791 by Elizabeth **Newbery**. Aladdin was absorbed into children's literature as one of (Benjamin) **Tabart**'s *Collection of Popular Stories for the Nursery; Newly Translated and Revised from the French, Italian, and Old English Writers* in 1804–9.

The fairy tale from the French has a similar history. Some of the fashionable stories by Madame d'Aulnoy from her *Contes des fées* (from 1697), such as 'The Blue Bird' (the source of 'Prince Charming' in pantomimes), were translated into English in 1699; others followed in 1707, including 'The Yellow Dwarf'. The stories were very popular, although the first edition for children did not appear until 1773—Francis **Newbery**'s *Mother Bunch's Fairy Tales. Published for the Amusement of . . . Little Masters and Misses*.

Cinderella, Little Red Riding Hood, Puss in Boots, and Sleeping Beauty first appeared in the stories of Charles Perrault. His *Histories ou contes du temps passé* (later known as *Contes de ma mère l'Oye*) were translated from the French under the name of Robert **Samber** (but in reality by Guy **Miège** (1644–1718)) and published in 1729 as *Histories, or Tales of Past Times. Told by Mother Goose*. These tales have a long and complicated publishing history, which suggests that the attraction of the book for children was perceived from the outset. However, the strength of the didactic movement of the 18th c. is demonstrated by the fact that 'Mother Goose' appeared in bilingual 'educational' editions from *c.*1741. Again, some of these stories were widely disseminated through the work of Benjamin Tabart.

Other early translations which drifted towards the children's market were La Fontaine's *Fables* [II.g.7] and the German Friedrich de la Motte Fouqué's 'gilded image of medieval Christendom and knight-errantry in fabrications of compelling if superficial quality' (Thwaite 1972: 107); the latter's *Sintram and His Companions* (1814, translated in 1820 by Julius **Hare** (1795–1855)), was a favourite of Charlotte Yonge and Louisa May Alcott as children.

Most early translations *specifically for children* had overt moral and educational purposes. The standard introduction to Homer in English schools for several centuries was a translation of Fénelon's *Les Aventures de Télémaque* (1699) as *The Adventures of Telemachus the Son of Ulysses* (also 1699). Foremost amongst moral tales was the Countess de Genlis's *Veillées du château* (1784; as *Tales of the Castle*, 1785); the inset stories are based on fact, as the Countess did not approve of fairy tales.

Characteristic of the 18th-c. sugaring of the didactic pill was *The Young Misses Magazine* (1761) translated from Madame Leprince de Beaumont's *Magasin des enfans, ou dialogues entre une sage gouvernante et plusieurs de ses élèves* (1756), which included the first English version of 'Beauty and the Beast'. Arnaud Berquin took a similar approach: *L'Ami des enfans* (1782–3) came into English as *The Children's Friend* (from 1783).

iii. Classics of the Nineteenth Century In 1797, Samuel Taylor Coleridge wrote to Thomas Poole: 'Should children be permitted to read romances and relations of giants and magicians and genii? . . . I have formed my faith in the affirmative.' Such thinkers found somewhat unlikely allies in the brothers Jacob Ludwig Carl and Wilhelm Carl

Grimm, whose scholarly *Kinder- und Hausmärchen* (i: 1812, ii: 1814) was first translated into English by Edgar **Taylor** (1793–1839) and his family in 1823 as *German Popular Stories*. 'We had', Taylor wrote, 'the amusement of some young friends principally in view', and the book was illustrated by George Cruikshank. The 200 tales, which included 'The Frog Prince', 'Hansel and Gretel', and 'Snow White', were variously modified for children's supposed sensibilities, and while the majority of editions for children have been retellings, there have been recent distinguished translations by Brian **Alderson** (1978) and Jack **Zipes** (1987). Alderson noted in his 'Afterword': 'It seems to me that the translator should never forget that his original stemmed not from a scholar's study but from a storyteller talking to his listeners' (Alderson 1978: 188). The history and criticism of the stories is discussed in Jack Zipes's *The Brothers Grimm* (Zipes 1988).

Lesser-known followers of the Grimms included Ludwig Bechstein with his German folk-tales, translated in 1854 as *The Old Storyteller*, and Wilhelm Hauff with collections of fairy stories translated from the 1840s. Bechstein's tales have been adapted for children as recently as 1962.

Other notable additions to the folk-tale treasury included an abridged version of the *Pentamerone*, translated in 1848 by J. E. **Taylor** with the somewhat improbable title, *The Pentamerone or the Story of Stories, Fun for the Little Ones*. Peter Christen Asbjørnsen and Jørgen Moe's collection of Norse folk-tales (1841–4) was translated by Sir George Webbe **Dasent** (1817–96) in 1859 as *Popular Tales from the Norse*, as an adult text. The stories, although never as popular as the German stories, brought the troll into English fiction, and versions of many of them appeared in Andrew Lang's 'Colour Fairy Books' from 1889.

Perhaps the most direct influence of translated stories on children (and some critics claim it to have been the most decisive) was that of Hans Christian Andersen [II.0.4.ii], although he maintained that he wrote for both adults and children. Some indication of the way in which the tide was turning against the evangelicals was the appearance of *five* translations of Andersen's work in 1846. These were *Wonderful Stories for Children* by Hans Christian Anderson [*sic*], translated by Mary **Howitt** (1799–1888), *Danish Fairy Legends and Tales*, translated by Caroline **Peachey**; and *A Danish Story Book*, *The Nightingale and Other Tales*, and *The Shoes of Fortune and other Tales*, all translated by Charles **Boner** (1815–70). Brian Alderson has noted that the tales 'became one of the most widely read children's books in Victor-

ian England' (Alderson 1982: 1), and that the first translations made many changes to suit the sentimental taste of the period. There was also, he notes, an 'almost universal failure amongst 19th c. translators in England to capture Andersen's quintessential *manner* as a storyteller: his casting of many of the narratives into a conversational mode and hence the various colloquialisms, abruptnesses, and ironic asides that constantly recur'. Similarly, Andersen's humour, which helped 'to give the stories that quality which had not been met with in children's books before . . . tended to be overlooked or excluded from early translations' (Alderson 1982: 5).

Not until 1893 with R. Nisbet **Bain**'s (1854–1909) translation did, in Alderson's opinion, an 'enthusiast . . . think carefully about what needed to be done'; 'modern' translations began with M. R. **James**'s *Forty Stories* in 1930; other notable editions have been those of Paul **Leyssac** (*It's Perfectly True! and Other Stories*, 1937) and Naomi **Lewis** (*Hans Andersen's Fairy Tales*, 1981).

Several major 19th-c. texts have become classics in the sense that they have entered the cultural public domain, and have been freely adapted in several media. Some, like *The Swiss Family Robinson*, set trends; others, like *Heidi*, reflected them; others, like *Struwwelpeter*, satirized them.

Der schweizerische Robinson (Zurich, 1812–13), the most influential of all Robinsonnades, demonstrates the internationalism of great myths. Defoe's *Robinson Crusoe* was an international bestseller in the 18th c., and the first adaptation for children appeared in 1768. Johann Wyss's development of the concept has a long and complex translation history. It was first translated into French in 1814 by Madame de Montolieu, who added much material. *The Family Robinson Crusoe*, possibly translated by William **Godwin** (1755–1836), ostensibly from the German (although it featured some of Madame de Montolieu's work), appeared in the same year. *The Swiss Family Robinson* was adopted as the title in 1818. The book inspired Captain Marryat's *Masterman Ready* (1841–42) which was in turn a seminal book for 70 years of boys' stories.

Heidis Lehr-und Wanderjahre by Johanna Spyri (1881) first appeared in English in two volumes, as *Heidi's Early Experiences* (1884) and *Heidi's Further Experiences* (1884). The book was characteristic of a blend of domestic realism and (generally) female wish-fulfilment which was widely popular, and seen in books such as *Little Women* (1868) and *Little Lord Fauntleroy* (1886), through to *Pollyanna* (1913).

Didacticism survived well into the 19th c.; in 1844, a young German doctor, Heinrich Hoffmann, searching for a Christmas present for his young son, could find nothing but 'moralizing stories, beginning and ending with admonitions like "the good child must be truthful"'. His riposte, a collection of ironically exaggerated cautionary tales, was hugely successful: *Lustige Geschichten und drollige Bilder* was published in 1845. The title *Der Struwwelpeter* was adopted for the third edition, and an English version, based on the sixth edition, was published in Leipzig in 1848 as *The English Struwwelpeter; or, Pretty Stories and Funny Pictures for Little Children*. The satirical tradition it established still survives.

Quite apart from these major books, German has had an unacknowledged influence. Wilhelm Busch's *Max und Moritz: Eine Bubengeschichte in sieben Streichen* (1865) had illustrations which were formative in the development of modern comics and cartoon films (Perry and Aldridge 1971: 96). At the other end of the scale, Christoph von Schmid's *Das Blumenkörbchen* (1823), translated as *The Basket of Flowers* (1833), has been described by Humphrey Carpenter as the 'archetypal Sunday School book . . . one of the most popular reward books throughout the 19th c., and, astonishingly, still in print for use in African missions in 1972' (Carpenter and Prichard 1984: 49).

'Of all sorts of make-believe,' observed John Goldthwaite, '*Pinocchio* is the most passionate . . . [It is] the most perfect Christian parable since *The Pilgrim's Progress*' (Goldthwaite 1996: 185, 187). Anne Lawson **Lucas** suggests that 'one of the most extraordinary qualities of *Pinocchio*, which makes it especially available to reinterpretation, is its essential ambiguity' (Lucas 1996: p. xlv). Certainly with *Le Avventure di Pinocchio: storia di un burattino* 'Carlo Collodi' (Carlo Lorenzini) produced an enduring work of popular fiction. It was first published as a serial between 1881 and 1883 in *Il Giornale per i Bambini*, and as a book in 1883; the first English translation, by Mary E. **Murray**, was in 1892. A new definitive translation by Ann Lawson Lucas appeared in 1996 [see II.m.11].

iv. The Twentieth Century In the 20th c. individual texts and series have been equally influential, although very few in number. Perhaps the most impressive group has been Scandinavian; children's literature has a higher status in these countries than in the UK, and this may be reflected in the serious themes that they pursue, although this has sometimes been masked by the translations.

The Nobel Prize winner Selma Lagerlöf [II.o.10.ii] produced a semi-educational travelogue, *Nils Holgerssons undebara resa genom Sverige* (1906–07), which with its sequel was translated as *The Wonderful Adventures of Nils* by Velma Swanson **Howard** (first published in the USA—i: 1907, ii: 1911). It is generally accepted as a classic of its kind.

Major contemporary figures include Tove Jansson, a Finn writing in Swedish, whose *Kometjakten* (1946) was translated into English as *Comet in Moominland* by Elizabeth **Portch** (1951). This book and its sequels (many of them translated by Thomas **Warburton**) created a new mythology and carry a gently ecological-mystical undertone.

The most successful Swedish writer has been Astrid Lindgren [II.o.10.ii], greatly respected in Sweden, and much translated, notably in the old Soviet Union. Her most famous book, *Pippi Långstrump* (1945), came into English in Britain in 1954 (translated by Florence **Lamborn**) as *Pippi Longstocking*; there have been several sequels. These fantasies of a powerful, anarchic child have been criticized (ironically enough) on the grounds of sexism, but it has been suggested by Maria Nikolajeva that critics have failed to see the extensive irony in the books. They are 'anti-power, anti-conventional, anti-totalitarian . . . With her deep insight into the mechanism of tyranny, she is the Orwell of children's literature' (Nikolajeva 1996: 41). As Lindgren's principal translator, Patricia **Crampton**, has noted, 'quite a few authors writing in a "language of limited diffusion", like Swedish, are prepared to sacrifice a phrase here, an idea there, in order to make their books more acceptable in the world's major language. Not her' (Crampton 1989: 21). As a result, the English translations are regarded by experts as particularly authentic.

This Swedish tradition has been maintained by contemporary writers such as Peter Pohl, whose prizewinning postmodernist story of contemporary Stockholm life, *Janne, min vän* (1985) was translated into English by Laurie **Thompson** as *Johnny My Friend* in 1991.

From the Norwegian, Alf Prøysen has had considerable success with a rather slighter fantasy series featuring the occasionally diminutive Mrs Pepperpot. The stories have appeared in various selections in English; the first, *Little Old Mrs Pepperpot* (1959) was translated by Marianne **Helweg** from *Kjerringa som ble så lita som ei teskje* (1957). From the Danish, one of the most influential children's books to deal with World War II has been Anne Holm's *David* (1963; translated by L. W. **Kingsland** as *I Am David*, 1965).

There have been some outstanding German contributions to British children's culture in the 20th c. The earliest was the animal tale *Bambi* (1923) by 'Felix Salten' (Siegmund Salzmann), which appeared in English in 1928, with a foreword by John Galsworthy. *Emil and the Detectives*, as we have seen, was an extremely influential tale of children capturing a petty criminal, and it has political over- tones: Kästner's books were burnt by the Nazis in 1933. However, these have been dwarfed by the commercial success, as both adult and children's book, of Michael Ende's *Die Unendliche Geschichte* (translated by Ralph **Manheim** as *The Neverending Story*, 1979). A few of the outstanding books from one of the most productive eras of German children's literature (1955–70) also found their way into English, including Hans Peter Richter's *Wir waren dabei* (1962; translated by Edite **Kroll** as *I Was There*, 1973), which deals the author's experiences in the Hitler Youth.

French children's literature has similarly pro- vided a small but significant corpus. Possibly the most enduring character has been Babar the ele- phant, who first appeared in 1931 in *L'Histoire de Babar, le petit éléphant* (as *The Story of Babar, the Little Elephant*, 1934). The first seven books in the series were written by Jean de Brunhoff, and many more have been produced since 1946 by his son Laurent. (Such was Babar's popularity that in 1941 Enid Blyton published *The Babar Story Book* 'from stories by Jean de Brunhoff'; the journal *Junior Bookshelf* was moved to despair: 'What in heaven's name can she have done to it? Did de Brunhoff's fine prose need rewriting?') The 1930s also saw the ingenious satire on politics and war, *Patapoufs et Filifers* (1930) by André Maurois; it is interesting that this essentially pacifist work was published in wartime Britain (as *Fattipuffs and Thinifers*, 1941).

Since the war, important examples have been the remarkable thriller *Le Cheval sans tête* (1955; as *A Hundred Million Francs*, 1957) by Paul Berna, and the work of the major children's author René Guillot, such as *Les Compagnons de la fortune* (1950; as *Companions of Fortune*, 1952), and of the illustrator Tomi Ungerer.

But the influence of French has been strongest through the cartoon book, or, perhaps more justly, in view of their extent and content, graphic novels. René Goscinny and Albert Uderzo's *Astérix*, the rebellious Gaul, first appeared in *Pilote* in 1959, and the ingenious translations by Anthea **Bell** have a well-deserved cult following. For all their knock- about farce, these books are remarkably subtle, and in a way display the art of the translator at its best. More conventional, although perhaps no less ingenious in his parody of popular culture, has been the Belgian writer-artist Georges Remi, who, as 'Hergé', first chronicled his indefatigable boy detective Tintin in the newspaper *Le Vingtième* in

1929. Books, and the first English versions, first appeared in 1930.

The fact that other outstanding translations of the century could be listed in a couple of paragraphs is significant. Certainly there have been outstand- ing original texts such as Reiner Zimnik's *Der Kran* (Switzerland, 1956; translated by Marion **Koenig** as *The Crane*, 1969); occasional notable books from Russia, such as Yuri Korinetz's *There, Far Away, Beyond the River* (1967, translated 1973); and rarities such as the Eskimo text, translated by the author, **Arkoosie**, *Harpoon of the Hunter* (1970) or the self- translation from the Irish by Ré **Ó Laighléis** of his *Ecstasy Agus Scéalta Eile* (*Ecstasy*, 1995).

v. The Current Situation In the last few decades, there have been considerable efforts to promote genuine internationalism, yet the traffic remains largely one way, despite the work of the Inter- national Board on Books for the Young, and the International Research Society for Children's Liter- ature. Closer European integration has led only to the bland concept of europublishing—which has required writers and artists (especially) to 'dena- tionalize' their works in order to gain large, eco- nomic, print-runs (Bell 1985).

Nor are the prospects very good. As Klaus Flugge, the founder of the Andersen Press (now part of Random House) and a committed publisher of translations, said in 1994: 'British children's book publishing has dominated the European market since the 1960s . . . [and] the British have more or less turned their back on foreign books for children' (Flugge 1994: 209); he continues 'Even the name of an author or artist militates against their success in England. The fact that it is difficult to pronounce names like Nöstlinger and Velthuijs has made both of these international prize winners more and more difficult to sell in this country' (p. 212). Mainstream publishers have been known to disguise the fact that books *are* translations.

Currently, the most powerful children's list in Britain, Penguin, while featuring an estimated 2500 titles, includes only around 50 translations; Julia Eccleshare's 1993 edition of *Children's Books of the Year*, which selects around 200 books, lists only Claude Gutman's *Fighting Back* and Annie Schmidt's *Minnie* as translated books (Eccleshare 1993).

Both of these were published by Turton & Chambers. This company, founded by the British writer Aidan Chambers and the Australian book- seller David Turton in 1989, has published 12 trans- lations, with slightly more success than major companies. Chambers's view is that to be worth translating, a book must be unusual (and most, of course, are not), and the unusual book has a limited appeal regardless of its origin. The establishment of the biennial Marsh Award for Children's Literature in Translation in 1996 has not so far encouraged experiment. This award, funded by the British Arts Council, is 'intended to bring attention to the quality and diversity of translated fiction [and to] encourage more translations'. It is unfortunate that the first winner, Christine Nöstlinger's *A Dog's Life*, was a 1990 translation from the German, now out of print—which was seen by specialists in the field to be 'well written but not greatly distinguished . . . and not distinctively Austrian' (Hill 1996: 22). (Even the umlaut is missing from Nöstlinger's name on the cover!) It is paradoxical, therefore, that of the five winners between 1981 and 1990 of the only major award for children's translation—the Astrid Lindgren Translation Prize, awarded by the Inter-national Federation of Translators—two, Patricia Crampton and Anthea Bell, were British.

The history of translation of children's books into English, then, is one of influential titles rather than of quantity, but, as Chambers points out, translation is culturally as important as ever: 'Reading ourselves into the minds of people who don't share our language is one way to increase the possibility of communication across the barriers of geography and nationality' (Chambers 1993: 1). As children's literature has always been concerned with education, this seems to many to be its vital educational role for the 21st c.

Translators of children's books are notoriously invisible; in the early years they seem to have been regarded as unremarkable hacks; latterly, publishers have sometimes been at some pains to ignore the fact that a book was a translation. If translators are not named in the above text, it is because they have not been traced.

5. ORAL LITERATURE
Ruth Finnegan

i. Introduction The issues in translating oral literature are those of all translation, but with additional problems due to the specific properties of oral texts. These properties are not as unusual as they may at first appear, for it is now recognized that many literary genres have been composed, delivered, or transmitted by oral means rather than, or as much as, through writing. Examples include south Slav sung epic [II.e.10.ii], southern African praise poetry [II.a.4], Somali lyrics, the Finnish *Kalevala* [II.o.iii], Australian Aborigine songs (Berndt 1976; Strehlow 1971), South Pacific dance dramas or laments from Papua New Guinea (Finnegan and Orbell 1995), and the sung poetry, spoken narratives, or orated speeches/sermons of peoples throughout the world, past and present (examples and references in Finnegan 1982; 1992a; 1992b; Firth 1990; Sherzer 1990; Tedlock 1984). But the processes involved in translating such examples are often either quietly ignored or relegated to some mysterious black box labelled 'orality'.

My focus here is on the specific issues of translating from the oral, but let me first reiterate that there are also all the usual problems of translation. Whether consciously or not, translators cannot avoid taking a position on familiar controversies like the nature of language, text, or the 'equivalences' of translation; the arguably contending pulls of information transfer, of artistry, of meanings for differing audiences or historical contexts; the politics of publication and selection; figurative and poetic expression, layers of meaning, intertextuality. Obvious as they seem, such issues do need emphasizing in view of the still common—but ill-founded—stereotype of oral forms as falling within a simplified model of communal and unchanging 'oral tradition', radically contrasted to 'normal' (i.e. western) literature. But oral literature too is characterized by artfulness and originality, and there is no clear and absolute divide between it and written literature. Translating it is as complex and controversial as for other literary genres.

ii. Inter-Cultural Translating Differences and unfamiliarities between the original and target cultures affect all inter-cultural translation and are certainly not confined to translation from the oral. But it is notable that a large proportion of translations from genres explicitly recognized as oral come originally from non-western cultures, principally those with colonial backgrounds. Unsurprisingly their translators have often reflected and reinforced contemporaneous stereotypes of 'the primitive', 'the African', etc. Sometimes this is through a linguistic style associated with childish, crude, or uneducated expression, sometimes through framing the translations as examples of expected 'primitive' or 'early' genres ('myth', 'epic', 'tradition' being especially popular) and/or by very free versions conveying romanticizing evocations of the mystical, mysterious, or archaic. Attempts to represent the unfamiliar linguistic structures of, say, African languages by un-English word-for-word equivalences are also sometimes tolerated in ways that would be unthinkable in translating European languages, thus confirming readers in their 'probable view that African oral literature is very inferior stuff' (Andrzejewski 1965: 100; similarly Tedlock, 1971, on translations from Native American literatures).

Such translations therefore need to be read with an awareness of cultural/historical assumptions (such as those sketched above) which may lie behind translators' renderings. A more recent trend, especially within the social sciences, is to comment extensively on the political and ethical issues that arise where translators hold greater power than the original authors through their nationality, culture, or educational background, and thus to be particularly sensitive to any suggestion of exploiting or conveying inferior images of the original authors through the terminologies, stylistics, or mode of distribution of these translations.

iii. Translating from Oral to Written

In oral literature, performance and delivery properties are not contingent extras, but intrinsic to the meaning, form, and artistry of the original. Two translation processes are therefore being undertaken: not just from one language to another, but also from an oral to a written mode. Scheub brings this out in his discussion of the audience's role and the expressive qualities in Xhosa story-telling in southern Africa:

How does one effectively translate the verbal and non-verbal elements of such a tradition to the written word? . . . It is impossible to consider the verbal elements of the performance in isolation from the non-verbal, yet there is no useful way of transferring the non-verbal elements to paper.   (Scheub 1971: 31)

Similarly, Fine (1984) identifies the problems of translating from a source medium (performance) which represents aural (linguistic and paralinguistic), visual, kinesic, artefactual, proxemic (i.e. issues of interpersonal spacing), and perhaps tactile elements, to a receptor medium (writing) with more limited channels for communicating. Inevitably, these non-verbal elements are underplayed in written translations.

Translators sometimes tackle this through such devices as additional notes, 'stage directions', special typographical devices (see below), or at least some acknowledgement of the problem. Many, however, apparently ignore such issues, giving the tacit impression that the (written) translation represents a comparably 'texted' original.

But while specific performance features vary according to culture, language, genre, or performer, *some* such elem-ents are always likely both to be present in the original and to be missed in written translations.

Features especially likely to be screened out in writing include the artistic/poetic qualities in genres whose accepted conventions include music, the arts of the speaking or singing voice, visual effects, enactment, or audience participation. Translations also often give an impression of oral narrative as typically involving little development of individual personality—failing to transmit the vivid characterization and inner feelings that can be represented in performance but are near-impossible to convey directly in writing. There is, besides, no neutral way in which unverbalized subtleties like atmosphere, emotion, tension, irony, differing voices, and detached 'meta-' reflection can be directly translated into written words, whereas oral performers can communicate these through speed, pitch, volume, pace, facial expression, gesture, emphasis, nuance, dramatization, repetition, and direct interactions between performer and audience. Onomatopoeic effects play a relatively small part in written genres, but form a rich resource in some oral literatures. 'Ideophones' are much used in African story-telling—special words which directly convey an idea through sound, like the Zulu *khwi*, representing turning round suddenly, or the Thonga *peswa-peswa* of a lady walking with high-heeled shoes (see Finnegan 1970: 64 ff.). All these effects are removed or radically diminished in writing. Further, the performance situation as a whole contributes to the work. Thus meanings which might be clearly evident to the original audience (or certain sections of it) may not be directly expressed in words, all the more uncapturable by translators where there are deliberate ambiguities or layers of meaning. And while translators can scarcely undertake to reproduce every detail of performance, they may have to deal with genres where *several* performers play significant roles in the piece as actually delivered—providing musical support, for example, or echoing, challenging, or intertwining with each other. Translators can only with difficulty indicate this plurality, given our single-line typographical conventions which highlight one 'lead' performer only. Other voices slip off the page.

Such instances may appear merely 'secondary', to be brushed aside when the translator gets down to the 'text proper'. But there is now a greater appreciation that such features may be of the essence, and that ignoring them in written translations risks changing or diminishing the sense and impact of the original.

iv. Transcribing A translator often comes to the original after it has already been transcribed from dictation or tape into writing—i.e. into a form that ostensibly does offer that 'text proper' for translation. But its transcribers have already inevitably made a series of choices, such as how to deal with 'interruptions', repetitions, performance features, and multiple voices, or how to apply written conventions of orthography, punctuation, paragraphing, or layout (no mere mechanical matter). Transcription is far from a transparent or automatic representation of its 'original', and the transfer from an oral to written form is already one kind of translation.

Particularly relevant for translators of oral literature is the decision of whether to transcribe the piece 'as verse' or 'as prose'. For an oral genre the answer may be controversial. Thus there has been a major revision in approaches to Native American narratives, once classed as prose but now increasingly transcribed as verse. Dell Hymes, a leading figure in this reassessment, argues that 'All the collections that are now in print must be re-done. They do not show the structure of the texts they present . . . Hidden within the margin-to-margin printed lines are poems, waiting to be seen for the first time' (Hymes, in Sherzer and Woodbury 1987: 19). If it *is* transcribed as verse, this means further decisions about line and verse demarcation. Musical elements (sung or instrumental), or utterances like sobs, shouts, or yodels are essential in some genres but may or may not appear in transcriptions. The many possible variants in the choice of dictation / recording situation and the scope and mode of transcription are thus not mere technical details, but likely to significantly affect the translator's original 'text' and its eventual translation.

For recently recorded forms, the translator may be responsible for transcription as well as translation, and it is now established good practice to append some explanation of the strategies used. But often the translator is faced with the transcriptions of others, and in practice tacitly accepts the text as given.

Some classic texts like the Homeric epics [II.i.2] or the *Song of Roland* [II.g.3] have arguably been transcribed from actual or putative oral delivery. The written forms are now in effect established as the accepted texts. There is perhaps little to be gained by speculating about their ultimate origins, though it is worth noting that insofar as they are claimed to be in some sense 'oral' this also implies that features of that presumed 'oral original' have inevitably been affected by its encapsulation in writing. Recent scholars (e.g. Coleman 1996) also draw attention to the aural features associated with public reading or delivery in much classical and medieval literature—features which pose issues for translators about identifying and delimiting the unit for translation.

v. Presenting Translations from Oral Texts Translators naturally present texts following the conventions and genres of their own culture (in practice most translations discussed in this volume are for a western or western-educated readership). But the question of how to apply these conventions is not an uncontroversial one. The translator must make decisions about, for example, the title of a translated piece (oral forms often do not have titles, yet we expect them in written works); attributing authorship (again a normal written expectation but sometimes—not always—more complex or multiple for oral forms); or its format as prose or poetry. Printed formats may also implicitly—but sometimes controversially—signal that translations are reproducing particular genres familiar from western literature such as 'poem', 'children's literature', or 'epic'.

Further, while the model of a fixed, bounded, and stable text has been the dominant framework for approaching literature (until, that is, the recent concept of computer 'soft' text), this is more problematic for oral literature. The precise boundaries of a 'work' and what is central or permanent to its 'text' may be elusive. For example, should translations of the fluid and in a sense endless Yoruba *oriki* praises (Barber, in Barber and Farias 1989) be presented as delimited texts? Should stories about the same protagonists (but told at different times or by different authors) be systematized into an integrated narrative? Translators and editors may decide to publish potentially linked performances from different occasions in the form of sustained texts, under such headings as, say, 'epic', 'mythological cycle', or 'song cycle': one possible strategy, but not without controversy (as for example in the arguments over 'epic' in south-central Africa—see references in Finnegan 1992a: 151). Such translations may then become accepted as unquestionably falling into these ostensibly definitive—but perhaps debatable—categories.

It is normally assumed that translations will take a written form. But since performance features transfer so poorly into print-based texts, some argue that translations should better (or additionally) be presented through audio or video recordings or by live renderings. Dell Hymes *performed* his translation of a Native American (Chinookan) story, emphasizing that some re-creative element was unavoidable and oral delivery as good a way as any to convey this (Hymes 1975; see also Yai, in Baiber and Farias 1989).

Other translators try to represent at least some performance elements through print- or graphic-based media. Musical transcriptions and visual illustrations can give some impression of immediacy and individual personality, with the sequential dynamics of performance sometimes represented through a series of photographs (as in Scheub on Xhosa story-telling (Scheub 1977)). Attempts are occasionally made to capture gesture and movement through dance-transcription systems.

Special typographical representations are also sometimes exploited to indicate performance features. Writers associated with the journal *Alcheringa/Ethnopoetics* in particular have developed print-based devices to indicate such delivery arts as timing (pauses, lengthening syllables, etc.), volume, intensity or stress in speaking, tonal contours, gestures, and audience participation. As an example, the following short extract about the pursuit and capture of 'White Shumeekuli' illustrates Dennis Tedlock's layout for his 'performable translations' of Zuni narrative. Though such formats are not universally favoured or practicable, it is illuminating to consider the weaker impression that this version would give if set out in plain printed prose.

. . . he was far ahead, the White Shumeekuli was fa——r
    ahead of them.
They kept on going until
they came near Shuminnkya.
Someone was herding out there.
He was herding, his sheep were spread out (*sweeping gesture*
    toward the east) when
they came along there shouting.
(*chanting*)
    'THE——RE GOES OUR WHITE SHU——MEEKULI
    RUNNING A WA——Y
    WHOEVER IS OUT THERE PLEASE HELP US
CATCH HIM FOR US!'
That's what they were shouting as they kept after him.
(*in a low voice*) 'Ah yes, there's a Yaaya dance today,
    something must've happened.'
That's what the herder was thinking about.
They were coming closer.
After a time their Shumeekuli
(*looking westward*) came into view.
He was still running.
The herder stood

under a tree (*indicates an imaginary tree in front of him*)
where he was going to pass (*indicates a path from the west past
    the tree*)
and waited for him there (*stands beside the tree facing west*).
Then
going straight on
the Shumeekuli headed for the place (*indicates the path again*)
where the herder was standing.
Sure enough, just as he
came up past the TREE
the herder CAUGHT him (*grabbing with both arms*) for them.
(*facing the audience again*) There he caught him . . .

(Tedlock 1983: 26–7)

Here capitalization indicates louder voice; lines on two levels are chanted with an interval of about three half-tones between them; repeated letters and dashes show lengthening; and when the text is set in poetic lines (as here) each line is delivered as a unit followed by a brief pause.

vi. Conclusion No more than with any other form of translation are there agreed 'solutions' as far as oral literature is concerned. But most specialists would now accept that the translation of oral literary forms means facing these kinds of issue, and that since translation is an active and interpretive rather than mechanical process, a translator's choices should be made explicit.

In the light of the issues faced by its translators, perhaps some term other than 'oral literature' might seem more apt—'performed art' perhaps (for the controversies, see Finnegan 1992a: 9 ff.). The term 'literature', however, remains useful in focusing on the literary qualities shared between the many literatures of the world and on translators' established strategies for tackling these, while 'oral' draws attention to additional dimensions raised by its active performance. That terminology also reminds us that many literary forms of the past and present in practice partake in some sense or other of oral qualities in their origins, their processes of composition, or their current forms of distribution (not just those aurally rich examples of the past but also forms like the lyrics of popular music in contemporary culture). The issues raised here thus have resonances for translation more generally. Weighing the implications of oral forms can lead to the recognition that the creative choices made by translators have an even wider range than is generally recognized.

For further discussion and references, see especially Andrzejewski 1965; Donaldson 1979; Finnegan 1992a, esp. ch. 9; Scheub 1971; Swann 1992; Tedlock 1971.

REFERENCES FOR PART I

AALTONEN, S. (1996), *Acculturation of the Other: Irish Milieux in Finnish Drama Translation*, Joensuu, Finland.

ALDERSON, B., tr. (1978), *The Brothers Grimm: Popular Folk Tales*, London.

—— (1982), *Hans Christian Andersen and His Eventyr in England*, Wormley, UK.

ALI, M. J. (1981), *Scheherazade in England: A Study of Nineteenth-Century English Criticism of the Arabian Nights*, Washington, DC.

ANDRZEJEWSKI, B. W. (1965), 'Emotional Bias in the Translation and Presentation of African Oral Art', *Sierra Leone Language Review*, 4: 95–102.

ANON. (1834), 'State of the French Drama', *Quarterly Review*, 51(101): 177–212.

ANON. (1836), 'French Novels', *Quarterly Review*, 56(111): 65–131.

ANON. (1868), 'Glimpses at Foreign Literature (I): George Sand', *Belgravia*, 5: 156–60.

ARNOLD, M. (1861), *On Translating Homer*, London.

ARROWSMITH, W., and SHATTUCK, R., eds. (1961), *The Craft and Context of Translation: A Critical Symposium*, Austin, Tex.

BAKER, M. (1996a), 'Linguistics and Cultural Studies: Complementary or Competing Paradigms in Translation Studies?', in *Übersetzungswissenschaft im Umbruch: Festschrift für Wolfram Wilss*, Tübingen, 9–19.

—— (1996b), 'Corpus-Based Translation Studies: The Challenges That Lie Ahead', in *Terminology, LSP and Translation: Studies in Language Engineering, in Honour of Juan C. Sager*, Amsterdam and Philadelphia, 175–86.

BALDWIN, T. W. (1944), *William Shakspere's Small Latine & Lesse Greeke*, 2 vols., Urbana, Ill.

BARBER, K., and FARIAS, P. F. DE M., eds. (1989), *Discourse and Its Disguises: The Interpretation of African Oral Texts*, Birmingham.

BARNSTONE, W. (1993), *The Poetics of Translation: History, Theory, Practice*, New Haven, Conn.

BARRATT, A. (1984), 'Works of Religious Instruction', in A. S. G. Edwards, ed., *Middle English Prose: A Critical Guide to Major Authors and Genres*, New Brunswick, NJ.

—— (1992), *Women's Writing in Middle English*, New York.

BARRET-DUCROCQ, F., ed. (1992), *Traduire l'Europe*, Paris.

BARTHES, R. (1966), *Critique et vérité*, Paris.

BASSNETT, S. (1980), *Translation Studies*, London; rev. edn. London and New York, 1991.

—— (1981), 'The Translator in the Theatre', *Theatre Quarterly*, 10: 37–48.

—— (1985), 'Ways Through the Labyrinth', in Hermans (1985: 87–102).

BATES, E. S. (1943), *Intertraffic: Studies in Translation*, London.

BATTEUX, C. (1760), *Principles of Translation. Written Originally in French*, Edinburgh.

BEER, J., ed. (1989), *Medieval Translators and Their Craft*, Kalamazoo, Mich.

BEHN, A. (1993), *The Works of Aphra Behn*, ed. J. Todd, vol. iv, Columbus, Oh.

BELL, A. (1985), 'Translator's Notebook: The Naming of Names', *Signal, Approaches to Children's Books*, 46: 3–11.

BELL, R. (1991), *Translation and Translating: Theory and Practice*, London and New York.

BELLOC, H. (1931), *On Translation*, Oxford.

BENJAMIN, W. (1968), 'The Task of the Translator', in his *Illuminations*, tr. H. Zohn, New York; repr. London, 1973.

BENNETT, H. S. (1965), *English Books and Readers 1558–1603*, Cambridge.

—— (1969), *English Books and Readers 1475–1557*, rev. edn., Cambridge.

—— (1970), *English Books and Readers 1603–40*, Cambridge.

BENNETT, J. A. W. (1986), *Middle English Literature*, ed. and completed D. Gray, Oxford.

BERK-SELIGSON, S. (1988), 'The Impact of Politeness in Witness Testimony: The Influence of the Court Interpreter', *Multilingua*, 7(4): 441–39.

—— (1990), *The Bilingual Courtroom: Court Interpreters in the Judicial Process*, Chicago and London.

BERMAN, A. (1992), *The Experience of the Foreign: Culture and Translation in Romantic Germany*, tr. S. Heyvaert, Albany, NY.

—— (1995), *Pour une critique des traductions: John Donne*, Paris.

BERNDT, R. M. (1976), *Love Songs of Arnhem Land*, Melbourne.

BIRD, P. A. (1988), 'Translating Sexist Language as a Theological and Cultural Problem', *Union Seminary Quarterly Review*, 42: 89–95.

BLOOM, H. (1975), *A Map of Misreading*, New York.

BLUNT, J. H., ed. (1873), *The Myroure of Oure Ladye*, Early English Text Society, ES 19, London.

BOLGAR, R. R. (1954), *The Classical Heritage and Its Beneficiaries*, Cambridge.

BONNEFOY, Y. (1990), *Entretiens sur la poésie, 1972–1990*, Paris.

BOURDIEU, P. (1991), *Language and Symbolic Power*, ed. J. Thompson, tr. G. Raymond and M. Adamson, London.

—— (1993), *The Field of Cultural Production*, tr. R. Nice et al., London.

BOUTCHER, W. (1996), 'Vernacular Humanism in the Sixteenth Century', in J. Kraye, ed., *The Cambridge Companion to Renaissance Humanism*, Cambridge.

BRISSET, A. (1990), *Sociocritique de la traduction: théâtre et altérité au Québec*, Montreal.

BRODSKY, J. (1974), 'Beyond Consolation', *New York Review of Books*, 7 Feb. 1974, 14.

BROOKS, P. (1985), *The Melodramatic Imagination: Balzac, Henry James, Melodrama and the Mode of Excess*, New York.

BROSSARD, N. (1983), *These Our Mothers, or: The Disintegrating Chapter*, tr. B. Goddard, Toronto.

BROWER, R. A., ed. (1959), *On Translation*, Cambridge, Mass.

BURKERT, W. (1987), *Ancient Mystery Cults*, Cambridge, Mass.

BURNSHAW, STANLEY (1989), *The Poem Itself*, New York [1st edn. 1960].

CALLAHAN, D. (1993), 'Material Conditions for Reception: Spanish Literature in England 1920–1940', *New Comparison*, 15: 100–9.

CAMERON, D. (1992), *Feminism and Linguistic Theory*, 2nd edn., New York.

CAMPBELL, G. (1789), *The Four Gospels, Translated from the Greek. With Preliminary Dissertations, and Notes Critical and Explanatory*, London.

CARPENTER, H., and PRICHARD, M. (1984), *The Oxford Companion to Children's Literature*, Oxford.

CATFORD, J. C. (1980), *A Linguistic Theory of Translation: An Essay in Applied Linguistics*, London [1st edn. 1965].

CATULLUS (1969), *Catullus*, tr. C. Zukofsky and L. Zukofsky, London.

CHAMBERLAIN, L. (1992), 'Gender and the Metaphorics of Translation', in Venuti (1992: 57–74).

CHAMBERS, A., ed. (1993), *Stories in Translation: A Penguin Booklist*, London.

CHEKHOV, A. (1959), *Plays*, tr. E. Fen, Harmondsworth, UK.

—— (1962), *Six Plays*, tr. R. Corrigan, New York.

—— (1978), *The Cherry Orchard*, tr. T. Griffiths, London.

CHEYFITZ, E. (1991), *The Poetics of Imperialism: Translation and Colonization from 'The Tempest' to Tarzan*, New York and Oxford.

CHOMSKY, N. (1965), *Aspects of the Theory of Syntax*, Cambridge, Mass.

COHEN, J. M. (1962), *English Translators and Translations*, London.

COLEMAN, J. (1996), *Public Reading and the Reading Public in Late Medieval England and France*, Cambridge.

COLGRAVE, B., and MYNORS, R. A. B., eds. (1969), *Bede's Ecclesiastical History of the English People*, Oxford.

CONLEY, C. H. (1927), *The First English Translators of the Classics*, New Haven, Conn.

COPELAND, R. (1991), *Rhetoric, Hermeneutics and Translation in the Middle Ages: Academic Traditions and Vernacular Texts*, Cambridge.

COWLEY, A. (1656), *Pindarique Odes, Written in Imitation of the Stile & Manner of the Odes of Pindar*, London.

COWPER, W. (1785), 'Critical Remarks on Pope's Homer', *Gentleman's Magazine*, 610–13.

COX, F. (1997), 'Translating the *Aeneid* to the *Nouveau Roman*: Pierre Klossowski's *Aeneid*', *Translation and Literature*, 6(2): 203–15.

CRAMPTON, P. (1994), 'In Memory of George', *In Other Words*, 3: 51–2.

—— (1989), 'Astrid-trans-Lindgren', *Books for Keeps*, 59: 21.

CRYSTAL, D. (1997), *English as a Global Language*, Cambridge.

D'ABLANCOURT, N. P. (1640), *Les Annales de Tacite: première partie: contenant la vie de Tibère*, Paris.

DAN, J. (1986), 'Midrash and the Dawn of Kabbalah', in G. H. Hartmann and S. Budick, eds., *Midrash and Literature*, New Haven, Conn., 127–39.

DANIELL, D. (1994), *William Tyndale: A Biography*, New Haven, Conn.

DARTON, F. J. H. (1982), *Children's Books in England: Five Centuries of Social Life*, 3rd edn., rev. B. Alderson, Cambridge [1st edn. 1932].

DAVIS, R. B. (1955), *George Sandys, Poet-Adventurer: A Study in Anglo-American Culture in the Seventeenth Century*, London.

DAY, R. A. (1966), *Told in Letters: Epistolary Fiction before Richardson*, Ann Arbor, Mich.

D'HULST, L. (1992), 'Sur le rôle des métaphores en traductologie contemporaine', *Target*, 4(1): 33–51.

DELISLE, J. (1977), 'Les Pionniers de l'interprétation au Canada', *Meta*, 22(1): 5–14.

—— (1980), *L'Analyse du discours comme méthode de traduction*, Ottawa.

—— (1987), *Translation in Canada*, Ottawa.

—— and WOODSWORTH, J., eds. (1995), *Translators through History*, Amsterdam.

DE LOTBINIÈRE-HARWOOD, S. (1991), *Re-belle et infidèle: la traduction comme pratique de réécriture au féminin / The Body Bilingual: Translation as Rewriting in the Feminine*, Montreal and Toronto.

DENHAM, J. (1656), *The Destruction of Troy: An Essay upon the Second Book of Virgils Aeneis*, London.

DERRIDA, J. (1985), 'Roundtable on Translation', tr. Peggy Kamuf, in C. McDonald, ed., *The Ear of the Other*, New York.

DEUTSCH, B., and YARMOLINSKY, A. (1923) *Contemporary German Poetry*, London.

DEVEREUX, E. J. (1983), *Renaissance English Translations of Erasmus: A Bibliography to 1700*, Toronto.

DONALDSON, T. (1979), 'Translating Oral Literature: Aboriginal Song Texts', *Aboriginal History*, 3: 62–83.

DOUGLAS, G. (1957–64), *Virgil's Aeneid Translated into Scottish Verse by Gavin Douglas*, ed. D. F. C. Coldwell, 4 vols., Edinburgh and London.

DRYDEN, J. (1956), *The Works of John Dryden*, ed. E. N. Hooker and H. T. Swedenberg, Jr., vol. i, Berkeley and Los Angeles.

—— (1958), *The Poems of John Dryden*, ed. J. Kinsley, vol. iii, Oxford.

DUBUC, R. (1978), *Manuel pratique de terminologie*, Montreal.

DUNSTER, S. (1712), *The Satires and Epistles of Horace, Done into English, with Notes*, 2nd edn., London.

DURNING, R. E. (1969), *Margaret Fuller, Citizen of the World*, Heidelberg.

EBEL, J. G. (1967), 'A Numerical Survey of Elizabethan Translations', *Library*, 5th ser., 22: 104–27.

—— (1969), 'Translation and Cultural Nationalism', *Journal of the History of Ideas*, 30: 593–62.

ECCLESHARE, J. (1993), *Children's Books of the Year*, London.

ELAM, K. (1980), *The Semiotics of Theatre and Drama*, London.

ELIOT, G. (1850), unpublished letter of 3 Dec. 1850 (private collection).

ELIOT, T. S. (1932), *Selected Essays 1917–32*, London.

—— (1960), *The Sacred Wood: Essays on Poetry and Criticism*, London; 1st edn. 1920.

ELLIS, R. (1982), 'The Choices of the Translator in the Late Middle English Period', in M. Glasscoe, ed., *The Medieval Mystical Tradition in England*, Exeter, 18–46.

—— ed. (1991a), *The Medieval Translator*, ii, London.

—— ed. (1991b), *New Comparison*, 12 ('Translation in the Middle Ages') [*The Medieval Translator*, 3].

—— and EVANS, R., eds. (1994), *The Medieval Translator*, iv, Exeter.

—— and TIXIER, R., eds. (1996), *The Medieval Translator*, v, Turnhout.

—— WOGAN-BROWNE, J., MEDCALF, S., and MEREDITH, P., eds. (1989), *The Medieval Translator*, i, Cambridge.

FARDY, B. D. (1984), *Jerry Potts: Paladin of the Plains*, Langley, BC.

FARWELL, B. (1988), *A Biography of Sir Richard Francis Burton*, London and New York.

FAWCETT, P. (1997a), *Translation and Language: Linguistic Approaches Explained*, Manchester.

—— (1997b), 'Macerated Malraux: A Study of *La Voie royale* in Translation', in K. Simms, ed., *Translating Sensitive Texts: Linguistic Aspects*, Atlanta, Ga., and Amsterdam.

FIELD, R. (1989), 'From *Ipomedon* to *Ipomedon A*: Two Views of Courtliness', in Ellis et al. (1989: 135–41).

FINDLATER, R. (1967), *Banned! A Review of Theatrical Censorship in Britain*, London.

FINE, E. C. (1984), *The Folklore Text: From Performance to Print*, Bloomington, Ind.

FINNEGAN, R. (1970), *Oral Literature in Africa*, Oxford.

—— ed. (1982), *The Penguin Book of Oral Poetry*, Harmondsworth, UK.

—— (1992a), *Oral Traditions and the Verbal Arts: A Guide to Research Practices*, London.

—— (1992b), *Oral Poetry: Its Nature, Significance and Social Context*, 2nd edn., Bloomington, Ind.

—— and ORBELL, M., eds. (1995), *South Pacific Oral Traditions*, Bloomington, Ind.

FIRTH, R. (1990), *Tikopia Songs: Poetic and Musical Art of a Polynesian People of the Solomon Islands*, Cambridge.

FISCHER-LICHTE, E., et al., eds. (1990), 'The Dramatic Touch of Difference: Theatre Own and Foreign', *Forum Modernes Theater*, 2.

FLORIO, J., tr. (1910), *Essays of Michael Lord of Montaigne*, eds E. Rhys and A. R. Waller, 3 vols., London.

FLUGGE, K. (1994), 'Crossing the Divide: Publishing Children's Books in the European Context', *Signal: Approaches to Children's Books*, 75: 209–14.

FOSTER, J. R. (1927), 'The Abbé Prévost and the English Novel', *Proceedings of the Modern Language Association of America*, 42: 443–64.

FOWLER, H. W., and FOWLER, F. G. (1931), *The King's English*, 3rd edn., Oxford.

FRANCE, P., and GLEN, D., eds. (1989), *European Poetry in Scotland: An Anthology of Translations*, Edinburgh.

FRANCIS, P. (1743), *The Odes, Epodes, and Carmen Seculare of Horace*, vol. i, London.

FRANCKLIN, T. (1753), *Translation, a Poem*, London.

FRANTZEN, A. J. (1990), *Desire for Origins: New Language, Old English and Teaching the Tradition*, New Brunswick, NJ, and London.

FRAWLEY, W. (1984), *Translation: Literary, Linguistic and Philosophical Perspectives*, London and Toronto.

FRAYN, M., with C. HAMPTON and T. WERTENBAKER (1989), *Platform Papers*, Royal National Theatre, London.

FREIWALD, B. (1991), 'The Problem of Trans-lation: Reading French Feminisms', *TTR*, 4 (2): 55–68.

FUSELI, H. (1793), review of W. Cowper, *The Iliad and Odyssey of Homer*, *Analytical Review*, 15: 1–16.

GALLANT, C. (1990), 'L'Influence des religions catholique et protestante sur la traduction des textes sacrés à l'intention des Micmacs dans les provinces maritimes: du livre des prières de l'abbé Maillard (1710–1762) à la traduction des Évangiles par Silas Tertius Rand (1810–1889)', *TTR*, 3 (2): 97–109.

GARIOCH, R. (1980), *Collected Poems*, Manchester.

GARNETT, R. (1991), *Constance Garnett: A Heroic Life*, London.

GENTZLER, E. (1993), *Contemporary Translation Theories*, London and New York.

GODARD, B. (1988), 'Preface', in *Lovhers* by N. Brossard, tr. B. Godard, Montreal.

—— (1995), 'A Translator's Diary', in S. Simon, ed., *Culture in Transit: Translation and the Changing Identities of Quebec Literature*, Montreal.

GOLDTHWAITE, J. (1996), *The Natural History of Make Believe*, New York.

GOREAU, A. (1980), *Reconstructing Aphra: A Social Biography of Aphra Behn*, New York.

GRAHAM, J. F. (1981), 'Theory for Translation', in M. Gaddis Rose, ed., *Translation Spectrum: Essays in Theory and Practice*, Albany, NY.

—— ed. (1985), *Difference in Translation*, Ithaca, NY, and London.

GRAY, A., tr. (1932), *Arrows: A Book of German Ballads and Folksongs Attempted in Scots*, Edinburgh.

—— tr. (1949), *Sir Halewyn: Examples in European Balladry and Folk-Song*, Edinburgh and London.

—— tr. (1954), *Four and Forty: A Selection of Danish Ballads Presented in Scots*, Edinburgh.

GREEN, R. F. (1980), *Poets and Princepleasers: Literature and the English Court in the Late Middle Ages*, Toronto, Buffalo, and London.

GREENFIELD, S. B. (1966), *A Critical History of Old English Literature*, London.

GRIFFITH, E. (1769), *The School for Rakes*, London.

GRIFFITHS, M. (1985), 'Presence and Presentation: Dilemmas in Translating for the Theatre', in T. Hermans, ed., *Second Hand: Papers on the Theory and Historical Study of Literary Translation*, ALW-Cahier, 3: 161–83.

HABICHT, W. (1989), 'Shakespeare and Theatre Politics in the Third Reich', in H. Scolnicov and P. Holland, eds., *The Play out of Context: Transferring Plays from Culture to Culture*, Cambridge, 110–21.

HAGEDORN, N. L. (1988), '"A Friend to Go Between Them": The Interpreter as Cultural Broker during Anglo-Iroquois Councils, 1740–70', *Ethnohistory*, 35 (1): 60–80.

—— (1994), '"Faithful, Knowing, and Prudent": Andrew Moncour as Interpreter and Cultural Broker, 1740–1772', in M. C. Szasz, ed., *Between Indian and White Worlds*, Norman, Okla.

HALE, T. (1998), 'Roman Noir', in M. M. Roberts, ed., *A Handbook to Gothic Literature*, London and Basingstoke, 189–95.

HAMMOND, G. (1993), 'The Authority of the Translated Word of God: A Reading of the Preface to the 1611 Bible', *Translation and Literature*, 2: 52–67.

HANNA III, R. (1996), '"Vae Octuplex", Lollard Socio-Textual Ideology, and Ricardian-Lancastrian Prose Translation', in R. Copeland, ed., *Criticism and Dissent in the Middle Ages*, Cambridge, 244–63.

HANNAY, M. P., ed. (1985), *Silent but for the Word: Tudor Women as Patrons, Translators and Writers of Religious Works*, Kent, Oh.

—— (1990), *Philip's Phoenix: Mary Sidney, Countess of Pembroke*, New York and Oxford.

HARE, S., ed. (1995), *Allen Lane and the Penguin Editors 1935–1970*, Harmondsworth, UK.

HARVEY, K. (1998), 'Translating Camp Talk: Gay Identities and Cultural Transfer', *The Translator*, 4 (2): 295–320.

HAYWOOD, E. (1721), *Letters from a Lady of Quality to a Chevalier. Translated from the French*, London.

HELBO, A. (1987), *Theory of the Performing Arts*, Amsterdam.

HERMANS, T., ed. (1985), *The Manipulation of Literature: Studies in Literary Translation*, London.

—— (1996), 'Norms and the Determination of Translation', in R. Alvarez and C.-A. Vidal, eds., *Translation, Power, Subversion*, Clevedon, UK.

HEYLEN, R. (1993), *Translation, Poetics and the Stage: Six French Hamlets*, London.

HIGMAN, F. (1993), 'Ideas for Export: Translations in the Early Reformation', in J. R. Brink and W. F. Gentrup, eds., *Renaissance Culture in Context: Theory and Practice*, Aldershot, UK.

HILL, C. (1993), *The English Bible and the Seventeenth-Century Revolution*, Harmondsworth, UK.

HILL, R. (1996), 'Children's Books in Translation: The Marsh Award', *Books for Keeps*, 101: 22.

HITCHMAN, J. F. (1867), 'Decline of the Drama', *Belgravia*, 2: 57–65.

HOFSTADTER, D. A. (1997), *Le Ton beau de Marot*, New York and London.

HOLMES, J. S. (1988), *Translated! Papers on Literary Translation and Translation Studies*, Amsterdam.

HOMEL, D., and SIMON, S., eds. (1988), *Mapping Literature: The Art and Politics of Translation*, Montreal.

HONIG, E. (1985), *The Poet's Other Voice: Conversations on Literary Translation*, Amherst, Mass.

HORGUELIN, P. (1981), *Anthologie de la manière de traduire*, Montreal.

HUDSON, A., ed. (1978), *Selections from the English Wycliffite Writings*, Cambridge.

—— (1988), *The Premature Reformation*, Oxford.

HYMES, D. H. (1975), 'Folklore's Nature and the Sun's Myth', *Journal of American Folklore*, 88: 345–69.

IBSEN, H. (1964), *Ghosts and Other Plays*, tr. P. Watts, Harmondsworth, UK.

IMRIE, M. (1992), 'Verso: la politique de traduction d'un éditeur britannique', in F. Barret-Ducrocq, ed., *Traduire l'Europe*, Paris, 129–33.

INCHBALD, E. (1798), *Lovers' Vows: A Play in Five Acts . . . From the German of Kotzebue*, London.

IONESCO, E. (1958a), *Four Plays*, tr. D. Allen, New York.

IONESCO, E. (1958b), *Plays*, i, tr. D. Watson, London.

JACOBSEN, E. (1958), *Translation: A Traditional Craft. An Introductory Sketch with a Study of Marlowe's 'Elegies'*, Copenhagen.

JAMES VI OF SCOTLAND (1955), *Poems*, ed. J. Craigie, i, Edinburgh and London.

JAMES, L. (1963), *Fiction for the Working Man, 1830–50*, Oxford.

JENKYNS, R. (1980), *The Victorians and Ancient Greece*, Oxford.

JOBE, R. (1996), 'Translation' in P. Hunt, ed., *International Companion Encyclopedia of Children's Literature*, London, 519–29.

JOHNSON, S. (1905), *The Lives of the Poets*, ed. G. B. Hill, Oxford.

JONES, R. F. (1953), *The Triumph of the English Language: A Survey of Opinions concerning the Vernacular from the Introduction of Printing to the Restoration*, London.

JONES, W. (1970), *The Letters of Sir William Jones*, ed. G. Cannon, Oxford.

JOUVE, N. W. (1991), *White Woman Speaks with Forked Tongue: Criticism as Autobiography*, London and New York.

KADISH, D. Y., and MASSARDIER-KENNEY, F., eds. (1994), *Translating Slavery: Gender and Race in French Women's Writing, 1783–1823*, Kent, Oh.

KAHN, L. G. (1963), 'Bürgerliche Stil und bürgerliche Übersetzung', in J. J. Störig, ed., *Das Problem des Übersetzens*, Darmstadt; first pub. 1935.

KAPP, Y. (1972), *Eleanor Marx*, 2 vols., New York.

KARTTUNEN, F. (1994), *Between Worlds: Interpreters, Guides, and Survivors*, New Brunswick, NJ.

KELLY, L. (1979), *The True Interpreter: A History of Translation Theory and Practice in the West*, Oxford.

KERENYI, C. (1955), 'The Mysteries of the Kareiroi', tr. R. Manheim, in J. Campbell, ed., *The Mysteries: Papers from the Eranos Yearbooks*, New York, 32–63.

KING, G. (1978), *Garden of Zola: Émile Zola and His Novels for English Readers*, London.

KIRKCONNELL, W. (1967), *A Slice of Canada: Memoirs*, Toronto.

KLEIN, H. (1995), 'Anthologies of German Poetry in Translation Published in Britain 1930–1990', in H. Kittel, ed., *International Anthologies of Literature in Translation*, Berlin, pp. 56–83.

KNOX, R. (1949), *On Englishing the Bible*, London.

—— (1957), *On English Translation*, Oxford.

KOHFELDT, M. L. (1985), *Lady Gregory: The Woman behind the Irish Renaissance*, New York.

KOSKO, B. (1994), *Fuzzy Thinking: The New Science of Fuzzy Logic*, London.

KOWZAN, T. (1975), *Littérature et spectacle*, Paris and The Hague.

KRONTIRIS, T. (1992), *Oppositional Voices: Women as Writers and Translators in the English Renaissance*, London and New York.

LACY, N. J., ed. (1986), *The Arthurian Encyclopedia*, Woodbridge, Suffolk.

LATHROP, H. B. (1967), *Translations from the Classics into English from Caxton to Chapman 1477–1620*, New York; 1st edn. 1932.

LAVIOSA, S. (1997), 'How Comparable Can Comparable Corpora Be?', *Target*, 9 (2): 289–319.

LEFEVERE, A. (1975), *Translating Poetry: Seven Strategies and a Blueprint*, Assen and Amsterdam.

—— (1992a), *Translation, Rewriting and the Manipulation of Literary Fame*, London and New York.

—— (1992b), *Translation / History / Culture*, London and New York.

—— and BASSNETT, S., eds. (1990), *Translation, History and Culture*, London and New York.

LEGGE, M. D. (1963), *Anglo-Norman Literature and Its Background*, Oxford.

L'ESTRANGE, R. (1678), *Five Love Letters from a Nun to a Chevalier*, London.

LEVINE, S. J. (1991), *The Subversive Scribe: Translating Latin American Fiction*, St Paul, Minn.

LEWIS, D. (1969), *Convention: A Philosophical Study*, Cambridge, Mass.

LOEWENSTEIN, J. (1996), 'Humanism and Seventeenth-Century English Literature', in J. Kraye, ed., *The Cambridge Companion to Renaissance Humanism*, Cambridge, 269–93.

LOUW, B. (1993), 'Irony in the Text or Insincerity in the Writer: The Diagnostic Potential of Semantic Prosodies', in M. Baker, G. Francis, and E. Tognini-Bonelli, eds., *Text and Technology: In Honour of John Sinclair*, Amsterdam, 157–76.

LOWELL, ROBERT (1961), *Imitations*, New York/London.

LUCAS, A. L. (1996), 'Introduction' in *The Adventures of Pinocchio*, by C. Collodi, Oxford, pp. vii–xlvi.

LUCAS, E. V. (1900), Prefatory Note to the One-Volume Edition, in *The Story of Burnt Njal*, tr. G. W. Dasent, London.

LYNE, R. (1996), 'Golding's Englished *Metamorphoses*', *Translation and Literature*, 5: 183–200.

MCCONICA, J. K. (1965), *English Humanists and Reformation Politics under Henry VIII and Edward VI*, Oxford.

MACHAN, T. W. (1985), *Techniques of Translation: Chaucer's Boece*, Norman, Okla.

MACPHERSON, J. (1760), *Fragments of Ancient Poetry, Collected in the Highlands of Scotland, and Translated from the Galic or Erse Language*, Edinburgh.

—— (1762), *Fingal, an Ancient Epic Poem*, London.

MASON, I. (1994), 'Discourse, Ideology, and Translation', in A. Shunnaq and M. Heliel, eds., *Language, Discourse and Translation in the West and Middle East*, Amsterdam and Philadelphia, 23–34.

MATTHIESSEN, F. O. (1931), *Translation: An Elizabethan Art*, Cambridge, Mass.

MESCHONNIC, H. (1973), *Pour la poétique II*, Paris.

MILNES, R., *et al.* (1974), 'The Translator at Work', *Opera*, 26: 951–62, 1056–64.

—— (1975), 'The Translator at Work', *Opera*, 27: 242–50, 738–42.

MINNIS, A. J. (1988), *Medieval Theories of Authorship: Scholastic Literary Attitudes in the Later Middle Ages*, 2nd edn., Aldershot, UK.

MITCH, D. F. (1992), *The Rise of Popular Literacy in Victorian England: The Influence of Private Choice and Public Policy*, Philadelphia.

MONTESINOS, J. F. (1973), *Introducción a una historia de la novela en España en el siglo XIX: seguida del esboza de una bibliografía de traducciones de novelas (1800–1850)*, 3rd edn., Madrid.

MORGAN, E. (1972), *Wi the Haill Voice: 25 Poems by Vladimir Mayakovsky Translated into Scots*, Oxford.

MORLEY, H. (1887–95), *An Attempt towards a History of English Literature*, 11 vols., London.

NABOKOV, V. (1955), 'Problems of Translation: *Onegin* in English', *Partisan Review*, 22 (4): 496–512.

NEILL, W. (1992), *Tales frae the Odyssey o Homer Owreset intil Scots*, Edinburgh.

NEWMARK, P. (1981), *Approaches to Translation*, Oxford.

—— (1988), *A Textbook of Translation*, London.

NICOLL, A. (1955), *A History of English Drama, 1660–1900*, iv: *Early Nineteenth Century*, rev. edn., Cambridge.

NIDA, E. A. (1964), *Towards a Science of Translating, with Special Reference to Principles and Procedures Involved in Bible Translating*, Leiden.

—— and Taber, C. (1969), *The Theory and Practice of Translation*, Leiden.

NIKOLAJEVA, M. (1996), *Children's Literature Comes of Age: Toward a New Aesthetic*, New York.

NIRANJANA, T. (1992), *Siting Translation: History, Post-Structuralism, and the Colonial Context*, Berkeley, Calif.

NORBROOK, D. (1994), 'Lucan, Thomas May and the Creation of a Republican Literary Culture', in K. Sharpe and P. Lake, eds., *Culture and Politics in Early Stuart England*, Basingstoke.

NØRGAARD, H. (1958), 'Translations of the Classics into English before 1600', *Review of English Studies*, n.s. 9: 164–72.

NORTON, G. P. (1984), *The Ideology and Language of Translation in Renaissance France and Their Humanist Antecedents*, Geneva.

NOTT, J. (1787), *Select Odes, from the Persian Poet Hafez*, London.

—— (1795), *The Poems of Caius Valerius Catullus, in English Verse*, London.

OITTINEN, R. (1993), *I am Me—I am Other: On the Dialogics of Translating for Children*, Tampere, Finland [Acta Universitatis Tamperensis, ser. A, vol. 385].

OLDHAM, J. (1987), *The Poems of John Oldham*, ed. H. F. Brooks with R. Selden, Oxford.

ORME, N. (1989), *Education and Society in Medieval and Renaissance England*, London and Ronceverte, Va.

PATTERSON, A. (1991), *Fables of Power: Aesopian Writing and Political History*, Durham, NC.

PATTERSON, L. (1991), *Chaucer and the Subject of History*, London.

PAVIS, P. (1992), *Theatre at the Crossroads of Culture*, London and New York.

PEARSALL, D. (1977), *Old English and Middle English Poetry*, London and Boston, Mass.

PENGUIN BOOKS (1985), *Fifty Penguin Years*, Harmondsworth, UK.

PENNYCOOK, A. (1994), *The Cultural Politics of English as an International Language*, London.

PENROD, L. K. (1993), 'Translating Hélène Cixous: French Feminism(s) and Anglo-American Feminist Theory', *TTR*, 6 (2): 39–54.

PENTLAND, D. (1993), 'North American Languages of Canada, 1534–1900', *Facsimile*, 10: 5–15.

PERRY, G., and ALDRIDGE, A. (1971), *The Penguin Book of Comics*, London.

PHILIPS, K. (1729), *Letters from Orinda to Poliarchus*, 2nd edn., London.

PLANCHÉ, J. R. (1872), *The Recollections and Reflections of J. R. Planché*, 2 vols., London.

POLLARD, A. W., ed. (1911), *Records of the English Bible: The Documents relating to the Translation and Publication of the Bible in English, 1525–1611*, Oxford.

POPE, A. (1967), *The Twickenham Edition of the Poems of Alexander Pope*, ed. J. Butt, vol. vii, London.

POUND, E. (1954), *Literary Essays of Ezra Pound*, ed. T. S. Eliot, London.

—— (1973), *Selected Prose 1909–1965*, London.

PYM, A. (1995), 'Schleiermacher and the Problem of *Blendlinge*', *Translation and Literature*, 4 (1): 5–30.

RAAB, F. (1964), *The English Face of Machiavelli: A Changing Interpretation 1500–1700*, London.

RADICE, W., and REYNOLDS, B., eds. (1987), *The Translator's Art: Essays in Honour of Betty Radice*, Harmondsworth, UK.

RAHILL, F. (1967), *The World of Melodrama*, University Park, Penn.

REMLEY, P. G. (1996), *Old English Biblical Verse: Studies in Genesis, Exodus and Daniel*, Cambridge.

RICH, T. (1940), *Harington and Ariosto: A Study in Elizabethan Verse Translation*, New Haven, Conn.

RICHARDS, I. A. (1953), 'Towards a Theory of Translating', in A. F. Wright, ed., *Studies in Chinese Thought*, Chicago, 247–63.

ROBINSON, D. (1991), *The Translator's Turn*, Baltimore, Md.

ROBINSON, D. (1996), *Translation and Taboo*, De Kalb, Ill.

ROBINSON, D. ed. (1997), *Western Translation Theory from Herodotus to Nietzsche*, Manchester.

ROWELL, G. (1956), *The Victorian Theatre, 1792–1914: A Survey*, Oxford.

ROY, C. (1993), 'A Sociolinguistic Analysis of the Interpreter's Role in Simultaneous Talk in Interpreted Interaction', *Multilingua*, 12 (4): 341–63.

SAVORY, T. H. (1957), *The Art of Translation*, London.

SCHEUB, H. (1971), 'Translation of African Oral Narrative-Performances to the Written Word', *Yearbook of Comparative and General Literature*, 20: 8–36.

—— (1977), 'Body and Image in Oral Narrative Performance', *New Literary History*, 8: 345–67.

SCHULTE, R., and BIGUENET, J. (1992), *Theories of Translation: An Anthology of Essays from Dryden to Derrida*, Chicago and London.

SCOTT, H. (1984), 'Louky Bersianik's *L'Euguélionne*: Problems of Translating the Critique of Language in the New Quebec Feminism', Master's thesis, Concordia University, Montreal.

SHARPE, K. (1994), 'The King's Writ: Royal Authors and Royal Authority in Early Modern England', in K. Sharpe and P. Lake, eds., *Culture and Politics in Early Stuart England*, Basingstoke.

SHERZER, J. (1990), *Verbal Art in San Blas*, Cambridge.

—— and WOODBURY, A. C., eds. (1987), *Native American Discourse: Poetics and Rhetoric*, Cambridge.

SIMON, S. (1992), 'The Language of Cultural Difference: Figures of Alterity in Canadian Translation', in Venuti (1992: 159–76).

—— (1994), *Le Trafic des langues: traduction et culture dans la littérature québecoise*, Montreal.

—— ed. (1995), *Culture in Transit: Translation and the Changing Situation of Quebec Literature*, Montreal.

—— (1996), *Gender in Translation: Cultural Identity and the Politics of Transmission*, London and New York.

SIMPSON, P. (1993), *Language, Ideology and Point of View*, London and New York.

SINCLAIR, J. (1996), 'The Search for Units of Meaning', *Textus*, 9: 75–106.

SKINNER, Q. (1996), *Reason and Rhetoric in the Philosophy of Hobbes*, Cambridge.

SMITH, G. G., ed. (1904), *Elizabethan Critical Essays*, 2 vols., Oxford.

SMOLLETT, T., tr. (1755), *The History and Adventures of the Renowned Don Quixote*, London.

SPENDER, D. (1992), *Living by the Pen: Early British Women Writers*, New York and London.

STEINER, G., ed. (1966), *The Penguin Book of Modern Verse Translation*, Harmondsworth, UK.

—— (1975), *After Babel: Aspects of Language and Translation*, Oxford.

STEINER, T. R. (1975), *English Translation Theory, 1650–1800*, Assen, Neth.

STRATFORD, P. (1977), *Bibliography of Canadian Books in Translation: French to English and English to French*, Ottawa.

STREHLOW, T. G. H. (1971), *Songs of Central Australia*, Sydney.

SWANN, B., ed. (1992), *On the Translation of Native American Literatures*, Washington and London.

SWANTON, M., tr. (1993), *Anglo-Saxon Prose*, London and Rutland, V.

TEDLOCK, D. (1971), 'On the Translation of Style in Oral Narrative', *Journal of American Folklore*, 84: 14–33.

—— (1983), *The Spoken Word and the Work of Interpretation*, Philadelphia.

THIRLWALL, J. C. (1966), *In Another Language: A Record of the Thirty-Year Relationship between Thomas Mann and His English Translator, Helen Tracy Lowe-Porter*, New York.

THWAITE, MARY F. (1972), *From Primer to Pleasure in Reading*, London [1st edn. 1963].

TOLLES, W. (1940), *Tom Taylor and the Victorian Drama*, New York.

TOURY, G. (1995), *Descriptive Translation Studies and Beyond*, Amsterdam and Philadelphia.

TROUSDALE, M. (1976), 'Recurrence and Renaissance: Rhetorical Imitation in Ascham and Sturm', *English Literary Renaissance*, 6: 156–79.

TYTLER, A. F. (1978), *Essay on the Principles of Translation*, ed. J. F. Huntsman, Amsterdam and Philadelphia.

VELTRUSKY, J. (1977), *Drama as Literature*, Lisse, Neth.

VENUTI, L., ed. (1992), *Rethinking Translation: Discourse, Subjectivity, Ideology*, London and New York.

—— (1995a), *The Translator's Invisibility*, London and New York.

—— (1995b), 'Translation, Authorship, Copyright', *Translator*, 1: 1–24.

—— (1996), 'Translation, Heterogeneity, Linguistics', *TTR*, 9 (1): 91–115.

—— (1997), 'The American Tradition', in M. Baker, ed., *Routledge Encyclopedia of Translation Studies*, London and New York.

VINAY, J.-P., and DARBELNET, J. (1958), *Stylistique comparée du français et de l'anglais: méthode de traduction*, Paris.

VIZETELLY, E. (1904), *Émile Zola: Novelist and Reformer*, London.

VOLOSHINOV, V. N. (1973), *Marxism and the Philosophy of Language*, tr. L. Mateyka and I. R. Titunik, New York.

VON FLOTOW, L., ed. (1988), *Ink and Strawberries*, Toronto.

—— (1991), 'Feminist Translation', *TTR*, 4(2): 69–85.

WADENSJÖ, C. (1992), *Interpreting as Interaction: On Dialogue Interpreting in Immigration Hearings and Medical Encounters*, Linköping, Sweden.

WALDRON, R. (1988), 'Trevisa's Original Prefaces on Translation: A Critical Edition', in E. D. Kennedy, R. Waldron, and J. S. Wittig, eds., *Medieval English Studies Presented to George Kane*, Woodbridge, UK, pp. 285–99.

WATSON, N. (1995), 'Censorship and Cultural Change in Late-Medieval England: Vernacular Theology, the Oxford Translation Debate, and Arundel's Constitutions of 1409', *Speculum*, 70: 822–64.

WEDEKIND, F. (1980), *Spring Awakening*, tr. E. Bond, London.

WEISSBORT, D. (1989), *Translating Poetry: The Double Labyrinth*, Iowa City.

WERTENBAKER, T. (1989), *Platform Papers*, Royal National Theatre, London.

WHIBLEY, C. (1909), 'Translators', in A. W. Ward and A. R. Waller, eds., *The Cambridge History of English Literature*, iv, Cambridge.

WILDE, O. (1973), *The Complete Works of Oscar Wilde*, London and Glasgow.

WILLIAMS, M. (1992), 'Ideology, Point of View, and the Translator', *Turjuman*, 1 (1): 75–94.

WOODSWORTH, J. (1994), 'Aladdin in the Enchanted Vaults: The Translation of Poetry', *Textual Studies in Canada. The 'Aux Canadas' Issue: Reading, Writing, and Translation*, 5: 105–15.

—— (1997), 'Doña Marina, Interpreter and Cultural Intermediary', *Circuit*, 53: 22–3.

WRIGHT, J. (1663), *Sales Epigrammatum: Being the Choicest Disticks of Martials Fourteen Books of Epigrams*, London.

—— (1694), *Country Conversations*, London.

YATES, F. A. (1934), *John Florio: The Life of an Italian in Shakespeare's England*, Cambridge.

ZIM, R. (1987), *English Metrical Psalms: Poetry as Praise and Prayer, 1535–1601*, Cambridge.

ZIPES, J. (1988), *The Brothers Grimm*, New York.

ZUBER, O., ed. (1980), *Language of Theatre: Problems in the Translation and Transposition of Drama*, Oxford.

ZUBER, R. (1995), *Les 'Belles Infidèles' et la formation du goût classique*, Paris; 1st edn. 1968.

Part II

Translated Literature

a. African Languages

1. INTRODUCTION

Literature in African languages encompasses both oral and written literary traditions. Much of the writing in African languages remains untranslated into English, and a number of writers have pinned their literary hopes upon writing in African languages rather than in English, notable amongst them Ngũgĩ wa Thiong'o [I.a.6.i]. Translation has been a notable feature, however, in a number of African language literatures, but from English, French, or Russian *into* African languages, following the ubiquitous exemplars of a hundred years of Bible translation. While creative prose writing in many African languages is a by-product of the colonial era, prose and verse writing in certain African languages stems from an earlier period when a number of African societies were fully engaged with the intellectual world of Islam and Arabic-language-based scholarship [see II.b]. Chronicles, poetry, treatises on theology, and government, both in Arabic and in African languages, circulated widely, for example, in the Western Sudan in the 18th and 19th c. Some of this material is available in English translation. In Ethiopia the development of prose-writing in Ge'ez was closely linked with the Ethiopian Christian Church both in hagiographical religious writing and in royal chronicles.

Major surveys of oral literature in Africa have been undertaken by Ruth Finnegan (1970) and more recently by Isidore Okpewho (1992). These studies have offered an overview of the genres of oral literature in the first case and, in the second, issues that have more recently arisen in the study of oral literature. Finnegan's later work (1992) has summarized many of the trends and issues in relation to oral literary studies generally in Africa and

well beyond—the problematic nature of choices about translating into prose or verse, close translation or gist, text alone or text with a description of performance, among other issues [see I.c.5]. Two major bibliographies (Görög-Karady 1992; Scheub 1977) provide an overview of the field.

A focus upon written literary traditions along with their links to parallel oral forms has been provided by two wide-ranging survey volumes. The first, by Albert Gérard, concentrates upon the development of written literature in a number of African societies. The later compendium, edited by B. W. Andrzejewski et al., surveys oral and written literatures widely across the continent, with a greater concentration upon Anglophone Africa than Francophone or Lusophone Africa. This imbalance has been rectified in a book by Alain Ricard which provides a new integrated overview of African literatures, bringing together oral and written literatures, and working across the boundaries which have hitherto divided Francophone Africa from Anglophone Africa and writing in African languages from writing in English or French.

Perhaps the most accessible of African oral literary traditions, and the most easily presentable to a foreign audience, has been the oral narrative. From the beginning of the colonial era, officials and missionaries took an interest in oral narratives. One view was that to govern it was necessary to understand, and that oral narratives provided the necessary key to such cultural understanding. Spare-time activity could readily involve 'collecting tales'. Sometimes, such tales were published as written down, often in sketchy outline by a local scribe, or retold in the 'translator's' own words (see Courlander 1973). The richness and ubiquity of oral narrative traditions in Africa are such that, while the translated narrative may be more easily accessible, the aesthetics and nature of performance within which the narratives are embedded are lost in the bald translation. Elements of performance, of the creativity of the artist within the continuities of the tradition, and the social significance of the narrative in context became the focus of attention in studies which presented the translated texts. For this reason, most English translations of African oral narratives are embedded in extensive commentary and annotation both upon the text and upon the performer(s) of the text.

The presentation of African-language literatures was the purpose behind the founding of a series, the Oxford Library of African Literature, in which a number of studies of oral narrative traditions were published. In this series, and in other volumes, the authors present texts with discussion of the performers, their audiences, and the context. But interests vary from writer to writer. Some focus upon the narratives and a sociological interpretation of their content (Al-Shahi and Moore 1978; Evans-Pritchard 1967; Mbiti 1966; Ross and Walker 1979; Seitel 1980); others are particularly interested in the performance event; others again are interested in the performer and his or her artistic creativity (e.g. Scheub 1975); some veer towards a socipsychological interpretation of the narratives (Cancel 1989; Jackson 1982; Zenani 1992), a popular focus for French scholars also. An issue for each writer is the degree to which the English translation should reflect the style and language of the original. Most translators opt for a simple, straightforward style of English. While there is a risk of appearing stilted and odd, Ruth **Finnegan**, E. E. **Evans-Pritchard**, and John S. **Mbiti** are effective in their versions, with Harold **Scheub**'s rendering of Zenani being particularly vivid and lively.

African epic traditions have been a focus for research and the publication of English translations. Narratives which relate the exploits of a culture hero, often involved in struggles in the world of the supernatural as well as that of mortals, present particular problems of presentation and translation. An oral tradition seldom has a single authoritative version. *Griots* (bards) and narrators each put their own spin, and that of the interests they represent, on the parts of the epic they favour. Equally, any particular rendering may be as fragmentary as any other. The translator is faced with many issues in attempting to figure a way to render a 'text'. In addition to the issue of content, many epic narratives incorporate a wide variety of styles and registers of language; prose narrative may be interspersed with song, chant may break into dance, instrumental music may act as counterpoint to verbal delivery. In most studies, an original transcribed text is paired with a close translation, and the whole is set in extensive textual footnotes and contextual introductions.

Perhaps the best known of the epic traditions is that of Sunjata, the founding figure of the Mande-speaking peoples of West Africa, spread across Senegal, Gambia, Guinea, and Mali. *Griots* across this part of West Africa sing of the exploits of Sunjata and his encounters with his enemy Sumanguru. Gordon **Innes** provides three verse texts from the Gambian tradition, along with other historical narratives of a similar kind, and John W. **Johnson** presents a Malian version with its original text [see II.a.3.iii]. The English translation of a French version by Djibril Tamsir Niane [II.a.3.iii] is a prose recension of the story rather than a translation of an African-language original.

The proliferation of versions in a variety of formats is taking place in other epic traditions. The story of Shaka is retold, for example, by R. M. **Kunene**, and a number of English translations of Thomas Mofolo's written Sesotho version are to be found in D. P. **Kunene** (1981), and in Mofolo (1931). Other epic traditions are rendered in Morris (1964), Huntingford (1965), Biebuyck (1969; 1978), and Hale (1990), which compares a written with an oral recension of the history of the great king of Songhai, Askia Mohammed.

Poetry is perhaps the richest and most varied genre of African oral literature. It is here that the translator is often most taxed in rendering in English the flavour and content of the original. Again, the pattern is in the main for the translation to be embedded in extensive annotation and commentary, although some anthologies have relied more upon the text to stand for itself (Beier 1966; Finnegan 1978; Mapanje and White 1983; Opland 1992). Some of the densest and most crafted of all poetry is to be found in the many traditions of praising. Royal praise traditions have tended to require extensive annotation to allow the reader of the English translation access to the imagery and the cultural references hidden in the texts (Cope et al. 1968; Hodza and Fortune 1979). Yet complexity of imagery and denseness of expression are by no means limited to royal praises. There are other genres of oral poetry, some associated with ritual practices such as the Ifa divination poetry among the Yoruba, or the funeral dirges among the Akan, which are equally complex.   GF

128

TRANSLATIONS AND STUDIES   Al-Shahi, A., and Moore, F. C. T., *Wisdom from the Nile: A Collection of Folkstories*, Oxford, 1978 · Andrzejewski, B. W., Pilaszewicz, S., and Tyloch, W., eds., *Literatures in African Languages: Theoretical Issues and Sample Surveys*, Cambridge, 1985 · Beier, Ulli, *African Poetry*, Cambridge, 1966 · Biebuyck, Daniel P., *The Mwindo Epic from the Banyanga*, Berkeley, Calif., 1969 · *Hero and Chief: Epic Literature of the Banyanga, Zaire Republic*, Berkeley, Calif., 1978 · Cancel, Robert, *Allegorical Speculation in an Oral Society: The Tabwa Narrative Tradition*, Berkeley, Calif., 1989 · Cope, Trevor, Stuart, James, and Malcolm, Daniel, *Izibongo: Zulu Praise-Poems*, Oxford, 1968 · Courlander, Harold, *Tales of Yoruba Gods and Heroes*, New York, 1973 · Evans-Pritchard, E. E., *The Zande Trickster*, Oxford, 1967 · Finnegan, Ruth, *Oral Literature in Africa*, Oxford, 1970 · ed., *The Penguin Book of Oral Poetry*, London, 1978 · *Oral Traditions and the Verbal Arts: A Guide to Research Practices*, London, 1992 · Gérard, Albert, *African Language Literatures*, London, 1981 · Görög-Karady, Veronika, *Bibliographie annotée: littérature orale d'Afrique noire*, Paris, 1992 · Hale, Thomas J., *Scribe, Griot and Novelist: Narrative Interpreters of the Songhay Empire*, Gainesville, Fla., 1990 · Hodza, A. C., and Fortune G., *Shona Praise Poetry*, Oxford, 1979 · Huntingford, G. W., *The Glorious Victories of Amda Seyon, King of Ethiopia*, Oxford, 1965 · Jackson, Michael, *Allegories of the Wilderness: Ethics and Ambiguity in Kuranko Narratives*, Bloomington, Ind., 1982 · Kunene, D. P., tr., *Thomas Mofolo: Chaka*, London, 1981 · Kunene, R. M., *Emperor Shaka the Great*, London, 1979 · Mapanje, Jack, and White, Landeg, eds., *Oral Poetry from Africa: An Anthology*, Harlow, 1983 · Mbiti, John S., *Akamba Stories*, Oxford, 1966 · Mofolo, Thomas, *Chaka, an Historical Romance*, tr. F. H. Dutton, Oxford, 1931 · Morris, H. F., *The Heroic Recitations of the Bahima of Ankole*, Oxford, 1964 · Okpewho, Isidore, *African Oral Literature: Backgrounds, Character and Continuity*, Bloomington, Ind., 1992 · Opland, Jeff, *Words That Circle Words: A Choice of South African Oral Poetry*, Parklands, South Africa, 1992 · Ricard, Alain, *Littératures d'Afrique noire: des langues au livres*, Paris, 1995 · Ross, Mabel H., and Walker, Barbara, *'On Another Day . . .': Tales Told among the Nkundo of Zaire*, Hamden, Conn., 1979 · Scheub, Harold, *The Xhosa Ntsomi*, Oxford, 1975 · *Bibliography of African Oral Narratives, Proverbs, Riddles, Poetry and Song*, Boston, Mass., 1977 · Seitel, Peter, *See So That We May See: Performances and Interpretations of Traditional Tales from Tanzania*, Bloomington, Ind., 1980 · Zenani, Nongenile Masithathu, *The World and the Word: Tales and Observations from the Xhosa Oral Tradition*, Madison, Wis., 1992.

For Additional references, see II.a.2–4.

2. EAST AFRICAN LANGUAGES

Noteworthy English translations of literatures from East Africa commenced in the second half of the 19th c., mainly by missionaries, and primarily from Swahili, the *lingua franca* of the region and now the national language of Tanzania and Kenya. Significant contributions in this field came from two missionaries resident on the Swahili coast: Bishop Edward **Steere** (d. 1882), of the Universities Mission to Central Africa based in Zanzibar, and the Revd W. E. **Taylor** (d. 1927), of the Church Missionary Society based in Mombasa.

i. Tales and Other Prose Steere published in 1870 a collection of tales, 'as told by natives of Zanzibar', containing original oral texts with a page-by-page English translation. It was a pioneering effort, though he himself acknowledges the compilation of 'the late M. Jablonsky . . . for a long time acting French consul in Zanzibar' which, unfortunately, was written down in Polish and not published. Steere's *Swahili Tales* is also notable for its introduction, which discusses the sources, style, and songs contained in the tales.

Some tales are said to have had their provenance in the stories of the *Arabian Nights* [II.b.5], and in Swahili legends; Steere sees similarities also with some 'well-known English tales', though there is no suggestion that the latter were imported into East Africa. The last part of one tale ('Sultan Darai'), for example, closely resembles 'Puss in Boots', while in another ('Sultan Majnun') the hero has a name ('sit-in-the-kitchen') 'as nearly like Cinderella as may be'. In terms of style, Steere distinguishes three types, basing his criteria, it seems, on the number and use of Arabic words in the tales. There is, first, 'the best and purest language of Zanzibar'; followed by a 'dialect spoken by a class less refined and educated, less exact in its style and with more Arabic words'; and, finally, a court dialect whose style 'is more Arabic in its forms and vocabulary than the rest, and is characteristically represented by a strict translation of an Arab story'. While the translation does not reflect this division, it is noticeable that a number of both Arabic and Swahili words are retained in the English translation. Examples include greeting phrases, *sabalkheri / masalkheri* ('good morning/ evening'); names of currencies, *dirham* and *deenar*; and words whose cultural content is not easily translatable: *kanzu* (a gown worn by Muslim men), *hodi* (a formulaic request for permission to enter a house or place), *kitoweo* (a relish, usually fish or meat, served with the main dish), *joho* (a ceremonial robe).

Steere remarks on the inclusion of songs in the tales which the audience is required to sing along with the narrator, and he comments on the presence of non-Swahili, but Bantu, words in the songs, a fact indicative of the influence of the mainland on Zanzibar in this genre. *Swahili Tales* also contains a poem of the legendary Swahili hero Fumo Liongo, and the beginning of the story of the prophet Job.

Equally significant is the Revd Taylor's *African Aphorisms*, subtitled *or Saws from Swahili-land*, published in 1891. Like Steere, Taylor acquired deep knowledge of the people, their language and customs through his friendship with them. His relationship with two Swahili scholars—Mwalimu Sikujua, an accomplished poet, and Hemedi Muhammad, a man with a 'quick ear' for distinguishing sounds—was particularly fruitful. This enabled Taylor to collect what he himself refers to as 'a large collection of the best of Swahili poetry, ancient and modern', among which were the poems of the celebrated Mombasa poet Muyaka bin Mwinyi Haji (d. 1840). Another outcome of this relationship was the volume of proverbs containing over 600 Swahili proverbs, with an appendix of grammatical notes. Each proverb is translated, contextualized, and, where appropriate, compared to others, either Swahili or English. Footnotes elaborate on the meaning of significant words or historical allusions. It is thus not surprising that a scholar of Swahili earlier this century, Alice Werner, remarked in an obituary on Taylor that the volume 'should never have been allowed to go out of print, both for the sake of the proverbs themselves and the notes, which besides elucidating many obsure points in Bantu grammar are full of interest from other points of view' (see Frankl and Omar 1993: 40).

While the *Aphorisms* were being published, another volume was in the making which also came to acquire an interesting place in Swahili scholarship, especially in the understanding of the Swahili world and identity. In the 1890s Carl Velten, a German linguist and administrator in the then Tanganyika (now Tanzania), asked a group of Africans to write down the customs and traditions of their people. They did so in Swahili, using the Arabic script. The overall coordinator was Mtoro bin Mwinyi Bakari, a scholar who is said to have been 'a master of Swahili prose' (King, in Bakari 1981: p. viii). Velten compiled the material, transliterated it into the roman script, translated it into German, and published it in Göttingen in 1903. A selection was translated into English by Lyndon **Harries** (1965), and a full translation from the Swahili original was published in 1981 as *The Customs of the Swahili People*. It was a posthumous publication in the name of J. W. T. **Allen** as editor

and translator; a number of his colleagues contributed a preface, notes, and appendices in his memory. One of them, Noel King, places in perspective the content and contribution of the book, stating that the volume revealed to the European rulers a human dimension of the people they were governing, their culture, and viable ways of life other than their own. King elaborates:

... the *Desturi* was one of the lone voices to tell them that African and other civilizations ... had to be taken into account if historians were to capture something of the greatness and tragedy of the human race. In a way, it [the book] did for the academic world what Africa through Picasso and others did for the world of art or what jazz did for the world of music. (Bakari 1981: p. xi)

A bold claim, perhaps, but it is one which is indicative of the significance of Bakari's work.

Other works of this period which could be considered as precursors to Swahili prose were the chronicles of the various city-states of the East African coast. These are accounts of local rulers and dynasties, narrated from the perspectives of the writers. Some parts have been rendered into English (**Freeman-Grenville** 1962; **Werner** 1915); their literary aspects have been discussed by Rollins (1983), who points out that the narration also, at times, carries verses of poetry appropriate to the events.

ii. Poetry Swahili poetry has received considerable attention from Western scholars, making it by far the most accessible genre in English. Some volumes contain extensive texts and translations of both classical and modern poems: Knappert on religious as well as secular poetry (1971; 1972; 1979); a survey of some major classical poems and their forms by Harries (1962); Allen (1971) on the form *-utendi*—utilized mainly (though not exclusively) for epic narratives; Abdulaziz (1979) on the poems of Muyaka Haji mentioned earlier; and, with a more specialized focus, Shariff (1983) on dialogic poems; Topan (1974) on the emergence of the free verse in Swahili poetry; and Biersteker and Shariff (1995) on war poems.

As an illustration of the genre one can take a religious classical poem composed in the early 19th c. by Sayyid Abdalla Nassir (d. 1820) on the glory and then decline of Pate, a city on an island off the coast of northern Kenya. Nassir called the poem *al-Inkishafi*, a title with the basic meaning of 'the uncovering' but which has been translated by W. **Hichens** (1939) as 'The Soul's Awakening' and by James de Vere **Allen** (1977) as 'Catechism of a Soul'. The ruins of Pate evoke in the poet deep reflections on the transitoriness of life, thus connecting the impoverishment of the city to issues of morality. Although this was, and still is, a common theme in Swahili Islamic poetry, its treatment by Nassir has resulted in a work of art which W. E. Taylor commended as 'a great, if not the greatest religious classic of the race' (in his introduction to Stigand 1915: 11).

Three major translations exist of the text: the two by Allen and Hichens just mentioned, and, the earliest, by Taylor (given in Stigand 1915). Each represents an interpretation of the poem by its generation: a 'classicist' one by Taylor; a formal scholastic one by Hichens; and a culturally insightful one by Allen, with an introduction by a Swahili academic, Ali Mazrui.

iii. **Drama** Drama, in its Western sense, is of relatively recent importation to East Africa. Although Swahili playwrights have written many plays over these three decades on a wide variety of themes and issues, only a handful have actually been translated into English (though the traffic in the other direction is quite common, particularly in relation to Ngũgĩ's works). Of these, the most renowned is *Kinjeketile* (1969) by Ebrahim Hussein of Tanzania, which also has the distinction of having been the first full-length play written in Swahili. It depicts the rebellion of the tribes in southern Tanganyika against German oppression. A prophet named Kinjeketile is possessed by a spirit, Hongo, who gives him medicine to make the people impervious to German guns and bullets. The medicine is water—*maji* in Swahili; hence the name of the rising: the Maji Maji rebellion (1905–7). Although the existence of Kinjeketile is historically documented, Hussein makes it clear in his introduction to the play that the hero 'is not an historical evocation of the real man' but 'a creature of the imagination'. All the same, the main events of the play follow closely the oral narratives documented by historians. In this lies also the novelty of Hussein's approach, that of writing a play based on documents of oral history. When the Swahili version of the play was first performed in Dar es Salaam in 1970, it was perceived as an artistic enactment of the first nationalistic fight for freedom.

Several features emerge from a comparison of the original version of the play with its translation. As the play has been rendered into English by the playwright himself (then a university student at Dar es Salaam), the translation reflects what he himself deems essential (or indeed possible) to convey to an English-speaking audience. The introduction to the English version, for example, is briefer: an elaborate explanation in Swahili on the production of the play (inclusive of a diagram) is shortened to a 'note' of two sentences in English; does Hussein assume that an English-speaking producer has no need of detailed direction in this regard? An explanation on the use of standard Swahili and dialect variations is omitted as the issue is not relevant in the translated version. Although the impact of such code-switching is lost in English, Hussein feels obliged to replace it by other means to indicate Kinjeketile's state of being possessed by Hongo. In the Swahili original, Kinjeketile spoke dialectical Swahili in his normal state and standard Swahili when possessed; in the English translation, his normal (prose) speech is replaced by verse when possessed.

Finally, mention must be made of works on oral literature of specific peoples in East Africa which contain English translations of the texts; among them are volumes on the Maasai (Kipury 1983), the Gikuyu (Kabira and Mutahi 1988), the Kamba, the Kalenjin (Chesaina 1991), the Luo (Onyango-Ogutu and Roscoe 1974), the Embu (Mwaniki 1971), and the Swahili (Topan 1972). **FMT**

Translations and Studies Abdulaziz, M. H., *Muyaka: 19th Century Swahili Popular Poetry*, Nairobi, 1979 · Allen, J. W. T., ed. and tr., *Tendi: Six Examples of a Swahili Classical Verse Form*, New York, 1971 · Bakari, Mtoro bin Mwinyi, *The Customs of the Swahili People*, ed. and tr. J. W. T. Allen, Berkeley, 1981 · Biersteker, Ann, and Shariff, Ibrahim Noor, eds., *Mashairi ya vita vya Kuduhu. War poetry in Kiswahili exchanged at the time of the Battle of Kuduhu*, East Lansing, Mich., 1995 · Chesaina, C., *Oral Literature of the Kalenjin*, Nairobi, 1991 · Frankl, P. J. L., and Omar, Yahya, 'W. E. Taylor (1856–1927): Swahili Scholar Extraordinary', *South African Journal of African Languages*, 13 (1993), Supplement 2, 37–41 · Freeman-Grenville, G. S. P., *The East African Coast: Select Documents from the First to the Earlier Nineteenth Century*, Oxford, 1962 · Harries, Lyndon, *Swahili Poetry*, Oxford, 1962 · ed., *Swahili Prose Texts: A Selection from the Material Collected by Carl Velten from 1893 to 1896*, London, 1965 · Hussein, Ebrahim, *Kinjeketile*, Dar es Salaam, 1970 · Kabira, Wanjiku, and Mutahi, Karega wa, *Gikuyu Oral Literature*, Nairobi, 1988 · Kipury, Naomi, *Oral Literature of the Maasai*, Nairobi, 1983 · Knappert, Jan, *Swahili Islamic Poetry*, 3 vols., Leiden, 1971 · *A Choice of Flowers: An Anthology of Swahili Love Poetry*, London, 1972 · *Four Centuries of Swahili Verse*, Nairobi, 1979 · Mwaniki, H. S. K., *Ndai, Ng'ano na Nthimo iria Ukua wa Aembu: Traditional Riddles, Proverbs and Stories of the Embu People*. Nairobi, 1971 · Nasir, Sayyid Abdalla, *al-Inkishafi: A Soul's Awakening*, tr. W. Hichens, London, 1939; rep. Nairobi, 1972 · *al-Inkishafi: Catechism of a Soul*, tr. James de Vere Allen, Nairobi, 1977 · Onyango-Ogutu, B., and Roscoe, Adrian, *Keep My Words*, Nairobi, 1974 · Rollins, Jack D., *A History of Swahili Prose*, Leiden, 1983 · Shariff, Ibrahim N., 'The Function of Dialogue Poetry in

Swahili Society', D.Ed. dissertation, Rutgers University, 1983 · Steere, E., *Swahili Tales as Told by Natives of Zanzibar*, London, 1870 · Stigand, C. H., *A Grammar of Dialectic Change in the Kiswahili Language*, Cambridge, 1915 · Taylor, W. E., *African Aphorisms or Saws from Swahili-land*, London, 1891; rep. 1924 · Topan, Farouk M., 'Oral Literature in a Ritual Setting: The Role of Songs in a Spirit Mediumship Cult of Mombasa, Kenya', Ph.D. dissertation, University of London, 1972 · 'Modern Swahili Poetry', *Bulletin of the School of African and Oriental Studies*, 37, 1 (1974), 175–87 · Werner, Alice, 'A Swahili History of Pate', *Journal of African Society*, 14 (1915), 148–61, 278–97, 392–413.

3. WEST AFRICAN LANGUAGES

i. Written Texts While English translations of African oral literary traditions are numerous, there are few English translations of creative writing in African languages. A translation appeared in 1968 by Wole **Soyinka** of a novel written in Yoruba in 1938 by D. O. Fagunwa. The richly evocative translation was entitled *The Forest of a Thousand Daemons*. Fagunwa's Yoruba novels were a major influence upon the development of later Yoruba writing. The first part of the story follows the hero, Akara-Ogun, on a journey of encounters with fantastical beings in the forest. Each encounter is a challenge where the hero is faced with defeat. The second part of the book brings a group of travellers through a similar series of trials and adventures, accompanied by Akara-Ogun, until they finally return with a message to their town of origin. The story is replete with conundrums, puzzles, and unexplained symbols. There are few other translations of African-language texts extant, while original writing in English has thrived in West Africa. Ricard (1995) reports English translations of a Twi novel published in Accra entitled *Bediako, the Adventurer* by Victor **Amarteifio** (1965) with lengthy digressions in the English version absent from the Twi original, and a translation from Ewe of a playscript entitled *The Fifth Landing Stage* by Kwesi **Fiawoo** (1943). Both these works were translated by their authors.

ii. Oral Poetry and Song Within Yoruba oral literature many genres have been the object of scholarly study. Many of these studies contain English translations of representative texts. Yoruba hunters' songs, *ijala*, form the subject of a study by S. A. **Babalola**, which provides some fifty songs in Yoruba and in English translation praising great hunters and the animals they hunt, with substantial commentary upon style, performance, and content. The boundaries between genres are fluid, and the act of praising, so integral to *ijala*, is also reflected in the utterance of *oriki*, praise, with its own characteristic use of language (Barber 1991). A further study which presents English translations of substantial Yoruba literary texts is that of Wande **Abimbola** (1975; 1976), in which he presents the texts associated with the Yoruba divination system, Ifa.

Categories of oral literature associated with other ritual contexts are also available in English translation through the work of J. K. **Nketia**, whose readable and vivid translations of Ghanaian Akan dirges are set alongside the original texts and a detailed musicological discussion and musical transcription. Kofi **Awoonor**'s study of Ghanaian Ewe poetry provides English translations of poems by the oral poet, Apalo, and two others, but without the Ewe originals. Awoonor is a poet who renders Ewe poetry with great skill and creativity in English, as in the following short text:

I am at home to reveal matters to you.
Dunyo asks, who doesn't understand?
Let the chorus come here.
The trader who goes to the market
Must come home. So he said
I shall go and see my homeland.
I go to see my people.
And he was encircled.
If I rise I linger indoors
Not knowing death has removed all my kinsmen.
He has locked the doors and hid the keys.
He built a smithy-shop for me.
The followers of Adzima, I was asleep
When song called me.
Dunyo says I am only singing.
I will linger upon this song
Till it drives me into sorrow.

A concentration upon performance characteristics, and in particular the musical accompaniment, is mirrored in a study by Dan Ben-Amos (1975) of storytelling in Benin, Nigeria, which provides close literal translations of the original texts.

iii. Oral Narratives Oral narrative traditions in West Africa have been extensively researched and, to a lesser extent, made available in English translation. One of the most substantial collections of narratives was made at the beginning of the 20th c. by Frank Edgar working in Hausa-speaking areas of northern Nigeria. His three volumes of Hausa texts were translated into smoothly readable English by A. N. **Skinner** (1969). Graham **Furniss**'s overview of Hausa literature (1996) provides a number of English translations of poetry, song and genres of popular culture along with summaries of some creative prose-writing in Hausa. The translations are accompanied by the Hausa originals and are embedded within commentary and discussion of the social and cultural context within which such texts are produced. H. A. S. **Johnston** (1966) presents a selection of translated Hausa stories.

Many studies of oral narratives provide extensive discussion of the process of storytelling, the artistry involved, and the creative process, in addition to the presentation of translated texts. Ruth **Finnegan** divides her study of Limba story-telling from Sierra Leone into a first part that discusses the tradition, followed by 100 stories engagingly translated in a vivid and clear English style (1967). Marion **Kilson**'s study of Mende tales (1976), also from Sierra Leone, focuses upon the structural characteristics of tales about the two most common protagonists in trickster stories in Mende society, royal antelope and spider. The English translations of again about 100 tales reflect the short sentences of the Mende originals, creating something of a staccato effect. The attempt to represent the performance effect of the oral original sometimes leads to English translations with 'stage instructions' and representations of the audience's involvement. D. J. **Cosentino** presents such a study in relation to another body of Mende tales (1982).

The epic of Sunjata has perhaps received more attention from translators and commentators than any other part of the oral literature of West Africa. The epic is known widely across the Mande-speaking world, particularly Senegal, Gambia, Guinea, and Mali. A significant rendering of the epic in metropolitan languages was the retelling by Djibril Tamsir **Niane** in French (1960) of a version heard in Siguiri in Guinea. An English translation appeared in 1965, clearly not a transcription and translation but a retelling in Niane's own words of what he had heard. The English version is fluent and readable and captures something of the oral presentational style. The two other major English versions of the epic were of a more scholarly nature (there are other French versions). Gordon **Innes** published in 1974 the transcriptions and English translations of three recorded versions from the Gambia. Accompanied by extensive annotation and introduction, the translation follows closely the original Mandinka. A similar approach with extensive folklorist annotation and comment came from a later publication by John W. **Johnson** (1986), presenting close translations of texts that had been recorded in Mali from a *griot* named Fa-Digi Sisoko.

No oral recording of the epic tells exactly the same story, and each text presents not only a particular slant on the narrative but also different episodes, plots and sub-plots. The epic tells of the life and exploits of the eponymous hero in a time long past; born a cripple, he manages as a youth to demonstrate prodigious strength and rise up and walk. Forced into exile by jealous brothers, he eventually returns to rescue his country, Manding, from the oppressive rule of the king, Sumanguru. With supernatural forces at his command, Sumanguru is a formidable enemy, and after repeated battles of great armies and countervailing magical forces, the downfall of Sumanguru is engineered through the finding of his secret by Sunjata's sister, who has charmed her way into his private quarters. After the defeat of Sumanguru the epic goes on to speak of the expansion of Manding under Sunjata until it becomes a great empire of the Western Sudan.

J. P. **Clark**'s book (1977) on another epic, the Ozidi saga from south-western Nigeria, derives from his collection of narratives in his language, Ijo, relating to a narrative that is performed during a week of festival in which the stories are interwoven with song, dance-dramas, music, and eating and drinking. In order to capture the nature of the original, Clark first used his talents as a poet and playwright to prepare a stage play and film of the saga. His later volume retains the representation of audience participation in their questions and exclamations along with the English translation of the prose narrative. The eponymous hero swears to exact revenge on those who have killed his father, and the episodes that make up the saga are fighting tales in which Ozidi kills the assassins. He goes on to defeat a number of further threatening monsters, including the Smallpox King, armed with diseases, and the Scrotum King, a seven-headed monster, all of whom are armed with supernatural powers. On his side, Ozidi is aided by Oreame, a witch-grandmother, who provides the countervailing powers to defeat these forces.

A new edition of two Sunjata texts translated by Innes has been published by Penguin (Suso and Kanute 1999), and much work has been done, and is still under way, in Francophone and Anglophone Africa on other epic traditions (see e.g. Bird et al. 1974; Innes 1976; Jablow 1971; Goody 1972; Hale 1990).

For discussion of some of the available anthologies, bibliographies and surveys of African language literatures and works which address theoretical issues, see I.c.5; II.a.1.

GF

TRANSLATIONS AND STUDIES   Abimbola, Wande, *Sixteen Great Poems of Ifa*, Paris, 1975 · *Ifa: An Exposition of the Ifa Literary Corpus*, Ibadan, 1976 · Amarteifio, Victor, *Bediako, the Adventurer*, Accra, 1965 · Awoonor, Kofi, *Guardians of the Sacred Word: Ewe Poetry*, New York, 1974 · Babalola, S. A., *The Content and Form of Yoruba Ijala*, Oxford, 1966 · Barber, Karin, *I Could Speak until Tomorrow: Oriki, Women and the Past in a Yoruba Town*, Edinburgh, 1991 · Ben-Amos, D., *Sweet Words: Story-Telling Events in Benin*, Philadelphia, 1975 · Bird, Charles et al., eds., *The Songs of Seydou Camara I: Kambili*, Bloomington, 1974 · Clark, J. P., *The Ozidi Saga*, Ibadan, 1977 · Cosentino, D. J., *Defiant Maids and Stubborn Farmers: Tradition and Invention in Mende Story Performance*, Cambridge, 1982 · Fagunwa, D. O., *The Forest of a Thousand Daemons*, tr. Wole Soyinka, London, 1968 · Fiawoo, Kwasi F., *The Fifth Landing Stage*, London, 1943 · Finnegan, Ruth, *Limba Stories and Story-Telling*, Oxford, 1967 · Furniss, Graham, *Poetry, Prose and Popular Culture in Hausa*, Edinburgh, 1996 · Goody, J., *The Myth of the Bagre*, Oxford, 1972 · Hale, Thomas J., *Scribe, Griot and Novelist: Narrative Interpreters of the Songhay Empire*, Gainesville, Fla., 1990 · Innes, Gordon, *Sunjata: Three Mandinka Versions*, London, 1974 · *Kaabu and Fulaadu: Historical Narratives of the Gambian Mandinka*, London, 1976 · Jablow, Alta, *Gassire's Lute: A West African Epic*, New York, 1971 · Johnson, John W., *The Epic of Son-Jara: A West African Tradition*, Bloomington, Ind., 1986 · Johnston, H. A. S., *A Selection of Hausa Stories*, Oxford, 1966 · Kilson, Marion, *Royal Antelope and Spider: West African Mende Tales*, Cambridge, Mass., 1976 · Niane, D. T., *Sundiata: an Epic of Old Mali*, tr. G. D. Pickett, London, 1965 · Nketia, J. H., *Funeral Dirges of the Akan People*, Achimota, Ghana, 1955 · Ricard, Alain, *Littératures d'Afrique noire: des langues aux livres*, Paris, 1995 · Skinner, A. N., *Hausa Tales and Traditions: An English Translation of 'Tatsuniyoyi na Hausa', originally compiled by Frank Edgar*, vol. i, London, 1969; vols. ii and iii, Madison, Wis., 1977 · Suso, B., and Kanute, B., *Sunjata*, London, 1999.

4. LANGUAGES OF SOUTH AFRICA

South Africa was very well served by collectors of folklore active in the 19th c., largely missionaries, persons associated with mission education, or colonial administrators. Publications by W. H. I. **Bleek** (on Zulu, Khoi and San), Henry **Callaway** (Zulu), Édouard **Jacottet** (Southern Sotho), James **Stuart** (Zulu), and George McCall **Theal** (Xhosa) remain pioneering classics in the field. Southern Sotho poems, tales, and riddles had been included in French works by the missionary Eugène **Casalis** published in 1841 and 1859, and translated into English in 1861, but Bleek (1827–75) led the way in producing works devoted to South African folk literature. Working first among the Zulu from 1853 and later on Khoisan languages in Cape Town, he assembled material for a series of books under his own name and in collaboration with his sister-in-law, Lucy **Lloyd**, and his daughter, Dorothea Bleek. The manuscript of his work on Zulu is dated 1857, 'thirty chapters of Zulu traditions and customs in the original language with an English translation and notes'; his anthology of Nama tales first appeared in 1864, based on unpublished material collected and translated into German by the missionary G. Krönlein; and his work with San informants later in the same decade led to collections of tales and songs by Lloyd and Bleek (1911) and Dorothea Bleek (1923). Recently Stephen **Watson** has produced a volume of new translations of songs from the Bleek collection (1991).

Callaway (1817–90) produced in 1868 a pioneering collection of Zulu tales taken down from dictation. He offered it to the reader as a volume of 'Zulu Native Literature,—if we may be allowed to apply such a term to that which has hitherto been stored only in the mind and imparted to others orally'. The book contained copiously annotated texts and translations, including a number of variants of tales. This was followed by an acclaimed collection of Zulu testimonies on religion, including many mythical narratives, heroic legends, and accounts of customs and traditions. Jacottet and Theal both produced early collections of folk-tales. Theal (1837–1919) published separately some of the texts of Xhosa folk-tales he assembled, but his major volume of 1886 presented 21 tales in translation only. It included a chapter on 'Proverbs and Figurative Expressions'. 'It is with a view of letting the people we have chosen to call Kaffirs describe themselves in their own words, that these stories have been collected and printed,' he wrote in his Preface. Jacottet (1858–1920) published two volumes of Sotho tales, the first of which appeared in translation in 1908. Stuart (1868–1942) collected Zulu folk-tales, but alone among these early folklorists he assembled a major corpus of 19th-c. praise poetry. Stuart's 258 Zulu poems, taken down from dictation, were all translated by Daniel **Malcolm**; Trevor Cope selected 26 of these for his annotated edition of 1968. Malcolm's translation of Stuart's collection of Zulu proverbs appeared in the early 1950s.

Native collectors of folklore were very active from early on. Much of the material they assembled was published in early newspapers and books. The vast majority of this vernacular material is not available in English; an exception is the collection by Sol **Plaatje** of 732 Tswana proverbs, which was issued in 1916. Plaatje did not collect these from informants, but produced them from memory while staying in England; a further 400 proverbs he subsequently collected from oral sources remain unpublished (Willan 1984: 333–5).

These early translations of folklore were produced for a variety of motives. Native authors like Plaatje frequently expressed a desire 'to save from oblivion' the lore they recorded, but Willan also ascribes to Plaatje a political motive: his collection of proverbs was 'a statement of the cultural worth and integrity of his native language' (Willan 1984: 192). The missionaries and civil servants were often involved in the burgeoning international study of folklore that led to the formation of a South African Folk-Lore Society in 1879, only one year after its parent society was formed in London, with Lucy Lloyd as secretary. An understanding of native folklore could also aid the process of conversion: as Callaway put it, 'We cannot reach any people without knowing their minds and mode of thought; we cannot know these without a thorough knowledge of their language.'

Throughout the 20th c. a steady stream of African folklore in English has appeared, most eminently in four of the volumes of the Oxford Library of African Literature that presented South African texts with facing translations: three dealt with praise poetry, Schapera (1965) on Tswana, Cope (1968) on Zulu, and Damane and Sanders (1974) on Southern Sotho, one, Scheub (1975) on Xhosa, treated folk-tales. In addition to those works already mentioned, most of the major oral genres and most of the languages are now represented in translation through works such as Baumbach and Marivate (Tsonga, 1973), Manqondo (Xhosa, 1978), and Zenani (Xhosa, 1992) on tales; Gunner and Gwala (Zulu, 1991) and Sitole (Xhosa, 1996) on poetry; Blacking (Venda, 1967), Tracey (Zulu, 1948), and Weinberg (Zulu, 1984) on songs; Dunning (Zulu, 1946) and Nyembezi (Zulu, 1954) on proverbs; and Msebenzi (Zulu, 1938) on historical legend with poetry. Finally, translations based on collections in the field include Van Warmelo (1930) on Ndebele tales, poems, and proverbs, and the general anthologies of Tracey (1967) on tales and Opland (1992) on oral poetry. Unrepresented in this list are translations of speeches, a dominant genre in oral tradition, and specimens of Northern Sotho lore.

The picture is far more sparse and sporadic when we consider written literature, despite the fact that Xhosa literature appears in print from 1837 in news-papers and 1906 in books, and Southern Sotho literature from 1863 in newspapers and from 1907 in books. There has been no systematic translation of works of written literature from any of the vernacular languages, most of the classics remain untranslated, and chance or missionary content seems to play as much of a role in determining suitability for translation as literary or historical significance (perhaps because the histories of the literatures still await proper definition). Indeed, only one author, Thomas Mofolo, is represented by more than one work, and only Mofolo again has had any work translated more than once: Mofolo's *Moeti oa Bochabela* (1907), the first Sotho novel, is available in H. **Ashton**'s translation as *The Traveller of the East*, and his historical novel about the Zulu king Shaka is available in the translations of F. H. **Dutton** and Daniel **Kunene**. The first Zulu novel, John Dube's historical *Insila ka Tshaka* (1930), can be found in J. **Boxwell**'s translation as *Jeqe the Bodyservant of King Tshaka*; the first Venda novel, the symbolic *Mafangambiti* (1956), written by the prolific T. N. Maumela, appeared in translation in 1985; and one of the earliest Xhosa novels, Enoch Guma's pious *U-Nomalizo* (1918), which its first reader called 'revolutionary in its treatment of romantic love in a culture where marriages are family arrangements', is available in a translation by S. J. **Wallis**. Perhaps the greatest Xhosa novel, A. C. Jordan's *Ingqumbo Yeminyanya* (1940, The Wrath of the Ancestors), has been translated into both English (by Jordan's widow) and Afrikaans.

Florence **Friedman** has produced translations of poems by the greatest Zulu poet, B. W. Vilakazi; one of the greatest Xhosa poets, J. J. R. **Jolobe**, translated his own prize-winning historical narrative, *UThuthula*, in 1938, to which he later added his translation of three more of his poems to form *Poems of an African*. Poems by various Xhosa poets, including the title poem by Jolobe, are assembled in Kavanagh and Qangule's *The Making of a Servant and Other Poems* (1971), but there are no other translations of published vernacular poetry, and none at all of any vernacular dramas, short stories, histories, or ethnographies. Strikingly absent from this list are any translations from the work of perhaps the greatest figure in South African oral or written literature, the Xhosa oral poet and author S. E. K. Mqhayi (1875–1945). However, the obscure academic publication *Mqhayi in Translation* contains W. G. **Bennie**'s abridged translation of Mqhayi's autobiography *UMqhayi waseNtabozuko* as well as John Knox **Bokwe**'s translation of two chapters of Mqhayi's classic novel *Ityala lamawele* (1914, The Case of the Twins) prepared in 1919.

Translations or versions of South African folklore are readily accessible, but written literature in the vernacular languages, neglected by scholars and translators alike, still attracts scant respect. [For Afrikaans writing see the following entry.]

JO

TRANSLATIONS AND STUDIES Baumbach, E. J. M., and Marivate, C. T. D., *Swihitani swa Xironga: Xironga Folk-tales*, Pretoria, 1973 · Blacking, John, *Venda Children's Songs: A Study in Ethnomusicological Analysis*, Johannesburg, 1967 · Bleek, Dorothea F., *The Mantis and His Friends: Bushman Folklore*, Cape Town, 1923 · Bleek, W. H. I. *Reynard the Fox in South Africa; or, Hottentot Fables and Tales, Chiefly Translated from Original Manuscripts in the Library of His Excellency Sir George Grey, K.C.B.*, London, 1864 · *Zulu Legends*, ed. J. A. Engelbrecht, Pretoria, 1952 · Callaway, Henry, *Nursery Tales, Traditions, and Histories of the Zulus, in Their Own Words, with a Translation into English, and Notes*, Springvale, Pietermaritzburg/London, 1868; rep. 1970 · *Izinyanga Zokubala; or, Divination, as Existing Among the AmaZulu, in Their Own Words*, Springvale, 1871; repr. *The Religious System of the AmaZulu*, London, 1884 and Cape Town, 1970 · Casalis, Eugène, *The Basutos, or Twenty-Three Years in South Africa*, London, 1861; repr. Cape Town, 1965 · Cope, Trevor, *Izibongo: Zulu Praise Poems*, Oxford, 1968 · Damane, M., and Sanders, P. B., *Lithoko: Sotho Praise-Poems*, Oxford, 1974 · Dube, John, *Jeqe the Bodyservant of King Tshaka (Insila ka Tshaka)*, tr. J. Boxwell, Lovedale, SA, 1951 · Dunning, R. G., *Two Hundred and Sixty-Four Zulu Proverbs, Idioms, etc., and the Cries of Thirty-Seven Birds*, Durban, 1946(?) · Guma, Enoch S., *Nomalizo or 'The Things of This Life Are Sheer Vanity'*, tr. S. J. Wallis, London, 1928 · Gunner, Liz, and Gwala, Mafika, *Musho! Zulu Popular Praises*, Johannesburg, 1991 · Jacottet, E., *The Treasury of Basuto Lore*, London, 1908 · Jolobe, J. J. R., *Thuthula: A Poem Translated from the Xhosa by the Author*, London, 1938 · *Poems of an African*, Lovedale, SA, 1946 · Jordan, A. C., *The Wrath of the Ancestors*, tr. Priscilla P. Jordan, Lovedale, SA, 1980 · Kavanagh, R., and Qangule, Z. S., *The Making of a Servant and Other Poems*, Johannesburg, 1971 · Lloyd, Lucy, and Bleek, W. H. I., *Specimens of Bushman Folklore*, London, 1911 · Malcolm, D., and Stuart, J., *Zulu Proverbs*, Pietermaritzburg, 1950(?) · [Manqondo, Mncinane,] *Iintsomi ZasemaMpondweni: Folk-tales from Mpondoland*, ed. and tr. J. V. Cantrell, Pretoria, 1978 · Maumela, T. N., *Mafangambiti: The Story of a Bull*, tr. Diana McCutcheon and Norman Tshikovha, Johannesburg, 1985 · Mofolo, Thomas, *Chaka: An Historical Romance*, tr. F. H. Dutton, Oxford, 1931 [rev. edn. 1949] · *The Traveller of the East*, tr. H. Ashton, London, 1934 · *Chaka the Zulu*, tr. F. H. Dutton [rev. edn. London, 1949] · *Chaka*, tr. Daniel P. Kunene, London, 1981 · Mqhayi, S. E. K., *Mqhayi in Translation*, ed. Patricia E. Scott, Grahamstown, 1976 · Msebenzi, *History of Matiwane and the amaNgwane Tribe as Told by Msebenzi to His Kinsman Albert Hlongwane*, tr. N. J. van Warmelo, Pretoria, 1938 · Nyembezi, C. L. Sibusiso, *Zulu Proverbs*, Johannesburg, 1954 · Opland, Jeff, *Words That Circle Words: A Choice of South African Oral Poetry*, Johannesburg, 1992 · Plaatje, S. T., *Sechuana Proverbs with Literal Translations and Their European Equivalents*, London, 1916 · Schapera, I., *Praise-Poems of Tswana Chiefs*, Oxford, 1965 · Scheub, H., *The Xhosa 'Ntsomi'*, Oxford, 1975 · Sitole, Bongani, *Qhiwu-u-u-la!! Return to the Fold: A Collection of Bongani Sitole's Xhosa Oral Poetry*, ed. and tr. Russell H. Kaschula and Mandlakayise C. Matyumza, Pretoria, 1996 · Theal, George McCall, *Kaffir Folklore: A Selection from the Traditional Tales Current among the People Living on the Eastern Border of the Cape Colony*, London, 1886; repr. Westport, Conn., 1970 · Tracey, Hugh, *'Lalela Zulu': 100 Zulu Lyrics*, Johannesburg, 1948 · *The Lion on the Path and Other African Stories*, London, 1967 · Van Warmelo, N. J., *Transvaal Ndebele Texts*, Pretoria, 1930 · Vilakazi, Benedict Wallet, *Zulu Horizons*, tr. Florence Louie Friedman, Johannesburg, 1973 · Watson, Stephen, *Return of the Moon: Versions from the/Xam*, Cape Town, 1991 · Weinberg, Pessa, *Hlabelela Mntwanami: Sing, My Child! Zulu Children's Songs*, Johannesburg, 1984 · Willan, Brian, *Sol Plaatje: A Biography*, Johannesburg, 1984 · Zenani, Nongenile Masithathu, *The World and the Word: Tales and Observations from the Xhosa Oral Tradition*, tr. Harold Scheub, Madison, Wis., 1992.

5. AFRIKAANS

Afrikaans, one of the world's youngest languages, developed from Dutch and a variety of other languages spoken at the southernmost tip of Africa in the 17th c. Its development as a literary language is intertwined with its speakers' struggles for political emancipation from former Dutch and British colonizers. Once Afrikaans gained official recognition alongside English in 1925, it became the language of the 'oppressor', the ruling National Party which took over political power in 1948. Thus started the deliberate development of one minority language at the expense of the other indigenous South African languages—a situation that was only rectified when the National Party was defeated by the African National Congress in 1994.

In a relatively short time Afrikaans writers joined the ranks of the world's best in all literary genres. The most translated Afrikaans poet is Breyten Breytenbach; while authors such as Etienne Leroux, Hennie Aucamp, Dalene Matthee, Elsa Joubert, Jeanne Goosen, and Mark Behr have won international acclaim through translation. Representative translations are listed in the bibliography. Of all the Afrikaans authors, André P. Brink is clearly the most renowned (Toerien 1993). In many respects Brink is a controversial figure, especially in South Africa, where he is the man many conservative Afrikaners love to hate: the man who put Afrikaans literature on the international literary map, but who at the same time exposed many of the injustices perpetrated by his own people against black South Africans; the man who popularized in his novels the struggles of the oppressed to liberate themselves, but who simultaneously found himself caught in the crossfire between black and white extremists. It has been said that Brink's portrayal in his novels of erotic themes across the colour-line (forbidden by one of the cornerstones of apartheid, the Immorality Act), as well as of violence and racial prejudice, has been a deliberate tactic to capture the attention of the outside world and so ensure personal gain.

However, although his literary-political motives may be suspect, his contributions to literature and translation cannot be ignored, for Brink's work spans more than 30 years of literary production. Between 1962 and 1991, he produced no less than 10 best-sellers which he himself translated into English. The English translations were used as mediating source texts for translations into other languages. Brink was awarded the Central News Agency literary prize twice—for both Afrikaans and English works—and he also received the prestigious Martin Luther King Memorial Prize in 1980.

The reason for Brink's success is twofold. First, he was one of the most influential Afrikaans writers to emerge during the cultural renewal of the 1960s, an Afrikaans movement not confined to Afrikaans literature but which influenced the whole social fabric of South Africa, challenging many social taboos and prejudices and assailing the literary, moral, religious, and political conventions of the Afrikaner. He admits that he chose to write in Afrikaans because he believed that by means of his writing he could join the struggle to liberate blacks from oppression by whites, as well as fellow Afrikaners from the constricting ideology of apartheid (Brink 1983).

Secondly, his novel Kennis van die Aand (1973, Looking on Darkness) was the first Afrikaans novel ever to be banned (in 1975) by the previous government's Publication and Recreational Activities Act of 1963. Although this meant that his voice was silenced in his own country and in his own language, a disaster for any minority writer, it secured his career as a politically committed novelist and translator. Within one year of the banning, Kennis van die Aand had been translated into six languages, and another novel, 'n Oomblik in die Wind (1975, An

Instant in the Wind), had appeared. Three years later Gerugte van Reen (1978, Rumours of Rain), as well as 'n Droë Wit Seisoen (1979, A Dry White Season), appeared.

A multitude of critics have discussed Brink's original work, but hardly any reference can be found to his translations (Kruger 1999). According to Brink himself (Brink 1983: 113–14), translating his novels has involved 'rethinking' and 're-feeling [them] in the framework of a new language ... Afrikaans, like French, ... is much more at ease with superlatives and emotions. In English the threshold of overstatement is reached much more readily; valid emotionalism in Afrikaans soon becomes unbearable in English.' Working on the translation of Kennis van die Aand influenced writing 'n Oomblik in die Wind to such an extent that some of the preliminary passages of the latter were actually written first in English. Although a first draft then appeared in Afrikaans, he used his notes as a guide to rework the book into English. In the process some episodes contained in the Afrikaans draft fell away while some new ones emerged spontaneously. He then worked on both texts interchangeably before completing the novel in English. From that text a final Afrikaans version was prepared, 'each language impos[ing] its own demands on the final shape of the work'.

It is obvious from Brink's translations that his main aim was accessibility and the accommodation of his target readership: all the English translations can be regarded as texts in their own right. Both An Instant in the Wind and A Chain of Voices portray 18th-c. Cape society and politics, and wherever appropriate, Brink explains foreign concepts and adds information, e.g. as regards place names and geographical location. However, one notes that, as self-translator, Brink was able to take liberties with his texts that outsiders would not have been allowed.

In Kennis van die Aand the main character and narrator, Josef Malan, a 'coloured' man, tells his story in Standard Afrikaans. In order to accomplish the multi-perspectivity that has become Brink's trademark, sections occur in which other 'coloured' characters speak 'Kaapse Afrikaans', a dialect spoken by 'coloured' people in the Cape Town area. In the translation, Looking on Darkness, Brink clearly tried to create an equivalent dialect in English for these characters, a contrived 'Capey English' which is functionally adequate but falls far short of the original.

The candid use of foul and vulgar language (by 'coloured' characters in Kennis van die Aand in particular), and the portrayal of sex and violence which contributed shock value to the Afrikaans originals, also somehow seem tempered in English translation. In general, however, all of Brink's translations are rendered in fluent English, and his unconventional style guarantees the target reader not only gripping reading but also an insight into the psyche of the Afrikaner and the political situation in South Africa during the apartheid era.   AK

AUCAMP, HENNIE   Ferguson, I., *House Visits: A Collection of Short Stories*, Cape Town, 1983.

BEHR, MARK   Behr, Mark, *The Smell of Apples*, London, 1995.

BREYTENBACH, BREYTEN   Hirson, D., *In Africa Even the Flies Are Happy: Selected Poems 1964–1977*, London, 1978.

BRINK, ANDRÉ P.   (All titles are self-translated, and have been published in popular editions such as Penguin.) *Looking on Darkness*, London, 1974 · *An Instant in the Wind*, London, 1976 · *Rumours of Rain*, London, 1978 · *A Dry White Season*, London, 1979 · *A Chain of Voices*, London, 1982.

GOOSEN, JEANNE   Brink, André P., *Not All of Us*, Strand, 1992.

JOUBERT, ELSA   Joubert, Elsa, *Poppie Nongena*, New York, 1985.

LEROUX, ETIENNE   Eglington, C., *Seven Days at the Silbersteins*, London, 1964.

MATTHEE, DALENE   Matthee, Dalene, *Circles in a Forest*, London, 1984.

STOCKENSTROM, WILNA   Coetzee, J. M., *The Expedition to the Baobab Tree*, London, 1983.

SEE ALSO   Brink, A. P., *Mapmakers: Writing in a State of Siege*, London, 1983 · Kruger, A., *Southern African Bibliography of Translation, Interpreting, Lexicography and Terminology*, rev. edn., Pretoria, 1999 · Toerien, B. J., *Afrikaans Literature in Translation: A Bibliography*, Cape Town, 1993.

b. Arabic

1. INTRODUCTION

The history of literary translation from Arabic into English is divisible into three distinct but overlapping phases, corresponding approximately with the evolution of the geo-political relationship of the English-speaking and Arabic-speaking worlds. The first phase lasted from the middle of the 17th to the end of the 18th c. During the first part of this period, the Ottoman empire was still perceived as a major military and religious threat to Christian western Europe: the Ottomans had occupied the Balkans and even twice laid siege to Vienna, in 1529 and 1683. It was in this context that Arabic, as the religious language of Islam, first became established as a subject of study in European universities, and that the earliest English translations of the Koran into English were completed.

Towards the end of this period—and certainly by the time of the Napoleonic occupation of Egypt in 1798—the Ottoman threat had receded, and we see the beginnings of the second phase of the relationship, when serious European academic interest in Arabic medieval literature of all kinds began. This interest, which arose as Europe began to assume an important and eventually dominant economic and political role in the Middle East and North Africa, manifested itself as much in the scholarly editing of manuscripts as in their translation, but the two activities tended to go hand in hand throughout the 19th and early 20th c., and have continued to do so up to the present day.

Whilst this academic tradition has produced many fine translations of classical works (many of them, it must be said, esoteric), it has been swamped in recent years by the output of the third phase, which began after World War II and coincided with the coming to political independence of the Arab world. This period has seen the translation into English of an abundance of modern Arabic literature in all genres. Unlike the productions of the second phase, the translations come without any academic apparatus and are not part of any grand literary-historical scheme: they stand on their own as individual examples of foreign literature in translation. Until the mid-1970s most of this work was published in specialist series, and much of the credit for putting it on the map goes to Denys **Johnson-Davies**, general editor of Heinemann's Arab Authors series. By the 1990s, however, Arabic literature in English translation had ceased to be a purely minority interest. It is now common for mainstream publishers to publish it, particularly since the fillip given to the field by the award in 1988 of the Nobel Prize for Literature to the elder statesman of Egyptian letters, Naguib Mahfouz [II.b.7].

There is no introductory work which surveys and exemplifies the full range of Arabic literature in English translation. However, introductory works on Arab literary history often contain much translation along the way. The best general introduction to the classical period is still the now rather dated but frequently reprinted *A Literary History of the Arabs* by R. A. **Nicholson**. This work presents a general literary history from about 500 CE (the date of the earliest surviving Arabic poetry) to the turn of the 20th c., though literature after the Napoleonic occupation of Egypt is dealt with only cursorily. Almost every page is enlivened by examples of Nicholson's own, often spirited translations of poetry and prose.

As to survey works which deal with the modern period, three deserve mention. The first survey in

English, J. A. **Haywood**'s *Modern Arabic Literature 1800–1970*, contains 12 translated extracts of various genres, as well as much translation of poetry within the text. Although in literary-historical terms the work is superficial, the translations do give a flavour of the range of modern Arabic literature. The more substantial works of M. M. **Badawi**, *A Short History of Modern Arabic Literature*, and P. **Cachia**, *An Overview of Modern Arabic Literature*, as well as treating some of the knotty problems of Arabic–English translation (e.g. in Cachia's book the use of colloquial Arabic in literary works), also contain exhaustive bibliographies of anthologies and single-author works in English translation.

The translations, and translation histories of some of the most celebrated works of classical Arabic literature, the *Mu'allaqāt* (Suspended Odes), the *Muqaddimah* (Prolegomena) and the *Alf Layla wa Layla* (Thousand and One Nights) are dealt with in separate articles below. But a large number of other works from the classical period, which belong to the second phase of Arabic–English literary translation, are also readily available, and a few of the most accessible will be mentioned here. They have been selected for their availability and inherent interest for the general reader, and to demonstrate the range of the 'golden age' of Arabic literature.

One of the most celebrated of the works of the medieval Arab geographers is the *Riḥla* (Journey) of the Moroccan Ibn Baṭṭūṭa (1304–69). Ibn Baṭṭūṭa set out in 1325 on a pilgrimage to Mecca. It was a long journey: over the next 25 years he reached every corner of what Muslims of his time regarded as the civilized world: Arabia, the Levant, Persia, East Africa, Ceylon, India, China, and the East Indies. The account of his journeys, whilst of no great literary moment, is a fascinating description of 14th-c. civil society, and a compendium of information on the peoples, curiosities, and sights he encountered. The *Riḥla* has been translated into English in four volumes by H. A. R. **Gibb**, but is also available in a single-volume abridged version.

Another, very different testament to the times in which its author lived is the *Kitāb al-I'tibār* (lit. 'book from which lessons may be drawn') of Usāmah Ibn Munqidh (1095–1188), translated into English by P. K. **Hitti**. Written in a matter-of-fact, first-person style, this book is a Syrian officer's memoirs of battles with the Crusaders, with lengthy and occasionally fantastical digressions on such matters as 'the Frankish character' (including their 'lack of jealousy in sexual affairs'(!)), 'strange stories of holy men', and 'adventures with lions and other wild animals'. The colloquial style of the Arabic text bears witness to the Syrian dialect of its author, and Hitti makes a good job of translating it. As an account of one short period of the Crusades seen from the Arab side, this work is a salutary antidote to the routine western portrayal of the Muslim defenders of the Holy Land as murderous, merciless savages.

Quite different in tone and purpose again is the Andalusian Ibn Ḥazm's treatise on courtly love *Ṭawq al-Ḥamāma*, which has been translated into both English (twice) and French. Ibn Ḥazm (994–1064) was by training a philosopher and theologian, but this did not inhibit him from writing at length, and apparently from first-hand experience, on such delicate matters as the nature, signs, and types of love, love letters, the union of lovers, and the reasons why lovers part, the whole classified with a philosopher's rigour into 30 or more separate chapters, and leavened with plentiful examples of the author's own poetry. The most stylish English translation, recently reprinted, is A. J. **Arberry**'s *The Ring of the Dove*.

The Iraqi polymath nicknamed al-Jāḥiẓ (776–869) ('the pop-eyed'), a massive figure of early medieval Arabic literature, wrote prolifically on every conceivable philosophical and social topic of his day, and has a place in Arabic letters somewhat analogous to that of Francis Bacon in English literature. Although much of his output remains untranslated, a few of his less technical, epistolary writings are available in English, notably the short *Kitāb al-Qiyān*, or *Epistle on Singing Girls* (translated by A. F. L. **Beeston**), an amusing satirical study of the manners, morals, and wiles of the coquettes of the Baghdad court.

Sīrat 'Antar (lit. 'the life of Antar') is a popular story-cycle, comparable to the *Thousand and One Nights*. The story is based around the figure of the half-African pre-Islamic Arabian poet 'Antara ibn Shaddād, transmogrified into an epic narrative about a medieval African slave who champions Islam and its Prophet and, by bravery and force of arms, becomes ruler of the world. But the ferocious scenes of combat are balanced by a unifying and healing strand in the narrative: Ham, Shem, and Japheth, the begetters of the human race, rediscover their primeval brotherhood and are reunited by a magic sword. A portion of the *Sīrat 'Antar*—the original is of huge length—which deals with Antar's adventures in Yemen, Africa, and Spain has been translated by H. T. **Norris**.

Finally, mention should be made of one of the most remarkable works in medieval, and indeed the whole of, Arabic literature, the *Risālat Ḥayy ibn*

Yaqẓān fī Asrār al-Ḥikma al-Mashriqiyya (lit. 'the epistle of Alive son of Awake concerning the secrets of oriental wisdom') by Ibn Ṭufayl (born near Granada, d. 1185), and most recently translated into English by L. E. **Goodman**. Because of its philosophical content, this is perhaps one of the most accessible works of Arabic literature for the western reader. On a deserted Indian island a child is miraculously born with no mother and father. His name is Alive son of Awake, and he is adopted and suckled by a gazelle. By observing and reflecting on his surroundings, he grows and prospers, and discovers by the exercise of pure reason the secrets of the physical and metaphysical universes. Secluding himself in a cave, he succeeds in separating his intellect from his surroundings by contemplating God, and uniting that intellect with Him. At this point Asāl, a devout man from a neighbouring inhabited island, arrives and teaches Alive language. Asāl is astonished to discover that the philosophical system Alive has developed, once he has the words to express it, transcends his own religion, and indeed all others. Asāl takes him to the neighbouring inhabited island, ruled over by King Salamān, and

he is given the task of spreading the word of his transcendent philosophy. But he fails. Pure truth is unsuited to the vulgar tastes of the populace; they seem only capable of receiving it in the form of the revealed religions. The two philosophers abandon their project and return to their desert island to live the superior and divine life to which only true philosophers can aspire.

There have been many interpretations of this story. The most plausible, in the intellectual context in which its author lived, is that it seeks to identify the goal of rationalist philosophy as 'pure' religion. The purpose seems to be to show the supreme capabilities of human intelligence, which can sense and come to know the divine, as well as the merely material, without the need for any exterior motivating force. From this point of view, the story anticipates an idea which St Thomas Aquinas put forward a hundred years later, namely that the perfection of human nature requires that the active intellect should not be external to man. This remarkable work thus foreshadows a religious-philosophical debate which, in medieval Europe, was to rage for two centuries.												CH

GENERAL WORKS   Badawi, Muhammad M., *A Short History of Modern Arabic Literature*, Oxford, 1993 · Cachia, Pierre, *An Overview of Modern Arabic Literature*, Edinburgh, 1990 · Haywood, John A., *Modern Arabic Literature 1800–1970*, London, 1971 · Nicholson, Reynold A., *A Literary History of the Arabs*, Cambridge, 1907 [frequent reps.].

TRANSLATIONS OF INDIVIDUAL WORKS   Arberry, Arthur J., *The Ring of the Dove: A Treatise on the Art and Practice of Love*, London, 1953 · Beeston, Alfred F. L., *The Epistle on Singing Girls of Jāḥiẓ*, Warminster, 1980 · Gibb, Hamilton A. R., *Ibn Baṭṭūṭa: Travels in Asia and Africa*, London, 1929; frequently rep. · Goodman, Lenn E., *Ibn Ṭufayl's Ḥayy ibn Yaqẓān: a Philosophical Tale*, New York, 1972, 2nd edn., 1983 · Hitti, Philip K., *An Arab-Syrian Gentleman and Warrior in the Period of the Crusades: Memoirs of Usāmah Ibn-Munqidh*, London, 1929; rep. 1987 · Norris, Harry T., *The Adventures of 'Antar*, Warminster, 1980.

2. THE KORAN

i. Introductory   The Koran (*Qur'ān*) is the Muslim scripture, and contains the divine revelations recited in Arabic by Islam's Prophet, Muhammad (*c.*570–632 CE), preserved in fixed, written form. The revelation of the Koran occurred over a 22-year period, beginning *c.*610 in the west Arabian city of Mecca, continuing in the city of Medina after Muhammad's emigration there in 622, and ending shortly before his death some ten years later. The Koran is the central document of the Islamic faith for all Muslims worldwide (approximately 1 billion people), whatever their native language.

Muslim tradition has it that Muhammad, a scion of the noble Meccan house of Quraysh, was illiterate. The transmission of the Koran during his lifetime and for two decades after his death was largely oral; its 'collection', from 'scraps of parchment and

leather, tablets of stone, ribs of palm branches, camels' shoulder-blades and ribs, pieces of board, and the breasts of men', and the establishment of a canonical written text, was a lengthy process, begun under the third Caliph 'Uthmān ibn 'Affān (644–56). The elimination of variant readings and the establishment of the codex used by the vast majority of Muslims today was a gradual process which, it is now thought, may have taken about three centuries.

Muslims believe that the Koran is the final expression of God's will and purpose for man. Its central message is that human salvation can only be achieved through man's absolute subservience to Him. Through a combination of quasi-ecstatic exhortation, overt prescription, and exemplificatory and allegorical example, the Koran lays down the principles and rules of human conduct. These prescriptions eventually provided the fundament of Islamic law (*sharīʿa*). The text is divided into 114 individually named *sūrah*s ('chapters'), e.g. *sūrat al-baqara* 'the Chapter of the Cow', each of which is divided into numbered *āyāt* ('verses'). Except for the short prayer-like opening, the ordering of the *sūrah*s is traditionally in roughly descending order of length, not chronological order of revelation. Although the text of the Koran is not poetry according to the Arabian definition of that term (and Muhammad specifically stated that he was not a poet), the syntax and phrasal patterning of many of the early *sūrah*s have a poetic 'feel' to them, and the verses of all *sūrah*s, early or late, are (sometimes, it must be admitted, rather loosely) end-rhymed.

The language and style of the Koran are *sui generis* within Arabic literature, and are considered by Muslims to be the literal words of God, and therefore inimitable (the doctrine of *iʿjāz*). Distinct literary styles, however, can be clearly distinguished in a revelation which extended over 22 years. The early Meccan *sūrah*s (about one-third of the total) often begin with a cryptic-sounding oath, and have short verses similarly reminiscent of oracular utterance. The language is impassioned and sweeping, and the vision of what lies in store for believers and unbelievers vivid and apocalyptic. The later Meccan *sūrah*s, in which the language is more reflective and serene, have a pronounced narrative, allegorical content. Figures and stories familiar from the Jewish Torah and the Christian gospels (e.g. Noah, Moses and Pharoah, Lot, Joseph and his brothers, Zacharias, Mary and Jesus) are adduced to point up the message that Muhammad's revelation stands at the end of an ancient monotheistic tradition, which it both concludes and subsumes. The Medinan *sūrah*s, which are the latest, the longest, and the most prosaic, contain the detailed rules for the personal conduct and social organization of the by now established Muslim community, mixed with much polemic against its enemies.

Exegesis (*tafsīr*) of the Koran was from the early period of Islam an important branch of learning, but the possibility of translations into other languages was at first not even considered—there was simply no need. At several points the Koran itself states that it is in a 'clear Arabic tongue'; evidently its intended audience was just those who spoke that language. It was only after Islam spread outside Arabia that the problem of the comprehension of the text by non-Arabic-speaking Muslims arose. In any case, there was the doctrinal obstacle to translation alluded to above: the text of the Koran is

considered by Muslims to be a 'miracle' (*muʿjiza*), the literal word of God, revealed through his Messenger, and *ipso facto* orthodox opinion has it that translation by any mere human into another language would be blasphemous [see I.c.3.iii]. This difficulty was eventually circumvented by the device of describing translation of the Koran as translation of its 'meanings' (Ar. *maʿānī*), i.e. by treating the translation as a species of commentary or interpretation. Hence the title of one of the most popular English versions, by the Muslim convert Marmaduke **Pickthall**, is 'The Meaning of the Glorious Koran' (which, in one recent bilingual edition, even contains a reproduction of a letter in Arabic from the Islamic Research Academy of al-Azhar University, Cairo, certifying that the 'translation of the meanings' is 'sound'). Nowadays Muslim translators often bear witness to the doctrinal significance of the Arabic text by arranging it interlinearly or side by side in columns with their translation.

ii. Translation History The Koran has been translated into most of the languages of Europe and Asia, and many African languages. The first translation into a European language was by an Englishman, **Robert of Ketton** (*fl.* 1143) (Robertus Ketenensis, also known as Robertus Retinensis, 'Robert of Reading'), who made a translation into Latin in Spain in 1143, first printed in Basel in 1543. The first English-language translation, 'The Alcoran of Mahomet', a retranslation of an earlier French version, was done by Alexander **Ross** (1591–1654), theologian, schoolmaster, and royal chaplain, and appeared in 1649. The first English translation done directly from the Arabic was by George **Sale** (?1697–1736), and published in London in 1734. This version, which has gone through many editions, was reprinted as recently as 1973. It remained the only English translation by a non-Muslim until a new translation by the Revd J. M. **Rodwell** (1808–1900) appeared in 1861. New translations into English by non-Muslims were subsequently published by Edward Henry **Palmer** (1840–82), and in the 20th c. by Richard **Bell,** Arthur John **Arberry**, and Thomas Ballantine **Irving**.

The frank purpose of early Koran translators was to refute Muslim religious arguments. The subtitle of Ross's translation, 'newly Englished, for all that desire to look into the Turkish vanities', gives an indication of this attitude, which went hand in hand with the translation of Christian religious texts into Arabic for missionary purposes. The adversarial stance towards Islam continued through the 18th and 19th c.: in 1734 Sale, in the preface to his translation, opines that 'how criminal soever Muhammad may have been in imposing a false religion on mankind, the praises due to his real virtues ought not to be denied him'; and as late as the mid-19th c., Rodwell's introduction echoes this patronizing tone. Beginning with the work of the Cambridge Arabist Palmer, a less religiously partisan, more academically rigorous approach develops, and we begin to read discussions of the linguistic and cultural difficulties involved in Koranic translation for a non-Muslim English-speaking audience.

To date, there have been more than 30 translations of the Koran into English by Muslims, the first appearing in the 1860s, perhaps the most enduring and popular of which is by 'Abdullah **Yusuf** '**Ali**. Almost all of these translations were done by Muslims from the Indian subcontinent, where the need for English translations was pressing. The major exceptions are two: the English Muslim Pickthall's translation already referred to, published in 1930, and that by the Iraqi scholar N. J. **Dawood** for Penguin Classics. Pickthall's translation is one of the most widely available and popular. Like Pickthall's, Dawood's version, first published in 1956, did not include the Arabic text, but editions with the Arabic text on facing pages are now available for both translations.

iii. Translations and Translation Issues Several of the English translators have felt free to rearrange the *surahs* in ways other than the traditional one. Rodwell orders the material according to what can be gleaned from the Muslim sources about when particular *surahs* were revealed, and makes use of the occasional datable historical allusions which occur in some of the later *surahs*. Bell attempts a more radical reworking which, whilst preserving the traditional order, indicates where discontinuities in the text, and other internal textual evidence (e.g. irregularities of rhyme), suggest that the original redactors may have cobbled together fragmentary revelations which date from different periods to form unities which never existed historically— resulting in what he describes as the 'dreary welter of the Qur'ān so often deplored by Western writers' (and what Arberry calls 'its [apparently] random nature' and 'inconsequence'). In early editions of his translation, Dawood followed a roughly chronological order, and his main reason for rejecting the traditional one was again that, from the reader's point of view, it lacks continuity and coherence—a view with which it is difficult to disagree. Editions of Dawood since 1990, however, when the bilingual edition was first published, have reverted to the traditional sequence. The reason for the change seems to have been that orthodox Muslim sentiment would not accept an Arabic text, even in bilingual format, which did not follow the time-honoured sequence.

The style of the English used by translators has varied with what was felt, at the time they did their translations, to be rhetorically appropriate and functionally equivalent. Compare, for example, the following three versions of two of the opening verses of *surah* 12, *surat yūsuf* ('the Chapter of Joseph'), one of the relatively straightforward Meccan 'narrative' *surahs*. The original layout of the translations has been preserved.

Rodwell (1861):

. . . When Joseph said to his father, 'O my father! verily I beheld eleven stars and the sun and the moon—beheld them make obeisance to me!'

He said, 'O my son! tell not thy vision to thy brethren, lest they plot a plot against thee: for Satan is the manifest foe of man.'

Arberry (1955 edn.):

When Joseph said to his father, 'Father, I saw
eleven stars, and the sun and the moon; I saw them
    bowing down before me.'
He said, 'O my son, relate not they vision
to thy brothers, lest they devise against thee
some guile. Surely Satan is to man
    a manifest enemy.'

Dawood (1995 edn.):

Joseph said to his father: 'Father, I dreamt of eleven stars and the sun and the moon; I saw them prostrate themselves before me.'

'My son', he replied, 'say nothing of this dream to your brothers, lest they plot evil against you: Satan is the sworn enemy of man.'

Rodwell's is a fairly literal rendering, and, unsurprisingly given his clerical training and the period he lived in, the style is a pastiche of the English of the King James Bible [see II.c.2], full of vocabulary and grammatical structures which were obsolescent if not already obsolete in the written English of the mid-19th c. (e.g. 'verily', 'beheld', 'brethren', 'make obeisance', 'tell not thy vision' in the short extract above). Arberry's version, done a century later, has something of the same flavour, even though he specifically states in his introduction that he has tried 'to compose clear and unmannered English, avoiding the "Biblical" style favoured by some of my predecessors'. The unusual layout of Arberry's translation is meant to convey 'some faint impression . . . of [the Koran's] dramatic impact and most moving beauty'. Dawood's version, on the other hand, is written in idiomatic contemporary English, in early editions without verse numbers, and is laid out in the manner of a modern prose work. In justification, he states in his introduction that 'in adhering to a rigidly literal rendering of Arabic idioms, previous translations have, in my opinion, practically failed to convey both the meaning and the rhetorical grandeur of the original'.

As has been pointed out, however, the Koran encompasses several distinct Arabic styles, and there are *sūrah*s in which the more literal if rather mannered 'poetic' approach of Arberry succeeds better than the plain prose of Dawood. Compare their renderings of verses 5–9 of *sūrah* 55, *sūrat al-raḥmān* ('The Chapter of the Benificent'), an early Meccan *sūrah*:

Arberry:

> The sun and moon to a reckoning
> and the stars and the trees bow themselves;
> and heaven—He raised it up and set
>   the Balance.
>   (Transgress not in the Balance,
> and weigh with justice, and skimp not in the Balance.)

Dawood (1956 edn.):

> The sun and the moon pursue their ordered course. The plants and the trees bow down in adoration. He raised the heaven on high and set the balance of all things, that you might not transgress it. Give just weight and full measure.

Here Dawood's version, clear though its meaning is, ignores certain structural features of the Arabic—notably the thrice repeated word *mīzān*, 'balance', which is predicated of both the organization of the universe and human action. The translation dilutes the semantic coherence of the Arabic, and the final sentence, 'Give just weight . . .', seems to come as a banal and unnecessary afterthought to what has gone before. Arberry's translation, though somewhat stilted, follows more closely the repetitive phrasing of the original, and brings out more clearly the point that human actions are just as subject to the immutable, eternal forces of divine 'balance' as the non-rational universe. More recent editions of Dawood have substituted 'that balance' for 'it' in the third sentence, perhaps in an attempt to reflect the importance of the word *mīzān* in the Arabic.

Both Arberry's and Dawood's translations, different in approach though they are, are bold attempts at a re-creation of the text in English. By and large, other recent English translations, especially those by Muslims who perhaps feel they have to remain as faithful to the original as possible, have tended to espouse 'literal' translation, by which is meant the reproduction in English of the phrasing and syntax of the Arabic, however unnatural-sounding—at times incomprehensible—the result.

At a trivial level, this simply produces a kind of distracting, un-English foreigner-speak, as when Joseph ('the Chapter of Joseph', verse 33) says that if he is seduced by women's wiles, he will become (Pickthall's translation) 'of the foolish'; and if his shirt is torn from behind (verse 27), it will be clear that his attempted seducer is lying and that he is 'of the truthful'.

More seriously, this kind of doctrinally inspired literalism can on occasion produce a translation in which the words are English, but the typically loose concatenation of the Arabic clauses, if reproduced in the translation, tends to obscure the meaning of whole passages. Compare the following literal (Pickthall), and liberal (Dawood) translations of verse 24 of 'the Chapter of Jonah'. In the Arabic, a comparative structure is used to make a simile: the life of human beings is similar to that of crops in the sense that they are just as subject to divine intervention—a variation on the familiar 'man proposes, God disposes' theme.

Pickthall:

> The similitude of the life of the world is only as water which We send down from the sky, then the earth's growth of that which men and cattle eat mingleth with it till, when the earth hath taken on her ornaments and is embellished, and her people deem that they are masters of her, Our commandment cometh by night or by day and We make it as reaped corn as if it had not flourished yesterday. Thus do We expound the revelations for people who reflect.

Dawood (1995 edn.):

> This present life is like the rich garment with which the earth adorns itself when watered by the rain We send down from the sky. Crops, sustaining man and beast, grow luxuriantly: but as its tenants begin to think themselves its masters, down comes Our scourge upon it, by night or in broad day, laying it waste as though it did not blossom but yesterday. Thus do We make plain Our revelations to thoughtful men.

It was pointed out earlier that Koranic translations are considered by Muslims to be interpretations of the 'meanings' of the text. This has left open to Muslim translators the possibility of producing translations which reflect a particular sectarian or other bias, and which can on occasion stray very far from the literal meaning of the Arabic. This possibility has been thoroughly exploited in some widely available translations, though one example will have to suffice here. The main Shi'ite sect, which regards the fourth Caliph 'Ali, the Prophet's cousin and brother-in-law, together with his line of descent, as the only legitimate successors of the Prophet and (therefore) leaders of the Muslim community, routinely back-projects this article of faith onto its translations. Compare, for example, (*a*) the orthodox Pickthall's translation with (*b*) that of the Shi'ite S. V. Mir **Ahmad Ali** of chapter 42, verse 23, in which the reward of those who believe and do good works is being described (present writer's italics; material not present in the Arabic and supplied by the translator is placed in brackets):

(*a*) 'Say (O Muhammad, unto mankind): I ask of you no fee therefor, save lovingkindness among *kinsfolk* . . .'
(*b*) 'Say (O Muhammad): "I do not ask of you any recompense for it (the toils of prophetship), save love of *(my) relatives* . . ." '

Thus Pickthall interprets the verse as meaning that God is instructing Muhammad to tell mankind that the price of dwelling eternally in paradise is treating one's family well, which, contextually, seems the intended meaning; but the Shi'ite version has Muhammad saying that the reward for the toils of his prophet-hood is that mankind must love members of *his* (Muhammad's) family—that is, by implication, 'Ali and his line of descent. Many similar examples could be cited of sectarian, rationalist, or modernist bias in Muslim English translations.

The question of which English translation of the Koran is the 'best' is unanswerable. What should the criteria be? Of the modern translations which have stood the test of time, Arberry's is at one end of a cline in which reproducing, however dimly, the rhythmic and sonorous qualities of the original is seen as paramount; Dawood's is at the opposite end, in which simplicity and transparency of meaning are all. But for all translators there are many verses whose meaning is ambiguous or simply obscure. Many Arabs would contend that Arberry set himself a hopeless task, in that so much of the majesty and aesthetic appeal of Koranic Arabic resides in its sound: the Koran was after all not written as a book, but revealed as an oral recitation (the meaning of the word *Qur'ān*) to a real audience, a circumstance to which the frequently vocative, second person style bears witness. Like calligraphy in the visible world, Koranic cantillation in the audible one became one of the great Islamic arts. In that sense, the orthodox Muslim view seems correct: the Koran—at least in regard to one of its most fundamental aspects, the language-dependent nature of its performance—is finally inimitable, and untranslatable.   CH

TRANSLATIONS   *The Koran, commonly called The Alcoran of Mohammed, Translated into English Immediately from the Original Arabic; with Explanatory Notes, taken from the most Approved Commentators. To which is Prefixed A Preliminary Discourse*, tr. George Sale, London, 1734 [rep. 12 times between 1764 and 1844; rep. 1882–6 with a new critical apparatus by E. M. Wherry (numerous reps., up to 1973); rep. with an introduction by Revd G. Margoliouth, Everyman 1909, rep. 20 times to 1963] · *The Koran: Translated from the Arabic, the Sūrahs arranged in Chronological Order, with Notes and an Index*, tr. J. M. Rodwell, London, 1861 [2nd edn. 1876; 3rd edn. 1909, often rep. to 1963; Everyman, 1992] · *The Qur'ān*, tr. E. H. Palmer, 2 vols., Oxford, 1880 [2nd edn. 1900, often rep. to 1965] · *The Meaning of the Glorious Koran: An Explanatory Translation*, tr. M. M. Pickthall, London, 1930 [frequent reps., London and New York; Everyman, 1992] · *The Holy Qur'ān: an Interpretation in English, with the Original Arabic Text in Parallel Columns, a Running Rhythmic Commentary in English, and Full Explanatory Notes*, tr. 'Allama 'Abdullah Yusuf 'Ali, Lahore, 1934–7 [frequent reps.] · *The Qur'ān*, tr. Richard Bell, 2 vols., Edinburgh, 1937–9 · *The Koran Interpreted*, tr. A. J. Arberry, 2 vols., London, 1955 [frequent reps., including World's Classics] · *The Koran*, tr. N. J. Dawood, Harmondsworth, 1956 [Penguin; several revised edns, with parallel text from 1990] · *The Holy Qur'ān, with English Translation of the Arabic Text and Commentary According to the Version of the Holy Ahlul-Bait. With Special Notes from Ayatullah Agha Haji Mirza Pooya Yadzi on the Philosophic Aspects of Some Verses*, tr. S. V. Mir Ahmad Ali, Karachi, 1964 [frequent reps.] · *The Noble Qur'ān*, tr. T. B. Irving, Vermont/Leicester, 1992.

SEE ALSO   anon., 'Bibliography of Translations of the *Qur'ān* into European Languages', in A. F. L. Beeston et al., eds., *Arabic Literature to the End of the Umayyad Period*, Cambridge, 1983, pp. 502–20 · anon., 'Al-Ḳur'ān', in H. A. R. Gibb et al. eds., *Encyclopedia of Islam*, new edn., Leiden, 1986, v. 400–32.

3. THE *MU'ALLAQĀT*

The *Mu'allaqāt* are a collection of ancient Arabian odes, generally reckoned to be seven in number, although some commentators extend their number to nine or ten. The odes of five poets—Imru' al-Qays, Ṭarafa, Zuhayr, Labīd, and 'Amr—appear in all the commentators' collections, but there is no

unanimity on the number or even the identity of the others. None of the odes can be dated with precision, but they are all thought to have been composed in Arabia before Islam (i.e. during the first half of the 6th c. CE or earlier), although they were only collected together some two to three centuries later. They are the earliest surviving examples of ancient Arabic poetry, although many aspects of their structure suggest that they do not stand at the beginning of a tradition, but rather represent a tradition in full flower. But this tradition was an oral one, and no prototypes or precursors have come down to us.

The *Muʿallaqāt* were among the first Arabic literary works to attract the attention of European orientalists in the 18th and 19th c. Caussin de Perceval published a translation into French in 1847–8, and the great Arabist Theodor Nöldecke translated five of the odes into German in 1899–1901. The first English translation appeared earlier, in 1783, by William 'Asiatic' **Jones** (1746–94) [II.l.2.i]. Though now obsolete, and in places inaccurate, in its time this translation was a huge step forward in the study of ancient Arabian poetry. C. J. **Lyall** (1845–1920) published in 1894 an edition and commentary on the poems which is still a landmark of Arabic philological scholarship, but he never completed a full English translation; a translation of some excerpts was published in his *Translations of Ancient Arabian Poetry* in 1885. The next complete English translation was by Capt. F. E. **Johnson** of the Royal Artillery, assisted by a certain Shaikh Faizullahbhai of Bombay, and published in 1894. In the words of a later translator, A. J. **Arberry**, 'it adheres firmly to the tradition of the schoolboy's Latin crib and is understandably, and deliberately, without the least literary value'. A worthier attempt was that of those well-known Edwardian partisans of Arab political causes Lady Anne **Blunt** (1837–1917) and Wilfrid Scawen **Blunt** (1840–1922). They conceived of their work as a continuation of the free, self-consciously 'literary' approach espoused by Edward FitzGerald, translator of the *Rubāʿiyyāt* ('Quatrains') of the Persian poet Omar Khayyâm, which had proved enormously popular with the Victorian reading public [II.q.2.iv]. Alas, the Blunts' translation failed to ignite the same public enthusiasm; unlike FitzGerald's translation, which went through countless reprints and became a cultural icon in its own right, the Blunts' book has never been reprinted. In the modern period, translations of individual odes have frequently appeared in students' introductory works (e.g. Alan **Jones**'s *Early Arabic Poetry*, vol. ii) or in monographs (e.g. Suzanne Pinkney **Stetkevych**'s *The Mute Immortals Speak*), but the only complete recent translation of the *Muʿallaqāt* is that of Arberry, *The Seven Odes*. Since this is the only English translation which is now easily available and which is aimed at the general reader, some consideration of its approach and merits will be briefly attempted here.

The first point which needs to be made is that the *Muʿallaqāt* are ferociously difficult to translate. Their vocabulary is archaic, and as far removed from modern literary Arabic as Chaucer's English is from that of today. There are many verses whose meaning is obscure even to Arab literary experts. The style of this ancient poetry is *sui generis* too, succinctly characterized by Arberry as exhibiting 'pregnant brevity and epigrammatic terseness'. But the problem for the translator is not merely philological and stylistic; the ancient world of deserted Bedouin encampments which the poems typically evoke, the desert flora and fauna which they describe so meticulously, and not least the arcane tribal lore and traditions which underpin the sentiments expressed, are all totally foreign to the western reader's poetic sensibility. Moreover, the structure, topoi, and development typical of ancient Arabian poetry are quite unlike those of any ancient western models, such as Greek or Latin verse, with which the educated western reader might be familiar.

On the page, Arberry's translations read elegantly enough, even if the mannered and faintly archaic idiom (reminiscent of some of the English Romantics) occasionally jars. But perhaps the major—in fact the unsurmountable—difficulty confronting the translator, and recognized by Arberry, is how to reflect the structural characteristics of the Arabian ode. There may be more than 60 rigidly isometric monorhymed couplets. This was an exacting prosodic discipline for the poet, and its importance underlines the incantatory, auditory aspect of poetry in the non-literate society of ancient Arabia. Rhyme and metre were intrinsic to—were in fact the defining characteristics of—all poetry. In the hands of a master, this rigidity of structure could create an almost unbearable tension, as the listener waited for yet another line-concluding rhyme which both fitted the metrical scheme and completed the sense with that inevitability of *le mot juste* which is the mark of great poetry. But in a translation it is impossible to reflect this crucial characteristic. A second major problem is the richness and precision of the Arabic lexicon in many contexts—the description of desert animals is an obvious one. Here the danger is that the fine distinctions carried by the Arabic terms become blurred as the translator is forced into flaccid paraphrases.

To conclude, two extracts from Arberry's translations, the first from Imruʾ al-Qays's *muʿallaqa* and the second from that of Labīd, will serve to illustrate both Arberry's translation style and some of the problems—the foreignness of the topoi, the apparent banality of the similes—which have been mentioned. The first extract is the famous opening of Imru' al-Qays's ode, in which the poet, in stereotypical fashion, depicts himself and two riding companions coming across a deserted camp-site which he had once inhabited:

Halt, friends, both! Let us weep, recalling a love and a
    lodging
by the rim of the twisted sands between Ed-Dakhool and
    Haumal,
Toodih and El-Mikrat, whose trace is not yet effaced
for all the spinning of the south winds and the northern
    blasts;
there, all about its yards, and away in the dry hollows
you may see the dung of antelopes spattered like pepper-
    corns.
Upon the morn of separation, the day they loaded to part,
by the tribe's acacias it was like I was splitting a colocynth;
there my companions halted their beasts awhile over me
saying, 'Don't perish of sorrow; restrain yourself
    decently!'
Yet the true and the only cure of my grief is tears out-
    poured:
what is left to lean on where the trace is obliterated?

The second extract, from the *mu'allaqa* of Labīd, is a camel description:

Is such my camel? Or shall I liken her to a wild cow, whose
    calf
the beasts of prey have devoured, lagging, though true
    herd-leader?
Flat-nosed, she has lost her young, and therefore unceas-
    ingly

circles about the stony waste, lowing all the while
as she seeks a half-weaned white calf, whose carcass the
    grey robber-wolves
in greed unappeasable have dragged hither and thither;
they encountered her unawares, and seized her little one
    from her,
and of a truth the arrows of Fate miss not their mark.

Are the *Mu'allaqāt* great poetry? There is no doubt that, judged by the exacting standards of the indigenous connoisseur, they are indeed supremely fine poems technically; and beyond their purely technical excellence, they have achieved in the Arab world the status of cultural icons, and for centuries exerted a powerful grip on the Arab poetic imagination. Needless to say, however, the desert chivalry and derring-do they depict, and the lyricism and pastoral images they contain, are almost completely lost in translation. Read by an English reader lacking any remotely relevant frame of reference, the *Mu'allaqāt* appear for the most part arcane, or merely quaint. This is a great pity. In the original, some of the animal descriptions have the bleeding muscularity and sharpness of line of, say, the animal poems of Ted Hughes; the desert storms make one think of the work of Turner, the English painter; and there is an occasional hint of a Rabelaisian appetite for drinking and womanizing which the pastel shades of Arberry's English fail to reflect. For these rude life forces to show through, we would need somehow radically to recreate the poems, rather than translate them in the conventionally accepted sense: a forlorn hope.   CH

FULL TRANSLATIONS *The Moallakat or Seven Arabian Poems, which were suspended on the Temple at Mecca; with a translation and arguments*, tr. William Jones, London, 1783 [rep. in *The Works of Sir William Jones*, ed. Lord Teignmouth, London 1807, x. 1–193] · *The Seven Poems suspended in the Temple at Mecca*, tr. Capt. F. E. Johnson, London, 1894 · *The Seven Golden Odes of Pagan Arabia*, tr. Lady Anne Blunt and W. S. Blunt, London, 1903 · *The Seven Odes: The First Chapter in Arabic Literature*, tr. A. J. Arberry, London, 1957.
SELECT PARTIAL TRANSLATIONS *Translations of Ancient Arabian Poetry*, tr. Charles James Lyall, London, 1885 · *A Literary History of the Arabs*, by Reynold Nicholson, London, 1907 [frequent reps.] · *Translations of Eastern Poetry and Prose*, tr. Reynold Nicholson, Cambridge, 1922 · *Early Arabic Poetry*, vol. ii: *Select Odes*, tr. Alan Jones, Reading, 1996 · *The Mute Immortals Speak: Pre-Islamic Poetry and the Poetics of Ritual*, by Suzanne Pinkney Stetkevych, Ithaca, NY, London, 1993.

4. THE *MUQADDIMAH*

The *Muqaddimah*, or 'Introduction', conventionally translated as 'The Prolegomena', was written by Ibn Khaldun (1332–1406) of Tunis towards the end of his life. The title of the work refers to the fact that it is meant as an introduction to a much larger work, the *Kitāb al-'Ibar* (lit. 'Book of Examples' or 'Universal History'). Standard modern editions of the *Muqaddimah*, in Arabic or English translation,

include Book I of the larger work. Ibn Khaldun was a colourful, many-faceted court politician and intellectual who pursued a varied career as chamberlain, secretary, and envoy of various local north African rulers, and in later life as a scholar, teacher, and magistrate.

The *Muqaddimah* is an 'introduction' to the study of human history, in which the central aim is uncovering the causes of the fall of civilizations. The *Kitāb al-'Ibar* is meant to illuminate with concrete examples the more analytical approach of the *Muqaddimah*. In writing the *Muqaddimah*, Ibn Khaldun had no models to fall back on. He himself had been classically trained in the Koranic sciences and Islamic jurisprudence, and was fully conversant with the Arabo-Muslim philosophical tradition of rationalist speculation. But Ibn Khaldun rejects this in favour of a (in his view) more soundly based species of philosophical speculation grounded in empiricism. He was well aware that, in the Muslim society of his time, his was a revolutionary approach, and one which required a new style of discourse. Thus he developed his own distinctive vocabulary for many new concepts, or extended the meaning of old ones, e.g. *'ilm al-'umrān*, 'the science of civilization' (= roughly modern 'sociology'), *'aṣabiyya*, 'group spirit' (a quality he considered intrinsic to human societies, and the strength of which was a prime factor in their efflorescence, survival, and eventual fall).

Ibn Khaldun is an atypical, indeed a unique figure in Arabo-Muslim cultural history. He had no forerunners and no intellectual successors. A translation of part of the *Muqaddimah* into Turkish was done in 1730 (and eventually published in Cairo in 1859), but it was only in the 19th c., and in Europe, that the full significance of his work was realized. The French orientalist Quatremère produced the first complete Arabic edition of the *Muqaddimah* in 1858, and this was closely followed by the first translation into a European language, French, by William MacGuckin de Slane in 1863–8. As for translations into English, a few passages appeared in Reynold **Nicholson**'s *Translations of Eastern Poetry and Prose* (1922), and an abridged translation by Charles **Issawi**, under the title *An Arab Philosophy of History*, appeared in 1950. The first complete English translation, in three volumes by Franz **Rosenthal**, was published in 1958. An abridged and edited version of the latter was published in 1967.

In the introduction to his translation, Rosenthal comments that a philosophical work like the *Muqaddimah* can be translated in one of three ways: as literally as the second language permits; more radically, using a modern phraseology and style; or by recasting it in the form it might have had, had it been written by a contemporary author. The (to western tastes) rather flowery, convoluted Arabic prose style is less salient in a work of this type, in which the demands of clear exposition, rather than rhetorical artifice, predominate. Rosenthal comments: 'It is true, as has often been remarked, that Ibn Khaldun did not always adhere strictly to the

accepted norms and rules of classical Arabic, which were artificial to him and remote from the speech habits of his time. But Ibn Khaldun's long, rolling, involved sentences, his skilful and restrained application of rhetorical figures, and his use of a large, though not farfetched vocabulary, make it indeed a pleasure to read the *Muqaddimah*, or to hear it read aloud.' (Almost the whole of the original work was prepared in the form of lectures to be read aloud.)

The translation strategy adopted by Rosenthal is a mixture of the first and second approaches: he attempts a contemporary idiom, but does not depart radically from the source text. Where he does, interpolated material is placed in brackets. Often, this is simply to make the literal sense of the text clearer, since Ibn Khaldun was extremely fond of long sentences in which it is not always clear even in the original to which noun or nouns the following pronouns were referring. Also, clause and sentence linkage at this period in the history of Arabic was less explicitly expressed than it is now. If an English reader is fully to grasp the meaning, the translator sometimes has to interpret the sense of conjunctions which can have several different meanings. Compare, for example, the two translations below of a passage on the organization of labour in a society. The first translation (the present writer's) is literal, in particular as regards sentence cohesion, in which the Arabic particles *wa* and *fa*, which can mean any of 'and', 'but', 'so', 'then' (or nothing at all), are left untranslated in the text; the second, more idiomatic translation is Rosenthal's, in which the linkages which he has supplied to interpret these ambiguous particles are capitalized. Where they have been omitted from the translation and simply replaced by a punctuation mark, they are indicated by §. For ease of comparison, the sense groups have been numbered:

Literal translation:

(1) *wa* the reason for this is that it is known *wa* it is established that one individual cannot satisfy his needs independently of others (2) *wa* that they all cooperate in their civilization to do this (3) *wa* what is produced through the cooperation of the group of them is sufficient to satisfy the need of their number several times over (4) *fa* sustenance in wheat, no one individual by himself can produce his ration (5) *wa* if six or ten are delegated to produce it including a blacksmith, and carpenter to make the tools, and an oxman, and a ploughman, and a harvester, and the rest, *wa* they are distributed each to his task . . .

Rosenthal's translation (II. 271):

(1) § The reason for this is that, as is known and well established, the individual human being cannot by himself obtain all the necessities of life. (2) § All human beings

must co-operate to that end in their civilisation. (3) BUT what is obtained through the co-operation of a group of human beings satisfies the need of a number many times greater (than themselves). (4) § FOR INSTANCE, no one, by himself, can obtain the share of wheat he needs for food. (5) BUT when six or ten persons, including a smith and a carpenter to make the tools, and others who are in charge of the oxen, the ploughing of the soil, the harvesting of the ripe grain, and all the other agricultural activities, undertake to obtain food and work toward that purpose either separately of collectively . . .

One of the main translation problems is in Ibn Khaldun's extensive technical vocabulary, briefly alluded to above. This is chiefly because the cultural milieu which he uses to provide the examples for his exposition, with which any Arabo-Muslim reader would have been familiar, is remote from European experience. The key term 'aṣabiyya, mentioned earlier, which Rosenthal renders 'group spirit', is a famous example. Ibn Khaldun uses it to refer to the cohesiveness of any community or body politic, and it has been rendered in the various European translations 'esprit de corps' (MacGuckin de Slane), 'Gemeinsinn', and even, more implausibly, 'Nationalitätsidee' (Kremer). The word's original meaning was 'spirit of kinship', and it was used in pre-Islamic society to refer to feelings of community based on tribal consanguinity. In Ibn Khaldun's usage it becomes the force which impels any group of human beings to assert themselves politically in order to gain supremacy over another. Once established in power, Ibn Khaldun contends, the ruling group tends to detach itself from this

rude cohesive force and substitute other forces of coercion to maintain its hegemony, which by their nature (in Ibn Khaldun's view) are not as strong. The classic case of this, although Ibn Khaldun does not say so directly, was the spread of Islam. Initially it was the 'aṣabiyya of the Arabs as an ethnic group which carried all before it; subsequently, the purely religious element which they brought with them, Islam, gradually assumed dominance as a means by which the ruling group stayed in power as the primary, ethnic 'aṣabiyya correspondingly waned.

Rosenthal's translation is a superb piece of scholarship: smooth, flowing, and idiomatic but at the same time remarkably faithful to the erudite, didactic tone of the original. Its main disadvantage for the general reader is precisely that it is a scholarly edition with the normal scholarly apparatus, which results in three unwieldy and expensive hardback volumes. The single-volume abridgement of Rosenthal by Dawood (available in paperback) achieves its concision by the judicious cutting of a certain amount of repetition, reducing the multiple examples Ibn Khaldun sometimes uses to illustrate his argument, and omitting some of the information which could be regarded as standard background information of the time (e.g. geography, scientific principles). The result is a compact yet accurate epitome of Ibn Khaldun's magnum opus (in contrast to the rather disjointed and 'bitty' feel of Issawi's selections), a work which Arnold Toynbee described as 'undoubtedly the greatest work of its kind that has ever yet been created by any mind in any time or place'. CH

TRANSLATIONS *Translations of Eastern Poetry and Prose*, tr. Reynold Nicholson, Cambridge, 1922 · *An Arab Philosophy of History: Selections from the Prolegomena of Ibn Khaldun of Tunis (1332–1406)*, tr. Charles Issawi, London, 1950 [frequent reps.] · *Ibn Khaldûn: The Muqaddimah: An Introduction to History*, tr. Franz Rosenthal, 3 vols., London, 1958 [2nd edn. 1967, frequent reps.] · *Ibn Khaldûn: An Introduction to History: The Muqaddimah*, tr. Franz Rosenthal, ed. N. J. Dawood, London, 1967; rep. 1978, 1987.

5. THE *THOUSAND AND ONE NIGHTS*

While the *Iliad* attracted the attention of British poets and scholars of the first rank [II.i.2], the *Thousand and One Nights* was less well served by its English translators and was mangled in partial, incompetent, or even fraudulent translations and commentaries. The Arabic story collection was a book which in several important senses was made by its first French translator. Antoine **Galland** (1646–1715), the first person to translate the medieval story collection into a European language, rescued the stories from obscurity and low regard in the Arab lands. The stories only became

popular in the Near East after the publication of Galland's 12-volume *Les Mille et une nuits* (1704–17). Galland also established what became the widely accepted (though erroneous) long canon of stories, for the earliest Arabic manscripts of *Alf Layla wa Layla* did not include such stories as 'The Seven Voyages of Sinbad', 'Ali Baba', and 'The Ebony Horse'. These were collected by Galland from various sources, in order to plump his collection out. It even seems possible that some of the stories included in Galland's collection were not translated, but rather composed by him. Certainly, no

Arabic originals have ever appeared for such stories as 'Aladdin' and 'Prince Ahmed and the Peri Banou'.

Galland's translation was immensely successful in France and competed in popularity with the fairy stories of d'Aulnoy and Perrault [I.c.4.ii]. (Neither the French fairy tales nor the Arabian tales were originally intended to be read by children. Such stories had their first successes with adult audiences, but since there was so little literature directed at children in the 18th c. it was inevitable that children read them too.) Even before the French edition was complete, an anonymous Grub Street translation into English of the earliest volumes appeared in 1705 or 1706, and by about 1721 the whole of the Galland translation had been rendered into English. The capable, anonymous translator echoed the courtliness of Galland's prose ('Sister, says Dinarzade, it must be owned that the more you speak, the more you surprise and satisfy . . .'). He also reproduced the glosses that Galland was accustomed to insert within the body of his translation—Galland had had no hesitation in 'improving' on his Arabic original, removing coarse expressions, expanding and deleting as he thought fit. The Grub Street translation and subsequent adaptations and modernizations of it held the field for over 100 years. Addison, Steele, Johnson, Beckford, Austen, Coleridge, De Quincey, Tennyson, Gaskell, Thackeray, Dickens, and hundreds of other novelists and poets were inspired by it and made innumerable overt and covert references to its stories in their writings.

The 19th-c. translations made directly from the Arabic turned out to be less inspiring. Translators who chose to work directly on the Arabic, rather than to adapt Galland, faced a difficult choice between four printed texts which diverged quite widely. Stories from the Ottoman period (i.e. from the 16th c. onwards) had been added by Arab and Indian compilers to the original core of medieval stories, and these additions were drawn from a wide variety of sources. The material came from all over the Islamic world and included folk epics, wonder tales, fairy stories, wisdom literature, mystical teaching tales, historical fragments, pornography, and much else besides. There was therefore no homogeneity in the style, content, or meaning of what was being translated. Additionally, of course, translators tried to find Arabic originals for the stories which were in Galland's translation but which had not appeared in the early manuscripts of the Nights. In some cases they were successful, but only in some; Burton was to go to the bizarre lengths of having one of the Galland stories translated into Hindustani, so that he could catch the story's authentic flavour when he retranslated it back into English.

The earliest translations from Arabic into English were attempted in India. Jonathan **Scott** (1754–1829) claimed to have accomplished the task. However, it is clear that his *Arabian Nights Entertainments* (1811) was very closely based on Galland's French with only occasional additions and emendments. Next Henry **Torrens**, a government official in India, translated the first 50 'nights'. However, Torrens's Arabic was not marvellous and his heart was not really in the task he had set himself. So, when he heard of the appearance of Lane's translation, he abandoned his own.

Edward William **Lane** (1801–76) had spent the years 1825–8 in Egypt. His *Manners and Customs of the Modern Egyptians* (1836) was the first literary result of that sojourn. It can be argued that he undertook his translation (from the somewhat literary Bulaq, or Cairo version) as a pretext for a second lengthy treatise on Middle Eastern manners and customs presented in the guise of endnotes. Prudery and erratic literary judgement led him to exclude a lot of the stories in whole or in part. His prose style was rather ponderous and sub-Biblical: 'And it came to pass that their father died, and the Sultan mourned for him, and, turning his regards towards the two sons, took them into his favour, invested them with robes of honour, and said to them, Ye two are invested in your father's office . . .' Nevertheless, Lane was an excellent Arabist (and the compiler of what is still the best Arabic–English dictionary), and those stories which were translated by him were translated accurately.

The polyglot John **Payne** (1842–1916), who also translated the French poet Villon, was accustomed to make his translations while riding about on the top of a London bus. In the 1870s he turned his attention to the *Nights*. Payne's translation, which included all the obscene passages, even if it sometimes toned them down, was published for subscribers only. Unlike Galland, Lane, and Burton, Payne was interested in the *Nights* as literature rather than as a manual on Middle Eastern *mœurs*, and he turned the often rather crude Arabic into artistic if rather mannered English: 'As for this that thou sayest, it may not be that I should cast away either the lamp or the ring; nay thou seest that which it did with us of good, whenas we were ahungered . . .'. His work has rarely been reprinted and has not received the attention it deserves.

The subtitle of Sir Richard Francis **Burton**'s translation claimed that it was 'Plain and Literal'. It was neither. Burton (1821–90) was a fan of Sir Thomas Urquhart and of the latter's vocabulary-expanding translation of Rabelais [II.g.5.i]. There were at least two other factors behind Burton's use of outré vocabulary. First, his own translation often followed his friend Payne's translation rather closely, something Burton did his best to disguise by finding where possible synonyms for the words used by Payne. Secondly, Burton, unlike most other translators, strove (unsuccessfully) to achieve the rhetorical and rhythmic effects of the *saj'*, or rhymed prose, which Arabic authors had used for highlights in the narrative: 'Thereupon sat a lady bright of blee, with brow beaming brilliancy, the dream of philosophy, whose eyes were fraught with Babel's gramarye and her eyebrows were arched as for archery . . .'. Burton also seems to have thought that, though some of the original stories were agreeably erotic, they were not erotic enough; he went out of his way to exaggerate their obscenity and made wholly unwarrantable additions to his original. His footnoting was eccentric and sometimes salacious. Burton was helped in his translation by a number of distinguished Arabists and, for all its many and glaring faults, his translation holds the field as the best translation of the *Thousand and One Nights*—considering the work in the widest sense, including not just the relatively small corpus of 35 or so tales in the earliest substantially surviving manuscripts, but the swollen, ragbag compendium of hundreds of medieval and later additions.

Across the Channel Joseph-Charles Mardrus (1868–1949) produced the first integral French translation since Galland in the years 1900–4. Mardrus was steeped in the imagery and locutions of *fin-de-siècle* literature, and his translation made it seem as though the anonymous medieval authors were imbued with similar values. Powys **Mathers** translated Mardrus's French into English in 1923. His translation of Mardrus reads very well, and remains popular with readers today. It is therefore a pity that Mardrus's translation of the Arabic is so appalling. It is full of elementary blunders and strange translating strategies. While the translation is at times madly literal, at other times the 'translation' is a mere fiction.

N. J. **Dawood**'s Penguin translation of a selection

of stories from the *Nights* includes several stories which are not strictly part of the collection. It is somewhat flat, and it leaves out all the poetry. Several European translators of the *Nights* have decided to omit the poetry from their translations, either because they judged it to be boring or because it was difficult to translate. Classical Arabic poetry, which depends heavily on puns and other forms of word-play, is indeed peculiarly difficult to translate [see II.b.3]. Nevertheless, omission of the poetry from some stories renders them almost meaningless, as in some cases the story was designed as nothing more than a frame for the poetry it contained. The original Arab audiences seem to have regarded poems as high points in the narration rather than as decorative irrelevancies.

Things improved with Husain **Haddawy**'s 1990 translation of Mahdi's scholarly text-critical Arabic edition, which had been published in 1984. Haddawy's translation is accurate, lively, and based on a properly edited manuscript, and this combination of qualities is something which none of its predecessors can boast of. It accurately reproduces the vivid and concretely detailed storytelling style of the original. However, since it is a translation of the earliest authentic manuscript, it contains only 35 stories and inevitably omits many of the stories which are familiar nursery staples. In a second volume Haddawy has gone on to translate 'Sinbad' and 'The Story of Qamar al-Zaman and His Two Sons' from the Arabic of the rather literary Bulaq text, while he has had perforce to translate 'The Story of Ali Baba and the Forty Thieves' and 'The Story of Aladdin and the Magic Lamp' from Galland's French. The recent *Arabian Nights Entertainment*, edited by Robert Mack, is a lightly modernized version of that found in Henry Weber's three-volume *Tales of the East* (1812), which was in turn a modernized version of the Grub Street translation. Mack's edition is useful for stories which are not included in Haddawy's volumes, and useful too in offering the text which so inspired two centuries of English literature. RI

TRANSLATIONS *Les Mille et une nuits*, tr. Antoine Galland, 12 vols., Paris, 1704–7 · *Arabian Winter-Evenings' Entertainments or Arabian Nights' Entertainments*, tr. anon., London, 1706–21 · *A New Translation of the Thousand Nights and a Night: Known in England as the Arabian Nights' Entertainments*, tr. Edward William Lane, London, 1838–42 · *The Book of the Thousand Nights and One Night*, tr. John Payne, London, 1882–4 · *The Book of the Thousand Nights and One Nights: A Plain and Literal Translation of the Arabian Nights' Entertainments*, tr. Richard Francis Burton, 10 vols., Benares (= Stoke Newington), 1885–6 · *Supplemental Nights to the Book of the Thousand Nights and a Night*, tr. Richard Francis Burton, 6 vols., Benares (= Stoke Newington), 1886–8 · *The Book of the Thousand Nights and One Night, Rendered from the Literal and Complete Version of Dr. J. C. Mardrus*, tr. Powys Mathers, 4 vols., London, 1923 · *Tales from the Thousand and One Nights*, tr. N. J. Dawood, London, 1973 [Penguin] · *The Arabian Nights, based on the Fourteenth-Century Syrian Manuscript, edited by Muhsin Mahdi*, tr. Husain Haddawy, New York, 1990 · *The Arabian Nights, ii: Sinbad and Other Popular Stories*, tr. Husain Haddawy, New York, 1995 · *Arabian Nights Entertainments*, tr. anon., ed. Robert L. Mack, Oxford, 1995.

SEE ALSO   Borges, J. L., 'The Translators of *The 1001 Nights*', in *Borges: A Reader*, ed. E. R. Monegal and A. Reid, New York, 1981 · Caracciolo, P., ed., *The Arabian Nights in English Literature: Studies in the Reception of The Thousand and One Nights into British Culture*, Basingstoke/London, 1988 · Irwin, R., *The Arabian Nights: A Companion*, London, 1994 · Macdonald, D. B., 'A Bibliographical and Literary Study of the First Appearance of the *Arabian Nights* in Europe', *Literary Quarterly*, 2 (1932), 387–420.

6. MODERN LITERATURE

i. Background The starting-point for an account of modern Arabic literature has traditionally been regarded as 1798, the date of Napoleon's invasion of Egypt. The 19th c. saw much of the Middle East being systematically exposed to European ideas and influence on a large scale for the first time, and the resulting re-examination of traditional Islamic society had major implications for most areas of Arab life—political, economic, social and educational. Associated with these developments were changes of major importance for the development of modern Arabic literature, including the growth of a new reading public, the rise of indigenous journalism, and the development of a new, simpler Arabic prose style. In both poetry and prose, authors were re-examining traditional Arabic literary conventions, while at the same time the growth of translation from western languages was making European literary forms known to a newly literate public. The resulting literary and cultural renaissance (*nahḍa* in Arabic) reached its high point in the last third of the 19th c. and was effectively complete by the time of World War I; by then, poetry had seen the flourishing of a vigorous 'neoclassical' movement, while in prose traditional Arabic literary forms had been all but replaced by the western novel, short story, and drama.

ii. Fiction Before World War II The development of modern Arabic literature was slow to make an impact on the West, and the first work to attract significant attention outside the Middle East was the first part of Ṭāhā Ḥusayn's *al-Ayyām* (1929, The Days). One of the best-loved works of modern Arabic literature, the work—essentially an autobiography written in the third person—tells the story of the upbringing and education of a blind boy in an Upper Egyptian village. Its importance was recognized by the appearance in 1932 of an English translation by E. H. **Paxton**, as well as translations into other European languages; two further volumes of Ṭāhā Ḥusayn's autobiography, which appeared in Arabic in 1939 and 1967 respectively, have also been translated into English, by Hilary **Wayment** and Kenneth **Cragg** respectively.

Stylistically, *al-Ayyām* (particularly the first volume) is an idiosyncratic work, which blends the parallelisms typical of classical Arabic prose with eccentricities peculiar to the author. These problems pose formidable problems for the translator, and Paxton in particular fails on occasion to cope successfully with them, at times attempting to imitate the author's repetitions and parallelisms in an almost slavish fashion; unfortunately, the idiosyncrasies which give Ṭāhā Ḥusayn's Arabic its charm in English often sound merely quirky.

Although Ṭāhā Ḥusayn's work was the first to attract western attention, some earlier fiction has since been translated into English. Al-Muwayliḥī's *Ḥadīth ʿĪsā ibn Hishām* (1892–1902, The Tale of ʿĪsā ibn Hishām) stands at the end of a great tradition, as perhaps the last great Arabic work to be written as a series of *maqāmāt*—a classical narrative form involving the use of rhymed prose; as such, it presents problems for the translator quite different from those of most modern fiction. Roger **Allen**'s vigorous translation entitled *A Period of Time*, with its copious notes and introduction, will serve the English-speaking reader as an excellent introduction to the cultural developments of the period as well as to the work itself. Astonishingly, only 20 or so years separate al-Muwayliḥī's work from the first genuine Arabic novel with a contemporary plot: Muḥammad Ḥusayn Haykal's *Zaynab* (1913), written while the author was studying in Europe. Both in the original Arabic and in J. M. **Grinsted**'s English translation, however, this sentimental story of peasant love and life, which reflects the author's nostalgia for his home country, has a somewhat dated feel to it.

More appealing are the four novels of Tawfiq al-Ḥakīm—all autobiographically based, reflecting a trend already established by Ibrāhīm al-Māzinī's *Ibrāhīm al-Kātib* (1931, Ibrahim the Writer), translated by M. **Wahba**. Of al-Ḥakīm's novels, three are available in English translation: *ʿAwdat al-Rūḥ* (1933, Return of the Spirit), translated by W. **Hutchins**; *ʿUṣfūr min al-Sharq* (1938, Bird of the East), translated by R. Bayly **Winder**; and *Yawmiyyāt Nāʾib fī al-Aryāf* (1937, Diary of a Country Prosecutor), translated by A. S. **Eban**. From a structural point of view the last is by far the most accomplished, being noteworthy for some of the most pungent social criticism to be found in the pre-1952 Arabic novel; both *Return of the Spirit* and *Bird of the East*, by contrast, are marred by a lack of artistic unity which no translator can disguise. The nationalist element in the former, however, has ensured its continuing popularity, not least with the late Egyptian president Nasser; while the latter is an important early example of a work illustrating a group of themes revolving around the clash of values between East and West. These themes—often deriving from the experiences of Arabs studying in the West—were subsequently developed by a number of authors, both from Egypt and from elsewhere in the Arab world: among other examples may be mentioned the Egyptian Yaḥyā Ḥaqqī's *Qindīl Umm Hāshim* (1942, The Saint's Lamp), translated by M. M. **Badawi**; and the Sudanese al-Ṭayyib Ṣāliḥ's *Mawsim al-Hijra ilā al-Shimāl* (1966, Season of Migration to the North), translated by Denys **Johnson-Davies**. The quality of the English translations of these works is generally competent, though Hutchins's version of *Return of the Spirit* sometimes tries to follow the distinctive syntax and word order of the original Arabic too closely, with unidiomatic results. By contrast, Badawi's version of *The Saint's Lamp* occasionally gives the impression of attempting to solve translation problems by simply leaving out the phrase in question—a strategy which is unlikely to worry the non-Arabist reader particularly, but which may well prove irritating to those able to consult the original text.

iii. Fiction Since World War II

The development of the Arabic novel and short story since World War II has seen an increasing sophistication of technique and diversity of theme, against an evolving political background that has often been reflected in literary trends. Many of these trends are exemplified in the works of the Arab world's best-known writer, the Nobel prize-winner Najīb Maḥfūẓ, whose works are discussed below [II.b.7]. The first main trend, towards 'commitment' (Arabic *iltizām*), had its origins in a combination of political and social developments, and is best exemplified in 'Abd al-Raḥmān al-Sharqāwī's *al-Arḍ* (1954, The Land), translated into English by Desmond **Stewart** and recently described as 'arguably the most widely known work of modern Arabic fiction both inside and beyond the Near and Middle East' (Robin Ostle, introduction to *Egyptian Earth*, tr. Desmond Stewart, 1990). The book revolves around themes of power and corruption and is unashamedly socialist in tone. An important means of conveying authenticity is the use of Egyptian colloquial in the dialogue sections, a technique which al-Sharqāwī extends through the use of different dialects which vary with the speaker: though Stewart's translation reads smoothly and easily, subtleties of this sort are almost inevitably lost in his English version.

No other 'committed' Arabic novel of comparable power to *al-Arḍ* exists in an English version, the realism of this phase of Arabic prose writing being best appreciated by the English reader through translations of collected short stories by writers such as Yūsuf Idrīs—many of whose best stories are available in English. Equally at home in Cairo and in the Egyptian countryside, and with an eye for the foibles of human nature unsurpassed among modern Egyptian writers, Idrīs's first collection, *Arkhaṣ Layālī* (1954, The Cheapest Nights), translated by Wadida **Wassef**, caused controversy from the time of its appearance. Idrīs's writing is marked not only by a stark realism but also by an entirely distinctive use of language, which often goes well beyond the simple use of colloquial Egyptian in dialogue, importing features of the colloquial dialect even into the narrative passages. Although Idrīs has been generally well served by his English translators, many of these features are almost inevitably lost, or partly lost, in English translation.

The atmosphere of 'commitment' which dominated Arabic literature in the 1950s had already begun to be eroded by the mid-1960s as the idealism of the 1952 Egyptian Free Officers' Revolution gave place to disillusionment. The new mood was exemplified in Egypt by the writings of a group of authors often known as the 'generation of the sixties', among the principal members of which were Ṣun 'Allāh Ibrāhīm, Jamāl al-Ghīṭānī, and Yūsuf al-Qa'īd. Translations of works by all these authors are available in English, including the work that possibly best exemplifies the new mood: Ṣun 'Allāh Ibrāhīm's novella *Tilka al-Rā'iḥa* (1966, That Smell), translated into English by Denys Johnson-Davies, an autobiographically inspired example of Arabic 'prison literature' in which the protagonist—newly released from jail—drifts aimlessly around Cairo, vainly attempting to forge relationships with the people who inhabited his past. Johnson-Davies's English version faithfully recaptures the spirit of the original, whose cynicism and explicit depiction of sexual themes caused outrage on first publication, but which remains an effective chronicle of the monotony of life of the Cairo lower classes.

Particularly demanding from the translator's point of view are the works of Jamāl al-Ghīṭānī, whose frequent use of 'intertextuality' poses particular difficulties—the translator being faced not only

153

with the usual linguistic and cultural problems of translating from Arabic but also with the task of translating, within the same work, from a number of styles, some of which may involve complex historical allusions. A particularly good example is provided by what is generally regarded as al-Ghīṭānī's finest work, the novel al-Zaynī Barakāt (1971), which incorporates texts by the medieval historian Ibn Iyās and other material written in his style, into a work painting an allegorical picture of the corruption of contemporary Egypt. Farouk **Abdel-Wahab**'s translation copes with these problems admirably, his polished and elegant English well capturing the changes in linguistic register of the original Arabic, including a suitable measure of 'archaic' language at appropriate points.

Less successful is Peter **O'Daniel**'s version of the later Waqā'i' ḥārat al-Za'farānī (1976, Incidents in Za'frani Alley), in which al-Ghīṭānī pastiches newspapers and other contemporary material; although reasonably accurate, O'Daniel's version occasionally betrays signs of carelessness or haste—for example, in his rendering into English of the Arabic tense system. The presentation of the volume is also markedly inferior to that of Zayni Barakat. The same contrast between the standards of publication of a major western publishing-house and the Cairo-based General Egyptian Book Organization may be observed by comparing the English translations of Yūsuf al-Qaʿīd's two novels al-Ḥarb fī barr Miṣr (1978, War in the Land of Egypt) and Akhbār 'Izbat al-Manīsī (1971, News from the Meneisi Farm); although both are competently done, and both include useful and perceptive introductions or afterwords, **Abdel-Messih**'s version of News from the Meneisi Farm gives the impression at times of needing a good sub-editor to iron out the frequent unidiomatic expressions and inappropriate registers of the English.

An entirely distinctive voice in modern Arabic literature (though closely associated with the 'generation of the sixties') is Idwār al-Kharrāṭ, who has gained a reputation as a notoriously difficult author to translate. Al-Kharrāṭ's command of the subtleties of the Arabic language far outstrips that of most of his contemporaries, and his meandering style often produces an effect akin to a prose poem. Frances **Liardet**'s translations of Turābuhā Za'farān (1986, City of Saffron) and Yā Banāt Iskandariyya (1990, Girls of Alexandria) have, however, rightly acquired a reputation as two of the most successful translations into English of a modern Arabic author; in her translations—for which she received the co-operation of al-Kharrāṭ himself—she succeeds in making the author's unique vision her own

and expressing it in an English idiom so finely crafted that the reader is seldom conscious of reading a translation at all.

Although many of the most interesting recent developments in Arabic prose writing have been undertaken in Egypt, other parts of the Arab world have also seen a growth in the production of innovative fiction, only a fraction of which has so far been translated into English. Among the most ambitious is the Saudi 'Abd al-Raḥmān Munīf's five-volume Mudun al-Milḥ (1984, Cities of Salt), which chronicles the progress of a Bedouin community into the oil-rich but western-dominated 20th c. and provides a major challenge to the translator through sheer volume alone; the first three volumes have been carefully and lovingly rendered into English by Peter **Theroux**, providing a quite different perspective on the Middle East from that of most Egyptian novels of the same period.

Liardet's translations of al-Kharrāṭ's novels are rare examples of works translated and published purely for their literary and artistic merit. In the limited market for modern Arabic literature in English translation, commercial considerations also play an important role—readers' tastes being influenced to an appreciable extent by the fashion of the moment. One example of this phenomenon may be found in the mushrooming of translations of works by Najīb Maḥfūẓ following his award of the Nobel Prize for literature in 1988, another in the boom in translations of writing by women in the last few years. An excellent introduction to the growth, and intricate variety, of feminist writing in Arabic over the last century may be found in the anthology Opening the Gates: A Century of Arab Feminist Writing, edited by Margot Badran and Miriam Cooke. Fashion is of course no guarantee of excellence, either in an original work or in a translation: the popularity in translation of works by Nawāl al-Saʿdāwī—including a number of works of fiction translated into English by her husband, Sharif **Hatata**—undoubtedly owes more to admiration for her courage as an outspoken feminist than to the opinions of the literary critics. Moreover, not all recent translations of women's fiction have themselves received critical approval. The need for translators to acquire an adequate understanding of the problems involved in translating from Arabic to English, and the technical skills necessary to solve them, are well illustrated by comment on the Arab Women Writers Series, edited by Fadia Faqir and recently discussed at some length in an article by Hilary Kilpatrick (1996). Kilpatrick's review of the four translations so far published in this series includes much material of wider relevance to translators of contemporary Arabic literature, and indeed to translators from other languages also.

iv. Drama The western influences which led to the gradual substitution of the novel and short story for traditional Arabic prose narrative forms also bore fruit in the establishment of western-style drama in the Middle East. The first experiments along these lines took place in Beirut in 1847; but for most of the 19th and early 20th c. productions were largely confined to farce and melodrama, together with free adaptations of western plays. Moves towards the establishment of a serious Egyptian theatre started with the efforts of Muḥammad Taymūr, Anṭūn Yazbak, and Ibrāhīm Ramzī around the time of World War I, and reached fruition with Tawfīq al-Ḥakīm, who dominated the Egyptian theatre from the 1930s until well after the Free Officers' Revolution in 1952.

Although early 'intellectual' plays such as *Ahl al-Kahf* (1933) and *Shahrazād* (1934) remain among the most interesting of Tawfīq al-Ḥakīm's works, many were written to be read rather than acted, and recent translators have tended to focus on his later works, which—from the early 1960s—show the influence of techniques derived from avant-garde western theatre. Outstanding among these works is *Yā Ṭāli' al-Shajara* (1964, The Tree Climber), the first play by al-Ḥakīm to show the influence of the Theatre of the Absurd. The play is characterized by lively and fast-moving dialogue, the freshness and lively tone of which is well captured by Denys Johnson-Davies, whose translation has been successfully produced on the English stage.

Al-Ḥakīm's dramatic output also includes a series of plays on social themes published in the late 1940s and early 1950s, the most successful of which is *Ughniyat al-Mawt* (1947, Song of Death)—perhaps the most accomplished one-act play in Arabic. The work revolves around the conflict between traditional and modern values, a theme which recalls the setting of the earlier novel *Yawmiyyāt Nā'ib*. The play is again characterized by fast-moving dialogue between characters talking at cross purposes—a feature which poses particular problems for the translator; although Johnson-Davies's translation captures the general mood well, the wide cultural gap between the play's setting and the intended audience at times makes his rendering seem a little stilted.

A perennial problem for Arab dramatists has been the choice of 'classical' or 'colloquial' Arabic as a medium of communication. Most of al-

Ḥakīm's drama, designed for the armchair at least as much as the stage, was written in 'classical' Arabic (though sometimes 'translated' into colloquial when staged); but newer generations of Arab playwrights, more politicized in outlook, have increasingly employed the colloquial, even in print. Although these questions continue to be hotly debated, and although they inevitably face the translator with sharp questions of the appropriate register to adopt, much of the passion they arouse among sections of the Arab cultural elite is inevitably lost in any translated version.

As with the novel, recent drama has been characterized by an increasing tendency towards experimentation, while at the same time theatre production has become increasingly linked with television. There has also been a sharp rise in theatrical activity outside Egypt. An excellent idea of the diversity of contemporary Arab theatre, both in theme and provenance, may be gained from the anthology of *Modern Arabic Drama*, edited by S. K. **Jayyusi** and Roger Allen, which includes vigorous translations of plays from Egypt, Lebanon, Palestine, Syria, Kuwait, Iraq, and Tunisia, each play carrying the name of two translators—a technique which Jayyusi has also used to good effect in the field of poetry (see below). Particularly welcome is the inclusion of no fewer than three plays by writers from Syria, a country where dramatic innovation has recently been particularly—and perhaps unexpectedly—conspicuous.

v. Poetry Modern Arabic poetry falls into three fairly well-defined though overlapping phases: 'neoclassical' (mostly written between the last third of the 19th c. and World War I), 'romantic' (mostly written between the two world wars), and 'modernist'. Each of these styles of poetry presents particular problems for the translator. Whereas neoclassical poetry generally preserves the strict metrical and rhyme schemes of medieval Arabic poetry, presenting corresponding problems of translation, the 'romantic' style was heavily influenced by western romantic poetry, not only in poetic attitudes but also, to an extent, in its adoption of a wider variety of poetic forms. Translated into English, such poems tend to sound at best old-fashioned, at worst like pastiches of western romantic poetry—as in many of the examples in **Arberry**'s *Modern Arabic Poetry* (1950).

It is perhaps partly for this reason that comparatively little neoclassical and romantic poetry has been translated into English. Most poetry translated recently dates from the period following World War II, when poets began to adopt modernist techniques derived from the West, including the use of prose poetry and various forms of free verse. As with the novel, the choice of material to be translated has occasionally been influenced by political as well as by literary considerations, among the best-known poetry of this era in English being that of the Palestinian poets Maḥmūd Darwīsh, Samīḥ al-Qāsim, and others. Of these, it is perhaps Darwīsh whose work has the most universal and immediate appeal. In addition to the several volumes of his poetry available in English, his autobiographically based prose poem *Dhākira lil-Nisyān* (1995, Memory for Forgetfulness), set during the Israeli bombardment of Beirut, has been sensitively and vigorously translated into English by Ibrahim Muhawi. Much Palestinian literature has inevitably been coloured by political events, but any suspicion that this literature is monolithic will be quickly dispelled by a glance at Salma Khadra Jayyusi's lovingly compiled *Anthology of Modern Palestinian Literature* (1992) (which includes prose passages as well as poetry).

Complete volumes of works by some other individual modern Arab poets have appeared in English (including Adūnīs, the most adventurous and iconoclastic), but the English-speaking newcomer to the field is probably best served by the several anthologies available, for example those of Boullata, Asfour, Khouri and Algar, al-Udhari, and Jayyusi. Although these anthologies are all generally accurately and competently translated, Jayyusi's *Modern Arabic Poetry: An Anthology* again has the edge, if only because of its size and scope. Jayyusi's policy of having all translations reworked by an English-language poet has been criticized by some as the first stage on the road to 'translation by committee'; but in practice the resulting translations—the majority of which preserve the authenticity of the original in an idiomatic and readable English poetic style—appear to have justified the technique. Although predominantly based on poetry from after World War II, Jayyusi's anthology also contains a selection of poetry from earlier periods of modern Arabic poetry; her perceptive preface and introduction draw attention to some of the problems of translating these works and serve as a useful poetic complement to Kilpatrick's observations on translating Arabic fiction.   PGS

ANTHOLOGIES   Abdel-Wahab, Farouk, *Modern Egyptian Drama*, Minneapolis, 1974 · Arberry, Arthur J., *Modern Arabic Poetry: An Anthology with English Verse Translation*, London, 1950 · Asfour, John Mikhail, *When the Words Burn: An Anthology of Modern Arabic Poetry 1945–1987*, Dunvegan, Ont., 1988 · Badran, Margot, and Cooke, Miriam, *Opening the Gates: A Century of Arab Feminist Writing*, London, 1990 · Boullata, Issa J., *Modern Arab Poets 1950–1975*, Washington, DC, 1976 · Jayyusi, Salma Khadra, ed., *Modern Arabic Poetry: An Anthology*, New York, 1987 · *Anthology of Modern Palestinian Literature*, New York, 1992 · Jayyusi, Salma Khadra, and Allen, Roger, eds., *Modern Arabic Drama: An Anthology*, Bloomington / Indianapolis, 1995 · Johnson-Davies, Denys, *Modern Arabic Short Stories*, London, 1967 · *Egyptian Short Stories*, London, 1978 · *Egyptian One-Act Plays*, London, 1981 · *Arabic Short Stories*, London, 1983 · Khouri, Mounah, and Algar, Hamid, *An Anthology of Modern Arabic Poetry*, Berkeley, Calif., 1975 · Manzalaoui, Mahmoud, ed., *Arabic Writing Today: The Short Story*, Cairo, 1968 · *Arabic Writing Today: The Drama*, Cairo, 1977 · al-Udhari, Abdullah, *Victims of a Map*, London, 1984 · *Modern Poetry of the Arab World*, Harmondsworth, 1986.

DARWĪSH, MAḤMUD [MAHMOUD DARWISH]   Muhawi, Ibrahim, *Memory for Forgetfulness*, Berkeley, Calif., 1995.

al-GHIṬĀNĪ, JAMĀL [GAMAL al-GHITANI]   Abdel-Wahab, Farouk, *Zayni Barakat*, London, 1988 · O'Daniel, Peter, *Incidents in Zafrani Alley*, Cairo, 1988.

al-ḤAKĪM, TAWFĪQ [TEWFIK al-HAKIM]   Eban, A. S., *The Maze of Justice*, London, 1947 · Hutchins, W., *Return of the Spirit*, Washington, DC, 1985 · Johnson-Davies, D., *The Tree Climber*, London, 1966 · *Fate of a Cockroach: Four Plays of Freedom* [includes *Song of Death*], London, 1973 · Winder, R. Bayly, *Bird of the East*, Beirut, 1966.

ḤAQQĪ, YAḤYĀ   Badawi, M. M., *The Saint's Lamp and Other Stories*, Leiden, 1973.

HAYKAL, MUḤAMMAD ḤUSAYN [MOHAMMED HUSSEIN HAIKAL]   Grinsted, J. M., *Zainab*, London, 1989.

ḤUSAYN, ṬĀHĀ [TAHA HUSSEIN]   Cragg, Kenneth, *A Passage to France*, Leiden, 1976 · Paxton, E. H., *An Egyptian Childhood: The Autobiography of Taha Hussein*, London, 1932, repr. 1981 · Wayment, Hilary, *The Stream of Days*, Cairo, 1943.

IBRĀHĪM, ṢUN'ALLĀH [SONALLAH IBRAHIM]   Johnson-Davies, Denys, *The Smell of It and Other Stories*, London, 1971.

IDRĪS, YŪSUF   Wassef, Wadida, *The Cheapest Nights and Other Stories*, London, 1978.

al-KHARRĀṬ, IDWĀR [EDWAR al-KHARRAT]   Liardet, Frances, *City of Saffron*, London, 1989 · *Girls of Alexandria*, London, 1993.

al-MĀZINĪ, IBRĀHĪM 'ABD al-QĀDIR   Wahba, Magdi, *Ibrahim the Writer*, Cairo, 1976.

MUNĪF, 'ABD al-RAḤMĀN   Theroux, Peter, *Cities of Salt*, New York, 1989 · *The Trench*, New York, 1993 · *Variations on Night and Day*, New York, 1993.

al-MUWAYLIḤĪ   Allen, Roger, *A Period of Time*, Oxford, 1992.

al-QAʿĪD, YŪSUF   Kenny, Olive, Kenny, Lorne, and Tingley, Christopher, *War in the Land of Egypt*, London, 1986 ·
    Abdel-Messih, Marie-Thérèse F., *News from the Meneisi Farm*, Cairo, 1987.
ṢĀLIḤ, al-ṬAYYIB [TAYEB SALIH]   Johnson-Davies, Denys, *Season of Migration to the North*, London, 1969.
al-SHARQĀWĪ, ʿABD al-RAḤMĀN   Stewart, D., *Egyptian Earth*, London, 1962.

SEE ALSO   Kilpatrick, H., 'Primary Problems in Translating Contemporary Arabic Novels', *Edebiyât*, 7 (1996), 126–52.

7. NAGUIB MAHFOUZ

Described by some as the world's greatest living novelist and also as the most creative and prolific literary figure in the Arab world today, the Egyptian writer Naguib Mahfouz (Najīb Maḥfūẓ) has produced over 30 novels and several anthologies of short stories and plays in a wide range of narrative styles. Though his early works are characterized by realism and attention to detail with Cairo urban life as the focus, more recently Mahfouz's prose style has looked back to the traditional narrative modes of Arabic and its classical literary tradition, rather than to the European models which he had previously used and adapted.

Mahfouz was widely read in the Middle East, where he was extremely influential in the development of the novel long before he received international recognition. In 1988 he became the first Arab writer to be awarded the Nobel Prize for Literature. Eclectic in his choice of themes, Mahfouz writes in several genres: social realism in 1947 in *Zuqāq al-Midaqq* (Midaq Alley) and again in 1956 with the Cairo Trilogy; *roman noir* in 1949 in *Al-Liṣṣ wal-Kilāb* (The Thief and the Dogs) and in 1951 in *Bidāyah wa-Nihāyah* (The Beginning and the End); psychoanalysis; metaphysics; allegories, as in 1959 in *Awlād Ḥāratinā* (Children of Gebelawi). His themes of alienation, political failure, and moral responsibility can be found in much contemporary fiction.

The Cairo Trilogy consists of *Bayn al-Qaṣrayn* (Palace Walk), *Qaṣr al-Shawq* (Palace of Desire), and *Al-Sukkariyyah* (Sugar Street). This established Mahfouz's fame, and earned him recognition outside Egyptian literary circles. In this trilogy he portrays the rising spirit of Egyptian nationalism and the struggle to escape from British hegemony. The publication of a French translation of the first two parts of the trilogy is said to have been an important factor in the decision of the Nobel Committee to award Mahfouz the prize.

With the exception of a limited readership, the West has been relatively unaware of Naguib Mahfouz's importance as a 'wielder of language' until comparatively recently, despite the fact that some of his work had previously been translated in England and in France. In *The Politics of Dispossession* (1995) Edward Said discusses the apparent reluctance of major US publishers to commission translations from Arabic. Whether Mahfouz's 'global recognition' will change this remains to be seen.

His receipt of the Nobel Prize has meant that after 1988 large American publishers, notably Doubleday, introduced Mahfouz to a new readership, replacing the dribble of academic translations by Middle Eastern publishing houses and particularly by the American University Press in Cairo. It is worth noting, however, that several of the recent publications are in effect no more than new editions of existing translations which have received critical acclaim. Examples include *Al-Summān wal-Kharīf* (1962), translated as *The Autumn Quail* by Roger **Allen** and published in 1985 by the American University Press, and then republished in 1990 by Doubleday, and *Midaq Alley*, translated by Trevor **Le Gassick** in 1974 for the publishing house Three Continents, and republished in 1992 by Doubleday. *Layālī alf Laylah* (1979) is a work described (el-Enany 1993) as a 'dark reworking' and the 'only modern treatment that lives up to the imaginative challenge' of the classic *Thousand and One Nights* [II.b.5]. This was translated as *Arabian Nights and Days* 'with great feeling' by Denys **Johnson-Davies** and was the winner of the *Independent* Foreign Literature Award in 1995.

Mahfouz's use of standard Arabic in his dialogues is a characteristic feature of his style, and this facilitates the task of the translator, the handling of dialect being notoriously complex in translation. When dealing with colloquialisms, the translator can choose to neutralize, by the use of standard English. This can be the only option which does not affect the overall pragmatic coherence of the text. In contrast, the use of Americanisms in some of the translations which were commissioned by American publishers, for example the interjections 'okay' and 'buster' which are in *Palace of Desire*, may disorientate the non-American reader. Another strategy noted in various translations is the use of more generic equivalents in English to translate Egyptian Arabic. Examples of this can be found in Catherine **Cobham**'s translation of *Malḥamat al-Ḥarāfīsh* (The Harafish) where a *riyal*, a coin of a specific value, becomes simply a 'coin', and where formulas invoking the name of God or His Prophet are secularized. It can be argued that the fluency of the translation amply compensates for any loss of specific meaning and connotations that this approach involves.

The English translations of Mahfouz's work vary not so much in terms of 'quality' as in the degree of 'foreignization' or 'domestication'. Many of these translations include glossaries in order to explain culture-bound terms and concepts, and thereby make the books more accessible to the foreign reader. In *The Autumn Quail* Roger Allen opts for keeping some of the terms which are not intrinsically culture-bound in their Arabic transliteration, as for example in the case of *Shari'a Ibrahim* (Ibrahim Street). In *Mirāyā* (1972), which he translated as *Mirrors*, Allen also makes extensive use of footnotes. The novel, built around a series of frames, is embedded in Egyptian political life and contains numerous references to historical figures and the main political parties, which in all likelihood are unfamiliar to the English reader. But however informative and useful the many footnotes might be for the reader of the translation, they can also be rather intrusive. The presence of numerous footnotes can, in addition to breaking the flow of the narrative, thwart any attempt to transcend the specificity of the setting, not doing justice to the universal transcultural significance of the original text.

The reader of English translations of Arabic fiction, notably when confronted with sensitively faithful translations, might be misled and see poeticisms in certain expressions and greetings which in fact are standard in Arabic, and which do not indicate the use of a particularly flowery style by the original author. For instance, in Anthony Burgess's review (*The Independent*, 10 May 1995) of *Palace of Desire*, W. **Hutchins** and L. and O. **Kenny**'s translation of the first part of the Cairo Trilogy, undue emphasis is placed on the use of idioms such as the Arabic greeting 'You've brought light into our home'. In fact, this is a fairly standard welcome.

In the following passage, Catherine Cobham uses both neutralization and foreignization. A generic term, *cart*, is given as the equivalent of the more colloquial Arabic *Karu*, whilst in another instance *ṭa'miya* is kept in the English text. It would have been possible to translate *ṭa'miya* by *felafel*, a term which is more 'universal', more likely to be familiar to the English reader, and which also belongs to Egyptian Arabic.

But it wasn't just for a night.

They would leave the house at dawn and slip back in as night fell. During the day they drove the cart from one district to another and ate lentils, beans and *ta'miya*; at night they floated about in cotton and silk, lounged on divans on the ground floor, and slept in a luxurious bed reached by a short flight of ebony stairs. Fulla stroked curtains, cushions, carpets, and exclaimed, 'Our life was just a nightmare!'

At night through the carved lattices the alley looked a gloomy place, haunted by wretched phantoms. 'Divine wisdom is hard to comprehend,' muttered Ashur sadly. (*The Harafish*, p. 46)   MS-C

TRANSLATIONS   Abadir, Akef, and Allen, Roger, *God's World*, Chicago, 1973 · Allen, Roger, *Mirrors*, Chicago, 1977 · *Autumn Quail*, tr. revised by John Rodenbeck, London/New York, 1990 · Awad, Ramses, *The Beginning and the End*, London/New York, 1990 · Cobham, Catherine, *The Harafish*, London/New York, 1993 · el-Enany, Rasheed, *Respected Sir*, London, 1986; London/New York, 1990 · el-Gabalawi, Saad, 'Al-Karnak' in his *Three Egyptian Novels*, New York, 1988 · Hashem, Malak, *The Day the Leader Was Killed*, Cairo, 1989 · Henry, Kristen, and al-Warraki, Narriman, *The Beggar*, London/New York, 1990 · Hutchins, William, and Kenny, Olive *Palace Walk*, London/New York, 1990 · *Palace of Desire* (with Lorne M. Kenny), London/New York, 1991 · *Sugar Street* (with Angele Boutros Samaan), London/New York, 1992 · Johnson-Davies, Denys, *The Time and the Place and Other Stories*, London/New York, 1991 · *The Journey of Ibn Fattouma*, London/New York, 1992 · *Arabian Nights and Days*, Cairo, 1994; London/New York, 1995 · Kenny, Olive, *Wedding Song*, London/New York, 1990 · Le Gassick, Trevor, *Midaq Alley*, Washington, DC, 1974; London/New York, 1992 · and Badawi, Mustafa, *The Thief and the Dogs*, tr. revised by John Rodenbeck, London/New York, 1990 · Liardet, Frances, *Adrift in the Nile*, London/New York, 1993 · Moussa-Mahmoud, Fatma, *Miramar*, London, 1978; Cairo, 1985 · Selaiha, Nehad, *One-Act Plays*, i, Cairo, 1989 · Sobhi, Soad, with Fattouh, Essam, and Kenneson, James, *Fountain and Tomb*, Washington, DC, 1988.

SEE ALSO   el-Enany, R., *Naguib Mahfouz: The Pursuit of Meaning*, London, 1993 · Le Gassick, T., 'The Arabic Novel in Translation' in R. Allen, ed., *The Arabic Novel since 1950*, Cambridge, Mass., 1992.

c. The Bible

1. THE BIBLE IN ENGLISH

i. Nature of the Bible What is known as 'the Bible' is in fact a library of religious writings spanning a period of more than 1000 years, representing a wide variety of cultural contexts and of literary genres, and originating in three languages, Hebrew, Aramaic, and Greek. The collection provides the basic canon of sacred writings of the Judaeo-Christian tradition.

Its major component is the Hebrew Bible, comprising 24 books of varying length (subdivided in English Bibles into 39). Substantial parts of two of these books (Daniel 2:4–7:28; Ezra 4:8–6:18; 7:12–26) and one isolated verse in another (Jeremiah 10: 11) are in Aramaic, the rest in Hebrew. Christians habitually refer to these books as the Old Testament (OT), but for Jews this term is not acceptable since it implies a Christian 'takeover' of the Hebrew Bible as merely prolegomena to their own Scriptures.

The New Testament (NT) consists of 27 Christian writings of the 1st c. CE, written in the common Greek of the period, though with a variety of styles and levels of linguistic sophistication.

Translation of the various writings which make up the Bible is significantly affected by their status as 'Scripture' [see I.c.3]. They thus constitute a canon of authoritative writings regarded by members of the Jewish and Christian religions as in a different category from other literature and, despite their manifestly human authorship, as conveying in some sense the 'Word of God'. Other Hebrew and Greek writings from the Jewish world and from early Christianity, while they may be valued for their literary and religious qualities, are not 'Scripture'.

There are, however, certain Jewish writings (of later date than the OT books) which, while never part of the Hebrew Bible, were particularly valued in some early Christian circles. These are known as the Apocrypha, and are included in some English translations of the Bible. These books were preserved in Greek, not in Hebrew, even though many of them came from Hebrew or Aramaic originals. Their status is defined in Catholic theology as 'deutero-canonical' (i.e. authoritative on a lower level than that of the canonical books of the OT). Protestants generally treat them as of less importance.

ii. Bible Translation before Translation into English Translations of the Hebrew Scriptures became necessary by the 3rd c. BCE, when many Jews no longer understood Hebrew. Translation into Greek (the lingua franca of the Eastern Mediterranean) was focused in the large Jewish community of Alexandria. At first there were various individual translations, but by the end of the 2nd c. BCE a standard collection, known as the Septuagint, was widely accepted. It was the Septuagint which was in effect the Bible of the first Christians, and which is copiously quoted in the NT. It is not the product of a single translation project, and the styles adopted for the various books differ considerably, some of them departing quite freely from the Hebrew text as we know it. Different manuscripts of the Septuagint witness also to considerable variations in the accepted Greek text. Later Greek versions of the Hebrew Bible were essentially revisions of the Septuagint, some (notably that of Aquila) much more literal.

In Palestine and further east, Aramaic was the prevalent language among Jews, and a variety of Aramaic versions of the Hebrew Bible, known as targums [II.j.1.ii], were produced around the same period, though it was many centuries before any sort of standard Aramaic text was established. Targums are typically much more free and expansive even than the Septuagint, and sometimes contain quite substantial interpolations. They are the witness to a developing and quite creative interpretative tradition within Jewish worship and preaching.

Translation of both Hebrew Bible and NT into Latin began very early in the Christian era, and again a variety of independent versions were soon in use. Towards the end of the 4th c., however, St Jerome was commissioned by Pope Damasus to revise existing translations so as to produce a standard Latin version of the whole Bible, the Vulgate, which became the accepted text of the Latin Church, so that relatively few manuscripts of earlier Latin versions survive.

Translation into Syriac followed a similar course, with the early 5th-c. Peshitta version supplanting earlier Syriac translations, some of which had been in existence since the 2nd c. The other major versions translated directly from the Greek are the Coptic versions deriving from the 3rd and 4th c. Subsequent translations into Gothic, Armenian, Ethiopic, and Georgian are known as 'secondary versions', since they were made not from the original language but from one of the earlier translations.

The character of these various early translations varied considerably. While some were the work of scholars such as Jerome, with a formidable knowledge of relevant languages, most are not associated with any named translator. The motive of the translators was generally more religious than literary: to make the sacred texts accessible to worshippers who did not know the original languages. The written Aramaic targums, for instance, were a development from the practice in the synagogue of giving an oral, and in most cases probably extempore, Aramaic interpretation after the Hebrew text had been read.

Such versions are not likely to be marked by verbatim accuracy, and the character of many of the surviving versions from the Septuagint onwards indicates that this was not always the primary concern of the anonymous translators. This was to be a significant factor when the Bible began to be translated into English, since it was Latin rather than Greek which dominated western Europe, while Hebrew was little known among European Christians of the late Middle Ages.

iii. The Problem of Textual Transmission To return to 'the original text' is, however, no easy matter when we are dealing with ancient texts passed on in manuscript form before the days of printing. In Bible translation the issue of textual criticism is particularly important and complex.

Until the middle of the 20th c., the earliest surviving manuscripts of the Hebrew Bible dated from the 9th c. CE, i.e. over 1000 years later than even the latest books of the Hebrew Bible were written. But the discovery of the Dead Sea Scrolls, together with a number of other recent discoveries, have now made available to us manuscripts of the Hebrew text written 1000 years and more earlier. The result has been to confirm the care with which the text had been preserved, even though a number of differences have emerged.

In addition to Hebrew manuscripts, there are full manuscripts of the Septuagint and other versions from the 4th c. CE onwards, and partial texts which are even earlier. These often offer a significantly different reading from the Hebrew text tradition, but this is as likely to be due to the freedom exercised by the Greek translator as to a variant Hebrew text to which he had access.

In the case of the NT the time-scale is less extended. There are complete Greek texts of the NT from the 4th c., and many earlier papyri of parts of it have survived, some from as early as the middle of the 2nd c. In all, we have over 5000 Greek manuscripts of the NT, though the majority of these are later and of lesser value. There is also a wide variety of manuscript evidence for the early versions in Latin, Syriac, and Coptic, as well as numerous citations from the NT books by early Christian writers whose works are preserved. The NT is thus vastly better attested than any other ancient literature. The works of Tacitus [II.n.10.iv], by contrast, survive in only two incomplete manuscripts written many centuries after his time, between them covering only about half of what he is known to have written.

But a large quantity of manuscripts means a large range of variants, since no two manuscripts are exactly alike. Most of the variants are of minor importance, matters of spelling or grammar, or of stylistic variation. Where there are differences of substance, in most cases experts are in little doubt which represents the original, but there remain a significant number of variants where translators must make a choice as to the words to be rendered, or as to whether or not to include a portion of text, which may be as little as one word but may be a whole verse or two. There is room here for sincere disagreement even among those who are well versed in the discipline of textual criticism, and English versions of the Bible may and do differ accordingly.

Many of the most important Biblical manuscripts have been discovered relatively recently, and the whole science of textual criticism has become far more sophisticated and, one hopes, more responsible. Translations of the Bible made before the present century are likely therefore to be based on less reliable texts. The need for constant retranslation arises not only from the development of the English language but also from the growing availability of evidence for the original texts themselves.

iv. Early English Translations In medieval England Latin was the language of literate people. Direct access to the Bible was restricted in practice to the clergy and monastic orders, and their Bible was the Latin Vulgate.

Perhaps the earliest renderings of Biblical texts into English are in the Old English poems of **Cædmon**. These are sometimes based on the Bible, and amount virtually to free metrical versions of parts of the Biblical text [see I.b.1.ii]. Translations of parts of the Bible into Old English are said to have been produced in the early 8th c. by Bishop Aldhelm of Sherborne (Psalms) and by Bede (John's Gospel), but these have not survived. Probably the earliest actual translations preserved are those inserted between the lines of the Latin text of medieval manuscripts, notably the Northumbrian version inserted by **Aldred** into the Lindisfarne Gospels in the 10th c.

The first extant independent Old English version of the gospels, known as the Wessex Gospels, comes from the 10th c., as does Ælfric's translation of Genesis to Judges [I.b.1.ii]. But with the Norman Conquest translations into English virtually ceased, as Norman French became the language of the literate.

In the 14th c. Richard **Rolle** (c.1300–1349) produced a prose version of the Psalms in his south Yorkshire dialect, together with a verse-by-verse commentary, and copies of this work were made in other dialects [see I.b.1.i]. An anonymous Middle English version of parts of the NT for use in monasteries is also preserved from the 14th c.

But it was John **Wyclif** (c.1330–1384) and his associates who first attempted to put an English Bible in the hands of lay people. Wyclif, master of Balliol College, Oxford, was a 'reformer before the Reformation'. His attacks both on the privileges of the Church and on such Catholic doctrines as transubstantiation earned him the Pope's condemnation for heresy. His guiding principle was the supreme authority of the Bible. The 'Wyclif' translation is probably mostly not by Wyclif himself, but the project was at the heart of his aim to restore the Bible's authority in the life of Church and nation. It

was based not on the original languages (which were not available then in England) but on the Latin Vulgate, which it translates so literally as to be sometimes almost unintelligible to those who do not know Latin. A revised version, produced after Wyclif's death probably by his secretary John **Purvey** (c.1353–c.1428), shows more respect for English idiom; the reviser's prologue states his aim as 'to translate after the sentence and not only after the words . . . and if the letter may not be followed in the translating, let the sentence ever be whole and open [plain].'

The Lollard movement which arose from Wyclif's work provoked fierce opposition from the Church establishment. A provincial synod convened by the Archbishop of Canterbury in 1408 issued the 'Constitutions of Oxford' which forbade the production or use of vernacular Bibles without a bishop's approval. But the revised translation (rather than the earlier Wyclif version) continued nonetheless to be widely read and circulated. It was, in effect, *the* English Bible throughout the 15th and early 16th c. [see also I.b.1.v].

v. The Sixteenth Century Two major factors separate later English translations from those of the 14th c. The first was the rediscovery in European scholarship of the Hebrew and Greek languages, and the growing availability of Biblical texts in the originals. The second was the invention of printing.

The first printed Hebrew Bible appeared in 1488, and the first printed Greek NT in 1516. The materials were therefore available for a translation from the originals to be printed in English, and William **Tyndale** (1494–1536) [I.b.2.iv] was the first to take up the opportunity. As one of the foremost champions of the Reformation in England, Tyndale was constantly engaged in controversy, and spent his last 12 years in exile on the Continent, where he was eventually burnt as a heretic. His English NT was printed in 1526, not in England, where there was still strong official hostility to a vernacular Bible (particularly one suspected of 'Lutheran' connections), but at Worms, from where it was smuggled into England, where it met with an enthusiastic black market.

The German connection is significant, since only four years earlier Martin Luther had printed the first German NT. Much of the cross-reference and comment which accompanies Tyndale's translation is clearly based on Luther's. But the translation is Tyndale's own, based on Erasmus's 1522 Greek NT, and using a vigorous, idiomatic English style which was to be the basis of all subsequent English translations until the 20th c.

Tyndale is by far the most significant figure in the story of the translation of the Bible into English. In addition to his NT, he also began the translation of the Hebrew Bible. He published the Pentateuch in English in 1530, and prepared translations of some other books which were subsequently incorporated into 'Matthew's Bible' (see below). But he devoted more time to revising his NT; the extensively revised 1534 edition became the definitive text on which subsequent translators drew.

The first complete English Bible to be printed (in 1535) was the work of Tyndale's friend and associate Myles **Coverdale** (1488–1568) [I.b.2.iv]. Its title-page describes it as 'translated out of Douche [German] and Latyn into Englishe', as Coverdale made no claim to be an expert in Hebrew and Greek. But his NT was essentially Tyndale's, revised in the light of German versions, while his OT incorporated elements of Tyndale's and Luther's work based on the originals. It was his version of the Psalms, subsequently incorporated in the Great Bible of 1539, which became the Psalter of the Book of Common Prayer.

Matthew's Bible (1537) was compiled by Tyndale's associate John Rogers, writing under a pseudonym. It is in fact the work of Tyndale, as far as he had reached (including the unpublished parts of the Hebrew Bible), the rest being drawn from Coverdale. It is notable as the first English translation to be published 'with the king's most gracious licence'. Bible translation had at last received official approval.

The stage was thus set for an 'authorized version', which was to be placed in every church in the land, so that 'your parishioners may most commodiously resort to the same and read it'. Coverdale was entrusted with the task of revising the Matthew Bible for this purpose, and the resultant version, issued with a preface by Thomas Cranmer, is known as the Great Bible (1539). This remained the officially recognized Bible until the reign of Elizabeth I. It was in all essentials the work of two men, Tyndale and Coverdale.

But it had one significant weakness. Apart from those Hebrew books which Tyndale had translated, the rest of the OT (Coverdale's work) was not based on the Hebrew text. This was one of the motives for an extensive revision which was eventually published as the Geneva Bible of 1560 (so called because it was first printed in Geneva, and was the work of men closely associated with the Reformation movement on the Continent). This translation was not, as hitherto, the work of one man, but of a group of scholars—the first English 'committee translation'. Its popular title,

'the "Breeches" Bible', derives from its translation of Genesis 3: 7, where Adam and Eve sewed fig-leaves together to make themselves 'breeches'.

The Geneva Bible was an immediate success, and quickly supplanted the Great Bible not only in private use but in church as well. This was the Bible of the Elizabethan Church, and of Shakespeare. An official revision of the Great Bible, the Bishops' Bible of 1568, never seriously competed with the Geneva Bible in general usage.

vi. The King James Bible [see also II.c.2] James I (James VI of Scotland) did not share the general enthusiasm for the Geneva Bible, largely on account of the notes published along with the text which were felt to be partisan. So at the Hampton Court Conference summoned in the year after his accession it was agreed to produce a new version, without commentary, 'to be read in the whole Church, and none other'. The work was entrusted to a large group (47 in all) of the best scholars available, who between them represented a range of theological opinion, and so could not be stigmatized as producing a partisan text.

The King James Bible of 1611 (popularly known in Britain as the Authorized Version (AV); this title, even if a little misleading, is so well established that it will be used from here on) claims to be 'newly translated out of the original tongues', but the translators did not start from scratch. The following clause in the title adds 'with the former translations diligently compared and revised', and they were in fact instructed to take the Bishops' Bible of 1568 as the basis of their work. The phrases of Tyndale's NT can often be heard, though they tended generally to revise in a more literal direction. But their preface ('The Translators to the Reader', unfortunately not included in most modern editions) makes it clear that they did much more than merely revise the Bishops' Bible (which, after all, was not based directly on the Hebrew text in many OT books), working in detail from the original texts.

The translators, well aware of the range of possibilities both in the reading of the original text and in the understanding of its words, added marginal notes, not of the 'commentary' type which the king disliked, but to indicate reasonable alternative renderings. In answer to the criticism that such notes undermined the reader's confidence in the text, they replied that 'they that are wise had rather have their judgments at liberty in differences of readings, than to be captivated to one, when it might be the other'.

They chose to avoid 'concordance' translation, whereby the same English word is always used for the same word in the original. Indeed, they seem to have set some store by variety in style, so that at times they vary the English renderings of a given word where the same word would have conveyed the sense perfectly well.

In these and other ways the AV marked a significant advance on earlier versions, so that even without royal backing it would probably have supplanted even the Geneva Bible in both public and private use. Given the king's strong endorsement as well, it was assured of success. The term 'Authorized Version' is not quite accurate, since it was never (like the Book of Common Prayer) imposed by Act of Parliament, but the clause 'appointed to be read in churches' on its title page indicates its quasi-official status. For English-speaking Protestants from the mid-17th c. until 1881 there was, in effect, only one English Bible.

There is, however, one major weakness which the 1611 version shares with all its predecessors, and which is no fault of its translators. The Hebrew and Greek texts available in the 16th and early 17th c. were much inferior to what is available today, and at many points the words rendered by King James's translators are not what is now agreed to be the original text. This problem is particularly serious in the NT, for which they were dependent on the Greek text issued by Stephanus in 1550. This text, misleadingly known as the Received Text (*Textus Receptus*), was based on the few Greek manuscripts then available, which were late in date, and represented the 'Byzantine' type of text which most scholars now believe to be a revision (and in some places expansion) of the original. In a few places no Greek text at all was available, and Stephanus' text is taken from the Vulgate, translated back into Greek. The most notorious example is the Trinitarian text in 1 John 5: 7, which occurs in no Greek manuscript before the 15th c., where it is clearly derived from the Latin. The discovery of earlier texts and the advances in textual criticism mean that there are now serious textual questions to be set against the undoubted literary qualities of the AV.

The above discussion may have suggested that Bible translation into English was an exclusively Protestant enterprise. Certainly Protestants took the lead, but a Catholic response began with the publication of the Rheims NT in 1582, followed by the OT published at Douai in 1610. This Douai Bible was deliberately based not on the Hebrew and Greek but on the Vulgate, the version prescribed by the Council of Trent. Its style was so much based on the Latin as to be quite obscure, and a major revision was undertaken by Bishop Challoner in the 18th c. A further revision of the Douai-Challoner

NT, known as the Confraternity Version, was published in America in 1941.

vii. Translations in the Nineteenth and Early Twentieth Centuries

The AV had no significant rival for 270 years. There were of course a number of individual efforts at Bible translation, some of them worthy attempts to update the AV (including one by John **Wesley** in 1768), others quite eccentric. But none made much lasting impression.

But the AV, for all its good qualities, inevitably became dated in two respects: in addition to the increase of knowledge about the Hebrew and Greek texts noted above, there was also the fact that no language stands still, and the 'Biblical language' of 1611 became increasingly remote from ordinary speech. And of course even the AV was not faultless even in its own time. So a Revised Version (RV) was produced in 1881 (NT) and 1885 (OT) by a committee set up by the Convocation of Canterbury, drawing on the best biblical scholarship of the time.

A parallel revision process was carried out in America, and the two committees kept in touch with each other's work, but the American revisers were not prepared to follow such strictly conservative guidelines as the British. The resultant American Standard Version (ASV) of 1901 is thus of recognizably similar character to the RV, but not identical (notably in its use of 'Jehovah' instead of 'the LORD' to represent the divine name).

The RV was deliberately a 'revision', not a new translation. Its compilers aimed to keep as close as possible to the familiar wording, even retaining 'all archaisms, whether of language or construction, which though not in familiar use cause a reader no embarrassment and lead to no misunderstanding'. Where errors needed to be corrected, or the language was now misleading, they aimed still to follow the style and diction of the AV as closely as possible. On one point, however, they clearly felt differently from the 1611 translators, in that they aimed wherever the context allowed to use the same English rendering for the same original word.

One feature of the new version which to us seems commonplace, but which was a major contribution to intelligent understanding, was the layout of the printed text. Instead of each verse being printed as a paragraph in itself, with no indication of where a new section began, the RV printed the text in sense-paragraphs (though retaining verse-numbers for reference). In the poetical books and in some other poetical material (though surprisingly not in the prophetic books) the text was set out in lines rather than printed like prose.

In the reconstruction of the text to be translated,

the RV represents a huge leap forward and was welcomed as such by most Biblical scholars of the time (though with lively exceptions such as the redoubtable Dean Burgon, whose fury at the loss of such familiar texts as the Trinitarian formula in 1 John 5: 7 knew no limits). It was widely accepted as the 'proper' text to use in schools and colleges. But the pedantic and archaic style of translation resulting from the revisers' principles was not calculated to excite the reading public, and it seems never to have caught the public imagination. The AV remained most people's Bible.

But the principle of retranslation was now recognized, and during the first half of the 20th c. many new versions began to appear. Most of them were the work of individuals, and could claim no official status. The following list of versions published before 1950 may give some idea of the gradual opening of the floodgates: *The Twentieth Century New Testament* (1902); R. F. **Weymouth**, *The New Testament in Modern Speech* (1903); F. **Fenton**, *The Holy Bible in Modern English* (1903); J. **Moffatt**, *The New Testament: a New Translation* (1913; complete Bible 1928); Jewish Publication Society version (1917); E. J. **Goodspeed**, *The New Testament: an American Translation* (1923; complete Bible 1927); G. W. **Wade**, *The Documents of the New Testament* (1934); C. B. **Williams**, *The New Testament in the Language of the People* (1937); *The New Testament in Basic English* (1941); R. A. **Knox** (1945; complete Bible 1949); *The New World Translation* of Jehovah's Witnesses (1950; complete Bible 1953).

Two of these versions may be singled out for special mention. Moffatt's vigorous version (which sometimes reflects Scottish rather than English idiom) made a decisive break from 'Bible English', and introduced many for the first time to a Bible in which the characters spoke like real people. Like all individual translations it is at the mercy of the translator's preferences and ideas: it may be questioned whether it helps many ordinary readers to find at the beginning of the Gospel of John, 'The Logos existed in the very beginning, the Logos was with God, the Logos was divine', while the introduction of Enoch into the text of 1 Peter 3: 19 is a rather wild scholarly guess.

Moffatt's version remained a solo effort, with no authority but his own. Ronald Knox's version, on the other hand, received the official endorsement of the Catholic hierarchy, and so stood alongside the Douai Bible as an official version. Like the Douai, it is a translation of the Vulgate, though with careful attention throughout to the original languages. Knox explained his principles in an important book, *On Englishing the Bible* (1949). Prominent

among them is the desire, while writing natural English, to avoid being merely contemporary. Rather he aimed to produce such good, timeless English that it would not seem dated even in 200 years' time. Time will tell, but unfortunately for Knox's version it was only another 20 years before a much more widely read Catholic translation, the Jerusalem Bible, appeared.

But while this wealth of individual Bible translations were being produced, the inadequacy of the more 'official' RV (and its American counterpart) was increasingly felt, and a movement began towards a more extensive revision in the AV tradition. The result was the 'Revised Standard Version' (RSV) of 1946 (NT; whole Bible 1952), a revision by an American committee of the ASV.

The committee's aim was a thorough revision which nonetheless retained the 'qualities which have given to the King James Version a supreme place in English literature'. The RV and ASV had retained the archaic verb endings ('-est', '-eth') and the use of 'thou' instead of the singular 'you'; the new version abandoned these archaisms, except for retaining 'thou' where God is addressed. The ASV's use of 'Jehovah' was dropped again in favour of 'the LORD'. Clearly obsolete forms of expression were replaced, and the language has an altogether more modern feel, though it is far from colloquial. Poetic material was set out more consistently in lines, and in other ways the typography was brought into the 20th c., as with the use of quotation marks for direct speech.

The careful attention to developments in textual criticism which marked the RV was carried further in its successor. One interesting feature is the appearance 13 times in Isaiah of notes attributing the reading adopted to 'One ancient Ms.'. This is the great Isaiah scroll from Qumran, discovered in 1947 and published just in time for the committee to take it into account. Since this text is more than 1000 years earlier than the Masoretic manuscripts on which previous translators had had to depend, it marks a significant move forward in translating the Hebrew Bible, comparable with the influence of the great 4th-c. codices on the RV of the NT.

Updated readings of the Hebrew and Greek texts and (relatively unadventurous) attempts to introduce more modern idiom inevitably attracted conservative criticism and vilification of the new version, including the widespread assertion that its translators were determined to undermine the divinity of Christ. Looking back now, it is hard to see what the fuss was about, since the RSV is far more conservative and reassuringly familiar in its language than most more recent versions (each of which in its turn has received the same treatment). But the long dominance of the AV had encouraged a resistance to change which the archaic style of the RV had not seriously threatened, but which now awoke with vigour.

viii. From the New English Bible to the Present Day

The RSV was still essentially in the tradition of Bible translation going back to Tyndale. It was a revision, not a new translation. We have noted above some more radically new translations in the first half of the 20th c., but these remained individual contributions. There was still no genuinely new translation by a representative body commanding wide recognition.

The New English Bible (NEB: NT 1961; whole Bible 1970) was the pioneer. The committee which produced it was set up jointly by many of the Protestant Churches in Britain, and included many of the most respected Biblical scholars of the day. They were 'free to employ a contemporary idiom rather than reproduce the traditional "biblical" English', and were assisted by a panel of 'trusted literary advisers'. The resultant style is certainly 'new', though many ordinary readers have found it too literary, even 'donnish'. But its publication marked a new era in English Bible translation. Many others soon followed. There follows a list, in chronological order and with minimal descriptions, of the more important committee or 'official' translations (of very varied character) up to the time of writing. (In most cases the NT was published first; dates given are for the whole Bible.)

Jerusalem Bible (1966), a new Catholic translation based on the French Bible de Jérusalem: stylistically elegant, and widely used by Protestant readers. A New Jerusalem Bible (1985), following a new edition of the Bible de Jérusalem in 1973, is the work of Henry **Wansbrough**, with an even more readable style than its predecessor, and making significant steps toward inclusive language (see II.c.1.xiii).

New American Bible (1970), produced by members of the Catholic Biblical Association for the Roman Catholic bishops of America: more formal style; the NT, rather hastily prepared, was replaced by a new translation in 1987.

New American Standard Bible (1970), a conservative attempt to update the ASV of 1901: English style sacrificed to literal translation; little used outside America.

Good News Bible (1976; also known as Today's English Version), produced under the auspices of the United Bible Societies and designed to be suitable for those for whom English is a second language; it uses language which is 'natural, clear,

simple and unambiguous', following the principle of 'dynamic equivalence' (as advocated in the works of Eugene A. Nida [see. II.c.1.xi]); the result is a vigorous and uncluttered style, which has been particularly welcomed among younger people for whom 'Bible English' is an unfamiliar language.

New International Version (1978), translated by a committee representing the evangelical constituency primarily in North America, but with an Anglicized version: a moderately contemporary style which reads well in public or in private; currently the bestselling version in English; an inclusive-language edition of the NT published in Britain in 1995.

New King James Version (1982), preserving the textual features of the AV, but with modernized language and spelling: a rather quixotic enterprise, inspired by the dominance of the KJV in America, and a backlash against modern textual criticism.

New Jewish Version (1985), replacing the Jewish Publication Society Bible of 1917: a totally new translation, on the 'idiom for idiom' rather than 'word for word' principle.

Revised English Bible (1989), a radical revision of the NEB, with a much improved style and fairly consistently inclusive language.

New Revised Standard Version (1989), the latest in the line of versions derived from the AV: a very extensive revision of the RSV, with the last of the 'thou's' removed and with the most comprehensive attention to inclusive language yet attempted.

Following the lead of the NEB most recent committee versions, while drawn up by Biblical scholars, have profited from the help of literary consultants. This feature, together with the continuing advances in Biblical scholarship and textual criticism, means that Bible translation has entered a quite new phase since 1960. No previous generation (not even those of Tyndale and of the AV) has been so well served by versions which both communicate effectively and may be relied on to convey the original sense as nearly as it can be ascertained. (It should be noted, however, that not all translations aim to be idiomatic [see below, xi].)

Alongside these committee or 'official' versions, the spate of individual versions has continued. Even to list them would be impossible. I mention just two which have been influential.

J. B. **Phillips**, aware that young people no longer understood 'Bible English', produced his famous Letters to Young Churches in 1947 and completed the NT in 1958 and Four Prophets in 1963. His style is lively paraphrase, sometimes colloquial to the point of inelegance, but vigorous and arresting. In the days before the Good News Bible, Phillips filled a significant gap, particularly for younger readers, and is still widely read today.

A more idiosyncratic paraphrase is the Living Bible of Kenneth **Taylor** (1971), in very colloquial American idiom, and giving clear expression to the author's conservative theology. ('The theological lodestar in this book has been a rigid evangelical position.') But as a result of aggressive marketing it has probably been more widely read than any other individual version in recent years.

All these versions are, or intend to be, in 'standard English' (though transatlantic variations have made 'Anglicized editions' of some primarily American versions necessary). But attempts have also been made to translate the Bible or parts of it into non-standard English, such as *The Gospels in Scouse* and *Chapters from the New Testament translated into the Wensleydale Tongue*.

Some such versions are relatively light-hearted, but a more serious and scholarly version is W. L. Lorimer, *The New Testament in Scots* (Penguin, 1983), based on a lifetime of study of the Scots language [see I.a.6.ii]. Here is Matthew 5: 14–15: 'Ye are the licht o the warld. A toun biggit on a hill-tap canna be hoddit; an again, whan fowk licht a lamp, they pit-it-na ablò a meal-bassie, but set it up on the dresser-heid, and syne it gies licht for aabodie i the houss.'

Translations have also been made into various forms of Pidgin English [see I.a.6.i]. Here are the first four beatitudes from Matthew 5: 3–6 in a West African pidgin, as translated by the Mill Hill Fathers in Cameroon: 'Bless he live for people whe them de poor for heart;—na country for Heaven he go be them own. Bless he live for people whe them get strong heart;—them go chop country. Bless for people whe them de cry;—them go cool them heart. Bless for them people whe them de hungry for be holy;—them heart he go full up.'

ix. Translations of the Psalms Both because of their poetic character and because of their central place in corporate worship, the psalms have attracted the attention of many translators in addition to those working on the Bible as a whole. A fascinating range of such translations are surveyed and sampled in D. Davie's *The Psalms in English*. Only a few versions can be mentioned here, restricted to those who have translated the whole psalter rather than selected psalms. Such translations have in general been designed for corporate worship rather than for private reading.

Traditional Hebrew poetry, which does not rhyme, depends essentially on the parallelism of lines rather than on a regular metre. It is typically (but not always) set out in pairs of lines, where there is often a balance or contrast between the two members. This structure lends itself to the 'Anglican chant', a development from medieval plainsong in which pairs of lines of respectively four and six notes allow the singers to fit in wording of quite variable length and metre by singing all words on a monotone until the final three or five syllables of the line are reached. Coverdale's version of the Psalms, incorporated into the *Book of Common Prayer*, is designed for such chanting, with each verse printed as two lines divided by a colon.

Until the 20th c. Coverdale's psalter was unchallenged in Anglican worship, despite its sometimes quaint archaisms. In 1966 a Revised Psalter appeared, produced by an Archbishops' Commission on which musicians and poets significantly outnumbered Hebraists, and which included T. S. **Eliot** and C. S. **Lewis**. It was a very conservative revision, and had only limited use before the production of the *Alternative Service Book* in 1980 took away any general demand for a revision of the Prayer Book Psalter.

The psalter printed in the *Alternative Service Book* is the Liturgical Psalter, originally translated for the Australian Prayer Book of 1977. While the *Alternative Service Book* has been widely criticized for its 'committee language', its psalter has been more favourably accepted as a sensitive rendering in restrained modern idiom, one which both reads well in itself and at the same time is not so distant from Coverdale's style as to alienate the regular worshipper. The gradual erosion of chanting in Anglican worship suggests that this may be the last version in that tradition.

But not all English-speakers are Anglicans, and in Scotland in particular a vigorous tradition of metrical psalms has produced versions which are closer to traditional English poetry in metre and rhyme. An early attempt (1551) by Thomas **Sternhold** (d. 1549) and John **Hopkins** (d. 1570) has been widely criticized for its pedestrian style and contrived versification, though it held a place in popular use even after other and better versions were available. Of much greater literary merit was another early version by Sir Philip **Sidney** (1554–86) and his sister Mary **Herbert**, Countess of Pembroke (1561–1621), but this long remained unpublished and never had the popular appeal of Sternhold and Hopkins. Whereas they had put all the psalms into the same rather monotonous metre, the Countess made a point of using many different poetic metres and stanza patterns.

The best-known metrical psalter is Nahum **Tate** (1652–1715) and Nicholas **Brady** (1659–1726), *A New*

Version of the Psalms of David fitted to the Tunes used in Churches (1698), using eight different metres which could be sung to familiar hymn tunes. The level of poetry achieved is not even, but some abiding favourites in modern hymn-books started life as Tate and Brady paraphrases ('Through all the changing scenes of life'; 'As pants the hart for cooling streams'). Their version long remained for many *the* metrical psalter.

A different approach to the use of psalms in worship in modern times arose from the French *Bible de Jérusalem* (1955), in which 'special attention was paid to the rhythmic structure of the poetry of the psalms, and this allowed a sung or recited psalmody to be fashioned'. An English version was published in 1963 as *The Psalms: A New Translation, Translated from the Hebrew and Arranged for Singing to the Psalmody of Joseph Gelineau*. The Gelineau Psalms thus offer a much freer poetic form than the constraints of either Anglican chant or the metrical psalters allow, and the result is an arresting, vigorous, and authentic rendering which, even without musical performance, perhaps gets the modern reader as close as possible to the 'feel' of the Hebrew psalms.

A literary version in blank verse, not designed for worship, was produced for Penguin Classics by Peter **Levi** (*The Psalms*, 1976). Levi, while not claiming to be a Hebrew scholar, declares his first loyalty to be to the Hebrew text, the English language coming second. One unfortunate decision was to use 'God' (rather than the traditional 'the Lord') for the divine name Yahweh, which results in some very odd language. Thus Psalm 50 begins: 'God, God is God. | God spoke . . .'. The familiar 'Bless the Lord, O my soul' which begins and ends Psalm 103 gives way to the more prosaic 'My spirit, praise God'.

x. The Text to Be Translated We have noted that some English versions were made from the Latin (notably Wyclif, Coverdale, Douai, Knox), and even today many translations made into African, Asian, and Latin American languages are made from an English version by translators who do not know Hebrew and Greek. But modern English translations are themselves routinely based on the Hebrew and Greek. The question which remains, however, is which Hebrew and Greek texts should be used.

The dramatic increase in known manuscripts and advances in text-critical method mean that we are not now in the position of the AV translators who had to depend on only a few late manuscripts. The translator who is not an expert in textual criti-

cism may with a great deal of confidence work from the currently published critical texts. But where manuscript evidence is divided critics are sometimes not in agreement, and a translator must take sides over the omission or inclusion of a suspect verse, or over which of two words is more likely to have been in the original text. At such times at least a basic acquaintance with the highly specialized science of textual criticism is needed.

A helpful innovation introduced into the United Bible Societies' edition of *The Greek New Testament* is a rating of each disputed reading from A to D, where A indicates the editors' virtual certainty over the text they have chosen to print, while D indicates a high degree of doubt. This Greek NT was designed for use by translators, who are thus allowed to share the textual critics' dilemmas and to know where they may responsibly part company from them. A companion volume, B. M. Metzger's *A Textual Commentary on the Greek New Testament* (1971), explains in layman's terms the basis on which each decision was made, and the reasons for disagreements among the editors. With such helps the translator is on much firmer ground. Nothing comparable exists for the Hebrew text, where the issues and methods are quite different.

xi. Literal versus 'Dynamic' Translation [see also I.a.3] Any translator is faced with the competing demands of the desire, on the one hand, to be as faithful as possible to the original and, on the other, to produce a version which communicates well and is a pleasure to read. The more disparate the structures of the languages involved, the greater this tension becomes.

But for the Bible translator there is the additional feature that the very words of the text to be translated are regarded by some of the potential readers, and perhaps by the translators themselves, as the product of divine inspiration. The form, as well as the content, of the original may thus come to be regarded as sacrosanct, the only acceptable version being one which mirrors as closely as possible the grammatical structures and lexical range of the Hebrew or Greek text [see I.c.3]. Such an attitude resembles the Muslim insistence that there can never be a 'translation' of the Koran, only interpretations, since it is the Arabic text itself which is the locus of divine inspiration [see II.b.2.i].

A recent example of a translation which deliberately reproduces the features of Hebrew language rather than using natural English idiom is E. **Fox**'s *The Five Books of Moses* (1996). Fox follows the principles of Martin Buber, which are conveniently set out in a recent English translation of some of his writings, *Scripture and Translation* (1994). Buber believed that the impact of a text, particularly of the Biblical text, cannot be reduced merely to its 'meaning', but that the form and sound of the words are equally important, and must be retained in a translation. The result, as found in Fox's translation, is intentionally 'foreign' to the English ear, and aims to impress with its strangeness rather than to eliminate the cultural and linguistic distance between the original text and the modern reader. To translate merely 'sense for sense' is to lose the power of the original.

A less literary concern probably underlies those translations, ancient and modern, which are generally characterized as excessively literal (such as Aquila's Greek OT, the first Wyclif translation, or the New American Standard Bible). Such versions intentionally subordinate natural idiom to the 'faithful' reproduction of the sacred text. The alternative is 'paraphrase', a label used often as a term of disapprobation: 'paraphrase' allows the translator's own ideas to intrude into the text, so that on this view the authority of the original is relativized.

Against this literalistic tendency stands the theory of translation which has come to be known as 'dynamic equivalence', a term especially associated with the work of Eugene A. Nida, which has come to prominence particularly in the context of the continuing enterprise of translating the Bible into the thousands of languages which so far have no Bible version. On this view it is not the form of the text which matters, but its content, and it is the translator's responsibility to render that sense into the target language in whatever way will best communicate to native speakers of that language, without regard to such matters as the grammatical structure, word order, vocabulary, or cultural features of the original. Translations produced under this philosophy are typically more free, readable, and elegant, and can fit more comfortably into the cultural context of the intended readers, but are often suspected of having adulterated the sacred text.

The Good News Bible, produced for the Bible Societies, was a self-conscious paradigm of 'dynamic equivalence'. But in fact virtually all English versions of the last half-century have accepted the principle of translating idiom for idiom rather than word for word, even though the degree of freedom exercised has varied. Thus even the relatively conservative New International Version, regarded by some as veering towards literalism, while it lists as its first concern 'the accuracy of the translation and its fidelity to the thought of the biblical writers' (notice 'thought', not 'words'), also

affirms that 'faithful communication of the meaning of the writers of the Bible demands frequent modifications in sentence structure and constant regard for the contextual meanings of words'. The resultant translation claims, with considerable justification, to be in 'clear and natural English'.

One special factor affecting the Bible translator is the fact that the texts being translated were written in a period of widespread illiteracy, and many of them were probably designed originally for public reading. And even today, while most books are translated for private reading, Bible translators have to reckon with the fact that their work is likely to be read out in church. Some translation committees have therefore wisely made a point of having their proposed translations read aloud before agreeing them. Within a typical congregation there will be those who love the reassuring old words of the AV as well as those whose concern is to hear language which communicates directly in lively, contemporary style. The translator who has an eye to public reading must try to balance these conflicting demands.

xii. Conservatism Conservatism, in the sense of resistance to change, seems to affect people in matters of religion more readily than in other areas. Thoroughly modern people with radical political views may nonetheless be staunch advocates of the AV and the Book of Common Prayer. This is a hurdle which every Bible translator must face.

Shortly after *Good News for Modern Man* was published, in an English-speaking service at a remote hill-station in Nigeria, the leader of the service read a passage from the new version (which had been designed for precisely that sort of situation where English was at best a second language) and then put the book down saying, 'Now we will hear it from the real Bible'; he proceeded to read the same passage from the AV. This devotion to the AV as the 'real Bible' is still to be found in many English congregations, after decades of 'better' translations being freely available. The language of the Bible is expected to be the English of the 16th c. The colloquial language which Tyndale employed so that the Scriptures would be accessible to the ploughboy has thus become with time the esoteric language of religion, and the more remote it becomes from ordinary speech the more it is revered as the proper hallmark of the sacred.

The task of Bible translation is much easier where there is no existing version to be supplanted. A translator who had been commissioned to produce a dynamic new translation for a tribe in Zaïre who already had a Bible version, translated from the AV and quite remote from the current form of the language, related how he read out his fresh, new, colloquial version with pride, and people commented favourably on how easy it was to understand, but then remarked that of course it wasn't the Bible. There are many who expect the Bible, as sacred writings, not to sound like ordinary literature even in translation, and who value it for its very remoteness from everyday speech.

But the Bible, or most of it, was not written in a special 'holy' language. The Hebrew prophets spoke in vigorous contemporary idioms and the New Testament writers used what is sometimes called 'market Greek'. A translation which is to do justice to the intention of the original writers must put intelligibility before the maintenance of traditional language which no longer communicates effectively.

xiii. Inclusive Language In the latter part of the 20th c. the traditional English use of 'men' to mean 'people', 'he' as a pronoun for an unspecified person of either sex, etc. has become increasingly unacceptable, and Bible versions have been adapted accordingly. Thus while the RSV, the Jerusalem Bible, the NEB, and the New International Version had used the 'generic masculine', their revisions in the 1980s and 1990s have gone to great lengths to be inclusive wherever the original did not appear to be gender-specific [see I.a.5.iv].

Such accommodation to modern sensibilities is easily lampooned as 'trendy' and 'politically correct', but it is in fact a matter of good translation. Thus the Greek *anthropos* (human being), while it is masculine in form, is clearly differentiated from *aner* (a male person), and to use the same English term 'man' for both was always liable to distort the sense. It has taken modern sensitivity to exclusive language to alert us to the poverty of the English language in this respect, and to send us in search of better ways of conveying the sense of the original.

But of course Hebrew and Greek also use generic masculine pronouns and terms of address such as 'brothers' when clearly the whole Church community is in view. Today many female readers feel excluded by such terms, and so if a translator continues to offer literal (masculine) renderings, the effect is actually to misrepresent the Biblical writers, who did not have only males in mind.

On the other hand, there is sometimes room for debate over whether the original did intend to be inclusive. The patriarchal culture which lies behind much of the masculine language of the Bible is itself also part of the data to be translated, and it is a question how far the translator may properly obscure it.

There are certain well-tried devices to avoid gender-specific language, such as turning singular generic statements into the plural (and thus substituting 'they' for 'he'), or using the first or second person in place of the third where the context allows the sense to be conveyed in this way. Words like 'people', 'humanity', or 'mortals' can be used in place of 'man', 'men', or 'mankind'. But there is the danger that by reducing the range of vocabulary available the translation may be made less elegant, for example by too many uses of 'people' in a short space. And there are disputes as to how far English idiom is yet ready to accept terms like 'humans', 'humankind', or whether it allows a 'whoever' to be followed by a 'they'. Usage is fluid, and judgements as to what is currently acceptable will vary. But the issue will not go away, and it is hard to imagine any new translation from now on perpetuating the generic masculines of the traditional versions.

There are further problems for the Bible translator in this area. 'Fishers of men' (Mark 1: 17) is a well-loved phrase, and aptly echoes the preceding mention of 'fishermen'. It is hard to see how an inclusive version can retain the familiar phrase, or match the elegance of the word-play. Or what of Jesus' regular self-designation as 'the Son of Man', a phrase which literally means a human being? If 'the son of man' is Psalm 8:4 becomes 'human beings', what are we to do with Hebrews 2:6, where on the basis of that verse the writer sees the psalm as pointing to Jesus? Even with generous use of footnotes, such issues are not easily resolved, and the Bible translator does not have the luxury of writing a commentary on his or her text!

All this is to do with Biblical ways of speaking about people. Feminist discomfort with masculine language referring to God has not yet been reflected in mainstream Bible translation. This theological debate is a different issue from the exclusion of half the human race by the use of generic masculine pronouns, and translators have not so far seen it as their business to address it.   RTF

REFERENCES

(Translations of the Bible into English have been detailed in the text, and are not listed again here.)

Ackroyd, P. R., Evans, C. F., Lampe, G. W. H., and Greenslade, S. L., eds., *The Cambridge History of the Bible*, 3 vols., Cambridge, 1963–70, esp. vol. ii, pp. 338–491 ('The Vernacular Scriptures'); vol. iii, pp. 141–74 ('English Versions of the Bible 1525–1611'), pp. 361–82 ('English Versions since 1611') · Bruce, F. F., *History of the Bible in English*, 3rd edn., Oxford, 1978 · Buber, M., and Rosenzweig, F., *Scripture and Translation*, Bloomington, Ind., 1994 · Daniell, D., *Tyndale's New*

Testament 1534: A Modern-Spelling Edition, New Haven, Conn., 1989 · *Tyndale's Old Testament: A Modern-Spelling Edition*, New Haven, Conn., 1992 · Davie, D., ed., *The Psalms in English*, London, 1996 · Duthie, A. S., *Bible Translations, and How to Choose Between Them*, Exeter, 1985 · Hammond, G., *The Making of the English Bible*, New York, 1983 · Hargreaves, C., *A Translator's Freedom: Modern English Bibles and Their Language*, Sheffield, 1993 · Herbert, A. S., ed., *Historical Catalogue of the Printed Editions of the English Bible 1525–1961*, London/New York, 1968 · Knox, R. A., *On Englishing the Bible*, London, 1949 · Lewis, J. P., *The English Bible from KJV to NIV*, Grand Rapids, Mich., 1982 · Nida, E. A., *Toward a Science of Translating*, Leiden, 1964 · Nida, E. A., and Taber, C. R., *The Theory and Practice of Translation*, 2nd edn., Leiden, 1982 · Robinson, D., *Translation and Taboo*, DeKalb, Ill., 1996 · Robinson, H. W., ed., *The Bible and Its Ancient and English Versions*, Oxford, 1940 · 'Versions' (by various authors), *The Anchor Bible Dictionary*, vol. vi, pp. 787–851, New York, 1992.

2. THE AUTHORIZED VERSION AND ENGLISH LITERATURE

It is a matter of sometimes derisive notice among both religious and literary historians of the English Bible that the AV has been occasionally praised as an 'inspired' translation. Not only did scholars such as James Scholefield and Benjamin Jowett in the 19th c. share this view, but their accolades helped give rise to a more popular (and naïve) partisanship in the 20th c. Yet in the lesser literary sense of the adjective, the AV had already been granted an 'inspired' and inspirational status by many of the most eminent poets, dramatists, novelists, and essayists in the English language. Thomas Babington Macaulay's oft-quoted conviction that the AV was 'a book, which, if everything else in our language should perish, would alone suffice to show the whole extent of its beauty and power' (1828) finds echoes from Jonathan Swift (1712) to T. H. Huxley (1870). English authors as diverse as Wordsworth, Shelley, Ruskin, Francis Thompson, and George Orwell acknowledged an 'inspirational' literary influence of the Authorized translation.

It is not always easy to characterize with useful precision the nature of the professed influence of the AV upon these and many other notable English writers who at various times have sung the praises of this long-standing translation. Also, it must be admitted that the praise is not universal. Distinguished modern Christian writers and apologists such as C. S. Lewis and T. S. Eliot have resisted both traditional adulation of the AV and the claim by both writers and critics that it has been, especially stylistically, a prime model or foundation for English prose. Lewis, for example, acknowledged the AV as a source of profound importance, but denied that this has much to do with any special literary properties of the translation, even in such an AV associated writer as Bunyan. Further, Lewis sturdily resisted the idea that the Bible could be considered as literature apart from its role as religious authority. On this point he had the weighty concurrence of T. S. Eliot, who insisted that 'the Bible

has had a *literary* influence upon literature *not* because it has been considered as literature, but because it has been considered as the report of the Word of God' (1935).

Yet other notable moderns, standing well outside the conventions of faith, have argued the opposite case, both acknowledging and sometimes resenting a deep literary influence of the AV upon their own work. Two examples must suffice. Unexpectedly, perhaps, the writing of D. H. Lawrence is arguably among the most heavily salted by the AV of all modern British writers (e.g. *David, The Man Who Died, Apocalypse, The Rainbow*), and he knew it. He consciously imitated AV Biblical parallelism even in his anti-Christian prose, so that like Jack, in his *The Boy in the Bush*, it may fairly be said of him that even though 'he had no use for Christianity proper . . . the Bible was perhaps the foundation of his consciousness'. Correspondingly, in *The Summing Up* (1938), Somerset Maugham complained that the AV had indeed been an altogether persistent but 'very harmful influence on English prose', its 'oriental' and 'alien imagery' a lamentable encrustation upon the purity of 'plain, honest English speech'. Of these divergent reports, which is most to be believed, and what are the essential literary qualities of the AV?

The explicit desire of the AV translators 'that the Scripture may speak like itself, as in the language of Canaan, that it might be understood even of the very vulgar' (1611 Preface) has been mistaken by some as suggesting that its formulations reflect common spoken English of the day. Unsurprisingly, there is little to confirm such rhetorical and syntactical magniloquence in early 17th-c. vernacular; the AV phrase, like its Hebrew original, is intonation of public oratory—not difficult for ordinary folk to understand, but not in any way intended to be mimetic of their natural patterns of speech.

The AV translators intended their work in the first instance for public reading: the 1611 text was produced in an oversized folio only, to be used in churches for lections. Smaller sizes, designed for study or private use, appeared only in later editions (quartos, for study, after 1612–13; duodecimos in Roman type for private use after 1617). The AV was punctuated rhetorically, employing far more commas and colons than a text for silent reading could possibly require, reminding us that from its publication until modern times, even in families, the text would usually be read aloud. A plain, literal style is indeed what the translators attempted, but also an oratorical quality of delivery, having the dignity of public discourse. Here the enhanced parallelism, varied synonyms, and emphatic rhy-thms of the AV set it apart from the intended study format of Tyndale or the annotated Geneva versions (Norton, 1993). An oral / aural context of familiarization has clearly contributed substantially to the memorabil-ity of the AV, and its oratorical cadence and fine (though plain) phrasing has continued to make its locutions memorable, often persistently memor-able, even for those for whom religious reasons for the Bible's authority have long been abandoned. No other English translation is so successfully orator-ical, and none carries so easily, in its turn of phrase, 'the weight of glory'. Hence, none is so likely, bidden or not, to be found hidden in the heart.

Lewis and Eliot were adult converts, and came to the Bible after their ear for language was formed; Lawrence and Maugham, like many another, lost their faith only after their childhood AV tuition in grand, plain speech had been engrafted too deep to expunge. For generations of English speaking writ-ers, from later 17th-c. poets to American, African, and many another postcolonial novelist still writing today, it is the formation of a Lawrence which tells the general tale. George Orwell's narrator in *Coming Up for Air*, who gets the Bible in 'big doses' through his childhood, who saw AV 'texts on every wall' and who 'knew whole chapters of the Old Testament by heart', could say for many: 'Even now my head's stuffed full of bits out of the Bible.' It is doubtful, in a time without a standard translation and especially without one designed for public reading, whether any such memorability—at least of language and style—will long trouble the minds of secular writers.

Since 1611, then, poets have typically taken the question of translation seriously, and Bible transla-tion no less seriously than any other. One need only consider Marlowe's Doctor Faustus, or Goethe's, for each of whom wilful mistranslation of the Bib-lical text was a prelude to their devil's contract and ultimate damnation. In the case of the AV, Eng-lish poets grew by degrees to venerate it as no

other, and to see it as an exemplary literary model.

In the beginning, overt connection to the AV was somewhat restrained. John Donne used the Latin Vulgate, annotated Hebrew and Greek texts, and a variety of English translations, and it is difficult to know what role was played by the AV in his proclam-ation that St Paul was a more powerful orator than Cicero, David a better poet than Virgil. George Herbert, who still more than Donne was familiar with the AV as a public text for lections and ser-mons, echoed something of its plain grandeur in his own verse, collected appropriately by himself in a volume entitled *The Temple*. But it is John Milton, thoroughly immersed in the AV, whose conviction of the literary superiority of the Bible first (and for-matively) attaches itself to the AV translation as well as the originals. Yet even Milton used his 1612 AV more as a crib to the Latin, or Hebrew and Greek, than as in its own formulations authorita-tive. Bunyan, who knew much of the AV by heart, departed from it often, precisely in order more accurately to reflect common speech.

By the 18th c. most British writers were AV-saturated from birth, and some were willing to look upon it as authoritative for literary style and English usage. Swift, who like Donne and Herbert was an Anglican clergyman, thought the AV and the Book of Common Prayer the signal achievements of Eng-lish translation, and the AV translators in particular 'masters of English style'. At the end of the century, William Blake echoes the AV throughout his poetry, all the more so perhaps when he was inverting the content of the Bible to create his own myth; he too thought of the AV as 'having been translated as well as written by the Holy Ghost' (1803). Wordsworth hailed the AV in 'Ecclesiastical Sonnet XXIX' as a 'transcendent boon', Coleridge thought the AV Old Testament in particular 'the true model of simplicity of style'. Charlotte Brontë's novels are richly textured with AV lan-guage—many of her characters may be said to 'speak' it. Similarly, John Ruskin said that to the AV Bible he owed 'the first cultivation' of his 'ear in sound' (1889). Matthew Arnold, first formal advo-cate of the study of the Bible 'as literature', saw the Book of Isaiah in particular 'as a literary work of the highest order' and 'by virtue of the [AV] translation . . . a monument of the English language at its best' (1872). So great a weight of canonical literary opin-ion secured for the AV an unshakeable literary authority well into the 20th c., as instanced still in *The Great Code* of Northrop Frye.

It is not to be wondered at that among those for whom in the early years of life the AV was the 'book of books' its authority should prevail in matters

171

both of style and of narrative substance. Nor is it surprising that adult converts such as Lewis or Eliot should be more concerned for the matter than for the idiom of their English Bibles. Yet when contemporary literary critics such as Robert Alter and George Steiner still cite the AV as an outstanding capturing of the beauties of Biblical poetry or as an unparalleled register of sublimity in English style, they bear witness to an achievement in English translation which, for its perdurability, sustained critical acclaim, and general cultural influence, can hardly be said to have an equal. Here is one instance, surely, where translation by committee created no camel.   DLJ

REFERENCES   Alter, R., *The Art of Biblical Poetry*, New York, 1985 · Eliot, T. S., 'Religion and Literature', in *Selected Prose*, ed. J. Hayward, Harmondsworth, 1953 · Frye, N., *The Great Code*, Toronto/New York, 1982 · Jeffrey, D. L., *A Dictionary of Biblical Tradition in English Literature*, Grand Rapids, Mich., 1992 · Lewis, C. S., 'The Literary Impact of the Authorized Version', in his *They Asked for a Paper*, London, 1962 · Norton, D., *A History of the Bible as Literature*, 2 vols., Cambridge, 1993 · Steiner, G., *After Babel: Aspects of Language and Translation*, Oxford, 1975.

d. Celtic Languages

1. INTRODUCTION

Despite their shared Celtic inheritance and a measure of comparable historical experience, the Celtic cultures of Ireland, Gaelic Scotland, and the Isle of Man, and of Wales, Cornwall, and Brittany, are distinct, both linguistically and psychologically. They have given rise to a plurality of Celtic literatures. Strictly speaking, 'Celtic literature' in the singular ought to apply solely to undifferentiated 'Celts'— who could only have existed in a past time well before the beginnings of the surviving literatures. In practice, however, 'Celtic literature' is commonly used as a shorthand for the literature(s) of Celtic peoples in historical times, including the present.

In fact there are good reasons for taking this liberty. In the medieval context the shared 'Celtic heritage' is still powerfully enough present to make comparative treatment illuminating. In the modern period genetic similarity is less significant, but comparability is ensured for two other reasons. First, the relationship which each of the Celtic languages and cultures has with those of a dominant non-Celtic neighbour—English (or French, in the case of Brittany)—shows fundamental and illuminating similarities. Secondly, Celtic literature (like Celtic film, Celtic music, and perhaps some other arts) has to a significant extent been nurtured by Celtic writers, scholars, and readers acting in concert, or in a spirit of Celtic solidarity, or at least mutual consciousness. Moreover, such notions as 'the Celtic Fringe' and 'the Celtic mind' are well-established constructs in the wider English-speaking world, whose persuasiveness and ideological thrust creates a third sort of Celtic unity, which can reinforce or be reinforced by the home-grown unities.

Of the individual Celtic literatures, those of Ireland and Wales attained written form very early— in the post-Roman period and the early Christian milieu—due to the adoption, unusually early and widely, of writing in the vernacular languages. This in its turn was a function of the existence, side by side and influencing one another, of a monastic Church culture and a secular court culture. The bulk, variety, and literary value of these medieval Celtic literatures is very considerable.

While in some respects they invite comparison with Old English and Old Norse saga and myth and poetry [II.0.1–2], the Irish and Welsh literary traditions can also be viewed independently through time, since they show remarkable continuity in the face of Viking, Norman, and later incursions. Equally, they had the power to assimilate and put their own stamp on many of the innovations and fashions which have affected western European literature from the late Middle Ages to the present day—from romance and courtly love through to romanticism and modernism. They are the big fish in the Celtic pool.

Scotland's contribution in the early period is subsumed within that of Ireland and Wales. Gaelic Scotland was at one with Gaelic Ireland in cultural organization and literary consciousness in the Middle Ages. The literary legacy of 'Welsh' (properly 'Brythonic') Scotland, i.e. the old kingdoms of Pictland and Strathclyde, is seen dimly as the 'Old North' of the heroic age remembered in medieval Welsh literature. While the Brythonic element disappeared early from Scotland, the Gaelic literary tradition, employing the 'classical Irish' language of the professional literati, flourished throughout the late Middle Ages in

Gaelic-speaking parts of the country. Specifically Scottish Gaelic literature—more thoroughly popular, orally based vernacular literature—can be found from the 16th c. onwards, and started to appear in published form in the 18th c.

Of the other Celtic literatures, an early Breton literature can be inferred but has not survived. Carols and other religious poetry survive from the late Middle Ages. There are ballads from the 18th c., and popular tales from the 19th. There was a revival and there is a modern, intellectual output as in the other currently spoken Celtic languages. A considerable amount of translation from Breton into French exists, but very little into English, especially of contemporary literature. Exceptions include Tom **Taylor**'s *Ballads and Songs of Brittany*, Edith **Rinder**'s *Legendary Romances and Folk-Tales of Brittany*, and, for modern poetry, the Breton contributions to Thomas Rain **Crowe**'s *A Celtic Resurgence*. (This work also contains specimens of contemporary writing translated from Cornish and Manx.)

Cornish, like Breton, shows examples of a late medieval religious literature. Because the language died out in the 17th c., contemporary Cornish literature counts as revived as well as revivalist literature. An authoritative account of the traditional literature can be found in Brian **Murdoch**'s *Cornish Literature*.

Manx literature is late and fragmentary; but since Manx survived until well into the present century some Manx folk-tales, ballads and popular songs have been preserved. Translations are provided in e.g. A. W. **Moore**'s *Carvalyn Gailckagh* and the same author's *Manx Ballads and Music*.

While scholars of English literature used to invoke 'Celtic origins' rather freely to explain away texts and themes and traits which seemed otherwise inexplicable, there are only scattered indications that specific Celtic texts were actually translated into English in the late Middle Ages and early modern period. It was really from the mid-18th c. onwards that Celtic literature became fashionable, at a time when a Celtic past quite suddenly appeared to offer a novel and exciting alternative mythological landscape to the artificiality of Arcadia, and fed a lively interest in native antiquity which related ultimately to developments in popular consciousness of a specific British identity. The willingness of Welsh scholars like Lewis **Morris** to provide translations and commentary, and of English men of letters like Thomas Gray to study and promote them, gave the English-speaking world such figures as the Bard and the Druid, in addition to specimens of ancient poetry from an age of conspicuous heroism and emotional response.

There were misconceptions aplenty. 'Celtic' and 'Scandinavian' mythology sometimes got mixed up; and the druids as a Celtic priesthood became associated with the megalithic structures of Stonehenge and Avebury which really belonged to a far earlier, pre-Celtic past. Moreover, there was a bogus element in the Celtic texts that became available. For this demand for texts with 'Celtic' qualities (which were identifiable, even if their characteristics would only become fully contextualized when the Romantic Movement got under way) stimulated some native Celts to gild the lily, or supply artificial blooms: most notoriously, James 'Ossian' **Macpherson** [II.d.4], whose well-calculated (or perhaps fortunate) interpretation of the mood of the times had a powerful effect in creating for Celtic literature an atmosphere of 'Celtic Twilight' which was not a prominent feature in the authentic texts. On the other hand, the ructions caused by these controversial 'translations' eventually stimulated Scots, Irish, and Welsh scholars to take a greater interest in the authentic traditions, and to make these available, through translation, to the wider literary public. This was largely how the practice of translating Celtic literature into English became established.

Another burst of Celticism took place in the later 19th c. Whereas the earlier one had gloried in and identified with the resistance of the ancient Britons to Continental (Roman) imperialists, there was now an ethos that preferred to identify with the conquerors, whether Roman or Saxon, and sought to minimize the Celtic past or eliminate it from the record of British history. As a counter to this imperialist ethos, cultural or political resistance movements manifested themselves within the Celtic countries, and an intellectual *cum* artistic one in the country as a whole. Scientific scholarship in Celtic Studies had in the meantime become established in the university system. The enhanced range and reliability of Celtic material available from this source provided the fuel, and political hopes and fears provided the flame, for a fresh surge of interest in the Celtic heritage, both within the Celtic countries and more generally. Once again, the raw ingredients were served up with a complex seasoning of promotion and resistance, romanticism and positivism, charlatanry and purism and politics.

An important complication since the first days of Celticism has been the development of localized Irish, Welsh, and Scottish Gaelic frames of literary reference, in which the destinies of individual Celtic literatures have become variously entangled with those of their local Anglophone counterparts, as part of Irish, Welsh, and Scottish 'literary scenes'.

The Celtic partner influences writing in English, and the English partner influences what is produced in the Celtic language.

Yet the pan-Celtic vision continues to be attractive, on at least two planes. There is still plenty of life in the tradition of seeing the Celtic contribution to literature as containing distinctive or unique features worth bringing together. This tradition tends to emanate from outside the Celtic homelands. It also tends to have a scholarly flavour, and links to comparative literary study, ethnology, and archaeology; but new variants have also developed, such as the currently powerful appetite for 'Celtic wisdom', under such headings as 'Celtic Christianity' and 'Celtic paganism'.

At the same time, the European Union contains a constellation of minority languages whose vitality depends to a greater or lesser extent on the knowledge that each is not alone and all face comparable social, political, and intellectual challenges. In this world, pan-Celtic festivals, journals, and anthologies have an important role. It is paradoxical that, despite EU support for communication and literary translation between its minority languages, they tend to require the intervention of the majority languages, like English, to get their messages across to wider audiences. But this in its turn exposes the world of English literature to an element of what Bobi Jones has recently called the 'literature of discomfort'—from the un-cosy, subversive, 'wild' side of the world's cultural street. *Plus ça change...* WG

CELTIC ANTHOLOGIES Crowe, Thomas Rain, ed., *A Celtic Resurgence*, Cullowhee, NC, 1997 · Jackson, Kenneth Hurlstone, ed., *A Celtic Miscellany*, rev. edn., Harmondsworth, 1971 [Penguin] · Koch, John T., and Carey, John, eds., *The Celtic Heroic Age*, rev. edn., Andover, Mass., 1997 · Matthews, Caitlin, and Matthews, John, eds., *The Encyclopedia of Celtic Wisdom: The Celtic Shaman's Source-Book*, London, 1996 · Sharpe, E. A., and Mathay, J., eds., *Lyra Celtica: An Anthology of Representative Celtic Poetry*, rev. edn., Edinburgh, 1924.
BRITTANY Bryce, Derek, *Celtic Folk Tales from Armorica*, rev. edn., Felinfach, Wales, 1997 · Hemon, Roparz, *Christmas Hymns in the Vannes Dialect of Breton*, Dublin, 1956 · Rinder, Edith W., *The Shadow of Arvor: Legendary Romances and Folk-Tales of Brittany*, Edinburgh, n.d. [c.1920] · Taylor, Tom, *Ballads and Songs of Brittany*, London/Cambridge, 1865.
CORNWALL Ellis, Peter B., *The Cornish Language and Its Literature*, London, 1974 · Murdoch, Brian, *Cornish Literature*, Cambridge, 1993.
ISLE OF MAN Moore, A. W., *Carvalyn Gailckagh* ['Gaelic Carols'], Douglas, IOM, 1891 · *Manx Ballads and Music*, Douglas, IOM, 1895.
SEE ALSO Jackson, K. H., *Studies in Early Celtic Nature Poetry*, Cambridge, 1935 · Price, E., ed., *Celtic Literature and Culture in the Twentieth Century*, Cardiff, 1997 · Williams, J. E. C., ed., *Literature in Celtic Countries*, Cardiff, 1971.

2. EARLY IRISH/GAELIC

Early Irish (Gaelic) literature, in prose, is conventionally divided, by modern scholars, into four cycles of tales: the Ulster, Fionn (or Fenian), mythological, and king or historical cycles. However, the 12th c. *Book of Leinster* classifies these stories according to the type of tale involved—stories of deaths, visions, voyages, etc. A mixture of the two kinds of classification allows for inclusiveness.

The Ulster cycle concerns the Ulaid, a powerful tribe from the north of Ireland (whence 'Ulster'), and their territorial conflicts with the Connachta from the west. The great warrior of the Ulaid was Cú Chulainn ('the Hound of Culann'; often 'Cuchulain' in English spelling), while the Connacht forces were led by the wild queen Medb (meaning 'intoxication'; often 'Maeve' in English spelling). *Táin Bó Cuailnge* (The Cattle Raid of Cooley) is the best-known tale of the Ulster cycle, and deals with Medb's raid on the Ulaid to carry off a prized bull, the Donn of Cooley, in what is today Co. Louth. This tale of Cú Chulainn's almost single-handed defence of Ulster (the Ulstermen were laid low through a curse laid on them by the goddess Macha) is the Irish equivalent of the Anglo-Saxon *Beowulf* [II.0.1] or the Finnish *Kalevala* [II.0.3]; and it has inspired many translations and adaptations. The tale is preserved in the *Book of Leinster* and (an earlier version) in the *Book of the Dun Cow* (11th c.). The earlier (and starker) recension was translated by Winifred **Faraday** in 1904. The *Book of Leinster* version was translated by Standish Hayes **O'Grady** in 1898, and by Joseph **Dunn** in 1914. Lady **Gregory** also based her retelling in *Cuchulain of Muirthemne* on this version, attractive to her and to others because its narrative is more coherent than that in the *Book of the Dun Cow*. When Thomas **Kinsella** undertook his powerful translation of the *Táin* in 1969 he followed the earlier version, clarifying obscurities and bridging gaps, mostly from the *Book of Leinster* redaction of the tale.

Cú Chulainn first enters English literary discourse as Cuthullin, through the Scottish James Macpherson's *Fingal* (1762) and *Temora* (1763) [II.d.4.ii]. Macpherson mixed up the Ulster and the Fionn (or Ossianic) cycles, but the windswept bleakness and brooding heroism of his atmospheric and loose paraphrases of Irish (and Gaelic) heroic lays became fashionable and initiated a first wave of Celticism. Macpherson claimed (wrongly) that Scottish literature pre-dated Irish—in fact in the centuries prior to c.1650 the two geographical areas shared a common literary heritage—and this assertion spurred Irish and Anglo-Irish literati and scholars to investigate and translate the Ulster and Fionn cycles. Sylvester O'Halloran questioned the authenticity of Macpherson's versions, and he in turn inspired Standish James O'Grady (the cousin of the translator of the *Táin* of 1898) to write a series of 'histories' of Ireland's heroic phase, including the *History of Ireland: Cuculain and his Contemporaries* (1880), a key work in the emergence of a second phase of Celticism, known as the Irish Literary Revival, embracing the works of W. B. Yeats, Lady Gregory, and J. M. Synge, and also, more popularly, termed 'the Celtic Twilight' (or, in James Joyce's mocking phrase in *Finnegans Wake*, the 'cultic twalotte').

The Ulster cycle entered English and Anglo-Irish literary consciousness emphatically in the surging anapaestic energy of Thomas Moore's song 'Avenging and Bright' in his *Irish Melodies* (1808–24). In a note Moore says that his lyrics were inspired by a translation of the story of Deirdre and the sons of Uisnech made by Theophilus **O'Flanagan** in the *Transactions of the Gaelic Society* (1808). This tale, *Longes mac nUislenn* (The Exile of the Sons of Uisliu) belongs to the Ulster cycle. A pre-tale of the *Táin* (it explains how some Ulaid are with Medb's forces), this harrowing story of impetuous love, exile in Scotland, and revenge has a classical simplicity and force. It was translated by Thomas **Stott** (1755–1829), who worked from a manuscript crib supplied by William Neilson, the scholar and northern radical, as *The Song of Deardra* (1825). The poet and antiquary Sir Samuel **Ferguson** (1810–86) translated the story in 1834 as part of his *Hibernian Nights' Entertainments* for the *Dublin University Magazine*. Kinsella's *The Táin*, the work of a major modern Irish poet, communicates the drive and surge of the original, its brusque violence, its brisk narrative intercut with sharp exchanges. This translation was an inspiration for other writers, poets, and musicians, and played no little part in the revival of Irish literature, art, and learning that took place in the 1970s and 1980s.

The world of the Ulster cycle, essentially the world of the La Tène Iron Age Celts as described by Diodorus Siculus and Caesar, informs a good deal of Irish writing in English, whether direct translations or adaptations. W. B. Yeats's Cuchulain cycle of plays (amongst which are *The Green Helmet*, 1910 and *The Only Jealousy of Emer*, 1919) draw upon this body of material, as does the very different *The Faith Healer* (1979) by the playwright Brain Friel.

The Fionn (Fenian or Ossianic) cycle is centred on the mythical hero Fionn mac Cumhaill, his son, Oisín (whence Ossian), and other members of Fionn's warrior band, or *fian*, known familiarly as the Fianna. The provenance of this cycle, in its earliest phases, is Munster and Leinster; its warriors live a nomadic, open-air life; and the stories are permeated with magic, romance, and the beauty of the natural world. The tales were told—and localized—all over Ireland and Scotland. By the 12th c. the framework of the cycle and a substantial body of literature was established; *Acallam na Senórach* (The Colloquy of the Ancients) is a compendium of this lore, in prose and verse. Set at the time of St Patrick, the stories are told to the saint and his clerics by the survivors of the pagan past, who recall the glories of life as members of Fionn's Fianna, before Christianity.

Once again it was Macpherson who introduced, in sadly mutilated fashion, this material to the English-speaking world (and beyond—Napoleon treasured his copy of *Ossian*). The most famous tale of this cycle is *Tóraigheacht Dhiarmada agus Ghráinne* (The Pursuit of Diarmaid and Gráinne), which tells of the flight of the young lovers of the title from the aging Fionn mac Cumhaill. It has similarities with the Deirdre story, but it belongs more emphatically to the world of myth: Diarmaid, for instance, is killed by a boar, an otherworld animal, who is really his brother. The tale was edited and translated by Standish Hayes O'Grady for the Ossianic Society (established to promote research on the cycle) in 1855, and inspired the poet Austin Clarke's version *The Vengeance of Fionn* (1917) and Lady Gregory's play *Grania* (1911). Other tales of this cycle include *Feis Tighe Chonáin*, edited and translated by Nicholas **O'Kearney** in 1855, which W. B. Yeats used in *Fairy and Folktales of the Irish Peasantry* (1888), and Lady Gregory in her compilation of Fionn materials in *Gods and Fighting Men* (1904). This cycle, in its mixture of pagan and Christian world-views, its creation of a world which is outside normal society and therefore to some degree liberated from its constraints, its evocation of the persistent incursions of the world of magic and of faery, had a formative influence on the mood and structure of writings as various as James Joyce's *Finnegans Wake* (1939), Flann O'Brien's *At Swim-Two-Birds* (1939), and Eoghan Ó Tuairisc's *The Week-End of Dermot and Grace* (1964).

The mythological cycle is an assembly of materials, loosely grouped together for convenience, because they display a predominantly mythic content, although all the cycles show such elements to some degree. This cycle contains tales dealing with the gods of pagan Ireland and their adversaries: the Tuatha Dé Danann (the Tribes of the Goddess Danu) and the Fomoiri (the People from Under the Sea). The main tales of this cycle are: *Cath Maige Tuired* (The Battle of Mag Tuired), dealing with the battle between the entities referred to above at Moytirra in modern Co. Sligo, and translated by Whitley **Stokes** in the *Revue Celtique*, 12 (1895), and later by Elizabeth **Gray**; and *Tochmarc Étaíne*, concerning the loves of Étaín and Midir across different reincarnations, translated by Osborn **Bergin** and Richard **Best** in *Ériu*, 12 (1934–8). W. B. Yeats made use of The *Battle of Mag Tuired* and the Étaín story in the play *The Shadowy Waters* (1906) and the poem 'The Two Kings' (1906).

Linked to the mythological cycle but more satisfyingly grouped as a tale-type of the 'voyage' kind are the *immrama* or voyage-tales, amongst which is the 8th-c. *Voyage of Bran*, telling how Bran travels to the otherworld at the invitation of a beautiful woman of the *sídh* or world of faery. This tale was edited and translated by Kuno **Meyer** in 1895, and the folklorist and comparative anthologist Alfred Nutt wrote a commentary in 1897. A companion voyage tale is *Immram Curaig Maíle Dúin* (The Voyage of Mac Dúin's Boat), translated by P. W. **Joyce** in *Old Celtic Romances* (1879) and providing the basis for Louis MacNeice's play *The Mad Islands* (1962) and Paul Muldoon's poem 'Immram' in *Why Brownlee Left* (1980).

The historical (also known as the king) cycle of tales dates from between the 9th and 12th c. and deals with personages (mythic and historical) and incidents (often wars) that have assumed, by the time of composition, dynastic or territorial significance. *Cath Maige Rath* (The Battle of Moira), which survives in a 12th c. redaction, deals with a battle that took place near Moira in present-day Co. Down in 637 CE. The tale's import concerns the need for centralized authority, and provides a sanction to the winning side by making the battle a victory over paganism. The rebel, Congal of Ulster, became the hero of Samuel Ferguson's verse translation in *Congal* (1872), which drew upon the edition and translation by the scholar John

O'Donovan in 1842 for the Irish Archaeological Society.

The battle of Moira was so fierce that its tumult drove the sub-king Suibne (Sweeney), from Rasharkin in modern Co. Antrim, into a frenzy. His madness and his exploits all over Ireland and Scotland; his sojourn in the wilderness living off cress, nuts, and water; his sorrow—all form the content of *Buile Shuibne* (The Frenzy of Sweeney). The tale was edited and translated by J. G. **O'Keeffe** (1913) and this edition was used by Flann O'Brien in his Sweeney passages in *At Swim-Two-Birds* (1939). Seamus **Heaney**, who grew up in Sweeney's old kingdom, translated the tale in *Sweeney Astray* in a vigilant and bony English, which communicates a bare and penitential beauty.

Most of the tales from the cycles contain long passages of poetry which reveal the elegance, concision, and emotional impact of early Irish verse. A body of early lyric poetry survives from the monastic life of the Irish Church of the 9th and 12th c. Many of these poems are famous for their impressionistic sketches of the natural world, which is bathed in a luminous radiance. These poems were edited and translated by Kuno Meyer in *Selections from Ancient Irish Poetry* and by Gerard **Murphy** in *Early Irish Lyrics*. Amongst the best known of these poems are 'The Blackbird at Belfast Lough' and 'Pangur Bán', both translated by Frank **O'Connor** in *King, Lords and Commons* (1959).

Much of the verse of the formally trained bardic poets had an official and institutional function, which did not, however, entirely remove it from a semi-hieratic arena of activity. Poetry was regarded as an elevated form of knowledge, and the bardic poets were fully conscious of their power and dignity. Their ascendancy, as a class, was notable between c.1200 and 1600; nevertheless they traced their pedigree back to practitioners (or reputed practitioners) such as Colum Cille, the saint of Derry, or Colman mac Léníní from Cloyne in Cork. Famous families, renowned in poetry, emerged: the O'Dalys of Cork, the O'Higginses of Sligo, the O'Husseys of Fermanagh, the MacNamees of Tyrone. These poets, and many others, were edited and translated by Osborn Bergin in various journals, collected in *Irish Bardic Poetry*. James Clarence **Mangan** (1803–49) made a brilliant translation of an ode by Eochaidh O'Hussey in 1846. Eugene **O'Curry**, the Gaelic scholar from Clare, provided Mangan with a crib for his translation of Feargal Mac Award's lament for the O'Neills and the O'Donnells buried in Rome.

After the Tudor conquest the Gaelic order, which sustained this learned caste of bardic poets, went into decline, but in the process produced a series of poets in the 17th c. who are notable for their originality and ferocity. Amongst these are Pádraigín Haicéad (d. 1654) and Dáibhí Ó Bruadair (?1625–98), both translated by Michael **Hartnett**.   RW

ANTHOLOGIES   Deane, Seamus, ed., *The Field Day Anthology of Irish Writing*, 3 vols., Derry, 1991 · Gregory, Lady Augusta, *Gods and Fighting Men*, London, 1904 · Greene, David, and O'Connor, Frank, eds., *A Golden Treasury of Irish Poetry*, London, 1967 · Hull, Eleanor, *A Text Book of Irish Literature*, 2 vols., Dublin, 1906 · Jackson, Kenneth Hurlstone, *A Celtic Miscellany*, London, 1951 · Kinsella, Thomas, ed., *The New Oxford Book of Irish Verse*, Oxford, 1986 · Leahy, A. H., *Heroic Romances of Ireland*, London, 1905–6 · Murphy, Gerard, *Early Irish Lyrics*, Dublin, 1956 · O'Grady, Standish Hayes, *Silva Gadelica*, London, 1892 · Sigerson, George, *Bards of the Gael and Gall*, London, 1897.
ULSTER CYCLE   Dunn, Joseph, *The Ancient Irish Epic Tale Táin Bó Cúailnge*, London, 1914 · Faraday, Winifrid, *The Cattle-Raid of Cualnge*, London, 1904 · Gregory, Lady Augusta, *Cuchulain of Muirthemne*, London, 1902 · Kinsella, Thomas, *The Táin*, Dublin, 1969; rep. London, 1970.
FIONN CYCLE   Clarke, Austin, *The Vengeance of Fionn*, London, 1917 · O'Grady, Standish Hayes, *Tóruigheacht Dhiarmada agus Ghráinne*, Dublin, 1855.
MYTHOLOGICAL CYCLE   Gray, Elizabeth, ed., *Cath Maige Tuired*, London, 1982 · Meyer, Kuno, and Nutt, Alfred, eds., *The Voyage of Bran*, London, 1895–7.
HISTORICAL CYCLE   Dillon, Myles, *The Cycles of the Kings*, Chicago, 1946 · Ferguson, Samuel, *Congal*, Dublin/ London, 1872 · Heaney, Seamus, *Sweeney Astray*, London, 1983 · O'Keeffe, J. G., ed., *Buile Shuibhne*, London, 1913.
POETRY   Bergin, Osborn, ed., *Irish Bardic Poetry*, Dublin, 1970 · Hartnett, Michael, *Ó Bruadair and Haicéad*, Oldcastle, 1985, 1993 · Meyer, Kuno, *Selections from Ancient Irish Poetry*, London, 1911 · Murphy, Gerard, *Early Irish Lyrics*, London, 1956.

SEE ALSO   Alspach, R. K., *Irish Poetry from the English Invasion to 1798*, Philadelphia, 1943 · Cronin, M., *Translating Ireland*, Cork, 1996 · Dillon, M., *Early Irish Literature*, Chicago, 1948 · O'Rahilly, T. F., *Early Irish History and Mythology*, Dublin, 1946 · Welch, R., *A History of Verse Translation from the Irish 1789–1897*, Gerrards Cross, Bucks, 1988.

3. MEDIEVAL WELSH

i. *The Mabinogion* The collection of 11 stories which go under the modern name of *The Mabinogion* is most English readers' first encounter with medieval Welsh literature. It boasts the earliest Arthurian tale, as well as three Arthurian romances, an assortment of native tales, and the jewel in the crown, the linked *Four Branches of the Mabinogi*. These tales have been the inspiration for numerous English works of children's literature, fantasy, and historical romance, as well as providing themes for poets such as David Jones, Anthony Conran, and Gillian Clarke.

The Mabinogion was given its current name by its first major translator, Lady Charlotte **Guest** (1812–95), who generalized a scribal error into a blanket term for the collection; the title is now firmly entrenched. Guest, *née* Bertie, daughter of the Earl of Lindsey, married into a Welsh iron-making family. She took her new surroundings seriously, teaching herself and her children Welsh and embarking on her translations with the linguistic and scholarly help of such experts as John **Jones** (Tegid) and Thomas **Price** (Carnhuanawc). Her translations, which may have amounted mainly to the artistic shaping of her collaborators' literal versions, appeared first in 1838–49, and then in a popular edition in 1877, having already, by her own testimony, been widely and well received.

Her translations are in the romantic 'historical' prose of the 19th c., and sit well in a century immersed in Scott. There are some misunderstandings of the original (inevitable, given that scholarly work on the tales was in its infancy), but overall her versions are roughly faithful, written in the fluid and comfortable style of a storyteller. She has perhaps too often smoothed the texts to a graceful norm. There is little effort made to reproduce differences in style between individual tales, or indeed to reproduce some of the stylistic devices which make the originals so vibrant.

For that the public would have to await the classic translation of Gwyn **Jones** and Thomas **Jones**. As with Guest's work, this is widely regarded as a classic in its own right, its archaic but inviting diction coupled with a bold attempt to reproduce stylistic features of the original when possible. The Joneses create a marvellous medieval panorama, ready for world consumption. They do not shrink, for instance, before the occasional terseness of the original. Instead, they use this to the translation's advantage: 'Meat for thy dogs and corn for thy horse, and hot peppered chops for thyself, and wine brimming over, and delectable songs before thee' ('Culhwch and Olwen'); 'And towards the middle of the clearing, lo, the pack that was pursuing it over-taking it and bringing it to the ground' ('Pwyll').

These translators benefited from scholarly advances, and recent good editions of texts, but also from their collective backgrounds. Thomas Jones was a fine Welsh scholar, while Gwyn Jones is a notable author of novels, short stories, and essays in English, as well as an authority on Norse and medieval English literature. It is this combination of scholarly and literary verve which gives their translation at once an authority and an appeal which has yet to be matched.

Their 'rigorously accurate' work, with its 'archaic' tone (Ford, *The Mabinogi*), has not struck all readers alike, and some have found in it a stumbling-block. Two American translators have provided a modern audience with modern English versions. Patrick K. **Ford** aimed his work particularly at university students, and sought to avoid 'quaintness', in *The Mabinogi and other Medieval Welsh Tales*. His version is curiously lifeless, and despite its desire to breathe modern life into the tales, leaves them uninspiring. There is also a tendency (sometimes perhaps based on the translator's scholarly work) to over-read particular words, and invest them with too specific or contentious a meaning.

Jeffrey **Gantz** has produced the better version in contemporary English, a competent, fluid telling of the tales, mostly accurate, readable, and popular with students. There are some idiosyncrasies, including the rendering of names from the original ('Gronw' appears as 'Goronwy', for instance), but its accessibility as a Penguin Classic makes it likely to remain in the forefront of translations of *The Mabinogion*.

ii. Poetry Medieval Welsh poetry finds its world celebrity in Dafydd ap Gwilym (*c.*1315–*c.*1370). His work comes towards the end of the medieval period, and after the end of Welsh independence, yet it encapsulates much of the technique of earlier periods, while catapulting it to new heights. Dafydd formalized the *cywydd*, a verse form of seven-syllable lines in couplets with rhyming stressed and unstressed syllables, and extensive use of the intricate internal sound-patterning called *cynghanedd*. While the metrical virtuosity of this form makes translation formidable, Dafydd's range of subject matter—love, nature, and good-humoured self-mockery—have made him irresistible.

The earliest major translators, Sir H. Idris **Bell** and his son David **Bell**, mainly attempted to reproduce the couplet scheme, but with a loose syllable count and no attempt to reproduce the stressed/unstressed pattern of the rhymes. Their work is pleasant and readable, but suffers from a slightly flowery and dated tone. It also misses the feel of Dafydd altogether: the words are there, but one could be reading anyone. By contrast, Gwyn **Williams** in *The Burning Tree* opted for free verse, which allowed him multiple methods for catching Dafydd's voice. These translations were the first to make Dafydd well known outside Wales, and for long remained the best available.

Two poets working in the 1960s attempted to grapple with verse-forms closer to Dafydd's own. Joseph P. **Clancy**, in *Medieval Welsh Lyrics*, used the seven-syllable line with a stressed/unstressed alternation in line-ending, but no overt rhyme. While occasionally losing some of the strict sense of the originals, these translations are strikingly accurate and go some way to revealing Dafydd's voice in English. Clancy internalizes the techniques of the medieval poet and takes full advantage of the potential afforded by translation of bringing something new into the language. This is particularly true of Dafydd's use of the *sangiad*, an interjection or interruption in the line, which other translators have been tempted to smooth out:

> I bumped, by jumping badly,
> My shin, and how my leg hurt,
> Against, an ostler left it,
> The side of a noisy stool.

Clancy's delight in Dafydd's brio comes out in full force in the comic poems, like 'The Girls of Llanbadarn', where, as so often, the ease of reading hides a complexity of ornamentation present also in the translation:

> Passion doubles me over,
> Plague take all the parish girls!
> Because, frustrated trysting,
> I've had not a single one.
> No lovely longed-for virgin,
> Not a wench nor witch nor wife.

The other major translator to opt for closer stylistic adherence is Anthony **Conran**. Although his *Penguin Book of Welsh Verse* includes only eight of Dafydd's poems, Conran attempts for these and other *cywyddau* to recreate the metre more fully in English, employing seven-syllable lines and alternating end-rhymes:

> A fine gull on the tideflow,
> All one white with moon or snow,
> Your beauty's immaculate,
> Shard like the sun, brine's gauntlet.

While this often produces brilliant poems (best is

his rendition of the later Iolo Goch's poem on Owain Glyndwr's house at Sycharth), some of the intensity of line which Clancy manages to capture is lost in the rhyme scheme.

Rolfe **Humphries**, too, in *Nine Thorny Thickets* (1969) worked close to the original form, though with rather wider license on the sense. His poems have a great swing to them and are full of life and something of Dafydd's devilry. His introduction is the thing to note, with its strong defence of poetic translations: 'Translators should swashbuckle a bit more than we do. So here I am now, look you, a poet translating a poet, not some frayed but polite border functionary wearily exchanging the worn scrip of one republic for that of another.'

The most recent of Dafydd's translators have resoundingly failed to swashbuckle. Richard **Loomis**'s translations of the whole corpus of Dafydd is literal, no more and no less, a good student's key but no scintillating read. More prosaic still is Rachel **Bromwich**, whose translations are now the most widely known through publication in Penguin. To be fair, these appear alongside the originals, but still do little to reveal Dafydd's mastery to the outside world. Despite her severe advocacy of prose translation in her introduction, Bromwich's own renderings are sometimes curiously wide, especially when tempted out of strict prose by a still rosier style. She often needlessly supplies extra information, masking the original, as in the insertions in 'The Wind': 'most reckless in the world, [though] without foot or wing'; 'Tell me, [my] devoted jewel'. To experience the glories of the *cywyddwyr* in English, one must still go to Williams, Conran, or, for the best balance of sense and poetry, Clancy.

Williams and Conran have both also translated a representative selection of other medieval Welsh verse, but Clancy has provided quantity and depth for both the later period in *Medieval Welsh Lyrics* and especially for the earlier period in *The Earliest Welsh Poetry* (1970). This provides a full survey of the court poets of the 12th and 13th c., as well as excellent versions of the earlier dramatic lyrics in *englyn* form, and of some of the earliest poetry in Welsh, the praise poems of Taliesin and Aneirin.

Aneirin's *Gododdin*, ostensibly a work of the 6th c., is contentious in its origins and form, and is well known to English-language audiences through, for instance, its use by David Jones. Translators have had to deal with choices of how to represent not only the verse but also its overall structure. Clancy's 1970 translation, which once again aims at presenting the poetic voice of the original while retaining much of the literal sense, adopts Ifor Williams's reconstructed poem from the edition in *Canu Aneirin* (1938). While a brilliant work of scholarship, Williams's presentation of the text aimed at an original which is probably unrealizable, and translators who follow him, such as Clancy or A. O. H. **Jarman**, tidy the text still further into a misleading coherence. Clancy's is the poet's translation while Jarman's is the scholar's, but both are attractive as a first experience of the work.

Kenneth H. **Jackson** provided a prose translation of most of the work in *The Gododdin: The Oldest Scottish Poem* (1969). Jackson's prose translations elsewhere tended to be those of a fine poet *manqué*, but here his struggles for sense and no more leave little impression of either form or poetry, however useful as scholarship. Joseph P. Clancy's most recent translation in *The Triumph Tree* (1998) is a fairly thorough revision of his 1970 work, and structurally presents as fully as possible a translation of *The Gododdin* as it actually appears in the manuscript (something no edition of the poem yet does). Poetically he has turned towards a stricter literalism, but the translation retains much of the original poetic power, and is the best place to experience the shape and feel of this, one of the oldest of Welsh poetic works.   TC

PROSE   Ford, Patrick K., *The Mabinogi and Other Medieval Welsh Tales*, Berkeley, Calif., 1977 · Gantz, Jeffrey, *The Mabinogion*, Harmondsworth, 1976 [Penguin] · Guest, Lady Charlotte, *The Mabinogion*, 3 vols., London, 1838–49; one-vol. edn. London, 1877; rep. Cardiff, 1977 · Jones, Gwyn, and Jones, Thomas, *The Mabinogion*, London, 1948 [Everyman, 1949; rev. edn., 1974].

POETRY: ANTHOLOGIES   Clancy, Joseph P., *Medieval Welsh Lyrics*, London/New York, 1965 · *The Earliest Welsh Poetry*, London/New York, 1970 · Clancy, T. O., ed., *The Triumph Tree: Scotland's Earliest Poetry, AD 550–1350*, Edinburgh, 1998 · Conran, Anthony, *The Penguin Book of Welsh Verse*, Harmondsworth, 1967 [Penguin]; revised as *Welsh Verse*, Bridgend, Wales, 1992 · Jones, Gwyn, *Oxford Book of Welsh Verse in English*, Oxford, 1977 · Williams, Gwyn, *The Burning Tree*, London, 1956 · *Welsh Poems: Sixth Century to 1600*, London, 1973.

DAFYDD AP GWILYM   Bell, H. Idris, and Bell, David, *Dafydd ap Gwilym: Fifty Poems*, London, 1942 · Bromwich, Rachel, *Dafydd ap Gwilym: A Selection of Poems*, Llandysul, 1982 [subsequently Penguin, 1985] · Humphries, Rolfe, *Nine Thorny Thickets: Selected Poems by Dafydd ap Gwilym* (with four translations by Jon Roush), Kent, OH., 1969 · Loomis, Richard Morgan, *Dafydd ap Gwilym: The Poems*, Binghamton, NY, 1982.

GODODDIN   Jackson, Kenneth H., *The Gododdin: The Oldest Scottish Poem*, Edinburgh, 1969 · Jarman, A. O. H., *Aneirin: Y Gododdin: The Earliest British Heroic Poem*, Llandysul, Wales, 1988.

SEE ALSO   Stephens, M., ed., *The Oxford Companion to the Literature of Wales*, Oxford, 1986; rev. as *The New Companion to the Literature of Wales*, Cardiff, 1998.

4. SCOTTISH GAELIC

i. Beginnings Amongst the earliest external references to Gaelic literature are Middle Scots compositions which include caricatures of Gaelic bards as seen through Lowland eyes. Significantly, the Scots makars chose to make their Highland counterparts speak in pseudo-Gaelic gobbledegook, and showed little curiosity about the content of Gaelic literature. Admittedly, they referred occasionally to the past position of Gaelic as the court language of pre-Norman Scotland; and it is clear with hindsight that there were certain corridors of communication between Gaelic and English, ranging from family history to popular song and tale; but the 'official' position was one of imperviousness to the literary tradition of their uncivil Highland counterparts.

An awakening of Lowland interest in Gaelic culture took place in the mid-18th c. Contributory factors included a desire to know the Highlander. Amongst other things, in the aftermath of the political and religious strife of the Jacobite period the Highlander had come to represent Scotland in English opinion, and educated Scots tended to try to keep up with English thinking. At the same time, the belligerent role of Highlanders in the Risings of 1715 and 1745 had become intertwined with wider Scottish anxieties about Scottish identity in the wake of the Union of the Parliaments. And Scotland was not exempt from a growing antiquarian curiosity about ancient Britain, with attendant speculation about the races who had peopled the British Isles in the past, and about their descendants in more recent times.

Then in 1756 Jerome **Stone** (1727–56) published in the *Scots Magazine* an English version of a Gaelic heroic ballad with an accompanying letter in which he drew attention to 'a great number of poetical compositions . . . some of them of very great antiquity, whose merit entitles them to exemption from the unfortunate neglect, or rather abhorrence, to which ignorance has subjected that emphatic and venerable language in which they were composed'. This excited considerable interest, appearing, as it did, at a time when similar discoveries in early Welsh and Irish (and indeed in Norse) literature were coming to the attention of the educated British readership.

ii. Ossian Unfortunately, whatever general or scholarly interest might have been sparked by ingenuous activities of this sort was overwhelmed by the appearance in 1760 of James 'Ossian' **Macpherson**'s (1736–96) *Fragments of Ancient Poetry*, swiftly followed by the same author's *Fingal* (1762) and *Temora* (1763), attributed to the legendary bard Ossian. These largely fabricated productions chimed with external literary expectations, stimulating and then feeding an insatiable taste for a mood of melancholic brooding over an heroic past. Fingal and Ossian captivated Europe more completely than any British literary characters since King Arthur.

They also generated controversy at home, for Macpherson's claims were by no means universally accepted. But the argument was fought on several fronts, and the glare of publicity simply added to the confusion. Thus the prize of international prestige, the fact that some prominent sceptics were English, and the fact that Irish critics were claiming Fingal and Ossian as Irishmen, conspired to make it a point of Highland and Scottish honour to defend their authenticity against all comers. As a result of all this, 'Ossian' spawned imitators (e.g. Revd Dr John **Smith**, whose *Sean Dana . . . Ancient Poems of Ossian, Orrann, Ullin, &c* (1787), contained the Gaelic 'originals' of the 'translations' he had included in his *Galic Antiquities*). Again, 'Ossianic' compositions found their way into the printed anthologies of Gaelic poetry that were now beginning to appear (e.g. in John Gillies's *Collection of Ancient and Modern Gaelic Poems and Songs*, 1786), and hence actually became a part of Gaelic literature and literary trad-ition, despite the fact that their metre, language, and tone were outlandish from the Gaelic point of view. This twin legacy of uncertain credentials and 'Celtic gloom' continued to corrode both external perceptions and native literary values for a century or more. Awareness of the external admiration for Ossian destabilized in various ways the critical faculties of those who wrote on Gaelic literature and those who went out to collect it in the field: e.g. Marjorie Kennedy-Fraser, whose influential *Songs of the Hebrides* (1909) sacrificed the strong passion of the originals for mist and whimsy.

In fact, the polemics, obfuscation, triumphalism,

and so forth of the Ossianic controversy had in time given way to a calmer mood of curiosity as to what Gaelic literature really contained: e.g. Thomas **Hill**'s *Antient Erse Poems* (1784) and Mathew **Young**'s *Antient Gaelic Poems* (1787). Even Dr Johnson, Macpherson's arch-detractor, and James Boswell were asking their Highland hosts for literal translations of real Gaelic poems and songs during their Highland trip in 1773, and the same genuine curiosity can be found in the accounts of many other visitors to the Highlands. Indeed, it is worth adding that the rescue of genuine Gaelic MSS of the late Middle Ages, and equally the stimulus to collect orally preserved Gaelic balladry and other forms of vernacular Gaelic literature, owes a great deal to the excitement generated by 'Ossian'. Amongst these activities we may note a second wave of 'translation' of Gaelic material, which has received a better press than Macpherson's efforts: when Jacobitism and the 'Forty-Five became respectable, men like James **Hogg** and Walter **Scott** composed poetic versions of translations of Gaelic songs— e.g. in Alexander Campbell's *Albyn's Anthology* (1816–18)—as part of a reinterpretation of the past that saw the Highlander fully integrated into the 19th-c. Scottish identity.

iii. Nineteenth Century The scholarly investigation of earlier Gaelic literature (as of the other Celtic literatures) had been part of the heroic project of the antiquarian Edward Lhuyd, whose *Archaeologia Britannica* appeared in 1707. That thread was not picked up again until in 1811–12 the Highland Society of Scotland encouraged the Gaelic scholar Ewen MacLachlan to examine the old Gaelic manuscripts in their possession. And it was only in 1861 that the collaboration of the Scottish historian William Forbes Skene and the Gaelic scholar Revd Thomas MacLauchlan resulted in the publication of a full transcription and translation of the contents of the early 16th-c. *Book of the Dean of Lismore*.

Almost simultaneously, Gaelic folk-tales became widely available when John Francis **Campbell** of Islay (1822–85) brought out the four volumes of *Popular Tales of the West Highlands*, whose translations owed their blend of colloquial and archaic elements partly to contemporary theories about the antiquity of folk-tales and partly to earlier translations like Lady Charlotte Guest's *Mabinogion* [II.d.3.i]. The demand for Gaelic tales and legends, once established, remained strong; a notable contribution was contained in Lord Archibald **Campbell**'s series *Waifs and Strays of Celtic Tradition* (1889–95).

Meanwhile, the elucidation of the Gaelic manuscript tradition continued with Revd A. Cameron's *Reliquiae Celticae* (1892–4), which brought the bardic eulogies and elegies of the hereditary poetic families to the public attention. By then Celtic had become a university subject in Scotland, and a tradition of scrupulous scholarship and authoritative publication had been established, though the milestone of the foundation of a Scottish Gaelic Texts Society, whose aim, to bring out definitive editions of the principal poets of the 16th, 17th, and 18th c., was not reached until 1937. The popular song tradition did not receive much attention until the present century, but works like John Lorne **Campbell**'s *Hebridean Folksongs* have redressed the balance in more recent times. For a variety of reasons the Scottish tradition of Celtic scholarship has in general proved itself relatively open to providing English translations—partly, no doubt, from a wish (as John Murdoch put it) to 'insist on contributing our share to the literature of the world', and partly to correct obstinate misconceptions about the Gael.

For very many ordinary Highlanders, of course, the 19th c. was an age of clearances and emigration, social disintegration and upheaval. The literature of the period tended to be avoided by scholars as an embarrassment—fragmented and degenerate by comparison with the brilliance of the 'Golden Age' that had preceded it. Eventually, however, a political resistance developed, and Gaelic confidence revived in the 1870s and 1880s with the Land Agitations and Crofters' Wars. Renewed external interest and internal confidence combined to enable a modest Gaelic literary revival to take place. Gaelic-Scots solidarity, and to some extent pan-Celtic outreach, dictated that English translations would play their part in this revival, to a greater extent than occurred in Ireland or Wales.

iv. Twentieth Century This sense of bilingual solidarity was reciprocated from the Scots side in the interwar period. In the context of the Scottish Renaissance Hugh **MacDiarmid** promoted and translated the greatest 18th-c. Gaelic poet, Alasdair mac Mhaighstir Alasdair, Douglas **Young** promoted and translated the contemporary poet Sorley MacLean, and George Campbell **Hay** moved freely between Gaelic and Scots in his compositions and translations. A tradition was being forged. A significant publication in the emergence of the present-day version of this bilingual tradition was *Four Points of a Saltire* (1970), in which Gaelic and Scots poets were featured side by side. This tradition, backed up by a flourishing Celtic-Scots folk music axis and the growth of a culture of poetry-readings, remains important to the present. As part of the same cultural circumstances, Gaelic poets have become used to preparing English versions of their poetry for mixed audiences, and translation has been important in widening the appeal and reputation of Gaelic poets like Sorley MacLean and Derick Thomson.

At the same time, not all recent Gaelic poetry has been translated. Insofar as one can distinguish between 'contemporary traditional' poets and a modern intellectual movement, the former are less likely to feel the need to translate their work into English. Equally, however, some of the latter are concerned to avoid becoming bilingual—as opposed to Gaelic—poets. The same is true—or more so—as regards prose-writing. Whereas Angus Robertson brought out his pioneering novel *An t-Ogha Mór* (1913) in English (*The Ogha Mor*, 1924), and Iain Crichton Smith has transposed material from his *An t-Aonaran* (The Loner) (1979) into English, the ethos of the well-developed short-story tradition, and of the novel, biography, and autobiography in Gaelic, is in general a more deliberately self-sufficient one, and external interest has not so far developed a sufficient momentum to demand translation.

To sum up, the contemporary English-speaking reader interested in Gaelic is served by translations of a fair selection of the major vernacular poets of the 17th and 18th c. These vary from bombastic 19th-c. renderings to the austere, scholarly English of the Scottish Gaelic Texts Society, where a high degree of fidelity is usually present but translators' graces are sometimes less in evidence. The same is true of the often anonymous traditional literature (dating in its composition from the 16th to the 19th c.), of which a representative selection is now available in scholarly editions and anthologies. More recently, the contemporary, original work of the 19th c. has been rediscovered and found to be more varied and sophisticated and less barren than was previously allowed. Finally, modern poetry,

which has been the most intensively cultivated branch of literary composition in Gaelic in recent times, has likewise attracted more translators than any other.

As to character and quality, some of the earliest translations were seriously inadequate linguistically, and others were rendered misleading by their authors' zeal to make them conform to actual or imagined external expectations. From the point of view of a modern reader, even the scholarly translations of the 19th c. are too often bedevilled by a penchant for archaism, whether high-flown and windy or quaint and folksy. Scholars of the 20th c. like W. J. **Watson** (1865–1948) evolved an Olympian style with a timeless authority which was appropriate enough for the older court poetry, but less so for less formal genres. Alexander **Carmichael** (1832–1912) hit a resonant note when preparing his versions of folk prayers and charms to appear in *Carmina Gadelica* (1901). A high level of scholarly comprehension has not always been proof against stylistic misapprehension: George **Calder**'s (1859–1941) 'verse' translations of William Ross must count amongst the most egregious ever seen in the English language. Over the last quarter-century, a more low-key approach has emerged amongst Gaelic translators. The scholars have played an important role in this, e.g. in the normative tale and song translations provided by John **MacInnes** and others in *Scottish Studies, Tocher*, and to accompany the musical publications of the School of Scottish Studies in Edinburgh. At a more exacting level, Sorley **MacLean**'s translations, both of his own work and of pre-20th-c. Gaelic poets, are on a different plane: luminous and monolithic. Derick **Thomson**'s translations of his own work reflect the word-play and thought-play of his Gaelic versions in a masterly way. Iain Crichton **Smith**'s translations of Duncan Bàn Macintyre and other traditional Gaelic poets have discrimination and bite, and represent a serious attempt to come to terms with the challenge of providing literary translations of Gaelic poetry.   WG

ANTHOLOGIES (PRE-20TH-C. POETRY) Cameron, Alexander, *Reliquiae Celticae*, Inverness, 1892–4 · Campbell, Alexander, *Albyn's Anthology, or a Select Collection of the Melodies and Vocal Poetry Peculiar to Scotland and the Isles . . .*, 2 vols., Edinburgh, 1816–18 · Campbell, John Lorne, and Collinson, Francis, *Hebridean Folksongs*, 3 vols., Oxford, 1969–81 · Carmichael, Alexander, *Carmina Gadelica: Hymns and Incantations with Illustrative Notes . . .*, 2 vols., Edinburgh, 1901 [several rev. edns. with 4 further vols.] · McLauchlan, Thomas, and Skene, William Forbes, *The Dean of Lismore's Book: A Selection of Ancient Gaelic Poetry*, Edinburgh, 1862 · Meek, Donald E., *Tuath is Tighearna: Tenants and Landlords*, Edinburgh, 1996 · Ó Baoill, Colm, and Bateman, Meg, *Gàirnan Classach / The Harp's Cry*, Edinburgh, 1994 · Pattison, Thomas, *The Gaelic Bards and Original Poems*, 2nd edn., Glasgow, 1890 · Thomson, Derick S., *Gaelic Poetry in the Eighteenth Century: A Bilingual Anthology*, Aberdeen, 1993.
ANTHOLOGIES (20TH-C. POETRY) MacAulay, Donald, ed., *Nua-Bhardachd Ghàidhlig: Modern Scottish Gaelic Poems*, Edinburgh, 1976 · MacLean, Sorley, Hay, George Campbell, Neill, William, and MacGregor, Stuart, *Four Points of a*

Saltire, Edinburgh, 1970 · Whyte, Christopher, ed., *An Aghaidh na Sìorraidheachd/In the Face of Eternity*, Edinburgh, 1991.

ANTHOLOGIES (TALES)   Campbell, John F., ed., *Popular Tales of the West Highlands, Orally Collected . . .*, 4 vols., 2nd edn., Paisley, 1890–3 · Mackay, John G., ed., *More West Highland Tales*, 2 vols., Edinburgh, 1940–60.

OSSIANICA   Macpherson, James, *Fragments of Ancient Poetry, Collected in the Highlands of Scotland, and Translated from the Galic or Erse Language*, Edinburgh, 1760 · *Fingal. An Ancient Epic Poem, in Six Books . . .*, London, 1762 · *Temora, an Ancient Epic Poem, in Eight Books . . .*, London, 1763 · Smith, John, *Galic Antiquities: Consisting of a History of the Druids . . . and a Collection of Ancient Poems, Translated from the Galic . . .*, Edinburgh, 1780 · *Sean Dana . . . Ancient Poems Collected in the Western Highlands and Isles*, Edinburgh, 1787.

MACGILLEAIN, SOMHAIRLE [SORLEY MACLEAN]   *Dàin do Eimhir agus Dàin eile* [Poems to Eimhear and Other Poems], Glasgow, 1943 · *Reothairt is Contraigh/Spring Tide and Neap Tide: Selected Poems 1932–72*, Edinburgh, 1977 · *O Choille gu Bearradh/From Wood to Ridge: Collected Poems in Gaelic and English*, Manchester, 1989.

MAC IAIN DEORSA, DEORSA [GEORGE CAMPBELL HAY]   Byrne, Michel, ed., *Collected Poems and Songs of George Campbell Hay*, Edinburgh, 1999.

MAC THOMAIS, RUAIRIDH [DERICK THOMSON]   *Creachadh na Clàrsaich/Plundering the Harp: Collected Poems 1940–1980*, Edinburgh, 1982 · *Smeur an Dòchais/Bramble of Hope*, Edinburgh, 1991.

SEE ALSO   Gillies, W., ed., *Ris a' Bhruthaich: The Criticism and Prose Writings of Sorley MacLean*, Stornoway, 1985 · Ross, R. J., and Hendry, J., eds., *Sorley MacLean: Critical Essays*, Edinburgh, 1986 · Thomson, D., *An Introduction to Gaelic Poetry*, London, 1974.

5. MODERN IRISH (GAELIC)

i. Pre-Twentieth-Century Writing Postclassical Gaelic literature begins amid the profound social, political, and cultural upheavals of the 17th c. in Ireland, and Seathrún Céitinn (Geoffrey Keating) is a key transitional figure of the period. In 1723 Dermod **O'Connor** (dates unknown) published a controversial translation of Keating's *Foras Feasa ar Éirinn* (1630s, General History of Ireland). Keating was a continentally educated Co. Tipperary priest of Norman stock who, some time in the 1630s, produced this lengthy, polemical history in response to the writings of unsympathetic English commentators on Ireland. Unpublished in the original until the 19th c., it became the most popular prose work in the postclassical Gaelic manuscript tradition of the 17th to the 19th c. Several English translations in manuscript form preceded O'Connor's version. This takes considerable liberties with the original, adding to it and subtracting from it at will, more in the manner of a medieval adapter than an 18th-c. scholarly translator. He was roundly criticized for this by his contemporaries.

Despite a tantalizing reference in Edmund Spenser's *A View of the Present State of Ireland* (1596) to certain unnamed Gaelic poems which Spenser had 'caused . . . to be translated unto [him]', the earliest substantial body of Irish verse in English translation extant dates from almost two centuries later. The preface to the seminal dual-language *Reliques of Gaelic Poetry* (1789) by Charlotte **Brooke** (d. 1793) contains some conscientious musings on the problems of verse translation. Unfortunately,

this theoretical scrupulousness did not, in practice, save her versions of various Gaelic 'heroic poems, odes, elegies and songs' from being infected by the inflated exclamatory style of late 18th-c. 'Celticism', as pioneered by Thomas Gray and James Macpherson [II.d.4.ii].

Among Brooke's many 19th-c. heirs the two translators who made the greatest impression on Irish literature in English were Sir Samuel **Ferguson** (1810–86) and James Clarence **Mangan** (1803–49). Ferguson was an energetic and prolific polemicist with strong views on the problems of translating Gaelic literature. His *Lays of the Western Gael* (1865) includes over 20 'Versions from the Irish', mostly from the postclassical Gaelic song tradition. 'Cean Dubh Deelish', whose title is a transliteration of the Irish for 'dear black head', has been widely admired for its effective replication of the rhythm, meaning, and emotional tug of the original:

> Put your head, darling, darling, darling,
> your darling black head my heart above;
> Oh, mouth of honey, with the thyme for fragrance,
> Who, with heart in breast, could deny you love?

Unlike Ferguson, James Clarence Mangan knew little or no Irish and relied on literal 'cribs' provided by contemporary Gaelic scholars. Gaelic literature was one among many sources of inspiration for Mangan, who was fascinated by the notion of translation. His enigmatic, extravagant, and contradictory nature is perfectly reflected by his translation practices, taken as a whole. His best-known version from the Irish, 'My Dark Rosaleen', begins:

> Oh my Dark Rosaleen
> Do not sigh, do not weep
> The priests are on the ocean green
> They march along the deep.

It is an expanded, incantatory reworking of 'Róisín Dubh', a popular love-song generally construed as an allegorical expression of fidelity to Ireland.

In 1890 Douglas **Hyde** (1860–1949) published a collection of prose translations from Irish folklore, *Beside the Fire*. Aiming for a literal reproduction of the Irish idioms of his source material, Hyde chose to translate into the Hiberno-English vernacular of rural Ireland. W. B. Yeats lauded this refreshing alternative to the 'formal eighteenth-century style' of previous translators whose 'horses were always steeds and their cows kine'. Hyde also translated a large body of poetry from the Irish song tradition, maintaining the same translation policy. The most celebrated of his six-part presentation of 'The Songs of the Province of Connaught' is *The Love Songs of Connaught* (1893). It includes his translation of the anonymous 'Mo Bhrón ar an bhFarraige' ('My Grief on the Sea'), which the writer and translator Frank **O'Connor** described as 'the perfect translation of a great poem from one language into another'.

Notable among recent collections of Irish poetry in translation is *An Duanaire: Poems of the Dispossessed 1600–1900* (1981), an anthology of 100 poems edited by Seán Ó Tuama with translations by the poet Thomas **Kinsella**, which was an Irish bestseller. Kinsella's stated aim was to provide readable translations 'of the greatest possible fidelity of content', conveying 'all images and ideas occurring in the Irish' and none which did not. In this, despite a small number of mistranslations, he largely succeeded.

Brian Merriman's *Cúirt an Mheán-Oíche* (1780, The Midnight Court) is the most celebrated comic poem in the Irish language. This bawdy extravaganza which runs to over 1000 lines has attracted the attention of a host of translators. The most successful and popular version, by Frank O'Connor (included in *Kings, Lords and Commons*, 1959) captures much of its antic energy in a headlong rush of rhyming tetrametric couplets which closely resembles the prosody of the original.

ii. Twentieth-Century Prose Relatively few literary works produced since the beginning of the language revival movement in the late 19th c. have been translated into English. The modern prose texts which achieved the greatest popularity in

English translation belong to what is known as the 'Literature of the Blaskets'. During the first half of this century the remote Blasket islands, off the south-west coast of Ireland, attracted the attention of numerous scholars of literature, philology, and anthropology, both native and foreign. One by-product of this attention was a number of autobiographies written or dictated by members of this largely non-literate community. The most immediately and enduringly popular of these is Muiris Ó Súilleabháin's (Maurice O'Sullivan) *Fiche Blian ag Fás* (1933, Twenty Years a-Growing), published in English translation by M. L. **Davies** and George **Thomson**. The book's success was facilitated by E. M. Forster's enthusiastic introduction to the first of many editions of the book in the World's Classics series. Ó Súilleabháin had rather more formal education than Tomás Ó Criomhthainn (Tomás O'Crohan), whose magesterially stark account of island life, *An tOileánach* (1929, The Islandman), was translated with faithful economy in 1937 by Robin **Flower**. Bryan **McMahon**'s *Peig* is a translation into idiomatic Kerry English of the the vivid, sometimes overly dramatic, account of her life originally dictated in Irish by the exceptionally gifted storyteller, Peig Sayers, and first published in 1936.

Two of the most popular works in the canon of Irish literature in English were in fact originally written in Irish. These are Flann O'Brien's parody of the Blasket books and other 'peasant' autobiographies, *The Poor Mouth* (1973), and Brendan **Behan**'s boisterous political satire, *The Hostage* (1958). In the introduction to his otherwise effective translation of *An Béal Bocht* (1941) Patrick C. **Power** acknowledges the difficulty of reproducing in English some of O'Brien's bilingual wordplay and his mocking of specific stylistic tics of O'Crohan and others. Behan produced the translation of his own play, *An Giall*; many of the elements of music-hall, audience engagement and topical reference in the standard text of *The Hostage*, however, derive from Joan Littlewood's energetic adaptation of the play for the London stage later the same year.

This century's most celebrated Gaelic writer of creative fiction, Máirtín Ó Cadhain, is almost unknown outside Irish-speaking circles. While most of his mature work awaits translation, Eoghan Ó **Tuairisc**'s *The Road to Brightcity* translates a selection of early short stories from the 1930s and 1940s. The most memorable of these are grim tales of rural hardship, initially inspired by the social realism of Maxim Gorky. Ó Tuairisc's precise but informal idiom is surprisingly faithful to Ó Cadhain's richly textured Irish. On occasion he quietly curbs the author's tendency towards verbosity but strains to find Hiberno-English equivalents for some of the more highly wrought passages in the original.

iii. Twentieth-Century Poetry

Ó Cadhain's poetic contemporaries have been equally ill-served by English translators. Modern poetry in Irish came of age with a generation of poets who began publishing in the late 1930s and early 1940s. Yet Máirtín Ó Direáin's *Tacar Dánta / Selected Poems* of 1981, translated with measured deference by Douglas Sealy and Tomás Mac Síomóin, was the first solo anthology to introduce the work of a poet of this generation to readers of English. It marked a decisive turn towards translation in a poetic community who, unlike their Scottish counterparts [II.d.4.iv], were unused to presenting their work bilingually. The watershed publication for a younger generation of poets who came of age since the 1970s was *An Tonn Gheal: The Bright Wave* (1986). This anthology showcased the work of six poets accompanied by translations by 14 of their English-writing peers, whose notion of translation ranged from the faithful to the fanciful. In his foreword the anthology's publisher, the poet / novelist / dramatist Dermot Bolger, stressed his preference for the translation of the spirit rather the letter of the original, and this sentiment has underwritten much subsequent translation.

The Bright Wave was published in tandem with a volume by Nuala **Ní Dhomhnaill** in English translation. Ní Dhomhnaill is by far the most celebrated of the younger generation. She has been translated into a variety of languages and in English has benefited from the attentions of what has been described as a 'veritable procession of linguistic suitors'. *Nuala Ní Dhomhnaill: Selected Poems* (1986) contains some 50 translations by Michael **Hartnett** and a handful by the poet herself. Hartnett's translations are on the whole accurate and persuasive in their blunt literalness, though they occasionally sacrifice fluency for fidelity. Ní Dhomhnaill's own translations are equally plain-spoken. *Pharaoh's Daughter* (1990), on the other hand, draws on the skills of 13 different translators, all but one of whom are well-known Irish poets who write in English. The translating strategies are extremely varied, ranging from the unshowy fidelity of Hartnett, Eiléan **Ní Chuilleanáin**, and Seamus **Heaney** to freewheeling versions by Medb **McGuckian** and Paul **Muldoon**. These latter contributed to the frustration expressed by certain reviewers at the difficulty of discerning Ní Dhomhanill's true voice amidst the chorus of more familiar accompanists. This reception notwithstanding, Paul Muldoon was the choice of translator for Ní Dhomhnaill's third dual-language collection, the punningly titled *The Astrakhan Cloak* (1992) (the Irish word for 'translation' is *aistriúchán*).

Several other poets of Ní Dhomhnaill's generation have also produced dual-language collections in the wake of *The Bright Wave*, and this tendency has undoubtedly resulted in a wider Irish readership for Gaelic poetry. Concern has been expressed, however, that the degree of 'future translatability' may become a subconscious factor influencing original composition. It is worth noting that one of the most consistently interesting and iconoclastic of contemporary poets, Biddy Jenkinson, has refused to succumb to the temptation of translation: 'I prefer not to be translated into English in Ireland. It is a small rude gesture to those who think that everything can be harvested and stored without loss in an English-speaking Ireland.'   CMGL

ANTHOLOGIES   Bolger, Dermot, ed., *An Tonn Gheal: The Bright Wave* [various translators], Dublin, 1986 · Brooke, Charlotte, *Reliques of Irish Poetry*, Dublin, 1789 · Ferguson, Samuel, *Lays of the Western Gael*, London, 1865 · Hyde, Douglas, *Beside the Fire*, Dublin, 1890 · *Love Songs of Connaught*, Dublin, 1893 · Kinsella, Thomas, tr., and Ó Tuama, Seán, ed., *An Duanaire 1600–1900: Poems of the Dispossessed*, Dublin, 1981 · Mangan, James Clarence, and O'Daly, John, *The Poets and Poetry of Munster*, Dublin, 1849 · O'Connor, Frank, *Kings, Lords and Commons*, London, 1959.

BEHAN, BRENDAN   Behan, Brendan, *The Hostage*, London, 1958.

CÉITINN, SEATHRÚN [GEOFFREY KEATING]   O'Connor, Dermod, *The General History of Ireland collected by the Learned Jeffrey Keating D.D. . . . Faithfully Translated . . . By Dermod O'Connor*, London, 1723.

NÍ DHOMHNAILL, NUALA   Hartnett, Michael, *Selected Poems*, Dublin, 1986 · Various, *Pharaoh's Daughter*, Oldcastle, Ireland, 1990 · Muldoon, Paul, *The Astrakhan Cloak*, Oldcastle, Ireland, 1992.

O'BRIEN, FLANN   Power, Patrick, *The Poor Mouth*, London, 1973.

Ó CADHAIN, MÁIRTÍN   Ó Tuairisc, Eoghan, *The Road to Brightcity*, Dublin, 1981.

Ó CRIOMHTHAINN, TOMÁS [TOMÁS O'CROHAN]   Flower, Robin, *The Islandman*, Dublin, 1937.

Ó DIREÁIN, MÁIRTÍN   Mac Síomóin, Tomás, and Sealy, Douglas, *Selected Poems / Tacar Dánta*, Newbridge, Ireland, 1981.

Ó SÚILLEABHÁIN, MUIRIS [MAURICE O'SULLIVAN]   Llewelyn Davies, Moya, and Thomson, George, *Twenty Years a-Growing*, Oxford, 1933 [World's Classics].

SAYERS, PEIG McMahon, Bryan, *Peig: The Autobiography of Peig Sayers of the Great Blasket Island*, Dublin, 1973.

SEE ALSO Cronin, M., *Translating Ireland*, Cork, 1996 · Welch, R., *A History of Verse Translation from the Irish 1789–1897*, Gerrards Cross, Bucks, 1988.

6. MODERN WELSH

i. Pre-Twentieth-Century Writing Welsh literature entering its latest (last?) era of greatness, even as Welsh speakers decline to a mere fifth of the population; English, an aggressive language threatening Welsh with extinction yet the sole and native tongue of the majority of the Welsh, and the second language of the world; English and Welsh producing literatures the serious incompatibility of which is typified by the untranslatability of Welsh strict-metre poetry, a culturally definitive and resilient form as resourcefully modern as it is ancient [see II.d.3.ii]; neighbouring cultures that inhabit radically different time-zones, so that an English reader finds it difficult not to patronize a Welsh modernism that seems little better than a belated romanticism: these, and many other, factors constitute the invisible force-field of translation from Welsh into English in the 20th c. They also ensure that this intercultural activity has been supercharged with political implications and accordingly entangled in a skein of contrasting tropes, with translation variously figuring as colonization or freedom struggle, selling out or buying in, an act of cultural betrayal or an honourable ambassadorial service, as internationalist in spirit or as intra-national—the healing suture of a linguistically divided nation.

Things were rather simpler in past centuries, partly because Welsh-language society was numerically and socially so much more powerful, and partly because the Celtic revivals periodically hosted by English culture during the 18th and 19th c. were predominantly antiquarian in character and generated little interest in recent or contemporary literature. Consequently it was not until the latter decades of the last century that such classics of religious culture as Morgan Llwyd's *Llyfr y Tri Aderyn* (1653, The Book of the Three Birds), Ellis Wynne's *Gweledigaetheu y Bardd Cwsg* (1703, The Visions of the Sleeping Bard), and the hymns, poems, and prose works of William Williams, Pantycelyn (1717–91) began to appear in English. Of these writers it was Wynne who attracted the most illustrious translators, his *Visions* being tackled first by the irrepressible George **Borrow** (1860) and later by the great poet T. Gwynn **Jones** (1940).

Intrinsically strong through it was, Welsh-language culture in the 19th c. continued to seem unappetizing to its neighbour. A parochially Non-conformist literature, stiff with piety and propriety, appealed little to the imperial England that had, after all, invented and perfected Victorianism. When translated into painfully correct English, even the dialect-enriched novels of a genius like Daniel Owen—the first and perhaps still the greatest of Welsh novelists—could seem intellectually inbred, technically laboured, and whimsically homespun. Fortunately, however, the 1963 version of Owen's *Gwen Tomos* is appreciably better than 19th-c. attempts to translate *Rhys Lewis* and *Enoc Huws*.

ii. Anthologies Early last century, the religious culture anatomized by Owen with a mixture of respect, affectionate humour, and scathing exasperation had produced in the mystical Methodist Ann Griffiths a hymn-writer of ecstatic originality. Sadly, little of this is captured even in well-meaning translations, and, similarly, little except the frailties of lyricists like Ceiriog, Alun, or Islwyn seems ever to appear in English. A sprinkling of such materials, soggy with predictable sentiment, may be found in John **Jenkins**'s anthology *The Poetry of Wales* (1873), designed in part to confirm Arnold's racial thesis that the Celts are spiritual and artistic while the Saxons are materialistic philistines. A more personal (and persistently recurring) motive for translation—racially mixed parentage—is explicitly affirmed by Edmund O. **Jones**, in his preface to *Welsh Lyrics of the Nineteenth Century* (1896), a collection whose badness (like that of his *Welsh Poets of Today and Yesterday*, 1901) may be due in part to his effort to reproduce the metre of the original lyrics.

The eccentric Irish scholar A. P. **Graves** (Robert Graves's father) underpinned his *Welsh Poetry, Old and New* (1912) with conscientious scholarly research, and in 1926 published his *English Verse Translations of the Welsh poems of Ceiriog Hughes*. Equally conventional, but redolent of period charm, is *Translations from the Welsh* (1913), a bilingual text by Francis **Edwards** who, like Graves, timidly acknowledges the extraordinary renaissance that was then newly under way in Welsh poetry, as university education gave poets access both to the antiquity of their native tradition and to the cosmopolitanism of European culture. The eminent scholar H. Idris **Bell** tried to communicate the excitement of this resurgence to English readers, first in *Poems from the Welsh* (1913) and then (with C. C. **Bell**) in *Welsh Poems of the Twentieth Century*, competent translations concluding with an excellent, substantial essay on the development of Welsh poetry from earliest times to the present.

Bell provided the model for the classic anthologies that eventually followed. Of these, Anthony **Conran**'s *Penguin Book of Welsh Verse* [II.d.3.ii] was a landmark volume, epic in scope, original in conception, and innovative in its stylistic and formal experimentations. Inspired by Gwyn **Williams**'s pioneering 1950s translation of medieval Welsh poetry, Conran set out to convey the continuity and greatness of the Welsh poetic tradition from the 6th c. to the present, and his volume—appearing towards the end of a decade in which Wales had been galvanized by political and cultural nationalism and in which Welsh youth had been mobilized by the ageing Saunders Lewis to save a rapidly declining language—made a powerful impression both within Wales and without.

Only a fifth of Conran's collection was devoted to modern Welsh poetry, whereas in 1982 the distinguished American translator Joseph P. **Clancy** added a complete volume, *Twentieth-Century Welsh Poems*, to his two earlier translations from Welsh poetry of the earliest and classical periods [II.d.3.ii]. Prefaced by an outstanding historical essay on the social antecedents and political contexts of modern Welsh poetry, Clancy's volume in every way constitutes an authoritative text, spanning the several successive phases of Welsh poetry this century— the great originators (T. Gwynn Jones, W. J. Gruffydd), the brilliant revisionist work of the second generation (R. Williams Parry, T. H. Parry-Williams, Saunders Lewis, Gwenallt), the arresting talents that matured after World War II (Waldo Williams, Euros Bowen, Alun Llywelyn-Williams, Bobi Jones), and a sample from the 1970s generation. R. Gerallt **Jones**'s excellent bilingual text, *Poetry of Wales 1930–1970*, had already covered much of this ground, but aimed only to supply an English text that would help readers make sense of the accompanying Welsh poem. Gwyn Jones selected the best available translations of modern poetry (including versions by such as George Borrow) when compiling his attractive *Oxford Book of Welsh Verse in English* (1977).

iii. Twentieth-Century Writers Conscious that an anthology failed to do justice to a major writer's work, Clancy collaborated with Gwyn **Thomas** in 1982 to produce the latter's bilingual *Living a Life*. In this volume Thomas's wry colloquialism, and accessible, anti-bardic style contrasts vividly with the bravura

conceits, the impassioned rhetoric of spiritual affirmation, and the dazzle of language in the constantly adventuring poetry of Bobi Jones, for instance. Clancy then went on to publish Saunders Lewis's *Selected Poems*, attempting (with some success) to do justice to a poetry that was magisterially controlled, classically precise, sacramentally disposed.

Founder-member and long-time president of Plaid Cymru, controversial cultural ideologue, a poet, dramatist, and novelist of genius, and charismatic both as political leader and as the artificer of a national tradition, Saunders Lewis is easily the most imposing figure in 20th-c. Welsh culture. There are two excellent English-language compilations of his work (*Presenting Saunders Lewis* and *Saunders Lewis: A Presentation of His Work*), while Clancy has translated a dozen of his plays, published in four volumes. The religious faith that underwrites the Catholic Lewis's work is a characteristic feature of modern Welsh poetry, and has tended to alienate a largely secularized English readership as evidenced by some reactions to the translated work of the powerful sacramental-symbolist poet Euros Bowen.

Written in marvellously tangy Welsh, Kate Roberts's fiction is both resonantly local and European in stature. Although somewhat thinned and subdued, her great stories remain recognizably powerful in stylish translations by Wyn **Griffith** and others, and in Clancy's imposing *The World of Kate Roberts*. First privately printed in Cardiff, Griffith's translation of *Y Byw Sy'n Cysgu* (1956, The Living Sleep), and Idwal **Walters** and John Idris **Jones**'s translation of *Traed Mewn Cyffion* (1936, Feet in Chains) reached a wider audience when reissued by Corgi.

The North Wales quarrying districts of some of Roberts's most celebrated work are more indulgently treated in the attractive fiction of T. Rowland Hughes, available in Richard **Ruck**'s fluent translations. In turning to the South Wales mining valleys with *William Jones* (1946), Hughes further underlined the fact that Welsh-language culture was not consignable either to one region of Wales or to the rural 'gwerin' (the idealized *volk*) as implicitly suggested in such classics of nostalgic pastoral reminiscence as Hugh Evans's *Cwm Eithin* (1931, The Gorse Glen) and D. J. Williams's *Hen Dŷ Ffarm* (1953, The Old Farm House, brilliantly translated for a Council of Europe Series by the poet Waldo **Williams**), and in part even in W. J. Gruffydd's *Hen Atgofion* (1936, The Years of the Locust). The conservatism of such writing was anathema to a novelist such as John Rowlands, whose quintessentially 1960s novel, *Ieuenctid yw*

Mhechod (1965, A Taste of Apples), shocked the culture with a frank picture of a minister's sexual misconduct.

Important aspects of the Welsh past have been treated in powerfully popular form in Marion Eames's *Y Stafell Ddirgel* (1969, The Secret Room) and *Y Rhandir Mwyn* (1972, Fair Wilderness), and in E. Tegla Davies's flawed masterpiece about the Tithe Wars, *Gŵr Pen y Bryn* (1923, The Master of Pen Y Bryn). As well as representing a younger generation's impatience with a romantic national-ist ideology of the Middle Ages, Wiliam Owen Roberts's Marxist deconstruction of history in *Y Pla* (1987, Pestilence) is illustrative of the utterly dis-tinctive versions of postmodernist fiction currently issuing from Wales, as is Robin Llywelyn's strange fantasia, *O'r Harbwr Gwag i'r Cefnfor Gwyn* (1994, From Empty Harbour to White Ocean). A forerun-ner of such fiction was Caradog Prichard's night-marish and phantasmagoric portrait of a North Wales quarrying community, *Un Nos Ola Leuad* (1961, One Moonlit Night). Probably the greatest Welsh novel of the century, it was freely translated, with considerable panache, by Menna **Gallie**, and more soberly and dependably by Philip **Mitchell**.

Short fiction has been a form particularly attractive to modern Welsh-language writers, and their work has been well represented in a number of English-language anthologies of Welsh short stories of the 20th c.

Welsh poetry has been brilliantly remaking itself over the last 20 years. It was conveniently show-cased, and discussed, in a special Welsh issue of *Modern Poetry in Translation*. The fierce political conscience that characterizes much of this writing is one feature of the work of Menna Elfyn, whose Welsh version of *écriture feminine* has attracted attention worldwide. She has also broken with tradition in working closely with other poets (including Gillian **Clarke**, Nigel **Jenkins**, and R. S. **Thomas**) to produce two notable bilingual collec-tions of her own poems: *Eucalyptus* and *Cell Angel*.

Still rich in talent and exhilaratingly alive to the contemporary, Welsh-language culture is incom-parably stronger than those of the other, related, Celtic communities. Ironically, however, it is its very self-sufficiency, combined with its edgy need for eternal vigilance, that makes it significantly less attractive, and amenable, to translation into a rival English than is theirs.   MWT

ANTHOLOGIES   Bell, H. I., and Bell, C. C., *Welsh Poems of the Twentieth Century*, Wrexham, 1925 · Clancy, Joseph P., *Twentieth-Century Welsh Poems*, Llandysul, 1982 · Conran, Anthony, *The Penguin Book of Welsh Verse*, London, 1967 [rev. and expanded as *Welsh Verse*, Bridgend, 1986] · Johnston, Dafydd, ed., *Modern Poetry in Translation*, Welsh Issue (Spring, 1995) · Jones, R. Gerallt et al., *Poetry of Wales, 1930–70*, Llandysul, 1974.

BOWEN, EUROS   Bowen, Euros, *Poems*, Llandysul, 1974 · Davies, Cynthia, and Davies, Saunders, ed., *Euros Bowen: Priest-Poet*, Penarth, 1993.

DAVIES, E. TEGLA   Watkins, Nina, *The Master of Pen y Bryn*, Swansea, 1975.

EAMES, MARION   Garlick, Elin, *Fair Wilderness*, Swansea, 1976 · Phillips, Margaret, *The Secret Room*, Swansea, 1975.

ELFYN, MENNA   Clarke, Gillian et al., *Cell Angel*, Newcastle upon Tyne, 1996 · Conran, Tony et al., *Eucalyptus*, Llandysul, 1995.

EVANS, HUGH   Humphreys, E. Morgan, *The Gorse Glen*, Liverpool, 1948.

GRIFFITHS, ANN   Ryan, John, *The Hymns of Ann Griffiths*, Caernarfon, 1980.

GRUFFYDD, W. J.   Lloyd, D. Myrddin, *The Years of the Locust*, Llandysul, 1976.

HUGHES, T. ROWLAND   Ruck, Richard, *From Hand to Hand*, London, 1950 · *William Jones*, Llandysul, 1953 · *Out of Their Night*, Llandysul, 1954 · *The Beginning*, Llandysul, 1969.

JONES, BOBI   Clancy, Joseph P., *Selected Poems of Bobi Jones*, Llandysul, 1987.

LEWIS, SAUNDERS   Clancy, Joseph P., *The Plays of Saunders Lewis*, 4 vols., Swansea, 1985 · *Selected Poems of Saunders Lewis*, Cardiff, 1993 · Jones, Alun R., and Thomas, Gwyn, eds., *Presenting Saunders Lewis*, Cardiff, 1973 · Jones, Harri Pritchard, *Saunders Lewis: A Presentation of his Work*, Springfield, Ill., 1990.

LLYWELYN, ROBIN   Llywelyn, Robin, *From Empty Harbour to White Ocean*, Cardiff, 1996.

OWEN, DANIEL   Harries, E. R., and Williams, T. Ceiriog, *Gwen Tomos*, Wrexham, 1963 · Harris, James, *Rhys Lewis*, Wrexham, 1888 (rev. 1915) · Vivian, Claude, *Enoc Huws*, 1895.

PRICHARD, CARADOG   Gallie, Menna, *Full Moon*, London, 1973 · Mitchell, Philip, *One Moonlit Night*, Edinburgh, 1995.

ROBERTS, KATE   Clancy, Joseph P., *The World of Kate Roberts*, Philadelphia, 1991 · Griffith, Wyn, *Tea in the Heather*, Ruthin, 1968 · *The Living Sleep*, Cardiff, 1976 [reissued London, 1981] · Griffith, Wyn et al., *A Summer Day*, Cardiff, 1946 · Walters, Idwal, and Jones, John Idris, *Feet in Chains*, Cardiff, 1977 [reissued London, 1980].

ROBERTS, WILIAM OWEN   Roberts, Elizabeth, *Pestilence*, London, 1991.

ROWLANDS, JOHN   Ruck, Richard, *A Taste of Apples*, London, 1966.

THOMAS, GWYN   Clancy, Joseph P., and Thomas, Gwyn, *Living a Life*, Amsterdam, 1982.

WILLIAMS, D. J.   Williams, Waldo, *The Old Farmhouse*, London, 1961; rep. Carmarthen, 1987.

189

e. Central and East European Languages

1. ARMENIAN

i. Introduction The translation movement in Armenia began immediately after the invention of the Armenian alphabet (406 CE), at the initiative of St Mesrop Mashtots and St Sahak Part'ew, both of whom took an active part in the undertaking. Translations played a significant role in broadening the scope of the Armenian mind and in enriching the Armenian language. They provide a vivid reflection of Armenia's cultural relations with other peoples over the centuries. Armenian written literature begins with the translation of the Bible (413). The Armenian Church sanctified the translators, commemorating them annually on 11 October on the Feast of the Holy Translators.

ii. Legends and Folk-Tales The oral literature is older than the written, and folk poetry has flourished in Armenia for the past 2000 years. *Armenian Legends and Poems*, compiled and illustrated by the painter and poet Zabelle C. **Boyajian**, presents the most comprehensive chrestomathy of Armenian legends, folklore, and poetry, with a study, 'Armenia: Its Epics, Folk-Songs, and Medieval Poetry', by Aram Raffi, son of the novelist Raffi. Folk-tales were collected by ethnographers as part of a patriotic movement to save the Armenian nation, divided between two rival empires, from extinction, and to give it a new dignity and pride. They were published under the title *Hay zhoghovrdakan Hek'iat'ner* by the Armenian Academy of Sciences in 15 volumes (Erevan, 1959–), and selections from these volumes are available to the English reader in three anthologies: *Apples of Immortality*, by Leon **Surmelian**; *Armenian Folk-Tales and Fables*, by Charles **Downing** (pseudonym of C. J. F. Dowsett), and *Three Apples Fell from Heaven*, by

Mischa **Kudian**. These tales take the reader into the bazaars of the Caucasus and of the Near East or among the camp-fires of caravan roads. In their vivid authentic national colouring they give the reader a comprehensive picture of the mythology, popular beliefs, daily life, and social relations of Armenians.

In the 7th c. the Arabs repeatedly invaded Armenia, subjugating the people and exacting heavy taxes. In the middle of the 9th c., however, the Armenians were able to establish their independence, and the struggles leading to that victory produced a cycle of epics known collectively as the *Sasountsi David* or *Sasna dsřer* (David of Sassoun or Daredevils of Sassoun). The story of Sassoun, associated with a mountain region in south-western Armenia, now part of Turkey, was discovered by Archbishop Garegin Servandztean in 1873 and published in Constantinople in 1874. Two English translations of the national epic are available: *David of Sassoun: The Armenian Folk Epic in Four Cycles: The Original Text*, by Artin K. **Shalian**, and *Daredevils of Sassoun: The Armenian National Epic*, by Leon Surmelian. The version by Surmelian, novelist and professor of English at California State College, is racy and vivid, and preserves the forthright, colloquial tone of the original. In his introduction to the epic the translator sums up the appeal of the epic thus: 'Only a country like Armenia, caught between East and West and wholly belonging to neither, a battleground of world empires, of Christendom versus Islam, and a mediator between two seemingly irreconcilable civilizations and ways of life, yet uniting more than separating—only Armenia, I say, could produce Sassoun.'

iii. Prose and Poetry before 1900 The poetry of Grigor Narekatsi (951–1003) remains not only the most extraordinary achievement of his period but a monument of Armenian literature. In the scope and breadth of his intellect and poetic inventiveness, and in the brooding, visionary quality of his language, Narekatsi is a poet of world stature. His *Matean Oghbergout'ean* (1673, Book of Lamentations) establishes him as a poet of the rank and order of St Augustine, Dante, and Edward Taylor. The *Book of Lamentations*, translated by Mischa Kudian, is at once a dialogue with God and with the self; the poet's struggle is metaphysical and existential. Narekatsi's descent into the caverns of the human heart and soul becomes a confrontation with man's fallenness and the nature of human frailty:

> even if the seas change to salty ink,
> and the forests of reeds are cut into pens
> and the boundless fields spread with parchments
> I could but finish writing a fraction
> of my lawlessness.

Like St John of the Cross, Narekatsi's journey through the soul's dark night is full of anguish that oscillates between hope and fear, faith and doubt. Poetic utterance is an act of penitence:

> I, but breathing dust, became patronizing,
> I, vocal clay, became imperious,
> I, contemptible earth, became condescending,
> I, negligible ash, climbed high . . .
> I, rational mud, shone with the flush of anger.

The poets of the medieval period reveal a growing humanism and secularity. While Nerses Shnorhali (1102–73) celebrates the Divine Light, a poet like Frik (c.1234–1315) is astonishingly modern. He confronts a universe governed not by God but by some random force called Fate, which is at best morally neutral. Frik's poetry is characterized by a strong humanism and a restless hubris that refuse to accept human misery and the arbitrariness of life's injustice: 'The unlucky man is a slave of the wealthy | and the poor man becomes a prisoner | like the candle burning | in church to serve Christ.' A good selection from all these poets is found in the anthologies of Diana **Der Hovanessian** and Aram **Tolegian**.

The sense of a dynamic correspondence between sexual passion and the lushness of the natural world is encountered in Yovhannes T'lkourantsi and Nahapet Kouchak as presented by James R. **Russell** and Diana Der Hovanessian respectively.

> When you cry, the larks cry,
> my open rose, my lark.

> When you cry, it's rosewater,
> rosewater, not salt.

The above verse by Sayat–Nova (*fl.* 1740–95), a Romantic by European standards, embraces the world's body in a way that is at once erotic and transcendental, affirming a unity of body and soul. The same poet who says to his lover: 'You are a fire, dressed in fire', exclaims: 'Love God, Love the soul, Love Lovers.'

Raffi (1837–88) and Petros Dourian (1851–72) are poets of a darker, melancholic romanticism who realise in nature the predicament of man's estrangement, the tragic nature of human fate, and the mysterious whirlpool of the unconscious. In Raffi's 'Lake Van', the surreal austerity of the night lake under the moon triggers the poet's collective sense of the suffering of the Armenian past. For Petros Dourian, the imminence of his early death at 21 forced a bitter confrontation with the meaning of nothingness: 'the whole world is nothing but a mockery of God.'

The works of the two foremost satirists in the Armenian language, Hakop Paronian and Ervand Otian, are available in English. Paronian's *Paghtasar aghbar* (1886, Uncle Balthazar) and *Medsapativ Mouratskanner* (1887, Honourable Beggars) depict with humour and satire family and official life in Armenia. *The Honourable Beggars*, a masterpiece about human greed and vanity, edited and translated by Mischa Kudian, was adapted into a play by Jack Antreassian. Ervand Otian's *Ênker B. P'anjouni* (1914, Comrade Panchoonie), translated by Jack **Antreassian**, is a savage attack on the misuse of language and more specifically political rhetoric.

Several works of Armenian dramatists are available to the English reader. *Char Voki* (1894) by Alexander Shirvanzade was translated by the playwright and director Nishan **Parlakian** as *Evil Spirit*, with an introductory essay by Edward Allworth. The second author, Levon Shant's, most admired play, *Hin Astouadsner* (1909), translated as *The Ancient Gods* by Anne **Boranian**, is a drama based on the conflict between the hedonistic and spiritual forces influencing man.

iv. Twentieth Century The turbulence of the turn of the century had a considerable impact on the flourishing of Armenian literature. Siamanto, Daniel Varouzhan, and Grigor Zohrab responded at first with a fervent nationalism to the climate of momentary optimism following 1908, when the Young Turks took power and promised a more democratic government. Shortly afterwards, on the eve of the 1915 massacres in which they perished, they cried out with uncontrolled outrage and grief.

In *The Lost Voices of World War I: An International Anthology of Writers, Poets and Playwrights*, edited by Tim Cross, V. Nersessian presents three major authors who were victims of the genocide. The first two poets, Siamanto and Daniel Varouzhan, wrote poetry of epic proportions. Their poetry recreates the myths and legends of the past and embodies the fullness and fertility of the land that subsumes the consciousness of a people and defines the timelessness of their homeland. Siamanto's *A Handful of Ash* and Varouzhan's *Oriental Bath* and *The Flickering Lamp*, rendered into English by Diana Der Hovanessian and Marzbed **Margossian**, have enduring power. In a poem called 'The Tiller', Varouzhan bathes the farmers in a divine light, and their life-giving labour becomes a mystical vision:

> Sow, ploughman, sow, for the sacred host,
> the wafer of God. Let seeds of light flood
> through your hand. Tomorrow the body of Christ
> will ripen in each milky spike.

Grigor Zohrab is the founder of the realistic short story in western Armenian literature. Of his 41 published short stories, a selection, *Khghtchmtank'i Dzayner* (1909, Voices of Conscience), were translated by Jack Antreassian, with an introduction by Michael Kermian.

Hovannes Toumanian, the national poet of Armenia, is available to the English reader in such translations as Mischa Kudian's *The Bard of Loree: Selected Works of Hovhannes Toumanian*, the *Selected Works* by Dorian **Rottenberg**, and *Once There Was and Was Not* by Virginia A. **Tashjian**. A prolific and multi-faceted writer, Vahan T'ot'ovents is known to English readers by his best-known work *Kyank'ě hin Hṙomeakan tchanaparhi Vra* (1933, Life on the Old Roman Road) under the title *Scenes from an Armenian Childhood*, translated by Mischa Kudian. An autobiographical work, this presents a series of pictures from an Armenian childhood in the 1880s, with each one exactly and lyrically turned to catch the essence of a childhood experience. From family life the book broadens to include a view of the street, the neighbours, rural scenes. The whole world of Asia Minor is revealed with striking clarity and precision. In addition Mischa Kudian has translated a collection of short stories by T'ot'ovents, *Tell Me, Bella*.

After the 1915 massacres, literary activity among the Armenians moved from Constantinople to Paris and Beirut. Among the writers in Paris Shahan Shahnour, also known in French literary circles as Armen Lubin, is regarded as the most original and powerful novelist of the French diaspora. In his major work *Nahanjě Aṙants Ergi* (1929, Retreat Without Song), he resorted to shock tactics in an effort to shake Armenians out of their apathy and torpor; some of his deliberately provocative comments led to stormy protests at the desecration of sacred values. Another volume of his stories, *The Tailor's Visitors*, explores the Armenian mood and psyche shortly after the Dispersion against the backdrops of Istanbul (his birthplace) and Paris (his adopted city). The stories, which he describes as an illustrated history of the Armenians, fluctuate between the old and newly emerging schools of writing, with a great deal of satire and allegory.

Gostan Zarian, a contemporary of Shahnour, produced works of astonishing variety in French, Russian, Italian, and Armenian. The genre in which he excelled was the diary form, with long autobiographical divagations, reminiscences, and impressions. The finest of these *Antsordě ev ir Chamban* (1926–8) and *Bankoopě ev mamouti oskornerě* (1931–4) are available in English translation by Ara **Baliozian** as *The Traveller and His Road* and *Bancoop and the Bones of the Mammoth*. The first is a diary covering the years 1922–5; the central theme of the book is Armenia, her past splendour and present misery.

The rich storehouse of Armenian imaginative writing, locked for many readers behind what Osip Mandelstam described as the 'iron picket-fence of the Armenian alphabet', has thus been made passionately alive for the first time to the English-speaking world. Diana Der Hovanessian, Ara Baliozian, Mischa Kudian, Leon Surmelian, C. J. F. Dowsett, and Jack Antreassian—and others not mentioned in this brief article—have made the voices of the past speak with immediacy and urgency. The translations sampled here read with a fluency and an intensity that create a sense of an unfolding journey. The English writer and author of the novel *Ararat*, D. M. Thomas, found 'the beauty and abundance of Armenian poetry a revelation'.

However, the poet and translator Leon Surmelian, after writing some of the most beautiful poetry in Armenian, was later prompted to switch to English, explaining: 'I find it impossible to write creatively in two languages. . . . I lost the battle of the Armenian language in order to win for myself the battle of the Armenian spirit—which is more important.' Abandoning 'the most beautiful language I have ever heard' to write in English was not an easy thing to do. But, 'to serve his people', 'sacrifices' had to be made.   VN

ANTHOLOGIES   Antreassian, Jack, ed., *Ararat: A Decade of Armenian-American Writing*, New York, 1969 · Basmadjian, Garig, *Armenian-American Poets: A Bilingual Anthology*, Detroit, 1976 · Blackwell, Alice Stone, *Armenian Poems Rendered into English Verse*, Boston, Mass., 1917 [rep. 1978] · Boyajian, Zabelle, C., *Armenian Legends and Poems*, with an introduction by the Viscount Bryce, and a contribution by Aram Raffi, London, 1916; 2nd edn., 1958 · Cross, Tim, ed., *The Lost Voices of World War One: An International Anthology of Writers, Poets and Playwrights*, London, 1988 · Der Hovanessian, Diana, and Margossian, Marzbed, *Anthology of Armenian Poetry*, New York, 1978 · Downing, Charles, *Armenian Folk Tales and Fables*, London, 1972 · Kudian, Mischa, *Three Apples Fell from Heaven: A Collection of Armenian Folk and Fairy Tales*, London, 1969 · ed., *Soviet Armenian Poetry*, London, 1984 · Shalian, Artin, *David of Sassoun: The Armenian Folk Epic in Four Cycles*, Athens, OH, 1964 · Surmelian, Leon, *Apples of Immortality: Folktales of Armenia*, Berkeley, Calif., 1966 · *Daredevils of Sassoun: The Armenian National Epic*, London, 1966 · Tashjian, Virginia A., *Once There Was and Was Not: Armenian Tales Retold*, Boston, 1966 · Tolegian, Aram, *Armenian Poetry Old and New: A Bilingual Anthology*, Detroit, 1979.

ANTREASSIAN, ANTRANIG   Antreassian, Jack, *The Cup of Bitterness and Other Stories*, New York, 1979 · *Death and Resurrection*; New York, 1988.

DAVTAK, K'ERTOGH   Dowsett, C. J. F., *Elegy on the Death of the Great Prince Juanser*, Erevan, 1986.

ISSAHAKIAN, AVETIK   Kudian, Mischa, *Avedik Issahakian: Selected Works. Poetry and Prose*, Moscow, 1976.

KOUCHAK, NAHAPET   Der Hovanessian, Diana, *Come Sit Beside Me and Listen to Kouchak: Medieval Armenian Poems of Nahapet Kouchak*, New York, 1984 · Dowsett, C. J. F., 'Armenian: An Enquiry into the Theme of Lover's Meetings and Partings at Dawn in Poetry', in Arthur T. Hatto, ed., *EOS*, The Hague, 1965 · Osers, Ewald (with Levon Mkrtchian), *A Hundred Hayrens*, Erevan, 1979.

NAREKATSI, GRIGOR   Kudian, Mischa, *Lamentations of Narek: Mystic Soliloquies with God*, London, 1977.

OTIAN, ERVAND   Antreassian, Jack, *Comrade Panchoonie*, New York, 1977.

PARONIAN, HAKOP   Kudian, Mischa, *Honourable Beggars*, London, 1978 · Megerditchian, Ervant D., *Uncle Balthazar: A Comedy in Three Acts*, Boston, 1933.

SAYAT–NOVA   Dowsett, C. J. F., *Sayat Nova: An Eighteenth-Century Troubadour*, Louvain, 1997.

SHAHNOUR, SHAHAN   Kudian, Mischa, *Retreat Without Song*, London, 1982 · *The Tailor's Visitors*, London, 1984.

SHANT, LEVON   Baytarian, Hagop, *The Princess of the Fallen Castle*, Boston, 1929 · Boranian, Ann, *The Ancient Gods*, La Verne, Calif., 1987.

SHIRVANZADE, ALEXANDER   Parlakian, Nishan, *For the Sake of Honour*, New York, 1975 · *The Evil Spirit*, New York, 1980.

TLKOURANTSI, YOVHANNES   Russell, James R., *Yovhannes Tlkourantsi and the Medieval Armenian Lyric Tradition*, Atlanta, Ga., 1987.

T'OT'OVENTS   Kudian, Mischa, *Tell me, Bella*, London, 1972 · *Scenes from an Armenian Childhood*, London, 1980.

T'OUMANIAN, HOVHANNES   Kudian, Mischa, *The Bard of Loree: Selected Works of Hovhannes T'oumanyan*, London, 1970.

ZARIAN, GOSTAN   Baliozian, Ara, *The Traveller and his Road*, New York, 1981 · *Bancoop and the Bones of the Mammoth*, New York, 1982.

ZOHRAB, GRIGOR   Antreassian, Jack, *Voice of Conscience: The Stories of Krikor Zohrab*, New York, 1983.

SEE ALSO   Baliozian, A., *The Armenians: Their History and Culture*, New York, 1980 · Ishkhanyan, R., ed., *The Armenian Literature in Foreign Languages*, Erevan, 1971 [lists Armenian authors translated into English between 1800 and 1920] · Nersessian, V., *Armenia*, Oxford, 1993 · 'Armenian Literature', 'Bible', 'The Sasun Cycle, Alexander Romance', and 24 biographies of Armenian authors, in R. B. Pynsent and S. I. Kanikova, eds., *The Everyman Companion to East European Literature*, London, 1993 · *A Bibliography of Articles on Armenian Studies in Western Journals, 1869–1995*, London, 1997.

For English translations of Armenian poetry and prose, reviews and criticism, consult *Ararat: A Quarterly* (New York, 1960–); *Raft: Journal of Armenian Poetry and Criticism* (Cleveland, OH, 1987–); and *Review of National Literatures*, 13 (1984), ed. V. Oshagan, devoted to Armenia.

2. BULGARIAN

Bulgarian literature traces its origins back to the 9th c. and is the oldest of the literatures written in the Slavonic languages. Its early, almost exclusively religious flowering under Tsar Simeon (893–927) is intimately connected with the country's Christianization and with the adoption by the Church of the language spoken by the common people. Despite this early 'Golden Age' and a second flowering in the 13th c., the country's subjugation, first to the rule of Byzantium and then, for nearly 500 years, to the Ottoman empire, means that modern Bulgarian literature dates only from the middle of the

19th c. Over this 150-year period it has distinguished itself particularly in the more concise forms: the folk-song, the short story, the pithy proverb, and the lyric poem.

The history of the translation of modern Bulgarian literature into English is short and, when compared with translation into other European languages such as French, German, and Russian, both patchy and lacking in volume. Patterns of publication may be identified, but there exists no well-established, clearly perceived tradition of Bulgarian–English translation. Each new translated work has to start afresh, standing alone, independently and often self-consciously bearing the whole weight of the culture it represents. Other than from the second-hand bookstalls of Sofia, and for brief periods following the publication of each new publication, translations are not readily accessible.

From the early 1860s, when the American missionary Elias **Riggs** published a translation of nine Bulgarian folk-songs together with a selection of Bulgarian proverbs in *The American Presbyterian and Theological Review* (1863–4), until the outbreak of World War I, just three major works of Bulgarian literature were translated and published in the English-speaking world: a shortened version of Ivan Vazov's historical novel *Pod igoto* (1889–90, Under the Yoke), which, in its first edition, predated the work's publication in book form in Bulgarian; Henry **Baerlein**'s *The Shade of the Balkans*, a collection of Bulgarian proverbs and folk-tales, many translated via the German; and a truncated, much sanitized rendition by M. W. **Potter** of Zahari Stoyanov's memoirs *Zapiski po bulgarskite vustaniya* (1884–92, Pages from the Autobiography of a Bulgarian Insurgent), which were largely devoted, like Vazov's novel, to the failed Bulgarian uprising of April 1876.

Published at approximately 10-year intervals, each of these three works owed its existence to British public interest in Bulgaria stimulated by political rather than purely literary concerns. *Under the Yoke*, translated by the Slavophile scholar William **Morfill**, who later published an English-language grammar of Bulgarian and eventually became Oxford University's first professor of Russian, appeared at a time when political events in Bulgaria were often in the headlines. Baerlein's anthology, compiled and translated with the assistance of the poet Pencho **Slaveikov** and the aspiring journalist E. J. **Dillon**, owed its creation to public concern over Turkish suppression of the Ilinden uprising in Macedonia in May 1903. Similarly, the publication in 1913 of Potter's translation of

Stoyanov's memoirs was in no small measure stimulated, like the second edition of *Under the Yoke* (1912), by the outbreak of war in the Balkans. (Although both English editions of Vazov's novel contained a 'Translator's Note', neither made mention of the translator's name.)

Between 1914 and the end of World War II, both in Britain and America, translations of Bulgarian literature—exclusively short works: folk-songs, ballads, poems, and stories—appeared as isolated publications in journals, or in general anthologies of 'world literature'. In America, stories like Ivan Vazov's *Ide li?* (1889, Is He Coming?) appeared in Dodd Mead's series *The Best Continental Short Stories of 1923–24*, while Elin Pelin (pseudonym of Dimitur Ivanov) and Yordan Yovkov were both represented in the 1924–5 volume with *Krai vodenitsata* (1903, Beside the Mill) and *Eski-Arap* (1916), respectively.

In Britain, from the mid-1920s, the specialist journal *The Slavonic Review* also published the occasional translation from Bulgarian. Elin Pelin's early stories *Doushata na ouchitelya* (1904, The Dominie's Soul) and *Pechena tikva* (1904, Stewed Pumpkin) both appeared in translations by N. B. **Jopson** in 1926/7 and 1932/3 respectively. Two further stories by Elin Pelin, *Vetrenata melnitsa* (1902, The Windmill) and *Zanemelite kambani* (1928, The Bells That Would Not Ring), the first translated by the young Bulgarianist scholar Vivian de S. **Pinto**, and the second by Valentina **Jukova**, appeared in volumes for 1947–8 and 1948–9.

In Bulgaria a similarly irregular publication pattern may be observed, particularly in the 1930s. In the postwar period, however, Bulgarian governmental subsidies for foreign-language publication stimulated a sudden increase in the volume of translation, both of poetry and of prose. Publication of individual poems in journals eventually led to single- and multi-author collections. The greatest poets, who had also written least, Hristo Botev and Nikola Vaptsarov, both revolutionaries who had met violent and early deaths, were the most frequently translated. Of the early verse translations, those by Peter **Tempest**, a graduate in Russian from Oxford who married and settled in Sofia, living there between 1949 and 1962, have best stood the test of time. His Vaptsarov collection, *Selected Poems*, was published in London as early as 1953, and his monumental *Anthology of Bulgarian Poetry*—over 500 pages covering the 9th to the 20th c., published by Sofia Press in 1980—stands as a lasting witness to his dedication and achievement. More recently, Ewald **Osers** has produced distinguished, restrained translations in an attractively presented series published in London by Forest Books. The series includes works by a variety of poets—including Elisaveta Bagryana, Ivan Davidkov, Blaga Dimitrova, and Geo Milev—translated by a variety of hands. In North America, isolated poems by different authors have appeared in journals such as *Books Abroad* (1969, Lyubomir Levchev translated by Vladimir **Phillipov**), and also in short volumes published by small presses such as Don **Wilson**'s volume *Hush, You Nightingales!* with translations of poems by Andrei Filipov, Stefan Gechev, Konstantin Pavlov, and Alexander Shurbanov.

In prose the postwar increase in production showed initially in shorter works published primarily in journals such as *Free Bulgaria*, *Bulgaria*, and *Bulgaria Today*. The most important journal for literature in translation was *Obzor*, a quarterly for literature and the arts, which appeared in Sofia between 1967 and the early 1990s and remains the most significant single repository of Bulgarian literature in English. Later, especially after the establishment of the Foreign Languages Press and Sofia Press, came multi-author prose anthologies such as *In the Fields: Bulgarian Short Stories* (1957) and *Bulgarian Short Stories* (1960), containing works rendered almost exclusively by Marguerite **Alexieva**, doyenne of Bulgarian prose translators into English. To Alexieva also belong a new and unabridged rendering of *Under the Yoke*—this she translated together with her sister, Theodora **Atanassova**—the single-author anthologies *Elin Pelin: Short Stories* and *The White Swallow and Other Stories* (Yordan Yovkov), and a multitude of other major translations. Her greatest achievement is a stylistically sustained rendering of Anton Donchev's *Vreme razdelno* (1964, Time of Parting), set in the 17th c. and telling of the forced Islamization of the Bulgarian population.

Other significant prose publications outside Bulgaria include Michael **Holman**'s lively rendering of Nikolai Haitov's spirited short-story cycle *Divi razkazi* (1967, Wild Tales), John **Burnip**'s rich and rigorously faithful translation of Yordan Yovkov's two cycles *Vecheri v Antimovskiya Han* and *Staroplaninski legendi* (1928 and 1927, The Inn at Antimovo and Legends of Stara Planina), and Robert **Sturm**'s immensely readable version of Viktor Paskov's novella *Balada za Georg Henih* (1988, A Ballad for Georg Henih). The most representative anthology is the Twayne collection of 36 stories by 29 authors and nearly half as many translators, *Introduction to Modern Bulgarian Literature*.

The best overall single-volume introduction to the spirit and content of Bulgarian life and letters—ancient and modern, poetry and prose—remains the unashamedly romantic compilation *The Balkan Range: A Bulgarian Reader*. A labour of love created by the Bulgarian émigré historian Nikola **Roussanoff** in collaboration with the Canadian poet John Robert **Colombo**, it was published in Toronto in 1976 to mark the centenary of the April uprising and thereby to echo one of the recurring themes in Bulgarian literature of the modern period.   MJH

ANTHOLOGIES Alexieva, Marguerite, Drenkov, Petko, and Florin, Sider, *In the Fields: Bulgarian Short Stories*, Sofia, 1957 · Alexieva, Marguerite, and Mintoff, Marko, *Bulgarian Short Stories*, Sofia, 1960 · Baerlein, Henry, *The Shade of the Balkans: Being a Collection of Bulgarian Folksongs and Proverbs*, London, 1904 · Colombo, John Robert, and Roussanoff, Nikola, *Under the Eaves of a Forgotten Village: Sixty Poems from Contemporary Bulgaria*, Toronto, 1975 · *The Balkan Range: A Bulgarian Reader*, Toronto, 1976 · Kirilov, Nikola, and Kirk, Frank, eds., *Introduction to Modern Bulgarian Literature: An Anthology of Short Stories*, New York, 1969 · Leonidov, Rumen, ed., *An Anthology of Contemporary Bulgarian Poetry*, Sofia, 1994 · MacGregor-Hastie, Roy, *Modern Bulgarian Poetry*, Sofia, 1975 · Meredith, William, ed., *Poets of Bulgaria*, London, 1988 · Pridham, Radost, *A Gift from the Heart: Folk Tales from Bulgaria*, Cleveland, OH, 1967 · Pridham, Radost, and Morris, Jean, *The Peach Thief and Other Bulgarian Stories*, London, 1968 · Tempest, Peter, *Anthology of Bulgarian Poetry*, Sofia, 1980 · Tonchev, Belin, ed., *Young Poets of a New Bulgaria*, London, 1990 · Walker, Brenda, and Tonchev, Belin, *The Devil's Dozen: Thirteen Bulgarian Women Poets*, London, 1990 · Wilson, Don, *Hush, You Nightingales! Four Bulgarian Poets*, Canton, Conn., 1993.

BAGRYANA, ELISSAVETA Ireland, Kevin, *Ten Poems, in the Original and in an English Translation; Her Life and Work in Photographs; Authors and Critics on Bagryana*, Sofia, 1970 · Walker, Brenda, Borissov, Valentine, and Tonchev, Belin, *Penelope of the Twentieth Century*, London, 1993.

BOTEV, HRISTO Ireland, Kevin, *Poems*, Sofia, 1974 · Mincoff, Marco, ed., *Poems*, Sofia, 1955.

DAVIDKOV, IVAN Osers, Ewald, *Fires of the Sunflower*, London, 1988.

DIMITROVA, BLAGA Boris, Niko, and McHugh, Heather, *Because the Sea Is Black: Poems of Blaga Dimitrova*, Middletown, Conn., 1989 · Pridham, Radost, *Journey to Oneself*, London, 1969 · Walker, Brenda, Tonchev, Belin, and Levchev, Vladimir, *The Last Rock Eagle*, London, 1992.

DONCHEV, ANTON Alexieva, Marguerite, *Time of Parting. A Novel*, London, 1967.

195

GERMANOV, ANDREI   Colombo, John Robert, and Roussanoff, Nikola, *Remember Me Well*, Toronto, 1978.

HAITOV, NIKOLAI   Holman, Michael, *Wild Tales*, London, 1979.

IVANOV, DIMITUR [ELIN PELIN]   Alexieva, Marguerite, *Short Stories*, Sofia, 1965.

KONSTANTINOV, ALEKO   Salter, Francis, *Bai Ganiu: The Incredible Tales of a Contemporary Bulgarian*, in *Canadian Slavic Studies*, 3 (1, 3, 4) (1969); 4 (1, 2, 4) (1970); 5 (1, 2, 3) (1971).

LEVCHEV, LYUBOMIR   Colombo, John Robert, and Roussanoff, Nikola, *The Left-Handed One*, Toronto, 1977 · Osers, Ewald, *Stolen Fire*, London, 1986.

MARKOV, GEORGI   Brisby, Liliana, *The Truth That Killed*, London, 1983.

MILEV, GEO   Osers, Ewald, *The Road to Freedom*, London, 1988 · Tempest, Peter, *September*, Sofia, 1961.

PASKOV, VIKTOR   Sturm, Robert, *A Ballad for Georg Henih*, London, 1990.

RADICHKOV, YORDAN   Tempest, Peter, *Hot Noon*, Sofia, 1970.

STANEV, EMILYAN   Alexieva, Marguerite, and Stankov, Zdravko, *The Stranger and Other Short Stories*, Sofia, 1967.

STOYANOV, ZAHARI   Potter, M. W., *Pages from the Autobiography of a Bulgarian Insurgent*, London, 1913.

TALEV, DIMITUR   Alexieva, Marguerite, *The Iron Candlestick*, Sofia, 1964 · Kolin, Nadia, *Ilinden: A Novel of the Macedonian Rebellion 1903*, Sofia, 1966 · Shipkov, Michail, *The Bells of Prespa*, Sofia, 1966.

VAPTSAROV, NIKOLA   Osers, Ewald, *Nineteen Poems*, London/New York, 1984 · Tempest, Peter, *Selected Poems*, London, 1953 · Tempest, Peter, and Filipov, Vladimir, *Nikola Vaptsarov. Poems*, Sofia, 1984.

VAZOV, IVAN   Alexieva, Marguerite, and Atanassova, Theodora, *Under the Yoke*, Sofia, 1955 · Molhova, Jana, *Selected Stories*, Sofia, 1967 · [Morfill, William,] *Under the Yoke*, London, 1893 [rep. London, 1912].

YOVKOV, YORDAN   Alexieva, Marguerite, and Mincoff, Marco, *The White Swallow and Other Short Stories*, Sofia, 1965 · Burnip, John, *The Inn at Antimovo; Legends of Stara Planina*, Columbus, OH, 1990.

SEE ALSO   Holman, M., 'Bulgarian Literature in English: The First British Translations', in *Purvi mezhdounaroden kongres po bulgaristika. Dokladi: Bulgarskata literatoura i svetovniyat literatouren protses* ii, Sofia, 1983, 506–19 · 'Ivan Vazov's *Under the Yoke*: The First English Translation', in *Anglo-Bulgarian Symposium, London, 1982: Proceedings II*, SSEES, University of London, 1985, 161–71 · Manning, Cl., and Smal-Stocki, R., *The History of Modern Bulgarian Literature*, Westport, Conn., 1974 · Matejic, M. et al., *A Biobibliographical Handbook of Bulgarian Authors*, Columbus, OH, 1981 [also lists English translations] · Moser, C., *A History of Bulgarian Literature 865–1944*, The Hague, 1972.

3. CZECH AND SLOVAK

i. Czech: Medieval to Baroque There is a continuous tradition of writing in Czech from the late 13th c. onwards, but the first English translations only begin to appear during the 19th c.

Various Latin works from Bohemia, such as those of the reformer Jan Hus, reached scholarly readers of course. Jan Dubravius' treatise on fishponds, *De piscinis* (1547), is cited in Izaak Walton's *The Compleat Angler*. Later the Latin writings of the Protestant exile Comenius (Jan Amos Komenský), spread throughout Europe. He stayed briefly in London; there were English versions of his pioneering school textbooks [see I.c.4.ii]. In his Czech prose masterpiece, *Labyrint světa a ráj srdce* (1631, The Labyrinth of the World and the Paradise of the Heart), a pilgrim through life finds the world to be a chaotic labyrinth where people delude and mistreat one another. A praiseworthy English translation appeared in 1901, by the Austro-Hungarian diplomat Count Francis Lützow (1849–1916); it was quickly reissued in Dent's Temple Classics. (Matthew Spinka's later version handles the expressive baroque mix of Latinate style and vernacular idiom rather less happily.)

ii. Before 1918 The first volume of translations from Czech was produced by Sir John Bowring (1792–1872), a Benthamite politician with Baltic mercantile interests. His *Cheskian Anthology* of 1832 is a pioneering effort indeed, containing medieval verse, pseudo-medieval verse (now taken to be a 19th-c. forgery), folk-songs, and contemporary poetry, including a group of sonnets from Jan Kollár's cycle *Slávy dcera* (1824, Daughter of Slavia). Bowring also produced Russian, Polish, Serbian and Hungarian volumes of this kind, using French or German cribs. He offers a Herder-like view of 'natural' poetry and national culture.

Unlike Bowring, Albert Wratislaw (1821–92), an English headmaster apparently related to the Counts Vratislav, did indeed learn Czech, and he maintained lifelong contacts with Bohemia. One of his best books (warmly reviewed at the time in the *Athenaeum*) is his translation, evidently family-inspired, of Václav Vratislav z Mitrovic's *Příhody* (1599, The Adventures of Baron Wenceslas Wratislaw of Mitrowitz), an account of an embassy to Constantinople and its captivity by the Turks. In his *The Native Literature of Bohemia in the Fourteenth Century* (1878) Wratislaw also translated specimens of key medieval texts.

The London *Athenaeum* printed a series of brief annual surveys of contemporary Czech literature, but there were few other 19th-c. translators. Sir Walter William **Strickland** (1851–1938), an anti-imperialist naturalist-traveller with anarchist leanings, issued obscure volumes of Vítězslav Hálek, Emanuel Bozděch and Svatopluk Čech. In Chicago, a centre of Czech immigrants, Frances **Gregor**'s version of Božena Němcová's classic rural novel *Babička* (1855, The Grandmother) appeared in 1891.

iii. 1918–1948 Soon after the break-up of Austria-Hungary in 1918, Paul **Selver**, a translator who worked at the Czechoslovak embassy, made a strong impact with Karel Čapek's drama *R. U. R. Rossum's Universal Robots* (1920), whose early productions ushered the word 'robot' into the English language. Despite its cuts and errors, Selver's version has often been reprinted, alongside Karel and his brother Josef Čapek's *Ze života hmyzu* (1921, The Insect Play). A complete but uninspired new version by Claudia **Novack-Jones** was issued in 1990 by the Catbird Press in America, in *Toward the Radical Center: a Karel Čapek Reader*, the first volume in an ambitious Čapek series. Selver went on to translate Čapek's whimsical *Anglické listy* (1924, Letters from England), which also achieved favour, and some of the *Povídky z jedné a z druhé kapsy* (1929, Tales from Two Pockets). Norma (Bean) **Comrada**'s complete Catbird version shows how tricky it is to convey the chatty texture of these philosophically humorous half-detective stories. Otakar Vočadlo, a university teacher of Czech for a while in London, found other translators for Čapek amongst his pupils. Dora **Round** translated *Kniha apokryfů* (1945, Apocryphal Stories). Robert **Weatherall**, with his Czech wife, Marie, translated the trilogy of novels *Hordubal, Povětroň, Obyčejný Život* (1933–4, Hordubal, Meteor, An Ordinary Life, also reissued by Catbird). Their version of the Dystopian science-fiction novel *Válka s mloky* (1936, War with the Newts) was more recently replaced with a rather similar-quality version by Ewald **Osers**, a prolific translator who came to England from Czechoslovakia in 1938. Čapek's anti-totalitarian play *Bílá nemoc* (1937, The White Plague) has also been retranslated, by University of California professor Michael **Heim**.

However, Čapek is eclipsed today by Jaroslav Hašek, also first translated by Selver. (Both are in turn eclipsed by Franz Kafka, but he wrote in German.) With his zany blarney, and mixture of idiotic and astute behaviour, Švejk, the hero of Hašek's farcical war-, army-, church- and state-debunking novel *Osudy dobrého vojáka Švejka* (1921–3, The Good Soldier Švejk), has become a somewhat dubious image for the Czech mentality. Selver's readable, if slightly abridged 1930 text gave way in 1973 to a new version by a former ambassador to Prague, Sir Cecil ('Joe') **Parrott**. This is complete and unexpurgated (though 'rude words' are not in fact all that prominent in the original), but Parrott's dialogue is all too often wooden and uneasy in register: 'There are some revolvers, Mrs Müller, that won't go off even if you bust yourself. There are lots of that type. But for his Imperial Highness I'm sure they must have bought something better. And I wouldn't mind betting, Mrs Müller, that the chap who did it put on smart togs for the occasion.' Selver's dialogue may sometimes be a little more demotic, but it also lacks virtuosity: 'There's some revolvers, Mrs Müller, that won't go off, even if you tried till you was dotty. There's lots like that. But they're sure to have bought something better than that for the Archduke, and I wouldn't mind betting, Mrs Müller, that the man who did it put on his best clothes for the job.'

Other interwar authors received scant attention. Jaroslav Durych's Catholic historical novel *Bloudění* (1929, Wandering) was translated by Lynton A. **Hudson** as *Descent of the Idol*, but never reprinted. The left-wing avant-garde only received any perceptible response many years later. Today there is some recognition of Jan Mukařovský's structuralist aesthetic writings, partly available in translation, alongside the works of his Russian-born contemporary Roman Jakobson, himself resident in Czechoslovakia during those interwar years.

The next author to make a brief impact in English, from the 1940s on, was the émigré novelist Egon Hostovský, with some encouragement from Graham Greene. Twisted Spoon Press in Prague have recently issued a translation of his novel *Žhář* (1935, The Arsonist). A praiseworthy attempt by Karel **Brušák** with Stephen **Spender** to translate the crucial 19th-c. romantic Karel Hynek Mácha's poem *Máj* (1836, May) inevitably fails (like several others) to do this somewhat untranslatable masterpiece justice.

iv. 1948 to the Present A good number of English translations published after the 1948 Communist takeover were issued in Prague; by no means all of these are socialist propaganda. For example, Němcová's *Babička* (see above) reads well in its second version, entitled *Granny*, by Edith **Pargeter** (better known as Ellis Peters, author of a successful series of medieval whodunits). Her Heinemann version of Jan Neruda's *Povídky malostranské* (1877,

Tales of the Malá Strana), called *Tales of the Little Quarter*, has its faults, but Heim's recent version, entitled *Prague Tales*, also diminishes Neruda's subtleties. Notable also is Pargeter's Prague edition of *Konec starých časů* (1934, The End of the Old Times) by the original prewar prose-writer Vladislav Vančura, whose *Rozmarné léto* (1926, Capricious Summer) is better known abroad, through Jiří Menzel's film of the same name.

Menzel also filmed Bohumil Hrabal's short novel *Ostře sledované vlaky* (1965, Closely Observed Trains), published in Pargeter's translation in 1968. Hrabal can at times be quite a tough nut for translators. The manic, stop-less monologue of *Taneční hodiny pro starší a pokročilé* (1964, Dancing Lessons for the Older and More Advanced) has been tackled recently by Heim, mostly effectively (but note the shift in the title, *Dancing Lessons for the Advanced in Age*). Heim has also—more unevenly—translated some of Hrabal's stories, and a not quite definitive text of the philosophical novella *Příliš hlučná samota* (1980, Too Loud a Solitude). In translating Hrabal's comic *Bildungsroman* about a waiter, *Obsluhoval jsem anglického krále* (1980, I Served the King of England), the Canadian Paul **Wilson** reins back Hrabal's virtuoso garrulity and loses accuracy in the process. His text reads well, but also simplifies, and not merely by pruning synonyms or detail. In Wilson's words the ex-waiter protagonist says, near the end of the book: 'how we deal with our own death is the beginning of what is beautiful, because the absurd things in our lives, which always end before we want them to anyway, fill us, when we contemplate death, with bitterness and therefore beauty.' The original says something more like this: 'dealing with this death is the beginning of thinking in the beautiful and about the beautiful, because savouring the absurdity of that road which anyway ends with a premature departure, this enjoyment and experiencing of one's ruination,—this fills a person with bitterness, and therefore beauty.' James **Naughton** has tried to be more scrupulous, in his versions of *Postřižiny* (1976, Cutting It Short), *Městečko, kde se zastavil čas* (1978, The Little Town Where Time Stood Still), and a selection from *Dopisy Dubence* (1995, Letters to Dubenka).

The most famous postwar Czech novelist today is Milan Kundera, resident in France since 1975. Clearly he now has far more readers internationally than he ever had in Czech. His first novel, *Žert* (1967, The Joke), centres around a disillusioned young Communist's joke which backfires with unpleasant consequences; Ludvík embarks subsequently on a futile act of sexual revenge. In the first English version, by David **Hamblyn** and Oliver **Stallybrass**,

published in 1969, shortly after the invasion, the chapters had been reordered, wrecking the author's choreography of points of view. A second version, by Heim (1982), has now been further revised by the author. Kundera presents his translators with few real difficulties, even when he centres discussion on a native term such as *lítost* (basically 'regret'). His literary register is mostly middle-of-the-road; he aims at clarity, within a realm of ironic authorial play. Sensitized to translators' vagaries, Kundera began scrutinizing the French texts of his works until he felt able to declare them equal in status to the original Czech. His characters often puzzle over (in)authenticity: the individual versus history, memory versus amnesia, love versus sex. Later novels, blending a somewhat mirage-like or ambivalent sense of the documentary with narrative play and essayistic commentary, include *Kniha smíchu a zapomnění* (1981, The Book of Laughter and Forgetting) and *Nesnesitelná lehkost bytí* (1985, The Unbearable Lightness of Being), both translated by Heim. His last Czech-language novel, *Nesmrtelnost* (1990, Immortality), was translated by Columbia-based Peter **Kussi**. His latest work is in French.

Josef Škvorecký's novels of youth, jazz, and socio-political sarcasm have also been widely available in translation. He emigrated to Canada, following the 1968 invasion. Soon afterwards *Zbabělci* (1958, The Cowards), a de-solemnizing account of wartime adolescence, was issued in a good version by Jeanne **Němcová**. His more densely crafted novella *Bassaxofon* (1967, The Bass Saxophone) was also well served by Káča **Poláčková-Henley**. Paul Wilson has done commendable service with his panoramic novels *Mirákl* (1972, The Miracle Game) and *Příběh inženýra lidských duší* (1977, The Engineer of Human Souls). It is a pity that *Tankový prapor* (1971, The Tank Battalion), with its entertaining use of rude language, is titled in English *The Republic of Whores*.

Ivan Klíma, successful for many English readers with his accessible, quizzically evocative short-story volumes and novels, has been translated by various hands. Ludvík Vaculík's key post-Stalinist novel, *Sekyra* (1966, The Axe), and post-Kafkaesque novel, *Morčata* (1977, The Guinea Pigs), both briefly reached Penguin status. Various postwar writers on Jewish themes have also been translated, especially Jiří Weil, Ladislav Fuks, and Arnošt Lustig. The racy, effervescent, and sometimes original novelist Vladimír Páral has unluckily made little impact in English. Younger significant writers such as Daniela Hodrová or Alexandra Berková still lack solo debuts, but Michal Viewegh's more immediately accessible, slimly sardonic post-Velvet

Revolution novel *Výchova dívek v Čechách* (1994, Bringing Up Girls in Bohemia) is nicely translated by the couple 'A. G. Brain' (Alice and Gerald **Turner**). Alexandra **Büchler** has recently edited (and part-translated) a useful prose anthology, *This Side of Reality* (1996), issued by Serpent's Tail.

v. Poetry and Drama The most successful poet in English has been Miroslav Holub, first translated by a Prague-based New Zealander, Ian **Milner**, with his wife Jarmila—and also by George **Theiner**, who produced the excellent Penguin anthology *New Writing in Czechoslovakia*, and later worked for *Index on Censorship*. Holub's Penguin *Selected Poems* of 1967 were introduced by A. Alvarez, who had interviewed him while preparing the broadcasts printed in *Under Pressure* (1965). Holub is admired for his scientific, ironic, anti-totalitarian approach, but his translators sometimes miss vital nuances. Respect (with lamely insufficient knowledge) is paid to the older, difficult Vladimír Holan, first attempted by the Milners, and for some rankable with a Rilke. The lighter-toned 1984 Nobel prize-winner Jaroslav Seifert now seems pretty much forgotten by English readers. Younger poets such as Sylva Fischerová have received only sporadic attention.

In post-war drama, only Václav Havel's absurdist plays have made any long-term impact. His 1960s plays *Zahradní slavnost* (1963, The Garden Party) and *Vyrozumění* (1965, The Memorandum) were soon performed in Vera **Blackwell**'s translations, and briefly analysed in Martin Esslin's *The Theatre of the Absurd* (1968). There is a noticeable tendency for Havel's dialogue to become bland in translation. Later plays, including the one-acter *Audience* (1975, Audience) and *Pokoušení* (1986, Temptation), were translated by various hands—a couple of his one-acters have alternative American versions by Jan **Novak**. Today, however, 10 years after the 1989 'Velvet Revolution' and his first election as president, Havel's plays have slightly sunk from view. 'Dissident' literature has lost its Iron-Curtain mystique.

vi. Slovak Literature in Slovak, written in its modern form since last century, and close to Czech, is still badly neglected by translators. Volumes from America include some pre-1918 stories of Martin Kukučín and Timrava (Božena Slančíková), translated by Norma Leigh **Rudinsky**, and Jozef Cíger Hronský's best-known novel *Jozef Mak* (1933), by Andrew **Cincura**. Ladislav Mňačko made a brief impact with his anti-Stalinist *Ako chutí moc* (1967, The Taste of Power), translated by Paul **Stevenson**. Peter **Petro** produced an abridged version of Dominik Tatarka's anti-Stalinist *Démon súhlasu* (1956, The Demon of Conformity) and the younger dissident Martin M. Šimečka's autobiographical *Žabí rok* (1985, The Year of the Frog). Slovakia split from the Czech Republic in 1993. Picador's recent East European anthology *Description of a Struggle* (1994) offers individual stories by Ján Johanides, Pavel Vilikovský, Dušan Mitana and Rudolf Sloboda. The poet Miroslav Válek has been translated by Osers, in *The Ground Beneath Our Feet* (1996) and James **Sutherland-Smith** has edited an exploratory poetry anthology *Not Waiting for Miracles* (1993).

JN

ANTHOLOGIES   Theiner, George, ed., *New Writing in Czechoslovakia*, Harmondsworth, 1969.

ČAPEK, KAREL   Heim, Michael Henry, *The White Plague*, in *Cross Currents*, 7, Ann Arbor, Mich., 1988 · Osers, Ewald, *War with the Newts*, London, 1985 · Selver, Paul, *R.U.R.*, London, 1923 [several reps.] · Weatherall, Marie, and Weatherall, Robert, *Hordubal, Meteor, An Ordinary Life*, London, 1934–6.

CÍGER HRONSKÝ, JOZEF   Cincura, Andrew, *Jozef Mak*, Columbus, OH, 1985.

COMENIUS [KOMENSKÝ], JAN AMOS   Lützow, Francis (Count), *The Labyrinth of the World and the Paradise of the Heart*, London, 1901 · Spinka, Matthew, *The Labyrinth of the World and the Paradise of the Heart*, Chicago, 1942; rep. Ann Arbor, Mich., 1972.

HAŠEK, JAROSLAV   Parrott, Cecil (Sir), *The Good Soldier Švejk and His Fortunes in the World War*, London, 1973 · Selver, Paul, *The Good Soldier Schweik*, London, 1930.

HAVEL, VÁCLAV   Blackwell, Vera, *The Memorandum*, London, 1967 · *The Garden Party*, London, 1969 · Blackwell, Vera, Novak, Jan, and Theiner, George, *Selected Plays 1963–83*, London, 1992 · Theiner, George, *Temptation*, London, 1988.

HOLAN, VLADIMÍR   Eshleman, Clayton, with Annette Smith and František Galan, *A Night with Hamlet*, in C. Eshleman, ed., *Conductors of the Pit*, New York, 1988 · Milner, Ian, and Milner, Jarmila, *Selected Poems*, Harmondsworth, 1971.

HOLUB, MIROSLAV   Milner, Ian, and Theiner, George, *Selected Poems*, Harmondsworth, 1967 · Milner, Ian, and Milner, Jarmila et al., *Poems Before and After*, Newcastle upon Tyne, 1990.

HRABAL, BOHUMIL   Heim, Michael Henry, *The Death of Mr Baltisberger*, Garden City, NY, 1975 · *Too Loud a Solitude*, London, 1991 · *Dancing Lessons for the Advanced in Age*, New York, 1995 · Naughton, James, *Cutting It Short* and *The Little Town Where Time Stood Still*, London, 1993 · *Total Fears (Letters to Dubenka)*, Prague, 1998 · Pargeter, Edith,

A Close Watch on the Trains [subsequently *Closely Observed/Watched Trains*], London, 1968 · Wilson, Paul, *I Served the King of England*, London, 1989.

KLÍMA, IVAN   Osers, Ewald, *Love and Garbage*, London, 1990 · Wilson, Paul, *My Golden Trades*, London, 1992.

KUKUČÍN, MARTIN   Rudinsky, Norma Leigh, *Seven Slovak Stories*, Cleveland, OH, 1980.

KUNDERA, MILAN   Heim, Michael Henry, *The Book of Laughter and Forgetting*, New York, 1980 · *The Unbearable Lightness of Being*, New York, 1984 · rev. by the author and Aaron Asher, *The Joke*, New York, 1992 · Kussi, Peter, *Life Is Elsewhere*, New York, 1974 · *The Farewell Party*, New York, 1976 · *Immortality*, New York, 1992 · Rappaport, Suzanne, *Laughable Loves*, New York, 1974.

MÁCHA, KAREL HYNEK   Brušák, Karel, with Stephen Spender, *May*, Canto ii, in *Review 43*, 2, London, 1943 · Naughton, James, *May*, Canto iii, in *Yazzyk Magazine*, 4, Prague, 1995.

MŇAČKO, LADISLAV   Stevenson, Paul, *The Taste of Power*, London, 1967.

NĚMCOVÁ, BOŽENA   Pargeter, Edith, *Granny*, Prague, 1962.

NERUDA, JAN   Heim, Michael Henry, *Prague Tales*, London, 1993 · Pargeter, Edith, *Tales of the Little Quarter*, Melbourne, 1957.

PÁRAL, VLADIMÍR   Harkins, William, *Catapult*, Highland Park, NJ, 1989.

SEIFERT, JAROSLAV   Osers, Ewald, *The Selected Poetry*, London, 1986.

ŠKVORECKÝ, JOSEF   Němcová, Jeanne, *The Cowards*, New York, 1970 · Poláčková-Henley, Káča, *The Bass Saxophone*, Toronto, 1977 · Wilson, Paul, *The Engineer of Human Souls*, Toronto, 1984 · *The Miracle Game*, Toronto, 1991.

TIMRAVA [BOŽENA SLANČÍKOVÁ]   Rudinsky, Norma Leigh, *That Alluring Land: Slovak Stories*, Pittsburgh, 1992.

VACULÍK, LUDVÍK   Poláčková(-Henley), Káča, *The Guinea Pigs*, New York, 1973 · Šling, Marian, *The Axe*, London, New York, 1973.

VIEWEGH, MICHAL   Brain, A. G. (Alice and Gerald Turner), *Bringing Up Girls in Bohemia*, London, 1997.

SEE ALSO   Kovtun, G. J., *Czech and Slovak Literature in English*, Washington, DC, 1988 [detailed bibliography] · Naughton, J., 'Czech Literature in Britain: from Bowring to Strickland', in E. Schmidt-Hartmann and S. B. Winters, eds., *Großbritannien, die USA und die böhmischen Länder 1848–1938*, Munich, 1991, 107–17 · *Traveller's Literary Companion to Eastern and Central Europe*, Brighton, 1995 [selected bibl., updates Kovtun].

4. GEORGIAN

Very little Georgian literature has been translated into English, even though Georgian (first recorded in 430 CE) is one of the world's oldest and richest literary languages, and has scores of medieval texts and many modern poets and prose writers whose importance and aesthetic merits are comparable with the best of the major European cultures. Torn from the orbits first of Iran, then of the Arabs and Byzantium, to be isolated from Europe by Iranian, Turkic, and finally Russian hegemony, Georgia's language and culture were virtually unknown except to a few Italian missionaries in the 17th c. Only at the beginning of the 19th c. did the first western scholars take an interest in the language and then the literature. Hitherto, only a little seepage had occurred: for instance, *The Tale of Varlaam and Josaphat* known to early modern English derives from a Greek version of the original Sanskrit text which was almost certainly transmitted from oriental to western languages by an 11th-c. Georgian translation.

At the end of the 19th c. the siblings Oliver (1864–1948) and Marjory **Wardrop** (1869–1909) travelled in Georgia, met Prince Ilia Chavchavadze, a leading luminary and writer, and learnt the language. Marjory Wardop's prose translation of Georgia's national verse epic-romance, attributed to Shota Rustaveli and dated to around 1220, *Vepkhvist'qaosani* (The Knight in the Panther's Skin), is reasonably accurate and stylistically unsurpassed. Unfortunately, this and a translation of Chavchavadze's rather Tennysonian narrative poem *Gandegili* (1883, The Hermit) was all that Marjory Wardrop achieved before her untimely death. Oliver Wardrop produced a fine version of the most important work of the abortive Georgian 18th-c. renaissance, the chain of fables by Sulkhan-Saba Orbeliani, *Tsigni sibrdzne-sitsruisa* (1720, The Book of Wisdom and Lies).

The Wardrops were followed by a number of scholars, largely in the field of Biblical studies, medieval history, and literature. Their close reading of Georgian texts has resulted in a series of magnificent translations of much of the prose of Georgia's 'Golden Age' from the 10th to early 13th c., when Georgia was an independent, unified kingdom, flourishing between the break-up of the Byzantine empire and the Mongol invasion. The work of David Marshall **Lang** in selected passages from the lives of the Georgian fathers and saints is particularly accurate and well written.

In 1921, when the Bolsheviks invaded

independent Georgia, western scholars and representatives fled the country. In Europe the Georgian diaspora was too small to spark much interest, although a few poets were published in French and a few novels in German. All we can find in English is an abridgement, in an article by Z. **Avalishvili**, of a passion, *Tsigni da ts'ameba ketevan dedoplisa* (1625, The Martyrdom of Queen Ketevan), written by King Teimuraz I.

Until the death of Stalin virtually no Georgian literature was translated into English within the USSR, or under Soviet auspices. In the thaw of the 1960s Venera **Urushadze**, a Georgian who had spent much of her life in the USA, translated, with the help of Kevin **Crosley-Holland**, the whole of Rustaveli and on her own produced a huge anthology of Georgian poetry, chiefly 19th-c., in English verse. The translations are so vague, the English so florid, and the verse such doggerel that the originals are barely recognizable: the best one can say of Urushadze is that she is a pastiche of Mrs Hemans prompted by motifs from the Georgian romantics (Aleksandre Chavchavadze and Nikoloz Baratashvili). Apart from David Marshall Lang in Britain, R. H. **Stevenson** in America produced two scholarly versions of major medieval texts.

Georgian novelists of the Soviet period often prepared a parallel Russian version of their texts, and this prompted the Moscow authorities to produce a number of English versions from these Russian texts. The English was done by Georgians or Russians, and the work of English experts failed to produce readable, idiomatic prose. Furthermore, these editions had internal propaganda purposes: few copies left the USSR. At least, however, a few stories by Mikheil Javakhishvili and a novel by Konstantin Gamsakhurdia (though not the best of his *œuvre*) can be found in English.

In the 1970s the coming of English lectors and scholars to Tbilisi resulted in renewed interest. Donald **Rayfield** has translated a number of poems (long and short) by Vazha Pshavela, and the Tabidze cousins. These translations were, however, published in Tbilisi and not marketed abroad. Most important is the work of Kathleen **Vivian**, who has retranslated *The Knight in the Panther's Skin* from better canonical texts and with better professional assistance, has gone on to translate the later parts of the Georgian chronicle, and has been able to publish these in fine editions in western Europe.

Other translations are hard to find. Academic scholarship has led to a full and accurate version of the early part of the Georgian Chronicles (c.800–1000, by various hands, attributed to Leont'i Mroveli) by Professor R. W. **Thompson**, and in Charles **Dowsett**'s monograph on the mainly Armenian poet Sayat-Nova (*fl.* 1740–95) [II.e.1.iii] there is much on Sayat-Nova's Georgian poems. Otherwise today's achievements are scant. The witty Georgian texts of scenarios for the puppet plays by Rezo Gabriadze have been circulated as programmes for visitors to the Edinburgh Festival, while western feminists (such as Goldie Blankoff-Scarr) have drawn attention, with lines quoted in translation, to today's Georgian women poets. French, German, and Italian publishers have produced a number of important Georgian novels (with limited critical acclaim), but English-language publishers are resolutely insular. From today's impoverished and chaotic Georgia the only source of literature in English translation is, alas, quotation in political journals such as *Amnesty International* or *Index on Censorship*.

The most extensive range and quantity of Georgian literature in translation so far will be found in Donald Rayfield's *The Literature of Georgia: A History*, a work whose 364 pages are one-fifth quotation, given the inaccessibility for the reader of Georgian texts in translation.

Georgian folklore was, until 1994, just as poorly represented in English. Kevin **Tuite**'s anthology of Georgian folk poetry (with a little from the related Kartvelian languages Svan and Mingrelian), in its scholarship and its poetic flair, despite its mere 147 pages, can claim to be the most impressive presentation so far of Georgian culture to the English-speaking world. PDR

ANTHOLOGIES Lang, David Marshall, *Lives and Legends of the Georgian Saints*, London, 1956 · Rayfield, Donald, 'Georgian Poetry' [introd. and trs.], in *The Elek Book of Oriental Verse*, ed. K. Bosley, London, 1979, 182–90 · 'The Heroic Ethos in Georgian and Russian Folk Poetry', *Slavonic and East European Review*, 56 (1978), 505–21 [contains translations] · 'The Soldier's Lament: Folk Poetry in the Russian Empire 1914–1917', *Slavonic and East European Review*, 66 (1988), 66–90 [contains trs.] · Tuite, Kevin, *An Anthology of Georgian Folk Poetry*, London/Madison, NJ, 1994.

BIBLICAL TEXTS Blake, R. P., 'Ancient Georgian Versions of the Old Testament', *Harvard Theological Review*, 19 (1926), 271–97.

CHRONICLES Thompson, R. W., *The Georgian Chronicle (I)*, in his *Rewriting Caucasian History*, Oxford, 1996 · Vivian, Kathleen, *The Georgian Chronicle: The Period of Giorgi Lasha*, Amsterdam, 1991.

ROMANCE Lang, D. M., *The Balavariani* [c.1000, adaptation possibly from Arabic, attributed to Ekvtime Atoneli],

London, 1966 · Stevenson, R. H., *Amiran-Darejaniani* [*c*.1125, attributed to Mose Khoneli], Oxford, 1958 · Wardrop, O., *Visramiani*, [*c*.1150, anonymous adaptation from Farsi], London, 1914.

CHAVCHAVADZE, ILIA   Wardrop, Marjory, *The Hermit*, London, 1895.

GAMSAKHURDIA, K'ONST'ANT'INE   Eristavi, V., *The Hand of a Great Master*, Moscow, 1959 · Various, *Mindia, Son of Hogay*, Moscow, 1961.

JAVAKHISHVILI, MIKHEIL   anon., 'Too Late', in *Mindia, Son of Hogay*, Moscow, 1961.

JUGHASHVILI, IOSEB [STALIN]   Rayfield, D., 'Stalin as Poet' [six poems], *Poetry and Nation Review*, 41 (1984), 44–7.

ORBELIANI, SULKHAN-SABA   Vivian, Kathleen, *The Book of Wisdom and Lies*, London, 1982 · Wardrop, Oliver, *The Book of Wisdom and Lies*, London, 1894.

RUSTAVELI, SHOTA   Stevenson, R. H., *The Lord of the Panther-skin*, Albany, NY, 1977 · Vivian, Kathleen, *The Knight in the Panther Skin*, London, 1977 · Wardrop, Marjory, *The Man in the Panther's Skin*, London, 1912; rep. 1966.

SAYAT-NOVA   Dowsett, Charles, *Sayat'-Nova: An Eighteenth Century Troubadour*, Louvain, 1997.

TABIDZE, GALAK'T'ION   Rayfield, Donald, *Ten Poems*, Tbilisi, 1975.

TABIDZE, T'ITSIAN   Rayfield, Donald, 'Georgian Poetry: Titsian and Galaktion Tabidze', *Modern Poetry in Translation*, 18 (1974), 11–13.

TEIMURAZ I, KING   Avalishvili, Z., 'Teimuraz I and His Poem *The Martyrdom of Queen Ketevan*', *Georgica*, 4 (1937), 17.

VAZHA-PSHAVELA   Rayfield, Donald, *Three Poems: Aluda Ketelauri, Host and Guest, The Snake Eater*, Tbilisi, 1981 · *Aluda Ketelauri*, in *Modern Poetry in Translation*, 2nd ser., 1 (1983), 116–32.

SEE ALSO   Barrett, D., *Catalogue of the Wardrop Collection and of Other Georgian Books and Manuscripts in the Bodleian Library*, London, 1978 · Lang, D. M., *Catalogue of Georgian and Other Caucasian Printed Books in the British Museum*, London, 1962 · Rayfield, D., *The Literature of Georgia: A History*, Oxford, 1994; rev. edn., London, 1999 [includes translated quotations from a wide range of Georgian authors].

5. HUNGARIAN

i. The Foreignness of Hungarian Literature 'The Magyar language stands afar off and alone,' remarks Sir John Bowring (1792–1872) [see II.e.3.ii], the first translator of Hungarian literature into English, in the preface to his 1830 volume *Poetry of the Magyars*. 'The study of other tongues will be found of exceedingly little use towards its right understanding.' This linguistic isolation is central to any understanding of Hungary's literature and its place in the European tradition to which, partly by circumstance, and partly by an act of national will, it subscribes. It conditions the expectations of its writers, it reflects the vicissitudes of the Hungarians as a nation, it determines their psy- chological co-ordinates and explains their ambitions.

One by-product of linguistic isolation is the practice of translation itself, particularly in the field of poetry. Most notable translators have worked with Hungarian collaborators, either friends or scholars known to them or those provided by the Hungarian branch of PEN. This collaborative process of translation is described in some detail by Frederick **Turner** in an essay entitled 'The Journey of Orpheus: On Translation' which forms part of his Introduction to *Foamy Sky: The Major Poems of Miklós Radnóti*. Turner and Zsuzsanna **Ozsváth** work through a three-stage process. In the first Ozsváth reads the poem twice in Hungarian, once as she might at a poetry reading, once to bring out the verse form. From these Turner is able to 'ascertain the meter, tone, cadence, and often the emotional colour of the original'. In the second Ozsváth provides a word-by-word translation to establish the syntactic order and idiom, 'even when they make very strange sentences in English'. The third stage is a close reading of the poem as it is situated in its own language and culture. At this point Turner produces a draft version which he presents to Ozsváth, and which is then discussed and redrafted. Referring to Radnóti's own view of translation as enacting the myth of Orpheus, Turner elaborates this into an *ur*-language theory which resembles Walter Benjamin's at some points. This account describes a particularly thorough process, but it is essentially the same as others have followed for both poetry and prose.

ii. The Political Context of Translation Literature has enjoyed a very high status in Hungary, its prestige being underlined by the fact that Árpád Göncz, President of the Republic from 1990, is not only a fine playwright and short story writer but is himself a prize-winning translator of modern American fiction. In international terms, however, while achievements in music, photography, cinema, mathematics, and various branches of the sciences and humanities have enjoyed great prestige, Hungarian literature remains relatively unknown. The general Hungarian conviction is that, but for linguistic isolation and the inadequacy of translation, literature, and particularly poetry, would be recognized as the nation's most valuable contribution to European culture. Because of this, particularly in the postwar period, considerable cultural resources have been pressed into service to redress this balance. The political significance of this is complex and has not always been readily recognized by readers abroad.

The major institutions for commissioning and publishing translations since the war have been the publishers Corvina and the English-language magazine *The New Hungarian Quarterly*, both of which have survived, albeit in slimmed-down versions, the changes of 1989, the latter reverting to its pre-Communist name, *The Hungarian Quarterly*. While both these organs operated, as they had to, under the direct patronage of the state, they did so in a climate determined by the post-1956 consensus according to which, by the powers of nod and wink, Hungarian literature attained a considerable (and, in Eastern European terms, enviable) degree of autonomy. All the same, certain subjects were liable to censorship of one kind or another: the events of 1956 itself for instance, the Russian presence, the condition of Hungarian minorities in surrounding countries, and the work of expatriate writers, to name a few. These cultural issues were inextricably wound into the political fabric, were influenced by political views and exerted influence in turn.

This was particularly the case in the 1950s and mid-1960s, even abroad and especially after 1956. When W. H. Auden, for example, writing the foreword to Ilona Duczynska and Karl Polanyi's important anthology of Hungarian 'Populist' writing, *The Plough and the Pen* (1963), ventured the opinion that Ferenc Juhász's poem 'The Boy Changed into a Stag Cries Out at the Gate of Secrets' (1955) was 'one of the greatest poems' written in his time, he did so without any knowledge of the original Hungarian and was utterly reliant on Kenneth **McRobbie**'s translation. Furthermore, though he no doubt had read Duczynska's 'Introduction to the Hungarian Populists', he might have not been fully aware of the extent to which it provided a specifically Marxist reading of 20th-c. Hungarian literature that wholly ignored other equally important movements and presented a rather partisan view of politics, including the 1956 revolution. Auden was, in other words, working in the dark.

Juhász's poem was later retranslated by David **Wevill** as 'The Boy Changed into a Stag Clamours at the Gate of Secrets' for the Penguin Modern

European Poets series in 1970, where a selection of Juhász's work was coupled with poems by Sándor Weöres. Juhász was clearly of the Populist or *népies* group of writers: Weöres, though too large a figure to be accommodated by any single tendency, is usually allied with the *urbánus* or Urban group. In its first phase the Communist system in Hungary had regarded the *urbánus* poets as bourgeois individualists and shut down their magazines, the chief of which, *Újhold* or New Moon, was banned in 1948. Beside Weöres, this group included the major figures of Ágnes Nemes Nagy, János Pilinszky, and Iván Mándy. None of them got a mention in *The Plough and The Pen*.

iii. Aspects of Hungarian Writing Hungarian literature cannot easily be characterized by one or other tendency, since there are strong elements of realism and romanticism in the works of various poets and novelists of the 19th c. Of the major 19th-c. and early 20th-c. Hungarian novelists Mór (anglicized variously as Moritz, Maurice, and Maurus) Jókai enjoyed particular success at the turn of the century with a whole series of novels and short stories published in England and America. The works of Kálmán Mikszáth were also readily available.

Beyond this it might be useful to draw attention to the Hungarian search for an epic work comprehensive enough to articulate the patterns of the nation's history and imagination in a single sweep. The 19th-c. verse drama *Az ember tragédiája* (The Tragedy of Man) by Imre Madách has generally assumed this role. Madách published it in 1861, and it was first performed on stage in 1883. It traces the dream of Adam from the fall, through 15 historical episodes. The firm belief in the value of this play has produced a series of translations, only a tiny fraction of which have ever been published. The work is undoubtedly remarkable and, fulfilling as it does so many of the appropriate epic functions, it is cause for perennial regret that it has never enjoyed the international success which its admirers feel it deserves. The published translations into English have enjoyed a degree of critical success without making a significant breakthrough into the world canon. All have their virtues and their faults, being directed to different purposes, some presenting the work as literature, others as an actable play.

There is a characteristically Hungarian dialectic between the garrulous and the concise which, in terms of translation, tends to favour the latter. Many of the major figures of Hungarian literature were immensely productive virtuosic writers: Sándor Petőfi, the great 19th-c. Romantic poet, left behind a mass of poems, as did his friend János Arany. In the 20th c. the poet Ferenc Juhász, the exiled poet and philosopher essayist Győző Határ, the contemporary writers of fiction, Péter Esterházy, Péter Nádas, and László Krasznahorkai are all producers of vast, highly structured works. The sheer productivity of a novelist and short-story writer like the prewar Gyula Krúdy is staggering. His *Adventures of Sindbad*, a selection of his proto-magic realist stories was published in 1998. Nádas's *Emlékiratok könyve* (1986, The Book of Memories) has been acclaimed by many as a great work and was certainly a cult book in both Hungary and Germany, but there were demurring voices in England. Krasznahorkai's monumentally black but humorous work *Az ellenállás melankóliája* (1989, The Melancholy of Resistance) is currently in translation.

iv. Difficulties of Translation As far as poetry goes, the sad fact is that certain of the major Hungarian writers have, so far, proved untranslatable. Edwin Morgan has produced some credible and lively Petőfis but hardly enough to establish him as more than a reputation. Morgan's versions of the great poet Attila József are exciting but do not, at the time of writing, constitute a complete volume. As for Endre Ady, his short fiction has been well translated but his poetry, which played such an important part in Hungarian literature, lacks adequate interpreters. The bulk, and therefore to a great extent the true achievement, of Sándor Weöres's poetry and drama remains out of reach. Morgan's versions are the enticing best we have.

In prose fiction, the great prewar humorist Frigyes Karinthy, while popular, particularly in the late 1930s—his best-known work, *Utazás a koponyám körül* (1937, A Journey Round My Skull), was a humorous account of his own operation for a brain tumour—inevitably lost something in the cultural transplantation. Two outstanding postwar writers, István Örkény and Iván Mándy, are so intrinsically part of the Budapest milieu that their black humour and lyricism have so far lost some of their edge in translation. Géza Ottlik, whose seminal work *Iskola a határon* (1959, School on the Frontier) so influenced Péter Esterházy, is deeply embedded in the consciousness of Hungarian readers. Unfortunately, Budapest does not yet exist in the European mind as distinctly as do Vienna or Prague. Örkény's *Egyperces novellák* (1984, One-Minute Stories) is a wonderful exercise in the grotesque, and Mándy's terse, dreamlike, melancholy lyricism is as close as prose fiction can get to poetry. Albert **Tezla**'s

selection of his short stories, *On The Balcony* goes some way towards making him available.

Neither Esterházy nor Nádas, considered to be the major postmodern novelists of the late 20th c., have quite made the mark in English their Hungarian public must have hoped for: none, at least, has as yet executed the quantum leap to the Márquez or Kundera level. Esterházy is a funny, lyrical, experimental writer, whose *A szív segédigéi* (1986, Helping Verbs of the Heart) appeared in a popularly available and critically praised translation by Michael **Heim** and formed part of a series of fictions under the general title *Bevezetés a szépirodalomba* (1986, lit. 'an introduction to literature'). His other novels, such as *Hrabal könyve* (1990, The Book of Hrabal), continue to be translated into various languages including English, but some of his wry, complex jokes require a Budapest audience. Ádám Bodor's darkly surreal short stories, *Az Eufrátesz Babilonnál* (1985, The Euphrates at Babylon), reflecting the conditions of Transylvania under Ceausescu, were beautifully translated but did not attract much critical attention. His best work, *Sinistra körzet* (1992, Sinistra District) has yet to find a translator. One of the finest novelists of the previous generation, Miklós Mészöly, is represented by *Once There Was a Central Europe*, a selection of his short stories, 'video clips', and essays.

There are the great success stories, of course. Ferenc Molnár's reputation was most firmly established by his 'legend in seven scenes', *Liliom* (1909). Adapted by Rogers and Hammerstein, it gained immense popularity as the musical *Carousel*. His *A Pál utcai fiuk* (1907, The Paul Street Boys), telling the story of a group of schoolboys in Budapest, is a Hungarian, possibly—as it has been claimed—a world juvenile classic. The novels of the great prewar poet, journalist, and essayist Dezső Kosztolányi have also been fortunate. Kosztolányi wrote only five novels, and three of them, *Néro, a véres költo* (1922, lit. 'Nero, the bloody poet', but available as *Darker Muses*), *Édes Anna* (1926, Anna Édes), and *Pacsirta* (1924, Skylark), are available in English translation. Others international successes include Tibor Déry's novel, *Niki: egy kutya története* (1956, Niki: The Story of a Dog), which appeared in three popular editions in England after the Hungarian uprising. Two more Déry collections followed. Of these the three novellas under one cover, *The Giant; Behind the Brick Wall; Love*, translated by Ilona **Duczynska** and Kathleen **Szász**, was the most praised. The pre-eminent modern example of success is György Konrád's first novel, *A látogató* (1969), translated by Paul **Aston** as *The Case Worker*, which immediately established the author's international reputation, to the extent that he became an important intellectual spokesman for his generation.

v. Anthologies For the general reader anthologies will form the first introduction to the work of Hungarian writers, chiefly poets. These may be of the pan-European or eastern European sort, such as *Child of Europe*, edited by Michael March, *The Poetry of Survival*, edited by Daniel Weissbort or *The Faber Book of Modern European Poetry*, edited by A. Alvarez. One of the most striking results of Hungarian missionary enterprise was the publication of the key anthology *Modern Hungarian Poetry*, edited by Miklós Vajda, which, while it may be limited by including only those translations that had already been published by *The New Hungarian Quarterly*, does contain most of the important poets of the century, translated by the best of the available English and American poets, including Richard **Wilbur**, Charles **Tomlinson**, Peter **Redgrove**, Michael **Hamburger**, Laura **Schiff**, and George **MacBeth**.

The *Old Hungarian Literary Reader*, edited in 1985 by Tibor Klaniczay, provides an excellent introduction to Hungarian literature from the 11th to the 18th c., both poetry and prose, the translators including G. F. **Cushing**, the most important British scholar of Hungarian literature of the last 40 years, who was also the translator of one of the

most important 20th-c. texts: the Populist poet Gyula Illyés' lyrical and seminal study of the conditions of Hungarian agricultural life in the 1930s, *A puszták népe* (1936, People of the Puszta).

The major new anthology of 20th-c. Hungarian poetry is the much-praised *The Colonnade of Teeth* (1996), edited by George **Gömöri** and George **Szirtes**, which includes, importantly, poets living abroad, among them a number from Hungarian minorities in neighbouring countries. Individual collections by some of the major poets of the mid- to late century such as Gyula Illyés, Miklós Radnóti, István Vas, György Faludi, Sándor Weöres, János Pilinszky, Ágnes Nemes Nagy, László Nagy, István Csoóri, Ottó Orbán, Dezso Tandori, Imre Oravecz, György Petri, and Zsuzsa Rakovszky have all been well received in translation.

Meanwhile, the grand projects continue. The enormous first volume of *In Quest of the Miracle Stag*, an anthology of Hungarian poetry from the 13th c. to the present, edited by Adam **Makkai** (who has also contributed copiously as a translator), is a work of vast energy, though the very compendiousness of the project, first conceived in the 1960s, results in rather mixed quality. Corvina have also continued to publish a steady stream of anthologies in English of modern short stories, novellas, and plays, many of which contain translations of high quality.

GS

ANTHOLOGIES Alvarez, A. ed., *The Faber Book of Modern European Poetry*, London, 1992 · Bowring, John, *Poetry of the Magyars*, London, 1830 · Dávidházy, Péter et al., *The Lost Rider*, Budapest, 1997 · Duczynska, Ilona, and Polányi, Karl, eds., *The Plough and the Pen*, London, 1963 · Gömöri, George, and Szirtes, George, *The Colonnade of Teeth*, Newcastle upon Tyne, 1996 · Kabdebó, Tamás, *Hundred Hungarian Poems*, Manchester, 1976 · Klaniczay, Tibor, ed., *Old Hungarian Literary Reader*, Budapest, 1985 · Makkai, Adam, *In Quest of the Miracle Stag*, Budapest / Chicago, 1996 · March, Michael, *Child of Europe*, London, 1990 · Morgan, Edwin, and Wevill, David, *Penguin Modern European Poets: Sándor Weöres and Ferenc Juhász*, London, 1970 · Vajda, Miklós, ed., *Modern Hungarian Poetry*, New York, 1977 · Weissbort, Daniel, ed., *The Poetry of Survival*, London, 1991.

ADY, ENDRE Sollosy, Judith, *Selected Shorter Fiction*, Budapest, 1994.

BODOR, ÁDÁM Aczél, Richard, *The Euphrates at Babylon*, Edinburgh, 1992.

CSOÓRI, SÁNDOR Domokos, Mátyás, ed., *Barbarian Prayer*, Budapest, 1989.

DÉRY, TIBOR Duczynska, Ilona, and Szász, Kathleen, *The Giant; Behind the Brick Wall; Love*, London, 1964 · Hyams, Edward, *Niki: The Story of a Dog*, London, 1958 · Szász, Kathleen, *The Portuguese Princess*, London, 1966.

ESTERHÁZY PETER Heim, Michael, *Helping Verbs of the Heart*, New York, 1990 · Sollosy, Judith, *The Book of Hrabal*, London, 1993.

GÖNCZ, ÁRPÁD Wilson, Katharina M., and Wilson, Christopher J., *Homecoming and Other Stories*, Budapest, 1991.

ILLYÉS, GYULA Cushing, George, *People of the Puszta*, Budapest, 1967 · Kabdebó, Thomas, and Tábori, Paul, eds., *Selected Poems*, London, 1971.

JÓKAI, MÓR BAIN, R. NISBET, *A Hungarian Nabob*, London, 1898 · *Tales from Jókai*, London, 1904 · Kennard, Mrs H., *The Man with the Golden Touch*, Budapest, 1963 · Szabad, Emeric, ed., *Hungarian Sketches in Peace and War*, Edinburgh, 1854.

JÓZSEF, ATTILA Bátki, John, *Selected Poems and Texts*, Cheadle Hulme, 1973 · Kabdebó, Tamás, ed., *Attila József: Poems*, London, 1966 · Hargitai, Peter, *Perched on Nothing's Branch: Selected Poems*, Talahassee, Fla., 1986.

KARINTHY, FRIGYES Duckworth Barker, Vernon, *A Journey Round My Skull*, London, 1939.

KONRÁD, GYÖRGY Aston, Paul, *The Case Worker*, New York / London, 1969 · Sanders, Ivan, *The City Builder*, New York / London, 1977 · *The Loser*, New York, 1982, London, 1983.

KOSZTOLÁNYI, DEZSŐ   Aczél, Richard, *Skylark*, London, 1993 · Fadiman, Clifton, *Darker Muses*, Budapest, 1990 · Szirtes, George, *Anna Édes*, London/New York, 1991.

KRÚDY, GYULA   Bátkí, John, *Sunflower*, Budapest, 1997 · Szirtes, George, *Adventures of Sindbad*, Budapest/London, 1998.

MADÁCH, IMRE   Horne, J. C. W., *The Tragedy of Man*, Budapest, 1963 · MacLeod, Ian, *The Tragedy of Man*, Edinburgh, 1993 · Mark, Thomas, *The Tragedy of Man*, Boulder, Co., 1989 · Sanger, C. P., *The Tragedy of Man*, London, 1933 · Szirtes, George, *The Tragedy of Man*, London/Budapest/New York, 1988.

MÁNDY, IVÁN   Tezla, Albert, *On The Balcony*, Budapest, 1988.

MÉSZÖLY, MIKLÓS   Tezla, Albert, *Once There Was a Central Europe*, Budapest, 1997.

MIKSZÁTH, KÁLMÁN   Bingham, Clifton, *The Good People of Palócz*, London, 1893 · Worswick, B. W., *St Peter's Umbrella*, London, 1900; rep. 1966.

MOLNÁR, FERENC   Glazer, Benjamin F., *Liliom*, New York/London, 1945 · Rittenberg, Louis, *The Paul Street Boys*, Budapest, 1994.

MÓRICZ, ZSIGMOND   Adams, Bernard, *Relations*, Budapest, 1997 · Cushing, George, *Seven Pennies and Other Short Stories*, Budapest, 1988.

NÁDAS, PÉTER   Sanders, Ivan, with Goldstein, Imre, *The Book of Memories*, London/New York, 1997.

NAGY, LÁSZLO   Connor, Tony, McRobbie, Kenneth, et al., *Love of the Scorching Wind*, Oxford, 1974.

NEMES NAGY, ÁGNES   Berlind, Bruce, *Selected Poems*, Iowa City, Iowa, 1980 · Maxton, Hugh, *Between: Selected Poems of Ágnes Nemes Nagy*, Budapest/Dublin, 1988.

ORAVECZ, IMRE   Berlind, Bruce, *When You Became She*, Grand Terrace, Calif., 1994.

ORBÁN, OTTÓ   Berlind, Bruce, *The Journey of Barbarus*, Pueblo, Colo., 1997 · Szirtes, George, ed., *The Blood of the Walsungs*, Newcastle upon Tyne, 1993.

ÖRKÉNY, ISTVÁN   Heim, Michael, and Györgyey, Clara, *The Flower Show; The Toth Family*, New York, 1982 · Sollosy, Judith, *One Minute Stories,* Budapest/Sydney, 1994.

OTTLIK, GÉZA   Szász, Kathleen, *School at the Frontier*, New York, 1966.

PETRI, GYÖRGY   Wilmer, Clive, and Gömöri, George, *Night Song of the Personal Shadow*, Newcastle upon Tyne, 1991.

PILINSZKY, JÁNOS   Csokits, János, and Hughes, Ted, *The Desert of Love*, London, 1976 · Jay, Peter, *Crater*, London, 1978 · Jay, Peter, and Major, Eva, *Conversations with Sheryl Sutton*, Manchester/Budapest, 1992.

RADNÓTI, MIKLÓS   George, Emery, *The Complete Poetry*, Ann Arbor, Mich., 1980 · Ozsváth, Zsuzsanna, and Turner, Frederick, *Foamy Sky: The Major Poems of Miklós Radnóti*, Princeton, NJ, 1992 · Wilmer, Clive, and Gömöri, George, *Forced March: Selected Poems*, Manchester, 1979.

RAKOVSZKY, ZSUZSA   Szirtes, George, *New Life*, Oxford, 1995.

TANDORI, DEZSO   Berlind, Bruce, *Birds and Other Relations, Selected Poems*, Princeton, NJ, 1986.

VAS, ISTVÁN   Szirtes, George, ed., *Through the Smoke*, Budapest, 1989.

VÖRÖSMARTY, MIHÁLY   Zollman, Peter, *The Quest: Csongor and Tünde*, Budapest, 1996.

WEÖRES, SÁNDOR   Vajda, Miklós, ed., *Eternal Moment: Selected Poems*, London/Budapest and St Paul, Minn., 1988.

SEE ALSO   Czigány, M., *Hungarian Literature in English Translation Published in Great Britain, 1830–1968*, London, 1969 · *The Oxford History of Hungarian Literature*, Oxford, 1984 · Klaniczay, T., *A History of Hungarian Literature*, Budapest, 1983.

6. POLISH POETRY

i. Introduction Even as late as the sixth decade of the 20th c., writing about Polish poetry in English translation would have been an easy task: the subject could have been dismissed in a sentence, stating that the few translations available, mainly in obscure publications, had deservedly passed almost unnoticed. Now, the bare enumeration of the individual volumes and anthologies of Polish poetry in translation—never mind the periodicals and journals—would have taken up the whole of this entry.

So why has Polish poetry suddenly achieved its present status, endorsed by such eminent critics and poets as Al Alvarez, John Bayley, Donald Davie, Seamus Heaney, Edwin Morgan, and Tom Paulin? The British intellectuals, critics, and poets, cosily safe in liberal Britain, became mesmerized by the courage of intellectuals and writers behind the Iron Curtain. Secondly, the large Polish expatriate community provided translators: Czesław **Miłosz**, Bogdan **Czaykowski**, Adam **Czerniawski**, Jan **Darowski**, Andrzej **Busza** and Stanisław **Barańczak**. But most importantly, good poetry flourished in postwar Poland.

ii. Kochanowski 'The run-of-the-mill translator in our day translates only his contemporaries or near-contemporaries,' Davie has caustically observed in his foreword to Czerniawski's translation of *Treny* by the 16th-c. poet Jan Kochanowski. The 19th-c. polymath John **Bowring** [see II.e.3.ii] was certainly not run-of-the-mill: his anthology *Specimens of the Polish Poets*, the first such collection in English, includes a selection from *Treny*. Kochanowski's sequence of elegies on the death of his very young daughter, published in 1580, is an acknowledged masterpiece, yet English-language readers justifiably ignored Bowring's lame translation of its fragments, as they ignored the first full version by Dorothea P. **Radin**, a polished 'poetical' academic exercise, published as part of *Poems by Jan Kochanowski* (1928). Then, in 1995–6, three more versions suddenly appeared: by Michał **Mikoś** entitled *Laments*, by Seamus **Heaney** (with Barańczak) also entitled *Laments*, and by Czerniawski under its original title, *Treny*.

Mikoś has produced another academic exercise, which however lacks the stylistic consistency and technical accomplishment of the Radin version; the Heaney translation has the fluency of a Heaney poem but is marred by Barańczak's dogmatic thesis (inherited from Brodsky) that a translation must at all costs faithfully preserve the original's rhyming and rhythmical structures. As Davie observed in another context, the professional poet as translator realizes that 'in translating rhymed verse the rhyme is the first thing to go, and metre the second: whereas the amateur . . . cannot be sure of having poetry at all unless he has these external features'. To achieve this goal the translators have been constrained to pad and to import phrases and images that Kochanowski did not and would not have employed. Contrariwise, Czerniawski clings to the thesis that, whatever the Surrealists and other irrationalists might say, meaning, taken in its widest sense, its primary in poetry. His translation is therefore semantically faithful but structured more loosely, and he even renders the concluding discursive poem into prose. Here are two samples for comparison (Heaney–Barańczak expand to 38 words against Czerniawski's 27 words and the original's 26):

> The void that fills my house is so immense
> Now that my girl is gone. It baffles sense:
> We all are here, yet no one is, I feel;
> The flight of one small soul has tipped the scale.
>
> (Heaney-Barańczak)

> Your flight, my dearest, caused
>   This vast emptiness in my house.
> We are a crowd yet no one's here:
>   One tiny soul and so much is gone.
>
> (Czerniawski)

iii. Nineteenth-Century Poetry Bowring, like Moses, could not proceed to the promised land, but unlike Moses, didn't even have the chance to glimpse it. His anthology ends with the Polish Enlightenment, which, although it has many good things to its credit, is no match for the achievements of the 19th-c. poets Adam Mickiewicz, Juliusz Słowacki, and Cyprian Kamil Norwid. Słowacki is the English translator's nightmare in that his narrative poems are modelled on Byron's and his poetic plays on Shakespeare's. And yet his imagination is very much his own. He is a master of the Polish language, especially of its music and colour—which means another nightmare task for translators. No wonder no satisfactory translations of his poetry or plays exist. Norwid is a modernist forebear on a par with Baudelaire, Dickinson, Hopkins, and Hölderlin, and for that very reason a formidable challenge for translators. Christine **Brooke-Rose** has produced the best renderings of a couple of Norwid's lyrics ('Pilgrim' and 'Autumn'); the most comprehensive selection of them is in Czerniawski's bilingual *Poezje/Poems* and his anthology *The Burning Forest*.

Mickiewicz, generally acknowledged to be the outstanding Polish poet, presents different problems. The father of Polish romanticism, he is also a lucid, witty classicist. His *Sonety krymskie* (1826, Crimean Sonnets) pay tribute to Edmund Burke's sublimity and terror, while the *Ballady i romanse* (1822, Ballads and Romances) are Polish equivalents of Goethe's versified narratives, Keats's 'La Belle Dame Sans Merci', and Coleridge's 'The Ancient Mariner'; his language has the freshness and innocence of Wordsworth's *Prelude*, his poetic drama *Dziady* (1832, The Forefathers' Eve) is a match for Goethe's *Faust*. All these await competent translators [for the plays, see II.e.8.i]. As for the epic *Pan Tadeusz (Master Tadeusz)*, its translator would require the transparency, brilliance, and versifying virtuosity possessed by the author of *The Rape of the Lock*.

There are in fact five English versions of *Pan Tadeusz*. Mickiewicz published it in Paris in 1834 and already by 1885 Maude Ashurst **Biggs** had issued the first English translation, *Master Thaddeus*. In her introduction she hopes 'to introduce for the first time into this country an image of the thoughts and feelings of a people, whose literature is only neglected because they have no recognized position among nations', while in his introduction the editor, W. R. Morfill, wisely observes that rhyming couplets of 13 syllables have not been greatly favoured by English poets, and also notes that Miltonic blank verse ('which allows the translator to be more literal by emancipating him from . . . the tags of rhyme') established the standard medium for epic poetry, an example followed by Henry Francis Cary in his influential translation of Dante's *Divine Comedy* [II.m.2.ii]. But Mickiewicz's tragical-comical-historical-pastoral romp in the Lithuanian countryside has little in common either with Dante's 'dark wood' or Milton's account 'of man's first disobedience'; and while the Biggs translation achieves at times a stately dignity, it cannot compete with Milton's grandeur just by placing words in the wrong order.

Or, given its novelistic plot, is the poem more like one of Walter Scott's romantic tales, and should it therefore be rendered in prose? This was the decision of George Rapall **Noyes** in 1917. But that solution is not quite right either. Mickiewicz's work is undoubtedly a poem, and this prose rendering proves it. In the prose version the pace of the action—and Mickiewicz is superb at handling complex narrative, as well as Homeric similes—gets bogged down in quaint and lengthy poeticisms. Watson **Kirkconnell** and Kenneth **MacKenzie** bravely attempt to reproduce Mickiewicz's masterly rhyming couplets, but Kirkconnell has to confess despairingly in his Translator's Preface: 'compulsory [sic] liberty has been the occasional concocting of a new phrase in order to secure any rhyme at all . . . and there are instances where no amount of juggling with the synonyms of every word in a sentence will provide a chiming pair.'

Remarkably, all these translations are very faithful to an original linguistically abundant and rich in metaphor. Davie's *The Forests of Lithuania*, being a Poundian distillation of Mickiewicz's epic, necessarily fails the faithfulness test but confirms the intuitively convincing thesis that only poets have the necessary qualifications for translating poetry. A truism perhaps. Here is his version of Mickiewicz's defence of the beauties of Lithuanian forests, addressed to a couple of his characters yearning for Italy:

> Linking hands
> (That's leaves) the trees and bushes stand
> Like dancers, maid and man, around
> The married pair in middle ground,
> Two that for straightness, hue and height
> Surpass their sylvan neighbours quite;
> The silver birch, the well-loved bride,
> Her man the hornbean by her side.
> Grave seniors sit some way apart
> To watch their progeny disport,
> Matronly poplars, hoary beech
> Who gazing find no need of speech;
> And a moss-bearded oak that bears

> The weight of full five hundred years
> Rests, as on tombstones overthrown,
> On his own forebears turned to stone.

Contradicting his own thesis quoted above, Davie skilfully turns Mickiewicz's 13-foot lines into Marvellian rhyming octosyllables with a superbly managed concluding couplet; his rivals, shackled by their pedestrian rhymes, confound the opulence, vividness, and spontaneity of the original so elegantly caught by Davie. But alas, Davie's version is in its brevity but a synopsis of the original and is, this time in conformity with his thesis, mostly in blank verse.

iv. Twentieth-Century Poetry Davie's *Forests of Lithuania* notwithstanding, it was through the publication in 1968 of *Selected Poems* by Zbigniew Herbert (in a translation by Miłosz and Peter Dale **Scott**) and A. Alvarez's vigorous championing of Herbert's poetry that for the first time ever a Polish poet gained recognition in England and America. His 'Elegy for Fortinbras' won general admiration both as a portrayal of power-politics and as a tribute to Shakespeare. Two further volumes of his poetry, another *Selected Poems* and *Report from the Besieged City* (both translated by John and Bogdana **Carpenter**), followed. Herbert is a fastidious stylist and ironist, delighting in complex Latinate sentences, characteristics which his translators have not always been able to handle satisfactorily.

Czesław Miłosz, himself a very prolific and gifted translator of modern English-language poetry (under German occupation in Warsaw he was translating Shakespeare and T. S. Eliot), had his own poetry translated into English first by himself but increasingly by others, notably by Robert **Hass** and Robert **Pinsky**, and his *The Collected Poems 1931–1987* appeared in 1988 after he was awarded the Nobel Prize. Miłosz may have translated *The Waste Land*, but his poetic and ideological sympathies are essentially traditionalist. His translators are not therefore faced with the problem (all too conspicuous in the case of an innovative poet like Norwid) of having to bring out the strangeness and oddity of the originals—a task translators normally fudge for fear of being accused of linguistic incompetence or dottiness. Hass and Pinsky, the translators of Miłosz's Blakean 'Naive Poems', declare: 'No translation into English [of this sequence] has been published because the author believed it was untranslatable, a fact which we may have succeeded in demonstrating.' Miłosz in fact has perversely produced his own version of this engaging sequence—markedly inferior to that of his American translators.

Sixteen years after Miłosz, the poet Wisława Szymborska was awarded the Nobel Prize in 1996. Her poems had first become available in book form in English in 1981 in *Sounds, Feelings, Thoughts*, a selection translated by Magnus J. **Krynski** and Robert A. **Maguire**. This was followed in 1990 by Czerniawski's *People on a Bridge* and in 1996 by Barańczak and Claire **Cavanagh's** *View with a Grain of Sand*. Her poems are mainly witty and sombre poetic fables, requiring the translators to match her intelligence, elegance, and verbal dexterity. Success here has inevitably been patchy.

Undoubtedly the outstanding Polish living poet is Tadeusz Różewicz. From his debut immediately after World War II he has maintained his position as the most innovative poet, with an enormous range of themes and stylistic and formal models. Many contemporary Polish poets, Herbert amongst them, have learnt from him. His English translators include Krynski, Maguire, Victor **Contoski**, and Czerniawski. Here the translator's main problem is how to cope with Różewicz's minimalist poetics— how to avoid either 'poeticizing' the bareness

or alternatively, how not to treat the simple simplistically.

In his introduction to *The Oxford Book of Verse in English Translation* Charles Tomlinson tetchily complains of the 'depressing translation boom of recent years'. Judging by the parsimonious way in which he has selected translations from eastern European countries (a fragment of the Davie *Forests of Lithuania* and Herbert's 'Elegy on Fortinbras' is all that the Poles get, as against endless retranslations of Horace and Ovid), translations from these languages are presumably the targets of his distaste. At the same time J. Plamenatz, the Oxford political scientist, pontificates that western European nations 'had languages adapted to the . . . consciously progressive civilization to which they belonged. They had . . . philosophers, scientists, artists and poets . . . of "world" reputation. . . . The case with the Slavs, and later with the Africans and Asians, has been quite different.'

Should this turn out to be the prevailing opinion, the future of Polish poetry in English translation looks bleak, unless another Cold War saves the day.

ACz

ANTHOLOGIES Alvarez, A., ed., *The Faber Book of Modern European Poetry*, London, 1992 · Barańczak, Stanisław, and Cavanagh, Claire, *Polish Poetry of the Last Two Decades of Communist Rule*, Evanston, Ill., 1991 · Bowring, John, *Specimens of the Polish Poets*, London, 1827 · Busza, A., and Czaykowski, B., *Gathering Time: Five Modern Polish Elegies*, Mission, BC, 1983 · Carpenter, Bogdana, ed., *Monumenta Polonica: the First Four Centuries of Polish Poetry*, Ann Arbor, Mich., 1989 · Conquest, Robert, ed., *Back to Life: Poems from Behind the Iron Curtain*, London, 1958 · Czerniawski, Adam, *The Burning Forest: Modern Polish Poetry*, Newcastle upon Tyne, 1988 · Filip, T. M., and Michael, M. A., *A Polish Anthology*, London, 1944 · Gillon, A., and Krzyzanowski, J., eds., *Introduction to Modern Polish Literature*, 2nd edn., New York, 1982 · Miłosz, Czesław, *Post-War Polish Poetry*, 3rd edn., Berkeley, Calif., 1983 · Peterkiewicz, J., and Singer B., *Five Centuries of Polish Poetry*, 2nd edn., London, 1970 · Pirie, D., *Young Poets of New Poland*, London, 1993 · Umadevi [Dynowska W.], Schandra, H., and Bhatt, B., *The Scarlet Muse: An Anthology of Polish Poems*, Bombay, 1944 · Weissbort, Daniel, ed., *The Poetry of Survival*, London, 1991.

HERBERT, ZBIGNIEW Carpenter, Bogdana, and Carpenter, Jan, *Selected Poems*, Oxford, 1977 · *Report from the Besieged City*, Oxford, 1987 · Miłosz, Czesław, and Scott, Peter Dale, *Selected Poems*, Harmondsworth, 1968.

KOCHANOWSKI, JAN Czerniawski, Adam, *Treny*, Katowice, 1996 · Havermale, H. H., et al., *Poems of Jan Kochanowski*, Berkeley, Calif., 1928 · Heaney, Seamus, and Barańczak, Stanislaw, *Laments*, London/New York, 1995 · Mikoś, Michal, *Laments*, Warsaw, 1995.

MICKIEWICZ, ADAM Biggs, Maude Ashurst, *Master Thaddeus*, London, 1885 · Davie, Donald, *The Forests of Lithuania*, Hull, 1959 · Kirkconnell, Watson, *Pan Tadeusz*, Toronto, 1962 · MacKenzie, Kenneth, *Pan Tadeusz*, London, 1964 · Noyes, George Rapall, *Pan Tadeusz*, London, 1917.

MIŁOSZ, CZESŁAW Various translators, *The Collected Poems* (1931–1987), New York/London, 1988.

NORWID, CYPRIAN CAMIL Brooke-Rose, Christine, 'Twelve Poems', *Botteghe Oscure*, 3 (1958), 191–9 · Czerniawski, Adam, *Poezje/Poems*, Kraków, 1986.

RÓŻEWICZ, TADEUSZ Contoski, Victor, *Unease*, St Paul, Minn., 1980 · Czerniawski, Adam, *They Came to See a Poet*, London, 1991 · Krynski, Magnus J., and Maguire, Robert A., *'The Survivor' and Other Poems*, Princeton, NJ, 1976.

SZYMBORSKA, WISLAWA Barańczak, Stanisław, and Cavanagh, Claire, *View with a Grain of Sand*, New York/London, 1996 · Czerniawski, Adam, *People on a Bridge*, London, 1990 · Krynski, Magnus J., and Maguire, Robert A., *Sounds, Feelings, Thoughts: Seventy Poems*, Princeton, NJ, 1981.

SEE ALSO Czerniawski, A., ed., *The Mature Laurel: Essays on Modern Polish Poetry*, Bridgend, Wales, 1991 [with comprehensive bibliography of translations] · Miłosz, C., *The History of Polish Literature*, London, 1969.

7. POLISH FICTION

Ever since Adam Mickiewicz wrote his novel in verse, *Pan Tadeusz* [II.e.6.iii], Polish writers have tended to use the longer prose narrative as a means of recapturing a lost order. In its mature form, that of the 19th-c. realist—or as the Poles say 'Positivist'—novel, the form of that narrative has often recalled the epic, with the occasional excursion into the romance and idyll. For the translator, this has often meant having to contend with a literary form generically different from its Russian, European, or British cousin. Civic-minded, indebted to a cultural ethos serving a 'nobleman's democracy', the Polish novel has often been weighed down by a moralizing didacticism. To the imposition of epic scope and civic instruction would be added other burdens, especially in the modern period: those of a poetic lyricism and philosophical discourse.

i. Seventeenth to Nineteenth Centuries Of the predecessors of the modern Polish novel, the English reader has access only to the 17th-c. *Pamiętniki* (Memoirs) by Jan Pasek, a work that has been admirably, even heroically, served by the translator Catherine S. **Leach**. Leach's reconstruction of the Pasek memoir in all its baroque pomposity, hilarity, and braggadocio is a *tour de force* of literary archaeology. Yet its very strength, an archaeological exactitude that led the translator to model the idiom on that of British memoirists such as Samuel Pepys, also has the effect of archaizing the work in such a way as to deprive it of its all-important immediacy, gained through an uncanny intimacy of tone based on oral narration. While Pasek's self-irony is always naïvely unintentional, Leach's swashbuckling narrator sometimes seems to wear a peruke and to speak in a drawing-room lisp.

A lack of irony, on the other hand, can also spoil the game. Authors of the Polish Enlightenment, for example, will sound merely like epigones of their French and British contemporaries without that proper shade of irony that, in the Polish variant, seems always to stop short of cynicism. For all its commendable fidelity to the original, Thomas H. **Hoisington's** translation of Ignacy Krasicki's *Mikołaja Doświadczyńskiego przypadki* 1776 (The Adventures of Mr Nicholas Wisdom), lacks at times the elegance, based on a careful phrasing and understatement, the indulgent smile, and the light-slippered footwork that has earned the Krasicki work its status as a classic.

The 19th-c. novel is known to English readers largely through the work of Henryk Sienkiewicz.

Jeremiah **Curtin's** translations of Sienkiewicz's historical trilogy (*Ogniem i mieczem*, 1884, With Fire and Sword; *Potop*, 1886, The Deluge; *Pan Wołodyjowski*, 1887–8, Pan Michael) are no longer in print, nor should they be revived in their present form. While not a novelist to be compared with the masters of European realism, Sienkiewicz, whose historical novels are better treated as Homeric epics in prose, was at least a careful stylist. The Curtin translations lack any sense of style but are at least faithful to the original. The same cannot be said of those of Curtin's successor, W. S. **Kuniczak**, the American novelist who has dedicated himself to making Sienkiewicz accessible to the broad public. The motive of greater accessibility is possibly the only argument that can be made in defence of his *Trilogy*, which has provoked strong criticism on the part of those who remain unmoved by the rationalizations in favour of what can at best be termed a loose paraphrase and at worst a clumsy imitation that adds little to, and in fact mostly diminishes, the original.

The greatest work of late 19th-c. Polish prose is *Lalka* (1890, The Doll) by Bolesław Prus, a rare example of a work that attempts a novel of character but that fails, for all its (by Polish standards) innovation in terms of psychological exposition, to overcome those problems discussed earlier. Prus's translator, David **Welsh**, by resorting to an excessive literalism, passes on the author's handling of the literary conventions uncritically. The fault here lies neither solely nor even principally with the translator. The impasse is caused by a forking of novelistic conventions, one that cannot be overcome except perhaps by a recourse to adaptation.

ii. Twentieth Century Modernism in Poland, as elsewhere on the Continent, rejected these inherited burdens. The modernist novel, represented above all by Stanisław Ignacy Witkiewicz, Bruno Schulz, and Witold Gombrowicz, liberated from its moralizing, didactic, compensatory tasks, allowed simultaneously for the exploration of aesthetic form and for investigations into pure being as it exists primally, in isolation from the notion of any national or collective identity.

Witkiewicz's huge modernist novel *Nienasycenie* (1927, Insatiability) is quintessentially a novel of language. As in Gombrowicz's *Ferdydurke*, the prose is constantly imperilled by the very ontological traumas it describes: here garrulity, density, and an infinitely convoluted syntax act as the last sigh of an expiring subjectivity. Two English versions, both by Louis **Iribarne**, exist: the first (1977) in a scholarly edition, the second (1996) in a freer version, bordering on adaptation, that aims for a more contemporary idiom. The earlier edition sought to contain the book's madness, as reflected in its monumental verbal onanism, within a studied and formal prose—to spare the prose, in other words, the effects of the book's underlying nihilism. The later edition casts off the pretence in favour of a chaotic rant, mirroring the book's schizoid form and above all its hero, whose schizophrenic ravings we have apparently been reading.

The best known of the modernists is Witold Gombrowicz, and the least well served in translation. Three of Gombrowicz's four major novels, all written in Polish, were translated into English from either French or German and, in one case, from both! Eric **Mosbacher's** version of the arch-modern *Ferdydurke* (1938), for all its brio, gives an altogether false impression of the author's unconventional style. Although wildly eccentric, Gombrowicz is something of an exception to the rule: a writer of *le mot juste*. The lack of care in the Mosbacher translation—and his is not the only one guilty of such recklessness—suggests that the translator was deaf to Gombrowicz's special use of language. By slackening the syntax and flattening out cadence on behalf of comic farce, by depriving passages of their formal shaping, their rhythmic contour as they cheerfully and in nihilistic fashion make a mockery of the very premise of formal discourse, Mosbacher conveys a different world, one subject to a moralizing satire in which the author's words are somehow spared the subversion. Worse still, Mosbacher's translation is a severely bowdlerized version of both the 1938 and a later revised edition (published posthumously by Kultura (Paris), 1969). The logic behind the deletions would seem to have been aimed at thinning out both the pure verbal nonsense and the metafictional elements. In a novel that foregrounds language and the process of its own creation so provocatively and programmatically, such cuts are especially injurious to the novel's integrity.

Bruno Schulz has at least been translated from the Polish by the competent and by and large scrupulous hand of Celina **Wieniewska**. However, by mistitling the English edition of Schulz's first major prose work *The Street of Crocodiles* instead of adopting the original title, *The Cinnamon Shops* (*Sklepy cynamonowe*, 1934), the publishers seriously distort the work's thematic focus. Similarly, the addition of the story 'The Comet' to the original 12 is an unpardonable licence, denying the collection, which can be seen as a loosely structured novel, its proper closure and possibly depriving the work of an allusion to a narrative structure inherited from Jewish sources. And this brings us to one of the two main failings of the Wieniewska version: its failure to resonate, on the local level of diction and imagery especially, the subtly interwoven allusions to Jewish ritual and mythology. The other omission is equally injurious. The Wieniewska translation, for all its attention to the work's visual and narrative logic, remains deaf to the submerged poetry of Schulz's prose. Denied the experience of being affected by Schulz's cadences that shape emotion and meaning as surely as anecdote, especially in their ability to elevate the mundane, the reader might well see in this writer a slightly more lyrical folklorist of the *shtetl*; but if cadence is allowed to shape the writer's paragraphs and if the tone is allowed to move up and down the register, from comic grotesque to the sublime to expirations of a deadly boredom, then the book can be seen for what it is: a 'lower demiurgy' that can, through its sheer poetic energy, transform the world into a 'new Genesis'.

Postwar Polish fiction has been generally well served by a new generation of American translators: Michael **Kandel** (Stanisław Lem), Richard **Lourie** (Alexander Wat, Tadeusz Konwicki), Lillian **Vallee** (Wat, Gombrowicz), and Madeline **Levine** (Miron Białoszewski, Ida Fink, Czesław Miłosz). Although none of the prose works translated by them enjoys the prestige of the three discussed earlier, the English-language careers of their authors are at least safe in the hands of those who work directly from the Polish and who command a knowledge of the literary tradition from which they come.   LI

GOMBROWICZ, WITOLD   Mosbacher, Eric, *Ferdydurke,* London/New York, 1961 [new edn., New York, 1967].

KRASICKI, IGNACY   Hoisington, Thomas H., *The Adventures of Mr Nicholas Wisdom*, Evanston, Ill., 1992.

PASEK, JAN   Leach, Catherine S., *Memoirs of the Polish Baroque*, Berkeley, Calif., 1976.

PRUS, BOLESŁAW (pseud. ALEKSANDER GŁOWACKI)   Welsh, David, *The Doll*, New York, 1972.

SCHULZ, BRUNO   Wieniewska, Celina, *The Street of Crocodiles*, New York, 1963 [Penguin, 1977].

SIENKIEWICZ, HENRYK   Kuniczak, W. S., *The Trilogy* (*With Fire and Sword; The Deluge; Fire in the Steppe*), New York, 1991.

WITKIEWICZ, STANISŁAW IGNACY   Iribarne, Louis, *Insatiability*, rev. edn., Evanston, Ill., 1996.

8. POLISH DRAMA

Several impediments have hindered the translation of Polish drama into English. Foremost among these is the preponderance of verse drama. With a few notable exceptions in the modern period, the 'great tradition' of Polish drama has been the work of poets who took up the dramatic form as masters of poetic form and often as bardic figures in search of a literary form capable of doing justice to a historical violation on a grand scale, namely the loss of nationhood. A poetic idiom did not help to overcome the barrier posed by a somewhat obscure subject-matter dealing with national history.

Poetry affects not only the dramatic idiom. Ever since Mickiewicz, Polish playwrights have given us drama after drama in which violent history is shown as something that can only be engaged in poetic visions, in dreams. This has often dictated a theatrical form that is non-illusionistic, mythopoeic, expressionist *avant la lettre*. For the translator, therefore, both the verbal *and* the stage idiom have seemed intractably beyond transfer, especially into a theatrical culture that is perhaps not accustomed to seeing archetypal figures wrestle on the stage, ineffectively but magnificently, with the demons of history and politics.

i. Sixteenth to Nineteenth Centuries From the drama written before the romantics, only one has ever been translated into English: a precious 16th-c. Renaissance tragedy, *Odprawa posłów greckich* (1578, The Dismissal of the Grecian Envoys) by Poland's great classical poet, Jan Kochanowski. Based on classical models of dramaturgy, until recently this chamber work has been accessible to English readers only in a horribly outdated version published in 1928. That version by George Rapall **Noyes** et al. suffers from an archaic diction and a strained syntax.

Now a new version by Charles S. **Kraszewski**, published as a playscript in a more stageable idiom, exists. Here we have the other extreme: the play's intellectual brilliance and formal elegance are sacrificed to vulgarity. In Chorus I, for example, an ode to youth's folly, the translator has the poet say:

> As it is, they think with gut and cod,
> While reason takes a nod . . .

Lost is the play's tragic irony that arises when a highly polished discourse is deliberately counterpointed by history's at times brutal indifference to poetry.

In the romantic search for a heroic dimension in the face of a historical debacle, the dramatic monologue often served as the chief instrument for dramatizing the hero's reinvention of self that is the condition for action. As handled by poets Adam Mickiewicz, Juliusz Słowacki, and Zygmunt Krasiński, the monologue never becomes so stylized as to turn the act of mythic self-creation into allegory or bathos. Nothing could be more fatal to this drama than to allow the sublime self-dramatizations in verse to lose the gestural qualities of voice. That illusion of voice, especially in the best of these dramas, Mickiewicz's *Forefathers' Eve, Part III*, is managed through a diction and phrasing that is astonishingly supple, natural, lyrical yet magisterial in its range.

The English-speaking world knows this drama—if at all—through translations, by various hands, that have been recently revised or retranslated and collected into one volume (*The Polish Romantic Drama*, 1977). This volume contains two of the famous triad, Mickiewicz's *Dziady, Część III* (1832, Forefathers' Eve, Part III), and *Nieboska komedia* (1833, The Undivine Comedy) by Krasiński (regrettably, Słowacki's *Kordian*, 1834, is omitted in favour of another Słowacki drama). These translations, even though benefiting from emendations by editor-translator Harold B. **Segel**, do little to advance the cause of Polish romantic drama in English. The most grievous damage is done to Mickiewicz's masterpiece. The decision by the original translators (Noyes et al., 1944) to cast the play in rhymed verse effectively strips the speech of any claim to dramatic plausibility. The addition of epithets merely for the sake of cadence; the tendency toward a prolix expansion of line in order to effect a rhyme; the quick recourse to a conventionalized romantic idiom ('I beat my hand upon my bleeding breast' for the poet's 'I bloodied my fists on my own chest')—all diminish the dramatic power of Mickiewicz's line. But an even greater harm is done by the inattention to the poet's careful use of phrasing—in the musical sense—to dramatically shape the monologues into set pieces. In the play's famous monologue known as 'The Great Improvisation', Konrad's poetic speech actually effects the hero's transformation of self into myth. Yet the only English translation by which this archetypal romantic drama is known—a text so seminal as to be called the Polish *Hamlet*—

mostly elevates the discourse to romantic bathos.

ii. Twentieth Century

Between the romantics and the moderns stands the transitional figure of Stanisław Wyspiański. His turn-of-the-century drama in verse *Wesele* (1901, The Wedding) is entirely about a defeated poetry, yet one in which poetry is ironically vindicated on the purely theatrical level. Now, paradoxically, the obstacle posed by the poetic idiom becomes the means of the translator's triumph. The translator would be fully justified in turning the script into what it truthfully was intended to be: a libretto, fully gestural, operatic. To wrest from this quintessential poetic drama a surrealistic but folksy comedy of manners and morals, as the version by Gerard T. **Kapolka** inadvertently does, surrenders the play to the very adversary the drama vehemently opposes: the prose of banality. More, not less, poetic ornament is required here.

The moderns would continue this movement away from poetry toward a more *theatricalized* poetic form. The immediate heir to Wyspiański's theatricality was Stanisław Ignacy Witkiewicz, and in Daniel C. **Gerould** the English reader is fortunate to have a translator who fully grasps the performative, gestural aspect of this playwright's idiom. His renditions of Witkiewicz's stage speech recognize its libretto-like character: a stage speech reduced to one of many formal motifs in a type of theatrical composition borrowed from abstract art. Gerould, appreciating the weight exerted by the verbiage in a Witkiewicz drama, works hard to make it theatrical; he is especially inventive in those dramas where the performance is realized through a deliberate glut of verbal and theatrical signs. *The Shoemakers* (a co-translation, involving, besides Gerould, C. S. **Durer**, of *Szewcy*, 1931–4) is a *tour de force* of linguistic inventiveness aimed, like the play's shifts in style and tonal register, at theatricalizing the language.

Similarly, Witold Gombrowicz's translators have had to face this very Polish kind of intellectualizing in the face of forces hostile to essence. Krystyna **Griffith-Jones** and Catherine **Robins** have succeeded in conveying the satirical, grotesque manner of *Ivona, księżniczka Burgunda* (1935, Ivona, Princess of Burgundia) but, through a somewhat cavalier attention to the playwright's wording, have perhaps diluted the role of the formal imperative that this playwright saw as *the* behavioural drive, an imperative in which language is the main determinant. In the case of *Ślub* (1953, The Marriage), critics praised the translator Louis

Iribarne for playing up the lexical-stylistic shifts used by Gombrowicz to show the manipulation by and of language that allows for various tyrannies in interhuman relations. Yet the didactic element of Gombrowicz's original text, his explication of his 'interhuman church', remains perhaps that play's intractable element, in both its translation and its staging. For the English edition of Gombrowicz's third and last play, *Operetka* (1966, Operetta), Iribarne freely augmented, through rhyme and pastiche, the already libretto-like text on behalf of its operatic stylization, of what is essentially a parody of a parody (the operetta form).

Presumably to overcome this sort of intellectuality and to ensure a more stageable idiom, several of Sławomir Mrożek's major plays have been englished through collaborations involving a native speaker and a professional with some experience with the form, or through outright adaptation. Pre-eminent among these is *Tango* (1964), a classic of the postwar Polish stage and well represented in the European repertory. The 1968 version by Ralph **Manheim** and Teresa **Dzieduszycka** shows a mastery of English idiom, the phrasing is manageable for stage actors, and the discursive passages are left intact. A second 1968 translation by Nicholas **Bethell**, adapted by Tom **Stoppard**, despite emendations aimed at quickening the pace and contemporizing the idiom, is unnecessarily reckless with the playwright's meaning. All too frequently the play's deadly philosophical and political subtext is overlooked in favour of sexual farce.

As in Gombrowicz, much of the scenic dynamic in a Mrożek play depends on the purely linguistic construction as a determinant of action. It is precisely this that is lost, however, in the English translation of *Emigranci* (1974, The Emigrants). While more idiomatic than the version it replaces (by Teresa **Wrona** and Robert **Holman**), the newly authorized stage version by Canadian playwright Henry **Beissel** (who adapted the play from the French rather than from the original Polish) is less sensitive to the purely formal power of language to shape reality. To a far greater extent than in other Mrożek plays written before *The Emigrants*, the pathos derives from a mutual and painful exposure of the myth-making power of language as the latter conceals the primal terrors. Mrożek is not served well in a translation that attempts, through a greater stage realism, to root the motivations in a psychology of alienation.

The last playwright to form the modern canon, the poet Tadeusz Różewicz, continues the Wyspiańskian project of burying the poetic—read: mythic, visionary—in a theatrical form that is, ironically, exquisitely poetic. The early *Kartoteka* (1960, Card Index) and the later *Białe małżeństwo* (1974, Mariage Blanc) both use poetry to bury poetry. Różewicz's translator, the poet Adam **Czerniawski**, handles the paradox well. Różewicz's deliberate flattening of the tone, his use of such devices as pastiche, concatenation, and glossolalia—all devices aimed at bulldozing both stage illusionism and the poetic theatre into the grave of history—are faithfully reproduced in English, yet the translations also know when to be lyrically tender. Often this stylistic levelling is achieved at the expense of a certain naturalness in the handling of English idiom. But this too works to the playwright's advantage: it contributes to the alienating oddity that makes Różewicz's language such a powerful tool on the stage: traces for a carbon-dating of a spent civilization.   LI

GOMBROWICZ, WITOLD Griffith-Jones, Krystyna, and Robins, Catherine, *Yvona, Princess of Burgundia*, New York, London, 1969 · Iribarne, Louis, *The Marriage*, New York, 1969, London, 1970 · *Operetta*, London, 1971.

KOCHANOWSKI, JAN Kraszewski, Charles S., *The Dismissal of the Grecian Envoys*, Studio City, Calif., 1994 · Noyes, George Rapall et al., *Poems*, Berkeley, Calif., 1928.

MICKIEWICZ, ADAM Noyes, George Rapall et al., ed. and tr., *Forefathers' Eve, Part III*, in *Polish Romantic Drama*, ed. Harold B. Segel, Ithaca, NY/London, 1977.

MROŻEK, SŁAWOMIR Beissel, Henry, *The Emigrants*, New York, 1984 · Bethell, Nicholas, adapted by Tom Stoppard, *Tango*, London/New York, 1968 · Manheim, Ralph, and Dzieduszycka, Teresa, *Tango*, New York, 1968 · Wrona, Teresa, with Robert Holman, *Émigrés*, London, 1976.

RÓŻEWICZ, TADEUSZ Czerniawski, Adam, *The Card Index and Other Plays*, New York/London, 1969 · *Mariage Blanc*, London/New York, 1983.

WITKIEWICZ, STANISŁAW IGNACY Gerould, Daniel C., and Durer, C. S., *The Madman and the Nun and Other Plays*, Seattle/London, 1968.

WYSPIAŃSKI, STANISŁAW Kapolka, Gerard T., *The Wedding*, Ann Arbor, Mich., 1990.

9. ROMANIAN

i. Nineteenth Century The earliest example of Romanian literature in English translation, and the first scholarly account of the Romanian language by a Briton—probably a Scot—appears to occur in M. A. **Bruce-Whyte**'s *Histoire des langues romanes et de leur littérature*, published in Paris in 1841. The work was translated into French and published in France because the author was resident there and, according to Bruce-Whyte, the subject interested the French more than the English. In his chapter 'Analyse de la langue valaque', Bruce-Whyte gives a Romanian poem (with a verse translation in English) which he claims came from the mouth of a shepherd. It was in fact a poem written by an 18th-c. Wallachian nobleman, Ienachiţă Văcărescu, and entitled 'Amărâta turturea' (The Moping Dove).

A stimulus to the British public's interest in the peoples and culture of south-eastern Europe was given by the Crimean War. Writers were quick to satisfy the demand for background information, and accounts of journeys made to the area were rapidly printed. It was at this time that Romanian literature received attention through the anthologies of E. C. **Grenville Murray** and Henry **Stanley**. Grenville Murray was an illegitimate son of the second Duke of Buckingham and Chandos, and he combined a diplomatic career with freelance journalism. He describes in his anthology, *Doine, or the National Songs and Legends of Roumania*, how in the summer of 1853 he was convalescing on the island of Prinkipo and passed the time translating Romanian folk-ballads. The anthology contains prose versions of 33 poems, 18 of which are from the collection of folk-poetry gathered by Vasile Alecsandri and published in 1852 and 1853 in Paris. The collection has an appendix with six 'national' airs of Romania arranged for the piano.

More ambitious in scope is Henry Stanley's *Rouman Anthology*, containing the Romanian text of 45 poems with 16 English versions. Eight of the Romanian poems are folk-ballads from Alecsandri's collection; the remainder include 17 original poems by Alecsandri, 9 by Dimitrie Bolintineanu, and 4 by Grigore Alexandrescu. The book, finely printed with vignettes and ornamental borders based on Byzantine manuscript decoration, was, in the words of Stanley's father, 'too dear and too little adapted for the general taste here to have much circulation'.

Of greater impact on the English-speaking world were the collections of Romanian folk-poetry made by the Romanian writer Elena Văcărescu (Hélène Vacaresco). These were translated into

English by Carmen **Sylva**, the pen-name of Elizabeth, the first Queen of Romania, under the title *The Bard of the Dimbovitza: Romanian Folk-Songs Collected from the Peasants*.

ii. Twentieth Century The activity of Marcu Beza, a member of the Romanian legation in London and lecturer in Romanian at the University of London's School of Slavonic and East European Studies from 1919 to 1930, exerted a major influence on the translation of Romanian literature into English. His own *Doda: A Study of Macedonian Life* appeared in Lucy **Byng**'s sensitive translation in 1925, and he encouraged her also to translate one of the few Romanian novels of the 19th c., Duiliu Zamfirescu's *Viaţa la ţară* (1894, Life in the Country) which appeared in 1926 under the title *Sasha*. In 1930, Liviu Rebreanu's novel *Pădurea Spânzuraţilor* (1922, The Forest of the Hanged), based partly on his brother's experience as a Transylvanian Romanian in the Austro-Hungarian army during World War I who attempts to desert to his fellow nationals, is caught and hanged, was vividly translated by Alice **Wise**. Remarkably, in the same year appeared in London *Poems of Mihail Eminescu*, translated by the suffragette E. Sylvia **Pankhurst** with the help of I. O. **Stefanovici**, who had already translated some Mark Twain into Romanian and was working on Emerson's essays. Pankhurst discovered in Eminescu (1850–89) a kindred spirit in dislike of contemporary decadence and social injustice, and she sent her translations to her friend George Bernard Shaw. His comment in his preface to the volume, 'the translation is astonishing and outrageous: it carried me away', was suitably ambiguous.

Nothing of note from Romanian literature was translated during World War II. The imposition of Communist rule in Romania in 1945 and the consequent subordination of writers to the Party's dictates meant that only literature which satisfied the approved literary method of 'socialist realism' could appear. Mihail Sadoveanu's *Mitrea Cocor* (1949) was a notorious example of the genre. The picaresque adventures of the eponymous peasant hero of the novel and the realization of his ambitions after the Soviet occupation of Romania in 1944 found their way into an anonymous English translation of 1953 with a preface by Jack Lindsay. Equally subservient in his early work to 'socialist realism' was Petru Dumitriu. The first two volumes of his trilogy *Boiarii* (1955–6, The Boyars) were published in spirited translations by E. **Hyams** and Norman **Denny** respectively as *Family Jewels* and *The Prodigals*. The novels chronicle, in Galsworthy manner,

the fortunes of a landed family over the years 1860–1948.

As Romania began to assert its autonomy from the Soviet Union in the early 1960s, so contacts with the West were developed. These treaties opened the door for British and American scholars and writers to visit Romania and meet Romanian colleagues. Until the overthrow of Communist rule in 1989, this traffic was preponderantly one-way, with Romanian writers often finding it irritatingly difficult to secure a passport from their authorities; but their work became increasingly better-known to the English-speaking world through the efforts of a number of dedicated translators and publishers. In Britain, the publishing activity of Peter Jay and his Anvil Press, Brenda Walker and her Forest Books, and Neil Astley at Bloodaxe Books in Newcastle have done much to promote a familiarity with contemporary Romanian writing through authors such as Ana Blandiana, Nina Cassian, Daniela Crâsnaru, Mircea Dinescu, Paul Goma, and Nichita Stănescu. The last of these is a unique voice in contemporary poetry, exploring the relationship between self and language. The representative selection by Petru **Popescu** and Peter **Jay** is the first, and still the most eloquent, translation of these difficult compositions. By contrast, Marin Sorescu's verse ironizes the human condition in a simple language whose accessibility lends itself easily to translation. The universality of his work is reflected in its relative popularity with translators. The volumes of poetry and drama translated by Andrea **Deletant** and Brenda **Walker**, and of verse by John **Deane**, catch the colloquiality of Sorescu's language.

At the same time, English speakers were introduced to many of the accomplished writers of the interwar years. The creative richness of this period is illustrated in the poetry of Tudor Arghezi, sensitively translated by Michael **Impey** and Brian **Swann** in 1976, in the Symbolist verse of George Bacovia, skilfully rendered by Peter Jay in a sadly little-known translation in 1980, and in the artistry of Mircea Eliade's storytelling, expertly conveyed by Mac Linscott **Ricketts**. These translations of individual writers have been supplemented by anthologies, the first of which to appear in Britain and the United States was edited by Roy **MacGregor-Hastie** in 1969 under the auspices of UNESCO. This anthology of 20th-c. Romanian poetry was the first such collection to be published in Britain, and contains a judicious selection of verse in accurate translation. *An Anthology of Contemporary Romanian Poetry*, translated by Andrea Deletant and Brenda Walker, is distinguished by its attempt to retain the metre and harmony of the originals, while the publication in 1987 of *The Biggest Egg in the World*, versions of Sorescu by poets including Seamus **Heaney**, Michael **Longley**, and Paul **Muldoon**, was evidence of a growing association between Romania and Ireland. This was strengthened by John Fairleigh's edition of contemporary Romanian verse in vibrant translations by Irish poets, Heaney and Muldoon being joined by Derek **Mahon** and others. This volume is virtually a work of creative literature in its own right.

DD

ANTHOLOGIES   Deletant, Andrea, and Walker, Brenda, *Anthology of Contemporary Romanian Poetry*, London, 1984, Chester Springs, Penn., 1990 · *Silent Voices: An Anthology of Contemporary Romanian Poetry*, London, 1986 · Fairleigh, John, *When the Tunnels Meet*, Newcastle upon Tyne, 1996 · Grenville Murray, E. C., *Doine, or the National Songs and Legends of Roumania*, Hertford, UK, 1854 · MacGregor-Hastie, Roy, *Anthology of Contemporary Rumanian Poetry*, London/Chester Springs, Penn., 1969 · Stanley, Henry, *Rouman Anthology*, Hertford, UK, 1856 · Sylva, Carmen, *The Bard of the Dimbovitza: Romanian Folk-Songs Collected from the Peasants*, London, 1892 [several reps.].

ARGHEZI, TUDOR   Impey, Michael, and Swann, Brian, *Selected Poems*, Princeton, NJ, 1976.

BACOVIA, GEORGE   Jay, Peter, *Plumb: Lead*, Bucharest, 1980.

BEZA, MARCU   Byng, Lucy, *Doda: A Study of Macedonian Life*, London, 1925 · *Sasha*, London, 1926.

BLANDIANA, ANA   Alexe, Gheorge, *Don't Be Afraid of Me: Collected Poems*, Detroit, 1985 · Jay, Peter, and Cristofovici, Anca, *The Hour of Sand: Selected Poems 1969–89*, London, 1990.

CARAGIALE, ION LUCA   Knight, Frida, *The Lost Letter and Other Plays*, London, 1956 · Tappe, Eric, *Sketches and Stories*, Cluj-Napoca, 1979.

CASSIAN, NINA   Deletant, Andrea, and Walker, Brenda, *Call Yourself Alive: The Love Poems of Nina Cassian*, London, 1988; Chester Springs, Penn., 1989 · Schiff, Laura, *Lady of Miracles*, Berkeley, Calif., 1983 · Smith, William Jay, *Life Sentence: Selected Poems*, London/New York, 1990 · Walker, Brenda, with Nina Cassian, *Cheerleader for a Funeral*, London, 1992.

CRÂSNARU, DANIELA   Adcock, Fleur, *Letters from Darkness*, Oxford/New York, 1991.

DINESCU, MIRCEA   Deletant, Andrea, and Walker, Brenda, *Exile on a Peppercorn: The Poetry of Mircea Dinescu*, London/Boston, 1985.

DOINAŞ ŞTEFAN AUGUSTIN   Jay, Peter, and Nemoianu, Virgil, *Alibi and Other Poems*, London, 1975.

DUMITRIU, PETRU   Denny, Norman, *The Prodigals*, London, 1962 · Hyams, E., *Family Jewels*, London, 1961.

ELIADE, MIRCEA   Ricketts, Mac Linscott, *Youth without Youth*, Columbus, OH/London, 1989 · Ricketts, Mac Linscott, and Stevenson, Mary Park, *The Forbidden Forest*, Notre Dame, Ind., 1978 · Stevenson, Mary Park, *The Old Man and the Bureaucrats*, Notre Dame, 1979.

EMINESCU, MIHAI   MacGregor-Hastie, Roy, *The Last Romantic: Mihail Eminescu*, Iowa City, 1972 · Pankhurst, E. Sylvia, *Poems of Mihail Eminescu*, London, 1930.

GOMA, PAUL   Clark, Angela, *My Childhood at the Gate of Unrest*, London/Los Angeles, 1990.

POPESCU, PETRU   Telford, Carol, Jay, Peter, and Popescu, Petru, *Burial of the Vine*, London, 1975.

REBREANU, LIVIU   Grandjean, P., and Hartauer, S., *The Uprising*, London, 1964 · Hillard, A., *Ion*, London, 1965 · Wise, A. V., *The Forest of the Hanged*, London, 1967.

SADOVEANU, MIHAIL   anon., *Mitrea Cocor*, London, 1953.

SORESCU, MARIN   Deane, John F., *The Youth of Don Quixote*, Dublin, 1987 · Deletant, Andrea, and Walker, Brenda, *Let's Talk About the Weather . . . and Other Poems*, London/Boston, 1985 · *The Thirst of the Salt Mountain: A Trilogy of Plays*, London/Boston, 1985 · Deletant, Dennis, *Vlad Dracula the Impaler: A Play*, London, 1987 · Dragnea, Gabriela, Friebert, Stuart, and Varga, Adriana, *Hands Behind My Back: Selected Poems*, Oberlin, OH, 1991 · Hamburger, Michael, *Selected Poems, 1965–1973*, Newcastle upon Tyne, 1983 · Heaney, Seamus et al., *The Biggest Egg in the World*, Newcastle upon Tyne, 1987.

STĂNESCU, NICHITA   Carlson, Thomas C., and Poenaru, Vasile, *Bas-Relief with Heroes: Selected Poems, 1960–1982*, Memphis, Tenn., 1988 · Popescu, Petru, and Jay, Peter, *The Still Unborn about the Dead*, Iowa City, 1974, London, 1975.

SEE ALSO   Bruce-Whyte, M. A., *Histoire des langues romanes et de leur littérature*, Paris, 1841 · Carlton, C. M., and Perry, T. A., *Romanian Poetry in English Translation: An Annotated Bibliography and Census of 249 Poets in English (1740–1989)*, supplement to *Miorita: A Journal of Romanian Studies*, 12 (1988) · Steinberg, J., *Introduction to Rumanian Literature*, New York, 1966.

10. SERBO-CROAT

i. Introduction Translation of works in Serbo-Croat into English has been haphazard. Three factors may be identified as playing a role: the general cultural climate (as in the case of 19th-c. interest); political factors seen by publishers as potentially favouring sales; and the commitment of individuals—both translators and publishers—to a particular author. Investigation reveals a substantial amount of translation, as shown by the dedicated work of Professor Vasa D. Mihailovich of the University of North Carolina, who has initiated an invaluable series of bibliographies.

It goes without saying that the quality of these translations varies greatly, and that many have simply informative value. Nevertheless, there is a striking contrast between the amount of material that has been translated and the degree to which individual writers are known in the English-speaking world. Even a writer of the substance of Ivo Andrić, who was awarded the Nobel Prize for Literature in 1961, is barely known—although he has fared better since the war in his native Bosnia drew new attention to his work. One of the finest contemporary European writers, Danilo Kiš, is well known in Europe, particularly in France, but unfamiliar to most English readers, despite some excellent translations of his works.

It is interesting and perhaps surprising that one or two contemporary poets have had a relatively greater success, for all the intrinsic difficulties of translating poetry: in the case of Vasko Popa and Ivan V. Lalić this may be explained in part by the dedication and quality of their respective translators, but also perhaps because the audience for translated poetry is a restricted, self-selected one.

The main difficulties in translating from Serbo-Croat into English are structural and cultural. On the one hand conventions of word order and verbal systems differ considerably; on the other, literature in the Yugoslav lands has often had a clearly political function, and many references are hard to convey without copious footnotes.

ii. The Oral Tradition The first aspect of literature in Serbo-Croat to receive the attention of the outside world was the oral tradition. In the climate of the romantic movement, when thinkers such as Herder saw the 'common people' as embodying the true spirit of a nation, popular literature became fashionable at the end of the 18th and beginning of the 19th c. A traditional song, 'Hasanaginica' ('The Wife of Hasan-aga'), published by an Italian

traveller, Alberto Fortis, in 1778, caught the attention of Goethe, who made his own version of the song. The added weight of Goethe's name guaranteed a new impetus: the song was 'translated' into many European languages, including a rather poor version by Sir Walter **Scott**. In the course of the 19th c. some 15 newspaper articles were devoted to the South Slav oral tradition, illustrated by copious examples, and seven volumes of translations.

There was a further period of interest when Serbia was in the news during World War I. In the 1930s two American scholars, Milman **Parry** and Albert **Lord**, trying to explain the genesis of Homeric epic, collected songs in Serbo-Croat-speaking areas and evolved from them their 'oral-formulaic' theory of oral composition. Of the most recent collections, that of Anne **Pennington** and Peter **Levi** is of interest, as Levi has endeavoured to create a language to convey the stylization of the original songs, while Vasa **Mihailovich** has attempted to reproduce their rhythms; the translations of John **Matthias** have been widely praised and the latest collection, translated by Geoffrey **Locke**, contains some of the most readable versions yet made.

iii. Written Literature One of the first important works to be translated from Serbo-Croat into English in the 20th c. was *Gorski vijenac* (1847, The Mountain Wreath) by the 19th c. Montenegrin poet Petar Petrović Njegoš. The translator was John **Wiles** and the work has acquired a special patina with the passing of time. Vasa Mihailovich's 1986 version of the poem is more accessible to contemporary readers. Njegoš's philosophical poem, *Luča mikrokozma* (1845, The Ray of the Microcosm), was translated into English at much the same time by the Serbian scholar Ana **Savić-Rebac**, who made versions in several European languages.

There were sporadic individual efforts of this kind in the first half of the 20th c., but systematic work did not get under way until the period of Communist rule, 1945–90, when it was fostered by the government in order to increase awareness abroad of the presence of Yugoslavia on the world stage. This work was initially carried out by native speakers of Serbo-Croat, with varying degrees of success. Later on, native speakers of English, who happened to find themselves in Yugoslavia, began to be involved. Important work was also done by exiles from Yugoslavia, particularly those living in the United States. As time went on, the activity became increasingly professional and translations of literary merit began to be produced.

The first systematic approach to the translation of Yugoslav literatures into English dates from the 1960s, when the award of the Nobel Prize for Literature to Ivo Andrić in 1961 gave the activity added momentum. Two major works by Andrić appeared in the 1950s, *Travnička hronika* (1958, Bosnian Story) and the great panoramic novel of Bosnian history, *Na Drini ćuprija* (1959, The Bridge over the Drina), and other works appeared in the 1960s. New translations of several works were published in 1992, to mark the centenary of his birth. The importance of his account of historical processes in the region was recognized during the 1992–5 wars, and his works became recommended reading for British officers serving in Bosnia. A writer of equivalent stature from Croatia, Miroslav Krleža, also began to be translated in the 1960s, *Povratak Filipa Latinowicza* (1932, The Return of Philip Latinovicz) being the best known of his works in English.

In the course of the 1970s and 1980s, most of the significant poets and prose writers in the Serbo-Croatian language were translated into English. Perhaps the greatest success was achieved by the poet Vasko Popa, with some 10 volumes including a selection published by Penguin in 1969 and the substantial *Collected Poems* published by the Anvil Press in 1996. Popa has been very well translated by Anne Pennington in England and the poet Charles **Simic** in the United States. His work has been widely admired, among others by Ted Hughes, who wrote the introduction to the Penguin volume. While full of resonances in the original, Popa's diction and phrasing are deceptively simple and thus rewarding for the translator, particularly for those like Pennington and Simic who understand so many of the references.

The other poet to have achieved a real presence in the English-speaking world is Ivan V. Lalić, with American versions again by Simic and British versions of all Lalić's collections admirably translated by Francis **Jones**. Both men are professional, creative individuals whose translations read like poems in their own right.

As far as prose is concerned the picture is disheartening: many works which achieve prominence in their own language are translated into English, indeed there is sometimes competition among publishers for the rights. But, even where the publisher invests considerable effort in promoting a work, for the most part it has little impact. A case in point is Milorad Pavić's *Hazarski rečnik* (1988, A Dictionary of the Khazars), which was a best-seller in several European countries.

Even the wars in former Yugoslavia have not really changed the situation: it seems that the British and American reading public prefer to read their own journalists' impressions rather than works by writers from the region. Recently translated works include the Serbian classic *Seobe* (1929, Migrations), by Milos Crnjanski (Tsernianski in the English translation), who lived much of his life in exile in London and works by the Croatian writers Slavenka Drakulić and Dubravka Ugrešić from Croatia, and, Slobodan Selenić, and Vladimir Arsenijević from Serbia. Several works by Bosnian writers have been translated, including an anthology of poets from Bosnia and a collection of stories by Isak Samokovlija. It remains the case that there is a wealth of interesting material translated from Serbo-Croat, published usually in very short print runs and languishing in libraries, waiting to be discovered by the more adventurous reader.

ECH

ORAL TRADITION   Goy, E. D., *Zelen bor/A Green Pine: An Anthology of Love Poems from the Oral Poetry of Serbia, Bosnia and Hercegovina*, Belgrade, 1990 · Locke, Geoffrey N. W., *The Serbian Epic Ballads: An Anthology*, Belgrade, 1997 · Matthias, John, and Vuckovic, Vladeta, *The Battle of Kosovo*, Athens, OH, 1987 · Mihailovich, Vasa D., and Holton, Milne, *Songs of the Serbian People*, Pittsburgh, 1997 · Pennington, Anne, and Levi, Peter, *Marko the Prince: Serbo-Croat Heroic Songs*, London, 1984.

ANDRIĆ, IVO   Edwards, Lovett, *The Bridge over the Drina*, London, 1959 · Hawkesworth, Celia, *The Days of the Consuls*, London, 1992; rep. as *Bosnian Chronicle*, London, 1996 · *The Damned Yard* [and short stories by various translators], London, 1992 · with Andrew Harvey, *Conversation with Goya; Bridges; Signs*, London, 1992 · Hitrec, Joseph, *Bosnian Chronicle*, New York, 1963 · *The Pasha's Concubine* [selected stories], New York, 1968, London, 1969 · Johnstone, Kenneth, *Bosnian Story*, London, 1958 · *Devil's Yard*, London, 1962 · Willen, Drenka, *The Vizier's Elephant* [selected stories], New York, 1962.

ARSENIJEVIĆ, VLADIMIR   Hawkesworth, Celia, *In the Hold*, London, 1996.

CRNJANSKI, [TSERNIANSKI] MILOŠ   Heim, Michael Henry, *Migrations*, New York, 1994.

DRAKULIĆ, SLAVENKA   anon., *Marble Skin*, 1995 · Bursac, Ellen Elias, *Holograms of Fear*, New York, 1991 · Pribićević-Zorić, Christina, *The Taste of a Man*, London, 1997.

KIŠ, DANILO   Hannaher, William, *Garden, Ashes*, London, 1985 · Heim, Michael Henry, *The Encyclopedia of the Dead*,

New York, 1989 · Mannheim, Ralph, *Hourglass*, New York, 1990 · Mikić-Mitchell, Duška, *A Tomb for Boris Davidovich*, New York, 1980.

KRLEŽA, MIROSLAV   Depolo, Zora, *On the Edge of Reason*, London, 1959 · *The Return of Philip Latinovicz*, London, 1959, New York, 1969 · various, *The Cricket Beneath the Waterfall and Other Stories*, New York, 1972.

LALIĆ, IVAN   Jones, Francis R., *The Works of Love*, London, 1981 · *Last Quarter*, London, 1987 · *Passionate Measure*, Dublin, 1989 · *A Rusty Needle*, London, 1996 · *Fading Contact*, London, 1997 · Simic, Charles, *Fire Gardens*, New York, 1970 · *Roll Call of Mirrors*, Middletown, Conn., 1988.

NJEGOŠ, PETAR PETROVIĆ   Mihailovich, Vasa D., *The Mountain Wreath*, Ervine, NC, 1986.

PAVIĆ, MILORAD   Pribićević-Zorić, Christina, *The Dictionary of the Khazars*, New York, 1988, London, 1989 · *Landscape Painted with Tea*, New York, 1990.

POPA, VASKO   Pennington, Anne, *Selected Poems*, Harmondsworth, 1969 [Penguin] · *Earth Erect*, London, 1973 · *Collected Poems 1943–1976*, Manchester/New York, 1978 · *The Blackbirds' Field*, Oxford, 1979 · with Andrew Harvey, *The Golden Apple*, London, 1980 · *Collected Poems* (rev. and expanded by Francis Jones), London, 1997 · Simic, Charles, *The Little Box*, Washington, DC, 1970 · *Homage to the Lone Wolf: Selected Poems*, Oberlin, 1979.

SAMOKOVLIJA, ISAK   Hawkesworth, Celia, and Pribićević-Zorić, Christina, *Tales of Old Sarajevo*, London, 1997.

SELENIĆ, SLOBODAN   Petrović, Jelena, *Premeditated Murder*, London, 1996.

UGREŠIĆ, DUBRAVKA   Hawkesworth, Celia, *Have a Nice Day*, London, 1995 · *The Culture of Lies*, London, 1998 · *The Museum of Unconditional Surrender*, London, 1998 · Hawkesworth, Celia, and Heim, Michael Henry, *The Jaws of Life*, London, 1991 · Heim, Michael Henry, *Fording the Stream of Consciousness*, London, 1990.

SEE ALSO   Mihailovich, V. D., *A Comprehensive Bibliography of Yugoslav Literature in English*, Columbus, OH, 1984; supplements 1988, 1992.

11. UKRAINIAN

Since its medieval antecedent Kyivan (Kievan) Rus' fell to the Tartars of Batu in 1240, Ukraine has enjoyed only brief periods of independence, being dominated by the Polish-Lithuanian commonwealth, the Russian empire, the Austro-Hungarian empire, Poland, and the USSR. This situation resulted in the fact that, besides publications in the old Ukrainian language, works of old Ukrainian literature also appeared in Polish, Russian, Latin, and German. Thereafter while the first literary work in modern Ukrainian was published at the end of the 18th c. by I. Kotliarevs'kyi, many writers who were Ukrainian by birth still wrote only or also in other languages, such as Russian, German, Polish, and French. In this article only English translations of literary works written in Ukrainian (old and modern) or in its predecessor—Old Church Slavonic with elements of the Kyivan Rus' vernacular—will be considered.

Ukrainian literary works have reached the English-speaking world through three main channels shaped by different ideologies. One was created by Ukrainian émigré communities living in English-speaking countries since the end of the 19th c. and, in large numbers, since the end of World War II. Ukrainian communities in the USA, Canada, Britain, and Australia have promoted works of Ukrainian literature through their publishing houses and journals, with the aim of demonstrating to the world Ukrainian cultural distinctiveness from Russia and Poland at a time when free creativity was suppressed by the Soviet regime in Ukraine.

This publishing activity was regarded as anti-Soviet by the USSR authorities, and several Moscow and Kyiv (Kiev) publishing houses and journals were ordered to start printing in English works of Ukrainian classics and writers regarded as 'progressive' by the regime, with the aim of carrying out what Soviet jargon described as 'counter-propaganda activities', fighting 'Ukrainian bourgeois nationalism' and promoting the 'achievements of the power of the Soviets'. Finally, some translations from Ukrainian were done by individual English-language translators (often in collaboration with Ukrainian intellectuals) with the emphasis on their aesthetic rather than political values.

Among old Ukrainian literary works of the Kyivan Rus' period written in Old Church Slavonic with elements of the vernacular, *Slovo o polku Ihorevi* (late 12th c., The Tale of Ihor's Campaign) has been most widely rendered in English (17 translations, according to R. Zorivchak). In 1898 it was translated in New York by J. A. **Joffe** as *The Song of Prince Igor's Band*. W. **Kirkconnell** and C. H. **Andrusyshen** published their translation, *The Tale of the Campaign of Ihor*, in 1963 in the anthology *The Ukrainian Poets, 1189–1962*, which encompasses eight centuries of the development of Ukrainian

219

literature. Among other translated works of early Ukrainian literature are *Slovo o zakoni i blahodati* (Sermon on Law and Grace), written by Ilarion between 1037 and 1050 and translated by N. L. **Icker**, Nestor's 12th-c. *Povist' vremennykh lit* (The Tale of Bygone Years), translated by S. H. **Cross** and O. P. **Sherbowitz-Wetzor**, and Simon's and Polikarp's *Kyivo-Pechers'kyi pateryk* (1215–30, The Paterik of the Kyivan Caves Monastery), translated by M. **Heppell**.

Works of Ukrainian baroque literature written in old literary Ukrainian are under-represented in English. An untitled poem of Hryhorii Skovoroda (1722–94) was translated by Vera **Rich** in 1994. The Easter drama *Slovo o zburenniu pekla*, published anonymously in the late 17th c., was first translated by I. **Makaryk** as *About the Harrowing of Hell* in 1989.

Among 19th c. Ukrainian writers, Taras Shevchenko was the first to be translated into English and the one who has been represented most fully. A few lines from his poem *Kavkaz* (1845, The Caucasus) were translated in *The Alaska Herald* by A. **Honcharenko** (A. Humnyts'kyi, 1832–1916) as early as 1868. In 1964 all the Ukrainian poems of Shevchenko were published in a translation by C. H. **Andrusyshen** and W. **Kirkconnell**. Among other translators of Shevchenko's poetry are W. R. **Morfill** (1834–1909), E. L. **Voynich** (1864–1960), C. A. **Manning**, J. **Weir**, and V. **Rich**.

Translations of other Ukrainian 19th-c. and 20th-c. classics include Ivan Franko's poems and novels, Lesia Ukraiinka's poems and plays, Marko Vovchok's *Marusia* (1871) translated in the 1880s by C. W. **Cyr** from the French version co-authored by P.-J. Stahl, and novels by Mykhailo Kotsiubyns'kyi.

The best Ukrainian 20th-c. prose is represented in translation by, among others, Volodymyr Vynnychenko, Mykola Khvyliovyi, Valerian Pidmohyl'nyi, Ivan Bahrianyi, and Valerii Shevchuk. Among the best 20th-c. poets, those better represented in English are Pavlo Tychyna, B. I. Antonych, Lina Kostenko, Vasyl' Holoborod'ko, and Ivan Drach, while drama is represented by Mykola Kulish and Ivan Kocherha.

The most significant recent translation of work published in Ukraine in the 1980s and 1990s is the anthology *From Three Worlds: New Ukrainian Writing*. The authors included in it are united in their rejection of political struggle by means of literature. A modernist, apolitical, and aesthetic approach to literature is what representatives of the 1960s literary movement Valerii Shevchuk and Vasyl Holoborod'ko have in common with Evhen Pashkovs'kyi and Oleksandr Irvanets', who

belong to the following generation. The motif of young Ukrainians seeking a niche for a 'normal' life free of politics, despite constant provocation of such political involvement by the dying Soviet communist regime, is present in Volodymyr Dibrova's 1990 short stories *Pisni Bitlz* (translated as *Beatles Songs* by J. **Brasfield** and P. H. **Davies**) and, especially, Iurii Andrukhovych's 1989 *Sviato aktyvnoho spohliadannia* (translated as *Observation Duty* by C. M. **Sochocky** and G. **Parker**). To Andrukhovych's young hero, who returns home wounded after having had to fight in Afghanistan on the Russian side, both sides of the conflict are foreign. However, he is back in Ukraine not to campaign but to observe normal everyday life. According to young Ukrainian writers, this normality comes from the West, where they look for their inspiration, and certainly not from Russia. This very important point Andrukhovych, Dibrova, the poet Viktor Neborak, and others often stress in the works published in the anthology. Andrukhovych uses all possible external channels of information, trying to access the 'civilized world' while avoiding restrictions imposed by the Russian ideological machine on his country. Similarly, Dibrova's secondary-school pupils listen to the BBC World Service charts and are crazy about the Beatles and other western bands, whose songs they record on 'thick old X-ray films . . . at the . . . record studio over on Red Army Street, not far from the public baths' (p. 24).

Translators, however, often miss the authors' point when rendering passages on the young generation of Ukrainians' western orientation at the expense of Russian culture, perhaps because this point clashes with the intention of the publisher. The anthology is part of the New Russian Writing series which is marketed for English-language readers mainly interested in new developments in *Russian* culture. Therefore, the intention of the publisher is to promote Russian culture and not to deny it, as some authors and their heroes represented in the collection seem to do. The publisher clearly believed that Ukrainian literature could only be accepted by the reader of the translation through its association with Russian. Hence translators sometimes found Russian connotations where they did not exist in the original; Sochocky and Parker at one point even explain the Ukrainian word *kurkul* to the English-language reader through the Russian *kulak* (p. 224). The emphasis of the original on young intellectuals' tendency to avoid Russian cultural sources and look for inspiration westwards is often obscured in the translation. For example, the detective novel which

Andrukhovych's hero reads *in Polish*, because the author is anxious to point to his ability to access information in a foreign language other than Russian, becomes a 'Polish detective novel' in translation (p. 214). In general the anthology is lasting evidence of the fact that, as had often been the case in the past, five years after Ukraine's independence Russian culture was still a channel through which Ukrainian culture could pass to be accepted by the Anglo-Saxon world.   OS

ANTHOLOGIES   Andrusyshen, C. H., and Kirkconnell, W., *The Ukrainian Poets, 1189–1962*, Toronto, 1963 · Franklin, Simon, *Sermons and Rhetoric in Kievan Rus'*, Cambridge, Mass., 1989 · Hogan, Ed, ed., *From Three Worlds: New Ukrainian Writing*, Boston, Mass., 1996.

ANTONYCH, BOHDAN IHOR   Rudman, M., Nemser, P., and Boychuk, B., *Square of Angels*, Ann Arbor, Mich., 1977.

BAHRIANYI, IVAN   Davidovich, S., and Gregorovich, A., *The Hunters and the Hunted*, Toronto, 1954.

DRACH, IVAN   Kunitz, S. et al., *Orchard Lamps*, New York, 1978.

FRANKO, IVAN   Hnidyj, A., *Moses and Other Poems*, New York, 1987 · Weir, J., and Dalway, C., *Stories*, Kyiv, 1972.

HOLOBOROD'KO, VASYL'   Stefaniuk, Myrosia, *Icarus With Butterfly Wings and Other Poems*, Toronto, 1991.

ILARION   Ickner, N. L., 'Sermon on Law and Grace', *Comitatas*, 9 (1978).

KHVYL'OVYI, MYKOLA   Luckyj, George S. N., *Stories from the Ukraine*, New York, 1960.

KOCHERHA, IVAN   May, W., *Yaroslav the Wise*, Kyiv, 1982.

KOSTENKO, LINA   Naydan, Michael M., *Selected Poetry: Wanderings of the Heart*, New York, 1990.

KOTSIUBYNS'KYI, MYKHAILO   Carynnyk, M., *Shadows of Forgotten Ancestors*, Littleton, Colo., 1981.

KULISH, MYKOLA   Luckyj, G. S. N., and Luckyj, M., *Sonata Pathetique*, Littleton, Colo., 1975.

NESTOR   Cross, S. H., and Sherbowitz-Wetzor, O. P., *The Russian Primary Chronicle: Laurentian Text*, Cambridge, Mass., 1953.

PIDMOHYL'NYI, VALERIAN   Luckyj, G. S. N., and Luckyj, M., *A Little Touch of Drama*, Littleton, Colo., 1972.

SIMON AND POLIKARP   Heppell, M., *The Paterik of the Kievan Caves Monastery*, Cambridge, Mass., 1989.

SHEVCHENKO, TARAS   Andrusyshen, C. H., and Kirkconnell, W., *The Poetical Works of Taras Shevchenko, the Kobzar*, Toronto, 1964 · Voynich, Ethel Lilian, *Six Lyrics From the Ruthenian of Taras Shevchenko . . .*, London, 1911.

SHEVCHUK, VALERII   Kholmogorova, Victoria, *The Meek Shall Inherit . . .*, Kyiv, 1989.

SKOVORODA, HRYHORII   Rich, Vera, 'Little Bird, Whose Flanks Shine Goldly . . .', *Ukrainian Review*, 4 (1994).

TYCHYNA, PAVLO   Various translators, *Selected Poetry*, Kyiv, 1987.

UKRAIINKA, LESIA   Rich, Vera, *Lesya Ukrainka*, Toronto, 1968.

VOVCHOK, MARKO [AND STAHL, P.-J.]   Cyr, C. W., *Maroussia: A Maid of Ukraine*, New York, 1890.

VYNNYCHENKO, VOLODYMYR   Prokopov, Theodore S., *Selected Short Stories*, Wakefield, NH, 1991.

f. East Asian Languages

1. CHINESE: INTRODUCTION

Translations of classical or traditional Chinese literature have been more influential on and familiar to an English-language readership than works of the modern or contemporary period, and the entries here focus on renderings from the substantial body of that literature into English. There is no attempt to be exhaustive in what follows; the aim is rather to provide some signposts which indicate the shape Chinese literature has taken in English, concentrating on the three principal literary genres of poetry, the essay, and the classical novel.

The standard introduction for many years has been *An Anthology of Chinese Literature*, edited by Cyril **Birch**, which appeared in two volumes, spanning Chinese literature from early times to the present day. This anthology, which the editor in his introduction calls 'the most comprehensive in the English language', incorporated poetry, drama, Buddhist allegory, historical writing, autobiographical writing, letters, essays, and excerpts from two classical novels, as well as a section on modern literature. There is, of course, much more to Chinese literature. Two other genres for which significant numbers of English translations exist are drama and short fiction. Sources for these are given in the bibliography.

Anthologies of Chinese literature in English do not restrict themselves to materials which would be considered purely literary in a western sense. The separation of literature from historical and philosophical writings in the Chinese tradition is a relatively new phenomenon. The ideal of the male educated élite, the literati, was a combination of government official, poet, and philosopher. Reflecting this broader understanding, the prose volume of *Gems of Chinese Literature* by Herbert

A. **Giles** (1845–1935) [see II.f.2.i; II.f.3.ii] included pieces from the philosophers Confucius and Mencius. Birch includes a section titled 'Zhuangzi (Chuang Tzu) and Others on Death', as well as early historical writings. What is presented here and in similar volumes is a broadly defined corpus of material based in large part on a received tradition taken from Chinese sources, a compendium of the literary heritage of educated Chinese through the ages, albeit with some exceptions and varying emphases.

In the late 1960s and early 1970s, perhaps in line with social trends and popular educational theories of the times, the emphasis for anthologists of Chinese literature in English had become subjective and experiential. As William McNaughton put it in his introduction, the aim of *Chinese Literature: An Anthology from the Earliest Times to the Present* (1974) was to 'help its reader to feel what it was like to be inside a Chinese skin in 500 BC . . . 300 AD . . . 1890 . . . 1949 . . . and beyond'. The approach reflects a particular western inclination in seeking to understand cultures beyond its own; the goal, at least as expressed, is to meet the other culture on its own terms.

Entering the 1990s, we begin to see the way in which new theories of translation and academic trends, particularly American academic trends, influence translation practice and anthology choice. The (Chinese) canon is challenged on its own ground. The introduction to the *Columbia Anthology of Traditional Chinese Literature* states: 'This collection contains many exciting pieces never published in English and others scarcely known even in China, but richly deserving of fuller recognition.' The point of view is very much centred on what Chinese literature will be in English and on the needs of the English-language readership: 'Anthologists and literary historians who emphasize only standard genres and élite writers are responsible for perpetuating a false image of what Chinese literature might be for our own age.'

Since the early 1950s, the Foreign Languages Press in Beijing has published translations of Chinese literature in other languages, including English. The magazine *Chinese Literature* and series of anthologies, full-length translations, and excerpts from a wide range of literature, classical as well as modern, are sold in hotels, tourist spots, and dedicated bookshops all over China; these translations have certainly played a role in the popular conception of the literature held by English-speaking readers. The work of the prolific translation team of Gladys and Hsien-yi **Yang** has greatly contributed to the reputation of these titles.

This discussion would not be complete without some mention of the many and influential translations of philosophical works. Since the translation by the missionary-translator James **Legge** (1815–97) of the classic works known as the *Four Books,* and later efforts in collaboration with the Chinese scholar **Wang** Tao (1828–97), philosophical works have been as influential in English translation as the strictly literary corpus. For a generation of readers in the 1960s and 1970s, the wisdom of the East was embodied in the thoughts of Confucius, Laozi (Lao Tzu), and Zhuangzi (Chuang Tzu). The two-volume *Sources of Chinese Tradition*, edited by William Theodore de Bary, Wing-tsit Chan, and Burton **Watson**, was standard fare, while single-volume translations of the philosophers, both of

the so called Great Tradition (mainstream Confucian) and of the little traditions (prominently Buddhist and Taoist) by Arthur **Waley**, Watson, D. C. **Lau**, and others were also popular texts for the cultural awakening to the East of a new generation. A special place on both a scholarly and popular level must be accorded to the various English translations of the *Yijing* (I Ching), most commonly called *The Book of Change* in English. It has been presented as a work of philosophy (Cary **Baynes**'s 1967 translation of Richard **Wilhelm**'s German rendering), a book for 'practical use in divination' (**Blofeld**, 1963), and a popular fortune-telling manual, as in the 1974 Bantam New Age Book, proclaimed 'a new interpretation for modern times'.

As ancient wisdom couched in obscure and often enigmatic language open to a variety of interpretations, Chinese philosophical works have lent themselves to many renderings by those who neither read nor speak Chinese, but proceed from what is termed an 'affinity' with the work in question, to offer their own rendering on the basis of the many translations available. A recent example is the translation of the *Dao de jing* (Tao te ching) by Stephen **Mitchell**, a respected Biblical scholar and long-time student of Zen, but not a sinologist. The *Dao de jing* has had a special appeal: it is said to be the second most translated book in the world after the Bible.

Note on transliteration Though the pinyin system is now commonly used in the media and most works on modern Chinese topics, many scholarly works on traditional literature continue to employ the old Wade–Giles system. Where necessary for understanding, and particularly in the case of names or titles in common use, both forms are given in the following entries.   JKW

TRANSLATIONS   de Bary, William Theodore, with Wing-tsit Chan and Burton Watson, *Sources of Chinese Tradition*, New York, 1960 · Baynes, Cary, *The I Ching or Book of Change*, New York, 1950 · Birch, Cyril, ed., *Stories from a Ming Collection*, New York, 1958 · *Anthology of Chinese Literature*, 2 vols., New York, 1965–7 · *Scenes for Mandarins*, New York, 1995 · Blofeld, John, *The Book of Change*, London, 1965 · Giles, Herbert A., *Strange Stories from a Chinese Studio*, New York, 1908 · *Gems of Chinese Literature: Prose*, London/Shanghai, 1884; rev. edn., 1923 · Lau, D. C., *Lao Tzu: Tao Te Ching*, 1963 · Lau, Joseph S. M., and Ma, Y. M., eds., *Traditional Chinese Stories: Themes and Variations*, New York, 1978 · Legge, James, *The Four Books*, Hong Kong, 1861 · Liu, Jung-en, *Six Yuan Dramas*, London, 1972 · McNaughton, William, ed., *Chinese Literature: An Anthology from the Earliest Times to the Present*, Tokyo, 1974 · Mair, Victor, ed., *The Columbia Anthology of Traditional Chinese Literature*, New York, 1994 · Mitchell, Stephen, *Tao Te Ching: A New English Version*, London, 1989 · Owen, Stephen, *An Anthology of Chinese Literature: Beginnings to 1911*, New York, 1996 · Waley, Arthur, *The Analects of Confucius*, New York, 1938.

2. CHINESE POETRY

i. Introductory In the current corpus of Chinese classical literature in translation, poetry predominates as a genre. This fact in itself testifies to a difference between the traditional Chinese and English conception of the purposes served by literature. In the classical Chinese tradition the highest literary status was in fact accorded to non-fiction prose, or *wen*, which covers such diverse categories as letters, travel essays, memoirs, *pièces d'occasion*, book prefaces, petitions, memorials, and epitaphs [see II.f.3]. The well-known saying 'Poetry is for the expression of personal feelings; prose is a vehicle of the Way' explains succinctly why prose was given a higher standing in the classical tradition: as a vehicle of the Way, it served a much larger social and moral purpose, and was therefore a much more important part of the cultural framework in traditional China. This is not to say that poetry was unpopular; quite the contrary. Poetry-writing was a favourite pastime for all educated men, for it was the genre which, sanctioned by tradition, gave expression to the emotions of the private man. The fact that until the 1920s all well-educated Chinese could and did write classical poetry is an important one to bear in mind, for it gives us a clear picture of the nature of its original readership: the intended readers were themselves poets who had an intimate knowledge of the rules of prosody.

One can see how impossible it is to replicate this relationship between poet and audience outside the tradition in which every educated man was a sound poet. Yet despite this handicap, as well as the fact that prose enjoyed a higher status in the Chinese tradition, poetry looms far larger than any other genre in the westerner's conception of classical Chinese literature. Though in the initial period westerners in China were guided by the norms of the Chinese literary tradition, as the translations reached a wider English readership the interest of non-sinologists obviously shifted the balance towards poetry. In 1947 Robert **Payne** called poetry 'the finest flower' of Chinese culture.

The first substantial volume of Chinese poetry in English translation still in use is *The She-King*, produced by James **Legge** (1814–97) in 1871 in Hong Kong; Legge's romanized title of the book betrays the influence of a southern Chinese dialect. *Shi jing*, the first collection of Chinese poetry, dates back to 1000 BCE. One of the oldest classics in the Chinese cultural tradition, it is also the most heavily annotated and commented upon, and enjoys the highest status in the poetic tradition. A major characteristic of the old commentaries is to interpret all love songs as political allegory, and to treat the collection as essential reading for good government. Legge's translation, with a detailed explanation of the commentaries and copious notes, falls very much within the native traditional treatment of this collection. His decision to follow mostly the explications of the 12th-c. scholar Zhu Xi shows a definite—Bernhard Karlgren called it 'unfortunate'—conservatism. The edition now commonly available, with the translations in delineated prose, was published in 1871; in 1876 a new edition in verse was published, probably in recognition of the norms of English poetry. In producing two entirely different versions of *The She-King*, Legge was the first English translator of classical Chinese poetry to seek concrete solutions to the perennial problems of balancing the requirements of scholarship and prosody. But ultimately Legge's interest in this work was culturally rather than literarily oriented: *The She-King* was part of his project to translate the bulk of the Confucian canon. This perhaps also explains why the existence of the verse translation of *The She-King* is not widely known.

ii. Nineteenth-Century Translations It was two of Legge's near-contemporaries who produced the early English anthologies of Chinese poetry: *Poeseos Sinensis Commentarii: On the Poetry of the Chinese* (1830) by John Francis **Davis** (1795–1890) and *Gems of Chinese Literature: Verse* by Herbert A. **Giles** (1845–1935), in which the poems are selected and presented as a body of *belles lettres*. Davis, one-time governor of Hong Kong, expressed his wish to remedy the 'indifferent reception' of Chinese literature in the West by 'a careful selection of the best subjects, and by treating these in such a manner as shall interest the greatest number of tasteful and cultivated readers'. His translation approach is one of flexibility: according to the needs of individual poems, they are rendered into 'prose translations' (delineated), 'metrical versions', or 'avowed paraphrase'.

However, what most strikes the present-day reader is Davis's choice of material. Much of what is collected here would come under the category of verse rather than poetry. Davis admits to a strong preference for tea-picking ballads and devotes considerable space to them. Verses gleaned from works of fiction and drama are also included here, as are 10 poems on London written by the late-Qing scholar Wang Tao. In contrast, there is very little high poetry in this slim volume. Few of the important poets of the classical tradition are represented, nor is any poet mentioned by name. One may thus conclude that what struck Davis as 'the best subjects' to represent 'the poetry of the Chinese' had little resemblance to the Chinese poetic tradition itself. In all probability Davis based his selection mostly on material he came across as a student of the language. The Chinese poetic tradition was after all not a burden he had to carry, and he could therefore assume that what interested him would similarly interest his intended English readership.

Herbert Giles also had in mind 'the requirements of a general public', in whose interest he decided to eliminate unpronounceable names and difficult allusions. In contrast to Davis, Giles's choice of material makes it clear that he was familiar with the norms and standards of classical poetry. His translations are set firmly in an English cultural and literary framework: the verse forms and metres were all familiar to their intended readers, while the use of Greek, Latin, and Italian allusions was obviously considered to be an advantage in the days of the book's publication. The following lines from the poem 'Yao's Advice' show how anglicization could lead to rather doubtful effects:

> With trembling heart and cautious steps
> Walk daily in fear of God. . . .

These are certainly the words of a Victorian missionary rather than those of an ancient Chinese poet. However, perhaps too much has been made of Giles's old-fashioned style in recent decades. Most translators function within their contemporary cultural framework, projecting the vision of their times onto the translated material, and therein lies their appeal to their readers. Such was the case with Giles. Though the fact that he had spent long years in China probably accounted for the conservatism of his literary tastes compared with his English contemporaries, the awareness that he was translating material from ancient times would have justified the use of antiquated poeticism for the translator as well as his readers.

iii. 1900–1950 Let us now return briefly to the *Shi jing*. The post-Legge translations of this poetry collection clearly illustrate the fast-changing poetic and translation norms. Two of the most notable are *The Book of Songs* by Arthur **Waley** and *The Book of Odes* by Bernhard **Karlgren**. Though thoroughly acquainted with the tradition of treating love songs in this collection as political allegory, Waley decided to present them as folk-poetry with explanatory notes aimed at the average reader, while the scholarly textual notes formed a separate volume. Moreover, he broke up the original structure of the collection and grouped his translations along thematic lines. The new-found interest in folk literature in Europe—which had an impact on China—provided the background to Waley's bold translation decisions. Working in the modernist tradition, he forsook regular metre and rhyme and relied instead on 'sprung rhythm' and an extensive range in terms both of vocabulary and of register. He also made liberal use of English literary devices. The following excerpt from Waley's *The Book of Songs* shows an unmistakable Shakespearean echo:

> The Lady: The cock has crowed;
> It is full daylight.
> The Lover: It was not the cock that crowed,
> It was the buzzing of those green flies.
> The Lady: The eastern sky glows;
> It is broad daylight.
> The Lover: That is not the glow of dawn,
> But the rising moon's light.

That Waley has effectively been the only translator of Chinese literature to reach a large, non-specialist audience testifies to his literary talent and the soundness of his method. Karlgren, on the other hand, took a distinctly academic approach and produced a complete, word-for-word rendition between 1942 and 1946. Scholarship was to take precedence over all else, including poetry. While it had little influence outside sinological circles, it was a significant landmark as an academic translation in which poetic elements became the least of the translator's concerns. As the field of sinology grew, this emphasis on knowledge over poetry became an increasingly obvious trait.

Despite the small proportion of Chinese poetry available in English translation, there is no denying its influence on the 20th-c. English poetic tradition. How Ezra **Pound** translated the Chinese poems (via the American Japanese scholar Fenollosa's notes) collected in *Cathay* as part of the imagist movement—a revolt against the nature and function prescribed for Anglo-American poetry—is now a familiar story. Pound's experiments with translating from the Chinese were followed by other imagist poets, notably Amy **Lowell**. What is interesting, however, is that this successful cross-cultural fertilization resulted from something of a misconception. Deprived of its phonological and structural elements, the extremely regulated classical Chinese poetry struck Pound and other imagist poets as quintessentially imagery-based. They used it as a model to free their own poetry from the constriction of tradition, without realizing that this model was in fact strictly confined by rules within the Chinese tradition. The Anglo-American poets' innocence of that tradition allowed them to construe Chinese poems according to their particular needs. This is just one example of how forces for change came from within the host culture, and outside elements were only catalysts. Viewed in this light, academic discussions about the 'accuracy' of Pound's translations, or rather his deficiencies therein, are somewhat beside the point. The following excerpt from a partial translation entitled 'Old Idea of Choan by Rosoriu' illustrates what most attracted the Imagists:

Birds with flowery wing, hovering butterflies
   crowd over the thousand gates.
Trees that glitter like jade,
   terraces tinged with silver,
The seed of a myriad hues,
   a network of arbours and passages and covered ways,
Double towers, winged roofs,
   border the network of ways:
A place of felicitous meeting

The case of the Imagists is doubly interesting in that the results of the cross-cultural fertilization played a part in the development of the new Chinese literary tradition around 1919. Hu Shi (1891–1962), the advocate for a Chinese literary revolution, was inspired by the Imagists' manifesto and sought to model a new Chinese poetry on such ideas without realizing that classical Chinese poetry—the tradition he tried to overthrow—was an essential part of the Imagists' frame of reference. Events thus came full circle.

iv. Since 1950 How an individual poet can get a new lease of life in translation or achieve a status unimaginable within his own culture is amply demonstrated by the case of Han Shan (Cold Mountain) in English translation. An esoteric and minor poet in the Chinese tradition, Han Shan has the rare honour of being one of the few Chinese poets to have their complete works available in English. Though Arthur Waley was the first to bring him to the attention of English readers (27 poems published in *Encounter*, September 1954), it was Gary **Snyder** who, both through the immediacy and vitality of his language and through his Americanization of the Han Shan legend, turned this minor poet into a Beat cult figure. Seen through Snyder's eyes, Han Shan had an irresistible appeal to a new generation of Anglo-American readers brought up on modernist poetics and enthralled with eastern religion and philosophy. It is significant that the major translators of Han Shan—Snyder, Burton **Watson**, and Red **Pine** (an American who went to live in Taiwan)—all had a strong interest in Zen Buddhism. The case of Han Shan shows beyond any doubt that translated literature which appeals to a wide public has a life uniquely its own within the framework of its host culture. That a strong Japanese connection served both Pound and Snyder in their production of translations from the Chinese—work which had the strongest impact on its host culture so far—is a matter worth exploring, for it may reveal the literary and cultural inclinations of the English-speaking world.

It must be pointed out that Cold Mountain achieved an individual—some would say iconic—status in English because of very special circumstances; most English translators of classical Chinese poetry are governed by Chinese evaluations of individual poets. Thus the most frequently translated poets are the giants of the Tang (618–907) and Song (960–1279) dynasties—Li Bai (Li Po), Tu Fu, Wang Wei, Bai Juyi, and Su Dongpo. In their selection of poems, translators are often guided by popular Chinese poetry anthologies such as *Three Hundred Tang Poems* (translated by Witter **Bynner** and **Kiang** Kang-hu as *The Jade Mountain*). Though there is no longer any prejudice against the so-called derivative poetic sub-genres such as *ci* lyrics and *qu* songs as in the days of Wylie, the poetry of the Tang dynasty—commonly accepted as the zenith in the development of regulated verse-forms—remains a strong focal point for many translators.

It is the usual practice for translators and editors to adhere strictly either to the classical or to the modern Chinese poetic tradition in their selection of material for publishing, but we have an exception in *The White Pony* edited by Robert Payne. Divided according to dynastic sections, the bulk of the book is devoted to classical poetry up to 1911, with a slim last section on modern poetry written in the vernacular. The obvious question is: how does one show in translation the immense difference in language as well as poetic form between the two traditions? This book does not provide an answer, for one can hardly tell from the translations that there is a difference. However, it is noteworthy as a ground-breaking work which tries to bridge China's two diverse poetic traditions, and also as a work produced by group effort. The translators for the majority of the poems are not credited because too many people (all Chinese) had worked on one poem.

Since the 1960s Chinese poetry in English translation has been dominated by the works of academics in Chinese studies. Many translations are made to satisfy the needs of university courses, and it is natural for translators who are first and foremost teachers to concentrate on the meaning of words and lines and the poet's status in the Chinese tradition rather than on the sense of poetry. The ground-breaking *Sunflower Splendour*, which includes classical poetry from the earliest records to the 1950s, reveals both the strength and the weakness of such collaborative academic efforts. While it remains the most comprehensive and one of the most informative anthologies of its kind, as translated *poetry* the works in this volume are very uneven. This generation of translators were educated in a different way from their predecessors, and their careers in academe impose upon them conditions vastly different from the prewar era. Such objective circumstances are bound to have an impact on literary translation. On the whole academic translators of today lack the strong classical grounding of Legge, the superb sense of prosody of Giles, and the literary ingenuity of Waley.

There are outstanding exceptions to this generalization. David **Hawkes** illustrates, with his *Songs of the South* (1959), *A Little Primer of Tu Fu* (1965), and particularly the poems in *The Story of the Stone* (1973–80), how the best of his generation can combine academic expertise with a sure sense of prosody; these works are a *tour de force* showing the diversity in style and translation approaches one person can command. In Burton Watson's many translations, the beauty of Chinese poetry (and prose) shines through because of the natural ease of his use of language, as is shown in his translation of Su Dongpo's *ci* lyric 'To the Tune of "Partridge Sky"':

Mountains shine through forest breaks, bamboo hides the wall;
withered grass by small ponds, jumbled cicada cries.
White birds again and again cut across the sky;
faint scent of lotus shining pink on the water.

Beyond the village,
by the old town walls,

with goosefoot cane I stroll where late sunlight turns.
Thanks to rain that fell at the third watch last night
I get another cool day in this floating life.

Ultimately, if we look at individual translations, it is the talent of the translators that matters the most. The trend of postwar education as well as the structuring of academic institutions are not conducive to the prospering of poetry, translated or otherwise. It is perhaps worth noting that both Hawkes and Watson voluntarily curtailed a 'normal' academic career to devote themselves to translating.

With the current trend of privileging factual knowledge over literary sensitivity, Chinese poetry in translation—increasingly conceived by university presses as textbook material—will eventually become little more than a teaching tool. While the problem is not limited to poetry in translation, it suffers considerably more than other genres because this trend leads to a further segregation of an already small readership. In reducing the importance of the poetic elements in translation—be it by design or because of limited talent—we run the risk of completely marginalizing translated Chinese poetry in its host culture. One way of instilling life into translated poetry is through co-translation. Collaboration between native Chinese scholars and Anglo-American poets has borne fruitful results in many cases; the works of **Lowell**/**Ayscough** and Bynner/Kiang in the 1920s are good examples. Kenneth **Rexroth** and Ling **Chung** (1970s) as well as C. H. **Kwok** and Vincent **McHugh** (1950s) also testify to the success of such collaboration. However, such efforts are still the exception rather than the rule.

Despite the high hopes for cross-cultural communication expressed by many translators, the reception of literature in translation is conditioned almost exclusively by the host culture's literary and cultural norms, and its needs and expectations. It is for this reason that the brave but sometimes misguided efforts of many mainland Chinese academics at translating classical poetry for an English readership are not discussed here.   EH

ANTHOLOGIES Bynner, Witter, and Kiang Kang-hu, *The Jade Mountain*, London, 1929 · Cranmer-Byng, L., *A Lute of Jade*, London, 1909 · Davis, John Francis, *Poeseos Sinensis Commentarii: On the Poetry of the Chinese*, London, 1830 [new edn. 1870; rep. New York, 1969] · Giles, Herbert A., *Gems of Chinese Literature: Verse*, London/Shanghai, 1884 [rev. edn. London, 1923] · Graham, A. C., *Poems of the Late T'ang*, Harmondsworth, 1965 [Penguin] · Hawkes, David, *Songs of the South*, London, 1959 · Karlgren, Bernard, *The Book of Odes*, Stockholm, 1944 · Legge, James, *The She-King*, London, 1871; rep. Hong Kong, 1965 · Liu, Wu-chi, and Lo, Irving Yucheng, eds., *Sunflower Spendor: Three Thousand Years of Chinese Poetry*, Bloomington, Ind., 1975 · Lowell, Amy, and Ayscough, Florence, *Fire-Flower Tablets*, London/Cambridge, Mass., 1922 · Payne, Robert, ed., *The White Pony*, New York, 1947 · Pound, Ezra, 'Cathay', in his *Selected Poems*, London, 1928 · *Renditions* (Hong Kong), 11 and 12 and 21 and 22, special numbers on classical Chinese poetry (1979, 1984) · Rexroth, Kenneth, and Chung, Ling, *The Orchard Boat*, New York, 1972 · Turner, John, *A Golden Treasury of Chinese Poetry*, Hong Kong, 1989 · Waley, Arthur, *The Book of*

Songs, London, 1937 · Watson, Burton, *The Columbia Book of Chinese Poetry: from Early Times to the Thirteenth Century*, New York, 1984.

HAN SHAN [COLD MOUNTAIN]   Pine, Red, *The Collected Songs of Cold Mountain*, Port Townsend, Wash., 1983 · Snyder, Gary, *Riprap and Cold Mountain Poems*, San Francisco, 1969 · Watson, Burton, *Cold Mountain: 100 Poems by the T'ang Poet Han Shan*, New York, 1965.

LI PO and TU FU   Cooper, Arthur, *Li Po and Tu Fu*, London, 1973 · Hawkes, David, *A Little Primer of Tu Fu*, Oxford, 1967.

WANG WEI   Robinson, G. W., *Poems of Wang Wei*, London, 1973.

SEE ALSO   Khan, P., 'Han Shan in English', *Renditions*, 25 (1986), 140–75 · Pfister, L., 'James Legge's Metrical *Book of Poetry*', *Bulletin of the School of Oriental and African Studies*, 60 (1997), 64–85 · Wong, Siu-kit, and Lee, Ka-shu, 'Three English Translations of the *Shi Jing*', *Renditions*, 25 (1986), 113–39 · Wylie, A., *Notes on Chinese Literature*, Shanghai, 1867.

3. CHINESE PROSE

i. Introduction The first translations from the Chinese by westerners were of philosophical texts, poetry, and drama; free-standing prose essays did not come under their pens. The reasons are not hard to imagine. The philosophical texts encapsulated Chinese wisdom; Chinese poems and plays had novelty value, and a unity which enabled them to be appreciated independently. Prose compositions, being discursive, were to a much greater degree embedded in the historical discourse of the nation, rather like islands whose mass is invisible under the sea: they needed a lot of explaining. Even those compositions which were relatively self-contained had their drawbacks. Leaving aside the Jesuit order active in the 17th c., it was not until well into the 19th c. that westerners resident in China acquired sufficient knowledge of the language to translate Chinese literature. By that time the art of the essay was so well developed and widely practised in the West that the Chinese counterpart did not seem very remarkable, especially as those examples most readily available owed their celebrity to virtues that in the first place were difficult for foreigners to appreciate, and in the second place would be lost in translation.

The Chinese had always valued aesthetic qualities—tone, rhythm, mood, nuance—over thought content. Independent penetrating thought, satire and humour, honest self-analysis, graphic description of human habitations and customs were low on their list of priorities. It was not that those qualities did not exist (though some were rare); it was that they were not normally brought together in the prose composition. The most natural place for the description of local personages and surroundings, for instance, was the notes and jottings of scholar-officials which made no pretensions to literary art. Chinese 'essays' that appealed more to western tastes and interests came to light in the

20th c., exhumed by native Chinese scholars who had by then been exposed to the western essay.

Chinese prose compositions intended to be read for pleasure, as opposed to those written for utilitarian or instructive purposes, took their place alongside verse in the 3rd c. CE, and have been esteemed as a kind of *belles lettres* ever since, but the forms they took were different from the 'essay' founded in Europe by Montaigne [II.g.5.ii]. They were framed as letters, prefaces, discussions, expositions, accounts, biographies, obituaries, etc., so dividing territory that the European essay could range over at will. Anthologies of the most admired pieces were compiled from age to age. In the 19th c. the most popular surviving anthologies that potential translators would have encountered were *Guwen guanzhi* (1695) and *Guwen cilei zuan* (1779), which incorporated pieces from the earliest times but had a bias towards the orthodox 'Eight Prose Masters of the Tang and Song'. The Chinese educated élite had been brought up on these, but to the foreign students these unannotated texts must have been formidably difficult, as indeed they are now to native readers, for whom translations into the modern vernacular are supplied. The few westerners who did grapple with them were aware that their artistic qualities too were not easily transferred. Herbert **Giles** (1845–1935) quoted the Revd Arthur Smith to the effect that the great writers of the Song dynasty (10th–13th c.) had 'an indescribable loftiness of style, which resembles expression in music' (Giles 1923: p. iv). Undeterred, however, by that consideration, Giles published the first anthology of Chinese prose in English translation in 1884 as the first part of *Gems of Chinese Literature*; this part was extended to 286 pages in the revised edition of 1923, which (thanks to reprints in Taiwan and the USA) may still be found.

In the 20th c. competence in the Chinese language shifted from the resident 'China hands' (as

Giles was originally) to university-trained sinologists, and at the same time native Chinese scholars acquired enough English to do the job of translation, but prose continued to be neglected in favour of other branches of literature. Translations of essays appeared only incidentally in scholarly monographs, and that usually as excerpts. An apparent exception was E. D. **Edwards**'s *Chinese Prose Literature of the T'ang period*, but the non-fictional prose consisted mainly of notes on curiosities; it contained no extended essays. The non-academic English reader looking for Chinese prose literature to read was not served again until the second half of the century, when new anthologies were published.

Western translators, perhaps inevitably, have followed Chinese scholars and critics in their selection of material. When a change in cultural values took place in China, as it did most notably in the 1920s, this change was therefore reflected in the works translated, though the process was slow. The new canon leaned heavily towards writers of the late 16th to 18th c. who had previously been considered unorthodox, if not downright heretical. Fittingly, it was a Chinese scholar, **Lin** Yutang, who introduced the new canon indirectly but very influentially with his *The Importance of Living* (1938), which in setting out his own attitude to life quoted his favourite authors extensively. Despite the fact that his translations were only fragments, their impact on the English-speaking public must have been considerable: the book was reprinted 20 times up to 1960 (see below).

ii. Herbert A. Giles Given that the readership for the academic monographs which have incorporated translations of Chinese essays is very small, we shall concentrate here on anthologies intended for the general reader. The first of those, as noted, was produced by Herbert Giles. Giles worked without the aid of the fully annotated modern editions which serve the present-day translator of classical prose so well. Hence he was prone to mistakes in interpreting both words and situations—the latter because classical Chinese is so economical in its use of words that when and by whom something is done or said is often not indicated but left to the reader to divine. Since his *Gems* was first compiled while the Chinese empire was still in being, statesmen, rulers, and sages figure more prominently among his authors than the virtues of their compositions justify. He was also fond of archaisms which must have seemed strained even in the Victorian age. But despite all their drawbacks, some of his translations remain unsurpassed when judged as freestanding compositions, bound to, yet emancipated from, the original: they have a life of their own, and embody a mood or passion that inspires the right choice of words. Giles's best efforts would have gone down very well at public readings, for in addition to finding the right words, his sense of prosody was superlative: his syllables fall naturally into metrical feet, without becoming ersatz verse. His own boldness and vigour may make him overplay his hand, yet the reader can rarely complain about the results. To give one example, from Ouyang Xiu's 'Zuiweng ting ji' (The Old Drunkard's Arbour), the bare phrase *shui luo er shi chu* (water falls and stones surface) is rendered as 'the naked boulders of the lessening torrent': the powerful stresses of the trochees help to make it a magnificent climax to the sequence of which it is part.

Giles gave pride of place to the four acknowledged masters of the Tang and Song dynasties: Han Yu, Liu Zongyuan (Liu Tsung-yuan), Ouyang Xiu (Ouyang Hsiu), and Su Shi (Su Shih), also known as Su Dongpo (Su Tung-p'o). He was wise to do so, for they were all masters of oratory and rhetoric, albeit controlled and sometimes subdued. In overt oratory, as with Han Yu's mock-heroic 'Ji eyu wen' (The Crocodile of Ch'ao-chou), Giles demonstrated skills that later translators never learnt, and was Han Yu's match. He equally excelled in the picturesque and burlesque. Considering that he worked to all appearances unaided, his achievements were remarkable.

iii. Anthologies of the 1960s and 1970s It was a very different picture of Chinese prose that English readers got from Lin Yutang when in 1960 he realized the promise implicit in *The Importance of Living* and produced a proper anthology of Chinese prose (with a few poems thrown in for good measure) under the title *The Importance of Understanding*. Of the four masters mentioned above, two (Han Yu and Ouyang Xiu) did not appear at all; Liu Zongyuan was granted one composition, an appreciation of nature; and Su Dongpo was represented not by his studiously crafted set pieces but by his unstudied occasional animadversions. The heights were commanded by the freethinkers Li Zhuowu (Li Chuo-wu), Jin Shengtan (Chin Sheng-t'an), Yuan Hongdao (Yuan Hung-tao), Zhang Dai (Chang Tai), and above all Li Yu (also known as Li Liweng). They had been resurrected in China by the new generation of intellectuals seeking precursors to themselves, companions in insubordination. Lin Yutang had given material assistance to that revolution in taste with the magazines he edited in Shanghai in the early 1930s. Lin himself, however, was devoted less to insubordination than to the 'familiar style' of writing they practised: conversational, amiable, direct, and indiscreet. In keeping with that style, their subject-matter favoured the personal and domestic, concentrating on the pleasures and pains of life and avoiding matters of state. So to the list of free spirits and eccentrics he added his own favourite good talkers, some of whom, it must be said, strike one as merely garrulous, like Shi Zhenlin (Shih Chen-lin).

All this had a bearing on Lin Yutang's translation practice, as he felt that his fellow feeling gave him the privilege of interpreting for the author as for a friend: 'In translating an author, you practically engage to speak for him in a new language, and you cannot do so unless you are speaking for an old friend, so to speak' (Lin 1960: 19). 'Speaking for', as opposed to 'speaking as', was indeed the hallmark of Lin's translations. Where the author's and translator's tone, mannerisms, and proclivity coincided, as with the whimsical Jin Shengtan and the argumentative, mercurial Li Yu, this worked very satisfactorily, but the assimilation of writers of a different bent was too cosy. To compound the problem, English was after all a second language for Lin, and though he wrote it fluently and faultlessly he was only able to command the middle range: the vulgar and comical and the grand and sententious were beyond him. Nevertheless, he accomplished what he set out to do, namely to make known to English readers a new range of homely, relaxed, good-humoured prose literature to set alongside the sage, artful, and high-flown.

The freethinkers mentioned above found a permanent place in the pantheon. Monographs on them in English have been published which include translations in whole or part of their essays; for instance *Pilgrim of the Clouds: Poems and Essays by Yuan Hung-tao and His Brothers* by Jonathan **Chaves**, and *The Invention of Li Yu* by Patrick **Hanan**. It is probably in this format that an author's prose is most readily appreciated by the lay reader, for such books can supply the much-needed context of the author's life, times, intellectual concerns, and other writings (few if any Chinese literary men wrote prose essays exclusively). Hanan's book is a model of balance between explanation and quotation, and his translations, while following the wording of the original very closely, nevertheless stay within the bounds of normal English diction.

The classical tradition still had its defenders, however. Volume I of Cyril **Birch**'s *Anthology of Chinese Literature* allocated its comparatively little space for prose to the famous four, Han, Liu,

Ouyang, and Su, with Han Yu getting the lion's share. This was a sensible preference, for the selection bore witness to Han Yu's superior intellect. His translator, J. K. **Rideout**, had obviously entered into close communion with his subject, and he brings out Han's strengths well, in particular his wit. We have him to thank for translating the otherwise neglected piece 'Song qiong wen' (Farewell to Poverty), in which the author relents in his decision to expel the demons which keep him poor, because they also keep him honest. Rideout's dignified but graphic language finds the right level; as nearly as practicable, he 'speaks as' his author.

At the same time, the 'minor tradition' of Chinese prose gets a look-in in volume ii of Birch's *Anthology*, in his own translation of excerpts from Li Yu's *Xianqing ouji* (Random Relaxations). Evidently owing his place in the anthology to his universal appeal, this sybarite who excelled in extracting uncommon pleasure from common things is justly served by Birch's easy and seamless renderings.

Chronologically speaking, the next anthology to consider is Shih Shun **Liu**'s *Chinese Classical Prose: The Eight Masters of the T'ang-Sung Period*. This is in a sense an attempt to recapture control of the agenda from foreign hands, as may be inferred from the translator's reference to 'this sampling in English of what the Chinese people for centuries have truly regarded as "deathless prose" '. It is a useful book because of its extensive coverage and its printing in parallel of the Chinese text, but the selection proves that what might be significant in terms of the Chinese heritage may not be very significant to those who do not share that heritage. Furthermore, there is nothing very 'deathless' about the language of the translator.

iv. Anthologies of the 1990s Birch's *Anthology* remained a presence to be reckoned with when the next generation of anthologies was produced in the 1990s. Apart from operating their own schemes, these new anthologies seemed consciously to fill gaps left by Birch. The two very bulky general anthologies edited by Victor **Mair** and Stephen **Owen** are likely to satisfy demand for this kind of publication in the immediate future. Occasional and informal prose compositions take up 250 pages of Mair's 1317-page anthology and a similar proportion of Owen's 1152 pages. In the same years the editors of *Renditions* in Hong Kong produced two special issues, 'Classical Prose' (1990) and 'Classical Letters' (1994), which also aimed to fill in a perceived gap in English translations of Chinese prose literature.

All these recent collections have been able to draw upon the extensive apparatus of modern scholarship, including excellent new Chinese monolingual dictionaries. Consequently they exhibit very few obvious mistakes in interpretation. In addition, in the case of *Renditions*, intensive editing ensures a high standard of precision in the choice of words. In general the translators of this generation attempt to retain all the stylistic features of the original, and differ only in the degree to which their individual command of English allows them to do so expertly and elegantly. With some honourable exceptions, their own English style is not as smooth as that of Birch's generation.

The selections of Mair and Owen are based on generic groupings and 'family' relationships. The *Renditions* selections lean towards native preferences, in that all the pieces they include have educated Chinese tastes for generations, but at the same time are selected on individual merit, with an eye to what can be immediately appreciated by non-Chinese readers. The 'Classical Letters' collection fills the widest gap in English translations: letters occupy a much more central place in the Chinese than in the western canon, by virtue of the fact that they offer a free form for observations that the established categories of prose cannot accommodate. The Mair and *Renditions* pieces are translated by different hands, but Owen has translated everything himself. Fortunately he is a meticulous scholar, and has a sure sense of style.

No single composition is included in all the successive anthologies noted above, so comparison of renderings cannot be complete, but one skit on boot-licking, framed as a letter, significantly, occurs in four of them. Two sentences from this letter, 'Bao Liu Yizhang shu' (In Reply to Liu Yizhang) by Zong Chen (Tsung Ch'en, 1525–60), can illustrate the translators' different styles. The first sentence is spoken by the gatekeeper to the supplicant who arrives at a high official's residence at crack of dawn to seek audience. The original is *He keren zhi qin ye* (How diligent a visitor you are!). The successive translations are:

Giles: You are in a fine hurry, you are!
Lin: Are you out of your mind?
Mair: You're very persistent, aren't you?
Kane: Persistent, aren't you? (*Renditions*)

The second sentence is spoken by the supplicant to his acquaintances on emerging from the audience with the high official. The original is *Xianggong hou wo hou wo* (His Excellency received me very favourably, very favourably). This is translated as:

Giles: He treated me very kindly, very kindly indeed!
Lin: I was received royally, most royally.
Mair: His Lordship is so good to me! Oh, he's so good to me!
Kane: His Lordship treated me with great kindness! Great kindness!

Giles's renderings have his typical vigour and flourish. Lin's are the most context-sensitive, in that they accentuate—and somewhat exaggerate—the tone of the utterance. 'Are you out of your mind?' perhaps inclines too far towards American colloquial usage, but his choice of 'royally' strikes exactly the right note. Mair and Kane favour modern plainness in the first sentence in the use of 'persistent', with Kane achieving greater force by using fewer words. Mair injects more emotion into the second utterance, making it sound effeminate. Kane's version is very similar to Giles's, only slightly closer in rhythm to the Chinese. Since Giles also throws in an illuminating comparison with Juvenal's *Satires* with his translation, he should take the overall honours in this little competition, but he makes too many slips elsewhere in the same piece to avoid being superseded.

Giles and Lin gave generous space to prose in their books not only because of its important place in the source literature but also because of their own high esteem for the 'essay' as an art form. But their view was inadequate, being either ill-informed or biased. What is desirable now is a general history of the Chinese essay with copious illustrations that would give an idea of the development of the genre and rescue anthology pieces from their isolation.   DEP

TRANSLATIONS   Birch, Cyril, ed., *Anthology of Chinese Literature*, 2 vols., New York, 1965–7 · Chaves, Jonathan, *Pilgrim of the Clouds: Poems and Essays by Yuan Hung-tao and His Brothers*, New York, 1978 · Edwards, E. D., *Chinese Prose Literature of the T'ang period, AD 618–906*, London, 1937, 1938 · Giles, Herbert A., *Gems of Chinese Literature*, Shanghai, 1884, London, 1923 · Hanan, Patrick, *The Invention of Li Yu*, Cambridge, Mass., 1988 · Lin Yutang, *The Importance of Living*, London, 1938 · *The Importance of Understanding*, Cleveland, OH/New York, 1960 · Liu Shih Shun, *Chinese Classical Prose: The Eight Masters of the T'ang-Sung Period*, Hong Kong, 1979 · Mair, Victor, ed., *The Columbia Anthology of Traditional Chinese Literature*, New York, 1994 · OWEN, STEPHEN, *An Anthology of Chinese Literature: Beginnings to 1911*, New York, 1996 · *Renditions* (Hong Kong), 33 and 34, special nos. on classical prose (1990) · *Renditions*, 41 and 42, special nos. on classical letters (1994).

4. CHINESE FICTION

i. Introductory Premodern Chinese novels are a treasure trove not sufficiently explored by western readers primarily because they are not yet well represented in English translation. The first Chinese novel to be translated into English was *Haoqiu zhuan* (17th c., The Fortunate Union), a romantic novel which ends happily with a brilliant scholar marrying a beautiful, chaste girl. Translations of this novel appeared as early as 1761 (Thomas **Percy**) and 1829 (John Francis **Davis**). However, this represents an anomaly in the history of Chinese literary translations. Most translators subsequently concentrated on the famous six canonic novels. Since the 1910s, these works have been variously translated and retranslated.

There are several reasons for the scarcity, as well as unpopularity among western readers, of translations of Chinese novels. In addition to the difficulties presented by the language, these novels are often voluminous and episodic and contain formal features unfamiliar to western readers. For example, poetry is an essential feature of most premodern Chinese novels. Translators handle this formal feature in several different ways: some delete all the poems in order to tighten the narrative, others translate the poems selectively and in free verse; only the most meticulous translate all the poems into English rhyming verse. But since poetry serves important functions in description, presentation, and commentary, translations that leave out the poems are impoverished.

ii. The Six Classic Novels Of the six classic novels, *Sanguo zhi yanyi / San-kuo chih yen-i* (published *c*.1522, The Romance of the Three Kingdoms) is a historical epic portraying heroes and events during the tumultuous period from 190 to 280 CE. Probably compiled by Luo Guanzhong / Lo Kuan-chung (*c*.1330–1400), it combines historical records with popular materials, transforming them into a masterpiece filled with ingenious plots and complex characters. The first English translation, by C. H. **Brewitt-Taylor**, appeared in 1925. Although he covered the entire 120 chapters of the original, Brewitt-Taylor's prose is somewhat archaic and he omits some verses from his translation.

In 1976, Moss **Roberts** published a partial translation covering chapters 20 to 85 of the novel, with summaries in italics to help bridge the missing episodes. Although this updated abridged translation soon became a widely used classroom text, it

was not until 1991 that Roberts published a complete translation that did justice to the excellence of the novel. This latest version translates the verses into English rhyme while rendering the dialogues and drama in a lively fashion.

Shuihu zhuan / Shui-hu chuan (early 16th c., Water Margin), attributed to Shi Nai'an (1296–1370), was possibly of collective authorship. Though based on historical events, it displays even more fictionalizing elements than does *Three Kingdoms*. It relates the story of the formation—and subsequent honourable surrender to the government—of a group of 108 outlaw-heroes. While the complete version of *Water Margin* contains 120 chapters, the novel can be found in versions of 100, 110, and 115 chapters, as well as in a truncated 70-chapter version which ends very differently from all the longer versions. Both Pearl S. **Buck**'s and J. H. **Jackson**'s translations were based on the novel's 70-chapter version. Though not entirely accurate, their translations are readable and have each been reprinted several times.

Sidney **Shapiro**'s 1981 translation is the most complete to date, combining the 70-chapter and the 100-chapter editions. Shapiro follows the shorter version in translating the first 70 chapters, cutting the poems and deleting redundant details in the final 30 chapters. Except for these modifications, he is largely faithful to the original text. He avoids archaic formalism, opting for a clean prose that is more accessible to the general reader. The illustrations accompanying Shapiro's translation—fine woodcuts selected from a Ming dynasty edition—help to convey the flavour of the novel. John and Alex **Dent-Young**'s 1994 rendering of chapters 1–22 differs from previous translations of *Water Margin*. They translate in full, including most of the verses, and their translation is based on the most complete version of the novel. It is lively and very accessible to the general reader.

Xiyou ji / Hsi-yu chi (published 1592, Journey to the West), attributed to the Ming writer Wu Cheng'en / Wu Ch'eng-en (*c*.1500–82), is the most entertaining of the six classics. In this 100-chapter novel combining history, fantasy, satire, and allegory, the famous Tang monk embarks on a pilgrimage to India to obtain Buddhist Scripture. He and his animal disciples must overcome many ordeals before completing their mission.

As Arthur **Waley** and Anthony **Yu** have pointed out, the two early English versions of the novel,

Timothy **Richard**'s *A Mission to Heaven* and Helen M. **Hayes**'s *The Buddhist Pilgrim's Progress*, are but brief adaptations. Waley was the first to translate this picaresque novel more faithfully. His *Monkey: Folk Novel of China*, an instant success on publication in 1943, was reprinted many times. George **Theiner**'s *The Monkey King*, based on a Czech translation, has many inaccuracies and is much less known than Waley's.

Of all the translations of premodern Chinese novels, Waley's *Monkey* is perhaps the most popular and widely read in the West. Demonstrating a remarkable capacity to render the dialogue and narrative with vitality and humour, Waley recreated the narrator's tone in bringing to life such memorable characters as Monkey, Pigsy, and Sandy. These names, coined by Waley, are now familiar to many Western readers. His enthusiastic and fluid storytelling notwithstanding, Waley's translation is not very accurate and has many omissions. He left out, for example, almost all the poems; and although he attempted to convey the entire story structure, he actually translated quite selectively, approximately 20 chapters in all—and those only partially.

In contrast to Waley's version, Anthony Yu's *Journey to the West* is a complete translation and includes an extensive introduction, informative notes, and an index. Distinguished by its extreme fidelity to the original, it allows the reader to perceive the novel not merely as a work of entertainment but as satire and religious allegory.

Jin Ping Mei / Chin P'ing Mei (published *c*.1617), also in 100 chapters, is the first Chinese novel of manners written by a single author under the pseudonym of Xiaoxiao Sheng (the Scoffing Scholar). It relates the rise to prosperity and subsequent decline of the household of a middle-class man and his six wives. Clement **Egerton**'s *The Golden Lotus* is a translation of the entire Chongzhen (1628–44) edition of the novel. Although Egerton omitted many verses and translated the more erotic passages into Latin, on the whole his translation is fairly readable; the Latin passages appear in English in the 1972 edition. Bernard **Miall** based his 1939 translation on Franz **Kuhn**'s abridged German version. Though readable, Miall's version has many errors and omits the erotic passages entirely.

David Tod **Roy**'s *The Plum in the Golden Vase* is the first volume of a projected five-volume annotated translation of the same work. Based on the fuller Wanli (1573–1620) edition of the novel, Roy's translation is meticulous and highly readable. In addition, *The Plum in the Golden Vase* includes much useful editorial material. Overall, this skilful

translation promises to supersede previous English versions.

The 18th-c. author Wu Jingzi / Wu Ching-tzu's 55-chapter satiric novel *Rulin waishi / Ju-lin wai-shih* (*c*.1750, The Scholars) targets phoney scholars as well as the much-abused civil service examination and official recruitment system. While ridiculing opportunistic office-seekers, it praises genuine Confucian scholars. Episodic in structure, this novel incorporates a good deal of autobiographical material. The English translation by **Yang** Hsien-yi and Gladys **Yang** includes a list of principal characters, some interesting illustrations, and a useful appendix explaining the examination system and official ranks. Though an accurate translation, it is quite literal and lacks the eloquence of the original.

Honglou meng / Hung-lou meng (published 1792, The Dream of the Red Chamber) is the most admired of all these novels by Chinese readers. It was primarily authored by Cao Xueqin / Ts'ao Hsüeh-ch'in (*c*.1715–63/64), who died after finishing the first 80 chapters. The remaining 40 chapters were completed by Gao E / Kao E (*c*.1740–*c*.1815), an inferior writer. Depicting the initial success and later decline of a prominent family, this novel of manners highlights the ill-fated romantic love between the young hero and one of his female cousins. Both encyclopedic and lyrical, it is a profound work resonating with philosophical, religious, and political significance.

Chi-chen **Wang**'s 1929 translation is a significantly condensed version. His second and enlarged edition of 1958 doubled the number of stories included, but still represents a much-abridged version of the first 80 chapters. Although readable, it focuses only on the main storyline and paraphrases much of the original. Florence and Isabel **McHugh**'s 1958 English retranslation of Franz Kuhn's German translation is likewise abridged, but full of errors as well.

By contrast, David **Hawkes** and John **Minford**'s five-volume translation, *The Story of the Stone*, sets a new standard for the translation of Chinese novels. The first—and most significant—80 chapters were translated by Hawkes, the last 40 by Minford. Though not completely free of minor inaccuracies, this translation is excellent in diction, tone, and style. A true *tour de force*, it recreates the panoramic fictional world in its entirety, successfully rendering the elegant language and lively conversations of the original into English.

Confronting the novel's textual inconsistencies, Hawkes consulted several different editions to find the best possible version. He chose rhymes, instead of the usual free verse, for all the poems in the work. The marvellous 'Won-Done Song' in chapter 1 is but one example of the many beautifully rendered poems:

Men all know that salvation should be won,
But with ambition won't have done, have done.
Where are the famous ones of days gone by?
In grassy graves they lie now, every one . . .

Hawkes's and Minford's achievement is so superior that Yang Hsien-yi and Gladys Yang's translation, *A Dream of Red Mansions*, seems pale in comparison.

iii. Non-canonical Classical Novels In addition to the novels of the canon, a number of other good novels have been translated. For example, Dong Yue / Tung Yüeh's *Xiyou bu/Hsi-yu pu* (1641, A Supplement to Journey to the West) was translated by Shuen-fu **Lin** and Larry **Schulz** under the title *The Tower of Myriad Mirrors*. With its description of Monkey's dream journey, this novel provides a satirical allegory rich in psychological, sociopolitical, and religious dimensions. Accurately translating the novel in its entirety, Lin and Schulz employ a fluid language to bring out the liveliness of the story. Their translation includes an informative introduction.

Rou putuan / Jou p'u-t'uan (1657, The Carnal Prayer Mat) by the 17th-c. writer Li Yu (1610/11–1680) is a 20-chapter erotic novel with comic and moral overtones. Richard **Martin**'s 1963 English retranslation of Franz Kuhn's German version takes considerable liberty in rearranging the order of chapters: it begins, for example, with chapter 2 and ends with chapter 1 of the original. While readable, it omits many poems and contains a number of inaccuracies.

It was not until 1990, with the publication of Patrick **Hanan**'s excellent translation, that Li Yu's ingenious novel received its due. Hanan restored the original order of chapters and translated the novel in full, including the commentaries attached to the end of each chapter. His translation captures the novel's humour and original flavour, while skilfully rendering the poems into English rhymes. Hanan also provides an informative introduction and useful notes.

Few western readers are familiar with *Xingshi yinyuan zhuan/Hsing-shih yin-yüan chuan* (published *c.*1661, Marriage as Retribution Awakening the World), a 100-chapter vernacular classic of the 17th c. by an unknown author. Primarily noted for its portrayal of a henpecked husband and his termagant wife and concubine, this novel also uses social

satire to target a broad range of concerns. It is highly entertaining, due to its vivid characterization and colourful language.

Chi-chen Wang published a pioneering partial translation and summary of the first 20 chapters in 1982. A decade later, Glen **Dudbridge** meticulously translated chapters 68–9. With only partial translations of this novel available at present, Eve Alison **Nyren**'s first volume of a projected complete translation entitled *The Bonds of Matrimony* is particularly welcome. Containing a full translation of the first 20 chapters, *The Bonds of Matrimony* is very readable and preserves the drama of the original. Unfortunately, it has numerous omissions, and some serious mistranslations.

Li Ruzhen/Li Ju-chen's 100-chapter *Jinghua yuan/Ching-hua yüan* (1828, Flowers in the Mirror) combines mythology and history with adventure and fantasy. An allegorical satire of an imaginary journey, it may be compared to Swift's *Gulliver's Travels*. However, it does not lend itself easily to translation due to the author's fondness for puns and lengthy discourses on the Chinese language. **Lin** Tai-yi's much-abridged 1965 translation version was intended for the general reader. She compressed dialogues and narratives, and deleted passages on Chinese language, history, and poetry. Synopses of untranslated portions are indented in the text to make the narrative flow more smoothly. In his 1973 anthology, H. C. **Chang** translated the episode on the Women's Kingdom from chapters 32–7. His translation is more accurate, and he gives clear explanations in the notes concerning the passages he has omitted.

Wu Jianren/Wu Chien-jen's (a.k.a. Wu Woyao/Wu Wo-yao) 108-chapter *Ershinian mudu zhi guai xianzhuang/Er-shih-nian mu-tu chih kuai-hsien-chuang* (1909, Strange Happenings Eyewitnessed in the Last Twenty Years), a famous social satire told in the first person, reveals many examples of social and political ills in late Qing society, Shih Shun **Liu**'s 1975 translation is abridged but readable.

Among the late Qing novels, the best known in the West is Liu E's 20-chapter *Laocan youji/Lao-ts'an yu-chi* (1906, Travels of Lao Ts'an). The author criticizes incompetent officials and corruption, and outlines ideas on political reform and moral philosophy. Famous for its simple but elegant prose, this novel also features magnificent descriptions of Chinese landscapes and music. Harold **Shadick**'s translation, first published in 1952, set a fine example for future translators. Complete and accurate, his translation is successful in capturing the flavour of the original.

Another good example of translation outside the canon is Patrick Hanan's *The Sea of Regret: Two Turn-of-the-Century Chinese Romantic Novels* (1995). Hanan's translation includes both Fu Lin's short novel *Qin hai shi/Ch'in hai shih* (1906, Stones in the Sea) and Wu Jianren's *Hen hai* (1906, The Sea of Regret), written in response to Fu Lin's work. *Stones in the Sea* is, according to Hanan, the first true 'I-novel' in Chinese literature. Influenced by *The Dream of the Red Chamber*, both novels depict romantic love set against the backdrop of the Boxer rebellion of 1900. Hanan's excellent and lucid translation includes an introduction and notes.

To conclude, the trend in the translation of pre-modern Chinese novels is largely moving toward a more responsible and scholarly approach. Many earlier translators (who were not experts in Chinese literature) and publishers of translations adapted the original texts in order to cater to western readers' tastes and moral standards, often at the expense of textual integrity as well as the author's style and intentions. Such translations provide readers with a superficial and often erroneous understanding of Chinese novels and culture. Beginning in the 1970s scholar-translators such as Hawkes, Yu, Hanan, and Roy greatly elevated the standard for translation, aiming for comprehensive, faithful English versions that sufficiently preserve the style and flavour of the original. Through careful research into the textual and contextual backgrounds of the novels, these translators convey to readers not only the author's intentions but also the various socio-cultural factors at play.

iv. Modern Novels Compared with their pre-modern counterparts, modern Chinese novels have received far more attention from translators. The prolific writer Lao She's (pseud. Shu Qingchun/Shu Ch'ing-ch'un) renowned proletarian novel *Luotuo Xiangzi/Lo-t'uo Hsiang-tzu* (1937, Camel Xiangzi/Rickshaw) was poorly rendered by Evan **King**, who cut, rewrote, and changed the ending. Jean M. **James**'s meticulous and skilful translation supersedes King's and surpasses **Shi** Xiaoqing's. In 1980 **James** also published a translation of Lao She's *Er Ma* (1935, Ma and Son). Lao She's satiric allegory *Maocheng ji/Mao-ch'eng chi* (1932, Cat Country) was first translated by James E. **Dew**, then more successfully by William A. **Lyell,** Jr. Ba Jin/Pa Chin's (pseud. Li Feigan/Li Fei-kan) famous *Jia* (1933, Family), a sentimental novel of tragedies caused by the traditional family, was first made accessible to western readers through Sidney **Shapiro**'s abridged translation, then reprinted with supplemental parts translated by **Lu** Kuang-huan and introduction by Olga Lang. Ba Jin's *Han ye/Han-yeh* (1947, Cold Nights), translated by Nathan K. **Mao** and **Liu** Ts'un-yan, is a sophisticated work of psychological realism. *Weicheng/Wei-ch'eng* (1947, Fortress Besieged), a satirical comedy of manners and the only novel written by Qian Zhongshu/Ch'ien Chung-shu, perhaps modern China's most learned author, was carefully translated by Jeanne **Kelly** and Nathan K. Mao. *Jinsuo ji/Chin-so chi* (1943, The Golden Cangue, masterfully written and translated by Eileen **Chang**, a.k.a. Zhang Ailing/Chang Ai-ling) is one of the best novellas in world literature. Eileen Chang has also translated into English her two masterpieces, *Yang ge/Yang-ko* (1954, The Rice-Sprout Song) and *Chidi zhi lian/Ch'ih-ti chih lien* (1954, Naked Earth).

YW

The Six Classic Novels (in chronological order)

Sᴀɴɢᴜᴏ ᴢʜɪ ʏᴀɴʏɪ/Sᴀɴ-ᴋᴜᴏ ᴄʜɪʜ ʏᴇɴ-ɪ [Three Kingdoms]   Brewitt-Taylor, C. H., *Romance of the Three Kingdoms*, 2 vols., Shanghai; rep. Rutland, Vt., 1959 · Roberts, Moss, *Three Kingdoms: China's Epic Drama*, New York, 1976 · *Three Kingdoms: A Historical Novel*, Berkeley, Calif., 1991.

Sʜᴜɪʜᴜ ᴢʜᴜᴀɴ/Sʜᴜɪ-ʜᴜ ᴄʜᴜᴀɴ [Water Margin]   Buck, Pearl S., *All Men Are Brothers*, 2 vols., New York, 1933; rep. 1948, 1957 · Dent-Young, John, and Dent-Young, Alex, *The Broken Seals: Part One of the Marshes of Mount Liang*, Hong Kong, 1994 · Jackson, J. H., *Water Margin*, 2 vols., Shanghai, 1937 · Shapiro, Sidney, *Outlaws of the Marsh*, 2 vols., Bloomington, Ind., 1981.

Xɪʏᴏᴜ ᴊɪ/Hsɪ-ʏᴜ ᴄʜɪ [Journey to the West]   Theiner, George, *The Monkey King*, London, 1965 · Waley, Arthur, *Monkey*, London, 1942 [Penguin, 1961] · Yu, Anthony, *The Journey to the West*, 4 vols., Chicago, 1977–83.

Jɪɴ Pɪɴɢ Mᴇɪ/Cʜɪɴ P'ɪɴɢ Mᴇɪ [The Golden Lotus]   Egerton, Clement, *The Golden Lotus*, 4 vols., London, 1939, New York, 1972 · Miall, Bernard, *Chin P'ing Mei: The Adventurous History of Hsi Men and His Six Wives*, London, 1939; rep. London, 1962 · Roy, David Tod, *The Plum in the Golden Vase, or Chin P'ing Mei*, i: *the Gathering*, Princeton, NJ, 1993.

Rᴜʟɪɴ ᴡᴀɪsʜɪ/Jᴜ-ʟɪɴ ᴡᴀɪ-sʜɪʜ [The Scholars]   Yang, Hsien-yi and Yang, Gladys, *The Scholars*, Peking, 1957.

Hᴏɴɢʟᴏᴜ ᴍᴇɴɢ/Hᴜɴɢ-ʟᴏᴜ ᴍᴇɴɢ [Dream of the Red Chamber]   Hawkes, David, and Minford, John, *The Story of the Stone*, 5 vols., London, 1973–86 [Penguin] · McHugh, Florence, and McHugh, Isabel, *The Dream of the Red*

Chamber, New York, 1958 · Wang, Chi-chen, *Dream of the Red Chamber*, London, 1929 · *Dream of the Red Chamber*, New York, 1958 · Yang, Hsien-yi, and Yang, Gladys, *A Dream of Red Mansions*, 3 vols., Peking, 1978.

Other Premodern Novels

ANON. (Haoqiu zhuan) Davis, John Francis, *The Fortunate Union*, 2 vols., London, 1829 · Percy, Thomas, *Hau Kiou Choaan, or the Pleasing History*, 4 vols., London, 1761.

ANON. (Xingshi yinyuan zhuan) Dudbridge, Glen, 'Women Pilgrims to T'ai Shan: Some Pages from a Seventeenth-Century Novel', in Susan Nanquin and Chün-fang Yü, eds., *Pilgrims and Sacred Sites in China*, Berkeley, Calif., 1992 · Nyren, Eve Allison, *The Bonds of Matrimony: Hsing-shih yin-yüan chuan. A Seventeenth-Century Chinese Novel* (vol. i), Lewiston, NY, 1995 · Wang, Chi-chen, 'Marriage as Retribution', *Renditions*, 17 and 18 (1982), 46–94.

DONG YUE / TUNG YÜEH Lin, Shuen-fu, and Schulz, Larry J., *The Tower of Myriad Mirrors: A Supplement to Journey to the West*, Berkeley, Calif., 1978.

FU LIN Hanan, Patrick, 'Stones in the Sea', in *The Sea of Regret: Two Turn-of-the-Century Chinese Romantic Novels*, Honolulu, 1995.

LI RUZHEN / LI JU-CHEN Chang, H. C., 'The Women's Kingdom', in H. C. Chang, ed., *Chinese Literature: Popular Fiction and Drama*, Edinburgh, 1973 · Lin, Tai-yi, *Flowers in the Mirror*, Berkeley / Los Angeles, Calif., 1965.

LI YU Hanan, Patrick, *The Carnal Prayer Mat*, New York, 1990 · Martin, Richard, *Jou Pu Tuan (The Prayer Mat of Flesh)*, New York, 1975.

LIU E Shadick, Harold, *The Travels of Lao Ts'an*, Ithaca, NY, 1952.

WU JIANREN / WU CHIEN-JEN Hanan, Patrick, 'The Sea of Regret', in *The Sea of Regret: Two Turn-of-the-Century Chinese Romantic Novels*, Honolulu, 1995 · Liu, Shih Shun, *Vignettes from the Late Ch'ing*, Hong Kong, 1975.

Modern Novels

BA JIN / PA CHIN Lang, Olga, ed., *Family*, Garden City, NY, 1972 · Mao, Nathan K., and Liu, Ts'un-yan, *Cold Nights*, Hong Kong / Seattle / London, 1978 · Shapiro, Sidney, *The Family*, Peking, 1958.

CHANG, EILEEN Chang, Eileen, *The Rice-Sprout Song*, New York, 1955 · *Naked Earth*, Hong Kong, 1956 · *The Golden Cangue*, in *Modern Chinese Stories and Novellas 1919–1949*, ed. Joseph S. M. Lau et al., New York, 1981.

LAO SHE Dew, James, *Cat City*, Ann Arbor, Mich., 1964 · James, Jean M., *Rickshaw*, Honolulu, 1979 · *Ma and Son*, San Francisco, 1980 · Lyell, William A., Jr., *Cat Country: A Satirical Novel of China in the 1930s*, OH, 1970 · Shi, Xiaoqing, *Camel Xiangzi*, Bloomington, Ind. / Beijing, 1981.

QIAN ZHONGSHU / CH'IEN CHUNG-SHU Kelly, Jeanne, and Mao, Nathan K., *Fortress Besieged*, Bloomington, Ind. / London, 1979.

5. JAPANESE: INTRODUCTION

Japanese literature has a long and distinguished history, beginning before the 8th c., and continuing until the present day. The traditions developed quickly, so that the earliest anthology of Japanese court poetry, the *Man'yōshū* (Anthology of Ten Thousand Leaves), which dates from this early period, represents one of the first and greatest peaks of expression in the history of Japanese poetry. Poetry remained until the 20th c. the most valued means of self-expression in Japanese literature. Genres that might roughly be said to correspond to our notions of fiction and drama also came to take on considerable importance, but poetry long remained the most significant literary form.

European travellers, mostly from Spain and Portugal, began to arrive in Japan in the 16th c., and as they learnt the language, some took an interest in Japanese literature. A few sections from classical works were translated, notably into Portuguese, but the closing of Japan to the outside world in the

early 17th c. cut any significant literary contacts. In general, it can be said that translations into English of Japanese literature, both classical and contemporary, only began in earnest towards the end of the 19th c., when British and Americans began to visit Japan.

The first serious translators of Japanese literature, who had Victorian models before them, tended to seek to recreate the Japanese originals they encountered using familiar and comfortable models, ranging from Shakespeare to Tennyson. By the 20th c., however, new developments in English and continental literature (some of them, in the field of poetry, through the imagist interest in Japanese *haiku*) allowed translators to come to shape their English versions in an increasing consonance with the originals.

On the whole, translations made from the Japanese in this century have been undertaken by those with a sustained interest and sympathy for the culture and arts of this complex civilization. The greatest of the modern translators—a list that would surely include Arthur **Waley**, Donald **Keene**, Ivan **Morris**, and Edward **Seidensticker**—

all maintained a continuing interest in Japanese civilization that reveals itself in their artfully constructed English versions of works in both prose and poetry.   JTR

ANTHOLOGIES   Gessel, Van C., and Matsumoto, Tomone, eds., *The Shōwa Anthology: Modern Japanese Short Stories*, New York/Tokyo, 1985 · Hibbett, Howard, ed., *Contemporary Japanese Literature: An Anthology of Fiction, Film, and Other Writing*, New York, 1977 · Keene, Donald, ed., *Anthology of Japanese Literature, from the Earliest Era to the Mid-Nineteenth Century*, New York, 1955 · ed., *Modern Japanese Literature: An Anthology*, New York, 1956 · Morris, Ivan, ed., *Modern Japanese Stories*, Rutland, Vt., 1962.

6. JAPANESE POETRY

i. Classical The earliest known English translation of any substantial body of Japanese poetry is *Japanese Odes, or Stanzas by a Century of Poets* by F. V. **Dickins** (1838–1915), published in London in 1866, a complete rendition of an anthology called *Hyakunin isshu*. Originally compiled by Fujiwara no Teika (1162–1241) and adopted by the influential Nijō school of poets as a canonical text, the *Hyakunin isshu* had, by the mid-19th c., long been familiar to ordinary Japanese as a popular card-game. It was natural that Dickins, a naval physician assigned to Japan, should decide to test his command of the Japanese language by translating the anthology.

All of the 100 poems that make up the *Hyakunin isshu* are written in the 5-7-5-7-7-syllable form known as *tanka* (also called *uta*, *waka*, *misohito-moji*). Dickins, who had practically no predecessors to guide him, translated these poems in four to eight lines each. Here, for example, is the poem of Princess Shikishi (d. 1201): 'Tamano'o yo taenaba taene nagaraeba shinoburu koto no yowari mozo suru', which, without frills and with considerable fidelity to the grammar, may be translated: 'String of beads, if you must break, break; if you last longer, my endurance is sure to weaken' (Sato, *String of Beads*). Dickins rendered it:

Of my life or soon or late the thread,
  The withering thread perforce must snap:
I almost would 'twere now, I dread
Of longer life the sure hap—
  The secret of our love displayed,
For e'er our happiness low laid.

In his preface to *Japanese Odes*, Dickins spoke of 'allusions' and 'metaphorical expressions' as impeding the rendition of 'the original with exactitude'. In this instance the 'string of beads' stands for life, and the poem is written on one of the set topics, 'love to be endured'—a conceit that a particular kind of love for someone must not be revealed but be 'endured' alone. It is obvious that Dickins's extravagant

version resulted in large measure from his decision to incorporate all such things in the translation.

The varying numbers of lines Dickins gave to his translations, on the other hand, apparently derived from his view (correct, as it turns out) of this verse form as unlineated. Thus, instead of speaking of the number of lines, he described the tanka as having, 'on an average, thirty characters or syllables'—a description which, as a phonetic paraphrase of the *formal* name of the tanka, *misohito-moji*, '31 characters', is accurate.

But Dickins's view of the tanka as unlineated was in time overtaken by that of the form as a five-line poem that was held by both of the two leading Japanologists of the day, William George **Aston** (1841–1911) and Basil Hall **Chamberlain** (1850–1935). Indeed, when Dickins published a thoroughly revised translation of the *Hyakunin isshu* in the *Journal of the Royal Asiatic Society* in 1909, the Shikishi poem came out as:

> My life's thread precious,
>   if it must snap, now let it,
>   endure I cannot
> this love within me hidden,
> nor e'er my love betray.

The new translation is arranged in a 5-7-5-7-7-syllable formation, and the five-line, 5-7-5-7-7-syllable format is what Dickins applied throughout the anthology, wherever he could. (During the 43-year interval he had abandoned rhyme. As he had correctly noted in *Japanese Odes*, 'nothing in the nature of rhyme can be detected in [tanka].') Dickins, by then a reader of Japanese at Bristol, took this dramatic step apparently because he was dissatisfied with the results of his colleagues in the field: Chamberlain rendered tanka into rhyming quatrains, and Aston into five unrhymed lines of varying lengths.

In any event, because of its neatness the form Dickins created, including the indentation of the two five-syllable units, would win a number of adherents among future American scholar-translators, including Laurel Rasplica **Rodd** with Mary Catherine **Henkenius** in their *Kokinshū* and Helen Craig **McCullough** in her *Kokin Wakashū*. Both books are complete translations of the first imperial anthology of Japanese verse, compiled *c.*910, in which practically all the IIII poems assembled are tanka.

In 1961 Earl **Miner**, with Robert H. **Brower**, published *Japanese Court Poetry*, which the authors described as 'the first extended treatment in a Western language' of the genre and which gave a fresh impetus to serious study of classical Japanese verse. In it the poem by Shikishi (here called Shokushi) re-emerged as:

> O cord of life!
> Threading through the jewel of my soul,
>   If you will break, break now:
> I shall weaken if this life continues,
> Unable to bear such fearful strain.

Miner's approach, because it produced, as here, translations notable for what may be called a flexible formalism and an apparent ability to stand on their own as poems, has exerted considerable influence. At the same time, the 'monumental' seriousness of *Japanese Court Poetry* has also led to the kind of criticism that may not have been raised in the earlier days—with Dickins and Chamberlain, for instance—when greater leeway was accepted in verse translation. The criticism is focused on *amplification*.

If one takes out all the words whose counterparts do not exist in the original of Shikishi's poem, Miner's translation can be whittled down to: 'cord of . . . jewel . . . If you break, break . . . I shall weaken if this . . . continues . . . strain.' But even if amplification to this extent is justifiable because of poetic convention and implied context, does it not destroy the lean sinuosity of the original? It is apparently with this question in mind that Mark Morris, who argues that the tanka is a one-line poem, has termed the Miner translation a 'Baroque imagist lyric'.

No doubt giving a set 'form' is greatly attractive when translating verses written in fixed forms such as tanka. But in English translation from Japanese, amplification has another meaning. Japanese, a polysyllabic language, tends to say much less than English in the same number of syllables. This is clear in one of the more recent translations of the *Hyakunin Isshu* that are fitted into the 5-7-5-7-7-syllable, five-line format—the one by Steven D. **Carter** in his *Traditional Japanese Poetry* (1991):

> Like a string of jewels,
>   break now—shatter, my life!

> For if I live on
>   I must surely lose the strength
> to conceal my secret love.

Here, the first five-syllable unit, which in the original is a metaphor and forms a vocative, is turned into a simile. Then the metaphor is explained, creating redundancy. Where a word *tayuru* ('break') is repeated, a different word, 'shatter', is brought in. And the phrase *shinoburu koto* ('to endure' or 'endurance') is drawn out to 'the strength to conceal my secret love'. All of this is done, evidently, to gain syllables.

Dickins aside, the initial reactions to Japanese poetry were dismissive. Aston, who arrived in Japan as an interpreter for the British legation and went on to write the first comprehensive history of Japanese literature in a western language, observed that the early Japanese poets' decision to concentrate on the tanka form had 'fatal consequences', causing generations of poets that followed to produce 'nothing more substantial than aphorisms, epigrams, conceits, or brief exclamations'. As for the even shorter form, the 5-7-5-syllable *haiku* (originally called *hokku*), he said, 'it would hardly be necessary to notice this kind of composition at all' were it not for the fame of Matsuo Bashō (1644–94) and his disciples.

Similarly, Chamberlain, long a philologist in the employ of the Imperial University of Tokyo, termed the rules for the *renga* 'puerile' in their 'minuteness', adding that it was supremely 'absurd' that the whole sequence 'gave no continuous sense'. The renga is a verse form that alternates 5-7-5- and 7-7-syllables up to 50 times and in a 'disjunctive' mode, as Miner put it in the first major attempt to explain the form in a non-Japanese language, *Japanese Linked Poetry*.

It is ironic then that each of these three forms—tanka, haiku, and renga—has since attracted the attention, special and general, of foreign poets. The tanka prompted the American poet Adelaide Crapsey (1878–1914) to devise the poetic form of the 'cinquain'. The renga's very disjunctive mode of versification proved fascinating enough to Charles Tomlinson and three other European poets for them to get together in the late 1960s to work out their own sequence. The haiku, or what Aston called 'this kind of composition', is now accepted worldwide. Each form, however, came with many cultural assumptions and prosodic requirements, necessitating explications along with translations.

We have glimpsed the complexities of the tanka. To see what the haiku as initially conceived and composed was like, let us look at the most famous haiku, a composition by Bashō: 'Furuike ya kawazu tobikomu mizu no oto', which Chamberlain, who usually translated haiku into unrhymed couplets of iambic tetrameter, rendered in a single line: 'The old pond, aye! and the sound of a frog leaping into the water'. As it happens, this translation is among the most accurate, both in grammatical construction and in line formation. The question is: to what extent does it convey the original?

The haiku started out as the opening unit of the renga, a verse sequence composed by a group of people (hence its original name of *hokku*, 'opening phrase'). As such it was required to offer a salutation and specify the time (season) of composition. When the court-oriented orthodox renga was displaced by the more down-to-earth variety, these requirements were retained, with the addition of a third element, *haikai* ('humour'), which may be ribald or crude, reliant on puns or allusive twists.

With the 'pond/frog' haiku, the salutation lies, possibly, in the self-deprecation of Bashō saying to his guests that his abode is so humble all he can offer for entertainment is the sound of frogs jumping into a none-too-attractive pond in his garden. The season is indicated by the frog, which represents spring. Humour? In classical or orthodox tanka, reference to frogs required reference to their croaks. By referring to the sound the frog makes as it plunges into the water, Bashō has created a humorous twist.

The way in which such background knowledge enhances the reading of haiku prompted R. H. **Blyth** to write a multi-volume explication of haiku. There are several other notable book-length explications, but Blyth's remains unsurpassed, although his thesis that 'haiku is Zen', which is his greatest appeal, may be questioned. By the time Blyth prepared his last volume on the subject, the haiku had become such a popular international poetic form that he was able to append a chapter called 'World Haiku'. So it may be appropriate to cite his proposal for 'the ideal haiku form in English'.

Such a form should consist, Blyth said, of 'three short lines, the second a little longer than the other two; a two-three-two rhythm, but not regularly iambic or anapaestic; rhyme avoided, even if felicitous and accidental'. His own translations do not often follow that prescription, though this one does:

> The old pond;
> A frog jumps in:
> The sound of the water.

There are of course those who believe in the need for the English translation or an English haiku to reflect the 'original form'—in this instance, a three-line, 5-7-5-syllable format. One such is Kenneth **Yasuda**, who in *The Japanese Haiku* also stressed the need to use a rhyme scheme:

> Ancient pond unstirred
> Into which a frog has plunged,
> A splash was heard.

Still, the collections of haiku translated by various hands, such as Sato's *One Hundred Frogs* and Bowers's *The Classic Tradition of Haiku*, show that haiku translations have been flexible, beginning with one-line translations by Lafcadio **Hearn** (1850–1904). This and the brevity of the form may account for the ready acceptance of the haiku as a one-line poem when the argument to that effect was put forward in the 1970s. Today, at least in English, one-line haiku are common, though the general acceptance of the one-line form remains in doubt.

Before the tanka, which dates from the 7th c., became the preferred and predominant form, there were some longer forms, notably the *chōka*, which repeats the 5-7-syllable unit three or more times, indefinitely, and often ends with a 7-syllable unit. Japan's oldest extant (and some say greatest) anthology, the *Man'yōshū*, compiled in the second half of the 8th c., assembles about 4500 verses written in various forms, and there is no doubt that one great attraction of this book lies in verses written in the supple chōka form.

However, as a result of a curious set of circumstances, interest in the chōka dwindled, and at the end of the 19th c. the three verse forms of tanka, renga, and haiku were virtually the only vehicles available to the Japanese poets. (There was also *kanshi*, verse in Chinese, which until the mid-19th c. carried greater prestige than verse in the indigenous language. Burton **Watson** has translated the most in this genre, beginning with his two-volume set, *Japanese Literature in Chinese*.)

ii. Modern In 1882 the first serious attempt was made to move beyond the traditional verse forms, by adopting longer, 'western-style' forms. Once begun, the development of new poetic forms was fast. By the 1910s the Japanese counterpart to 'free verse'—which essentially means poems not using any discernible syllabic patterns while using 'colloquial' as opposed to 'literary' language—had firmly taken root. And by the end of the 1930s many of the more original, 'modern' poems had been written in the new genre, usually grouped as *shi* (which simply means 'verse' or 'poem') and treated separately from tanka, haiku, and renga, which continue to be written.

Still, even though a large selection from the oldest anthology, the *Man'yōshū*, was translated as early as 1940, by a committee of Japanese scholars and the English poet Ralph **Hodgson**, English translation of substantial bodies of shi had to wait until 1957 when two anthologies appeared, evidently in connection to the International PEN conference held in Japan: *An Anthology of Modern Japanese Poetry*, by **Kōno** Ichirō and **Fukuda** Rikutarō, and *The Poetry of Living Japan*, by **Ninomiya** Takamichi and D. J. **Enright**.

And if according individual poets separate volumes marks a turning-point, it took another dozen years before English translators began to show a more serious interest in shi. In 1969 Graeme **Wilson** translated Hagiwara Sakutarō (1886–1942) in *Face at the Bottom of the World and Other Poems*, and Cid **Corman** and **Kamaike** Susumu, Kusano Shimpei in *Frogs and Others*.

Since then two dozen modern poets have attracted similar attention, including those whom many regard as the four greatest: Takamura Kōtarō (1883–1956), in Sato's *Chieko and Other Poems*, Hagiwara, in Sato's *Howling at the Moon*, Miyazawa Kenji (1896–1933), in Sato's *Spring and Asura*, and Nishiwaki Junzaburō (1894–1982), who has been translated by Yasuko **Claremont** in *Gen'ei* (1991) and by Hosea **Hirata** in *The Poetry and Poetics of Nishiwaki Junzaburō* (1995).

The following is Hagiwara's poem 'Sickly Face at the Bottom of the Ground' in Sato's translation:

> At the bottom of the ground a face emerging,
> a lonely invalid's face emerging.
>
> In the dark at the bottom of the ground,
> soft vernal grass-stalks beginning to flare,
> rats' nest beginning to flare,
> and entangled with the nest,
> innumerable hairs beginning to tremble,
> time the winter solstice,
> from the lonely sickly ground,
> roots of thin blue bamboo beginning to grow,
> beginning to grow,
> and that, looking truly pathetic,
> looking blurred,
> looking truly, truly, pathetic.
>
> In the dark at the bottom of the ground,
> a lonely invalid's face emerging.

This is representative of Hagiwara, the first poet to express modern neurosis and angst through images contemplated by an 'invalid fearful of diseases', as a contemporary put it.

Miyazawa, in contrast, described rural life through a combination of an almost insouciant trust in the unity of scientific knowledge and religious (Buddhist) belief and a profound sense of humour and drama. Here is one of his untitled poems, again in Sato's translation:

> Since the doctor is still young,
> they say he doesn't mind jumping out of bed at night,
> discounts drugs for them, and doesn't do
> complicated things like injections
> or anything that desecrates nature too much.
> I think that's why they like him.
> By the time this doctor finally comes to feel
> just as the villagers do,
> and work as an integral part,
> he'll have fallen behind in new techniques
> and at the lecture of the county doctor's society
> he'll curl up small, a perpetual listener.
> Such is the effect of this sunlight,
> water, and the transparent air.
> Every time I pass here by train,
> I try to imagine what kind of person he is.
> Because, presiding over this beautiful hospital,
> he has a face like a chameleon,
> I feel very sorry for him.
> Four or five persons have bowed.
> Now the doctor quietly returns the bow.

Among the poets who established their reputations in postwar Japan, the more frequently translated include Yoshioka Minoru, Tamura Ryūichi, Tanikawa Shuntarō, Ōoka Makoto, Shiraishi Kazuko, Takahashi Mutsuo, and Yoshimasu Gōzō.

Today the two anthologies of Japanese poetry from ancient to modern times, completed 17 years apart, *The Penguin Book of Japanese Verse*, by Geoffrey **Bownas** and Anthony **Thwaite**, and the far larger *From the Country of Eight Islands*, by Burton Watson and Sato, remain in print. There are, in addition, a sizeable number of anthologies with a more limited scope, such as *Postwar Japanese Poetry*, by Harry **Guest**, Lynn **Guest**, and **Kajima** Shōzō, *A Play of Mirrors: Eight Major Poets of Modern Japan*, by **Ōoka** Makoto and Thomas **Fitzsimmons**, and *Burning Giraffes*, by James **Kirkup**.

Given the normally small runs of books of translated poems, it is hard to assess what influences modern Japanese poetry is having through English translation. But continued additions, including a planned historical survey of Japanese women poets, suggest considerable interest in Japanese poetry, both classical and modern.   HS

ANTHOLOGIES   Blyth, R. H., *Haiku*, i, Tokyo, 1949 · *A History of Haiku*, ii, Tokyo, 1964 · Bowers, Faubion, ed., *The Classic Tradition of Haiku: An Anthology*, New York, 1996 · Bownas, Geoffrey, and Thwaite, Anthony, eds., *The Penguin Book of Japanese Verse*, Harmondsworth/Baltimore, 1964 · Dickins, F. V., *Japanese Odes, or Stanzas by a Century of Poets*, London, 1866 · 'A Translation of the Japanese Anthology Known as Hyakunin Isshiu, or Hundred Poems by a Hundred Poets', *Journal of the Royal Asiatic Society*, 1909 · Carter, Steven D., *Traditional Japanese Poetry*, Stanford, Calif., 1991 · Guest, Harry, Guest, Lynn, and Kajima Shōzō, *Postwar Japanese Poetry*, Baltimore, 1972 · Kōno, Ichirō, and Fukuda, Rikutarō , *An Anthology of Modern Japanese Poetry*, Tokyo, 1957 · Kirkup, James, *Burning Giraffes: An Anthology of Modern and Contemporary Japanese Poets in Translation*, Salzburg, 1996 · McCullough, Craig Helen, *Kokin Wakashū*, Stanford, Calif., 1985 · Ninomiya, Takamichi, and D. J. Enright, *The Poetry of Living Japan*, London, 1957 · Nippon Gakujutsu Shinkōkai [Japanese Classics Translation Committee] with Ralph Hodgson, *The Man'yōshu*, Tokyo, 1940; rep. 1969 · Ōoka, Makoto, and Fitzsimmons, Thomas, eds., *A Play of Mirrors: Eight Major Poets of Modern Japan*, Rochester, NY, 1987 · Rodd, Laurel Rasplica, with Mary Catherine Henkenius, *Kokinshū*, Princeton, NJ, 1984 · Sato, Hiroaki, and Watson, Burton, *From the Country of Eight Islands: An Anthology of Japanese Poetry*, New York, 1981; rep. 1984 · Watson, Burton, *Japanese Literature in Chinese*, 2 vols., New York, 1975–6.

HAGIWARA SAKUTARŌ   Sato, Hiroaki, *Howling at the Moon: Poems of Hagiwara Sakutarō*, Tokyo, 1978; rep. Los Angeles, 1998 · Wilson, Graeme, *Face at the Bottom of the World and Other Poems*, Tokyo/Rutland, Vt., 1969.

KUSANO SHINPEI   Corman, Cid, and Kamaike Susumu, *Frogs and Others*, Tokyo, 1969.

MIYAZAWA KENJI   Sato, Hiroaki, *Spring and Asura: Poems of Kenji Miyazawa*, Chicago, 1973 [subsequently expanded as *A Future of Ice: Poems and Stories of a Japanese Buddhist, Miyazawa Kenji*, San Francisco, 1989].

NISHIWAKI JUNZABURŌ   Claremont, Yasuko, *Gen'ei*, Sydney, 1991 · Hirata, Hosea, *The Poetry and Poetics of Nishiwaki Junzaburō*, Princeton, NJ, 1995.

SHIKISHI   Sato, Hiroaki, *String of Beads: Complete Poems of Princess Shikishi*, Hawaii, 1993.

TAKAMURA KŌTARŌ   Sato, Hiroaki, *Chieko and Other Poems of Takamura Kōtarō*, Honolulu, 1980 [subsequently expanded as *A Brief History of Imbecility: Poetry and Prose of Takamura Kōtarō*, Honolulu, 1992].

SEE ALSO   Brower, R. H., 'Japanese', in W. K. Wimsatt, ed., *Versification: Major Language Types*, New York, 1972 · Brower, R. H., and Miner, E., *Japanese Court Poetry*, Stanford, Calif., 1961 · Miner, E., *Japanese Linked Poetry*, Princeton, 1979 · Mostow, J. S., *Pictures of the Heart: The* Hyakunin Isshu *in Word and Image*, Honolulu, 1996 · Sato, H., *One Hundred Frogs: From Renga to Haiku to English*, Tokyo/New York, 1983 [one chapter published independently as *One Hundred Frogs*, New York, 1996].

7. JAPANESE FICTION

i. Classical By happy coincidence, the most important work in Japanese literary history is also the work of prose narrative that has inspired the most translations into English. *Genji monogatari* (early 11th c., The Tale of Genji), produced by a woman of the imperial court known to us as Murasaki Shikibu, describes the meteoric and mercurial career and loves of the 'shining' Prince Genji. Not only does the tale serve as a guidebook to proper aesthetic achievements (in this early court period, nothing superseded the 'rule of taste', as the British japanologist Sir George Sansom once wrote), but by the end of its 54th and final chapter it has also ratified the doctrine of decline and evanescence so characteristic of Japanese sensibility. In that sense, *The Tale of Genji* is the supreme literary manifestation of the dual propensities toward celebration and desolation witnessed among the Japanese.

The first complete translation of the *Genji* into English was done between 1925 and 1932 by Arthur **Waley**, whose style and approach not only typify the attitudes of his day but set the standard for translations from Japanese for many decades to come. Waley exoticized the text, scrupulously refusing ever to visit Japan lest it should spoil the idealized image of the place that Lady Murasaki's work had fashioned in his mind. At the same time he adopted something of an imperialistic attitude toward the tale, imposing his own interpretations on thorny passages, freely cutting sections his own artistic tastes judged inferior, and expanding upon those he felt the author had not fully shaped. This dual interaction with the text, swinging between reverent (but distant) admiration and a thinly veiled sense of the need to control it for its own good, was characteristic of translator attitudes toward Japanese literature for much of this century. While many in the postwar period who read Waley's *Genji* admit to feeling more that they are visitors at the Victorian court than at the Heian palace, the impact of this first rendition has been enormous. In fact, the modern Japanese language has changed in so many fundamental ways from the language of the 11th c. that many educated Japanese of the 1920s and 1930s confessed they found it easier

241

to understand the Waley translation than the Murasaki original.

While several generations of Japan experts and curious readers were weaned on the Waley version of *Genji*, the western scholarly community after World War II grew increasingly uneasy about the liberties Waley had taken with the text. It was, therefore, inevitable that a new translation would be done, and perhaps a natural culmination of an illustrious career as translator of many modern and some premodern Japanese texts that Edward G. **Seidensticker** should undertake it. Seidensticker's translation was published in 1976 by Alfred A. Knopf, and has to all intents and purposes displaced the Waley version.

Seidensticker's *Genji* is unquestionably more faithful to the original text. But, as Edwin Cranston of Harvard University has noted in his comparative review of the translations: 'Like Waley, Seidensticker has a consistent vision of the work he is translating. It is a drier, brisker, more quotidian vision, but it is consistent. . . . Seidensticker's great virtue is that he presents the entirety of Murasaki's masterpiece, and sticks closer to its text. . . . [But] there is still room for more: a more ample and luscious translation, more poetic and less brisk—something very like Waley, but with less embroidery and a more responsible attitude toward the integrity of the text.' Some of the differences in approach to translating the text can be seen through a comparison of the Waley and Seidensticker versions of the tale's opening sentence. The earlier rendition gives: 'At the Court of an Emperor (he lived it matters not when) there was among the many gentlewomen of the Wardrobe and Chamber one, who though she was not of very high rank was favoured far beyond all the rest . . .' Seidensticker offers: 'In a certain reign there was a lady not of the first rank whom the emperor loved more than any of the others.' Waley clearly provides more than is justified by the original; Seidensticker provides a little less than the rhythms of Lady Murasaki demand.

It almost seems as though Seidensticker is paying penance for (or perhaps even doing some overcorrection of) some of his earliest translations from the 1950s, when he was under the sway of the Waley philosophy of doctored translation and paid less attention to fidelity. His renditions of classical diaries and modern short stories (including a markedly truncated version of 'The Izu Dancer' by Kawabata Yasunari) were certainly governed more by a concern for how things sounded in English than by how closely they resembled the originals. But by the 1960s, as he focused his talents on several of the most important modern novels, including

Kawabata's *Yama no oto* (1950, The Sound of the Mountain) and Tanizaki Jun'ichirō's *Sasameyuki* (1948, The Makioka Sisters), he had become convinced that the original authors could be trusted to tell their own stories. The masterful translations that resulted from this change of attitude were proof that the purpose of translation had been more clearly defined by those who did it best and most frequently.

The final chapter has yet to be written on the translation of *The Tale of Genji*. Seidensticker allowed an abridgment containing only 12 chapters from the first section of the tale to be published in 1985 for classroom use, and Helen **McCullough**, a translator of numerous classical works and a scrupulously faithful follower of original texts, produced a volume called *Genji and Heike* that includes 10 chapters taken from across the scope of the Genji tale and also provides selections from her complete translation of the early 13th-c. military epic *Heike monogatari* (The Tale of the Heike). At the time of writing Royall **Tyler**, who has translated a number of medieval nō plays, is working on a complete retranslation of the *Genji* for Penguin. It is worth noting that *Genji* and *Heike* are the chief among only a handful of Japanese literary works that have been graced with more than one translation; a shortage of qualified translators (on the European Continent many of the translations of Japanese fiction that appear are taken not from the original Japanese but from a published English translation) and a finite reading audience severely limit the publication of translations of Japanese prose works.

A generation or so of readers drew their mental pictures of Japan from the Waley translation of *Genji*, and it must have been difficult for those accustomed to the delicate sensibilities of that classical text to watch Japan in the 1930s begin to betray every exotic expectation the tale had constructed in their minds. For obvious reasons, interest in Japanese literature waned in the middle of this century. Ironically, however, the need to contain Japanese military aggression concomitantly produced a generation of western soldiers who became intrigued by the subtle nuances of the language they had studied at military academies so that they could interrogate captured soldiers; once they moved in to occupy defeated Japan, they grew enamoured of what they saw of Japanese culture through the ruins of the landscape. The scholarly and somewhat antiquarian tastes of the British gentlemen who studied Japan after its opening to the West in the late 19th c. were replaced by this first generation of American warrior-cum-scholar types who tackled the task of introducing Japanese literature to the West with something like missionary zeal.

The first full translation of a Japanese literary text to appear after the war was Wm. **de Bary**'s version of Ihara Saikaku's *Kōshoku gonin onna* (1686; Five Women who Loved Love). This raucous and sardonic collection of stories about women who are willing to sacrifice social position and life itself in their pursuit of passion certainly served as a useful corrective to the florid image generated in western minds by *The Tale of Genji*, but it must have baffled many readers who could not reconcile such contradictory glimpses behind the screens of Japanese culture.

Though de Bary's translation captures little of the stylistic intricacy or poetic felicity of the original, still it opened the doors to more translations of literature produced by the 'former enemy'. Although the emergence of a small reading audience interested in contemporary Japan resulted in a shift in focus to 20th-c. literature, many fine translations from premodern works were undertaken as well. Notable among them are several renditions of the 17th-c. haiku master Matsuo Bashō's travel journal, *Oku no hosomichi* (1694, The Narrow Road to the Deep North), the medieval historical tales translated by Helen and William McCullough, and a number of prose pieces which the Japanese call *zuihitsu* ('miscellaneous writings'), including Ivan **Morris**'s complete annotated translation of *Makura no sōshi* (11th c., The Pillow Book), by Sei Shōnagon, a lady of the court who was a contemporary of Lady Murasaki, and the priest Yoshida Kenkō's medieval musings on the decline in civilization titled *Tsurezuregusa* (1332, Essays in Idleness), transformed into English by Donald **Keene**.

ii. Modern A solid boost to the international reputation of Japanese literature came as a result of the tireless efforts of novelist Kawabata Yasunari, who, as president of the Japan PEN Club, toiled to make the first International PEN conference held in Japan in 1957 a forum for the introduction of Japanese literature to the world. The success of that gathering, combined with the publication of Donald Keene's landmark collection, *Modern Japanese Literature: An Anthology*, paved the way for a spate of translated novels and short stories. By the early 1970s western readers were able to talk about a 'Big Three' among modern Japanese novelists—Tanizaki Jun'ichirō, Kawabata Yasunari (who in 1968 became the first Japanese author to receive the Nobel Prize for Literature), and Mishima Yukio, and Knopf had established itself as the leading publishing house for contemporary Japanese fiction in translation.

One of the first modern novels in translation to make a significant positive impact upon the reputation of Japanese fiction in the West was Edwin **McClellan**'s elegant, seamless rendition of Natsume Sōseki's 1914 novel, *Kokoro*. The novel, one of the undisputed masterpieces of the modern age, is a powerful examination of the dark depths of the human heart and the price that must be paid when expanded individual freedom leads to greater opportunities to betray and destroy others. Sōseki lived in London for a few years at the turn of the century and was thoroughly versed in the traditions of the British novel, but his writings repeatedly examined the toll that modernization was taking on traditional moral values. McClellan's translation of this moving novel is remarkable in that it strays scarcely a whit from the original text, and yet manages to convey the unrestrained power of Sōseki's writing in an eloquent English idiom. The achievement is all the more impressive when compared with an earnest but ultimately lifeless attempt by a native Japanese to translate *Kokoro* in 1941.

The 1960s and 1970s were, indeed, something of a Golden Age in the translation of Japanese fiction into English. Throughout this period, the overwhelming majority of translations were undertaken by American academics, many of whom had direct personal ties with the Japanese authors they were translating. Keene, for instance, developed a lifelong friendship with Mishima and translated several of his best plays into English. He ceded most of the author's novels to others, but reserved for himself *Utage no ato* (1960, After the Banquet), containing some of Mishima's most fully-etched characters.

Seidensticker and Keene both worked out special arrangements with their American universities to give them at least half of each year in Japan, where they frequently socialized with Kawabata, Tanizaki, and many of the other leading authors of the day. Though such personal relationships always run the danger of colouring critical judgements, the fine-tuned analytical skills of these scholar-translators allowed them to use their personal understanding of the authors' aims to enrich their translations of the fiction. Both men, in fact, stepped in after Mishima's sensational suicide by *seppuku* in 1970 to rescue the project of translating his final tetralogy when the first two volumes did not live up to their expectations, and Seidensticker himself agreed to translate the final volume.

Translation was most assuredly driven by the personal tastes of the translators and the interpersonal associations they had with Japanese authors in the 1960s and 1970s, most particularly since this was the period before the advent of the literary agent in Japan. Translation agreements (often not even written into formal contracts until after western publishers were drawn into the deal) were frequently reached over drinks or through the mail, which at times worked to the disadvantage of an unknown Japanese author at the mercy of a translator whose English stylistic skills he or she could not evaluate. Endō Shūsaku, who achieved a sizeable international following because of the Christian motifs in novels such as *Chimmoku* (1966, Silence) and *Samurai* (1980, The Samurai), hired one of his several translators on the basis of a clumsily phrased letter written in Japanese by a neophyte freshly admitted to a graduate programme in Japanese literature.

One of the most prolific, diverse, and reliable translators of Japanese fiction in the postwar period is John **Bester**, whose work has ranged from Enchi Fumiko's portrayal of female oppression in *Onnazaka* (1957, The Waiting Years) to 1995 Nobel prize winner Ōe Kenzaburō's *Man'en gannen no futtoboōru* (1967), translated as *The Silent Cry*, and Ibuse Masuji's harrowing but ultimately invigorating account of the Hiroshima bombing, *Kuroi ame* (1966, Black Rain). Also deserving mention for their durability as literary works in English are E. Dale **Saunders**'s version of the Kafkaesque existential novel *Suna no onna* (1962, The Woman in the Dunes) by Abe Kōbō, and John **Nathan**'s brash,

demanding translation of Ōe Kenzaburō's *Kojinteki na taiken* (1964, A Personal Matter).

It would seem, at the time of writing, that the Golden Age for the translation of Japanese fiction has passed. Literary agents now stand as a barrier between author and translator, demanding their cut and requiring translators to settle for a pre-established fee rather than a share in royalties, and spoiling the personal relationship so crucial to success in any segment of Japanese society. Readership has also waned, and fewer translated novels from Japan are discussed in the major American or British literary reviews. Certainly part of the blame must be placed on a decline in the quality of contemporary fiction in Japan, where the appeal to a popular audience has resulted, as it has in so many other parts of the world, in a general dumbing-down of style as well as content. One must look long and hard for a writer today whose sense of literary tradition extends back further than the 1960s, and most often the cultural referents—if they are to be found at all—are the Beatles and the sexual revolution. While a reader may understandably have tired of all those cherry blossoms and sleeves damp from tears, of suicides both despairing and honourable, and of delicate portraits of subtly shifting emotions given precedence over plot twists, one has to wonder whether it is worth the effort to translate into English a novel that could as easily have been written by a 20-year-old American misfit in Cleveland as by a Japanese clone of the same in Kanagawa.　　　　　　　　　　　　　　VG

ABE KŌBŌ　Saunders, E. Dale, *The Woman in the Dunes*, New York, 1964.

ANONYMOUS　McCullough, Helen C., *The Tale of the Heike*, Stanford, Calif., 1988 · McCullough, William H., and McCullough, Helen C., *A Tale of Flowering Fortunes: Annals of Japanese Aristocratic Life in the Heian Period*, Stanford, Calif., 1980.

ENCHI FUMIKO　Bester, John, *The Waiting Years*, Tokyo, 1971.

ENDŌ SHŪSAKU　Gessel, Van C., *The Samurai*, London/New York, 1982 · Johnston, William, *Silence*, Tokyo, 1969.

IBUSE MASUJI　Bester, John, *Black Rain*, Tokyo, 1969.

IHARA SAIKAKU　de Bary, William Theodore, *Five Women Who Loved Love*, Rutland, Vt., 1956, London, 1969.

KAWABATA YASUNARI　Seidensticker, Edward G., *The Izu Dancer and Other Stories*, Rutland, Vt., 1974 · *Sound of the Mountain*, New York/London, 1970.

MATSUO BASHŌ　Yuasa, Nobuyuki, *The Narrow Road to the Deep North*, Harmondsworth, 1966 [Penguin].

MISHIMA YUKIO　Gallagher, Michael, *Spring Snow*, New York/London, 1972 · *Runaway Horses*, New York/London, 1973 · Keene, Donald, *After the Banquet*, New York/London, 1963 · Saunders, E. Dale, and Seigle, Cecilia Segawa, *The Temple of Dawn*, New York, 1973, London, 1974 · Seidensticker, Edward G., *The Decay of the Angel*, New York, 1974.

MURASAKI SHIKIBU　McCullough, Helen C., *Genji and Heike*, Stanford, Calif., 1994 · Seidensticker, Edward G., *The Tale of Genji*, New York, 1976 [abr. edn. New York, 1990] · Waley, Arthur, *The Tale of Genji*, London/Boston/New York, 1925–32 [several reps.].

NATSUME SŌSEKI　McClellan, Edwin, *Kokoro*, Chicago, 1957 · Sato, Ineko, *Kokoro*, Tokyo, 1941.

ŌE KENZABURŌ　Bester, John, *The Silent Cry*, Tokyo, 1974 · Nathan, John, *A Personal Matter*, New York, 1968.

SEI SHŌNAGON　Morris, Ivan, *The Pillow Book of Sei Shōnagon*, 2 vols., New York, 1967.

TANIZAKI JUN'ICHIRŌ　Seidensticker, Edward G., *The Makioka Sisters*, New York, 1957.

YOSHIDA KENKŌ　Keene, Donald, *Essays in Idleness: The Tsurezuregusa of Kenko*, New York, 1967.

SEE ALSO   Cranston, E., 'The Seidensticker Genji', *Journal of Japanese Studies*, 4 (winter 1978), 1–25 · Fowler, E., 'Rendering Words, Traversing Cultures: On the Art and Politics of Translating Modern Japanese Fiction', *Journal of Japanese Studies*, 18 (winter 1992), 1–44.

8. JAPANESE DRAMA

i. Introduction Although Japanese theatre has an ancient heritage, with performing traditions going back as far as the 6th c. or earlier, the first preserved literary texts that have attracted wide approbation, both in modern Japan and, in translated form, around the world, can be said to occur with the flowering of the *nō* drama around 1400 in the work of the great playwright, actor, and theoretician Zeami Motokiyo. The nō (the term, which is often translated as 'accomplishment' and is sometimes romanized as noh), spare, poetic, often highly spiritual in its aesthetics, remained the most influential form of theatre down to the 17th c., at which point it came also to exert an important influence on the development of the puppet theatre and kabuki, popular forms of theatre enjoyed by the urban merchant classes. Inroads of western artistic influences in the latter half of the 19th c. and after, including the prestige assigned by Japanese theatregoers to the works of Shakespeare, Ibsen, and Chekhov, led to fixing the 'classical' repertoire of older forms and the creation of a modern Japanese theatre, which in turn spurred on the creation of a genuine avant-garde in the 1970s and after. Useful, sometimes eloquent translations of works from all these genres and periods now exist.

It was not always so. Japan's peculiar historical development, which led to her remaining cut off from world civilization from the 1630s to the middle of the 19th c., permitted little of significance in the way of theatrical influences to enter from other Asian and European theatres or literature. Nor were there opportunities for Japanese theatre to become known in the West. Visitors to Japan before this period, particularly the Catholic missionaries from Spain and Portugal, did record their responses to theatrical performances in the 1500s, but the language barrier was such that no translations were made during this early period.

The Japanese theatre thus developed in virtual isolation until the latter half of the 19th c., when Japanese travelling to Europe began to observe theatrical productions in London, Paris, New York, Berlin, and elsewhere, while Europeans and Americans residing in Japan began to attend the theatre and develop a lively interest in the texts of the various dramas they encountered. This enthusiasm was by no means limited to English-speaking enthusiasts and translators. Those wishing to gain a fuller understanding of the development of Japanese drama in translation need to examine the work of such early figures as Noël Péri, a notable French enthusiast, as well as the work of a number of German writers and translators.

In the early period of translation, which began in the 1880s and continued until the mid-1930s and the beginning of World War II, there appear to have been two major barriers to overcome. The first generation of those who attempted translations were often observers who were resident in Japan for other purposes. Many of these early figures, such as England's Basil Hall **Chamberlain** (1850–1935), William George **Aston** (1841–1911), Frederick V. **Dickins** (1838–1915), and Frank **Brinkley** (1841–1912), were educators or government officials sent to work in Japan; some, like Brinkley, stayed on and developed new careers. Most of them learnt the Japanese language well. Highly educated, and at a time when literature, particularly classical Greek and Latin literature, still remained a central part of a gentlemen's education, these early translators observed the diverse forms of theatre then performed in Japan through the glasses of their own enthusiasms and prejudices. True, their residence in Japan convinced them that Japan had a high culture; her drama was therefore not to be dismissed as mere ethnography. By the same token, in attempting to find a literary language in which to cast their translations, they chose a kind of dignified theatrical diction comfortable to them and their first readers but perforce very distant indeed from the beauty and spirit of the language of the original texts.

ii. The Nō Theatre It is therefore not surprising that more often than not many early translators chose nō, the most classical and 'literary' of Japanese theatrical forms, as the appropriate genre in which to undertake their first experiments. Many of these were first published in the *Transactions of the Asiatic Society of Japan* and similar scholarly journals of the period.

Early experimental translations of the type described above were eclipsed by the work of two men, both of whom approached the nō theatre with differing interests. The first of them, the American

Ernest **Fenollosa** (1853–1908), resident in Japan for more than a decade and passionately interested in the Japanese arts, studied nō chanting and dancing with Umewaka Minoru, a great performer of the period, and then attempted to translate the plays he studied for performance. After Fenollosa's death, his papers and draft translations were given over to the young American poet Ezra **Pound**. Pound reworked the translations, edited Fenollosa's essays, and published in 1916 *'Noh' or Accomplishment: A Study of the Classical Stage of Japan* under both their names. Despite occasional inaccuracies in translation and in some ways a certain tendentiousness typical of Pound, the collection remains even now highly regarded as a brilliant introduction to the beauties of the poetry of medieval Japanese theatre.

Actually, Pound's book was not the first. A collection by the English scientist Marie C. **Stopes** and her Japanese collaborator, Professor Sakurai Jōji, reflects her enthusiasm for nō gained during a visit to Japan. Entitled *Plays of Old Japan: the Nō*, the book, published in London in 1913, contains both thoughtful essays and quite accurate translations of the three plays she chose to render into English. Nevertheless, Pound's versions revealed a genuine poetic flair and quickly established a lasting interest among Western readers in this form of Japanese drama.

Pound included translations of 15 plays, including those based on incidents in two of the great works of Japanese prose literature, the *Genji monogatari* (Tale of Genji) and the *Heike monogatari* (Tale of the Heike) [see II.f.7.i]. Four years later, in 1921, Arthur **Waley** published his even more influential *Noh Theatre of Japan*, in which he included 19 translated plays, with only six duplicating those in the Fenollosa/Pound volume. Within a relatively short space of time, English-language readers had access to some 28 dramas from the canon of roughly 240 plays which remain in the modern repertoire.

Unlike Fenollosa, who first approached the form in terms of performance, Arthur Waley, at that time an employee of the British Library, read these theatrical texts as literature and, by treating them as such, helped raise their prestige both in Japan and in the West. Despite the fact that he never saw nō performed, Waley's extraordinary linguistic skills in both languages give his translations an elegance and profundity wonderfully appropriate to the originals.

In the postwar period, a number of important contributions enlarged still further the number and quality of translations of nō available in English. First, the Japanese government, with a conviction that Japanese culture needed to be better understood and appreciated in Europe and the United States, undertook to reestablish a series of translations and commentaries on classical Japanese literature begun before the war. The series of plays, rendered into English by an apparently anonymous committee of translators and issued under the auspices of the Nippon Gakujitsu Shinkōkai (Japan Society for the Promotion of Scientific Research) in three volumes, 10 plays to each volume, made other central texts available in excellent English and with the kind of annotations that showed for the first time the intertextuality inherent in the form, since poems and references from a whole corpus of medieval Chinese and Japanese literary and religious texts make appearances in the dramatic texts themselves.

Many of the subsequent translations undertaken came from the academic community. Donald **Keene**, whose importance remains overwhelming in the field of translated Japanese literature and drama, continued to make English versions available. In his *20 Plays of the Nō Theatre*, he and his students produced a volume of plays that read with a special grace, yet contain the necessary scholarly apparatus to allow the plays to be properly examined in terms of their literary and cultural milieu. Newer translations in this vein, such as Kenneth **Yasuda**'s *Masterworks of Nō Theatre* and the *Japanese Nō Dramas* of Royall **Tyler**, one of Donald Keene's most distinguished students, carry on this tradition.

Finally, the increasing number of scholars and performers working with Japanese colleagues on the literary and performance history of nō have produced translations attuned to performance values, such as those undertaken by Karen **Brazell**, Richard **Emmert** (under the auspices of the National Noh Theatre in Tokyo), and **Shimazaki** Chifumi. Indeed, the very canon itself, now being reexamined in Japan, is being expanded in English by a volume of new translations of plays less often performed in modern times by Mae **Smethurst**.

Kyōgen ('mad words'), the comic interludes performed between the nō plays in a traditional day's programme, are charming and thoroughly effective stage pieces which show at best modest literary aspirations, since much of their effective humour lies in situation and movement. A volume of translations prepared in 1938 by Shio **Sakanishi**, at that time an employee of the Library of Congress in Washington, DC, served for many years as the most convenient and accomplished introduction to the form. This collection has been supplemented in recent years by the work of Don **Kenny** and others, English-speaking performers whose long residence in Japan has helped them to approach the translation of the form with warmth and skill. The volume by Carolyn Anne **Morley**, *Transformations, Miracles, and Mischief: The Mountain Priest Plays of Kyōgen*, published in 1993, provides a group of particularly effective translations.

iii. Bunraku and Kabuki The puppet theatre (first known as jōruri and, since the 19th c. most often referred to as bunraku), reached its first flowering with the dramas of Chikamatsu Monzaemon (1653–1724), sometimes described by early enthusiasts as 'the Shakespeare of Japan', a service, of course, to neither dramatist. Many of the greatest and most enduring dramas of Japan's Tokugawa period (1600–1868) were first written to be performed by narrators and puppets. These plays, however, were soon taken over by the all-male troupes of actors performing kabuki, so that, in a real sense, the same works remain classics in both performing genres.

Early attempts to translate these texts were coloured in the minds of the translators by a certain distaste for what, in their Victorian vision, they took to be the unhappy excesses of emotion to be found there. They also found it difficult to match the original language with what they considered to be an appropriately decorous style in English.

The play which immediately attracted the greatest attention was the 1748 11-act drama by Takeda Izumo and his colleagues concerning the vendetta of the 47 rōnin (masterless samurai), *Chūshingura* (The Treasury of Loyal Retainers). One of the earliest attempts to render this mammoth and exciting work into English was entitled *Chiushingura or The Loyal League*, translated by Frederick V. Dickins [see II.f.6.i]. Calling his version 'a Japanese Romance', Dickins made use of the original text with some skill, writing out the narrator's comments as prose passages connecting the dialogue, so that the play reads rather like a novel. Dickins chose to adopt a level of language that, certainly for today's readers, seems stilted and self-consciously 'literary', and he has also omitted the kind of telling detail that makes the original so powerful. One look at the now standard 1971 translation by Donald Keene shows the difference immediately. Keene's language is tougher, the exchanges far more telling.

The Dickins translation, whatever its real merits and its faults, served for many years as the only roughly complete version of this famous drama available in English. The British poet John Masefield, in writing his own dramatic version of the vendetta which he entitled *The Faithful*, first produced in 1915, mentions how he learnt the details of the story from Dickins's English rendering, and this

translation was much cited for a considerable time. Several English versions by Japanese translators were published in Tokyo early in the century but gained limited circulation in the West.

Along with *Chūshingura*, the plays of Chikamatsu also received early attention, but the difficulties of rendering these poetic and lengthy texts into English resulted in paraphrase or summary versions of the original. Among the most widely available of these versions was a collection by the Japanese translator Asatarō **Miyamori**, a faculty member at Tokyo's Keio University, entitled *Masterpieces of Chikamatsu*, published in England in 1926. His versions attempt to give the flavour of the works, although in a manner more redolent of Shakespearean language than of the sort of poetry to be found in the originals. Still, Miyamori's work remains even now the only source in English concerning the contents of several of Chikamatu's major works. The British playwright Peter Oswald, in his 1996 drama *Fair Ladies at a Game of Poem Cards*, mentions that he read this version, which, strangely, 'wasn't set out like a play, but like an account of a play: mainly narration, some reported speech'. Miyamori's strategy thus allowed Oswald to create virtually a new work of art.

It was not until the postwar period that, again thanks to the talents and energies of Donald Keene, English-language readers were able to grasp for the first time the dramatic effectiveness of Chikamatsu as a major dramatist on the world stage. Keene's collection *Major Plays of Chikamatsu*, first published in 1961, reveals in English for the first time the lyric thrust of such love-suicide plays as *Sonezaki shinjū* (1703, Love Suicides at Sonezaki) or *Shinjū ten no Amijima* (1721, The Love Suicides at Amijima), and the volume contains as well the only full translation of a Chikamatsu history play (the preferred genre during the playwright's lifetime), the outlandish and heroic *Kokusenya Kassen* (The Battles of Coxinga), written in 1715.

Nevertheless, it must be said that the literature of the puppet theatre and kabuki has scarcely been touched. James **Brandon**, an expert on kabuki performance, has made available in his 1975 *Kabuki: Five Classic Plays* superior versions of such keys of the classical repertory as Tsuruya Namboku's *Sakura hime Azuma bunshō* (1817, The Scarlet Princess of Edo) and Takeda Izumo's *Ichinotani futaba gunki* (1751, The Battle at Ichinotani). Stanleigh **Jones** has created fine versions of two other works by Takeda Izumo and his stable of writers, the 1746 *Sugawara denju tenarai kagami* (Sugawara and the Secrets of Calligraphy) and *Yoshitsune senbon zakura* (1747, Yoshitsune and the Thousand Cherry Trees).

Still missing are translations in English of such major works as Namboku's most representative work, *Tōkaidō Yotsuya Kaidan* (The Ghost of Yotsuya), or any complete version of a play by Kawatake Mokuami, the last great dramatist of kabuki, who died in 1893. The translations we do possess have revealed, however, that the twin arts of kabuki and the puppet theatre, however singled out they may be for their theatrical and scenic splash, make use of texts composed at the highest level of skill and sophistication. In their disparagement of the 'excesses' of these plays, the early Victorian translators were prisoners of their own genteel traditions.

iv. The Modern Theatre Kabuki, nō, and the puppet theatre continued into the 20th c. and still retain their popularity among devotees of the theatre. Nevertheless, their repertories have become fixed, and any new experiments in the genre are now the exception rather than the rule.

By the turn of the century young Japanese playwrights, inspired by western examples, began writing modern dramas that, as in Europe and the United States, depended on purely spoken dialogue. By the 1920s, evocative plays were being written by such important figures as the novelists Tanizaki Jun'ichirō and Arishima Takeo. Talented young playwrights, such as Kishida Kunio and Murayama Tomoyoshi, went to Europe to study and learn at first hand the art of the modern theatre. European translators, however, were little attracted to these experiments, perhaps because they seemed insufficiently 'exotic'. A few collections of translations were published during the interwar years by Japanese translators anxious to show off the developments of the movement, but these achieved limited circulation and often betrayed a certain stiffness, since the translators were working out of, not into, their own language. It was not until the 1970s that adequate transla-

tions of modern Japanese theatre began to appear. Even so, only one or two works by the two most prominent dramatists in the early postwar period, Kinoshita Junji and Tanaka Chikao, have yet achieved translation. The most extensive work in making these dramas available in translation has been done by David **Goodman**, whose interest in the Marxist theatre of the interwar period produced a gripping English-language version of Kubo Sakae's *Kazanbaichi* (The Land of Volcanic Ash), a play first produced in 1938.

The political difficulties of the 1960s in Japan, first over the renewal of the Japan–US Security Treaty, then the Vietnam war, brought about the development of an avant-garde theatre that stood in opposition to what a number of talented writers and directors now came to see as a staid if left-wing mainstream modern theatre movement. Inspired by Beckett, Ionesco, and what they termed certain powerful 'irrational' elements in traditional Japanese theatre, these playwrights ranged widely in their individual views. Important translators such as Donald Keene have given wide exposure to the absurdist dramas of Abe Kōbō. The efforts of David Goodman, Robert **Rolf**, and John **Gillespie** have made a strong case for the power of the idiosyncratic visions of such writers as Betsuyaku Minoru, Shimizu Kunio, and Kara Jūrō. Indeed, despite the fact that many of the most important of these experimental works from the last 20 years remain to be translated, interested readers can gain a better sense of the state of Japanese theatre since the middle 1960s than of that of any other period.

The long and diverse history of the Japanese theatre still remains to some extent in the shadows; what we have shows a level of literary creativity that deserves a good deal more exploration.

JTR

Nō AND KYŌGEN   Fenollosa, Ernest, and Pound, Ezra, *'Noh' or Accomplishment: A Study of the Classical Stage of Japan*, London, 1916 [subsequent American reps.] · Keene, Donald, ed., *Twenty Plays of the Nō Theatre*, New York, 1970 · Morley, Carolyn Anne, *Transformation, Miracles, and Mischief: The Mountain Priest Plays of Kyōgen*, Ithaca, NY, 1993 · Nippon Gakujitsu Shinkokai [Japanese Society for the Promotion of Scientific Research], *Japanese Noh Drama*, 3 vols., Tokyo, 1955–60 · Sakanishi, Shio, *Kyōgen: Comic Interludes of Japan*, Boston, 1938 [as *The Ink-Smeared Lady and Other Kyōgen*, Rutland, Vt./Tokyo, 1960] · Smethurst, Mae, *Dramatic Representations of Filial Piety: Five Noh in Translation*, Ithaca, NY, 1998 · Stopes, Marie C., *Plays of Old Japan: The Nō*, London, 1913 · Tyler, Royall, *Japanese Nō Dramas*, London/New York, 1992 [Penguin] · Waley, Arthur, *The Nō Plays of Japan*, London, 1921; rep. New York, 1954 · Yasuda, Kenneth, *Masterworks of Nō Theatre*, Bloomington/Indianapolis, 1989.
BUNRAKU AND KABUKI   Brandon, James, *Kabuki: Five Classic Plays*, Cambridge, Mass., 1975; rep. Honolulu, 1992 · Dickins, Frederick Victor, *Chiushingura, or the Loyal League* (by Takeda Izumo et al.), London, 1880 · Jones, Stanleigh, *Sugawara and the Secrets of Calligraphy* (by Takeda Izumo et al.), New York, 1984 · *Yoshitsune and the Thousand Cherry Trees* (by Takeda Izumo et al.), New York, 1993 · Keene, Donald, *Major Plays of Chikamatsu*, New York, 1961 · Miyamori, Asatorō, *Masterpieces of Chikamatsu, the Japanese Shakespeare*, London, 1926.

MODERN Goodman, David, *Land of Volcanic Ash* (by Kubo Sakae), Ithaca, Ny, 1986 · Rolf, Robert T., and Gillespie, John K., *Alternative Japanese Theatre: Ten Plays*, Honolulu, 1992.

SEE ALSO Ortolani, B., *The Japanese Theatre*, Leiden, 1990; rep. Princeton, NJ, 1995 [with bibliography of translations].

9. KOREAN

While modern Korean literature began to emerge in the years preceding Japan's annexation of Korea (1910), translation of Korean literature into English only really began in the 1940s with the pioneering work of Lee In-su, although a few isolated publications can be found before this, including the work of James S. **Gale**. After liberation from Japan in 1945 and the Korean war (1950–3), Koreans soon realized that their literature was unknown abroad for lack of translation. One early attempt to remedy this was an anthology *Korean Verses*, published by the Korean Poets' Association in Seoul in 1961. This included translations by Lee In-su, **Kim** Jong-gil, **Zong** In-sob, **Ko** Won, and other pioneers. In 1960, Peter **Hyun** published an anthology *Voices of the Dawn* in London, and in 1964 Peter H. **Lee** began his long career in the field, publishing *Poems from Korea* in Honolulu. Lee's more recent work is widely used in the academic study of Korean literature abroad.

The greatest problem has always been the difficulty of finding a publisher. Innumerable translations remain buried in back numbers of such papers and periodicals as the *Korea Times*, the *Korea Journal*, and more recently the Korea Foundation's *Koreana* or Korean PEN's *Korean Literature Today*. Translation by people whose native tongue is English, standard for most countries' literature, has always been the exception in Korea. A few missionaries and Peace Corps workers, having mastered Korean to a certain degree, have worked hard on translating in their spare moments. Starting in the 1960s, Richard **Rutt** worked mainly on the older poetry known as *sijo*, which led to the publication of *The Bamboo Grove* in 1971. In the 1970s he was joined in translating by Edward W. and Genell Y. **Poitras**, Daniel **Kister**, and Kevin **O'Rourke**, all of them producing numerous translations of fiction and poetry. Still active in the 1990s, Kevin O'Rourke displays a true poet's skills in his anthology *Tilting the Jar, Spilling the Moon*, as well as in his versions of such poets as So Chong-ju and the classic Lee Kyu-bo. David **McCann** has concentrated on So Chong-ju, while serving as one of the very rare non-Korean professors of Korean Literature in the world. The sudden death in 1995 of Marshall R. **Pihl** of the University of Hawaii was a grave loss. His *The Korean Singer of Tales* was a major achievement. Since 1990,

Brother **Anthony** of Taizé, working mainly in collaboration with **Kim** Young-moo, has published a number of volumes of contemporary poetry, including Ku Sang, Kim Kwang-kyu, So Chong-ju, and Ch'on Sang-pyong.

The majority of translations have been made by Koreans, usually professors in English departments of Korean universities, among them the poet Kim Jong-gil with his *Slow Chrysanthemums*, poems by Korean masters of classical Chinese. Other such professors include **Kim** Jaihiun, **Lee** Sung-il, **Chung** Chong-wha, and **Suh** Ji-moon, who have published many volumes of translations in Korea and abroad. Now living in the United States, **Chun** Kyung-ja has produced some particularly noted work.

Korean fiction is fortunate to have found a highly professional team of translators in Bruce and Ju-Chan **Fulton**. They have translated short stories and novellas that represent some of the best modern Korean writing. Their recent publications have made a significant breakthrough: thanks to them, for the first time Korean writers, particularly women, are being widely read in the West for what they have to say to a world audience.

Over the last 20 years, the Korean government has established funding agencies to encourage translation of Korean literature and publication abroad. The most significant work has been done by the Korean Culture and Arts Foundation. The non-governmental Daesan Foundation, established in 1992, runs a parallel programme. Concerns of national prestige and dreams of a Nobel Prize naturally underlie these acts of cultural patronage, which allow books to be published but have no power to make people read them. The decision by the Harvill Press to include Yi Mun-yol's *The Poet* (1995) among their titles represented a major step in the recognition of Korean literature, for it was the first time that a major international publisher had taken the initiative in commissioning a translation from the Korean.

There are indications that in future important work will be done by people of Korean descent living in English-speaking countries. Some will address the needs of the academic readership involved in East Asian Studies, while others will make Korean literature available to a wider public.

The valuable contribution made by JaHyun **Kim Haboush** in *The Memoirs of Lady Hyegyong* on the academic side, or the work of the translator Walter **Lew** as the editor responsible for the first number (1995) of the review *Muae* in New York, testify to this.

The Bibliography below can only indicate a few titles, for the translators named above have all published numerous volumes, and there are many others who might have been named if space had allowed. There is unfortunately no full up-to-date bibliography of Korean literature in translation available, although a CD-Rom Bibliography of Korean Studies made at Harvard includes as much information as possible.   AS

ANTHOLOGIES   Chung, Chong-wha et al., *Modern Korean Literature 1905–1960*, London, 1995 · Fulton, Bruce, and Fulton, Ju-chan, *Words of Farewell: Stories by Korean Women Writers*, Seattle, 1989 · *Wayfarer: New Fiction by Korean Women*, Seattle, 1997 · Kim, Jaihiun, *Classical Korean Poetry*, Berkeley, Calif., 1994 · Kim, Jong-gil, *Slow Chrysanthemums*, London, 1987 · Lee, Peter H., ed., *Anthology of Korean Literature: From Early Times to the Nineteenth Century*, Honolulu, 1982 · ed., *Modern Korean Literature: An Anthology*, Honolulu, 1990 · Lee, Sung-il, *The Wind and the Waves: Four Modern Korean Poets*, Berkeley, Calif., 1989 · O'Rourke, Kevin, *Tilting the Jar, Spilling the Moon*, Dublin, 1993 · Pihl, Marshall R., *The Korean Singer of Tales*, Cambridge, 1994 · Pihl, Marshall R., Fulton, Bruce, and Fulton, Ju-chan, *Land of Exile: Contemporary Korean Fiction*, New York, 1993 · Rutt, Richard. *The Bamboo Grove: An Introduction to Sijo*, Berkeley, Calif., 1971.

CH'AE MAN-SIK   Chun, Kyung-ja, *Peace under Heaven*, New York, 1991.

CHONG CHI-YONG   Kister, Daniel A., *Distant Valleys: Poems of Chong Chi-yong*, Berkeley, Calif., 1994.

HWANG SUN-WON   Suh, Ji-moon, and Pickering, Julie, *The Descendants of Cain*, Armonk, NY, 1997.

HYEGYONG, LADY   Kim Haboush, JaHyun, *The Memoirs of Lady Hyegyong*, Berkeley, Calif., 1996.

KIM NAMJO   McCann, David R., and Sallee, Yee, *Hyunjae: Selected Poems of Kim Namjo*, Ithaca, NY, 1993.

KO UN   Brother Anthony of Taizé and Kim, Young-moo, *The Sound of My Waves: Selected Poems by Ko Un*, Ithaca, NY, 1991.

KU SANG   Brother Anthony of Taizé, *Wastelands of Fire: Selected Poems by Ku Sang*, London, 1990.

PARK KYONG-NI   Tennant, Agnita, *Land: A Novel*, London, 1996.

YI MUN-YOL   Chung, Chong-wha, and Brother Anthony of Taizé, *Yi Mun-yol: The Poet*, London, 1995.

g. French

1. INTRODUCTION

There are probably more translations into English from French literature than from any other. French was, with Latin, the main literary language of England after 1066, but by the 13th c. French romances were being translated. Later medieval translations of note include **Chaucer**'s *Romance of the Rose*, **Malory**'s *Morte Darthur*, and the anonymous version of Mandeville's travels [see I.b.1]. Since the Renaissance, the flood of translations from French has not abated, though French literature has at times been somewhat eclipsed by Italian, German, Russian, and others, and has not exerted as great an influence on high culture as the Greek and Latin classics. Among the high points in this tradition are the translations of Montaigne, of the 18th-c. *philosophes*, of the symbolist poets, of Proust, and of a galaxy of 20th-c. thinkers. In the 19th c., translation of lurid French plays and novels held a central place in British popular culture, to the dismay of many critics [see I.b.4].

French language and literature were not a significant part of most school and university syllabuses until the late 18th c. at earliest, but French has always been a language known by many educated people, women as well as men, in Britain and Ireland. As a result, translators can often count on some familiarity with the original on the part of readers. Many poetry translations are published in bilingual editions, inviting judgement and comparison, and the example of Baudelaire—and to a lesser extent La Fontaine and Mallarmé—demonstrates how translators may be attracted in great numbers to try their skills on a well-known work.

There are inevitably, given the amount of material, gaps in the account offered here of translations from French. One significant area where translations once found readers is the fiction of the 17th and 18th c., from the immense romances of Mademoiselle de Scudéry and her contemporaries, to Fénelon's once best-selling educational novel *Télémaque* (c.1695), of which there were several different 18th-c. translations, including some in verse. A particular favourite (with Walter Scott among others) was Lesage's picaresque *Gil Blas* (1715–35); this was translated anonymously on its first appearance, and then by the young Tobias **Smollett** (1721–71), whose 1749 translation went through numerous editions over the following 150 years and more.

Even *Gil Blas* is little read today, however, and apart from the tales of Diderot and Voltaire [see II.g.8], only two novels of the period have retained a following and found new translators in any numbers. Madame de Lafayette's *La Princesse de Clèves* (1678) has had several modern translations, from an elegant if cavalier version by Nancy **Mitford** (London, 1950, later Penguin Classics) to the scrupulous rendering by Terence **Cave** (Oxford, 1992). Choderlos de Laclos's fascinatingly ambiguous *Les Liaisons dangereuses* (1782, Dangerous Connections) has also been translated several times in the 20th c., among others by Richard **Aldington** (London, 1924).

The various prose writings of François-René de Chateaubriand were very popular in the 19th c., but have proved less so since then. His *Génie du*

Christianisme (1802, The Genius of Christianity), and particularly the short tale *Atala* included in it, found many translators (*Atala* was even turned into verse). The 20th c. has seen versions of *Atala* and its companion piece, *René*, and Robert **Baldick**'s selection from the remarkable *Mémoires d'outre-tombe* (1849–50, Memoirs from Beyond the Grave) was published in Penguin Classics in 1965, but apparently without great success. Among other 19th-c. prose writers not discussed below who have attracted readers in English translation, one might pick out Benjamin Constant, whose subtle story *Adolphe* (1821) has been translated several times, and Ernest Renan, whose controversial *Vie de Jésus* (1863, Life of Jesus) once found readers all over Europe.

Apart from La Fontaine, there is little to be said about the translation of French poetry from 1600 to 1850, however massive the original production may have been. The satires, epistles, and other poems of Nicolas Boileau were translated in the 18th c., when he was seen as the leading figure in French classical criticism, but have attracted little attention more recently. Poets as significant as the early 17th-c. Théophile de Viau and Malherbe and the victim of the Revolution André Chénier have been translated only fragmentarily, in anthologies. Similarly, while there were 19th-c. and early 20th-c. versions of the poems of the romantics, Alphonse de Lamartine, Alfred de Vigny, Marceline Desbordes-Valmore, and Alfred de Musset, these do not match the prominence once accorded these poets in either quantity or quality. Their prose writings and plays [see I.b.4] have proved more attractive to translators and publishers.

Of the pre-Baudelaire 19th-c. poets, the two most significant today are Victor Hugo and Gérard de Nerval. Hugo's plays, and some of his novels [see II.g.9], have been much translated, but his poetry, though some of it appeared in English in the 19th c., remains curiously neglected; there is, however, an imaginatively translated selection by the poet Harry **Guest**, *The Distance, the Shadows* (London, 1981). The enigmatic Nerval has proved more fascinating. As well as translations of his poetic prose, notably Norman **Glass**'s 1972 version of the *Voyage*

en Orient (1851, Journey to the Orient), there have been several attempts at his small and challenging body of verse. The version of *Les Chimères* (1853, The Chimeras) by Derek **Mahon** (1982, Penguin 1996) stands out for its force and beauty.

While many anthologies of modern French poetry in translation exist, not so many attempt to cover the whole tradition. Of those listed below, the first three are single-author, monolingual collections in verse, conforming all too readily to the poetic expectations of their period (or indeed an earlier one). The fullest is that of Alan **Conder**, the fruit of 30 years' work originating in the desire to translate the whole of the *Oxford Book of French Verse*; it comes with recommendations from Louis Cazamian and Walter de la Mare. Wilfred **Thorley**'s collection is interesting in that he attempts to translate in appropriate period style, though from about 1750 onwards he settles into a fairly elaborate premodern diction. The Penguin volume offers a broad choice of original poems with plain prose versions at the foot of the page.

One field not considered here, and in which there has been a good deal of translating activity, is the modern theatre. One or two texts have attracted repeated translation, notably the two highly theatrical but contrasted pieces, Alfred Jarry's *Ubu roi* (1896, King Ubu) and Edmond Rostand's *Cyrano de Bergerac* (1897); the latter now exists in a Scots version by Edwin **Morgan** (1992). Their near-contemporary Paul Claudel, by contrast, has been little translated, even though he is one of France's leading playwrights. No doubt his vast poetic dramas frighten off British directors, who have been very willing to stage most of the other major French dramatists of the 20th c. The plays of Jean Cocteau, Jean Giraudoux, Albert Camus, Jean-Paul Sartre, Eugène Ionesco, and Samuel Beckett [II.g.14], for instance, have been much performed and published in English, but only rarely retranslated. A surprising success was enjoyed in the 1950s and 1960s by the many plays of Jean Anouilh, two of them in translations by Christopher **Fry**, who also did a fine version of Giraudoux's *La Guerre de Troie n'aura pas lieu* (1935) as *Tiger at the Gates* (1956).   PF

ANTHOLOGIES Carrington, Henry, *Anthology of French Poetry, 10th to 19th Centuries*, London/New York, 1900 · Conder, Alan, *Cassell's Anthology of French Poetry*, London, 1950 [as *A Treasury of French Poetry*, New York, 1951] · Thorley, Wilfred, *Fleurs-de-Lys: A Book of French Poetry Freely Translated into English Verse*, London, 1920 · Woledge, Brian, Brereton, Geoffrey, and Hartley, Anthony, *The Penguin Book of French Verse*, Harmondsworth, 1975 [previously published as 4 vols., 1961, 1958, 1957, 1959].

2. TROUBADOURS AND TROUVÈRES

i. The Challenge of the Troubadours The troubadours and trouvères flourished in the two halves of what is now France from the end of the 11th c. until the end of the 13th c., the troubadours writing in the southern *langue d'oc* (often known as Provençal), the trouvères in the northern *langue d'oïl*. Links exist between them, since the troubadours influenced the work of the trouvères, the latter adopting many of the lyric forms and tropes of the former. Traditionally, English readers came to the troubadours through Dante's references and tributes to them in the *Divine Comedy* [II.m.2]. Interest in Dante and his circle was rekindled by the Brotherhood of pre-Raphaelite artists and poets, including Dante Gabriel Rossetti [II.m.4.iv]. Part of the fascination with the troubadours is that their texts bear eloquent testimony to a highly civilized culture which flourished and was then suppressed by the Albigensian Crusade in the 13th c.; theirs is a lost art, a lost civilization, that can be romanticized as the origins of western culture as we know it.

The large majority of translators prefer to concentrate on the troubadours. There are a number of reasons for this, besides the significance to an English audience of cultural transmission through Dante and his circle. The two languages are sufficiently different to affect the process of translation. The *langue d'oïl* is manifestly the medieval version of modern French: anyone with competence in that language can comprehend the lyrics of the trouvères, in much the same way as any competent reader of modern English can comprehend Chaucer. The lyric forms of the trouvères are often imitated in English, including American English; a surge of imitations of form rather than specific content appeared at the end of the 19th c. So the characteristics of the art of the trouvères are familiar to us; and it is this familiarity which deters translators.

The troubadours, on the other hand, present an exciting challenge to the translator: to recover a lost art, to make new (Ezra Pound's catchphrase) a highly influential body of texts, to decode the hidden, mystic, or political meanings of *trobar clus* (or 'coded' poetic composition), and all this in a language which is remarkable for its fluidity as well as its fluency. The troubadours' art was above all ludic and performative. Their playfulness with language, the sense of fluid inventiveness finding forms, finding tropes, finding turns of phrase, is immensely appealing. The language is rich and various, but not yet fixed in orthography, syntax, or rules of versification.

In 1912 Walter Morse Rummel published a musical edition of *Neuf chansons de troubadours des XIIe et XIIIe siècles*. It included songs by both troubadours and trouvères. This edition stands at a pivotal moment between 19th-c. and 20th-c. approaches to translation, and it illustrates the specific issues the translator of the troubadours and trouvères has to address. These hinge largely on whether the medieval text should be deemed a 'literary' text or a musical score; and whether the modern translator can translate music, versification and meaning in a unified fashion, when such a cohesive high art form no longer exists. Does s/he translate for musical performance or create the equivalent of troubadour song in words only? Rummel's edition highlights the tension between sensitivity to the medieval cultural context and consideration for a modern audience.

ii. Early Twentieth Century: Ezra Pound Published a few years before Rummel, Barbara **Smythe**'s *Trobador Poets: Selections from the Poems of Eight Trobadors* represents the culmination of 19th-c. translations which seek to domesticate the foreignness of the source language and its cultural context. Smythe rendered troubadours into a minor Georgian idiom, which is easy on the ear, but which can turn the most exquisite lines in the source text into banal versification. Thus Bernart de Ventadorn's 'Can vei la lauzeta mover | De joi sas alas contra.l rai' becomes:

> Whene'er I see the lark take flight
> And soar up towards the sun on high
> Until at last for sheer delight
> It sinks, forgetting how to fly,
> Such envy fills me when I see
> All those whom love thus glad can make,
> I marvel that the heart of me
> With love and longing does not break.

By making these lyrics accessible to an English-speaking audience she erases the specific qualities of the source texts. It could be said that in his translations for Rummel's edition Ezra **Pound** adopted the same tactic. Yet he emerges as the crucial translator of Provençal poetry, a key figure for their promulgation in English and American 20th-c. culture, and an eminent influence on many translators who follow him.

Although Pound remains the major modern translator of the troubadours, without whom much of the succeeding work might never have been attempted, his translations are not consistently accessible to a contemporary readership. After his initial encounters with medieval Provençal, as in *The Spirit of Romance* or the Rummel musical edition, where he still uses a *fin-de-siècle* diction learnt from Rossetti and Swinburne, he tends to exaggerate the sense of the remoteness both of the culture and of the source language. He also attempts to imitate precisely the complexities of troubadour versification; so that he produces experimental blueprints for the innovative modern poet, introducing 'new' prosodic techniques into modernist discourses, rather than producing readable texts. This is particularly true of his translations of Arnaut Daniel, to be found in bilingual edition in *The Translations* (1970). Here is an example:

Sweet cries and cracks
    and lays and chants inflected
By auzels who, in their Latin belikes,
Chirm each to each, even as you and I
Pipe toward those girls on whom our thoughts attract;
Are but more cause that I, whose overweening
Search is toward the noblest, set in cluster
Lines where no word pulls wry, no rhyme breaks gauges.

(Doutz brais e critz,
Lais e cantars e voutas
Aug del auzels qu'en lur latins fant precs . . .)

Used in the target language 'auzels' suggests the quality of a lost world of troubadour love and song, still perceptible but not quite graspable; it foregrounds the foreignness of the troubadour text and the culture it represents. This tactic is not so evident in his poetic sequence 'Langue d'Oc' (1918), which is reprinted in the *Collected Shorter Poems* (1968). Yet even here the immediacy of the speaker's voice is counterbalanced by the inclusion of deliberate archaism, e.g.

> I remember the young day
> When we set strife away,
> And she gave me such gesning,
> Her love and her ring.

This sequence represents a distillation and culmination of Pound's earlier work on the troubadours. The originals are reworked to create the illusion of verisimilitude, but actually these poems are 'yet more elaborate masks' of the modernist poet, representing his condensed summary of troubadour art [see also II.f.2.iii and II.m.4].

iii. Modern Translators When Pound first discovered medieval troubadours, most scholarly editions were by European philologists, which presented a double barrier to the general reading public. Now there are a number of excellent scholarly editions with original texts and with prose

translations and editorial apparatus in English. Alan Press's *Anthology of Troubadour Lyric Poetry* remains, however, the most accessible bilingual text for the general reader. It provides an intelligent selection of texts which indicates the range of troubadour art, and prints clear prose translations alongside the original Provençal lyrics. An example of the trend towards presenting medieval culture through the lens of contemporary cultural concerns is the habit of publishing poetry by women separately to compensate for their exclusion from 'standard' anthologies; for example Meg **Bogin**'s *The Women Troubadours*. Bogin gives clear, readable blank verse translations, which are intended, like Press's, to make the original more accessible to the general reader.

Frederick **Goldin**'s *Lyrics of the Troubadours and Trouvères* is a bilingual text which is more comprehensive than most, with a good selection of trouvère lyrics as well as troubadour works. His is an ambitious volume, which attempts to combine scholarship with an attempt to help the reader to become a better reader of the originals, and at the same time to suggest through his blank verse translations the complexities of the original performances in their specific social settings. Like a number of translators he resorts to footnotes to explain the subtleties of the cultural ethos of the *cansons*, which complicates the reader's response considerably.

James J. **Wilhelm**'s solution is to publish his translations (again both of troubadours and trouvères) as freestanding poetic translations, with a selection of original texts at the end of the book. His translations achieve the difficult task of rendering the lyrics in a range of styles which utilize both modern American English, and a lightly archaic diction, while sustaining rhyme, metre, and versification; and yet remaining close to the original meaning. For example, his version of Machaut's 'Blanche com lys, plus que rose vermeille' avoids the excesses of Poundian archaisms, while retaining a convincingly medieval feel to it:

> White as a lily, redder than a rose,
> More splendid than a ruby oriental,
> Your beauty I regard; no equal shows
> white as a lily, redder than a rose.

Anthony **Bonner**'s *Songs of the Troubadours* is comparable in its presentation of freestanding translations, which retain a feel of the medieval historical context while offering fluent blank-verse versions. Despite Bonner's desire to encourage the reader to return to the source texts, the translations are highly readable in English, with a minimum of helpful explanatory endnotes. Bonner openly acknowledges Ezra Pound's influence on his work, as does his contemporary Paul **Blackburn**.

Blackburn, working in a Poundian tradition, adopts many of the linguistic habits and gestures of Pound, and develops his approaches to produce what is arguably the most worthwhile of all translations of the troubadours in English. A poet in his own right, but also a talented linguist, he, like Pound, retains a sense of the remoteness, the difference and the inaccessibility of the culture these lyrics represent. His interest in the craft of versification, which equals that of Pound, solves the problem of translating verse structures and patterns not by imitating them, but by converting them into open-field, free, blank verse. He has also learnt

from Pound the tactic of combining different discourses, so that some medieval words are retained and translated within the line; yet very strong, colloquial, contemporary words and phrases are also introduced. In this stanza from Marcabru we find a double anachronism: Dante is quoted, but the line also alludes to Eliot's *The Waste Land*. The effect is a voice firmly rooted in its remote context, yet speaking assuredly to its postmodern, contemporary audience:

> Lord, how they enjoy it!
> 'I had not thought there were so many'
> whose sole delight is in wickedness, that
> grows and grows worse in its excess.
> but what summons me to be an enemy is
> that this bitch *likes* to hear me roar and cry.
>
> HMD

TRANSLATIONS   Blackburn, Paul, *Proensa: An Anthology of Troubadour Poetry*, Berkeley, Calif., 1978 · Bogin, Meg, *The Women Troubadours*, New York, 1976 · Bonner, Anthony, *Songs of the Troubadours*, London, 1973 · Goldin, Frederick, *Lyrics of the Troubadours and Trouvères*, New York, 1973 · Nichols, Stephen G., Galm, John A., and Giamatti, A. Bartlett, *The Songs of Bernart de Ventadorn*, Chapel Hill, NC, 1965 · Pound, Ezra, *Literary Essays*, rev. edn., London, 1960 · *Collected Shorter Poems*, 2nd edn., London, 1968 · *The Spirit of Romance*, London, 1910 [rev. edn., 1970] · *The Translations of Ezra Pound*, 2nd enlarged edn., London, 1970 · Press, Alan, R., *Anthology of Troubadour Lyric Poetry*, Edinburgh, 1971 · Rummel, Walter Morse, *Neuf chansons de troubadours des XIIᵉ et XIIIᵉ Siècles*, London, 1912 · Smythe, Barbara, *Trobador Poets: Selections from the Poems of Eight Trobadors*, London/New York, 1911 · Wilhelm, James J., *Medieval Song: An Anthology of Hymns and Lyrics*, London, 1972.

3. MEDIEVAL LITERATURE

The earliest translations of medieval French texts were primarily of short stories, either comic or serious: fabliaux, lays (by Marie de France and others), and short narratives such as *Aucassin et Nicolette* and the *Chastelaine de Vergi*. One of the earliest to be printed is the lay of *Oiselet*, which was translated by John **Lydgate** (under the title *The Churl and the Bird*) and printed by William Caxton around 1478 [see I.b.1.vi]. But it was not until the last years of the 18th c. that most readers could begin to enjoy the literary production of medieval France. The publication in 1779–81 of Legrand d'Aussy's four volumes of short stories entitled *Fabliaux ou contes du XIIᵉ et du XIIIᵉ siècle* led to the appearance in 1786 of *Tales of the XIIth and XIIIth Centuries from the French of M. Le Grand*, an anonymous collection of prose translations of fabliaux, but also including texts such as Marie de France's *Lanval*, the *Chastelaine de Vergi*, and *Aucassin et Nicolette*. In 1796 and 1800 Gregory L. **Way** published *Fabliaux or Tales*, 'metrical translations' of 26 tales taken from Legrand, including Marie de France's *Guigemar*, the lays of *Oiselet*, *Aristote*, *Narcissus* and *Graelent*, the *Vair Palefroi* and other stories. In 1815 these transla-

tions were reissued in three volumes by George **Ellis**, who himself had published in 1805 *Specimens of Early English Metrical Romances*, containing adaptations of nine of Marie de France's lays (not *Guigemar*, *Lanval*, or *Chevrefoil*).

Whether in prose or verse, these early translations are often no more than paraphrases of the original. But they are charmingly done and still a pleasure to read. Moreover, they introduced the English-speaking public to some of the best-loved medieval stories, which have continued to attract translators. For versions which are accurate and faithful to the original, one has to wait at least until the second half of the 19th c.

As so much of the early French output was in verse, translators have to begin by deciding whether to render the original in verse, which naturally necessitates some textual liberties, or in prose, which itself can vary in its degree of fidelity. The most translated of all Old French texts, the *Chanson de Roland* (Song of Roland), has, over nearly 150 years, been rendered into English in a bewildering variety of versions. The oldest, dating from 1854, is by A. C. **Marsh** (whose name appears only as 'the author of *Emilia Wyndham*'). Although rather a paraphrase of the original, this is quite an effective prose rendering. In 1880 John **O'Hagan** produced a version in rhyming couplets written in very archaic language. As time went by, translations, often published on both sides of the Atlantic, became more accurate and scholarly: e.g. Isobel **Butler** (1904, etc.), Jessie **Crosland** (1902, 1924), Arthur S. **Way** (1913), Leonard **Bacon** (1914, 1919), and C. K. **Scott Moncrieff** (1919).

A very effective and much-appreciated translation of the *Song of Roland* is Dorothy L. **Sayers**'s Penguin Classic of 1957. The battle she describes between County Roland and the Paynims is expressed in a language which makes full use of archaisms and poetic licence, but it undoubtedly has its own charm: 'The County Roland is mighty of his mood' (1. 2066); 'He plucks his beard right angerly and wroth' (1. 2414). In recent years there has been a movement towards student-oriented versions which enable the reader to follow the text more or less word by word (e.g. Robert **Harrison**, 1970; D. D. R. **Owen**, 1972; Howard S. **Robertson**, 1972; Frederick **Goldin**, 1978; Gerard J. **Brault**, 1978). In 1990 a translation by Glyn S. **Burgess** replaced Sayers's version in the Penguin Classics series.

One text in particular has attracted translators, the love story *Aucassin et Nicolette*. Appearing first in 1786 and then amongst G. L. Way's metrical versions (unusually, in view of its alternating passages of verse and prose, presented as one long poem of 769 decasyllabic lines), it was very much in demand by the end of the 19th c. Numerous translations appeared in both Britain and the USA: A. R. **Macdonough** (1880), F. W. **Bourdillon** (1887), Andrew **Lang** (1887), E. J. **Wilkinson** (1887), M. S. **Henry** (1896), and E. E. **Hale** (1897). Bourdillon's version was particularly successful, and Lang's translation, which passed through a huge number of printings, the last as late as 1957, caught the popular imagination. The prose sections in *Aucassin* are normally rendered in fairly accurate and down-to-earth style, but the heptasyllabic verse sections have produced extremely archaic renderings. As late as 1971 Pauline **Matarasso** began her Penguin Classics version with the words 'Who would hear a goodly lay | Of a dotard old and grey | Parting fair young lovers twain'. One early translation which still reads well today is that by Laurence **Housman** (1902), and more recently Glyn S. Burgess has produced a translation aimed at a scholarly audience (1988).

In 1910 and 1911 Eugene **Mason** published in Everyman's Library two influential collections:

Aucassin & Nicolette and Other Mediaeval Romances and Legends and *French Mediaeval Romances from the Lays of Marie de France*. Although stylistically archaic, even for the time in which they were written, these volumes were not superceded for 70 or 80 years. Some of Marie de France's lays had already been made known to the general public by A. W. E. **O'Shaughnessy** (1882), Jessie L. **Weston** (1900), and Edith **Rickert** (1901), but Mason was the first to provide all 12. He also included with Marie's poems two anonymous lays, *Espine* and *Graelent*, together with *La Fille du Comte de Pontieu* and the *Chastelaine de Vergi*.

Marie de France, France's first major woman writer, has continued to find favour with translators. In 1963 Patricia **Terry** included in her *Lays of Courtly Love in Verse Translation* very effective verse translations of *Laüstic*, *Chevrefoil*, *Les Deus Amanz*, and *Eliduc* (revised and expanded in 1995 to include *Lanval*). In 1978 a blank-verse rendering of the *Lais* was published by Robert **Hanning** and Joan **Ferrante**, and in 1986 a prose version by Glyn S. Burgess and Keith **Busby** appeared in Penguin Classics.

Although accepted as France's greatest writer of Arthurian romance, Chrétien de Troyes remained, until recently, surprisingly little translated. For many years the only available translation was that by William W. **Comfort**, first published in 1914 (*Chrétien de Troyes: Arthurian Romances*). In 1975 this volume was re-issued with a new Introduction by D. D. R. Owen, who in 1987 replaced it in Everyman's Library with a translation which, unlike that of Comfort, includes the *Perceval*. Comfort's style was effective, but rather old-fashioned, even for its day, especially when rendering conversations. Both his and Owen's translations are based on W. Foerster's editions, but in 1990 David **Staines** produced a translation of all five Arthurian romances based on the copies by the scribe Guiot (*The Complete Romances of Chrétien de Troyes*). Also based on Guiot is William W. **Kibler**'s Penguin Classics translation, published in 1991 under the title *Chrétien de Troyes: Arthurian Romances* (*Erec et Enide* is translated by Carleton W. **Carroll**). Staines is the only translator to include the disputed *Guillaume d'Angleterre*. All these translations are in prose, but one can point to impressive translations into verse of *Yvain* (1975) and *Perceval* (1985) by Ruth H. **Cline**, as well as to an excellent rendering in verse of *Philomena*, another of Chrétien's disputed texts, by Patricia Terry in *The Honeysuckle and the Hazel Tree*.

A lengthy and much-admired text from the thirteenth century is *Le Roman de la rose* ('The Romance of the Rose'), begun by Guillaume de Lorris and completed by Jean de Meun. Geoffrey **Chaucer** translated part of this romance into English, probably in the 1360s [see I.b.1.iv]. The *Rose* was translated into English verse by Harry W. **Robbins** in 1962 and into good, accurate prose by both Charles **Dahlberg** (1971) and Frances **Horgan** (1994).

Amongst translations of the various versions of the important Tristan legend one can point to those by Alan S. **Fedrick**, *Beroul: The Romance of Tristan* (Penguin Classics, 1970), A. T. **Hatto** (version by Thomas in *Gottfried von Strassburg, Tristan*, Penguin Classics, 1960), and Renée L. **Curtis** (translation of part of the prose Tristan under the title *The Romance of Tristan*, World's Classics, 1994). A translation of

Beroul's version with facing text has also been published by Norris J. **Lacy** (1989). Similarly, Stewart **Gregory** has published translations of Beroul (1992) and Thomas (1991). The publication of texts with facing English translation is very much to be encouraged. Other recent examples are *The Romance of Yder* (Alison **Adams**, 1983), *Le Pèlerinage de Charlemagne* (Jean-Louis G. **Picherit**, 1984, Glyn S. Burgess, 1988, 1998), *Raoul de Cambrai* (Sarah **Kay**, 1992), Marie de France, *Fables* (Mary Lou **Martin**, 1984) and *Espurgatoire Seint Patriz* (Michael J. **Curley**, 1993) and *Le Jeu d'Adam* (Wolfgang **Van Emden**, 1996). [For troubadour and *trouvère* poetry see II.g.2.]   GB

Translations

Translations cited and clearly identified above have been omitted from this bibliography.

Tales of the XIIth and XIIIth Centuries, from the French of M. Le Grand, tr. anon., 2 vols., London, 1786 · *Fabliaux or Tales, abridged from French Manuscripts of the XIIth and XIIIth Centuries by M. Le Grand*, tr. Gregory Lewis Way, 2 vols., London, 1796–1800 [new edn. in 3 vols. by G. Ellis, 1815] · *Specimens of Early English Metrical Romances*, tr. George Ellis, 3 vols., London, 1805 [2nd edn., rev. by J. O. Halliwell, Bohn, 1848] · *Aucassin & Nicolette and Other Mediaeval Romances and Legends*, tr. Eugene Mason, London/New York, 1910 [Everyman] · *French Mediaeval Romances from the Lays of Marie de France*, tr. Eugene Mason, London/New York, 1911 [new edn., as *Lays of Marie de France and Other Legends*, Everyman, 1954] · *Lays of Courtly Love in Verse Translation*, tr. Patricia Terry, New York, 1963 [rep. and expanded as *The Honeysuckle and the Hazel Tree: Medieval Stories of Men and Women*, Berkeley/Los Angeles/London, 1995] · *Aucassin and Nicolette and Other Tales*, tr. Pauline Matarasso, Harmondsworth, 1971 [Penguin].

4. POETRY 1450–1620

i. Introduction The period 1450–1620 saw the final flowering, with Charles d'Orléans and François Villon, of the late medieval French rondeau and ballade, their replacement, with Pierre de Ronsard and the Pléiade, by Renaissance forms, and the decline of these latter under the influence of 17th-c. classicism. Translation is instrumental in these changes. Although the Pléiade's aim of recreating a classical poetry in France cannot, insists Joachim Du Bellay, be achieved by translation, but only by imitation in its various forms (emulation, assimilation, reminiscence, allusion . . .), nevertheless the line between translation and imitation, whether of Horace or of Petrarch, is difficult to draw [see I.a.3], and the Pléiade practise both, just as they are in turn translated and imitated by contemporary English poets bent on the same patriotic endeavour. Two entire 16th-c. poetical works, Du Bellay's *Antiquités de Rome* (1558, *Ruins of Rome*) and Guillaume de Salluste du Bartas's *Semaines* (1578, *The Divine Weeks and Works*), and many individual poems were translated during this period; more often, French influences are assimilated into English poetry and, while pervasive, remain elusive.

At last Malherbe came, as Boileau famously put

it, and ended 'ronsardizing' in France and England for two centuries. The revival of the early French poets in England in the 1820s, initiated in a series of articles for the *London Magazine* by the translator of Dante, Henry Francis **Cary** (1772–1844) [see II.m.2.ii], if anything pre-dates that in France, and is again intimately associated with the aspirations of new generations of poets, romantic and Pre-Raphaelite. Versions by Dante Gabriel **Rossetti** (1828–82), **Swinburne**, and Andrew **Lang** (1844–1912), already anthologized by 1900, established, too, the style of translation which would prevail for the next half-century, whereby the translator departs from the argument of his text only to satisfy its formal requirements, by means—inversions, archaisms—which are also felt to enhance its old-world charm. Modernizing tendencies are already apparent in **Yeats**, however; and by 1950 it is generally agreed that a plainer approach will better render the freshness of the early poets. Verse versions become freer, prose renderings proliferate, as do dual-text and annotated editions. Varied readerships, too, are accommodated, from students whose first resort will be the *Penguin Book of French Verse*, with its comprehensive choice of texts and prose renderings, to readers who prefer the literary translations of the Oxford and Penguin anthologies of Charles Tomlinson and George Steiner. C. H. **Sisson**'s versions, meanwhile, suggest that working poets still find inspiration in the early French poets.

ii. Late Medieval Poetry Charles, Duke of Orleans, is remembered particularly for a handful of rondeaux ('The year has put his cloak away' c.1450), whose charm and difficulty for the translator lie in their combination of formal rigour, allegorizing of emotion, and atmosphere of springtime and enchantment. The largest selections (Henry **Carrington**, Cedric **Wallis**) are not the most available nor the best rendered; but Brian **Woledge** and Ralph Nixon **Currey** choose and translate with distinction.

In Villon, the combination is rather of a rigorous form with an unruly content. This tension—between the form of the *Testament* (1461, a sequence of octaves punctuated by ballades) and the mercurial blend of pathos, ribaldry, and defiance with which Villon reviews his disorderly life—resists translation. Nevertheless, unknown before Cary introduced him, Villon was soon the most familiar of the early French poets, thanks especially to Rossetti's haunting, if archaizing, version of the famous refrain 'But where are the snows of yesteryear?', and his eloquent lament for lost love 'Two we were, and the heart was one'. Swinburne's tastes are broader, although excessive archaisms ('Meseemeth . . .') and a striving for musicality sometimes obscure his meaning. At his best, he renders Villon with unsurpassed deftness: 'Look in again when your flesh troubles you,' says the pimp to the departing client.

The Oxford and Penguin anthologies include a fine selection of further ballades, from Basil **Bunting**'s spirited *danse macabre* to Tom **Scott**'s translations 'intil Scots' ('Ay, whaur are the snaws o langsyne?'). Disappointing omissions, however, are John Millington **Synge**'s lilting prose adaptations and William Ernest **Henley**'s (1849–1903) irresistible ballade in thieves' jargon ('It's up the spout and Charley Wag . . .') (reprinted in Lewis, 1928).

These are episodes, however, and best understood within the context of the complete *Testament*, itself repeatedly translated since 1878. Of the post-1945 verse renderings, Harry Bertram **McCaskie**'s is urbane, Norman **Cameron**'s persuasively archaic. The most available is Peter **Dale**'s *tour de force* for Penguin. His critics allege deviation from the original, an overindulgence in sexual innuendo, and a neglect of musicality ('We two live in nothing

bigger | Than one heart . . .'); nevertheless his version is both dashing and metrically exact. Galway **Kinnell**'s prose translation is accurate, Anthony **Bonner**'s free-verse rendering fluent and faithful, although based on a superseded French edition, as are all the pre-1974 versions. Most include Villon's other poems, the French text, and notes. John Howard **Fox**'s indispensable commentary and prose translation, while incomplete, reflect the latest scholarship, as does Barbara **Sargent-Baur**'s scrupulous and unrhymed version, which, while at times puzzling the ear, at others achieves an easy lyricism ('Two we were, and had but one heart . . .').

iii. The Sixteenth Century Clément Marot—of whom echoes may be found in Wyatt, Surrey, and Spenser—has always been better known for his witty and elegant court verse than for his more personal and satirical *Épîtres* (Epistles) of 1538. He remains little translated, but the selections in Carrington, Alan **Conder** and Currey nevertheless give some sense of his celebrated *badinage* and his charm. One short poem is also given in numerous inventive translations in Douglas A. Hofstadter's extraordinary essay, *Le Ton beau de Marot*.

Maurice Scève, precursor, like Marot, of the Pléiade and author of the first sequence of Petrarchan love poems [see II.m.4.ii] in France (*Délie*, 1544), was unknown in England before Cary's recommendation of him as offering 'fine things, somewhat in the way of our own Donne'. He is rarely translated, doubtless because his very qualities—a compression of thought and expression, out of which emerges, radiant and resolving, an enigmatic image—resist reworking. Wallace **Fowlie**'s selection is generous but his prose renderings are sometimes literal to the point of obscurity. Geoffrey **Brereton**'s prose versions for Penguin are judicious, Sisson's single translation masterly.

Du Bellay, second only to Ronsard among the Pléiade poets, composed while in Rome his major sonnet cycles, *Les Antiquités de Rome* (1558), a meditation upon its ruins, and *Les Regrets* (1558), a satirical and elegiac portrait of life in the papal city. Melancholy, introspective, a poet's poet, he was an early influence on Edmund **Spenser**, whose complete version of the *Antiquités* as *Ruines of Rome*, with its accompanying *Songe ou Vision* as *The Visions of Bellay*, catches Du Bellay's allusiveness and his elevated rhetoric, but not his complexity of tone, nor—since Spenser adopts the emergent English sonnet form in place of the French (with its more insistent octave rhyme scheme *abba abba*)—his incantation on Rome's name. Ezra **Pound**'s version of the third sonnet (1909) fails, too, to conjure with the name of Rome, but renders finely the ironies of mutability ('Tiber alone, transient and seaward bent | Remains of Rome . . .').

The *Regrets*, neglected by the Elizabethans, have been much translated since, especially the sonnet in which Du Bellay contrasts the Rome of his exile with his native Anjou. G. K. **Chesterton** may lose some of its finer nuances, but he imitates to perfection the last line, with its opening out towards the 'quiet kindness of the Angevin air'. Sisson's version ends on a disconcerting up-beat; and indeed he emphasizes throughout the ironies of this sonnet, which needs, however, to be read in context, as one of a sequence, meticulous in form but complex in tonality and reference, which Sisson's own complete translation makes accessible to the 20th-c. English reader.

The intensity of Louise Labé's 24 sonnets (1555), in which Petrarchan conventions are adapted to communicate a woman's experience of passion, has long won her a place in the anthologies, as well as (since 1947) several full translations. The most recent, scholarly, and available, by Graham Dunstan **Martin**, combines fluency and accuracy with a modern diction. Alta Lind **Cook**, at her best, achieves both simplicity and lyricism ('If in my arms I held him close to me | Binding him fast as ivy binds the tree'), as does Frances **Lobb** ('Sweeter than life would seem that death to me'). But the exigencies of the sonnet form at times encourage convoluted inversions, stilted diction, or, in the case of Frederic **Prokosch**, embellishments ('this wild incessant heart' for 'l'esprit'), inspired more by Labé's urgency than by the Petrarchan register through which she expresses it.

Ronsard, 'paragon of poets' (in the words of William Drummond of Hawthornden), was well known in contemporary England and Scotland for his philosophical and polemical verse. It was his early love poems, however, which more often inspired imitations (Alexander **Montgomerie**, 1545–98) or plagiarisms (Thomas **Lodge**, 1558–1625), few of which reappear in modern anthologies. More revealing of his influence on his contemporaries are the discreet echoes caught in Shakespeare, Herrick, even Marvell.

Even before Cary's revival of Ronsard, **Keats**, who shared a publisher with Cary, had attempted a free translation, which was to enjoy a long career in the anthologies, but whose most haunting lines ('Love poured her beauty into my warm veins') demonstrate above all how one poetic imagination may inform another.

Waddington's selections from Lang and others encourage a view of Ronsard as the poet of wine

and roses. The 20th c. sees also, however, the appearance of more comprehensive editions, plainer in style and more scholarly in approach (Curtis Hidden **Page**, Charles **Graves**), as well as of several complete translations of Ronsard's late *Sonnets for Helen* (1578). The modernizing typography of Humbert **Wolfe**'s version, the best of these latter, is, however, deceptive: archaisms, elaborate syntax, and highly wrought diction persist, which, while at times they evoke the dark splendour of Catherine de' Medici's court (the setting for these sonnets), more often obfuscate. Nevertheless, Ronsard's late Petrarchan radiance ('Lately as dreaming on a stair I stood') is also caught.

Ronsard's most recent translator, Nicholas **Kilmer**, includes scientific poems in his excellent selection. He promises, too, versions intended for readers 'from a culture less patient with poetry'; and indeed, the anthology pieces in particular, liberated from strict formal constraints, emerge fresh and spare, as in the lines mourning the death of a young girl: 'I bring you my tears, this vase of milk | this basket filled with flowers.' Nevertheless, in his eagerness to avoid what he sees as cliché, Kilmer renounces, however voluntarily, its consolations and sometimes its music.

Brereton's prose renderings for Penguin remain an invaluable resource, a starting-point from which, in true Renaissance fashion, the reader can venture forth, gathering from every new version which presents itself its choicest blooms. If, after browsing among the numerous translations of Ronsard's most familiar sonnet, we find that, as envisaged by Du Bellay, it is an imitation ('When you are old and grey and full of sleep') which haunts the memory, this is no doubt because Yeats, like Keats, defines himself, and Ronsard too, by his departures.

Du Bartas's vast, encyclopedic, and didactic Christian epic, *La Semaine* (1578), in Josuah **Sylvester**'s (c.1563–1618) complete translation (*The Divine Weeks and Works*), was the most-read French poem in Renaissance England. So conclusively, however, did Du Bartas's cosmology and his overblown style subsequently fall from favour that he is known in England today only as an influence on Milton.

Translators have long shown a preference for the conventional. Agrippa d'Aubigné, Du Bartas's fellow Huguenot, is represented by the occasional love sonnet, while his great epic poem *Les Tragiques* (1616), a bitter, apocalyptic account of the French religious wars, remains untranslated. Théophile de Viau's idiosyncratic vignettes of the natural world (1621) have inspired only a 17th-c. extract, and an appreciation of his 'music of blowing leaves and walking birds' (Swinburne); whereas Philippe Desportes's polished but facile sonnets in the Petrarchan manner (1573) are everywhere in the anthologies.

Poets neglected elsewhere are given a voice in the Penguin *French Verse*. There is evidence of revaluation, too, in Sisson's anthology, which includes both Jean-Baptiste Chassignet's baroque

meditations on mortality (1594) and François de Malherbe's 'Consolation to M. du Perier' (1594), famous for its eloquent lament for a lost daughter ('And, a rose, she has lived like a rose for a morning'), but also because it displays those classical perfections which, for Boileau, announce Racine and La Fontaine, and consign to oblivion the unruliness of the early French poets.   AMS

ANTHOLOGIES [and studies which include translations]   Brickell, Alfred, ed., *Few, but Roses*, London, 1924 · Carrington, Henry, *Anthology of French Poetry*, London/New York, 1900 · Cary, Henry Francis, *The Early French Poets*, London, 1846; rep. 1923 · Conder, Alan, *Cassell's Anthology of French Poetry*, London, 1950 · Currey, R. N., *Formal Spring*, London/New York/Toronto, 1950 · Lang, Andrew, *Ballads and Lyrics of Old France*, London, 1872 · Sisson, C. H., *Collected Translations*, Manchester, 1996 · Steiner, George, ed., *The Penguin Book of Modern Verse Translation*, Harmondsworth, 1970 · Tomlinson, Charles, ed., *The Oxford Book of Verse in English Translation*, London, 1980, 1983 · Waddington, Samuel, ed., *The Sonnets of Europe*, London, 1886 · Woledge, Brian, Brereton, Geoffrey, and Hartley, Anthony, eds., *The Penguin Book of French Verse*, Harmondsworth, 1966–80 · Wyndham, George, *Ronsard and La Pléiade*, London, 1906.

CHARLES, DUC D'ORLÉANS   Wallis, Cedric, *Rondels*, London, 1951.

DU BARTAS, GUILLAUME DE SALLUSTE   Sylvester, Josuah, *The Divine Weeks and Works*, ed. Susan Snyder, Oxford, 1979.

DU BELLAY, JOACHIM   Sisson, C. H., *The Regrets*, Manchester, 1984 · Spenser, Edmund, 'Ruines of Rome' and 'The Visions of Bellay', *Poetical Works*, London [numerous edns.].

LABÉ, LOUISE   Cook, Alta Lind, *Sonnets*, Toronto, 1950 · Lobb, Frances, *The Twenty-Four Love Sonnets*, London, 1950 · Martin, Graham Dunstan, *Sonnets*, Edinburgh, 1973 · Prokosch, Frederic, *Love Sonnets*, New York, 1947.

MAROT, CLÉMENT   Hofstadter, Douglas A., *Le Ton beau de Marot*, New York/London, 1997.

RONSARD, PIERRE DE   Graves, Charles, *Lyrics*, Edinburgh/London, 1967 · Kilmer, Nicholas, *Poems*, Berkeley/Los Angeles/London, 1979 · Page, Curtis Hidden, *Songs and Sonnets*, Boston/New York, 1903, 1924 · Wolfe, Humbert, *Sonnets for Helen*, London, 1934, 1972.

SCÈVE, MAURICE   Fowlie, Wallace, *Sixty Poems*, New York, 1949.

VIAU, THÉOPHILE DE   Stanley, Thomas, 'Sylvia's Park', 1651 [rep. in *Thomas Stanley: Poems and Translations*, ed. G. M. Crump, Oxford, 1962] · Swinburne, Algernon Charles, 'Théophile', in *Collected Works*, xiii, ed. E. Gosse and T. J. Wise, London/New York, 1926.

VILLON, FRANÇOIS   Bonner, Anthony, *The Complete Works of François Villon*, New York/London 1960 · Bunting, Basil, 'Villon' and 'The Well of Lycopolis', in his *Collected Poems*, London, 1968 · Cameron, Norman, *François Villon: Poems*, London, 1952 · Dale, Peter, *Villon*, London, 1973 [subsequently Penguin] · Fox, John, *Villon: Poems*, London, 1984 · Kinnell, Galway, *The Poems of François Villon*, Hanover, NH/London, 1982 · Lewis, D. B. Wyndham, *François Villon: A Documented Survey*, London, 1928 · Lowell, Robert, 'The Great Testament' (five extracts), in his *Imitations*, New York, 1962, London, 1962; rep. 1971, 1984 · McCaskie, H. B., *The Poems of François Villon*, London, 1946 · Payne, John, *The Poems of Master François Villon of Paris*, London, 1878 · Rossetti, Dante Gabriel, 'The Ballad of Dead Ladies', etc., in his *Poems*, London, 1870 · Saklatvala, Beram, *Complete Poems of François Villon*, London/New York, 1968 [Everyman] · Sargent-Baur, Barbara, *François Villon: Complete Poems*, Toronto/Buffalo/London, 1997 · Swinburne, Algernon Charles, 'From the French of Villon', in his *Poems and Ballads*, 2nd ser., London, 1878 · Synge, J. M., 'Prayer of the Old Woman Villon's Mother' and 'An Old Woman's Lamentation', in his *Poems and Translations*, London, 1912; rep. 1962 · Wilbur, Richard, 'Ballade of the Ladies of Time Past' and three others, in his *New and Collected Poems*, London/Boston, 1988.

SEE ALSO   Prescott, Anne L., *French Poets and the English Renaissance*, New Haven, Conn./London, 1978.

5. RENAISSANCE PROSE: RABELAIS AND MONTAIGNE

i. Rabelais The comic romances of François Rabelais (*Pantagruel*, 1532; *Gargantua*, 1534/5; *Le Tiers Livre*, 1546, The Third Book; *Le Quart Livre*, 1548–52, The Fourth Book), having been spurned for their vulgarity and obscurity by classical taste, emerged

as French classics by the 19th c. Their carnivalesque variety of language, where many voices and speech types jostle in a polyphony which may or may not offer a serious 'message', offers a notable challenge to the translator.

The classic version of Rabelais is the work of two translators, neither of whom wrote English as a fully native language. The first three books were translated in the mid-17th c. by Sir Thomas **Urquhart** (c.1605–1660), a late representative of Scottish Renaissance learning and a royalist combatant in the Civil Wars and in his writings (which also include curious treatises and pamphlets). His work was continued some 30 years later by the French Protestant émigré Pierre le Motteux (Peter **Motteux**) (1660–1718), translator of *Don Quixote* [II.k.5], who translated the *Quart Livre* and the probably inauthentic fifth book. Today, both translations have a period quality, but they are vastly different.

Urquhart's rendering is rich, inaccurate, at times barely comprehensible. It is oddly literal, sometimes virtually transcribing the definitions in Cotgrave's 1611 French–English dictionary: thus 'flamants' (flamingos) becomes 'reddish, long-billed, stork-like, scrank-legged sea-fowles'. This version is more elaborate than the original, but it is racy too, often preserving the directness of Rabelais's storytelling voice. From the opening chords—'Most Noble and Illustrious Drinkers, and you thrice precious Pockified blades'—Urquhart offers a pleasure comparable to that of Rabelais.

Motteux makes fewer mistakes than Urquhart over Rabelais's meaning. At the same time, he is freer and less respectful. Where Urquhart can be gravely ponderous, Motteux plays with the text, modernizing it and recasting it in the new, witty Restoration style. While his dialogue is often rapid and entertaining, his narrative, set alongside Urquhart's, can seem discordantly flippant. Thus 'Pantagruel restait tout pensif et mélancolique' becomes 'Pantagruel seemed metagrabolized, dozing, out of sorts, and as melancholick as a cat'. Nevertheless his version has life and has acquired a firm place as the continuation of the greater Urquhart.

There have been several more recent attempts to replace the much-loved Urquhart–Motteux translation. That of W. F. **Smith**, an example of what has been called the Victorian Tudor style, is from its first words ('Drinkers very illustrious') a highly literal, archaizing version, as well as being a well-annotated work of scholarship. Although a limited edition, it leaves some 'offensive' chapters (e.g. *Gargantua*, 13) in the original French.

A much more widely read translation is that of J. M. **Cohen**. He recasts the text in acceptable modern English, avoiding archaisms (except for comic effect) and shortening Rabelais's sometimes sprawling sentences. He is unembarrassed in his rendering of obscenities, and his text reads cheerfully: its opening words are: 'Most noble boozers, and you my very esteemed and poxy friends—for to you, and you alone my writings are dedicated.' Cohen's translation is generally more lively, more accurate, and less prudish than that of Samuel **Putnam**, first published in a private edition. This was the basis for Putnam's *The Portable Rabelais*, a selection with extensive linking commentaries, which eventually replaced Cohen in the Penguin Classics. Another American translator, J. **Le Clercq**, produced a modernized Rabelais for a private edition, a somewhat cavalier version, incorporating explanatory material into the text and remodelling Rabelais's sentences.

More important than any of these is the fully annotated translation of the *Complete Works* by the 16th-c. scholar Donald M. **Frame**, who states that he has tried to write 'what I think Rabelais would (or at least might) have written if were using [American] English today'. In reality, this version is fairly far removed from modern speech, as can be seen from his translation of the opening: 'Most illustrious topers, and you, most precious poxies, for to you, not to others, my writings are dedicated.' It can, however, be recommended for its accuracy.

The other recent American translation of Rabelais, by Burton **Raffel**, is less accurate in detail; there are quite frequent misreadings, potentially obscure allusions are dropped, and explanatory or decorative phrases are added. It is, however, written in a lively and frequently inventive modern idiom, and of the modern translations comes nearest to equalling the verve of Urquhart–Motteux, as in the portrait of Brother John in *Gargantua* xxvii: 'a true monk if ever there monked one since the days when monks first practiced monking through this unmonkish world of ours, and in all breviary matters a priest right up to his teeth'.

ii. Montaigne Of the other important prose writings of Renaissance France, the only one to have had a major impact on English-language culture—leaving aside the special case of Calvin—is the *Essais* (1580–95) of Michel de Montaigne. For over 300 years only two complete renderings of the *Essais* existed, the second of which was largely responsible for Montaigne's great popularity with English-speaking readers.

The first version of the essays ranks among the classics of English translation. First published in 1603, it was the work of the grammarian John **Florio** (c.1553–1625), son of an Italian Protestant refugee in England [I.b.2.v]. His Montaigne is dedicated to a group of noble ladies, but his dedication speaks of translation as 'female' (and therefore defective) in relation to the male original. Even so, he claims to have enriched the English language and defies his critics to do better.

Florio's inaccuracy and floridity have often been criticized (Yates 1934). He makes mistakes, to be sure, and in places his version is obscure through following the original too closely. For most modern readers his Elizabethan English is difficult. But the most criticized feature of his translation is its amplification of the text, its fondness for symmetrical constructions, to word-play far removed from the frequent plainness of the original. Even so, his English often offers good equivalents for Montaigne's liveliness, metaphors, and wit. Almost every page contains happy expressions such as 'The world runs all on wheels' or 'I cannot settle my object; it goeth so unquietly and staggering, with a kind of natural drunkenness' (from 'Du repentir', Of Repenting).

Florio's version of Montaigne's 'Des cannibales' (Of the Cannibals) is famously quoted by Gonzago in Shakespeare's *Tempest*, and his translation was appreciated by Ben Jonson. It was not reprinted after 1632, however, and was to be eclipsed by that of Izaak Walton's friend the poet Charles **Cotton** (1630–87) [see II.g.6.3]. First published in 1685–6, this was often reissued, sometimes with substantial revisions, the last major new edition being that of William Carew **Hazlitt** in the late 19th c.

Cotton's version is marked by the change in English prose of the mid-17th c. It is somewhat more accurate and more intelligible than Florio's. One notes a tendency to tone down metaphor and word-play, and to introduce symmetries which are absent from the original. In general, it presents a Montaigne who writes in a graceful, easy, and witty style which recommended it to the contemporaries of Pope and Johnson, but was appreciated too by the English romantics.

Cotton's Montaigne formed the basis for a partly new translation with a valuable introduction by Jacob **Zeitlin** in 1934–6, but this quite respectable version seems never to have been reprinted. And indeed, although reissued more than once in the first half of the 20th c., Cotton had virtually disappeared from circulation by the second half. Meanwhile, the neglected Florio had returned in triumph at the end of the 19th c., when there was a growing taste for archaizing translation. Reintroduced by Henry Morley (1885/6) and George Saintsbury (1892–3), Florio's Montaigne was frequently re-issued in the 20th c. Sometimes it appeared in selections, and the spelling and para-graphing might be modernized, but it was never substantially revised.

Two new translations appeared in the 1920s. First the American George B. **Ives**, who had criticized his predecessors' looseness, produced his own 'fig-leaf' translation, where the risqué passages are left in French. In other respects, his version is somewhat more accurate than Florio's or Cotton's, but it is flat and wordy, and shows a tendency to generalized archaism. At almost the same time E. J. **Trechmann** published his translation. While praising Florio and Cotton, Trechmann speaks of the need for a *modern* Montaigne, preserving the vigour and humour of the original. His translation, however, though it is an honest account written in fairly unpretentious English, fails almost as much as Ives's to match the liveliness and wit of the original.

In 1958 Donald M. **Frame** published a new translation of Montaigne's *Complete Works*. As later with his Rabelais, Frame aimed to capture the 'living natural quality of [Montaigne's] style' as if he had been writing in English today. But this is far from being a modern Montaigne. For the most part Frame tries to preserve the style of the original by sticking close to the syntax, and the result is often obscure and awkward. It is, however, a more accurate rendering than the selected *Essays* produced by J. M. **Cohen** for Penguin Classics in 1958. True to Cohen's usual principles, this is a domesticated version. Montaigne's quirkiness and liveliness are smoothed out, and his meaning is often rendered only approximately. To readers who might be put off by a more exact rendering or by the older English of Florio, it offers a somewhat modernized Montaigne whose syntax and paragraphing make for relatively easy reading.

Cohen's selection was superseded in Penguin Classics in 1993 by the complete translation of the eminent scholar M. A. **Screech**. Though Screech insists in his fine introduction on the need to produce a readable text, he eschews the cavalier domestication practised by Cohen. His version is scholarly, scrupulous, accurate, with full notes and commentaries. Modern expressions are generally avoided in favour of a fairly 'timeless', lightly archaic English, and the text often lacks the verbal pleasures offered by Florio or Cotton.

A particular problem for the translator of Montaigne is the treatment of the quotations, mainly Latin, with which the text is studded and which set up a many-voiced dialogue across the centuries. Florio and Cotton give Latin and English in the text, translating verse by verse. Hazlitt in his revision replaces the verse translations with prose footnotes, a practice followed by Ives and Cohen.

Trechmann and Frame give English translations only, in verse where appropriate, whereas Screech gives both Latin and English in the text, with prose translations of the verse.

It is hard to illustrate translating styles from a brief passage, but here are versions of two sentences from 'On Repentance' by Florio, Cotton, and Screech respectively:

So do we attribute savage shapes and ougly formes unto divels. As who doeth not ascribe highraised eye-browes, open nostrils, a sterne frightful visage, and a huge body unto Tamberlaine, as is the forme or shape of the imagination we have fore-conceived by the bruite of his name?

Therefore it is that we give such savage forms to demons: and who does not give Tamerlane great eye-brows, wide nostrils, a dreadful visage, and a prodigious stature,

according to the imagination he has conceived by the report of his name?

That is why we give savage shapes to demons. And who does not give Tamburlaine arching eyebrows, gaping nostrils, a ghastly face and an immense size proportionate to the idea we have conceived of him from the spreading of his name?

For those who know Montaigne, he is a writer for today, yet no one has attempted to translate him into truly idiomatic modern English. Indeed, he and Rabelais are among the authors whom many modern readers prefer in ancient garb. Newer versions, though easier to read, better presented, and often more accurate, seem not to possess the charm (a somewhat spurious and élitist charm perhaps) of the English language written at the time of Shakespeare and the King James Bible.   PF

MONTAIGNE   *The Essayes, or Morall, Politike and Millitarie Discourses of Lo. Michaell de Montaigne*, tr. John Florio, London, 1603 [20th-c. reprints in Everyman, etc.] · *Essays of Michael Seigneur de Montaigne*, tr. Charles Cotton, London, 1685–6 · *The Essays of Michel de Montaigne*, tr. Charles Cotton, ed. William Carew Hazlitt, London, 1877 [frequent reps.] · *The Essays of Montaigne*, tr. George B. Ives, Cambridge, Mass., 1925 · *The Essays of Montaigne*, tr. E. J. Trechmann, London, 1927 · *The Essays of Michel de Montaigne*, tr. Jacob Zeitlin, New York, 1934–6 · *The Complete Works of Montaigne: Essays, Travel Journal and Letters*, tr. Donald M. Frame, Stanford, Calif., London, 1957–8 · *Essays*, tr. J. M. Cohen, Harmondsworth, 1958 [Penguin] · *The Essays of Michel de Montaigne*, tr. M. A. Screech, London, 1991 [subsequently Penguin].

RABELAIS   *The First Book of Mr Francis Rabelais* [containing *Gargantua* and *Pantagruel*], tr. Thomas Urquhart, London, 1653 · *The Works of F. Rabelais M.D., or the Lives . . . of Gargantua and Pantagruel*, tr. Thomas Urquhart and Peter Motteux, London, 1693–4 [much rep. in the 20th c., e.g. Everyman] · *The Five Books and Minor Writings*, tr. W. F. Smith, London, 1893 · *The Complete Works of Rabelais*, tr. Jacques Le Clercq, New York, 1944 [Random House Modern Library] · *The Portable Rabelais*, tr. Samuel Putnam, New York, 1946 [subsequently Viking/Penguin] · *The Histories of Gargantua and Pantagruel*, tr. J. M. Cohen, Harmondsworth, 1958 [Penguin] · *Gargantua and Pantagruel*, tr. Burton Raffel, New York, 1990 · *The Complete Works of François Rabelais*, tr. Donald M. Frame, Berkeley/Los Angeles/London, 1991.

SEE ALSO   Brown, H., *Rabelais in English Literature*, Cambridge, Mass., 1933 · Yates, F., *John Florio: The Life of an Italian in Shakespeare's England*, Cambridge, 1934.

6. CLASSICAL DRAMA

i. Introduction This entry is devoted principally to the three playwrights, Corneille, Racine, and Molière, who have dominated the translation of French classical drama, to the exclusion of many outstanding plays by other authors. Théophile de Viau's strangely exciting *Pyrame et Thisbé* (1623), for example, seems never to have found a translator, and only a few plays of such major writers as Jean Rotrou or Jean Mairet exist in English. Nevertheless, perhaps because of his brother Pierre's fame, some of Thomas Corneille's plays have been translated; his *Ariane* (1672), for instance, exists in at least two versions.

As far as the major 18th-c. dramatists are concerned, there were many contemporary transla-

tions of the now unperformed plays of Voltaire (e.g. versions of *Alzire*, *Mérope*, and *Zaïre* by the playwright Aaron **Hill** (1685–1750)), but very little since. Beaumarchais's comedies *Le Barbier de Séville* (1775, The Barber of Seville) and *Le Mariage de Figaro* (1782, The Marriage of Figaro) have been quite often translated, the latter in the first instance as *The Follies of a Day* (1785) by Thomas **Holcroft** (1745–1809), who learnt the play from performances in order to do so. The Beaumarchais plays and two comedies by Marivaux both figure in Penguin Classics, the former translated by John **Wood** (1964) and the latter by David **Cohen** in a volume entitled *Up from the Country* (1980). Marivaux, once underestimated, is now admired as the creator of beautifully written and unsettling comedies; as such, he has recently begun to find sympathetic translators for the stage.

ii. General Questions A crucial problem is that of dramatic verse. With few exceptions. 17th-c. French tragedy and 'serious' comedy are written in rhyming couplets. The 12-syllable alexandrines carry strong stresses on the sixth and twelfth syllables, but are otherwise without the steady stress pattern characteristic of English poetry; they owe much of their shape and vigour to rhyme. With one or two partial exceptions such as Robert David **MacDonald**'s 1985 translation of Racine's *Phèdre*, it has proved virtually impossible to transfer this form successfully into English verse drama. The result tends to be a long, thumping line falling into two short halves, as in the ludicrous opening of D. **Johnston**'s 1873 version of Corneille's *Le Cid*:

> Frankly, without reserve, does my Elvira tell
> The very words to me which from my father fell?

The choice is therefore usually between prose, blank verse, and heroic couplets—or a mixture. Prose has not been much used for tragedies except in self-avowed cribs. It was the norm for Molière's verse comedies until about 1900, but since that time more translators have used verse, exploiting the comic potential of the couplet. In English, rhyme stands out more eye-catchingly than in French; Molière's rhymes are not usually comic in their own right, but the same is not so true of those of Tony **Harrison** or Liz **Lochhead**.

Because of its comic potential, after the brief flourishing of the rhyming couplet in English verse tragedy around 1670, rhyme was generally eschewed in the translation of tragedy. Translators have tended to be guided by the belief that blank verse occupies the same position in English as the alexandrine in French, even though the results sometimes read like pale pastiches of Shakespeare. In recent years, however, some have dared to take the risks of rhyme; the results are mixed, but often more memorable than those of their blank-verse competitors.

A second feature, common to all theatre translation, is the pull towards adaptation, particularly when a stage production is envisaged [see I.c.2.iv]. Such was the case with most 17th- and 18th-c. translations. At this time, French theatre had its admirers and imitators, but the British, proudly aware of their own traditions and often scornful of French culture, did not shrink from improving on the originals. Thus Matthew **Medbourne**'s 1670 version of Molière's *Tartuffe* is described as 'rendered into English with much addition and advantage'.

On the whole, tragedies were not too drastically altered, though Edmund **Smith**'s *Phaedra and Hippolytus* (1709) gave Racine's *Phèdre* a happy ending, with Hippolytus escaping death to marry his beloved, and William **Whitehead**'s well-received *The Roman Father* (1750) eliminated the Curiace family entirely from Corneille's *Horace*. Molière's comedies and Corneille's *Le Menteur* (1644, The Liar) were treated with even less respect, often being simply quarried for material. To quote one example among dozens, the very successful *Amphitryon* (1690) of John **Dryden** is avowedly based in part on Molière and Plautus; it translates Molière freely from time to time, but is essentially Dryden's own play.

After about 1800, translations were done for the study or schoolroom rather than the stage, and accuracy became more important than actability. The 20th c., however, has seen a revival of the theatrical fortunes of the French classics, and thus a return to adaptation and transposition to other times and places, particularly in the case of Molière.

Tragedy, less obviously tied to 17th-c. reality, has not been so much transposed. There have, however, been bold attempts to overcome the perceived remoteness of Racine's world by situating his tragedies nearer to the audience's experience. One of the freest and most remarkable, Craig **Raine**'s '1953', based on *Andromaque*, takes Racine's tragedy of the Trojan War and rewrites it in the aftermath of a World War II in which the Axis powers have triumphed. The effect, enhanced by Raine's violently inventive language, is electrifying.

iii. Pierre Corneille Corneille wrote 32 plays, but translations have clustered around five or six tragedies and *The Liar*. His greatest success, *Le Cid*, was published and played in English in 1637, almost simultaneously with the original; the translator, John **Rutter** (*fl.* 1635), was working for the Earl of Dorset, Lord Chamberlain to Charles I's French queen. His translation, in serviceable blank verse, is reasonably accurate, except that it omits whole scenes and speeches. It was plagiarized by John **Ozell** (d. 1743) as *The Heroic Daughter* (1714).

The Restoration brought a group of estimable versions in heroic couplets, the best being those of the 'matchless Orinda', the poet Katherine **Philips** (1631–64). Her *Pompey* (a translation of *La Mort de Pompée*, 1644) was played in Dublin and published in 1663, followed the next year by a rival version by 'certain persons of honour' (the best known being the poet Edmund **Waller** (1606–87)). Then came two versions of *Horace* (1641), one from Izaak Walton's friend Charles **Cotton** (1630–87), the other from Katherine Philips. Philips died before completing hers, and the final act was translated in cavalier fashion by Sir John **Denham** (1615–69).

Philips's translations are remarkably scrupulous for their time: they are clearer and closer to Corneille's vigorous rhetoric than the fluent text of the 'persons of honour'. Here is the defiant Camille in her *Horace* (iv.6):

> Give me, Barbarian, then, a heart like thine;
> And since my thoughts I can no more disclaim,
> Restore my Curtius, or excuse my flame;
> All my delight with his dear life is fled,
> I loved him living and lament him dead.

Cotton's *Horace*, never acted it seems, adds the translator's own songs and Greek-style choruses after each act; these tend to counter the martial heroism of the original. In other respects his is an eloquent yet conscientious rendering, and his final act was preferred to Denham's for the second edition of Mrs Philips's *Horace*.

Thereafter there were versions of several Corneille tragedies, including the actor-manager Colley **Cibber**'s adaptations of *Le Cid* (*The Heroick Daughter*, 1718) and *Cinna* (*Cinna's Conspiracy*, 1713), but little of value was produced for the next two centuries. The late 19th and early 20th c. saw some verse translations written in a stilted, archaic style which robs them of all vitality. All these translators wrote for the reader rather than the spectator, and this was also true of three writers of the mid-20th c., Lacy **Lockert**, Samuel **Solomon**, and John **Cairncross**, who all translated a number of plays with reasonable accuracy, mainly confining themselves to the same group of plays (*Le Cid*, *Horace*, *Cinna*, *Polyeucte*, *The Liar*, and one or two more).

Lockert's versions, in blank verse with occasional rhyme, are extravagantly archaic and often awkward. Solomon also mixes blank verse and rhyme; his translations are closer to modern English than Lockert's, and they have their moments, though the general effect is plain and rather lifeless. Cairncross, finally, translated six plays for Penguin Classics, including for the first time *L'Illusion comique* (1636, The Comic Illusion). He uses a fairly flexible blank verse, putting a premium on intelligibility; the language is of the 'timeless' variety, having recourse to archaisms, and tending to play down Corneille's powerful rhetoric.

Here are their three versions of Augustus's famous lines in the final scene of *Cinna*:

> Is it not enough, O heaven. Hath fate, to harm me
> One of my people still left to seduce? . . .
> Though to its efforts it joins aid of hell,
> I am earth's master and my own as well.   (Lockert)

> Gods! is this not enough? has harsh fate yet
> Some intimate of mine it would subvert?
> To aid it, let hell's banners be unfurled:
> I'm master of myself as of the world.   (Solomon)

> My cup is full. O gods, can hostile fate
> Still find one of my house to lead astray?
> Let it join forces with the powers of hell.
> I'm master of myself as of the world.   (Cairncross)

Rather more satisfactory than any of these are a number of translations of individual plays made with a view to stage production. For instance, Ranjit **Bolt** has rendered *The Illusion* and (more freely) *The Liar* into inventive rhyming couplets, Noel **Clark** also uses rhyme, though somewhat less convincingly, in his versions of three tragedies, and there is a sturdy and accurate blank-verse translation of *Horace* by the poet Alan **Brownjohn**. On the whole, though, Corneille has benefited less than Racine or Molière from the 20th-c. move to revive French classical drama in English performance.

iv. Jean Racine Racine, with his unique blend of formality, passion and musicality, is often considered 'untranslatable'. The 17th and 18th c. saw versions, free or faithful, of all his tragedies, all of them condemned as 'wretched travesties' by Katherine Wheatley (1956). Certainly, none is as true to the spirit of the original as the best Corneille translations, but even so, two of them enjoyed a considerable reputation.

In his *Titus and Berenice* of 1677, the playwright Thomas **Otway** (1652–85) reduces *Bérénice* (1670) to three acts, alters the action and motivation, and both cuts and expands Racine's dialogue. He avowedly aimed for a natural, simple style, and his translation avoids the bombast which creeps into many versions of Racine. His play has moments which almost match the original, as when his Titus declares:

> No, madam, no: my heart, since I must speak,
> Was ne'er more full of love or half so like to break.

Soon afterwards, unfortunately, Racine's terse 'Sortons, Paulin, je ne lui puis rien dire' is padded out to become:

> Oh, the dismal secret will not come . . .
> Away, Paulinus, e're i'm quite undone.
> My speech forsakes me, and my heart's all stone.

The Distrest Mother by Ambrose **Philips** (1674–1749), a version of *Andromaque* (1667), enjoyed a great success for at least a century. Philips alters the structure of Acts IV and V, sentimentalizes Racine, stressing the pathos around Andromache, and includes improving reflections. The style is generally decorous, though lapsing into bombast for the 'fury' of Orestes; the overall impression, in spite of some accurate and inventive renderings, is of a Racine lacking in fire.

All of the other 18th- and 19th-c. translations of individual plays are mediocre or worse, except perhaps for a worthy and very faithful account of *Athalie* (1691) by William **Duncombe**. This was not destined for the stage, and was the first and probably the best of many ensuing translations of this Biblical tragedy.

The first attempt at a complete Racine, meant for reading rather than acting, was produced by Robert Bruce **Boswell** in 1889–90 and seems to have done service for several decades. It is in sub-Shakespearean blank verse, somewhat archaic in diction, and not particularly faithful either to Racine's literal meaning or to his dramatic rhetoric. The 20th c. has seen several more volumes of complete or selected tragedies, including several by the translators of Corneille discussed above. Lacy Lockert's versions, entirely rhymed, sacrifice even more to an archaizing poetic style than his Corneille; Samuel Solomon's are done with care, but his periodic recourse to rhyme often lets him down; Cairncross seems more at home with Racine than Corneille and gives an accurate line-by-line translation, though without much magic or music.

There are also smaller selections, all in blank verse, all true to Racine's literal meaning, by the American George **Dillon**, the British scholars R. C. **Knight** and Kenneth **Muir**, and the poet C. H. **Sisson**. Dillon's is avowedly as literal as possible; he keeps close to Racine's turns of phrase in a fairly modern and natural-sounding English, but the padding-out of the verse leads to a certain flatness. Knight, a noted Racine specialist, also preserves a good deal of the original phrasing, the metaphors and the rhetorical effects. Muir, whose translations were performed under the direction of G. Wilson Knight, aims for what he calls a 'neutral diction'; to avoid monotony, he favours run-over lines at the expense of Racine's powerful one- or two-line formulations. None of these versions really catches fire; without being wildly archaic, they are a good deal less modern than that of Sissons, whose faithful, plain, somewhat understated yet moving translations avoid the spurious eloquence of much blank verse.

Racine has in fact attracted several poets as translators in the 20th c. The first was John **Masefield**, who in his *Berenice* and his adaptation of *Esther* (1689) accomplished the feat of drastically simplifying Racine to excellent effect, as when three lines in *Bérénice* become:

> And if, as sometimes happens, I am late,
> I find her weeping.

Much more recently, Douglas **Dunn** has produced a free version of *Andromaque* for radio production in inventive modern English with fairly rough rhythms, in couplets which rhyme quite unobtrusively. Somewhat more stageable and faithful to the letter of Racine's text is the *Andromache* of Eric **Korn**, written in a modern idiom (which shocked some spectators at the Old Vic in 1988) and avoiding the tum-ti-tum effect of so much blank verse.

It is, however, *Phèdre* (1677) which has been the biggest draw, inspiring poets as different as Robert **Lowell**, Tony **Harrison**, Derek **Mahon**, and Ted **Hughes** (and at the time of writing a new translation in Scots by Edwin **Morgan** is announced). Mahon, writing for the Dublin theatre, mixes rhyme and blank verse somewhat arbitrarily; he sometimes misses the meaning, and his language veers between the prosaic and the poetic, the modern and the timeless, but his translation has a vigorous theatricality. Hughes's unrhymed free translation, made for acting, is sinewy and strong, often underlining Racine's meaning; the rhythms are deliberately prosaic, only occasionally rising to Racine's grandeur.

Lowell's and Harrison's are both written in couplets. Harrison, in his *Phaedra Britannica*, attempts to make the ferocious irrationality of the original more real to modern theatregoers by transposing the play to the 19th-c. British empire in India, with Phèdre as a Memsahib hounded by the Hindu gods. Lowell stays with ancient Greece, but his characters speak violent post-romantic English poetry. He apologizes in his preface for his 'heavy touch' and his version has been criticized for turning Racine into melodrama, but like Harrison's it is impressive in performance.

Both Lowell and Harrison spell out vividly what is often merely implicit in the original. Where Phèdre in Act I, sc. 4 speaks of the 'égarements' (aberrations) of her mother, Lowell writes:

> Oh Venus, murdering Venus! love
> gored Pasiphaë with the bull.

and Harrison, less explicitly perhaps:

> Mother! Mother! driven by the dark gods' spite
> beyond the frontiers of appetite.
> A *judge*'s wife! Obscene! Bestialities
> Hindoos might sculpture in a temple frieze!

It is a moot question whether it is possible in English to combine the 'propriety' maintained by Sisson and the power communicated by these exuberant adaptations.

v. Molière (Jean-Baptiste Poquelin) Molière has been more translated than either of the tragic playwrights. In his case adaptation has been commoner than translation, since close translations of his comedies, especially his verse masterpieces, have often struck British audiences as rather unfunny.

Early adaptations tend to be very free indeed, giving the play a new setting, radically reworking the plot and enlarging the cast. Splendid comedies such as William **Wycherley**'s *The Plain Dealer* (1677, based on *Le Misanthrope*, 1666) or Henry **Fielding**'s *The Mock Doctor* (1732, based on *Le Médecin malgré lui* 1666) are in large part original compositions. The tendency in these plays is towards a cruder humour than Molière's.

The early 18th c. saw two prose translations of virtually the whole body of Molière's comedies. The first, published in six volumes under the name of the indefatigable translator John Ozell in 1714, seems to have had little success and is now very rare. It is, however, a distinctly literal version, no doubt meant for reading, and offers quite lively renderings of some of the short prose comedies. Then in 1739, having previously published a shorter selection, the scientist Henry **Baker** (1698–1774) and the clergyman James **Miller** (1706–44) produced a revised and enlarged *Works of Molière* with facing English and French texts. The prose translation is reasonably accurate and quite racy in places (the peasant speech in *Don Juan* is well rendered); frequently reprinted or plagiarized, it was still available in Everyman's Library until well into the 20th c., in spite of its period language.

Molière translation went into the doldrums in the 19th c., when his plays ceased to attract British playgoers. Towards the end of the century there were a number of rather mediocre prose collections, all apparently made to be read, not acted. The most respected of these is the six-volume *Dramatic Works of Molière* by Henri **van Laun**. In 1908 the American Curtis Hidden **Page** broke new ground by including clear and sometimes vigorous verse translations of *Tartuffe* (1664/9) and *Le Misanthrope* in his collection of eight plays.

A fascinating sign of the return to a stage Molière is the *Kiltartan Molière* of Lady Augusta **Gregory** (1852–1932), made for the Abbey Theatre in Dublin [see I.a.5.i]. Her text follows the development of three prose comedies quite closely, but renews the dialogue in Irish terms: thus *L'Avare* (1668, The Miser) opens with the words: 'What ails you and what is vexing you, Elise, and you having given me your word you would never break with me?'

The innumerable 20th-c. adaptors of Molière are often much freer. In the 1930s F. **Anstey** published nine comedies 'freely adapted for the English stage'; *Les Fourberies de Scapin* (1671, The Rogueries of Scapin) is in fact quite faithfully rendered, whereas *Tartuffe* is radically recast, to no great advantage. Anstey's dialogue lacks verve, unlike that of the actor Miles **Malleson**, who achieved great success after 1945 with his entertaining adaptations, such as *The Slave to Truth*. Here, while following the plot of *Le Misanthrope* quite closely (though sentimentalizing the ending), Malleson breaks up the dialogue to produce a rapid cut-and-thrust effect quite different from Molière's more sedate tone. More recently there have been far more daring adaptations, for instance Martin **Crimp**'s *Misanthrope* played at the London Young Vic in 1996 or Ranjit Bolt's brilliant transposition of *Les Femmes savantes* (1672) as *The Sisterhood* (1989).

As for close translations, there are two postwar British collections, both entirely in prose, the 10 plays produced for Penguin Classics by John **Wood**, and the *Six Prose Comedies* of George **Graveley**, later revised and enlarged by Ian **Maclean**. Graveley is generally more accurate but also stiffer than Wood, but neither version convinces as a potential stage text. Similarly working in prose, the American Albert **Bermel** has produced in his *Actor's Molière* some very plausible versions, both translations and adaptations, of the prose comedies.

The *Don Juan* of Christopher **Hampton**, compared with those of Wood and Graveley, is lively, modern, and somewhat free. Where Graveley's peasant Pierrot at the beginning of Act II says 'What a ringmarole of frippery these court folks does put on', and Wood's 'What a sight of contraptions those courtiers do be a wearin' ', Hampton simplifies it successfully to 'What a pantomime' (Bermel offers 'Yow, these nobles, what a load o' crapdiddle on 'em'). Hampton has also done a blank-verse *Tartuffe*, a close rendering and a success on stage. Choosing rather to use couplets, the poet Richard **Wilbur** produced admired versions of *Tartuffe*, *Le Misanthrope*, and *The School for Wives* (L'École des femmes, 1662). For all their virtues of accuracy and wit, these sometimes succumb to the monotony of the form; as stage versions they seem less satisfactory than the *Tartuffe* and *School for Wives* of Ranjit Bolt, also in couplets, but consistently entertaining and modern in tone. Perhaps the most remarkable of all the verse translations is Tony Harrison's free version of *Le Misanthrope*. Set in modern Paris, this is a remarkable rendering, conveying the serious tensions of the play while finding witty equivalents for the satire, as in Clitandre's self-praise at the beginning of Molière's Act II:

> Assured and polished, and a handsome creature
> (my teeth, I think my most outstanding feature)
> my sportsman's figure and my splendid gear
> easily made me *Best-Dressed Man* last year.

Finally, the years since 1945 have seen many translations or adaptations of Molière into Scots [see I.a.6.ii]. The pioneer was Robert **Kemp**, whose blank-verse version of *L'École des femmes*, *Let Wives Tak Tent*, transfers the play to a richly realized 17th-c. Edinburgh. Here and in Liz Lochhead's outrageously rhyming *Tartuffe*, set in middle-class Glasgow, or in the fine translations of Hector **MacMillan**, the idiomatic style and the *realia* of modern Scotland give a bite to Molière's dialogue which is sometimes lacking in English translations.   PF

CORNEILLE, PIERRE   *The Cid*, tr. John Rutter, London, 1637 · *Pompey*, tr. Katherine Philips, Dublin, 1663 · *Pompey the Great*, tr. 'certain persons of honour', London, 1664 · *Horace*, tr. Katherine Philips, London, 1669 [in her *Poems*, with final act by J. Denham; 2nd edn. 1710 with final act by C. Cotton] · *Horace*, tr. Charles Cotton, London, 1671 · *The Mistaken Beauty, or The Lyar*, tr. anon., London, 1685 · *Cinna's Conspiracy*, adapted from *Cinna* by Colley Cibber, London, 1713 · *The Heroick Daughter*, adapted from *Le Cid* by Colley Cibber, London, 1718 · *The Roman Father*, adapted from *Horace* by William Whitehead, London, 1750 · *The Chief Plays of Corneille*, tr. Lacy Lockert, Princeton, NJ, 1952 · *Moot Plays of Corneille*, tr. Lacy Lockert, Nashville, Tenn., 1959 · *Seven Plays*, tr. Samuel Solomon, New York, 1969 · *The Cid, Cinna, The Theatrical Illusion*, tr. John Cairncross, Harmondsworth, 1975 [Penguin] · *Polyeuctus, The Liar, Nicomedes*, tr. John Cairncross, Harmondsworth, 1980 [Penguin] · *The Liar* and *The Illusion*, tr. Ranjit Bolt, Bath, 1989 · *Le Cid, Cinna, Polyeuct*, tr. Noel Clark, Bath, 1993 · *Horace*, tr. Alan Brownjohn, London, 1996.

MOLIÈRE [JEAN-BAPTISTE POQUELIN]   *Tartuffe*, tr. Matthew Medbourne, London, 1670 · *The Works of M. de Molière*, tr. John Ozell, 6 vols., London, 1714 · *The Works of Molière, French and English*, tr. Henry Baker and James Miller, 10 vols., London, 1739 [much rep., including a selection in Everyman, 1929, 1956] · *The Dramatic Works of Molière*, tr. Henri van Laun, 6 vols., Edinburgh, 1875–6 · *The Affected Misses* [and other plays], tr. Curtis H. Page, 2 vols., London, 1908 · *The Kiltartan Molière*, tr. Lady Augusta Gregory, Dublin, 1910 · *Four Molière Comedies, Freely Adapted for the English Stage*, tr. F. Anstey, London, 1931 · *Six Prose Comedies of Molière*, tr. G. Graveley, London, 1956 [rep. Oxford, 1968, rev. and augmented by Ian Maclean, Oxford, 1989, World's Classics] · *The Slave of Truth*, tr. Miles Malleson, London, 1957 · *The Misanthrope and Other Plays*, tr. John Wood, Harmondsworth, 1959 [Penguin] · *Five Plays*, tr. John Wood, Harmondsworth, 1963 [Penguin] · *Tartuffe*, tr. Richard Wilbur, London, 1964 · *The Misanthrope*, tr. Richard Wilbur, London, 1967 · *The School for Wives*, tr. Richard Wilbur, New York, 1971 · *The Misanthrope*, tr. Tony Harrison, London, 1973 · *Don Juan*, tr. Christopher Hampton, London, 1974 · *Let Wives Tak Tent* (*L'École des femmes*), tr. Robert Kemp, Glasgow, 1983 [first perf. 1947] · *Tartuffe*, tr. Christopher Hampton, London, 1984 · *Tartuffe*, tr. Liz Lochhead, Edinburgh, 1985 · *The Actor's Molière*, tr. Albert Bermel, 4 vols., New York, 1987 · *Tartuffe, The Sisterhood*, tr. Ranjit Bolt, Bath, 1991 · *The Misanthrope*, tr. Martin Crimp, London, 1996 · *The School for Wives*, tr. Ranjit Bolt, London, 1997.

RACINE, JEAN   *Titus and Berenice*, tr. Thomas Otway, London, 1677 [modern edn., *The Works of Thomas Otway*, ed. J. C. Gooch, Oxford, 1932, vol. i] · *The Distrest Mother* [*Andromaque*], tr. Ambrose Philips, London, 1712 · *Athaliah*, tr. William Duncombe, 1722 · *The Dramatic Works of Jean Racine: A Metrical English Version*, tr. Robert Bruce Boswell, 2 vols., London, 1889–90 · *Berenice*, tr. John Masefield, London, 1922 · *Esther*, adapted and partly translated by John Masefield, London, 1922 · *The Best Plays of Racine*, tr. Lacy Lockert, Princeton, NJ, 1936 · *Racine's Mid-Career Tragedies*, tr. Lacy Lockert, Princeton, NJ, 1958 · *Five Plays*, tr. Kenneth Muir, London, 1960 · *Three Plays of Racine*, tr. George Dillon, Chicago, 1961 · *Phaedra*, tr. Robert Lowell, New York, 1961 · *Iphigenia, Phaedra, Athaliah*, tr. John Cairncross, Harmondsworth, 1963 [Penguin] · *Andromache, Britannicus, Berenice*, tr. John Cairncross, Harmondsworth, 1967 [Penguin] · *Complete Plays*, tr. Samuel Solomon, 2 vols., London, 1967 · *Phaedra Britannica*, tr. Tony Harrison, London, 1975 · *Four Greek Plays*, tr. R. C. Knight, Cambridge, 1982 · *Phedra*, tr. Robert David MacDonald, Oxford, 1985 · *Britannicus, Phaedra, Athaliah*, tr. C. H. Sisson, Oxford, 1987 [World's Classics] · *Andromache*, tr. Eric Korn, New York, 1988 · *Andromache*, tr. Douglas Dunn, London, 1990 · *1953*, a version of Racine's *Andromaque* by Craig Raine, London, 1990 · *Racine's Phaedra*, tr. Derek Mahon, Oldcastle, Ireland, 1996 · *Phèdre*, tr. Ted Hughes, London, 1998.

SEE ALSO   Attridge, D., 'Dryden's Dilemma, or, Racine Refashioned: The Problem of the English Dramatic Couplet', *Yearbook of English Studies*, 9 (1979), 55–77 · Canfield, D. F., *Corneille and Racine in England*, New York, 1904 · Harrison, T., 'Molière Nationalized', *Revue de l'Histoire du Théâtre* (1973), 169–86 · Peacock, N., *Molière in Scotland*, Glasgow, 1993 · Wheatley, K. E., *Racine and English Classicism*, Austin, Tex., 1956.

7. LA FONTAINE

Although Jean de la Fontaine (1621–95) is the author of a rich and varied body of writing, he is known in English for one masterwork only. The *Fables* (1668–93), a subtle, varied, witty reworking of Aesop and other fabulists, seem quintessentially French, but in their freedom offer a wonderful opportunity to the poet-translator. Written primarily for adults, they have often been treated as children's literature, and like the *Histoires ou contes du temps passé* (1697, usually entitled *Mother Goose Tales* in English) of Charles Perrault [I.c.4.ii], have been endlessly rewritten for English-speaking children. Unlike Perrault, they have also given birth to many adult translations, all of which inevitably reinflect and not infrequently simplify these subtle fables in line with the preconceptions of particular readers or periods (see Rubin 1995).

Early renderings by John **Dennis** (1657–1734—in his *Miscellanies of 1693*) and particularly by the author of the *Fable of the Bees*, Bernard de **Mandeville** (?1670–1733), recast a few fables in jolly octosyllables in the manner of Butler's *Hudibras*—Mandeville used the charming title *Aesop Dress'd* for his versions. The first more or less complete translation was published over a century later by Robert **Thomson** (*fl.* 1790–1810). His verse lacks the terseness and subtlety of the original, but gives a truer idea of it than the cavalier version of John **Matthews** (1755–1826) with its satirical topical references. Neither of these had anything like the success of the much-reprinted complete American translation by Elizur **Wright** (1804–85), very much a children's version done mainly in short, over-regular lines with obtrusive rhyming, as seen in the opening of 'The Two Doves':

> Two doves once cherished for each other
> The love that brother hath for brother.

The translation by Charles Dickens's collaborator Walter **Thornbury** (1828–76), is similarly mechanical in rhythm, bringing in superfluous elements to pad out its rhyming couplets.

The 20th c. has seen several attractive verse translations (the *Fables* are also sometimes reduced to prose in children's books). Only the most interesting of these can be mentioned here. In his complete *Fables* of 1931, Rupert Brooke's friend, the scholar and art patron Edward **Marsh**, aims to stay close to La Fontaine while often transposing him to an English setting. The tone is in places rather poetically archaic and the dialogue a little old-fashioned, but there are many neat humorous touches and the translation retains much of its appeal. Another complete version published in America the previous year, that of Joseph **Auslander** (vol. i) and Jacques **Le Clercq** (vol. ii) is considerably freer in its approach, adopting a variety of verse-forms; both translators, but particularly Le Clercq, pad out the original, bringing in extra jokes, but in so doing they lose much of La Fontaine's rapidity and homogenize his sometimes brutal changes of tone.

A more remarkable complete version is that published in 1954 by the poet Marianne **Moore**, whose La Fontaine speaks with a distinctive voice, deliberate, rather literary, but sometimes homespun too. Staying close to the original rhyme schemes, she avoids excessive rhythmical regularity; her distinctiveness can be seen in the closing lines of 'The Oak and the Reed':

> The bulrush bent, but not the tree.
> Confusion rose to a roar,
> Until the hurricane threw prone
> That thing of kingly height whose head had all but
>   touched God's throne—
> Who had shot his root to the threshold of Death's door.

The principal recent translations are all selections. Two of them, made by academics and published by university presses, have not achieved wide circulation. Francis **Scarfe**'s bilingual *100 Fables* is an accurate line-by-line version, often inventive if a little tending to archaism; it lacks something of La Fontaine's lightness of touch, but in 'The Wolf and the Lamb', for instance, the different voices in the dialogue are well caught. Norman R. **Shapiro**'s *Fifty Fables*, also bilingual, has similar qualities, though in this case the demands of fairly strict adherence to La Fontaine's rhyme scheme results in a good deal of padding and a rather dead feel in places.

Two other attractive translations, both more modern in style and less concerned to echo the form of the original, are aimed at a wider audience. The fuller is that by Christopher **Wood**, which includes nearly half the 240 fables in both French and English as well as copious notes. Wood is perhaps too fond of the octosyllable, but his translation makes excellent use of the stylistic and prosodic freedom offered by La Fontaine and is full of memorable touches, both witty and musical. The shorter Penguin Classic by James **Michie** (with a pleasant introduction by Geoffrey Grigson) is sharp and down-to-earth, full of familiar good humour;

Michie likes to use short rhyming lines but his lively verse generally avoids the pitfalls of doggerel. Here are his and Wood's versions of the opening of 'The Wolf and the Stork':

> Wolves are gluttonous feeders.
>   This wolf, readers,

> Gobbled so fast that a bone got stuck in his craw
>   And he thought he was going to die.   (Michie)

> Wolves eat wolfishly. One such
> bon viveur ate so much
> a bone stuck in his throat. He thought he'die.   (Wood)
>
>   PF

TRANSLATIONS   *Some Fables after the Easie and Familiar Method of M. de la Fontaine*, tr. Bernard de Mandeville, London, 1703 [rev. edn. as *Aesop Dress'd*, 1704] · *La Fontaine's Fables. Now First Translated from the French*, tr. Robert Thomson, Paris, 1806 · *Fables from La Fontaine, in English Verse*, tr. anon. [John Matthews], London, 1820 · *The Fables of La Fontaine*, tr. Elizur Wright, Boston, Mass., 1841 · *The Fables of La Fontaine*, tr. Walter Thornbury, London, 1867 · *The Fables of Jean de la Fontaine*, tr. Joseph Auslander and Jacques Le Clercq, 2 vols., New York, 1930 · *The Fables of Jean de La Fontaine*, tr. Edward Marsh, London/New York, 1931 [later Everyman] · *The Fables of La Fontaine*, tr. Marianne Moore, New York, 1954 · *Selected Fables*, tr. Marianne Moore, London, 1955 · *Selected Fables*, tr. James Michie, Harmondsworth, 1979 [Penguin] · *100 Fables*, tr. Francis Scarfe, London/Paris, 1985 · *Fifty Fables of La Fontaine*, tr. Norman R. Shapiro, Urbana, Ill./Chicago, 1985–8 · *Selected Fables*, tr. Christopher Wood, Oxford, 1995 [World's Classics].

SEE ALSO   Rubin, D. L., 'Refabulations', in A. L. Birberick, ed., *Refiguring La Fontaine: Tercentenary Essays* Charlottesville, Va., 203–22.

8. THINKERS 1630–1780

With the exception of Descartes, no writers of 17th- and 18th-c. France have entered the mainstream of English-language philosophy. But several French thinkers of the period have exerted a great influence, often through translation, on English-speaking culture. Apart from the authors discussed below, one might cite: the disenchanted *Maximes* (1665–78) of La Rochefoucauld, translated for instance by Aphra Behn as *Seneca Unmasqued* (1685) [see I.b.3.iii]; the *Caractères* (1688–94) of his fellow-moralist La Bruyère, also translated more than once; the multi-volume *Histoire naturelle* (1749–1804, Natural History) of Georges-Louis Leclerc de Buffon and his collaborators; and the great compilation of Abbé Raynal, *Histoire des deux Indes* (1770–80, History of the Two Indies), with its subversive contributions by Diderot.

i. Descartes René Descartes is now seen as a founding figure of modern philosophy, but only a few of his works were translated in his own day. The *Discours de la méthode* (1637, Discourse on Method) appeared in 1649 in an anonymous version that is scrupulous and agreeable to read, though the passage of time has rendered it less useful. The following year saw a faithful version (again anonymous) of *Les Passions de l'âme* (1649, The Passions of the Soul), but the *Meditations* (1641), first published in Latin, had to wait until 1680 for an English translation.

Then came a long gap until 1850, when John **Veitch** inaugurated modern Descartes translation

with his version of the *Discourse*, soon followed by the *Meditations* and selections from the *Principia* (1644). These did service for decades, but for much of the 20th c. the standard Descartes, and the most complete, was that of Elizabeth S. **Haldane** and G. T. R. **Ross**. Containing the first translation of the Latin *Regulae* (1628, Rules for the Direction of the Mind), this is a fairly literal, rather heavyweight rendering. Criticized for inaccuracy, it has now been replaced by the *Philosophical Writings of Descartes*, translated by John **Cottingham**, Robert **Stoothoff**, and Dugald **Murdoch**, with the correspondence translated by Anthony **Kenny**.

This translation is careful and accurate; unlike Haldane and Ross, who mix the Latin and French sources, the authors translate the *Meditations* directly from the Latin. In places it falls some way short of Descartes's eloquence, though the version of the *Meditations* catches the jagged insistence of the original better than most. Interestingly, Robert Stoothoff chooses to translate the famous 'Je pense, donc je suis' in the *Discours* as 'I am thinking, therefore I exist' rather than the more usual 'I think, therefore I am'. The anonymous translator of 1649 is the only one to render Descartes's 'être' uniformly as 'to be'.

The simplest words ('be', 'think', etc.) pose difficult problems of interpretation. It is not surprising, then, that it is often philosophers who have translated selections or individual works (e.g. the *Discourse on Method, Optics, Geometry and Meteorology* (1965) of Paul J. **Olscamp** and the *Meditations on First*

Philosophy (1979) of Donald A. **Crews**). In their selection, Elizabeth **Anscombe** and Peter Thomas **Geach** are very aware of terminological problems and try to solve some of these by giving the French or Latin original in brackets. In his *Philosophical Writings* Norman **Kemp Smith** goes further than most, possibly too far, in interpreting and clarifying Descartes. The Americans John J. **Blom** and Lowell **Bair** have also produced useful selections; both show lapses of understanding, but Bair's is the more fluent. Arthur **Wollaston**'s Penguin selection, which includes the *Meditations* done from the French, is a more literary account; he adapts Descartes's syntax more than most to the demands of readability, and is sometimes cavalier in his approach.

ii. Pascal Blaise Pascal, Descartes's younger contemporary, wrote on scientific and religious questions. His attack on the Jesuits, *Lettres provinciales* (1656–7, Provincial Letters), has been translated more than once, but his influence abroad is essentially due to his disturbingly eloquent apologia for Christianity, the *Pensées* (Thoughts). This remained unfinished at his death in 1662, and there is no certainty about the correct ordering of the fragments it contains. The many translations have followed the different orders contained in successive editions.

The first edition of 1670 was the basis of the quite vigorous 1688 translation by Jos. **Walker** and the more verbose but often reprinted version by Basil **Kennett** (1674–1715). More recently, the edition by Léon Brunschvicg, regarded as authoritative in the first half of the 20th c., was well translated (though with occasional errors) by W. F. **Trotter**, and J. M. **Cohen** produced a fluent rendering of the Pléiade edition of J. Chevalier. Both of these offer a relatively coherent ordering of the fragments.

It is revealing that Cohen was replaced in Penguin Classics after a mere five years by Alban **Krailsheimer**'s scrupulous rendering of the 1951 edition of Louis Lafuma, which reproduces the order of one of the two copies made after Pascal's death. More recently, Honor **Levi**'s World's Classics volume follows the 'second copy' used in Philippe Sellier's authoritative edition. This translation, though generally reliable, does not include the complete text and is not entirely accurate in detail.

Current critical opinion prefers such 'authentic' editions. Attempts to reconstruct Pascal's intended order may be thought more user-friendly; a useful compromise is provided by Lafuma's 1952 Delmas edition, which regroups all the fragments in the 27 files created by Pascal. This is the basis for the translations of John **Warrington** (partly a reworking of Trotter) and of Martin **Turnell** (one of the most eloquent versions).

iii. Montesquieu Charles de Secondat, baron de Montesquieu, was the author of the witty epistolary novel *Lettres persanes* (1721, Persian Letters) and the essay *Considérations sur les causes de la grandeur des Romains et de leur décadence* (1734, Reflections on the Causes of the Greatness and Decline of the Romans). Both of these important texts were twice translated in the 18th c., the former first by John **Ozell** in 1722, the latter perhaps by Tobias **Smollett** in one instance. There are several modern versions of the *Letters*, including an accurate and scholarly one by C. J. **Betts**, and David **Lowenthal** has done a reliable translation of the *Considérations*. But it is Montesquieu's massive master-work, *De l'esprit des lois* (1748, The Spirit of the Laws), which has most marked English-speaking culture.

In 1750, the Irish-born writer Thomas **Nugent** (1700–72) published his *Spirit of Laws* with Montesquieu's approval. This version has worn well, being frequently republished over the following two centuries, often with minor revisions. It is a confident and eloquent translation, true to the spirit of the original, but allowing itself freedom to rephrase and sometimes clarify the French text. By contrast, the 1988 version by Anne M. **Cohler**, Basia Carolyn **Miller**, and Harold Samuel **Stone** follows Montesquieu's text very closely even in such matters as sentence structure, though it is not always as accurate as Nugent on points of meaning. This edition, filling out the numerous footnotes in line with modern norms, can be recommended to students of Montesquieu's thought.

iv. Voltaire Born a few years after Montesquieu, Voltaire (François-Marie Arouet) wrote prolifically and became hugely famous in his lifetime. The majority of his works were translated into English as they appeared. There were also English collected works. The first, directed by Tobias Smollett and Thomas **Francklin**, and containing critical notes by Smollett which 'correct [Voltaire's] mistakes', began to appear in 1761; there were many editions in the next two decades, and a luxurious one with some new translations attributed to a mysterious William F. **Fleming** was issued at the beginning of the 20th c. In 1779, the year after Voltaire's death, came a further 14-volume set, with sound versions of fuller texts, from a team directed by William **Kenrick**.

In his day Voltaire was known as France's leading dramatist, poet, and historian. Most of his plays were produced on the London stage, but have

271

hardly been translated since the 18th c. The epic *La Henriade* (1728) was rendered into insipid blank verse by John **Lockman** (1698–1771), but rhyming couplets were preferred for the Smollett edition and for the vigorous if old-fashioned translation produced in 1797 on subscription by Charlotte Maria **Bury**, who also did one of the three early translations of Voltaire's notorious mock-epic *La Pucelle* (1755, The Maid of Orleans).

The various historical works were highly popular in the 18th c. (they take pride of place in the collected editions), and have occasionally been attempted in more modern times, notably the *Histoire de Charles XII* (1731, History of Charles XII), well translated by Antonia **White** (1976), and *Le Siècle de Louis XIV* (1751, The Age of Louis XIV), translated with other historical texts in a valuable edition by J. **Brumfitt** (1966).

Since 1800, however, Voltaire has figured in translation overwhelmingly through his philosophical tales. There are exceptions such as the *Dictionnaire philosophique* (1764, Philosophical Dictionary), often translated in whole or in part in the early 19th c. and subsequently by H. I. **Woolf** (1924), Peter **Gay** (1962, a full, if free version), and Theodor **Besterman** (1971, Penguin Classics). Besterman, the editor of Voltaire's correspondence, has also done a *Select Letters* (1963), and there have been versions of other philosophical works, notably the *Lettres philosophiques* (1734, Philosophical Letters)—which were in any case originally published in English in 1733. But translators have flocked above all to *Zadig* (1748), *Candide* (1759), and the other *contes*, so much so that it is only possible here to mention a few names.

The translations from the Smollett edition have sometimes been reprinted, with revisions, but the first modern version of a collection of tales was done in 1891 by Robert Bruce **Boswell**, translator of Racine [II.g.6.iv]—a rather leaden performance. A lighter touch is shown by William **Walton** in 1900 in the first rendering of the complete tales, but this version too is lacking in bite. In more recent times there have been several good selections. John **Butt**'s Penguin versions tend to eliminate Voltaire's sharp disjointedness in favour of an elegant fluency, but most collections adopt a more literalist approach. This is true of the translations of Donald M. **Frame** and Roger **Pearson**, both of which score highly in different ways, Pearson being more convincing in the dialogue. An earlier World's Classics version by Joan **Spencer**, now replaced by Pearson, steers an elegant middle course between literalism and readability. The novelist Richard **Aldington**'s stylish versions of

Candide and other stories have been much admired and reprinted. Of the many versions of *Candide* alone, one might single out the scrupulous yet agreeable translation of Lowell **Bair**.

Finally there have been some useful anthologies of Voltaire's essays, dialogues, and other philosophical works. That of Joseph **McCabe**, presented in the best-selling Thinker's Library, offered new translations of the more committed writings, including a good account of the important *Traité de la tolérance* (1762, Treatise on Tolerance). More recently, David **Williams** has published reliable new translations of the *Political Writings*, notably the dialogues entitled *A.B.C.* Paul **Edwards** and Christopher **Thacker** both offer copiously commented selections of extracts translated by various hands.

v. Rousseau Like Voltaire, the Genevan Jean-Jacques Rousseau had a huge impact on his contemporaries, not least in Britain. Within 10 years his first important work, the *Discours sur les sciences et les arts* (1751, Discourse on the Sciences and the Arts), had been translated by three different hands, and even his little pastoral opera, *Le Devin du village* (1752, The Village Soothsayer), was twice translated, once by the musicologist Charles **Burney** as *The Cunning Man* (1766).

The Works of J. J. Rousseau, published a few years before his death, brought together translations of most of the major works by William **Kenrick** (?1725–1779). It is a paradox that Kenrick, described by the *DNB* as a 'superlative scoundrel', should have been partly responsible for the wave of high-minded British Rousseauism, above all through his spirited if free renderings of the novel *La Nouvelle Héloïse* (1761, Eloisa) and the treatise on education, *Émile* (1762, Emilius). *Eloisa*, for all its huge contemporary success, has never been retranslated in its entirety, and Kenrick's version was reissued as recently as 1989 (an abridged version, in a new and more accurate translation by Judith H. **McDowell**, 1968, unfortunately omits nearly half the text, including many essential 'digressions'). The 1995 reprint of *Emilius*, however, adopts the rival version made by Montesquieu's translator Nugent, which sticks more closely to Rousseau's phrasing.

There have been two modern versions of *Émile*. The often reprinted Everyman version by Barbara **Foxley** interprets, simplifies, and paraphrases for elegance, whereas that of Allan **Bloom** is fiercely literal. Thus where Foxley translates Rousseau's opening blast as 'God makes all things good, man meddles with them and they become evil', Bloom sticks closely to the original constructions:

'Everything is good as it leaves the hand of the Author of things; everything degenerates in the hands of man.'

It is Rousseau the political thinker who has attracted most modern translators. Since 1893 there have been at least a dozen versions of *Du contrat social* (1762, The Social Contract) and almost as many of his crucial *Discours sur l'inégalité* (1755, Discourse on Inequality). For the most part these give a quite accurate account of Rousseau's thought. All inevitably involve a degree of interpretation; the enigmatic and paradoxical formulations call for elucidation, and while versions such as those of Maurice **Cranston** aim 'to put this text into intelligible English', the serious student of Rousseau's thought will probably fare better with an annotated edition such as those of Christopher **Betts** and Charles M. **Sherover**. Betts and Cranston are the only translators to render the famous 'L'homme est né libre' literally as 'Man was born free', which carries different, more historical connotations than the traditional 'Man is born free'.

Rousseau has also been influential as an autobiographer, but here the translation history is more patchy. The *Confessions* (1782–9), published too late to be included in Kenrick's collection, were translated anonymously and rather clumsily by two different hands; these translations continued to be reissued, often abridged, until well into the 20th c. Of their successors, the most satisfactory for the general reader is an anonymous translation of the unabridged text, first published *c.*1890 and often reissued; as compared with this, the Penguin Classics version of J. M. **Cohen**, while characteristically readable, fails to render the specificity of Rousseau's style. There have also been two recent versions of his beautiful swan-song, *Rêveries du promeneur solitaire* (1782, Reveries of the Solitary Walker), by Charles **Butterworth** (1979) and by Peter **France** (Penguin Classics, 1979).

An important new American initiative is the *Collected Writings* launched by the University Press of New England in 1990. Five volumes had appeared by 1996, including not only the political writings but the first-ever translation of the fascinating *Rousseau juge de Jean-Jacques* (1776, Rousseau Judge of Jean-Jacques) and a new and very close translation of the *Confessions*. This is an edition for scholars; some little-known texts and fragments are included, and there are extensive notes and introductions. Some older translations are reused; the authors of the new translations, Judith R. **Bush**, Christopher **Kelly**, and Roger D. **Masters**, favour a literalist approach, even at the cost of 'some awkwardnesses', and indeed obscurity. They aim to offer 'a

standard reference for scholarship' with texts 'that have not been deformed by the interpretive bias of translators or editors'. Given the nature both of translation and of Rousseau's thought, however, a definitive version hardly seems possible.

vi. Diderot   Denis Diderot's fate has been different from that of Voltaire and Rousseau. Apart from the *Encyclopédie*, few of his major works were widely known in his lifetime, though there were translations of several individual works. His masterpiece, the dialogue *Le Neveu de Rameau* (begun *c.*1760, Rameau's Nephew), was first published in France in a retranslation from Goethe's German version. But in the 20th c. his many-sided genius has been fully recognized and his protean work much translated.

Since his works are mainly short texts in a vast variety of forms, translations have usually been selections. The first, by Beatrix L. **Tollemache** (1893), gives elegant renderings of shortish texts on aesthetic questions; more complete texts of this kind are now available in a useful and reliable version by Geoffrey **Bremner**. Two of the great works on art criticism, the *Salons* of 1765 and 1767, are included in the two-volume *Diderot on Art*, translated somewhat flatly, and with quite a few misreadings, by John **Goodman**.

For the 'philosophical' Diderot, Margaret **Jordan**'s rather wooden and far from accurate 1916 versions of the early works was complemented in 1937 by the important collection of materialist writings translated and introduced with a strong Marxist emphasis by Jean **Stewart** and Jonathan **Kemp** as *Diderot Interpreter of Nature*. The political writings, to which more attention has recently been given, are well represented in a volume by John **Hope Mason** and Robert **Wokler**, which includes the first translation of Diderot's commentary on the *Nakaz* of Catherine the Great.

Two wide-ranging American collections are the large but rather bitty volume of excerpts chosen by Lester G. Crocker and well translated by Derek **Coltman**, and—the best general selection—an attractive volume translated by Jacques **Barzun** and R. H. **Bowen**, the former being responsible for a fine translation of *Rameau's Nephew* (first translated into English in abridged form by John **Morley** as an appendix to his 1878 *Diderot and the Encyclopedists*).

Diderot's fictional writings have attracted some good translators. Of the versions of his Gothic novel *La Religieuse* (1760, The Nun), that by Leonard **Tancock** is the most fluent and energetic, though it does not quite render Diderot's breathless style. Elsewhere, Tancock couples a lively and faithful translation of *Rameau's Nephew* with a version of the scientific dialogues *Le Rêve de d'Alembert* (1769, D'Alembert's Dream), where he treads a tricky path between modern readability and historical scruple. P. N. **Furbank** has published an attractive if not always accurate rendering of several short stories and dialogues. But the greatest success is perhaps the rendering of Diderot's remarkable Sternian anti-novel *Jacques le fataliste* (begun *c*.1771, Jacques the Fatalist) by Michael **Henry**; superseding a quite respectable translation by J. Robert **Loy**, this very accurate account communicates much of

the verve, inventiveness, and variety of the original. Here is Henry's rendering of Diderot's narrator in full provocative flow:

The name William is neither heroic nor common. And it's the same with Bugger. Bugger without qualification is neither the famous cartwright nor one of his boring ancestors, nor one of his boring descendants. In all honesty, how can a person's name be in good or bad taste? The streets are full of hounds called Pompey. So cast off your irrational false sense of propriety, or I shall have to deal with you like Lord Chatham dealt with Parliament: 'Shh ... ugar, Sugar, Sugar', he said to them. 'What do you find so funny about that?   PF

DESCARTES, RENÉ   *A Discourse of a Method for the Well-Guiding of Reason and the Discovery of Truth in the Sciences*, tr. anon., London, 1649 · *The Passions of the Soule*, tr. anon., London, 1650 · *Six Metaphysical Meditations*, tr. William Molyneux, London, 1680 · *A Discourse on Method* [with the *Meditations* and a selection from the *Principles*] tr. John Veitch, London, 1912[Everyman; 1st edns. 1850, 1853] · *Philosophical Works*, tr. Elizabeth S. Haldane and G. T. R. Ross, 2 vols., Cambridge, 1911 [frequent reps.] · *Philosophical Writings*, tr. Norman Kemp Smith, London, 1952 · *Philosophical Writings*, tr. Elizabeth Anscombe and Peter Thomas Geach, London, 1954 · *Essential Works of Descartes*, tr. Lowell Bair, New York, 1961 · *The Essential Writings*, tr. John J. Blom, New York, 1977 · *The Philosophical Writings of Descartes*, tr. John Cottingham, Robert Stoothoff, Dugald Murdoch, 2 vols., Cambridge, 1984–5 [additional vol. of the correspondence, tr. Anthony Kenny, pub. 1991].

DIDEROT, DENIS   *Diderot's Thoughts on Art and Style*, tr. Beatrix L. Tollemache, London, 1893 · *Diderot's Early Philosophical Writings*, tr. Margaret Jourdain, Chicago/London, 1916 · *Diderot, Interpreter of Nature*, tr. Jean Stewart and Jonathan Kemp, London, 1937 [several later edns.] · *Jacques the Fatalist and His Master*, tr. J. Robert Loy, New York, 1959 · *Rameau's Nephew and Other Works*, tr. Jacques Barzun and R. H. Bown, Indianapolis, 1964 · *Rameau's Nephew and d'Alembert's Dream*, tr. Leonard Tancock, Harmondsworth, 1966[Penguin] · *Diderot's Selected Writings*, tr. Derek Coltman, New York/London, 1966 · *The Nun*, tr. Leonard Tancock, Harmondsworth, 1972 [Penguin] · *Jacques the Fatalist*, tr. Michael Henry, Harmondsworth, 1986 [Penguin] · *Political Writings*, tr. John Hope Mason and Robert Wokler, Cambridge, 1992 · *This Is Not a Story, and Other Stories*, tr. P. N. Furbank, Oxford, 1993 [World's Classics] · *Selected Writings on Art and Literature*, tr. Geoffrey Bremner, London, 1994[Penguin] · *Diderot on Art*, tr. John Goodman, 2 vols., New Haven, Conn./London, 1995.

MONTESQUIEU, BARON DE   *Persian Letters*, tr. John Ozell, London, 1722 · *Reflexions on the Causes of the Grandeur and Declension of the Romans*, tr. anon., London, 1734 · *The Spirit of Laws*, tr. Thomas Nugent, London, 1750 [frequent reps.] · *Persian Letters*, tr. J. Robert Loy, New York, 1961 · *Persian Letters*, tr. George R. Healy, Indianapolis, 1964 · *Considerations on the Greatness of the Romans and their Decline*, tr. David Lowenthal, New York, 1964 · *Persian Letters*, tr. C. J. Betts, Harmondsworth, 1973[Penguin] · *The Spirit of the Laws*, tr. Anne M. Cohler, Basia Carolyn Miller, and Harold Samuel Stone, Cambridge, 1988.

PASCAL, BLAISE   *Monsieur Pascal's Thoughts, Meditations and Prayers*, tr. Jos. Walker, London, 1688 · *Thoughts on Religion and Other Subjects*, tr. Basil Kennett, London, 1704 · *The Thoughts of Blaise Pascal*, tr. C. Kegan Paul, London, 1885 · *Thoughts*, tr. W. F. Trotter, London, 1904 [later Everyman] · *Pensées: Notes on Religion and Other Subjects*, tr. John Warrington, London, 1960[Everyman] · *The Pensées*, tr. J. M. Cohen, Harmondsworth, 1961[Penguin] · *Pensées*, tr. Martin Turnell, London, 1962 · *Pensées*, tr. Alban Krailsheimer, Harmondsworth, 1966[Penguin] · *Pensées and Other Writings*, tr. Honor Levi, Oxford, 1995 [World's Classics].

ROUSSEAU, JEAN-JACQUES   *Eloisa*, tr. William Kenrick, 4 vols., London, 1761 [rep. 1989] · *Emilius and Sophia*, tr. William Kenrick, 3 vols., London, 1762 · *Emilius*, tr. Thomas Nugent, 2 vols., London, 1763 [rep. Taipei and Bristol, 1995] · *The Works of J. J. Rousseau*, tr. William Kenrick, 10 vols., London, 1773–4 · *The Confessions*, tr. anon, London, *c*.1896 [later Everyman] · *Émile, or Education*, tr. Barbara Foxley, London, 1911 [Everyman, frequent reps.] · *The Social Contract and Discourses*, tr. G. D. H. Cole, London, 1913[Everyman, frequent reps.] · *Confessions*, tr. J. M. Cohen, Harmondsworth, 1953 [Penguin] · *The Social Contract*, tr. Maurice Cranston, Harmondsworth, 1968 [Penguin] · *Émile*, tr. Allan Bloom, New York, 1979 [Basic Books, then Penguin] · *A Dissertation on Inequality*, tr. Maurice Cranston, Harmondsworth, 1984[Penguin] · *Of the Social Contract*, tr. Charles M. Sherover, New York, 1984 · *The Collected Writings of Jean-Jacques Rousseau*, tr. Roger D. Masters, Judith R. Bush, and Christopher Kelly, 5 vols. to date, Hanover, NH, 1990– · *The Social Contract: Discourse on Political Economy*, tr. Christopher Betts, Oxford, 1994 [World's Classics].

VOLTAIRE, [FRANÇOIS-MARIE AROUET]   *The Works of M. de Voltaire*, tr. Tobias Smollett and others, 25 vols., London,

1761–65 [numerous reps., including an updated 20-vol. luxury version in London and New York, 1901 and reprints] · *The Works of M. de Voltaire*, tr. William Campbell, J. Johnson, et al., under the direction of W. Kenrick, 14 vols., London, 1779–81 · *Zadig and Other Tales*, tr. Robert Bruce Boswell, London, 1891 · *The Whole Prose Romances*, tr. William Walton, London/Philadelphia, 1900 · *Selected Works*, tr. Joseph McCabe, London 1911 · *Candide and Other Romances*, tr. Richard Aldington, London/New York, 1927 [frequent reps.] · *Candide*, tr. John Butt, Harmondsworth, 1947 [Penguin] · *Candide*, tr. Lowell Bair, New York, 1959 [Bantam] · *Candide, Zadig, and Selected Stories*, tr. Donald M. Frame, 1962 · *Zadig; L'Ingénu*, tr. John Butt, Harmondsworth, 1964 [Penguin] · *Candide and Other Stories*, tr. Joan Spencer, Oxford, 1966 [World's Classics] · *Selections*, ed. Paul Edwards, New York, 1989 · *Candide and Other Stories*, tr. Roger Pearson, London/New York, 1992 [Everyman and World's Classics] · *Political Writings*, tr. David Williams, Cambridge, 1994 · *Selected Writings*, ed. Christopher Thacker, London, 1995 [Everyman].

SEE ALSO   France, P., 'Rousseau's Confessions in English', *Franco-British Studies*, 2 (1986), 27–39.

9. NINETEENTH-CENTURY FICTION

i. Translation and the Canon The 19th c. in France saw an explosion in the production of prose fiction and in the fiction-reading public. Technological and sociological changes led to the appearance of the *roman feuilleton* (serialized novel), which appealed to a mass readership. At the same time the novel, previously seen as a disreputable genre, gained a new artistic status as a means of depicting and exploring the world. The genre diversified and changed rapidly, passing through a kaleidoscopic series of manifestations which can be labelled—though very crudely—romantic, realist, naturalist, symbolist, and so on.

Much of this production was translated into English, though this was often resisted on moral or political grounds [see I.b.4.iv]. The transfer followed different patterns: sometimes, as with Alexandre Dumas *père*, there was a massive immediate response, followed perhaps by disaffection, whereas elsewhere translation followed long after composition (e.g. the Polish writer Potocki's *Manuscrit trouvé à Saragosse*, written c.1800 but only rediscovered in the 20th c. and translated to considerable acclaim by Ian **MacLean** in 1996 as *The Manuscript Found at Saragossa*). In general the translated canon has followed that in France; there are few acknowledged classics crying out for translation.

There is today a retrospective critical consensus that Stendhal, Balzac, Hugo, Flaubert, and Zola dominate 19th-c. French fiction; this entry will be mainly concerned with them. But they emerge from a huge mass of fiction-writers, many of whom have been translated more than once. One might name such important figures as François-René de Chateaubriand, Benjamin Constant, Prosper Mérimée, Jules Barbey d'Aurevilly, or Joris-Karl Huysmans [see I.b.4.iv]. In particular there are seven figures—other than the five discussed more fully below—who were (and in some cases still are) massively popular in French and in English.

Perhaps the most popular in the mid-19th c. were the blockbuster novels of Eugène Sue and Alexandre Dumas. Sue's low-life thriller *Les Mystères de Paris* (1842–3, The Mysteries of Paris), translated, retranslated, and published in many editions, was a major literary event of the mid-century [see I.b.4.iii]. Dumas, the master of romance, has enjoyed a longer-lived popularity; such novels as *Le Comte de Monte Cristo* (1844, The Count of Monte Cristo) and *Les Trois Mousquetaires* (1844, The Three Musketeers) were translated almost immediately and have been retranslated or reissued constantly ever since, sometimes in adapted form, as children's stories, or as comics. On a world scale, Dumas is no doubt one of France's most famous novelists. At the turn of the century, when he enjoyed his greatest vogue, new editions came at the rate of five or six a year, and there were collective editions of his novels in 1893–7 (60 vols), 1903–11 (56 vols), and 1910–11 (25 vols). Since then there have been few new translations (several World's Classics volumes edited by David Coward reprint early translations) but in 1996 Robin **Buss** broke new ground with a fresh version of *Monte Cristo* for Penguin.

George Sand's novels, particularly the edifying rustic stories such as *La Mare au diable* (1846, The Devil's Pool), were also very popular in their day, and most were rapidly translated. There were also collections of novels (though no complete works in English), but in the 20th c. Sand fell into a disfavour which has only recently begun to be dissipated by feminist criticism. A number of new translations have now appeared, from Eva **Figes**'s pioneering 1967 version of *La Petite Fadette* (1848) to three recent World's Classics volumes, including Sylvia **Raphael**'s 1994 version of Sand's important first novel, *Indiana* (1832).

Writing later in the century, Guy de Maupassant won a huge following in the English-speaking world as the 'French Chekhov'. Translation began in 1887, and by 1923 there were five different complete editions of the stories in English. Since then the vogue has subsided, but many of the stories are still available. His novels too, such as *Une vie* (1883, *A Life*), *Bel-Ami* (1885) and *Pierre et Jean* (1888), have been much translated. His main English translator was Marjorie **Laurie**, who tackled the complete works, though her translations in Penguin Classics have been successively replaced by those of H. N. P. **Sloman**, and then Roger **Colet** (*Selected Short Stories*, 1971).

Perhaps even more popular was Jules Verne. His adventure stories were easily absorbed into English literature, many of their innumerable young readers not even realizing that *Twenty Thousand Leagues under the Sea* (or *Seas*) was one of several translations of *Vingt mille lieues sous les mers* (1870). As is the way with children's books [see I.c.4], translators often remained anonymous and books were abridged or adapted. Verne is now increasingly treated as an adult writer in France, and this is echoed in the recent inclusion in the World's Classics list of William **Butcher**'s translations of *Le Tour du monde en quatre-vingts jours* (1871, Around the World in Eighty Days) and *Voyage au centre de la terre* (1864, Journey to the Centre of the Earth).

Finally, one should mention two late 19th-c. writers whose fame has lasted less well, but who in their day attracted many translators. Of Alphonse Daudet's many works, the only one to have retained something of its old popularity is the collection of Provençal stories, *Lettres de mon moulin* (1867, Letters from my Windmill). Anatole France's star has sunk even more decisively since the days when he won the Nobel Prize in 1921; in his day, most of his novels were translated, some of them several times, and there was an English complete works published in many volumes between 1908 and 1928.

ii. Stendhal Henri Beyle, known as Stendhal, claimed to write for the 'happy few' and for posterity. His translation history bears out the accuracy of this view. He has never won the immense readership of Balzac, Dumas, or Hugo, and although one or two of his youthful writings on Italy and music were translated almost immediately, for many years after his death in 1842 there were no translations at all. There is no complete works in English, the most ambitious venture being a collection of five titles done by C. K. **Scott Moncrieff**. Even so, *Le Rouge et le noir* (1830, The Red and the Black) and *La Chartreuse de Parme* (1842, The Charterhouse of Parma) have established Stendhal as one of Europe's greatest novelists.

Both these novels were first translated around 1900, two or three different translations of each being published before 1920. These are adequate, though tending to dilute Stendhal's characteristic staccato manner, but have been long forgotten. Scott Moncrieff's versions came in the 1920s and have remained in print; since the 1950s they have been rivalled by the two Penguin Classics translations of Margaret R. B. **Shaw**, and by the World's Classics volumes of Catherine **Slater** (for *Le Rouge*) and Margaret **Mauldon** (for *La Chartreuse*). *Le Rouge* has also been translated by Lowell **Bair**.

The Scott Moncrieff translations, which also include *Armance* (1827) and a version of the *Chroniques italiennes* (1829–36, Italian Chronicles), have not acquired the reputation of his Proust [II.g.13]. Nevertheless they are fine, spirited renderings, not entirely accurate on minor points of meaning, but giving a good account of the elegant, concise, yet sometimes moving style of the originals. Stendhal's abrupt paragraphing, sentence structure, and punctuation are retained to good effect. Scott Moncrieff's English has a period flavour, and he avoids all contractions such as 'He's'. He is particularly successful with the high-society scenes, including the court scenes in *La Chartreuse*; in this Italian novel he solves the problem of the intimate 'tu' form by having the heroine Clelia ask at a crucial point 'Hai mangiato?'

This is how Scott Moncrieff does the walk to the scaffold of Julien Sorel, hero of *Le Rouge*:

Fortunately, on the day on which he was told that he must die, a bright sun was gladdening the earth, and he himself was in a courageous mood. To walk in the open air was a delicious sensation for him, as is treading solid earth to a mariner who has long been at sea. 'There, all is well', he said to himself; I am not lacking in courage.

For the last sentence ('Allons, tout va bien, se dit-il, je ne manque point de courage'), Shaw has: 'There now, he said to himself, everything is going well . . . My courage isn't failing me'; Bair gives us: ' "I'm ready", he said to himself, "everything is going well, my courage hasn't failed me" ', whereas Slater translates: 'Here we go, everything's all right, he told himself, I'm not lacking in courage.'

The more recent translators offer a more modern and more natural-sounding English; they are sometimes surprisingly close to Scott Moncrieff, though none of them follows Stendhal's word order quite as closely. In her two translations Shaw is clumsy at times, lacking Scott Moncrieff's sharpness and elegance. Bair's *The Red and the Black* reads easily, but tends to add phrases to improve the flow or make the text easier to follow. Slater's version also adds the odd explanatory word, but is generally concise and readable, and Mauldon's *Chartreuse*, while the colloquialism jars at times, renders both dialogue and narration in a brisk, natural-seeming manner, though for some reason she too tends to normalize Stendhal's punctuation and syntax. In spite of his archaisms, Scott Moncrieff's versions have not really been superseded.

Other important works by Stendhal exist in English. H. L. R. **Edwards**'s translation of the unfinished novel *Lucien Leuwen* (1834–6) is generally adequate, though not always accurate and a little orotund in places. The autobiographical *La Vie de Henry Brulard* (1835, The Life of Henry Brulard), a favourite with Stendhalians, has been translated three times; the versions by Jean **Stewart** and B. J. C. G. **Knight**, and more recently by John **Sturrock**, both have their virtues, Stewart/Knight being more fluent, whereas Sturrock remains closer to the abrupt movement of Stendhal's text.

iii. Balzac Honoré de Balzac did not have to wait for popularity as long as Stendhal. Even if he did not enjoy the instant success of Dumas in French and in translation, the interlocking 89 fictional titles of his *La Comédie humaine* (1829–47, The Human Comedy) came before long to be recognized as the major literary monument of the century.

In many cases translation into English had to wait some decades, but by the end of the century there were three different collections of his works in English. The first, done single-handed by Katherine Prescott **Wormeley**, was not unjustly described by a contemporary reviewer as being written in 'clear and fluent English, reading not at all like a translation'. It was followed by another set, lavishly illustrated but not better translated, from Ellery **Sedgwick**, George B. **Ives**, and others, and then by a 40-volume edition, masterminded by George Saintsbury, with translations by Clara **Bell**, Ellen **Marriage**, James **Waring**, and R. S. **Scott**. Several volumes of this have had a long life, being adopted by Everyman's Library, and in some cases, such as Waring's version of one of Balzac's greatest novels, *La Cousine Bette* (1846, Cousin Bette), the old translation has worn well.

The 20th c. has seen no further attempts at a complete Balzac in English, but a large number of one-off translations, particularly of favourites such as *La Peau de chagrin* (1831, The Wild Ass's Skin) or *Eugénie Grandet*. One which deserves special mention is Rayner **Heppenstall**'s racy Penguin version of the melodramatic *Splendeurs et misères des courtisanes* (1838–47) as *A Harlot High and Low*. In addition there have been many selections of stories,

including the mock-medieval *Contes drolatiques* (1832–7, Droll Stories), which have been frequently translated.

Some translators have attempted several volumes, for instance Marion Ayton **Crawford**, whose Penguin translations are not entirely reliable and tend to domesticate Balzac's often idiosyncratic prose, and the Balzac scholar H. J. **Hunt**, whose four Penguin volumes include a sound version of the great *Illusions perdues* (1837–43, Lost Illusions). A freer but more impressive *Lost Illusions*, long since out of print, is that of the poet Kathleen **Raine**, whose beautiful phrasing seems at times to improve on the original. Where Balzac writes of the dead heroine: 'Sur le visage de Coralie étincelait cette fleur de beauté qui parle si haut aux vivants en leur exprimant un calme absolu' (translated literally by Hunt as 'On Coralie's face gleamed the bloom of beauty which speaks so eloquently to living people because it expresses absolute calm'), Raine writes: 'Coralie's face was radiant with that flower of beauty that speaks so eloquently to the living of perfect calm'. She has also done a *Cousine Bette*, though here one may prefer the scrupulous yet lively account from Sylvia Raphael.

Balzac's most popular novel is probably his prose *King Lear*, *Le Père Goriot* (1834–5). Translated in 1860 as *Daddy Goriot*, this has gone through a number of different versions. Those available at the end of the 20th c. include two recent translations, both successful, though in different ways. A. J. **Krailsheimer**'s is distinguished by its closeness to the original, but it is also stylish and vigorous, with lively renderings of the very varied dialogue passages. Burton **Raffel** is less accurate in detail, sometimes over-translating ('old dotards' for *vieillards*) or failing to catch the nuance of meaning ('businessman' for *rentier*, 'old workman' for *ancien employé*). He modernizes the text, translating proper names and either explaining or omitting over-specific cultural references; both his narrative and his dialogue are inventive and energetic, and he catches better than most what he calls the 'power and slashing, challenging emotion' of Balzac.

iv. Hugo Victor Hugo, even more than Balzac, was a massive presence in French 19th-c. culture; two million people attended his state funeral in 1885. His works in all genres were extensively translated into English; 1895 saw the publication of *The Novels of Victor Hugo*, translated by various hands, and Graham Robb in his *Victor Hugo: A Life* (1997) states that 'well over two million copies of Hugo's novels were in circulation in Britain before World War I'. Subsequently, the picture has been less rosy.

Many of his major novels, including *Les Travailleurs de la mer* (1866, Toilers of the Sea) and *L'Homme qui rit* (1869, The Laughing Man), exist only in old translations, inaccurate and abridged. As an exception, one must welcolme the valuable new version by Geoff **Woollen** of the anti-capital-punishment texts, including *Le Dernier Jour d'un condamné* (1829, The Last Days of a Condemned Man).

Even for Hugo's greatest novel, *Les Misérables* (1862), the situation is unsatisfactory. This has been several times translated, and often excerpted. The original 'authorized' version by F. C. L. **Wraxall** was much reprinted, sometimes in abridged form. It was followed by those of Charles E. **Wilbour** and Isabel F. **Hapgood**. All these 19th-c. translations have been reissued in the 20th c., especially Wilbour's. However, all of them, especially Hapgood's sometimes inaccurate rendering, show their age; none has the intense vitality which characterizes Hugo's prose at best. The one modern version is described by its translator Norman **Denny** as 'not a photograph but a slightly modified version of Hugo's novel, designed to bring its great qualities into relief by thinning out, but never completely eliminating, its lapses'. So Denny abridges the text, 'tones down' the rhetoric, and transfers digressions to appendices. The prose is simplified, and the syntax often remodelled in the name of readability; to give a small example, Hugo's 'Il suivait, entre deux rangées d'arbres, une large chaussée pavée ondulant sur des collines qui viennent l'une après l'autre, soulèvent la route et la laissent tomber, et font là comme des vagues énormes' is reduced to 'He followed a wide tree-lined road through a countryside where the small hills succeeded one another like waves of the sea'. The result may be felt to justify such high-handed treatment, but there is still no full modern translation of this, one of the great European novels.

Things are better with *Notre-Dame de Paris* (1831). The 19th c. saw several versions of this perennially popular story, soon known as *The Hunchback of Notre-Dame*. The first, unfortunately based on the first edition, is by William **Hazlitt**, son of the essayist [see I.b.4.iii]; in spite of its now antiquated English, it has been reprinted in the 20th c., for instance in Everyman's Library. J. Carroll **Beckwith**'s version, done for the *Novels* of, 1895 has also been reissued; it reads quite fluently, adding brief glosses as it goes, treating Hugo's syntax rather freely and sometimes failing to catch the meaning of the dialogue. Fortunately there are two good modern translations. A. J. Krailsheimer's is the more scrupulous, sticking quite closely to Hugo's syntax, avoiding unnecessary interpretation and

keeping explanation for the end notes. John Sturrock's earlier Penguin Classic is freer: tending to eschew archaism, it reads very naturally, especially the dialogue. It is odd that in 1996 Penguin chose also to reissue the more stilted and inaccurate 1965 translation of Walter J. **Cobb**.

Hugo's bulky novels share with those of Dumas a popularity which authorizes free reuse as well as translation proper. *Notre-Dame* in particular has spawned in English a great progeny of abridgement, adaptations, children's retellings, and comics.

v. Flaubert Some 20 years Hugo's junior, Gustave Flaubert was less popular in his day, but in the 20th c. has increasingly been seen as an unrivalled master. George Steiner, in *After Babel*, shows the difficulties posed for a translator by his many-layered, highly worked prose with its idiosyncratic syntax. The temptation is to normalize it in the name of readability; even if this is resisted and some equivalent is found for his extraordinary use of tenses, there still remains the challenge of doing justice to the sounds and rhythms of his prose.

The difficulty has not deterred translators. Even if his six major works were not immediately translated, all were available in English by the beginning of the 20th c., some in several versions. In the early 20th c., the gamey exoticism of *Salammbô* (1862), his novel of ancient Carthage, and of the metaphysical *La Tentation de Saint Antoine* (1874, The Temptation of Saint Antony) attracted a number of translators. But the undisputed favourite has been *Madame Bovary* (1856), his sardonic tragedy of provincial life.

One of the first in the field was Eleanor **Marx-Aveling** (1855–98), daughter of Karl Marx [see I.a.5.i]. Her plain version, though not attempting to match Flaubert's style, stands comparison with several of the later versions. Some of these, such as the American translations of Lowell Bair and Mildred **Marmur**, treat the text freely, often ignoring the syntax, but offer no compensating gain. The translations of J. Lewis **May** and of Gerard **Hopkins** both aim for an English style worthy of the original; in doing so, they reshape Flaubert's sentences, lightening them and making them flow more easily. The result is sometimes rather conventionally literary, but Hopkins in particular writes with freedom and flourish, producing a readable, very English-sounding text.

Rather closer to the original, but still tending to domesticate, is Alan **Russell**'s fluent 1950 version for Penguin. This was superseded in 1992 by a new translation from Geoffrey **Wall**, which seeks to reproduce some of the formal features of Flaubert's text, notably his punctuation and paragraphing. This 'foreignizing' version has real merits, but Wall is not always so careful with the meaning of the original and his version often sounds unnecessarily awkward. Take a small example from the seduction scene in Part II, chapter 9: 'The earth, reddish like powdered tobacco, absorbed the sound of their feet; and with the tips of their shoes, as they walked on, the horses pushed fallen pine-cones in front of them.' (Hopkins has: 'The earth, reddish in colour like snuff, deadened the noise of their horses' hooves, trundling pine-cones as they moved.')

Perhaps the most satisfying account is that of Francis **Steegmuller**. He too is not always precise in his rendering of Flaubert's meaning, he tends to interpret, and he treats the syntax quite freely. Nevertheless, his translation, as well as being highly readable, generally comes closer than the others to rendering the sense of Flaubert's narrative and dialogue, his irony, and his poetry.

Flaubert's second great novel of modern life, *L'Éducation sentimentale* (1869, The Education of the Feelings), is seen by many critics as his masterpiece, yet it has been comparatively little translated since the first rendering in 1898. Two of the modern versions, those of Anthony **Goldsmith** and Robert **Baldick**, are fairly similar, reasonably close to the original, but lacking distinction. The third, by Douglas **Parmée**, is free, stylish, and full of life, particularly in the dialogue. Goldsmith renders the beginning of the famous epilogue quite literally:

He travelled.
He knew the melancholy of the steamboat; the cold awakening in the tent; the tedium of scenery and ruins; the bitterness of interrupted friendships.
He came back.

Baldick's version reads like an edited version of this, but Parmée gives us:

He travelled.
Chilly awakenings under canvas; dreary mail-packets; the dizzy kaleidoscope of landscapes and ruins; the bitter taste of friendships nipped in the bud: such was the pattern of his life.
He came home.

After *Madame Bovary*, Flaubert's most translated work is *Trois contes* (1794, Three Tales). The first attempt, by George Burnham Ives, has stood the test of time as well as most of its successors. Of these, one should mention the fairly free but stylish 1923 version of Arthur **McDowall**, and in particular the excellent rendering by A. J. Krailsheimer, who translates very exactly to produce a readable text that conveys a good deal of Flaubert's personal

tone. Krailsheimer has also done fine translations of the grotesque epic of modern knowledge, *Bouvard et Pécuchet* (1881)—also available in a sound 1936 version—and of *Salammbô*, where again he improves upon all previous versions (the first, an accurate rendering by J. S. **Chartres**, was published, like the Marx-Aveling *Madame Bovary*, by Zola's publisher, Vizetelly).

Two further modern translations deserve a mention. There is a careful version of *The Temptation of Saint Antony* by Kitty **Mrosovsky**, which can be interestingly compared with the handsomely phrased, poetically archaic translation made by Lafcadio **Hearn** at the beginning of the century. And Francis Steegmuller has published an attractive selection from Flaubert's correspondence, which in its freedom and verve contrasts with the marmoreal prose of the novels.

vi. Zola The novels of Émile Zola, leader of the naturalist school, were and have remained immensely popular, both in France and abroad. In the last decades of the 19th c. they were also controversial because of their vulgar language and provocative descriptions of sexuality and low life. England was the scene of such a controversy.

The first English versions were made in America; from the mid-1870s numerous translations (many under the pseudonym John **Stirling**) were published, often shortly after the originals. Their popularity and perceived inadequacy led the publisher Henry Vizetelly to launch a large-scale translation in London. Subtitling all the books 'a realistic novel', he issued between 1884 and 1888 a total of 18 titles, 15 of them from Zola's great Rougon-Macquart series, an epic of French life under the Second Empire. These texts, rapidly translated by unnamed authors, billed as complete, but lightly expurgated, sold extremely well. Too well, so that a National Vigilance Association, outraged by *The Soil* (1888), a translation of Zola's shocking novel of peasant life, *La Terre* (1887), took Vizetelly to court. He gave an undertaking not to sell objectionable works, but was again prosecuted (and ruined) after he had reissued his Zola titles, incompletely bowdlerized by his son Ernest (who tells the story at length in his *Émile Zola*, 1904).

Ernest went on to 'edit' many of the earlier translations, bowdlerizing as he went, and to translate others for the first time; his translations are if anything less adequate than their not very brilliant predecessors. His brother Edward also translated Zola, producing in 1901 a remarkably unexpurgated version of Zola's 'Jack the Ripper' novel, *La Bête humaine* (1890), as *The Monomaniac*. Meanwhile, by a nice irony, the Lutetian Society had produced in 1894–5 an unexpurgated, but limited, edition of six very popular novels. The translators include such illustrious names as Ernest **Dowson**, Havelock **Ellis**, and Arthur **Symons**. Ellis's *Germinal* and Symons's *The Drunkard* (from *L'Assommoir*) have stayed in print, in revised versions; Symons's in particular is a fine eloquent rendering, though its dialogue inevitably seems outdated now.

In the 20th c. most of the Rougon-Macquart novels have been retranslated, in some cases several times, the most popular being *La Bête humaine*, his novel of prostitution, *Nana* (1880), the epic of a miners' strike, *Germinal (1885)*, and *L'Assommoir* (1877, sometimes *The Dram Shop*), his tragic story of drink and degradation in working-class Paris. In addition one should note the publication of several selections of short stories in translation, and the extreme popularity of his early horror story, the melodramatic *Thérèse Raquin* (1867). Considerations of space mean that the following brief remarks (and bibliographical information) are confined to two masterpieces, *Germinal* and *L'Assommoir*.

Both novels pose problems through their specialized vocabulary (especially for *Germinal*) and their systematic use of popular speech, including recondite slang, which in *L'Assommoir* in particular spreads from the dialogue to the narration, combining in an original way with an eloquent or painterly style. Translators comment on this; Leonard **Tancock**, for instance, who did several novels by Zola for Penguin Classics, says in his introduction to *L'Assommoir* that he has aimed for 'popular speech as timeless as I could make it'. His *Germinal*, treating the original with some freedom, reads in a lively and natural way, tending if anything to abbreviate. By contrast, Peter **Collier**'s later translation, staying closer to Zola's phrasing, occasionally over-translates, but does greater justice to Zola's powerful style.

For *L'Assommoir*, which Tancock translates in the same way as *Germinal*, an interesting comparison can be made between two versions, *The Dram Shop* by Gerard Hopkins and *L'Assommoir* by Margaret Mauldon. (The title of this novel, meaning 'the knocker-out', defies translation.) Hopkins offers a fluent, elegant text, treating Zola as freely as he had Flaubert; his dialogue reads convincingly on the whole, but he makes little effort to render the popular tone of some of the narration. Mauldon's translation is much more scrupulous, following both Zola's syntax and his changes of tone, but still producing a very readable text. Here are their versions of a passage near the end of the penultimate chapter:

But the drunks were in their element, and cared for nobody. Knives flashed from pockets, and the fun and feasting ended in bloodshed. Such women as there were walked quickly, while all around men prowled with wolfish eyes. The night grew thick and turgid with abominations. (Hopkins)

But right now the drunks were king of the castle, and didn't give a damn about the rest of the world. Christ! knives were being pulled out of pockets, the evening's little spree was winding up in bloodshed. Women walked fast, wary-eyed men prowled about, and the thickening night was big with dreadful deeds. (Mauldon) PF

BALZAC, HONORÉ DE Crawford, Marion Ayton, *Old Goriot*, Harmondsworth, 1951 · *Eugénie Grandet*, Harmondsworth, 1955 · *Cousin Bette*, Harmondsworth, 1965 · *The Chouans*, Harmondsworth, 1972 [all Penguin] · Heppenstall, Rayner, *A Harlot High and Low*, Harmondsworth, 1970 [Penguin] · Hunt, Herbert J., *Lost Illusions*, Harmondsworth, 1971 · *The Wild Ass's Skin*, Harmondsworth, 1977 · *Cousin Pons*, Harmondsworth, 1978 [all Penguin] · Krailsheimer, A. J., *Père Goriot*, Oxford/New York, 1991 [World's Classics] · Raffel, Burton, *Père Goriot (Old Goriot)*, New York, 1994 · Raine, Kathleen, *Cousin Bette*, London, 1948 · *Lost Illusions*, London, 1951 · Raphael, Sylvia, *Eugénie Grandet*, Oxford/New York, 1990 · *Cousin Bette*, Oxford/New York, 1992 [both World's Classics] · Saintsbury, George, ed., *La Comédie humaine*, tr. Clara Bell, Ellen Marriage, R. S. Scott, James Waring et al., 40 vols., 1895–8 [many vols. rep. in Everyman] · Sedgwick, Ellery, et al., *La Comédie Humaine*, 11 vols., London, 1895–6 · Wormeley, Katherine Prescott, *Balzac's Novels in English*, 7 vols., Boston, 1885–93, London, 1886–91.

FLAUBERT, GUSTAVE Bair, Lowell, *Madame Bovary*, New York, 1959 [Bantam] · Baldick, Robert, *Sentimental Education*, Harmondsworth, 1964 [Penguin] · Chartres, J. S., *Salambo: A Realistic Romance of Ancient Carthage*, London, 1886 · Earp, T. W., and Stonier, G. W., *Bouvard and Pécuchet*, London, 1936 · Goldsmith, Anthony, *Sentimental Education*, London, 1941 [Everyman] · Hearn, Lafcadio, *The Temptation of Saint Anthony*, London/New York, 1910; rep. 1932 · Hopkins, Gerard, *Madame Bovary: Life in a Country Town*, London, 1948 [World's Classics] · Ives, George Burnham, *Gustave Flaubert [Three Stories]*, New York/London, 1903 · Krailsheimer, A. J., *Bouvard and Pécuchet*, Harmondsworth, 1976 [Penguin] · *Salammbo*, Harmondsworth, 1977 [Penguin] · *Three Tales*, Oxford/New York, 1991 [World's Classics] · McDowall, Arthur, *Three Tales*, London, 1923 · Marmur, Mildred, *Madame Bovary*, New York, 1964 [Signet] · Marx-Aveling, Eleanor, *Madame Bovary: A Story of Men and Women*, London, 1886 [many reps.] · May, J. Lewis, *Madame Bovary: A Story of Provincial Life*, London/New York, 1928 · Mrosovsky, Kitty, *The Temptation of Saint Antony*, London, 1980 [Penguin, 1983] · Parmée, Douglas, *A Sentimental Education*, Oxford/New York, 1989

[World's Classics] · Russell, Alan, *Madame Bovary: A Story of Provincial Life*, Harmondsworth, 1950 [Penguin] · Steegmuller, Francis, *The Selected Letters of Gustave Flaubert*, London, 1954 · *Madame Bovary: Patterns of Provincial Life*, New York, 1957 [Everyman] · Wall, Geoffrey, *Madame Bovary: Provincial Lives*, London, 1992 [Penguin].

HUGO, VICTOR Artois, M. W., et al., *The Novels of Victor Hugo*, 28 vols., London, 1895 [20th-c. reps. of individual vols.] · Cobb, Walter J., *The Hunchback of Notre-Dame*, New York, 1965 [Signet; repr. Penguin, 1996] · Denny, Norman, *Les Misérables*, London, 1976 [later Penguin] · Hapgood, Isabel F., *Les Misérables*, 5 vols., New York, 1887 · *Notre-Dame de Paris*, 2 vols., London, 1899 · Hazlitt, William, *Notre Dame: A Tale of the 'Ancien Régime'*, 3 vols., London, 1833 [several reps.] · Krailsheimer, A. J., *Notre-Dame de Paris*, Oxford/New York, 1993 [World's Classics] · Shoberl, Frederic, *The Hunchback of Notre Dame*, London, 1833 · Sturrock, John, *Notre-Dame de Paris*, Harmondsworth, 1978 [Penguin] · Thomas, W. Moy, *The Toilers of the Sea*, 3 vols., London, 1866 [20th-c. reps. in Everyman and elsewhere] · Wilbour, Charles E., *Les Misérables*, 2 vols., London, 1887 · Woollen, Geoff, *The Last Days of a Condemned Man and Other Prison Writings*, Oxford/New York, 1992 [World's Classics] · Wraxall, Sir F. C. L., *Les Misérables*, 3 vols., London, 1862.

STENDHAL [HENRI BEYLE] Bair, Lowell, *The Red and the Black*, New York, 1958 [Bantam] · Edwards, H. L. R., *Lucien Leuwen*, London, 1984 [originally as 2 vols., *The Green Huntsman* and *The Telegraph*, London, 1951] · Lloyd, Lady Mary, *The Chartreuse of Parma*, London, 1901/2; rep. 1923 · Mauldon, Margaret, *The Charterhouse of Parma*, Oxford/New York, 1997 [World's Classics] · Scott Moncrieff, C. K., *The Works of Stendhal*, 6 vols., London/New York, 1925–8 [2nd edn. 1926–8, includes *On Love*, tr. Vyvyan Holland; later edns. of *The Charterhouse of Parma* and *Scarlet and Black* (later as *The Red and the Black*) in Everyman] · Shaw, Margaret R. B., *Scarlet and Black*, Harmondsworth, 1953 [Penguin] · *The Charterhouse of Parma*, Harmondsworth, 1958 [Penguin] · Slater, Catherine, *The Red and the Black*, Oxford/New York, 1991 [World's Classics] · Stewart, Jean, and Knight, B. C. J. G., *The Life of Henry Brulard*, London, 1958 [Penguin, 1973] · Sturrock, John, *The Life of Henry Brulard*, London, 1995 [Penguin].

ZOLA, ÉMILE (*Germinal* and *L'Assommoir*) anon., *The 'Assommoir': A Realistic Novel*, London, 1884 [rev. edn. as *The Dram Shop*, ed. E. A. Vizetelly, London, 1897] · *Germinal, or Master and Man: A Realistic Novel*, London, 1885 [rev. edn. ed. E. A. Vizetelly, London, 1901] · Collier, Peter, *Germinal*, Oxford/New York, 1993 [World's Classics] · Dowson, Ernest, et al., *Nana* [tr. V. Plarr]; *L'Assommoir* [tr. A. Symons as *The Drunkard*]; *Pot-Bouille* [tr. P. Pinkerton]; *La Curée* [tr. A. Teixeira de Mattos]; *La Terre* [tr. E. Dowson]; *Germinal* [tr. H. Ellis], 12 vols., London, 1894–5 [reps. of *L'Assommoir* and *Germinal* in Everyman] · Fitzgerald, S. J. Adair, *Drink; Adapted from 'L'Assommoir' of Émile Zola*, London, 1903 · Hopkins, Gerard, *The Dram Shop*, London, 1951 · Mauldon, Margaret, *L'Assommoir*, Oxford/New York, 1995 [World's Classics] · Tancock, Leonard, *Germinal*, Harmondsworth, 1954 [Penguin] · *L'Assommoir*, Harmondsworth, 1970 [Penguin] · Townsend, Atwood H., *L'Assommoir*, New York, 1962 [Signet] · Trask, Willard, *Germinal*, New York, 1962 [Bantam].

10. POETRY SINCE HUGO

Inevitably, for what has been one of France's most productive and exciting periods of poetry-writing, this entry has to be highly selective, concentrating on a small number of major French poets [for poetry written in French outside France, see II.g.16]. It cannot therefore deal with such important poets as Lautréamont or more recent figures such as Pierre Reverdy, Henri Michaux or Yves Bonnefoy. As a result, the work of certain fine translators (one thinks particularly of Mary Ann **Caws**, who has translated André Breton, Louis Aragon, and René Char) goes virtually unmentioned.

i. General Problems As one might expect, translation into English does not offer an entirely accurate reflection of the canon of French poetry as the French perceive it. Certain voices who have traditionally been considered the dominant voices of the period do not seem to have found many translators or readers (e.g. Paul Valéry), while others have had a 'visibility' which seems disproportionate (e.g. Jules Laforgue). In the latter case, this is largely

attributable to the influence of a crucial figure in the tradition, T. S. Eliot. It was Eliot, moreover, who remarked that the English-speaking poetry public is largely reticent about or deaf to 'the traditional merits of French classical poetry'—hence perhaps the relatively few translations of Valéry.

Translation of poetry seems to be peculiarly dependent on the somewhat limited and homogeneous nature of the poetry-reading public. This public tends to prefer texts that are different but not radically foreign, works which contain certain, at least, of the recognizable poetic features of the host culture (e.g. the poetry of Bonnefoy or Jean Follain). Moreover, it is from this public that translators often come, and when the translator is sensitive to the conventions of his or her own tradition and period, this can lead to a form of 'cultural ventriloquism', where the original is 'acclimatized' into whatever happens to be the dominant poetic idiom in English. An example is the 1927 translations of Stéphane Mallarmé by Arthur **Ellis**, which use forms like 'flow'rs' and 'fall'n' or give 'And build ye an high roof of silence o'er' for 'et bâtissez un grand plafond silencieux'.

In such cases the translations are marked (though sometimes interestingly, as with Arthur **Symons** translating Baudelaire and Mallarmé) by the 'poetic' voice of a period, a voice that is generally belated in terms of its own tradition, so that such translations tend to date quickly. By the same token, more recent translations that read well to us may do so because we recognize, if only subliminally, the cadences and preferences of major contemporary poets.

Added to this constraint in the cultural frame there are also formal problems. Certain types of text particular to the period—e.g. prose poems like Arthur Rimbaud's *Une saison en enfer* (1873, A Season in Hell) or *Illuminations* (published 1886), or poems such as those of Paul Eluard which use tropes like the litany—are apparently easier to render into English than poems that add complex formal constraints of poetic structure to those of meaning. For French poetry, even in the modern period, the 12-syllable alexandrine line poses a particular problem, given the central place it occupies in the tradition and the prosodic constraints with which it is associated.

The innumerable translations of French poetry in the modern period cover a spectrum ranging from the workmanlike and useful literal prose rendering, often alongside the original text (e.g. the anthologies edited by William Rees and Elaine Marks), to ambitious translations attempting to find poetic equivalents for complex rhythmical or structural phenomena. Seen positively, the translation of poetry is largely a labour of love. Though commitment does not prevent translators from making astonishing mistakes, the collections of translated French poems nearly always contain striking successes in individual lines, a sudden daring reworking or an extended metaphor, an inventive series of rhymes or even the accident of a powerful mistranslation. Yet every translation seems to strike more by its inadequacies than its successes, each one seeming to call for yet another.

Let us take as an example four versions of the last stanza of Rimbaud's famous but deeply enigmatic sonnet 'Voyelles' (Vowels):

O, suprême Clairon plein de strideurs étranges,
Silences traversés des Mondes et des Anges:
—O l'Oméga, rayon violet de ses yeux!

O, the last trumpet, loud with strangely strident brass,
The silences through which the Worlds and Angels pass:
O stands for Omega, His Eyes' deep violet glow.
(Norman **Cameron**)

O—the great Clarion, harsh with chords unproved,
The silences where worlds and angels moved;
O—Omega, blue lightnings of Her Eyes!
(Brian **Hill**)

O, supreme Clarion full of strange stridor,
Silences crossed by words and angels:
—O, the Omega, violet beam from His Eyes!
(Wallace **Fowlie**)

O, supreme Trumpet, harsh with strange stridencies,
Silences traced in angels and astral designs:
O . . . OMEGA . . . the violet light of His Eyes!
(Paul **Schmidt**)

If exactness is an important criterion, one might note here that only Hill gives the 'standard' French reading of the eyes being those of a woman, whereas the others offer an interesting 'misreading'—what one might call a Protestant Apocalyptic reading. One also notes that only Fowlie has made an effort to render Rimbaud's complex neologism *strideurs*, but even he has played safe by using an attested (though rare) word, 'stridor'. All four have tended to 'poeticize' and 'historicize' *clairon* (bugle, an instrument that only appeared in France in 1825), some choosing, perhaps rather timidly, the vague 'clarion', which has none of the modern and modernist military connotations of the French. None has respected systematically Rimbaud's typographical choices, notably capitalizations, or really come to terms with the complexity of the noun determination in his text; the use of definite articles in the translations appears rather random, or motivated by metrical considerations.

Cameron, unlike most translators, translates alexandrines by alexandrines, giving himself space, but becoming unnecessarily prolix in the process ('O stands for Omega'). The difficulties of rhyming translation are suggested by Hill's unfortunate 'chords unproved' and inexact 'moved' (why only in the past?). Yet the absence of rhymes, notably the linking of *étranges* and *Anges*, provokes nostalgia when a translation such as Fowlie's is set against the original. Having said this, and felt cruelly that the besetting sin of translators is often prudence, one cannot help but sympathize with their difficulties and be struck by their successes, if not here then elsewhere.

A further factor particularly affects translation from French. Because it is a prestigious European language, French has regularly been included in school syllabuses, particularly in the 20th c. (this may explain the very large number of dual-language publications of French poetry in translation). It is a language in which many poets have a grounding, often a good grounding. Thus some translators are themselves poets of considerable talent, for example Samuel **Beckett** (translator of Apollinaire, Eluard, and Rimbaud) or Kenneth **White** (Breton)—and for earlier periods David **Gascoyne** (Breton, Soupault, Char, Reverdy, etc.), Stephen **Spender** (Eluard), C. **Day Lewis** (Valéry), Arthur Symons (Verlaine, Mallarmé), or T. S. **Eliot**, who translated the *Anabase* (Anabasis) of St-John Perse, a poet also translated by W. H. **Auden**.

However, poets often translate only those poems with which they have real affinities, and to ends which are extremely complex, as in the classic case of Ezra **Pound**. The poems they choose to translate can, as a consequence, be relatively marginal in the canon, thus giving the English-speaking reader a partial view of the *œuvre* of the French poet. There is also a slight distortion in the reading process in that the reader tends to listen 'stereophonically' to two voices rather than one (Beckett *and* Rimbaud or Apollinaire).

Less powerfully individualized translators may present a broader, more faithful range of texts. It is not certain, however, that they give a better hearing for the individual poem, since their translations, as suggested above, are often unconsciously informed by somewhat restricted preconceptions about what is 'poetic'. Such preconceptions currently include English hesitations about too systematic a use of abstraction, modernist preference for the spoken language and economy, and 20th-c. reticence about inversions or 'straddled adjectives' such as 'faery lands forlorn'. To take one small example from an anthology, Edward **Lucie Smith** translates Aragon's line 'L'homme seul est un escalier' (The man alone is a staircase) as 'The man alone: a stair', replacing the verb 'est' by a paratactic structure. Such a translation is not a syntactical obligation but an aesthetic choice; it seems likely that this sort of preference will not stay with us and that the translation will age as a consequence.

ii. Individual Poets Of individual poets of the period—and only six can be discussed here, all of them from the late 19th or early 20th c.—the most challenging is undoubtedly the formidably hermetic Stéphane Mallarmé, whose prose poems are difficult enough, but whose later verse poems, dense, ambiguous, sonorous and elaborately crafted, seem to defy translation. Many translators have bravely attempted to echo Mallarmé's prosody, the first being Arthur Symons, whose richly jewelled versions of some early poems, notably the scene from *Hérodiade*, won Mallarmé's approval. More recently C. F. **MacIntyre**'s selection keeps quite close to the original ('inani bibelot

d'inanité sonore' becomes 'abolished bibelot empty and sonorous'), but in fact loses much of the sonority. There are two complete bilingual collections, both using rhyme, by Henry **Weinfield** and Keith **Bosley**, of which the latter is generally more satisfying. In a smaller selection done early this century, the art critic Roger **Fry** eschews both rhyme and metre, as does the Irish poet Brian **Coffey**, whose daring versions of a number of poems achieve a certain beauty in their refusal to explicate. The opposite strategy is followed by Charles **Chadwick**, whose bilingual edition offers an 'expanded prose translation which aims above all to make the sense of the poems clear'.

Equally popular is Paul Verlaine, whose distinctive music has rarely been matched in English. His erotic poems have attracted translators, the most successful being Alan **Stone**. The largest selection of his main body of work is the dual-language *Selected Poems* of Joanna **Richardson**, who seeks to imitate, sometimes with some difficulty, the forms of the original. So too do two older translators of smaller selections of Verlaine, C. F. MacIntyre and Brian Hill, who both keep quite close to the original text, not without success. However, MacIntyre is sometimes driven to awkward and archaic constructions, whereas Hill at best manages to come quite close to the rhythms and sonorities of the French.

For Arthur Rimbaud, there is a complete works with parallel translation by Wallace Fowlie, who offers a fairly literal rendering, with no attempt to convey the form of the original, at least as far as the poems in verse are concerned. A more recent monolingual volume by Paul Schmidt, where the verse is rendered fairly freely, is particularly successful with its sharp and inventive versions of the satirical poems. More controversially, Schmidt translates the prose poems of the *Illuminations* as free verse—but in any case his version of these and of *A Season in Hell* is freer and less incisive than the excellent translations of Enid Rhodes **Peschel**. Earlier translations of the verse poems include those of Norman Cameron and Brian Hill, both of whom achieve some successes, but their versions of 'Le Bâteau ivre' (The Drunken Boat) pale in comparison with the powerful and inventive translation done by Samuel Beckett in 1932 (which paved the way for recent translation by two other Irish poets, Derek **Mahon** and Ciaron **Carson**, 1995), or indeed with a fine Scots rendering by Alastair **Mackie**.

As for Paul Valéry, as already mentioned, there have been relatively few translations for a poet of his stature. This has, however, been partially compensated for by the remarkable achievement of

Jackson **Mathews**'s *Collected Works* in 13 volumes, of which a shortened form was published under the title *Paul Valéry: An Anthology*. Interesting translations of individual works include Mark Kinsley **Wardle**'s *Le Serpent* (with an introduction and warm recommendation from T. S. Eliot), and versions of *Le Cimetière marin* (The Graveyard by the Sea) by C. **Day Lewis**, Graham Dunstan **Martin**, and (in a rather dense Scots) Douglas **Young**.

Guillaume Apollinaire has generally been fortunate in his translators; there is, for instance, a notably vigorous translation by Samuel Beckett of 'Zone'. The best introduction to his work in English is probably Oliver **Bernard**'s *Selected Poems*, an expanded, bilingual version of an earlier Penguin selection, in which the translation often echoes the rhythms and forms of the original with striking success. By contrast, Anne Hyde **Greet**, in her full renderings of *Alcools* and *Caligrammes*, makes no sustained attempt to find equivalents for Apollinaire's hallucinating verse forms.

For Paul Eluard, there is no satisfactory selected poems, let alone a collected poems. The best general introduction is perhaps Alexander **Lloyd**'s sometimes inaccurate *Selected Writings*. Generally, translators have tended to specialize either in his political poems or in his justifiably famous love poetry. For the former, the most satisfactory introduction is probably the same translator's earlier *Selected Poems*. He has also produced a *Poésie ininterrompue* (Uninterrupted Poetry), while Marilyn **Kallet** has published a good *Last Love Poems*. Also of interest are Stephen Spender and Frances **Cornford**'s translations of *Le Dur Désir de durer* (The Hard Desire to Endure), and the even earlier *Thorns of Thunder* by Samuel Beckett and others, which contains a relatively large number of poems.

iii. Anthologies In the 20th c., in addition to the poets discussed above, the most translated authors include Louis Aragon, Yves Bonnefoy, André Breton, René Char, Pierre-Jean Jouve, Henri Michaux, Saint-John Perse, and Francis Ponge. All of these have found good translators, many of the best translations being published in journals rather than in separate volumes. Along with numerous other poets, they are also well represented in a variety of anthologies, most of them bilingual. Only some of the more recent of these—and those where poems are translated by poems—can be mentioned here, though it is perhaps worth noting one earlier collection, Cecily Mackworth's *A Mirror for French Poetry* (1947), which contains translation by many hands including T. S. Eliot, Vernon **Watkins**, Arthur Symons, David Gascoyne, Louis **MacNeice**,

and Aldous **Huxley** (Mallarmé's 'L'Après-midi d'un faune').

The most complete of the recent collections is Paul **Auster**'s *Random House Book of 20th-Century French Poetry*, though among the many French poets included only one is a woman. This anthology also contains the work of several poet-translators such as Wallace **Stevens**, David Gascoyne, John **Ashbery**, and Robert **Bly**. A similar British anthology, confined to poems written in the 15 or 20 years preceding publication in 1971, is the catholic selection edited by Simon Watson **Taylor** and Edward Lucie Smith, with translations by Samuel Beckett, Keith Bosley, Anthony **Rudolf**, and others. A much more recent collective publication is *The New French Poetry*, edited by David **Kelley** and Jean **Khalfa**, with many of the translations by Kelley. This offers longish poems or extracts from 'the new metaphysical poetry which has become an influential strand in recent French literature', and includes writers such as Louis-René des Forêts, Edmond Jabès, Gisèle Prassinos, and Jacques Réda.

As against these, there are collections where all the translations are the work of a single hand—with the obvious danger that differences between poets may be obliterated. Omitting the grand figures of the mid-century (Char, Jouve, Aragon, etc.), Serge **Gavronsky** and Graham Dunstan Martin both concentrate on the new voices of the 1960s, Gavronsky limiting himself to eight poets (fairly literally translated) and Martin casting his net wider and more adventurously. More recently Martin **Sorrell** (in his slightly misleadingly entitled *Modern French Poetry*) offers an idiosyncratic group of poets, from older figures such as Jules Supervielle or Jacques Prévert to newer poets such as Jean Daive or Anne-Marie Albiach. His 11 poets include (very unusually) five women, and he has since gone further to correct the traditional male-centred view in *Elles*, a bilingual collection of 17 women poets. All of these anthologies include many satisfying renderings, generally in a free verse which corresponds to the form of the original.

Finally, it is worth noting an important recent initiative, the Bloodaxe Contemporary French Poets edited by Timothy Mathews and Michael Worton. The series is devoted to complete poetic collections (not anthological extracts), which are given in French and in English poetic translation, accompanied by critical essays. The translations are often excellent, and the initial list of authors will give an idea of the canon of modern French poetry as currently conceived in Britain: Yves Bonnefoy, Aimé Cesaire, René Char, Paul Eluard, Eugène Guillevic, André Frénaud, Philippe Jaccottet, Gérard Macé, Henri Michaux.   PV and PF

ANTHOLOGIES   Auster, Paul, ed., *The Random House Book of 20th-Century French Poetry*, New York, 1984 · Fowlie, Wallace, ed., *Mid-Century French Poets*, New York, 1955 · Gavronsky, Serge, *Poems and Texts*, New York, 1969 · Kelley, David, and Khalfa, Jean, eds., *The New French Poetry*, Newcastle upon Tyne, 1966 · Macworth, Cecily, ed., *A Mirror for French Poetry* (1840–1940), London, 1947 · Marks, Elaine, *French Poetry from Baudelaire to the Present*, New York, 1962 · Martin, Graham Dunstan, *Anthology of Contemporary French Poetry*, Edinburgh, 1972 · Rees, William, *French Poetry, 1820–1950, with Prose Translations*, London, 1990 · Sorrell, Martin, *Modern French Poetry*, London, 1992 · *Elles: A Bilingual Anthology of Modern French Poetry by Women*, Exeter, 1995 · Taylor, Simon Watson, and Lucie Smith, Edward, eds., *French Poetry Today*, London, 1971.

APOLLINAIRE, GUILLAUME   Beckett, Samuel, *Zone*, Dublin, 1972 · Bernard, Oliver, *Selected Poems*, Harmondsworth, 1965 [Penguin, new edn. 1986] · Hyde Greet, Anne, *Caligrammes*, Berkeley, Calif., 1960 · *Alcools*, Berkeley, Calif., 1965.

ELUARD, PAUL   Beckett, Samuel, et al., *Thorns of Thunder*, London, 1936 · Kallet, Marilyn, *Last Love Poems*, Baton Rouge, La., 1980 · Lloyd, Alexander, *Selected Writings*, London, 1952 · *Selected Poems*, London, 1987 · *Unbroken Poetry*, Newcastle upon Tyne, 1996 [Bloodaxe Contemporary French Poets] · Spender, Stephen, and Cornford, Frances, *Le Dur Désir de durer*, London, 1950.

MALLARMÉ, STÉPHANE   Bosley, Keith, *The Poems*, Harmondsworth, 1977 [Penguin] · Chadwick, Charles, *The Meaning of Mallarmé*, Aberdeen, 1996 · Coffey, Brian, *Poems of Mallarmé*, Dublin/London, 1990 · Ellis, Arthur, *Stéphane Mallarmé in English Verse*, London, 1927 · Fry, Roger, *Poems*, London, 1936 · Huxley, Aldous, *L'Après-midi d'un faune*, London, 1936 · MacIntyre, C. F., *Selected Poems*, Berkeley, Calif., 1957 · Symons, Arthur, *Mallarmé: Poésies*, ed. Bruce Morris, Edinburgh, 1986 · Weinfield, Henry, *Collected Poems*, Berkeley, Calif., 1994.

RIMBAUD, ARTHUR   Beckett, Samuel, *Drunken Boat*, Reading, 1976 · Cameron, Norman, *Selected Verse Poems of Arthur Rimbaud*, London, 1942 · Fowlie, Wallace, *Complete Works with Selected Letters*, Chicago, 1966 · Hill, Brian, *The Drunken Boat: Thirty-Six Poems by Arthur Rimbaud*, London, 1952 · Mackie, Alastair, 'The Drucken Boat', in P. France and D. Glen, eds., *European Poetry in Scotland*, Edinburgh, 1989 · Peschel, Enid Rhodes, *A Season in Hell; The Illuminations*, New York, 1973 · Schmidt, Paul, *Complete Works*, New York, 1976.

VALÉRY, PAUL   Day Lewis, Cecil, *Le Cimetière marin/The Graveyard by the Sea*, London, 1946 · Kirkup, James, *La Jeune Parque/The Eternal Virgin*, Tokyo, 1970 · Martin, Graham Dunstan, *Le Cimetière marin/The Graveyard by the Sea*, Edinburgh, 1971 · Mathews, Jackson, *Collected Works*, 13 vols., London, 1957–75 · *Paul Valéry: An Anthology*, London, 1977 · Wardle, Mark Kinsley, *Le Serpent*, London, 1924 · Young, Douglas, 'The Kirkyaird by the Sea', in P. France and D. Glen, eds., *European Poetry in Scotland*, Edinburgh, 1989.

VERLAINE, PAUL   Elliot, Alistair, *Femmes, Hombres = Women, Men*, London, 1979 · Grant, Roland and Apcher, Claude, *Forty Poems*, London, 1948 · Hill, Brian, *The Sky Above the Roof: Fifty-Six Poems by Paul Verlaine*, London, 1957 · MacIntyre, C. F., *Selected Poems*, Berkeley, Calif., 1948 · Richardson, Joanna, *Selected Poems*, Harmondsworth, 1974 [Penguin] · Stone, Alan, *Men and Women: Erotic Works*, London, 1985.

SEE ALSO   Shields, K., 'Three Irish Translations of Rimband's "Bâteau ivre" ' *New Comparison*, 19 (1995), 167–82.

11. BAUDELAIRE

Charles Baudelaire's principal poetic works, *Les Fleurs du mal* (1857, Flowers of Evil) and the posthumously published *Petits Poèmes en prose* (1869, Little Poems in Prose), have been massively and regularly translated into English. There are some 40 published book-length translations, not to speak of innumerable publications in journals and anthologies or translations of the prose writings. Since 1890, when Stuart **Merrill** published *From the French: Pastels in Prose*, there has been no decade without a major translation, either in Britain or America.

The number of translations has probably been multiplied by a complex interaction between facets of his work and English-language culture. Aspects of this interaction include the influence on Baudelaire of the English-language Gothic tradition, in the person of Edgar Allen Poe, and his interest in its romantic antecedents, notably Thomas de Quincey (he translated both of these). Also important, no doubt, is the absence in the English-language tradition of a poet of similar stature who could function as an inheritor and transcender of romanticism, an opener of new spaces.

Baudelaire thus came to play a crucial role within the English poetic tradition, as is witnessed in the publication in 1905 of the *Poems in Prose* translated by Arthur **Symons** (1865–1945), who later produced a volume, once regarded as authoritative in spite of its extravagance, of the major part of his poetic output. Baudelaire seemed to the following generation to be opening up a new 'decadent' space, one of whose aspects was a form of Satanism (see the translations of Aleister **Crowley**). This concern for the essentially romantic side of the poet has tended

285

to obscure the rigour of his classical form and the subtlety of his rhythms.

There are so many translations, each with its good moments, that one cannot hope to do justice to them all. The bibliography has been extended to give a fairly complete listing of book-length translations; the anthology *Baudelaire in English*, edited by Carol **Clark** and Robert Sykes, gives samples of many translations as well as a helpful discussion of the translation history.

The full-scale translations of *Les Fleurs du mal* show a wide range of approaches to poetic translation. At one extreme there are the many rhymed translations, from that of F. P. **Sturm** to those of Philip **Higson** and Elliot R. **Ashe** and more recently those of Walter **Martin** and (sometimes) James **McGowan**. Others, such as those of Wallace **Fowlie** or Richard **Howard**, do not attempt systematically to respect such constraints, while others, such as those of Francis **Scarfe** and Carol Clark, offer useful prose versions. If one takes the last line of 'L'Albatros', three of these translations give respectively for 'Ses ailes de géant l'empêchent de marcher' the following:

Baulked by vast wings his very walk is lame   (Higson)

His giant wings keep him from walking   (Fowlie)

His giant wings impede him as he walks   (Scarfe)

In the first the final word seems imposed by a rhyme with 'aim', and an added 'very' is perhaps intended to give weight; the second is rhythmically awkward in a poetic translation; while the final one is satisfactory in terms of sense, it inevitably loses much of the sweep, the 'giant wings' of the French alexandrine with its medial cesura foregrounding 'géant'. As one would expect, all these translations have their successes and their weaker moments.

Perhaps the most heartening aspect of this story is the number of poets who have attempted to come to grips with this work, even perhaps to appropriate it. These include poets such as Edna St Vincent **Millay**, Laurence **Lerner**, Roy **Campbell** (who did a complete *Fleurs du mal*), and Michael **Hamburger**. There are perhaps two outstandingly exciting translations, though both are very partial. Robert **Lowell** offers an extremely fine, though much criticized, translation of a dozen poems, first included in his *Imitations*. Here is his opening of one the 'Spleen' poems:

> I'm like the king of a rain-country, rich
> but sterile, young but with an old wolf's itch ...

The same poem (LXXVII) is the site of one of the most interesting experiments in the field of published translation: the 31 versions or radical reworkings or imperial annexations of this one poem by Nicholas **Moore**, texts which show a remarkable knowledge of French language and culture and are accompanied by an essay 'On the Impossibility of Translation'.   PV

Translations (confined to separate publications of the poetry, for the most part bilingual editions) Aggeler, William, *The Flowers of Evil*, Fresno, Calif., 1954 · Campbell, Roy, *Poems of Baudelaire: A Translation of Les Fleurs du Mal*, London, 1952 · Clark, Carol, *Baudelaire: Selected Poems*, Harmondsworth, 1995 [Penguin] · Clark, Carol, and Sykes, Robert, eds., *Baudelaire in English*, London, 1997 [Penguin] · Conder, Alan, *Les Fleurs du Mal*, London, 1952 · Crowley, Aleister, *Little Poems in Prose*, London, 1928 · Dillon, George, and Millay, Edna St Vincent, *Flowers of Evil*, New York/London, 1936 · Duke, Francis, *The Flowers of Evil and Other Poems of Charles Baudelaire*, Charlottesville, Va., 1961 · Egan, Beresford, and Bower, Alcock, C., *Fleurs du Mal, in Pattern and Prose*, London, 1929 · Fowlie, Wallace, *Flowers of Evil, and Other Poems*, New York, 1964 · Friedman, Florence Louie, *Flowers of Evil: Les Fleurs du Mal*, London, 1962 · Goudge, John, *Selected Poems*, Walton-on-Thames, 1979 · H.C. [possibly Henry Curwen], *Some Translations from Charles Baudelaire, Poet and Symbolist*, London, 1894 · Hamburger, Michael, *Twenty Prose Poems of Baudelaire*, London, 1964; rev. edn., 1968 · Hemmings, F. W. J., *City Blues*, Melton Mowbray, 1977 · Higson, Philip, and Ashe, Elliot, R., *Baudelaire: The Flowers of Evil and All Other Authenticated Poems*, Chester, 1975 · Howard, Richard, *Les Fleurs du Mal*, Brighton, 1982 · Huneker, James, *The Poems and Prose Poems of Charles Baudelaire*, New York, 1919 · Kraetzer, Arthur F., *The Flowers of Evil*, New York, 1950 · Laver, J., ed., *Flowers of Evil, Translated into English Verse by Various Hands*, London, 1940 · Leakey, F. W., *Selected Poems from Les Fleurs du Mal*, London, 1997 · Leclercq, Jacques, *Flowers of Evil*, New York, 1958 · Lerner, Laurence, *Spleen*, Belfast, c.1966 · Lloyd, Rosemary, *The Prose Poems and La Fanfarlo*, Oxford, 1991 [World's Classics] · Lowell, Robert, *The Voyage and Other Versions of Poems by Baudelaire*, London, 1961 [originally in his *Imitations*] · McGowan, James, *The Flowers of Evil*, Oxford, 1993 [World's Classics] · MacIntyre, C. F., *One Hundred Poems from Les Fleurs du Mal*, Berkeley/Los Angeles, Calif., 1947 · Martin, Walter, *Complete Poems*, Manchester, 1997 · Matthews, Marthiel, and Matthews, Jackson, eds., *The Flowers of Evil*, London, 1955 · Merrill, Stuart, *From the French: Pastels in Prose*, New York, 1890 · Moore, Nicholas, *Spleen*, London, 1973, repr. 1990 · Richardson, Joanna, *Selected Poems*, Harmondsworth, 1975 [Penguin] · Scarfe, Frances, *Baudelaire*, Harmondsworth, 1961 [Penguin] · Scott, Cyril, *The Flowers of Evil*, London, 1909 · Shanks, Lewis Piaget, *Flowers of Evil*, New York, 1931 · Sturm, F. P., *The Poems of Charles Baudelaire*, London, 1906 · Symons, Arthur, *Poems in Prose*, London, 1905 · Les

Fleurs du Mal; Petits Poèmes en Prose; Les Paradis Artificiels, London, 1925 · Varese, Louise, *Paris; Spleen; 1869*, London, 1951 · Wagner, Geoffrey, *Selected Poems*, London, 1946; rep. 1971 · Walton, Alan Hull, *Selections from Baudelaire*, London, 1943.

12. TWENTIETH-CENTURY FICTION

i. The English-Language Canon A multitude of 20th-c. French novelists have achieved widespread recognition outside France. The latter part of this entry will focus on just a few major writers in order to illustrate some of the problems faced by the translator. But we should begin with a broader survey of the field, though again limiting ourselves to the outstanding figures.

Of the novelists born before 1880 and achieving recognition in the 20th c., Marcel Proust is the one whose stock currently stands highest; a separate entry is devoted to him [II.g.13]. André Gide has been an equally important writer for most of the 20th c.; a number of translators worked on his novels, but the standard translations for *Les Nourritures terrestres* (1897, Fruits of the Earth), *L'Immoraliste* (1902, The Immoralist), *Les Caves du Vatican* (1914, Vatican Cellars), *Les Faux-Monnayeurs* (1926, The Counterfeiters), and several other important books are those done with great flair and sensitivity by Dorothy **Bussy**, Lytton Strachey's sister and Gide's friend. Of the same generation, the very popular Colette has been extensively translated, some of her novels more than once; the uniform edition of her complete works in English contains several translations each by Antonia **White** (e.g. the Claudine series), Roger **Senhouse** (e.g. *Le Blé en herbe*, 1923, Ripening Corn), and Enid **Macleod** (e.g. *La Vagabonde*, 1910).

Of the writers born in the 1880s, François Mauriac has been the most popular in English. Almost all his novels were translated by a single translator, Gerard **Hopkins**, whose work supersedes earlier versions of individual novels. Mauriac's younger contemporary, Georges Bernanos, has fared less well, though there are translations of his major writings, including *Journal d'un curé de campagne* (1936, The Diary of a Country Priest) and *Sous le soleil de Satan* (1926, translated as *The Star of Satan*), both by Pamela **Morris**, and *La Joie* (1929, Joy) by Louise **Varese**.

The next decade brings Louis-Ferdinand Céline, for a long time an outlawed author in France because of his war record, and the equally sulphurous figure of Georges Bataille. All of Céline's major novels now exist in English; in particular there are rival versions by John **Marks** and by Ralph **Manheim** (who has translated five of the novels) of

the two great early anti-epics, *Voyage au bout de la nuit* (1932, Journey to the End of the Night) and *Mort à crédit* (1936, Death on Credit). Bataille, by contrast, was for a long time little translated, but his growing stature, at least in the academy, is reflected in more recent versions of *Histoire de l'œil* (1928, translated as *Story of the Eye*) and *Le Bleu du ciel* (1957, translated as *The Blue of Noon*).

The years between 1900 and 1920 produced a great array of novelists whose reputation was—and in some cases still remains—considerable in the English-speaking world. Samuel Beckett is the subject of a separate entry [II.g.14]. The case of Julien Green, the Franco-American writer is discussed below; the most important of his early interpreters was Oscar Wilde's son, Vyvyan **Holland**, who translated four novels.

Of Beckett's contemporaries, Jean-Paul Sartre, Albert Camus, Simone de Beauvoir, and André Malraux were particularly influential in the decades following World War II. Sartre's *La Nausée* (1938, Nausea), the fictitious diary of Antoine Roquentin, which exists in two translations, has kept its popularity. The short stories of *Le Mur* (1939, The Wall) were popular in English under the alluring title *Intimacy*, and the three novels of his unfinished series *Les Chemins de la liberté* (1945–9), translated by Eric **Sutton** and Gerard Hopkins, had their moment of glory in the postwar period. Simone de Beauvoir's semi-autobiographical *Les Mandarins* (1954, The Mandarins) was translated by Leonard **Friedman**, but has had less impact in English than her *Le Deuxième Sexe* [see II.g.15]. As for Malraux, the translations made almost immediately by Stuart **Gilbert** and Alastair **Macdonald** of his *La Voie royale* (1930, The Royal Way), *L'Espoir* (1937, translated as *Days of Hope*) and particularly *La Condition humaine* (1933, Man's Estate) have all lasted well. But the greatest success in the English-speaking world is no doubt Camus's *L'Étranger* (1938, The Outsider), which is discussed below; in addition, a 1960 edition of Camus's *Collected Fiction* brings together translations by Justin **O'Brien** of *La Chute* (1956, The Fall) and the story-collection *L'Être et le royaume* (1958, Exile and the Kingdom) and by Stuart Gilbert of *The Outsider* and the great fable *La Peste* (1947, The Plague).

Three writers born in the first decade of the century whose work is very different from that of

287

Sartre or Camus are Julien Gracq, Raymond Queneau, and Nathalie Sarraute. Gracq's elusive poetic tales, *Un balcon en forêt* (1958, Balcony in the Forest) and *Un beau ténébreux* (1945, A Dark Stranger), were both translated reasonably soon, though apparently with little public success, but his masterly *Le Rivage des Syrtes* (1951, The Opposing Shore) had to wait until 1993 for its translation by Richard **Howard**. Queneau's extraordinarily inventive *œuvre*, from *Le Chiendent* (1933, The Bark Tree), through *Pierrot mon ami* (1942, My Friend Pierrot) and *Zazie dans le métro* (1959, Zazie in the Metro), to *Les Fleurs bleues* (1965, translated as *From Blue to Blue*), has found a suitably inventive translator in Barbara **Wright**, whose sparkling versions now hold the field. Sarraute's numerous writings, including the path-breaking *Portrait d'un inconnu* (1948, Portrait of an Unknown Man), have likewise found a dedicated single translator in Maria **Jolas**.

Sarraute is the doyenne of the experimentalists grouped under the banner of the Nouveau Roman (New Novel), most of whose practitioners were born between 1912 and 1926. Translators have served these writers well in English. The case of the Nobel prize-winner Claude Simon is discussed below, as is that of Marguerite Duras, often associated with the Nouveau Roman (Duras's main translator is Barbara **Bray**, but some of her texts have been twice translated). The other most prominent writers in this group are Alain Robbe-Grillet and Michel Butor. Robbe-Grillet's challenging early novels, *Les Gommes* (1953, The Erasers), *Le Voyeur* (1955, The Voyeur), *La Jalousie* (1957, Jealousy), and *Dans le labyrinthe* (1959, In the Labyrinth), quickly found translators of the calibre of Richard Howard and Christine **Brooke-Rose**. Howard also translated Butor's *Degrés* (1960, Degrees), whereas his other early novels (still his best-known), *L'Emploi du temps* (1956, Passing Time) and *La Modification* (1957, Second Thoughts), were translated soon after their original publication by Jean **Stewart**.

More recent novelists, even those as fêted as Philippe Sollers or Catherine Clément, have not achieved such success in English. An exception to prove the rule is possibly provided by Georges Perec; the particularly fascinating formal challenges provided by Perec's *La Disparition* (1969, The Disappearance, translated as *A Void* in order not to use the letter 'e') and *La Vie mode d'emploi* (1978, Life, a User's Manual) have been well met by Gilbert **Adair** and David **Bellos** respectively. All along, there have have been many other French authors, much read in French and translated into English rather promptly and usually well, but little noticed

in English. Once published, their books are quickly remaindered.

Why original voices like those of Marguerite Yourcenar, Nathalie Sarraute, and Annie Ernaux are ignored calls for speculation beyond the scope of this discussion. While French literary theory [see II.g.15] is quickly translated and widely read (at least in universities), when writers such as Hélène Cixous and Julia Kristeva switch to fiction, they lose readers. Sometimes the content may be antipathetic to the very readers who come to French fiction because of their interest in French theory; on these grounds perhaps Sollers, Michel Tournier, and Marie Redonnet repel readers, especially women readers. More likely it is simply a matter of the market-place. Contemporary French writers must compete in translation with a large and rich selection of English-language writers. Why read J.-M.-G. Le Clézio when plots with relevant sites and issues can be concocted by Irving Stone and James Michener, or in French by the Canadian Anne Hébert or the Caribbean Patrick Chamoiseau? For in the USA and Canada, continental French novelists must compete also with Francophone writers [see II.g.16], who are strongly supported by well-organized blocks in the academy.

It must be added that in the USA translations routinely go out of print unless they are adopted as textbooks. Readers using libraries with adequate storage space will have no difficulty finding on the shelves the novels mentioned in this entry, but the same may not be true of bookshops. For the British scene, the recent Babel Guide to modern French fiction gives a fairly full listing of the titles available in 1996.

While by no means all the works of the writers mentioned above have been translated into English, one can say on the whole that they have all found at least competent—and in many cases excellent—translators, so that English speakers have been able to read acceptable re-expressions of what was written in French. The bilingual Green has preferred to let his French self be rendered by a second party, whereas Beckett has preferred self-translation. Proust, Céline, Sartre, Camus, and one or two others have been canonical long enough for some of their work to be retranslated, so that in a few cases the reader has a choice of versions.

In the market-place, French fiction has usually been the purview of trade publishers. However, certain university presses have also been involved in publishing these translations, and this may make a difference in translation strategy, because university presses may be more willing to let the original echo through. But by and large the norms for these translations have been the same as those for creative writing in English. In English, these authors tend to sound like contemporary English-language novelists.

Generally the translators have confidence in their own talent, and translate to fit their conceptualization of the original text. In the case of retranslation, we see more evidence of deference to the text, less normalization by the rhetorical standards current at the time. But this can run the gamut from an English novel with a little French colour to a French novel with English words. Such a gamut can be discerned also in one-time translations, as a closer look at some specific cases, all 'good' translations, will demonstrate. What the ensuing discussion suggests, however, is that it is the quality, indeed the mystique, of the French text that determines the popularity and posterity of the translation.

ii. Retranslation: Camus, Céline, Green The extremes come to the fore with Camus's *L'Étranger*, which has been translated three times, by Stuart Gilbert (1946), James **Laredo** (1981), and Matthew **Ward** (1988)—Gilbert being replaced by Laredo in the Penguin collection and by Ward in the Knopf list. Well before the late 1980s, it was clear that this short novel, in which the young white Algerian narrator Meursault recounts his killing of an Arab, was becoming a canonical text on school and college reading-lists. The reactions from readers of the French and readers of Gilbert's English made it equally clear to educators that students should be shown what Meursault was 'really' like, i.e. how Camus conceived him. It is interesting in this connection to compare the two versions used successively in the USA, those of Gilbert and Ward.

With Gilbert, Meursault is a young man of few attachments, a fatal victim of a single gratuitous act. He can recapitulate momentous occasions in high rhetoric. He is not unsympathetic. With Ward (who first encountered Meursault as a teenage reader of Gilbert's translation), Meursault is a self-absorbed creature whose bland exterior conceals considerable loathing for his fellow humans. He comes to have deep thoughts, but he expresses them in an ordinary register.

The closing lines of Parts 1 and 2 show this difference. Gilbert's Meursault regrets firing repeatedly on the Arab: 'And each successive shot was another loud fateful rap on the door of my undoing'. If, however, he can die as a scapegoat, he will have repaid his debt to society: 'all that remained to hope was that on the day of my execution there should be a huge crowd of spectators and that they should greet

me with howls of execration.' Ward's Meursault recognizes that his act was a mistake: 'And it was like knocking four quick times on the door of unhappiness'. His final wish is nearly that of the cocky criminal: 'I had only to wish that there be a large crowd of spectators the day of my execution and that they greet me with cries of hate'.

With *Voyage au bout de la nuit* by Céline, it is not clear why the publishing house which controlled the rights to John H. E. P. Marks's 1934 translation and reissued it in 1960 needed to commission Ralph Manheim's retranslation of 1983. Although Céline sets five of the 45 chapters in the USA, he himself learnt English early and well in Great Britain and worked with Marks on the translation. Most comparisons are inconclusive. The only place where Marks's and Manheim's divergence in interpretation comes sufficiently to the fore to influence readers is in Céline's poetic ending. Some 15 years have elapsed since the narrator, Bardamu, was swept away with the Pied Piper recruitment band to enlist in the army for World War I. Robinson, his familiar, shot fatally by the woman he abandoned, has been taken to the police station. The survivors have repaired to a bistro near the Seine. It is nearly dawn. Amidst the spilt drinks and sleeping drunks, Bardamu listens to the horn of a tugboat going downstream. For 'call' Céline has used 'appel', the word used in army recruitment, and for 'remove', 'emmener', the same verb he used for the moment of Robinson's death in the previous chapter. Céline's very last words are 'qu'on n'en parle plus'; (literal: 'let no one say anything more about it').

Was it the socio-political context that led Marks to end with a negative spin, and Manheim with a positive spin? In 1934, the Depression was at its worst, and Hitler was solidifying power; in 1983, the superpowers had each other on hold in the Cold War, and Manheim received a MacArthur Foundation award guaranteeing a comfortable income for the rest of his life. In any event, Marks concludes: 'Far in the distance the tugboat whistled; its call passed the bridge, one more arch, then another, the lock, another bridge, farther and farther . . . It was summoning all the barges on the river, every last one, and the whole city and the sky and the countryside, and ourselves, to carry us all away, the Seine too—and that would be the end of us.' Manheim, on the contrary, is reminiscent of Balzac's Rastignac, ambiguously defiant at the conclusion of *Le Père Goriot*: 'Far away, the tug hooted; calling the bridge, the arches one by one, a lock, another bridge, further, further away . . . It was calling to itself every boat on the river, every one, the whole town, and the sky and the country and us, all of it

289

being called away, and the Seine too, everything,—let's hear no more of all this.'

At the opposite end of the retranslation gamut is *Adrienne Mesurat* (1927), Julien Green's most successful and possibly best novel. It came early in his career, and in Henry Longan **Stuart**'s translation *The Closed Garden* (1928) was commercially successful also. A revision, rather than a retranslation, was commissioned for 1991 publication basically for archival reasons. That is, a major author's major work was largely unavailable in translation because librarians in the late 1920s thought Green would be merely a popular novelist, rather than a subject for academic scholarship. Moreover, in the meantime, Green's œuvre had been established. The revision by Marilyn **Gaddis Rose** restored omissions, probably inadvertent because their absence had not affected the meaning, but uncovered no inaccuracies. The revision also replaced the irrelevant English title with the French title.

When dealing with works of the 20th c., where semantic shift and regional variations have yet to reduce the comprehensibility of English translations from the first half-century, retranslation is seldom called for. The literary taste of such talented British translators as Gerard Hopkins, Vyvyan Holland, and Stuart Gilbert must have been capacious since they were able to harmonize their taste with assignments as varied as Mauriac, Green, Malraux, and Sartre. Readers outside the United Kingdom, if they noticed at all, expected French novels to sound British.

iii. The New Novel During the second half-century, more American translators have entered the scene, although not in the numbers encountered with Hispanic and Francophone literatures, and they have introduced a more American lexicon. Sometimes the Americanisms are totally misguided, as when Helen R. **Lane**, translating Claude Simon's *Triptyque* (1973, Triptych), changes the author's Brechtian interjection to 'BROADWAY DEPARTMENT STORE—THE CITY'S NEWEST . . . LATEST FASHIONS—FOR MEN AND WOMEN', undercutting the rural French setting.

The Simon passage, however, can move the discussion to the influence translation has had in the reception of French fiction since World War II. It is difficult to believe that the French New Novel would have stirred up the academic scene if its exemplars had not been translated by such remarkable translators as Richard Howard, Barbara Bray, Richard **Seaver**, and Samuel Beckett himself. They have certainly made writerly fiction popular with the academy.

The case of Simon is especially arresting, for it suggests, if it cannot prove, the limits of translation in the dissemination of literature. When Simon received the Nobel Prize in 1985, only Lane's *Triptych* and Daniel **Weissbort**'s version of *Leçon des choses* (1973, The World Around Us) were listed as still in print, although his US publisher immediately advertized the availability of Howard's translations of *Le Vent* (1947, The Wind), *La Route des Flandres* (1960, The Flanders Road), *Le Palace* (1962, The Palace, lit. The Grand Hotel), *L'Herbe* (1958, The Grass), *Histoire* (1967, Histoire), and *La Bataille de Pharsale* (1966, The Battle of Pharsalus). All of Howard's translations can be characterized as masterly, as can be Beryl and John **Fletcher**'s version of *Les Géorgiques* (1981).

Yet reader (and sales) response to Simon was nothing like that greeting Camus's acceptance of the Nobel (or Sartre's refusal of it!). Chiefly librarians paid attention. *The Flanders Road*, depicting the fall of France in May–June 1940, gives an inside, emblematic view of a major historical event. Howard recognized Simon's Faulknerian project and proceeded according to his own sense of the text and its visualizations. He does a remarkable job keeping the allusions consonant. What he does most effectively is intensify by inconspicuous abridgments (the French contains 96,720 words while the English contains 81,408). Here is the beginning with Cavalry Captain de Reixach's retreat: 'un instant l'éblouissant reflet de soleil accroché ou plutôt condensé, comme s'il avait capté attiré à lui pour une fraction de seconde toute la lumière et la gloire, sur l'acier virginal . . . Seulement, vierge, il y avait belle lurette qu'elle ne l'était plus' (47 words). Howard captures this as 'for an instant the sun's dazzling reflection caught or rather condensed all the light and the glory on that virginal steel . . . Only, it was a long time since she had been a virgin' (32 words).

When we return to that 'instant' at the end of the novel, the original and the translation are very close. Simon says: 'le paysage tout entier inhabité vide sous le ciel immobile, le monde arrêté figé s'effritant se dépiautant s'écroulant peu à peu par morceaux comme une bâtisse abandonnée, inutilisable, livrée à l'incohérent, nonchalant, impersonnel et destructeur travail du temps' (41 words). Howard follows: 'the whole landscape uninhabited under the motionless sky, the world stopped frozen crumbling, collapsing gradually disintegrating in fragments like an abandoned building, unusable, left to the incoherent, casual, impersonal and destructive work of time' (34 words).

Unlike Simon, whose works play on critical

historical crises, Marguerite Duras, between the phenomenal popular successes of the screenplay *Hiroshima mon amour* (1961) and *L'Amant* (1984, The Lover), focused on the apparently trivial. Yet she kept enlarging her circle of careful readers. In her case, unlike Simon's, where we can only attest that the translators are not to blame for readers losing patience, her translator, Barbara Bray, can be credited also with helping readers stay engaged amidst minute perceptions. *Emily L.* (1987) is an excellent example of Bray's flair. In this novel (*roman*) that is actually a concealed narrative (*récit*) with an implicit listener, there is a fragmented narration of a drunken couple from the Isle of Wight in their late 60s or early 70s who come to a small Breton resort. After the death of her infant daughter the woman had spontaneously written a poem of quiet despair. Bray had to recognize that this poem, which is discussed line by line by the frame narrator in the third person and in the past tense, is in fact Emily Dickinson's 'There is a certain slant of light'. Eventually the entire poem is paraphrased, glossed, and integrated with the characterizations. This does not mean that American readers find the novel easier to understand. It just gives readers of the English translation a more accessible set of clues than readers using the French text. The Duras case shows us also that a translator can 'clarify' a novel without removing its mystique.

Continental French fiction was well served by translation during the 20th c. Both mainstream and vanguard on the way to becoming mainstream found translators and publishers. A few French authors have continued to have a steady readership in English translation. Camus, Céline, and Duras for example, may well join Beckett and Green, as 'English' novelists. Yet we should keep in mind that the sifting of posterity is both unfinished and unstable. Inasmuch as French novelists have been assigned reliable translators, their works in translation, albeit stored in libraries, remain available for rediscovery. MGR

BATAILLE, GEORGES Matthews, Harry, *The Blue of Noon*, New York, 1978, London, 1979 · Neugroschel, Joachim, *Story of the Eye*, New York, 1977, London, 1979 [Penguin].

BEAUVOIR, SIMONE DE Friedman, Leonard M., *The Mandarins*, London, 1957.

BERNANOS, GEORGES Morris, Pamela, *The Diary of a Country Priest*, 1937 · *The Star of Satan*, London, 1940 · Varese, Louise, *Joy*, London, 1948.

BUTOR, MICHEL Howard, Richard, *Degrees*, New York/London, 1962 · Stewart, Jean, *Second Thoughts*, London, 1958 · *Passing Time*, London, 1961.

CAMUS, ALBERT Gilbert, Stuart, *The Outsider*, London/New York, 1946 [Penguin] · *The Plague*, London/New York, 1948 [Penguin] · Hapgood, David, *The First Man*, London/New York, 1995 [Penguin] · Laredo, Joseph, *The Outsider*, Harmondsworth, 1981 [Penguin] · O'Brien, Justin, *The Fall*, New York, 1956, London, 1957 · *Exile and the Kingdom*, New York, 1958 · Ward, Matthew, *The Stranger*, New York, 1988.

CÉLINE, LOUIS-FERDINAND (LOUIS-FERDINAND DESTOUCHES) Manheim, Ralph, *Death on the Instalment Plan* [later *Death on Credit*], New York/London, 1966 · *Castle to Castle*, New York, 1968, London, 1969 [Penguin] · *North*, New York/London, 1972 [Penguin] · *Rigodon*, New York, 1974 · *Journey to the End of the Night*, New York, 1983 · Marks, John H. E. P., *Journey to the End of the Night*, London/New York, 1934 [Penguin] · *Death on the Instalment Plan*, London/New York, 1938.

COLETTE, SIDONIE-GABRIELLE White, Antonia, Senhouse, Roger, Macleod, Enid, et al., *Uniform Edition of Works by Colette*, 17 vols., London, 1951 [several in Penguin].

DURAS, MARGUERITE Bray, Barbara, *The Sailor from Gibraltar*, London/New York, 1966 · *Destroy, She Said*, London/New York, 1970 · *The Lover*, London/New York, 1985 · *Blue Eyes, Black Hair*, London/New York, 1987 · *Emily L.*, London/New York, 1989 · Ellenbogen, Eileen, *The Rapture of Lol V. Stein*, London, 1967 · Seaver, Richard, *Moderato Cantabile*, New York, 1960; London, 1966 · *Hiroshima mon amour*, New York, 1961 · *The Ravishing of Lol V. Stein*, New York, 1968.

GIDE, ANDRÉ Bussy, Dorothy, *Strait Is the Gate*, London, 1924 [Penguin] · *The Counterfeiters*, London, 1928 [Penguin] · *Lafcadio's Adventures* [later *Vatican Cellars*], London/New York, 1928 [Penguin] · *The Immoralist*, New York/London, 1930 [Penguin] · *Two Symphonies* [*La Symphonie Pastorale* and *Isabelle*], London, 1931 [Penguin] · *Fruits of the Earth*, London, 1949 [Penguin] · *If It Die*, London, 1950 [Penguin].

GRACQ, JULIEN (LOUIS POIRIER) Howard, Richard, *Balcony in the Forest*, London, 1960 · *The Opposing Shore*, London, 1993 · Strachan, W. J., *A Dark Stranger*, London, 1951 · Varese, Louise, *The Castle of Argol*, London, 1951.

GREEN, JULIEN Green, Anne, *The Transgressor*, New York, 1957, London, 1958 · *Each in His Darkness*, New York/London, 1961 · Holland, Vyvyan, *The Dark Journey*, London/New York, 1929 · *The Strange River*, London/New York, 1932 · *The Dreamer*, London/New York, 1934 · *Midnight*, London/New York, 1936 · Stuart, Henry Longon, *The Closed Garden*, New York, 1928; rev. Marilyn Gaddis Rose, New York, 1991.

MALRAUX, ANDRÉ Gilbert, Stuart, *The Royal Way*, London, 1935 · Gilbert, Stuart, and Macdonald, Alastair, *Days of*

Hope, London, 1938 [Penguin] · Macdonald, Alastair, *Storm in Shanghai* [later *Man's Estate*], London, 1934 [Penguin] · Wale, Winifred Stephens, *The Conquerors*, London/Toronto, 1929.

MAURIAC, FRANÇOIS   Hopkins, Gerard, *The Collected Edition of the Novels of François Mauriac*, 17 vols., London, 1946–70 [2 vols. tr. by other hands; many novels subsequently in Penguin].

PEREC, GEORGES   Adair, Gilbert, *A Void*, London, 1994 · Bellos, David, *Life a User's Manual*, London/Boston, Mass., 1987 · *W, or the Memory of Childhood*, London/Boston, Mass., 1994.

QUENEAU, RAYMOND   Wright, Barbara, *Exercises in Style*, London, 1958 · *Zazie*, London, 1960 · *Between Blue and Blue*, London, 1967 · *The Bark Tree*, London, 1968 · *The Sunday of Life*, London, 1976 · *Pierrot Mon Ami*, London, 1988.

ROBBE-GRILLET, ALAIN   Brooke-Rose, Christine, *In the Labyrinth*, London, 1967 · Howard, Richard, *Jealousy*, New York/London, 1959 · *The Voyeur*, New York/London, 1959 · *The Erasers*, New York/London, 1966.

SARRAUTE, NATHALIE   Jolas, Maria, *Portrait of a Man Unknown*, London/New York, 1959 · *Tropisms*, London/New York, 1963 · *The Golden Fruits*, London/New York, 1967 · *Martereau*, London/New York, 1967 · *The Planetarium*, London/New York, 1967.

SARTRE, JEAN-PAUL   Alexander, Lloyd, *The Diary of Antoine Roquentin*, London, 1949; rep. 1962 · *Intimacy*, London, 1951 · Baldick, Robert, *Nausea*, Harmondsworth, 1965 [Penguin] · Hopkins, Gerard, *Iron in the Soul*, London, 1950 [Penguin] · Sutton, Eric, *The Age of Reason*, London, 1947 [Penguin] · *The Reprieve*, London, 1947.

SIMON, CLAUDE   Fletcher, Beryl, and Fletcher, John, *The Georgics*, Riverrun, NY, 1989 · Howard, Richard, *Grass*, New York, 1959 · *The Wind*, New York, 1959 · *The Flanders Road*, New York,. 1961 · *The Palace*, New York, 1963 · *Histoire*, New York, 1967 · *The Battle of Pharsalus*, New York, 1971 · Lane, Helen R., *Tryptich*, New York, 1979 · *Conducting Bodies*, Riverrun, NY, 1980 · Weissbort, Daniel, *The World Around Us*, Princeton, NJ, 1983.

SEE ALSO   Keenoy, R., Laluyaux, L., and Stanton, G., *The Babel Guide to French Fiction in Modern Translation*, London, 1996.

13. PROUST

Without Marcel Proust, not only is the western novel of the 20th c. barely imaginable; so also are 20th c. art, philosophy, and psychology. The list of interdisciplinary credits could go on and on. Virginia Woolf wrote that if major impressionist paintings were destroyed, they could be reconstructed from the descriptions in *A la recherche du temps perdu* (1913–27, Remembrance of Things Past). Psychology students learn about the 'Proust phenomenon' (a body memory sequence called 'involuntary memory'). Philosophy students do better with the arguments in philosophers like Bergson and Sartre if they know about Proust.

Despite our millennial obsession with history and memory which has been accompanied by a renewed interest in *Remembrance*, where history is concerned, Proust had a tunnel vision. *Remembrance* makes few references to epochal events. Only the Dreyfus Case, a linking subplot in *Le Côté de Guermantes* (The Guermantes Way), requires a forewarned reader, although there are passing mentions of the Franco-Prussian War, the Commune, and the Russo-Japanese War. True, the narrator's time frame goes from the era following the Franco-Prussian War to World War I and the immediate postwar period. Yet within this frame his life is conspicuously privileged and his own personal pursuits relatively trivial. His consciousness, however, whether waking, drowsing, or dreaming, contains far more than he can address. Proust is a master of synecdoche, so that with salient selected details he casts a net of interrelationships over every social class, even if it is the big fish of the aristocracy, *haute bourgeoisie*, and the arts he most wants to catch. Thus, Marcel the narrator, an asthmatic social climber who wants to be a writer, stumbles, sniffs, touches, and tastes the stimuli of memorable sensations. These give him back the past, and hence a subject for a novel he will write—unless, of course, it is the novel we have just finished reading. As readers, while enjoying someone else's non-threatening experiences, we have been absorbing a method for recognizing and exploiting our own involuntary memory sequences.

Obviously conveying the ineffable in words requires very careful writing, and Proust in the sections he was able to revise and copy-edit before his death uses language that is not only concrete and visualizable but charged with allusions, giving those reworked sections (roughly up to but not including *La Prisonnière*) (1923, The Captive)) the density of Symbolist poetry. This made the task of translating both burdensome and rewarding. A gifted British translator, Charles Kenneth **Scott Moncrieff**, who had previously published translations of *The Song of Roland* and *Beowulf*, was on hand, and translated before his own death the first six sections of *Remembrance* (1922–30, published as the first 11 English volumes) The final posthumous volume, *Le Temps retrouvé* (1927, The Past

Recaptured) received three translations, by Stephen **Hudson** (1932), Frederick Augustus **Blossom** (1932), and Andreas **Mayor** (1970).

Pierre Clarac and André Ferré prepared an edition, expected to be definitive, for Gallimard in 1954. From this edition Terence **Kilmartin**, using Scott Moncrieff's and Mayor's translations, completed a copy-editing and revision in 1981. Thereafter, two further critical editions were issued: Jean-Yves Tadié, aided by 14 colleagues, for Gallimard and Bernard Raffali for Robert Laffont, and in 1992 D. J. **Enright** re-revised the Kilmartin correction. In all of these cases Proust scholars restored probable additions and maintained variants in annotations. It was Clarac and Ferré who provided indexes not only of proper names, places, and historical references but of motifs also; these Kilmartin put in a separate handbook. In the meantime the Australian James **Grieve** completed a translation of *Du côté de chez Swann* (1913, Swann's Way) in 1982. It is accurate but it does not reveal the sense of style of the other English versions.

Reviewers of the newly published *A l'ombre des jeunes filles en fleur* ('Within a Budding Grove'), which received the Prix Goncourt in 1919, compared Proust to George Meredith and Henry James, reportedly to his immense pleasure. It could thus be legitimately maintained that when translated, Proust should be left in the early 20th-c. English of Scott Moncrieff as completed by Mayor. Kilmartin did. By his own testimony he was both respectful and fastidious. He corrected outright errors, smoothed the syntax where he believed his predecessor had calqued too reverently for comprehensibility. Enright restored also passages that had been consigned to appendices. In terms of style and accuracy, comparison among translations is usually inconclusive. Comparisons between any translation and the original, on the other hand, are very rewarding.

Scott Moncrieff, aptly called by Christopher Prendergast 'the true hero of the story', developed a narrative persona of considerable charm and used an appropriate rhetoric reminiscent of the narrator's favourite childhood author, George Sand. To bring out this persona, Scott Moncrieff usually heightened some features of his rhetoric, above all, the persona's pleasure in occasionally somewhat pretentious expressions, for example, obsolete expressions, and archaisms. (Indeed, as a translator of Latin, Old French, Italian, and French, including all of Stendhal's major works, Scott Moncrieff is always interpretative.)

It is highly doubtful that Scott Moncrieff removed or obscured any important cues brought to light by subsequent scholarship. Recent Queer Studies, for example, have highlighted the pervasiveness of elaborately coded yet unconcealed homosexuality markers in the novel. One such code, involving tea and tea parties, goes into effect as soon as the narrator's mother offers him a linden-leaf infusion and a madeleine pastry (a moulded sponge cake). The narrator specifies that his first swallow ('la gorgée mêlée des miettes de gâteau') brought him ecstasy. Scott Moncrieff, letting readers infer the mouthful of tea and sponge cake (*la gorgée*) from the preceding sentence, interprets as 'the warm liquid mixed with the crumbs'. Neither Kilmartin nor Enright makes a change. When the narrator compares this fleeting sensation to 'la même façon qu'opère l'amour', both Kilmartin and Enright keep Scott Moncrieff's 'the effect which love has'. But when the narrator finds his self-esteem enhanced as a result ('J'avais cessé de me sentir médiocre, contingent, mortel'), Kilmartin inserts a 'now' ('I had ceased now to feel'), and Enright removes it ('I had ceased to feel').

Whether French or English, the importance of the madeleine lies less in its shape, which could be seen as either male or female, than in its role in retrieving the narrator's body memory. This example is typical of Scott Moncrieff. He may have been interpretative, but he left metonyms intact. He resisted the cutting back on elaboration that verges on redundancy. On the other hand, there was no way he could render Proust's adroit use of grammatical gender. For example, for Swann the motif of the Vinteuil Sonata triggers illuminating memory sequences of pain and joy with a consequent self-awareness. Because the motif is *la petite phrase*, referred to as *elle*, all of these sequences are overtly eroticized—*in French*.

Nor is Scott Moncrieff's interpretative strategy misleading in dialogues. For example, when Oriane de Guermantes is taken aback when Charles Swann tells her and the narrator that he is mortally ill, Proust observes that she did not know 'la jurisprudence' of such situations. Scott-Moncrieff explains, she did not know 'the right line to take'. This scene shows also the pointlessness of modernizing. Oriane, realizing this revelation requires serious conversation, says 'venez déjeuner', which becomes 'come to luncheon', instead of the more current 'come have lunch' or 'come to lunch'.

Reading the resulting Scott Moncrieff/ Mayor/Kilmartin or Enright composite translation as a single translation, with all its unobtrusive indicators of 1920s high culture, is a satisfying experience in itself. Even more satisfying is when bilingual readers put *Remembrance* alongside

293

La Recherche for a stereoscopic reading. Such a reading experience shows that the gap between the two is not a site of discrepancies but an enrichment.

Although most of Proust's other writing has been edited and published, translations into English have been piecemeal. He has attracted some of the best French translators. For instance, Sylvia Townsend **Warner** and John **Sturrock** have translations of *Contre Sainte-Beuve* (1952, Against Sainte-Beuve); Terence Kilmartin, George D. **Painter**, and Ralph **Manheim** have translated some of the letters; Gerard **Hopkins** translated *Jean Santeuil* and parts of *Les Plaisirs et les jours* (1896, Pleasures and Days).   MGR

A LA RECHERCHE DU TEMPS PERDU   Enright, D. J., *In Search of Lost Time* (revision of Scott Moncrieff, Mayor as rev. by Kilmartin), London, 1992, New York, 1992–3 · Grieve, James, *In Search of Lost Time*, Canberra, 1982 · Scott Moncrieff, C. K., with Andreas Mayor, rev. Terence Kilmartin, *Remembrance of Things Past*, London, 1922–30; rep. 1970, 1981 [vol. i: *Swann's Way, Within a Budding Grove*; vol. ii: *The Guermantes Way, Cities of the Plain*; vol. iii: *The Captive, The Fugitive* (also *Sweet Cheat Gone*), *Time Regained* (also *Past Recaptured*)].

OTHER WRITINGS   Autret, Jean, with William Burford and Philipe J. Wolfe., *On Reading Ruskin* (Prefaces to *La Bible d'Amiens* (1904) and *Sésame et le lys* (1906)), New Haven, Conn., 1987 · Curtis, Mina, *Letters*, New York, 1949 · Gant, Roland, *The Veiled Wanderer: Letters to the Duc de Guiche*, London, 1949 · Hopkins, Gerard, *Jean Santeuil*, New York, 1946 · Kilmartin, Terence, *Selected Letters*, vol. ii, New York, 1989 · Manheim, Ralph, *Selected Letters*, vol. i, Garden City, NY, 1983 · Painter, George D., *Letters to His Mother*, London, 1956 · Varese, Louise, with Gerard Hopkins and Barbara Dupree, *Pleasures and Days*, Garden City, NY, 1957 · Sturrock, John, *Against Sainte-Beuve and Other Essays*, London, 1988 [Penguin] · Warner, Sylvia Townsend, *By Way of Sainte-Beuve*, London, 1984 [also published as *On Art and Literature, 1896–1919*, New York, 1958].

SEE ALSO   Prendergast, C., 'English Proust', *London Review of Books*, 8 July 1993.

14. BECKETT

Towards the end of his life Samuel Beckett appears to have reached a bilingual 'magma', as George Steiner puts it in *The New Yorker* (September 16, 1996), in which French and English shared an astutely impoverished lexicon. English was his first language; he remained aloof from the nationalistic bilingualism of his native Ireland. Like many who set out to be romance language scholars, his attachment to French can be assumed to have once been chiefly intellectual. Further, although scholars have determined from his papers that he 'began' writing in French in July 1946, it can be assumed that through his first works, especially *Waiting for Godot* and *Endgame*, his bilingualism must have been what linguists have sometimes termed a compound system. This means that he had in his language repertory two signs for every referent. His creative writing used either French or English depending upon the milieu and the task.

Eventually, after living the final 50 or so years of his life in France, his bilingual system may well have had a mixed 'magma' available. The record shows that he was the chief translator of his works, whether he wrote them first in French or English. After *Watt* (1945) he usually wrote first in French. The differences between his French and English versions are by no means great, yet they are sufficiently marked for some scholars to call the French his 'rough drafts'. Still if we judge from the texts themselves, he seems to have used an interpretive strategy, common enough with successful professional translators like Richard **Howard**, Ralph **Manheim**, or William **Weaver**. He conceptualizes the total text and composes the translation from his own cues in the 'original'. Be it French or English, the voice is always his.

He both adapts his texts and defers to them. Consider some excerpts from his self-translation of a nine-paragraph tribute to the paintings of his long-time friend Jack B. Yeats. In 1954, for a Paris publication, he asks: 'Quoi de moins féerique que cette prestigieuse facture comme soufflée par la chose à faire, et par son urgence propre?' (literally: 'What is less fairylike than this prestigious workmanship seemingly staggered by the task at hand, and by its own urgency?'). For the Dublin Exhibition in 1971, he asks; 'What less celt than this incomparable hand shaken by the aim it sets itself or by its own urgency?' While the English echoes the mood and direction of the French, another translator would probably be accused of lexical over interpretation—*féerique*, 'fairylike' becomes 'celt', and the *prestigieuse facture comme soufflée* (workmanship staggered by the task at hand) becomes 'incomparable hand shaken'. Inasmuch as *soufflée* is related to 'breath' and 'breeze', we can reasonably conjecture that Beckett was thinking of 'inspired' as well. This would be an instance of compression in English.

Elsewhere he advances what seems to be a reference to Irishness and W. B. Yeats: 'L'artiste qui joue son être est de nulle part. Et il n'a pas de frères', but neutralizes the specificity in his rendering. Instead of 'And he has no brothers', Beckett translates: 'The artist who stakes his being is from nowhere, hath no kith'.

In his drama translations he worked with the productions and adapted accordingly. For example, in transforming *En attendant Godot* (1952) into *Waiting for Godot* (1954) he accommodates London and New York audiences. Towards the end of the play, Vladimir and Estragon accompany their futile attempt to pull themselves up and away from Pozzo and Lucky with futile remarks like these:

ESTRAGON.	Nous irons dans l'Ariège.
VLADIMIR.	Où tu voudras.
POZZO.	Trois cents! Quatre cents!
ESTRAGON.	J'ai toujours voulu me ballader dans l'Ariège.
VLADIMIR.	Tu t'y balladeras.
ESTRAGON.	Qui a pété?
VLADIMIR.	C'est Pozzo.

This is how the dialogue was translated for London:

ESTRAGON.	We'll go to the Pyrenees.
VLADIMIR.	Wherever you like.
POZZO.	Ten shillings—A pound!
ESTRAGON.	I've always wanted to wander in the Pyrenees.
VLADIMIR.	You'll wander in them.
ESTRAGON.	(recoiling): Who belched?
VLADIMIR.	Pozzo.

For the New York audience, Beckett did not convert Pozzo's exclamation to dollars; he omitted it entirely, but with *Qui a pété?* he did not recoil: 'Who farted?' He did not expect either audience to recognize the Ariège. And he was taken with the euphony of 'wanted to wander'.

But plays nearly always get adapted during staging. What about his prose fiction, the novels (so to speak) of the trilogy *Molloy*, *Malone Dies*, and *The Unnamable*? Here the subtle rhetorical improvements truly make the translating seem like an excuse for bilingual copy-editing. *Molloy* was translated by Patrick **Bowles** with Beckett's collaboration; *Malone Dies* and *The Unnamable* he did himself. The French and English narrative voices are consistent. However, the English narrator is wittier and more learned: well-educated, well-bred, mentally disturbed, and down on his luck. For

example, Malone says, 'Que dis-je? je suis capable d'aller jusqu'à la Transfiguration, tel que je me connais, ou l'Assomption' (literally, 'What am I saying? I am capable of going on until the Transfiguration, such as I know myself, or the Assumption'). The self-directed irony is stepped up and compressed to 'Indeed I would not put it past me to pant on to the Transfiguration, not to speak of the Assumption' (179).

Towards the close of *Endgame*, Hamm's attempt to quote Baudelaire's *Recueillement* (Contemplation) in translation is probably lost on listeners who are not forewarned: 'You CRIED for night; it comes—[*Pause. He corrects himself.*] It FALLS: now cry in darkness'. However, in the fiction subtle allusions increase in density, complexity, and importance in the English, which represents, chronologically at least, Beckett's second thoughts. In a line of the *Unnamable* towards the beginning, the narrative voice tries to place itself and its own narrative in a sentence of 171 words with this kernel 37 words from the end of the sentence: 'I'll never know, which is perhaps merely the inside of my distant skull where once I wandered'. That line might be considered reminiscent of Poe and by extension of Baudelaire. The comparable sentence in French contains 195 words. Although we would say the English still translates closely, the *je ne saurai sans doute jamais* ('I shall doubtless never know') occurs after 113 words. Nine words intervene before *et qui n'est peut-être que l'intérieur de mon crâne* ('and which is perhaps only the inside of my distant skull'). Strung out in this way, no such allusion is cued. A reader is assaulted by the obsessive voice. It can be assumed that in going into English, Beckett not only compressed information but in so doing interwove intertextual allusions.

The intertextual complexity both within and surrounding Beckett is illustrated by the annual international bibliography of the Modern Language Association (*PMLA*). It duplicates the listing of Beckett scholarship in both the English and Foreign Languages volumes. The duplication, remarkably like an analogue of Becket's self-translation, shows how the language of the text attracts different, albeit overlapping, sets of readers who in turn respond to Beckett's own somewhat divergent extratextual cues. Readers sharing Beckett's bilingualism get to read somewhat different 'originals'.   MGR

COLLECTIONS *Collected Poems in English and French*, London/New York, 1977; 3rd edn., 1984 · *Collected Shorter Plays*, London/New York, 1984 · *The Complete Short Prose*, New York, 1995.
WORKS FIRST PUBLISHED IN FRENCH (translation by Beckett unless stated otherwise) *Waiting for Godot*, London/New York, 1954 (*En attendant Godot*) · *Molloy*, tr. with Patrick Bowles, London/New York, 1955 · *Malone*

Dies, London / New York, 1956 (*Malone meurt*) · *The Unnamable*, London / New York, 1958 (*L'Innommable*) · *Endgame*, London / New York, 1958 (*Fin de partie*) · *Poems in English*, London, 1961 · *Play*, London / New York, 1964 (*Comédie*) · *How It Is*, London / New York, 1964 (*Comment c'est*) · *Imagination Dead Imagine*, London, 1966 · *Come and Go*, London / New York, 1967 (*Va et vient*) · *No's Knife*, London, 1967 (*Textes pour rien*) · *The Lost Ones*, New York, 1972 (*Le Dépeupleur*) · *Mercier and Camier*, London / New York, 1974 (*Mercier et Camier*) · *Fizzles*, London / New York, 1976 (*Foirades*) · *Ill Seen Ill Said*, New York, 1981 (*Mal vu mal dit*) · *Eleutheria*, tr. Albert Bermel, New York, 1994.

Works First Published in English (translations by Beckett unless stated otherwise) *More Pricks than Kicks*, London, 1934 (*Bande et sarabande*, tr. Édith Fournier) · *Murphy*, London, 1938 · *Watt*, Paris, 1953 · *All That Fall*, London, 1957 (*Tous ceux qui tombent*) · *Krapp's Last Tape; Embers*, London, 1959, New York, 1960 (*La Dernière Bande*; *Cendres*) · *Happy Days*, New York, 1961; London, 1962 (*Oh les beaux jours*) · *First Love*, London, 1973; New York, 1974 (*Premier Amour*) · *Rockaby and Other Short Pieces*, New York, 1981 · *Worstward Ho*, New York, 1983; London, 1984 (*Cap au pire*, tr. Édith Fournier) · *Disjecta*, London, 1983; New York, 1984.

See also   Fitch, B. T., *Beckett and Babel: An Investigation into the Status of the Bilingual Work*, Toronto, 1988 · Friedman, A. W., Rossman, C., and Scheizer, D., *Beckett Translating / Translating Beckett*, University Park, Penn., 1987.

15. TWENTIETH-CENTURY THINKERS

i. Introduction Inherently interdisciplinary, the French tradition encourages fine writing in the arts and sciences generally, and, reciprocally, encourages systematic thought in the belles-lettres. As the 20th c. ends, French thought, including but not limited to anthropology, cultural studies, history, linguistics, literary theory and criticism, philosophy, and sociology, seems to have remained much more vital than French literature. The prestige of the latter was linked to a series of individuals who still seem to overshadow their successors. French thought, on the other hand, remained energetic and continues to energize western thought outside France. This energy is by no means spent, although the present discussion, given constraints of space, will focus chiefly on thinkers whose deaths have verified their appeal to posterity. (This will explain, if not excuse, the omission of thinkers such as Maurice Blanchot, Pierre Bourdieu, Gérard Genette, Jean-François Lyotard, Michel Serres, and Tsvetan Todorov.)

Consider the constellation starting with Ferdinand de Saussure and Henri Bergson and the less prominent figures Alexandre Kojève, Léon Brunschvicg, and Jacques Maritain and moving through the existentialism of Jean-Paul Sartre (as well as Gabriel Marcel and Maurice Merleau-Ponty). Existentialism in turn overlapped with the structuralism of Claude Lévi-Strauss, the semiotics of Roland Barthes, and the gallicized post-Heideggerianism of deconstruction and postmodernism in Michel Foucault and Jacques Derrida, not to mention the explosion of feminist philosophy led by Luce Irigaray. Every direction, while highlighting style, has focused on language and grammar, whether defined literally or metaphorically.

Transmission of this body of writing in the English-speaking world has relied largely on translation because teachers of French, although the first to receive French thought, tended to confine themselves simply to popularizing it, without engaging in translation. Critiquing and continuing it, including translating it, has brought scholars from the individual thinker's own discipline into the translators' community. The existence of such a body of translators may help explain why these translations have dated far less than those of belles-lettres [see II.g.12]. Most translators have also had the opportunity to consult the author. In almost every case, he or she could at least use English as a scholarly tool and hence could respond to queries. Further, the translations usually have translators' notes.

ii. Types of Translation It is certainly demonstrable that these translators defer to the texts and usually work with texts to which they have made an affective professional commitment. Typical is Alfonso **Lingis**, who has translated the major works of Emmanuel Levinas. Lingis prefaces his translation of *Autrement qu'être* (1974, Otherwise than Being) with this statement: 'the present English version, more than most philosophical translations, is a transposition of the original text, and does not wish to sever its dependence on and subordination to it'. In fact his translation conforms to the norm for this type of translation. These English translations, if not literal, still have a French stamp, regardless of when the translation was made. Further, the translators, recognizing that their texts were giving readers new spaces to think in, have brought a great many key terms into English either directly (e.g. the *volupté* and *jouissance* of Levinas and Irigaray) or by neologisms (e.g. from Heidegger via Sartre, *being-in-itself* and *being-for-itself*).

They have thus enriched the English language as well as its constituent cultures. Of late, many texts have been studied stereoscopically (i.e. with French original and English translation), so that the semantic gap between text and translation can be appreciated.

Indeed, avoiding special, even idiosyncratic terminology would seem to have been misguided. The translations of Saussure, the only scholar here who has been retranslated, are problematic on this score. His *Cours de linguistique générale* (1922, Course in General Linguistics) has received two successive translations: Wade **Baskin**, 1966, and Roy **Harris**, 1983. Both translators are confusing when they try to avoid Saussure's distinction between *langue* (language, tongue), *parole* (speech), and *langage* (language system). Saussure states: 'En séparant la langue de la parole, on sépare du même coup: 1° ce qui est social de ce qui est individuel; 2° ce qui est essentiel de ce qui est accessoire et plus ou moins accidentel.' Baskin writes, 'In separating language from speaking we are at the same time separating: (1) what is social from what is individual; and (2) what is essential from what is accessory and more or less accidental.' Harris writes, 'By distinguishing between language itself and speech, we distinguish at the same time: (1) what is social from what is individual, and (2) what is essential from what is ancillary and more or less accidental.' Terminology stays slippery when the translators encounter *langage*. According to Saussure, 'la langue, distincte de la parole, est un objet qu'on peut étudier séparément . . . Non seulement la science de la langue peut se passer des autres éléments du langage, mais elle n'est possible que si ces autres éléments n'y sont pas mêlés.' Baskin renders this as: 'Language, unlike speaking, is something that we can study separately. . . . We can dispense with the other elements of speech; indeed the science of language is possible only if the other elements are excluded.' Harris may be clearer here: 'A language system, as distinct from speech, is an object that may be studied independently . . . A science which studies linguistic structure is not only able to dispense with other elements of language, but is possible only if those other elements are kept separate.' It would have been preferable to insert Saussure's terms parenthetically. As it is, readers must check the French in order to appreciate Saussure's system.

The Saussure translations, however, are anomalous and atypical. Richard **Howard**, himself a leading translator of 20th-c. French literature and philosophy, sums up the desirable strategy in his preface to Richard **Miller**'s 1974 translation of *S/Z*

(1970) by Roland Barthes. Miller's decision to translate *lisible* and *scriptible* as 'readerly' and 'writerly' showed that the translator was 'properly concerned with his reader's comprehension, not his comfort'. Katrine Pilcher **Keuneman**, however, should be credited with trying to match Barthes's style when she translated the essays in *Critique et vérité* (1966, Criticism and Truth). Her translation, with scholarly apparatus more extensive than the text, is in fact a model for such translating. She follows conventions when appropriate, e.g. 'verisimilitude' (*le vraisemblable*), and 'good taste' (*le goût*); she coins when she must, e.g. 'asymbolia' (*l'asymbolie*), and 'plural language' (*la langue plurielle*); she stands by her decisions, e.g. 'categorical' (*apophantique*) and 'discourse' (*parole*).

iii. From Bergson to Cixous However it has come about, most translations discussed here are usually in print and still being read. Least read may be Bergson, although the French feminist Catherine Clément has recently been promoting him. His style won him the Nobel Prize for Literature and a seat in the French Academy. He is also the French thinker who took the most responsibility for his English translations: his works still typically contain a notice that he authorized the translation personally. For example, for *Matière et mémoire* (1896, Matter and Memory), still consulted by students of Proust, translators Nancy Margaret **Paul** and W. Scott **Palmer** thank Bergson for revising the translation in proof and 'for many suggestions . . . made while the book was in manuscript'.

At the opposite extreme is Sartre, apparently progressively disinclined to copy-edit and hence requiring his translators' indulgence and patience. While it might be an overstatement to claim that Carol **Cosman**'s translation of his massive, obsessive study of Flaubert *L'Idiot de la famille* (1972, The Family Idiot) rescued Sartre from writers' purgatory, the timing of the translation demonstrated the postmodernist debt to him. His last works not only overlapped with the early publications of, say, Derrida or Foucault but ideologically antedated them. Yet, it was not Cosman's contemporary lexicon that made Sartre sound contemporary. More than 30 years separate Cosman's *The Family Idiot* from Hazel **Barnes**'s translation of *L'Être et le néant* (1943, Being and Nothingness), yet Sartre's voice rings through both translators. The same prodigiously well-informed speaker expresses his strongly held opinions in a variety of ways, as he plays the parts he assigns to himself. In *The Family Idiot* he is still recognizably his old self while acting the parts of a nearly neutral novelist, a speculative psychologist, an opinionated cultural historian, and an impatient moralist. He watches himself watching the Other, following his earlier precept in *Being and Nothingness*: 'Let us consider this waiter in the cafe . . . All his behaviour seems a game . . . We need not watch long before we can explain it: he is playing at being a waiter in a cafe.'

The literary works of Simone de Beauvoir are receiving increasing study as a result of her position in feminism. Perhaps in a slight eclipse following Sartre's death, the popularity of *Le Deuxième Sexe* (1949, The Second Sex) continued despite its being overly interpreted and somewhat abridged. Published in 1952, just a year before translator Howard Madison **Parshley**'s death, the translation was reissued in 1989. Highly readable, it is incomplete and misleading. Parshley, a zoologist, normalized the philosophical lexicon. 'Réalité humaine' becomes 'human nature'; 'expérience vécue', 'women's life today'; 'pour-soi' and 'en-soi' are used interchangeably. Although de Beauvoir herself does not take up gender *qua* gender as it came to be used subsequently, she does refer to 'my' body, specifically a woman's body, and Parshley's adherence to pre-feminist rhetoric, where the third-person singular is always 'his', is reductive. (Patrick **O'Brian** translating *La Vieillesse* (1970, Coming of Age) does this as well.) A complete text is alleged to be in progress, but this has been alleged recurrently over the past 20 years.

More interesting because of their intersection with translation theory are the translations of Derrida and the postmodernists associated with him. The group of translators who gave them western currency through English helped to reorient the norms of translation. Prior to Gayatri **Spivak**'s 1976 translation of Derrida's *De la grammatologie* (1967, Grammatology), the prevailing ideal for translations was that they should sound as if written in the target language. Barnes's *Being and Nothingness* had been faulted for letting the French echo through the English. Richard Howard's translation of Foucault's *Histoire de la folie* (1961, Madness and Civilization) in 1966 (well before Sartre's *The Family Idiot* came out in French) may have read too smoothly to be appreciated for its originality. It is both invisible and domesticated, assimilating the text for the English-language general reader.

Spivak, albeit criticized, proved to most readers that the new rhetoric was linked to new content. Derrida had a new sound which Spivak echoes. Readers sensed that this foreignized translation was closer to the original. They took 'différance' with an 'a' into their critical lexicon and began to tolerate multiple reflexive verbs. Although this neo-

literalism was not to prevail in belles-lettres, especially in the trade press, it became increasingly the norm for the cluster of French writers associated with Derrida.

The theoretical infrastructure, systematized by Lawrence Venuti in his *The Translator's Invisibility* (1995), explained Lingis and Spivak after the fact as well as Alan **Sheridan**'s translations of *Écrits* (1966, 1972) by Jacques Lacan. Such an infrastructure was even more essential for the feminist philosophers whose innovations with syntax and lexicon were startling for French readers [see I.a.5.iv]. Examples include Leon **Roudiez**'s translations of *Les Pouvoirs de l'horreur* (1980, Powers of Horror) and *Les Histoires d'amour* (1983, Tales of Love) by Julia Kristeva, and any book by Luce Irigaray. Curiously, Hélène Cixous was popularized by hearsay long before Betsy **Wing** translated *La Jeune Née* (1975, The Newly Born Woman) which Cixous wrote with Catherine Clément. It was to be another decade before *La Venue à l'écriture* (1977), which she wrote with Madeleine Gagnon and Annie Leclerc, was translated by Sarah **Cornell**, Deborah **Jenson**, Ann **Liddle**, and Susan **Sellers** as *Coming to Writing*. The use of translator teams became standard for essay collections and readers.

iv. Two Examples: Foucault and Irigaray It is worth taking a closer look at Michel Foucault and then moving on to Luce Irigaray to see the challenges they presented, Foucault as a traditional stylist with covert cues and Irigaray as a deliberately divergent stylist. Both of these are thinkers whose every scrap gets translated quickly and closely.

Foucault's work has received a spectrum of dedicated translators from an astute 'anonymous' who translated *Les Mots et les choses* (1970, The Order of Things) to Robert **Hurley**, who corralled the team translating selections from the three-volume *Dits et écrits, 1954–88*. Foucault's translators, who include Alan Sheridan, Richard Howard, Charles **Ruas**, Donald F. **Bouchard**, Sherry **Simon**, and A. **Sheridan Smith** are uniformly reliable. Nevertheless, there are nuances in the French which they cannot render.

Foucault wrote to persuade, not to bewilder. However, in his exploitation of grammatical gender to reinforce semantics he appears to underscore sexual impulses, even sexual roles. At times, the harmony of passive ideas embodied in feminine nouns possessed or acted upon by masculine nouns empowered by transitive verbs exceeds coincidence. In *L'Archéologie du savoir* (1969, Archeology of Knowledge), fearing that he is an historian of ideas after all, Foucault laments:

Un historien [masculine] des idées [feminine] qui a voulu renouveler de fond en comble sa discipline [feminine]; qui a désiré sans doute lui donner cette rigueur [feminine] que tant d'autres descriptions [feminine], assez voisines, ont acquise récemment; mais qui, incapable de modifier réellement cette vieille forme [feminine] d'analyse [feminine], incapable de lui faire franchir le seuil [masculine] de la scientificité [feminine] . . . déclare, pour faire illusion [feminine], qu'il a toujours fait et voulu faire autre chose. Tout ce brouillard [masculine] nouveau pour cacher qu'on [one, referring back to the male historian] est resté dans le même paysage [masculine], attaché à un vieux sol [masculine] usé jusqu'à la misère [feminine].

Sheridan Smith is totally accurate, but English removes the sexual energy:

One who set out to renew his discipline from top to bottom; who wanted, no doubt, to achieve [instead of the literal 'give'] a rigour that so many other, similar descriptions have recently acquired; but who, unable to modify in any real way that old form of analysis, to make it cross the threshold of scientificity . . . declares that he had been doing, and wanted to do, something quite different. All this new fog just to hide what remained in the same landscape, fixed to an old patch of ground cultivated to the point of exhaustion [lit. 'wretchedness'].

Until Foucault uses *rester*, 'remain', an intransitive verb of (non)motion at the 'same landscape' fixed to an 'old patch of ground', every verb, all of them active, none linking, had a feminine noun as an object. Feminine nouns were even the objects of prepositions. A historian, then, is a man who, when he cannot make a feminine entity (ideas) follow his methodology, is forced to follow hers (because 'old forms of analysis' are feminine). Many more sexual analogies could be adduced, but these will suffice to show the undercurrent of Nietzschean resentment of the feminine.

When we move to Irigaray, we find work that has required a far greater degree of dedicated decoding. The decoding had to be largely intuitive, i.e. immersing oneself in the material until it just 'comes' to one. Indeed, trying to avoid 'one', as did Catherine **Porter**, who worked with Carolyn **Burke** to translate the epochal *Ce Sexe qui n'en est pas un* (1977, This Sex Which Is Not One) in 1985, is a problem encountered early in the translation. Since frustrating conventional syntax and register expectations is part of Irigaray's rhetorical strategy, Porter warns that a translator must 'never impose *one* reading on a text'. A feminine discourse, according to Irigaray, must stray from traditional logical argument, which she considers flawed and 'phallocentric'. The title essay of *This Sex Which Is Not One* has received three translations, all of them reliable. In choosing a translation readers should be guided by their opinion of the scholar's other work on Irigaray.

Is it paradoxical or ironic that, although made by *amateurs* in the French sense (aside from Richard Howard and Alan Sheridan), these translations are more satisfying (if not 'better') than many translations of belles-lettres? Translations of Derrida alone have evolved from Spivak's somewhat clumsy *Grammatology* in 1976 (a translation that propelled her own career as scholar) to Peggy **Kamuf**'s Derrida translations as an art form in her versions of *Donner le temps* (1991, Given Time) and *Spectres de Marx* (1993, Spectres of Marx). All of them, Howard and Sheridan included, have had a sense of mission. Although these translators have not necessarily gone without monetary compensation, it has almost never been their reason for translating. Most of them are recognized scholars who want to share with others the contributions of French thought. As English becomes increasingly international, French thinkers may well find their most durable posterity in English.   MGR

Translations

Barthes, Roland   Keuneman, Katrine Pilcher, *Criticism and Truth*, London, 1966 · Miller, Richard, *S/Z*, New York, 1974.
Beauvoir, Simone de   Parshley, Howard Madison, *The Second Sex*, New York, 1952; rep. 1989 · O'Brian, Patrick, *Coming of Age*, New York, 1972.
Bergson, Henri   Paul, Nancy Margaret, and Palmer, W. Scott, *Matter and Memory*, London, 1950.
Cixous, Hélène   Cornell, Sarah, Jenson, Deborah, Liddle, Ann, and Sellers, Susan, *Coming to Writing*, Boston, 1988 [French original written with Madeleine Gagnon and Annie Leclerc] · Wing, Betsy, *The Newly Born Woman*, St Paul, Minn., 1988 [written with Catherine Clément].
Derrida, Jacques   Kamuf, Peggy, *Given Time*, Chicago, 1992 · *Specters of Marx*, New York/London, 1994 · Spivak, Gayatri, *Grammatology*, Baltimore, 1976.
Foucault, Michel   anon., *The Order of Things*, New York, 1971 · Howard, Richard, *Madness and Civilization*, London/New York, 1967 · Hurley, Robert et al., *Ethics, Subjectivity, and Truth*, New York, 1997 · Sheridan Smith, A. M., *The Archaeology of Knowledge*, New York, 1972.
Irigaray, Luce   Alsbury, Randall, and Foss, Paul, 'That Sex Which Is Not One', in P. Foss and M. Morris, eds., *Language, Sexuality and Subversion*, Sydney, 1978 · Porter, Catherine, and Burke, Carolyn, *This Sex Which Is Not One*,

Ithaca, NY, 1985 · Reeder, Claudia, 'This Sex Which Is Not One', in Elaine Marks and Isabelle de Courtivron, eds., *New French Feminisms*, Brighton/New York, 1981.

KRISTEVA, JULIA   Roudiez, Leon, *Tales of Love*, New York, 1985, *The Powers of Horror*, New York, 1988.

LACAN, JACQUES   Sheridan, Alan, *Écrits*, New York, 1977.

LEVINAS, EMMANUEL   Lingis, Alfonso, *Otherwise than Being*, The Hague, 1974.

SARTRE, JEAN-PAUL   Barnes, Hazel, *Being and Nothingness*, New York, 1956 · Cosman, Carol, *The Family Idiot*, 5 vols., Chicago, 1985–94.

SAUSSURE, FERDINAND DE   Baskin, Wade, *Course in General Linguistics*, London, 1966 · Harris, Roy, *Course in General Linguistics*, London, 1983.

16. FRANCOPHONE WRITING OUTSIDE FRANCE

Francophone writing has been produced in various parts of the world, notably in the former French colonies in Africa and the Caribbean and in Canada. Each of these areas has its own social and political legacy, mirrored in its literature and hence passed on to the translator in the form of translation problems to grapple with. In Africa and the Caribbean, authors writing in French are using the language of the (former) colonizer. Power relationships and political struggles are played out in the language, manifesting themselves in 'Africanized' French and the use of Creole in Caribbean writing. The polyphony of Francophone texts, in contrast to the more homogeneous and codified literature of metropolitan France, raises questions of translatability. The situation in Canada has been different.

i. Canada What is now Quebec was historically a colony of France, but was lost to the English in the mid-18th c. English became the dominant culture and language. Those writing in French, in Quebec primarily, but also in other parts of the country such as the maritime provinces, are in fact writing in their native tongue, rather than the language of the colonizer. And yet it is a different French. During certain periods of political upheaval in particular, language has been used to signal the alienation of a minority people adrift in a continent of Anglophones. Canadian French is often peppered with English: English words imported into the French text, or English words in disguise, such as the *néveurmagne* (never mind) and *tchesteurfilde* (chesterfield) used by Jacques Ferron, and commented on by his translator Betty **Bednarski** (1989). Translators in Canada are dealing with the same diglossia, the same intersection of languages and cultures, that exist elsewhere in *la francophonie*, and hence have similar concerns about translatability.

In Canada, the translation of literature has a somewhat shorter history than other forms of translation [see I.b.6]. The first major French Canadian novel, Aubert de Gaspé's *Les Anciens Canadiens* (1863, The Canadians of Old), was translated, by Georgiana **Pennée** and later by Charles G. D. **Roberts**, in the 19th c. Activity was sporadic for nearly 100 years. One notable work during that time was Louis Hémon's classic, *Maria Chapdelaine* (1916), translated twice in 1921, by W. H. **Blake** and Andrew **McPhail**.

Translation of French Canadian literature came into its own in the 1960s, at a time when relations between French and English became increasingly tense. A group of English writers living mainly in and around Montreal sought to bring the writing of Quebec to the attention of their fellow English Canadians, doing so with conviction and a certain sense of mission. F. R. (Frank) **Scott** is an example. A professor of constitutional law and early member of the Canadian socialist movement, he was also a poet who translated out of political conviction. In the preface to his 1977 anthology, *Poems of French Canada*, he is explicit: 'Translation is not only an art in itself, it is also an essential ingredient in Canada's political entity.' He is noted for his translations of the poets Hector de Saint-Denys Garneau and Anne Hébert, as well as for his 1970 'dialogue' with Hébert on the subject of his translation of her poem 'Le Tombeau des rois'.

Translators of Francophone literature in Canada worked hard for a quarter of a century to bring the work of a minority culture to the attention of a wider readership at home and abroad. John Glassco's 1970 *Poets of French Canada in Translation* included the work of 47 poets, and Philip **Stratford** published in 1974 a collection of stories and, in collaboration with Michael Thomas, a collection of fiction and poetry entitled *Voices from Québec*.

Sheila **Fischman** is Canada's most prolific translator, credited with having single-handedly created a substantial body of work. She was co-founder of *Ellipse*, a magazine that since 1969 has published translations of poetry in both directions. Often a finalist and three times a winner of Canada's top prize for translation, she has translated some 60 titles since 1970, including the works of such illustrious Quebec writers as Hubert Aquin, Marie-Claire Blais, Roch Carrier, and Michel Tremblay.

The translation of Quebec's vernacular has generated much debate in the translation community. The brand of urban, working-class French spoken in Quebec is sometimes referred to as *joual*, a term which derives from the Québécois pronunciation of *cheval* (horse). It is typically laced with blasphemy and anglicisms. Previously considered 'an inferior dialect, a sub-language, a stigma of a people going nowhere' (Homel and Simon 1988: 56), *joual* came to be celebrated as a literary language in the 1960s by nationalist writers such as Tremblay. The question of how to translate this particular sub-language has always been open for discussion.

English-speaking theatregoers, in Canada and elsewhere, have long enjoyed Tremblay's plays, many of them translated by Bill **Glassco** and John **Van Burek**: *Les Belles-Sœurs* (1968, The Sisters-in-Law), *A toi, pour toujours, ta Marie-Lou* (1971, Forever Yours Marie-Lou), *Hosanna* (1973), to name a few. The translators have found reasonable equivalents for the colloquial and the profane and have made the plays work. And yet there is a sense that these translations fail to measure up to the originals, to convey their 'overtones of nationalism' (Bosley 1988: 141).

An interesting although quirky phenomenon is the translation of Tremblay into Scots by Bill **Findlay**, a Scot, and Martin **Bowman**, a Montrealer with Scottish origins. They took an interest in *Les Belles-Sœurs*, one of the first works of literature in which spoken Quebec dialect is used deliberately and for ideological purposes. First translated as *The Guid Sisters* in 1979, the play was staged in Glasgow in 1989, and subsequently in Toronto, New York, and Montreal. Findlay and Bowman felt that using Scots as a language of translation would be a means of developing the 'potentialities' of the Scots language. The example of Michel Tremblay was 'inspirational' to them because his commitment to the 'specificity of Quebec experience' had not prevented him from achieving international recognition (Findlay 1992: 139). The 'subversive' use of a degraded form of French, tainted with anglicisms and reflecting Quebec's alienation, appealed to them. They thought it appropriate, and more true to the letter and spirit of the original, to translate *Les Belles-Sœurs* into Scots. Findlay and Bowman have since translated several other plays by Tremblay and other Quebec playwrights.

Acadian literature, the product of French communities in eastern Canada, has its own challenges. Antonine Maillet, one of Canada's leading women of letters, is known for her idiosyncratic use of language. While not the only translator of Maillet's work, Philip Stratford stands out for his highly acclaimed *Pélagie: The Return to a Homeland*, his 1982 translation of Maillet's *Pélagie-la-Charette* (1979), as well as for his commentaries on the difficulties of translating so-called 'Acadian'. Maillet makes use of the multiple variations of Acadian, to which she adds her own accent and expression 'heavily laced with Rabelais, Perrault, Molière, folk tales'. Stratford does not attempt to find an equivalent regional English Canadian dialect, but instead uses what he calls 'Low Standard American English' (Simon 1995: 95).

Feminist translators have played a crucial role in bringing key innovative texts to the attention of an English-Canadian readership [see I.a.5.iii–iv]. More than most translators, perhaps, they have worked in partnership with the original authors and have closely interwoven their creative practices and theoretical reflection. The title alone of *Lovhers*, Barbara **Godard**'s translation of feminist author Nicole Brossard's *Amantes* (1980), illustrates the challenges faced by the Anglophone translator attempting to capture the subversive use of language to critique a male-centred society. Other translations by Godard include Brossard's *Picture Theory* (1982), which has the same title in English and numerous references to English texts.

Multiculturalism has had an increasing impact on writing in Canada. In Quebec, a number of new figures have emerged on the literary scene, bringing an added dimension to the work of the French–English translator. One example is Dany Laferrière, a Francophone writer of Haitian origin, whose native tongue is Creole and whose books are 'translations from the Creole that's in his head', as his translator David **Homel** has said (Simon 1995: 48). In *How to Make Love to a Negro*, Homel's translation of Laferrière's *Comment faire l'amour avec un nègre sans se fatiguer* (1985), Homel is forced to address the same difficulty confronted by translators of African and Caribbean writing: how to translate 'nègre' (see below). This was the first of several translations of Laferrière, including the award-winning *Cette grenade dans la main du jeune nègre est-elle une arme ou une fruit?* (1993, Why Must a Black Writer Write about Sex?). Homel brings his own background as an American exile immersed in Quebec society to the task of translating writing in which the Quebec experience is layered over the author's Haitian identity.   JWW

ii. Africa English translations of works by Francophone African writers have played a vital, if sometimes belated, role in making a recent literary production accessible first of all to Africanists in general, and then to a larger world readership. This was particularly important in the immediate post-war years, when the journal *Présence africaine* (founded in 1947) and the Société Africaine de Culture promoted translations in both directions (for example, Nkrumah into French and Tempels into English). However, despite the early promise of Léopold Sédar Senghor's *négritude* and other pan-African movements, there has been surprisingly little collaborative contact between the Francophone and Anglophone communities in Africa, and English translations have by and large followed on the heels of publishing successes of the original French.

Early landmark translations include Camara Laye's romanticized autobiographical narrative *L'Enfant noir* (1954, Dark Child) by James **Kirkup** and Ferdinand Oyono's witty *Une Vie de Boy* (1956, Houseboy) by John **Reed** in Heinemann's African Writers Series. A number of poetry anthologies, responding to the impact of Senghor's famous *Anthologie de la nouvelle poésie nègre et malgache de langue française* (1948), underlined the genre's appeal to the first generation of Francophone African writers; Ulli **Beier** and Gerald **Moore**'s *Poetry from Africa*, and John Reed and Clive **Wake**'s *Selected Poems* by Senghor, as well as their *Book of African Verse*, all published in 1964, led the way, followed by Reed and Wake's *French African Verse* (1972). These were widely used in English-speaking African schools and universities, and Heinemann especially have always made affordability and accessibility of their texts a priority.

With African writing, considerations of audience are as crucial to the translation as to the original text, although the intended readership, of course, shifts with translation. Since translators also have an editorial role as interpreters for a primarily western (or western-educated African) audience, explanatory footnotes and glossaries are common, but are usually kept to a minimum for the sake of readability. The translator's intervention thus tends to be downplayed, as if the translation itself did not have a bearing on the status of the text and its reception, which it obviously does—as when, for example, Katherine **Woods** in her rendering of Cheikh Hamidou Kane's *L'Aventure ambiguë* (1961, Ambiguous Adventure) translates 'ta négritude' as 'your being a Negro—your Negroness, if I may coin a word'. Heinemann have nonetheless been able to count on a number of consistently outstanding translators; Clive Wake's and Francis **Price**'s translations of Sembène Ousmane have been among

Heinemann's bestsellers, and Dorothy **Blair** and Marjolijn **de Jaeger** have helped to make Francophone African women writers (Mariama Bâ, Aminata Sow Fall, and Calixthe Beyala, among others) more widely available.

There are also problems with producing too elegant an English translation, since more recent Francophone novelists have employed strategies for resisting various forms of discursive assimilation (of which translation is unavoidably one form). Ahmadou Kourouma and Sony Labou Tansi, for example, have reinvented and 'africanized' the French language in a gesture of deliberate alienation of western readers that actively defies translation. It requires the imaginative vigour of a translator such as Clive Wake to get even close to the power of Labou Tansi's prose, and Nidra **Poller** admits in her translator's note to Kourouma's *Monnè, outrages et défis* (1990, Monnew) that she has effectively had to create a new language, 'a rather special Malinke–French–English where the notion of foreign words has been set aside'.   MS

iii. The Caribbean Caribbean writing raises a different set of linguistic problems. One of the important early translations, in Heinemann's corresponding Caribbean series, is that by Langston **Hughes** and Mercer **Cook** of Jacques Roumain's *Les Gouverneurs de la rosée* (1944, Masters of the Dew). The novel is rooted in the Creole cultural world, but the original French is written with a wider Francophone readership in mind, with a rather diluted Creole being retained for direct, colloquial speech, and used effectively by Roumain to signal shifts in narrative focalization. Despite a clever attempt to find an equivalent of his French in the English vernacular of the Deep South, and despite the enlistment of two distinguished African American writers, the translation often loses the cultural polyphony of the original because its English is too homogeneous [see II.a.6.i].

One notoriously difficult term to translate, for both African and Caribbean writing, is 'nègre'. If 'nègre' in a Creole context has lost the racial overtones of 'negro' in English ('nèg' is a very neutral term for a man), this is in large part due to Aimé Césaire's defiant reappropriation of the negativity of the term in his long poem *Cahier d'un retour au pays natal* (1939, Notebook of a Return to My Native Land), a seminal work in so many ways for Francophone Caribbean literature, and whose legacy every writer after him has had in some sense to negotiate. Its importance is signalled by the number of translations it has spawned, and in this case successive translations have changed with the times—the tentative 'negro lad' and 'darky' of Émile **Snyder**'s 1971 translation become the more outspokenly assertive 'nigger' (Clayton **Eshleman** and Annette **Smith**; Mireille **Rosello**).

These three editions of Césaire's poem all recognize the usefulness of having the French side by side with the English. The translations range from Snyder's Présence Africaine edition (which is rather stilted in trying to follow too closely the contours of the French) to Rosello's recent edition in the Bloodaxe series (which is further from the original, but consciously tries to reproduce the unsettling quality and the linguistic inventiveness of Césaire's language), with Eshleman and Smith somewhere in between. The example of the enigmatic neologism which is the last word of Césaire's *Cahier*, 'verrition' (coined from the Latin verb *verri*, meaning 'to sweep' or 'to scan'), is a good point of comparison. Snyder goes for (insufficient) comprehensibility with 'flick', Eshleman and Smith try to convey the turning motion suggested by the Latin etymology of the term with 'veerition', while Rosello attempts a bolder equivalent English neologism with 'revolvolution'. Both Rosello and Eshleman/Smith provide lengthy and very useful translator's notes.

Césaire's work has also had a significant impact on black consciousness movements worldwide, but particularly in the USA during the 1970s because of its obvious appeal as a powerful expression of social alienation and pan-African solidarity. Reaction to Césaire has come from a group of rebellious younger writers such as Raphaël Confiant and Patrick Chamoiseau, who have championed the articulation of a Creole cultural identity (a complex issue Césaire avoids). Their *créolité* could be seen as a more user-friendly version of Édouard Glissant's *antillanité*. Such attempts to express the cultural complexity of the Francophone Caribbean make translation all the more daunting, and it is only very recently that Glissant's novels and theoretical writings have been successfully tackled, by J. Michael **Dash**. French Creole has posed an even greater problem, simply because there are very few translators sufficiently conversant with different Creoles to be able to do justice to writers such as Joby Bernabé, and even then the question remains of which Anglophone-based Creole to translate into. With the growing interest in New World studies, American publishers have taken the lead in bringing out translations of Caribbean writers; the CARAF Books series at the University Press of Virginia now features works by Daniel Maximin, René Depestre, and Maryse Condé as well as Glissant. Similarly inspired, the Ubu Repertory Theatre in New York has been active in staging many original translations by Francophone Caribbean writers, in particular women playwrights such as Ina Césaire, Simone Schwarz-Bart, and Gerty Dambury.   MS

Canada

ANTHOLOGIES   *Ellipse: A Quarterly Review of Works in Translation*, Sherbrooke, Quebec, 1969– · Glassco, John, ed., *Poetry of French Canada in Translation*, Toronto, 1970 · Scott, F. R., *Poems of French Canada translated by F. R. Scott*, Burnaby, BC, 1977 · Stratford, P., ed., *Stories from Québec*, Scarborough, Ont., 1974 · Stratford, P., and Thomas, Michael, eds., *Voices from Québec*, Toronto, 1977.

AUBERT DE GASPÉ, PHILIPPE-JOSEPH   Pennée, Georgiana, *The Canadians of Old*, Quebec, 1864 · Roberts, Charles G. D., *The Canadians of Old*, New York, 1890.

BROSSARD, NICOLE   Godard, Barbara, *Lovhers*, Montreal, 1986 · *Picture Theory*, Montreal, 1991.

HÉMON, LOUIS   Blake, W. H., *Maria Chapdelaine: A Tale of the Lake St. John Country*, New York, 1921 · McPhail, Andrew, *Maria Chapdelaine*, Montreal, 1921.

LAFERRIÈRE, DANY   Homel, David, *How to Make Love to a Negro*, Toronto, 1987 · *Why Must a Black Writer Write About Sex?*, Toronto, 1994.

MAILLET, ANTONINE   Stratford, Philip, *Pélagie: The Return to a Homeland*, New York, 1982.

TREMBLAY, MICHEL   Findlay, William, and Bowman, Martin, *The Guid Sisters*, Toronto, 1988 · Van Burek, John, and Glassco, Bill, *Les Belles-sœurs*, Vancouver, 1974 · *Hosanna*, Vancouver, 1974 · *Forever Yours Marie-Lou*, Vancouver, 1975.

SEE ALSO   Bednarski, B., *Autour de Ferron: Littérature, traduction, altérité*, Toronto, 1989 · Bosley, V., 'Diluting the Mixture: Translating Michel Tremblay's *Les Belles-Sœurs*', *TTR* 1 (1988), 139–45 · Delisle, J., 'The Canadian Tradition', in M. Baker, ed., *Routledge Encyclopedia of Translation Studies*, London/New York, 356–65 · Findlay, B., 'Translating Tremblay into Scots', *Theatre Research International*, 17 (1992), 138–45 · Hébert, A., and Scott, F., *Dialogue sur la traduction*, Montreal, 1970 · Homel, D., and Simon, S., eds., *Mapping Literature: The Art and Politics of Translation*, Montreal, 1988 · Simon, S., 'The Language of Cultural Difference: Figures of Alterity in Canadian Translation', in L. Venuti, ed., *Rethinking Translation*, London/New York, 1992, 159–76 · ed., *Culture in Transit: Translating the Literature of Quebec*, Montrèal, 1995 · Stratford, P., *Bibliography of Canadian Books in Translation: French to English and English to French*, Ottawa, 1977.

Africa

ANTHOLOGIES   Beier, Ulli, and Moore, Gerald, *Poetry from Africa*, Harmondsworth, 1964 [Penguin]   ·   Reed, John, and Wake, Clive, *Book of African Verse*, London, 1964   ·   *French African Verse*, London, 1972.

BÂ, MARIAMA   Bodé-Thomas, Modupé, *So Long a Letter*, London, 1981.

BEYALA, CALIXTHE   De Jager, Marjolijn, *The Sun Hath Looked upon Me*, London, 1996.

FALL, AMINITA SOW   Blair, Dorothy, *The Beggar's Strike*, London, 1981.

KANE, CHEIKH HAMIDOU   Woods, Katherine, *Ambiguous Adventure*, London, 1972.

KOUROUMA, AHMADOV   Poller, Nidra, *Monnew*, San Francisco, 1993.

LAYE, CAMARA   Kirkup, James, *Dark Child*, New York, 1954.

OUSMANE, SEMBÈNE   Price, Francis, *God's Bits of Wood*, London, 1970   ·   Wake, Clive, *Xala*, London, 1976.

OYONO, FERDINAND   Reed, John, *Houseboy*, London, 1966.

SENGHOR, LÉOPOLD SÉDAR   Reed, John, and Wake, Clive, *Selected Poems by Senghor*, Oxford, 1964.

TANSI, SONY LABOU   Wake, Clive, *The Seven Solitudes of Lorsa Lopez*, Oxford, 1995.

Caribbean

CÉSAIRE, AIMÉ   Eshelman, Clayton, and Smith, Annette, *The Collected Poetry of Aimé Césaire*, Berkeley, Calif., 1983   ·   Rosello, Mireille, with Pritchard, Anne, *Notebook of a Return to My Native Land*, Newcastle upon Tyne, 1995   ·   Snyder, Émile, *Return to My Native Land*, Paris, 1971.

GLISSANT, ÉDOUARD   Dash, J. Michael, *The Ripening*, London, 1985   ·   *Caribbean Discourse: Selected Essays*, Charlottesville, Va., 1989.

ROUMAIN, JACQUES   Hughes, Langston, and Cook, Mercer, *Masters of the Dew*, London, 1974.

h. German

1. INTRODUCTION

Probably the earliest translation into English from a German source is the 9th-c. poem of the Fall of Man known as *Genesis B*; that the Anglo-Saxon was a translation was suspected in 1875 and proved with the discovery of the original in 1894. Contemporaneous translations in the later Middle Ages are rare: Robert Mannyng's *Handlyng Synne* has a version of the clearly German story of the Dancers of Kölbigk, but his source is far less clear. Only in the Reformation period does German literature become more influential in Britain. The writings of the Reformers themselves made a social impact, and in literary terms the presence of Luther's own hymns like 'A Safe Stronghold Our God Is Still' in the modern hymnary is indicative, whilst the cautionary tale of Faust provided the impetus for Marlowe's *Doctor Faustus*.

Another hiatus follows, however, until the 19th c., the one real interruption being the European phenomenon of Goethe's *Werther* (1774), translated probably from a French version in the first instance in 1779, and with a somewhat chequered translation history until well into the 19th c. [II.h.5.ii]. Goethe's other works and most of Schiller's took longer to become available, and it is probably true to say that their dramas (and those of Kleist) have never been very important in the repertoire of the English-language theatre.

In the early 19th c. the indefatigable **Carlyle** promoted and translated not only contemporary material—the works of the Romantics—but also earlier literature. Most of the works of the Romantics were translated—E. T. A. Hoffmann perhaps in the forefront [II.h.11.i]—as indeed were the poems

of Voss, for example, whose *Luise* enjoyed a vogue in spite of the translation. The medieval interests of the Romantics and the influence of Wagner gave rise to a certain interest in medieval epic and also—though it was not very far-reaching—in German Minnesang (Thomas Lovell **Beddoes** translated Walther von der Vogelweide) and in the romance (Dante Gabriel **Rossetti** and Henry Wadsworth **Longfellow** both offered versions of a story by Hartmann). Popular and children's literature was far more influential in the 19th c., with innumerable translations of the Grimms' *Kinder- und Hausmärchen* from the middle of the century; Heinrich Hoffmann's *Struwwelpeter* (1847) clearly appealed to the Victorians, and gave us beside Peter himself also Johnny Head-in-air, although Wilhelm Busch's best-known text, *Max und Moritz*, is less familiar [see I.c.4.iii].

Of the writers in the century now seen as most important, Heine [II.h.6] was translated frequently. Büchner [II.h.4.iii] first made an impact in the English-speaking world in the 20th c. Many of the prose writers of poetic realism were translated, but remained little known. Kant, Hegel, Feuerbach, Marx, Schopenhauer, and Nietzsche were widely (if selectively) translated. The best-known and most widely influential German-language works of the earlier 19th c., however, include the textually complex story by Johann Wyss translated as *The Swiss Family Robinson*, while towards the end of the century came another work for children, Johanna Spyri's *Heidi*; both works are still read [I.c.4.iii].

In the last two decades, there has been a major

project in the United States to provide comprehensive coverage of the canon of German literature in English, *The German Library in 100 Volumes*, which is nearing completion. Before that, the influence of and interest in German remained somewhat patchy. This may be tested by collections of poetry translated from the German. Angel Flores's anthology of translations from Hölderlin to Rilke covers 14 poets, with translators of the calibre of Edwin **Morgan**, Robert **Lowell**, Michael **Hamburger**, and Randall **Jarrell**, but other works contain few German writers. Charles Tomlinson's *Oxford Book of Verse in English Translation* (1980) includes seven German poets: Walther von der Vogelweide, Goethe, Schiller, Heine, Mörike, Rilke, and Celan, and interest has focused on these. Rilke's influence has been considerable, and he has been tackled by not inconsiderable poets from time to time, as well as by some of the less competent [II.h.14], whilst Celan's 'Death Fugue' has entered the poetic consciousness [II.h.13.iii]. Other German-Jewish poets have attracted attention too, including Nelly Sachs and Else Lasker-Schüler. A trilingual anthology actually produced in Germany and combining English, French, and German war poetry, *Ohne Hass und Fahne* (No Hatred and No Flag), marked an important breakthrough in the perception of war poetry in 1959, even though a German poem from World War I became in translation the best-known lyric of World War II, Hans Leip's 'Lili Marlene'.

Drama has been dominated in the 20th c. by Brecht and, after the war, Dürrenmatt and Frisch, although most of the naturalists and the expressionists have also been translated (and to them in terms of influence must be added the 19th-c. writer Georg Büchner). Schnitzler is sometimes performed, though one of his best-known plays, *Reigen* (1900), remains known through the medium of French in the film *La Ronde*. Beside Brecht and the two Swiss writers, the presence of other German works on the English-speaking stage has been somewhat uneven. In addition to the plays mentioned below [II.h.12], one should mention Rolf Hochhuth's *Der Stellvertreter* (1963, The Representative), which attracted attention partly because of its criticism of Pius XII. Hochhuth's play about Churchill and Sikorsky, *Soldaten* (1967, Soldiers), also had a temporary *succès de scandale*.

For 20th-c. fiction [II.h.11] a recent survey of the 100 best books of the century contained three German works only: Mann's *Death in Venice*, Kafka's *Metamorphosis*, and Remarque's *All Quiet on the Western Front*. [For an important, though less popular text, Hermann Broch's *Death of Virgil*, see I.a.5.i.] Many of Mann's works—in spite of massively flawed translations—have been widely read, and the same is true of Kafka, though the translations were better. Only one of Remarque's novels was ever really popular, but it may stand as representative for many other war—or rather, antiwar—novels which enjoyed varying degrees of success. After World War II, the writings of Hermann Hesse became very popular, and the postwar writers Heinrich Böll and Günter Grass have enjoyed some vogue, but other works that have been most widely read are by postwar authors less readily accepted in the literary canon, such as Hans Habe and H. H. Kirst. KL

ANTHOLOGIES   Deppe, Wolfgang, Middleton, Christopher, and Schönherr, Herbert, eds., *Ohne Hass und Fahne | No Hatred and No Flag | Sans haine et sans drapeau*, Reinbek bei Hamburg, 1959 · Flores, Angel, *An Anthology of German Poetry from Hölderlin to Rilke*, New York, 1960 · Stockley, V., *German Literature as Known in England 1750–1830*, London, 1929.

SEE ALSO   Morgan, B. Q., *A Bibliography of German Literature in English Translation*, Madison, Wis., 1922 (new edn., London/New York, 1965) · O'Neill, P., *German Literature in English Translation: A Select Bibliography*, Toronto/London, 1981.

2. MEDIEVAL LITERATURE

i. Early Translations   Of the books produced in the eight centuries between the earliest documents and the Reformation, the first to be translated and the most influential in English come from the very end of the period. The *Narrenschiff* (1494, Ship of Fools) by the Swiss Sebastian Brant was first adapted rather freely ('some tyme addynge some tyme detractynge') by Alexander **Barclay** in 1508 from the Latin of Jacob Locher. Although Barclay claimed to have used the German, it is doubtful whether he knew any. Both the story-cycle of *Till Eulenspiegel* (1515), appearing anonymously in its earliest form as *Howleglass* in the 16th c., and that of *Fortunatus* (1509), dramatized by Thomas Dekker in 1600, were translated from Low and High German originals.

Translations of Luther's works are clearly of major importance, in particular the catechisms and the hymns, ten of which were rendered (freely) into Scots in the *Gude and Godlie Ballatis* by the **Wedderburn** Brothers as early as 1567. A final 16th-c. translation is of the Frankfurt *Historia von D. Johann Fausten* (1587, Dr Faustus), rendered vigorously in 1592 by one **P.F.** with embellishments and an even greater stress on the ultimate damnation. P.F. interrupts a letter in the text purportedly from Faustus himself with the claim that he could himself 'open . . . the diuine opinion touching the ruling of this confused Chaos, farre more than any rude Germane Author, being possessed with the diuell'. Marlowe's play came just after.

ii. Modern Translations Translations of pre-Reformation German literature belong mainly to the late 19th and 20th c., with a renewed emphasis since 1945. The Bohn and Everyman series contained only a few relevant works, but Penguin Classics in Britain, and the university presses of North Carolina and Nebraska, as well as Garland and Camden House in the USA, have brought a great deal of medieval German literature to an English-speaking audience. Faced with the choice of whether or not to imitate medieval verse-forms, many 19th-c. translations (and some recent ones) were metrical, but prose is now favoured. There has also been a corresponding shift from pseudo-medievalism to a modern style in which knights are no longer 'right doleful of their cheer'. The use of modern prose is defensible, but something is always lost—not only the regularity of the verse, but in the case of the heroic epic also the impact of formulaic repetitions as part of a style that was perceptibly archaic when the works were written down.

iii. Heroic Poetry Translations from Old High German (750–1150) are rare. There are translations of contemporary Latin works, but in German only the brief heroic father/son conflict of the *Hildes-brandslied* (Lay of Hildebrand) has commanded much interest. The *Gospel-Book* of Otfrid has never been translated, perhaps because the material is too familiar and the verse too mannered, although there is more than one version of the Old Low German Gospel-poem the *Heliand*, with its heroic overtones and closer proximity to Anglo-Saxon.

Interest was captured first by the 13th-c. heroic epic the *Nibelungenlied*, the tale of Siegfried and the fall of the Burgundians. Thomas Carlyle played a part here, as did the enthusiasm for Wagner, and the 19th c. saw a plethora of translations, the earliest (by Jonathan **Birch** in 1848) in a verse-form close to the original. Birch did not use archaizing language, though later translators did, and the demands of verse often proved too much for them,

as when William Nanson **Lettsom** in 1850 had Hagen tell his men: 'into the blood yet deeper tread every fiery flake, | In sooth this feast of Kriemhild's is ghastly merry-make'. Excessive archaizing also mars Margaret **Armour**'s otherwise accurate prose translation, well-known for a long period after its inclusion in Everyman's Library, and welcomed in 1897 by Francis Thompson as 'authentic genius, brought home to me in my mother tongue'. It is hard now to see why, and it was replaced in 1957 by a modern prose version by D. G. **Mowatt** and Hugh **Sacker**; a little later came another for Penguin by A. T. **Hatto**. A translation of the sequel, *Div Chlage* (The Lament), appeared only in 1994.

The case of the slightly later sister-epic *Kudrun* (Gudrun) is paradigmatic. In 1889 Mary Pickering **Nichols** imitated the quatrain of the original (which has a greatly extended final half-line), but the effect of her brave attempt is irretrievably of someone unable to scan. The first Everyman text by Margaret Armour used a dubiously archaic prose in which kings hold 'high-tides' rather than feasts, but three recent translations (1987–92) use modern English. These bear witness to the value placed upon this 'women's epic' in German studies, although it has still not been given wider acknowledgement.

iv. Romance The first of the romances is usually reckoned to be Heinrich von Veldeke's Troy story, the *Eneas*, but three writers dominate the high Middle Ages. Hartmann von Aue's narrative works were translated in 1983 in a convenient prose version by Rodney W. **Fisher**, and the two Arthurian poems, *Erec* and *Iwein*, have been translated separately more than once. The adaptation by Thomas Mann in 1955 of Hartmann's *Gregorius* may lie behind the interest in that work—it is subtitled 'A Medieval Oedipus Legend' in the version by Edwin **Zeydel** and Bayard **Morgan** and 'The Good Sinner' in that by Sheema **Buehne**—but attention was paid first to Hartmann's *Der arme Heinrich* (Poor Henry), paraphrased as *Henry the Leper* (1846) by Dante Gabriel **Rossetti** and imitated by **Longfellow** in *The Golden Legend* (1851).

Interest in Wagner also stimulated late 19th-c. translations of Wolfram von Eschenbach and of Gottfried von Strassburg. Wolfram's *Parzival* was put into verse by Jessie L. **Weston**, the author of *From Ritual to Romance*, in 1894, but there are modern prose versions. Wolfram's other narratives, *Willehalm* and *Titurel*, though, have been translated only fairly recently, although *Willehalm* is one of the most interesting medieval texts, with themes of racial and religious tolerance. Gottfried's *Tristan*—

the rhetorical style of which is difficult—was put into prose by Weston in 1899, but the more recent and admirably clear prose text by A. T. Hatto is regularly cited even in German-language criticism.

Growing interest in the Arthurian world in fantasy and quest literature in the 1970s and 1980s may have prompted the increase in (usually) prose translations of later medieval romances (as well as some of the early so-called minstrel epics). J. W. **Thomas**'s numerous translations include prose versions of Wirnt von Gravenberg's *Wigalois* and of the massive and convoluted Gawain-story, *Diu Crône* (The Crown) by Heinrich von dem Türlein, and other chivalric romances are now available. The moralizing story of the farmer *Helmbrecht*, which deserves to be better known, has been translated twice, and a further work which deserves more recognition is the comic poem *Der Ring* (The Ring) by Heinrich Wittenwiler, published, interestingly, together with the 15th-c. Scots comic poem *Colkelbie Sow*.

v. The Lyric The best-known German lyric poetry of the Middle Ages is the *Minnesang*, and here metrical renderings outnumber prose. The stylized subject, intricate (internal) rhyme, and necessary loss of the musical dimension are inhibiting factors, but anthologies date back to Edgar **Taylor**'s *Lays of the Minnesingers* in 1825. The success rate of the translations varies, subject as they are to the temptations of overused participial forms, archaisms and imitations of the German rhyme: *sanc*/*spranc* tempts the translator to 'sang/sprang' though the latter word means 'dance'. That example (a rare slip) is from a good representative anthology by Margaret **Richey**, who is able to maintain, for example, the deliberately light tone of a poem like Walther's 'Under der linden' (Under the Linden-Tree), a *faux-simple* (and sometimet bowdlerized) erotic poem in the mouth of a village girl. Individual poets, too, have been treated separately, including Heinrich von Morungen and the enigmatic Tannhäuser, both in scholarly editions with commentaries. In the latter case, even a highly experienced translator like J. W. Thomas can be forced into involuntary echoes of McGonagall ('Friedrich, he well deserves the name! | No-one will ever match his fame'). There is no first-class edition of the most important of the lyricists, Walther von der

Vogelweide, although Ian **Colvin**'s selection *I Saw the World* is perhaps the best.

vi. Religious Literature The prose of the great mystics, Tauler, Seuse, and especially Meister Eckhart, now attracts increasing attention, although their difficult language (when they wrote in German) long presented a barrier. Eckhart's tractates and sermons are available in various versions, and interest in women's studies has led to two translations of *Das fliessende Licht der Gottheit* (The Flowing Light of Divinity) by Mechthild von Magdenburg. The anonymous *Theologia deutsch* (Theologia Germanica), however, a late 14th-c. devotional text in the same tradition of the submission of the soul to God, printed by Luther himself in 1518, was translated in the 1850s by Susanna **Winkworth**, was given a preface by Charles Kingsley, and enjoyed considerable popularity. There are modern translations of the important dialogue of the *Ackermann aus Böhmen* (Death and the Ploughman) by Johannes von Tepl, and it is worth mentioning, finally, a recently translated and quite different theological piece from the early 14th c., the German poetical version of the apocryphal *Life of Adam* by Lutwin, which has drawn the attention of specialists in pseudepigrapha.

vii. The Reformation Luther's writings (in German and Latin) have been translated on a regular basis, and we now have the monumental St Louis edition. Tractates by other reformers such as Zwingli, Bucer, and Melanchthon are well represented in the Library of Christian Classics, the Courtenay Reformation Library, and elsewhere, although historians are increasingly showing interest in politically radical reformers like Thomas Müntzer. There are as yet few translations of Catholic opposition writers such as Thomas Murner. One might expect the enormously prolific Hans Sachs to have been widely translated, but this is not the case, and relatively few independent translations are recorded, although a version of one of his Protestant tracts dates from 1648. W. **Leighton**'s verse renderings of some of the best-known *Fastnachtspiele* (Shrovetide plays) were described in 1910 as being 'now first done into English verse', and since then only *Der farendt Schuler im Paradeiß* (The Wandering Scholar from Paradise) has appeared fairly regularly.   BOM

ANTHOLOGIES   Baylor, Michael G., *The Radical Reformation*, Cambridge, 1991 · Bithell, Jethro, *The Minnesingers*, i, London, 1909 · Mitchell, A. F., ed., *The Gude and Godlie Ballatis*, Edinburgh, 1897 · Murdoch, Brian, *The Grin of the Gargoyle*, Sawtry, UK, 1994 · Richey, Margaret F., *Medieval German Lyrics*, Edinburgh, 1958 · Seagrave, Barbara, and Thomas, J. W., *The Songs of the Minnesingers*, Urbana, Ill., 1966 · Taylor, Edgar, *Lays of the Minnesingers*, London, 1825.
BRANT, SEBASTIAN   Barclay, Alexander, *The Shyp of Folyes of the Worlde*, London, 1509; rep. Edinburgh, 1874.

ECKHART   McGinn, Bernard, Tobin, Frank, and Borgstadt, Elvira, *Meister Eckhart: Teacher and Preacher*, New York, 1986 · Walshe, M. O'C., *Sermons and Treatises*, Shaftesbury, UK, 1979–87.

FAUST-BOOK   P.F., *The Historie of the Damnable Life and Deserved Death of Doctor John Faustus*, London, 1592.

FORTUNATUS   anon., *The History of Fortunatus*, London 1676 [from Frankfurt edn. of 1550].

GOTTFRIED VON STRASSBURG   Hatto, A. T., *Tristan*, Harmondsworth, 1960 [Penguin] · Weston, Jessie L., *Tristan*, London, 1899.

HARTMANN VON AUE   Buehne, Sheema Z., *Gregorius*, New York, 1966 · Fisher, Rodney W., *The Narrative Works*, Göppingen, Germany, 1983 · Zeydel, Edwin H., and Morgan, Bayard Q., *Gregorius*, Chapel Hill, NC, 1955.

HEINRICH VON MORUNGEN   Fisher, Rodney W., *Heinrich von Morungen: An Introduction to His Songs*, San Francisco, 1996.

HEINRICH VON DEN TÜRLIN   Thomas, J. W., *The Crown*, Lincoln, Neb./London, 1989.

JOHANNES VON TEPL [or SAAZ]   Maurer, K. W., *Death and the Ploughman*, London, 1947.

KUDRUN   Armour, Margaret, *Gudrun*, London, 1928 [Everyman] · Gibbs, Marion E., and Johnson, Sidney M., *Kudrun*, New York, 1992 · McConnell, Winder, *Kudrun*, Columbia, SC, 1992 · Murdoch, B. O., *Kudrun*, London, 1987 [Everyman] · Nichols, Mary Pickering, *Gudrun*, Boston/New York, 1889.

LAMENT OF THE NIBELUNGEN   McConnell, Winder, *The Lament of the Nibelungen*, Columbia, SC, 1994.

LUTHER, MARTIN   Pelikan, Jaroslav, et al., Martin Luther, *Works*, 55 vols., St Louis, 1955–66.

LUTWIN   Halford, Mary-Bess, *Eva und Adam*, Göppingen, Germany, 1984.

MECHTHILD VON MAGDEBURG   Galvani, Christiane M., *The Flowing Light of the Divinity*, New York/London, 1991 · Menzies, Lucy, *The Revelation*, New York, 1958.

NIBELUNGENLIED   Armour, Margaret, *The Fall of the Nibelungs*, London, 1897 [Everyman] · Birch, Jonathan, *Das Nibelungen Lied; or: the Lay of the Last Nibelungers*, Berlin, 1848 · Hatto, A. T., *The Nibelungenlied*, Harmondsworth, 1965 [Penguin] · Lettsom, William Nanson, *The Nibelungenlied: The Fall of the Nibelungers*, London, 1850 · Mowatt, D. G., and Sacker H., *The Nibelungenlied*, London, 1962 [Everyman].

SACHS, HANS   Leighton, W., *Merry Tales and Three Shrovetide Plays*, London, 1910 · Scoloker, Anthony, *Goodly Disputacion between a Christen Showmaker and a Papysshe Person*, London, 1648.

TANNHÄUSER   Thomas, J. W., *Tannhäuser: Poet and Legend*, Chapel Hill, NC, 1974.

THEOLOGIA GERMANICA   Winkworth, Susanna, *Theologia Germanica*, London, 1854.

TILL EULENSPIEGEL   anon., *A Merye Jest of a Man that was Called Howleglass*, London, 1528[?].

WALTHER VON DER VOGELWEIDE   Colvin, Ian G., *60 Poems: I Saw the World*, London, 1938.

WIRNT VON GRAFENBERG   Thomas, J. W., *Wigalois*, Lincoln, Neb./London, 1977.

WITTENWILER, HEINRICH   Jones, George Fenwick, *The Ring*, Chapel Hill, NC, 1956.

WOLFRAM VON ESCHENBACH   Gibbs, Marion E., and Johnson, Sidney, *Willehalm*, Harmondsworth, 1984 [Penguin] · Hatto, A. T., *Parzival*, Harmondsworth, 1980 [Penguin] · Weston, Jessie L., *Parzival*, London, 1894.

3. POETRY 1750–1850

i. Introduction An understanding of German poetry between 1750 and 1850 in its German and international contexts requires some consideration of periodization, and particularly of the differences in periodization between German literary histories published in Germany and those published elsewhere. The 18th c. in Germany is, as in Europe in general, the age of the Enlightenment. In contrast to literary histories of other European countries, 19th-c. German philology created a 'classical period' meant to represent an aesthetic high point of German literature and to articulate a new national consciousness most visible in the works of Goethe and Schiller in the late 18th and early 19th c. In essence this classical period of German literature is conceived as apolitical; it maintains a philosophy of aesthetic immanence and places an emphasis on 'aesthetic education'

(Schiller) as a direct response and alternative to the French Revolution. Romanticism shares some of these characteristics, but in a more radical form. German romanticism is a relatively short-lived phenomenon (1796/7–1832), and in spite of the fact that it is part of a general European movement, it has strong national connotations in and for Germany.

In order to understand the ideological function of the creation of a 'classical period' of German literature in the late 18th c., it is useful to look at the first stanza of Schiller's 'Ode an die Freude' (Hymn to Joy), perhaps his most famous poem due to its use in Beethoven's Ninth Symphony:

> Joy, thou goddess, fair, immortal,
> Offspring of Elysium,
> Mad with rapture, to the portal

Of thy holy fame we come!
Fashion's laws, indeed, may sever,
But thy magic joins again;
All mankind are brethren ever
'Neath thy mild and gentle reign.
(tr. E. Arnold-Foster, *Works*, iii, 25)

A reading of these lines as an example of 'classical' German literature would no doubt emphasize the importance of 'joy' as an ahistorical, eternal value best illustrated by antiquity. However, one could also read these lines as exemplary for the ideology of the Enlightenment, which still dominated the European scene in Schiller's day. The questioning of 'fashion's laws' is typical for enlightened tolerance. The line 'All mankind are brethren ever' openly articulates enlightened cosmopolitanism and is a clear anticipation of the French Revolution's ideal of fraternity.

ii. Schiller Johann Christoph Friedrich von Schiller led a largely unexciting life; he initially attended military school, then studied medicine and worked as an army physician, but eventually left the military in order to become a poet. In 1794, while working as a professor of history at the University of Jena, he became acquainted with Goethe [II.h.5], and towards the end of his life he moved to Weimar in order to be nearer to him. Best known for his theatre pieces (*Don Carlos*, *Wilhelm Tell*, *Die Jungfrau von Orleans* (The Maid of Orleans) [II.h.4.iii]) and aesthetic treatises, Schiller also produced a significant amount of poetry.

A concise overview of Schiller's life and work can be found in Thomas **Carlyle**'s very accessible and—despite its 'Calvinist strain' (Ewen 1932)—appealing *Life of Schiller*. Carlyle's biography offers an idealized but nevertheless friendly and fairly accurate portrait, stressing the hardships in Schiller's life as well as his enlightened optimism. By no means does Carlyle attempt to make Schiller into a national icon. Idealizing tendencies dominate in Schiller's English and American reception, especially in the first half of the 19th c., when he was far more popular than even Goethe. The early reception of Schiller in England and the USA is quite well documented. Due to the German ancestry of many Americans, Schiller reception and Schiller celebrations in the USA often had nationalist overtones—especially the festivities of Schiller's 100th birthday in 1859.

The most serious collection of Schiller's poetry is available in volume iii of *The Works of Friedrich Schiller*, edited by Nathan Haskell Dole, translated by E. P. **Arnold-Forster**, and published at the turn of the century simultaneously in England and the USA. This edition offers very careful translations of form as well as content, although the language may strike us today as antiquated. The translator downplays in a brief preface the importance of this translation, and hopes the edition may also be useful for Germans studying English.

The most ambitious contemporary translation of Schiller's work is without doubt the three-volume edition of *Friedrich Schiller: Poet of Freedom*. This edition of Schiller's works was published under the auspices of the Schiller Institute, which describes itself as an 'institute for republican foreign policy with a special interest in improving ties between the United States and western Europe'. The preface by translator William F. **Wertz**, Jr. leaves little doubt concerning its intentions: 'Humanity will not survive without a renaissance, precisely because it is only a renaissance which can defeat pragmatic philistinism, which currently dooms civilization.' Not surprisingly, Wertz emphasizes the 'idea content' of Schiller's poetry. The foreword to the third volume, which appeared shortly after the Berlin Wall fell, emphasizes the importance of the Schiller Institute as a 'major player' in the eastern European revolutions of 1989. Such comments are no doubt well-meaning, but unquestionably misleading regarding Schiller's current importance as well as the intentions behind his work. The translations are easy to read, but take a fair amount of liberty in comparison to the original text.

iii. Klopstock In addition to Schiller and Goethe, one other 18th-c. German poet has attracted attention outside of the German-speaking world. Friedrich Gottlieb Klopstock is best known for *Der Messias* (1748–73, The Messiah). This is an epic poem, a narrative of the life of Jesus Christ divided into 15 cantos. The poem is a deeply religious work strongly influenced by the author's pietist beliefs, although occasionally it manifests strains of Enlightenment thought. Numerous editions of English translations exist that date to the late 18th and early 19th c., although some pre-date Klopstock's completion of the text and are therefore fragmentary. Catherine **Head**'s English verse translation of 1826 (earlier editions were primarily in prose) is remarkably easy to read, and also contains a list of abridgements made by the translator in comparison to the German original.

iv. Hölderlin Johann Friedrich Hölderlin's poetry, as well as his entire *œuvre*, is difficult to classify within any particular literary period. Gerhart Hoffmeister echoes a common characterization of his work when he states that it constitutes a 'private neoclassical mythology' (Hoffmeister 1990), a description particularly apt for texts such as *Hyperion* (the first volume of which was published in 1797) and the epic poem *Brot und Wein* (1800–1, Bread and Wine). For all its reliance on the poetic forms of antiquity, however, Hölderlin's poetry was marked by romantic aesthetic and contemporary political convictions, and the same may be said of much of his poetry's reception in Germany and in the English-speaking world.

Hölderlin's pantheism, idealist philosophy, and sympathy for the French Revolution are evident in his poetry until and even after he began to suffer most acutely from schizophrenia (from approximately 1805). Michael **Hamburger** refers to the poems and fragments written during this period as Hölderlin's 'most "modern"', as they tend to rely on invocation rather than to 'present a sequence of arguments or metaphors' (Hamburger 1966). Even in these late years, however, Hölderlin's attention to language still evinces traces of the care taken in his own prior word-for-word translations of Sophocles and Pindar. Hamburger's translations and commentary emphasize these aspects of Hölderlin's poetic production rather than engaging in an idealization or mystification of the author.

Hamburger is responsible for translating nearly all of Hölderlin's poetical works into English, and his editions contain much reflection on how the art of translation alters and shapes poetry in general, and Hölderlin's unconventional lexical and rhythmic choices in particular. The techniques of hypostasis and apostrophe, for instance, that Hölderlin frequently employed are difficult to render not only into English but into a diction comprehensible in a contemporary cultural context. More than 50 years of engagement with Hölderlin's texts on Hamburger's part have, however, resulted in a body of English work exemplary for its position between a translation practice in which the expression of metre and vocabulary in meaningful English is privileged and one that prefers to preserve German's conciseness and abstraction above all. As Hamburger states, this position has evolved over years of work, as he has moved 'towards a kind of translation that is neither free imitation nor strict metaphrase . . . but something in between. . . . I do not appropriate my text to the extent of transposing it into my own idiom, my own favourite verse forms and my own favourite imagery, but treat it as a phenomenon different in kind from anything I could ever produce.' It is indeed the combination of Hölderlin's radical 'strangeness' with his rigorous adherence to Greek metrics and idea content that is communicated in Hamburger's seminal versions.

Here the beginning of his *Bread and Wine*:

Round us the town is at rest; the street, in pale lamplight, grows quiet
And, their torches ablaze, coaches rush through and away.
People go home to rest, replete with the day and its pleasures,
There to weigh up in their heads, pensive, the gain and the loss,
Finding the balance good; stripped bare now of grapes and of flowers,
As of their hand-made goods, quiet the market stalls lie.

v. Novalis Friedrich von Hardenberg took the pen name Novalis in 1799, on the publication of his first collection of fragments, *Blüthenstaub* (Pollen). His poetry retains that fragmentary quality which is a leading formal and substantial characteristic of romanticism in general and of early German romanticism in particular. The group of poets and authors with whom Novalis met and studied in Jena in the last years of the 18th c. was formative for a movement that took its aesthetic and philosophical cue from Rousseau and Shakespeare, among other non-Germans, but that has never been fully conceptualized away from its specifically German manifestation.

Carlyle, who brought much German poetry to an English-speaking audience, was Novalis's first English translator. His critical commentary exhibits the combination of awe and frustration common among German-speaking and foreign readers of Novalis alike. Novalis is 'a man of the most indisputable talent, poetical and philosophical' who is prone to engage in 'often too obscure speculations' that do not translate particularly well. While it is difficult to dispute the opacity of much of Novalis's poetry, Carlyle's translations, together with those of Mabel **Cotterell** and Charles **Passage**, render seminal works such as the 'Hymnen an die Nacht' (1800, Hymns to the Night) into a clear English that preserves Novalis's radical, even reactionary pantheism and idealism while communicating the qualities of self-reflection and self-criticism that are also present in his poetry.

As with Schiller's 'Ode to Joy', the 'Hymns to the Night' can be interpreted strictly in the context of a particular literary period (in this case, of early German romanticism) or in a wider sense, as part of a general political and historical movement (in this case, that of a reaction against Enlightenment thought). While the translators reviewed here do not analyse Novalis's position within romanticism, their tendency to adhere as closely as possible to

German diction and metre help indirectly to reveal the author's ability to challenge as well as to conform to an emerging aesthetics that intended to embrace and eventually to submerge all that was explicitly political in the wake of the French Revolution.

Perhaps the most interesting modern translations of Novalis's poetry are available within English-language studies such as Géza von **Molnar**'s *Romantic Vision, Ethical Context: Novalis and Artistic Autonomy* and Kristin **Pfefferkorn**'s *Novalis: A Romantic's Theory of Language and Poetry*. The partial and complete translations of poems offered by these scholars are presented within the context of specific arguments about Novalis's work, but their lack of 'objectivity' is acknowledged, and their interpretations bring Novalis and the early German romantics into the present in a lively and meaningful way.

vi. Mörike Relatively few of Eduard Mörike's works are available in English, but there are 40 poems in N. K. **Cruickshank**'s and G. F. **Cunningham**'s *Poems by Eduard Mörike*. After retiring from the clergy at the age of 39, Mörike devoted himself to poetry (especially after 1845), preferring classical metre and shunning explicit philosophical or political content. The cycle 'Bilder aus Bebenhausen' (1863, Pictures from Bebenhausen) is representative of his anti-didactic, symbol-oriented style and is in part responsible for his classification as a poet of the 'Biedermeier' period—although his work can also be located under the headings 'classical' and 'romantic'. Margaret **Mare** eschews most of these categories in favour of presenting Mörike's biography and several poems in *Eduard Mörike: The Man and the Poet*. Together with Helga **Slessarev**, author of the Twayne World Authors Series volume on Mörike (which also contains translations of several poems), Mare notes Mörike's interest in music. This was reflected in his composition of song lyrics, some of which are translated in a collection of authors of German *lieder* edited by J. W. **Smeed** in 1992.

vii. Conclusion Some additional German poets from the period 1750–1850 can be found in the few available anthologies of German poetry listed below. In general, judging by the small number of translations published in the last two decades, the interest in translating German poetry of this period seems to have diminished. A further desideratum would be a study placing the poetry discussed here in a European context, and exploring for instance the differences in periodization between German literary histories and their non-German counterparts. In a recent study of Goethe's poetry, David Wellbery has shown that the broader European conceptualization of romanticism may lead to interesting insights if applied to 'pre-romantic' German poetry, perhaps even leading to a new understanding of gaps and continuities between German classicism, Enlightenment thought, and European romanticism.   LJ and CN

Anthologies   Blackwell, Jeannine, Zantop, Susanne, et al., *Bitter Healing; German Women Writers 1700–1830: An Anthology*, Lincoln, Neb., 1990 · Flores, Angel, ed., *An Anthology of German Poetry from Hölderlin to Rilke in English Translation*, New York, 1960 [Anchor] · Gode, Alexander, Ungar, Frederick, et al., *Anthology of German Poetry through the 19th Century*, New York, 1964 · Hinze, Klaus-Peter, and Trawick, Leonard M., *An Anthology of German Literature of the Romantic Era and Age of Goethe*, New York, 1993 · Kaufmann, Walter, *Twenty German Poets: A Bilingual Collection*, New York, 1962 [Modern Library] · Thomas, J. W., *German Verse From the 12th to the 20th Century in English Translation*, Chapel Hill, NC, 1963.

HÖLDERLIN, FRIEDRICH   Hamburger, Michael, *Hölderlin: His Poems Translated By Michael Hamburger With a Critical Study*, London, 1942; rep. 1952 · *Selected Verse*, London, 1961; rep. 1986 · *Poems and Fragments*, London, 1966; rep. 1980 · Leishman, J. B., *Selected Poems of Friedrich Hölderlin*, London, 1954 · Middleton, Christopher, *Friedrich Hölderlin, Eduard Mörike: Selected Poems*, Chicago / London, 1972 · Sieburth, Richard, *Hölderlin: Hymns and Fragments*, Princeton, NJ, 1984.

KLOPSTOCK, FRIEDRICH GOTTLIEB   anon. (Catherine Head), *The Messiah: A Poem*, 2 vols., London, 1826.

MÖRIKE, EDUARD   Cruickshank, N. K., and Cunningham, G. F., *Poems by Eduard Mörike*, London, 1959 · Mare, Margaret, *Eduard Mörike: The Man and the Poet*, London, 1957 · Slessarev, Helga, *Eduard Mörike*, New York, 1970 · Smeed, J. W., ed., *Famous Poets, Neglected Composers: Songs to Lyrics by Goethe, Heine, Mörike and Others*, Madison, Wis., 1992.

NOVALIS (FRIEDRICH VON HARDENBERG)   Cotterell, Mabel, *Hymns to the Night*, London, 1948 · Géza, Molnar von, *Romantic Vision, Ethical Context: Novalis and Artistic Autonomy*, Minneapolis, 1987 · Hastie, W., *Hymns and Thoughts on Religion*, Edinburgh, 1888 · Hilty, Palmer, *Henry von Ofterdingen*, New York, 1964 · Passage, Charles E., *Hymns to the Night and Other Selected Writings*, New York, 1960 · Pfefferkorn, Kristin, *Novalis: A Romantic's Theory of Language and Poetry*, New Haven, Conn., 1988.

SCHILLER, JOHANN CHRISTOPH FRIEDRICH   Arnold-Foster, E. P., and Pinkerton, Percy E., *The Works of Friedrich*

Schiller, iii, Boston, Mass., 1902 · Carlyle, Thomas, *The Life of Friedrich Schiller: Comprehending an Examination of his Works*, London, 1845 · Wertz, William F. Jr., et al., *Friedrich Schiller: Poet of Freedom*, 3 vols., New York/Washington, DC, 1985–90.

SEE ALSO   Carlyle, T., 'Novalis', in *Critical and Miscellaneous Essays*, ii, London, 1869 · Ewen, F., ed., *The Prestige of Schiller in England 1788–1859*, New York, 1932 · Hoffmeister, G., ed., *European Romanticism: Literary Cross-Currents, Modes, and Models*, Detroit, 1990 · Parry, E. C., ed., *Friedrich Schiller in America: A Contribution to the Literature of the Poet's Centenary, 1905*, Philadelphia, 1905 · Wellbery, D., *The Specular Moment: Goethe's Early Lyric and the Beginnings of Romanticism*, Stanford, Calif., 1996.

4. DRAMA 1770–1850

i. Lessing The flowering of German drama in the late 18th c. particularly during the *Sturm und Drang* (Storm and Stress) period, which ran from 1771 to 1778—owes much to the philosophical and aesthetic work undertaken by Gotthold Ephraim Lessing, who led from the front insofar as he wrote several plays of his own. Although Lessing made a convincing case for German playwrights to adopt Shakespeare as their model rather than 17th-c. French dramatists such as Racine, English-speaking culture has largely failed to repay the compliment by translating or performing even his major works regularly.

Not that attempts have not been made. As early as 1786, J. J. **Johnstone** translated *Minna von Barnhelm* (1767) as *The Disbanded Officer*. Serious work began in 1878, with Ernest **Bell**'s translation of *Miss Sara Sampson* (1755), which Lessing titled in English, as *Sara*. Whilst it sounds Victorian, this is still lively enough to have helped make a success of Cheek by Jowl's touring production of the play in Britain in 1990. Bell also edited two volumes of Lessing's plays, published in 1900. They include his spirited account of *Minna von Barnhelm*, which is sometimes unfairly—and inaccurately—called the only German comedy. Other translations, by R. Dillon **Boylan**, of *Nathan der Weise* (1783, Nathan the Wise) and *Emilia Galotti* (1772) are informative but rather leaden and very much of their period.

Even allowing for less than inspired translation, it might well be argued that *Nathan the Wise* is more a philosophical treatise on religious tolerance than a vital piece of theatre. *Emilia Galotti* is better known and has been translated several times since the 1950s, especially in the USA. The fact that Lessing can work in English is shown by the accurate and energetic translation by Anthony **Meech** of *Minna von Barnhelm*, performed at Hull University in 1979.

ii. Sturm und Drang The leading playwright of the 1770s in Germany, Jakob Michael Reinhold Lenz, has been performed in Britain only sporadically. As so often with European dramatists,

the Gate Theatre in Notting Hill, London, and the Citizens Theatre, Glasgow, have pioneered Lenz's plays in Britain. *Die Soldaten* (written 1774–5, premièred 1863) exists in a translation by Robert David **MacDonald** as *The Soldiers*, which is stylish but has some rather self-conscious, dated expressions. *Der neue Menoza* (written 1776) has been performed as *The New Menoza* in a translation by Meredith **Oakes** which, although speakable, could have taken more risks. Lenz's best-known play is *Der Hofmeister* (1778), generally translated as *The Tutor*. The translation by Anthony Meech, as performed by the Gate and published in 1993, is more vigorous than that by Betty Senk **Waterhouse**, published in 1986, but might be more theatrically effective with a lighter ironical touch.

Other playwrights of the *Sturm und Drang*—apart from Lessing and Goethe—such as Friedrich Maximilian Klinger, Heinrich Wilhelm von Gerstenberg, Heinrich Leopold Wagner, and Friedrich Müller—have yet to appear in convincing English translations.

iii. Late Eighteenth and Early Nineteenth Centuries All the major plays by the leading German dramatist, Friedrich Schiller, exist in English translation. Schiller interested translators from the late 18th c. on. The earliest recorded, though not readily available, translation is that attributed to Lord **Woodhouslee** in 1795, *Die Räuber* (1781, The Robbers). Along with other translations published up to 1799, largely in small magazines, this has not stood the test of time.

The first easily obtainable edition, published in 1847, of *The Historical Dramas* contains translations of *Don Carlos* (read 1784, published 1787) by R. Dillon Boylan, *Maria Stuart* (1800) by Joseph **Mellish**, *Die Jungfrau von Orleans* (1801, The Maid of Orleans) by Anna **Swanwick**, and *Die Braut von Messina* (1803, The Bride of Messina) by A. **Lodge**. In 1901 an edition of Schiller's plays included tame, if not lame, translations of *Wallensteins Lager* (1799, The Camp of Wallenstein) by James **Churchill**, and of

Wilhelm Tell (1804) by Sir Theodore **Martin**. Another edition that year included *Fiesko* (1784), and *Kabale und Liebe* (1784, Love and Intrigue). The nearest to a translation credit in this 1901 George Bell edition is 'translated by various hands'—a regrettable but by no means unique case of enforced translator-invisibility.

This 1901 volume is also the first readily available edition of the translation by Samuel Taylor **Coleridge** of two parts of *Wallenstein* (1799–1800), *Die Piccolomini* and *Wallensteins Tod*, as *The Piccolomini* and *The Death of Wallenstein*. He made the translations, which are poetically superb, in 1800, from a prompter's copy in manuscript. Extra or altered passages which appeared in printed editions of Schiller's play (some 250 lines) were translated by G. F. **Richardson**, and included in the 1901 edition.

Recent significant translations include those by F. J. **Lamport** (convincing if not inspired), Robert David MacDonald (always stylish and resourceful), Jeremy **Sams** (who takes some short cuts to sound theatrically effective), Stephen **Spender** (whose translation is articulate but feels its age), and Hilary Collier **Sy-quia**, adapted by Peter **Oswald**, (whose efforts to retain metre lead to some stiffness).

Never afraid of intercultural or cross-genre adventures in the theatre, Heinrich von Kleist took a classical theme treated by Molière for his tragicomedy, *Amphitryon* (1807), which has appeared in an uninspiring translation by Marion W. **Sonnenfeld**. F. J. Lamport has given a livelier account of *Penthesilea* (written 1807, premièred 1876). These and two other major plays, *Prinz Friedrich von Homburg* (published 1821) and the comedy *Der Zerbrochene Krug* (1808), appear as *The Prince of Homburg* and *The Broken Jug* in a volume of translations by Martin **Greenberg**. His renderings convey the sense accurately without making one's pulse race. A funny, inventive, and accurate recreation of Kleist's comedy is the translation and adaptation into Yorkshire idiom by Blake **Morrison**, *The Cracked Pot*, first performed in 1995.

Also in 1995, a still unpublished translation of *Amphitryon* by Amanda **Holden** was performed at the Gate. A whole volume of Kleist, translated and edited by David **Constantine**, published in 1997, confirms Constantine's view: 'There are writers we cannot do without and Kleist is one of them.' His translations of *Amphitryon*, *The Broken Jug*, and *Prince Friedrich of Homburg* are academically convincing but may play less than overwhelmingly.

If the complexities of Kleist's dramatic language could be tackled with the same resourcefulness and

élan as prose works by Kafka—and Kleist himself— a major new dramatist would be (re)discovered for the English-speaking stage. The power of Kleist's elliptical but reverberating style was well realized in a screenplay, by James **Saunders**, of the prose work *Michael Kohlhaas* (published in full in 1810). The haunting poetry of *Das Käthchen von Heilbronn* (1810) emerged strongly from a translation as *Kate of Heilbronn* by Peter **Tegel**, which was broadcast in Britain on Radio 3 but remains unpublished.

From the 1920s onwards, the plays of Georg Büchner have been translated into English so many times that they have assumed almost as much importance to English-speaking as to German-speaking dramatists. Less than totally convincing translations of all three plays have been made by Geoffrey **Dunlop** and Victor **Price**. More recently, Howard **Brenton** and Jane **Fry** have made a dramatically effective translation of *Dantons Tod* (written 1835, premièred 1902, Danton's Death). Anthony Meech has rendered the comedy *Leonce und Lena* (written 1836–7, premièred 1895, Leonce and Lena) into English that is always plausible and often poetic.

Woyzeck (written as a dramatic fragment 1835–7, published in various forms 1879, 1922, 1967, first significant performance 1914) has been translated or adapted several times into English. A far-reaching adaptation, which includes original material, by John **Mackendrick** fills out the sparse text at the expense of Büchner's expressive lacunae. The version by Gregory **Motton**, also a playwright, is punchy and persuasive. Büchner's dramatically dense, allusive, and atmospheric language works well in English, and the success of Werner Herzog's 1979 film proves that close adherence to the content, whatever scene order is adopted, can form the basis of a dramatically resonant translation.

Though born in the same year as Büchner, 1813, Friedrich Hebbel is much less known in the English-speaking world. A useful volume of his plays, including *Judith* (published 1841), *Herodes und Mariamne* (1849, Herod and Mariamne) and *Gyges und sein Ring* (published 1856, Gyges and His Ring), translated by Marion W. Sonnenfeld, offers a plausible basis on which to build. His two best-known social dramas, *Maria Magdalene* (1846) and *Agnes Bernauer* (1855), have yet to be translated effectively, though images of King Candaules in *Gyges* have recently appeared in the film of Michael Ondaatje's *The English Patient* and the BBC television adaptation of Anthony Powell's *Dance to the Music of Time*.

Franz Grillparzer also re-creates classical sources in a modern, dramatic way in *Sappho* (1818), which Arthur **Burkhard** has translated, together with other plays well-known in the German-speaking theatre, including *Ein Bruderzwist in Habsburg* (written 1824, premièred 1872, Family Strife in Habsburg), *Des Meeres und der Liebe Wellen* (1831,

Hero and Leander), and *Medea* (1821), which forms the third part of his trilogy, *Das Goldene Vliess* (The Golden Fleece). Grillparzer's individual combination of historical realism and poetic allusion should prove no more an obstacle to sensitive translation than the plays of Schiller, which are much better known in English. AV

BÜCHNER, GEORG   Brenton, Howard, Fry, Jane, Mackendrick, John, and Meech, Anthony, *Complete Plays* [*Danton's Death*, *Leonce and Lena*, *Woyzeck*], London, 1987 · Motton, Gregory, *Woyzeck*, London, 1996.

GRILLPARZER, FRANZ   Burkhard, Arthur, *Family Strife in Habsburg*, Yarmouth Port, Mass., 1940/50 · *Sappho*, Yarmouth Port, 1953 · *Medea*, Yarmouth Port, 1956 · *Hero and Leander*, Yarmouth Port, 1962.

HEBBEL, FRIEDRICH   Sonnenfeld, W. Marion, *Three Plays*, Lewisburg, Pa., 1974.

VON KLEIST, HEINRICH   Constantine, David, *Selected Writings*, London, 1997 · Greenberg, Martin, *Five Plays*, New Haven, Conn., 1988 · Morrison, Blake, *The Cracked Pot*, London, 1996.

LENZ, JAKOB MICHAEL REINHOLD   MacDonald, Robert David, Meech, Anthony, and Oakes, Meredith, *Three Plays*, London, 1993 · Waterhouse, Betty Senk, *Five Plays of the Sturm und Drang*, Lanham, Md./London, 1986 [includes *The Soldiers* and *The Tutor*].

LESSING, GOTTHOLD EPHRAIM   Bell, Ernest, ed., *The Dramatic Works of G. E. Lessing*, 2 vols., London, 1900 [includes *Nathan the Wise* and *Emilia Galotti*, tr. R. Dillon Boylan, as well as *Sara* and *Minna von Barnhelm*, tr. Ernest Bell], London, 1900 · Bell, Ernest, *Sara*; Meech, Anthony, *Minna von Barnhelm*, Bath, UK, 1990.

SCHILLER, FRIEDRICH   Boylan, R. Dillon, *Don Carlos*, Lodge, A., *The Bride of Messina*, Mellish, Joseph, *Mary Stuart*, Swanwick, Anna, *The Maid of Orleans*, in *The Works of F. Schiller: Historical Dramas*, London, 1847 · Churchill, James, *Wallenstein's Camp*, Coleridge, Samuel Taylor, *The Piccolomini* and *The Death of Wallenstein*, Martin, Sir Theodore, *Wilhelm Tell* (rep. from 1894), in *Schiller's Dramatic Works*, London, 1901 · Lamport, F. J., *The Robbers; Wallenstein*, Harmondsworth, 1979 [Penguin] · MacDonald, Robert David, *The Robbers*, London, 1987 · *Mary Stuart and Joan of Arc*, London, 1995 · Sams, Jeremy, *Mary Stuart*, London, 1996 · Spender, Stephen, *Mary Stuart*, London, 1959/74.

SEE ALSO   *German Plays in English Translation: A Stocklist of Texts Available in Goethe-Institute Libraries*, London, 1997.

5. GOETHE

i. Introduction In his essay on *Alemannic Poetry* (1805), Johann Wolfgang von Goethe wrote that it was a great step towards culture for a nation when it translated foreign works into its own language. Later, he argued that the concept of national literature was out of date, speaking instead of *Weltliteratur*. And to one of his English translators, he wrote that 'whatever we might say about the inadequacy of translation, it is and will remain one of the most important and worthiest concerns in what goes on in the world'. Himself a translator of several works, in No. 299 of his *Maxims and Reflections* (1826) he less flatteringly compared translators to 'busy pimps', extolling the charms of some thinly veiled beauty, and exciting an irresistible urge for the original.

In his Notes and Essays on the *West-österlicher Divan* (1819, West-Eastern Divan), itself influenced by the Persian poet Hâfez [II.q.2.ii], Goethe developed a theory of translation that envisaged three ascending levels. First is the simple prose translation. By avoiding the technicalities of poetry, prose offers a direct way into the foreign text but also cul-

tivates a 'higher mood', and Goethe cited Luther's translation of the Bible as an example. (In his autobiography, book xi, Goethe commented that what was truly characteristic of a poet was what remained when he was translated into prose.) Secondly, the 'parodistic' level seeks equivalences in the target language for aspects of the text under translation. Finally, at the highest level, the translation strives to make itself identical with the original. Goethe called for such a translation to be made of the Sanskrit play *Śakuntalā* [II.l.2.v], which he had read in 1830 in de Chézy's bilingual French version.

Under the general editorship of Victor Lange, Eric A. Blackall, and Cyrus Hamlin, the Suhrkamp/Insel 12-volume edition of *Goethe's Collected Works* offers the modern reader an authoritative translation of his main texts. Yet some older translations remain important in their own right, and some have heavily influenced the reception of Goethe in the English-speaking world. In this entry, texts are discussed in chronological order of publication.

ii. Early Writings Goethe's earliest, and most Shakespearean, play, *Götz von Berlichingen* (1771), was translated into English by Sir Walter **Scott** in 1799 as *Goetz of Berlichingen with the Iron Hand*. Despite the extreme inaccuracy of Scott's translation, it captured much of the flavour of Goethe's play and helped mediate the 'Storm and Stress' style to England. In 1965 the play was adapted for the English stage, by the Yorkshire playwright John **Arden**, as *Ironhand*, 'in the nature of a free paraphrase' and with a modern audience in mind.

Certainly Goethe's most important work (other than *Faust*) in terms of its British and, indeed, European reception was *Die Leiden des jungen Werther* (1774). The first English translation, *The Sorrows of Werter* (1779), ascribed to Daniel **Malthus**, was made from the French version, and was quickly succeeded by other translations in 1786, 1789, 1799, 1801, 1802, and 1809, establishing Goethe as 'the author of *Werther*'. As well as the inevitable difficulties arising from a translation, Malthus's version is further marred by the omission of several important sections. On the other hand, the anonymous translator of 1786 inserts extra footnotes and discourses. John **Gifford**'s translation of 1789, also made from the French, is nevertheless much more accurate, and the anonymous translator of 1799 fails to improve on it. Although he even claimed to be a personal friend of Charlotte and Werther, William **Render** (1801) offered a version that deviates widely from the original and omits key passages, but it introduced *Werther* to America.

The cult of 'Wertherism', as young men began wearing the characteristic blue coat and yellow breeches of the hero and committing suicide, allegedly in imitation of Werther, was attacked by Thackeray in his famous parody of one of the most well-known scenes from the novel in his verses:

> Werther had a love for Charlotte,
> Such as words could never utter,
> Would you know how he first met her?
> She was cutting bread and butter.

Of modern translations, the version by Victor **Lange** (1949) can be recommended for clarity and accuracy.

iii. After the Italian Journey In 1786 Goethe undertook the first of his two visits to Italy, which played a vital role in helping him formulate his mature aesthetic theory. The first English translation of his *Italienische Reise* (1816–17) was undertaken by the Revd A. J. W. **Morrison** and Charles **Nisbet** as *Goethe's Travels in Italy* (1883), and included the final segment from his autobiography and the

music of an Italian ballad. Under the title *Italian Journey* (1962), the excellent translation by W. H. **Auden** and Elizabeth **Mayer** serves as an illustration of Goethe's continuing interest to major English poets in the 20th c., and has itself contributed to reshaping the reception of Goethe in the English-speaking world over the last 30 years.

The historical drama *Egmont* (1787), completed after Goethe's return from Italy, marks the shift from the early 'Storm and Stess' period to the classical aesthetic he had elaborated abroad, although he chose vigorous prose rhythms rather than blank verse. However, it remained untranslated until 1841, even though *Clavigo* (1774) and *Stella* (1776) both appeared in anonymous translations in 1798. More recently, the translations by Michael **Hamburger** and Frank **Lamport** can be recommended.

The tragedy *Iphigenie auf Tauris* (1787) represents the first major example of Goethe's classical style, and was translated by William **Taylor** (1765–1836) in 1793. As might be expected of the translator of the ballads of Bürger and Lessing's *Nathan der Weise* and the author of a three-volume *Historic Survey of German Poetry*, the translation offers a fine version of Goethe's play. In a letter to Goethe on 31 January 1829, H. Crabb Robinson wrote: 'The slow progress your works have till now been making among my countrymen has been a source of unavailing regret. Taylor's *Iphigenia in Tauris*, as it was the first, so it remains the best version of any of your longer poems.' For a modern translation, see John **Prudhoe**'s careful *Iphigenia in Tauris* or David **Luke**'s blank-verse rendering (in *Collected Works*, vol. viii).

On the flyleaf of *Iphigenie*, Goethe wrote, 'All human sins are redeemed by pure humanity.' The rounded and generous nature of Goethe's conception of humanity emerged in his *Römische Elegien*, a cycle of 20 poems in classical metre composed between 1788 and 1790 after his second visit to Italy. First translated into English in 1876 in Boston, the eroticism of the *Roman Elegies* hindered their distribution whilst adding to their fame; David Luke's bilingual version permits the reader uncensored access to the poet's experience of Roman churches, palaces, and boudoirs. But it is perhaps less the fact that, after Rome, portraits of Goethe show (as W. H. Auden claimed) 'the self-assured face of a man who has known sexual satisfaction' that matters, than the statement and enactment in these poems of an aesthetic summarized in a famous couplet (translated here by Michael Hamburger):

Only thus do I appreciate marble; reflecting, comparing,
See with an eye that can feel, feel with a hand that can see.

The translation (1827) by Charles **des Voeux** (1802–33) of the play *Torquato Tasso* (1790) was undertaken in Weimar during his stay there as a diplomat, and benefited from the encouragement of Goethe himself. John Prudhoe's translation offers a good modern version, as does the extremely accurate translation by Michael Hamburger.

Part of Goethe's response to the French Revolution, the epic poem *Hermann und Dorothea* (1797), was first translated by Thomas **Holcroft** (1745–1809) in 1801, but his choice of blank verse and trochees fails to do justice to Goethe's hexameters and Homeric epithets. Strangely enough, Goethe approved of Holcroft's version (letter to Holcroft of 29 May 1801); a prose version appeared in 1805. The hexameter version by David Luke remains faithful to the original text in almost all respects.

Although a complete translation of *Die Wahlverwandtschaften* (1809, Elective Affinities) was not made until 1854 (translated by R. D. **Boylan**), modern readers can choose between the versions by Judith **Ryan** (discussed by J. Hillis Miller in a review essay that raises many pertinent problems of translating Goethe's prose), which tends towards simplification, and by David **Constantine**, which tries to capture the subtle nuances of this difficult text.

Goethe's attempt to achieve a synthesis between Occident and Orient, the *West-Eastern Divan*, long eluded translators. Following the versions by John **Weiss** (1818–79) and Edward **Dowden** (1843–1913), John **Whaley**'s bilingual version of 1974 succeeds in conveying the formal economy and conceptual complexity of this cycle, characteristic of the compressed style of Goethe's late writings. For example, Whaley renders the first line of 'Selige Sehnsucht' ('Blessed Longing'):

> Sagt es niemand, nur den Weisen,
> Weil die Menge gleich verhöhnet,
> Das Lebendge will ich preisen,
> Das nach Flammentod sich sehnet

as:

> Tell it no one, only sages,
> For the crowd derides such learning:
> Life I praise through all the ages
> Which for death in flames is yearning.

iv. Autobiography, *Wilhelm Meister*, and Science
The history of the translations of his autobiography and of the two *Wilhelm Meister* novels exemplifies the extent to which Goethe has consistently suffered from mistranslation. Even before the first translation had appeared, Goethe's major autobiographical statement, *Dichtung und Wahrheit*

(1812–32, Poetry and Truth), was attacked by an anonymous critic in the *Edinburgh Review*, 26 (1816) as 'not unentertaining though disfigured by the most puerile vanity and affectation'. The first anonymous English translation, *Memoirs of Goëthe [sic] Written by Himself* (1824) did little to help Goethe's cause, based as it was on the poor French translation by Aubert de Vitry. In his *Essay on Goethe* (1828), Carlyle wrote: 'It is our duty also to remark, if anyone be still unaware of it, that the *Memoirs of Goethe*, published some years ago in London, can have no real concern with this Autobiography.' And when the translation by Parke **Godwin** (1816–1904), John Henry **Hopkins** (1820–91), Charles A. **Dana** (1819–97), and John S. **Dwight** (1813–93) was published in New York in 1846–7, Godwin's editorial note included the remark: 'Several years since there was what purported to be a translation published in London; but this was a disgraceful imposture.' Yet the situation was hardly improved by the 'free' translation, *The Autobiography of Goethe* (1848–9), by John **Oxenford** (1812–77). Oxenford criticized the American version for being 'not sufficiently faithful' but, as Godwin pointed out in the second edition of the American translation, Oxenford's version was 'not a new translation at all, but a bold appropriation of the American version . . . simply adding to the wrong the injustice of a false accusation'.

Despite persistent mistranslation, Goethe proved to be a major influence on Thomas **Carlyle**, who in *Sartor Resartus* dubbed him 'the Wisest of our Time'. Via Carlyle, Goethe exercised influence over such Victorians as Matthew Arnold and George Eliot. Although Carlyle did much to promote the cause of Goethe in England, his translations of the *Wilhelm Meister* novels still leave much to be desired. His versions of the *Lehrjahre* (1795–6, Wilhelm Meister's Apprenticeship), and of the *Wanderjahre* (1821/29, Wilhelm Meister's Travels) deviate seriously from the original, and perhaps reflect Carlyle's deeper ambivalence towards Goethe. In 1823, Carlyle described the *Apprenticeship* as 'a book which I love not, which I am sure will never sell, but which I am determined to print and finish. There are touches of the very highest, most ethereal genius in it; but diluted with floods of insipidity.'

As well as his activity as a poet (to say nothing of his duties at the Weimar court), Goethe undertook numerous investigations in the fields of botany, geology, metereology, and other sciences. He launched a campaign against Sir Isaac Newton's theory of colour, attacking Newton on methodological grounds as well as, more seriously, for

317

confusing the scientific phenomenon with the object of perception. Published in 1810, Goethe's *Zur Farbenlehre* (1810) was translated into English by Sir Charles **Eastlake** (1793–1865) as *Goethe's Theory of Colours*, but Goethe's other natural-scientific writings were only slowly translated. For example, 'Die Metamorphose der Pflanzen' (1799, 'The Metamorphosis of Plants') and his essay on Nature (1782, also attributed to Tobler) were translated by Agnes **Arber** in *Goethe's Botany* (1946).

v. Faust Translations of Goethe's lyric poetry and *Faust* deserve special consideration, not least because of the numerous translations that exist. Published in two parts (I, 1808; II, 1832), the composition of *Faust* stretched across almost the whole of Goethe's career. The range of stanzaic and metrical forms used in it—blank verse, doggerel (*Knittelvers*), and hymnic structures, as well as, in Part II, *ottava rima*, *terza rima*, and trimeters—pose a particularly difficult challenge to the translator. The first English translation from *Faust* was published in a review of Part I in the *Monthly Review*, 52 (1810), and in 1822 **Shelley** made translations of sections of the work. In 1823, Lord Francis Leveson **Gower** published *Faust: A Drama by Goethe* in verse, and Abraham **Hayward** offered in 1833 a prose translation, while Charles T. **Brooks** translated Part I using English equivalents of the German versification (1856). Bayard **Taylor**'s famous verse translation appeared in 1870–1. Of the 20th-c. versions, those by the poet Louis **MacNeice**, Bayard Quincy **Morgan** (a prose version that aimed to combine 'fidelity to sense with freedom of style'), Barker **Fairley** (in accurate but often flat prose), Philip **Wayne** (in rhymed verse that often sacrifices sense to sound), Stuart **Atkins** (in metered verse offering clarity and accuracy), and, most recently, the excellent translation by David Luke (in rhymed verse), offer different attempts to come to terms with Goethe's use of metre.

For example, from the second Night scene, when Faust himself attempts to translate the Bible, the lines

> Geschrieben steht: 'Im Anfang war das *Wort*!'
> Hier steck ich schon! Wer hilft mir weiter fort?
> Ich kann das *Wort* so hoch unmöglich schätzen,
> Ich muß es anders übersetzen,
> Wenn ich vom Geiste recht erleuchtet bin

are translated by Atkins, with commendable accuracy, as follows:

> It is written, 'In the beginning was the *Word*.'
> How soon I'm stopped! Who'll help me to go on?
> I cannot concede that *words* have such high worth

> and must, if properly inspired,
> translate the term some other way

and by Luke, with the advantage of reproducing the rhyme scheme, thus:

> In the beginning was the word: why, now
> I'm stuck again! I must change that; how?
> Is then 'the word' so great and high a thing?
> There is some other rendering,
> Which with the spirit's guidance I must find.

Fairley's essay of 1969–70 illuminates the difficulties facing the translator. Many lines from *Faust* have taken on a proverbial status in German, in a manner similar to Shakespeare's *Hamlet* in English, and it is not always possible to find a satisfactory equivalent for them. For example, 'Zwei Seelen wohnen, ach! in meiner Brust' is difficult to translate because, as Fairley pointed out, in English, souls don't dwell in bosoms.

vi. Lyric Poetry As far as Goethe's poetry is concerned, Whaley, himself an accomplished translator of Goethe, has foregrounded three main difficulties involved. First, the difference (as well as misleading similarity) between German and English; second, problems of prosody, such as the English preference for iambic metre and the German tendency towards trochees; and finally, such special characteristics as the use of the verb for rhyme, reflecting Goethe's emphasis on dynamic process. Nevertheless, Goethe's poetry has been widely and variously translated, most notably by Michael Hamburger (acclaimed by Ted Hughes as the best translator since Shelley), David Luke, and Christopher **Middleton** (*Collected Works*, vol. i). For example, Hamburger's version of Goethe's aesthetic credo in 'Natur und Kunst' ('Nature and Art') brings us close to the 'sound–look' relations of the original even as they remain unattainable in English translation: 'In der Beschränkung zeigt sich erst der Meister, | Und das Gesetz nur kann uns Freiheit geben'—'None proves a master but by limitation | And only law can give us liberty.' David Luke's prose translations (1964) printed at the foot of a representative selection of original texts offer a useful introduction to Goethe's poetry. And from an earlier era, **Longfellow**'s translation of 'Über allen Gipfeln ist Ruh' ('Under the tree-tops is quiet now!') serves as just one example of a famous poet translating an equally famous poem. According to E. M. Wilkinson, this text also illustrates the untranslatable element of Goethe's poetry—'the assimilation of experience into language without the intervention of conceptual thought'.   PCB

COLLECTED WORKS *Goethe's Collected Works*, ed. Victor Lange, Eric Blackall, and Cyrus Hamlin, 12 vols., Cambridge, Mass., 1983–9.

POETRY *Hermann and Dorothea*, tr. Thomas Holcroft, London, 1801 · *West-Easterly Divan*, tr. John Weiss, Boston, 1877 · *West-Eastern Divan*, tr. Edward Dowden, London/Toronto, 1913 · *Selected Poetry*, tr. David Luke, Harmondsworth, 1964 [Penguin] · *West-Eastern Divan*, tr. John Whaley, London, 1974 · *Roman Elegies*, tr. David Luke, London/New York, 1977 · *Roman Elegies*, tr. Michael Hamburger [*Collected Works*, i, 1983] · *Hermann and Dorothea*, tr. David Luke [*Collected Works*, viii, 1987].

DRAMA *Iphigenia in Tauris*, tr. William Taylor, Norwich, 1793 · *Clavigo*, tr. anon., London, 1798 · *Stella*, tr. anon., London, 1798 · *Goetz of Berlichingen, with the Iron Hand*, tr. Walter Scott, London, 1799 · [*Fragments from Faust*], tr. Percy Bysshe Shelley, *The Liberal*, 1 (1822) · *Faust: A Drama by Goethe*, tr. Francis Leveson Gower, London, 1823 · *Torquato Tasso*, tr. Charles des Voeux, London, 1827 · *Faust: A Dramatic Poem*, tr. Abraham Hayward, London, 1833 · *Egmont*, tr. anon., Boston, 1841 · *Faust: A Tragedy*, tr. Charles T. Brooks, Boston, 1856 · *Faust: A Tragedy*, tr. Bayard Taylor, Boston, 1870–1 · *Faust*, tr. Philip Wayne, Harmondsworth, 1949–59 [Penguin] · *Goethe's Faust, Parts I and II, an Abridged Version*, tr. Louis MacNeice, New York, 1952 · *Egmont*, tr. Michael Hamburger, in *The Classic Theatre*, ed. Eric Bentley, ii, New York, 1958 · *Faust*, tr. Stuart Atkins, New York, 1962, Cambridge, Mass., 1984 [*Collected Works*, ii, 1984] · *Faust*, tr. Bayard Quincy Morgan, New York, 1954 [pt. i], Indianapolis, 1964 [pt. ii] · *Ironhand*, adapted by John Arden, London, 1965 · *Iphigenia in Tauris*, tr. John Prudhoe, Manchester/New York, 1966 · *Egmont*, tr. F. J. Lamport, in his *Five German Tragedies*, Harmondsworth, 1969 [Penguin] · *Goethe's Faust*, tr. Barker Fairley, Toronto, 1970 · *Torquato Tasso*, tr. John Prudhoe, Manchester, 1979 · *Iphigenia in Tauris*, tr. David Luke [*Collected Works*, viii, 1987] · *Torquato Tasso*, tr. Michael Hamburger [*Collected Works*, viii, 1987] · *Faust*, tr. David Luke, Oxford, 1987–94 [World's Classics].

FICTION *The Sorrows of Werter*, tr. Daniel Malthus, London, 1779 · *Werter and Charlotte*, tr. anon., London, 1786 · *The Sorrows of Werter*, tr. John Gifford, London, 1789 · *The Letters of Werter*, tr. anon., Ludlow, 1799 · *The Sorrows of Werter*, tr. William Render, London, 1801, rep. Boston, 1807 · *Wilhelm Meister's Apprenticeship*, tr. Thomas Carlyle, Edinburgh/London, 1824 · *Wilhelm Meister's Travels, or the Renunciants*, tr. Thomas Carlyle, in his *German Romance*, iv, London, 1827 · *Elective Affinities*, tr. R. Dillon Boylan, London, 1854 · *The Sorrows of Young Werther*, tr. Victor Lange, London/New York, 1949 [*Collected Works*, xi, 1988] · *Elective Affinities*, tr. Judith Ryan [*Collected Works*, xi, 1988] · *Elective Affinities*, tr. David Constantine, Oxford, 1994 [World's Classics].

OTHER PROSE *Memoirs of Goethe: Written by Himself*, tr. anon., London, 1824 · *Goethe's Theory of Colours*, tr. Charles Lock Eastlake, London, 1840 · *The Auto-Biography of Goethe*, tr. Parke Godwin, John Henry Hopkins, Charles A. Dana, and John S. Dwight, New York, 1846–7 · *The Autobiography of Goethe*, tr. John Oxenford, London, 1848–9 · *Goethe's Travels in Italy: together with his Second Residence in Rome and Fragments on Italy*, tr. A. J. W. Morrison and Charles Nisbet, London, 1883 · *Goethe's Botany*, tr. Agnes Arber, Waltham, Mass., 1946 · *The Italian Journey, 1786–88*, tr. W. H. Auden and Elizabeth Mayer, London/New York, 1962.

SEE ALSO F. Barker, 'On Translating *Faust*', *German Life and Letters*, 26 (1969–70), 54–62 · Long, O. W., 'English Translations of Goethe's Werther', *Journal of English and Germanic Philology*, 14 (1915), 169–203 · Miller, J. Hillis, 'Translating the Untranslatable', *Goethe Yearbook*, 5 (1990), 269–78 · Whaley, J., 'On Translating the Quality of Goethe's Poetry', *Publications of the English Goethe Society*, 49 (1978–9), 131–63 · Wilkinson, E. M., 'Goethe's Poetry', *German Life and Letters*, 2 (1948–9), 316–29.

6. HEINE

By the mid-20th c. there were 250 publications in English of works by the 19th-c. poet Heinrich Heine, ranging from the massive 20-volume Heinemann edition of Heine's *Works* translated by Charles Godfrey **Leland** (1824–1903, using the pseudonym Hans Breitmann) et al., to various 'complete' editions or selections of the poetry and/or prose, to anthologies of German literature that include Heine as one of the representative figures.

As in German, the image of Heine in English varies widely. Heine's work presents challenges to conventional poetic and ideological categories, and his image in English depends considerably on how the translator responds to such matters as

Heine's elusiveness, his mixture of styles, and the irony he directs at just about everything from political symbols and poetic traditions to the intense emotions or objects of emotion expressed in his poems. It also depends on how the translator decides to treat Heine's views of Napoleon, the French Revolution, Hegel, Marx and Saint-Simon, the 'Hellenes' and the 'Nazarenes', the German nation, the Jewish people, and the relationship of literature to politics. And it depends no less on the selection of works included or excluded than on the translational strategies used to present those works.

The frequently reprinted *Poems of Heinrich Heine*,

Complete by Edgar A. **Bowring** (1829–1911) was the earliest attempt of this kind. Bowring omitted the prose, sought 'literal' translations of poetry in the 'original metres', and rewrote Heine for Victorian audiences using archaisms and an elevated register that deviated from Heine's more colloquial usage. His practice is ill-suited to the ironic wit of *Deutschland: Ein Wintermärchen* (1844, Germany: A Winter's Tale), where Heine's jibes at the romantic-nationalistic attachment to medieval legends become: 'Behold the wood of Teutoburg . . . Behold the classical marsh.' Bowring's diction and poetic norms appear better suited to Heine's *Buch der Lieder* (1827, Book of Songs), but he again misses the irony of poem 15 of *Lyrisches Intermezzo* (1823, Lyrical Intermezzo), 'Die Welt is blind | Die Welt ist dumm', when he rewrites 'beseligend brennen' (blissfully burning) as 'rapturously glowing,' though his approach still compares favourably with that taken by another important 19th-c. translator, Theodore **Martin** (1816–1909), who simply omitted the poem from his popular *Poems and Ballads*.

A different Heine appears in the 1855 Leland/Breitmann translation of the *Reisebilder* (1826–31, Travel Pictures). Leland's Heine writes prose and poetry, and the prose, more than the poetry, displays a colloquial style also found in later North American Heine translations. The translation, running to nine editions by 1882 and still in print in 1911, is part of the 1905 Heinemann edition. Unlike Bowring, Leland seems attuned to Heine's ironic style, retaining, for example, the deflations of German nationalist rhetoric in *Ideen. Das Buch Le Grand* (1827, Ideas: The Book of Le Grand), though Napoleon's 'world-renowned hat' sacrifices to convention the Hegelian overtones of 'welthistorisches Hüttchen' ('world-historical hat'). In 1864, Leland published a highly readable version of the *Book of Songs*, a book which has been retranslated and published at least seven more times.

The three-volume translation of Heine's *Poetical Works* by John **Payne** (1842–1916) exceeds Bowring in its use of archaism, but produces some surprising effects achieved by the ironic contrast between elevated style and satiric utterance. Payne's *Germany, A Winter's Tale* eschews semantic precision but conveys brilliantly the speaker's witty retort to censorious customs officials: 'My head's a twittering bird's nest full | of confiscateable ditties.' Mark **Twain** eschews semantic precision less felicitously when he interpolates the 'Loreley's gruesome work' into his weirdly gothic version of that poem.

Although not a 'complete' edition, Louis **Unter-**meyer's *Poems of Heinrich Heine*, first published in 1917, seems more accessible for later 20th-c. audiences than Leland, Bowring, or Payne, at least in North America where his translations reappear in subsequent collections. Untermeyer's remarks on Heine's Jewishness, his description of Heine as an 'unusually emotional and quick-tempered Oriental', sound eccentric now, but they have historic value, as does his defence of Heine and German culture against the antagonisms created by World War I. The 'oriental' image of Heine may explain why Untermeyer, whose elegant translations were often reprinted, decided to 'revise' Heine, if somewhat less obviously than Mark Twain, by omitting from the final lines of poem 27 in *Lyrical Intermezzo* the word 'never,' thereby removing the ironic treatment of the lover's 'loyalty' along with the speaker's spiteful wish upon her.

The 1934 Everyman's Library collection of *Poetry and Prose* presents a Heine that differs considerably from those mentioned thus far. Edited by Ernest Rhys, it includes the work of many, mostly British, translators. Rhys enlists Heine to promote a counter-tradition to Nazi versions of German literature. Along with popular early poems, standard for the English Heine, the volume also includes parts of longer, less frequently published, prose works, from the 1887 translation by Havelock **Ellis** (1859–1939) of *The Prose Writings of Heinrich Heine*. Excerpts from the *Geständnisse* (1854, Confessions), *Lutezia* (1854), *Über Religion und Philosophie in Deutschland* (1854, On Religion and Philosophy in Germany), and the long poem *Atta Troll* (1847) emphasize the internationalist Heine fascinated with Italy, France, and London, and with the status of Jews in Europe. An excerpt from *On Religion and Philosophy* claims that Jews, by preserving the Hebrew language, helped Luther translate the Bible and thus contributed to the rise of modern German language and culture.

The 1948 *Poetry and Prose of Heinrich Heine*, edited by Frederic **Ewen**, gathers '110 new translations by Aaron **Kramer**' along with work by Emma **Lazarus** (1849–1887), Untermeyer, Ewen, and others. Like the Everyman edition, but larger, this volume is similarly significant for its selection since, beyond the standard poetry, it emphasizes Heine's prose and includes infrequently published memoirs and letters. Section headings include the conventional 'Poems and Ballads', but also the unconventional 'Songs of Protest', 'The Story Teller', 'Religion, Art and Life', 'Israel', and 'Citizen of the World', an editorial act that, like Ewen's introduction 'Heinrich Heine: Humanity's Soldier', produces new rubrics for reading Heine in response to events in Europe.

Two important Heine translations appeared in 1982: Hal **Draper**'s *Complete Poems of Heinrich Heine* and the first of two volumes published in The German Library series, *Heinrich Heine: Poetry and Prose*, edited by Jost Hermand and Robert Holub. The German Library volumes provide an excellent overview of Heine's work by gathering many previous translations, including Emma Lazarus's remarkable translation of 'Fragen' (Questions) from the second *Nordsee* (North Sea) cycle of 1827, found in her 1881 *Poems and Ballads of Heine* (reprinted 1947 and 1950).

Hal Draper's *Complete Poems of Heinrich Heine*, produced over 30 years, is the first such attempt since Payne. Like his predecessors, Draper strives to reproduce Heine's metre and rhyme, but, unlike them, stresses the difficulty of reproducing Heine's shifts of 'tone', which depend on the mix of deceptive simplicity and the range in Heine's register that moves from low to high and back again. Draper's tone skilfully conveys the simple musicality, for instance, of poem 36 in *Lyrical Intermezzo*, 'Aus meinem grossen Schmerzen', translated as 'Out of my great unrest', and the subtle irony of poem 50, where it remains unclear whether or not the speaker includes his lover among those being mocked for their blindness to the nonsense they speak about love. Draper also seems less inclined than predecessors like Bowring or Untermeyer to 'sanitize' Heine, but seeks instead to reproduce the political and religious satire of the later poems. Whatever problems may exist in the Draper translation, it is likely to remain for some time a standard collection of Heine's poems.

Four recent translations also deserve mention. Produced by experienced scholars or translators, they make available in affordable and, in three cases, bilingual editions diverse selections of Heine's work: Ritchie **Robertson**'s translation of *Selected Prose*; Walter W. **Arndt**'s edition of Heine's *Songs of Love and Grief*; T. J. **Reed**'s reprinted version of *Deutschland, A Winter's Tale*, and a new Everyman *Heinrich Heine*, with translations by several hands, edited by T. J. Reed and David Cram.   JG

Translations   Arndt, Walter W., *Heinrich Heine: Songs of Love and Grief: A Bilingual Anthology Translated in the Verse Forms of the Original*, Evanston, Ill., 1995 · Bowring, Edgar Alfred, *The Poems of Heine, Complete*, London, 1858 [frequent reps. in 19th c.] · Bozmann, M. M., et al., *Prose and Poetry by Heinrich Heine*, ed. Ernst Rhys, London/New York, 1934 [Everyman] · Draper, Hal, *The Complete Poems of Heinrich Heine: A Modern English Version*, Boston, 1982 · Ellis, Havelock, *The Prose Writings of Heinrich Heine*, London, 1887 · Ewen, Frederic, Kramer, Aaron, et al., *The Poetry and Prose of Heinrich Heine*, ed. Frederic Ewen, New York, 1948 · Holub, Robert, et al., *Heinrich Heine: Poetry and Prose*, ed. Jost Hermand and Robert C. Holub, New York, 1982 · *Heinrich Heine: The Romantic School and Other Essays*, ed. Jost Hermand and Robert C. Holub, New York, 1985 · Lazarus, Emma, *Poems and Ballads of Heinrich Heine*, New York, 1881; rep. 1947, 1950 · Leland, Charles G. (Hans Breitmann), *Pictures of Travel*, Philadelphia, 1855 [repr. in 1905 edn.; *The Harz Journey* section, pp. 1–61, rep. in bilingual edn., New York, 1995] · *Heine's Book of Songs*, Philadelphia/New York, 1864 · Leland, Charles G., Brooksbank, Thomas, Armour, Margaret, et al., *The Prose and Poetical Works of Heinrich Heine*, 20 vols., London/New York, 1882–1905 · Martin, Theodore, *Poems and Ballads by Heinrich Heine*, Edinburgh/London, 1878 · Mustard, Helen, and Knight, Max, *Heinrich Heine: Selected Works*, New York, 1973 · Payne, John, *The Poetical Works. Now First Completely Rendered into English Verse in Accordance with the Original Forms*, 3 vols., London, 1911 · Reed, T. J., *Heinrich Heine: Deutschland, A Winter's Tale*, London, 1997 [rep. in bilingual edn. of his 1986 translation] · Reed, T. J., and Cram, David, eds., *Heinrich Heine*, London, 1997 [Everyman] · Robertson, Ritchie, *Heinrich Heine: Selected Prose*, London, 1993 [Penguin] · Twain, Mark (Samuel L. Clemens), 'The Loreley', in *A Tramp Abroad*, Hartford, Conn., 1880 · Untermeyer, Louis, *Poems of Heinrich Heine*, New York, 1917 [rev. edn., 1923, 3rd expanded edn., 1937].

7. KANT, HEGEL, AND ROMANTIC PHILOSOPHY

i. Philosophy of the Romantic Period German texts in the history of ideas from roughly 1750 to 1850 present several problems of classification. Philosophers prefer 'idealism' to refer to the philosophy that includes Kant and some of his contemporaries, while German cultural history divides the materials into 'German Classicism' (*Klassik*) and 'Romanticism', and British and French cultural historians tend to categorize some Classical authors as Romantics (Goethe, Schiller). Similarly, some texts central to aesthetics or philosophy then are now considered theology or literature (e.g. Feuerbach's *Das Wesen des Christentums*) (1841, The Essence of Christianity).

Recent anthologies all provide serviceable core texts. Ernst **Behler**'s *Philosophy of German Idealism* offers otherwise unavailable texts by Fichte, Jacobi, and Schelling, as well as the important and anonymous 'Oldest Systematic Program of German Idealism, 1797'. Timothy J. **Chamberlin**'s

Eighteenth-Century Criticism performs an equivalent service for aesthetics between Herder and Schiller; Leslie A. **Willson**'s *German Romantic Criticism* supplements the available repertoire for Romantic theorists. Lawrence S. **Stepelevich**'s *The Young Hegelians* is a stylistically diverse set of translations of texts that have not been translated since the 19th c., if at all.

Other seminal translations are worth brief notice. Alexander **Gode** offers an engaging translation of the *Abhandlung über den Ursprung der Sprache* (1770, Essay on the Origin of Language), by Johann Gottfried Herder. T. **Churchill**'s 1800 *Outlines of a Philosophy of the History of Man* (*Ideen zur Philosophie der Geschichte der Menschheit*, 1784–91) still accurately represents Herder's chief work. The anthology of *Selected Early Works* by Herder translated by Ernest A. **Menze** and Michael **Palma** is the first volume of a projected series, a magisterial, scientific translation.

Peter Lauchlan **Heath** and John **Lachs**'s translation of Johann Gottlieb Fichte's *Wissenschaftslehre* (Science of Knowledge), using 1794–95 and two 1802 versions, is notable for accurate philosophical terminology and sensitivity to Fichte's shifts between technical rigidity and a conversational tone. Three volumes (each with a German–English glossary) translated by Daniel **Breazeale** bring Fichte to a broad philosophical audience by attending to the popular diction of transcendental idealism.

Andrew **Bowie**'s translation of Friedrich Wilhelm Joseph von Schelling's *Zur Geschichte der neueren Philosophie* (1833/7, On the History of Modern Philosophy) is to the highest standards, fully informed by contemporaneous philosophical rhetoric. Schelling's *Ideen zur einer Philosophie der Natur* (1803, Ideas for a Philosophy of Nature) is equally well translated and annotated by Errol E. **Harris** and Peter Heath. Peter Lauchlan Heath renders the *System des transzendentalen Idealismus* (1800, System of Transcendental Idealism), an exceedingly difficult technical text, into modern scientific prose. Almost a critical edition, Douglas W. **Stott**'s version of *Die Philosophie der Kunst* (The Philosophy of Art, lectures given in 1804/5 but published first in 1859) is a magisterial, flowing translation of a systematic work which unites philosophy with art and religion.

Ludwig Feuerbach is most famous from the 1854 translation by George **Eliot** (1819–80) of *Das Wesen des Christentums* (1841, The Essence of Christianity); in a sometimes free (more British than German), but largely accurate rendering, Eliot catches the urgent mix of politics and theology that made the book a manifesto of the age.

ii. Immanuel Kant Kant spans ethics, aesthetics, and epistemology. His work has been much translated, notably by William **Hastie** (1842–1903), who worked his way through most of the short works in the 1890s. Virtually all will be superseded by the Cambridge Kant edition.

The major works each have several translations. J. M. D. **Meiklejohn**'s 1855/60 edition of the *Kritik der reinen Vernunft* (1781–7, Critique of Pure Reason) corrects some terminological problems from the earliest editions and remains in print because of the natural rhythm of its prose. F. Max **Müller** (1823–1900) retranslated it in 1881 to correct these context/grammatical problems in a considerably less natural rendering that aims at greater philosophical correctness. The most familiar modern translator, Norman **Kemp Smith**, built on the work of his two predecessors in 1929/1933; his translation is informed by his own reading of critical philosophy. Wolfgang **Schwarz** tries to clarify Kemp Smith's 'vacillating vocabulary' but succeeds mainly in offering a Kant for analytic philosophy. Werner S. **Pluhar** and Patricia **Kitcher** in 1996 elegantly accommodate variants between Kant's first two editions.

The most notable of the previous translations of the *Kritik der praktischen Vernunft* (1788, Critique of Practical Reason) were each issued with a cluster of other shorter works in ethics. Thomas Kingsmill **Abbott** (1829–1913) offered in 1879 a freer version in dated English, still in print but replaced by Lewis White **Beck**'s reliable and commonly available, if not always eloquent, 1949 version.

The *Kritik der Urteilskraft* (1790, Critique of Judgement) has had three main translations: a competent 1892 version by J. H. **Bernard** (1860–1927) with a glossary of important terms, some in idiosyncratic formulations (e.g. 'faculty of concepts' for the 'understanding'); James Creed **Meredith**'s 1911–28 two-volume version in more modern tone; and the vigorous and accurate 1987 modern version by Werner S. Pluhar, a firm and philosophically adequate rendering.

The *Prolegomena zu einer jeden künftigen Metaphysik* (1783, Prolegomena to any Future Metaphysics) has had several translations, starting with John **Richardson**'s 1819 compilation. Most notable are those by Paul **Carus** (1859–1919) in 1902, and Lewis White Beck (who also drew on the independent translation by Ernest Belfort **Bax**); each tends to isolate this work from the total corpus.

Die Metaphysik der Sitten (1787, Metaphysics of Morals) and the *Grundlegung zur Metaphysik der Sitten* (1785, Groundwork of the Metaphysics of Morals) are usually translated together. Thomas

Kingsmill Abbott did a version which is accurate in its period moralizing diction but underplays the philosophy; Lewis White Beck uses the latest editions to offer a correct and modern version. Most recently, James Wesley **Ellington** added a version in thoroughly modern English, with excerpts of the longer texts; Mary J. **Gregor**, in what is virtually a historical-critical edition of the complete *Metaphysics of Morals* that is accurate yet in straightforward English, replaces early excerpted versions.

Zum ewigen Frieden (1795, Perpetual Peace) has seen many translations as a popular programmatic piece. Mary Campbell **Smith**'s 1903 version makes it a Victorian plea for world peace, adding an introduction almost as long as the original; Lewis White Beck's 1957 version is drier, very accurate, and more consciously philosophical in tone.

Mary J. Gregor translated Kant's last two essays rigorously, capturing the firm tone of the mature critical scholar. Her 1974 version of *Anthropologie, in pragmatischer Hinsicht abgefasst* (Anthropology from a Pragmatic Point of View) incorporates notes from the 1799 version. She followed it in 1979 with *Der Streit der Fakultäten* (1798, The Conflict of the Faculties), a parallel-text version that conveys Kant's firm polemical tone. Lewis White Beck's selection of shorter essays, *On History*, replicates Kant's popular voice, capturing some of his original acid tone; in a second, widely available selection of *Political Writings*, Hugh Barr **Nisbet**'s translations somewhat level Kant's usages to the modern where Beck retains some period flavour in his diction.

Most existing translations will be rendered obsolete for philosophical purposes by the Cambridge Edition of the *Works* of Immanuel Kant, presently planned as 14 volumes (all the texts published by Kant during his lifetime, plus selections of the *Nachlass* and the *Opus postumum*), edited by Paul **Guyer** and Allen W. **Wood**. This project has started again from scratch to produce a set of Kant translations with consistent style and terminology, striking a balance between accuracy and intelligibility, and providing an English version transparent to the German one (they footnote difficulties rather than interpreting to achieve resolutions). The translators observe the evolution of Kant's terminology; reflecting the fact that Kant was thinking in both Latin and German, they uphold the equivalency of *Anschauung* and *intuitio*, and *Wahrnehmung* and *perceptio*. They also provide a bilingual glossary and quietly regularize usages in the smallest words (*lediglich* = solely; *gänzlich* = entirely), while often even replicating typographic conventions such as sentence breaks.

iii. Georg Wilhelm Friedrich Hegel The great difficulty in translations of Hegel is the status of the original texts, since many of the lecture series were not prepared for publication by the author. Such is the case for the *Vorlesungen über die Geschichte der Philosophie* (1805–31, Lectures on the History of Philosophy). E. S. **Haldane** and F. H. **Simson** prepared an accurate translation, as careful as the poor original edition allowed. T. M. **Knox** and A. V. **Miller**'s *Introduction to the Lectures on the History of Philosophy* offers variants and is cross-referenced to the Hoffmeister edition of the original text, a great help for scholars. A translation of the new 1993 critical edition by Robert F. **Brown** and J. M. **Stewart** with H. S. **Harris** follows the 1825–6 lecture transcripts; it is careful, modern, and accurate, yet lacks supplements included by Haldane and Simson.

The *Vorlesungen über die Philosophie der Religion* (1823–7, Lectures on the Philosophy of Religion) have had two translations: that of E. B. **Speirs** and J. Burdon **Sanderson**, characterized by a looseness of terminology and no textual criticism, superseded by that of Peter Crafts **Hodgson**, Robert F. Brown, and J. Michael Stewart, who worked from all three lecture versions (1824, 1827, and 1831) and adhered to the terminological glossary established by Hodgson's 'Trinity Hegel Translation Group'.

J. **Sibree**'s translation of the *Vorlesungen über die Philosophie der Weltgeschichte* (1837, Lectures on the Philosophy of History), the only 'complete' edition available, has been termed baroque for its general stuffiness and inventive (but not always correct) terminological distinctions. In 1957, Robert S. **Hartman** retranslated the introduction under the title *Reason in History*; he does not claim it as definitive, but it is much superior in general correctness and modern diction. Hugh Barr Nisbet's *Lectures on the Philosophy of World History (Introduction)* is a more literal, very correct rendering of the same text. All are superseded to some degree by Leo **Rauch**'s 1988 *Introduction to the Philosophy of History*, which adheres to the Hodgson group's consistent terminology.

The Logic of Hegel, the first part of the 1830 *Encyclopedia* (*Enzyklopädie der philosophischen Wissenschaften im Grundrisse*), which also exists in 1817 and 1827 versions, was first translated by William **Wallace** (1844–97) in 1872, then revised in 1892. It is in many ways so fluent that it seems not to be a translation, and, as he admits, so free that it often paraphrases. The most correct modern version, by Theodore F. **Geraets**, W. A. **Suchting**, and H. S. Harris, follows Hodgson's terminology in a philosophically precise and natural edition, superseding earlier ones. The second part of the *Encyclopedia* was translated correctly but less naturally as *Hegel's Philosophy of Nature* by A. V. Miller in 1970.

The *Phänomenologie* (*Phenomenology*, the third part of the *Encyclopedia*) is a torso left in several partial manuscripts. The oldest translation, dating from 1894, but still in print, is that by William Wallace: *Hegel's Philosophy of Mind* (1830), a translation of §§ 377–577. A very accurate variant version (from the 1817 Heidelberg version) is Steven A. **Taubeneck**'s *Encyclopedia of the Philosophical Sciences in Outline*. Michael John **Petry**'s *Berlin Phenomenology* translates an 1825 version in a bilingual volume that is short, well-edited, with a high claim to literalness. The most familiar version of the text, from 1807, was a forerunner to the *Encyclopedia*. The *Phänomenologie des Geistes* (Phenomenology of Spirit / Mind) is in print in two versions: J. B. **Baillie** did a version of *The Phenomenology of Mind* which preserves some of the oddnesses of Hegel's turn of phrase; A. V. Miller straightens out difficult passages in his *Hegel's Phenomenology of Spirit*, lightly modernizing them. Each version has its supporters, although Miller's may be more accessible to modern readers.

The *Grundlinien der Philosophie des Rechts* (1821, Philosophy of Right) has been continually re-edited and retranslated. J. Michael Stewart and Peter C. Hodgson have weighed in with a version, *Lectures on Natural Right and Political Science*, based on a newly discovered transcription by Peter Wannemann, using their preferred (and remarkably gender-free) terminology.

Two free Victorian translations of the *Vorlesungen über die Ästhetik* (1842, Philosophy of Fine Art) exist, both in need of replacement; neither is bad, only dated and occasionally idiosyncratic. Bernard **Bosanquet** (1848–1923) did the introduction in 1905; F. P. B. **Osmaston** (b. 1857) did a complete version in 1920, faithful (he says 'literal') to the tone and meaning of the original.

T. M. Knox offers a number of texts in straightforward and correct, if not always graceful, prose that is a little old-fashioned, with less verve than the originals; most serviceable are his *Early Theological Writings* and selections from the *Political Writings*. John W. **Burbidge** and George **di Giovanni**'s *The Jena System, 1804–5* captures the terse and sometimes twisted character of Hegel's technical prose—a masterpiece worked over by many hands with a firm editorial principle and deep knowledge of the source texts. And finally, Clark **Butler** and Christiane **Seiler** translated a large selection of *The Letters*; theirs is a lucid rendering of Hegel's varying diction with useful notes.   KA

ANTHOLOGIES   Behler, Ernst, ed., *Philosophy of German Idealism*, New York, 1987 · Chamberlin, Timothy J., ed., *Eighteenth-Century German Criticism*, New York, 1992 · Stepelevich, Lawrence S., *The Young Hegelians: An Anthology*, Cambridge, 1983 · Willson, A. Leslie, ed., *German Romantic Criticism*, New York, 1982.

FEUERBACH, LUDWIG   Eliot, George (=Marian Evans), *The Essence of Christianity*, London, 1854 [frequent reps.].

FICHTE, JOHANN GOTTLIEB   Breazeale, Daniel, *Fichte, Early Philosophical Writings*, Ithaca, NY, 1988 · *Foundations of Transcendental Philosophy [Wissenschaftslehre] nova methodo [1796/99]*, Ithaca, NY, 1992 · *Introductions to the 'Wissenschaftslehre' and Other Writings, 1797–1800*, Indianapolis, 1994 · Heath, Peter Lauchlan, and Lachs, John, *The Science of Knowledge: With the First and Second Introductions*, Cambridge, 1970; rep. 1982.

HEGEL, GEORG WILHELM FRIEDRICH   Baillie, J. B., *The Phenomenology of Mind*, London/New York, 1910 [rev. 1931; rep. 1965] · Bosanquet, Bernard, *The Introduction to Hegel's Philosophy of Fine Art*, London, 1905 · Brown, Robert F., and Stewart, J. M., with H. S. Harris, *Lectures on the History of Philosophy*, iii: *Medieval and Modern Philosophy*, Berkeley, Calif., 1990 · Burbidge, John W., and Di Giovanni, George, *The Jena System, 1804–5: Logic and Metaphysics*, Kingston, Ont., 1986 · Butler, Clark, and Seiler, Christiane, *Hegel: The Letters*, Bloomington, Ind., 1984 · Geraets, Theodore F., Suchting, W. A., and Harris, H. S., *The Encyclopaedia Logic, with the Zusätze*, Indianapolis, 1991 · Haldane, E. S., and Simson, Frances H., *Lectures on the History of Philosophy*, 3 vols., London, 1892–6; rep. Lincoln, Neb., 1995 · Hartman, Robert S., *Reason in History: A General Introduction to the Philosophy of History*, Englewood Cliffs, NJ, 1953 · Hodgson, Peter Crafts, Brown, Robert F., and Stewart, J. Michael, *Lectures on the Philosophy of Religion*, 3 vols., Berkeley, Calif., 1984–7 · Knox, T. M., *Early Theological Writings*, Chicago/Cambridge, 1948 · *Political Writings*, Oxford, 1964 · Knox, T. M., and Miller, A. V., *Introduction to the Lectures on the History of Philosophy*, Oxford, 1985 · Miller, A. V., *Hegel's Philosophy of Nature, Being Part Two of the Encyclopaedia of the Philosophical Sciences (1830)*, Oxford, 1970 · *Hegel's Phenomenology of Spirit*, Oxford, 1977 · Nisbet, Hugh Barr, *Lectures on the Philosophy of World History (Introduction)*, Cambridge, 1975 · Osmaston, F. P. B., *The Philosophy of Fine Art*, London, 1920 · Petry, Michael John, *The Berlin Phenomenology*, Dordrecht/Boston, 1981 · Rauch, Leo, *Introduction to the Philosophy of History*, Indianapolis, 1988 · Sibree, J., *Lectures on the Philosophy of History*, London, 1857; repr. New York, 1956 · Speirs, E. B., and Sanderson, J. Burdon, *Lectures on the Philosophy of Religion: Together with a Work on the Proofs of the Existence of God*, 3 vols., London, 1895 · Stewart, J. Michael, and Hodgson, Peter C., *Lectures on Natural Right and Political Science: The First Philosophy of Right: Heidelberg, 1817–1818, with Additions from the Lectures of 1818–1819*, Berkeley, Calif., 1995 · Taubeneck, Steven A., *Encyclopedia of the Philosophical Sciences in Outline, and Critical Writings*, New York, 1990 · Wallace,

William, *The Logic of Hegel [Wissenschaft der Logik]*, 2nd edn., London, 1950 [orig. 1872, rev. 1892] · *Hegel's Philosophy of Mind: Being Part Three of the Encyclopaedia of the Philosophical Sciences [1830]*, Oxford, 1990 [orig. 1894].

HERDER, JOHANN GOTTFRIED Churchill, T., *Outlines of a Philosophy of the History of Man*, London, 1800; abridged as *Reflections on the Philosophy of the History of Mankind*, Chicago, 1968 · Gode, Alexander, *On the Origin of Language*, New York, 1966; Chicago, 1986 · Menze, Ernest A., with Michael Palma, *Selected Early Works, 1764–1767: Addresses, Essays, and Drafts; Fragments on Recent German Literature*, University Park, Penn., 1992.

KANT, IMMANUEL Abbott, Thomas Kingsmill, *Kant's Critique of Practical Reason and Other Works on the Theory of Ethics*, London, 1879 · Bax, Ernest Belfort, *Kant's Prolegomena, and Metaphysical Foundations of Natural Science*, London, 1883 [rev. edn. 1891] · Beck, Lewis White, *Critique of Practical Reason, and Other Writings in Moral Philosophy*, Chicago, 1949 · *Foundations of the Metaphysics of Morals*, Chicago, 1950 · *Prolegomena to Any Future Metaphysics*, New York/London, 1950 · *Perpetual Peace*, New York, 1957 · Beck, Lewis White, et al., *On History*, New York, 1963 · Bernard, J. H., *Kant's Kritik [Critique] of Judgment*, London, 1892 · Carus, Paul, *Prolegomena to Any Future Metaphysics*, La Salle, Ill., 1902 [rev. James Wesley Ellington, Indianapolis, 1977] · Ellington, James W., *Ethical Philosophy: The Complete Texts of 'Grounding for the Metaphysics of Morals,' and 'Metaphysical Principles of Virtue', Part II of 'The Metaphysics of Morals'*, Indianapolis, 1994 · Gregor, Mary J., *Anthropology from a Pragmatic Point of View*, The Hague, 1974 · *The Conflict of the Faculties [Der Streit der Fakultäten]*, Lincoln, Neb. 1992, New York, 1979 · *The Metaphysics of Morals*, Cambridge, 1991 · Guyer, Paul, and Wood, Allen W., eds., *The Cambridge Edition of the Works of Immanuel Kant.*, 14 vols., Cambridge, 1992 [principal translators: Paul Guyer, David Walford, Ralf Meerbote, Mary J. Gregor, Allen W. Wood, George Di Giovanni, Günter Zöller, J. Michael Young, Karl Ameriks, Steve Naragon, Eckart Forster] · Meiklejohn, J. M. D., *Critique of Pure Reason*, London, 1855–60 · Meredith, James Creed, *Kant's Critique of [Aesthetic] Judgement*, 2 vols., Oxford, 1911, 1928 · Müller, F. Max, *Critique of Pure Reason*, London, 1881 [rev. edn. 1902] · Nisbet, H. B., *Kant: Political Writing*, Cambridge, 1970; rep. 1991 · Pluhar, Werner S., *Critique of Judgment*, Indianapolis, 1987 · Pluhar, Werner S., and Kitcher, Patricia, *Critique of Pure Reason*, Indianapolis, 1996 · Richardson, John, *Metaphysical Works of the Celebrated Immanuel Kant*, London, 1819 [vols. i and ii], 1836 [vol. iii] · Schwarz, Wolfgang, *Critique of Pure Reason*, Aalen, Germany, 1982 · Smith, M. Campbell, *Perpetual Peace: A Philosophical Essay*, London, 1903 · Smith, Norman Kemp, *Critique of Pure Reason*, London/New York, 1929 [rev. edn. 1933].

SCHELLING, FRIEDRICH WILHELM JOSEPH VON Bowie, Andrew, *On the History of Modern Philosophy*, Cambridge, 1994 · Harris, Errol E., and Heath, Peter, *Ideas for a Philosophy of Nature as Introduction to the Study of This Science, 1797 [Second Edition 1803]*, Cambridge, 1988 · Heath, Peter Lauchlan, *System of Transcendental Idealism [1800]*, Charlottesville, Va., 1978 · Stott, Douglas W., *The Philosophy of Art*, Minneapolis, 1989.

8. MARX

The works of Karl Marx have generally been translated to reflect political trends, mostly commingled with those of Friedrich Engels, producing some interesting results. Most notable is the number of chrestomathies assembled from letters and journalism as Marx's definitive statements on particular topics, selections usually ripped from context.

The first generation of translations began with Marx himself; he wrote in German, English, and French as part of his journalistic enterprise. His daughter/secretary, Eleanor **Marx-Aveling** (1855–98) [see I.a.5.i], and her husband, Edward Bibbins **Aveling** (1851–98), were involved in establishing definitive editions/translations of the important works.

The translation history of *Das Kapital* (1867, Capital) is exemplary. The Samuel **Moore** and Edward Bibbins Aveling version of *Capital* (3 vols.) dating from 1887 is a standard, later supplemented rather than revised; its language is period, and to today's ears a little antiquated. When, in 1928–30, Eden **Paul** and Cedar **Paul** retranslated *Capital* to make it

sound more scientific and modern, they still collated their version with Moore's. Moore's prose is serviceable and clear, e.g.: 'The progress of our investigation will show that exchange value is the only form in which the value of the commodities can manifest itself or be expressed.' The Pauls translate with a firmer sense of the philosophical consistency of Marx's intention—a regularization imposed on the text by hindsight and by the growth of international Marxism: 'The course of our investigation will show that exchange-value is the necessary phenomenal form of value, the only form in which value can be expressed.'

The most widely disseminated text by Marx is the *Communist Manifesto* of 1848. The Samuel Moore 1888 translation, using Engels's corrections and annotations from an 1890 edition, is the standard, replacing a very free 1850 translation by Helen **Macfarlane**, and several other international versions. Eden and Cedar Paul's version casts an interesting light on the history of Marxism. Their 1928 version was translated from the revised (1922) edition of Ryazanov's *The Communist Manifesto* (a Russian version, more 'scientific' by implication). Again, it is slightly less idiomatic and more consciously seeking to impress than is Moore's: where he lets the 'spectre of communism' be 'exorcised', they have it 'laid'; where his communists have 'assembled in London' to draft the *Manifesto*, theirs have 'foregathered'.

Because Marx's early reputation rested on politics, the political works became visible earlier than his economic manuscripts. The English versions of these political texts should be taken as the norm for the English diction preferred by Marx; the best later translations approximate the voice in editions of the English journalism put out by Eleanor Marx-Aveling. Salomea Wolfovna **Ryazanskaya**'s 1972 translation of *Articles from the 'Neue Rheinische Zeitung', 1848–49* includes newspaper dispatches written for a liberal paper by both Marx and Engels, about the revolutions of 1848 throughout Europe. They are straightforwardly written in modern newspaper prose.

A large part of Marx's journalism was on the Paris revolutions and civil wars. *Die Klassenkämpfe in Frankreich* (1858, The Class Struggles in France) exists in two translations. The earlier, done in 1923 by Henry **Kuhn**, is more mannered and antiquarian in tone, occasionally using non-English phraseology. The anonymous Moscow edition (ed. C. P. Dutt), much more natural and 'scientific', follows the conventions of the 20th-c. editions. *Der Achtzehnte Brumaire des Louis Napoleon* (1852, The Eighteenth Brumaire of Louis Bonaparte) is a set of newspaper dispatches on the 1851 coup; An earlier translation, by Daniel **De Leon** (1852–1914), was cautious and generally reliable; a later one, by Eden and Cedar Paul, is unabridged, and is characterized by their tendentious language and their engagement with contemporary polemics.

Die deutsche Ideologie (1845–6, The German Ideology) was first published in Moscow in three parts in 1932: *Feuerbach*, *The Leipzig Concilium (Bruno Bauer and Max Stirner)*, and *True Socialism*. The most commonly available older translation, by Roy **Pascal**, is reliable and clear (and has been lightly revised by C. J. Arthur); like most versions, it omits the second part. The equivalent translation of *Feuerbach* is by W. **Lough**, that of *True Socialism* by C. P. **Magill**. When the complete version was gathered in Moscow in 1964–5, the translation veered in the same direction as the Pauls', with a tendency to regularize terminology towards more modern Marxist norms. Annette **Jolin** and Joseph **O'Malley**'s *Critique of Hegel's 'Philosophy of Right*, a translation of *Zur Kritik der Hegelschen Rechtsphilosophie*

(1843), includes passages from Hegel in the T. M. Knox translation [II.h.7.iii]. Well-introduced and documented, it is a natural-sounding modern translation, demonstrating how Marx was at pains to clarify Hegel's obscure prose.

International attempts at a standard edition begin in the 1920s, issued in parallel editions from Moscow, London, Edinburgh, and New York (and eventually as far as Delhi). The final result is the *Marx–Engels Gesamtausgabe (MEGA)* (from the Marx–Engels Institute) or *Marx–Engels Complete Works (MECA)* (English edition by Eric Hobsbawm et al.). The international norm for 'official' Marxist terminology was set first in 1933, by a two-volume version edited by Clemens Palme **Dutt** that has been continuously available; the set is now 50 volumes, based on original manuscripts and cross-referencing extant translations. However, active discussion is proceeding about redoing the *MEGA* and its editorial techniques, now that the political imperatives of its editorial team have altered.

One other large set is available. In the 1920s, Saul Kussiel **Padover** tried to retranslate the German texts concentrating on the history, less in the vein of the scientific-Leninist Marx. His seven volumes focus on letters and journalism about individuals, including many portraits of people; they sound natural, in the tone of popular history.

The commonly available paperback editions combine retranslations with the Moscow editions, usually in excerpts that are straightforward and careful renderings, especially of the smaller essays. Most notable among these are T. B. **Bottomore**'s two sets of retranslations and those of Joseph J. O'Malley, Terrell **Carver**, David **McLellan**, Eugene **Kamenka**, David **Fernbach**, and Robert C. **Tucker**.

To supplement the available translations of the economic manuscripts of the pre-*Capital* era, David McLellan retranslates sections of *Marx's Grundrisse* (*Grundrisse der Kritik der politischen Ökonomie*, 1857–8) from the 1904 edition, hitting a medium between a popular and scientific tone. Terrell Carver's *Karl Marx: Texts on Method* offers an equally solid translation of the 1857 *Introduction* to the *Grundrisse* and the *Notes on Adolph Wagner* (1879–80).

Saul Kussiel Padover's *Letters of Karl Marx* offers a broad selection of letters over 46 years, translated in a natural tone (some in excerpt), yet recognizing Marx's evolution as he wrote to many different partners (whose letters are not included). The edition of *Selected Letters* translated by Ewald **Osers** preserves oddities in Marx's and Engels's mixed use of language (they switched among English, French, and German); the letters are also tied together with personal-historical notes as a kind of group biography. The Dona **Torr** *Correspondence*, like the later Moscow editions, excerpts the letters to underscore what Marx read and was interested in writing about, sacrificing the (fairly bourgeois) tone of the originals. KA

TRANSLATIONS anon. [Marx-Lenin Institute], *Literature and Art*, New York, 1947 · *Selected Correspondence*, Moscow, 1950 · *The German Ideology*, Moscow, 1964, London, 1965 · Bottomore, T. B., *Karl Marx: Early Writings*, New York, 1963 · Bottomore, T. B., and Rubel, Maximilien, eds., *Karl Marx: Selected Writings in Sociology and Social Philosophy*, London, 1956 · Carver, Terrell, *Karl Marx: Texts on Method*, Oxford/New York, 1975 · *Marx: Later Political Writings*, Cambridge, 1996 · De Leon, Daniel, *The Eighteenth Brumaire of Louis Bonaparte*, New York/Moscow, 1900 · Dutt, Clemens Palme, *Selected Works [of] Karl Marx and Frederick Engels*, Moscow/Leningrad/London, 1948 · *The Class Struggles in France (1848–50)*, London, 1895 [rev. edn. Moscow, 1952 and 1960] · Fernbach, David, et al., *Political Writings*, 3 vols., Harmondsworth, 1973–4 [Penguin] · Hobsbawm, Eric, et al., *Collected Works [of] Karl Marx, Frederick Engels*, 50 vols., London, 1975– · Jolin, Annette, and O'Malley, Joseph, *Critique of Hegel's 'Philosophy of Right'*, Cambridge, 1970 · Kamenka, Eugene, ed., *The Portable Karl Marx*, Harmondsworth, 1983 [Penguin] · Kuhn, Henry, *The Class Struggles in France, 1848–1850*, New York, 1924 · McLellan, David, *Karl Marx: Early Texts*, Oxford, 1971 · *Marx's Grundrisse*, 2nd edn., London, 1980 · Moore, Samuel, *Manifesto of the Communist Party*, Moscow, 1888 · Moore, Samuel, and Aveling, Edward Bibbins [corrected by Engels], *Capital: A Critical Analysis of Capitalist Production*, i, London, 1887 [rev. Ernest Untermann, adding vols. ii and iii, London, 1907; abridged by Aveling as *The Student's Marx*] · O'Malley, Joseph J., with Richard A. Davis, *Marx: Early Political Writings*, Cambridge, 1994 · Osers, Ewald, *Selected Letters: The Personal Correspondence, 1844–1877*, ed. Fritz J. Raddatz, Boston, 1981 · Padover, Saul Kussiel, *The Karl Marx Library*, 7 vols., New York, 1972–7 · *The Letters of Karl Marx*, Englewood Cliffs, NJ, 1979 · Pascal, Roy, *The German Ideology*, pts. i and ii, London, 1938 [rev. C. J. Arthur, New York, 1970] · Paul, Eden, and Paul, Cedar, *The Eighteenth Brumaire of Louis Bonaparte*, London, 1926 · *Capital: A Critique of Political Economy*, London, 1928 [vol. i] and 1930 [vol. ii] · *The Communist Manifesto of Karl Marx and Friedrich Engels*, London, 1930 · Ryazanskaya, S. W., *Articles from the 'Neue Rheinische Zeitung', 1848–49*, Moscow, 1972 · Torr, Dona, *Correspondence 1846–1895: A Selection with Commentary and Notes*, New York, 1934 · Tucker, Robert C., ed., *The Marx–Engels Reader*, New York, 1978 [orig. 1972].

9. NIETZSCHE

The work of Friedrich Nietzsche presents a special problem in translation, given its reliance on a large range of poetic and expository styles (informed by Nietzsche's study of rhetoric and poetics), and in the light of the state of the editions.

The first translations appeared soon after the original publications. *The Complete Works of Friedrich Nietzsche*, edited by Oscar **Levy** and translated by a rotating cast between 1909 and 1919, have been reissued almost continuously throughout the English-speaking world. Together with the *Selected Letters* (1920–22), translated by Anthony Mario **Ludovici** and published as part of the collection, they render Nietzsche into spirited but sometimes antiquarian English, not purporting to reflect the original German. The volumes are uneven in quality, but are still a period reference.

Two post-World War II translators, Walter **Kaufmann** and R. J. **Hollingdale**, provided greatly improved versions of all the published works. Hollingdale is the basis for most British editions (including Penguin), Kaufmann for US ones (Vintage/Modern Library). The two translated differently in style and idiom and did not intend to render developments in Nietzsche's rhetoric, although they translate philosophical terminology and rhetoric consistently.

An example from *Also Sprach Zarathustra* (1883–5, Thus Spoke Zarathustra) illustrates the differences among the three major versions in print. Thomas **Common** (in Levy) renders the start of Book 1.4 as:

Zarathustra, however, looked at the people and wondered. Then he spake thus: Man is a rope stretched between the animal and the Superman—a rope over an abyss. A dangerous crossing, a dangerous wayfaring, a dangerous looking-back, a dangerous trembling and halting.

Truer to the original verb constructions, Hollingdale emphasizes the parallels in 'going-down', 'going-over', 'going-across', and 'staying-still' that run throughout the original Book I:

But Zarathustra looked at the people and marveled. Then he spoke thus: Man is a rope, fastened between animal and Superman—a rope over an abyss. A dangerous going-across, a dangerous wayfaring, a dangerous looking-back, a dangerous shuddering and staying-still.

Kaufmann, however, chooses more poetic-biblical diction instead of the philosophical implications of the verb structures:

Zarathustra, however, beheld the people and was amazed. Then he spoke thus: Man is a rope, tied between beast and overman—a rope over an abyss. A dangerous across, a dangerous on-the-way, a dangerous looking-back, a dangerous shuddering and stopping.

Kaufmann will almost always take the biblical phrase (here, 'beheld', 'beast'), while Hollingdale prefers more straightforward constructions maintaining the sense of the underlying words ('looked at', 'animal'); Common often tries to efface the text's foreign origins.

Other second-generation translations also improve on early translations. Marion **Faber**'s 1984 version of *Menschliches, Allzumenschliches* (1878, Human, All Too Human) corrects Levy/Helen **Zimmern** by attending to Nietzsche's literary sources, giving it a notable vigour. Peter **Preuss**'s 1980 translation of *Vom Nutzen und Nachteil der Historie für das Leben* (1873, On the Use and Disadvantage of History for Life) is readable and widely available. Other single translations are still being published, as are various selections of letters. Christopher **Middleton**'s *Selected Letters* stand as a benchmark for stylistic rendering, readability, and reliability. Unique is H. L. **Mencken**'s 1920 englishing of the *Antichrist* (1895), still in print. He achieves his goal of rendering 'some flavour of Nietzsche's peculiar style' in English and catches its rhetorical nuances and stylized accents.

Giorgio Colli and Mazzino Montinari's new German edition (Nietzsche, *Werke: Kritische Gesamtausgabe*) began to appear in 1963. By the editors' deaths in 1986, all published texts, unpublished fragments, and correspondence had been re-edited, leaving most annotations outstanding and the autobiographical works and philological writings unedited. A 1980 paperback version in 15 volumes (Nietzsche, *Sämtliche Werke: Kritische Studienausgabe*) was re-edited to incorporate corrections; this version is the basis for simultaneous English, French, Italian, and Japanese editions, changing Nietzsche scholarship fundamentally.

Licensed as a complete set by the European publishers, *The Complete Works of Friedrich Nietzsche*, under the general editorship of Ernst **Behler**, is an English edition with significantly revised versions of familiar texts, incorporating fragments known heretofore only in part (in Kaufmann and Hollingdale's 1967 translation of *Die Wille zur Macht* (1895, The Will to Power), in Daniel **Breazeale**'s reliable translation of parts of the early notebooks, *Philosophy and Truth*, and in Sander **Gilman** et al.'s *Friedrich Nietzsche on Rhetoric and Language*), and eliminating the *Will to Power* as an independent 'text'. Behler's translators produce paired volumes, with the published writings for each era doubled by volumes of contemporaneous fragments. Taking the fragments as drafts of the published version reveals alternative formulations of key passages that make Nietzsche's intents clearer. The English edition is ahead of the German edition in publishing the Basel philological writings; its format for annotations and arrangement offer a more complete picture of the genesis, textual history, and reception of each text than do Colli–Montinari's.

Aside from the complete works, the volume of translations of *Unzeitgemässe Betrachtungen* (1873–6, Untimely Meditations) under the general editorship of William **Arrowsmith** is noteworthy. Taken from the Colli–Montinari *Gesamtausgabe*, it is reader-friendly, with annotations (e.g. biographies) on the same page as the texts.

Finally, an 'English translation' of what is probably a Nietzsche pastiche deserves comment because it resurfaces regularly to be re-authenticated or disputed: *My Sister and I*. Supposedly written by Nietzsche in the Jena insane asylum between 1889 and 1890 and offering lurid meditations on his childhood and on sex, it was allegedly discovered (1921) and translated (1927) by Oscar Levy. In 1951, a 'carbon copy' of this production (no German original) was 'found in a trunk' by Samuel Roth and published in Seven Sirens Press. In 1952, Levy's sister called it a fraud. It last surfaced in the mid-1980s (see the Amok Books edition's documentation), when some claimed that passages resembled unpublished fragments.   KA

TRANSLATIONS Arrowsmith, William, ed., *Unmodern Observations*, New Haven, Conn., 1990 · Behler, Ernst, ed., *Complete Works of Friedrich Nietzsche*, 20 vols., Stanford, Calif., 1995– [principal translators: Diana I. Behler, Ernst Behler, Richard T. Gray, Gary J. Handwerk, Bernd Magnus, Brittain Smith, Steven A. Taubeneck] · Breazeale, Daniel, *Philosophy and Truth: Selections from Nietzsche's Notebooks of the Early 1870s*, Atlantic Highlands, NJ/Brighton, UK, 1979 · Faber, Marion, with Lehmann, Stephen, *Human, All Too Human: A Book for Free Spirits*, Lincoln, Neb., 1984; rep. Penguin, 1994 · Gilman, Sander L., Blaire, Carole, and Parent, David J. *Friedrich, Nietzsche on Rhetoric and Language*, Oxford, 1989 · Hollingdale, R. J., *Twilight of the Idols/The Anti-Christ*, Harmondsworth, 1968 [Penguin] · *Thus Spoke Zarathustra: A Book for Everyone and No One*, Harmondsworth, 1969 [Penguin] · *Beyond Good and Evil: Prelude to a Philosophy of the Future*, Harmondsworth, 1973 [Penguin] · *Ecce Homo: How One Becomes What One Is*, Harmondsworth, 1979 [Penguin] · *Daybreak: Thoughts on the Prejudices of Morality*, Cambridge, 1982 · *Untimely Meditations*, Cambridge, 1983 · *Human, All Too Human: A Book for Free Spirits*, Cambridge, 1986 · *Birth of Tragedy out of the Spirit of Music*, Harmondsworth, 1993 [Penguin] · Kaufmann, Walter A., *The Portable Nietzsche*, New York, 1954 · *Basic Writings*, New York, 1966 · *The Gay Science: With a Prelude in Rhymes and an Appendix of Songs*, New York, 1974 · Kaufmann, Walter A., and Hollingdale, R. J., *The Will to Power*, New York, 1967 / London, 1968 · Levy, Oscar, ed., *The Complete Works of Friedrich Nietzsche*, 18 vols., London / Edinburgh, 1909–19; rep. New York, 1964, 1974. [There is some variance in volume numbers because, after several volumes had been issued, the publishers renumbered the set, including volumes already published, in order of original composition. Principal translators: William August Haussmann, Maximilian August Mügge, J. M. Kennedy, Anthony Mario Ludovici, Adrian Collins, Helen Zimmern, Paul Victor Cohn, Thomas Common, H. B. Samuel] · Levy, Oscar (?), *My Sister and I*, Los Angeles, 1951; rep. 1990 · Ludovici, Anthony Mario, *Selected Letters of Friedrich Nietzsche*, New York / Toronto, 1922 · Mencken, H. L., *Antichrist*, New York, 1920; rep. 1988 · Middleton, J. Christopher, *Selected Letters of Friedrich Nietzsche*, Chicago, 1969 · Preuss, Peter, *On the Advantage and Disadvantage of History for Life*, Indianapolis, 1980.

SEE ALSO   Behler, Ernst, 'Translating Nietzsche in the United States: Critical Observations on *The Complete Works of Friedrich Nietzsche*', in Kurt Mueller-Vollmer and Michael Irmscher, eds., *Translating Cultures, Translating Literatures: New Vistas and Approaches in Literary Studies*, Stanford, Calif., 125–46 · Rosenthal, Albi, 'Betrachtungen über eine Nietzsche-Sammlung in England', *Nietzsche-Studien*, 19 (1990), 479–87.

10. FREUD

The work of Sigmund Freud was known in English in a relatively complete edition before it was in German. That the texts have been available does not mean that the translations have met with general agreement.

The earliest translations were by Abraham Arden **Brill**, most of them being collected in *The Basic Writings of Sigmund Freud*. His translations, which date from as early as 1910, are lively and conversational, with interpolations designed to make Freud's work readable to a novice audience; at times they are almost free rewritings, deleting and combining sentences from the originals at will. However, the older generation still considers as most lively and readable the slightly later four- (later, five-) volume edition of *Collected Papers* by Joan **Riviere**, which is also the basis for Philip **Rieff**'s editions. At about the same time, Granville Stanley **Hall** translated the *Gravida* competently.

James **Strachey**'s *Standard Edition* (*SE*) (with Alix **Strachey** and Joan Riviere as major translators) is at the same time awe-inspiring and deeply flawed. Neither it nor the German editions include Freud's writings on physical science or more than a scattering of letters. The *SE* lines up essays by date of conception (not publication). Published works were reprinted with minor corrections, not re-edited according to the manuscripts. The text notes and other references reflect exemplary historical research, especially since they were completed before a biography was available. Each text is introduced by a bibliography of its earlier publications in both German and English, although with only restricted attempts to note differences between editions (or to collate variants).

The work was conducted in parallel with the activities of a 'Glossary Committee', suggested by Ernest Jones in the 1920s, which was given the task of finding consistent equivalents for Freud's technical vocabulary. As Strachey explains in the 'General Introduction' to the *SE*'s volume i, they tried to regularize the main terminology across texts, creating consistent, readable translations: thus *Wohlbefinden* (well-being) becomes 'health', obscuring a differentiation in common German between mental and physical health (*Gesundheit*) and the grounds for Freud's choice. This regularization, therefore, is simultaneously the core of the set's weakness.

For example, the committee created technical terms ('id' and 'ego' as Latin based nouns) for what Freud explicitly wrote in 'plain German' (*das Ich* and *das Es*, German pronouns turned nouns according to conventional grammar rules). Other choices made neutral English out of originally poetic or affect-laden words: Helmut Junker points to translations such as 'the recognized imperfections of some fellow-mortal' as changing the more poetic emphasis of the original 'ein in seiner Unvollkommenheit erkanntes Menschenkind' away from the person onto that person's failings—a distinct change of sentence rhythm and tone (Ornston 1992: 53). *SE* neologisms (such as 'to cathect' for *abreagieren*) reflect the élitism of the Bloomsbury translators rather than Freud's own attempts to write for a more general audience.

Some of the solutions Jones found were discussed with Freud (to Freud's disapproval). While these were effective in establishing terminology for psychoanalysis, they ignore crucial differences in traditional philosophical and scientific usages that Freud himself respected, such as that between 'idea' (*Idee*) and 'representation' (*Vorstellung*) reflected in the only essay that Freud himself wrote in English, the 1912 'Note on the Unconscious in Psychoanalysis'.

Considered historically, the Glossary Committee's decisions flatten the stylistic nuances and cultural references of Freud's writing. Strachey and his colleagues did not know the tradition of vigorous scientific writing in German at the time, nor its closeness to philosophical and literary texts of the time. Today's consensus sees the *SE* as a monument needing an overhaul, especially in light of the copious scholarship on Freud's reading habits [see Bettelheim 1983 and Ornston 1992 for detailed critiques of existing translations, and Grubrich-Simitis 1996 for new readings of the texts calling for retranslation]. The Sigmund Freud Copyrights began to expire at the end of the 1980s, but no translators have yet taken up the challenge.

Many of Freud's exchanges of letters with other correspondents exist in reasonably accurate editions. There is little chance of a complete edition of the letters until sealed archival materials are opened in the 21st c. Peter Gay's bibliographical essay in *Freud: A Life for Our Time* (1988) documents availability and coverage of the most important extant collections.

One updated edition is that of the Freud–Fliess letters translated by Jeffrey Moussaieff **Masson**, which significantly corrects the 1954 Eric **Mosbacher** and James Strachey translations. Masson restores cuts not indicated in the original version, adds letters, and renders Freud's voice effectively as the letters move between chat, literary allusion, and reports on current science. More recently, Peter T. **Hoffer** translated *The Correspondence of Sigmund Freud and Sandor Ferenzi* to the same standards, while A. J. **Pomerans** offered fine translations of heretofore unknown letters to Eduard Silberstein.

Two volumes fall outside the standard manuscript history. Robert **Byck** and his predecessors offer readable collections of *The Cocaine Papers*, Freud's printed scientific papers on the topic (not collected in German). Of special note is the 1987 translation of *A Phylogenetic Fantasy* by Axel **Hoffer** and Peter T. Hoffer, one of Freud's presumably lost papers on metapsychology that was rediscovered among other manuscripts, now carefully rendered into modern English. Like the Masson letters, this edition stands as a model for what could be achieved according to modern standards of editing and translating.   KA

TRANSLATIONS   Brill, A. A., *The Basic Writings of Sigmund Freud*, 6 vols., New York, 1938 [orig. 1910–18; rep. 1995] · *Leonardo da Vinci: A Psychosexual Study of an Infantile Reminiscence*, New York, 1922 · Brill, A. A., Breuer, Josef, and Freud, Sigmund, *Studies in Hysteria*, New York/Washington, DC, 1936 · Byck, Robert, *Cocaine Papers*, New York, 1974 · Hall, G. Stanley, *Delusion and Dream: An Interpretation in the Light of Psychoanalysis of 'Gravida', a Novel by Wilhelm Jensen*, New York, 1922 · Hoffer, Axel, and Hoffer, Peter T., *A Phylogenetic Fantasy: Overview of the Transference Neuroses*, ed. Ilse Grubrich-Simitis, Cambridge, Mass., 1987 · Hoffer, Peter T., *The Correspondence of Sigmund Freud and Sandor Ferenczi*, 2 vols., ed. Eva Brabant, Ernst Falzeder, and Patrizia Giampieri-Deutsch, Cambridge, Mass., 1993–6 · Masson, Jeffrey Moussaieff, *The Complete Letters of Sigmund Freud to Wilhelm Fliess, 1887–1904*, Cambridge, Mass., 1985 · Mosbacher, Eric, and Strachey, James, *The Origins of Psycho-Analysis: Letters to Wilhelm Fliess, Drafts and Notes, 1887–1902*, ed. Marie Bonaparte, Anna Freud, and Ernst Kris, New York/London, 1954 · Pomerans, A. J., *The Letters of Sigmund Freud to Eduard Silberstein, 1871–1881*, Cambridge, Mass., 1990 · Rieff, Philip, *The Collected Papers of Sigmund Freud*, 8 vols., New York, 1993 [orig. 10 vols., New York, 1963] · Riviere, Joan, *Collected Papers* [*Sammlung kleiner Schriften zur Neurosenlehre*], 4 vols., London, 1924–5 [2nd edn., 1933] · *Collected Papers*, 5 vols., London, 1950 · Strachey, James, ed., *The Standard Edition of the Complete Psychological Works of Sigmund Freud*, 24 vols., London, 1953–66 [various reps., London and New York; principal translators: James Strachey, Alix Strachey, Joan Riviere].

SEE ALSO   Bettelheim, B., *Freud and Man's Soul*, New York, 1983 · Grubrich-Simitis, Ilse, *Back to Freud's Texts: Making Silent Documents Speak*, tr. Philip Slotkin, New Haven, Conn., 1996 · Ornston, D., Jr., ed., *Translating Freud*, New Haven, Conn., 1992.

11. FICTION: NINETEENTH AND TWENTIETH CENTURY

i. The 19th-Century Novella If the 19th c. in most European literatures was the age of the novel, in German literature it was the age of the novella. This fact is reflected in the translation history of 19th-c. German fiction, with translators tending to translate selections of short prose works by different writers, with the names Heinrich von Kleist, E. T. A. Hoffmann, Gottfried Keller, and Theodor Storm figuring prominently in anthologies. Important 19th-c. anthologies include: *German Romance*, a four-volume collection edited by Thomas **Carlyle**, which contained a number of first translations into English of prose works of the German romantics, including Carlyle's own translation of E. T. A. Hoffmann's *Der goldene Topf* (1814, The Golden Pot); and *Tales from the German* by John **Oxenford** and C. A. **Feiling**. Significant 20th-c. collections are listed in the bibliography.

Key novellas translated repeatedly down the years include Kleist's *Das Erdbeben in Chili* (1810, The Earthquake in Chile) and Storm's *Immensee* (1854, translated more than 15 times) and *Der Schimmelreiter* (1888, The Rider on the White Horse). The translation histories of two 19th-c. German writers merit special discussion, however. They are E. T. A. Hoffmann, the great romantic writer whose dark tales anticipated and influenced the work of Edgar Allan Poe, and whose work has consistently attracted translators up to the present day; and, from the last decades of the century, Theodor Fontane, the one 19th-c. German novelist ranking alongside the European masters of the realist novel.

ii. E. T. A. Hoffmann Hoffmann's first translator was R. P. **Gillies**, who translated the first of Hoffmann's two novels *Die Elixiere des Teufels* (1816, The Devil's Elixirs) as early as 1824 and translated some of the short stories in the following years, including *Das Fräulein von Scuderi* (1820, Mademoiselle de Scudéry) in the collection *German Stories* of 1826. An essay by Walter Scott in the *Foreign Quarterly Review* of 1827 made Hoffmann well known in Britain, though at the same time this essay, along with Carlyle's introduction to his translation of *The Golden Pot* in the same year, spread the perception that Hoffmann was an unhealthy, morbid writer. One of Hoffmann's key short tales, *Der Sandmann* (1816, The Sandman), was included in Oxenford's anthology in 1844, and translations of other stories appeared in similar anthologies throughout the 19th c. as the Victorians developed a taste for the dark side of romanticism,

though cuts to Hoffmann's texts were still frequently made in translation. The enduringly popular *Nussknacker und Mäusekönig* (1819, Nutcracker and Mouse King) was first translated in 1853 and has since been retranslated (most notably by the distinguished translator Ralph **Manheim**) and adapted many times, becoming world famous through Tchaikovsky's ballet. By the 1880s Hoffmann's reputation in Britain and America was such that separate two-volume collections of tales were published on each side of the Atlantic: in the United States *Weird Tales*, translated by J. T. **Bealby**, and in Britain *The Serapion Brethren*, a translation by Alexander **Ewing** of *Die Serapionsbrüder*, Hoffmann's four-volume collection of tales published 1819–21.

But it was after World War II that Hoffmann's reputation really took off in the English-speaking world, and this is reflected in the fact that not only was *The Devil's Elixirs* newly translated by Ronald **Taylor** in 1963, but also at least 10 selections of the stories have been newly translated since the war, with translators concentrating on *The Golden Pot*, *Mademoiselle de Scudéry*, and *The Sandman*. Leonard J. **Kent** and Elizabeth C. **Knight**'s handsome two-volume *Selected Writings* is particularly important in that volume ii contains the first translation of Hoffmann's second, uncompleted novel *Lebensansichten des Katers Murr* (1819–21, The Life and Opinions of Kater Murr)—a good, modern American literary translation, though by their own admission the translators sometimes sacrifice literalness in the interests of readability. R. J. **Hollingdale**, in his Penguin Classic *Tales of Hoffmann* went further still, feeling the need to editorialize in order, as he put it, to increase the tempo and tighten up the original tales to suit the taste and aesthetic expectations of the modern reader. Another popular modern collection, Ritchie **Robertson**'s *The Golden Pot and Other Tales*, by contrast, is faithful to the original texts and renders them accurately and stylishly into modern literary English.

iii. Theodor Fontane Given Fontane's status as one the great novelists of European realism, it is surprising that, with two exceptions, the works of this chronicler of Prussian manners and morals in the 1880s and 1890s were not translated into English before the 1960s and 1970s. Commonly regarded as his masterpiece, the novel of adultery *Effi Briest* (1895) was first translated in 1913, but only in an unsatisfactory, abridged form, and a translation of

Irrungen, Wirrungen (1888, Trials and Tribulations) appeared in 1917.

But from the 1960s there has been a steady stream of new translations of these and other works. An undistinguished translation of *Effi Briest* by Walter **Wallich** was quickly followed and superseded by Douglas **Parmée**'s version which became a Penguin Classic and successfully captured the style of the original, without always being accurate. A new translation by Hugh **Rorrison** and Helen **Chambers** is fluent and accurate, with helpful notes which provide the English reader with insights into Fontane's subtle and allusive prose.

Irrungen, Wirrungen too has been retranslated twice, confusingly each time under a different title: by Sandra **Morris** as *A Suitable Match* and by Derek **Bowman** as *Entanglements*, the latter in particular a fine, sensitive translation of a subtle text. The bulk of other translations of Fontane's works have been done by American translators. The first of the Berlin novels, *L'Adultera* (1880), has been translated twice: by Gabriele **Annan** in the late 1970s and more recently by Lynn R. **Eliason**. The translation for the first time of *Cécile* (1887) and Fontane's long last novel *Der Stechlin* (1899, The Stechlin) in recent years marks a welcome extension of the Fontane œuvre in English, which is still far from complete.

iv. Franz Kafka If, to the English reader, much German realist prose fiction of the second half of the 19th c. (with the exception of Fontane) has something of a provincial feel about it, this certainly cannot be said of German fiction in the 20th c., which has produced a number of novelists of truly international stature, particularly in the first decades of the century.

At the time of his death in 1924, Franz Kafka had published only a handful of short prose works, including *Die Verwandlung* (1915, Metamorphosis), *Das Urteil* (1916, The Judgement), *In der Strafkolonie* (1919, In the Penal Settlement), the collection *Ein Landarzt* (1919, A Country Doctor), and *Ein Hungerkünstler* (1922, A Hunger Artist). It was the decision of his friend Max Brod to ignore Kafka's instruction that his (substantial) unpublished writings be destroyed and instead to edit and publish those works posthumously in the following years which provided the basis for Kafka's rise to be the most famous, most influential and most studied German-language writer of the 20th c. Brod published versions of the unfinished novels *Der Prozeß* (1925, The Trial); *Das Schloß* (1926, The Castle); the fragmentary novel *Der Verschollene*, given the title *Amerika* (1927) by Brod, and a selection of shorter

fiction entitled *Beim Bau der chinesischen Mauer* (1931, The Great Wall of China).

The first English translators of Kafka's works were Willa and Edwin **Muir** (the latter an important English novelist and poet in his own right), who translated all these posthumously published volumes in the 1930s [on Willa Muir see I.a.5.i]. These classic and often reprinted translations have been consistently praised, especially for the quality of the English style, with Ronald Gray remarking that the Muirs had 'turn[ed] Kafka's work into an English so natural that one might not suspect that he had written in any other language'.

Selling slowly at first, but finding a large readership from the 1940s on, it was not only the translations themselves which were influential. For Edwin Muir's introductions to the translations, beginning with the 'Introductory Note' to *The Castle* (1930), in which he likened the novel to John Bunyan's *Pilgrim's Progress*, were highly influential in disseminating Brod's essentially religious and allegorical interpretation of Kafka's works in the English-speaking world.

For all their brilliance and continuing popularity, the Muir translations have two drawbacks. First, it has become increasingly clear that they are not always accurate (Gray 1977; Hobson 1977–8), which is especially significant given that the worldwide interest in Kafka means that many Kafka commentators continue to be dependent on the English translations. And second, Brod's idiosyncratic original German editions of Kafka's manuscripts, on which the Muirs' translations were based, have since been superseded.

First attempts to produce so-called 'definitive editions' of *The Castle* and *The Trial* in the 1950s required the translation of substantial additional material, which was translated for the former by Ernst **Kaiser** and Eithne **Wilkins** and for the latter by E. M. **Butler**. *The Trial* was again translated by Douglas **Scott** and Chris **Waller** in 1977. In his introduction J. P. Stern highlighted the fact that this translation 'keeps close to the syntax and lustreless informality of the original'. But again the German text they were using was flawed.

It was not until the 1980s and 1990s that a truly definitive edition of all Kafka's writings appeared in German. This has led to a new translation of *Der Verschollene* (i.e. *Amerika*) as *The Man who Disappeared* by Michael **Hofmann** which is based on the original manuscripts and finally allows English-language readers to read the work for the first time in the form Kafka left it. Unfortunately the same cannot be said for Idris **Parry**'s new translation of *The Trial* (1994), which despite the availability of the definitive German edition still uses an unreliable version of the text; although more coherent, this perpetuates the false impression first created by Brod that the novel was less fragmentary than is in fact the case. A new translation of *The Castle* by Mark **Harman** which is based on the restored text was published in 1998.

Kafka's shorter works, both published and unpublished, have a similarly complex translation history. Early translations of the published works included *The Metamorphosis* by A. L. **Lloyd** and the *Country Doctor* collection by V. **Leslie**. Both were superseded—in America by the work of the Muirs, who published *The Penal Colony: Stories and Short Pieces* (including *Metamorphosis*) in 1948, and in Britain by the work of the translator pair Eithne Wilkins and Ernst Kaiser, whose volume *In the Penal Settlement*, contained most of the published stories, including *Metamorphosis*. The same pair then published a selection of the posthumous stories under the title *Wedding Preparations in the Country*. In 1960 an expanded version of the Muirs' early translations of the posthumous stories appeared as *Description of a Struggle and the Great Wall of China*, with the additional stories (published by Brod in 1936) translated by Tania and James **Stern**. All these translations from the posthumous writings were, however, based on unreliable texts edited by Brod.

Then in the 1970s, the great Kafka scholar Malcolm **Pasley** began the process of re-editing and retranslating the posthumous stories into English direct from the manuscripts, even before they had appeared in this definitive form in German. *Shorter Works*, volume i, appeared in 1973, containing major short posthumous works in order of composition (from 1991 under the title *The Great Wall of China and Other Short Works*). This was followed by *Description of a Struggle and Other Stories* in 1979, which contained further posthumous stories and fragments in translations by the Muirs, the Sterns, and Pasley himself. In 1992, Pasley completed the task of providing the English-speaking world with a reliable, accurate, and complete text of all of Kafka's short stories. *The Transformation (Metamorphosis) and Other Stories* contains Pasley's own translations of the stories published during Kafka's lifetime in order of publication.

The published stories in particular have attracted and continue to attract new translators. Thus, in 1981 J. A. **Underwood** anticipated Pasley's final volume of the published stories by publishing for the first time in a single volume all the stories Kafka published in book form. Of all these stories, *Metamorphosis* has been translated most often, particu-

larly in America, with Stanley **Corngold** publishing a version in 1972 and, more recently, Joachim **Neugroschel** and Stanley **Appelbaum** translating the story into modern, accurate American English. So the English reader now has a choice of modern and accurate translations of the stories, whilst the classic translations by the Muirs also remain in print. (Translation of the very important diary and letters are noted in the Bibliography below.)

v. Thomas Mann Thomas Mann not only is one of the best-known German novelists of the 20th c., but through his campaign against National Socialism during his period of exile in the United States became a symbol of opposition to Hitler's regime, gaining immense prestige and a large readership in America and throughout the world as a result.

Beginning with the translation of *Buddenbrooks* (1901) in 1924, Helen **Lowe-Porter**, appointed by Mann's American publisher, Alfred Knopf, became the sole (and remarkably speedy) copyright translator of almost all of Thomas Mann's lengthy works of fiction over the next two and a half decades, including *Der Zauberberg* (1924, The Magic Mountain), the tetralogy *Joseph und seine Brüder* (4 vols., 1933–42, Joseph and His Brothers), and *Doktor Faustus* (1947), as well as the early stories, most notably *Der Tod in Venedig* (1911, Death in Venice). The only exceptions were Mann's last two works, *Die Betrogene* (1953) translated by Willard R. **Trask** as *The Black Swan* and *Bekenntnisse des Hochstaplers Felix Krull* (1954, Confessions of Felix Krull, Confidence Man), translated by Denver **Lindley**.

Early reviewers, impressed by the relative readability of Lowe-Porter's English and no doubt by the sheer scale of the task, consistently praised her achievement, but from the 1950s on doubts were expressed about the accuracy of the translations, culminating in Timothy Buck's recent detailed study which led him to conclude that they constituted 'grossly distorted and diminished versions' of Mann's work, and that 'the loss, not only of accuracy but also of quality, is inestimable'. Not only was her grasp of German so shaky that she made countless elementary errors of comprehension, but she also made frequent omissions and additions and, especially in *Buddenbrooks*, unnecessarily simplified Mann's characteristic complex syntax.

But it was perhaps in *Death in Venice*, Mann's most widely read work in English, that the damage by Lowe-Porter was most significant and severe. For here her puritanism, which saw her tone down Mann's treatment of sexuality, especially homoeroticism, throughout his *œuvre*, was most disastrous. The result is a reworked, sanitized version of the text, in which Mann's subtle and ambiguous references to von Aschenbach's sexual desire for Tadzio are largely lost, culminating in Lowe-Porter's 'astonishing' omission (Buck) of the last sentence of the penultimate paragraph, which describes a final attempt by the dying von Aschenbach to follow Tadzio.

A more accurate translation of *Death in Venice* by Kenneth **Burke** had already been published by Knopf in 1925, but this was superseded by Lowe-Porter's version and was only reprinted once. It was only with the publication in 1990 of a new translation by David **Luke** (who had already published new translations of a selection of short works by Mann in 1970, but had been unable to include *Death in Venice* for copyright reasons) that a faithful and sensitive version of the novella became widely available in English. The continuing popularity of the story is testified to by the appearance of two recent new American translations by Clayton **Koelb** and Stanley Appelbaum.

In recent years Knopf has finally begun to publish new American translations of Mann's major novels by John E. **Woods**. *Buddenbrooks* appeared in 1994, *The Magic Mountain* in 1995, and *Doctor Faustus* in 1998. Whilst representing a vast improvement in capturing Mann's style and retaining his sentence structure, these translations still surprisingly suffer from lapses in comprehension of the German text.

vi. Robert Musil Musil, the author of the short novel *Die Verwirrungen des Zöglings Törleß* (1906, Young Törless) and a number of short stories, gained his place in world literature through his vast unfinished novel *Der Mann ohne Eigenschaften* (1930–1943, The Man Without Qualities). Set in 1913, the novel is a penetrating analysis of Austrian society on the eve of the collapse of the Habsburg empire in World War I. It was translated into English in the 1950s by Eithne Wilkins and Ernst Kaiser. Their translation of *Törleß* appeared in 1955, and selections of the stories appeared in the 1960s. Though not error-free, these translations have been well regarded by a whole generation of readers and commentators. But as with Kafka, the original German edition of *The Man Without Qualities* has been superseded by a new edition, published in 1978, which made a fuller, more informed selection from the vast amount of unpublished material relating to the novel which Musil left (the entire material is now available in German on CD-Rom). This has led in turn to a new translation of the novel by Sophie **Wilkins** and Burton **Pike**, the former responsible for the parts published by Musil him-

self, and the latter translating for the first time a selection (running to over 600 pages) from the unpublished material in the 1978 German edition. This more accurate and much fuller version of the novel allows the English reader to appreciate more fully Musil's plans for the continuation of the novel.

vii. Hermann Hesse Hesse, who won the Nobel Prize for Literature in 1946, is one of the most widely translated and widely read of 20th-c. German prose writers and attained something of a cult status amongst the hippie generation in the 1960s and 1970s, especially in the United States. His most important works include *Peter Camenzind* (1904), *Unterm Rad* (1906, Beneath the Wheel), *Demian* (1919), *Siddhartha* (1922), *Steppenwolf* (1927), *Narziß und Goldmund* (1930), and *Das Glasperlenspiel* (1943, The Glass Bead Game).

Starting with the translation of *Demian* in 1923, most of his subsequent works were translated into English shortly after their publication in German. In the 1950s Hilda **Rosner** translated two of the eastern books, *Siddhartha* and *Die Morgenlandfahrt* (1932, The Journey to the East), and in the late 1950s, Walter J. **Strachan** translated the early novels, *Unterm Rad*, as *The Prodigy* in 1957, and *Peter Camenzind*, in 1961, as well as completing a new translation of *Demian* in 1958.

The translation of Hesse's works reached a high point between 1963 and 1972: during that period, not only were further works translated, especially by Ralph Manheim, sometimes together with Denver Lindley, but almost all the previously translated works were retranslated, or, in the case of *Steppenwolf*, revised, and most remain in print.

viii. War Novels from Two World Wars German war novels generated by both world wars have frequently attracted both translation into English and a wide readership. The most famous and most widely read in English of all such novels is Erich Maria Remarque's novel of the life of a young soldier on the Western Front in World War I, *Im Westen nichts Neues* (1929, All Quiet on the Western Front). A translation of the novel by A. W. **Wheen** appeared in the same year in Britain, and a 'severely mutilated version' (Owen) of this translation known as the 'US Kindergarten edition' also appeared in America the same year, omitting many sections which the US editors found too strong. Wheen's translation has been shown to be full of 'blatant mistakes, mistranslations, misleading renditions' (Owen), not to mention additions, and it also failed to capture the feel of the language of soldiers at the front. A new translation by Brian **Murdoch** finally appeared in 1994 which succeeded in rendering Remarque's lucid and often colourful language accurately into modern English.

All of Remarque's subsequent novels were translated into English very shortly after they appeared in German, including his powerful novel about German soldiers in retreat in Russia in World War II, *Zeit zu leben, Zeit zu sterben* (1954, A Time to Live and a Time to Die). Other important German war novelists whose works were translated include Theodor Plievier, whose *Stalingrad* (1945) was translated in 1956, and Hans Helmut Kirst, whose series of novels about Gunner Asch began with *Null Acht Fünfzehn* (1954, Zero Eight Fifteen: The Strange Mutiny of Gunner Asch), translated in 1955.

ix. Postwar Classics: Böll and Grass Heinrich Böll and Günter Grass emerged by the 1960s as the major prose writers of postwar Germany. Almost the entire *œuvre* of each has been translated into English, and both gained truly international reputations, with Böll being awarded the Nobel Prize for Literature in 1972.

Böll began publishing short stories in 1947, and published his first novel, *Wo warst du, Adam?* (Adam, Where Were You?) in 1951. Other major novels include *Billiard um halbzehn* (1959, Billiards at Half Past Nine), *Ansichten eines Clowns* (1963, The Clown), *Gruppenbild mit Dame* (1971, Group Portrait with Lady), and perhaps his best-known work, in which he attacked the practices of a German tabloid

newspaper, *Die verlorene Ehre der Katharina Blum* (1974, The Lost Honour of Katharina Blum).

Translations of Böll's works began to appear in English in the mid-1950s. Mervyn **Savill** translated the early novels as well as the early collections of short stories, and P. **Bowles**'s translation of *Billiard um halbzehn* appeared in 1961. Thenceforward, Böll's major translator into English has been Leila **Vennewitz**. From the mid-1960s she translated almost all his works shortly after they appeared, and she also retranslated a number of the earlier works.

Günter Grass's, *Die Blechtrommel* (1959, The Tin Drum), the story of the drummer-boy Oskar who observes life around him in Danzig (now Gdansk in Poland) under National Socialism, catapulted its author to literary fame and remains not only Grass's greatest work but probably the most important postwar German novel. It was quickly translated into English by the American translator Ralph Manheim, who has since translated all Grass's subsequent works, including the two works which, together with *The Tin Drum*, made up the Danzig Trilogy—the short novel *Katz und Maus* (1961, Cat and Mouse) and the less successful long novel *Hundejahre* (1963, Dog Years). Other important works include *örtlich betäubt* (1969, Local Anaesthetic) and *Der Butt* (1976, The Flounder). Manheim's translations have been widely praised, though criticisms have been voiced about the frequency of omissions and a tendency to tone down Grass's often very colourful language. KL

ANTHOLOGIES Carlyle, Thomas, ed., *German Romance*, 4 vols., Edinburgh, 1827 · Gillies, Robert Pearse, *German Stories*, 3 vols., Edinburgh, 1826 · Flores, Angel, ed., *Nineteenth-Century German Tales*, New York, 1959 · Francke, Kuno, and Howard, W. G., eds., *German Classics of the Nineteenth and Twentieth Centuries*, New York, 1913–15; rep. 1969 · Kesten, Hermann, *The Blue Flower*, New York, 1946 · Oxenford, John, and Feiling, C. A., *Tales from the German*, London/New York, 1844.

BÖLL, HEINRICH Bowles, P., *Billiards at Half Past Nine*, London, 1961 · Savill, Mervyn, *Adam, Where Art Thou?*, London, 1951 · *The Unguarded House*, London, 1957 · Vennewitz, Leila, *The Clown*, London, 1965 · *Group Portrait with Lady*, London, 1973 · *And Where Were You, Adam?*, London, 1974 · *The Lost Honour of Katharina Blum*, London, 1975.

FONTANE, THEODOR Annan, Gabriele, *L'Adultera and The Poggenpuhl Family*, Chicago, 1979 · Bowman, Derek, *Entanglements*, Bampton, 1986 · Chambers, Helen, and Rorrison, Hugh, *Effi Briest*, London, 1995 · Cooper, William A., *Effi Briest*, New York, 1966 [first published in Francke and Howard, *German Classics*, xii, New York, 1913] · Eliason, Lynn R., *L'Adultera*, New York, 1990 · Hollingdale, R. J., *Before the Storm*, Oxford/New York, 1985 · Morris, Sandra, *A Suitable Match*, London, 1968 · Parmée, Douglas, *Beyond Recall*, London, 1964 · *Effi Briest*, Harmondsworth, 1967 [Penguin] · Radcliffe, Stanley, *Cecile*, London, 1992 · Royce, Katherine, *Trials and Tribulations*, New York, 1917 · Valk, E. M., *A Man of Honor*, New York, 1975 · Wallich, Walter, *Effi Briest*, London, 1962 · Zimmermann, Ulf, *Jenny Treibel*, New York, 1976 · Zwiebel, William L., *The Stechlin*, Columbia, SC, 1995.

GRASS, GÜNTER Manheim, Ralph, *The Tin Drum*, London, 1962 · *Cat and Mouse*, London, 1963 · *Dog Years*, London, 1965 · *Local Anaesthetic*, London, 1969 · *The Flounder*, London, 1978 · *The Rat*, London, 1987.

HESSE, HERMANN Creighton, Basil, *Steppenwolf*, London, 1929 [rev. Walter Sorell, New York, 1963] · Dunlop, Geoffrey, *Narziss and Goldmund*, London, 1971 [orig. *Death and the Lover*, London/New York, 1932] · Friday, N. H., *Demian*, New York, 1923 · Manheim, Ralph, *Rosshalde*, New York, 1970 · *Knulp*, New York, 1971 · Manheim, Ralph, and Lindley, Denver, *Stories of Five Decades*, New York, 1972 · Molinaro, Ursule, *Narcissus and Goldmund*, New York,

1968 · Roloff, Michael, *Peter Camenzind*, New York, 1969 · Roloff, Michael, and Lebeck, Michael, *Demian*, New York, 1965 · Rosner, Hilda, *Siddhartha*, New York, 1951 · *The Journey to the East*, London, 1956 · Savill, Mervyn, *Magister Ludi* [*The Glass Bead Game*], London, 1949 · Strachan, Walter, *The Prodigy* [*Unterm Rad*], London, 1957 · *Demian*, London, 1958 · *Peter Camenzind*, London, 1961 · Vennewitz, Leila, *Narcissus and Goldmund*, London, 1993 · Winston, Richard, and Winston, Clara, *The Glass Bead Game*, New York, 1969.

HOFFMANN, E. T. A.　Bealby, J. T., *Weird Tales*, 2 vols., New York, 1885; rep. 1970 · Bullock, Michael, *Four Tales*, London, 1962 · Cohen, J. M., *Eight Tales of Hoffmann*, London, 1952 · Ewing, Alexander, *The Serapion Brethren*, 2 vols., London, 1886–92 · Gillies, R. P., *The Devil's Elixir* [*sic*], Edinburgh, 1824 · Hollingdale, R. J., with Stella and Vernon Humphries and Sally Hayward, *Tales of Hoffmann*, Harmondsworth/New York, 1982 [Penguin] · Kent, Leonhard J., and Knight, Elizabeth C., *Selected Writings*, 2 vols., Chicago, 1969 · Kirkup, James, *Tales of Hoffmann*, London, 1966 · Manheim, Ralph, *Nutcracker*, New York, 1984 · Passage, Charles E., *Three Märchen of E. T. A. Hoffmann*, Columbia, SC, 1971 · Robertson, Ritchie, *The Golden Pot and Other Tales*, Oxford, 1992 [World's Classics] · St Simon, Mrs, *Nutcracker and Mouse King*, New York, 1853 · Taylor, Ronald, *The Devil's Elixirs*, London, 1963.

KAFKA, FRANZ　Appelbaum, Stanley, *The Metamorphosis and Other Stories*, New York, 1996 · Corngold, Stanley, *The Metamorphosis*, New York, 1972 · Greenberg, M., and Arendt, H., *The Diaries of Franz Kafka 1914–1924*, London/New York, 1949 · Harman, Mark, *The Castle*, New York, 1998 · Hofmann, Michael, *The Man Who Disappeared* [*America*], Harmondsworth, 1996 [Penguin] · Kaiser, Ernst, and Wilkins, Eithne, *In the Penal Settlement: Tales and Short Prose Works*, London, 1949 · *Wedding Preparations in the Country and Other Posthumous Prose Writings*, London, 1954 · Kresh, J., *The Diaries of Franz Kafka 1910–1913*, London/New York, 1948 · Leslie, V., *The Country Doctor*, Oxford, 1945 · Lloyd, A. L., *The Metamorphosis*, London, 1937 · Muir, Willa, and Muir, Edwin, *The Castle*, London/New York, 1930 [definitive edn., tr. W. and E. Muir, Eithne Wilkins, and Ernst Kaiser, London, 1953] · *The Great Wall of China*, London, 1933 · *The Trial*, London/New York, 1937 [rev. edn. with additional chapters tr. E. M. Butler, London, 1956] · *America*, London, 1938 · *The Penal Colony: Stories and Short Pieces*, New York, 1948 · *Description of a Struggle and the Great Wall of China*, London, 1960 [incorporating *Description of a Struggle*, tr. Tanya and James Stern, New York, 1958, later reissued as *Description of a Struggle and Other Stories*, with additional translation by Malcolm Pasley, Harmondsworth, 1979] · Neugroschel, Joachim, *The Metamorphosis and Other Stories*, New York, 1993 · Parry, Idris, *The Trial*, Harmondsworth, 1994 [Penguin] · Pasley, Malcolm, *The Great Wall of China and Other Short Works*, Harmondsworth, 1991 (orig. *Shorter Works*, i, London, 1973) [Penguin] · *The Transformation (Metamorphosis) and other Stories*, Harmondsworth, 1992 [Penguin] · Scott, Douglas, and Waller, Chris, *The Trial*, London, 1977 · Stern, J., and Duckworth, E., *Letters to Felice*, New York, 1973, London, 1974 · Stern, T., and Stern, J., *Letters to Milena*, New York/London, 1953 · Underwood, J. A., *Stories 1904–1924*, London, 1981 · Winston, R., and Winston, C., *Letters to Friends, Family and Editors*, New York, 1977, London, 1978.

KIRST, HANS HELMUT　Kee, Robert, *Zero Eight Fifteen: The Strange Mutiny of Gunner Asch*, London, 1955.

KLEIST, HEINRICH VON　Greenberg, Martin, *The Marquise of O. and Other Stories*, New York, 1960 [rev. edn. 1973] · Luke, David, and Reeves, Nigel, *The Marquise of O—, and Other Stories*, Harmondsworth, 1978 [Penguin].

MANN, THOMAS　Appelbaum, Stanley, *Death in Venice*, New York, 1995 · Burke, Kenneth, *Death in Venice and Other Stories*, New York, 1925; repr. 1965 · Koelb, Clayton, *Death in Venice*, New York, 1994 · Lindley, Denver, *Confessions of Felix Krull, Confidence Man*, New York/London, 1955 · Lowe-Porter, Helen, *Buddenbrooks*, New York/London, 1924 · *The Magic Mountain*, New York, 1927 · *Death in Venice*, London, 1928 · *Stories of Three Decades*, New York/London, 1936 · *Doctor Faustus*, New York, 1948 · *Joseph and His Brothers*, New York, 1948 · Luke, David, *Death in Venice and Other Stories*, London, 1990 · Trask, Willard R., *The Black Swan*, New York/London, 1954 · Woods, John E., *Buddenbrooks*, New York, 1994 · *The Magic Mountain*, New York, 1995 · *Doctor Faustus*, New York, 1998.

MUSIL, ROBERT　Kaiser, Ernst, and Wilkins, Eithne, *The Man without Qualities*, 3 vols., London, 1953–60 · *Tonka and Other Stories*, London, 1965 · *Young Törless*, London, 1965 · *Five Women*, New York, 1966 · Wilkins, Sophie, and Pike, Burton, *The Man without Qualities*, 2 vols., London, 1995.

PLIEVIER, THEODOR　Robinson, H. Langmead, *Stalingrad*, London, 1956.

REMARQUE, ERICH MARIA　Lindley, Denver, *A Time to Love* [sic] *and a Time to Die*, London, 1954 · Murdoch, Brian, *All Quiet on the Western Front*, London, 1994 · Wheen, A. W., *All Quiet on the Western Front*, London [abr. version, Boston], 1929.

STORM, THEODOR　Jackson, Dennis, *The Dykemaster*, London, 1996 · Skelton, Geoffrey, *The White Horseman, Beneath the Flood*, London, 1962 · Wright, James, *The Rider on the White Horse and Selected Stories*, New York, 1964.

SEE ALSO　Buck, T., 'Loyalty and Licence: Thomas Mann's Fiction in English Translation', *Modern Language Review*, 91 (1996), 898–921 · Gray, R., 'But Kafka Wrote in German', in A. Flores, ed., *The Kafka Debate: New Perspectives For Our Time*, New York, 1977, 242–52 · Hobson, I., 'The Kafka Problem Compounded: Trial and Judgment in English', *Modern Fiction Studies*, 23 (1977–8), 511–29 · Keenoy, R., and Mitchell, M. eds., *The Babel Guide to German Fiction in English Translation*, London, 1997 [contains bibliography of German fiction translated in the UK since 1950] · Owen, C. R., 'All Quiet on the Western Front: Sixty Years Later', *Krieg und Literatur*, 1 (1989), 41–8.

12. DRAMA SINCE 1880

i. Naturalism The most important playwright, and the one most often translated—though not always strictly 'naturalist'—is Gerhart Hauptmann. An interesting though patchy translation by the 19 year-old James **Joyce** of *Vor Sonnenaufgang* (1889, Before Sunrise) stands out, particularly against conscientious but uninspiring translations by Ludwig **Lewisohn** of *Vor Sonnenaufgang* (as *Before Dawn*), *Die Weber* (1893, The Weavers), *Der Biberpelz* (1893, The Beavercoat), *Der rote Hahn* (1901, The Conflagration), *Fuhrmann Henschel* (1899, Drayman Henschel), *Rose Bernd* (1903), and *Die Ratten* (1911, The Rats). A translation of *The Weavers*, by Frank **Marcus**, performed at the Roundhouse, London, in the late 1970s, fails to find a convincingly realistic idiom in English.

ii. Expressionism One of the playwrights regarded as expressionist to have been widely translated in the English-speaking area is Georg Kaiser. Two volumes of his plays exist in plausible translations by B. J. **Kenworthy**, H. F. **Garten**, and Elizabeth **Sprigge**. Several major plays from a vast output are represented here, including *Von Morgens bis Mitternachts* (1917, From Morning to Midnight) *Die Bürger von Calais* (1917, The Burghers of Calais), *Die Koralle* (1917, The Coral), *Gas I/II* (1918, 1920), *Oktobertag* (1928, One Day in October) and *Das Floss der Medusa* (1942, The Raft of the Medusa). Ernst Toller is the only other dramatist of this movement to have been frequently translated into English and often performed—most recently at the Royal National Theatre, London. This was a performance of *Die Maschinenstürmer* (published 1922) in a translation by Ashley **Dukes** called *The Machine Wreckers*, originally published in 1923, which is more laborious than the alert translation by Peter **Tegel**, as performed at the Half Moon Theatre and on radio. Vera **Mendel**'s translation of *Masse-Mensch* (1921), published in 1934 as *Masses and Man*, reflects its period. *Hinkemann* (1924) has appeared in a solid translation by J. M. **Ritchie**, retaining the German title.

iii. Early to Mid-Twentieth Century Whilst not frequently translated or performed, the plays of Carl Sternheim, which mostly depict the middle classes in various stages of moral—and physical—undress, are important social satires, for which equivalents in English are difficult to find. Published translations by, for example, M. A. L. **Brown**, M. A. **McHaffie**, J. M. Ritchie, and J. D. **Stowell** of plays like *Bürger Schippel* (1913, Paul Schippel, Esq.),

Die Hose (1911, The Bloomers), *Der Snob* (1915), and *Das Fossil* (1925) lack the ironic edge of the version made of *Die Hose* by the playwright C. P. **Taylor** as *The Knickers*, which was performed in Scotland in the 1970s.

An important pre-Brecht playwright, whose work did not fully emerge in theatre-effective translations until the early 1990s, when her work was translated by Elisabeth **Bond-Pablé** and Tinch **Minter**, is Marieluise Fleisser. Her two major plays, *Fegefeuer in Ingolstadt* (1926) and *Pioniere in Ingolstadt* (1929), were memorably translated as *Purgatory in Ingolstadt* and *Pioneers in Ingolstadt* for production at the Gate Theatre, London in 1991. Likely to work in English with a similar combination of poetic allusiveness and irony is *Die Wupper* (written 1909, performed 1919), the major play by Else Lasker-Schüler, which—astonishingly—remains untranslated, unperformed, and unpublished in English. This cannot just be because its title would be *The River Wupper*.

The most important and frequently translated dramatist of this period is Frank Wedekind. Writers of the calibre of Edward **Bond**, working with Elisabeth Bond-Pablé, as well as the poets, Ted **Hughes** and Stephen **Spender**, have made trenchant translations of several plays, including *Frühlingserwachen* (published 1891, Spring's Awakening). The Bonds have also made idiomatic and dramatically effective translations of *Erdgeist* (1895, Earth Spirit) and *Die Büchse der Pandora* (1906, Pandora's Box). The two plays are usually combined into *The Lulu Plays*. Steve **Gooch** has made a convincing translation and adaptation of both the Lulu plays and of *Der Marquis von Keith* (1901, The Marquis of Keith). Anthony **Vivis** has translated Wedekind's mime play (without dialogue), *Die Kaiserin von Neufundland* (1897, The Empress of Newfoundland).

iv. Bertolt Brecht Drama by Brecht, or, more accurately perhaps, by Brecht & Co., has dominated contemporary theatre for the past 50 years or so. The Brecht industry shows no signs of winding down. That said, the publication in 1994 of John Fuegi's *The Life and Lies of Bertolt Brecht* has highlighted allegations that many, if not most, of the plays credited to Brecht were co-written principally with lover-colleagues, such as Elisabeth Hauptmann, Margarete Steffin, and Ruth Berlau, who are sometimes, but not always, credited as collaborators.

Given that various nettles are grasped, not least

that of the creative role of collaborators and the re-creative role of accurate and theatre-friendly translations, Brecht plays look likely to maintain their supremacy in the theatre. His work has been widely performed in the original in the German-speaking theatre, and all the major plays, as well as the minor plays and most of the adaptations, have been translated into English and produced frequently in all English-speaking territories, notably Britain and the USA.

Pioneering translations by Eric **Bentley**, who befriended and supported Brecht during his American exile, are generally considered less than convincing for theatre performance. Scholarly and conscientious translations by John **Willett** and Ralph **Manheim** (who was also a well-known translator of Günter Grass and Louis-Ferdinand Céline [II.g.12.ii]) have helped establish Brechtian theatre. The indispensable *Collected Plays*, volume i of which appeared in 1970, has now reached volume x. John Willett's critical books, including *The Theatre of Bertolt Brecht*, which dates from 1959, are invaluable to anyone studying or planning to direct Brecht plays, as well as being useful guides for translators.

Some 40 plays or adaptations are credited to Brecht, translations of which are published in the *Collected Plays*. Whilst academically sound, these translations may not always be the first choice of theatre directors looking for dramatic individuality and edge in English. Among the most important or interesting are:

Die Dreigroschenoper, (1928), translated as *The Threepenny Opera* by Ralph Manheim and John Willett; *Mann ist Mann* (1926), translated as *Man Equals Man* by Gerhard **Nellhaus**; *Aufstieg und Fall der Stadt Mahagonny* (1930), translated as The *Rise and Fall of the City of Mahagonny* by W. H. **Auden** and Chester **Kallman**; *Leben des Galilei* (1943), translated as *Life of Galileo* by John Willett; *Mutter Courage und ihre Kinder* (1949), translated as *Mother Courage and Her Children* by Ralph Manheim; *Der Gute Mensch von Sezuan* (1941), translated as The *Good Person of Szechwan* by John Willett; *Der Aufhaltsame Aufstieg des Arturo Ui* (1943), translated as The *Resistible Rise of Arturo Ui* by Ralph Manheim; *Der Kaukasische Kreidekreis* (1954), translated as *The Caucasian Chalk Circle* by James and Tania **Stern** with W. H. Auden; and *Die Tage der Kommune* (1956), translated as *The Days of the Commune* by Clive **Barker** and Arno **Reinfrank**.

In recent years a number of writers known principally for their own original plays have written translations or versions from so-called literal translations, building on work by W. H. Auden and Chester Kallman. One of the most persuasive of these translation-adaptations is George **Tabori**'s version, in stylized Elizabethan language, of *Arturo Ui*. Hanif **Kureishi** (*Mother Courage*), Michael **Hofmann** (*The Good Person of Sichuan*), and David **Hare** (*Life of Galileo, Mother Courage*) have all provided texts which play well in the theatre. Robert David **MacDonald**, who has also written plays of his own, has memorably translated *The Threepenny Opera* and, for Glenda Jackson's theatre swan-song, *Mother Courage*, complete with the f-word—an entirely appropriate decision. Jean **Benedetti**, Steve Gooch, Michael **Hamburger**, and Peter Tegel, among others, have also made effective translations.

v. Austrian Playwrights Though not as popular now as in the earlier part of this century, Hugo von Hofmannsthal has had a number of plays as well as libretti translated into English. A representative selection of his plays was published in Britain in 1963/64. Among these are stylish translations of such plays as *Elektra* (with music by Richard Strauss, 1909), *Das Salzburger grosse Welttheater* (1922, The Salzburg Great World-Theatre), *Der Turm* (1927, The Tower), *Der Rosenkavalier* (1911, The Knight of the Rose), *Arabella* (1933), and *Der Schwierige* (1921, The Difficult Man) made by Michael Hamburger, Christopher **Middleton**, Willa **Muir**, and Vernon **Watkins** respectively.

Johann Nestroy's best works are too specifically Viennese in idiom to translate effectively, and one can therefore understand, as well as admire, spirited adaptations, such as Tom **Stoppard**'s of *Einen Jux will er sich machen* (1842) as *On The Razzle*. Arthur Schnitzler also often uses Viennese dialect in his plays, but the greater universality of their content and approach has made them better known in this country, and they generally communicate well to an audience in the theatre, whether translated or adapted. An articulate and persuasive translation of *Anatol*, a sequence of seven one-act plays (1910), by Michael **Robinson**, as well as several renderings of Schnitzler's best-known play, *Der Reigen* (1920), a cycle of 10 dialogues usually translated as *La Ronde*, by John **Barton**, Sue **Davies**, Frank and Janet **Marcus**, and Charles **Osborne**, have helped establish Schnitzler's presence in British theatre. Several of his numerous one-act plays, including *Paracelsus* (1899) and *Der grüne Kakadu* (1899, The Green Cockatoo) have been translated by G. J. **Weinberger**. Tom Stoppard has made theatrically compelling versions of *Liebelei* (1895, Dalliance) and of *Das weite Land* (1911, Undiscovered Country). Schnitzler's best comedy, *Professor Bernhardi* (1912) has yet to be convincingly translated.

This is also true of Karl Kraus's play *Die Letzten*

Tage der Menschheit (published in its final form in 1926). This 800-page drama in 220 scenes has appeared as *The Last Days of Mankind* in a translation by Alexander **Gode** and Sue Ellen **Wright**. Still to be published is the energetic translation made in 1983 by Robert David MacDonald for a performance by the Citizens Theatre, Glasgow.

More recently, the plays of Peter Handke have made a considerable impact in their English translations, although the renderings of such plays as *Publikumsbeschimpfung* (1966), *Selbstbezichtigung* (1966), *Weissagung* (1966), *Kaspar* (1968), *Das Mündel will Vormund sein* (1969), *Der Ritt über den Bodensee* (1971) and *Die Unvernünftigen sterben aus* (1973)— translated by Michael **Roloff** respectively as *Offending the Audience, Self-Accusation, Kaspar, My Foot My Tutor, The Ride across Lake Constance,* and *They Are Dying Out*—allow room for future translation of a more idiomatic and theatrically effective nature. As with Kleist [II.h.4.iii], Handke's dramatic language is complex and self-referential. The degree of recreation in Ralph Manheim's translation of *Über die Dörfer* (1981) as *The Long Way Round* for a recent production at the Royal National Theatre failed to make the text convincing in English.

Among other contemporary Austrian playwrights who have been rendered into English are the following: Ernst Jandl, whose play *Aus der Fremde* (1980) was memorably translated as *Out of Estrangement* by Michael Hamburger; Elfriede Jelinek, whose post-Ibsen play, *Was Geschah nachdem Nora ihren Mann verlassen hatte,* was translated by Tinch Minter as *What Happened after Nora Left Her Husband;* Felix Mitterer, several of whose plays, including *Stigma* (1982) and *Sibirien* (1989), have been translated by Margit **Kleinman** and Louis **Fantasia**; and Peter Turrini, whose play *Josef und Maria* (1980) has appeared in Britain in a translation by David **Roger**. After his death Thomas Bernhard's drama continues to exercise considerable fascination in German-speaking theatre. Translations exist of several plays, including *Ein Fest für Boris* (1970) and *Der Theatermacher* (1985), translated respectively as *A Party for Boris* and *Histrionics* by Peter **Jansen** and Kenneth **Northcott**. An English translation by Neville and Stephen **Plaice** of *Die Macht der Gewohnheit* (1974, The Force of Habit) at the RNT in the early 1970s was unfairly dismissed. Other strong plays, such as *Die Jagdgesellschaft* (1974), translated by Gitta **Honegger** in the USA as *The Hunting Party,* have so far failed to assert themselves in Britain.

vi. Mid- to Late Twentieth Century Two playwrights who are known in Britain principally for only one play are Wolfgang Borchert, known for *Draussen vor der Tür* (first performed on radio in 1947), which has been plausibly translated by David **Porter** as *The Man Outside,* and was retranslated for a radio broadcast in 1997, by Robert **Walker**; and Carl Zuckmayer, whose play *Der Hauptmann von Köpenick* (published 1931) was given a very playable adaptation by John **Mortimer**.

Ödön von Horváth, the Hungarian who wrote in German, is much better known in Britain for a wide selection of plays, thanks largely to highly speakable and accurate translations by Christopher **Hampton**. Horváth's most popular play, *Geschichten aus dem Wienerwald* (1931), was published as *Tales from the Vienna Woods* after a successful production at the RNT. It was followed by equally striking productions at the RNT and the Hammersmith Lyric, respectively, of *Don Juan kommt aus dem Krieg* (written 1936, premièred 1952) as *Don Juan Comes Back from the War,* and of *Glaube, Liebe, Hoffnung* (1936), translated as *Faith, Hope and Charity*. In the USA, renderings of plays such as *Kasimir und Karoline* (1932), *Der jüngste Tag* (1937, Judgement Day), as well as *Figaro lässt sich scheiden* (1937, Figaro Gets a Divorce), have all been published. Kenneth **McLeish**, an energetic and gifted translator who died suddenly before Christmas 1997 at the age of 57, has also made a lively and idiomatic translation of *Zur schönen Aussicht* (written 1929, premièred 1969) as *The Belle Vue*.

Two Swiss dramatists who have made a big impact in English are Max Frisch and Friedrich Dürrenmatt, both now dead. Solid English translations by Michael **Bullock** have helped establish both, and more risk-taking renderings of Dürrenmatt by James **Kirkup** have helped ensure greater enduring interest in his work in English-speaking theatre. The best-known works by Dürrenmatt include *Der Besuch der alten Dame* (1956), usually translated as *The Visit, Die Physiker* (1962, The Physicists), *Der Meteor* (1966, The Meteor), and *Play Strindberg* (1972). Frisch's best-known plays include *Die chinesische Mauer* (1946, The Great Wall of China) and *Biedermann und die Brandstifter* (1958, The Fire-Raisers), as well as *Andorra* (1961) and *Biographie* (1968).

One of the most cogent political playwrights of recent years, who has had two major plays translated into English, is Peter Weiss. His outstanding success in Britain was the *Marat/Sade* (1964) in a translation by Geoffrey **Skelton**, adapted into rhymed verse by Adrian **Mitchell**, produced originally with great success by Peter Brook at the Royal Shakespeare Company in 1965 and recently revived at the Royal National Theatre by Jeremy

Sams. *Die Ermittlung* (1965) has been translated with appropriately chilling sobriety by Alexander **Gross**, as well as by Ulu **Grosbard** and Jon **Swan**, in both cases as *The Investigation*. Weiss's *Vietnam Diskurs* (1968) also exists in translation, though both this and the original play are of mainly historical interest now.

Thanks largely to sensitive translations in the USA by Carl **Weber** and in Britain by Marc **von Henning**, Heiner Müller, also dead, has begun to emerge in the English-speaking theatre as a dramatist of austere power who combines a poetic technique with a political agenda. The 1987 visit of Robert Wilson's production of Müller's *Hamletmaschine* (1979) to the Almeida Theatre, London, helped establish a status confirmed by other plays translated into English. *Der Auftrag* (1981, The Mission), *Quartett* (1982), *Verkommenes Ufer Medematerial Landschaft mit Argonauten* (1983, Waterfront Wasteland Medea Material, Landscape with Argonauts), and *Volokolamsker Chaussee I–V* (1985, Volokolamsk Highway) have helped Müller achieve at least a name in Britain, as well as the USA.

Manfred Karge, also a so-called Brecht-pupil, has made a considerable impact with two plays: *Jacke Wie Hose* (1982, translated as *Man to Man*) and *Die Eroberung des Südpols* (1986, The Conquest of the South Pole).

Among playwrights to emerge from Bavaria, apart from Brecht and Fleisser, Rainer Werner Fassbinder, Franz Xaver Kroetz, Kerstin Specht, and Martin Sperr all work well in English, which transmutes their differing combinations of lyrical and dramatic qualities into language which has usually resulted in successful productions. Translations by Denis **Calandra**, Steve Gooch, and Anthony Vivis (Fassbinder), Roger **Downey**, Jack Gelber, Steve Gooch, Michael Roloff, Katharina **Hehn**, and Anthony Vivis (Kroetz), Tinch Minter and Guntram H. **Weber** (Specht), and Anthony Vivis (Sperr) have helped establish these dramatists in the theatre.

Among the early plays by Kroetz which often caused riots in middle-class audiences and consternation in the Press, *Stallerhof* (1972), translated as *Farmyard* by Roger Downey, is characteristic. Kroetz rewrote another early play, *Lieber Fritz* (1975), as *Der Drang* (1994), translated in 1995 as *Desire*. One of his most successful plays in performance, in the USA and Britain, was *Wer Durchs Laub Geht* (1981), translated as *Through the Leaves*. More recently, his plays *Das Nest* (1975) and *Bauern Sterben* (1985, Dead Soil), have been well reviewed in theatre productions in Britain.

Whilst better known as a film-maker, Rainer Werner Fassbinder has made a considerable impact in Britain and the USA with theatre texts such as *Die Bitteren Tränen der Petra von Kant* (1971) and *Bremer Freiheit* (1971), translated as *The Bitter Tears of Petra von Kant* and *Bremen Coffee*, respectively. His fellow-Bavarian Martin Sperr has not made the breakthrough in Britain that his poetically charged social realism warrants, but he did achieve success with the Gate Theatre production in 1995 of *Jagdszenen aus Niederbayern*, translated by John **Grillo** and Anthony Vivis as *Hunting Scenes from Lower Bavaria*. Kerstin Specht's allusive stage poetry has yet to establish itself fully in the English-speaking theatre, but the translation of *Das Glühend Männle* (1989) as *The Little Red-Hot Man* has given her a foothold.

Two other major dramatists, Gerlind Reinshagen and Botho Strauss, have begun to have an impact in the English-speaking cultural world. Strauss's plays in published English translation include *Gross und Klein* (1978), translated by Anne **Cattaneo** as *Big and Little*, *Der Park* (1984) and *Die Fremdenführerin*, translated as *The Tour Guide* by Carl Weber and as *The Tourist Guide* by Tinch Minter and Anthony Vivis. Despite a notable production in Glasgow in 1971 of *Leben und Tod der Marilyn Monroe* (1970, The Life and Death of Marilyn Monroe), of *Sonntagskinder* (1976, Sunday's Children) in Derby in 1988, and of *Die Clownin* (1986, The Clown) at the RNT Studio in 1995, Reinshagen's work has yet to assert itself fully in print in Britain, although *Eisenherz* (1982), translated by Sue-Ellen **Case** as *Ironheart*, has appeared in the USA.   AV

BERNHARD, THOMAS   Honegger, Gitta, *The Hunting Party*, New York, 1990 · Jansen, Peter, and Northcott, Kenneth, *A Party for Boris*, London, 1991 · *Histrionics*, London, 1991 · Plaice, Neville, and Plaice, Stephen, *The Force of Habit*, London, 1976.

BRECHT, BERTOLT   Benedetti, Jean, *A Respectable Wedding*, London, 1970; rep. 1980 [with *The Beggar, or the Dead Dog*, tr. Michael Hamburger] · Bentley, Eric, *Baal*, in *Early Plays*, ed. E. Bentley, New York, 1964 · Brenton, Howard, *The Life of Galileo*, London, 1963 · Gooch, Steve, *The Mother*, London, 1978 · Hare, David, *Mother Courage and Her Children*, London, 1995 · Hofmann, Michael, *The Good Person of Sichuan*, London, 1989 · Manheim, Ralph, and Willett, John, eds., *Bertolt Brecht: Collected Plays*, London, 1970– [for details of translators see above] · Tabori, George, *The Resistible Rise of Arturo Ui*, London, 1972 · Tegel, Peter, *Baal*, London, 1979.

DÜRRENMATT, FRIEDRICH   Bowles, Patrick, *The Visit*, London, 1956 · Kirkup, James, *The Meteor*, London, 1973 · *Play*

Strindberg, New York, 1973 · Nellhaus, Gerhard, *Four Plays*, London, 1958, New York, 1964 [*Romulus the Great, The Marriage of Mr Mississippi, An Angel Comes to Babylon, The Physicists*].

FASSBINDER, RAINER WERNER   Calandra, Denis, *Plays*, New York, 1985 · Esslin, Renata, and Esslin, Martin, et al., *Shakespeare the Sadist*, London, 1977 [*Shakespeare the Sadist*, by Wolfgang Bauer, translated by Renata and Martin Esslin; *Bremen Coffee*, by Rainer Werner Fassbinder, translated by Anthony Vivis; *My Foot My Tutor*, by Peter Handke, translated by Michael Roloff, *Stallerhof*, by Franz Xaver Kroetz, translated by Katharina Hehn] · Gooch, Steve, *Cock-Artist, Gambit International Theatre Review*, 39–40, London, 1982 [also includes *The Mission* by Heiner Müller, translated by Stuart Hood, and *Home Work*, by Franz Xaver Kroetz, translated by Steve Gooch] · Vivis, Anthony, *The Bitter Tears of Petra von Kant* and *Blood on the Neck of the Cat*, Oxford, 1984.

FLEISSER, MARIELUISE   Bond-Pablé, Elisabeth, and Minter, Tinch, *Plays by Women*, vol. ix, ed. Annie Castledine, London, 1991 [*Purgatory in Ingolstadt* and *Pioneers in Ingolstadt*].

FRISCH, MAX   Bullock, Michael, *Four Plays*, London, 1969; rep. 1974 [*The Great Wall of China, Don Juan, Philipp Hotz's Fury, Biography*].

HANDKE, PETER   Roloff, Michael, *Plays*, i, London, 1997 [*Offending the Audience, Kaspar, My Foot My Tutor, The Ride across Lake Constance*, and, with the collaboration of Carl Weber, *They Are Dying Out*].

HAUPTMANN, GERHART   Joyce, James, *Before Sunrise*, Canoga Park, Calif., 1978 · Lewisohn, Ludwig, *The Dramatic Works*, 2 vols., London, 1913 · Marcus, Frank, *The Weavers*, London, 1980.

HOFMANNSTHAL, HUGO VON   Hamburger, Michael, et al., *Selected Plays and Libretti*, London, 1963.

HORVÁTH, ÖDÖN VON   Dixon, Richard, Downey, Roger, and Foster, Paul, *Four Plays*, New York, 1986 · Hampton, Christopher, *Tales from the Vienna Woods*, London, 1977 · *Faith, Hope and Charity*, London/Boston, 1989 · *Don Juan Comes Back From the War*, London, 1989 · McLeish, Kenneth, *The Belle Vue*, London, 1996.

JANDL, ERNST   Hamburger, Michael, *Out of Estrangement*, Cambridge, 1987.

JELINEK, ELFRIEDE   Minter, Tinch, *What Happened After Nora Left Her Husband*, in *Plays by Women*, x, ed. Annie Castledine, London, 1994.

KAISER, GEORG   Garten, H. F., Kenworthy, B. J., and Sprigge, Elizabeth, *Plays*, 2 vols., London, 1971–81.

KARGE, MANFRED   Minter, Tinch, and Vivis, Anthony, *The Conquest of the South Pole*, London, 1988 · Vivis, Anthony, *Man to Man*, London, 1988.

KRAUS, KARL   Gode, Alexander, and Wright, Sue Ellen, *The Last Days of Mankind*, New York, 1974.

KROETZ, FRANZ XAVER   Downey, Roger, *Through the Leaves and Other Plays*, New York, 1992 · Gelber, Jack, et al., *Farmyard and Four Other Plays*, New York, 1976.

LASKER-SCHÜLER, ELSE   Bennett, Beate Hein, *IandI [IchundIch]*, in *The Divided Home/Land: Contemporary German Women's Plays*, ed. Sue-Ellen Case, Ann Arbor, Mich., 1992.

MITTERER, FELIX   Fantasia, Louis, and Kleinman, Margit, *Siberia and Other Plays: Stigma, Visiting Hours, Dragonthirst, There's Not a Finer Country*, Riverside, Calif., 1994.

MÜLLER, HEINER   Henning, Marc von, *Theatremachine*, London, 1995 · Weber, Carl, *Hamletmachine and Other Texts for The Stage*, New York, 1984 · *Explosion of a Memory*, New York, 1989.

REINSHAGEN, GERLIND   Case, Sue-Ellen, and Teraoka, Arlene A., *Ironheart*, in *The Divided Home/Land*, ed. Sue-Ellen Case, Ann Arbor, Mich., 1992.

SCHNITZLER, ARTHUR   Marcus, Frank, and Marcus Janet, *La Ronde*, London, 1982 · Robinson, Michael, *Anatol*, Bath, 1989 · Stoppard, Tom, *Dalliance* and *Undiscovered Country*, London, 1986 · Weinberger, G. J., *Paracelsus and Other One-Act Plays*, Riverside, Calif., 1995.

SPECHT, KERSTIN   Weber, Guntram H., *The Little Red-Hot Man*, in *The Divided Home/Land*, ed. Sue-Ellen Case, Ann Arbor, Mich., 1992.

SPERR, MARTIN   Vivis, Anthony, *Tales From Landshut*, London, 1969.

STERNHEIM, CARL   Brown, M. A. L., et al., *Scenes from the Heroic Life of the Middle Classes*, London, 1970.

STRAUSS, BOTHO   Cattaneo, Anne, *Big and Little*, New York, 1979 · Minter, Tinch, and Vivis, Anthony, *The Tourist Guide*, in *Plays International*, vol. ii, 10, ed. Peter Roberts, London, 1987 · *The Park*, Sheffield, 1988 · Weber, Carl, *The Tour Guide*, in *Drama Contemporary: Germany*, ed. Carl Weber, Baltimore, 1996.

TOLLER, ERNST   Dukes, Ashley, *The Machine Wreckers*, London, 1923 [new edn. 1995] · Mendel, Vera, *Masses and Man*, London, 1934 · Ritchie, J. M., and Stowell, J. D., *Vision and Aftermath: Four Expressionist War Plays* [incl. *Hinkemann*], in *German Expressionism*, ed. J. M. Ritchie, London, 1969.

TURRINI, PETER   Roger, David, *Joseph and Mary*, in *Gambit International Review*, 39–40 ed. Steve Gooch and Julian Hilton, London, 1982.

WEDEKIND, FRANK   Bond, Edward, and Bond-Pablé, Elisabeth, *Plays*, London, 1993 · Hughes, Ted, *Spring Awakening: A New Version*, London, 1995 · Spender, Stephen, *The Lulu-Plays and Other Sex Tragedies*, London, 1972/81 · Vivis, Anthony, *The Empress of Newfoundland*, Cambridge, 1982.

WEISS, PETER   Baxandall, Lee, and Skelton, Geoffrey, *Two Plays*, New York, 1970 · Gross, Alexander, *The Investigation*, London, 1966 · Skelton, Geoffrey, and Mitchell, Adrian, *Marat/Sade*, London, 1969.

ZUCKMAYER, CARL   Mortimer, John, *The Captain of Köpenick*, London, 1971.

341

13. POETRY SINCE 1850

i. Anthologies and the Creation of a Canon Very little of the poetry written in the early years of this period, by poets such as Theodor Fontane, Gottfried Keller, or Conrad Ferdinand Meyer, has been translated into English. For the 1880s and 1890s the picture changes somewhat; a wide selection of poetry from this period is contained in *Contemporary German Poetry* (1923), a monolingual anthology by Babette **Deutsch** and Avrahm **Yarmolinsky**, which includes naturalist, post-symbolist, impressionist, and early expressionist poetry in translations from the work of Detlev von Liliencron, Stefan George, Rainer Maria Rilke, Else Lasker-Schüler, and many others. It also illustrates the more contemporary poetry of the time, attempting to give a picture of the 'confusion' of Germany's expressionist and post-expressionist poets such as Georg Heym, Georg Trakl, Paul Zech, Yvan Goll, and Gottfried Benn.

Deutsch and Yarmolinsky state that their intention is to produce English poems rather than absolutely accurate translations, and so they have omitted work they consider too fragmented to lend itself easily to translation into the more disciplined forms expected by English readers. This rather narrow view of the English reader of foreign poetry gives rise to a conservative approach to translation as something which should produce a culturally adapted result. Nevertheless, though this approach has inevitably resulted in lacunae—Theodor Storm is not included, nor are Hugo von Hofmannsthal or Hermann Hesse—there is no doubt that the book's skilful translations and useful introduction and notes have played a part in introducing German poetry of the late 19th c. to the poetry-reading public in Britain and America.

Anthologies of translations have always been important for making German poetry visible to the English-speaking reader, and none more so than those of Michael **Hamburger**. His 1962 bilingual collection with Christopher **Middleton** covers poetry from 1910 to 1960, providing translations of excellent quality, as well as a substantial introduction, thus giving a valuable picture of modern German poetry in this century.

Later bilingual collections by Hamburger have been similarly important; *East German Poetry* (1972) includes translations from Bertolt Brecht, Peter Huchel, Johannes Bobrowski, Reiner Kunze, and others by Hamburger and a number of other translators, including Ruth and Matthew **Mead** and Christopher Middleton. Hamburger's 1976 anthol-

ogy contains translations of poems by August Stramm, Hans Arp, Ernst Jandl, Günter Kunert, and Peter Handke as well as more frequently translated poets such as Lasker-Schüler, Benn, and Brecht.

Though Hamburger's is the name most closely associated with the anthologizing of 20th-c. German poetry in English translation, several other collections are worthy of mention. Agnes **Stein**'s 1979 monolingual collection contains her translations of poetry by Günter Eich, Hilde Domin, Erich Fried, and Günter Kunert, and Ewald **Osers**'s 1976 anthology, Milne **Holton** and Herbert **Kuhner**'s 1985 collection of Austrian poetry and P. **Daniel** and J. **Diethart**'s 1992 anthology of Austrian Jewish poetry all contain important work. Patrick **Bridgwater**'s anthology of 1963 contains prose translations, fascinating in their own right for their compromise between closeness to the original and conformity to English syntax. Several journals such as *Agenda* (1994) and *Lines Review* (1991) have produced special issues on German poets in translation, and *Dimension2* from the University of Texas at Austin frequently publishes translations of work by such poets as Huchel, Celan, and Ernst Meister.

ii. Major Translators Though academics may read poems in the German original, constrained only by what they know and by what is available, it is for most English readers the translator who determines what is read. For poetry since 1850, some of the most important translators have been Hamburger, Middleton, and the Meads, though most of their work is in fact confined to later poets of the period. Middleton, besides editing and co-translating with Hamburger the 1962 anthology, has translated three collections of poems by Günter Grass in collaboration with Hamburger. Though the two translators approach the act of translation very differently, both reject free imitation, which Hamburger has often called a 'springboard' from which to launch one's own work. And in fact Hamburger has been criticized for the closeness of his translations to the original. Michael Hulse (1972) feels that such closeness only works with poets to whose style and sensibilities Hamburger is attuned, such as Celan and Huchel. Hamburger himself has said that he always chooses those poems of a particular poet which he feels he can convey well. This suggests that much of what we read as German poetry in Hamburger's English translations has been filtered through Hamburger's own personality and preferences. It is fortunate that he is a translator of such eclectic taste and enormous versatility. Since the 1960s he has translated the work of Hans Magnus Enzensberger, much of it in collaboration with the author, and it is perhaps with Enzensberger and Celan, as well as with Hölderlin, that he is especially associated.

Other translators, too, are associated with particular poets. Ruth and Matthew Mead are especially known for their excellent translations of Bobrowski, though they have also translated Elisabeth Borchers (1969) and a number of lesser-known poets.

Michael **Bullock** has translated many German plays as well as poetry by Goll and Karl Krolow, but it is perhaps his translations of Krolow which are most successful and best known.

Ewald Osers is another prolific and important translator of the poetry of this period, who has given us English versions of Rose Ausländer, Reiner Kunze, and others.

Though few German poets of the period have been translated by more than two different translators, there are several noteworthy exceptions. Rilke and Brecht have been translated many times. Benn's work has found various translators, including Deutsch and Yarmolinsky. Goll, Hesse, Grass, and Krolow have appeared in a number of translations. Erich Fried, who, like many other German poets, fled to England after the rise of Nazism, has appeared in several collections. Celan, in spite of Hamburger's close association with his work, has in fact appeared in a large number of collections, several of them by others. Enzensberger's work has frequently appeared in his own translations (e.g. 1981), besides those by Hamburger and others. Christian Morgenstern, who, with his fondness for word-play, one might expect to be extremely difficult to render into another language, has also found a number of expert translators in England and America. Nelly Sachs has been translated by both Hamburger and the Meads, as well as a number of other translators, Trakl by Robert **Bly**, Middleton, and several others, and Kirsch is another poet who has attracted translators in recent years: collections include those by Wayne **Kvam** in America, and, in England, collections by Wendy **Mulford** and Anthony **Vivis** and by Margitt **Lehbert**.

iii. Problems of Translation Much of the debate on the nature of translation is in essence a discussion of how faithful or free it is, and whether it seeks equivalence of language, cultural detail, style, or

effect. In translating German poetry from the period since 1850, differences in tradition, background knowledge, philosophy, social habits, and expectations are not very great. The languages involved are both Germanic, close in syntax, word category, and even in lexis. In addition, the period in question is historically and culturally at least in part very close to our own; many historical events are shared, as are many geographical and social facts. The gap to be bridged in translation is thus relatively small.

A good illustration of the closeness possible is provided by translations of Celan's 'Todesfuge', of which there are many versions, including those by John **Felstiner**, Middleton, and Hamburger. Felstiner's version exploits the syntactic and lexical closeness of the German and English languages, gradually introducing more and more of the original German into the English version. This is possible because of the similarity of German *golden*, *Haar, Meister, aschen* to English words and because the German words can be made to fit into the English syntax. But even without such fusing of languages, an almost exact syntactic and lexical match is possible, as in Hamburger's 1988 version. And even if the poem cannot carry the same connotations or allusions in English, it does relate to a historical situation—that of the Nazi concentration camps—with which the English reader is acquainted and thus much of its meaning can be conveyed.

This is sometimes less straightforward. Enzensberger's poems, for example, often relate to specific cultural and social aspects of modern German life, to traditions and customs that Germans take for granted, and which Enzensberger is concerned to question. Because, like much contemporary poetry in both Germany and England, these poems aim to create in the reader a sense of the general application of particular experience, a translator should not reduce the particular too much. But some things are not readily comprehensible to the English reader. An explanation of Enzensberger's reference to 'Münchhausen's theorem' is incorporated into Hamburger's translation (1994: 105), for example, because Baron Munchhausen, for all that Raspe's version of his adventures first appeared in English, will not be as familiar to an English as to a German reader. And if, sometimes, the connotations fail, so that, for example, *ein Geruch nach Birken* (a smell of birches) in the bathroom will not call forth hair preparations as readily as it does to a German reader, the cultural gap is bridgeable by the English reader with a little imagination.

Many cultural phenomena are more difficult to

convey because not only do they lack an exact correspondence in English but they are not susceptible to explanation or a brief embedding in context. Hamburger's translation of *Sahneschnitzel mit Gurkensalat* (pork cutlets in cream sauce with cucumber salad) transforms this typically German meal into the typically English 'steak and chips', thus making it clear that the whole poem has been brought into an English context.

In spite of the similarities between German and English lexis and syntax, there are many differences. Compounds such as Celan's *Todesfuge*, on which Felstiner comments at some length, are common in German and beloved of poets, but difficult to render in English. In this case Felstiner himself opts for 'deathfugue', Hamburger for 'death fugue', and Middleton for 'fugue of death'. Each has different connotations, not quite those of the original. Trakl's *Mohnaugen* is clumsily rendered by Deutsch and Yarmolinsky as 'poppied eyes', unfortunately suggesting 'pop-eyes'. And what of Ausländer's *Mutter Sprache*, instead of the usual *Muttersprache* (mother tongue)? Ausländer's German suggests an apposition because a compound would be written as one word. This is lost in English, where Jean **Boase-Beier** and Anthony Vivis have no alternative but 'mother tongue'.

There are differences, too, in the formation of new words, for example verbs from adjectives. When August Stramm has 'tief stummen wir', the verb *stummen*, though unusual, fits into a pattern of similar derivations such as *grünen, scheuen, sichern*, as well as prefixed derivations such as *verstummen*. Both these types are less common in English, and Hamburger's 'deeply we dumb' has an artifice that the original does not.

Differences in syntax and word order cause even more difficulty, especially when there is deviation in the German text. Ernst Meister typically changes syntax, as in 'In den Äther speit Gold | ein raubender Fisch' ('Into the ether a ravaging fish spews gold') where one would expect 'ein raubender Fisch speit Gold'. This unusual word order is not kept by Richard **Dove**, and in fact any change in word order in English would be far more striking than in German where it is more flexible. Yet German word order can be mirrored successfully in English. The beginning of Hamburger's rendering of a poem by Huchel:

> That from the seed of men
> No man
> and from the seed of the olive tree
> No olive tree
> Shall grow

is a very close structural rendering of

> Dass aus dem Samen des Menschen
> Kein Mensch
> Und aus dem Samen des Ölbaums
> Kein Ölbaum
> Werde.

Uncommon in English, the preposed *that*-clause sounds very German, yet it works well. Hamburger's trick is to tie the Germanic syntax to a rhythm taken over almost exactly from the original poet. Thus he avoids the odd mismatch of German syntax and English rhythm that often makes too close a structural rendering sound like translationese. Few other translators manage so well to keep the German visible in the translation.

Above all, there are differences in the way the two languages can be stylistically manipulated. German, with its transparency of lexis (*Übersetzen*, 'carrying over', as opposed to 'translation'), is much more amenable to lexical jokes based on this transparency than English, where the preference is for puns which rest on homophony, polysemy, assonance, and alliteration. This makes translation of a poet like Morgenstern (*der Werwolf, des Weswolfs, dem Wemwolf*) especially difficult, and indeed even the superbly inventive Walter **Arndt** resorts to explanation here.

There are differences in poetic tradition, too, whether seen as the distinction between German *Weltanschauung* and English concern with the particular or as a distinction between the English and German reactions against romanticism. A reflection of this is the contrast between the extended metaphor common in many German poets, such as Krolow and Meister, and the tendency of English poetry to favour less complex metaphors or to embed long ones in first-person narrative, making them less obviously and heavily allegorical. This is a difficult problem for a translator; Dove, translating Meister, tends to keep the original long metaphors intact, as does Bullock in his translations of Krolow.

Other differences relate to the conventions of poetic form. A complete absence of punctuation has been common in German poetry since the early 1960s, and is found in poems by Domin, Fried, Borchers, Kirsch, and many others, perhaps as a way of subverting the strict punctuation rules of German, certainly as a method of creating additional ambiguities. This is uncommon in contemporary English poetry (though Adrian Mitchell's is an exception), and an exact rendering can look rather self-conscious, just as an exact rendering of the fragmented poetry of the early part of this century can (as Deutsch and Yarmolinsky pointed out) be difficult in a tradition unused to it. It may also carry connotations that the original did not have. Ausländer's lack of punctuation creates a subdued, compressed ambiguity, and that of Borchers signals an intellectual expression of doubt; neither suggests an exuberant or hectoring flouting of convention, and to translate so as to make them look like poets in the tradition of e.e. cummings would be wrong.

Just as punctuation can carry different connotations, so can morphological processes such as word formation. Because compounds are quite possible in English (and far more common than in a language such as French) it is a temptation to keep them, but is 'deathfugue' really the same as *Todesfuge*? Will Meister's *Schädelstätte* carry the same connotations as Dove's English 'skull-hill', or would 'place of skulls', the name used in the English

translation of the Bible, though linguistically less close, be culturally closer? A serious problem of attempting to show the reader the original rather than converting it to something familiar is that this may distract attention away from the poem itself by appearing to foreground the language. Foregrounding is a familiar poetic strategy and has a counterpart in the strategy for reading it; a heavily foreignized poem may trigger this strategy inappropriately when, in the original, language was subdued.

It is between such pitfalls of closeness and distance that translation of German poetry from this period must inevitably move. In spite of the recent increase of interest in foreignizing translation, in the end only a reading public educated in accepting the foreign will want poetry translations which show the original rather than posing as English poems.   JB-B

ANTHOLOGIES   Bridgwater, Patrick, *Twentieth Century German Verse*, London, 1963 · Daniel, Peter, and Diethart, Johannes, eds., *If the Walls Between Us Were Made of Glass: Austrian Jewish Poetry*, Vienna, 1992 · Deutsch, Babette, and Yarmolinsky, Avrahm, *Contemporary German Poetry*, London, 1923; rep. New York, 1969 · Hamburger, Michael, ed., *East German Poetry: An Anthology*, Manchester, 1972 · *German Poetry 1910–1975: An Anthology*, New York, 1976 · Hamburger, Michael, and Middleton, Christopher, *Modern German Poetry*, London, 1962 · Holton, Milne, and Kuhner, Herbert, *Austrian Poetry Today*, New York, 1985 · Osers, Ewald, *Contemporary German Poetry*, Cambridge, 1976 · Stein, Agnes, *Four German Poets*, New York, 1979.

AUSLÄNDER, ROSE   Boase-Beier, Jean, and Vivis, Anthony, *Mother Tongue*, Todmorden, UK, 1995 · Osers, Ewald, *Selected Poems*, London, 1977.

BENN, GOTTFRIED   Ashton, E., ed., *Selected Writings*, London, 1976.

BOBROWSKI, JOHANNES   Mead, Ruth, and Mead, Matthew, *From the Rivers*, London, 1975.

BORCHERS, ELISABETH   Mead, Ruth and Mead, Matthew, *Elisabeth Borchers*, New York, 1969.

CELAN, PAUL   Felstiner, John, *Paul Celan: Poet, Survivor, Jew*, London, 1995 · Hamburger, Michael, *Paul Celan: Poems*, Manchester, 1980 [expanded edns. 1988, 1990] · Hamburger, Michael, and Middleton, Christopher, *Selected Poems*, London, 1972 [Penguin].

ENZENSBERGER, HANS MAGNUS   Enzensberger, Hans Magnus, *The Sinking of the Titanic*, Manchester, 1981 · Hamburger, Michael, *Poems*, Newcastle upon Tyne, 1966 · Hamburger, Michael, and Enzensberger, Hans Magnus, *Selected Poems*, Newcastle upon Tyne, 1994.

FRIED, ERICH   Hood, Stuart, *100 Poems without a Country*, London, 1990.

GOLL, YVAN   Bullock, Michael, and Schulte, Rainer, *Selected Poems*, Dallas, 1981.

GRASS, GÜNTER   Hamburger, Michael, and Middleton, Christopher, *Selected Poems*, London, 1966 · *Poems of Gunter Grass*, London, 1969 [Penguin] · *In the Egg*, London, 1977.

HESSE, HERMANN   Manheim, Ralph, *Crisis: Pages from a Diary*, New York, 1975.

HUCHEL, PETER   Hamburger, Michael, *Selected Poems*, Manchester, 1974.

KIRSCH, SARAH   Kvam, Wayne, *Conjurations*, Athens, OH, 1985 · Lehbert, Margitt, *Winter Music: Selected Poems*, London, 1992 · Mulford, Wendy, and Vivis, Anthony, *The Brontës Hats*, Cambridge, 1991.

KROLOW, KARL   Bullock, Michael, *Invisible Hands*, London, 1969.

KUNZE, REINER   Osers, Ewald, *With the Volume Turned Down*, London, 1973.

MEISTER, ERNST   Dove, Richard, *Not Orpheus: Selected Poems*, Manchester, 1996.

MORGENSTERN, CHRISTIAN   Arndt, Walter, *Songs from the Gallows: Galgenlieder*, London, 1993.

SACHS, NELLY   Hamburger, Michael et al., *O The Chimneys: Selected Poems*, New York, 1967; rep. 1969 · Mead, Ruth, Mead, Matthew, and Hamburger, Michael, *The Seeker*, New York, 1970.

TRAKL, GEORG   Middleton, Christopher, ed., *Selected Poems*, London, 1968 · Wright, James, and Bly, Robert, *Twenty Poems*, Madison, Wis., 1961.

SEE ALSO   Hulse, M., 'German Poetry in Recent English Translation', *Modern Poetry in Translation*, n.s. 1 (1972), 193–206.

14. RILKE

Perhaps more than any other 20th-c. German poet, Rainer Maria Rilke makes creative use of the inherent features of German, its word order, genders, subjunctives, the freedom with which it allows words to be combined or changed from one part of speech to another. This alone means that translating his poetry is a formidable challenge. Despite (because of?) this, he has attracted many translators, and continues to do so: there have been at least 13 complete English versions of the *Duineser Elegien* (1923, Duino Elegies) since 1972, five of them since 1990.

The various translators demonstrate a wide variety of approaches to the translation of poetry from Walter **Arndt**'s 'form-true' versions to Robert **Lowell**'s *Imitations* of 1962. They also rehearse the age-old argument about what is 'more essential', poetic substance or poetic structure. Arndt, with J. B. **Leishman**, insists that the relationship between form and content is so intimate in Rilke that translations that ignore form are 'not so much a failed achievement as a failure to try'.

For Lowell, however, strict adherence to rhyme scheme and metre is for 'taxidermists' and M. D. **Herter Norton** calls rhyme and metre the 'more *technical* elements of form . . . whereas image, symbol, type of language, express the *intrinsic* qualities of the poetic idea'. Herter Norton's translations, however, demonstrate the shortcomings as poetry of translations which lack the tension between content and formal structure that fuels the originals. The poet W. D. **Snodgrass** (*After Experience*, 1958) seems to have used Herter Norton's work as a crib for his own fine versions of the first 10 *Sonette an Orpheus* (1923, Sonnets to Orpheus), which show how small changes can transform a plodding literal version into poetry.

Leishman has translated almost everything Rilke wrote and always tries to reproduce all features. For that, the English-speaking world must be grateful to him. However, to achieve this he sometimes has to go to lengths of recherché vocabulary and un-English structures which at best can be described as ingenious, at worst grotesque, backing up Lowell's 'taxidermist' gibe. Frequent rebarbative adverbs like 'paralyticly' or 'unhomesickly' make one wish he had concentrated on quality rather than quantity.

Another approach to the major rhymed collections, *The Sonnets to Orpheus* and *Neue Gedichte* (1907–8, New Poems, the most accessible of Rilke's mature work and the least often translated—*obscurité oblige!*), is a half-way house which retains rhyme where it is possible without strain, otherwise using assonance or no rhyme at all. C. F. **MacIntyre** and Leslie **Norris** and Alan **Keele** demonstrate this approach in their translations of *The Sonnets to Orpheus*, as does Stephen **Cohn** in his very readable recent version of *New Poems*. At their most successful, Leishman and Arndt reveal more of the original, but over a whole collection the reader will find Rilke more approachable through Cohn or MacIntyre.

The *Duino Elegies*, with their unrhymed, flexible lines, and vatic profundity, have proved irresistible to translators. One of the oldest versions, the collaboration between Leishman and Stephen **Spender**, is still a standard against which others must be judged. Although their idiom sounds less modern than Rilke's, they do have a convincing overall poetic tone. They seem to feel at home in Rilke's world and, as Roy Woods says, they often manage to reproduce 'something of his surprising language'. At times, however, they can overdo it. Lines like 'high up-beating | our heart would out-beat us' have a precious obscurity which is not Rilke's.

More recent translators go for a plainer style. C. F. MacIntyre is generally down-to-earth and clear, perhaps too down-to-earth for some tastes. The avoidance of portentousness can easily stumble into prosaic insipidity, as in Norris and Keele's failure to reproduce the grand gesture of the opening of the tenth *Elegy*: 'One day, when I recover from this appalling insight'. Probably the clearest and most consistently readable of this type is that by Stephen **Mitchell**.

A freer approach is Stephen Cohn's. The liberation from a close, line-by-line correspondence allows for flowing English. Of all translators he is the most vivid, often concretizing where other translators use abstractions which lack the physical force of the original, for example 'the nosing beasts' for 'die findigen Tiere'. On the other hand, the temptation of this approach to expand and explain sometimes loses the precision and tautness of the original, occasionally even the sense.

A much bolder venture is that of David **Young**, who has sought an overall equivalent structure in the triadic line of William Carlos Williams. This is a very flexible instrument in rendering the flow of Rilke's poetic thought, even though it does lack some tone colours, especially the grandest and the most lapidary. The vocabulary has a vividness close to Cohn's and a determined modernity which is unafraid (very occasionally too unafraid?) of colloquialism:

Those who got lucky early
    creation's
        spoiled darlings
a chain of mountains
    peaks and ridges
        red in the morning light
of all creation
    the blossoming godhead's
        pollen

This, despite what some commentators maintain, is still translation and not a Lowellian imitation. By creating an English equivalent to Rilke's poetic language and structures, it works as a whole and thus allows the reader who does not know German to experience the *Elegies* as a unified poem in a way that some which stay closer to Rilke's coat-tails do not.

MM

TRANSLATIONS   Arndt, Walter, *The Best of Rilke*, Hanover, NH, 1989 · Cohn, Stephen, *Duino Elegies*, Manchester, 1989 · *Neue Gedichte/New Poems*, Manchester, 1992 · Herter Norton, M. D., *Translations from the Poetry of Rainer Maria Rilke*, New York, 1938 · *Sonnets to Orpheus*, New York, 1942 [both now Norton paperback] · Leishman, J. B., *Sonnets to Orpheus*, London, 1936 · *New Poems*, London, 1939 [later Penguin *Selected Poems*] · Leishman, J. B., and Spender, Stephen, *Duino Elegies*, London, 1939 · MacIntyre, C. F., *Sonnets to Orpheus*, Berkeley/Los Angeles, 1960 · *Duino Elegies*, Berkeley/Los Angeles, 1961 · Mitchell, Stephen, *The Selected Poetry of Rainer Maria Rilke*, New York, 1980 [Picador 1987] · Norris, Leslie, and Keele, Alan, *The Sonnets to Orpheus*, Columbia, NY, 1989, London, 1991 · *The Duino Elegies*, Columbia, 1992 · Young, David, *Duino Elegies*, New York/London, 1978.

SEE ALSO   Woods, R., *Through a Glass Darkly: Poetry of R. M. Rilke and Its English Translations*, Trier, 1996.

i. Greek

1. INTRODUCTION

This introduction briefly describes available collections and selections of translations from Greek literature. Translation from the Greek begins in England about the middle of the 16th c.; its practitioners have been so numerous and of such stature in the history of English letters that the results can only be treated selectively in the anthologies discussed below and, indeed, in many of the sections on individual authors and genres which follow.

Most of this introduction inevitably occupies itself with general anthologies of classical Greek literature in translation. But a few collections and series are more comprehensive in one direction or another. *The Penguin Book of Greek Verse*, compiled by C. A. **Trypanis**, is unusual in representing the full chronological range of Greek literature down to the present, running from Homer to Odysseus Elytis. The prose translations at the foot of the page are not, however, intended to be read separately; they are of the standard type in this Penguin series, and no more than functional.

Belonging to an earlier era, the eight volumes of the Dent *Library of Greek Thought* represented an ambitious attempt to cover classical Greek literature in the widest possible sense. The translated sections from Greek writers of almost all descriptions occupy many hundreds of pages in all, organized into volumes on *Greek Astronomy* (edited by Sir T. L. Heath), *Greek Economics* (M. L. W. Laistner), *Greek Geography*, and so on. The English versions are practical; those interested in Greek writing beyond the literary will find here at least a selection of the material they need. (This may be the place to mention incidentally a major translation from a Greek text which is not discussed elsewhere in this volume, the translation by Stephen **MacKenna** of the *Enneads* of the neo-Platonist philosopher Plotinus (published 1917–30); this was MacKenna's life-work and has sometimes been considered one of the few great English-language translations of the 20th c.)

For exclusively literary material, some of the comprehensive 19th-c. collections of English poets are generous in their coverage of translations. The best-known is Alexander Chalmers's *Works of the English Poets from Chaucer to Cowper*, in 21 volumes, of which the last three (depending on the edition) are devoted to translations mainly from the classics. Translations from the Greek are preponderantly 18th-c. and include Francis **Fawkes**'s Theocritus, Anacreon, Bion, and Moschus, Thomas **Cooke**'s Hesiod, and Alexander **Pope**'s Homer.

Two long-running series should be mentioned. Bohn's Classical Library (1848–1913), in 116 volumes, is now largely superseded by later translations, though some of the volumes include still useful selections of historical work. The best known and easily the most comprehensive of 20th-c. series of this kind is the Loeb Classical Library, founded in 1912 and containing parallel texts of Greek and Latin authors. The Loeb translations usually have no pretensions to other than practical virtues, but are reliable guides to meaning. These small, green-covered volumes, covering almost all extant Greek literature, have been a welcome resource to many a student faced with a difficult passage to translate. The stiff and antiquated English of the (invariably prose) translations is occasionally updated as revised editions are issued [see I.b.6.vii].

General 20th-c. anthologies and collections are

here treated roughly in date order. Two collections of work by several hands are Oates and Murphy's *Greek Literature in Translation* and the Howe–Harrer *Greek Literature in Translation*. The translations in each case are many, but not especially various: most are by classical scholars of the 50 years before the volumes appeared. The verse translations in particular are usually very dated. Hamilton's *Greek Portrait* is painted with some interesting touches, but inferior 19th- and 20th-c., especially Edwardian, translators figure much too prominently. Higham and Bowra's *Oxford Book of Greek Verse in Translation* was conceived as a crib to the selections in the *Oxford Book of Greek Verse* (1930), and was so used by students. Existing translations are sometimes printed, often altered 'to bring them nearer the Greek'; these include work by historical figures such as Thomas **Moore**. But most of the translations are 20th-c., and over a third are by classical scholars, beginning with the editors themselves. Their work has been characterized by Donald Carne-Ross as 'horrid evidence of what happens when people whose only claim is that they can read Greek, try to write English'.

L. A. and R. W. L. **Wilding**'s *A Classical Anthology* gives parallel texts and prose translations from some 40 authors, covering 'celebrated' passages and others of which the editors 'are particularly fond'. But the translations, 'entirely subordinate to the text', are confessedly 'inadequate'. In contrast, F. L. **Lucas**'s *Greek Poetry for Everyman*, later issued as *Greek Poetry*, is intended for the entirely Greek-less, and no Greek text is included. Half the volume is taken up by Homer. Lucas's translations—many of them previously published—are based on a six-foot line deriving from ballad metre for virtually all the originals. They rarely possess any conviction, and as English verse are often unbelievably bad (as in the *Anacreontea*—'Of the Gods and these other matters none knows the verity—| No man that lived before us, no man that yet shall be'). Collections of modern translation by several hands are at least more varied; but Bernard Knox's 866-page *Norton Book of Classical Literature*, two-thirds of which is made up of Greek material, is as conservative in its choices as could well be imagined. The translators are for the most part American academics whose translations have been tried and tested in the college classroom among non-specialists. The few excursions into the work of writers known as poets in their own right are directed towards the safely dead (Ezra **Pound**, Robert **Lowell**).

Three more recent anthologies of historical translations can be recommended, in each case with some reservations. Richard Stoneman's *Daphne into Laurel: Translations of Classical Poetry from Chaucer to the Present* is a largish collection arranged chronologically. There are excerpts from the usual major texts and some interesting finds among minor ones. Brevity of samples whets the appetite and also creates space for numerous translators, but is in other ways a restriction. Adrian Poole and Jeremy Maule's *Oxford Book of Classical Verse in English Translation* will often be the first place to turn for a full sample of poetic translations from the Greek. The editors aim to print 'the best of classical verse in the best of English translations'. Fortunately, the second criterion turns out to be much more important than the first, and obviously eccentric emphases result among the classics—for example, a mere seven translations of Aeschylus against thirteen of the *Anacreontea*. Greek poetry occupies 225 of the 532 selections, up to the sixth c. CE, and the organization is by classical author. 'Translation' is interpreted very loosely indeed, so that poems and passages 'imitated' from or even 'inspired' by the classical text appear frequently. This is a generous selection in a number of ways, and ideal for browsing even by specialists—many of the inclusions are unexpected, some positively recherché. The editors' ways of choosing their texts are too eclectic to make it a reliable reference work in the ordinary sense, however—it will not necessarily reveal, for example, what the standard translations of a given Greek poet are.

Michael Grant's *Greek Literature in Translation* (also under the title *Greek Literature: An Anthology*) extends more widely among Greek writers to the historians, novelists, philosophers, and orators as well as poets. Its range of English translators is more restricted, however: while some 18th- and even 17th-c. translators appear, the emphasis is very heavily on those working in the 100 years before Grant's anthology, especially the last 50, and many of these are secondary or merely academic talents. The editorial matter is more perfunctory than in Grant's earlier *Latin Literature*.

There are several collections of classical Greek drama in translation, sometimes making use of previously published work. The Grene and Lattimore *Complete Greek Tragedies* (sometimes known as the 'Chicago' tragedies) has served for many years as a student resource. Its original nine-volume format has been adapted in reprints and the translations contained, by various modern hands, have also appeared as individual volumes. The more notable ones are discussed below in the entries on Aeschylus [II.i.3], Sophocles [II.i.4], and Euripides [II.i.5]. The same applies to the following volumes, which involve translators such as those mentioned: Oates and O'Neill's *Complete Greek Drama* (prose and verse translations by R. C. **Trevelyan**, Richard **Aldington**, E. P. **Coleridge**, Gilbert **Murray**); Robert W. Corrigan's *Classical Tragedy, Greek and Roman* (Tony **Harrison**, Dudley **Fitts**, Robert **Fitzgerald**); L. R. Lind's *Ten Greek Plays in Contemporary Translations* (Louis **MacNeice**, Rex **Warner**, Richard Aldington); Lane Cooper's *Fifteen Greek Plays* (Gilbert Murray, Robert **Whitelaw**, B. B. **Rogers**); and Dudley Fitts's *Four Greek Plays* (Dudley Fitts, Robert Fitzgerald, Louis MacNeice). A single-handed collection of Greek drama in translation is F. L. Lucas's *Greek Drama for Everyman* (London, 1954), containing the complete Aeschylus, two plays by Sophocles and Euripides,

one by Aristophanes, and extracts from and summaries of other plays and fragments.

Finally, two other kinds of collection. Charles Tomlinson's *Eros English'd: Classical Erotic Poetry in Translation from Golding to Hardy* is an interesting 'thematic' anthology which includes, among the Greeks, Sappho, Homer, the Homeric Hymns, Philostratus, Theocritus, the *Anacreontea*, Bion, Moschus, and others. It has glosses and cross-references to other versions of the same passage or poem included. Robin Sowerby's *The Classical Legacy in Renaissance Poetry* is not a collection at all, but a textbook; the number of translated poems and passages by Renaissance English poets he includes for discussion means, however, that it can almost be used as one.   SG

ANTHOLOGIES   Chalmers, Alexander, ed., *The Works of the English Poets from Chaucer to Cowper*, 21 vols., London, 1810 · Cooper, Lane, ed., *Fifteen Greek Plays*, New York, 1943 [rev. and enlarged edn. of Cooper's *Ten Greek Plays*, 1929] · Corrigan, Robert W., ed., *Classical Tragedy, Greek and Roman: 8 Plays in Authoritative Modern Translations Accompanied by Critical Essays*, New York, 1990 · Fitts, Dudley, ed., *Four Greek Plays*, New York, 1960 · Grant, Michael, ed., *Greek Literature in Translation: Translations from Greek Prose and Poetry*, Harmondsworth, 1973 [Penguin; rep. 1977 as *Greek Literature in Translation*; rev. 1990; frequent reps.] · Grene, David, and Lattimore, Richmond, eds., *The Complete Greek Tragedies*, 9 vols., Chicago, 1953–9 [rep. in many formats subsequently, in selections and single vols.] · Hamilton, Sir George Rostrevor, ed., *The Greek Portrait: An Anthology of English Verse Translations from the Greek Poets*, London, 1934 · Higham, T. F., and Bowra, C. M., eds., *The Oxford Book of Greek Verse in Translation*, Oxford, 1938 · Howe, G., and Harrer, G. A., ed., *Greek Literature in Translation*, New York, 1924 [rev. 1948] · Knox, Bernard, ed., *The Norton Book of Classical Literature*, New York, 1993 · *Library of Greek Thought, The*, 8 vols., London, 1923–4 · Lind, L. R., ed., *Ten Greek Plays in Contemporary Translations*, Boston, 1957 · Lucas, F. L., *Greek Poetry for Everyman*, London, 1951 [Everyman; rep. 1966 as *Greek Poetry*] · Lucas, F. L., *Greek Drama for Everyman*, London, 1954 [rep. 1967 as *Greek Drama for the Common Reader*] · MacKenna, Stephen, *Plotinus: The Enneads*, London, 1917–30 [with contributions by B. S. Page; rev. Page 1956 and subsequently, several reps.]. · Oates, Whitney J., and Murphy, C. T., eds., *Greek Literature in Translation*, New York, 1914 · Oates, Whitney J., and O'Neill, Eugene Jr., eds., *The Complete Greek Drama*, New York, 1938 · Poole, Adrian, and Maule, Jeremy, eds., *The Oxford Book of Classical Verse in English Translation*, Oxford, 1995 · Sowerby, Robin, *The Classical Legacy in Renaissance Poetry*, London, 1994 · Stoneman, Richard, ed., *Daphne into Laurel: Translations of Classical Poetry from Chaucer to the Present*, London, 1982 · Tomlinson, Charles, ed., *Eros English'd: Classical Erotic Poetry in Translation from Golding to Hardy*, London, 1992 · Trypanis, C. A., *The Penguin Book of Greek Verse*, Harmondsworth, 1971 [several reps.] · Wilding, L. A., and Wilding, R. W. L., *A Classical Anthology: A Selection from the Greek and Roman Literatures*, London, 1955.

2. HOMER AND OTHER EPICS

i. The *Iliad* and the *Odyssey* before Pope The Homeric epics (*c.*725–700 BCE) are among the most translated works in English, and English has more versions of them than any other language. Unlike *Beowulf* [II.o.1] or *The Song of Roland* [II.g.3], they have had no periods of eclipse and rediscovery. The moral grandeur of their presentation of heroism, and their lucid definition of tragic choice, have secured them a place at the centre of a humane education from classical Greece onwards, and generations of readers who could not read them in Greek have reached out to them in translation.

Although the story of the epics is easy enough to

convey, the poems bring certain problems for the translator. The most obvious is length: each has 24 books of 700-odd lines. Many would-be translators have ground to a halt at the end of book i, while others have only worked on the most famous passages, like the touching scene of Hector's farewell to Andromache in *Iliad* vi. As a result, there are far fewer translations of the epics as a whole than of their parts, and still fewer translators have completed both poems. The *Iliad* and *Odyssey* are in any case so unlike each other that no translator succeeds with them equally.

Another problem is the challenge of Homer's

Greek hexameter. This is the product of oral story-telling, and it shows the formal characteristics of verse that is constructed at the moment of recitation. It has insistent patterning (there are formulaic ways of arming a warrior or striking him down), fixed epithets (Achilles is 'swift-footed' even when seated), speeches repeated verbatim, and lengthy catalogues. Any translator who is faithful to these characteristics risks giving them more prominence than they had in the original, particularly in prose, where their function cannot be guessed at. And the translator who is not daunted by these problems still has to confront the most essential one: how to make Mycenaean heroes credible for his own age and time.

The most successful translations have been those where the translators allowed themselves considerable freedom. Famous among these is the Renaissance version of George **Chapman** (c.1559–1634), who translated the Iliad into 'fourteeners', the long-line ballad metre which afforded his inventiveness full scope (1598–1611). Chapman's great strength is his enthusiasm for Homer, amounting to 'idolatrie'. What the translator needs is the same largeness of spirit: 'Poesie is the flower of the Sunne, and disdains to open to the eye of a candle' (Preface). He writes with drive and conviction, his excitement spilling over into marginal glosses ('a simile most lively expressive'), and with a wealth of hyperbole. Chapman is entirely at home in the Iliad's world of extravagant power and clashing princes, and he identifies unreservedly with Achilles. This leads him into difficulties at the end of the story, however, when it becomes clear that Achilles' intransigence and self-regarding wrath are just what Jove deplores. He deals boldly with the quiddities of Homeric Greek, relishing compound epithets (Vulcan is 'heaven's great both-foot-halting God'), coining many new words, and resolving textual problems to his own loud satisfaction. His 14-syllable line has room for all Homer's figures of speech and plenty of new ones, as well as explanations in parentheses. At its best, as in Achilles' rejection of the embassy in Iliad ix, it has great rhetorical power.

The defect of all this energy is its disorderliness. Chapman's figures of speech often overwhelm their subject: they develop into mixed metaphors or contort themselves into word-play (a quarrel is a 'wreathing of wraths'). It is difficult to read many lines without getting diverted from the narrative thread. At such times, the fourteener shows its worst characteristic, a weak garrulity; we feel the translator is saying too much, and has not decided what matters most. When Chapman's style

becomes so elaborate that he puts parentheses in parentheses, we must regret his boast that he did not consult 'with any one living' save in one or two places, and that the last 12 books were translated in 'less than fifteen weeks'.

Although he declared that the fourteener was the only possible metre for translating Homer, in his Odyssey (1614–15) he returned to 10-syllable rhyming couplets. Perhaps this was a response to the difference between the poems, and the more domestic setting. Certainly the effect is quieter and more philosophical; but without the extra space afforded by the long line, his expression is even more crabbed and obscure. He is as convinced of his own philosophical interpretation of Ulysses' fate as he was of Achilles', but he now feels free to abandon the Greek entirely to make his point. As he traces the journey of this 'absolute man' through 'many afflictions', he loudly praises in the glosses his 'continued pietie . . . through all places, times and occasions', and enthusiastically blackens his hero's enemies, deliberately reversing the honorific epithets which Homer freely bestows even on the suitors and Polyphemus. A Jacobean taste for 'high sentence' obtrudes sometimes comically into the narrative ('To cold Bath-bathers hurtfull is the wind,' observes Nausicaa), and Chapman often invokes the theory of humours (Ulysses is 'no moist man'). More serious is the incursion of the Jacobean revenge ethic. Instead of checking Eurycleia's rapture over the slaughtered suitors, Chapman's Ulysses encourages her to 'vent [her] joyes' freely, travestying an episode that shows Homer's heroic ethic at its impartial best.

Chapman's Odyssey is thus more of a historical oddity than his Iliad, though it can still be enjoyed for particular episodes (Ulysses' book v landing in Phaeacia has often been praised). Its buccaneering attitude to the language can be relished, too: the work is full of neologisms. Taken together, the two translations are a moving glimpse of the literalism of the Renaissance, when heroes were taken to be patterns for real-life princes. Chapman dedicates the Iliad to Prince Henry, to 'furnish [his] youth's groundwork' with a 'princely president [precedent]'.

These translations dominated the field until the Restoration, when there was a new wave of confident translation [see I.b.3]. As more and more of the classic authors were rendered into English, Chapman's ungraceful 10-syllable couplet became the 'heroic' couplet, replete with formulae and elevated language, not unlike Homer's own. Many poets wrote in the same idiom, and learned from each other's work, in a serial effort that culminated in a whole library of translated classics (Virgil, Horace, Ovid, Lucretius, Juvenal). John **Denham** (1615–69) translated Sarpedon's speech to Glaucus in *Iliad* xii in the elegant new style and helped make this a *locus classicus* for the heroic creed. John **Dryden** turned to Homer after his magisterial *Aeneid* and translated *Iliad* i before he died, in a vigorous and sceptical style that set a new standard. William **Congreve** attempted the lamentations in *Iliad* xxiv, perhaps attracted by their relation to heroic drama, and many others worked on episodes of pathos (Hector's farewell to Andromache), satire (Thersites), or mischief (Juno's seduction of Jupiter).

The only translators to attempt both poems complete, however, were the courtier John **Ogilby** (1600–76) and the philosopher Thomas **Hobbes**. Ogilby's translations are magnificent books: handsome folios with full-plate engravings, which came into the hands of Alexander Pope as a boy and held him entranced. As poetry, however, they are merely basic, in a hapless jog-trot rhythm: 'The drooping Trojans Hearts with Joy revive, | When him they saw in safety come alive.' The versions of Hobbes are so burlesque that they only raise the question whether their comedy is deliberate or accidental. His Patroclus asks, 'Must we be all so far from home destroy'd, | And lie for dog's-meat on the Trojan coast?' Perhaps the great philosopher did not think poetry worth more effort.

ii. Pope's Homer The classic translation that was built on all the preceding versions, and shows how carefully its author scrutinized them for translating hints, is by Alexander **Pope**. In his preface, one of the most dazzling works of all translation criticism, Pope pays tribute to the 'daring fiery Spirit' that animates Chapman's version, which is 'something like what one might imagine Homer himself would have writ before he arrived at Years of Discretion'. But his own aim is to bring the art of translation to maturity, and he spends more than 10 years of his poetical prime working on the two epics, progressing regularly through more than 20,000 lines of Greek.

Pope's first loyalty is to 'that Rapture and Fire' which so carries the reader away that 'no man who has a true Poetical spirit is Master of himself' when reading Homer. True translation means preserving this energy; so Pope worries much less than later translators about literal equivalence, and takes numerous freedoms with the text, clearing out hindrances that might detract from its impact, and highlighting whatever shows Homer at his Homeric best. The epic is a 'wild paradise' of creativity in which the translator offers to clear the vistas for us.

His second loyalty is to literature: Homer is 'like a copious nursery which contains the seeds and first productions of every kind'. Since the epics have given life to so much other poetry, Pope can repay Homer in his own coin for what he loses in translation. When he comes to a simile adapted by Virgil, or a speech reworked by Ovid or Milton, Pope translates with reference to its later appearance, and gives a critical assessment of the exchange in a footnote ('It is much the same Image with that of Milton . . . tho' apply'd in a very different way').

For the first time, then, the reader is given a translation that could be mistaken for an original work: the verses race along, uncompromised in clarity, for book after book. The iambic pentameter ('heroic') couplet solves a number of problems that will plague later translators: it is nicely balanced between public and individual utterance, and it is the acknowledged metre of classical translation, so that it automatically brings with it an elevated atmosphere. It is particularly well adapted to fluent narration (it falls easily into verse paragraphs) and to speech, where it lends rhetorical point and compression.

Pope's heroic language can still be direct: he tells the story of 'mighty Chiefs untimely slain; | Whose Limbs unbury'd on the naked Shore | Devouring Dogs and hungry Vultures tore'. But it encompasses philosophy too, as Achilles meditates on Patroclus' ghost: ''Tis true, 'tis certain; Man, tho' dead, retains | Part of himself; th'immortal Mind remains.' And it is equally effective with pathos, as Priam kneels to Achilles and begs him to remember his own father: 'Those silver Hairs, that venerable Face; | His trembling Limbs, his helpless Person, see! | In all my Equal, but in Misery!'

It is the similes, however, which give Pope most scope for his art, and he rejoices in the evidence that Homer's world is not so far from Virgil's or his own, whether the comparison is between the collapse of the Greek wall and a boy's sandcastle, or an army gathering together and bees in swarm:

> As from some Rocky Cleft the Shepherd sees
> Clust'ring in Heaps on Heaps the driving Bees,
> Rolling, and black'ning, Swarms succeeding Swarms,
> With deeper Murmurs and more hoarse Alarms.

> *(Iliad ii)*

His greatest pleasure is in making the sound fit the sense, as in the comparison of Hector to a falling boulder:

> From Steep to Steep the rolling Ruin bounds;
> At ev'ry Shock the crackling Wood resounds;

Still gath'ring Force, it smoaks; and, urg'd amain,
Whirls, leaps, and thunders down, impetuous to the Plain:
There stops—So Hector . . .

(*Iliad* xiii)

The Scylla and Charybdis of translating Homer, as Pope sees it, are a strained sublimity and a platitudinous flatness. He aims to progress like Homer himself, with an 'unaffected and equal majesty'; if he has a fault, however, it is to err on the side of grandeur. He is uncomfortable with episodes showing the levity of gods and goddesses, although for Homer levity is not incompatible with seriousness. He cannot enter into the spirit of Olympian quarrels, or Juno's seduction of Jupiter in book xiv, to distract him from the battlefield. He is also uncomfortable with similes taken too openly from rural life: when Ajax is compared to an ass, stubbornly resisting a beating, Pope transmutes him into a 'slow Beast with heavy Strength indu'd', though he honourably reinstates the offending word in his footnote. The French critics of the period used similes like this as evidence that Homer was primitive and inferior to Virgil, and Pope cannot let down his defences; though he insists that in Greek or Hebrew, the word 'is of Dignity enough to be employed on the most magnificent Occasions'.

His engagement with critics, however, means that the reader has a double pleasure in Pope's edition: the footnotes amount to some of the finest close criticism of a major text in the 18 c. Always elegantly phrased, witty, heartfelt, and learned by turns, his notes confront all the major issues raised by taking an alien classic seriously.

The success of his *Iliad* meant that it was incumbent upon Pope to produce a companion *Odyssey*. This time, however, he took advantage of the widespread facility in producing heroic couplets to farm half the work out to two collaborators, Elijah **Fenton** (1683–1730), who undertook four books, and William **Broome** (1689–1745), who undertook eight. Pope then scrutinized and improved their verse before publication, 'to make the whole as finished and spirited' as he was able.

The final product is surprisingly homogeneous, and is perhaps best understood as a literary version of what was commonly done by painters and their studio assistants. But it suffers from a lower poetic temperature than its great predecessor, and from the intractable problem of finding the right note for a poem less insistently heroic. Indeed, the *Odyssey* is full of the 'low' items the age found ludicrous in poetry: as Fenton wrote to Broome before translating *Odyssey* xx, 'How I shall get over the bitch and

her puppies, the roasting of the black puddings . . . and the cowheel that was thrown at Ulysses' head, I know not.' Although Pope says in the Postscript that 'great pains' were taken to be 'easy and natural' in the translation, there are moments where a mock-epic discrepancy threatens, or epic diction hardens into pomposity. (The cowheel becomes 'that sinewy fragment . . . [to which] | The well-horn'd foot indissolubly join'd.')

Overall, however, Pope's *Odyssey* has the same virtues as his *Iliad*. It is rapid, clear, and fully annotated. When Homer takes Ulysses down to the underworld for a series of scenes with Elpenor, Ajax, Agamemnon, and Achilles that has haunted western literature, Pope's translation rises to the fascination of the subject; when Ulysses is finally reunited with his old father, it overflows with pathos:

Trembling with agonies of strong delight
Stood the great son, heart-wounded with the sight:
He ran, he seiz'd him with a strict embrace,
With thousand kisses wander'd o'er his face,
I, I am he; oh father rise! behold
Thy son with twenty winters now grown old;
Thy son, so long desir'd, so long detain'd,
Restor'd, and breathing in his native land.

(*Odyssey* xxiv)

iii. After Pope Byron said that no one would put down Pope's translations save to pick up the original, but he was Pope's only admirer among the romantics. The growing aversion to heroic diction at the end of the 18th c., and the preference for blank verse over couplets, led to a more puritan view of translation. It now seemed false to make such an ancient text rhyme, and the translator's role was to submit to his author in every detail. In this climate, William **Cowper** could promise to create the first truly faithful portrait of Homer. He prefaces his translations with the assurance, 'I have omitted nothing; I have invented nothing.'

The result is a relatively thin-textured *Iliad*, in which Cowper's sincere admiration for his author jostles with his obvious discomfort with the battlefield ethos. The ghost of Milton ventriloquizes in his blank verse, entangling his grammar and producing laborious inversions (the Satnio is a 'smooth-sliding river pure') or scholarly eccentricities ('Ades' for Hades). He prefers Homer's similes, particularly the pastoral ones, to the battle scenes they illuminate, and he is much more confident with female speakers than male (as in Andromache's book xxii lament).

It might be expected that Cowper's sensibility would show to better effect in his *Odyssey*, but he has the same problems as his predecessors in finding the appropriate style. When Nausicaa asks her father for a cart, she says: 'Sir! wilt thou lend me of the royal wains | A sumpter-carriage?' He acknowledges in a note that she actually calls him 'pappa! a more natural style of address, and more endearing', but he 'feared to hazard' a word so 'familiar'. Helen, too, elicits an awkward primness as 'a wanderer from the matrimonial bed'; the only passages where Cowper finds his vein are pastoral descriptions, like the gardens of Alcinous (book vii). Otherwise the translation, in its lack of energy and invention, betrays the state of depression from which Cowper set out to distract himself.

Although he had so little success in practice, Cowper's formulation of the problem confronting Homer's translators is classic: when the translator has been 'drenched and steeped' in the original, he must 'distinguish between what is essentially Greek, and what may be habited in English' and put his loyalty to English before Greek. 'If we copy [Homer] too closely . . . instead of translating we murder him.'

This warning went unheeded in the 19th c., which renewed the debate about fidelity in a formalist spirit. What did it mean to be 'true' to the original Greek? For many, well-trained in scansion, it meant fidelity to Homer's hexameter, and J. G. Lockhart's (1794–1854) specimen of Homer in English hexameters initiated decades of experiment. Unfortunately, Homer's metre depends on quantity (long and short syllables) where English depends upon stress: English hexameters therefore have much too insistent a rhythm ever to be taken for their Greek equivalent, and they remain a self-conscious allusion to antiquity, even in the hands of Matthew **Arnold**, who included some specimens in his admirable lectures 'On Translating Homer'. This is how he presents the moment when Achilles' horse magically speaks:

Sudden he bowed his head, and all his mane, as he bowed it,
Streamed to the ground by the yoke, escaping from under the collar;
And he was given a voice by the white-armed Goddess Hera.
'Truly, yet this time will we save thee, mighty Achilles!'

Laborious as this metre was, there were at least half a dozen attempts to render the entire *Iliad* or *Odyssey* in hexameters, the last in 1945. Perhaps the most fluent of them was by J. Henry **Dart** (1817–87), in response to Arnold.

Another 19th-c. school of thought emphasized Homer's antiquity and primitivism. He was given a

medieval tint (William **Morris**), or Spenserian naïvety (P. S. **Worsley**, 1835–66). He was assimilated to the Old Testament (G. **Musgrave**, 1798–1883) or Anglo-Saxon epic (F. W. **Newman**, 1805–97). Newman went so far as to say that a translation should be 'quaint' (though not 'grotesque'). Arnold's lectures vigorously denounced this attempt to make Homer stranger than he was: the qualities to be retained at all cost were Homer's nobility, plainness, and rapidity [see I.c.1.iii]. Many new translators rallied to the call, but only the Earl of **Derby** (1799–1869) won a wide audience, for his stately *Iliad* in blank verse: 'Of Peleus' son, Achilles, sing, O Muse, | The vengeance, deep and deadly.'

By the end of the century the attempt to represent Homer as poetry at all was being abandoned, and fidelity to his subject-matter seemed all that could be achieved. The medium was a stilted prose with Biblical colouring, as practised in the *Iliad* of A. **Lang**, W. **Leaf** and E. **Myers** (1882), and the *Odyssey* of S. H. **Butcher** and A. Lang (1879), which established itself as the standard Homer well into the twentieth century. Samuel **Butler** mounted an eccentric challenge, based on the presumption that the *Iliad* had been written by a Greek with a pro-Trojan bias, and the *Odyssey* by a woman, who portrayed herself in the text as Nausicaa. But the only prose version to escape eccentricity on the one hand and Biblical ponderousness on the other was an American one by George Herbert **Palmer** (1846–1926), whose *Odyssey* conveys his pleasure in the original in natural language: 'Tell of the storm-tossed man, O Muse, who wandered long after he sacked the sacred citadel of Troy.'

The pace of translation has not slowed in the 20th c. If the early translations erred on the side of sublimity, modern ones err on the side of fidelity, with nothing added. They win an immediate audience because their subject-matter is unmistakably fascinating; but their flat style quickly palls, and they are succeeded by new versions destined to be supplanted in their turn. English (as opposed to American) translators have largely favoured prose. A. T. **Murray**'s Loeb translation, written to accompany the Greek, was the last archaizing version; thereafter prose translations were addressed to readers unfamiliar with the Greek world, and aspired to some of the pace and realism of the novel. W. H. D. **Rouse**'s versions of both epics are adventure stories, to hold the attention of schoolboys; the *Odyssey* of T. E. **Shaw** (T. E. Lawrence) displays an insider's knowledge of the archeology and anthropology of the region in a selfconscious idiom. More tolerable to read at length are E. V. **Rieu**'s unpretentious Penguin translations, which have been followed by Martin **Hammond**'s fusty *Iliad* and Walter **Shewring**'s more colloquial *Odyssey*. Two shortened versions preserve more of the energy of the original: the *Iliad* of I. A. **Richards**, written with foreign readers of English in mind and Barbara Leonie **Picard**'s versions of both epics for children.

American translators have largely preferred five- or six-beat blank verse to prose. It suffers from the perennial problem of blank verse in being more obvious to the eye than the ear, but it conveys Homer's rapidity and plainness, if not often his nobility. The great success in this style is Robert **Fitzgerald**'s *Odyssey*, with its lively movement and flexible tone ('the first version to make the Butlerian thesis plausible that the Homer of the *Odyssey* was a woman'). Fizgerald's manner suits the *Iliad* less well, but his two translations have supplanted the more turgid versions of Richmond **Lattimore**. His most recent challenger is Robert **Fagles**, who has created a fast-moving and colloquial Homer for performance as well as private reading. In the age of audio books, Homer's public can be auditors again (*Odyssey*: 13 hrs. 10 mins.).

All of these modern versions require a good deal of effort from the reader: they present enough of the original for us to guess how much better Homer must be. It is worth commenting, therefore, on two rogue 'translations' which might stimulate any reader to a sharper sense of what goes missing: Robert **Graves**'s lively prose *Iliad*, which breaks into poetical 'ballads' at high points; and the ongoing version of chosen episodes by Christopher **Logue**. Logue abandons line-by-line fidelity to reconstruct the underlying epic concepts; although his Homer is more primitive than noble, his sense of the heroic scale and the endemic violence of the epics is revelatory.

There is an excellent anthology, *Homer in English* by George Steiner, which allows the reader to sample the whole history of Homeric translations (and many other works based on Homer).

iv. Homeric Hymns These are not devotional hymns, but sophisticated retellings of various myths associated with the gods. They date from the 8th to the 6th c. BCE and were long attributed to Homer. They were translated by Chapman with hyperbolic verve, in rudimentary rhyming coup-

lets. Congreve has a sophisticated version of the 'Hymn to Venus'; in **Shelley**, however, they found a greater poet, equally at home with hyperbole and myth. His is the classic version, elegant and lucid, in heroic couplets, or ottava rima (*Hermes*). A. S. **Way** produced an overwrought translation clogged with epithets in a pseudo-Renaissance manner; but the version by Thelma **Sargent** is fluent and readable.

v. The Battle of the Frogs and the Mice (Batrachomyomachia) This short mock-epic, formerly attributed to Homer, describes a battle between frogs and mice in the style of the *Iliad*. It is probably an Alexandrian pastiche (3rd or 2nd c. BCE). Chapman lost the comic discrepancy between matter and manner in his cumbrous version, but in the heyday of the English mock-epic, Thomas **Parnell** (1679–1718) translated it with deft assurance. His heroic couplet version was given additional polish by Pope, and was never superseded, though Cowper's attempt in blank verse has a mock-Miltonic charm.

vi. Hesiod: Theogony, Works and Days Hesiod's *Works and Days* was first translated by Chapman with his usual mixture of poetic energy and intrusive scholarship. Thomas **Cooke** (1703–56) added the *Theogony* to his version, in undistinguished heroic couplets. Charles **Elton** (1778–1853) translated *Works and Days* into couplets and the *Theogony* into sub-Miltonic blank verse, noting important parallels with Homer and the Bible. 20th-c. versions have been deliberately scholarly: that of Richmond Lattimore has a summary on the facing page, and R. M. **Frazer**'s attempts line-for-line equivalence. There is a careful prose paraphrase with full notes by M. L. **West**, and a clear and fluent version in blank verse by D. **Wender**.

vii. Musaeus: Hero and Leander 'Musaeus' is the traditional name of the author of this late classical love story (5th c. CE). The most dazzling account of the poem is by Christopher **Marlowe**, a paraphrase rather than a translation, laced with sensuality and wit. This version was completed by Chapman. No other translation compares, although J. **Sterling** achieved some smart phrasing and sub-Popean gallantry in his version, and E. **Arnold**'s version, dedicated to Browning, has a mild charm. FR

ILIAD *Homer's Iliads*, tr. George Chapman, London, 1598–1611 [ed. Allardyce Nicoll, New York, 1956] · *Homer His Iliads Translated*, tr. John Ogilby, London, 1660 · *Sarpedon's Speech to Glaucus*, tr. John Denham, London, 1668 · *Homer's Iliads in English*, tr. Thomas Hobbes, London, 1676 · *Priam's Lamentation and The Lamentations of Hecuba, Andromache, and Helen*, tr. William Congreve, London, 1693 · *The First Book of Homer's Iliads*, tr. John Dryden, London, 1700 · *The Iliad of Homer*, tr. Alexander Pope, London, 1715–20 [Penguin, 1996: 1743 edn.] · *The Iliad and Odyssey of Homer*, tr. William Cowper, London, 1791 · 'The Twenty-Fourth Book of Homer's Iliad', tr. J. G. Lockhart,

Blackwood's Magazine, Mar. 1846 · *The Iliad of Homer*, tr. F. W. Newman, London, 1856 · *Homer's Iliad*, tr. Earl of Derby, London, 1862, 1864 · *The Iliad of Homer*, tr. J. Henry Dart, London, 1865 · *The Iliad of Homer*, tr. A. Lang, W. Leaf, and E. Myers, London, 1882 · *The Iliad of Homer*, tr. Samuel Butler, London, 1898 · *The Iliad*, tr. A. T. Murray, London, 1924–5 · *The Story of Achilles*, tr. W. H. D. Rouse, London, 1938 · *The Wrath of Achilles, The Iliad of Homer Shortened and in a New Translation*, tr. I. A Richards, New York, 1950 · *The Iliad*, tr. E. V. Rieu, London, 1950 [Penguin] · *The Iliad of Homer*, tr. Richmond Lattimore, Chicago, 1951 · *The Anger of Achilles, Homer's Iliad*, tr. Robert Graves, New York, 1959 · *The Iliad*, tr. Barbara Leonie Picard, London, 1960 · *Patrocleia*, tr. Christopher Logue, Lowestoft, 1962; *Pax*, London, 1967; *War Music*, London, 1988; *Kings*, London, 1991 · *The Iliad*, tr. Robert Fitzgerald, New York, 1974 [World's Classics] · *The Iliad*, tr. Robert Fagles, New York, 1990 [Penguin, 1991].

ODYSSEY   *Homer's Odysses*, tr. George Chapman, London, 1614–15 · *Homer His Odysses Translated*, tr. John Ogilby, London, 1665 · *Homer's Odysses in English*, tr. Thomas Hobbes, London, 1677 · *The Odyssey of Homer*, tr. Alexander Pope [with William Broome and Elijah Fenton], London, 1725–6 · *The Iliad and Odyssey of Homer, Translated into English Blank Verse*, tr. William Cowper, London, 1791 · *The Odyssey of Homer*, tr. P. S. Worsley, Edinburgh, 1861–2 · *The Odyssey of Homer*, tr. G. Musgrave, London, 1865 · *The Odyssey of Homer*, tr. S. H. Butcher and A. Lang, London, 1879 · *The Odyssey of Homer, Done into English Verse*, tr. William Morris, London, 1887 · *The Odyssey of Homer*, tr. George Herbert Palmer, Cambridge, Mass., 1891 · *The Odyssey of Homer*, tr. Samuel Butler, London, 1900 · *The Odyssey*, tr. A. T. Murray, London, 1919 · *The Story of Odysseus*, tr. W. H. D. Rouse, London, 1932 · *The Odyssey of Homer*, tr. T. E. Shaw [T. E. Lawrence], London, 1932 · *The Odyssey*, tr. E. V. Rieu, London, 1946 [Penguin] · *The Odyssey*, tr. Barbara Leonie Picard, Oxford, 1952 · *The Odyssey*, tr. Robert Fitzgerald, New York, 1961 · *The Odyssey*, tr. Richmond Lattimore, New York, 1965 · *Homer, the Odyssey*, tr. Walter Shewring, Oxford, 1980 [World's Classics] · *The Odyssey of Homer*, tr. Robert Fagles, New York, 1997.

HOMERIC HYMNS   *The Crowne of all Homers Workes*, tr. George Chapman, London, ?1624 · *The Third Volume of the Works of Mr. William Congreve*, by William Congreve, 1710 · *Posthumous Poems*, P. B. Shelley, London, 1824 · *Poetical Works*, P. B. Shelley, London, 1839 (2nd edn.) · *The Homeric Hymns*, tr. A. S. Way, London, 1934 · *The Homeric Hymns*, tr. Thelma Sargent, New York, 1973.

BATRACHOMYOMACHIA   *The Crowne of all Homers Workes*, tr. George Chapman, London, ?1624 · *Homer's Battle of the Frogs and Mice*, tr. Thomas Parnell, London, 1717 · *The Iliad and Odyssey of Homer*, tr. William Cowper, London, 1791.

HESIOD   *The Georgics of Hesiod*, tr. George Chapman, London, 1618 · *The Works of Hesiod*, tr. Thomas Cooke, London, 1728 · *The Remains of Hesiod the Ascraean*, tr. Charles Elton, London, 1812 · *Hesiod*, tr. Richmond Lattimore, Ann Arbor, Mich., 1959 · *Hesiod: Theogony and Works and Days*, tr. D. Wender, Harmondsworth, 1973 [Penguin] · *The Poems of Hesiod*, tr. R. M. Frazer, Norman, Okla., 1983 · *Hesiod: Theogony and Works and Days*, tr. M. L. West, Oxford, 1988.

MUSAEUS   *Hero and Leander*, tr. Christopher Marlowe, London, 1598 · *The Divine Poem of Musaeus*, tr. George Chapman, London, 1616 · *The Loves of Hero and Leander*, tr. J. Sterling, Dublin, 1728 · *Hero and Leander*, tr. E. Arnold, London, 1873.

SEE ALSO   Arnold, Matthew, *On Translating Homer*, London, 1861 · Bartlett, P., 'The Heroes of Chapman's Homer', *Review of English Studies*, 17 (1941), 257–75 · Bush, J. N. D., 'English Translations of Homer', *PMLA*, 41 (1926), 335–41 · 'Musaeus in English Verse', *MLN*, 43 (1928), 101–4 · Kelly, L. G., *The True Interpreter: A History of Translation Theory and Practice in the West*, Oxford, 1979 · Lord, G. D., *Homeric Renaissance: The Odyssey of George Chapman*, London, 1956 · Mack, M., ed., *Alexander Pope: The Iliad of Homer*, London, 1967 · *Alexander Pope: The Odyssey of Homer*, London, 1967 · Mason, H. E., *To Homer through Pope: An Introduction to Homer's 'Iliad' and Pope's Translation*, London, 1972 · Sowerby, R., 'The Augustan *Odyssey*', *Translation and Literature*, 4 (1995), 157–82 · Steiner, G., *Homer in English*, London, 1996 [Penguin] · Webb, T., *The Violet in the Crucible: Shelley and Translation*, Oxford, 1976.

3. AESCHYLUS

i. Early Translations In his dedicatory poem to Shakespeare's First Folio Ben Jonson invokes 'thund'ring Æschilus', but few readers would have heard more in the name than a distant rumble. The oldest of the Greek tragedians took much longer than Sophocles and Euripides to enter the English literary imagination. Until the last decades of the 18th c. Aeschylus was as well known for his valour against the Persians at the battle of Marathon as for

the seven extant plays attributed to him (his authorship of *Prometheus Desmotes* (*c.*456 BCE, Prometheus Bound) is now seriously disputed). 'For not alone he nurs'd the Poet's flame, | But reach'd from Virtue's Hand the Patriot's Steel', wrote William Collins in his 'Ode to Fear' (1746). A few years earlier, in *Joseph Andrews*, Henry Fielding had given Parson Adams an eccentric enthusiasm when he put an Aeschylus into his pocket.

There were good reasons for keeping him at arm's length. Aeschylus presents the reader, let alone the translator, with the most daunting difficulties. The choral lyrics essential to Greek tragic drama are more prominent in his plays than in those of his successors, extending sometimes over hundreds of lines, as for example in the entry song of *Agamemnon* (458 BCE), or the lament shared by Orestes, Electra, and chorus over the tomb of the dead king in *Choephori* (458 BCE, The Libation-Bearers). These lyrics are densely metaphoric, bristling with polysyllabic compound adjectives, visionary and elliptical to the point of opacity (especially in the *Agamemnon*). Throughout the plays complex thoughts are expressed in burly and visceral figures of speech, which are not segregated in the choral songs but infiltrate the speech of the actors. Indeed, speech is rarely far from song. Along with his contemporary Pindar, Aeschylus represents, it has been argued, an archaic, magical view of the world and the role of language in it, 'before the intellectual chasm between signifier and signified has opened up. A word for him seems still to be a vision' (C. J. Herington, *Poetry into Drama*, 1985).

No wonder then that for more than 250 years following the first edition of his works (Venice, 1518)—severely maimed by omission of the end of *Agamemnon* and beginning of *Choephori*—he remained much more of a mystery to English readers than Sophocles and Euripides. The sole exception was the *Prometheus*, which was known through Latin translation. In 1663 Thomas Stanley's edition established a more solid presence and the accompanying Latin translation and commentary made him more widely accessible. (For Ezra Pound, Stanley's Latin shamed all attempts at preserving the force of its great original in English.) It was only in 1773 that the first complete play appeared in English, with a *Prometheus* by Thomas **Morell** (1703–84). One reviewer justly complained that it was not 'impregnated with the fire of Aeschylus'. Nor was there much of a sacred flame in evidence four years later, when Robert **Potter** (1721–1804) published the first complete translation. Wistful thoughts of the great English poets who might have translated Aeschylus before this gravitate towards the names of Marlowe and Milton (and later of Hopkins, whose own formal and stylistic innovations owe much to Aeschylus and Pindar). But the honour of ushering Aeschylus into English belongs to Potter, a Norfolk clergyman.

Potter's verse is of negligible merit. The best that can be said of it is that the choral lyrics read like a poor man's Thomas Gray, a sub-sublime. Potter did in fact take Gray's part against Johnson, who then snubbed him and called his translation 'verbiage'. Yet Potter's translation had a notable success, and helped him to the ecclesiastical preferment that had at least partly provided its motive. He went on to produce complete versions of the other two tragedians, but it was the Aeschylus for which he was best known. While his Sophocles had to share the field with Francklin's [II.i.4.ii] and his Euripides with Wodhull's [II.i.5.ii], his Aeschylus had no rivals until the 1820s, and even then it managed to hold its own through the century, being reprinted as late as 1892. Potter's Aeschylus, like Francklin's Sophocles and Wodhull's Euripides, represents the advent of the 'routine' verse translation which adapts its source text to the contemporary poetic conventions most amenable to most readers. (The three were printed together in 1809 as a standard five-volume set entitled *The Greek Tragic Theatre*.) Potter's choice of blank verse for the Greek hexameter and rhymed lyrics for the choral metres was one of the norms for well over a century; the other was unabashed prose.

ii. Nineteenth Century In 1766 Thomas Francklin had described Aeschylus as 'noble and sublime, but at the same time wild, irregular and frequently fantastic'. In other words, just the sort of natural genius to be taken up by the next generation. In the 19th c. Aeschylus at last came into his own, ranking close to or even above Sophocles and Euripides. He was renowned in particular for Prometheus, the iconic figure of political defiance, intellectual invention, and social altruism, whose impact on Shelley and Byron is manifest in, for example, *Prometheus Unbound* and *Manfred*. Also for the *Oresteia*, its radical enquiry into the origins of culture and the possibilities of progress; both Marx and Wagner were ready to admire him.

The 100 years from the 1820s to the 1920s see a deluge of translations, both routine verse and prose crib. Most of the names are now merely a matter of history. There were several complete translations and many versions of the two most popular plays, *Agamemnon* and *Prometheus*. An end-point can be marked by Gilbert **Murray**'s (1866–1957) relentlessly rhymed *Oresteia* of 1928, or his belated complete Aeschylus of 1952. But Murray's verse was always belated, and this whole strenuous era—from Potter to Murray—has little to draw the reader back to it.

A handful of items are still worth attention. There are some charms in Edward **FitzGerald**'s (1809–83) privately printed *Agamemnon*, but their winsomeness has little to do with the original. A better case can be made for the alexandrines of

Benjamin Hall **Kennedy** (1804–89), famed for his Latin primer; his break with blank verse modestly anticipates by some 50 years the welcome new flexibility of Louis **MacNeice** and others in the 1930s. His rendering has been claimed as the first that is 'recognizably Aeschylean' (Green 1968).

We get a stronger sense of what the 19th c. admired in Aeschylus from Elizabeth Barrett **Browning**'s fluent but sinewy versions of *Prometheus Bound*, the first in 1833 and a second, entirely revised, in 1850. Her preface rejects an idea of the classical as 'regular, and polished, and unimpassioned'. Aeschylus joins hands with Shakespeare against Racine to provide the model for a new romantic aesthetic based on 'vehement imaginativeness'. It may be true that Aeschylus' language 'writhes beneath its impetuosity', but this is the inevitable adjunct of passion. In the conception of Prometheus it finds a steadying focus: 'one of the most original, and grand, and attaching characters ever conceived by the mind of man', without whom Milton could never have conceived his Satan (nor, one might add, his Samson). Later in the century the young Gerard Manley **Hopkins**, whose version of some 40 lines of Prometheus' speech survives, declared the play 'immensely superior to anything else of Aeschylus . . . really full of splendid poetry'.

Robert **Browning** started translating the Greeks in the 1870s, but it was Euripides' two Heracles plays that claimed his attention before he turned to the *Agamemnon*. To say that it does not make for easy reading would be an understatement. Browning himself asserted the desirability of a translator being 'literal at every cost save that of absolute violence to our language', and of furnishing the reader 'with the very turn of each phrase in as Greek a fashion as English will bear'. Many readers snorted that English would *not* bear it. 'He has trampled upon his mother-tongue as with the hoofs of a buffalo,' bellowed the *Spectator*. And if there is such a thing as 'absolute violence to our language', then lines such as this may well perpetrate it: 'At night began the bad-wave-outbreak evils'. There is a well-known crack by W. B. Stanford that it is a good thing the Aeschylus is there to explain what Browning meant.

Yet the difficulty Browning sought to preserve is the difficulty of his original, as he partly described it himself—'all the artistic confusion of tenses, moods, and persons, with which the original teems'. If the translation is something of a nightmare, the same might be said of its original. One could apply to Browning's own manner the phrase he finds for the thwarting of Iphigeneia's utterance

at the moment of her sacrifice: 'violence bridling speech'. One reader at least recognized the real force in such moments: 'In passages where the terrible almost trenches on the grotesque . . . he is almost the only one of our poets who is thoroughly at home in this perplexing borderland of beauty and deformity' (F. A. Paley in the *Athenaeum*). The controversy incited by Browning's *Agamemnon* bears on many of our own current debates about the rival obligations of translation to domesticate or foreignize.

iii. Twentieth Century Ezra Pound admired Browning but deplored his *Agamemnon*. 'A search for Aeschylus in English is deadly, accursed, mindrending,' he complained. He tried to involve T. S. Eliot in an *Agamemnon* but it came to nothing, though 'Sweeney Agonistes', *Murder in the Cathedral*, and *The Family Reunion* testify to the impact of Aeschylus on Eliot's imagination. But the modernist contempt for slack poeticism, the jettisoning of rhyme and embrace of *vers libre*, the example of Hopkins, all these contribute to the changed climate out of which in the 1930s there emerge two important versions. From its vigorous opening alexandrines Louis MacNeice's *Agamemnon* shows a new interest in variegating verse-forms. Though more colloquial translations now make it sound more polite than it once did, it still commands respect for its astuteness ('Honest Dealing' is a good alternative, at l. 772, to the more predictable choice of 'Justice' or 'Righteousness', for *Dikē*), and there is an edge to the diction that leaves lines clear in the memory: 'Dark angel dowered with tears', 'Manshambles, a floor asperged with blood'. The other fine version from the 1930s is of the whole trilogy. It has never been as widely known because it is embedded within a full edition of the Greek text, with introduction and commentary. Yet George **Thomson**'s close, reliable reading is touched with a proper grandeur and an ear for shifting rhythmic effect.

The story of Aeschylus in English after 1945 is partly the story of all Greek tragedy in translation. In the immediate postwar decades the market for students and general readers was dominated by the Chicago Complete Greek Tragedies, which offered a popular *Oresteia* by Richmond **Lattimore**, and by Penguin Classics, for whom Philip **Vellacott** supplied a complete Aeschylus in two volumes. The painstaking but cumbersome Lattimore has proved more durable than the tame Vellacott, whose *Oresteia* has now been displaced by Robert **Fagles**'s, admired by many for its high voltage and deplored by some for its excess:

here she waits
the terror raging back and back in the future
the stealth, the law of the hearth, the mother—
Memory womb of Fury child-avenging Fury!

Further competition is now provided by Kenneth **McLeish** and Frederic **Raphael**, who have followed up an *Oresteia* produced on BBC television in 1979 as *The Serpent Son* with all the plays in two volumes, and by *Oresteias* from Hugh **Lloyd-Jones**, David **Grene**, and Wendy Doniger **O'Flaherty**, and from Michael **Ewans**. Mention must also be made of the three plays inevitably overshadowed by the others. Lively versions of *Persai* (472 BCE, The Persians), *Hepta epi Thebas* (467 BCE, The Seven against Thebes), and *Hiketides* (?463 BCE, The Suppliants) can be found in the Oxford University Press series The Greek Tragedy in New Translations, instigated by the influential critic and poet William **Arrowsmith**.

The two poets best known for other good reasons who have tried to give us an Aeschylus for the end of the 20th c. are Robert **Lowell** and Tony **Harrison**. Lowell's posthumously published *Oresteia* is a sad disappointment. Working from Lattimore's translation ('so elaborately exact'), Lowell's distinctive voice can be heard only at rare moments—the Herald on the misery of Troy, for instance: 'lice scissored through our groins, clean'. His earlier *Prometheus Bound* treats the source text more freely, in prose rather than verse. The result is thoroughly undramatic, but there are passages of crazed, hypnotic intensity, the voice of a mind on the edge of a world—'and then suddenly, the head of Cronus, my own head, and the heads of all the gods were broken spheres, all humming and vibrating with silver wires'. Lowell too modestly confesses: 'I think my own concerns and worries and those of the times seep in.'

Harrison's *Oresteia* was composed for a historic production by Peter Hall at the National Theatre in London in 1981. It is one of several productions in the last 20 years, of the *Oresteia* and other Greek tragedies, that support the (controversial) argument that for all the inevitable anachronisms, theatrical performance can provide a truer 'translation' of an ancient Greek text than any mere words on the page. (The double version by Grene and O'Flaherty, 'unabridged' and 'acting', also derives from production in the theatre.) Harrison is the leading example in English of the theatre-poet for whom the translation of Greek (and other foreign-language) drama is inseparable from performance. He has an emphatic note that his *Oresteia* is 'written to be performed, a rhythmic libretto for masks, music, and an all male company'.

Harrison's *Oresteia* contests the conventions that assign Greek tragedy to high culture. So many of the words to which translations too easily lean have been drained of all menace: a word like 'goddess', for instance, with its ethereally fading sibilance, or a phrase such as 'the envy of the gods'. Our ears need to be shocked by something raw and blunt, like 'she-god' and 'god-grudge'. Instead of mellifluously singing 'Cry Sorrow, sorrow—yet let good prevail!' (Vellacott), Harrison's chorus blurt 'Batter, batter the doom-drum, but believe there'll be better!' The diction is craggy with consonants, unabashed alliteration, and thudding compounds; the rhythms are popular, earthy, carnival. Delving into the past of his own language for 'that ghostly alliterative Anglo-Saxon-cum-ballad metric', Harrison's own strong rhythms express the defiance he finds at the heart of Greek tragedy: 'My brain can tell me life isn't worth living, I would like to die; but my heart beats on . . . That rhythmical thing is like a life-support system.' (Astley 1991)

There will always be those ready to say that Aeschylus is (like Pindar) 'untranslatable'—or at least more untranslatable than Sophocles and Euripides. Thus Hugh Lloyd-Jones, for instance, who concedes that his own version has no pretensions to literature and can justly be called 'pasta without sauce'. There is certainly a need for such scholarly cribs, but Aeschylus also needs poets and critics prepared to take outrageous risks. The ingredients for a fair pasta *with* sauce can be found, diversely, in Browning, MacNeice, Thomson, Lloyd-Jones, Fagles, and Harrison.   ADBP

COMPLETE PLAYS   *The Tragedies of Aeschylus*, tr. Robert Potter, Norwich, 1777 · *The Complete Plays of Aeschylus*, tr. Gilbert Murray, London, 1952 · *Aeschylus I: Oresteia*, tr. Richmond Lattimore, Chicago, 1953 · *Aeschylus II: The Suppliant Maidens and The Persians*, tr. Seth G. Benardete; *Seven against Thebes and Prometheus Bound*, tr. David Grene, Chicago, 1956 · *The Oresteian Trilogy*, tr. Philip Vellacott, Harmondsworth, 1956 [Penguin] · *Prometheus Bound and Other Plays* (*The Suppliants, Seven against Thebes, The Persians*), tr. Philip Vellacott, Harmondsworth, 1961 [Penguin] · *Aeschylus: Plays*, tr. Kenneth McLeish and Frederic Raphael, 2 vols., London, 1991.

THE ORESTEIA   *The Oresteia*, ed. and tr. George Thomson, Cambridge, 1938 · *The Oresteia*, tr. Hugh Lloyd-Jones (as separate plays), Englewood Cliffs, NJ, 1970 · *The Oresteia*, tr. Robert Fagles, London, 1976 [Penguin] · *The Oresteia*, tr. Robert Lowell, New York, 1978 · *The Oresteia*, tr. Tony Harrison, London, 1981 · *The Oresteia: A New Translation for the Theatre*, tr. David Grene and Wendy Doniger O'Flaherty, Chicago/London, 1989 · *The Oresteia*, tr. Michael Ewans, London, 1995.

SINGLE PLAYS   *The Agamemnon*, tr. Edward Fitzgerald [privately printed, 1865] · *The Agamemnon*, tr. Robert Browning, London, 1877 · *The Agamemnon*, tr. Benjamin Hall Kennedy, Cambridge, 1878 · *The Agamemnon*, tr. Louis MacNeice, London, 1936 · *Persians*, tr. Janet Lembke and C. J. Herington, Oxford/New York, 1981 · *Prometheus Bound*, tr. Elizabeth Barrett Browning, London, 1833 [rev. edn. London, 1850] · *The Prometheus Bound*, ed. and tr. George Thomson, Cambridge, 1932 · Robert Lowell, *Prometheus Bound, derived from Aeschylus*, London, 1970 · *Prometheus Bound*, tr. J. Scully and C. J. Herington, Oxford/New York, 1975 · *Seven against Thebes*, tr. A. Hecht and H. H. Bacon, Oxford/New York, 1974 · *Suppliants*, tr. Janet Lembke, Oxford/New York, 1975.

SEE ALSO   Astley, N., ed., *Tony Harrison*, Newcastle upon Tyne, 1991 · Brower, R. A., 'Seven Agamemnons', in R. A. Brower, ed., *On Translation*, Cambridge, Mass., 1959 · Green P., 'Some Versions of Aeschylus: A Study of Tradition and Method in Translating Poetry', in his *Essays in Antiquity*, London, 1968 · Pound, E., 'Translators of Greek', in T. S. Eliot, ed., *Literary Essays*, London, 1954.

4. SOPHOCLES

i. Problems of Translation   There is a revealing moment of protest in the first complete translation (1729, in prose) of the seven extant tragedies of Sophocles. At the climax of the play named after her, Electra urges her brother on to kill their mother, Clytemnestra, with a terrible cry: 'Strike her again, if you have the strength.' This was too much for the translator George **Adams**, 'late of St. John's College, Cambridge' (?1698–?1768), who complained in a footnote: 'The characters which Sophocles here gives Orestes and Electra are too cruel.' Alongside this we can set an anecdote told by Bernard Knox of a modern-day performance at which Electra's cry brought a middle-aged man to his feet with an answering shout of 'Bravo! Bravo!'—before he sank back with embarrassment.

This moment may not have been quite what George Eliot had in mind when she praised Sophocles for his 'delineation of the great primitive emotions'. But savagery is an essential component of Sophoclean tragedy. Until the 20th c. translation and interpretation sought to gloss over the violence contained by the shapely dramatic forms commended by Aristotle. Sophocles evoked words such as 'sweetness', 'royal', 'noble serenity', 'hieratic'; he was associated with restraint, authority, piety. An establishment man, surely, even a bit of a gentleman, and certainly the creator of one character of unimpeachable moral stature—Antigone. Adams finds the cruelty an aberration because the plays are mainly to be valued for their moral instruction; they 'teach men to reduce their passions to subjection to their reason'.

The real Sophocles does not translate so easily. Both action and diction carry a perpetual sense of the ominous, of the unsaid or the not yet said (and certainly not yet fully comprehended). A single quiet word or phrase can suggest a whole dark future, as when Aegisthus at the end of *Electra* (?418–410 BCE) speaks of the troubles of the clan, 'both now *and to come*'. This sense of nervous anticipation grows out of the minute subtleties of word order as well as the gathering menace of the action. The translator needs to rise to the moments of heightened utterance, for chorus and actor alike, when Ajax and Antigone prepare themselves for death, or the self-blinded Oedipus emerges from the palace, or the old men of Colonus reflect that it is best never to have been born. Such moments often attract free-standing translation: the first of these in C. S. **Calverley**'s (1831–84) plangent Victorian 'Speech of Ajax', for instance, and the last in versions by A. E. **Housman**, Thomas **Hardy** and W. B. **Yeats**. Yet no less important are the slivers of anxiety that colour the apparently plainer passages of dialogue and narrative, as when the characters in *Trachiniae* (?457–430 BCE, *The Women of Trachis*) keep insisting that now they all know the *whole* truth.

ii. Sixteenth to Nineteenth Centuries   Sophocles passes into the English literary imagination in the 16th c. Though he was not as popular as Euripides, their names were regularly linked by the Tudor humanists. Sidney cites Sophocles' Ajax as 'a more familiar insight into anger' than anything one can learn from the Schoolmen, and speaks of him as one of 'the great Captaines of Sweete Poesie'. But the only translations to be published before 1700 were Thomas **Watson**'s (?1557–1592) *Antigone* (?441 BCE) (into Latin, 1581), and Christopher **Wase**'s (1627–90) royalist *Electra* of 1649, an optimistic attempt to find parallels between the houses of Atreus and Stuart.

It is in the 18th c. that translation begins in earnest, with the publisher Bernard Lintott's ambition to issue the whole of Greek tragedy in English at a volume a month. This bore modest fruit with an anonymous *Ajax* (?450–440 BCE) in 1714 (in which Lewis **Theobald** (1688–1744) or Nicholas **Rowe** (1674–1718) may have had a hand), followed by an *Electra* and an *Oedipus Tyrannus* (?430–425 BCE) from the capable but uninspired pen of Theobald, who would later edit Shakespeare. But the series never got beyond three, and although Swift's friend Thomas **Sheridan** (1687–1738) published a *Philoctetes* (409 BCE) in 1725 and Adams his complete prose version a few years later, it was only in 1759 that the market really began to open up, with the first full presentation in English verse of 'the Shakespeare of antiquity', as the dedication to the Prince of Wales blazoned him: the translator was Thomas **Francklin** (1721–84). The same year saw the englishing of Père Brumoy's *Théâtre des Grecs* by Charlotte **Lennox** (1720–1804) (and friends), similarly dedicated; it included *Oedipus Tyrannus*, *Electra*, and *Philoctetes*.

In 1766 a second edition of Francklin's worthy, mild, fluent version was prefaced with a weighty 'Dissertation on Antient Tragedy', and it held sway for many years, being reprinted by John Morley in the Universal Library as late as 1886. The alternatives included complete renditions, decent and dull, by Robert **Potter** (1721–1804), Thomas **Dale** (1797–1870), and Lewis **Campbell** (1830–1908). The Victorian Sophocles is too high-minded to inspire much living translation, though the sonorous versions by Sir George **Young** (1837–1930) and Sir R. C. **Jebb** (1841–1905) still command respect, and mention should be made of Edward **FitzGerald's** (1809–83) skilful conflation of the two Oedipus plays.

One of the defining 'translations' of Sophocles for the Victorian imagination was more and other than a matter of words. This was a performance of *Antigone* by Helen Faucit in 1845–6, in London, Dublin, Edinburgh, and elsewhere, in a version by William **Bartholomew** (dates unknown) with music by Mendelssohn. Thomas De Quincey saw it as a symbolic event; the classics were being democratized, no longer the monopoly of a social élite. He recorded the general rapture that welcomed this vision of the antique: 'What perfection of Athenian sculpture! the noble figure, the lovely arms, the fluent drapery! What an unveiling of the ideal statuesque!' This was Greek tragedy made flesh—or better, an ideal synthesis of flesh, stone, and drapery.

Matthew Arnold was the most influential spokesman for the highly moralized view of Greek tragedy which pervades Victorian translations of Sophocles (see in particular his preface to *Merope* (1857)). He too thinks in terms of sculpture exercis-

ing its hypnotic effect on 'the riveted gaze of the spectator'. Sophocles is good for us (as Euripides and Shakespeare are not), because, in the famous formulation in the sonnet 'To a Friend', he 'saw life steadily, and saw it whole'. His tragedies conduct us to 'a state of feeling which it is the highest aim of tragedy to produce, to a *sentiment of sublime acquiescence in the course of fate, and in the dispensation of human life*'. This is catharsis with a distinctly Victorian aura. Dressed in the liturgical and quasi-Biblical diction of the 19th-c. translations, this produces, as E. M. Forster mockingly puts it in *The Longest Journey*, the idea of Sophocles 'as a kind of enlightened bishop'.

iii. Twentieth Century The story of Sophocles in the 20th c. is one of progressive liberation from this petrifying idealism. In so far as the modernists turn their attention to Greek tragedy, it is Euripides and to a lesser extent Aeschylus who initially catch their attention. Yeats did produce a *King Oedipus* staged at the Dublin Abbey Theatre in December 1926. But the rhythmical prose of the dialogues is limp, and the long verse lines of the choral odes if anything limper. More robust are the independent lyrics Yeats translated around the same time: the two great visionary songs from the *Oedipus at Colonus* (401 BCE), and the brief hymn to passion 'From the Antigone'.

But one of the major modernists *does* eventually grapple with Sophocles. In the years after 1945 that he spent incarcerated in St Elizabeth's Asylum for the Criminally Insane, Ezra **Pound** produced a version of *The Women of Trachis*, and worked with Rudd Fleming on a version of the *Electra* only published after his death. They are both extraordinary works, at once reckless and shrewd, and certainly calculated to raise the blood pressure of the strait-laced philologist. They elude simple verdicts of success or failure; like Browning's *Agamemnon* [II.i.3.ii] and Harrison's *Oresteia* [II.i.3.iii], they contest unthinking assumptions about the obligations of the translator to fluency and transparency.

Pound's choice of *The Women of Trachis* is itself significant. It is a shocking play, brimming with violence and sexual rapacity. It had needed a thorough laundering when Thomas Broughton adapted it in his libretto for Handel's *Hercules* (1744). No wonder the Victorians shunned it. Yet for all Pound's distance from Arnold, what they both admire in Sophocles is the combination of tumultous passion and formal mastery. Or as Pound has it, in the upper case to which he makes his Heracles rise, in climactic recognition that he is not dying in mere meaningless agony,

what
SPLENDOUR
IT ALL COHERES.

To characterize Pound's Sophocles one might invoke the phrase with which his chorus greet the wreckage of Heracles' once mighty body: 'A splendour of ruin'. Pound sets out to ruin the coherence of diction, style, and tone to which most translations aspire. The distance between song and speech is not minimized but exacerbated. The archaic idioms into which the Trachinian chorus melt can summon up a ghostly dignity:

> Phoebus, Phoebus, ere thou slay
> and lay flaked Night upon her blazing pyre,

or

> Tears green the cheek with bright dews
> pouring down.

In both plays there are passages of high lyric pathos, sustained by a rhythmic pulse too rarely heard in (ostensibly) verse translation, most notably in the wonderful scene in *Electra* in which the protagonist keens over the ashes of the brother she supposes to be dead:

> naught into naught, zero to zero
> to enter beside thee
> our fortune equal
> death endeth pain.

Yet the relief of song is constantly disrupted by the uncouthness of speech. In the midst of Electra's tender prayer, she bursts into the colloquial—'that bitch of a mother'. Pound puts comparable vulgarities into the mouth of Deianeira in *The Women of Trachis*, such as led one commentator to call her 'a brassy, cocksure guttersnipe' (Richmond Lattimore). But the degrading of speech is not mainly a matter of characterization. It is true that there is a zany eclecticism to some of the language—'Thebes-burg', 'Nope', 'Arf a mo', Ma'am!' But there is also a healthy and effective directness: 'Don't weasel to me.' For all the objections to which Pound's method and practice are open, there is an important sense in which his translations relive, through their own dislocations of tone, the collision of voices and desires, and the search for a design that can give them all meaning, such as power the action of Sophocles' texts: both splendour *and* ruin.

Nevertheless *The Women of Trachis* remains the least-known of the extant plays to the general reader. Of the two plays that draw most directly on Homer, *Ajax* has lost some of its earlier prestige, while *Philoctetes* has attracted more attention,

including a recent version by Seamus **Heaney** for the Field Day Theatre Company, entitled *The Cure at Troy*. This makes less overt reference to the world of contemporary Irish politics than Tom **Paulin**'s vigorous and resourceful *The Riot Act*, a version of *Antigone* also produced by Field Day (see Roche 1988). But Heaney's reworking of a story about a long-nursed wound and its miraculous healing gathers an inevitable resonance from the context of its composition. Heaney reimagines the figure of Heracles in the play's resolution as 'the voice of reality and justice', to which the crippled warrior must attend if he is to learn, as the chorus semi-sentimentally suggest, that 'the half-true rhyme is love'.

Over the centuries it is *Antigone* and *Oedipus Tyrannus* that have attracted most attention from translators, critics, and performers alike. There have been strong modern versions of both from Dudley **Fitts** and Robert **Fitzgerald** and, more recently, from Robert **Fagles**. *Oedipus at Colonus* has often been inserted between them to produce the set of 'three Theban plays'. Timberlake **Wertenbaker**, for example, provided a lean, acute script for performance by the Royal Shakespeare Company in 1991. Since 1945 the Theban plays have been widely read in the relevant volume of the Chicago Complete Greek Tragedy (there is a particularly effective *Oedipus at Colonus* by Robert Fitzgerald, first issued independently in 1941), and a Penguin version by E. F. **Watling** (1947), now superseded by a distinctly more full-blooded one from Robert Fagles.

From the mid-1980s onwards there has been a flurry of rival accounts: one might single out the integrated 'trilogy' by Stephen **Spender** which conjures up moments of radiance to express, for example, the passing of Oedipus:

> Light within light, invisible—music
> In music, silence. Calm
> Of utter peace, the god within the storm.

Variations on this trio of plays have included a well-respected set from H. D. F. **Kitto**, which forgoes the logic of retaining *Oedipus at Colonus* with its Theban kin and replaces it with the more consistently dramatic *Electra*. Another option is to offer the two Oedipus plays as a diptych. For a 1996 Royal National Theatre production Ranjit **Bolt** composed a rhymed version which he hoped would prove 'some sort of inadequate analogue for the wonderful sonority of the Greek', but its cool skills struck many auditors as too light for the task in hand.

Sophocles' most notable recent success in the British theatre goes well beyond the limits of what is normally thought of as translation. Tony **Harrison** builds *The Trackers of Oxyrhynchus* round the sizeable fragment of a satyr play, the *Ichneutae* (?455–410 BCE) only recovered from the sands of Egypt by the papyrologists Hunt and Grenfell in 1907. Harrison brings the satyrs and their play back to life and develops a swingeing debate about the cultural ownership of Greek tragedy; this culminates in the violent revenge of the disinherited satyrs of the modern world on behalf of their mythic archetype, Marsyas:

Aeschylus, Sophocles, gerroff our backs.
We're hijacking Culture and leaving no tracks.

Harrison's remarkable play, like his *Oresteia*, does not leave the classical source where it found it.

Meanwhile back in the more tranquil domain of the Loeb parallel-text editions, Hugh **Lloyd-Jones** now offers the reader an accurate guide to the literal meaning, no more and no less, including, with all the many other fragments, the four hundred lines or so of the *Ichneutae*. ADBP

COMPLETE PLAYS *The Tragedies of Sophocles*, tr. George Adams, London, 1729 · *The Tragedies of Sophocles*, tr. Thomas Francklin, 2 vols., London, 1759 · *The Tragedies of Sophocles*, tr. Robert Potter, London, 1788 · *The Tragedies of Sophocles*, tr. Thomas Dale, 2 vols., London, 1824 · *The Tragedies of Sophocles*, tr. Lewis Campbell, London, 1883 · *The Dramas of Sophocles*, tr. Sir George Young, Cambridge, 1888 · *The Tragedies of Sophocles*, tr. Sir R. C. Jebb, Cambridge, 1904 · *The Theban Plays*, tr. E. F. Watling, Harmondsworth, 1947 [Penguin] · *Electra and Other Plays*, tr. E. F. Watling, Harmondsworth, 1953 [Penguin] · *Sophocles I: Oedipus the King*, tr. David Grene; *Oedipus at Colonus*, tr. Robert Fitzgerald; *Antigone*, tr. Elizabeth Wyckoff, Chicago / London, 1954 · *Sophocles II: Ajax*, tr. John Moore; *The Women of Trachis*, tr. Michael Jameson; *Electra* and *Philoctetes*, tr. David Grene, Chicago / London, 1957 · *Sophocles*, ed. and tr. Hugh Lloyd-Jones, 3 vols., Cambridge, Mass. / London, 1994–6 [Loeb].

TWO OR MORE PLAYS *Oedipus Tyrannus, Electra, Philoctetes*, tr. Charlotte Lennox, in *The Greek Theatre of Father Brumoy*, 3 vols., London, 1759 · *The Downfall and Death of King Oedipus*, by Edward FitzGerald, London, 1880 · *Sophocles: Three Tragedies (Antigone, Oedipus the King, Electra)*, tr. H. D. F. Kitto, Oxford, 1962 · *Electra, Antigone* and *Philoctetes*, tr. Kenneth McLeish, Cambridge, 1979 · *The Three Theban Plays*, tr. Robert Fagles, New York / London, 1982 · *The Oedipus Trilogy: A Version*, by Stephen Spender, London, 1985 · *The Thebans*, tr. Timberlake Wertenbaker, London, 1992 · *The Oedipus Plays*, tr. Ranjit Bolt, Bath, 1996.

SINGLE PLAYS *Ajax*, tr. anon., London, 1714 · *Antigone*, tr. Thomas Watson (into Latin), London, 1581 · *An Imitative Version of Antigone*, tr. William Bartholomew, London, 1848 · *Antigone: An English version*, tr. Dudley Fitts and Robert Fitzgerald, New York / London, 1939 · *The Riot Act: A version of Sophocles' Antigone*, tr. Tom Paulin, London, 1985 · *Sophocles' Antigone: A New Version*, tr. Brendan Kennelly, Newcastle upon Tyne, 1996 · *Electra*, tr. Christopher Wase, The Hague, 1649 · *Electra*, tr. Lewis Theobald, London, 1714 · *Electra*, tr. Ezra Pound and Rudd Fleming, Princeton, NJ, 1989 · [*Ichneutae*] Tony Harrison, *The Trackers of Oxyrhynchus*, London, 1990 · *Oedipus, King of Thebes*, tr. Lewis Theobald, London, 1715 · *A Free Translation of the Oedipus Tyrannus*, tr. Thomas Maurice, in *Poems and Miscellaneous Pieces*, London, 1779 · *King Oedipus: A Version for the Modern Stage*, by W. B. Yeats, London, 1928 · *Oedipus Tyrannus: An English version*, tr. Dudley Fitts and Robert Fitzgerald, New York / London, 1951 · *Philoctetes*, tr. Thomas Sheridan, London, 1725 · *The Cure at Troy: A Version of Sophocles' Philoctetes*, by Seamus Heaney, London, 1991 · *Sophocles, Women of Trachis: A Version*, by Ezra Pound, London, 1956.

EXTRACTS 'What man is he that yearneth', tr. A. E. Housman, in his *Odes from the Greek Dramatists*, ed. Arthur W. Pollard, London, 1890 · 'Colonus' Praise' and 'From "Oedipus at Colonus"', 'From the "Antigone"', tr. W. B. Yeats, in his *Collected Poems*, London, 1933 · 'Speech of Ajax', tr. C. S. Calverley, in *Verses and Translations*, London, 1961 [1st edn. 1862] · 'Thoughts from Sophocles', tr. Thomas Hardy, in his *Complete Poetical Works*, ed. Samuel Hynes, vol. iii, Oxford, 1985.

SEE ALSO De Quincey, T., 'The Antigone of Sophocles as represented on the Edinburgh Stage' (1846), in his *Collected Works*, ed. David Masson, x, Edinburgh, 1889 · Mason, H. A., 'The Women of Trachis and Creative Translation', in J. P. Sullivan, ed., *Ezra Pound: A Critical Anthology*, Harmondsworth, 1970 · Roche, A., 'Ireland's Antigones: Tragedy North and South', in M. Kenneally, ed., *Cultural Contexts and Literary Idioms in Contemporary Irish Literature*, Gerards Cross, UK, 1988.

5. EURIPIDES

The youngest of the three great Greek tragedians, Euripides has always seemed the most amenable to English readers, less formidably alien than Aeschylus, less mysterious than Sophocles. This is partly because there is more to choose from; the

accidents of history have preserved 19 plays, several more than those of the other two combined.

But it is also the angle at which Euripides stands to the orthodoxies of his own world that makes him more accessible. In antiquity his drama had been a source of controversy, of admiration and irritation. The perplexity reflects the often violent conflicts within the plays themselves, both of attitude, opinion, and belief and of form, style, and tone. They scorn the formal integration recommended by Aristotle. Their choral lyrics often possess a seductive, centrifugal quality that threatens to lift them out of their dramatic context. (There is a legendary story, retold by Sidney in his *Apology*, of Athenian prisoners melting the hearts of their Syracusan captors with some verses of Euripides.) Yet the plays also subject to the sharpest analysis the power of all forms of language to charm and persuade and transform the relations of strength and weakness.

i. Fragmentary Translation The sense of disintegration formally embodied in his drama encourages translators to pick and choose. This helps to account for the high proportion in English of free-standing translations of particular lyrics and passages. Near the beginning of the 18th c., for instance, Laurence **Eusden** (1688–1730) versified part of one chorus from the *Medea* (431 BCE), and right at the end Thomas **Campbell** (1777–1844) did another. In the 19th c. Thomas Love **Peacock** and Elizabeth Barrett **Browning** turned their hands to lyrics on 'Love' from *Hippolytus* (428 BCE) and *Troades* (415 BCE, The Trojan Women) respectively, while John Addington **Symonds** (1840–93) found a defiant premonition of late Victorian godlessness in a fragment from *Bellerophon* (c.438–28 BCE). Shortly after World War I **H. D.** (Hilda Doolittle) marks an historic breakthrough with her keen-edged choruses, untainted by Victorian poeticism, from the *Iphigeneia in Aulis* (?405 BCE) and the *Hippolytus*.

Through the previous centuries many short translations were transplanted and embedded within other texts. Readers of Roger **Ascham**'s (1515/16–1569) *Toxophilus* found themselves regaled with some lines from *Heracles* (?c.417 BCE) in praise of the archer, in jaunty fourteeners. To demonstrate the influence of *Iphigeneia in Aulis* on the quarrel scene between Brutus and Cassius in *Julius Caesar*, Charles **Gildon** (1665–1724) rendered the whole passage between Agamemnon and Menelaus into English. Later in the 18th c. Charles Burney included in his *General History of Music* a grandly lugubrious extract from a choral lyric in *Medea* by his friend Samuel **Johnson**. (For all the instances in this and the preceding paragraph, see Poole and Maule 1995.)

The tradition of translating independent fragments goes back to the very origins of Greek tragedy's passage into English culture in the 16th c. The key figure here is Erasmus, whose influence on Tudor education can scarcely be overestimated. In 1506 he published Latin translations of two Euripides plays, *Hecuba* (?425–4 BCE) and *Iphigeneia in Aulis*, dedicating them to William Warham, Archbishop of Canterbury. For Erasmus the real value in these texts was encapsulated in brief detachable verses which embodied an idea, belief, attitude, gesture, or image. These little nuggets of wisdom were collected from a wide range of classical authors in his popular Latin *Adages*, which was issued in expanding editions from 1505 to 1540, and frequently reprinted and translated until the end of the next century. There are many references to the Greek tragedians, but most of all to Euripides. He passed into English, therefore, not only in the shape of complete plays but also, perhaps even more so, through these exemplary utterances, bathed in Erasmus' reflection and commentary—the image of a Polyxena or an Iphigeneia saying 'Farewell dear light', as she turns to face her death, for example.

ii. Sixteenth to Nineteenth Centuries Though Sophocles' name was frequently linked with that of Euripides by the Tudor humanists, there is no question which of the two was the livelier figure in the mind of the educated reader. It is no accident that the only two translations of whole plays into English to have survived from the 16th c. are both of Euripides. In many ways they complement each other. The first is a private version in prose of *Iphigeneia in Aulis* by Lady Jane **Lumley** (c.1537–1576/7), made about 1550 but unpublished until 1909. The other is *Jocasta*, a play put on at Gray's Inn in 1566 by two clever young laywers, George **Gascoigne** (c.1534–1577) and Francis **Kinwelmersh** (d. ?1580). Indirectly derived from *Phoenissae* (412–408 BCE, The Phoenician Women) via an Italian version by Lodovico Dolce, it is more memorable for the stage-images it creates, of the blind Oedipus led by his daughter Antigone, for instance, than for the verse itself. It was an experiment that failed to catch on, and until the later 18th c. most English readers who experienced Greek tragedies at all as complete dramas would have done so in Latin translations such as those by Erasmus or the Scots humanist George Buchanan (1506–82).

Buchanan's *Medea* of 1544 was followed by an influential *Alcestis* (438 BCE) performed before Queen Elizabeth in the 1560s, and his own best drama rewrites *Iphigeneia in Aulis* as the scriptural tragedy of Jephtha and his daughter (*Jephthes*, 1554).

Ascham praises it in his *Scholemaster* (1570) as the rare instance of a modern drama 'able to abyde the trew touch of *Aristotles* preceptes, and *Euripides* examples'. A century later its influence is evident in the one great example in English of a scriptural tragedy based on Greek models: Milton's *Samson Agonistes* (1671). One notes a continuing attraction in the troubled images of sacrifice which so many of Euripides' tragedies embody and examine.

Until the early 20th c. the English Euripides was mainly a soft-hearted creature. Elizabeth Barrett Browning gushed a mid-Victorian admiration for 'Euripides, the human, | With his droppings of warm tears'. A hundred years earlier Thomas **Morell** (1703–84) had struck an only slightly drier note in the preface to his *Hecuba* (1749), when he admired a dramatist 'guided in his Compositions rather by the Motions of an humane and tender Heart, than the Dictates of a laborious and studious mind'. Some years earlier Richard **West** (d. 1726) expressed bewilderment that his own *Hecuba*, freely adapted from its Euripidean source, should have met with so little success at Drury Lane: 'I thought it would prove an elegant Entertainment for a polite Assembly.' He had surely been on the right lines. A charming tearfulness long dominates the idea of Euripides in English. In 1915 the popular translations of Gilbert **Murray** (1866–1957) prompted this American growl from John Jay Chapman: 'The sentimentalism of this British school when it fondles Greek intellect is like Agave with the head of Pentheus in her arms.'

Euripides shared in the general Hellenic revival at the end of the 18th c., when, like Sophocles and Aeschylus, he enjoyed his first complete translation into English verse. That of Michael **Wodhull** (1740–1816) appeared in 1782 (he calls one of the plays *The Phoenician Damsels*, which gives a fair flavour), and that of Robert **Potter** (1721–1804) in 1781–3. The exiguous literary merits of these versions scarcely advanced his reputation, and the belated enthusiasm with which Aeschylus was welcomed into English also reduced his prestige.

The younger romantics certainly turned to the Aeschylean Prometheus for inspiration, but other outcasts and rebels could also attract them. **Byron** found time in his *Hours of Idleness* (1807) for a version of the chorus from *Medea* expressing sympathy for 'the exile's silent tear'. And **Shelley** seized with glee on the boisterous figure of the Cyclops: 'Stranger, I laugh to scorn Jove's thunderbolt.' His decision to translate the sole surviving example of a complete satyr play (*Cyclops*, ?412 BCE) may appear an eccentricity. But it is perhaps unsurprising that in the troubled years after Waterloo he should have

been drawn to what William Arrowsmith, himself a fine translator of the play, has described as 'a farce of ideas, a gay and ironic flirtation with the problem of civilized brutality'.

The 19th c. agreed that Euripides was the most modern of the tragedians—analytical, sceptical, agnostic, or even atheist—and hence of course 'the least of the three' (Jenkyns 1980). Though **Swinburne** protested his abhorrence, it failed to mask considerable debts; his *Erechtheus* (1876) is based on the lost Euripides play of that name (422 BCE), and massively influenced by *Hecuba*. A more candid and generous response came from Robert **Browning**, who shared with his wife, Elizabeth Barrett, an enthusiasm for 'Euripides the human', and some years after her death translated the two plays centred on Heracles. Both are enclosed within a larger framing narrative through which comment and interpretation are expressed—*Alcestis* in *Balaustion's Adventure* (1871) and *Heracles* in *Aristophanes' Apology* (1875). The former is particularly effective in the way it 'novelizes' the drama of a wife's self-sacrifice and her husband's guilt, turning it into a recognizably Victorian marital crisis, happily resolved by the muscular, Christ-like figure of Heracles: 'So, in a spasm and splendour of resolve, | All at once did the God surmount the man.'

Towards the end of the century the 'intellectual' element in Euripidean drama suggested his kinship with Ibsen and Shaw—Euripides the Rationalist, to borrow the title of a book by A. W. Verrall (1895). But the *fin de siècle* had something for every one, including a version of Euripides the Aesthete, sponsored by Walter Pater. His essay 'The Bacchanals of Euripides' (1889) helped to focus a new kind of attention on *The Bacchae* (405 BCE) which it has never since lost.

iii. The Twentieth Century Though Pater confessed to 'a real shudder at the horror of the theme', his admiration for the blither aspects of Dionysus contributed to the idea of Euripides as a sensitive soul. In 1902 this was taken over by Gilbert Murray, whose influential translations began with a volume containing *The Bacchae* and *Hippolytus*, shortly followed by *The Trojan Women*, *Electra*, and *Medea*. For Murray *The Bacchae* is to Euripides what for so many readers of the time *The Tempest* was to Shakespeare, a final testament to his beliefs about art and life. The play becomes an allegory of Euripides' escape from the sordid politics of Athens and 'Those haggard, striving, suspicious men' (a distinctly Yeatsian scorn). For Murray the play offers the assurance that 'The Kingdom of Heaven is within you—here and now'. The quasi-Biblical tone of his own translation can be gauged from the opening words he puts in the mouth of his Dionysus: 'Behold, God's Son is come unto this land.'

Though Murray also turned his hand to Aeschylus and Sophocles, it was his Euripides that made him, in T. S. Eliot's words, 'the most popular Hellenist of his time'. Murray's aspirations to poetry moved Eliot to righteous indignation: this was nothing more than 'a vulgar debasement of the eminently personal idiom of Swinburne'. Better, for Eliot, the unadorned prose crib which would not deceive the Greekless reader into supposing that Medea beglamours herself with a late Victorian veil of words as in: 'I dazzle where I stand | The cup of all life shattered in my hand.'

For the 20th c. the real challenge has been at last to see Euripides steadily and see him whole, in all the fluctuations of tone that distinguish him so sharply from Sophocles. H. D. brought a new lucidity of diction and line to her *Choruses from the Iphigeneia in Aulis and the Hippolytus* (1919):

> I crossed sand-hills.
> I stand among the sea-drift before Aulis.
> I crossed Euripos' strait—
> Foam hissed after my boat.

And in 1937 she produced a sumptuous full-length version of *Ion* (c.411 BCE), interspersed with commentary. But it is only in the years after 1945 that the plays really shake themselves free from Murray's mellifluous shackles. In particular, the five volumes of the Chicago Complete Greek Tragedy present the reader with the full array of 19 plays by various hands (of varying ability). Taken as a whole, these are a good deal livelier than the competing versions offered by Penguin, all from the pen of Philip **Vellacott**. Penguin have begun the process of replacing these with versions in dignified but speakable prose by John **Davie**.

Amongst the complete Chicago translations, the five by William **Arrowsmith** stand out. Arrowsmith was an ardent, impatient propagandist for living translation (not only of the classics), and the moving spirit behind a rival series from Oxford University Press (The Greek Tragedy in New Translations), which he inaugurated with a fine *Alcestis*. Arrowsmith's idea was to create partnerships of poet and scholar who would work on a play in tandem (or more rarely be found in one person, like himself). Though the series ran into difficulties, it

has produced some resourceful examples which live up to Arrowsmith's high ideals—a *Hecuba* and an *Electra* by Janet **Lembke** and Kenneth J. **Reckford**, for instance.

Euripides has always proved more of an incitement to writers in English than Aeschylus or Sophocles. He has also proved attractive to actors and directors. In the 20th c. *Medea* has proved an unsurprisingly popular vehicle for stars such as Sybil Thorndike, Judith Anderson (for whom Robinson **Jeffers** composed an acclaimed version in 1946), and more recently, on both sides of the Atlantic, Diana Rigg. Tony **Harrison** has cannibalized to extraordinary effect Euripides (amongst others) in the libretto for his *Medea: A Sex-War Opera*, commissioned but unperformed by the New York Metropolitan Opera. And Brendan **Kennelly** has also rewritten a *Medea* in a series of plays for women that includes new versions of *The Trojan Women* and Sophocles' *Antigone*.

Recent decades have seen an efflorescence of versions derived from Euripides and designed for performance. There have been in particular some notable *Bacchaes*, including an Africanized and politicized version by Wole **Soyinka** (commissioned but unperformed by the English National Theatre) and a sprightly, elegant account by Derek **Mahon**, the opening lines of which announce a promising sense of mischief (in marked contrast to Murray's, above):

> My name is Dionysus, son of Zeus
> and Semele, Cadmus' eldest daughter. Whoosh!
> I was delivered by a lightning-flash . . .

An arresting fantasia created by Caryl **Churchill** and David **Lan**, *A Mouthful of Birds*, takes *The Bacchae* as its point of departure. Lan has also contributed a more conventional *Ion*, and effective productions of this and other lesser-known plays such as *The Phoenician Women* (by the Royal Shakespeare Company in 1995–6) have supported the case for seeing translation as a matter for the theatre no less than for the study [see I.c.2].

Relishing the impossibility of categorizing the most mercurial of the Greek tragedians, John Jay Chapman observed: 'Sometimes he seems like a religious man, and again, like a charlatan. Of course he was neither. He was a playwright.' Plays which present with such force the sheer shiftiness of words and the world will prove congenial to translation for some time to come.   ADBP

COMPLETE PLAYS   *The Tragedies of Euripides*, tr. Robert Potter, 2 vols., London, 1781–3 · *The Nineteen Tragedies and Fragments of Euripides*, tr. Michael Wodhull, 4 vols., London, 1782 · *Euripides I: Alcestis*, tr. Richmond Lattimore; *The Medea*, tr. Rex Warner; *The Heracleidae*, tr. Ralph Gladstone; *Hippolytus*, tr. David Grene, Chicago/London, 1955 ·

Euripides II: The Cyclops and *Heracles*, tr. William Arrowsmith; *Iphigeneia in Tauris*, tr. Witter Bynner; *Helen*, tr. Richmond Lattimore, Chicago/London, 1956 · *Euripides III: Hecuba*, tr. William Arrowsmith; *Andromache*, tr. John Frederick Nims; *The Trojan Women*, tr. Richmond Lattimore; *Ion*, tr. R. F. Willetts, Chicago/London, 1958 · *Euripides IV: Rhesus*, tr. Richmond Lattimore; *The Suppliant Women*, tr. Frank William Jones; *Orestes*, tr. William Arrowsmith; *Iphigeneia in Aulis*, tr. Charles R. Walker, Chicago/London, 1958 · *Euripides V: Electra*, tr. Emily Townsend Vermeule; *The Phoenician Women*, tr. Elizabeth Wyckoff; *The Bacchae*, tr. William Arrowsmith, Chicago/London, 1959.

TWO OR MORE PLAYS *Hecuba and Iphigeneia in Aulis*, tr. Desiderius Erasmus (into Latin), Paris, 1506 · *Hippolytus and Bacchae*, tr. Gilbert Murray, London, 1902 · *Alcestis and Other Plays* (*Hippolytus* and *Iphigeneia in Tauris*), tr. Philip Vellacott, Harmondsworth, 1953 [Penguin] · *Bacchae and Other Plays* (*Ion, Helen, Women of Troy*), tr. Philip Vellacott, Harmondsworth, 1954 [Penguin] · *Medea and Other Plays* (*Heracles, Hecuba, Electra*), tr. Philip Vellacott, Harmondsworth, 1963 [Penguin] · *Orestes and Other Plays* (*The Children of Heracles, Andromache, The Suppliant Women, The Phoenician Women, Iphigeneia in Aulis*), tr. Philip Vellacott, Harmondsworth, 1972 [Penguin] · *The War Plays: Troades, Helen and Iphigeneia at Aulis*, tr. Don Taylor, London, 1990 · *Alcestis and Other Plays* (*Medea, Children of Heracles, Hippolytus*), tr. John Davie, Harmondsworth, 1996 [Penguin].

SINGLE PLAYS *Alcestis*, tr. George Buchanan (into Latin), Paris, 1556 · [*Alcestis*] Robert Browning, *Balaustion's Adventure; Including a Transcript from Euripides*, London, 1871 · *Alcestis: An English Version*, tr. Dudley Fitts and Robert Fitzgerald, 1936 · *Alcestis*, tr. William Arrowsmith, New York and London, 1974 · *The Bacchae of Euripides: A Communion Rite*, by Wole Soyinka, Oxford, 1973 · [*The Bacchae*] Caryl Churchill and David Lan, *A Mouthful of Birds*, London, 1986 · *The Bacchae: after Euripides*, by Derek Mahon, Loughcrew, 1991 · *Cyclops*, tr. Percy Bysshe Shelley, in his *Posthumous Poems*, London, 1824 · *Electra*, tr. Gilbert Murray, London, 1905 · *Electra*, tr. Janet Lembke and Kenneth J. Reckford, New York/Oxford, 1994 · *Erechtheus*, by Algernon Charles Swinburne, London, 1876 · *Hecuba: A Tragedy*, by Richard West, London, 1726 · *Hecuba*, tr. Thomas Morell, London, 1749 · *Hecuba*, tr. Janet Lembke and Kenneth J. Reckford, New York/Oxford, 1991 · [*Heracles*] Robert Browning, *Aristophanes' Apology; including a transcript from Euripides*, London, 1875 · *Hippolytus*, tr. Rex Warner, London, 1949 · *Hippolytus: a version*, tr. David Rudkin, London, 1980 · *Ion*, tr. H.D. [Hilda Doolittle], London, 1937 · *Ion: A New Version*, tr. David Lan, London, 1994 · *Iphigeneia in Aulis*, tr. Lady Jane Lumley [c.1550], Chiswick, 1909 · *Iphigeneia in Tauris*, tr. Gilbert West, in *Odes of Pindar*, London, 1749 · *Iphigeneia in Tauris*, tr. Richmond Lattimore, New York/London, 1974 · *Medea*, tr. George Buchanan (into Latin), Paris, 1544 · *Medea*, tr. Gilbert Murray, London, 1906 · *Medea: after Euripides*, by Robinson Jeffers, New York, 1946 · *Medea: A Sex-War Opera*, by Tony Harrison, in his *Theatre Works 1973–1985*, Harmondsworth, 1986 [Penguin] · *Medea: A New Version*, tr. Brendan Kennelly, Newcastle upon Tyne, 1992 · [*The Phoenician Women*] George Gascoigne and Francis Kinwelmersh, *Jocasta*, in Gascoigne, *A Hundreth Sundrie Flowres Bounde up in One Small Poesie*, London, 1573 · *The Trojan Women*, tr. Gilbert Murray, London, 1905 · *The Trojan Women: A New Version*, tr. Brendan Kennelly, Newcastle upon Tyne, 1993.

EXTRACTS 'Translation from the Medea of Euripides', by George Gordon, Lord Byron, in his *Hours of Idleness*, London, 1807 · *Choruses from the Iphigeneia in Aulis and the Hippolytus of Euripides*, by H.D. [Hilda Doolittle], London, 1919 · 'Euripides', in *The Oxford Book of Classical Verse in Translation*, ed. Adrian Poole and Jeremy Maule, Oxford, 1995.

SEE ALSO Chapman, J.J., 'Euripides and the Greek Genius', in his *Greek Genius and Other Essays*, New York, 1915 · Eliot, T. S., 'Euripides and Professor Murray' (1920), in his *Selected Essays 1917–32*, London, 1932 · Jenkyns, R., *The Victorians and Ancient Greece*, ch. 5, 'Tragedy', Oxford, 1980.

6. ARISTOPHANES

Until the discovery in the 20th c. of substantial papyrus fragments and one whole play of Menander, the *Dyskolos* ('The Peevish Man') of 316 BCE, Greek comedy survived only in the 11 extant plays of Aristophanes written between 425 and about 388 BCE. Greek drama generally, and Aristophanes in particular, was hardly translated at all before the 18th c., since the culture of the Renaissance and 17th c. was predominantly Latin-based. It was not until the 19th c., in the heyday of Greek studies in Britain and the Continent, that Aristophanes was read widely and frequently translated. And it was not until 1837 that the first complete translation was made into (undistinguished) English, by C. A. **Wheelwright** in 'familiar blank verse'.

Nevertheless, the few earlier translations have considerable historical and some intrinsic interest, because their authors have attempted to translate the Greek poet into the living idiom of their times. The earliest is the *Plutus* by Thomas **Randolph** (1605–35), rendered as *A Pleasant Comedie, Entituled, Hey for Honesty, Down with Knavery* (1651). Randolph was a literary disciple of Ben Jonson, and the address of Plutus, the god of riches, to his gold,

'Good Morrow to the Morne next to my Gold', echoes the opening line of Jonson's *Volpone*. His blank verse resembles that written for the stage in his time, and his language is, in the words of Jonson's requirement for comedy, 'such as men do use'.

Thomas **Stanley** (1625–78) included a translation of the *Clouds* in his *History of Philosophy* (1655), 'Added (not as a Comical Divertisement for the Reader, who can expect little in that kind from a subject so ancient, and particular, but) as a necessary supplement to the Life of Socrates'. This expresses very much a philosopher's interest (marked by some of the marginalia) in the comic poet's indictment of the great philosopher, made in 423, in which he appears as the representative of the new learning of the sophists. It is possible to glimpse some of the difficulties early translators faced because of the state of the text. Some speeches are wrongly attributed; some remarks that are obviously asides have been misunderstood. Stanley often curtails the Greek. He does not bother with many of the specifically Greek 'particularities' (to use the word of his own headnote); references to Greek institutions such as the passing of resolutions in the assembly are omitted. On the other hand, he sometimes sensibly anglicizes, as in the case of a dialogue which depends for its humour on a confusion between measures of metre and weight.

SOCR.   What have you most mind to learn,
        Measures, or Verse, or Rhyme?
STREPS. By all means Measures.
        For I was cheated by a Meal man lately
        Two pecks
SOCR.   That's not the thing that I demand;
        I'd know which you conceive the fairest
        measure
        The Trimeter, or the Tetrameter.
STREPS. The fairest Measure in my mind is a Bushel.

He cuts down the lyrical choral element and omits altogether the *parabasis*, the long speech in which the poet breaks the dramatic illusion to harangue the audience directly upon some matter of personal or topical interest. (The topicality of Aristophanes' comedy, much of it political, has always been a problem for translators.) Finally, Stanley baulks at Aristophanic indecency. There is not so much of it in the *Clouds*, but a section in which Socrates explains how thunder is a kind of meteorological farting is omitted. Nevertheless this version, written in verse, is often lively, clear, and sharply comic; boorish ignorance and pretentious sophistry are effectively ridiculed.

Henry **Burnell** (dates unknown) published in 1659 a prose version of the *Plutus*, one of the easiest plays with the least amount of indecency, with some explanatory notes and an introductory essay on wealth that turns Aristophanes into a Christian moralist. Lewis **Theobald** (1688–1744) translated the *Plutus* and the *Clouds* in 1715. Henry **Fielding** together with William **Young** (dates unknown) produced a version of the *Plutus* 'with large notes explanatory and critical' in 1742. Fielding and Young, like Theobald before them, translate into prose. In the preface, an affinity is noted between the dialogues of Plato and the plays of Aristophanes, both writers being remarkable for 'that Attic Purity of Language', a characteristic often lost sight of by later translators. The urbanity of the version is reflected in the elegant turns of the opening speech:

O Jupiter, and all ye Gods! what a vexatious thing it is to be the Slave of a mad Master! For, be the Servant's Advice never so excellent, if his Master takes it into his Head not to follow it, the poor Domestic is by Necessity forced to partake all the bad Consequences.

As might be expected of a translation in which the author of *Tom Jones* had a part, Aristophanic comic banter is relished and the delivery of the conversation is emphatic:

Odso! Master, I will tell you the best Method in the World to deal with him. I will put this Fellow to the most execrable End imaginable: for, having led him up to a Precipice, there leaving him, away I go—that tumbling from thence, the Gentleman—may break his Neck.

The result is an elegant, racy, and witty version that deserves to be better known. Not the least of its attractions is the extensive running commentary accompanying the text. Here issue is often taken with the French translation of Mme Dacier, Theobald is mocked for his dependence upon the French rather than the Greek and for his squeamishness about farting, the textual endeavours of Richard Bentley are ridiculed, Potter's *Antiquities* is cited to elucidate historical points, the puns and parodies that must defeat any translator are explained, and the artistic beauties of the original are enthusiastically highlighted.

The translations of the 19th c. are marked by two new interrelated aims: accuracy and metrical equivalence. **Swinburne**, introducing a 40-line version in anapaestic heptameters of a chorus from the *Birds*, sought 'to renew as far as possible for English ears the music of this resonant and triumphant metre, which goes ringing at full gallop as of horses who "dance as 'twere to the music | Their own hoofs make" ':

All best good things that befall men come from us birds,
   as is plain to all reason:
For first we proclaim and make known to them spring,
   and the winter and autumn in season;
Bid sow, when the crane starts clanging for Afric, in
   shrill-voiced emigrant number,
And calls to the pilot to hang up his rudder again for the
   season, and slumber;

In Aristophanes, Swinburne also says, 'the highest qualities of Rabelais were fused and harmonised with the supremest gifts of Shelley'. This is a very testing combination for a translator. In the century of Shelley it is the lyricism of the Greek that is best translated. This may account for the popularity of the *Birds*, the most lyrical and fantastic and the least topically political or indecent of the plays. John Hookham **Frere** (1769–1846), who translated four plays, writes verse with a truly fluent lyrical swing.

Ye children of Man! Whose life is a span,
Protracted with sorrow from day to day,
Naked and featherless, feeble and querulous,
Sickly, calamitous creatures of clay!
Attend to the words of the Sovereign Birds
(Immortal, illustrious, lords of the air),
Who survey from on high, with a merciful eye,
Your struggles of misery, labour and care.   (814–23)

The version by Oscar **Wilde** of the chorus in the *Clouds* is another reminder of the strong aesthetic appeal of Aristophanes' choral odes:

Cloud-maidens that float on for ever,
   Dew-sprinkled, fleet bodies, and fair,
Let us rise from our Sire's loud river,
   Great Ocean, and soar through the air
To the peaks of the pine-covered mountains where
     the pines hang as tresses of hair.

Frere is less happy with the comic banter in the *Birds*. As for the most earthy Rabelaisian element, when this occurs in the plays he translated, it is simply bowdlerized, or subjected to euphemism.

In the case of the *Lysistrata* [see also I.a.2.iii], in which the women of Athens and Sparta unite to bring an end to the war between their states by agreeing to deny their menfolk any sexual services, the indecent element is not incidental but central to the plot. Hence the play was scarcely translated at all, until a version in prose anonymously trans-

lated and privately published in 1896 (presumably before Wilde's trial) in a limited edition of 100 copies. This publication is notorious for its inclusion of the comically grotesque and wildly indecent illustrations of Aubrey Beardsley. Its prose is direct and not without a certain aesthetic pleasure; in the words of the translator, later identified as Samuel **Smith**, 'we can still catch glimpses of the ribald melancholy, the significant buffoonery, and the grotesque animality'. It may be compared with the verse translation of Benjamin Bickley **Rogers** published in 1878, who was clearly embarrassed by the content of the original. *Lysistrata* in Rogers advises 'We must abstain—each—from the joys of Love' (124), whereas Smith renders the Greek directly: 'Well, we must abstain from—Penis.' Smith regarded the play as a 'Rabelaisian protest' against the Peloponnesian war during which it had been written. The *Lysistrata* of 1896 may be regarded as a Rabelaisian protest against Victorian values.

In some respects Aristophanes may be said to have come into his own in the second half of the 20th c. His anarchic absurdist fantasies exert a strong imaginative appeal. *Lysistrata*, for example, valued not only for its frank and liberating indecency but as a potent anti-war protest, has been energetically translated by Douglas **Parker** in 1964 and creatively adapted to current circumstances by Tony **Harrison** in his verse translation of 1992:

Then they try to castrate us by stopping wars.
Domestic leniency, believe you me,
first it's sensuality, then it's CND.

There are racy versions of the nine old comedies of Aristophanes by Kenneth **McLeish**, and versions in direct prose of the three plays featuring women by Jeffrey **Henderson**, both sets of translations being generously provided with notes on context and performance. Mention should also be made of the translations made for the Penguin Classics by David **Barrett** and Alan **Sommerstein**. They use prose for the greater part, rendering the choruses in jaunty verse that may not embody the lyric virtuosity of the Greek but nevertheless has a kind of comic brio of which Aristophanes would have approved.   RS

TRANSLATIONS   [*Plutus*] *A Pleasant Comedie, Entituled Hey for Honesty, Down with Knavery*, tr. Thomas Randolph, London, 1651 · *The Clouds*, tr. Thomas Stanley, in *The History of Philosophy, The Third Part. Containing the Socratick Philiosophers*, London, 1655 · *The World's Idol: Plutus*, tr. H.H.B [Henry Burnell], London, 1659 · *The Clouds: A Comedy*, tr. Lewis Theobald, London, 1715 · *Plutus: or the World's Idol*, tr. Lewis Theobald, London, 1715 · *Plutus, the God of Riches*, tr. Henry Fielding and William Young, London, 1742 · *The Comedies of Aristophanes*, tr. C. A. Wheelwright, 2 vols., Oxford, 1837 · *The Birds of Aristophanes*, tr. John Hookham Frere, Malta, 1839 [with other 19-th c. versions in *Aristophanes: The Plays*, 2 vols., London, 1909; Everyman, frequently rep.; also with Frere's version of *The Acharnians*,

The Knights and The Frogs in World's Classics, ed. W. W. Merry, Oxford, 1907, frequently rep.] · Studies in Song, by Algernon C. Swinburne, London, 1880 [for his 'Grand Chorus of Birds from Aristophanes', rep. in editions of his poems] · Odes from the Greek Dramatists, ed. Arthur W. Pollard, London, 1890 [contains Oscar Wilde's versions of choral odes from the Clouds, rep. The Oxford Book of Classical Verse in Translation, ed. Adrian Poole and Jeremy Maule, Oxford, 1995] · The Lysistrata of Aristophanes ('now first wholly translated into English [by Samuel Smith] and illustrated with eight full length drawings by Aubrey Beardsley'), London 1896 [facsimile rep. New York, 1967] · Aristophanes with the English Translation of Benjamin Bickley Rogers, 3 vols., London/Cambridge, Mass., 1924 [Loeb] · Lysistrata, tr. Douglass Parker, in vol. ii of The Complete Greek Comedy, 3 vols., Ann Arbor, Mich., 1961–4 · The Wasps, The Poet and the Women, The Frogs, tr. David Barrett, Harmondsworth, 1964 [Penguin] · Lysistrata, The Acharnians, The Clouds, tr. Alan H. Sommerstein, Harmondsworth, 1973 [Penguin] · The Knights, Peace, Wealth, tr. Alan H. Sommerstein; The Birds, The Assemblywomen, tr. David Barrett, Harmondsworth, 1978 [Penguin] · The Common Chorus: A Version of Aristophanes' Lysistrata, tr. Tony Harrison, 1992 · Plays, 2 vols., tr. Kenneth McLeish, London, 1993 · Three plays by Aristophanes: Staging Women [Lysistrata, Women at the Thesmophoria, Assemblywomen], tr. Jeffrey Henderson, London/New York, 1996.

SEE ALSO   Lord, L. E., Aristophanes: His Plays and Their Influence, Boston, 1922 · Rechner, L., Aristophanes in England: Eine literarhistorische Untersuchung, Frankfurt, 1914.

7. LYRIC, PASTORAL, AND EPIGRAM

'"Greek lyric poetry" is a conventional catch-all term' (West 1993: p. vii). The following discussion ranges somewhat more widely even than this loose category, and covers, in effect, all shorter forms of ancient Greek poetry, or in other words ancient Greek poetry excluding the epic, didactic, and dramatic. In order of their treatment below, this includes most importantly: poems in the subjective personal lyric tradition created by Alcaeus and Sappho and continued in the Anacreontea; the hymnal/choral poems of Pindar and Callimachus; and the pastorals of Theocritus and his followers Bion and Moschus. A final section deals with the large collection of short poems known as the Greek Anthology or the Palatine Anthology; this overlaps to some extent with other sections because translations of selections from this collection often include work by such poets as Sappho and Anacreon.

For much of this poetry, 'translation' has often meant something more like 'reconstruction' because the available texts are often fragmentary. Translators have not only rendered the words they possess, but guessed or imagined what the rest of the text might have said, including this in their versions too. Some modern versions, indeed, are based on Greek texts which themselves reflect considerable and sometimes superseded editorial conjecture, leading to translations at a further remove from the originals. The more successful 'reconstructive' translators have a responsible approach in which textual defects are made good by the imagination, and square brackets, or other symbols, are supplied around the added material by scholarly convention.

i. **Personal Lyric** Three similarly titled modern anthologies attempt to represent the full range of the lyric tradition: Richmond **Lattimore**'s Greek Lyrics, M. L. **West**'s Greek Lyric Poetry, and Andrew M. **Miller**'s Greek Lyric: An Anthology in Translation. The prolific Lattimore's substantial volume includes some clear successes, but some disasters too; and the attempt at 'close approximations' of metres leads on occasion to at least two obvious defects: metres which make no sense in English, and extreme prosaicism.

West's chronological organization takes his treatment down to 450 BCE by way of some 40 different poets, major and minor, some of them represented only by a line or two. This makes the volume an easily affordable introduction to a large sample of material, though the affordability is achieved at the cost of confusingly crowded page layout. But the translations have little or no poetic life. West apologizes himself for using expressions that 'have an old-fashioned air': this is pervasive, and seldom justified on the claimed grounds that such expressions 'correspond better to the Greek concept'.

Miller's selection of poets is shorter, but his aims are no more ambitious; he disavows any intention of capturing 'the aesthetic qualities and stylistic effects of the texts', leaving him only with 'the poems' conceptual content and . . . formal organization'—with the elements, that is, in which the poetic life of these texts seems least likely to inhere. Nor are the translations always a good guide to meaning, for Miller silently incorporates small-scale conjectures.

Two further collections have a smaller range.

Guy **Davenport**'s *Archilochos, Sappho, Alkman*, offering fairly comprehensive translation of these three poets only, gives us a self-consciously modern Archilochus who uses expressions such as 'longable for' and 'jackass', and a hazily romantic Sappho ('spirit, for Sappho, shines from matter; one embraces the two together, inseparable', Davenport's introduction tells us). The Alcman section consists principally of an interesting batch of four alternative versions of the *Hymn to Artemis of the Strict Observance* (respectively, literal; musical; imaginatively reconstructing the lost sections; and 'faithful').

David **Mulroy**'s *Early Greek Lyric Poetry* is conceived on different lines, and presents a different kind of selection in a different way, designed to show the textual history of a cross-section of Greek lyric verse. Many of the texts come from papyrus fragments of recent discovery. A short section of continuous descriptive prose on each of 20 poets provides an account of the provenance of the relevant poems and fragments which have come down to us, in chronological order of availability (in the quotations of grammarians, scholiasts, etc.) or discovery. This account is interspersed with translations not only of the verse but often of the context in which it is quoted. Hence, for example, in the 'Anacreon' section, Mulroy includes an Anacreontic text which is quoted by Dio Chrysostom in one of his lectures; Mulroy renders the words with which Dio Chrysostom introduces it as well as the text as found in this source. These translations are of no special excellence, but the historical overview Mulroy provides is readily approachable by non-specialists.

Sappho's difficult simplicity has attracted many translators. There are a number of pre-20th-c. versions, usually far removed, in their ornamentation and elaboration, from what would now be thought of as characteristic of Sappho. Such writers as Ambrose **Philips** (1674–1749), Matthew **Green** (1696–1737), and Francis **Fawkes** (1721–77) also struggle to construct anything that sounds metrically plausible as an equivalent for the Sapphic stanza. One 20th-c. translator deserves special notice: A. E. **Housman**, the classical scholar, produced a very few versions of Sappho which at least as English poems are striking and successful. They can be found in editions of his collected verse or in the Jay–Lewis anthology mentioned below.

For the rest, only some of the more major modern Sapphos are noticed here—none is standard—together with an anthology which allows a fuller range of work to be readily sampled. Mary **Barnard**'s version of 100 Sapphic poems and frag-

ments reflects Ezra Pound's influence, and firmly rejects sentimentality and 'prettiness'. Another of the better-known translations of a generation or so ago is Willis **Barnstone**'s complete parallel-text *Sappho*. This has merits of a functional kind, but seldom develops much poetic energy; its rhythms, in particular, are those of prose. Barnstone takes too few risks, for example in refusing a potentially arresting image or metaphor in favour of a conventional one. Jeffrey M. **Duban**'s *Ancient and Modern Images of Sappho: Translations and Studies in Archaic Greek Love Lyric* is original in a number of respects. This is an anthology of love lyric, containing a selection from Sappho, to which are added translations from Archilochus and Ibycus. Most of the volume consists of editorial matter of some utility, the extensive notes including among other things previous translations and excerpts from critical discussions, and the introduction reviewing a full range of recent translations. Duban's renderings themselves use rhyme and metre throughout.

Diane **Rayor**'s *Sappho's Lyre: Archaic Lyric and Women Poets of Ancient Greece* is one of the most poetically adept of modern versions. It is the most complete representation of classical Greek women poets in translation available, and carries a helpful introduction. Rayor tries to use 'our modern poetic idiom', retains 'the ancient images', re-creates sound and tempo effects (though not metres) where possible, and devises a simple system to indicate how and where the texts are incomplete. The principles are admirable, the practice often effective—by no means always, partly owing to a very uncertain grasp of modern idiom. There are translations of many fragments of which little can really be made, too, but this is the price at which the comprehensiveness of the collection is bought. Josephine **Balmer**'s *Sappho: Poems and Fragments* is one of the most recent versions and is a complete one. Balmer's interpretations and textual reconstructions are responsible, but the versions tend to the prosaic, and are often surpassed by Rayor's.

Perhaps the most interesting way of reading Sappho in English is not in a single translation but in an anthology. The most recent attempt to produce such a volume is Peter Jay and Caroline Lewis's *Sappho through English Poetry*. The translations and imitations run from the 17th c. to the present in just 50 pages; more could have been included, especially of 20th-c. work. But this is not a straightforward anthology of translations, for the editors intend to 'sketch how Sappho has fared in English'. So the rest of the book is given over to 'myths, meditations, and travesties' more or less directly concerned with Sappho.

The tradition in which Sappho's poems are written issues later in the *Anacreontea*, a collection of lyrics once attributed to Anacreon but now taken to belong to many different poets and indeed periods. There is a core group of a dozen or so poems which have tended to be thought of as the essential part of the collection by English translators, and with these, though many versions are available, the single classic translation by Abraham **Cowley** (1618–67) should suffice for all but specialized purposes. Cowley's *Anacreontiques* (1656) seem to result from a happy match of temperaments between original and translator—though it is also true that Cowley abandons his original on occasion. Dr Johnson describes them as 'paraphrastical translations' and 'rather pleasing than faithful'; the pleasure, as he sees it, lies in their permanently attractive wit. Johnson observes apropos of these 'songs dedicated to festivity and gaiety' that 'men have been wise in many different modes; but they have always laughed the same way' (*Life of Cowley*). Cowley's Anacreon has not lost his charm, even if the charm is of a kind we are less than fully familiar with today. Cowley's successors—none matching his appeal—are many, including over the next 150 years John **Addison**, Ambrose Philips, Francis Fawkes, David **Urquhart**, and the Irish writer Thomas **Moore** (*Odes of Anacreon*, 1800; in its eighth edition by 1810).

ii. Pindar and Callimachus Pindar has been more than most Greek lyric poets the despair of English translators. His subject-matter has proved wholly unassimilable to the English tradition, though what were perceived as his particular kinds of poetic energy were an inspiration to 17th- and 18th-c. poets. The three *Pindarique Odes* (1656) by Abraham Cowley [see I.b.3.ii; I.c.1.iv] are not translations, but are sometimes said to give the best indication available in English verse of Pindar's manner, and were certainly influential in popularizing it. Cowley adopts this manner for its flexible combination of classical monumentality and distance with the play of developing, modulating thought, questioning and qualifying over the varying line-lengths. The subjects of Cowley's Pindarics have no connection with Pindar's writings.

The drawbacks of earlier 20th-c. Pindars are readily visible in the Arthur S. **Way** version of 1922, a rhymed, metrical period piece now in parts scarcely readable ('while I laud a horse that thrice can vaunt . . . to fellow-burghers courteous', *Olympian* xiii). Two almost exactly contemporary parallel-text alternatives to the Loeb are C. J. **Billson**'s and Lewis R. **Farnell**'s (in 'rhythmical prose with literary comments'). Geoffrey S. **Conway**'s complete *Odes of Pindar* is stiff, sometimes impossibly artificial in expression (from 'word of sooth' to 'false-wrought tales'); its utility lies in the copious and reliable explanatory material it provides. Richmond Lattimore's version of 1947 frankly acknowledges the difficulties translators face while claiming that 'at his dazzling best, Pindar is perfectly clear'. Lattimore is usually as clear as possible (sometimes not very), but what is crippling is the lack of a suitable poetic idiom.

Pindar's contemporary Callimachus, most of whose surviving works are hymnal lyrics, has been infrequently but regularly englished since the 18th c. Easily the most interesting treatment is Diane Rayor and Stanley **Lombardo**'s *Callimachus: Hymns, Epigrams, Select Fragments*, which elicits conspicuously modern poetry from the apparently unpromising material.

iii. Pastoral There are both historical and modern translators of Theocritus, the modern in some quantity, but his heterogeneous corpus has not proved amenable to anglicization in any period. One of the main stumbling-blocks has been the artificial mixture of dialects or voices: attempts to reproduce them in Scots or local dialects of English have been comically quaint or vulgar. The best translations are of individual texts. Striking early englishings of six Theocritus idylls were published by '**E.D.**' in 1588. They are in fourteeners influenced by Arthur Golding's Ovid [II.n.6.iii]. There is little to be said for John **Fell**'s or John **Dryden**'s 17th-c. versions. The complete rendering by Thomas **Creech** (1659–1700) is more to some tastes: it is 'bold, humorous, and direct' (Wells 1988), but also careless, even sometimes inept. Francis Fawkes is at least more accurate than some predecessors, and provides extensive notes; but this version is apt to seem quaint, and is now forgotten.

The trouble is that the same can be said of most of the more modern translations. The Victorians are notably partial to Theocritus' wistful moods—Elizabeth Barrett Browning writes of his songs 'Of the sweet years, the dear and wished-for years' (*Sonnets from the Portuguese*, i)—and some of the numerous 19th-c. versions have their points. The 'Infant Hercules' by Leigh **Hunt**, in couplets, is an early example. Andrew **Lang** (1844–1912) writes a prose graceful in spite of its attempt at fidelity, but it is still prose. The work of the gifted amateur C. S. **Calverley** (1831–84) looks very much a period piece in, for example, its fastidious periphrases (for 'Not on an o'erfull stomach' read 'hungrily'); but the failure to construct a plausible language for Theocritus is nothing new.

This complaint is not applicable to one of the standard 20th-c. translations, that contained in A. S. F. **Gow**'s scholarly edition of Theocritus, but only because nothing is ventured—Gow 'has no higher aim than to show in tolerable English' what he takes to be the meaning. He leaves to others the 'attempt to reproduce the compost of artificial dialect, far-fetched vocabulary, and constant novelty of expression which constitutes Theocritus' style'. A few later translators have undertaken this task (Robert **Wells** in his dull Penguin edition ducks it). Douglas P. **Hill** deploys a variety of metres considerably greater than Theocritus' and produces pleasant music not of remarkable authenticity.

Three modern American versions are worthy of note. In the most recent of them, Daryl **Hine**'s of 1982, Theocritus is characterized as 'at once the most musical and the most picturesque of Greek poets, the scholar's delight and the translator's despair'. This translation is metrically a *tour de force*. The relentless quantitative dactyls can be most effective locally:

Doesn't she know Aphrodite was madly in love with a
   cowherd?
Tending his flocks in the mountains of Phrygia she in the
   woodland
Loved her Adonis, and there in the woodland lamented
   his passing.

                         (Idyll xx)

But they do not satisfy indefinitely. Hine is aware that these translations are also more rhythmical than their source texts, and therefore 'untrue to the Greek [but] true to English'. The translations by Barriss **Mills** and Anna **Rist**, both well received, use different poetic manners. Mills's 'fairly literal rendering' in a 'not too strict' syllabic metre is certainly 'idiomatic'—aggressively so at times:

    'Slut!' I said. 'So I'm not good enough
    for you? You like some other sweetheart
    better? Well, go cuddle up
    to your other friend.'

                         (Idyll xiv)

But this is not wholly representative. In other poems Mills's longer lines, and less colloquial vocabulary, work better, at times achieving an unpretentious grace. Rist aims for an overall 'ease and harmony of flow' at the expense of 'consistency in rendering the form'. Her vocabulary is certainly far-fetched, with one character in Idyll xv employing the expression 'bogey get you' in conjunction with a word such as 'scoundrels'. In saying that she finds no plausible

voice for an English Theocritus, one is saying only what is true of all his translators down the centuries, to varying but always considerable degrees.

Only a few historically interesting translations and imitations of the later pastoral poets Bion and Moschus are mentioned here. One of the earliest is by the poet Richard **Crashaw**, whose version of the First Idyll of Moschus ('Cupid's Cryer') is in an attractive, tripping measure. The cantabile quality of these Greek poems is often the attraction for translators, as it is for John **Oldham** (1653–83). Oldham imitated Moschus' Idyll iii (the *Epitaphios Bionis*) in his poem *Bion*, and Bion's Idyll i (*Epitaphios Adonidos*) in his *Lamentation for Adonis*. Ezra Pound challenged readers to find 'in English another passage of melody sustained for so long' as in *Bion*, which takes the form of an elegiac tribute to the poet John Wilmot, Earl of Rochester. 18th-c. versions of various parts of Bion and Moschus abound—for instance by Thomas **Cooke** (1724), Richard **Polwhele** (1786), and Edward **Dubois** (1799). There are also plenty of easily available modern cribs. But the most important English poem which springs out of late Greek pastoral is an imitation, of Moschus' *Epitaphios Adonidos* by **Shelley**. Shelley's *Adonais: An Elegy on the Death of John Keats* (1821) is too well known to need comment here.

Finally, A. **Holden**'s *Greek Pastoral Poetry* conveniently provides in a modern Penguin edition complete verse translation of all three poets discussed in this section. Holden has a shrewd sense of the apparently inevitable restraints an English translator of this poetry is under and works within them, avoiding dialect and attempting a 'colloquial force', avoiding metre but using free verse rhythms which work when read aloud. These unpretentious translations are supplemented by useful notes.

iv. The Greek Anthology In the 1st c. BCE the poet Meleager of Gadara made a collection of 'epigrams'—i.e. short poems in elegiac couplets—by 46 other poets, under the title *The Garland* (or *Wreath*). This became the nucleus of later collections which eventually came to form the so-called *Greek Anthology*, containing over 6,000 'epigrams' from a total of about 1,500 years (600 BCE–900 CE) and from a large number of poets ranging from the well-known (Sappho, Anacreon, Simonides) through the obscure to the anonymous. Although the relevant notion of 'epigram' here is primarily 'inscription', the variety of subjects is wide; a proportion of the collection is humorous or satirical. But as a whole these epigrams are most unlike those in the English poetic tradition, which stems rather from the wit and point of Martial's Latin [II.n.7.v]. In fact, there is little in English verse that approaches the manner of these Greek poems, described by a reviewer of one recent translation in these terms:

What exhausts the imagination is the minute range of the effective variations of tone, of rhythm, and of theme on which all these poems depend . . . the climax that the rhythm of English verse imposes on a short epigram is the bump of a hammer where the poem was conceived as the dying notes of a guitar.

It is unsurprising, then, that the dozens of translations from the *Greek Anthology* can show only limited success even collectively.

This account is limited to standard comprehensive editions of translations, and examples of recent and more readily available versions. (Well-known 20th-c. translators whose work on the *Greek Anthology* is not discussed below include W. H. D. **Rouse** and Richard **Aldington**.) Some of the largest collections of translations are the Bohn literal prose versions by George **Burges** (with some verse translations by others); J. W. **Mackail**'s 400-page *Select Epigrams*, a parallel-text edition with surprisingly successful prose translations; Shane **Leslie**'s urbane and witty prose translation *The Greek Anthology*; and the five-volume Loeb edition with translations by W. R. **Paton**. By the early 20th c. it was universal practice to divide the *Anthology* into 16 books; these sections contain different kinds of poems—Book VI, for example, dedicatory epigrams, Book VIII the epigrams of St Gregory the Theologian, mainly about tomb-robbers.

Two typically slim modern selections are Dudley **Fitts**'s *From the Greek Anthology: Poems in English Paraphrase* and Robin **Skelton**'s *Two Hundred Poems from the Greek Anthology*. Each supplies some 150–200 epigrams and displays the variety of the *Anthology* in a unified way, but the approaches contrast. Skelton's versions are conservative in form, rhymed or near-rhymed and 'basically iambic or trochaic'. Fitts, who considers he has 'not really undertaken translation at all . . . [but] simply tried to restate in my own idiom what the Greek verses have meant to me', eschews regularity of stanza form and rhyme. On a comparable scale, William J. **Philbin**'s *To You Simonides: Epigrams and Fragments from the Greek* is divided into 'thematic' sections; its 300 translations are unfussy, often neat. The volume has never attracted much attention, but the translations make pleasant enough browsing. Some translators select thematically from the *Anthology*: Michael **Kelly**'s *Jousts of Aphrodite: Erotic Verse Translated from the Original Greek* is a single-handed collection of about 100 of its erotic poems. It aims at deliberate and provocative modernity, but is written in a language no one has ever spoken and is sometimes hapless in its phraseology ('Why should I gush indiscretely | any further?').

But a clear recommendation can be offered, finally, for *The Greek Anthology and Other Ancient Epigrams*, a substantial Penguin collection of some 850 *Greek Anthology* poems translated by a range of modern hands. Peter **Jay** is the editor and sometimes the translator. The standard is high, but then the translators include such writers as Ezra **Pound**, Edwin **Morgan**, Peter **Porter**, Christopher **Logue**, Alistair **Elliot**, and Kenneth **Rexroth**. Over half the translations were made expressly for this collection. As well as being the most easily available translation of the *Anthology* in selection, this is the only multiple-translator collection. For browsing purposes, it is the one with which to start. Though inevitably variable in approach and degree of success, these translations include at least some examples of the best that can be done with this poetry in 20th-c. English; they are often interesting, sometimes compelling. Jay attempts (vainly perhaps) to signal editorially the degree of distance between translation and source text; he also includes notes, a glossary of proper names, a bibliography, and other useful supplementary material.   SG

ANTHOLOGIES   Davenport, Guy, *Archilochos, Sappho, Alkman: Three Lyric Poets of the Late Greek Bronze Age*, Berkeley, Calif., 1980 · Lattimore, Richmond, *Greek Lyrics*, Chicago, 1960 [incorporates some previously published translations by Lattimore] · Miller, Andrew M., *Greek Lyric: An Anthology in Translation*, Indianapolis, 1996 · Mulroy, David, *Early Greek Lyric Poetry*, Ann Arbor, Mich., 1992 · West, M. L., *Greek Lyric Poetry: A New Translation*, Oxford, 1993 [World's Classics].

SAPPHO AND ANACREON   *Anacreontiques*, tr. Abraham Cowley, in his *Poems*, London, 1656 [rep. in edns. of Cowley's poems] · *Sappho: A New Translation*, tr. Mary Barnard, Berkeley, Calif., 1958 · *Sappho: Lyrics in the Original Greek with Translations*, tr. Willis Barnstone, New York, 1965 · *Ancient and Modern Images of Sappho: Translations and Studies in Archaic Greek Love Lyric*, tr. Jeffrey M. Duban, Lanham, Md., 1983 · *Sappho's Lyre: Archaic Lyric and Women Poets of Ancient Greece*, tr. Diane Rayor, Berkeley, Calif., 1991 · *Sappho: Poems and Fragments*, tr. Josephine Balmer, Newcastle upon Tyne, 1992 · *Sappho through English Poetry*, ed. Peter Jay and Caroline Lewis, London, 1996.

PINDAR AND CALLIMACHUS   *Pindarique Odes*, tr. Abraham Cowley, in his *Poems*, London, 1656 [rep. in edns. of

Cowley's poems] · *Pindar in English Verse*, tr. Arthur S. Way, London, 1922 · *The Odes of Victory*, tr. C. J. Billson, 2 vols., Oxford, 1928–30 · *The Works of Pindar*, tr. Lewis R. Farnell, 3 vols., London, 1930–2 · *The Odes of Pindar*, tr. Richmond Lattimore, Chicago, 1947 · *The Odes of Pindar*, tr. Geoffrey S. Conway, London, 1972 [Everyman] · *Callimachus: Hymns, Epigrams, Select Fragments*, tr. Stanley Lombardo and Diane Rayor, Baltimore, 1988.

PASTORAL *Sixe Idyllia*, tr. 'E.D.', Oxford, 1588 · *Cupid's Cryer*, in Richard Crashaw, *Steps to the Temple*, London, 1646 [rep. in edns. of Crashaw's poems] · *Bion* and *The Lamentation for Adonis*, in John Oldham, *Some New Pieces*, London, 1681 [subsequently in Oldham's *Works*, etc.] · *The Idylliums of Theocritus with Rapin's Discourse of Pastorals*, tr. Thomas Creech, London, 1683 · *Miscellany Poems*, London, 1684, and *Sylvae; or, the Second Part of Poetical Miscellanies*, by John Dryden et al., London, 1685 [Dryden's four translations from Theocritus can also be found in most larger collected edns. of his poems] · *The Idylliums of Moschus and Bion*, tr. Thomas Cooke, London, 1724 · *The Idylliums of Theocritus*, tr. Francis Fawkes, London, 1767 · *The Idyllia, Epigrams, and Fragments, of Theocritus, Bion, and Moschus, with the Elegies of Tyrtaeus*, tr. Richard Polwhele, 2 vols, Exeter, 1786 [several reprints] · *The Wreath; Composed of Selections from Sappho, Theocritus, Bion, and Moschus*, tr. Edward Dubois, London, 1799 · *Foliage*, by Leigh Hunt, London, 1818 [Hunt's Theocritus is reprinted in later edns. of his poems] · *Adonais*, by Percy Bysshe Shelley, Pisa, 1821 [rep. in all standard edns. of Shelley's work] · *Theocritus Translated into English verse*, tr. C. S. Calverley, Cambridge, 1869 [rep. to 1913] · *Theocritus, Edited with a Translation and Commentary*, tr. A. S. F. Gow, 2 vols, Cambridge, 1950 · *The Idylls of Theocritus in English Verse*, tr. Douglas P. Hill, Eton, 1959 · *The Idylls of Theokritos: A Verse Translation*, tr. Barriss Mills, West Lafayette, Ind., 1963 [and reprints]. · *Greek Pastoral Poetry: Theocritus, Bion, Moschus, The Pattern Poems*, tr. Anthony Holden, Harmondsworth, 1974 [Penguin] · *The Poems of Theocritus*, tr. Anna Rist, Chapel Hill, NC, 1978 · *Theocritus: Idylls and Epigrams*, tr. Daryl Hine, New York, 1982 · *Theocritus: The Idylls*, tr. Robert Wells, Manchester, 1988 [Penguin from 1989].

THE GREEK ANTHOLOGY *The Greek Anthology*, tr. G[eorge] Burges, London, 1848 [Bohn] · *Select Epigrams from the Greek Anthology*, tr. J. W. Mackail, London, 1890 [parallel texts; rep. 1906, 1911, 1913, etc.; rev. 1940] · *The Greek Anthology*, tr. W. R. Paton, 5 vols., London, 1916–26 [Loeb] · *The Greek Anthology*, tr. Shane Leslie, London, 1929 · *From the Greek Anthology: Poems in English Paraphrase*, by Dudley Fitts, London, 1957. [The fullest collection of Fitts's translations. Two earlier volumes incorporated here are his *One Hundred Poems from the Greek Anthology*, 1938, and *More Poems from the Greek Anthology*, 1941] · *Two Hundred Poems from the Greek Anthology*, tr. Robin Skelton, London, 1971 · *To You Simonides: Epigrams and Fragments from the Greek*, tr. William J. Philbin, Dublin, 1973 · *The Greek Anthology and Other Ancient Epigrams: A Selection in Modern Verse Translations*, ed. Peter Jay, London, 1973 [Penguin from 1981, rep. 1986] · *Jousts of Aphrodite: Erotic Verse Translated from the Original Greek*, tr. Michael Kelly, London, 1986.

SEE ALSO Baumann, M., *Die Anakreonteen in englischen Übersetzungen; ein Beitrag zur Rezeptionsgeschichte der anakreontischen Sammlung*, Heidelberg, 1974 · Hutton, J. 'The First Idyll of Moschus in Imitations to the Year 1800', *American Journal of Philology*, 49 (1928), 105–36 · Kerlin, R. T., *Theocritus in English Literature*, Lynchburg, Va., 1910 · Revard, S. P., 'Cowley's *Anacreontiques* and the Translation of the Greek Anacreontea', in *Acta Conventus Neo-Latini Torontoensis*, ed. A. Dalzell et al., Binghamton, NY, 1991, 595–607.

8. CLASSICAL PHILOSOPHY

Classical Greek philosophy is dominated by two profound thinkers of the 4th c. BCE, who pose sharply divergent challenges to translators. Plato, striving to depict and sustain the enquiring spirit of his mentor, Socrates, composed almost entirely in literary dialogues which span a gamut of styles from casual conversation to visionary myth-telling. By contrast, the ideas of Plato's greatest pupil, Aristotle, are contained in treatises designed functionally for teaching and study in his school, the Lyceum: their language is typically terse, and often technical, though shot through with reflective sagacity. The writings of earlier Greek philosophers (known collectively as Presocratics) survive only in reports and isolated quotations: their translation history is accordingly more limited, and will be considered briefly in the final part of this article.

i. Plato The history of English translations of Plato falls into three broad phases: the pioneering activity of the 18th c., whose versions soften the argumentative acuity of the originals with stylistic suaveness; the 19th c.'s production of academic translations which show increasing concern for accuracy, but less for literary finesse; and the expanded popularity of Platonic translations in the 20th c., during which a gradual bifurcation developed between renderings for the general reader and those espousing stricter fidelity to philosophical specifics.

It is perhaps surprising that scarcely any Platonic dialogues were translated into English before the 18th c. In contrast to the Continent, where late Renaissance Platonism produced translations into French and Italian, Platonizing currents in English thought, including the Christian Platonism of the 17th-c. Cambridge Platonists, derived largely from the reading of Latin translations. Of genuine Platonic works, only the *Apology* (Socrates' defence speech) and *Phaedo* were put into English (anonymously, in 1675) prior to 1700. Together with *Euthyphro* and *Crito*, these form a group of works, permeated by an intense commitment to ethical rationality, which throughout the 18th c. were the most popular Platonic dialogues for their depiction of Socrates, in the final days of his life, as a moral hero. But early versions of them, such as those in the selection of nine dialogues translated, again anonymously, in 1710 (and, revealingly, not from Greek but from André Dacier's flowing French of 1699), tend towards a graceful inexactitude which loses the close weave of Plato's text.

The first complete English Plato emerged from 1759 onwards in a series of versions by Floyer **Sydenham** (1710–87) and, subsequently, Thomas **Taylor** (1758–1835): the completed edition, incorporating a revision of H. **Spens**'s dour *Republic* (originally 1763), appeared in 1804. Despite shortcomings, Sydenham's nine dialogues have vivacious touches, and more fluency than the ponderous tone preferred by Taylor. The latter imprinted on the whole enterprise a heavily Neoplatonist conception of the philosopher as theological 'hierophant' leading his readers upwards towards the transcendent—apt, perhaps, for allegorical myths, but not for the cut-and-thrust of argument. As pioneers, Sydenham and Taylor deserve indulgence, but John Stuart Mill was justified in describing their edition as 'full of faults, and often with difficulty understood even by those who can read the original' (*Monthly Repository*, 8, 1834).

Taylor was an acquaintance of Blake and other romantics, and the appearance of this first complete translation coincided with the arousal of romantic interest in Plato the idealist, the spiritualist, and the creator of myths. One result of this was the version of the *Symposium* (or *Banquet*) produced by **Shelley** in a few days in summer 1818 (published posthumously, in doctored form). Shelley's only predecessor, Sydenham, troubled about 'gross indecency', had disguised the dialogue's homoerotic atmosphere by manipulation (e.g. adolescent boyfriends of older men become 'mistresses') and textual truncation. Shelley allows homosexual sentiments clear expression, though he mutes some allusions to physical gratification. He adopts a general tone of erotic idealism, thereby partly missing the stylistic shifts in characterization of the assorted speakers, but capturing something of the special elevation of Diotima's esoteric message to Socrates, in which

love becomes the channel of access to immutable reality. Shelley's translation, though superseded for philosophical purposes, remains a telling specimen of heady romantic Platonism.

A few years after this, however, a more rationalistic view of Plato reasserted itself in the translations-cum-summaries of nine dialogues ('very full abstracts', he called them) made by John Stuart **Mill**. Only four were published, in 1834–5—one, the *Apology*, a complete translation. The acumen of these abridgements makes one regret that Mill, whose study of Plato was assiduous, did not produce fuller versions. Mill interpreted Plato as above all the philosopher of the enquiring, undogmatic intellect; he therefore concentrated on works characterized by dialectical open-endedness. While not aspiring to literary refinement, Mill's summaries do convey the probing thrust of Socratic conversation, and avoid the laxity which mars earlier versions. Moreover, his judicious hints about the shape of the arguments could still be consulted with profit by interested readers.

From the mid-19th c. onwards Plato's status was enhanced by his increased prominence in the syllabuses of the public schools and universities. As well as spawning numerous mediocre versions, many of them 'cribs', this process led to what, through several revisions, has proved the most widely used Platonic translation of all, by the Oxford scholar Benjamin **Jowett** (1817–93). Jowett handles Platonic dialogue in a less archaizing manner than many predecessors; his achievement of a consistent tone is a prime reason for the translation's lasting appeal, and compensates for some lapses in accuracy. But this consistency has some negative consequences. There is a kind of 'professorial' uniformity of register to Jowett's Plato which flattens out the differences between, at the extremes, colloquial humour and mythopoeic earnestness. Yet Jowett's accomplishment in opening up the whole of Plato to English readers was a major cultural service.

The 20th c. has seen Plato's works become recognized not only as foundational texts for western thought, but also as enticingly written 'novellas' of the mind in search of (self-)knowledge. A strikingly enlarged readership has resulted: 20th-c. translations of Plato's central work, the *Republic*, run into double figures, whereas the 19th c. produced only two full versions. The myriad expressive nuances of Plato's use of dialogue, and his perpetually intriguing characterization of the ironic Socrates, lend his writing a depth which goes beyond its explicit conceptual content. Yet the more one sees in Plato, the starker becomes the dilemma of translation.

While some translators have given high priority to literary artistry and dramatic force, the generally linguistic-cum-analytic cast of modern Anglophone philosophy has created a contrary pressure towards greater literalism. If philosophy is embedded in the fabric of particular languages, we will get nearer to the ideas of the past, it can be argued, the closer we adhere to earlier thinkers' own categories and idioms of thought.

While a dichotomy between the literal and the literary affects many areas of translation, it has peculiar force in relation to texts which harness (as Plato's paradigmatically do) conceptual strictness with psychological subtlety. The issue can be highlighted through comparison of the translations of the *Republic* by Francis **Cornford** and Allan **Bloom**. Bloom, who happily admits to 'a slavish . . . sometimes cumbersome, literalness', frequently retains Greek phraseology, while Cornford unapologetically gives the arguments a modern air. Bloom offers, for example, 'What is the fair?' (reproducing a Greek locution), where Cornford has 'What does "honourable" mean?' Underlying the stylistic is the ideological. Bloom, influenced by the conservative political philosopher Leo Strauss, aspires to 'understand the ancient authors as they understood themselves', and hopes to liberate readers of the *Republic* from the tyranny of modern values. Cornford, who dismisses literalism as 'grotesque and silly' (and hence becomes an anti-model for Bloom), tries to build bridges between ancient and modern thinking, and to maximize the accessibility of Plato to non-specialists.

There are things to be said on both sides of this divide, since all translation must negotiate between opening ourselves to difference and assimilating others to our own frameworks of experience. Cornford, given to abbreviating and 'tidying' Plato's text, creates a brisk effect which can make the Platonic Socrates sound too familiar, too businesslike. Bloom, on the other hand, not only tolerates awkwardness but virtually contradicts the very idea of translation (see his reference to 'the tyranny of the translator'!). If, as he claims in his Preface, 'the only possible sources of clarification or connection' in a translation are 'the original terms', why or how *translate* at all? Bloom's own practice inevitably falls short of this specious ideal. Besides, his literalism generates errors of interpretation.

To some extent, of course, this dichotomy can be resolved in terms of readerships. Cornford's precedent is emulated in, for example, various Penguin Classics volumes of Plato, including H. D. P. **Lee**'s informal *Republic*, or Robin **Waterfield**'s transla-

tions, also including the *Republic*, for World's Classics. These all belong to a tradition which sees some 'modernization' of Plato's conceptual language as appropriate. Waterfield's style is exceptionally fluent, and he is more conscious than most of the rich metaphorical streak in Plato. Among a substantial range of late 20th-c. translations of Plato, his are an attractive option for the general reader, though the series by R. E. **Allen**, which aims to be the first complete, single-handed Plato since Jowett's, provides a more staid, slightly old-fashioned, and much less well-annotated alternative. Of somewhat older versions, those by G. M. A. **Grube** are still worth reading for their plain and direct manner. With the partial exception of Paul **Shorey**'s lively *Republic*, Plato volumes in the Loeb series are now extremely dated.

In a decidedly different category is the Clarendon Plato Series, which seeks to treat Platonic language with the scrupulousness required by professional philosophers and their students. The result is a consistently high standard where technicalities are concerned, but considerable variation in overall approach, for instance between the neat, lucid rendering of *Phaedo* by David **Gallop** and the stiff version of *Gorgias* by Terence **Irwin** (which sacrifices English sense to would-be-Greek idiom).

Although Plato's later works, in which the figure of Socrates becomes less important, are mostly greyer in philosophical character, several can reward a broader readership. (This is an area where Cornford was a pioneer, though his versions are no longer the first choice for non-specialists.) *Theaetetus*, an inexhaustibly fascinating quest for a definition of knowledge, is one of Plato's masterpieces: the translation by Margaret **Levett**, measured rather than sparkling, transmits much of the work's intellectual and dramatic adroitness. *Phaedrus* is a dialogue which displays Plato's brilliant ability to use (and parody) a spectrum of styles: its exploration of the nature of rhetoric has been rendered with some panache by Alexander **Nehamas** and Paul **Woodruff**. *Timaeus*, with its mixture of cosmology, anthropology, and the Atlantis myth, was once Plato's most influential work: Desmond Lee's translation is the most readable yet produced. Finally, Plato's last, longest, and driest work, the *Laws*, most of which is the outline of a legal code, poses formidable stylistic challenges. Here a sharp dichotomy in translation methods reappears. Trevor **Saunders**'s Penguin version is prepared to resort to slight paraphrase in the interests of explanatory clarity, while Thomas **Pangle**'s translation is similar in motivation to, if a little less hidebound than, Bloom's *Republic*.

ii. Aristotle Because Platonic and Aristotelian phases in western thought have tended not to coincide, the history of translations of Aristotle into English might be expected to diverge from the patterns already traced for Plato. But that turns out not to be so. Fluctuations in the appeal of Aristotelianism prior to 1800 made virtually no difference in this matter, since Aristotle's works were read almost exclusively by those capable of using Latin translations (less often the original Greek). In fact, with a single exception, English versions of Aristotle before the 19th c. are rarer than those of Plato. The exception is the *Poetics*, a key text of literary and aesthetic neoclassicism, which produced four 18th-c. English versions, one of them, by Thomas **Twining** (1735–1804), a remarkably assured rendering of the elliptical Greek, made all the more valuable by its fine interpretative essays. Beyond this, however, Aristotle received scant early attention from English translators—little more, indeed, than occasional reworking of versions in other modern languages. The *Rhetoric*, for instance, despite its pertinence to neoclassical interests, was available only in the pithy résumé by the philosopher Thomas **Hobbes**, which gives the work's skeleton without its flesh. Even the *Nicomachean Ethics* was not seriously tackled before 1797, when the historian John **Gillies** (1747–1836) translated it complete (together with the *Politics*). Gillies's rendering has a period refinement too elegant to be authentic. Yet his version reveals some alertness to the direction and logic of the philosopher's arguments, and his urbanity is less distracting than the note of piety later struck by several Victorian translators of the work.

Although the mid-19th c. saw a revival of Plato partly at Aristotle's expense, the period as a whole generated a noteworthy increase in English translations of the latter, even if, after Thomas **Taylor**'s nine-volume Aristotle (1806–12)—less cloying than his Plato (see above), but vitiated by a clumsiness that betrays deficient comprehension—no one later in the century attempted to do for Aristotle what Jowett did for Plato. Victorian versions often leaned towards a solemnity, sometimes underpinned by Christianizing readings, which missed the sinewy vigour of Aristotelian thinking and gave the philosopher an undeserved reputation for aridity. Yet Aristotle's treatises were now becoming much more readily available in English, including a large range in the popular Bohn's Classical Library; and the works most widely known, partly under the influence of Oxford 'Greats'—the *Nicomachean Ethics*, *Politics*, *Rhetoric*, and *Poetics*—each attracted several translations. But 19th-c.

progress in Aristotelian scholarship was slow to impinge upon translations. It is not until we reach F. H. **Peters**'s *Nicomachean Ethics* of 1881 that we meet a version, written with firm command, whose accuracy still enjoys respect.

In the 20th c., translations of Aristotle have been fewer than those of Plato, chiefly because the austere compression of the former's works makes them less appealing than the imaginative richness of his teacher's dialogues. But Aristotle has been well enough served. Pride of place is taken by the 'Oxford translation', *The Works of Aristotle*, under the general editorship of the great Aristotelian scholar Sir David **Ross**. Such a large venture, which appeared in 12 volumes (1908–52) and involved some 20 hands, was inevitably uneven in quality; there were anomalies, too, between the treatment of similar terms and ideas across different works. But the set as a whole established new standards for the rendering of Aristotle into an unpretentious English prose which balanced reasonable reliability (for its time) with concern for the needs of readers to whom raw Aristotelian technicalities would have been indigestible. Among the highlights—still unsurpassed—were Ross's own poised versions of both *Nicomachean Ethics* and *Metaphysics*, and the sprightly, erudite rendering of the multifarious *History of Animals* by the polymathic Sir D'Arcy Wentworth **Thompson** (1860–1948).

The Oxford translation has now been revised and corrected, with some versions replaced altogether, in a new edition by Jonathan **Barnes**: this is unquestionably the primary resource for anyone who wants access to the entire Aristotelian corpus in English. Of the 23 volumes of Aristotle in the Loeb series, a number are imperfectly trustworthy, and the parallel-text format anyhow suits students of the Greek better than general readers. Beyond this, the abundance of individual translations makes a survey impossible. One work alone, the *Poetics*, has been attempted more than 20 times since 1900: a notable treatment is that by M. E. **Hubbard**, who protests against making Aristotle speak 'a version of the higher Babu', and holds a nice balance, if occasionally too self-consciously, between Aristotelian idiosyncrasy and English idiom. As the one shortcoming of the revised Oxford translation is the absence of annotation, it may be worth singling out—at representative points on the spectrum of Aristotle's interests—the versions of the *Nicomachean Ethics* by Terence **Irwin**, the *Rhetoric* by George **Kennedy**, and the *Physics* by Robin **Waterfield**, all of which provide careful explanatory help.

Translators of Aristotle do not face the same

dilemma between the literal and the literary as translators of Plato; but they cannot avoid hard choices. The Clarendon Aristotle series, sister to the Clarendon Plato (above), subordinates other considerations to conceptual precision, whose achievement is assisted by glossaries and extensive philosophical commentary. Yet even here the tensions intrinsic to translation can be discerned. This is piquantly shown by the two editions of Barnes's version of *Posterior Analytics*, a complex disquisition on the logic of scientific reasoning. In the first edition, Barnes wryly acknowledges a 'blinkered pursuit of literalness' which tries to maximize one-to-one correspondences between translation and original. In the second, he explains his decision to rewrite the translation without much of its previous 'dog English': he now recognizes that, beyond a certain point, laborious literalism stands in inverse ratio to real fidelity, since it occludes, rather than promoting, the possibility of understanding. Despite this, Barnes continues to hanker after the illusory purity of a translation free of interpretation, and one-to-one correspondence continues to be a fetish for many translators of ancient philosophy.

iii. The Presocratics Finally, backwards in time to the earliest Greek philosophers, the Presocratics, whose works, owing to their meagerly fragmentary survival, have mostly been the preserve of specialists. This is unavoidable, but a pity, since we are dealing here not only with extraordinary thinkers but also with some extraordinary writers. The scope of Presocratic writings (6th–5th c. BCE) stretches from the riddling apophthegms of Heraclitus, the first great aphorist, via the vatic poetry of Parmenides and Empedocles, and the satirical bite of Xenophanes' verse, to the formal prose of Anaxagoras and Democritus. (The most famous of Presocratics, Pythagoras, probably wrote nothing, despite the spurious so-called 'golden verses', a set of moral maxims often translated into English since the 17th c.) Readers must, however, be prepared to encounter the ideas of these figures in the dismembered and embedded state in which they have been cited by later authors.

Translations of the Presocratics began to appear in the late 19th c., building on the collections of source material made by German scholars. The earliest of real note were by John **Burnet** (1863–1928), incorporated in his historical account, *Early Greek Philosophy*, and written in a uniformly robust late Victorian prose for all the authors concerned. Since then, detailed scholarship has greatly elucidated a difficult field, and modern readers can turn to more than one publication for illumination. For those requiring exegetical assistance, *The Presocratic Philosophers* of G. S. **Kirk**, J. E. **Raven**, and M. **Schofield**, editions of individual authors in the Phoenix Presocratics series, and Richard **McKirahan**'s *Philosophy before Socrates* all provide copious explanatory materials. For those seeking a cleaner approach to the material, Jonathan **Barnes**'s Penguin, *Early Greek Philosophy*, presents the Presocratics' tattered remains with admirable immediacy. Without skirting round difficulties, Barnes tries hard to achieve renderings which preserve the varying forms of language used by these pioneers in both philosophical and scientific theorizing.

The 20th c. has seen undeniable progress in the quality of translations of classical Greek philosophy, and the last 50 years have enjoyed a healthy multiplication of versions, especially of Plato, which has given these texts much wider currency. While there is, as I have emphasized, a broad dichotomy between more fluent renderings for the general reader and more literal treatments for the student of philosophy, it would be regrettable if this distinction were to become schematic. It is a besetting weakness of more literal versions that they reproduce elements of Greek idiom which cannot be properly understood except, self-defeatingly, with a knowledge of Greek itself. At the same time, freer versions can easily produce a spurious, complacent assimilation of ancient to modern ways of thinking. As this contrast suggests, the problems of translation in this area are a reflection of larger issues in our relationship to the past. The greatest challenge, therefore, facing future translators of classical Greek philosophy is to render its ideas in ways which respect the integrity of their intellectual contexts and cultural perspectives, while opening up those contexts and perspectives to renewed experience in the present.   SH

ARISTOTLE   *A Briefe of the Art of Rhetorique*, tr. Thomas Hobbes, London, 1637 [and later edns.] · *Aristotle's Treatise on Poetry*, tr. Thomas Twining, London, 1789 [2nd edn., 1812; rep. Farnborough, 1972] · *Aristotle's Ethics and Politics*, tr. John Gillies, London, 1797 · *The Works of Aristotle*, tr. Thomas Taylor, London, 1806–12 · *The Nicomachean Ethics of Aristotle*, tr. F. H. Peters, London, 1881 [many later edns.] · *The Works of Aristotle*, various translators, ed. W. D. Ross, Oxford, 1908–52 [rep. as *The Complete Works of Aristotle: the Revised Oxford Translation*, ed. Jonathan Barnes, Princeton, NJ, 1984; major works from 1st edn. in Richard McKeon, ed., *The Basic Works of Aristotle*, New York, 1941] ·

'Clarendon Aristotle Series', Oxford, 1962– [includes *Posterior Analytics*, tr. Jonathan Barnes, 1975, 2nd edn., 1994] · Aristotle's *Poetics*, tr. M. E. Hubbard, in D. A. Russell and M. Winterbottom, eds., *Ancient Literary Criticism*, Oxford, 1972 [rep. in *Classical Literary Criticism*, Oxford, 1989, World's Classics] · *Aristotle: Nicomachean Ethics*, tr. Terence Irwin, Indianapolis/Cambridge, 1985 · *Aristotle on Rhetoric*, tr. George Kennedy, New York, 1991 · *Aristotle: Physics*, tr. Robin Waterfield, Oxford, 1996 [World's Classics].

PLATO　*Plato His Apology of Socrates and Phaedo*, tr. anon., London, 1675 · *The Works of Plato Abridged*, tr. anon., London, 1701 · *The Works of Plato*, tr. Floyer Sydenham and Thomas Taylor, London, 1804 [individual versions 1759 onwards] · *The Symposium*, tr. Percy Bysshe Shelley, 1818 [rep. in doctored form, 1840 and subsequently, including Everyman; original version in J. A. Notopoulos, *The Platonism of Shelley*, Durham, NC, 1949, which also contains Shelley's *Ion*] · 'Notes on Some of the More Popular Dialogues of Plato', with partial translations, by John Stuart Mill, published in the *Monthly Repository*, 1834–5 [see J. M. Robson and F. E. Sparshott, eds., *Essays on Philosophy and the Classics by John Stuart Mill*, Toronto, 1978; vol. xi of Toronto collected edition of Mill's works] · *The Dialogues of Plato*, tr. B. Jowett, Oxford, 1871 [later edns.] · *Plato, Theaetetus*, tr. M. J. Levett, Glasgow, 1928; rev. edn. in Miles Burnyeat, *The Theaetetus of Plato*, Indianapolis/Cambridge, 1990 · *Plato, Republic*, tr. Paul Shorey, London/New York, 1930 [Loeb] · *The Republic of Plato*, tr. Francis Cornford, Oxford, 1941 [many reprints] · *Plato: The Collected Dialogues*, ed. Edith Hamilton and Huntington Cairns, Princeton, NJ, 1961 · *Plato, The Republic*, tr. H. D. P. Lee, Harmondsworth, 1965 [Penguin: the series contains the same translator's *Timaeus*, and several other useful volumes] · *The Republic of Plato*, tr. Allan Bloom, New York, 1968 · *Plato, The Laws*, tr. Trevor Saunders, Harmondsworth, 1970 [Penguin] · 'Clarendon Plato Series', Oxford, 1973– [includes *Phaedo*, tr. David Gallop, 1975, rep. World's Classics, 1993; *Gorgias*, tr. Terence Irwin, 1979] · *Plato, Republic*, tr. G. M. A. Grube, Indianapolis, 1974 [rev. edn., 1992] · *The Laws of Plato*, tr. Thomas Pangle, New York, 1980 · *The Dialogues of Plato*, tr. R. E. Allen, New Haven, Conn., 1984– · *Xenophon: Conversations of Socrates*, tr. Hugh Tredennick and Robin Waterfield, Harmondsworth, 1990 [Penguin; contains the philosophically much blander Socratic writings of Plato's older contemporary Xenophon; for earlier translations see D. R. Morrison, *Bibliography of Xenophon's Socratic Writings 1600-Present*, Pittsburgh, 1988] · *Plato, Republic*, tr. Robin Waterfield, Oxford, 1993 [World's Classics, 1994. Other World's Classics Plato translations include *Gorgias* and *Symposium* by Waterfield, *Protagoras* by C. C. W. Taylor, and *Apology, Euthyphro, Crito* by David Gallop] · *Plato Phaedrus*, tr. A. Nehamas and P. Woodruff, Indianapolis/Cambridge, 1995 [various other Plato translations issued by the same publisher, most recently in *Plato: Complete Works*, ed. J. M. Cooper, 1997].

PRESOCRATICS　*Early Greek Philosophy*, by J. Burnet, London, 1892 [several later edns.] · *The Presocratic Philosophers*, tr. G. S. Kirk, J. E. Raven, and M. Schofield, Cambridge 1957 [2nd edn., 1983] · 'The *Phoenix* Presocratics': supplementary volumes of *Phoenix*, Toronto, 1984– [containing translations of individual thinkers] · *Early Greek Philosophy*, tr. Jonathan Barnes, Harmondsworth, 1987 [Penguin] · *Philosophy Before Socrates*, tr. Richard McKirahan, Indianapolis/Cambridge, 1994.

SEE ALSO　Dover, K. J., 'Expurgation of Greek Literature', in his *The Greeks and Their Legacy*, Oxford, 1988, pp. 270–91 · Evans, F. B., 'Platonic Scholarship in Eighteenth-Century England', *Modern Philology*, 41 (1943) 103–10 · Turner, F. M., *The Greek Heritage in Victorian Britain*, New Haven, Conn., 1981.

9. ATTIC ORATORY

The surviving corpus of Greek oratory (i.e. the practical application of public speaking, as distinct from the theoretical art of speaking, or rhetoric) consists mainly of works composed by the ten members of the canon of Greek, or better (since they all practised at Athens in Attica) Attic orators during the 5th and 4th c. BCE: Antiphon, Andocides, Lysias, Isocrates, Isaeus, Aeschines, Demosthenes, Lycurgus, Hyperides, and Dinarchus.

With the exception of Isocrates and Demosthenes, the orators have held little interest for translators until relatively recent times. Classical oratory was virtually unknown in the Middle Ages, and its rediscovery in the Italy of the Renaissance naturally centred on Cicero. But the moral and political content of certain works by Isocrates and Demosthenes eventually led to their translation, firstly into Latin by scholars such as George of Trebizond and then into German, French, and English. Three pieces by Isocrates were especially popular. *To Nicocles*, a discussion of monarchical duties addressed by Isocrates to a royal pupil, was translated in 1531 by Thomas **Elyot** (1490–1546), who admired Isocrates' practical morality and prose style. The *Nicocles*, an address by the prince to his subjects on the principles of government, followed in 1534. *To Demonicus*, an essay on practical morality, was translated in 1557 by John **Bury** and in 1585 by R. **Nuttall**. In 1580 Thomas **Forrest** translated all three pieces in an expansive style from the Latin version of Hieronymus Wolf.

Further forays were made into the Isocratean

corpus in the 16th and 17th c., including the translation of the *Demonicus* for use in schools by John **Brinsley**, but it was not until 1752 that the complete works of Isocrates (except for then-unpublished parts of the *Antidosis*) were translated by Joshua **Dinsdale**. Soon after, in 1778, the historian John **Gillies** published a selection of elegant, if not always precisely accurate translations of Lysianic and Isocratean speeches. Two of these (Lysias' *Funeral Oration* and Isocrates' *Panegyricus*) may be found in the 1966 collection of *Greek Orations* edited by W. R. **Connor**, which otherwise consists of translations from the Loeb series and the *Demosthenes* of A. W. **Pickard-Cambridge** (see below). One other translation of Isocrates worthy of mention is that of the first ten speeches by A. H. **Dennis** and J. H. **Freese** for the Bohn Library (1894).

Demosthenes, acknowledged by critics ancient and modern as the greatest orator of antiquity, has naturally received the most attention from commentators and translators, in particular his series of speeches delivered against the imperialist Philip II of Macedon (the so-called *Philippics*), the three speeches also against Philip in support of Olynthus (the *Olynthiacs*), and his masterpiece, *On the Crown*, spoken in defence of Ctesiphon against Demosthenes' great rival Aeschines in 330 BCE. The nationalistic fervour displayed by Demosthenes imbues these speeches with a timeless, inspirational quality that makes them choice material for scholars and politicians of all eras. Thus the *Olynthiacs* and *Philippics* were first translated into English in 1570 by Thomas **Wilson** (*c*.1525–1581), the leading humanist and author of *The Arte of Rhetorique*, to serve as propaganda against the imperialism of Philip of Spain. The parallel with the situation concerning their original target is apparent, and passages from the *Philippics* were later used for a similar purpose against Napoleon by Pitt the Younger.

The 19th c. in particular saw numerous translations of Demosthenes, beginning with a selection of speeches in two volumes by Thomas **Leland**. This included Aeschines' *Against Ctesiphon*, delivered at the same trial as Demosthenes' *Crown* speech, and Dinarchus' *Against Demosthenes*. The Crown trial speeches were also translated by J. **Biddle** in 1881. Other translations of Demosthenic speeches include Henry, Lord **Brougham**'s rendition of the *On the Crown*, the five volumes by C. R. **Kennedy**, and, lastly, the two volumes of *Public Orations* by A. W. Pickard-Cambridge, which bring us into this century. Kennedy is especially worthy of note, a London barrister who produced an accurate translation which paid close attention to points of law.

Until the 20th c. the works of the other members of the canon were studied essentially as models of Greek prose style, the intricacies of Greek periodic sentence structure furnishing excellent examples for composition, but making close yet readable translation a difficult task. However, a version of Isaeus' speeches by William **Jones** (1746–94) was published in 1779, and two of Hyperides' speeches were translated in 1893 by F. G. **Kenyon**, who had published the recently discovered papyrus containing the *Against Philippides* in 1891.

Many of the translations referred to above are now largely inaccessible and of interest primarily to specialists. But modern readers of the orators have various more recent sources of translation available to them. Foremost among these is the Loeb Classical Library, which contains the entire corpus of Attic orators in 15 volumes, by 12 translators. This parallel-text series not only makes the less well-known orators accessible, but does so by translations that generally adhere closely to the originals, though some of them are now beginning to feel rather dated. The two unfortunately titled volumes of *Minor Attic Orators* should not deter the potential reader, since they contain some important examples of the orator's craft, such as Antiphon's *On the Murder of Herodes*, Andocides' *On the Mysteries*, Lycurgus' *Against Leocrates*, and Hyperides' *Funeral Speech*.

The first port of call for translations of classical texts in Britain is usually the Penguin Classics series. Unfortunately, the oratorical canon is poorly served by the Penguins, with the exception of *Greek Political Oratory* by A. N. W. **Saunders** (an earlier volume on the Crown trial has been deleted). This useful and varied selection contains (in addition to Thucydides' *Funeral Speech*) Andocides' *On the Mysteries*, Lysias' *Against Eratosthenes*, Isocrates' *Panegyricus* and *Philip*, and 10 speeches from Demosthenes' set of *Philippics*. The translations are sometimes rather loose, but in the tradition of the Penguins they are highly readable.

Another collection of speeches may conveniently be noted here, that of Kathleen **Freeman**, whose main purpose is to illustrate various Athenian legal procedures, such as those dealing with homicide, violence, and property rights, by means of the speeches delivered at the trials. To this end she provides lucid translations of 15 forensic speeches (though some not in their entirety) from the works of Antiphon, Lysias, Isaeus, and the Demosthenic corpus. Freeman's selection has now been revised and updated by Christopher **Carey**. Antiphon's speeches appear in the collections of sophistic material edited by R. K. Sprague (tr. J. S. **Morrison**) and by M. **Gagarin** and P. Woodruff (tr. Gagarin).

Finally, there are various modern commentaries now beginning to appear on individual speeches and selections of speeches which include translations. These reflect the great flowering of interest in recent years in the study of the classics in translation, and of the orators as important sources for legal, social and political history. Like the Loebs, the translations tend to be functional renderings of the texts for those with little or no Greek rather than elegant versions, and indeed the author of one of the best of them, Douglas **MacDowell** (in his edition of Demosthenes' *Against Meidias* speech), actually assumes some knowledge of Greek in his readers. His commentary is keyed to the Greek text, as is that of Ian **Worthington**, who provides a readable translation (though reliant on J. O. **Burtt**'s Loeb version) of the three surviving speeches of

Dinarchus. The pioneering series in the field of commentaries keyed to the translation is that published by Aris and Phillips of Warminster, which now includes selected speeches of Antiphon and Lysias (tr. M. **Edwards** and S. **Usher**) and Isocrates (tr. Usher), all of Andocides (tr. Edwards), Demosthenes' *Crown* speech (tr. Usher), and the *Against Neaera* attributed in the manuscripts to Demosthenes but in fact written by Apollodorus (tr. Carey).

The renewed interest in the Attic orators as sources for Athenian culture has, then, created a demand for up-to-date commentaries and accurate but readable translations. To fulfil the latter need Michael Gagarin has initiated a series entitled *The Oratory of Classical Greece*, a complete translation of the canon which is to be published by the University of Texas Press. The first volume on Antiphon and Andocides, prepared by Gagarin himself and MacDowell, was published in 1998.   ME

ANTHOLOGIES   *The Orations of Lysias and Isocrates*, tr. J. Gillies, London, 1778 · *Demosthenes* [vol. ii containing Aeschines' *Against Ctesiphon* and Dinarchus' *Against Demosthenes*], tr. T. Leland, 2 vols., London, 1819 · *Minor Attic Orators I: Antiphon and Andocides*, tr. K. J. Maidment, Cambridge, Mass., 1941 [Loeb] · *The Murder of Herodes* [containing Antiphon 1 and 5, Lysias 1, 3–4, 7–8, 12, 23–4, 32, Isaeus 8, Demosthenes 54–5, 59], tr. K. Freeman, London, 1946 · *Minor Attic Orators II: Lycurgus, Dinarchus, Demades, Hyperides*, tr. J. O. Burtt, Cambridge, Mass., 1954 [Loeb] · *Greek Orations* [containing Lysias 2 and parts of Isocrates 4, tr. J. Gillies, and selections from the Loeb and Pickard-Cambridge translations of Isocrates, Demosthenes, Aeschines and Hyperides], ed. W. R. Connor, Ann Arbor, Mich., 1966 · *Greek Political Oratory* [containing Andocides 1, Lysias 12, Isocrates 4, 5, Demosthenes 1–6, 8–9, 15–16], tr. A. N. W. Saunders, Harmondsworth, 1970 [Penguin] · *Greek Orators I: Antiphon and Lysias* [containing Antiphon 5 and Lysias 1, 10, 12, 16, 22, 24, 25], ed. and tr. M. Edwards [Antiphon] and S. Usher [Lysias], Warminster, UK, 1985 · *Trials from Classical Athens* [containing Antiphon 1, 5–6, Lysias 1, 3, 10, 32, Isocrates 20, Isaeus 3–4, Demosthenes 35, 37, 54–5, 57, 59, Hyperides 3], tr. C. Carey, London, 1997.

AESCHINES   *The Speeches of Aeschines*, tr. C. D. Adams, Cambridge, Mass., 1919 [Loeb].

ANDOCIDES   *Greek Orators IV: Andocides*, ed. and tr. M. J. Edwards, Warminster, UK, 1995.

ANTIPHON   *Antiphon*, tr. J. S. Morrison, in R. K. Sprague, ed., *The Older Sophists*, Columbia, NY, 1972 · *Early Greek Political Thought from Homer to the Sophists* [containing Antiphon's *Tetralogies* and fragments of his own defence speech, *Truth, Concord, Proems* and *Art of Rhetoric*], tr. M. Gagarin and P. Woodruff, Cambridge, 1995.

DEMOSTHENES   *Demosthenes. The three Orations . . . in favour of the Olynthians . . . with those fower Orations titled . . . against king Philip of Macedonie*, tr. T. Wilson, London, 1570 · *The Oration of Demosthenes upon the Crown*, ed. and tr. Henry, Lord Brougham, London, 1840 [rev. in Sir John Lubbock's *Hundred Books*, London, 1893] · *The Orations of Demosthenes*, tr. C. R. Kennedy, 5 vols., London, 1852–70 [Bohn] · *The Chersonese Oration*, tr. Henry, Lord Brougham, in his *Works*, vii, Edinburgh, 1872 · *The Two Orations On the Crown*, tr. J. Biddle, Philadelphia, 1881 · *Demosthenes: Against Midias*, tr. C. A. M. Fennell, Cambridge, 1882 · *Demosthenes: The Olynthiacs and Philippics*, tr. O. Holland, London, 1901 · *The Public Orations of Demosthenes*, tr. A. W. Pickard-Cambridge, 2 vols., Oxford, 1912 · *Demosthenes*, tr. J. H. Vince, C. A. Vince, A. T. Murray, N. W. DeWitt, and N. J. DeWitt, 7 vols., Cambridge, Mass., 1926–49 [Loeb] · *Demosthenes: On the Crown*, tr. J. J. Keaney, ed. J. J. Murphy, New York, 1967 · *Demosthenes: Against Meidias*, ed. and tr. D. M. MacDowell, Oxford, 1990 · *Greek Orators VI: Apollodoros Against Neaira* [Demosthenes] 59, ed. and tr. C. Carey, Warminster, UK, 1992 · *Greek Orators V: Demosthenes On the Crown*, ed. and tr. S. Usher, Warminster, UK, 1993.

DINARCHUS   *A Historical Commentary on Dinarchus*, tr. I. Worthington, Ann Arbor, Mich., 1992.

HYPERIDES   *Hyperides: Philippides and Athenogenes*, tr. F. G. Kenyon, London, 1893.

ISAEUS   *Isaeus*, tr. Sir W. Jones, Oxford, 1779 [vol. ix of Jones's collected works] · *Isaeus*, tr. E. S. Forster, Cambridge, Mass., 1927 [Loeb].

ISOCRATES   *To Nicocles*, tr. Sir T. Elyot, London, 1531 · *Nicocles* [*The Doctrinal of princes made by the noble oratour Isocrates*], tr. Sir T. Elyot, London, 1534 · *To Demonicus* [*The Godly aduertisement or good counsell of the famous orator Isocrates, intitled Paraenesis to Demonicus*], tr. J. Bury, London, 1558 · *To Nicocles, Nicocles, To Demonicus* [*A perfite Looking Glasse of all Estates: most excellently and eloquently set forth by the famous and learned Oratour Isocrates*], tr. T. Forrest, London, 1580 · *To Demonicus* [*The good Admonition of the sage Isocrates to young Demonicus*], tr. R. Nuttall, London, 1585

· *To Demonicus*, tr. J. Brinsley, London, 1622 · *Archidamus, or the councell of warre*, tr. T. Barnes, London, 1624 · *The Orations and Epistles of Isocrates*, tr. J. Dinsdale, revised by the Rev. Mr. Young, London, 1752 · *Isocrates*, tr. A. H. Dennis and J. H. Freese, London, 1894 [Bohn] · *Isocrates*, tr. G. Norlin and L. Van Hook, 3 vols., Cambridge, Mass., 1928–45 [Loeb] · *Greek Orators III: Isocrates* [containing the *Panegyricus* and *To Nicocles*], ed. and tr. S. Usher, Warminster, UK, 1990.

LYSIAS   *Lysias*, tr. W. R. M. Lamb, Cambridge, Mass., 1930 [Loeb].

10. HISTORY

Herodotus of Halicarnassus, who in the course of writing the history of the victories of the Greeks in two campaigns over the Persians at Marathon in 490 BCE and Salamis in 480 investigated the history of the whole of the near east, and the Athenian Thucydides, who chronicled the history of the conflict between Athens and Sparta in the Peloponnesian War (431–404 BCE), have been the two most durable Greek historians for readers and translators. With their different conceptions of history, their different methods, world-views, and subjects, they have always been linked, compared, and contrasted, attracting rival devotees rather like Tolstoy and Dostoevsky. Their only rival in popularity might be the Athenian Xenophon, in two works that resulted from his own experiences as an Athenian general leading an expedition in Persia shortly after the Peloponnesian War. His *Anabasis*, which describes a heroic retreat after the expedition got into difficulties, has been commonly read in selections as a school text. His *Cyropaedia*, describing the education and career of the Persian ruler Cyrus the Younger, was a popular text in the Renaissance, though the strongly idealized portrait of Cyrus, who emerges as almost a philosopher-king, perhaps takes us beyond the realms of history. Of later historians writing in Greek, Polybius, who deals with Rome's rise to power, and Plutarch [II.i.11.i] have had the most currency, the latter being particularly popular in the Renaissance.

i. Herodotus The first translation of Herodotus, of the first two books only, appeared in 1584, attributed to Barnabe **Rich** (1542–1617). The translation is made from the Latin version of the Italian humanist Laurentius Valla, who also translated Thucydides in the 1440s; these early versions were the basis of the later Latin version accompanying the Greek text in the bilingual editions that became the norm for these historians, as for other Greek classics, until the 19th c. Rich is not concerned with accuracy; whole sentences are omitted, while more commonly he expands like other translators of this era. His is an englishing translation; Greek customs, institutions, and practices are familiarized, for

example high priests become bishops. But his version is lively, fanciful, and enthusiastic, capturing, in its naïve way, something of Herodotus' delight in telling a good story.

The first complete Herodotus in English was produced by Isaac **Littlebury** (dates unknown) in 1709; this version, probably also made from Valla's Latin, frequently misunderstands and curtails the Greek, and scarcely exceeds half the original's length. Where Littlebury does succeed, however, is in the general tenor of his style, which is simple, graceful, and plain, offering a decent equivalent in English of the narrative voice of Herodotus who writes 'speech as it is spoken' (it is recorded that he gave public recitations of his work) in a style wholly without literary or rhetorical affectation.

Yet Herodotus' language is an interesting amalgam of dialects, principally the Ionic and the Attic, and contains phrasing reminiscent of Homeric epic. This has led translators into archaizing tendencies, sometimes with echoes of Biblical phraseology and rhythms. The version of George **Rawlinson** (1812–1892) is scholarly and accurate; but like others of an archaizing kind it has not sufficient literary merit to recommend it to the modern reader in preference to the more graceful, consistent and readable versions in modern idiom by A. D. **Godley** (1856–1925) and Aubrey **de Selincourt**.

ii. Thucydides In the Renaissance and 17th c. the Greek historians were not read as widely as their Roman counterparts, Livy, Sallust, Caesar, and Tacitus [II.n.10], nor were they generally considered to be good stylistic models. Nevertheless it was the early period that saw one of the finest translations of any Greek or Roman prose writer when in 1629 the philosopher Thomas **Hobbes** published Thucydides, whom he calls in his preface 'the most politic historiographer that ever writ' [see I.b.2.vi]: He goes on to mention dismissively the mediocre 1550 version by Thomas **Nicolls** (dates unknown), the only previous one in English, which on Nicolls's admission had been made from the French of Claude de Seyssel, who in turn had translated from the Latin version of Valla.

Explaining on the title-page that his Thucydides is 'Interpreted with Faith and Diligence Immediately out of the Greek', Hobbes is asserting a fully justified claim to sound scholarship, for while the influence of the Latin can be seen in his vocabulary, he does not follow it where it deviates from the Greek. Nor does he follow the practice of earlier translators of the classics in englishing the unfamiliar customs and practices of the ancient world. His version is as accurate as the state of the Greek in his Renaissance text allowed. Yet there is nothing pedantic or stilted about it; translating at a time when the kingdom was beginning to see some of the strains that were to result in civil war, there is every reason to believe that he took seriously his own claim that Thucydides had written his history as a warning of the evils of democratic government. Like other early translators, Hobbes was also concerned to forge a modern style in living English.

In so doing, it can be said that he created something new in English prose. A friend and disciple of Bacon, he found the matter of the most scientific and analytical of the ancient historians deeply congenial, and in translating the matter faithfully he caught something of his manner. Thucydides' style has two distinct aspects. His narrative of events is written in a plain, straightforward, and workmanlike style, while in the speeches that, in the manner of nearly all the ancient historians, he composed for his protagonists and which contain the main burden of his political, social, and military analysis, the style is abstract, antithetical and condensed. Hobbes does not always manage to render the full complexity of the densely packed speeches, but he always gives a strong rendering of the main arguments, as might be suggested by the following extract from Pericles' oration on the Athenian dead:

For to famous men, all the Earth is a Sepulchre; and their Vertues shall be testified, not onely by the Inscription in Stone at home, but by an Unwritten Record of the Mind, which more then any Monument, will remain with every one for ever. In imitation therefore of these men, and placing Happiness in Liberty, and Liberty in Valour, be forward to encounter the dangers of War. (ii. 43)

Overall his style is plain, direct, muscular, analytical, expository prose without frills, ambiguities, or tropes that draw attention to themselves. As a disciple of Bacon, Hobbes had no difficulty in embracing Thucydides' characteristically antithetical mode of argument. His style marks a distinct break with the more ornate and florid style adopted by many Elizabethan writers for historical translation.

Hobbes's version stood the test of time. The superiority of its vigorous language to the more elegant and decorous but blander prose of the serviceable version by William **Smith** (1711–87) was apparent, for it was reissued with 'corrections' in the 19th c., when Thucydides was much studied in the public schools for his lessons in government, until it was superseded by two Victorian versions, the first by Richard **Crawley** (1840–93) and the second by Benjamin **Jowett** (1817–93), the Master of Balliol, who also translated Plato [II.i.8.i]. Crawley translates Thucydides with great clarity into stately and sonorous prose; his narrative is dramatic and intense, the speeches are delivered with vigour, emphasis, and a weighty oratorical force, that may be illustrated in the same passage from Pericles' funeral speech:

For heroes have the whole earth for their tomb; and in lands far from their own, where the column with its epitaph declares it, there is enshrined in every breast a record unwritten with no tablet to preserve it, except that of the heart. These take as your model, and judging happiness to be the fruit of freedom and freedom of valour, never decline the dangers of war.

Crawley's Thucydides has *gravitas* without being pompous. Jowett is less dramatic and emphatic and lacks Crawley's ringing turn of phrase, but his translation is very clear and conveys something of the high seriousness of the original. Rex **Warner**, in a prefatory note to his translation of 1954, pays tribute to his predecessors, noting that Crawley has taken over words and turns of phrase from Hobbes as he himself has consulted Crawley. Warner is modest in claiming for himself merely the virtue of modernity. Without the dignity, elegance, or intensity of Crawley's, his version is nevertheless admirably clear, accurate, and readable.

iii. Xenophon and Polybius The earliest somewhat wayward version of Xenophon's *Cyropaedia* made in 1537 by William **Barker** (*fl.* 1572) was reprinted several times before it was superseded by the more accurate version of Philemon **Holland** (1552–1637). Published in 1632 not long after Hobbes's Thucydides, this version takes us back into a previous age; it was, indeed, completed in 1620–1. Diffuse, enthusiastic, and florid, it makes a strong contrast with the sinewy rigour of Hobbes. In the preface to his translation of the *Cyropaedia* of 1728, Maurice **Ashley** (dates unknown) remarks: 'There is indeed a plainness and simplicity in this piece of Xenophon that may seem childish and contemptible to some judgements.' Ashley's elegant version, cool and restrained, is altogether more sober and urbane than Holland's. Equally urbane is the translation by Edward **Spelman** (d. 1767) of Xenophon's *Anabasis*. The best modern version is by Rex Warner.

The most readable of the early translations of Polybius is by James **Hampton** (1721–78), published between 1756 and 1772. Remarking on the obscurity and inelegance of Polybius' Greek, the translator frankly admits that he has sought to polish him up. He aims 'to spread one simple, grave and sober colouring over the whole work, to render the diction strong, expressive even and correct, and to give to the periods a roundness, a stability and varied cadence'. Insofar as he succeeds, his version is a great improvement on earlier translations in Eng-

lish (for example, the version in knotty though often lively prose of 1633 by Edward **Grimeston** (dates unknown)), even if it will not quite satisfy the modern reader's likely demand for accuracy in translation of historical texts. More accurate is the stately version by Evelyn **Shuckburgh** (1843–1906). The Penguin Polybius offers a substantial selection in the rhythms and vocabulary of contemporary English by Ian **Scott-Kilvert**.

Extracts in modern translations from the historians discussed here, and from other ancient historians, are available in *Readings in the Classical Historians*, ed. Michael Grant (New York, 1992).   RS

HERODOTUS   *The Famous Hystory of Herodotus*, tr. B. R., London, 1584 [rep. The Tudor Translations, London, 1924] · *The History of Herodotus*, tr. Isaac Littlebury, 2 vols., London, 1709 [rep. several times] · *The History of Herodotus*, tr. George Rawlinson, 4 vols., London, 1858–60 [later Everyman] · *Herodotus with an English Translation*, tr. A. D. Godley, 4 vols., London/New York, 1920 [Loeb] · *Herodotus: The Histories*, tr. Aubrey de Selincourt, Harmondsworth, 1954 [Penguin] · *Herodotus: The Histories*, tr. Robin Waterfield, Oxford/New York, 1998.

POLYBIUS   *The History of Polybius*, tr. Edward Grimeston, London, 1633 · *The General History of Polybius*, tr. James Hampton, 4 vols., London, 1756 · *The Histories of Polybius*, tr. Evelyn S. Shuckburgh, 2 vols., London, 1889 · *Polybius: The Rise of the Roman Empire*, tr. Ian Scott-Kilvert, selected with an introduction by F. W. Walbank, Harmondsworth, 1979 [Penguin].

THUCYDIDES   *Eight Bookes of the Peloponnesian Warre Written by Thucydides*, tr. Thomas Hobbes, London, 1629 [2nd edn., 1676; also in *The English Works of Thomas Hobbes of Malmesbury*, ed. Sir William Molesworth, London, viii, 1843; rep. Aalen, 1962; and in *Hobbes' Thucydides*, ed. Richard Grene, Chicago, 1968] · *The History of the Peloponnesian War by Thucydides*, tr. Richard Crawley, London, 1874 [later Everyman, 1910, and a substantial selection in World's Classics, often rep.] · *Thucydides: Translated into English with Introduction, Marginal Analyses, Notes and Indices*, tr. B. Jowett, 2 vols., Oxford, 1881 · *Thucydides: History of the Peloponnesian War*, tr. Rex Warner, Harmondsworth, 1954 [Penguin].

XENOPHON [OF ATHENS]   *The Eight Books of Xenophon, Containing the Institution, School and Education of Cyrus*, tr. William Barker, London, 1567 · *Xenophon: Cyropaedia*, tr. Philemon Holland, London, 1632 [rep. Newtown, Wales, 1936] · *Xenophon. Cyropaedia*, tr. Maurice Ashley, London, 1728 · *The Expedition of Cyrus with Notes Critical and Historical*, tr. Edward Spelman, London, 1742 · *Xenophon: The Persian Expedition*, tr. Rex Warner, Harmondsworth, 1949 [Penguin] · Sowerby, R. E., 'Thomas Hobber's Translation of Thucydides', *Translation and Literature*, 7.2 (1998), 147–69.

SEE ALSO   Burke, P., 'A Survey of the Popularity of Ancient Historians, 1450–1700', *History and Theory*, 5 (1966), 135–52 · Sowerby, R. E., 'Thomas Hobbes's Translation of Thucydides', *Translation and Literature*, 7.2 (1998), 147–69.

11. BIOGRAPHY, FICTION, AND OTHER PROSE

i. Plutarch's Lives Plutarch of Chaeronea, a Greek citizen of the Roman empire, was a wide-ranging writer whose works are the *Parallel Lives* on which his fame chiefly rests, consisting of 50 paired lives (25 Greek and 25 Roman), with in most cases an essay comparing the pair in question, and the *Moralia*, a large collection of essays and dialogues on a variety of topics. His humane Platonic philosophy made his works more acceptable than those of most pagan writers to the Christian fathers and to medieval thinkers: this guaranteed their preservation *in extenso* when so much classical literature was lost. His works were among the earliest to attract

attention with the revival of interest in the classics in 16th-c. England.

The first and most famous translation of the Lives into English was that by Sir Thomas **North** (*c*.1535–*c*.1601), published between 1579 and 1602/3. However, this was not made directly from the Greek, but was a version of the French translation by Jacques Amyot published in 1559. The importance of Amyot for English as well as French translation from the Greek is considerable. He was a true scholar as well as a translator. Nonetheless, he sometimes misunderstood his original, and North, a less scholarly writer, adds new errors. North's book became the standard for its generation, and indeed for 100 years; Shakespeare's Roman plays are heavily indebted to the information in, and often the phraseology of, North's Plutarch. A striking example is Enobarbus' description of Cleopatra in *Antony and Cleopatra* (II.ii): 'The barge she sat in, like a burnished throne . . .'. The passage in North's *Life of Antony* reads (in part):

she disdained . . . but to take her barge in the river of Cydnus, the poope whereof was of gold, the sailes of purple, and the owers of silver, which kept stroke in rowing after the sounde of the musicke of flutes, how-boyes, citherns, violls, and such other instruments as they play'd upon in the barge.

The baroque fantasies and conceits with which Shakespeare enriches this picture cannot conceal the lush exoticism of North's original, which is a very fair sample of his style, rich and intense without being ornate.

The classic version of the *Lives* is the translation from the Greek 'by several hands', edited by John **Dryden** and published in five volumes, 1683–86. Besides Dryden, who also contributed a Life of Plutarch, the translators include such names as Paul **Rycaut** (1628–1700), Thomas **Creech** (1659–1700), and Richard **Duke** (1658–1711). This translation has been very frequently reprinted ever since. It was re-edited in piecemeal fashion after the appearance of the French translation of the *Lives* (from 1694) by André Dacier, but continued to bear signs of haste and unevenness. This provided the motivation for the new translation published in six volumes in 1770 by the brothers John (1735–79) and William **Langhorne** (1721–72). In their preface the Langhornes castigated Dryden's version as 'full of errors, inequalities and inconsistencies . . . deficient in both learning and language', and promised a version in clear English, accompanied by historical notes, particularly for the benefit of young people.

This translation held the field for more than a century, and was reprinted more than 20 times in its entirety before 1900, as well as forming the basis of numerous individual volumes of selected lives. But in 1859 Arthur Hugh **Clough** (1819–61) published a revised version of the Dryden translation and added an introduction, in which he castigated the Langhornes' as 'dull and heavy'. A comparison of one passage from the *Life of Themistocles* will show the differences:

His behaviour is also commended with respect to the interpreter who came with the King of Persia's ambassadors that were sent to demand earth and water. By a decree of the people, he put him to death, for presuming

to make use of the Greek language to express the demands of the barbarians.　(Langhorne i. 288)

When the king of Persia sent messengers into Greece, with an interpreter, to demand earth and water, as an acknowledgement of subjection, Themistocles, by consent of the people, seized upon the interpreter, and put him to death, for presuming to publish the barbarian orders and decrees in the Greek language; this is one of the actions he is commended for . . .　(Clough i. 168–9, Everyman)

Clough's translation is more direct, in a more natural English word order, and remains very close to Dryden, only tidying up the pleonasm of 'subjection and obedience to him' into the one word 'subjection'. These qualities make Clough's translation much the most readable of the three today, despite its lack of annotation, and it quickly eclipsed the Langhornes' work.

The most reliable complete modern translation is that in the Loeb Classical Library (with facing Greek and scholarly apparatus) by Bernadotte **Perrin** in 11 volumes. However, the most accessible versions of Plutarch (in both the modern directness of their language and their ready availability) are now the several volumes of selected lives published by Penguin and arranged according to historical period rather than by Plutarch's pairing. *Fall of the Roman Republic: Six Lives* by Rex **Warner** is the first, followed by two volumes of Greek lives and another of Romans translated by Ian **Scott-Kilvert** and a volume of Spartan lives by R. J. A. **Talbert**.

ii. Plutarch's *Moralia* The more heterogeneous material of the *Moralia* has been less often translated, though one of the essays, 'Quyete of Mind', was translated as early as 1527 by Thomas **Wyatt** (1503–42) from a Latin version, of which there were already more than one. 'The Governance of Good Helthe', translated by an anonymous hand in *c*.1530, is another very early translation. Two translations by Thomas **Elyot** (*c*.1490–1546), 'The Education or Bringinge up of Children' and 'Howe one may Take Profite of his Enmyes', follow soon after. Elyot's aim was a moral one, as is clear from his description of his work: '*The Education of children*, which also I translated oute of the wise Plutarche, making men and women, which will follow those rules, to be wel worthy to be fathers and mothers' (*The Image of Governance Compiled of the Actes of Alexander Severus*, preface).

A few other individual treatises were also translated in the 16th c. and this same treatise, 'Of the Benefit we may Get from our Enemies', was translated from Latin into English by Henry **Vaughan** (1621–95) as part of his *Olor Iscanus* (1650); but in 1603 appeared the translation of the entire *Moralia* by Philemon **Holland** (1552–1637). He described this on the title-page as 'translated out of Greeke into English, and conferred with the Latine translations and the French . . . Whereunto are annexed the summaries necessary to be read before every treatise.' It was, then, a major scholarly undertaking, which though it uses the complete translation by Amyot, does so only as a scholarly adjunct and not—like North with the *Lives*—as a source.

The prolific Holland was 'the Translatour generall of his age' as the ecclesiastical writer Thomas Fuller called him. His elaborate style is rebarbative today, though the translation was reprinted in 1657, 1888, 1892, and 1912 (Everyman). Plutarch writes in simple, regular periods. Amyot had turned these into shorter sentences; but Holland follows the periodic structure of Plutarch in wordy fashion. The opening of 'The Education of Children' in the Loeb (which is close to the Greek) runs:

Let us consider what may be said of the education of free-born children, and what advantages they should enjoy to give them a sound character when they grow up. It is perhaps better to begin with their parentage first.

Holland has:

Forasmuch as we are to consider what may be said as touching the education of children free borne and descended from gentle bloud, how and by what discipline they may become honest and vertuous, we shall perhaps treat hereof the better, if we begin at their very generation and nativity.

Though Plutarch has one pleonastic phrase ('begin . . . first'), Holland's style relies for its ponderous flow on the use of pleonasm, and this is reflected in the enormous size of his translation (over 1,000 folio pages).

A more frequently reprinted translation is *Plutarch's Morals by Several Hands* with preface by Matthew **Morgan** (1652–1703), in five volumes. The translators include Thomas Creech, Ambrose **Philips** (1674–1749), and others less well known. This was revised by William **Goodwin** of Harvard in 1870. His revision consisted mainly of alterations to the punctuation in conformity with 19th-c. style. Some words were modernized (e.g. 'false persuasion' for the archaic 'misjudging'), and some perhaps superfluous phrases were eliminated. It was provided with an enthusiastic preface by R. W. Emerson, who asserted: 'It is the vindication of Plutarch'.

A few individual essays have also been translated, but they have never had the popularity of the *Lives*. The standard translation is that in the bilingual Loeb Classical Library by a variety of scholars (Frank Cole **Babbitt** did the first six volumes). It aims to remain as close to the Greek as possible and to provide a serviceable guide to Plutarch's sense, for the use of scholars and students. The most recent selections are by Rex Warner, Robin **Waterfield** and Ian **Kidd**, and Donald **Russell**. All of these convey an enthusiasm for Plutarch as a writer and thinker which the Loeb has no need to display. Of the two more recent, Waterfield and Kidd's is the more literal, while Russell writes in a graceful English which appears the authentic voice of Plutarch in an English guise.

iii. Fiction The Greek novel or romance has suffered a long period of neglect which has begun to be reversed in the last 20 years. The canon of the Greek romances consists of five works: Chariton's *Chaereas and Callirhoe*, Xenophon of Ephesus' *Ephesian Tale (Ephesiaca)*, Achilles Tatius' *Clitophon and Leucippe*, Longus' *Daphnis and Chloe*, and Heliodorus' *Ethiopian Story (Aethiopica)*. The dating of most of these works is uncertain, ranging from perhaps the 1st c. BCE for Chariton to the 3rd or 4th c. CE for Heliodorus. All the romances are elaborately plotted stories of young love thwarted and finally successful, full of shipwrecks, attacks by bandits, apparent deaths by murder, and executions miraculously survived.

The first to be translated into English was the *Aethiopica* of Heliodorus. Ja[mes] **Sanford** (dates uncertain) in 1567 appended an excerpt from it to *The Amorous and Tragical Tales of Plutarch*. As so often, Amyot had preceded the English translator, with a French version of 1547 appearing only a dozen years after the first printed Greek edition. In 1568/9 appeared Thomas **Underdowne**'s (*fl.* 1566–87) famous translation, made from an intermediate Latin version by Stanislaus Warschewiczki. This translation will have been known to Philip Sidney (who however was quite capable of reading it in Greek), and may have been a factor in his choice of the romance form for his *Arcadia* (begun about 1577), which is heavily indebted for its manner, and for many individual episodes, to Heliodorus (see Wolff 1912: 262–366).

Underdowne's translation is a splendid example of Elizabethan prose, delighting in rich vocabulary, alliteration, and balanced clauses, as in the following description of the aftermath of a fight:

To be brief, God shewed, a wonderfull sight in so short time, bruynge bloud with wine, ioyninge battayle with banketing, minglinge indifferently slaughters with drinkinges, and killing with quaffinges, providing suche a sight for the theeves of Egypt to pause at.

This translation has been frequently reprinted, and formed the basis of the modernized translation by F. A. **Wright**.

Other translations include the pompous and verbose verse translation by William **Lisle** (?1569–1637) and that of 'a person of quality' with Nahum **Tate** (1652–1715). Here is the latters' version of the famously abrupt opening sentence, which plunges the reader straight into the action without mediation or preamble:

The break of day had now dispersed the darkness, and the sun with earliest beams, guilded the summits of the mountains; when a troop of men, that had no living but by robberies, and rapine, appeared upon the promontory that elevates itself over one of the mouths of Nilus . . .

This runs smoothly but offers no essential improvement over Underdowne's vigorous version.

Translations in standard series are those of R. **Smith** (Bohn) and W. **Lamb** (Everyman); both lay less emphasis on style than on accuracy. A translation by the prolific American translator, Moses **Hadas**, appeared in 1957. The standard translation—very stylish in the manner of a modern novel—is now that by J. R. **Morgan** in the portmanteau volume edited by B. P. Reardon, *Collected Ancient Greek Novels*.

The next of the novels to be translated was Longus' *Daphnis and Chloe*, by Angell **Daye** (*c.*1550–after 1587). Again, Daye's translation is from Amyot's French, not the original Greek. Daye omitted the preface, rearranged some of the contents, and elaborated the phraseology to an amazing degree. Where Amyot has: 'mais ce baiser icy est toute autre chose; le pouls m'en bat, le coeur m'en tressaut, mon âme en languit et neantmoins ie desire la baiser derechef', Daye writes: 'but this kisse of far other efficacie and operation, by touch whereof, my pulse beateth, my heart trembleth, and my verie soule languisheth, all which notwithstanding, my suffizaunce of remedie resteth yet onely in kissing her'.

The next English translation is that of George **Thornley** (1657), which was reprinted with an introduction by George Saintsbury in 1893, and also forms the basis of the translation in J. M. Edmonds's Loeb volume of 1916. It is swift and lively, but tender and graceful (though George **Moore** called it 'dry and lumpy'):

[Lycenium] when she saw him itching to be at her, . . . slipping under, not without art, diverted him to her fancie, the place so long desired and sought. Of that which happened after, there was nothing done that was strange, nothing that was insolent; the Lady Nature and Lycenium shewed him how to do the rest.

This version held the field through the 18th and 19th c., though other versions appeared. Longus' succinct style and his somewhat titillating subject-matter made the book quite popular in the 20th c. George Moore's translation, *The Pastoral Loves of Daphnis and Chloe*, was published in 1924. Moore does not shy away from the sexual detail of the story: Lycoenium (another English spelling of the Greek Lykainion) explains to Daphnis: 'Chloe, when she will struggle with thee, will cry out, weep, and will bleed as if she had been killed'. Jack **Lindsay**'s 1948 translation, by contrast, has only 'will cry and weep as if wounded'. Moore's style in general contains more of the periodic grace and tender humour of the Greek than Lindsay's more modern, staccato version.

Longus is the only one of the novelists to have appeared in Penguin, and P. **Turner**'s translation is accurate enough. Moses Hadas's plain and functional translation of 1953 appeared in a composite volume with Xenophon of Ephesus and a work by Dio Chrysostom. The most up-to-date translation, in a rather informal style ('There's a city in Lesbos', 'What happened was this . . .', etc.), is that by Christopher **Gill** in Reardon's *Collected Ancient Greek Novels*.

The other three novels have been much less popular subjects for translation. The only Elizabethan version is that of Achilles Tatius by W. B[urton] (1575–1645, the elder brother of Robert Burton), though there had by this time been three French translations, as well as a Latin one by Annibale Croce: Burton's translation is based on the latter, not on the Greek, of which the first printed edition appeared only in 1601. It is faithful to the words and mood of the original. Burton may have been inspired to his work by Philip Sidney, who uses several motifs from Achilles in his *Arcadia*. Another Achilles, by Anthony **Hodges**, appeared in 1638, and was praised by Richard Lovelace in his prefatory verses as a match for Sidney's *Arcadia*. Hodges writes a colourful, limpid, rather poetic and graceful prose, and is able to convey the grotesque humour (which some critics have wrongly taken for ineptitude) of Achilles as well.

Plain cribs are R. Smith's 1848 version for Bohn and S. **Gaselee**'s 1917 version for Loeb. The standard version is now that by J. J. **Winkler** in Reardon's *Collected Ancient Greek Novels*, a consummate work of recreation of the style of Achilles and a literary *tour de force* in its own right. Winkler describes it as 'not a crib but a translation. It aims to give the 20th-c. English-speaking reader direct and immediate pleasures analogous to those experienced by Achilles' late 2nd-c. readers'. Thus he aims at a floridity of style that will 'astonish, beguile, repel and linger with a peculiar aftertaste', and at reproducing effects like alliteration, replacing puns by other puns, echoes of Greek classics by echoes of English classics: in 1.xv 'the bed of Dawn, the table of Tereus' (*Eous eunen, Tereos trapezan*) becomes 'Dawn's divan and Tereus' table'. In a court scene we have 'Get up from the bench, Mr President . . . You have no right to cast a vote against the wicked; today's decrees are tomorrow's dead letters.' On Leucippe's return Clitophon cries out, 'O tardy tidings! My happiness was delivered one day late. Marriage *post mortem*! Wedding after wake! Now Fortune presents me with a bride whose corpse she once refused to let me have in its entirety' (the alliterative phrases perhaps improve on the balanced, but not alliterative, clauses of the original).

Chariton was translated anonymously in 1764, via an Italian version. In 1939 appeared Warren E. **Blake**'s version, in what he called 'a brittle, modern idiom, designed to recapture as far as possible Chariton's abrupt and rapid-moving style'. Reardon's version of 1989 translates Chariton's *koine* into what he calls 'unaffected but not cheap English'. G. P. **Goold**'s 1995 Loeb version has the usual qualities of the Loeb series.

Xenophon was translated once (by Moses Hadas, 1953) before Graham **Anderson**'s version of 1989 (again in Reardon's collection). Anderson writes that 'a lively, polished translation would credit Xenophon with qualities that he does not possess'; he carries out with all modesty the task of reproducing Xenophon's monotonous and pedantic style, which has led some commentators to suppose that the text we have is no more than a summary, or a kind of 'screenplay' for extemporization.

iv. Aesop The Fables of Aesop have been extensively translated [see also I.b.3.v], with well over 70 versions listed in Foster's *English Translations from the Greek* since the version (from French) by William **Caxton** (*c.*1422–91). The English translations of Aesop occupy 16 columns in the British Library catalogue. However, care needs to be taken in distinguishing the versions. No authentic text of the original 5th-c.(?) author Aesop is extant. A collection of his fables was made in the 4th c. BCE by Demetrius of Phalerum, which was extant in the 10th c. CE but is now lost. Several later Greek prose collections of fables exist under his name. Two collections of fables in verse, made without knowledge of the prose collection but probably based on that of Demetrius of Phalerum, were composed by Babrius (Greek, 2nd c. CE) and Phaedrus (Latin, a freedman of Augustus, therefore early 1st c. CE).

Between 350 and 600 CE an otherwise unknown man called Romulus made a prose reworking in Latin of the fables of Phaedrus; this was reworked in Latin elegiacs by Walter the Englishman (*fl.* 1177), and it was this text that was usually translated under the name of Aesop in England. A compendium of all these works, entitled *Mythologia Aesopica*, was published by Isaac Nicholas Nevelet in 1610. [For translations of La Fontaine's French rewritings of Aesop, see II.g.7.]

Thus many works described as translations of Aesop turn out in fact to be translations from Latin, as for example Robert **Henryson**'s (*fl.* 1460–88) verse translation of a dozen fables into Scots (first printed 1570), or John **Ogilby**'s (1600–76) verse translation of 1651, a very expansive paraphrase. Christopher **Smart**'s (1722–71) posthumously published translation (1831) is among the first to make explicit that it is made from Phaedrus' Latin. Simon **Sturtevant**'s translation of 1602 ('for young schollers') is one of the earliest of school cribs, while William **Bullokar**'s translation from Latin of 1585 is a curiosity, being one of the first books to present a text in English according to what the author regarded as a rational system of English orthography (*Aesopz Fablz in tru Ortography with Grammar-notz*).

Caxton's Aesop is in fact closer to the Greek collections than many of his successors. It was made from a French version (1480) of a Latin collection of fables by Heinrich Steinhöwel (1476–7) which included the Life of Aesop from the Planudes recension, as well as four books of the Romulus collection, plus a number of other fables deriving directly from the Greek originals, as well as some where the source is a Latin version. Caxton's Aesop has been authoritatively edited by R. T. Lenaghan. Caxton keeps close to the French, even sometimes in syntax (e.g. 'took of the most best metes'), but also leaves out words and phrases. He adds doublets ('doubte ne drede' where the French has one verb), especially in the introductory morals of the fables.

The order of fables varies from one translation to the next, as does the amount of introductory material and reflective morals; but Sir Roger **L'Estrange**'s (1616–1704) translation from the Greek and other sources, which includes the Life of Aesop for the first time since Caxton, is an often-reprinted classic. Samuel **Croxall**'s (d. 1752) Aesop of 1722 is a similar compendium from a variety of Greek and Latin sources, more wordy than L'Estrange and with 'applications' of the fables often running to two paragraphs.

In 1848 Thomas **James** published a translation,

illustrated by Tenniel, which epitomizes both the scholarly problem, and the opportunities offered by 'Aesop' to a translator: it claims to present a free translation which reflects the styles of the various Greek and Latin authors on whom he drew. G. F. **Townsend**'s 1879 translation gives 300 fables, 'from the Greek', but sometimes omits the concluding morals. Vernon **Jones**'s translation of 1912 (with illustrations by Arthur Rackham and an introduction by G. K. Chesterton) is of the succinct school of Aesop translation, with morals in a single line. A selection of just over 200 fables, from various sources, is to be found in the Penguin by S. A. **Handford**. The 1939 edition of Aesop in Greek by A. Hausrath contains over 400 fables, but there is no complete English translation.

v. Lucian The miscellaneous nature of Lucian's satirical essays (written in the 2nd c. CE) has meant that few authors have undertaken complete translations; among the earliest are Thomas **Elyot**'s (c.1490–1546) 'Dialogue of Lucian and Diogenes of the Life Harde and Sharpe, and of the Lyfe Tendre and Delicate'; the anonymous 'Toxaris' of 1565, and a posthumously published selection of 1634 by Francis **Hickes** (1566–1631). The first complete translation is that produced in 1684 by Ferrand **Spence**, whose elaborate syntax ill reflects Lucian's snappy and ironic Greek. More readable is the version of a team of mostly minor translators assembled by Dryden, published in 1711; it is swift and graceful, and ably reflects Lucian's facetiousness. Thomas **Francklin** (1721–84), who also translated Sophocles [II.i.4], published a complete Lucian in 1780. This ponderous version deals ill with Lucian's humour: a note on the description of the Men in the Moon who make cheese out of honey and the milk in which they wash reads: 'Here Lucian is a little defi-

cient in point of memory. If they eat, as he tells us, nothing but frogs, what use could they have for cheese?'

At least 20 other complete or partial translations followed. The translation by H. W. and F. G. **Fowler** appeared in 1905 and is still a useful compendium, responsive to Lucian's style and able to make the reader laugh; but like many it is not altogether complete. The Loeb translation by A. M. **Harmon** contains all the works. 20th-c. selections include those by P. **Turner** (1961), B. P. **Reardon** (1965), and L. **Casson** (1962), all of which provide readable introductions to this author's work.

vi. Theophrastus Theophrastus' *Characters*, a collection of sketches of personality types (the miser, the superstitious man, etc), was first translated into English by John **Healey** (d. 1610) in the year of his death. Typically eloquent passages from 'The garrulous man' and 'The miser' are:

Garrulity is a slippery looseness, or a babling of a long inconsiderate speech . . . [The miser] basely parsimonious as he is, also being with his feast-companions doth exact and stand upon a farthing as strictly, as if it were a quarter's rent of his house.

A vigorous translation by several unidentified hands was published alongside an English version of the *Characters* of La Bruyère (who was heavily influenced by Theophrastus) in 1699. It also includes La Bruyère's essay on Theophrastus. A. J. **Valpy**'s lively version of 1831 was reprinted in 1992 by the Open Gate Press, accompanied by contemporary line-engravings of the associated physiognomies. In 1870 appeared a translation by the great Greek scholar R. C. **Jebb**, which aims to reproduce the Greek in plain decent English—more than a crib, less than a work of literature.   RJS

ANTHOLOGIES Reardon, B. P., ed., *Collected Ancient Greek Novels*, Berkeley, Calif., 1989.

ACHILLES TATIUS *The Most Delectable and Pleasant Historye of Clitophon and Leucippe*, tr. W. Burton, London, ?1597 [a unique copy, rep. 1923 with an introduction by S. Gaselee].

AESOP [There are sixteen columns of English translations of Aesop in the British Library catalogue. These are some of the major items] · *The Book of the Subtyl Histories and Fables of Esope . . .*, tr. William Caxton, London, 1484 [ed. R. T. Lenaghan, *Caxton's Aesop*, Cambridge, Mass., 1967] · *The Fables of Aesop Paraphras'd in Verse*, tr. John Ogilby, London, 1651 · *The Fables of Aesop*, tr. Roger L'Estrange, London, 1691–2 [often rep., e.g. Everyman, 1906] · *Fables of Aesop and Others*, tr. Samuel Croxall, London, 1722 · *The Fables of Phaedrus*, tr. Christopher Smart, London, 1765 [*Poetical Works*, vi, ed. Karina Williamson, Oxford, 1996] · *Aesop's Fables*, a new version, chiefly from original sources, tr. Thomas James, London, 1848 · *Aesop's Fables*, tr. G. F. Townsend, London, 1879 · *Aesop's Fables*, tr. V. S. Vernon Jones, London, 1912 · *Fables of Aesop*, tr. S. A. Handford, Harmondsworth, 1954 [Penguin].

CHARITON *The Loves of Chaereas and Callirhoe*, tr. anon., London, 1764 · *Chaereas and Callirhoe*, tr. Warren E. Blake, Ann Arbor, Mich., 1939 · *Chaereas and Callirhoe*, tr. B. P. Reardon, in *Collected Ancient Greek Novels* · *Chaereas and Callirhoe*, tr. G. P. Goold, Cambridge, Mass., 1995 [Loeb].

HELIODORUS *The Amorous and Tragicall Tales of Plutarch; whereunto is Annexed the Hystorie of Cariclea and Theagenes . . .*, tr. James Sanford, London, 1567 · *An Aethiopian Historie*, tr. Thomas Underdowne, London, 1569 [frequently rep., not always with acknowledgement, e.g. by William Barret, London, 1622; rev. F. A. Wright, London, 1924] · *The Faire*

Aethiopian, tr. William Lisle, London, 1631 [alternative title, 'The Famous Historie of Heliodorus, Amplified, Augmented and Delivered Paraphrasticaklly in Verse'] · *The Aethiopian History of Heliodorus*, tr. 'a person of quality' and Nahum Tate, London, 1685 · *The Adventures of Theagenes and Chariclia*, tr. anon., London, 1717 · *The Ethiopics*, tr. R. Smith, London, 1848 · *An Ethiopian Story*, tr. Walter Lamb, London, 1961 [Everyman] · *An Ethiopian Story*, tr. John Morgan, in Reardon, *Collected Ancient Greek Novels*, 1989.

LONGUS   *Daphnis and Chloe . . . Termed by the Name of the Shepheard's Holidaie*, tr. Angell Daye, London, 1587 · *Daphnis and Chloe, a most Sweet, and Pleasant Pastorall Romance for Young Ladies*, tr. G. Thornley, 1656 [rev. J. M. Edmonds, Cambridge, Mass., 1916, Loeb] · *The Pastoral Amours of Daphnis and Chloe*, tr. anon., London, 1720 · *The Pastoral Loves of Daphnis and Chloe*, tr. George Moore, London, 1924 · *Daphnis and Chloe*, tr. Jack Lindsay, London, 1948 · *Daphnis and Chloe*, tr. Moses Hadas, in *Three Greek Romances*, Indianapolis, 1953 · *Daphnis and Chloe*, tr. P. Turner, Harmondsworth, 1968 [Penguin] · *Daphnis and Chloe*, tr. Christopher Gill, in Reardon, *Collected Ancient Greek Novels*, 1989.

LUCIAN   [complete translations or collections; for individual works see the body of the text and Foster] · *Certaine Select Dialogues of Lucian*, tr. Francis Hickes, London, 1634 · *Works*, tr. Ferrand Spence, 4 vols., London, 1684 · *Workes* ('translated out of Greek by several eminent hands'), ed. John Dryden, London, 1711 · *Works of Lucian*, tr. Thomas Francklin, London, 1780 · *Works of Lucian*, tr. H. W. Fowler, and F. G. Fowler, 4 vols., Oxford, 1905 · *Works*, tr. A. M. Harmon, Cambridge, Mass., 1913–15 [Loeb] · *Satirical Sketches*, tr. P. Turner, Harmondsworth, 1961 [Penguin] · *Selected Satires*, tr. L. Casson, New York, 1962 · *Select Works*, tr. B. P. Reardon, Indianapolis, 1965.

PLUTARCH   [complete versions only; for individual lives or essays see the body of the text, and Foster's bibliography. Important items subsequent to Foster are included here in full] · *The Lives of the Noble Grecians and Romanes*, tr. Thomas North, London, 1579 [new Lives 1602, incorporated into new text 1603 with extra material; numerous reprints] · *The Philosophie, Commonly Called the Morals of Plutarch*, tr. Philemon Holland, London, 1603 · *Plutarch's Lives Translated from the Greek by Several Hands*, ed. John Dryden, London, 1683–6 [rev. Arthur Hugh Clough, 1859, many reprints] · *Plutarch's Morals, Translated by Several Hands*, London, 1684–94 · *Lives*, tr. John Langhorne and William Langhorne, London, 1770 · *Lives*, tr. Bernadotte Perrin, Cambridge, Mass., 1914–26 [Loeb] · *Moralia*, tr. F. C. Babbitt et al., Cambridge, Mass., 1927–69 [Loeb] · *Fall of the Roman Republic: Six Lives*, tr. Rex Warner, Harmondsworth, 1958 [Penguin] · *The Rise and Fall of Athens*, tr. Ian Scott-Kilvert, Harmondsworth, 1960 [Penguin] · *Makers of Rome*, tr. Ian Scott-Kilvert, Harmondsworth, 1965 [Penguin] · *The Age of Alexander*, tr. Ian Scott-Kilvert, Harmondsworth, 1973 [Penguin] · *Six Spartan Lives*, tr. R. J. A. Talbert, Harmondsworth, 1988 [Penguin] · *Moral Essays*, tr. Rex Warner, Harmondsworth, 1971 [Penguin] · *Essays*, tr. Robin Waterfield and Ian Kidd, Harmondsworth, 1992 [Penguin] · *Selected Essays and Dialogues*, tr. Donald Russell, Oxford, 1993.

THEOPHRASTUS   *Epictetus his Manuall and Cebes his Table, oute of the Greek Originall*, tr. John Healey, London, 1616 · *Characters . . . by Monsieur La Bruyere . . . with the Characters of Theophrastus*, tr. by several hands, London, 1699 [corrected edn. 1700; many subsequent reprints] · *Characters*, tr. A. Valpy, London, 1831; rep. 1992 · *The Characters of Theophrastus*, tr. R. C. Jebb, London, 1870 [new edn. by J. E. Sandys, 1909].

XENOPHON OF EPHESUS   *An Ephesian Tale*, in *Three Greek Romances*, tr. Moses Hadas, Indianapolis, 1953 · *An Ephesian Story*, tr. Graham Anderson, in Reardon, *Collected Ancient Greek Novels*, 1989.

SEE ALSO   Foster, F. M. K., *English Translations from the Greek: A Bibliographical Survey*, New York, 1918 · Wolff, S. L., *The Greek Romances in Elizabethan Prose Fiction*, New York, 1912.

12. MODERN GREEK

i. Introduction Exactly when modern Greek literature begins is a much-debated question. One approach (Beaton 1994) is to define it as literature since Independence (1821), but here what scanty reference is possible will be made to earlier periods in which the Greek language, in a form readable without difficulty by a speaker of the modern language, is used for literary purposes. In fact, some of the most vexed problems in translating from modern Greek concern the very terms in which Greek identity, long before the modern period, has been defined *vis-à-vis* the West, as a famous phrase from a poem by George Seferis shows.

In 'Neophytos the Cloisterer Speaks' (1955), Seferis has a medieval Cypriot saint speak of 'ton kaïmó tis Romiosínis'. The phrase has become almost as much a part of Greek public discourse as C. P. Cavafy's 'Waiting for the Barbarians'—but, unlike the latter, it is inward-looking and not readily translated. Coming from one of Greece's most distinguished translators (notably of *The Waste Land*), this can be no coincidence. The poem's setting and outlook confirm this: during the EOKA struggle against British rule, in which Seferis played a behind-the-scenes role, the poet adopts the persona of a saint who symbolizes Orthodox resistance to the medieval West and indignantly ends with the (only too translatable) words from *Othello*: 'You are welcome, sir, to Cyprus. Goats and monkeys!' The less translatable phrase cited earlier may by contrast be glossed as 'the sense of yearning or unfulfilment which is part of the condition of being an Orthodox Greek'. Before Independence, Greeks referred to themselves (and in certain contexts they still do), not as *Ellines* ('Hellenes') but as *Romioi* (from the word meaning 'Roman', by which the Byzantines identified themselves). *Romiosini* is a 19th-c. neologism, apparently coined by the major poet Kostis Palamas to give a name to an idea of Greece based less on the ancient heritage than on Orthodox Christendom, its medieval past and modern irredentist aspirations. Clearly, a rendering like 'Romanhood' would hardly pass muster, and the difficulty of the case (beyond the fact that Seferis' poem is rhymed) is perhaps most graphically shown by the fact that Edmund **Keeley** and Philip **Sherrard** omit the poem from their standard translation of Seferis.

If such difficulties attend the rendering of an English-influenced Nobel prize-winner, it is not surprising—even given the fact that modern Greek is rarely learnt by those not of Greek extraction— that coverage of the literature in adequate English translation in book form is patchy. In particular, the two founders of Greek poetry of the modern period, Dionysios Solomos and Andreas Kalvos, remain largely unattempted and deeply resistant to translation, while the giant among writers of fiction, Alexandros Papadiamantis, has seen the surface of his *œuvre* no more than scratched. With post-1945 and, especially, post-1960 writing, the picture is healthier (Philippides' bibliography lists translations, mainly in American periodicals). And Cavafy, Seferis, and more recently Yannis Ritsos have, through translations, had a discernible influence on the stance and tone of Anglo-American poetry since the 1940s.

ii. Before Independence The beginnings of written literature in the vernacular are marked by the poem *Digenes Akrites*, now agreed to be of the 12th c. Traditionally, since its rediscovery in 1875, referred to as an epic, this work is now agreed to be an amalgam of epic and romance elements, but there is still no consensus as to which of the two oldest manuscript versions is closer to the original. The fuller account of the story, in an archaizing and

solecistic Greek, is in the Grottaferrata version; the Escorial version, elliptical to the point that it has been held to constitute a series of loosely connected lays, is written in a form of the vernacular. The plain translations, with facing texts, of the two versions by Elizabeth **Jeffreys** and David **Ricks** allow ready comparison with works of the medieval West. The same may be said of Leontios Machairas' anti-Western 15th-c. *Chronicle* of Cyprus, whose literary qualities (visible in R. M. **Dawkins**' rendering) drew Seferis to it. Under Venetian rule, Crete saw a flowering of literature under western influence, from the late 14th c. to the fall of the island to the Ottomans in 1669, but translations are scarce, and in the case of the most celebrated work of all, Vitzentzos Kornaros's romance *Erotókritos* (early 17th c.; much reprinted and read under Ottoman rule), the only complete version, by Theodore P. **Stephanides**, can hardly be recommended.

The only Greek poetry of the Ottoman period with an abiding influence was oral folk poetry: of a very rich corpus, a selection, on modern editorial principles, sorely needs to be produced for the use of the comparative folklorist. In the meantime, the reader can obtain some idea of what so impressed Goethe in the Greek ballads by consulting G. F. **Abbott**'s rather quaint renderings. It remains a problem for any translator of later Greek poetry, however, that references to the ancient world and mythology are much more detectable, and more easily brought over into English, than the perhaps equally pervasive echoes of the folk-song tradition.

iii. Modern Literature Kostis Palamas is little read in Greece today, and his best verse is perhaps to be found in his shorter poems, but an idea of his ambition and cultural importance in *O Dodekálogos tou Yíftou* (1907, The Dodecalogue of the Gypsy) and *I Floyéra tou Vasiliá* (1910, The Emperor's Reed-Pipe) may be derived from the not unreadable fustian of Theodore P. Stephanides and George C. **Katsimbalis**. Part of the interest of these works is precisely to see how consciously Cavafy, the most influential of all modern Greek poets in Greece and abroad, reacted against them. Though E. M. Forster had written on Cavafy as early as 1919, it is with Cavafy's posthumous collected poems (1935), translated with dry and sympathetic wit by John **Mavrogordato**, that his reputation grew. The authoritative voice of Cavafy in English, however, is now the more colloquial one of Keeley and Sherrard—better suited, it is true, to the ironic historical poems than to those of passion, and tending to sacrifice the complex metrical and rhyming effects of the original. More formally ambitious, though very uneven, is Memas **Kolaitis**; while good versions of individual poems have been made by poets such as James **Merrill**, Robert **Pinsky**, and (an imitation, 'Rois Fainéants') W. H. **Auden** (it is in part the latter's preface to Rae **Dalven**'s less than adequate translation which has kept it in print).

Auden indeed spoke of 'a tone of voice' in Cavafy which survives translation. Such a tone has proved much less translatable in Cavafy's successors, with the great exception of Seferis. Translations of Angelos Sikelianos convey his vatic manner but not his warmth of language and formal ingenuity; the Nobel prize-winner Odysseus Elytis reveals in English something of his intricate imagery, and of his ambition, and the Selected Poems by various hands is a good introduction to his work; yet his etymological and formal gambits often fall flat when unsustained by the language of the ancient classics and of the Orthodox Church. Seferis' mode of high seriousness, not least because of its more familiar range of reference (Homer, Eliot) exercises a far more powerful spell over the reader of English: his collections, from his first free-verse book Mythistorema (1935) on, all preserve, in Keeley and Sherrard's painstakingly revised renderings, a voice of quiet authority. These translators can, as in the rhymed section of the long poem 'Kichli' (1947, 'Thrush'), rise to the often considerable formal challenges of Seferis' metrical poems, but they are typically too modest to do so.

Keeley's informal tone is perhaps most successful in his translations of Ritsos' shorter poems, which have brought a wide public in contact with an uneven but clearly major poet; and the complex dialogue between Ritsos' poems and those of Cavafy and Seferis is evident even in translation. Another major poet who comes over well in English is Takis Sinopoulos: the bleak power of his verse in the shadow of the civil war (1946–9) is clearest in John **Stathatos**' distinguished versions.

Modern Greek poetry's prestige has traditionally been, even at home, higher than that of prose, and space here permits only an identifying of prose landmarks: central works which have been (except where reservations are entered below) faithfully and readably translated. Outside the field of imaginative prose, but with a significant influence on Seferis and others, are the Memoirs of the Revolutionary general Yannis Makriyannis (written before 1864, pub. 1907). Georgios Vizyinos' half-dozen short stories (mostly from the 1880s) reveal great cultural and psychological complexity, and Andreas Karkavitsas' O Zitiános (1896, The Beggar) is Greek naturalism at its strongest. Alexandros Papadiamantis' rich short-story œuvre may stand with Chekhov's; Elizabeth **Constantinides**'s selection, however, is not particularly representative, and the renderings are somewhat wooden. Stratis Myrivilis' I Zoi en Táfo (1924, Life in the Tomb, substantially revised in later editions, on which Peter **Bien**'s translation is based) is a powerful testimony to World War I. Nikos Kazantzakis' many novels (some in unreliable translations from the French) have enjoyed a reputation abroad but not in Greece. Finally, three postwar novels of high ambition in contrasting modes, and which give the English-speaking reader a good idea of Greek fiction's diversity and strength, are: Kostas Tachtsis' only novel, To Tríto Stefáni (1962, The Third Wedding), covering the first half of the century, with unmatched irreverence and brio, through the eyes of two generations of middle-class women; Stratis Tsirkas' trilogy Akyvérnites Politeíes (1960–5, Drifting Cities), which views the war years in the Middle East on a large and diverse canvas inspired by Cavafy and Seferis; and Rhea Galanaki's O Víos tou Ismaíl Ferík Pasá (1989, The Life of Ismail Ferik Pasha), which, at the time of the collapse of Yugoslavia, tells with masterly narrative ambivalence the story of a (historical) Cretan who is captured by the Ottomans and eventually returns to his native island as an Egyptian general charged with the suppression of the 1866 rising. DBR

ANTHOLOGIES Abbott, G. F., Songs of Modern Greece, Cambridge, 1900 [bilingual] · Friar, Kimon, Modern Greek Poetry, New York, 1973 · Modern Poetry in Translation, 4 (1968) and 34 (1978); n.s. 13 (1998) [special issues].

CAVAFY, C. P. [K. P. KAVAFIS] Dalven, Rae, Complete Poems, New York, 1961 · Keeley, Edmund, and Sherrard, Philip, Collected Poems [rev. edn., Princeton, NJ, 1992] · Kolaitis, Memas, The Greek Poems, 2 vols., La Rochelle, NY, 1989 · Mavrogordato, John, Poems, London, 1951.

DIGENES AKRITES Jeffreys, Elizabeth, Digenis Akritis: The Grottaferrata and Escorial Versions, Cambridge, 1998 [bilingual] · Ricks, David, Byzantine Heroic Poetry, Bristol, 1990 [bilingual; Escorial version].

ELYTIS, ODYSSEUS Carson, Jeffrey, and Sarris, Nikos, Collected Poems, Baltimore, 1997 · Keeley, Edmund, et al., Selected Poems, London, 1991 · Keeley, Edmund, and Savidis, G. P., To Axion Esti, Pittsburgh, 1974 [bilingual].

GALANAKI, RHEA Cicellis, Kay, The Life of Ismail Ferik Pasha, London, 1996.

KARKAVITSAS, ANDREAS Wyatt, William F., Jr., The Beggar, New Rochelle, NY, 1982.

KAZANTZAKIS, NIKOS Bien, Peter, The Last Temptation, London, 1973 · Wildman, Carl, Christ Recrucified, London, 1992.

KORNAROS, VITZENTZOS   Stephanides, Theodore P., *Erotókritos*, London, 1985.

MAKHAIRAS, LEONTIOS   Dawkins, R. M., *Recital concerning the Sweet Land of Cyprus entitled 'Chronicle'*, 2 vols., Oxford, 1932 [bilingual].

MAKRIYANNIS, YANNIS   Lauderdale, H. A., *Makriyannis: The Memoirs of General Makriyannis*, London, 1966 [abridged].

MYRIVILIS, STRATIS   Bien, Peter, *Life in the Tomb*, London, 1977 [rev. edn., 1992].

PALAMAS, KOSTIS   Stephanides, Theodore P., and Katsimbalis, George C., *The Dodecalogue of the Gypsy*, London, 1974; Memphis, Tenn., 1975 · *The King's Flute*, Athens, 1982 [bilingual].

PAPADIAMANDIS, ALEXANDROS   Constantinides, Elizabeth, *Tales from a Greek Island*, Baltimore, 1987.

RITSOS, YANNIS   Keeley, Edmund, *Exile and Return*, London, 1989 · *Repetitions, Testimonies, Parentheses*, Princeton, NJ, 1990.

SEFERIS, GEORGE   Keeley, Edmund, and Sherrard, Philip, *Complete Poems*, Princeton, NJ, 1967 [rev. edn., Princeton, NJ, London, 1995; bilingual edn., London, 1982].

SIKELIANOS, ANGELOS   Keeley, Edmund, and Sherrard, Philip, *Selected Poems*, Princeton, NJ, 1979; rev. edn., Limni, Euboea, 1996 [bilingual].

SINOPOULOS, TAKIS   Friar, Kimon, *Landscape of Death*, Columbus, OH., 1979 [bilingual] · Stathatos, John, *Selected Poems*, London, 1981.

TAKTSIS, TAKTSIS [TACHTSIS]   Finer, Leslie, *The Third Wedding*, London, 1967 [Penguin, 1969].

TSIRKAS, STRATIS   Cicellis, Kay, *Drifting Cities*, 3 vols., New York, 1974 [1 vol., Athens, 1995].

VIZYINOS, GEORGIOS   Wyatt, William F., Jr., *My Mother's Sin and Other Stories*, Hanover, 1988.

SEE ALSO   Beaton, R., *An Introduction to Modern Greek Literature*, rev. edn., Oxford, 1999 [with guide to translations] · *Journal of Modern Greek Studies*, 8.1 (November 1990), special issue on translation · Philippides, D. M. L., *Census of Modern Greek Literature*, New Haven, Conn., 1990.

j. Hebrew and Yiddish

1. Hebrew   2. Yiddish

1. HEBREW

i. Introduction This entry is concerned with post-Biblical Hebrew literature. Until very recently this literature was written exclusively by Jews, and the enterprise of translating it was confined also, with a few notable exceptions, to Jewish circles. This enterprise has thus to be understood against the background of developments in Jewish social and cultural life in Britain and the United States.

Hebrew literature has a more or less continuous history since the Bible [II.c.1]. The discovery of the Dead Sea Scrolls dating from late Second Temple period (roughly 2nd c. BCE–1st c. CE) has illustrated vividly how creatively the language was used at that time. A little later it was adopted as the vehicle of the Rabbinic movement, which eventually became the dominant expression of Judaism until the 19th c. The main challenger to Rabbinism, the Karaite movement that first emerged in the late 8th c., also produced an important religious literature in Hebrew. During the Middle Ages the language was used not only for strictly 'religious' literature such as hymns, homilies and Biblical commentaries, but also for scientific and philosophical treatises and for popular edifying literature verging on belles-lettres. Especially in Spain and Italy there was a rich vein of secular poetry, interweaving classical Hebrew elements with influences from contemporary Arabic and Italian poetry respectively.

The 19th c. in Europe marks an important turning point. The Rabbinic movement, which had been running out of steam for some time, was experiencing a certain renewal, especially in eastern Europe, but it had also begun to be challenged by millenarian and revivalist movements. The accompanying literature tended to use traditional forms of Hebrew. At the same time, however, political

and social reforms gradually broke down the isolation of the Jewish communities and led to the adoption of other languages in everyday speech, education, general culture, and even the liturgical practice of the synagogue. These changes were at first more strongly felt in western Europe. In eastern Europe, where the political structures were slower to change, a strong secularist movement emerged that was committed to the Hebrew language. This was the Hebrew Enlightenment (*Haskalah*), and it soon gave rise to a Hebrew literature whose forms were borrowed from other European languages, including the novel, drama, and lyric and epic poetry.

The Zionist movement of national self-determination that arose at the end of the 19th c. inherited a strong element from the Haskalah, and eventually adopted Hebrew as the language of its schools and other institutions in Palestine. In the 20th c. Hebrew literature has gone from strength to strength. Meanwhile, the continuing trend to linguistic assimilation among Jews outside Israel, coupled with a widespread interest in Hebrew writing, have encouraged the development of translation, into English and many other languages. At first this activity was a spin-off from the Zionist movement, as was apparent in the type of literature translated, the often amateur character of the translations, and the limited forms of distribution. In time, however, more able translators rose to the challenge, and the overall standard is now higher. The existence of a government-funded Israel Institute for the Translation of Hebrew Literature has undoubtedly done a great deal for the propagation of Israeli Hebrew literature in translation, but it has to be said that generally speaking the quality of translations produced under its auspices is not really comparable to that of those published on the 'free market'. Few countries (if any) today of a comparable size can rival Israel in respect of the amount of its literature that is translated into foreign languages, and an impressive number of Israeli authors enjoy an international reputation.

This long continuous history, coupled with the existence of the Jews as a minority community in most countries, has important implications for the character of Hebrew literature and for its translation. Each stage of the literature has roots in what went before, but Hebrew writers also have close ties with other languages and literatures of their day. Many have been bilingual, and some have written in two or more languages. The translator has to be sensitive to these points of attachment, and has to be a discreet but insistent guide for his readers. Sometimes the connections work in the translator's favour: for example contemporary Israeli prose writing and poetry draw heavily on familiar European models. At other times they are a discouraging obstacle, as when the Hebrew texts are heavy with allusions to the Bible and Talmud, to medieval Arabic poetry or philosophy, or to spoken Yiddish.

ii. Rabbinic and Medieval Literature It was not until the late 18th c. that Jews in England felt the need to translate their religious literature. A key date indicating the first recognition of this need is the publication by Alexander Alexander of a Hebrew and English edition of the Pentateuch and *haftaroth* (prophetic lections) in London in 1785, the first time that a bilingual text was issued for Jewish use in England. It was followed a very few years later by another Hebrew–English Pentateuch, edited by David Levi. The English text of both editions is the Authorised Version, a testimony to the high regard accorded to this translation as an accurate rendering of the Hebrew paying due regard to the Jewish tradition of exegesis and commentary.

David **Levi** (1740/1742–1801) has been described as 'an intellectual giant' and 'the greatest English-born Jewish Hebrew scholar' (S. Daiches, in *Miscellanies of the Jewish Historical Society of England*, 1942). While eking out a precarious living as a hat-dresser, and with no formal education behind him, he produced a serious of scholarly works and translations of remarkable quality. His finest work as translator is found in his translations of the festival prayers of both the London Jewish denominations of his day (Sephardi and Ashkenazi). He has had many imitators and successors in this work, and today there is a bewildering number of translated liturgies, repre-

senting different liturgical rites and religious denominations, and very different approaches to the task of translation. From a translation point of view the most interesting is the 'Routledge *Mahzor*', which includes verse renderings of the hymns by such gifted translators as Nina Davis **Salaman** and the novelist Israel **Zangwill** (1864–1926). Recent prayer books have tended to tone down 'archaic' stylistic features without abandoning a certain stiff formality.

The following examples, from the opening of the well-known hymn *Adon 'Olam*, convey some idea of the evolution of Anglo-Jewish liturgical translation. They span nearly two centuries. It should be pointed out that all of these except the third, which is from a Liberal Jewish prayer-book, were printed as an aid to understanding the Hebrew rather than to be sung aloud.

> Universal Lord! who the sceptre sway'd,
> 'Ere creation's first wond'rous form was framed;
> When by his will divine, all things were made,
> Then—King! Almighty! was his name proclaimed!
>
> (David Levi)

> Lord of the world, He reigned alone
>   While yet the universe was naught.
>   When by his will all things were wrought,
> Then first his sovran Name was known.
>
> (Israel Zangwill, 'Routledge *Mahzor*')

> Eternal Lord, who reigned before
> There yet existed anything:
> When by his will the world was made,
> Already then his name was King.
>
> (John Rayner, *Gate of Repentance*, 1973)

> Eternal Lord who ruled alone
> before creation of all forms,
> when all was made at his desire
> then as the king was He revealed.
>
> (*Forms of Prayer*, 1977)

Since the rise of vernacular culture among the Jews in England was accompanied by a decline in enthusiasm for Rabbinic Judaism, which was broadly speaking the *chasse gardée* of professionals who had no need of translations, it was a very long time before even the main classics of rabbinic Hebrew culture were translated for Jewish use. The earliest translations were made by Christian scholars, sometimes for their own private use. For example, a translation of the first section of Moses Maimonides's great code of Jewish law by a Surrey curate, Ralph **Skinner**, dating from the early 1620s, is preserved in manuscript in Trinity College, Dublin. The early translators of Maimonides all seem to have been Christians. The first exception is a volume containing part of the Code, published under the name of Elias **Soloweyczik**, a Polish rabbi. A complete translation of the Code was eventually undertaken by the Yale University Press in the Yale Judaica Series, a remarkable publishing initiative which, together with a handful of other enterprises such as the Soncino Press and the Littman Library of Jewish Civilization, has enormously improved the availability of Jewish literature to English-readers.

The most important classical text of rabbinic Judaism is the Babylonian Talmud, and it is surprising how long it remained untranslated. Admittedly it is a complex and esoteric text, compiled in a mixture of Rabbinic Hebrew and Aramaic and in a strangely idiosyncratic and often technical style. Some extracts and individual tractates were published in the late 19th and early 20th c.; the first (and so far only) complete English translation is the Soncino Press translation (1935–52), by various translators under the general editorship of I. **Epstein**. This was a monumental undertaking, of a generally high scholarly and linguistic standard, which opened the Talmud up for the first time to a lay readership. The translations are lightly but helpfully annotated. In 1989 a new translation of the Talmud began to appear, with a much fuller commentary by the Israeli rabbi Adin **Steinsaltz**. This exciting initiative has the potential to introduce the Talmud to readers who lack the basic education without which the Soncino edition is not really of much use.

Soncino Press also published translations of other classic Rabbinic texts, such as the Midrash Rabba. Most of the disparate but interrelated works that together go by the name of Midrash have now been translated, although the standard of translation is very variable. The outstanding practitioner of this difficult genre is the American William **Braude**, who was adept at providing sufficient padding to make the highly elliptical and elusive rabbinic style accessible to modern readers.

The Christian contribution to rabbinics, which has already been mentioned, has persisted. The standard English translation of the Mishnah, one of the foundation documents of Rabbinic Judaism, is by Herbert **Danby**, who was a canon of the Anglican cathedral in Jerusalem. Other translations of Rabbinic works, such as those by Charles **Taylor**, R. Travers **Herford**, W. O. E. **Oesterley**, R. G. **Finch**, and G. H. **Box**, have stood the test of time less well, although they were useful in their day. Christian scholars are still involved in the translation of Rabbinic texts today, most notably in the new translation of the Aramaic Bible translation (the Targum [II.c.1.ii]), begun in the late 1980s and

still in progress. It is, however, impossible to give a comprehensive account of translations of this literature in such a small compass.

A special word is due about translations of medieval Hebrew poetry. The great Hebrew poets of Spain, such as Samuel ha-Nagid, Solomon Ibn Gabirol, Judah ha-Levi, and Moses Ibn Ezra, present an irresistible challenge to would-be translators, and have attracted flocks of them, some of whom have been strikingly successful in very different ways. The poems have strict metres and rhyme schemes, and the subject-matter and its treatment are both highly conventional. The language is artificial and far removed from everyday life (Hebrew was not even spoken when the poems were written), and the social and religious background are alien. In other words, they raise the same kind of issues for a translator as classical Greek and Latin poetry. The most ambitious and accomplished recent translations are those by Raphael **Loewe**, who follows very specific English models in the metaphysical poetry of the 17th c. In drawing on the resources of formal English poetry Loewe is following in the footsteps of earlier translators such as Alice (Mrs Henry) **Lucas**, Nina Davis Salaman, and Israel Zangwill. They are distinguished by their strongly philosophical flavour and their complexity of syntax and thought. At the other extreme, David **Goldstein** adopted a simple and direct modern style, avoiding formal elements like metre and rhyme and bringing the imagery of the originals to the fore. Both approaches are loyal to key features of the Hebrew poems; neither attempts to emulate the directness and liveliness of some of the recent translations of the Greek and Latin classics.

The following illustrations of these two approaches are taken from the exordium of a poem by Samuel ha-Nagid celebrating the raising of the siege of Lorca in 1042:

Send a carrier-pigeon, although she cannot speak,
With a tiny letter attached to her wings,
Sweetened with saffron-water, perfumed with
    frankincense.
And when she rises to fly away, send with her another,
So that, should she meet an eagle, or fall into a snare,
Or fail to make haste, the second will speed away.
And when she comes to Joseph's house, she will coo on
    the roof-top.
When she flies down to his hand, he will rejoice in her, as
    with a song-bird . . .

(David Goldstein)

A pigeon-herald send: though not a word
She speaks, tied to her wings shall be enscrolled
A minute message in rare perfume rolled,
And while she soars, send forth another bird

Lest she fall prey to hawk, or nets enfold;
Or, should she lag, her mate shall speed her wing
To Joseph's house, and o'er the housetops sing,
Till on his hand she lights, for him to hold
Like some pet songster, smiling, fondling . . .

(Raphael Loewe)

iii. Modern Literature It is hard to determine the moment of birth of modern Hebrew literature. The translation of the satirical work *Megalleh Temirin* (1819, Revealer of Secrets) by Joseph Perl (1773–1839) is subtitled 'the first Hebrew novel', but most critics would apply that description rather to *Ahavat Zion* (1853, Love of Zion), by Abraham Mapu, a historical romance set in the Biblical period. Hardly anything has been translated of the 19th-c. literature, which was produced mainly in Russia. Among the exceptions is Mendele Mokher Seforim (pseudonym of S. Y. Abramovitsh), a remarkable creative genius in both Hebrew and Yiddish, whose stories of Jewish life in the east European *shtetl* vividly conjure up a lost world have been often translated, mostly from the Yiddish.

Early in the 20th c., with the migration of Jewish intellectuals steeped in Hebrew culture from Russia and the adoption of Hebrew as the language of instruction in Zionist schools, a modern Hebrew literature began to take root in Palestine. Among the important figures of this period are Micha Yosef Berdyczewski, Uri Nissan Gnessin, who pioneered stream-of-consciousness techniques in Hebrew, and Josef Hayyim Brenner, a writer strongly influenced by Turgenev and Dostoevsky, who struggled to portray realistically the tormented psyche of the 'uprooted' young Zionist immigrants. Their self-conscious and inventive prose is not easy to translate, particularly now, at a remove of several generations, when both style and subject-matter seem very dated. Some of their stories are translated in the recent anthologies edited by A. Lelchuk and G. Abramson.

From the 1920s Palestine became established as the world centre of Hebrew literature. The towering figure among the prose writers of the period of the British Mandate (1920–48) was S. Y. Agnon, whose achievement was recognised with the joint award of the Nobel Prize for Literature in 1966, and with the translation of his writings into English and other languages. The outstanding English translator of Agnon and his contemporaries was I. M. **Lask**, by far the most prolific translator of Hebrew prose in his day. Lask's fluent but rather flat translations, which provided a whole generation of English readers with its idea of Palestinian Hebrew literature, concealed the stylistic richness

and subtlety of that literature. It must be said in mitigation that Agnon is one of the hardest of authors to translate, drawing as he does on a wide range of earlier, untranslated, and probably untranslatable literature in Hebrew and on the nuances of Yiddish speech. Since 1966 several other translators have tried their hand at Agnon, but he has not yet found a mediator worthy of him.

The last years of the British Mandate saw the rise of a new generation of Hebrew writers, deeply committed to and involved in the struggle for national independence. These writers, unlike their predecessors, were either born in Palestine or at any rate educated from childhood in the Hebrew language. Leading writers of this generation are S. Yizhar, Benjamin Tammuz, Aharon Megged, and Moshe Shamir. Such translations as were made of their stories and novels were drab efforts produced by enthusiasts with more interest in their political message than their literary qualities. An exception is the translation of Shamir's historical novel *Melekh Basar Vadam* (1954, King of Flesh and Blood), by David **Patterson**, a sensitive translator who lectured in Hebrew at Oxford; he subsequently also translated a novel by Brenner.

The generation of writers born in the 1930s, dominated by A. B. Yehoshua and Amos Oz, benefited from the awakening of an interest in Israeli writers among British and American publishers, stimulated only in part by the award of the the Nobel Prize to Agnon. This development led to an improvement in the level of translation, as well as making Hebrew writing accessible to a much larger public. Other writers of this and the following generation whose work has been published outside Israel include Yoram Kaniuk, Aharon Appelfeld, Yaakov Shabtai, the Arab writer Anton Shammas, and David Grossman. Gradually in recent years more women authors have begun to be translated, reflecting the quality and quantity of women's writing in Israel.

The same improvement has affected anthologies, particularly important because of the popularity of the short story and novella in Hebrew writing, and because a wider range of authors can be represented in them. Recent anthologies have begun to explore a wider canon of writers than that represented in earlier collections, including those who wrote in the early part of the century and those from a background in the Muslim world, who have generally been neglected previously in favour of writers with a European background (see particularly in this respect A. Alcalay, ed., *Keys to the Garden*). The influence of the state-sponsored translation institute is still strongly felt, however, not only in the choice of authors translated but particularly in the prominence of a small number of Israel-based translators, who tend to be out of touch with the nuances of the fast-changing English language and to impose a homogeneous character on the widely differing prose they translate. Two significant areas of contemporary Israeli literature that, despite all this energetic activity, have not yet fulfilled their potential in translation are drama and children's writing.

Poetry has been a rich seam in modern Hebrew literature, and a good deal of the 20th-c. poetry is available in translation, both in anthologies and in books of poems by individual poets. The abundant 19th-c. poetry, on the other hand, has fallen from favour and is hardly available at all in English. Although much of it is of doubtful worth, there are some poems that deserve to be rescued from obscurity.

The first outstanding modern Hebrew poet, by universal acclaim, is Hayyim Nahman Bialik, who left an indelible mark on Hebrew language and literature. Many of his shorter and a few of his longer poems have been translated, some several times over; but with few exceptions the translations do not do justice to the inventiveness of his language or to the complexities of his personality, although they do convey some impression of his nationalistic fervour and moral weight, which earned him the role of 'national poet' of the Zionist movement. Yet his personal poems are among his most touching and memorable. This excerpt from 'After My Death' is translated by Arthur C. **Jacobs**, who was a very sensitive translator from Hebrew:

> After I am dead
> Say this at my funeral:
> There was a man who exists no more.
>
> That man died before his time
> And his life's song was broken off halfway.
> O, he had one more poem
> And that poem has been lost
> For ever.

Bialik's contemporary Saul Tschernichovski, a more colourful and in many ways more exciting figure, is even less well served by his translators, although a small selection of his poems is in most anthologies.

The leading poets of the Mandate period in Palestine were Abraham Shlonsky, Natan Alterman, and Lea Goldberg. Goldberg's attractive and touching lyrics have been sensitively translated by Robert **Friend**, himself an English-language poet. Shlonsky and Alterman have been less fortunate in their translators, and their verse, tied as it often is to

a specific political and social situation, has not stood the test of time very well. The poets of this period, like their predecessors, seem to stand with one foot in Russia and Poland and the other in the Hebrew tradition going back to the Bible. The resulting synthesis can seem alien to English readers, particularly when yoked to rather earnest nationalist and socialist ideals. A notable exception is Uri Zvi Greenberg, a poet of more enduring stature, particularly in his laments for the victims of the Nazi genocide, a theme of much postwar Hebrew poetry but one which comes across with particular power in Greenberg's prophetic, Aeschylean style. Translations of Greenberg's poems can be found scattered in journals and anthologies, but his stature as one of the outstanding Hebrew writers of the present century has yet to be recognized with the publication of his collected poems in English. His poem 'With My God the Blacksmith', translated here by Dom **Moraes**, is analysed in the remarkable book *The Hebrew Poem Itself*, by Stanley Burnshaw, Ezra Spicehandler, and T. Carmi, in which Hebrew poems are made accessible to English readers not through translation but through analysis and explication:

> In all revelations my days flare like chapters of prophecy.
> Mass of metal, my flesh between them awaits the fire.
> Above looms my God the blacksmith, hammering
>   terribly.
> Each wound carved in me by Time splits into a fissure,
> Sparking out inward fire in flashes of memory.
>
> My fate controls me, till day has sunk in the west.
> When this battered mass, thrown back on the bed, lies
>   still,
> With a gaping wound for a mouth, which none has
>   dressed,
> Naked I say to my God: Thou hast wrought Thy will.
> Now it is night: of Thy goodness, let us rest.

Among the poets of the succeeding generation are several who are highly esteemed in Israel yet for one reason or another have not come across well in English. Others have made the transition with great success, particularly those who are closest to the English poetic tradition and furthest from the somewhat parochial political concerns of the Zionist milieu, such as Yehuda Amichai, T. Carmi, Dan Pagis, and Natan Zach. Amichai, though born in Germany, acknowledges a debt to Dylan Thomas, Auden, and Eliot. He is the most translated contemporary Israeli poet and the one who as a frequent visitor is best known in English-speaking countries. The volume of his collected poetry translated by Benjamin and Barbara **Harshav** is a considerable achievement. This short poem,

399

entitled 'Lament', is translated by the English poet Ted **Hughes**:

> Mr Beringer, whose son
> fell by the Canal, which
> was dug by strangers
> for ships to pass through the desert,
> is passing me at the Jaffa Gate:
>
> He has become very thin; has lost
> his son's weight.
> Therefore he is floating lightly
> through the alleys
> getting entangled in my heart
> like driftwood.

Carmi grew up in a Hebrew-speaking family in the United States, and spoke English as well as he spoke Hebrew, though he insisted he could not translate his own poetry. He had a very strong knowledge of and empathy with the Hebrew poetic tradition, stretching back to the Bible, and he spent several years editing a definitive anthology of it, accompanied by his own 'prose' translations. He had earlier cooperated with Ezra Spicehandler and Stanley Burnshaw on the interesting experiment (*The Hebrew Poem Itself*) of presenting Hebrew poems, in the original, for readers ignorant of the language.

Dan Pagis was born in the Bukovina, and went to Palestine at the age of 17. A survivor of the Nazi camps, he was particularly preoccupied with the theme of the Holocaust. Natan Zach, although born in the same year as Pagis, grew up in the Hebrew-speaking environment in Palestine, and his writing displays traces of the early familiarity with Hebrew speech patterns which is lacking in the poets who immigrated later in life. To an even greater extent than the poets just mentioned, Zach's writing marks a clear break with the ideological impulse, the literary allusiveness, and the eastern European influences that distinguish much earlier poetry, and is closer to the English milieu, which is one reason why it comes across well in translation.

During the past 20 years, while translation of Hebrew prose has flourished, translation of poetry appears to have receded. There have been few poetic anthologies to match the many anthologies of prose, and indeed an older practice of combining poetry and prose in a single anthology has declined. Recent volumes of individual poets have tended to be retrospectives of established poets.   NdeL

GENERAL ANTHOLOGIES   Carmi, T., ed., *The Penguin Book of Hebrew Verse*, Harmondsworth, 1981.

RABBINIC AND MEDIEVAL LITERATURE   Braude, William G., *The Book of Legends (Sefer ha-Aggadah): Legends from the Talmud and Midrash*, ed. H. N. Bialik and Y. H. Ravnitzky, New York, 1992 · *Forms of Prayer for Jewish Worship*, ed. the Assembly of Rabbis of the Reformed Synagogue of Great Britain, London, 1977– · *Gate of Repentance: Services for the High Holydays*, London, 1938 · Montefiore, C. G., and Loewe, H., *A Rabbinic Anthology*, London, 1938 · *Service of the Synagogue: A New Edition of the Festival Prayers with an English Translation in Prose and Verse*, London, 1906– · Singer, S., 'Early Translations and Translators of the Jewish Liturgy in England', *Transactions of the Jewish Historical Society of England*, 3, 59–71.

MISHNAH AND TALMUD   Danby, Herbert, *The Mishnah, Translated from the Hebrew*, Oxford, 1933 · Epstein, I., ed., *The Babylonian Talmud*, 35 vols., London, 1935–52 · *The Talmud: The Steinsaltz Edition*, New York, 1989– .

MIDRASH   Braude, William G., *Pesikta Rabbati: Discourses for Feasts, Fasts and Special Sabbaths*, New Haven, Conn./London, 1968 · Braude, William G., and Kapstein, Israel, *Pesikta de-Rab Kahana: R. Kahana's Compilation of Discourses for Sabbaths and Festal Days*, Philadelphia/London, 1975 · Braude, William G., and Kapstein, Israel, *Tanna debe Eliyyahu: The Lore of the School of Elijah*, Philadelphia, 1981 · Freedman, H., and Simon, M., eds., *Midrash Rabba*, 10 vols., London, 1939.

MEDIEVAL POETRY   Cole, Peter, *Selected Poems of Shmuel HaNagid*, Princeton, NJ, 1996 · Goldstein, David, *Hebrew Poems from Spain*, London, 1965 [reissued as *The Jewish Poets of Spain, 900–1250*, Harmondsworth, 1971 [Penguin] · Loewe, Raphael, *The Rylands Haggadah*, London, 1988 · *Ibn Gabirol*, London, 1989 · Lucas, Mrs Henry, *Songs of Zion by Hebrew Singers*, London, 1894 · Salaman, Nina, *Selected Poems of Jehuda Halevi*, Philadelphia, 1928 · Scheindlin, Raymond P., *Wine, Women, and Death: Medieval Hebrew Poems on the Good Life*, Philadelphia, 1986 · *The Gazelle: Medieval Hebrew Poems on God, Israel, and the Soul*, Philadelphia, 1991.

MODERN PROSE: ANTHOLOGIES   Abramson, Glenda, ed., *The Oxford Book of Hebrew Short Stories*, Oxford, 1996 · Alcalay, Ammiel, ed., *Keys to the Garden*, San Francisco, 1996 · Domb, Risa, ed., *New Women's Writing from Israel*, London, 1996 · Joseph, Herbert, S., ed., *Modern Israeli Drama; An Anthology*, Madison, Wis./London, 1983 · Lelchuk, A., ed., *Eight Great Hebrew Short Novels*, New York, 1983 · Michener, James A., ed., *Firstfruits: A Harvest of 25 Years of Israeli Writing*, Philadelphia, 1973 · Penueli, S. Y., and Ukhmani, A., eds., *Hebrew Short Stories: An Anthology*, 2 vols., Tel Aviv, 1965 · Ramras-Rauch, Gila, and Michman-Melkman, Joseph, eds., *Facing the Holocaust: Selected Israeli Fiction*, Philadelphia, 1985.

AGNON, S. Y.   Halkin, Hillel, *A Simple Story*, New York, 1985 · Lask, I. M., *The Bridal Canopy*, Garden City, NY, 1937 · Mintz, Alan, and Hoffman, Anne Golomb, *A Book That Was Lost and Other Stories*, New York, 1995 · Shapiro, Zeva, *Shira*, New York, 1989.

APPELFELD, AHARON Bilu, Dalya, *Badenheim 1939*, Boston/London, 1980 · Green, Jeffrey M., *The Immortal Bartfuss*, New York, 1988, London, 1995.

BERDYCZEWSKI, M. J. Super, A. S., *Miriam*, Tel Aviv, 1983.

BRENNER, Y. H. Halkin, Hillel, *Breakdown and Bereavement*, London, 1971 · Patterson, David, *Out of the Depths*, Boulder, Colo., 1992.

GROSSMAN, DAVID Rosenberg, Betsy, *See Under: Love*, London, 1991 · *The Book of Intimate Grammar*, London, 1994 · *The Zigzag Kid*, London, 1997.

HAZAZ, HAIM Halpern, Ben, *Mori Sa'id*, New York, 1956, London, 1957 · Levi, G., *Gates of Bronze*, Philadelphia, 1975.

KANIUK, YORAM Schachter, Joseph, *Himmo, King of Jerusalem*, New York/London, 1969 · Shapiro, Zeva, *The Acrophile*, New York, 1961 · *The Story of Aunt Shlomzion the Great*, New York, 1978 · Simckes, Seymour, *Adam Resurrected*, New York, 1971.

KENAZ, JOSHUA Bilu, Dalya, *After the Holidays*, San Diego, Calif., London, 1987 · *The Way to the Cats*, South Royalton, Vt., 1994 · Rosenberg, Betsy, *Musical Moment and Other Stories*, South Royalton, Vt., 1995.

MEGGED, AHARON Hodes, Aubrey, *Fortunes of a Fool*, London, 1962 · Louvish, Misha, *The Living on the Dead*, London, 1970 · Whitehill, Robert, and Lilly, Susan C., *Asahel*, New York, 1982.

MENDELE MOKHER SEFORIM Spiegel, M., *The Travels and Adventures of Benjamin the Third*, New York, 1968.

OZ, AMOS de Lange, Nicholas, *My Michael*, London/New York, 1972 · *Black Box*, New York/London, 1988 · *Fima*, New York/London, 1993 · *Don't Call it Night*, London, 1995, New York, 1996 · *Panther in the Basement*, London/New York, 1997.

PERL, JOSEPH Taylor, Dov, *Revealer of Secrets*, Boulder, Colo./Oxford, 1997.

SHABTAI, YAAKOV Bilu, Dalya, *Past Continuous*, Philadelphia, 1983 · *Past Perfect*, New York, 1987.

SHAMIR, MOSHE Kirson, R., *My Life with Ishmael*, London, 1970 · Patterson, David, *King of Flesh and Blood*, London, 1958 · Schachter, Joseph, *With his Own Hands*, Jerusalem, 1970.

SHAMMAS, ANTON Eden, Vivian, *Arabesques*, London, 1988.

SOBOL, JOSHUA Lan, David, *Ghetto*, with lyrics tr. and music arr. Jeremy Sams, London, 1989 · Rosenberg, Betsy, and Schlesinger, Miriam, *The Soul of a Jew: Otto Weininger's Last Night*, Tel Aviv, 1983.

TAMMUZ, BENJAMIN Budny, Mildred, and Safran, Yehuda, *Requiem for Na'aman*, New York, 1982 · Flantz, Richard, *The Orchard*, Providence, RI, 1984 · Parfitt, Y., and Budny, M., *Minotaur*, London, 1983 · Shachter, Joseph, *A Rare Cure*, Tel Aviv, 1981.

YEHOSHUA, A. B. Arad, Miriam, *Three Days and a Child*, New York/London, 1970 · Halkin, Hillel, *Mr. Mani*, New York/London, 1993 · Simpson, Philip, *The Lover*, New York, 1977, London, 1978.

YIZHAR, S. Louvish, Misha, *Midnight Convoy and Other Stories*, Jerusalem, 1969.

MODERN POETRY: ANTHOLOGIES Burnshaw, S., Carmi, T., and Spicehandler, E., eds., *The Modern Hebrew Poem Itself*, New York, 1966 · Dor, Moshe, and Zach, Natan, eds., *The Burning Bush, Poems from Modern Israel*, London, 1977 · Penueli, S. Y., and Ukhmani, A., eds., *Anthology of Modern Hebrew Poetry*, 2 vols., Jerusalem, 1966.

AMICHAI, YEHUDA Bloch, Chana, and Mitchell, Stephen, *The Selected Poetry of Yehuda Amichai*, Toronto, 1986 [expanded edn., Berkeley, Calif./London, 1996] · Harshav, Benjamin, and Harshav, Barbara, *Yehuda Amichai, a Life of Poetry, 1948–1994*, New York, 1994 · Hughes, Ted, *Amen*, London, 1978 · Lapon-Kandelshein, Essi, ed., *To Commemorate the 70th Birthday of Yehuda Amichai: a Bibliography of his Work in Translation*, Ramat Gan, Israel, 1994.

BIALIK, HAYYIM NAHMAN Efros, Israel, *Selected Poems*, New York, 1948 · Samuel, Maurice, *Selected Poems*, New York, 1926 · Snowman, L. V., *Poems from the Hebrew*, London, 1924.

CARMI, T. Mitchell, Stephen, *Selected Poems by T. Carmi and Dan Pagis*, London, 1976 · Moraes, Dom, and Carmi, T., *The Brass Serpent*, London/Athens, OH, 1964 · Schulman, Grace, *At the Stone of Losses*, Philadelphia, 1983.

GOLDBERG, LEAH Friend, Robert, *Selected Poems*, London, 1976.

PAGIS, DAN Mitchell, Stephen, *Poems*, London, 1972 · *Points of Departure*, Philadelphia, 1981.

TSCHERNICHOVSKI, SAUL Silbershlag, Eisig, *Saul Tchernichowsky, Poet of Revolt*, Bristol, 1968 · Snowman, L. V., *Tschernichovski and His Poetry*, London, 1929.

ZACH, NATAN Everwine, Peter, and Yasny-Starkman, Shulamit, *The Static Element*, New York, 1982 · Silkin, Jon, *Against Parting*, Newcastle upon Tyne, 1967.

SEE ALSO Goell, Y., *Bibliography of Modern Hebrew Literature in English Translation*, Jerusalem/New York, 1968 · Goldberg, I., *Bibliography of Modern Hebrew Literature in Translation*, Tel Aviv, 1979– .

2. YIDDISH

i. Selection Modern Yiddish literature originated in the early 19th c. and was, to a large extent, shaped by the multilingual and multicultural context that characterized central and eastern European Jewish civilization. This is reflected in the Yiddish language, which consists of old German dialects fused with elements from Hebrew / Aramaic and Slavic languages (Polish, Russian, and Ukrainian).

Dina Abramowitz (1967) noted that while in the half-century before 1945 some 80 English translations appeared in book form, the number of items for 1945–67 exceeded 200. The increasing number of English translations of Yiddish literature in the post-Holocaust period clearly indicates a growing interest in Yiddish culture among English readers. Abramovitz's bibliography consists of 217 entries of published Yiddish books in English translation and includes fiction, drama, memoirs, folklore, and essays. The translations show a much more comprehensive coverage of the three classic Yiddish writers than was previously the case. Sholem Aleichem is represented with 18 items, Y. L. Peretz with 13, and Mendele Moykher Sforim (Pseudonym of Sholem Y. Abramovitsh) with 4.

The establishment of an academic base for Yiddish studies at both Columbia and the Hebrew Universities in the early 1950s resulted in a scholarly approach to English translations of Yiddish literature. Increasingly, a new generation of scholars trained in the academic field of Yiddish participated in the editing, translating, and anthologizing of Yiddish literature. Most importantly, a handful of comprehensive anthologies of Yiddish prose and poetry in English translation, including scholarly introductions, has made a broad sample of Yiddish literature available to a general readership lacking knowledge of the language.

The first anthology was Helena **Frank**'s *Yiddish Tales*, published in 1912 and reprinted in 1975 as *The Modern Jewish Experience*. It was only the third work of Yiddish literature to be translated into English. Frank's primary motive was to present stories that 'have each its special note, its special echo from that strangely fascinating world so often quoted, so little understood . . . the Russian Ghetto.'

Frank's anthology became a model for Irving **Howe** and Eliezer **Greenberg**'s anthology *A Treasury of Yiddish Stories* (1954). What distinguished this anthology from Frank's *Yiddish Tales* was its ideological bias based on the view of the Jewish *shtetl* (small town) as the quintessential locus of Jewish virtues in 'the old world'. Howe and Greenberg

sought to resurrect 'a world that is no more', the title of I. J. Singer's Yiddish childhood memoir of 1946, by emphasizing what they considered the superior moral and spiritual values reflected in Yiddish literature. With all its shortcomings—that it created a *shtetl* image of Yiddish literature and excluded stories which did not fit into a social realist mould—this anthology succeeded in introducing a host of new Yiddish writers in English translation.

The most recent anthologies of Yiddish prose, *Yenne Velt: The Great Works of Jewish Phantasy and Occult* (1976) and *The Shtetl* (1979), both compiled and translated by Joachim **Neugroschel**, mark an important departure from the previous two anthologies by including pre-classic writers and a wider range of modern genres and styles.

Both *American Yiddish Poetry: A Bilingual Anthology* (1986), edited by Benjamin and Barbara **Harshav**, and *The Penguin Book of Modern Yiddish Verse* (1987), edited by Irving Howe, Ruth R. Wisse, and Khone Shmeruk, present the Yiddish text alongside literary rather than literal translations. In fact, these two anthologies represent the first comprehensive poetry anthologies in Yiddish since M. Bassin's two-volume *Finf hundert yor yidishe poezye* (1917, Five Hundred Years of Yiddish Poetry).

These two anthologies complement each other by emphasizing different aspects of modern Yiddish poetry. The *Penguin Anthology* focuses on Yiddish poetry as a mirror of a lost world by attempting to represent the most typically Jewish aspects of the Yiddish literary tradition. *American Yiddish Poetry*, on the other hand, highlights one branch of Yiddish poetry, the specifically modernist tradition as it developed in the USA from the 1910s to the 1970s. The focus is on the poet's individuality and aesthetic development as well as universal rather than specifically Jewish issues.

The bilingual format has also recently been employed in English translation of individual Yiddish poets, such as *Selected Poems of Yankev Glatshteyn*, translated by Richard J. **Fein**, and *The Fiddle Rose: Poems 1970–1972* by Abraham Sutzkever, translated by Ruth **Whitman**. Typically, this bilingual trend has been initiated by translators who often are poets in their own right. Simultaneously, in the USA the growing number of college courses on Yiddish subjects has increased the demand for more accurate text-oriented, scholarly editions of Yiddish literature. Recently, Yiddish women writers have been anthologized in *Found Treasures: Stories*

By *Yiddish Writers* and presented in bilingual editions of the works of Kadya Molodovsky, Malka Heifets-Tussman, and Rachel Korn.

ii. Translation In his book *A Bridge of Longing: The Lost Art of Yiddish Storytelling*, David G. Roskies offers interesting examples of how Isaac Bashevis Singer's stories steeped in traditional *yidishkeyt* (Jewishness) and utilizing the richness of Yiddish idioms, are stripped of their associative complexity in English translation. Pejorative references to Christianity are erased in the English translation of the story 'Zeidlus the Pope', in which the so-called *lehavdl loshn* (a language of distinction) is used to depict the *goyim* (Gentiles) in traditional negative stereotypes. By toning down this anti-Christian aspect of Singer's demonological narrators the translators lose their *raison d'être* as symbols of a traditional Jewish universe of good and evil.

Singer's rise to fame in America after the Holocaust was inaugurated by Saul **Bellow**'s excellent translation of the short story 'Gimpel tam' (Gimpel the Fool) into English in 1953. Singer originally serialized his Yiddish works in the *Forverts* (The Jewish Daily Forward) and later published these works in adapted English translations. Some of his work was published simultaneously in alternate versions in Yiddish and English, e.g. *Mayn tatns bezdn shtub* (1956) and *In My Father's Court* (1962). Increasingly Singer relied on a growing number of translators who enabled him to reach an international audience. Singer's work in other languages has with a few exceptions always been translated from the English version. However, English translations of Singer's work must be viewed as a 'second original', rather than as a faithful rendering of the original Yiddish text into English.

The multiple language components of Yiddish—that it draws from both Hebraic/Aramaic sources and from the coterritorial Germanic and Slavic languages—pose great challenges to the translator. Most English translation from the Yiddish is accompanied by a list of words of Hebrew and Yiddish origins with English explanations.

In addition to these culturally specific problems in translating from the Yiddish, two general approaches have resulted in very different types of translation. On the one hand there is the attempt to anglicize and smooth over the Yiddish original in a version which does not 'grind painfully on the English reader's ear', as Golda **Werman** puts it in her introduction to her translation of the stories of David Bergelson. On the other hand, there is the more literal translation of every turn and phrase in the original.

Even more important in translating Yiddish literature are specific issues of style and colloquiality. Modern Yiddish prose originated with S. Y. Abramovitsh's novels from the 1860s; they created an entirely new literary idiom out of spoken Yiddish. From its origin Yiddish literature excelled in its colloquial, down-to-earth qualities as a medium of parody, satire, and the carnivalesque. These inaugurated a radically new, multi-voiced literary style in Jewish literature.

To render the often highly crafted, multi-layered Yiddish literary speech patterns in English translation poses great challenges to the translator. In a recent translation of two novels by S. Y Abramovitsh, *Tales of Mendele the Book Peddler*, Ted **Gorelick** rendered *Fishke the Lame* 'by echoing the dialects found in English novels of the eighteenth and nineteenth centuries by such authors as Laurence Sterne and Charles Dickens, whose work influenced Abramovitsh'. This makes for a highly readable English text; however, it also creates a distance from the culturally specific Jewish sources to which the texts refers and with which it plays. In order to emulate more faithfully the oral quality of the Yiddish classics, Hillel **Halkin** fused modern and archaic style (including references to Jewish tradition in transliterated Hebrew) in his translation of Sholem Aleichem's *Tevye the Dairyman and the Railroad Stories*.

These problems of literary style are further exacerbated in the case of Yiddish poetry. In the introduction to his anthology of modern Yiddish poetry, Harshav sums up the two 'almost insurmountable difficulties' in translating Yiddish poetry:

1) the poetic value derived in Yiddish poetry from the play with synonymous alternatives and clashes between words from its component languages, since Yiddish still has a high degree of component-consciousness . . . and 2) the profusion of allusions, hints, and stylistic ironies relating to the codified worlds of its Hebrew heritage, Yiddish folklore, and Slavic realities—a background largely unfamiliar to English-speaking readers.

iii. Conclusion The Fund for the Translation of Jewish Literature established by the late Jewish historian Lucy Davidowicz has sponsored the above-mentioned English translations of Sholem Aleichem and Mendele Moykher Sforim in the series The Library of Yiddish Classics, as well as *The I. L. Peretz Reader* and An-Sky's *The Dybbuk and Other Writings*. These translations are accompanied by introductions and notes by leading scholars in the field. A continuation of this series, with translations of Yiddish writers Yankev Glatshteyn, Y. Y. Trunk,

Itsik Manger, and Sholem Aleichem, is currently being prepared by Yale University Press.

Except for *Three Great Jewish Plays* edited and translated by Joseph C. **Landis**, published in 1966, the rich Yiddish dramatic tradition has been virtually neglected in English translation. A planned volume of five Yiddish plays is currently being prepared for publication by Syracuse University Press edited by Nahma Sandrow.

The most urgent task for the translator of Yiddish literature today is to maintain some sense of cultural transmission and continuity. Irving Howe's 1974 proposal to establish 'a corps of experts who would maintain the tradition, who would have a sense of cultural aura and of cultural associations' seems to have a least partly been implemented as a result of the academization of Yiddish studies. However, this development has been accompanied by a loss of Yiddish literature's link to a vital Jewish cultural context and mass audience. English translations of Yiddish literature offer a very modest compensation for the rapid decline of Yiddish culture in the last two generations as a result of Jewish assimilation; the destruction of the central and eastern European Yiddish centres during World War II and in the Soviet Union in the early 1950s; and the nearly complete rejection of Yiddish in the State of Israel.   JS

ANTHOLOGIES   Forman, Frieda Raicus, Silberstein, Ethel, Swartz, Sarah, and Wolf, Margie, *Found Treasures: Stories by Yiddish Women Writers*, Toronto, 1994 · Frank, Helen, *Yiddish Tales*, Philadelphia, 1912 · Harshav, Benjamin, and Harshav, Barbara, *American Yiddish Poetry: A Bilingual Anthology*, Berkeley, Calif., 1986 · Howe, Irving, and Greenberg, Eliezer, *A Treasury of Yiddish Stories*, New York, 1954 · Howe, Irving, Wisse, Ruth R., and Shmeruk, Khone, eds., *The Penguin Book of Modern Yiddish Verse*, New York, 1987 · Landis, Joseph C., *Three Great Jewish Plays*, New York, 1966 · Neugroschel, Joachim, *Yenne Velt: The Great Works of Jewish Phantasy and Occult*, New York, 1976 · *The Shtetl*, New York, 1979.

ABRAMOVITSH, SHOLEM Y.   Gorelick, Ted, and Halkin, Hillel, *Tales of Mendele the Book Peddler*, New York, 1996.

ALEICHEM, SHOLEM   Halkin, Hillel, *Tevye the Dairyman and the Railroad Stories*, New York, 1987.

AN-SKY, S.   Werman, Golda, *The Dybbuk and Other Writings*, New York, 1992.

BERGELSON, DAVID   Werman, Golda, *The Stories of David Bergelson: Yiddish Short Fiction from Russia*, Syracuse, NY, 1996.

PERETZ, I. L.   Wisse, Ruth R., ed., *The I. L. Peretz Reader*, New York, 1990.

SINGER, ISAAC BASHEVIS   Blocker, Joel, and Pollet, Elizabeth, *The Penguin Collected Short Stories of Isaac Bashevis Singer*, New York/Harmondsworth, 1981 · Kleinerman-Goldstein, Channah, Gottlieb, Elaine, and Singer, Joseph, *In My Father's Court*, Philadelphia, 1966.

SINGER, I. J.   Singer, Joseph, *From a World That Is No More*, New York, 1946.

SUTSKEVER, ABRAHAM   Whitman, Ruth, *The Fiddle Rose: Poems 1970–1972*, Berkeley, Calif., 1990.

SEE ALSO   Abramovitz, D., *Yiddish Literature in English Translation; Books Published 1945–1967*, New York, 1967 · Hellerstein, K., 'Canon and Gender: Women Poets in Two Modern Anthologies', *Shofar*, 9 (1991) · Howe, I., 'Translating from the Yiddish', *YIVO-Annual*, 15 (1974) · Novershtern, A., 'Yiddish Poetry in a New Context', *Prooftexts*, 8, 3 (1988) · Roskies, D. G., *A Bridge of Longing: The Lost Art of Yiddish Storytelling*, Cambridge, Mass., 1995.

k. Hispanic Languages

1. INTRODUCTION

A knowledge of Spanish seems to have been fairly common among English aristocrats and men of letters in the 17th and 18th c. Apart from adaptations of Spanish plays by writers like Beaumont and Fletcher, there was considerable interest in the picaresque novel [II.k.6], the earliest example of which, the anonymous *Lazarillo de Tormes*, was translated in 1576 and may have been read by Shakespeare. This, like Quevedo's *Buscón*, has appeared in several modern versions. On the other hand, James **Mabbe**'s version of Mateo Alemán's immensely long though very vivid *Guzmán de Alfarache*, which first appeared in 1622, had to wait until 1924 for a reprint, and we still badly need a good modern version.

The best-known of all Spanish works is, of course, *Don Quixote*, which has remained a classic in English almost from its original publication [II.k.5]. **Shelton**'s lively though at times inaccurate translation (1612, 1620) was quick off the mark, and was followed by equally influential versions by **Motteux**, **Jarvis**, and **Smollett**. Of these early versions, the best is surely Jarvis's, and though there have been many modern versions, notably those by J. M. **Cohen** and Burton **Raffel**, none quite equals the elegance and precision of this gifted 18th-c. translator.

17th-c. Spanish theatre, though it contains many masterpieces, has for the most part had to wait until recently for any quantity of translations; however, one of the more pleasing features of the contemporary English stage has been the number of produc-

tions of classical Spanish plays, both in London and elsewhere, though not all of these versions have been published [II.k.4].

The 19th-c. romantic revival produced more travel books than translations. However, towards the end of the century a number of novels by Galdós [II.k.8] were published in now almost unreadable English versions. Better versions have only begun to appear in the last half-century, beginning with Gamel **Woolsey**'s fine translation of *La de Bringas*. By now, almost a dozen of his novels have been translated, including his masterpiece, *Fortunata y Jacinta*, and he has been the subject of serious studies by critics like V. S. Pritchett and C. P. Snow. Two equally fine, though less prolific, 19th-c. novelists have also been well translated: the Portuguese writer Eça de Queirós [II.k.14], and Galdós's Spanish contemporary Leopoldo Alas ('Clarín'), whose major novel, *La Regenta*, now exists in a superb version by John **Rutherford** [II.k.8].

20th-c. Spanish novelists and dramatists are more sparsely represented in English, apart from older writers like Cela and Juan Goytisolo. (Javier Marías is something of an exception here, perhaps because of his English connections.) Certainly, no recent Spanish novelist has had anything like the impact of the Portuguese writer José Saramago, and particularly of his novel *O Evangelho segundo Jesus Cristo* (1991), whose translation in 1993 revealed an author of genuine European stature [II.k.8].

Catalan literature [II.k.12] has always tended to

come a poor third in foreign estimation, compared with writing in Spanish and Portuguese. (Scandalously, it is omitted altogether from John Sturrock's otherwise excellent *Oxford Guide to Contemporary Writing*, 1996.) Yet its actual achievement, from the 13th-c. mystic Ramon Llull to the work of many talented 20th-c. poets and prose writers, is very considerable, and both the quantity and quality of modern English translations are impressive. Apart from translations of Llull himself, initiated in the 1920s by Allison **Peers**, there are several versions of the poems of Ausiàs March, surely the greatest European poet between Chaucer and Villon, as well as a fine translation of the extraordinary 15th-c. Valencian novel *Tirant lo blanc* by David **Rosenthal**. Coming to modern times, there are good versions of the poems of Riba, Espriu, and Ferrater as well as a number of excellent novels.

By far the most successful recent translations have been those of Latin American fiction [II.k.11]: the early stories of Borges and the so-called 'boom' writers of the Latin American novel: Fuentes, García Márquez, Rulfo, and Vargas Llosa. The novels of each of these have sold millions of copies. Nevertheless, their undoubted talents should not blind one to the work of less publicized writers like

Guimarães Rosa [II.k.15] and Juan Carlos Onetti, whose remarkable novels and stories, though long available in translation in the United States, have only recently begun to make an appearance in this country.

Spanish and Latin American poetry is on the whole well represented in translation; Portuguese less so, despite the early appearance of Richard **Fanshawe**'s splendid translation of Camões's *Lusiads* [II.k.13]. Among the older Spanish poets, however, there are some notable omissions: St John of the Cross, Luis de León, Góngora, and more recently Quevedo are all available in good translations; yet no one so far has produced a good selection of the poems of Garcilaso or Lope de Vega, though Geoffrey **Hill**'s fine paraphrases of several of Lope's sonnets in *Tenebrae* (1978) are a step in the right direction. By contrast, there is scarcely a major 20th-c. Spanish or Latin American poet who has not been translated—in the case of Lorca and Neruda many times over—and the influence of these poets and others on certain British and American poets has been considerable [II.k.10]. For translations of the younger Spanish poets, however, one needs to go to the little magazines, for example, to the special Spanish poetry number of *Agenda* published in the summer of 1997.   AT

ANTHOLOGIES Caracciolo-Trejo, E., *The Penguin Book of Latin American Verse*, Harmondsworth, 1971 · Cohen, J. M., *The Penguin Book of Spanish Verse*, Harmondsworth, 1954 [3rd edn., expanded, 1988] · Hammer, Louis, and Schyfter, Sara, *Recent Poetry of Spain: A Bilingual Anthology*, Old Chatham, NY, 1983 · St Martin, Hardie, *Roots and Wings: Poetry from Spain 1900–1975*, San Francisco/New York, 1976.

2. MEDIEVAL SPANISH LITERATURE

i. Early Translations: Sixteenth to Nineteenth Century Medieval English literature made its way into Spanish long before the current began to flow in the other direction: though it is possible that Chaucer came across Juan Ruiz's *Libro de Buen Amor* (c.1330, Book of Good Love) when he was in Spain in 1366, it was not until the late 1520s and early 1530s that translations and adaptations began, the first being Fernando de Rojas's dialogue novel *Tragicomedia de Calisto y Melibea* (c.1502, soon more generally known as *Celestina*) and Diego de San Pedro's sentimental romance *Cárcel de Amor* (1492, Prison of Love).

John **Rastell** (brother-in-law of Juan Luis Vives and a member of Sir Thomas More's circle, d. 1536) translated the first acts of *Celestina* and equipped them with a happy ending, publishing *A New Cõmodye in Englysh in Maner of an Enterlude c.*1530. The first extant translation of the complete work is

by James **Mabbe** (1572–c.1642), whose *The Spanish Bawd* was published in 1631. Mabbe's work has been used as the basis for a number of stage and radio productions (most memorably at Joan Littlewood's Theatre Workshop in London in 1958). Mabbe's style is ornate (unusually so for the 1630s), but his book still reads well, in some ways better than his 20th-c. successors. In two respects *The Spanish Bawd* falsifies its original: some sexually explicit phrases are smoothed over, and the Catholic setting (invocations of God and the Virgin, references to the Mass) is, in deference to Protestant sensibilities, replaced by classical mythology. These changes are now known to belong to the second phase of Mabbe's translation. The first phase, a manuscript version from the first decade of the century, is much closer to the Spanish.

Probably at the same time as Rastell was working

on his *Enterlude*, John Bourchier, Lord **Berners** (1467–c.1533) translated *Cárcel de Amor* and its short sequel (1495) by Nicolás Núñez. Berners used a French translation as the basis for his own, correcting it from the Spanish, but for Núñez's sequel he worked directly from the Spanish. He is for C. S. Lewis 'the last of the great medieval translators . . . Malory's equal' (Lewis 1954). His posthumously published translation is riddled with errors, but it gives a fair impression of San Pedro's style, and his book had a considerable influence on the evolution of Elizabethan prose style. San Pedro's first romance, *Arnalte y Lucenda* (c.1481), though not of the same quality as *Cárcel de Amor*, rivalled it in European popularity and far surpassed it in English. The translation by the Catholic apologist John **Clerk** (d. 1552), from Nicolas d'Herberay's French, published in 1543, was followed by three other versions, two of them greatly changed, by different hands between 1575 and 1660.

Although the first of the Spanish sentimental romances, Juan Rodríguez del Padrón's *Siervo libre de amor* (c.1440, Love's Free Slave), was never rendered into English, Juan de Flores's *Grisel y Mirabella* (c.1480) appeared in 1556 in a quadrilingual edition (French, Italian, Spanish—a retranslation from the Italian—and English). Like other editions of sentimental romances this proved popular, and it was reprinted four times. Another, much freer version was printed in 1606. Thus eight translations or free adaptations of sentimental romances were printed, in 17 editions, between 1543 and 1660. The vogue for this genre in England (much stronger initially than the popularity of *Celestina*: Mabbe's *Spanish Bawd* sold slowly) was soon reinforced by the demand for translations of chivalresque and pastoral romances (reaching its peak with *Don Quixote* [II.k.5]), and the growing interest in *Celestina* was accompanied by the popularity of the picaresque novels [II.k.6].

Late medieval Spanish fiction played a decisive part in the formation of Elizabethan taste and of the English novel, and not always through translations. The neo-Arthurian romance *Amadís de Gaula* (c.1495) was known in Elizabethan England well before the pamphleteer and dramatist Anthony **Munday** (1553–1633) published the first volume of his translation in 1590: Queen Elizabeth was already being called Oriana in the 1560s. In 1567 Thomas **Paynell** (d. 1576), sometime chaplain to Henry VIII, translated from French a florilegium of speeches and letters from *Amadís* and its sequels, and in 1571 Charles **Stewart**, son of the Regent of Scotland, began to translate the first book (he soon abandoned his task). Thus Anthony Munday's *The*

Ancient, Famous and Honourable History of Amadis de Gaule (published between 1590 and 1619, so in its later stages contemporary with Shelton's *Don Quixote*) was a response to an already established fashion. Munday worked from the French of Nicolas d'Herberay, who had amplified both the style and the content of the Spanish original, making it more rhetorical and adding erotic scenes. Munday, who elsewhere translated rather freely, in this work followed Herberay closely. The double process of translation inevitably leads away from the sense of the original at times, but the style is good, and this is still a readable romance.

Spanish poetry was much read in the England of the Tudors, and in Stuart Scotland and England, but it was not much translated. A curious exception is the version of the *Proverbios* of Íñigo López de Mendoza, Marquis of Santillana, with the glosses of the scholar Pero Díaz de Toledo. The *Proverbios* (1437) is a moral poem designed as a *speculum principis* for the heir to the Castilian throne. In the translation by the poet Barnabe **Googe** (1540–94) a century and a half later, it clearly had its relevance for Elizabethan England.

Translations of medieval Spanish works in the early 18th c. are a continuation of the previous century's work: John Shirley abridged Munday's *Amadís* in 1702, and five years later two versions of *Celestina*, one narrative and the other dramatic, appeared simultaneously. Captain John **Stevens** (d. 1726), translator and historian, included *The Bawd of Madrid* in a collection of four works (two of them picaresque novels), and an anonymous author or authors published *Celestina: or, the Spanish Bawd, A Tragi-Comedy* with another picaresque novel. Both are free versions, Stevens's throughout and the anonymous play in its second half. The *Tragi-Comedy* seems to adapt Mabbe's *Spanish Bawd*, but Stevens seems to have worked directly from the Spanish.

Until the beginning of the 19th c., English translators showed interest only in late medieval Spanish literature. It fell to Robert **Southey** (1774–1843) to make earlier works available to English-speaking readers. He had already published an abridged translation of *Amadís de Gaula* in 1803; it was reviewed in the same year by Walter Scott, whose own romances may have been influenced by *Amadís* and its successors. In 1808 he published *The Chronicle of the Cid*, a composite work mainly derived from the *Chrónica del famoso cavallero Cid Ruy Díaz Campeador*, a late medieval reworking of parts of the *Estoria de España* planned and directed by Alfonso X, the Wise, King of Castile 1252–84. Southey supplemented this by direct recourse to the *Estoria de España* (albeit in a late redaction printed in the 16th c.) and to the early 13th-c. epic the *Poema de Mio Cid*. The result is a splendid narrative, in a style that conveys the spirit of a vanished age while avoiding excessive archaism. V. S. Pritchett calls him 'one of the great masters of plain, flowing, and conversable prose narrative in our language' (*Chronicle* 1958). No full translation of the *Poema de Mio Cid* was to come for nearly 80 years, but Southey had opened up Spain's earlier medieval literature, and his example was followed. His predecessors had translated, retranslated, or adapted what was to them more or less contemporary literature. Southey did not (unlike Thomas Percy) use the term 'ancient poetry', but he knew that he was interpreting a bygone age.

Southey did not think highly of Spanish ballads ('infinitely and every way inferior to our own'), and he made only a little use of them in his *Chronicle*, but before long other translators rightly took a different view: Scott's biographer, the novelist John Gibson **Lockhart** (1794–1854), the traveller, MP, and hymn-writer Sir John **Bowring** (1792–1872), and the Scottish clergyman and prolific translator from Spanish and German James Young **Gibson** (1826–86). Henry Wadsworth **Longfellow**, Professor of Modern Languages at Harvard as well as the poet of *Hiawatha*, was captivated by some Spanish poems, recreating 'the Spanish ballad | of the noble Count Arnaldos' in *The Secret of the Sea* (1849). This was not Longfellow's first venture into medieval Spanish: in 1832 he had published in a magazine a version of Jorge Manrique's *Coplas por la muerte de su padre* (1479, Verses for His Father's Death), at once elegy and moral reflection, the one poem (apart from ballads) of 15th-c. Castile that is still widely read today. Longfellow's version is, like *The Secret of the Sea*, recreation rather than strict translation, and though there have in recent decades been accurate published translations, none really fills the gap.

ii. Modern Translations In the last quarter of the 19th c., what we may regard as modern translations from medieval Spanish begin, some aimed at the general reader, while in others the concept of a scholarly translation is dominant. Some older translations are reprinted or adapted (but often with a substantial introduction), but in the new ones accuracy is increasingly seen to be as important as readability. Moreover, the range of works made available is steadily widened: the first (though old-fashioned and unreliable) version of Juan Manuel's *exemplum* collection, *El Conde Lucanor* (1335), was published in 1868 and the first full translation of the *Poema de Mio Cid* in 1879. In 1882 the folklorist Henry Charles **Coote** (1815–85) appended to his translation of a monograph on the Seven Sages his English rendering (*Book of the Deceits and Tricks of Women*) of the *Libro de los engaños* (c.1253), the first substantial translation addressed primarily to scholars, and his example was soon followed. The second version of the *Poema de Mio Cid* (in verse, like the first) was published in 1897–1903, with an edition of the Spanish original and extensive notes, by the bibliophile and founder of the Hispanic Society of America, Archer M. **Huntington**.

20th-c. translations of medieval Spanish literature are numerous. Many works, including some of the major ones, have not been translated, but many have. The audience addressed varies: students, comparatists, the educated general reader—or, of course, more than one of these. In one remarkable case, a specialist audience is addressed for a practical reason: some of the laws in the *Siete partidas*, the encyclopedic legal code of Alfonso the Wise, are still in force in Louisiana, so partial translations were published in New Orleans in 1819–20, and over a century later the Comparative Law Bureau of the American Bar Association commissioned Samuel Parsons **Scott** to produce a full translation of this massive work.

Sometimes translations are inept, but more often they are serviceable, and a few are excellent: for instance, Joan **Evans**'s abridgement of *El Victorial* (early 1430s), a blend of chronicle, biography, and travel-book (1928), Keith **Whinnom**'s translation of two sentimental romances by San Pedro and Nuñez, which combines accuracy with a fine sense of the cadences of the original, and Roger **Wright**'s rendering of some 70 ballads (facing the originals) into English couplets. Wright chooses fidelity to the meaning rather than to the words; his versions are splendid performance texts.

The works most often translated are the *Poema de Mio Cid*, *Celestina*, the best-known ballads, and Juan Ruiz's *Libro de Buen Amor*. The last, despite its importance, is a late starter; the first generally available translation—by Rigo **Mignani** and Mario A. **Di Cesare**—did not appear until 1970 (it was followed by three others in the next eight years). Both this and the next translation, by Raymond S. **Willis**, use prose for the alexandrine lines of most of the original and verse for the inset lyrics, but they differ sharply in their aim: Mignani and Di Cesare give precedence to clarity and fidelity to the original, and their translation is designed to be read on its own, while Willis describes his version as a paraphrase (he sometimes omits a line), 'exclusively . . . an aid to understanding the Spanish'.

The first three translators of the *Poema de Mio Cid* (between 1879 and 1919) used verse, but their successors generally used prose, a striking exception being the American poet W. S. **Merwin**, whose poem reads splendidly, though sometimes at the expense of accuracy. The prose translation by Rita **Hamilton** and Janet **Perry**, now much the most widely known, is both readable and accurate, its only flaw being that epic epithets and other repeated phrases are sometimes omitted.

It has proved surprisingly difficult to achieve a successful modern English *Celestina*, and the great majority of the numerous stage and radio productions over the past 50 years have used adaptations of James Mabbe. There were five translations in the 1950s and 1960s; J. M. **Cohen**'s for Penguin Classics is the most widely known, but Phyllis **Hartnoll**'s for Everyman's Library is clearly the best: though lacking Mabbe's vigour, it is both accurate and readable.

Space allows only the briefest mention of good recent translations of other important works. Gonzalo de Berceo's mid-13th-c. *Milagros de Nuestra Señora* does not go well into English verse, so Richard Terry **Mount** and Annette Grant **Cash** have solved the problem with a prose translation broken up into lines that correspond to the original. A similar method is used by T. A. **Perry** for the mid-14th-c. *Proverbios morales* of Rabbi Šem Tob.

There are two translations of Juan Manuel's *El Conde Lucanor*, of which John **England**'s is the more successful, and Alfonso Martínez de Toledo's *Arcipreste de Talavera* (1438), part pungently written treatise, part collection of anecdotes, is effectively rendered by Lesley Byrd **Simpson**. Other works have been usefully translated: John Esten **Keller** has not only produced versions of several *exemplum* collections but has encouraged colleagues to translate *Amadís de Gaula* and the first indigenous Spanish romance, *El libro del cavallero Zifar* (c.1340, The Book of the Knight Zifar). There are still gaps, most obviously the major 13th-c. poems written in *cuaderna vía*, monorhymed alexandrine quatrains; the Mount and Cash *Miracles of Our Lady* is the first successful translation published in this area. Yet despite the gaps, English-speaking readers now have at least one adequate (or better) translation of most of the major works of medieval Spanish literature, and in some cases they have a choice of versions. They are not necessarily restricted to books: it is probable that more people have heard *Celestina* in English on the radio or seen it on the stage than have read all of the translations put together; and it is certain that—despite the availability of good translations of the *Poema de Mio Cid*—the majority of English-speakers owe their familiarity with the hero to the Charlton Heston film.   AD

ALFONSO X   *Las siete partidas*, tr. Samuel Parsons Scott, Chicago, 1931.

AMADÍS DE GAULA   *The Treasurie of Amadis of Fraunce*, tr. Thomas Paynell, London, 1567 · *The Ancient, Famous and Honourable History of Amadis de Gaule*, tr. Anthony Munday, London, 1590–1619 [abr. John Shirley 1702] · *Amadis of Gaul*, tr. Robert Southey, London, 1803 [two 20th-c. adaptations].

BALLADS   *Ancient Spanish Ballads, Historical and Romantic*, tr. John Gibson Lockhart, London, 1823 · *Ancient Poetry and Romances of Spain*, tr. John Bowring, London, 1824 · *The Cid Ballads and Other Poems and Translations from Spanish and German*, tr. James Young Gibson, London, 1887 · *Spanish Ballads*, ed. and tr. Roger Wright, Warminster, UK, 1987.

BERCEO, GONZALO DE   *Miracles of Our Lady*, tr. Richard Terry Mount and Annette Grant Cash, Lexington, Ky., 1997.

CHRONICLE   *The Chronicle of the Cid*, tr. Robert Southey, London, 1808 [rep. with introd. by V. S. Pritchett, New York, 1958].

DÍAZ DE GAMES, GUTIERRE   *The Unconquered Knight: A Chronicle of the Deeds of Don Pero Niño*, tr. Joan Evans, London, 1928.

FLORES, JUAN DE   *Histoire de Aurelio et Isabelle*, Antwerp, 1556 [quadrilingual edn. of *Grisel y Mirabella*].

JUAN MANUEL   *'El Conde Lucanor': A Collection of Mediaeval Spanish Stories*, ed. and tr. John England, Warminster, UK, 1987.

LIBRO DE LOS ENGAÑOS   *Researches Respecting the 'Book of Sindibâd'*, by Domenico Comparetti, tr. Henry Charles Coote, London, 1882 [contains Coote's tr. of the *Book of the Deceits and Tricks of Women*].

MARTÍNEZ DE TOLEDO, ALFONSO   *Little Sermons on Sin*, tr. Lesley Byrd Simpson, Berkeley, Calif., 1959.

POEMA DE MIO CID   *Poem of the Cid*, ed. and tr. Archer M. Huntington, New York, 1897–1903 [several reprints] · *The Poem of the Cid*, tr. W. S. Merwin, London, 1959 · *The Poem of the Cid*, ed. Ian Michael, tr. Rita Hamilton and Janet Perry, Manchester, 1975 [Penguin, 1984].

ROJAS, FERNANDO DE   *A New Cōmodye in Englysh in Maner of an Enterlude*, adapted John Rastell, London, c.1530 [several modern reprintings] · *The Spanish Bawd, Represented in Celestina: or, the Tragicke-Comedy of Calisto and Melibea*, tr. James Mabbe, London, 1631 [often reprinted, most recently ed. Dorothy S. Severin, Warminster, UK, 1987] · *The*

Spanish Libertines, tr. Captain John Stevens, London, 1707 [includes *The Bawd of Madrid*] · *Celestina: or, the Spanish Bawd. A Tragi-Comedy*, London, 1707 · *Celestina*, tr. Phyllis Hartnoll, London, 1959.

RUIZ, JUAN   *The Book of Good Love*, tr. Rigo Mignani and Mario Di Cesare, Albany, NY, 1970 · *Libro de Buen Amor*, ed. and tr. Raymond S. Willis, Princeton, NJ, 1972.

SAN PEDRO, DIEGO DE   *A Certayn Treatye most Wyttely Devysed . . . Entytled Lamant mal traicte de samye*, tr. John Clerk, London, 1543 · *The Castell of Loue, Translated out of Spanishe*, tr. John Bourchier, Lord Berners, London, *c*.1549 [facsimile rep., ed. William G. Crane, Gainesville, Fla., 1950] · *'Prison of Love', 1492, together with the Continuation by Nicolás Núñez, 1496*, tr. Keith Whinnom, Edinburgh, 1979.

SANTILLANA, MARQUÉS DE   *The Prouerbes of . . . Sir James Lopez de Mendoza, with the Paraphrase of Peter Diaz of Toledo*, tr. Barnabe Googe, London, 1579.

ŠEM TOB   *The 'Moral Proverbs' of Santob de Carrión: Jewish Wisdom in Christian Spain*, by T. A. Perry, Princeton, NJ, 1988 [includes Perry's tr. of the *Proverbios morales*].

SEE ALSO   Bryant, S. M., *The Spanish Ballad in English*, Lexington, Ky, 1973 · Lewis, C. S., *English Literature in the Sixteenth Century, Excluding Drama*, Oxford, 1954 · Martínez Lacalle, G., ed., Fernando de Rojas, *Celestine or the Tragick-Comedie of Calisto and Melibea*, London, 1972 · O'Connor, J. J., *'Amadis de Gaule' and Its Influence on Elizabethan Literature*, New Brunswick, NJ, 1970 · Randall, D. J. B., *The Golden Tapestry: A Critical Survey of Non-Chivalric Spanish Fiction in English Translation, 1537–1657*, Durham, NC, 1963.

3. SPANISH POETRY: SIXTEENTH AND SEVENTEENTH CENTURY

The greatest period in Spanish poetry runs roughly from 1530 to 1645—from the early poems of Garcilaso to the death of Quevedo—though the tradition is prolonged almost to the end of the 17th c. in the work of the remarkable Mexican poet Sor Juana Inés de la Cruz.

i. Garcilaso de la Vega Translations of Garcilaso de la Vega, the first major poet of the Spanish Renaissance, are surprisingly few: William **Drummond** of Hawthornden (1585–1649) adapts lines from Garcilaso and other 16th-c. Spanish poets in his own verses, though these do not amount to translations; in more recent times, James **Cleugh**'s version of the odes and sonnets—the only modern attempt at some of the longer poems—is marred by archaisms and mechanical rhythms. For a taste of Garcilaso's real power, one must go to the handful of sonnets translated, with equal brilliance, by Edwin **Morgan** and Laurence **Kitchin**. Both translators are amazingly resourceful in preserving the rhyme scheme and the fluency of the originals: Kitchin, on the whole, is more latinate than Morgan, but each is highly successful in his chosen mode, as is evident from their versions of Sonnet xxiii:

> Gather together from your happy spring
> fruits that are sweet before time ravages
> with angry snow the beauty of your head.
> The rose will wither as the cold wind rages,
> and age comes gently to change everything,
> lest our desire should change old age instead.
>
> (Morgan)

Now in your vernal joy store up a wealth
Of luscious fruit, before outrageous time

Covers the lovely summit deep in snow.
The rose will wither under windblown time,
All will be changed as age comes on by stealth.
He will make no exceptions, you should know.

> (Kitchin)

ii. St John of the Cross Of the two great 16th-c. religious poets, Luis de León and St John of the Cross (San Juan de la Cruz), the former has been relatively little translated. Aubrey **Bell**'s versions are accurate enough, though cast in what now seems a rather stilted diction; Willis **Barnstone**'s are much better, and manage to convey something of the austerity and the Horatian sweetness of the originals. St John of the Cross's poems, on the other hand, have frequently been translated, either in part or as a whole. Of the complete versions, Roy **Campbell**'s is still the best, though it suffers from an occasional lushness of diction; J. F. **Nims** bravely attempts a more modern idiom, but is sometimes inaccurate; Willis Barnstone varies between rhymed and unrhymed versions, and is less successful in the former; Lynda **Nicholson** is generally accurate, but many of her lines are rhythmically dead.

Compare, for instance, the following three versions of the second stanza of one of St John's best known poems:

> In safety, in disguise,
> In darkness up the secret stair I crept,
> (O happy enterprise)
> Concealed from other eyes
> When all my house at length in silence slept.
>
> (Campbell)

Blackly free from light
disguised and down a secret way
O lucky turn and flight!
in darkness I escaped,
my house at last was calm and safe.

(Barnstone)

In darkness and secure,
By the secret ladder and disguised,
O blessed venture!
In darkness and concealed,
My house in sleep and silence stilled.

(Nicholson)

Here, Nicholson's rhythm falters in the second line, where she quite unjustifiably replaces 'stair' by 'ladder'; Barnstone's version seems altogether too free, and his contorted expressions ('Blackly free from light', 'O lucky turn and flight') tend to destroy the naturalness of the original; Campbell's translation, on the other hand, scores on all counts: it is musically superb, stays close to the original, and modulates successfully into the slightly longer last line. Finally, there are excellent versions of individual poems by two outstanding contemporary poets: Seamus **Heaney**'s surprising introduction of a translation of 'Que bien sé yo la fonte' (How well I know that fountain) into his own long poem 'Station Island', and F. T. **Prince**'s versions of three poems, among them a reworking of '¡Oh llama de amor viva' (O living flame of love) in the stanza form of Crashaw's 'The Weeper'.

iii. Góngora Of the two great secular poets, Luis de Góngora and Francisco de Quevedo, it is Góngora who has attracted the most translations, beginning with Richard **Fanshawe** (1608–66), whose powerful version of Góngora's sonnet on the execution of Don Rodrigo Calderón has clear analogies with the fall of Strafford. Equally powerful, and uncompromisingly modern in their diction, are Robert **Lowell**'s versions—strictly speaking, 'imitations'—of two of Góngora's finest sonnets, grouped, along with two by Quevedo, under the heading 'The Ruins of Time'. Among more extensive translations, several are outstanding. Michael **Smith**'s selection of 37 sonnets, along with a number of ballads and short lyrical pieces, provides an excellent introduction to this marvellous poet, whose astonishing spectrum of registers is reflected in the versatility of the translations.

But the finest of the Góngora translations are those of his two long poems, the *Polifemo* (1613, Polyphemus) and the *Soledades* (1614, The Solitudes). The first exists in an excellent version by

Gilbert **Cunningham**, which almost miraculously preserves the *ottava rima* form and is remarkably faithful to Góngora's complex verbal constructions. Cunningham has also translated the *Soledades*, which had already appeared in an earlier version by E. M. **Wilson**. Both versions are equally fine, though there are interesting differences: where Cunningham gives one an admirably clear, sensitive, and technically skilful version of a difficult 17th-c. poem, Wilson does something more risky, but infinitely worth the attempt. Not only has he used his knowledge of 17th-c. English poetry to create verses which can stand in their own right; he also appears to have learnt from the example of William Empson, which he refers to in his preface—something which may account for the splendid terseness of lones like 'The ocean is not deaf. Our learning feigns'. Take their respective versions of this passage from the *First Solitude*:

Nor burrowed maze availed, nor rocky brow,
The peace of timorous coneys on the hill,
Become a shoulder's load and marvel now,
Their number trophy to the hunter's skill.

(Wilson)

Vainly the coney drills
His tortuous burrow in the roughest slope,
   Vainly for peace they hope,
These timorous dwellers in the highest hills,
Their trophies now a huntsman's shoulder cumber,
   Who boasts their lifeless number.

(Cunningham)

Here, Cunningham is closer to the overall musical pattern of the original, but Wilson reproduces more accurately the movement of syntax and the order in which the various components of the sentence are presented. Cunningham, for his part, constructs a more flowing sentence, yet Wilson, one could say, is 'truer' to the original in that he reflects more faithfully Góngora's tendency to use relatively colourless verbs, and his more distinctive syntax, while perfectly comprehensible, has the effect of slowing down the pace of one's reading very much as Góngora's own verse does.

Recently a new translation of the *Soledades* has appeared by Philip **Polack**. This, while closer to Cunningham than to Wilson, is a fine achievement in its own right and represents a complete rethinking of the original. The result is an extremely fluent version which stays remarkably close to the original and is noticeably more modern in its vocabulary than the other two—a sure sign of the enduring vitality of the poems.

411

iv. Quevedo Compared with Góngora, Quevedo, who was active in the first half of the 17th c., has been relatively little translated, despite a good beginning in the 17th c. with the vigorous version of 'La mosca' (The Fly) by Philip **Ayres** (1638–1712). Michael Smith's selection of 66 sonnets, plus a few longer poems, helps to fill the gap: these unpretentious and readable versions, while they sometimes fail to convey the subtlety of Quevedo's conceits, illustrate very well the extraordinary range of the originals. One particular sonnet, 'Miré los muros de la patria mía' (I looked at the walls of my native land), has been translated a number of times: by John **Masefield**, by Yvor **Winters**, and by Robert **Lowell**, as well as by Smith. The opening quatrain, in these four versions, goes as follows:

> I saw the ramparts of my native land,
> One time so strong, now dropping in decay,
> Their strength destroyed by this new age's way,
> That has worn out and rotted what was grand.

> (Masefield)

> I looked upon the old walls of my land—
> Once they were strong and now they fall away.
> Tired with the march of age, they may not stay—
> Their strength has vanished, and they scarcely stand.

> (Winters)

> I saw the musty shingles of my house,
> raw wood and fixed once, now a wash of moss
> eroded by the ruin of the age
> turning all fair and green things into waste.

> (Lowell)

> I saw the walls of my hometown,
> Strong one time, now crumbling away,
> Exhausted with the course of age
> That wears out now their brave display.

> (Smith)

One particular problem in these lines is that Spanish *patria* can mean 'fatherland' and 'birthplace' or 'ancestral home'. English has no single word which covers all these things, so that one has to decide which of the meanings one is going to emphasize. Smith takes the more intimate sense and produces a good translation which stays close to the original. Masefield, quite legitimately, takes the more general meaning: his version opens well, though by the third line it is beginning to falter a little. ('The new age's way' fails to convey the idea of movement implied in Spanish *carrera*, which is more like Smith's 'course'.) Winter's version, at first sight, is metrically more skilful than Mase-

field's, but by the third and fourth lines it is as if the original were being translated in half the space, so that everything has to be said twice over.

Lowell's version—again, characteristically, an 'imitation' rather than a strict translation—is another matter. He has taken various liberties with the original—not all, I think, justified—but the overall effect is certainly more memorable than any of the other versions. For one thing, it is the only one which comes near to matching the musical qualities of the original; for another, having decided on the more local meaning of *patria*, he has gone on to make the whole thing more intensely visual, as if he needed this extra concreteness in order to convey the power of what, in Quevedo, is more general and abstract. It is clear that, in his version, Quevedo's poem is being seen through a strong and idiosyncratic imagination, but at the same time one does not feel that he has betrayed Quevedo in the way that a more literal translation might well have done.

v. Sor Juana Inés de la Cruz The tradition of Spanish Renaissance verse virtually ends with the work of the 17th-c. Mexican poet Sor Juana Inés de la Cruz, which combines echoes of peninsular Spanish poetry with New World inflections over a remarkable range of material. Two of her poems, including the famous 'Hombres necios que acusáis' (Foolish men who accuse), exist in sprightly versions by Robert **Graves**, originally appended to a pioneering essay. But readers new to her work can now go to the splendid selection by Alan **Trueblood**, which not only includes a superb translation of Sor Juana's long, intensely erudite poem *Primero sueño* (First Dream) but copes ingeniously with her more demotic verses by translating them into the idiom of American blacks:

> Flasica, naquete día
> qui tamo lena li glolia,
> no vindamo pipitolia,
> pueque sobla la aleglia:
> que la Señola Malía
> a turo mundo la da.
> ¡Ha, ha, ha! &.

> Fanny, this mo'nin'
> we's full of glory,
> don' le's sell ladyfingers
> o' them almon' kisses.
> We've sumpin' better:
> Mary's fingers to kiss!
> Ha, ha, ha . . .!   AT

GARCILASO DE LA VEGA Cleugh, James, *Odes and Sonnets*, London, 1934 · Kitchin, Laurence, *Love Sonnets of the Renaissance*, London/Boston, Mass., 1990 · Morgan, Edwin, *Fifty Renascence Love-Poems*, Reading, UK, 1975.

GÓNGORA, LUIS DE Cunningham, Gilbert F., *The Solitudes*, Baltimore, 1968 · Fanshawe, Richard, two sonnets in his *Shorter Poems and Translations*, ed. N. W. Bawcett, Liverpool, 1964 · Lowell, Robert, two sonnets in his *Near the Ocean*, London, 1967 · Polack, Philip, *Soledades*, Bristol/London, 1997 · Smith, Michael, *Selected Shorter Poems*, London, 1995 · Wilson, E. M., *The Solitudes*, Cambridge, 1965 [first pub. Cambridge, 1931].

JOHN OF THE CROSS, ST Barnstone, Willis, *The Poems*, Bloomington/London, 1968 · Campbell, Roy, *The Poems*, London, 1951 [Penguin] · Heaney, Seamus, 'Que bien sé yo la fonte', in his *Station Island*, London/Boston, Mass., 1984 · Nicholson, Lynda, *The Poems*, in Gerald Brenan, *St John of the Cross: His Life and Poetry*, Cambridge, 1973 · Nims, John Frederick, *The Poems*, New York, 1959 [rev. edn., 1968] · Prince, F. T., three poems in his *Soldiers Bathing and Other Poems*, London, 1954.

JUANA INÉS DE LA CRUZ, SOR Graves, Robert, two poems in his *The Crowning Privilege*, London, 1955 · Trueblood, Alan, *A Sor Juana Anthology*, Cambridge, Mass./London, 1988.

LEÓN, LUIS DE Barnstone, Willis, *The Unknown Light: Poems*, New York, 1979 · Bell, Aubrey F. G., *Poems*, London, 1928.

QUEVEDO, FRANCISCO DE Ayres, Philip, 'La mosca', in his *Lyric Poems*, London, 1687 · Lowell, Robert, two sonnets in his *Near the Ocean*, London, 1967 · Masefield, John, 'Miré los muros de la patria mía', in his *The Story of a Round House*, London, 1912 · Smith, Michael, *On the Anvil*, Dublin, 1989 · Winters, Yvor, 'Miré los muros de la patria mía' in *Collected Poems*, Denver, 1960.

4. SPANISH GOLDEN AGE DRAMA

1. Introduction Of the dozen or so major dramatists who worked during what has come to be known as the Golden Age of Spanish Drama, only four have achieved any meaningful recognition in the English-speaking world. They are Miguel de Cervantes Saavedra, more frequently acclaimed of course as a writer of prose, Lope de Vega Carpio, generally hailed as the creator of the enduring form of the Spanish 'comedia', Tirso de Molina, the pseudonym of the Mercedarian Gabriel Téllez, and Pedro Calderón de la Barca, who brought the 'comedia' to a new level of dramatic and philosophical sophistication.

Such recognition was not only slow in coming. It has also been, for much of this century, partial. It was not that theatre critics would have had any difficulty in describing the works of these dramatists as classics of world theatre. But their appreciation was largely notional, given that only a minimal selection of the huge production of these writers was available in English. Moreover, those translations which did exist were rarely, if ever, performed. In 1992 Melveena McKendrick lamented the circumstance that 'the dramatic genius of sixteenth- and seventeenth-century Spain is virtually unrecognized outside the circle of Hispanic studies', concluding that 'not just two remarkable playwrights [Lope de Vega and Calderón] but a remarkable theatre to all intents and purposes still await discovery'.

It was, however, precisely the formalistic emphasis laid on Spanish Golden Age drama by a significant portion of Hispanist criticism between the mid-1950s and 1980 which encouraged the widespread belief that the uniqueness of the plays of Lope, Tirso, Calderón, and others would inhibit audience reception in English. Eric Bentley's stern riposte to this critical protectionism (1959), in which he asserts the indispensable universality of the Spanish 'comedia', initiated a stirring of interest that transcended the ambit of the professional *cognoscenti*. But the endeavour was hampered by the fact that these plays were rarely performed even in Spain, where contemporary theatre activity remained locked into the codes of political and social protest until the death of General Franco in 1975. The lack of an English-language performance tradition for Golden Age drama appeared justified by the absence of a similar tradition in Spain. In the words of Gary Taylor (1990), this lack of 'constant critical and theatrical reinfleshments inevitably make Shakespeare's characters seem more real for English-speaking peoples than the characters created by Euripides, Lope de Vega or Racine. But that seeming is, in the sweep of human culture, just a trick of perspective: a local illusion.'

ii. Calderón The fact that the 'comedia' did not attract early translators of the calibre of James **Mabbe** (*The Celestina*) [II.k.2.i] and Thomas **Shelton** (*Don Quixote*) [II.k.5.i] also served perhaps to disable its reception in English. Although Golden Age plays were liberally plundered by 17th-, 18th-, and 19th-c. dramatists in Germany, France, and England, the first recognizable English translations did not appear in print until relatively late. Notable

413

among these early renditions is *Eight Dramas of Calderón*, freely translated by the eminent Edward **FitzGerald** (1853). Although there is evidence of bowdlerization and some surviving traces of the sort of pomposity that the translator was able to erase from successive versions of the *Rubáiyát of Omar Khayyám* [II.q.2.4], generally speaking, the linguistic vivacity and rich recreation of Calderón's thematic complexity make these versions still readable today. Moreover, the fact that FitzGerald's age, like that of Calderón, was greatly preoccupied with the external manifestations of honourable conduct allows his translations to tackle the vexed question of the honour code in a way which still rings wholly true. These translations, reprinted in 1906, deserve resurrection.

FitzGerald chose his eight plays judiciously. Among them are works which have been successfully staged in the 1990s in English, including *El pintor de su deshonra* (c.1645, The Painter of His Own Dishonour), *Las tres justicias en una* (1623/30, The Three Judgments in One), *El alcalde de Zalamea* (c.1643, The Mayor of Zalamea), and *La vida es sueño* (1635, Life Is a Dream), to which FitzGerald gives the Shakespearean title *Such Stuff as Dreams Are Made Of*. In spite of its unpromising title, *Luis Pérez el gallego* (1644, Gil Pérez the Galician), one of Calderón's least known but most freewheeling works, is the most readable (and, indeed, probably most performable) of the translations contained within the anthology. This is undoubtedly because it is also one of the freest of the versions. There is always a danger that Calderón's linguistic complexity will degenerate into turgid and cryptic reworkings in English. Such is the occasional fate of Edwin **Honig**'s *Four Plays* (1961). What they lose in terms of beauty, however, they make up for in terms of verbal fidelity. These scholarly versions, including the richly numinous *La devoción de la cruz* (?1623–5, Devotion to the Cross) and the comic *La dama duende* (1629, The Phantom Lady) provide a good and reliable introduction to the variety and power of Calderón's theatre.

More in the line of FitzGerald than of Honig, in terms of his willingness to respond to the demands of the target rather than the source language, is the poet Roy **Campbell**. A noted Hispanophile, his version of one of Calderón's best-known tragedies, *El médico de su honra* (1635, The Surgeon of His Honour) is well crafted in terms of its dramatic shaping. Campbell's characteristically driving metre, however, is not entirely suited to the richly polymetric forms of the original, with the result that the English tends to sound strangely constrained in places.

The first useful anthology of Golden Age drama in English is to be found in *Spanish Drama*, edited by Angel Flores. John Gassner's brief preface, 'Spanish Drama in the World Theater', remains insightful, but the volume is more generally valuable in its provision of translations of rarely encountered plays. Among these are Lope de Rueda's *Las aceitunas* (published posthumously in 1567, The Olives), a fine example of the 'paso', or short farcical interlude, which was later to influence Cervantes in the development of his own 'entremeses' (interludes). Indeed, the inclusion of one of Cervantes' best-known interludes, *La guarda cuidadosa* (1615, The Vigilant Sentinel), allows the English-speaking reader to trace the early development of Golden Age theatre. In that sense, this volume fulfils an important function, although the translations of both the Lope de Rueda and Cervantes pieces (by Angel **Flores** and by Flores and Joseph **Liss** respectively) do little to capture the ironies and puns which characterize the rapidly moving dialogue of the originals.

As well as a number of more modern plays, *Spanish Drama* also contains four other Golden Age masterpieces: Lope de Vega's drama of political and ethical solidarity, *Fuenteovejuna* (c.1612–14), Calderón's *Life is a Dream*, Tirso de Molina's *El burlador de Sevilla* (c.1630, The Rogue of Seville), and *La verdad sospechosa* (1630, The Truth Suspected), the acknowledged masterpiece of the Mexican-born Juan Ruiz de Alarcón y Mendoza. The quality of the translations varies, but it has to be said that the general tendency on the part of the translators to respect the letter of the originals gives these versions an unfortunate wordiness. They are turgidly literary, rather than fully dramatic, pieces. Nevertheless, this book provides a useful English-language introduction to the historical development of the Spanish drama from Lope de Rueda to Federico García Lorca.

Another side to Calderón's dramatic art—his skilful exploitation of metatheatrical allegory in religious drama (the 'auto sacramental')—was revealed to an English-speaking audience in 1976, with George W. **Brandt**'s elegant translation of *El gran teatro del mundo* (c.1645, The Great Stage of the World). This is an exemplary translation in that it permits the values, linguistic and dramatic, of the original to speak for themselves whilst never allowing the English to buckle under the weight of Calderón's condensed poetic forms. Although English-language interest in Calderón was by then growing steadily, this translation was published by a university press, a clear indication that Calderón was not yet ready to be admitted into the accepted repertoire of performable foreign dramatists.

It was in 1981 that the decisive step was taken in this respect. That year saw the Cottlesloe production of Adrian **Mitchell**'s *The Mayor of Zalamea*, in a version specially commissioned by the National Theatre. The play was hailed as a 'blazing masterpiece' and 'a revelation', by *The Times* and *Daily Telegraph* respectively, views which echoed the universal acclaim of the critics. A limited edition of the translation was rushed out by Salamander Press to accompany the production, although it was subsequently reprinted in *Calderón: The Mayor of Zalamea, Life's a Dream and The Great Theatre of the World*, all adapted by Adrian Mitchell (*Life's a Dream* with the director John **Barton**) and all proven on stage. While Mitchell's work does not eschew the intellectual and spiritual complexities of Calderón's original pieces, he is also signally successful in bringing out what he calls in his Introduction the 'slow-burning passion' and 'lovely humour' of the Spaniard. Moreover, these are eminently fluent translations which seem to move effortlessly and seamlessly between a variety of verse forms.

The fact that all three of these plays were staged with remarkable success in a period of three years (1981–4) set the stage for the huge flowering of interest in the Spanish Golden Age which was to become one of the most notable movements in British theatre after 1990. But let us stay specifically with Calderón for the moment.

A number of new translations of Calderón, published and / or performed since the mid-1980s, confirm that he has now been accorded the status which his work deserves. Principal among these more recently published translations are the versions of Kenneth **Muir** and Ann L. **Mackenzie**. *Three Comedies* and *The Schism in England*, a translation of *La cisma de Inglaterra* (1627) contrive to be scholarly, elegant and entertaining, a good read as well as dramatic scripts which could form the basis of a successful performance. Their version of the *Casa con dos puertas mala es de guardar* (1629, House With Two Doors), where farce and a precursory sense of the absurd combine in one of Calderón's most fastmoving comedies, is especially successful in its recreation of the linguistic wit and verve which characterize the original.

The Schism in England was published by Aris and Phillips, a small academic press which has done much to further the cause of Spanish theatre, generally through the publication of bilingual editions with extensive introductions and annotations. The footnote is, of course, only of use to the translator

for the page rather than for the person who is working with a production in mind. It is hard to imagine A. K. G. **Paterson**'s *The Painter of His Dishonour* or Dian **Fox** and Donald **Hindley**'s *The Physician of His Honour* receiving successful stagings as they stand. But they are scholarly editions whose primary value lies in providing broad access to these important plays for an English-speaking audience.

There have been a number of major Calderón productions in the 1990s. Most significant among them was *Three Justices in One* (translated by Gwynne **Edwards** and included in his *Calderón: Plays One*. The play was performed by London's Gate Theatre as part of its award-winning Spanish Golden Age season (1991–2). Laurence **Boswell**, who was one of the directors of this season, and David **Johnston**, who provided two of the Lope de Vega translations, also produced a new version of *The Painter of Dishonour* for the Royal Shakespeare Company. The play, described in the *Guardian* as 'a strong story, big emotions, an operatic intensity; this is the real, right stuff', was published by in the same year by Absolute Classics.

One of Calderón's most successful and creative translators has been John **Clifford**. A Hispanist by training, a specialist in Calderón, this playwright has produced versions of *Schism in England* and *The Surgeon of His Honour*, among others. The Edinburgh Festival commissioned him to write a new version of *Life Is a Dream* for the 1998 Festival. Performed to critical acclaim, it has been published by Nick Herne. This is a version which is both taut and lyrical, a fine example of the translator ably rendering the spirit of this complex and rewarding play.

iii. Lope de Vega With the exception of one or two high-profile productions earlier in the century, the English-language trajectory of Lope de Vega has been very similar to that of Calderón. The celebrated Theatre Union production of *Fuenteovejuna* in Manchester in 1936, to raise funds for the Republican cause in the Spanish Civil War, was revived by Joan Littlewood's Theatre Workshop in 1955. Possibly inspired by the tone of contemporary relevance that Littlewood and Ewan MacColl found there, John **Osborne** executed his spirited and muscular version of *La fianza satisfecha* (?1612–?1615, A Bond Honoured), subsequently published by Faber in 1966. In terms of introducing Lope to the English-language theatre, more influential than Osborne's free adaptation was Jill **Booty**'s *Lope de Vega: Five Plays*. Translated into prose, these are quietly accurate, generally

415

readable renditions which, although clearly not acting versions as the translator claims, give a good account of Lope's prime qualities as a dramatist—narrative economy, a deft touch in characterization, a striking blend of lyricism and humour. Containing the five plays which would probably emerge from critical consensus as Lope's finest—*Peribañez y el comendador de Ocaña* (c.1605, Peribañez), *El castigo sin venganza* (1635, Punishment Without Revenge), *El caballero de Olmedo* (c.1615, The Knight from Olmedo), *Fuenteovejuna*, and *El perro del hortelano* (c.1613–15, The Dog in the Manger)—the book retains its status as a valuable vade-mecum.

It was 1989 which saw the first major professional production of a Lope play for a number of years. Once again, the play was Lope's most popular and best-known work, *Fuenteovejuna*. Once again the location was London's Cottesloe Theatre, and once again the translator was the poet Adrian Mitchell. Both production and translation were hailed by the press as a revelation, although Mitchell's version is less assured than his adaptations of Calderón. It is as if the spirit of Lope's rapidly moving dialogue, encrusted with jokes and punning references, has eluded him in a way that the more lofty writing of the later Calderón did not. The play was quickly published with *Lost in a Mirror*, the name which Mitchell gives to his forceful version of *El castigo sin venganza*.

More reliable translations of *Fuenteovejuna* and *The Dog in the Manger* were published by Victor **Dixon** in 1989 and 1990 respectively. Both of these translations are published with a full critical apparatus and have a deft colloquial touch which all too often eludes academic translators. One of the primary difficulties in translating Lope de Vega is coping with the rapidity of his writing, the highly condensed but beautifully turned line of his poetry, without losing the economy of each dialogue, each scene and of the play as a whole. This is exactly the pitfall into which Michael D. **McGaha**'s version of *Lo fingido verdadero* (c.1608, Acting Is Believing) falls, unable to cope with a play which combines in equal measure stringent wit and baroque linguistic complexity.

At the heart of the Gate Theatre's award-winning Spanish Golden Age season were Lope's *Lo fingido verdadero*, now translated as *The Great Pretenders* by David Johnston, and the same translator's adaptation of *The Gentleman from Olmedo*, recognized by many as Lope's greatest play, but previously only available in Booty's translation. Both plays enjoyed critical success and were subsequently published in one volume. Written in a free-flowing ballad metre, these are adaptations which are primarily intended for performance, and both Booty and McGaha provide a more reliable guide to the letter of the originals.

The same might be said both of Johnston's translation *Los locos de Valencia* (1590–5, Madness in Valencia) and Nick **Drake**'s poetic version of *Peribañez*, published together in 1998. This is a volume which gives a fascinating insight into Lope both as comic genius and subtle tragedian. In the case of *Madness in Valencia*, Johnston has taken the unusual step of providing alternative endings to the play: his own (the performed version) and Lope's original.

iv. Tirso de Molina It might be felt that Tirso de Molina has entered the English-speaking theatre on the coat-tails of his two more illustrious compatriots. But this is to do a grave disservice to the psychological complexity and deep moral intensity of his theatre. *The Rogue from Seville*, the English title generally given to his acknowledged masterpiece, *El burlador de Sevilla*, was of course already well known, even if only through its immense influence on successive generations of artists who brought their own creative talents to bear on its central paradoxes and tensions. It was Nicholas G. **Round**'s translation of *El condenado por desconfiado* (c.1624, Damned for Despair), published in 1986, which began to widen Tirso's appeal in English. This is an accomplished translation of the religious drama that is often seen as a companion piece to *El burlador*. It is published with an excellent introduction and well annotated. The same publishers—once again, Aris and Phillips—brought out Gordon **Minter**'s translation of *Don Gil de las calzas verdes* (1615, Don Gil of the Green Breeches) in the same format in 1991, although the comedy of this at times anarchic piece sometimes strains in this version. The same year also saw the publication of Frederick H. **Fornoff**'s translation of *La vida y muerte de Herodes* (?1612–?1615, The Life and Death of Herod), one of the least known of a series of plays which Tirso wrote on Biblical themes.

It is somewhat ironical, given Tirso's fecundity (second only to that of Lope de Vega), that the two major publications of the 1990s should be of plays already in print. Nick **Dear**'s *The Last Days of Don Juan* is a fast-moving, thoroughly enjoyable adaptation of *El burlador*, the principal change being that the trickster's servant Catalinón now becomes Catalina, thereby bringing the moral implications of his predatory nature closer to home. A more reliable guide to the narrative line of the original can be found in Gwynne Edwards' *The Trickster of Seville*. Laurence Boswell published the texts of his acclaimed productions of *Damned for Despair* and *Don Gil of the Green Breeches* in 1993, crediting Jonathan **Thacker** as co-translator.

v. Cervantes Interest in Cervantes as a dramatist has always been much less than the attention given to his prose works. He had an abiding interest in drama and frequently writes of his own love for the theatre. The same deftness of touch, both as a comic writer and tragedian, which characterizes his prose is also very much in evidence in a number of his plays. It was one of his early plays, *El cerco de Numancia* (1585, The Siege of Numantia), a stirring tragedy of patriotism and community solidarity, which first attracted the attention of translators into English. Perhaps the best known of a number of early versions of a play whose core values were easily adapted to the taste for melodrama which characterized late Victorian theatre is James **Gibson**'s *Numancia* (1885), a fascinating version which combines some of Cervantes' original simplicity with the more lurid expression of the penny dreadful. It was not until 1964 that Cervantes' most characteristic plays—the 'entremeses' (1615)—were published. These short pieces, Bosch-like, crowd the stage with richly drawn characters who between them create a magnificent and barbed tapestry of life in 16th-c. Spain. Edwin Honig's *Interludes: Cervantes* (1964) captures the *commedia dell'arte* feel of these eight pieces which were originally designed to be performed between the acts of a full-length play. The volume comes complete with an excellent introduction, including a translation of Cervantes' foreword to the original publication [see also II.k.5.iii].

Several Cervantes interludes have been successfully performed, both in English and Spanish, during the 1990s, and although there have been no new major publications of his plays in translation, interest is growing. The same period has seen Lope, Calderón, and Tirso established as major figures in the repertoire of the English-language theatre. For all of that, however, there are still literally hundreds of plays by these astonishingly prolific dramatists which remain to be discovered. What is clear is that the process of discovery has now begun in earnest.   DJ

ANTHOLOGIES   Flores, Angel, ed., *Spanish Drama*, New York, 1962.

CALDERÓN DE LA BARCA, PEDRO   Brandt, George W., *The Great Stage of the World*, Manchester, 1976 · Campbell, Roy, *The Surgeon of His Honour*, Madison, Wis., 1960 · Clifford, John, *Life Is a Dream*, London, 1998 · Edwards, Gwynne, *Calderón: Plays I*, London, 1994 · FitzGerald, Edward, *Eight Dramas of Calderón*, London, 1906 · Fox, Dian, and Hindley, Donald, *Calderón: El médico de su honra/The Physician of His Honour*, Warminster, UK, 1997 · Honig, Edwin, *Four Plays*, New York, 1961 · Johnston, David, and Boswell, Laurence, *The Painter of Dishonour*, Bath, 1995 · Mitchell, Adrian, *The Mayor of Zalamea; Life's a Dream; The Great Stage of the World*, Bath, 1981 · Muir, Kenneth, and McKenzie, Ann L., *Three Comedies*, Lexington, Ky., 1985 · *Calderón: La cisma de Inglaterra/The Schism in England*, Warminster, UK, 1990 · Paterson, A. K. G., *Calderón: El pintor de su deshonra / The Painter of His Dishonour*, Warminster, UK, 1991.

CERVANTES, MIGUEL DE   Gibson, James, *Numancia*, London, 1885 · Honig, Edwin, *Interludes, Cervantes*, New York, 1964.

LOPE DE VEGA   Booty, Jill, *Five Plays*, New York, 1961 · Dixon, Victor, *Fuenteovejuna*, Warminster, UK, 1989 · *The Dog in a Manger*, Ottawa, 1990 · Drake, Nick, and Johnston, David, *Peribañez/Madness in Valencia*, London, 1998 · Johnston, David, *The Great Pretenders; The Gentleman from Olmedo*, Bath, 1992 · McGaha, Michael, D., *Lo fingido verdadero/Acting Is Believing*, San Antonio, 1986 · Mitchell, Adrian, *Fuenteovejuna/Lost in a Mirror*, Bath, 1989 · Osborne, John, *A Bond Honoured: A Play*, London, 1966.

TIRSO DE MOLINA   Boswell, Laurence, and Thacker, Jonathan, *Don Gil of the Green Breeches*, Bath, 1993 · Dear, Nick, *The Last Days of Don Juan*, Bath, 1991 · Edwards, Gwynne, *El burlador de Sevilla/The Trickster of Seville*, Warminster, UK, 1986 · Fornoff, Frederick H., *La vida y muerte de Herodes/The Life and Death of Herod: A Christmas Tragedy and Epiphany*, New York, 1991 · Minter, Gordon, *Don.Gil de las calzas verdes/Don Gil of the Green Breeches*, Warminster, UK, 1991 · Round, Nicholas, G., *El condenado por deconfiado/Damned for Despair*, Warminster, UK, 1986.

SEE ALSO   Bentley, E., 'The Universality of the "Comedia" ', *Hispanic Review*, 27 (1959) [rep. in *The Playwright as Thinker*, New York, 1987] · McKendrick, M., *Theatre in Spain, 1490–1700*, Cambridge, 1992 · Taylor, G., *Reinventing Shakespeare*, London, 1990.

5. CERVANTES

i. Don Quixote: Up to 1900 The *Don Quixote* of Miguel de Cervantes is without doubt the most widely read of Spanish classics, a novel capable of engaging the reader at many levels, from sheer entertainment to the most profound reflections on human nature. The first part of Thomas **Shelton**'s version came out in 1612, seven years after part i of the original; his second part was published in 1620, five years after the completion of the novel. Shelton (*fl.* 1612) exploits the resources of Jacobean prose to the full: if at times he is more exuberant than the Spanish, the overall result is full of life, and he manages to convey a good deal of Cervantes' tone. Unfortunately, there are passages which he has clearly not understood. In the galley-slaves episode, for instance, he translates *la justicia, que es el mesmo rey* ('justice, which is the king himself') as 'the justice, who represents the king himself', and elsewhere there are signs of haste, as when he renders *en resolución* ('in short') as 'in resolution'.

The version by Peter **Motteux** (1660–1718), published almost three-quarters of a century later, is very different. It is more accurate, though only relatively so; while there are fewer errors, Motteux tends to paraphrase difficult passages: the result is often more natural than Shelton's laboured versions, though hardly satisfactory as a translation of the original. The greatest difference, however, is cultural: writing at the turn of the century, Motteux is able to benefit from the lucidity and matter-of-factness of Restoration prose. The result is a greater clarity in the descriptive passages and a more pointed kind of wit which is very much in keeping with the original. Occasionally, the kind of playfulness so evident in his earlier Rabelais translation [II.g.5.i] makes its appearance, usually very resourcefully, as when he translates the thieves' term *gurapas* (for galleys) as 'element-dasher'—almost certainly a coining of his own.

Motteux's version, then, has many merits, and thoroughly deserves the popularity which has kept it in print to the present day. However, it has a serious rival in the slightly later translation by Charles **Jarvis**, recently reprinted in World's Classics. In his lifetime, Jarvis (1678–1739) was better known as a painter than as a *littérateur*. (His portrait of Jonathan Swift now hangs in the National Portrait Gallery.) His knowledge of Spanish, however, seems to have been more than competent, and his version, unlike those of Shelton and Motteux, is very largely free from mistranslations. Moreover, he has an excellent and commendably economical prose style, with touches of Augustan vocabulary ('candour', 'alacrity', 'deportment'), which stays close to the original and manages to convey a good deal of its tone. The version of Tobias **Smollett** (1721–71), on the other hand, though often close to Jarvis, tends to broaden the tone, and for the most part is wordier in its solutions.

If Jarvis's is the best of the older English versions of *Don Quixote*, this is partly owing to the time it was written. By the early 18th c. the splendid idiosyncrasies of Elizabethan and Jacobean prose were far in the past and had been replaced by a more generally serviceable prose, developed by writers since Dryden and made standard by its currency in journals like the *Tatler* and the *Spectator*. Moreover, coming as it did just before the flowering of the 18th-c. novel with Smollett and Fielding, Jarvis's translation may be said to have avoided the transformation of the Cervantine manner into something altogether more English and more distant from the original.

Between 1775 and 1885, *Don Quixote* was retranslated at least four times: by Charles Henry **Wilmot** (*fl.* 1774), G. **Kelly** (*fl.* 1769), Mary **Smirke** (*fl.* 1818), and A. J. **Duffield** (1821–90). All these versions appear to have sunk without trace, though, if nothing else, they are signs of the continuing popularity of the novel itself. This is not the case with the remarkable version by John **Ormsby** (1829–95), first published in 1885, and recently revised by Joseph R. **Jones** and Kenneth **Douglas**. As Jones states in his preface to the Norton edition, 'Ormsby aimed his translation at the cultivated Victorian reader who could appreciate the echoes of classical English literary language and whose belletristic education allowed them to read archaic and dialectal prose with ease.' To a late 20th-c. reader, however, Ormsby's translation is not always easy to follow: in his quest for accuracy, he often introduces obscure Elizabethan words; more seriously, in attempting to reflect the syntax of the original, he frequently writes what amount to pseudo-Spanish sentences which bear little relation to natural English. Yet, to his credit, he regularly hits on the *mot juste*, so much so that many of his specific translations would be difficult to improve on. Thus, even though he takes accuracy to extreme lengths—an unusual fault among translators of *Don Quixote*—it is this very accuracy which has encouraged Jones and Douglas to revise his version, a task which has resulted in one of the most convincing of modern translations.

ii. Don Quixote: Twentieth Century For anything of comparable seriousness, one has to wait for Samuel **Putnam**'s version of 1945. This is in many ways an exemplary piece of work, done in full awareness of earlier translators—especially Ormsby—and backed by a series of very helpful notes. However, it does have its faults: though it perhaps rightly aims to attract the modern reader by stressing the colloquial side of the novel, this has the effect of reducing the strong rhetorical element of the original and thus producing too even a register. Not only this: one is often aware of a certain wordiness, partly the result of unnecessary connectives, as in the opening description of Don Quixote himself: 'This gentleman of ours was close on to fifty, of a robust constitution but with little flesh on his bones and a face that was lean and gaunt. He was noted for his early rising, being very fond of the hunt.' There is nothing here that would not pass on a rapid reading; however, more than once, the original is expanded—'with little flesh on his bones' (*seco de carnes*), 'a face that was lean and gaunt' (*enjuto de rostro*)—and the rhythm is partly destroyed by splitting the sentence. And finally, though Putnam's stress throughout is on the colloquial, when it comes to set speeches, like Marcela's magnificent tirade in part i, chapter 14, the sentences are often so convoluted that it is hard to imagine anyone, in however elevated a tone, actually speaking them.

J. M. **Cohen**'s version of 1950—probably the most widely read of all modern translations—errs in a different direction. Though it was obviously done with one eye on earlier translations—Jarvis in particular—the results are decidedly flat—almost as if it were a Lowest Common Multiple of existing translations. As a word-by-word rendering of the original it is accurate enough, but the prose is fairly lifeless by modern English standards and largely fails to convey the different registers of the original. This is not entirely Cohen's fault: what for Jarvis was living English for Cohen no longer is; in effect, Cohen has produced a translation which, though not deliberately archaizing, bears little relation to any form of modern English.

Can any modern translator do better? Walter **Starkie**'s version of 1954, though lively enough as far as it goes, takes the extreme course of abridging the original in the interests of modern taste. For anyone who wants an idea of the novel as a whole,

however, this is no solution: the cuts include much of what takes place in the household of the Duke and Duchess, as well as the episodes of the Canon of Toledo and Don Diego de Miranda. As Peter Russell noted, 'The general effect is to diminish the intellectual interest of the novel, to lessen its contact with the romances of chivalry and to make the Cervantine attitude to Don Quixote conform much more nearly to post-romantic English ideas of humour than it really does' (*Bulletin of Hispanic Studies*, 1955).

The one translator who *has* done better is Burton **Raffel**, whose excellent version of the novel was published in 1995. Raffel, already well known as a translator of Chrétien de Troyes and Rabelais [II.g.5.i], introduces his work on a note of honest doubt: 'No one can reproduce Cervantes' style in English. Not only is his prose uniquely magnificent, but the very music of Spanish, its syntactical structures, and the thrust and flavour of words, are literally untransportable into any other language.' The terms of this disclaimer are well chosen: the musicality of the original is indeed unique, and 'thrust and flavour' describes very well the experience of the reader as he makes his way through this massive text. Having said this, however, Raffel goes on to show just what a sensitive translator can do despite the inevitable distance from the language of the original. One of the virtues of his translation is that it attempts, as far as possible, to follow the syntax of the original without falling into any of Ormsby's excesses. Thus the sentence I have quoted from Putnam's version is rendered as follows: 'Our gentleman was getting close to fifty, but strong, lean, his face sharp, always up at dawn, and a devoted hunter.' What strikes one here is the sheer economy of Raffel's version: not so much a matter of following the original syntax point by point—he suppresses the semi-colon, for instance, after 'fifty'—but of achieving a more or less equivalent rhythm.

The same effect can be seen on a much larger scale in some of the set speeches, for example, in Marcela's great self-defence to which I referred earlier. Here, Raffel's translation, unlike Putnam's, is natural from beginning to end. This is partly a matter of vocabulary—'reproached' is better than 'reprehended', 'share my beauty' than 'lend them of my beauty'—but above all a question of rhythm: the whole speech flows, as does the original, and comes to rest on the mysterious final sentence, 'I am a remote fire, a sword seen from far off' (*Fuego soy apartado y espada puesta lejos*)—the effect of which Putnam completely loses.

Lastly, Raffel is immensely successful in dealing

with Sancho Panza's proverbs—a constant problem for translators since there are often no real equivalents in English. A passage like the following, for example, sounds completely spontaneous and needs no footnotes:

If you tell lies when you buy, your purse is bound to cry . . . And since I came into the world naked, I'll leave it the same way: nothing ventured, nothing gained—and suppose they really *were* lovers? What's it to me? What good is bacon if there's no pot to cook it in? Anyhow, can you put gates around a meadow? And besides, if they criticize God, who *won't* they criticize?

iii. Other Writings Translations of Cervantes' other works have an altogether more sporadic history. Apart from *Don Quixote*, the most frequently translated were the *Novelas ejemplares* (1613, Exemplary Novels), either as a whole or in part. The first English translation is roughly contemporary: the version by James **Mabbe** (1572–1642) of six of the twelve tales, published in 1640, though probably done some time earlier. Mabbe was an experienced translator, best known for his lively version of *La Celestina* [II.k.2]; his rendering of the *Exemplary Novels*, though it takes liberties no modern translator would allow, still reads extremely well and deserves to be reprinted.

Later translations, by Walter K. **Kelly** and N. **McColl**, can hardly be said to have survived; their archaic diction falls awkwardly between the two languages and they have never been reprinted. It is, in fact, only in the last quarter of a century that adequate translations of the *Exemplary Novels* have appeared, beginning with C. A. **Jones**'s Penguin selection of 1972. This is a fine version, done with great care and respect for the original, though, like Mabbe, it only includes six of the twelve stories. For a full version, one has to wait for the excellent four-volume translation of 1992, edited by B. W. **Ife** and done by a team of translators, including Ife himself. Though the different translators' criteria vary—some, for instance, are more colloquial than others—the overall achievement is very impressive, and this will clearly remain the definitive translation for some time to come.

Compared with *Don Quixote*, the *Exemplary Novels* present fewer difficulties to the translator: their registers remain more constant and their story-line is generally less complex. This is not the case with Cervantes' other fiction which, though very different from the *Quixote*, creates its own kind of problems. Hardly surprisingly, his pastoral novel *La Galatea* (1585) has not been translated since 1903. (There is an earlier version by G. W. J. **Gyll** which dates from 1867.) Though it is in many ways a fascin-

ating novel—among other things, it contains Cervantes' most explicit reflections on the nature of love—the amount of verse it includes is likely to discourage most potential translators, though a good modern translation would be something to set beside Sidney's *Arcadia*.

Cervantes' other full-length novel, *Los Trabajos de Persiles y Segismunda* (posthumously published in 1617, The Travails of Persiles and Segismunda), is another matter. This ambitious work, cast in the mould of the Byzantine novel, is now acknowledged to be one of Cervantes's masterpieces, though it is only with modern reassessments of the baroque that it has found anything like a steady readership. There is a contemporary translation from the French, published anonymously in 1619; the only relatively modern version, by Louise Dorothea **Stanley**, came out in 1856. This seems to have passed almost unnoticed—only to be expected, since both original and translation are poles apart from any possible Victorian taste. Nevertheless, times have changed, and it very much to be regretted that there is no really modern version of this unique example of 17th-c. fiction.

Cervantes' work as a dramatist, though neglected in his own lifetime, has recently attracted some distinguished translators, and several of his shorter plays have been successfully performed in English, Irish, and American theatres. Here one must distinguish between his full-length plays—largely unsuccessful at the time because cast in an older mode—and his short *entremeses* or interludes which brought him much greater acclaim. Of the former, *Numancia*—a verse play based on the siege of Numantia by the Romans—exists in a dignified but somewhat wooden version by Roy **Campbell**. By contrast, the interludes—there are eight of them—are based on scenes from everyday life, and owe a great deal to Cervantes' sense of comedy and to his unfailing ear for common speech. Some are written in verse, some in prose, and others in a mixture of the two. All eight have been very effectively translated by Edwin **Honig**, in versions which are eminently actable. Just as good, though in a rather different mode, are the two adaptations by the Irish poet Austin **Clarke**, *The Student from Salamanca* and *The Silent Lover*, in versions which are also very actable, and most recently, by Dawn L. **Smith**, in lively contemporary English. In Clarke's texts, the flexibility of the verse, as coming from a skilled practitioner, is entirely admirable, as is the faintly Irish diction, which one feels Cervantes himself would have appreciated:

Husband and wife should have their tiff-taff
On the twenty-second of June, for if
They knock about, curse, scraub and clout,
Showing their temper to St John,
At midnight when his feast is gone by,
They'll kiss, forget the words they said,
Turn round and make it up in bed.

Cervantes' influence on the modern novel in English is incalculable. It is most evident in his earliest imitators, Smollett and Fielding, though it continues to surface, often unpredictably, up to the present day. Walter Scott declared that Cervantes

was the storyteller who inspired him to become a writer; *Don Quixote* was one of Dickens's favourite books; G. H. Lewes read *Don Quixote* aloud and had George Eliot translate it 'like a good child'. The list could be extended to writers as diverse as Saul Bellow and Salman Rushdie. But perhaps it is most appropriate to end with another great novelist, Vladimir Nabokov, whose *Lectures on Don Quixote* (1983)—both idiosyncratic and acute—close with the following words: 'His blazon is pity, his banner is beauty. He stands for everything that is gentle, forlorn, pure, unselfish and gallant. The parody has become a paragon.'   AT

DON QUIXOTE   *The History of the Valorous and Wittie Knight-Errant Don Quixote of La Mancha*, tr. Thomas Shelton, London, pt. i, 1612, pt. ii, 1620; rep. London, 1896 · *The History of the Renown'd Don Quixote de la Mancha*, tr. Peter Motteux, London, 1700–3 [rep. Everyman] · *The Life and Exploits of the Ingenious Gentleman Don Quixote de la Mancha*, tr. Charles Jarvis, London, 1742 [rep. World's Classics] · *The History and Adventures of the Renowned Don Quixote*, tr. Tobias Smollett, London, 1755 [many reprints] · *The Ingenious Gentleman Don Quixote of La Mancha*, tr. John Ormsby, London, 1885 [rev. edn. New York, 1981] · *The Ingenious Gentleman Don Quixote de la Mancha*, tr. Samuel Putnam, New York, 1945 [later reprints] · *The Adventures of Don Quixote*, tr. J. M. Cohen, Harmondsworth, 1950 [Penguin] · *Don Quixote of La Mancha*, tr. Walter Starkie, London, 1954 [abr. version] · *The History of the Ingenious Gentleman Don Quijote de la Mancha*, tr. Burton Raffel, New York, 1995.
OTHER NOVELS AND SHORTER FICTION   *Exemplarie Novels: in Sixe Books*, tr. James Mabbe, London, 1640 [a selection] · *Exemplary Novels*, tr. C. A. Jones, Harmondsworth, 1972 [Penguin: a selection] · *Exemplary Novels*, tr. B. W. Ife et al., 4 vols., Warminster, UK, 1992 · *Galatea*, tr. G. W. J. Gyll, London, 1867 · *Galatea*, tr. H. Oelsner and A. B. Welford, Glasgow, 1901–3 · *The Travels of Persiles and Segismunda*, tr. anon. [from the French], London, 1619 · *The Wanderings of Persiles and Segismunda*, tr. Louise Dorothea Stanley, London, 1856.
PLAYS   *Eight Interludes*, tr. Dawn L. Smith, London, 1996 [Everyman] · *Interludes*, tr. Edwin Honig, New York, 1964 [Signet] · *The Siege of Numantia*, tr. Roy Campbell, in *Six Spanish Plays*, ed. Eric Bentley, New York, 1959 · *Two Interludes Adapted from Cervantes*, tr. Austin Clarke, Dublin, 1968.
SEE ALSO   Nabokov, V., *Lectures on Don Quixote*, ed. Fredson Bowers, London, 1985.

6. PICARESQUE NOVELS

The picaresque canon consists of three major works: the anonymous *Lazarillo de Tormes* (1554), Mateo Alemán's *Guzmán de Alfarache* (1599–1605), and Francisco de Quevedo's *La vida del Buscón* (The Life of a Swindler), written in 1605–6 but not published until 1626. Other important examples include two continuations of *Lazarillo* (1555 and 1620), as well as novels by Francisco López de Úbeda (*La pícara Justina*, 1605), Vicente Espinel (*Marcos de Obregón*, 1618), and *Estebanillo González* (1646). Several of Cervantes' *Novelas ejemplares* (1613, Exemplary Novels) also make use of picaresque material [see II.k.5.iii].

Spanish picaresque novels vary in form, but have some basic characteristics in common: they are generally pseudo-autobiographies of low-life characters who serve many masters in order to scrape a living. Two of the problems faced by English translators stem from this format. The low-life setting

causes difficulties of vocabulary, and the autobiographical format creates an ambivalent tone, especially when the protagonist writes as a repentant sinner. Other problems arise from the Spanish penchant for elaborate word-play, coupled with the translators' tendency to rely on French and Italian cribs.

Nevertheless, the Spanish picaresque has been well served by English translators, with nearly 100 separate editions by 26 named translators since 1576. Indeed, the pattern of publication, and the incidence of new translations, reflects the ebb and flow of Anglo-Spanish literary and diplomatic relations in the 17th c., the romantic period, the late 19th c., and the second half of the 20th c. (when the majority of new versions come from the USA).

The impact of the Spanish picaresque in England is due to three early translators: David **Rowland**

(b. ?1547), James **Mabbe** (1572–?1642), and John **Stevens**. Rowland came from an Anglesey family and appears to have studied at Westminster School and Oxford before travelling abroad, possibly in the service of Sir Thomas Gresham, to whom he dedicated his translation of *Lazarillo de Tormes* in 1576. Although Rowland evidently consulted a French version by Jean Saugrain (1561), he also used a Spanish edition of 1573. The result is remarkable for its accuracy, and for the skill with which it conveys the required mix of youthful innocence and worldly wisdom.

Rowland's translation, billed as 'a true description of the nature and disposition of sundry Spaniards', was reprinted 10 times by 1677, and from 1639 was issued together with an anonymous version of Juan de Luna's continuation (1620). Rowland's idiom was slightly archaic, even for 1576, and it eventually fell out of favour, but more than a dozen subsequent translators have struggled to equal his achievement, including Thomas **Roscoe**, Clements **Markham**, Mack **Singleton**, and William **Merwin**. Michael **Alpert**'s version for Penguin Classics is reliable but insipid. An attractive anonymous version was published by J. Bell in 1789, with an epilogue recounting Lazarillo's death in a hermitage.

James Mabbe's version of *Guzmán de Alfarache*, *The Rogue*, is one of the finest examples of English translation from Spanish. Mabbe was fellow and Bursar of Magdalen College, Oxford, and travelled widely on the Continent, often in the company of Sir John Digby, ambassador to Madrid. He published little original work, though he contributed some commendatory verse to Shakespeare's First Folio; but he produced outstanding versions of several works of Spanish fiction, including *The Spanish Bawd* [see II.k.2] and six of Cervantes's *Exemplary Novels*, together with treatises on devotional and political topics.

For his *Rogue* Mabbe used Barezzo Barezzi's Italian version (1606–15), as well as the Spanish original. Where he found the text obscure, he said so, and he was not averse to leaving some of it in Spanish. But the character, elegance, and rhythm of this work is astonishing, and no other English version comes close. Those of Arthur **O'Conner** (1812) and John Henry **Brady** (1821) are incomplete, being based on Lesage's French text, which was 'purgée des moralités superflues' ('cleansed of superfluous moralizing').

The Irishman John **Stevens** was not the first to attempt Quevedo's *Buscón*, but his version of 1707 made sufficient headway with this impossibly difficult text to get it established among English readers. It was revised and reissued in 1743 by a Spaniard, Pedro **Pineda**, and again in 1926 by Charles **Duff**, who recast the whole work and provided new translations of many passages. Stevens produced translations of several Spanish works, including Juan de Mariana's *History of Spain*, and a picaresque anthology called *The Spanish Libertines* (1707). Duff thought Stevens's Quevedo 'by far his best work', but even with the revisions *Paul the Spanish Sharper* now strikes one as ponderous. Michael Alpert's *Swindler* for Penguin Classics is much better: 'modern and colloquial, without being trendy'.

BWI

ANTHOLOGIES   *The Spanish Libertines*, tr. John Stevens, London, 1707 [includes *La pícara Justina*, *Celestina*, and *Estebanillo González*] · *The Spanish Novelists*, ed. and tr. Thomas Roscoe, London, 1832, 1880 [includes Roscoe's translation of *Lazarillo de Tormes* together with Juan de Luna's continuation, *Guzmán de Alfarache*, tr. John Henry Brady, and *El Buscón*, tr. John Stevens] · *Masterpieces of the Spanish Golden Age*, ed. Angel Flores, New York, 1957 [includes Mack Singleton's translations of *Lazarillo de Tormes* and *El Buscón*] · *Two Spanish Picaresque Novels* [containing *Lazarillo de Tormes* and *El Buscón*], tr. Michael Alpert, Harmondsworth, 1969 [Penguin].

EL BUSCÓN   *The Life of Paul the Spanish Sharper*, tr. John Stevens, in *The Comical Works of Don Francisco de Quevedo*, London, 1707.

GUZMÁN DE ALFARACHE   *The Rogue; or, The Life of Guzmán de Alfarache*, tr. James Mabbe, London, 1622 [modern reprints London/New York, 1924; New York, 1967].

LAZARILLO DE TORMES   *The Pleasaunt Historie of Lazarillo de Tormes*, tr. David Rowland, London, 1576 [modern reprints: Oxford, 1924, and ed. Gareth A. Davies, Newtown, Wales, 1991] · *Lazarillo de Tormes: His Fortunes and Adversities*, tr. Clements R. Markham, London/New York, 1908 · *The Life of Lazarillo de Tormes: His Fortunes and Adversities*, tr. W. S. Merwin, New York, 1962; Gloucester, Mass., 1964 [also rep. in *Great European Short Novels*, ed. Anthony Winner, New York, 1968].

MARCOS DE OBREGÓN   *The History of the Life of the Squire Marcos de Obregon*, tr. Algernon Langton, London, 1816.

7. SPANISH POETRY: NINETEENTH AND TWENTIETH CENTURY

19th-c. Spanish poetry is poorly represented in English, mainly because of the mediocrity of much of the poetry itself. However, there are at least two exceptions to this: José de Espronceda, the best of the first generation of Romantic poets, and Gustavo Adolfo Bécquer, the one major poet of the 1850s and 1860s. Espronceda's long poem, *El estudiante de Salamanca* (1836–7, The Student of Salamanca), has recently been translated by C. K. **Davis**, though his version is curiously archaic and might have been done by Lockhart or Longfellow. Twenty of Bécquer's poems were translated in 1927 by Rupert **Croft-Cooke**—a creditable effort for the time, though one lacks a version in a more modern idiom.

The 20th c., on the other hand, has been described with some justice as a new 'golden age' in Spanish poetry, and one is almost overwhelmed by the quantity of translations. To begin with the earlier poets: a selection of Antonio Machado, *Castilian Ilexes*, translated by Henry **Gifford** and Charles **Tomlinson** was published in 1963 and subsequently reprinted in Penguins. These are extremely effective versions, not least because they are largely done in William Carlos Williams's 'three-ply measure', a technique which, as Tomlinson himself says, avoids 'the rather facile rattle that occurs if one translates Spanish octosyllables into English with end rhymes'. A much larger selection has since appeared, translated with an excellent introduction by Alan **Trueblood**—less brilliant than the Gifford–Tomlinson versions, though resourceful and thoroughly reliable.

Another poet of the same generation, Juan Ramón Jiménez, has fared less well, partly because of the more abstract nature of his verse. The versions by J. B. **Trend** are too fulsome and uncertain in their idiom, even when revised by J. L. Gili. Of the other translations, much the best are those by Robert **Bly**, who at least finds a consistent idiom and manages to produce poems which read well in their own right.

Of the poets who began to write in the 1920s, much the most frequently translated has been Federico García Lorca. This is partly, one suspects, for non-literary reasons: his brutal death at a relatively early age became an obvious symbol for Republican supporters in Spain and abroad. Certainly, translations of his poems began to appear soon after his death, beginning with A. L. **Lloyd**'s much reprinted version of *Llante por la muerte de Ignacio Sánchez Mejías* (1935, Lament for the Death of a Bullfighter). The selection translated by J. L. **Gili** and Stephen **Spender** remains one of the best, though for readers with a little Spanish, Gili's literal prose renderings in his Penguin anthology are an indispensable key to the originals. An equally good American selection, published in 1959, contains some of the Spender–Gili translations, together with others by Langston **Hughes** and W. S. **Merwin**. More recently, the generous selection translated by Merryn **Williams**, which contains the first versions of the newly discovered *Sonnets of Dark Love*, includes some fine renderings of the longer poems—'Ode to Salvador Dalí' and 'Lament for Ignacio Sánchez Mejías'—and, despite the occasional error, is a considerable achievement.

Best of all is the comprehensive anthology edited by Christopher **Maurer**, originally published in the USA and recently made available in Britain. These versions, the work of a dozen translators including the editor, are of an unfailingly high standard and include not only work from all Lorca's published collections but also a group of uncollected poems, some of which have not been translated before. Maurer is also the translator of a much smaller, but attractive, selection of Lorca's poems and prose which includes two previously untranslated lyric sequences.

Lorca's two most popular collections, *Romancero gitano* (1928, Gypsy Ballads) and *Poeta en Nueva York* (1940), have been translated as a whole several times. *Gypsy Ballads*, to be sure, is a severe challenge to any translator: the Spanish ballad metre—octosyllabic, with assonance in the even-numbered lines—is virtually impossible to re-create in English. Words like 'spikenard' and 'pomegranate' inevitably sound more exotic than their originals, and Lorca's habit of introducing what amount to little poetic conceits lead him to feats of compression which are almost impossible to reproduce in another language. Nevertheless, a number of translators have risen to the challenge, with varying degrees of success. Take, for example, the following three versions of the opening lines of 'Romance de la luna, luna' (Ballad of the Moon, Moon):

> The moon came to the farrier's shop
> Wearing her bustle sprigged with nard.
> The little boy is staring at her,
> the little boy is staring hard.
> The moon is waving her white arms
> into the palpitating air,
> and shows, lascivious yet pure,
> her breasts of tin so hard and bare.
>
> (Roy Campbell)

The moon came to the smithy
in her bustle of spikenard.
The boy stares and stares at her.
The boy keeps staring hard.
In the agitated breeze
the moon makes her arms spin,
showing, lubricious and pure,
her breasts of hard tin.

(Robert G. Havard)

The moon came to the smithy
with her bustle of white rose.
The child looks at her,
and looks and looks.
In the agitated air
the moon moves her arm
and shows, pure, shameless,
her breasts of hard tin.

(Merryn Williams)

Here, to my mind, Williams gains by her very simplicity: she sensibly replaces 'spikenard' by 'white rose' and substitutes a common English word, 'shameless', for 'lubricious'. Havard, on the other hand, keeps 'spikenard' and 'lubricious' and pads out 'the moon moves her arms', presumably for the rhyme with 'tin'. Campbell takes rhyme much further: the result is a version which is rhythmically over-insistent and which leads to such intrusions as 'so hard and bare'. Havard's versions, it has to be said, are often resourceful and read well, despite occasional awkwardnesses, and are accompanied by some extremely helpful notes. Campbell's, by contrast, often fill out the originals quite unjustifiably, and, by insisting on full rhyme, destroy the much subtler effect of the assonance.

Poet in New York, though its meaning is often obscure, seems paradoxically easier to translate, partly because of its more expansive rhythms. Though the earlier translations tend to fall into a kind of sub-Whitmanesque, Merryn Williams's partial versions are outstanding, as is the rendering of the entire sequence by Greg **Simon** and Steven F. **White**, based on a new edition of the original text.

The other major poets of the so-called 1925 Generation—Jorge Guillén, Luis Cernuda, Rafael Alberti, Pedro Salinas, and Vicente Aleixandre—have all been translated, some better than others. *Cántico* (1965) contains some of the best of Guillén's poetry, translated by Richard **Wilbur**, W. S. Merwin, and others. (Wilbur's versions, in particular, are marvels of re-creation.) There is a good selection of the poems of Luis Cernuda, translated by Derek **Harris**, Anthony **Edkins**, and others; unfortunately, though the shorter poems

come off well, the longer, more discursive ones often seem flat and over-fluent, which the carefully poised originals are not. Alberti has been translated more than once: Ben **Belitt**'s versions are well chosen and reliable; they are partly eclipsed, however, by two quite outstanding translations, G. W. **Connell**'s rendering of the long sequence *Sobre los ángeles* (1929, Concerning the Angels)—probably Alberti's masterpiece—and Mark **Strand**'s superb anthology, *The Owl's Insomnia* (1973). Salinas, on the other hand, has not fared so well: the selection translated by Eleanor L. **Turnbull**, though pioneering for its time, is now decidedly outdated, and though better versions have appeared more recently in little magazines, there is still no more modern selection in book form. As for Aleixandre, who belongs chronologically to the 1925 Generation but whose reputation was slower in coming, there is a fine selection, well translated by Louis **Bourne**, published four years after Aleixandre was awarded the Nobel Prize for Literature.

Several good minor poets of the same period have also been translated. Dámaso Alonso, better known as a literary critic, was also an important precursor of the 'social realism' which came to dominate Spanish poetry in the 1950s and 1960s, and his best collection, *Hijos de la ira* (1944, Children of Wrath), has been very effectively translated by Elias **Rivers**. Miguel Hernández, who died in prison in 1942 at the age of 31, had all the makings of a major poet; his poetry, concentrated and expansive by turns, seemed for a long time to defy translation, but now there is a fine selection in English, very sympathetically translated by Don **Share** (1996).

The years immediately following the Civil War were not, on the whole, a good time for Spanish poetry: a number of the older poets continued to write, often in exile; the younger ones, on the other hand, seemed disoriented, still overshadowed by the 1925 Generation and failing to find an alternative tradition. The one exception to this is Blas de Otero, who published his first collection in 1942. Otero is a powerful, if uneven, poet who expresses the tensions between social and religious belief, often in forms of great violence. His sonnets—probably his best work—have often been compared with some justice to those of the great 17th-c. poet Francisco de Quevedo [II.k.3.iv], and some of these are included in the selection translated by Hardie **St Martin**.

More recently, a number of outstanding poets have emerged—José Ángel Valente, Claudio Rodríguez, Francisco Brines, Ángel Crespo, and, in a younger generation, Jaime Siles, Guillermo Carnero, and Andrés Sánchez Robayna. Though translations of most of these have appeared sporadically in little magazines, none has so far appeared in

book form, though all deserve to; only then will it be seen what a major contribution Spanish writers are making to contemporary European poetry.

AT

ANTHOLOGIES   Bourne, Louis, *Contemporary Poetry from the Canary Islands*, London/Boston, Mass., 1976 · Hammer, Louis, and Schyfter, Sara, *Recent Poetry of Spain: A Bilingual Anthology*, New York, 1983 · St Martin, Hardie, *Roots and Wings: Poetry from Spain 1900–75*, New York/London, 1976.

ALBERTI, RAFAEL   Belitt, Ben, *Selected Poems*, Berkeley/Los Angeles, 1966 · Connell, G. W., *Concerning the Angels*, London, 1967 · Strand, Mark, *The Owl's Insomnia*, New York, 1973.

ALEIXANDRE, VICENTE   Bourne, Louis, *The Crackling Sun*, Madrid, 1981.

ALONSO, DÁMASO   Rivers, Elias L., *Children of Wrath*, Baltimore, 1970.

BÉCQUER, GUSTAVO ADOLFO   Croft-Cooke, Rupert, *Twenty Poems*, Oxford, 1927.

CERNUDA, LUIS   Harris, Derek, Edkins, Anthony, et al., *The Poetry of Luis Cernuda*, New York, 1971.

ESPRONCEDA, JOSÉ DE   Davis, C. K., *The Student of Salamanca*, Warminster, UK, 1994.

GARCÍA LORCA, FEDERICO   Belitt, Ben, *Poet in New York*, New York, 1955 · Bly, Robert, *Selected Poems of Lorca and Jiménez*, Boston, 1973 · Campbell, Roy, *Lorca: An Appreciation of His Poetry*, London, 1952 · Gili, J. L., *Selected Poems*, Harmondsworth, 1960 [Penguin] · Havard, Robert G., *Gypsy Ballads*, Warminster, UK, 1990 [rev. edn., 1995] · Humphries, Rolfe, *The Poet in New York and Other Poems*, New York, 1940 · *Gypsy Ballads*, Bloomington, Ind., 1963 · Lloyd, A. L., *Lament for the Death of a Bullfighter*, London, 1937 [many reprints] · Maurer, Christopher, ed., *Selected Poems*, Harmondsworth, 1997 [Penguin] · *A Season in Granada*, London, 1998 · Simon, Greg, and White, Steven F., *Poet in New York*, New York, 1988 [Penguin, 1990] · Spender, Stephen, and Gili, J. L., *Poems*, London, 1939 · Spender, Stephen, Gili, J. L., et al., *Selected Poems*, New York, 1955 [many reprints] · Williams, Merryn, *Selected Poems*, Newcastle upon Tyne, 1992.

GUILLÉN, JORGE   Merwin, W. S., Wilbur, Richard, et al., *Cántico*, London, 1965.

HERNÁNDEZ, MIGUEL   Share, Don, *I have Lots of Heart*, Newcastle upon Tyne, 1996.

JIMÉNEZ, JAN RAMÓN   Bly, Robert, *Forty Poems*, Madison, Wis., 1967 · *Selected Poems of Lorca and Jiménez*, Boston, 1973 · Trend, J. B., *Fifty Spanish Poems*, Oxford, 1950 [rev. edn., by J. L. Gili, Penguin, 1974].

MACHADO, ANTONIO   Gifford, Henry and Tomlinson, Charles, *Castilian Ilexes*, Oxford, 1963 [Penguin, 1974] · Trueblood, Alan, *Selected Poems*, Cambridge, Mass./London, 1982.

OTERO, BLAS DE   St Martin, Hardie, *Twenty Poems*, Madison, Wis., 1964.

SALINAS, PEDRO   Turnbull, Eleanor L., *Lost Angel and Other Poems*, Baltimore, 1932.

8. SPANISH PROSE: NINETEENTH AND TWENTIETH CENTURY

Romantic Britain thought highly of Spain, but not of its contemporary literature. The perception of Spain as a country where the individual could be wild and free, where impending industrialization was not apparent, and where the romantic passions still operated unconstrained by the rationalism of the Enlightenment meant that anything which was modern in the country was left out of the picture. This archaizing view looked back to the literature of the Spanish Golden Age, to *Don Quixote* [II.k.5] above all, and only writing which appeared to accord with this image was validated.

This meant that 19th-c. Spanish writing, which was often struggling against precisely the forces idealized by foreign readers, was little translated at the time, and has been relatively little translated since. While most significant 19th-c. Spanish writers have had works translated, to a contemporary eye 19th-c. translations are generally undistinguished, and 20th-c. translations used not to be

much better. The best translation of a 19th-c. Spanish work is certainly John **Rutherford**'s version of Leopoldo Alas's magnificent *La Regenta* (1884–5). Rutherford rarely flags in rendering Alas's dense intrigue and acerbic picture of complacent, provincial Oviedo.

Pedro de Alarcón's *El sombrero de tres picos* (1874, The Three-Cornered Hat) has appeared in several versions, but it is soon apparent why new translations continue to appear. The original's relaxed, urbane tone is difficult to transpose into English without its appearing inconsequential. The best of many translations are the first anonymous one in 1886, relatively clear and lively, and that by Alexander **Tulloch** for Everyman. Robert **Graves** translated Alarcón's biting *El niño de la bola* (1880) as *The Infant with the Globe*, but it is not a brilliant effort. If even Graves was unable to avoid a laboured and orotund translation, it is not surprising that this fate has befallen many 19th-c. Spanish works in English.

425

Spain's most important 19th-c. novelist, Benito Pérez Galdós, suffered repeatedly in this respect. Where he is clear and conversational in Spanish, he was usually ponderous and stiff in English; where he is ironic and sharp in Spanish, he came across as long-winded and obvious in English. Recently, however, much better translations have begun to appear, notably Jo **Labanyi**'s translation of the multivalent *Nazarín* (1895), Charles **de Salis**'s handling of *Misericordia*, and Catherine **Jagoe**'s of the penetrating social fable *La de Bringas* (1884, That Bringas Woman). Gamel **Woolsey**'s translation of *La de Bringas* as *The Spendthrifts* is also spry and inventive, despite eliminating whole sentences. Agnes Moncy **Gullón**'s translation of Galdós's masterpiece, *Fortunata y Jacinta* (1886–7), however, gives the most extensive flavour of Galdós's rich social breadth.

After Spain lost its last American and Asian colonies in the war of 1898 with the USA, the pressures for modernization increased. In general, however, the modernizing impulse in Spain had to do battle with different forces (such as the powerful Roman Catholic Church) from those opposing the same impulse in English-speaking countries, and Spanish writers of this time were only fitfully perceived as relevant.

Miguel de Unamuno first appeared in English with a translation of his great, disputatious work of stream-of-consciousness philosophy, *Del sentimiento trágico de la vida en los hombres y en los pueblos* (1913, The Tragic Sense of Life in Men and Peoples), the vigour of which was well captured by J. E. Crawford **Flitch**. A tidier, but not more enjoyable, translation was later made by Anthony **Kerrigan** in the excellent Princeton University Press series of selected works by Unamuno. All of the translations in this series are praiseworthy; the most accessible is *Novel/Nivola*, also translated by Kerrigan, which contains the entertaining *Mist*, in which characters argue petulantly with the author (the original *Niebla*, 1914, pre-dated Pirandello's *Six Characters in Search of an Author* [II.m.12] by seven years).

José Ortega y Gasset has suffered less than Unamuno from the attitude identified by the pioneering Hispanist J. B. Trend: 'Contemporary men of letters in England are not as a rule prepared to admit that Spain as a country of the mind has any real existence' (*Nation and Athenaeum*, 1921). Ortega has had much of his work published in a standard format by Norton in the USA, albeit with great unevenness between the volumes. Of the many works translated, Ortega's eclectic, restless quality has been well caught in Philip W. **Silver**'s translation of *Sobre la razón histórica* (1979, On Historical

Reason). Of his major works, James **Cleugh**'s translation of *El tema de nuestro tiempo* (1923, The Modern Theme) copes well with such a dense work, which is unlike the oral and dynamic nature of most of Ortega's work. *La rebelión de las masas* (1929, The Rebellion of the Masses) has been best translated by Kerrigan. *La deshumanización del arte* (1925), was handled stolidly by Helene **Weyl** in *The Dehumanization of Art and Notes on the Novel*, and more fluently by Alexis **Brown** in *Velázquez, Goya and the Dehumanization of Art*.

The pungent and fascinating novelist Pío Baroja has always been ill served in translation. None of the translations of his works into English has been a real success. Typical are translations by Isaac **Goldberg** of *La busca* (1904) as *The Quest*, or by early Hispanist Aubrey **Bell** of *El árbol de la ciencia* (1911) as *The Tree of Knowledge*, in which Baroja's anti-bombastic and episodic panoramas of urban aimlessness and self-seeking deviousness, scratching poverty and quotidian routine, come out as too controlled and Edwardian.

The most-translated Spanish novelist ever, in terms of different titles, is Vicente Blasco Ibáñez, whose middlebrow novel *Los cuatro jinetes del Apocalipsis* (1916, The Four Horsemen of the Apocalypse) became an international bestseller, and subsequent Hollywood blockbuster; there followed a series of increasingly lavish films of his novels over the next 15 years. This also encouraged numerous translations, which were mostly rushed and clumsy. Better translations were done later, including those by Frances **Partridge** of *Sangre y arena* (1908, Blood and Sand) and *La maja desnuda* (1906, The Naked Lady). Blasco Ibáñez's more acclaimed, highly charged, naturalistic Valencian novels have proved difficult to turn into English; perhaps the best effort has been *The Holding*, the translation by Lester **Clark** and Eric Farrington **Birchall** of *La barraca* (1898).

Of the Spanish authors who emerged in the turbulent 1930s, Ramón Sender is the prose writer who has received most attention. Enthusiastically, if a little erratically, translated by the polymath zoologist and left-wing sympathizer Sir Peter Chalmers **Mitchell** as *Seven Red Sundays*, *Siete domingos rojos* (1932), was the first novel by a Spanish author to be published by Penguin. Of the rest of his work, the chilling *Epitalamio del prieto Trinidad* (1942) was reasonably done as *The Dark Wedding* by Eleanor **Clark**, and *La esfera* (1947), Sender's *La Nausée*, was translated competently by Felix **Giovanelli** as *The Sphere*.

Nobel prize winner Camilo José Cela's style is so guilefully colloquial it resists translation more than most. As Paul Ilie says, in the introduction to Frances **López Morillas**'s careful translation of Cela's dryly thoughtful travel book *Viaje al Alcarria* (1948, Journey to the Alcarria), 'Cela can combine in one expression not only an entire folkway, but a personal lyricism and a sly irony as well.' Despite these formidable barriers, translators have enjoyed the challenge. *San Camilo, 1936* (1969) has been skilfully translated by John **Polt**. Even the heavily colloquial *Mazurca para dos muertos* (1983) has been intelligently translated as *Mazurka for Two Dead Men* by Patricia **Haugaard**. *La familia de Pascual Duarte* (1942), an unsentimental and acrid representation of rural life, has been best translated by Anthony Kerrigan, but suffers, like Baroja's work, from the absence of a similar register in English. Cela's masterpiece, *The Hive* (*La colmena*, 1951), a witty, inventive, and magical tableau of 1940s Madrid, needs to have J. M. **Cohen** and Arturo **Barea**'s 1953 translation sharpened.

Juan Goytisolo has often been referred to as Spain's greatest living writer, and most of his work has been quickly translated into English. One of the very best translators of any era has been the splendid Gregory **Rabassa**, who has mostly worked with Spanish-American prose of the most demanding sort. Rabassa translated Goytisolo's *Señas de identidad* (1966) as *Marks of Identity*, a masterful effort at confronting the difficulties of Goytisolo's embattled dealing with what Spain meant to him. However, the best translations of both Goytisolo and

indeed contemporary Spanish prose have been those done by Peter **Bush** in his superb versions of Goytisolo's penetrating memoirs, *Coto vedado* (1985, Forbidden Territory) and *En los reinos de taifa* (1986, Realms of Strife), as well as the postmodern reverie of the novella *Cuarantena* (1991, Quarantine) and the high-spirited *La saga de los Marx* (1993, The Marx Family Saga).

Nowadays, the post-Franco re-entry of Spain into cultural respectability and even favour means that many successful Spanish novels are translated into English relatively quickly. The most heroic of these translations is that of Julián Ríos's kaleidoscopic *Larva: Babel de una noche de San Juan* (1984, Larva: Midsummer Night's Babel) translated by Richard Alan **Francis**, with assistance from Suzanne Jill **Levine** and Ríos himself. It might seem impossible to emulate the book's puns, multilingual ingenuity, and allusive word-play, but the translation conveys the polyglot vigour of the original brilliantly. The cumulative effect of the translators' inventiveness is such that the reading experience does indeed closely relate to that of reading the original. The most apparently impossible translation has become one of the most possible, in a way dedicated both to the possibilities and to the impossibilities of translation, the joy Ríos's work takes in language and the interwoven meanings of European cultures, the excitement of the felicitous double or triple meaning, and even the fun of the failed attempt. Babel is not so much our fate as our delight. DC

ALARCÓN, PEDRO DE   anon., *The Three-Cornered Hat*, London, 1886 · Graves, Robert, *The Infant with the Globe*, London, 1955 · Tulloch, Alexander, *The Three-Cornered Hat*, London, 1995 [Everyman].
ALAS, LEOPOLDO [CLARÍN]   Rutherford, John, *La Regenta*, London, 1984 [Penguin].
BAROJA Y NESSI, PÍO   Bell, Aubrey F. G., *The Tree of Knowledge*, London, 1928 · Goldberg, Isaac, *The Quest*, New York, 1922.
BLASCO IBÁÑEZ, VICENTE   Clark, Lester, and Birchall, Eric Farrington, *The Holding (La Barraca)*, Warminster, UK, 1993 · Partridge, Frances, *Blood and Sand*, London, 1958 · *The Naked Lady*, London, 1959.
CELA TRULOCK, CAMILO JOSÉ   Cohen, J. M., with Arturo Barea, *The Hive*, London, 1953 · Haugaard, Patricia, *Mazurka for Two Dead Men*, New York, 1992 · Kerrigan, Anthony, *The Family of Pascual Duarte*, Boston, Mass., 1964 · López Morillas, Frances, *Journey to the Alcarria*, Madison, Wis., 1964 · Polt, John, *San Camilo, 1936*, Durham, NC, 1991.
GOYTISOLO, JUAN   Bush, Peter, *Forbidden Territory: The Memoirs of Juan Goytisolo, 1931–1956*, London, 1989 · *Realms of Strife: The Memoirs of Juan Goytisolo, 1957–1982*, London, 1990 · *Quarantine*, London, 1991 · *The Marx Family Saga*, London, 1996 · Rabassa, Gregory, *Marks of Identity*, New York, 1969.
ORTEGA Y GASSET, JOSÉ   Brown, Alexis, *Velázquez, Goya and The Dehumanization of Art*, London, 1972 · Cleugh, James, *The Modern Theme*, London, 1931 · Kerrigan, Anthony, *The Rebellion of the Masses*, Notre Dame, Ind., 1986 · Silver, Philip W., *On Historical Reason*, New York, 1984 · Weyl, Helene, *The Dehumanization of Art and Notes on the Novel*, Princeton, NJ, 1948, 1968 [with 3 further essays].
PÉREZ GALDÓS, BENITO   Gullón, Agnes Moncy, *Fortunato and Jacinta*, Athens, Ga., 1986 [Penguin] · Jagoe, Catherine, *That Bringas Woman*, London, 1996 [Everyman] · Labanyi, Jo, *Nazarin*, Oxford, 1993 [World's Classics] · Salis, Charles de, *Misericordia*, Sawtry, UK, 1995 · Woolsey, Gamel, *The Spendthrifts*, London, 1951.
RÍOS, JULIÁN   Francis, Richard Alan, with Suzanne Jill Levine and the author, *Larva: Midsummer Night's Babel*, London, 1991.

SENDER, RAMÓN   Clark, Eleanor, *The Dark Wedding*, New York, 1943 · Giovanelli, Felix, *The Sphere*, New York, 1949 · Mitchell, Sir Peter Chalmers, *Seven Red Sundays*, Harmondsworth, 1936.

UNAMUNO Y JUGO, MIGUEL DE   Flitch, J. E. Crawford, *The Tragic Sense of Life in Men and in Peoples*, London, 1921 · Kerrigan, Anthony, *The Tragic Sense of Life in Men and Nations*, Princeton, NJ, 1972 · *Novel/Nivola*, Princeton, NJ, 1976.

SEE ALSO   Callahan, D., 'Material Conditions for Reception: Spanish Literature in England 1920–1940', *New Comparison*, 15 (Spring 1993), 100–9.

9. TWENTIETH-CENTURY SPANISH DRAMA

The two Nobel laureates of Spanish theatre, José Echegaray and Jacinto Benavente y Martínez, 1904 and 1922 respectively, are rarely represented either on the contemporary Spanish stage or in English-language translation. Both, however, along with the Alvarez Quintero brothers (Serafín and Joaquín), enjoyed some success on the English Edwardian stage. Faithful versions of two of Benavente's well-made plays can be found, however, in Angel Flores's *Spanish Drama* and Robert W. Corrigan's excellent anthology *Masterpieces of the Modern Spanish Theatre*. *Spanish Drama* offers a version of *Los intereses creados* (1907, The Bonds of Interest), Benavente's best-known work. Incidentally, there is also a version here of Echegaray's *El gran Galeoto* (1881, The Great Galeoto). Both plays, in unflattering versions, read like the museum pieces which they have in many ways become. William **Oliver**'s translation of *Las brujas del domingo* (1903, The Witches' Sabbath) in *Masterpieces* is, at least, fluent.

Also in *Masterpieces* is a translation of one of Antonio Buero Vallejo's early plays, the underrated *La tejedora de sueños* (1952, The Dream Weaver). Generally regarded as the most important dramatist of Spain's post-Civil War period, Buero has generally not been well served by his translators into English, and *The Dream Weaver* is no exception from this general rule, its wordiness detracting from the play's powerful dramatization of the Penelope legend. Marion Peter **Holt** has translated four of Buero's best-known plays. In one volume are *El sueño de la razón* (1970, The Sleep of Reason), *La fundación* (1974, The Foundation), and *En la ardiente oscuridad* (1951, In the Burning Darkness), while the masterly *Las Meninas* (1960) is published separately. These are competent translations, *The Foundation* being perhaps the most fluent. They are also copyrighted performance versions, although their suitability for this particular purpose is open to question (*The Sleep of Reason*, for example, was staged unsuccessfully at London's Battersea Arts Centre in 1991, although it is considered by many to be one of the finest plays to be written in postwar Spain). A competent version of Buero's *La doble*

historia del doctor Valmy (The Double Case-History of Dr Valmy) is available in Gwynne **Edwards**'s *Burning the Curtain: Four Revolutionary Spanish Plays*. Written in 1964, this powerful denunciation of police torture was denied its first performance in Spain until 1976, although it was premièred in English (in a different version, under the title given above) in 1967. Two of Buero's complex and rewarding historical plays are available from Aris and Phillips: *La detonación* (1977, The Shot) and *Un soñador para un pueblo* (1958, A Dreamer for the People), translated by David **Johnston** and Michael **Thompson** respectively. The case of Buero is one of translators rushing in where writers fear to tread. Simply, translators' fidelity to the original has not helped the cause of their dramatist. Buero has not enjoyed the success on the English-speaking stage that the quality of his plays deserves.

The same could be said of a number of other contemporary playwrights. In addition to Buero, Edwards' *Burning the Curtain* offers works by Francisco Ors, Jaime Salóm, and the enduring and prolific Alfonso Sastre. In the case of both Salóm's *Casi una diosa* (1993, Almost a Goddess) and Sastre's *Prólogo patético* (written 1950, Tragic Prelude) one could be forgiven for thinking that there is less to these plays than meets the eye. Ors's *Contradanza* (1980, Contradance) proved controversial at the time of its first staging, and its energy transfers well into English. Another useful anthology of earlier politically encoded drama is Patricia **O'Connor**'s *Plays of Protest from the Franco Era*. With the exception of Buero's *El tragaluz* (1967, The Skylight Window), deftly translated by Patricia O'Connor, these plays have not aged well.

The best-known dramatist of twentieth-century Spain is, of course, Federico García Lorca. Now one of the most performed of all foreign dramatists in English, he was largely unknown until 1986, when the relaxing of international copyright allowed new translations of his work to be written. In 1938 the eminent American poet Langston **Hughes** had produced an early version of *Bodas de Sangre* (1933, Blood Wedding), to which he had given the title *Fate at the Wedding*. It is a rhythmical and beautifully taut version, but languished in manuscript form until 1994. Had it been made public, the distended story of Lorca's reception in English might have been quite different. The officially sanctioned versions, by James **Graham-Luján** and Richard L. **O'Connell**, first published in Britain in 1959, had proved literally unspeakable. Many new versions of Lorca's theatre have been published in recent years, too numerous to list here, but a sure sign of the impact of his theatre. English-speaking audiences are now familiar with the trilogy of *Blood Wedding, Yerma* (1934) and *La casa de Bernarda Alba* (written 1936 but published posthumously, The House of Bernarda Alba), in versions by John **Edmunds**, Gwynne Edwards, Langston Hughes, Ted **Hughes**, David Johnston, Brendan **Kennelly**, and W. S. **Merwin** among others, and there is evidence of a growing interest in what some critics tend to refer to as the 'unknown Lorca'—the radically innovative works of a playwright who was deeply committed to experimentation. The reader's attention is drawn to John **London**'s *The Unknown Federico García Lorca*, an invaluable introduction to Lorca's alternative repertoire. It is worth noting that these are the first translations of Lorca's plays to be based on his manuscripts. Some of Lorca's shorter pieces are also available in Gwynne Edwards's *Lorca. Plays: Two*. Included in this edition is the play considered by many to be one of Lorca's finest: *Así que pasen cinco años* (1931, When Five Years Pass), an excursus into the complexities of time and the mysteries of sexual identity that is in turns lyrical and surreal.

Edwards's version struggles with Lorca's poetry, but the translation gives a good idea of the strength of this extraordinary play. Carlos **Bauer**'s *Federico García Lorca: The Public (El público*, written 1931) and *Play Without a Title (Comedia sin título*, written ?1936) will, however, only give the reader the faintest sense of the dramatic energy that courses through these richly innovative plays.

The enormous fascination that English-speaking audiences have felt for Lorca's theatre since 1986 has also allowed other Spanish dramatists to be rediscovered. Principal among these are the playwrights of the Golden Age. But Ramón María del Valle-Inclán is an important modern exception. His most anarchic plays—*Luces de Bohemia* (1920, Bohemian Lights), *Las comedias bárbaras* (1907–22, The Barbarous Comedies), and *Divinas palabras* (1933, Divine Words)—were all performed to great acclaim in the mid-1990s, and good scholarly versions of two of his greatest 'esperpentos', or grotesque farces, are available from Aris and Phillips. They are *Los cuernos de don Friolera* (1921, Mr Punch the Cuckold), in a fast-moving and witty version by Dominic **Keown** and Robin **Warner**, and *Lights of Bohemia*, by John **Lyon**, a much more readable version than that by the noted scholar Anthony N. **Zahareas**, with Gerald **Gillespie**. Unfortunately, the most readily available edition of Valle's plays, containing *Divine Words, Bohemian Lights*, and *Cara de Plata* (1922, Silver Face), translated by Maria **Delgado**, gives very little flavour of the linguistic inventiveness which so vividly characterizes the originals.   DJ

ANTHOLOGIES   Corrigan, Robert W., ed., *Masterpieces of the Modern Spanish Theatre*, New York, 1967 · Edwards, Gwynne, *Burning the Curtain: Four Revolutionary Spanish Plays*, London, 1995 · Flores, Angel, ed., *Spanish Drama*, New York, 1962 · O'Connor, Patricia, ed., *Plays of Protest from the Franco Era*, Madrid, 1981.

BUERO VALLEJO, ANTONIO   Holt, Marion Peter, *Three Plays*, San Antonio, Tex., 1985 · *Las Meninas*, San Antonio, Tex., 1987 · Johnston, David, *La detonación / The Shot*, Warminster, UK, 1989 · Thompson, Michael, *Un soñador para un pueblo / A Dreamer for the People*, Warminster, UK, 1994.

GARCÍA LORCA, FEDERICO   Bauer, Carlos, *The Public and Play Without a Title*, New York, 1983 · Edmunds, John, *Four Major Plays*, Oxford, 1997 · Edwards, Gwynne, *Lorca. Plays: One*; *Lorca. Plays: Two*, London, 1990 · Graham-Luján, James, and O'Connell, Richard L., *Three Tragedies*, London, 1959 [rep. Penguin, 1961] · *The Billy-Club Puppets. The Shoemaker's Prodigious Wife. The Love of Don Perlimplín and Belisa in the Garden. Doña Rosita the Spinster. The Butterfly's Evil Spell*, London, 1965 [rep. Penguin, 1970] · Hughes, Langston, and Merwin, W. S., *Blood Wedding and Yerma*, New York, 1994 · Hughes, Ted, *Blood Wedding*, London, 1996 · Johnston, David, *Blood Wedding*, London, 1989 · *Yerma and The Love of Don Perlimplín for Belisa in the Garden*, London, 1990 · Kennelly, Brendan, *Blood Wedding*, Newcastle upon Tyne, 1996.

VALLE-INCLÁN, RAMÓN MARÍA DEL   Delgado, Maria, *Valle-Inclan. Plays: One*, London, 1993 · Keown, Dominic, and Warner, Robin, *Esperpento de los cuernos de Don Friolera / The Grotesque Farce of Mr Punch the Cuckold*, Warminster, 1991 · Lyon, John, *Luces de Bohemia / Lights of Bohemia*, Warminster, UK, 1993 · Zahareas, Anthony N., and Gillespie, Gerald, *Luces de Bohemia / Bohemian Lights*, Edinburgh, 1976.

10. LATIN AMERICAN POETRY IN SPANISH

The great boom in Latin American writing began in the 1960s, in the wake of the intense international interest generated by the Cuban revolution of 1959. Within a few years, not only were writers such as Gabriel García Márquez, Jorge Luís Borges, Mario Vargas Llosa, and Julio Cortázar on bestseller lists around the world, but as fast as they produced new works, these were immediately translated, and the reputation of the translators, such as Gregory **Rabassa**, Helen **Lane**, or Suzanne Jill **Levine**, rose in parallel.

But the boom in Latin American writing mainly involved prose writers [see II.k.11]. Although the novel, short story, and essay have been extensively translated, poetry remained the Cinderella genre until recently. Some Latin American poets such as Pablo Neruda and César Vallejo are known in English, though the Nobel prize-winning writer Octavio Paz is probably better known outside Mexico for his prose than for his prodigious poetic output, despite the existence of some excellent translations, especially those produced in the 1960s by Muriel **Rukeyser**. The first Latin American writer to be awarded the Nobel Prize for Literature, in 1945, was the Chilean poet, Gabriela Mistral, but her work is surprisingly little known and only a few of her poems have appeared from time to time in anthologies. In 1994 Maria **Giacchetti** brought out a selection of Mistral's poetry in the series edited by the Chilean poet Marjorie Agosín for the New York-based White Pine Press, which has also produced selections of the poetry of other women writers. However, Neruda, Vallejo, and Paz remain the big three in English.

Interest in Latin American poetry emerged in the 1960s. Before that decade, readership was limited and highly specialized. In the 1960s, newly founded poetry journals such as *Stand*, edited by Jon Silkin, and *Modern Poetry in Translation*, edited by Ted Hughes and Daniel Weissbort, who all saw translation as fundamentally important, began to publish translations of previously unknown Latin American poets. Both Cape and Penguin promoted Latin American literature in particular. The *Penguin Book of Latin American Verse*, edited by E. Caracciolo-Trejo, came out in 1971, and Jean Franco started a series of editions of selected verse, entitled Penguin Latin American Poets. Both publishers favoured bilingual editions, with originals and translations on facing pages.

In 1970, Cape published a selection of translations of Neruda's poetry, by a team of distinguished poet-translators consisting of Anthony **Kerrigan**, W. S. **Merwin**, Alastair **Reid** and Nathaniel **Tarn**. Tarn had already translated Neruda's great poem, *Las alturas de Macchu Picchu* (1966, The Heights of Macchu Picchu), whilst Merwin had translated *Veinte Poemas de amor y una canción desesperada*) (1969, Twenty Love Poems and a Song of Despair), both published by Cape. The volume of *Selected Works* was approved by Neruda himself, and is a major landmark in the history of the translation of Latin American poetry in English, since it gave readers their first opportunity to read a wide range of Neruda's verse. The translations are sensitive and intelligent, and give readers some sense of the greatness of Neruda's writing, as well as some sense of his enormous linguistic and stylistic range. Anthony Kerrigan's translation of the famous 'Amor America (1400)' from the *Canto General*, for example, transforms Neruda's lyrical Spanish into powerful Anglo-Saxon rhythms:

> An Inca out of the slime, I
> touched the stone and said:
> Who
> is waiting there? And closed my hand
> around a fistful of empty glass.

Neruda's language is not easy to translate, densely symbolic as it is and full of references to Latin American history and pre-Columbian culture. It is also a language that has its own unique rhythms, and it is this aspect of the poetry that presents the greatest problem for translators. Ben **Belitt**'s dreadful version of the play *Fulgor y Muerte de Joaquín Murieta* (1967, Splendour and Death of Joaquin Murieta) is an example of what can happen when a translator seeks to reshape a text exclusively for American readers.

Neruda continues to be the most frequently translated of all Latin American poets, with a steady stream of translations appearing through the 1980s and 1990s. More recently, several US university presses have published translations of Latin American poets, perhaps in response to increased interest among students who want to study Latin American literature.

It is notable that so many of the translators of Latin American verse are themselves well-known poets. César Vallejo, the great Peruvian communist mystic, has been translated by Robert **Bly**, Ed **Dorn** and Gordon **Brotherstone**, and Clayton **Eshleman** among others. Bly has also translated Neruda, while Charles **Tomlinson** and Eliot

Weinberger have translated poetry by Octavio Paz. In 1971 Cape published a selection of Paz's poetry, entitled *Configurations*, with translations by a range of poets, including Muriel Rukeyser, Denise **Levertov**, Charles Tomlinson, Lysander **Kemp**, and John Frederick **Nims**. However, several of the best-known Latin American poets have failed to find English translators of much worth. Besides Gabriela Mistral, the great modernist poets like Rubén Darío and José Martí, the surrealist Vicente Huidobro, the Cuban rhythm poet Nicolás Guillén, or the Christian Marxist Ernesto Cardenal remain relatively unknown in English, despite the occasional attempt at translating some of their works by gifted, enthusiastic translators working with small presses. Jonathan **Cohen** translated some of Cardenal's early poems for Wesleyan University Press in 1984, but without any major impact. Earlier poets, such as Andrés Bello and José Joaquín Olmedo, whose early 19th-c. epics established the benchmark for later generations, are totally obscure beyond the continent of Latin America.

In the 1980s there was a surge of interest in Latin American women poets. In the preface to her anthology of contemporary Latin American women poets, *Woman Who Has Sprouted Wings*, Mary **Crow** claims that the incentive to produce the book derived from the almost total absence of translations of the work of many of Latin America's leading women poets, including Claríbel Alegría, Olga Orozco, Violeta Parra, Nancy Morejón, and Rosario Castellanos. Nora Weizer's anthology *Open to the Sun* was a similar undertaking, as was the collection edited by Marjorie Agosín and Cola Franzen, *The Renewal of the Vision*. Agosín and Franzen covered a 40-year period, from 1940 to 1980, and drew attention in their preface to the contribution of those women defined as 'our literary grandmothers', poets such as Alfonsina Storni, Juana de Ibarbourou, and Delmira Agostini. In the same year, a volume of the selected poems of Alfonsina Storni, translated by a team comprising Marion **Freeman**, Mary Crow, Jim **Normington**, and Kay **Short**, was published by White Pine Press. One of the main tasks of the translators of women poets was simply to introduce significant names to English readers, since most of the poets were unknown. Hence the large number of poets included in these anthologies, represented by only one or two of their poems.

The woman poet of Latin America whose work has become well known in English in recent years is the 17th-c. Mexican nun, Sor Juana Inés de la Cruz [II.k.3.v]. This is due in part to the revival of interest in her work in the wake of the feminist movement,

and partly also to Octavio Paz's magnificent biography of Sor Juana, which has now also been translated into English by Margaret Sayers **Peden** (1988). The coincidence of two women being the first poets of both Spanish America and English America led to comparisons being drawn between Sor Juana's poetry and that of Ann Bradstreet (c.1612–72), the New England poet. Working from translations of Sor Juana's works by Amanda **Powell**, Electa Arenal composed a play for two voices, combining the poetry of both women, that was first performed in San Francisco in 1979 and was instrumental in introducing Sor Juana to an English-language readership.

A great deal of translation of Latin American poetry is never published in book form, but appears in poetry magazines, in academic journals, or specialist Latin American studies journals, such as the *Latin American Literary Review*. Many of the books are published by small presses, in very restricted print runs. Yet despite the obscurity of many of the publications, the quality of translation is high, and Latin American poetry seems to appeal to English-language poets, not only to academics. This may be related to the fact that Latin American poetry is closely connected to the poetry of other traditions. Bello, for example, drew upon Virgil and the classical tradition in the composition of his epic *America* (first part appeared in 1823), the Latin American modernists were strongly influenced by European Symbolism, many 20th-c. poets have been inspired by French and Spanish Surrealism, and the impact of Walt Whitman on Latin American poetry in general is immeasurable.

The development of a genuinely Latin American poetry that has produced some of the greatest poets in the world has involved many literary transactions, with translation playing a crucial role. The links with traditions of Iberian Spanish poetry are, of course, strong, but just as American poets evolved their own styles and conventions that mark them out as completely different from British poets, so also have Latin American poets developed their own distinctive voices. French poetry, the poetry of eastern Europe, Afro-American music, pre-Colombian culture, the haiku, and Chinese image poetry have all been absorbed by Latin American writers and combined with Hispanic traditions and conventions. Poets like Mistral, Neruda, and Paz draw upon so many diverse sources that they can truly be said to be writing from within the melting-pot.

The impact of the Cuban revolution and the emergence of the myth of Latin America as a continent of revolutionaries, enhanced by the popularity of iconic figures such as Fidel Castro and Che Guevara, also led to the compilation of anthologies of revolutionary poets. *Our Word: Guerrilla Poems from Latin America* translated by Edward Dorn and Gordon Brotherstone was published in 1968, while in 1974 the Monthly Review Press brought out an anthology of *Latin American Revolutionary Poetry*, edited and mainly translated by Robert **Marquez**. Such anthologies brought together poetry that had often been published clandestinely and was not widely available even in Spanish, and also drew attention to the continued suffering of politically committed writers across the continent.

The history of translation of Latin American poets reflects changes in perception of the continent as a whole. Until the Cuban revolution brought Latin America into the spotlight, there was little interest in translating writers from across the continent. The impact of the revolution was such that many writers who were not necessarily in sympathy with the objectives of Fidel Castro and his marxist supporters also acquired a new popularity.

Jorge Luís Borges is a case in point, and although best known as a prose writer, his poetry has also been translated. The willingness of so many poets to translate Latin American writing may also have had political implications, particularly in the 1960s and early 1970s, and has certainly ensured that the standard of translation is high. The recent steady stream of translations published by small presses and by academic presses testifies to the growing interest in Latin American writing of the post-Cold War generation, and the selection of poets by translators also reflects this shift. Although Neruda, Paz, and Vallejo remain supreme, there is considerable interest in discovering women's poetry and the emphasis on political poetry of the previous generation has broadened to include a wider range of poets, including surrealists and religious writers. It may also be the case that the worldwide interest in magical realism, following the success of Latin American fiction, has also contributed to the resurgence of interest in the poetry of the continent.

SB

ANTHOLOGIES   Agosín, Marjorie, and Franzen, Cola, eds., *The Renewal of the Vision. Voices of Latin American Women Poets 1940–1980*, Cambridge, 1987 · Carracciolo-Trejo, E., ed., *The Penguin Book of Latin American Verse*, Harmondsworth, 1971 · Crow, Mary, ed., *Woman who has Sprouted Wings: Poems by Contemporary Latin American Women Poets*, Pittsburgh, 1987 · Dorn, Edward, and Brotherstone, Gordon, eds., *Our Word. Guerrilla Poems from Latin America*, London, 1968 · Marquez, Robert, ed., *Latin American Revolutionary Poetry*, New York/London, 1974 · Weizer, Nora, *Open to the Sun*, New York, 1978.

CARDENAL, ERNESTO   Cohen, Jonathan, *With Walker in Nicaragua and Other Early Poems 1949–1954*, Middleton, Conn., 1984 · *From Nicaragua with Love: Poems (1979–1986)*, San Francisco, 1986 · Pring-Mill, Robert, and Walsh, Donald, *Apocalypse and Other Poems*, New York, 1977.

GUILLÉN, NICOLÁS   Marquez, Robert, *Patria o Muerte? The Great Zoo and Other Poems*, New York/London, 1972 · Ortiz Carboneres, Salvador, *Nicolás Guillén's World of Poetry*, Centre for Caribbean Studies, University of Warwick, 1991.

HUIDOBRO, VICENTE   Weinberger, Eliot, *Altazor; or a Voyage in a Parachute (1919)*, St Paul, Minn., 1991.

JUANA INÉS DE LA CRUZ, SOR   Arenal, Electa, *This Life Within Me Won't Keep Still*, in *Reinventing the Americas*, ed. Belle Gale Chevigny and Gari Laguardia, Cambridge, 1986, pp. 158–203.

MISTRAL, GABRIELA   Dana, Doris, *Selected Poems*, Baltimore, 1971 · Giacchetti, Maria, *Gabriela Mistral: Selected Poems*, Fredonia, NY, 1993 · Hughes, Langston, *Selected Poems*, Bloomington, Ind., 1958.

NERUDA, PABLO   Belitt, Ben, *Splendor and Death of Joaquín Murieta*, London, 1973 · Merwin, W. S., *Twenty Love Poems and a Song of Despair*, London, 1969 · Reid, Alastair, *Fully Empowered*, London, 1976 · *Isla Negra*, London, 1982 · Tarn, Nathaniel, *The Heights of Macchu Picchu*, London, 1966 · *Selected Poems*, Harmondsworth, 1975 · *Pablo Neruda. Selected Works*, tr. Anthony Kerrigan, W. S. Merwin, Alastair Reid, Nathaniel Tarn, London, 1970.

PAZ, OCTAVIO   Rukheyser, Muriel, *Sun Stone*, New York, New Directions, 1963 · Rukeyser, Muriel, et al., *Configurations*, New York, New Directions, 1971 · Schmidt, Michael, *On Poets and Others*, Manchester, 1987 · Tomlinson, Charles, *Selected Poems*, Harmondsworth, 1979 · Weinberger, Eliot, *The Collected Poems of Octavio Paz 1957–1987*, New York, 1987 · *A Tree Within*, New York, 1988 · *Sunstone-Piedra de Sol*, New York, 1991.

STORNI, ALFONSINA   Freeman, Marion, *Alfonsina Storni: Selected Poems*, Fredonia, NY, 1987.

VALLEJO, CESAR   Bly, Robert, Wright, James, and Knopfle, John, *Twenty Poems*, Madison, Wis., 1962 · Brotherstone, Gordon, and Dorn, Ed, *Cesar Vallejo: Selected Poems*, Harmondsworth, 1976 [Penguin] · Brotherstone, Gordon, and Rubia Barcia, Jose, *The Complete Posthumous Poetry*, Berkeley/London, 1978. Eshleman, Clayton, *Poemas Humanos/Human Poems*, London, 1969 · Higgins, James, *Cesar Vallejo: A Selection of His Poetry*, Liverpool, 1987.

11. LATIN AMERICAN FICTION IN SPANISH

i. The Latin American Boom and the Changing Role of Translation The 1960s saw the boom in Hispanic American fiction in Europe and the English-speaking world. The Barcelona publishers Seix Barral were in no small way responsible for bringing an array of Latin American writers to prominence by awarding Jorge Luís Borges, Mario Vargas Llosa, Carlos Fuentes, and Guillermo Cabrera Infante their literary prizes. From the politically inimical Francoist Spain these authors bounced, through translation, into the forecourt of the Anglo-American publishing world. The Cuban Revolution, the exotic landscapes of Colombia, Cuba, Mexico, and Argentina, imagery and style dubbed 'magical realist', all these made for imaginative literature which could challenge tired social realism and give a sexy surface to the literary culture of societies whose revolutionary ferment seemed attractive to North American, British, or European societies wanting to move into another gear beyond Cold War politics, the disappointingly drab social democracies, the greyness of the Soviet bloc, or the grim violence of the war in Vietnam.

A fictional Latin America, distant and unknown, suddenly arrived in a variety of usually male guises, bristling with word-play and powerful storytelling, compelling and hallucinatory. As revolutionary situations ebbed and waned from the Southern Cone to Cuba, the writers themselves frequently moved to the lands where their work in translation was to flourish. Exiled writers, cosmopolitan intellectuals found solace in their enforced restlessness speaking and writing on behalf of their homelands to receptive western audiences eager for radical literary and political alternatives in Barcelona, Paris, or London. However, their words were translated, became something other, depended on the writerly choices of a significant group of translators. These translators at the time remained mainly hidden by the process of assimilation favoured by British and American traditions of publishing. Hispanic American narrators, it seemed, actually wrote in English. At least outside the confines of university colloquia, marginal journals and debates, translation was never the issue.

Over 30 years on, the politics of literary translation construe a different set of relationships between the Hispanic American and English-speaking worlds. For many the linguistic and cultural frontiers are blurred, whilst they are fiercely defended by others. In the USA and the UK, economic and political migration means that there are thousands of Spanish-speakers who are now also English-speaking US or UK citizens. Spanish threads its way through the American narratives of Sandra Cisneros or Junot Díaz and Cormack McCarthy and is published without footnote or translation. Writing takes place in varying degrees of fusion of Spanish and English, or separately in Spanish and English as new cultural identities are fashioned. Latin American narratives can emerge from Brooklyn or Shepherd's Bush as part of a new transnational, plurilingual literature.

Many of the 1960s and 1970s generation of Latin American writers now also live in the United States or Europe and engage in intercontinental travel, cosmopolitan living, and bilingual writing. Isabel Allende, Carlos Fuentes, Luis Sepúvelda, or Mario Vargas Llosa are at least as at home in their adoptive cities in the West as in their countries of origin. Some, like Guillermo Cabrera Infante, remain sentenced to exile. Such literary stars, living across frontiers but esconced in Manhattan or Knightsbridge, now find themselves confronted by new writers from massive migrations who often write in the language of power, albeit larded with Spanish. They are in need of multiple translation. Thus, the work of Sandra Cisneros is translated from English into Mexican Spanish for Mexico and chicano Spanish for the USA, where it was first written in English.

These new labyrinths of Spanish and English would have appealed to the first writer in the creation of the 'boom' in Latin American fiction in English translation, namely Jorge Luis Borges. After he was jointly awarded the Formentor Prize with Samuel Beckett in 1961, his short fictions became widely translated and his own reputation as an Anglophile reader of narratives from the Anglo-Saxon chronicles and poets to G. K. Chesterton, an admirer of esoteric philosophies from East and West *and* of gaucho culture and the city of Buenos Aires, made him attractive to 1960s readers, critics, and academics in search of new, fictional worlds. He is now an established canonical writer, and his stories have been translated many times; they have recently been published in a volume translated by Andrew **Hurley**. This tome is a good starting-point to consider how perspectives have changed on the literature of Latin America. Hurley dedicates his work to 'all translators—Borges included' and includes a five-page note on the translation of the stories in which he discusses Borges's idea of translations as part of an endless cycle of infinite possibilities where the idea of a 'definitive text' only appeals to the weary or the religious. His acknowledgements detail the involvement in the editing process of Margaret Sayers **Peden**, a leading North American translator, engaged by the publisher at a late stage, 'comparing the translation with the Spanish, suggesting changes that ranged from punctuation to "readings"'.

These comments which make the role of the translator visible have become a common feature in the publication of translations from Latin American literature. Helped by the fact that there is a strong, well-identified group of translators in the USA and in the UK, who now come together at professional meetings such as those held annually by the American Literary Translators' Association or at university symposia such as the early one at Binghamton in 1970, translators have become more confident in asserting their right to discuss their creative role in the imaginative transformation of the texts they have translated. This self-reflection is also prompted by the writing within the new discipline of Translation Studies. Suzanne Jill **Levine**, in *The Subversive Scribe*, describes how she translated the work of Cabrera Infante, Manuel Puig, Severo Sarduy, Bioy Casares as a committed feminist with particular ideas about the need to challenge the *machismo* of the writers she translates [see I.a.5.iv]. She also elaborates on her close collaborations with the writers she has translated, an experiment in participatory transformation. Carol **Maier** has written about her translations of the Cuban writer Octavio Armand. These theories can sometimes be driven by political considerations about the relationship between the so-called 'First' World and 'Third' World, as in the analysis of translations of testimonial literature: for instance, Anne **Wright**'s translation of Elizabeth del Burgos Debray's edited transcriptions of her Paris conversations with Rigoberta Menchú or the translation and critical framing of the work of Cuban writer Senel Paz, *Fresa y chocolate* (1992, Strawberry and Chocolate) as a response to Eurocentric criticism of his short stories and screenplay for the film of that name. Such debate has also been propelled by the work of Lawrence Venuti, who has generally concluded that literary translations have little impact on American culture, with the single exception of the authors of the Latin American boom who proved commercially profitable whilst 'forming a new canon of foreign literature in English as well as a more sophisticated American readership'. These translations altered the canon and encouraged writers like John Barth to experiment with narrative.

The critical work of translators has in part then made visible their mediation of Latin American texts, their role as interpreters and as initiators of projects. The convergence of a considerable body of writing and of three generations of thoughtful translators has led to the construction of a canon of Latin American work in English that has a noticeable impact on original writing in English.

ii. Borges Translation of Borges led the way. He was first on the scene in the 1960s in English. His short stories were translated by many hands, anthologized, and quickly drawn in by new university literature courses that were in the radical spirit of the time. Borges fitted well with Barthes and with disquisitions on the death of the author. He has been resurrected innumerable times by his translators. One of his early translators, Norman **di Giovanni**, with whom he collaborated closely for an extended period, created a particular form of English assimilation that smoothed out some distinctive features. This partnership worked well in a period that saw Borges's reputation rise, partly a result of his translator's assiduous cajoling of critics and publishers.

Andrew Hurley picks out the opening line of *Las ruinas circulares* (1940, The Circular Ruins) as one of the most famous lines in Spanish literature that has frequently been flattened in translation: 'Nadie lo vio desembarcar en la unánime noche' ('No one saw him disembark on the unanimous night'). It can serve as a good illustration of the interpretative adventure of translation of Latin American literature. The story tells of a man who imagines he is creating a world he is dreaming among the ruins of a temple in the jungle that has been laid waste by fire. Hurley defends the retention of 'unanimous' as an adjective that sounds equally odd in Spanish as it is in English. We can compare various versions of this opening sentence:

Nadie lo vio desembarcar en la unánime noche, nadie vio la canoa de bambú sumiéndose en el fango sagrado.

No one saw him disembark in the unanimous night, no one saw the bamboo canoe sink into the sacred mud. (Anthony **Bonner**)

No one saw him disembark in the unanimous night, no one saw the bamboo canoe sinking into the sacred mud. (James E. **Irby**)

No one saw him disembark in the unanimous night. No one saw the bamboo canoe running aground on the sacred mud. (Anthony **Kerrigan**)

Nobody saw him come ashore in the encompassing night, nobody saw the bamboo craft run aground in the sacred mud. (Norman di Giovanni)

No one saw him slip from the boat in the unanimous

night, no one saw the bamboo canoe as it sank into the sacred mud. (Andrew Hurley)

These variations give some idea of the different interpretations that will ensue in these translations: from Kerrigan's tactic of chopping up the long sentence, to di Giovanni's axing of the latinate, to Hurley's combination of the latinate with the softer, less dramatic verbs and prepositions. Sayers Peden has compared three of the earlier versions, pointing up the need to avoid the easy condemnation of errors as practised by the 'translation police' in the literary reviews and to concentrate on the interpretative moves of the translators through the narrative.

In this most circular of narratives, it is interesting to consider the translations of the words referring in the opening section to the fire that destroyed the original temple and which in the final paragraph destroys the protagonist dreamer. What we can see are shifts by translators who are aware of stylistic and thematic continuity and repetition in the story, who are aware at a later stage of previous translations of a modern canonical work, and who add their own echoes of modernity. Kerrigan is the first to use repetition and a Biblical language to match the ritual, mythopoeic resonances of Borges. Di Giovanni repeats 'flames', which palls in triplicate, and confuses issues by converting Kerrigan's banners into pennants after he has used 'sheets'. Hurley catches the repetition, the ominous ritual tone, and adds a contemporary historical note by introducing the word 'holocaust'. This gives the theme of circularity in Borges a further twist by virtue of the translator's interpretative move.

un templo que devoraron los fuegos antiguos / fueron destruidas por el fuego . . . vio cernirse contra los muros el incendio concéntrico . . . Caminó contra los jirones de fuego.

(a temple that the ancient fires destroyed / were destroyed by the fire . . . saw the concentric blaze threaten / hover against the walls . . . He walked against the tatters / strips of fire)

a temple which had been devoured by ancient fires / was destroyed by fire . . . the concentric fire licking the walls . . . He walked towards the sheets of flame.   (Bonner)

a temple long ago devoured by fire / were destroyed by fire . . . the concentric blaze close around the walls . . . He walked into the shreds of flame.   (Irby)

a temple, devoured by ancient conflagration / were destroyed by fire . . . the concentric conflagration close around the walls. He walked against the florid banners of the fire.   (Kerrigan)

a temple which was destroyed ages ago by flames / were destroyed by fire . . . the circling sheets of flame closing in on him . . . He walked into the leaping pennants of flame.   (di Giovanni)

a temple devoured by an ancient holocaust / were destroyed by fire . . . watched the concentric holocaust close in upon the walls . . . he walked into the tatters of flame.   (Hurley)

iii. **After Borges** After Borges came other writers who were to become literary figures in the English-speaking world and establish themselves with a healthy presence in bookshops and best-sellers' lists. They were associated largely with a group of North American translators. Gabriel García Márquez's *Cien años de soledad* (1967, A Hundred Years of Solitude), translated by Gregory Rabassa, made its mark throughout the world and still sells in its thousands 30 years later. The Colombian writer's change of style and change of translator led to a more recent sales triumph with *El amor en los tiempos del cólera* (1985, Love in the Time of Cholera), translated by Edith **Grossman**. The move to a more popular, less baroque style in his later work is mirrored in the transitions in the writing of Carlos Fuentes from *Terra Nostra* (1975) to *Viejo gringo* (1986, The Old Gringo), both translated by Margaret Sayers Peden, and of Mario Vargas Llosa from *Conversación en la catedral* (1970, Conversation in the Cathedral) to *La guerra del fin del mundo* (1982, The War of the End of the World), translated by Gregory Rabassa and Helen **Lane** respectively. This trio of writers has an international reputation through the English translation of their works and their own interventions in political and media life. They are cosmopolitan figures who have moved Latin American literature beyond the narrow circles of academic readers into the mass market, a fiction readily turned into theatre, film, television.

In their wake have come Isabel Allende and Laura Esquivel, whose novels—*La casa de los espíritus* (1982, The House of the Spirits) and *Como agua para chocolate* (1990, Like Water for Chocolate) respectively—have benefited from film tie-ins and rapidly became bestsellers in the United States, though sales were less high in the UK. These popularizing reworkings of the magical realist genre caught the mood of a market in search of Latin exotic in accessible, readable styles and created a Latin American presence in bookshops in the English-speaking world.

However, it would be wrong to suppose that such is the lot of all Latin American fiction in English translation. There are writers like Alejo Carpentier, in many ways the pioneer of magical

435

realism, much translated but never a powerful presence beyond universities. Juan Carlos Onetti's irony and bleak landscapes of the River Plate world of his invented Santa María have now been translated. It is a universe as Latin American and as coherent as Márquez's Macondo but without parrots and butterflies and with dirty back streets, grimy sex, and solitude, urban and unheroic. Little reviewed and with small sales, Onetti's turn has yet to come. The Cuban writer Lezama Lima is barely translated: *Paradiso*, the odd short story, yet hardly any of his striking literary essays. Yet both Onetti and Lezama are original stylists, creators of their own fictional worlds. The Uruguayan Felisberto Hernández has just one set of stories in translation. Where are the Honduran, Venezuelan, Ecuadorian, Costa Rican writers except in anthologies and small print runs from small presses? What do English readers know of Guatemalan writing beyond Miguel Angel Asturias?

Latin American fiction in English translation has broken through to the mainstream of the reading public: the combination of a determined group of translators and publishers, the historical conjuncture of the 1960s created a new literary taste that strongly affected domestic literary production. The growth of Hispanic culture in the United States ensures a base for that popular readership, fed by translation from Spanish and by Hispanic writing in English. New anthologies, the new collections of Latin American short stories and essays or new translations of different Hispanic Caribbean writing, and the new round of reprints or retranslations of Cortázar and Borges are indications that the millennium will see some old reputations consolidated. A configuration of younger translators, theoretically adroit and professionally trained, will no doubt bear the main responsibility for focusing the minds of publishers, big and small, on the many new Latin American voices still waiting to break their silence with English readers through the art of literary translation.   PB

ANTHOLOGIES   Alegría, Claribel, and Flakoll, Darwin J., *New Voices of Hispanic America*, Boston, 1962 · Bush, Peter, ed., *The Voice of the Turtle: An Anthology of Cuban Stories* [tr. P. Bush, Amanda Hopkinson, Andrew Hurley, et al.], London, 1997 · Cohen, J. M., ed., *Latin American Writing Today* [tr. J. M. Cohen, Jean Franco, Charles Tomlinson, et al.], New York, 1967 · Donoso, José, and Henkin, William A., eds., *TriQuarterly Anthology of Contemporary Latin American Literature*, New York, 1969 · González Echevarría, Roberto, ed., *The Oxford Book of Latin American Short Stories* [tr. Daniel Balderston, Luis Harss, et al.], New York, 1998 · Manguel, Alberto, ed., *Other Fires: Short Fiction by Latin American Women* [tr. S. J. Levine, A. Manguel, Giovanni Pontiero, et al.], Toronto, 1985.

ALLENDE, ISABEL   Bogin, Magda, *The House of the Spirits*, New York, 1985 · Peden, Margaret Sayers, *Of Love and Shadows*, New York, 1987 · *Eva Luna*, New York, 1988 · *The Infinite Plan*, New York, 1993 · *Aphrodisia*, New York, 1998.

ARMAND, OCTAVIO   Maier, Carol, *Refractions*, New York, 1994.

ASTURIAS, MIGUEL ÁNGEL   Flakoll, Darwin J., and Alegría, Claribel, *The Cyclone*, London, 1967 · Martin, Gerald, *Men of Maize*, New York, 1975 · Partridge, Frances, *The President*, London, 1963, as *El Señor Presidente*, New York, 1969 · Rabassa, Gregory, *Mulata*, New York, 1967, as *The Mulata and Mister Fly*, London, 1967 · *Strong Wind*, New York, 1969 · *The Green Pope*, New York, 1971 · *The Eyes of the Interred*, New York, 1972.

BORGES, JORGE LUÍS   Boyar, Mildred, and Morland, Harold, *Dreamtigers*, Austin, Tex., 1964 · di Giovanni, Norman Thomas, *The Aleph and Other Stories*, New York, 1970 · *Doctor Brodie's Report*, New York, 1972 · *Chronicles of Bustos Domecq*, with Adolfo Bioy Casares, New York, 1976 · *The Book of Sand*, New York, 1977 · *Six Problems for Don Isidro Parodi* (with Adolfo Bioy Casares), New York, 1981 · Hurley, Andrew, *Complete Fictions*, New York, 1998 · Kerrigan, Anthony, *Extraordinary Tales* (with Adolfo Bioy Casares), New York, 1971 · Kerrigan, Anthony, Reid, Alastair, Bonner, Anthony, et al., *Ficciones*, New York, 1962, as *Fictions*, London, 1962 · *A Personal Anthology*, New York, 1967 · Simms, Ruth L. C., *Other Inquisitions*, Austin, 1964 · Yates, Donald, and Irby, James E., *Labyrinths: Selected Stories and Other Writings*, New York, 1962.

CABRERA INFANTE, GUILLERMO   Gardner, Donald, and Levine, Suzanne Jill, *Three Trapped Tigers*, New York, 1971 · Hall, Kenneth (with the author), *Mea Cuba*, London, 1994 · Levine, Suzanne Jill, *View of the Dawn from the Tropics*, New York, 1978 · (with the author), *Infante's Inferno*, New York, 1984.

CORTÁZAR, JULIO   Blackburn, Paul, *End of the Game and Other Stories* [later as *Blow-Up and Other Stories*], New York, 1967 · *Cronopios and Famas*, New York, 1969 · Kerrigan, Elaine, *The Winners*, New York, 1965 · Levine, Suzanne Jill, *All Fires the Fire*, London, 1971 · Manguel, Alberto, *Unreasonable Hours*, Toronto, 1995 · *Bestiary*, London, 1998 [includes translations by Blackburn, Levine, and Rabassa] · Rabassa, Gregory, *Hopscotch*, New York, 1966 · *A Change of Light and Other Stories*, New York, 1980 · *We Love Glenda So Much*, New York, 1983 · *A Certain Lucas*, New York, 1984.

FUENTES, CARLOS   Hileman, Sam, *Where the Air Is Clear*, New York, 1960 · *The Death of Artemio Cruz*, New York, 1964 · *A Change of Skin*, New York, 1968 · Kemp, Lysander, *Aura*, New York, 1966 · MacAdam, Alfred, *Christopher*

Unborn, New York, 1989 · *The Crystal Frontier*, New York, 1997 · Peden, Margaret Sayers, *Terra Nostra*, New York, 1976 · *Burnt Water*, New York, 1980 · *Distant Relations*, New York, 1982 · *The Old Gringo*, New York, 1986.

GARCÍA MÁRQUEZ, GABRIEL Bernstein, J. S., *No One Writes to the Colonel and Other Stories*, New York, 1968 · Grossman, Edith, *Love in the Time of Cholera*, New York, 1988 · *Strange Pilgrims: Twelve Stories*, New York, 1993 · *Of Love and Other Demons*, New York, 1995 · Rabassa, Gregory, *One Hundred Years of Solitude*, New York, 1970 · *Leaf Storm and Other Stories*, New York, 1972 · *The Autumn of the Patriarch*, New York, 1976 · *Chronicle of a Death Foretold*, New York, 1982.

HERNÁNDEZ, FELISBERTO Harss, Luis, *Piano Stories*, New York, 1993.

LEZAMA LIMA, JOSÉ Rabassa, Gregory, *Paradiso*, Austin, Tex., 1974.

MENCHÚ, RIGOBERTA Wright, Ann, *I . . . Rigoberta Menchú: An Indian Woman in Guatemala*, ed. Elisabeth Burgos-Debray, London, 1984.

ONETTI, JUAN CARLOS Balderston, Daniel, *Goodbye and Other Stories*, Austin, Tex., 1990 · Bush, Peter, *No Man's Land*, London, 1994 · *Past Caring*, London, 1995 · *Farewells and Other Stories*, London, 1996 · *The Pit and Tonight*, London, 1999 · Caffyn, Rachel, *The Shipyard*, New York, 1968 · Caistor, Nick, *The Shipyard*, London, 1993 · Carpentier, Hortense, *A Brief Life*, New York, 1973 · Lane, Helen, *Let the Wind Speak*, New York, 1986.

PAZ, SENEL Bush, Peter, *Strawberry and Chocolate*, London, 1995.

PUIG, MANUEL Levine, Suzanne Jill, *Betrayed by Rita Hayworth*, New York, 1971 · *Heartbreak Tango*, New York, 1973.

SARDUY, SEVERO Levine, Suzanne Jill, *From Cuba With a Song*, New York, 1973 · *Cobra*, New York, 1975 · *Maitreya*, Hanover, NH, 1987.

SEPÚLVEDA, LUIS Bush, Peter, *The Old Man Who Read Love Stories*, New York/London, 1989.

VALENZUELA, LUISA Bonner, Deborah, *Other Weapons*, Hanover, NH, 1985 · Carpentier, Hortense, and Castello, Jorge, *Clara: Thirteen Short Stories and a Novel*, New York, 1976 · Costa, Margaret Jull, *Bedside Manners*, London, 1995 · *Symmetries (High Risk)*, London, 1998 · Lane, Helen, *Strange Things Happen Here*, New York, 1979 · *He Who Searches*, New York, 1987 · Rabassa, Gregory, *The Lizard's Tail*, New York, 1983 · Talbot, Tony, *Black Novel (With Argentines)*, New York, 1992.

VARGAS LLOSA, MARIO Kemp, Lysander, *The Time of the Hero*, London, 1962 · Lane, Helen, *Aunt Julia and the Script Writer*, New York, 1982 · *The War of the End of the World*, New York, 1984 · MacAdam, Arthur, *Who Killed Palomino Molero?*, New York, 1987 · Rabassa, Gregory, *The Green House*, New York, 1968 · *Conversation in the Cathedral*, New York, 1975.

SEE ALSO Borges, J. L., *Borges On Writing*, ed. N. T. di Giovanni, D. Halpern, and F. McShane, London, 1972 · Christ, R., 'Borges Translated', *The Nation*, 212, 9 (1 Mar. 1971), 282–4 · Felstiner, J., *Translating Neruda: The Way to Machu Picchu*, Stanford, Calif., 1980 · Howard, M., 'Stranger Than Ficción: The Unlikely Case of Jorge Luis Borges and the Translator Who Helped Bring His Work to America', *Lingua Franca* (June/July 1997), 40–9 · Levine, S. J., *The Subversive Scribe: Translating Latin American Literature*, St Paul, Minn., 1991 · 'Translation as (Sub) Version: On Translating Infante's Inferno', in L. Venuti, ed., *Rethinking Translation*, London, 1995, pp. 75–85 · Luis, W., and Rodríguez-Luis, J., eds., *Translating Latin America: Culture As Text (Translation Perspectives vi)*, Binghamton, NY, 1991 · Munday, J., 'The Caribbean Conquers the World?. An Analysis of the Reception of García Márquez in Translation', *Bulletin of Hispanic Studies*, 75 (1998), 137–44 · Payne, J., *Conquest of the New Word: Experimental Fiction and Translation in the Americas*. Austin, Tex., 1993 · Peden, M. S., 'The Arduous Journey', in W. M. Aycock, ed., *The Teller and the Tale: Aspects of the Short Story*, Lubbock, Tex., 1982 · 'Translating the Boom: The Apple Theory of Translation', *Latin American Literary Review*, 15, 29 (1987) · Rabassa, G., 'If This Be Treason: Translation and Its Possibilities', in W. Frawley, ed., *Translation: Literary, Linguistic, and Philisophical Perspectives*, Newark, NJ, 1984, pp. 21–9 · 'Words Cannot Express . . .: The Translation of Cultures', in W. Luis and J. Rodríguez-Luis, eds., *Translating Latin America: Culture as Text*, Binghamton, NY, 1991, pp. 35–44 · Wilson, J., *An A to Z of Modern Latin American Literature in English Translation*, London, 1989.

12. CATALAN LITERATURE

Catalan literature (which includes writing from Valencia and Mallorca) is rich in medieval texts, but for political reasons goes into eclipse from the 16th to the 19th c. It begins to gather weight again with the romantic revival and, despite the Civil War, is particularly strong in the 20th c.

By a strange stroke of fate, one of the first books to be printed by William **Caxton** (?1422–91) was his 1484 version of Ramon Llull's *Libre del orde de caval-* leria (Book of the Order of Chivalry or Knighthood). This, to be sure, was translated from the French; for translation direct from Catalan one has to wait for the 1920s and for the pioneering work of E. Allison **Peers**, whose own versions of Llull—the *Libre d'Amich e Amat* (1283/6, Book of the Lover and the Beloved), *Blanquerna* (1283/6), and the *Libre de les bèsties* (1288/9, Book of the Beasts)—first made this extraordinary figure available to modern English

437

readers. Peers's versions still read well, though the most authoritative translation is now Anthony **Bonner**'s *Selected Works*, and Mark D. **Johnston** has recently produced an excellent version of *The Book of the Lover and the Beloved*.

The 15th c.—in many ways the finest period of Catalan literature—is well represented in translation. The great Valencian poet Ausiàs March exists in three versions, though so far no one has come up with a satisfactory verse translation. Arthur **Terry**'s prose versions are mainly intended to help with the originals; Robert **Archer**'s translations—also in prose—are less literal, though very accurate, and deserve to be read in their own right; the three-volume verse translation, by Dominic **Keown** and others, is strangely archaizing, and tends to achieve its best effects where it is most simple.

The two prose masterpieces of the period, the anonymous *Curial e Guelfa* and *Tirant lo blanc*, by Joanot Martorell and Martí de Galba, have both been recently translated, the first in an excellent version by Pamela **Waley** and the second twice over, by David **Rosenthal** and Raymond **LaFontaine**. Neither Rosenthal nor LaFontaine is a medievalist, which accounts for a number of discrepancies in their versions; of the two, Rosenthal is more fluent, in that he bears the modern reader in mind, to the extent of omitting what he takes to be redundancies in the original. LaFontaine, on the other hand, works more as a philologist and remains faithful to the original, even to the extent of obscurity, though more of the original text survives in his version than in Rosenthal's.

For political and cultural reasons, there is a gap in Catalan literature beteen the end of the 15th c. and the beginning of the 19th c. Though the 19th-c. revival produced a number of masterpieces, notably in the poetry of Verdaguer, it is only with 20th-c. authors that translation begins to gather momentum again. All of the major poets who began to write shortly after the turn of the century have been translated at least in part. There is a good selection of Josep Carner, translated by Pearse **Hutchinson**, and a rather less comprehensive anthology of J. V. Foix, in versions by David Rosenthal. By contrast, J. L. **Gili**'s translations of Carles Riba—*Poems*, *Savage Heart*, and *Elegies of Bierville*—range widely over the work of this complex poet, often with great resourcefulness. Marià Manent, a minor but distinctive poet of the same generation, has been well translated by Sam **Abrams**, while Joan Salvat-Papasseit, an avant-garde poet who died young, exists in some fine versions by Dominic Keown and Tom **Owen**.

Of the poets who began to write in the 1930s,

much the most frequently translated has been Salvador Espriu. This is partly because of his undoubted stature as a poet, but also because of the popular success of his 1960 collection *La pell de brau* (The Bull Hide), whose meditation on the past and future of Spain struck a common chord at the time. *The Bull Hide* itself has been well translated by Burton **Raffel**; Kenneth **Lyons**'s selection is adequate, though some of the versions are awkward; best of all are the two much wider selections by Magda **Bogin** and Louis J. **Rodrigues**, both of which beautifully capture the tone of this austere and subtle poet.

Of the younger poets, the only one who has been translated to any extent is Gabriel Ferrater (Terry, 1967), a writer who is much concerned with 'the meaning of a life' and whose fluent poems show the influence of a number of English poets, from Hardy to Graves and Auden.

Partly because of the reluctance of most British publishers to take on works from minority languages, relatively few Catalan novels have been translated into English. Of those which *have*, however, three are outstanding, each belonging to a different generation. Víctor Català's *Solitud* (1905)—a story of great power and psychological penetration—exists in a good translation by David Rosenthal. Rosenthal has also translated Mercè Rodoreda's novel *La Plaça del Diamant* (1962, The Time of the Doves), the story of a working-class woman in the Barcelona of the 1930s and 1940s—perhaps the finest work of fiction to have appeared since the Civil War. And, coming to strictly contemporary writing, one must single out Judith **Willis**'s splendid version of Jesús Moncada's masterly first novel *Camí de sirga* (1988, The Towpath), a vivid account of the prosperity and decline of a small industrial town on the River Ebro.

To this one must add a couple of volumes of short stories: Joaquim Ruyra's *El rem del trenta-quatre* (The Long Oar), translated by Julie **Flanagan**, the work of a master from the early part of the century, and Pere Calders's Calvino-like stories, *La verge de les vies* (The Virgin of the Railway), in a version by Amanda **Bath**.

Contemporary Catalan theatre, though vigorous and many-faceted, has fared even less well in translation, mainly owing to difficulties in mounting performances. The one outstanding exception here is Salvador Espriu's *Primera història d'Esther* (1948, The Story of Esther), brilliantly translated by Philip **Polack**. Subtitled 'an improvisation for puppets', the original imagines the performance of a play on the Biblical episode of Esther in the small Catalan town of Sinera (Arenys de Mar), thus superimposing the Old Testament story on the world of Espriu's own childhood. Polack's masterstroke consists in adapting the play to a Welsh setting, and in introducing Welsh speech patterns into his text. Thus, 'Sinera' becomes 'Novareba' (Aberavon), and many of the personal names are cleverly transmogrified:

Pray for the town's dim-wits, an incomparable bunch under Drunken Jimmy's direction, the beggars who went from door to door, through streets and squares, asking for a little grudging charity, for whole generations. And for the wealthy families, now extinct, the Jeffreys, Griffiths, Powells and Lloyds. And for Mrs. Llywela James, who used to sit reading in a rickety chair . . .

Apart from this, a number of more recent Catalan plays have appeared in translation, mostly in little magazines. (For a full bibliography, see David George and John London, eds., *Contemporary Catalan Theatre*, Sheffield, 1996.) One play which has achieved book form is Sergi Belbel's *Després de la phija* (1993, After the Rain), translated by Xavier Rodríguez **Rosell**, David **George**, and John **London**, recently produced with considerable success at the Gate Theatre, London.

A full bibliography of translations from Catalan is contained in *Repertori bibliogràfic de traduccions d'obres literàries en català a d'altres llengües*, Barcelona, Institució de les Lletres Catalanes, 1995, and it should be noted that the Generalitat, or regional government, of Catalonia gives grants for translations of texts from Catalan. AT

ANON. Waley, Pamela, *Curial and Guelfa*, London, 1982.
BELBEL, SERGI Rosell, Xavier Rodríguez, George, David, and London, John, *After the Rain*, London, 1996.
CALDERS, PERE Bath, Amanda, *The Virgin of the Railway and Other Stories*, Warminster, UK, 1992.
CARNER, JOSEP Hutchinson, Pearse, *Poems*, Oxford, 1962.
CATALÀ, VICTOR Rosenthal, David, *Solitude*, London, 1966.
ESPRIU, SALVADOR Bogin, Magda, *Selected Poems*, London/New York, 1989 · Lyons, Kenneth, *Lord of the Shadow: Poems*, Oxford, 1975 · Polack, Philip, *The Story of Esther*, Sheffield, 1989 · Raffel, Burton, *The Bull-Hide*, Calcutta, 1977 · Rodrigues, Louis J., *Selected Poems*, Manchester, 1997.
FERRATER, GABRIEL Terry, Arthur, *A Small War and Other Poems*, Belfast, 1967.
FOIX, J. V. Rosenthal, David, *When I Sleep, Then I See Clearly: Selected Poems*, New York, 1988.
LLULL, RAMON Bonner, Anthony, *Selected Works*, Princeton, NJ, 1985 · Caxton, William, *Book of the Order of Chivalry or Knighthood*, Amsterdam, 1484 [rep. 1926] · Johnston, Mark D., *The Book of the Lover and the Beloved*, Warminster, UK, 1995 · Peers, E. Allison, *The Book of the Lover and the Beloved*, London, 1925 [rep. 1956] · *Blanquerna*, London, 1926 [many reprints] · *The Book of the Beasts*, London, 1927.
MANENT, MARIÀ Abrams, Sam, *The Shade of Mist*, Barcelona, 1992.
MARCH, AUSIÀS Archer, Robert, *A Key Anthology*, Sheffield, 1992 · Keown, Dominic, et al., *Selected Poems*, 3 vols., Valencia, 1986–93 · Terry, Arthur, *Selected Poems*, Edinburgh, 1976.
MARTORELL, JOANOT, and GALBA, MARTÍ DE LaFontaine, Raymond, *Tirant lo blanc*, Washington, DC, 1993 · Rosenthal, David, *Tirant lo blanc*, London/New York, 1984 [rep. Paladin].
MONCADA, JESÚS Willis, Judith, *The Towpath*, London, 1994.
RIBA, CARLES Gili, J. L., *Poems*, Oxford, 1964 [rev. edn., 1970] · *Savage Heart*, Oxford, 1993 · *Elegies of Bierville*, Oxford, 1995.
RODOREDA, MERCÈ Rosenthal, David, *The Time of the Doves*, New York, 1980.
RUYRA, JOAQUIM Flanagan, Julie, *The Long Oar*, Warminster, UK, 1994.
SALVAT-PAPASSEIT, JOAN Keown, Dominic, and Owen, Tom, *Selected Poems*, Sheffield, 1982.

13. CAMÕES

Known mostly for his epic of the Portuguese Discoveries, *Os Lusíadas* (1572, The Lusiads), comprising 10 cantos written in octaves chronicling Vasco da Gama's voyage to India, Luís de Camões also left a rich body of lyric poetry, ranging from sonnets to odes, canzons, madrigals, and sextines, which have rightly attracted the interest of translators and today are seen as equally important in evaluating his work.

The *Lusiads*, at first only attracting the attention of the neighbouring Spanish, was originally translated into English in 1655 by Sir Richard **Fanshawe** (1608–66), who had been secretary to the British ambassador in Madrid. Coinciding with new alliances between Portugal and England, it gained some acceptance, but the by then old-fashioned italianate stanzas of Fanshawe only really appealed to an intellectual minority. His translation, although in period English and difficult to read with ease nowadays, was a vigorous and faithful rendering providing one of the best examples of contemporary epic verse in English. Thus

> Mas um velho de aspeito venerando,
> Que ficava nas praias, entre a gente,
> Postos em nós os olhos, meneando
> Três vezes a cabeça, descontente

becomes

> But an Ould man of Venerable look
> (Standing upon the shore amongst the Crowds),
> His Eyes fixt upon us (on ship-board), shook
> His head three times, ore-cast with sorrows clowds.

It was not until the news of the Lisbon earthquake entered the imagination of the European public that travellers and poets visited Portugal and rediscovered its national epic. William Julius **Mickle** (1735–88), capturing the mood, produced what many politely described as a 'spirited' rendering of the cantos in 1776, *The Lusiad; or, The Discovery of India. An Epic Poem*. Seeing the work as a reflection of the importance of international commerce and free trade, he even went so far as to dedicate it to the East India Company. This version, abandoning octaves for heroic couplets, is a very free paraphrase which certainly catches the spirit of the poem; however, large tracts of it are pure invention, which increases its length and makes it unwieldy.

Threats to the Portuguese monarchy at the start of the 1800s prompted further interest in Portuguese affairs and so too a new translation by Lord **Strangford** (1780–1855) in 1803: he had a direct interest, having been first secretary to the British embassy in Lisbon and personally involved in the royal family's removal to Brazil. It was, however, much criticized by contemporary poets who did not see its relevance to the style of the day.

Although the romantics found the poet's biography of drama and adventure on the high seas sympathetic, no new version of the Lusiads appeared until the end of the century, when an engineer who had worked in Brazil, John James **Aubertin** (1818–1900), produced in 1878 one of the most faithful renderings of the original at the time. Thereafter, commemorations of the poet's death in 1880 led to the translation by Richard Francis **Burton** (1821–90), followed by a Spenserian verse rendering by Robert Ffrench **Duff**. Burton's attempts to adhere both to rhyme and literal rendering rather than maintain overall fidelity were counterproduct-ive because of the fussy and dated vocabulary employed. Thomas Moore **Musgrave**'s translation into blank verse was equally infelicitous.

Although there had been some interest in the sonnets in the 17th c. through William Hayley and later amongst the romantics, including Southey, it was only from the end of the 19th c. that real interest in Camões' other poetic output grew: Aubertin issued the *Seventy Sonnets of Camoens* in 1881 giving a polished, harmonious rendering, prompting Burton to produce his own version of *The Lyricks* in 1884, which suffered from the same fussiness of style as his *Lusiads*.

The best-known modern version of the *Lusiads* is the Penguin Classics edition by William C. **Atkinson**. Unfortunately, the prose rendering can only be considered as a paraphrastic adaptation, losing all sense of the rhythm and beauty of the verse original. Atkinson tries to justify this: 'It aims at rendering a service to the living, not pious tribute to the dead, and is concerned therefore with the substance, not the form, of the original.'

Far more satisfying is the convincing translation with introduction and notes by Leonard **Bacon**. This scholarly work maintains the best of the tradition of Camões translators and even satisfies the demands of rhyme with ease and accomplishment:

> But an old man of venerable air,
> Who on the seafront stood among the crowd,
> Turned his eyes towards us with a steady stare
> And thrice his head as one in grief he bowed.

Some attempts at putting the epic and lyric verse into more 20th-c. English by modern English poets have recently given new life to Camões. The excellent selection published by the Carcanet Press, *Luís de Camões: Epic and Lyric*, has extracts by Keith **Bosley** that fully capture the energy and harmony of the original while rejecting any archaisms.

A new edition of the *Lusiads* by Landeg **White** is certainly easy on the ear and shows how far a classic text can be transferred to the modern idiom. Unfortunately, purists may regard it as losing some of the 'grandeur' of the original:

> But an old man of venerable appearance
> Standing among the crowd on the shore,
> Fixed his eyes on us, disapproving,
> And wagged his head three times.

In addition, White's attempt to maintain a sense of rhyme in only the last couplet of each stanza does eventually begin to pall a little.   MH

TRANSLATIONS   *The Lusiad*, tr. Richard Fanshawe, London, 1655 [ed. with an introduction by Geoffrey Bullough, London, 1963] · *The Lusiad; or, The Discovery of India. An Epic Poem Translated from the Original Portuguese of Luis de*

Camoens, tr. William Julius Mickle, Oxford, 1776 · *Poems, from the Portuguese of Luis de Camoens: with Remarks on his Life and Writings*, tr. Lord Viscount Strangford, London, 1803 · *The Lusiad, an Epic Poem*, tr. Thomas Moore Musgrave, London, 1826 · *The Lusiad Books I to V*, tr. Edward Quillinan with notes by John Adamson, London, 1853 · *The Lusiad of Luis de Camoens*, tr. Sir T. L. Mitchell, London, 1854 · *The Lusiad; Translated into Spencerian Verse*, tr. R. ffrench Duff, London, 1880 · *Os Lusíadas (The Lusiads) Englished by Richard Francis Burton*, London, 1880–81 · *Seventy Sonnets of Camoens*, tr. J. J. Aubertin, London, 1881 · *The Lyricks: Sonnets, Canzons, Odes and Sextines. Englished by Richard F. Burton*, London, 1884 · *The Lusiads*, tr. Leonard Bacon, New York, 1950 · *The Lusiads*, tr. William C. Atkinson, Harmondsworth, 1975 [Penguin] · *Some Poems of Camões*, tr. Jonathan Griffin, London, 1976 · *Luís de Camões: Epic and Lyric*, tr. K. Bosley, London, 1989 · *The Lusiads*, tr. Landeg White, Oxford, 1997.

14. MODERN PORTUGUESE LITERATURE

The translating of Portuguese literature into English has been at best a very patchy process. The lack of any real canon of Portuguese literature means that translations into English have followed either sudden fashions in taste or the mere whim of translators themselves or their publishers. The lack of a large group of professional Portuguese–English translators is also a handicap, as a major part of the commissioned work to date derives from the pens of a select few. Even today, in the case of Saramago for example, a writer has to become famous on the Continent before critics wake up and publishers commission the work to be translated into English.

One can start with the 19th-c. realist novels of Eça de Queirós. Interest here is due to the analogy with French and Spanish writers, Eça's work fitting into the mould of the social satires of Balzac, Flaubert, and Galdós, as well as to the fact that Eça knew England well—some of his characters would be quite at home in an English novel. The peculiarity of his work lies in its descriptive tracts, its biting satire, and its flirtation with sexual elements with which he meant to shock his readers, including adultery, seduction by priests, child murder, and incest. The challenge to the translator lies in the accuracy of the descriptive imagery and some of the wit, but beyond that the translator needs no extra tricks: between them the poet Roy **Campbell** and Ann **Stevens** have done admirable work in covering his most interesting novels.

The lack of any translations of the more prolific writer and humorist Camilo Castelo Branco, who preceded Eça, is quite surprising, although one can see that his particular brand of humour and his subject matter may well be too narrow for the foreign reader. There is also a surprising lack of any translation of the realist poet Cesário Verde, a poet with a seminal influence on his 20th-c. successors, none being more indebted to him than Fernando Pessoa.

The unique poetry of Pessoa, a writer who was bilingual in English and Portuguese, lived in Durban as a child, and even wrote his own Shakespearean sonnets, has gradually grown in stature and now fascinates the world with its heteronymous personalities or *alter egos*. *Tabacaria* (1933, The Tobacconist's) is often seen as his defining work, as the first four verses can be taken as a definition of heteronymy itself. Two translators have made worthwhile efforts at projecting the sense of the poem. J. C. R. **Green** makes a closely literal attempt while managing to attain a fluidity and rhythmic rendering to engage the English reader. But this is not faithful to the real spirit and style of Pessoa, whose jerky, contradictory blank verse is best captured by the work of Suzette **Macedo**, wringing the last ounce of nihilism and contradiction from the piece in all its antithetical subtlety.

It was in the 1980s that Pessoa's importance was fully recognized, as within the space of three years Europe and America celebrated first the 50th anniversary of his death and then the centenary of his birth with international conferences and re-editions of his work. The 'espólio' (a chest full of scraps of paper) of his unpublished work was at last fully explored, and a new look at the real breadth of his work led to the start of critical editions, sometimes vastly and radically different from the established versions of 50 years' standing; at the same time his prose work, under the heteronym Bernardo Soares, was at long last given full attention. The Carcanet press brought out *A Centenary Pessoa* with translations by Keith **Bosley** for poetry and Bernard **McGuirk**, Maria Manuel **Lisboa**, and Richard **Zenith** for prose. The selection in this volume, dedicated to the memory of Jonathan **Griffin**, a pioneer in translating Pessoa, is without doubt the best insight into the world of Pessoa for any new English reader. Of the various versions of the *Livro do Desassossego* (1982, The Book of Disquietude), Richard Zenith's is by far the most scholarly. Jonathan Griffin's translations of Pessoa are an acquired taste (the largest collection can be found in the Penguin series): Griffin reworks Pessoa in many ways, attempting to put his verse into the vein of modern English poetry. For the purists, though, many of his renderings would be seen as reworkings or at best loose translations of the original lines.

Contemporary to Pessoa, the work of Mário de Sá-Carneiro (who is not normally considered a major writer) has nevertheless earned some respect from the translations of Margaret Jull **Costa**.

The 1930s and 1940s were a period belonging mainly to social realism, or neo-realism as it had to be called under the Salazar regime. Some works, such as *Retalhos da Vida dum Médico* (1953, Mountain Doctor) by the doctor Fernando Namora, have found their way into translation but with no great success. Miguel Torga, for a long time a writer not in vogue because of his rather austere vision of rural Portugal, has gained readers in France over the last 20 years and was even nominated for the Nobel prize. Ivana **Carlsen** manages to give a sensitive interpretation of his prose style, bringing out the full vigour of his close relationship with the land, its people, and their primary emotions in *Contos da Montanha* and *Novos Contos da Montanha* (1982, 1986, Tales from the Mountain).

In the 1960s in Portugal, as the Salazar regime continued its steady decline and resistance found a subversive yet clandestine voice, three writers stand out as significant in their different approaches to free speech and expression. One of these, Luís de Sttau Monteiro, a satirist and writer of wry humour, mocked the boring middle-class society of Lisbon, and the censors ignored the hidden political allegories as they laughed. His plays were passed over, but his novel *Angústia para o Jantar* (1961, The Rules of the Game) was eventually translated by Ann Stevens, the easy comic style and simple prose posing no great problems.

Jorge de Sena, an intellectual steeped in his own cultural heritage and the Renaissance, used medieval allegory as a cloak for his criticism in works such as *O Físico Prodigioso* (1977, The Wondrous Physician). His rich classical style, re-creating both the prose and poetry of another age, is unfortunately lost in Mary **Fitton**'s translation, which ends up more as a paraphrase, in the style of a jolly and fanciful tale by T. H. White.

The greatest of the three writers still producing works of significance very recently, José Cardoso Pires, has virtually escaped translation, apart from the *Balada da Praia dos Cães* (1982, Ballad of Dog's Beach) by Mary Fitton. This is quite astounding, since the pithiness of his prose style is equal in

stature to the baroque of José Saramago (see below), and in just as meaningful a way.

Women's writing in the seventies finds an excellent voice in *Novas Cartas Portuguesas* (1974, The Three Marias: New Portuguese Letters), a collection of letters, poems, and short stories documenting woman's role in a traditional society. The three co-authors, Maria Isabel Barreno, Maria Teresa da Horta, and Maria Velho da Costa, put this original work together to shock and to break moulds, and their three translators, Helen R. **Lane** for the prose and Faith **Gillespie** and Suzette Macedo for the poetry, do them full justice. It is a pity that their subsequent separate writings have not yet received the same treatment, but no doubt this will change as renewed interest in translation encourages more people, especially women, into the field.

The 1980s revealed the successful translation of another doctor-author, António Lobo Antunes, who like Namora displays a deep and critical insight into the real lives of individuals and their inner dramas. Richard Zenith, in his virtuoso translations, does not shy away from Antunes's use of imagery and idiomatic phrasing; it is easy to see how he is a favourite author amongst the English-speaking public with such works as *Explicação dos Pássaros* (1981, An Explanation of the Birds) and *Auto dos Danados* (1985, Act of the Damned). Elizabeth **Lowe** also gives a creditable rendering of *Os Cus de Judas* (1979, South of Nowhere).

In poetry, justifiable prominence has been given to Eugénio de Andrade, who shows his maturity in the prose poems of *Vertentes do Olhar* (1987, The Slopes of a Gaze), translated with keen sensitivity by Alexis **Levitin**.

It is perhaps only José Saramago, with his peculiar, creative prose style, who enjoys any major success today; nearly all his novels are already in English translation. The unfortunate death of his friend and translator, Giovanni **Pontiero**, has brought a halt to this, since he was without doubt the only person gifted enough to deal successfully with the problems of varying style, odd punctuation, and shifts in register, a form of prose which itself draws on the wealth of Portuguese literary history for so many of its 'musical' effects: this can be seen quite clearly in the various works, the best perhaps being *Memorial do Convento* (1982, Baltasar and Blimunda), *O Ano da Morte de Ricardo Reis* (1984, The Year of the Death of Ricardo Reis), and *A Jangada de Pedra* (1986, The Stone Raft).

Finally, it would not be fair to round off a look at modern Portuguese literature without considering the output of the African colonies, especially Angola and Mozambique. Michael **Wolfers** professionally presents the compelling drama of Luandino Vieira's *A Vida Verdadeira de Domingos Xavier* (1974, The Real Life of Domingos Xavier),

while David **Brookshaw**'s brave rendering of the animist-realist Mia Couto in *Vozes Anoitecidas* (1986, Voices Made Night) deserves special merit: the challenge of this author with his amazing neologisms and poetic prose is immense.   MH

ANTHOLOGIES   Bartes, A. R., *Portugal Through Her Literature: An Anthology of Prose and Verse*, Glastonbury, UK, 1972 · Costa, Margaret Jull, *The Dedalus Book of Portuguese Fantasy*, Sawtry, UK, 1995 · Macedo, Helder, and De Melo e Castro, E. M., *Contemporary Portuguese Poetry*, Manchester, 1978.
ANDRADE, EUGÉNIO DE   Levitin, Alexis, *The Slopes of a Gaze*, Tallahassee, Fla., 1992.
ANTUNES, ANTÓNIO LOBO   Lowe, Elizabeth, *South of Nowhere*, London, 1983 · Zenith, Richard, *An Explanation of the Birds*, London, 1992 · *Act of the Damned*, London, 1993.
BARRENO, ISABEL; DA HORTA, MARIA TERESA; VELHO DA COSTA, MARIA   Lane, Helen R., Gillespie, Faith, and Macedo, Suzette, *The Three Marias: New Portuguese Letters*, London, 1979.
COUTO, MIA   Brookshaw, David, *Voices Made Night*, London, 1990.
MONTEIRO, LUÍS DE STTAU   Stevens, Ann, *The Rules of the Game*, London, 1964.
NAMORA, FERNANDO   Ball, D., *Mountain Doctor*, London, 1956.
PESSOA, FERNANDO   Bosley, Keith, McGuirk, Bernard, et al., *A Centenary Pessoa*, Manchester, 1995 · Costa, Margaret Jull, *The Book of Disquiet*, London, 1991 · Green, J. C. R., *The Tobacconist*, Isle of Skye, 1975 · Griffin, Jonathan, *Selected Poems*, Harmondsworth, 1996 [Penguin] · Macedo, Suzette, *The Tobacconist's*, Lisbon, 1987 · Quintanilha, F. E. G., *Sixty Portuguese Poems*, Cardiff, 1971 · Rickard, Peter, *Selected Poems*, Edinburgh, 1971 · Watson, Iain, *The Book of Disquiet*, London, 1991 · Zenith, Richard, *The Book of Disquietude*, Manchester, 1991.
PIRES, JOSÉ CARDOSO   Fitton, Mary, *Ballad of Dog's Beach*, London, 1986.
QUEIRÓS, EÇA DE   Campbell, Roy, *Cousin Bazilio*, Manchester, 1992 · *The City and the Mountains*, Manchester, 1994 · Costa, Margaret Jull, *The Relic*, London, 1994 · Fedorchek, R. M., *Alves and Co.*, University Press of America, 1989 · Flanagan, Nan, *The Sin of Father Amaro*, Manchester, 1994 · McGowan, P., and Stevens, Ann, *The Maias*, London, 1986 · Stevens, Ann, *The Illustrious House of Ramires*, Manchester, 1992.
SÁ-CARNEIRO, MÁRIO DE   Costa, Margaret Jull, *Lucio's Confession*, London, 1994.
SANTARENO, BERNARDO   Vieira, Nelson H., *The Promise*, Providence, RI, 1981.
SARAMAGO, JOSÉ   Pontiero, Giovanni, *Baltasar and Blimunda*, London, 1988 · *The Year of the Death of Ricardo Reis*, London, 1992 · *The Gospel According to Jesus Christ*, London, 1993 · *Manual of Painting and Calligraphy: A Novel*, London, 1994 · *The Stone Raft*, London, 1994.
SENA, JORGE DE   Fitton, Mary, *The Wondrous Physician*, London, 1986.
TORGA, MIGUEL   Carlsen, Ivana, *Tales from the Mountain*, Fort Bragg, NC, 1991.
VIEIRA, LUANDINO   Wolfers, Michael, *The Real Life of Domingos Xavier*, London, 1978.

15. BRAZILIAN LITERATURE

Over 400 Brazilian literary works of all genres have been translated into English since 1886, and published in book form. The vast majority of such translations are novels, while short stories and poetry have usually appeared either in anthologies, most frequently of Latin American works, or in scholarly journals; very few plays have ever been translated into English. The greatest obstacle faced by the scholar or reader interested in Brazilian literature is the extreme difficulty in obtaining such translations. The older ones are out of print, even though some of them have been reprinted many times, and are usually to be located only at specialized libraries, whether in the English-speaking world or in Brazil. While modern translations are generally published in very small print runs, the tendency appears to be for new translations, and

even retranslations, of Brazilian works to come out every year.

The fact that the first translation of a Brazilian work appeared in 1886 means that no translations were published during the colonial period (1500–1822), and that most translations are of contemporary writers. However, what may be considered the very first Brazilian literary work, the epic *O Uruguay* (1769) by José Basílio da Gama, was translated into English by Sir Richard F. **Burton** (1821–90), who prepared copious notes and did careful research in order to carry out the translation, which is eloquent although sometimes biased in its attitudes. His wife, Isabel **Burton** (1831–96), tried to suppress the translation because she considered it anti-Jesuitical, and therefore offensive to her Catholic beliefs. She destroyed her husband's notes, but the manuscript surfaced much later at a library in California, and was published in 1982 as *The Uruguay: A Historical Romance of South America*, in a scholarly, bilingual edition.

Isabel Burton herself made the first translation of a Brazilian work into English. She translated *Iracema, lenda do Ceará* (1865), a novel belonging to the immediate postcolonial period, the best-known work by celebrated romantic writer José de Alencar, whose acquaintance the Burtons made in Brazil. Isabel Burton's translation, *Iraçéma, the Honey-Lips, a Legend of Brazil*, applies a delicate treatment to the star-crossed idyll between an Indian girl and a Portuguese soldier, one of the nationalistic themes exploited by Alencar.

Although a contemporary of late romantics, realists, naturalists, Parnassians and symbolists, José Maria Machado de Assis, the most celebrated of Brazilian writers, does not easily fit into any mould. His works are accurate, sometimes ironic descriptions of life in Rio de Janeiro, which during his lifetime was first the imperial and then the republican capital of Brazil, the heart of the era's genteel life. One of these descriptions is what may be considered his masterpiece, the novel *Memórias póstumas de Brás Cubas* (1881), the witty, sagacious memoirs of a typical upper-class city-dweller. William L. **Grossman**'s translation, first published in 1952 as *Epitaph of a Small Winner*, retains much of the original's humour and bite.

Many of Machado de Assis's works have been translated into English, including his best-known novel, *Dom Casmurro* (1900), whose main character's moodiness and jealousy made him notorious as the Brazilian Othello; this work has been translated twice, by Helen **Caldwell** and by Robert L. **Scott-Buccleuch**. Scott-Buccleuch's translation, published as *Dom Casmurro (Lord Taciturn)*, is a fine rendering, even if it omits nine chapters from the original, while the more complete translation by Caldwell reveals a perhaps excessive influence of her own views on Machado de Assis.

The first centenary of Brazilian independence, in 1922, heralded what is known as the modernist movement in the arts and literature. The movement's leader, Mário de Andrade, has had a few of his works translated into English, notably his novel *Macunaíma, o herói sem nenhum caráter* (1928, Macunaíma, the Hero Without a Character), which has greatly influenced Brazilian literature. This work is difficult for Brazilians because, attempting to unite Brazil, Andrade tried to bring together in it the modes of speech and slang of several parts of the nation, as well as their different cultures and ways.

Its translation into English, by E. A. **Goodland**, first published in 1984, on the other hand, is fluent and entertaining, adroitly using English slang together with Brazilian words to maintain the zest of the original.

Regionalism, a Brazilian literary movement which is the result of a reworking of naturalism and realism in the critical light of modernism, includes several Brazilian authors of great stature. Among them is Graciliano Ramos, a few of whose works have been translated into English, most remarkably his masterpiece, the short novel *Vidas secas* (1938), translated by Ralph Edward **Dimmick** in 1961 as *Barren Lives*. This is the harrowing tale of a tenant-farmer family's flight from the drought that plagues the Brazilian north-eastern hinterland. Although the translation has a few flaws, it succeeds in conveying the characters' numbness in the face of hardship and oppression.

Prominent amongst regionalist writers is João Guimarães Rosa, celebrated for having been able to escape previous formulas and for his aesthetic innovations in using the Portuguese language as spoken in Brazil. He was not a prolific writer, and most of his works have been translated into English. *Sagarana* (1946), Guimarães Rosa's collection of novellas, was translated in 1958 by Harriet **de Onís**, with very good results. His most notable work, *Grande Sertão: Veredas* (1956), was translated in 1963 by James L. **Taylor** and Harriet de Onís as *The Devil to Pay in the Backlands*. Faced with the task of rendering Guimarães Rosa's neologisms and word play into English, the translators opted for omitting several portions of the text in what turned out as a less than adequate translation. Guimarães Rosa's collection of short stories *Primeiras estórias* (1962, Early Stories) was translated by Barbara **Shelby** as *The Third Bank of the River and Other Stories* in 1968. This is a sensitive piece of work, and the story Shelby chose for the title of the volume points to the new dimension that Guimarães Rosa brought into Brazilian Literature.

The works of Jorge Amado, the best-known Brazilian writer outside Brazil, also belong to this tradition, particularly his early novels. However, it is translations of Amado's later novels that are most popular in English translation, although Brazilian critics have not granted them the same critical acclaim as early ones. Amado's recent novels are mostly colourful, humorous, and sensual, such as *Gabriela, cravo e canela* (1958) translated as *Gabriela, Clove and Cinnamon* by James L. Taylor and William L. Grossman, and *Dona Flor e seus dois maridos* (1966), translated as *Dona Flor and Her Two Husbands:*

A Moral and Amorous Tale by Harriet de Onís. These translations have been praised by critics, the more enthusiastic of whom have claimed that it is possible to get almost a whiff of the heroines' cooking just by reading the books.

An important theme of Brazilian literature, one that crosses over temporal barriers, is the Indian. *Iracema* and *Macunaíma* belong to this tradition, as does *Maíra* (1978) by Darcy Ribeiro, translated by E. A. Goodland with Thomas **Colchie**. This novel tells the story of an Amazonian Indian boy who is educated by Catholic priests, and of a white woman who finds refuge from her turmoil in the jungle. Their meeting allows the novelist to delve deeply into issues of cultural displacement in Brazil. Although the translation omits portions of the text and evens out some of the writing styles used by the author to give voice to the novel's different characters (Indians, whites, policemen, traders), it has maintained the poetry of the original, particularly in parts where the Indians tell their own legends.

Almost every work of Clarice Lispector, who may be thought of as the leading woman writer of modern Brazil and who has attained some prestige abroad, has been translated into English. Foremost among them is Giovanni **Pontiero**'s translation of the novella *A hora da estrela* (1977) as *The Hour of the Star*. In it, as in her work in general, Lispector opens a window into the feminine inner world: she gives the reader a glimpse into the soul of a desperately poor, uneducated young woman. In this translation, Pontiero's delicate pen provides the reader with delightful prose, as he did in all his other renderings of Lispector's works, such as of the novel *Perto do coração selvagem* (1944) which he translated as *Near to the Wild Heart*, and of the short stories *Laços de família* (1960), translated as *Family Ties*.

Only modern Brazilian poetry appears to have been translated into English. There are good anthologies by Elizabeth Bishop and Giovanni Pontiero, and a good selection of contemporary authors in fine translations was made by editor/translator John **Milton** for a special volume of *Modern Poetry in Translation* (1994). A remarkable example of Brazilian poetry in English translation is a bilingual edition of the poems of Cecília Meireles. Meireles is considered by many to be one of the leading Brazilian poets, and her poetry ranges from the grandeur of the epic to the softness of the lyric. This excellent selection, entitled *Poems in Translation*, was translated by Henry Hunt **Keith** and Raymond **Sayers**, and published in 1977. Also important is a selection of Manuel Bandeira's poems translated by E. **Flintoff**, and published as *Recife* in celebration of the poet's native town. Bandeira's poetry is at once modern, terse, and delicate, with a child's naïvety, qualities which shine through the translation.

Although a Brazilian theatre has existed since colonial times, only two popular modern comedies appear to have been translated into English. One, *O auto da Compadecida* (1956), by Ariano Suassuna, translated as *The Rogue's Trial* by Dillwyn F. **Ratcliff**, follows the traditions of Brazilian folk literature and theatre, rooted in Europe's mystery plays, and the translation retains much of its flavour. The other, *Apareceu a Margarida* (1973), by Roberto Athayde, is a monologue in which a disgruntled teacher addresses her students. Translated as *Miss Margarida's Way: Tragicomic Monologue for an Impetuous Woman*, it achieved a measure of success on the stage in New York. Although no translator is mentioned in the printed version, no humour seems to have been lost in the translation. HGB

ANTHOLOGIES Bishop, Elizabeth, and Brasil, Emanuel, eds., *An Anthology of Twentieth-Century Brazilian Poetry*, Middletown, Conn., 1971 · Milton, John, 'Special Feature: Modern Poetry from Brazil', *Modern Poetry in Translation*, n.s., 6 (1994–5) · Pontiero, Giovanni, *An Anthology of Brazilian Modernist Poetry*, Oxford, 1969.

ALENCAR, JOSÉ DE Burton, Isabel, *Iracéma the Honey Lips: A Legend of Brazil*, London, 1886.

AMADO, JORGE De Onís, Harriet, *Dona Flor and Her Two Husbands: A Moral and Amorous Tale*, London, 1986 · Taylor, James L., and Grossman, William L., *Gabriela, Clove and Cinnamon*, London, 1984.

ANDRADE, MÁRIO Goodland, E. A., *Macunaíma*, London, 1988.

ATHAYDE, ROBERTO anon., *Miss Margarida's Way: Tragicomic Monologue for an Impetuous Woman*, New York, 1977.

BANDEIRA, MANUEL Flintoff, E., *Recife (Poetry)*, Bradford, UK, 1984.

GAMA, JOSÉ BASÍLIO DA Burton, Sir Richard F., *The Uruguay: A Historical Romance of South America*, ed. Frederick C. H. Garcia and Edward F. Stanton, Berkeley, Calif., 1982.

GUIMARÃES ROSA, JOÃO De Onís, Harriet, *Sagarana*, New York, 1963 · Shelby, Barbara, *The Third Bank of the River and Other Stories*, New York, 1963 · Taylor, James L., and de Onís, Harriet, *The Devil to Pay in the Backlands*, New York, 1963.

LISPECTOR, CLARICE Pontiero, Giovanni, *Family Ties*, Austin, Tex., 1972 · *Near to the Wild Heart*, Manchester, 1990 · *The Hour of the Star*, Manchester, 1992.

MACHADO DE ASSIS, JOSÉ MARIA   Caldwell, Helen, *Dom Casmurro*, New York, 1993 · Grossman, William L., *Epitaph of a Small Winner*, New York, 1991 · Scott-Buccleuch, Robert, *Dom Casmurro (Lord Taciturn)*, London, 1992.

MEIRELES, CECÍLIA   Keith, Henry Hunt, and Sayers, Raymond, *Poems in Translation*, Washington, DC, 1997.

RAMOS, GRACILIANO   Dimmick, Ralph Edward, *Barren Lives*, Austin, Tex., 1984.

RIBEIRO, DARCY   Goodland, E. A., and Colchie, Thomas, *Maíra*, New York, 1984.

SUASSUNA, ARIANO   Ratcliff, Dillwyn F., *The Rogue's Trial*, Berkeley, Calif., 1963.

I. Indian Languages

1. INTRODUCTION

Translations from the Indian languages into English began in 1785 and were initially all from Sanskrit. They instantly caused a sensation, and were recognized as one of the most exciting cultural discoveries ever made by Europe. Within a couple of decades they had brought about what Raymond Schwab has called an Oriental Renaissance and J. J. Clarke Oriental Enlightenment. With the discovery of Sanskrit [II.l.2], which Sir William Jones in 1796 declared to be 'of wonderful structure, more perfect than the Greek, more copious than the Latin, and more exquisitely refined than either', the new discipline of comparative philology was born, which led to the conceptualization of the Indo-European family of languages. It was, as Schwab says, as if the two halves of the world had for the first time been joined together and the world made whole.

Such European discovery of India had been made possible by the efforts not of disinterested scholars but of missionaries and employees of the East India Company, which was at this stage advancing from trading in India to ruling over India. The Company paid handsomely for translations of Indian legal treatises and other utilitarian works, and for the compiling of dictionaries and grammars of the Indian languages; in 1800 it set up the College of Fort William in Calcutta to train its British employees in the Indian languages, and from the period when Warren Hastings was Governor-General (1772–85) it set out as a matter of policy to understand better the people of India so as to be able to rule them better.

Such a nexus between power and knowledge (in the correlation postulated by Michel Foucault) has provided the ideological basis of Edward Said's enormously influential *Orientalism* (1978). In his sweeping and homogenizing argument (in which 'the orient' means by and large the Middle East), Said has no space to register the great reversal in the orientalist project in India which occurred in 1835, exactly 50 years after the first translation from Sanskrit, when Lords Macaulay and Bentinck completely overturned the policy initiated by Hastings, and replaced the Indian languages with English as the vehicle of British rule. The defeat of the 'Orientalists' by the 'Anglicists' in this long-running battle was effectively sealed by Macaulay's notorious statement that 'a single shelf of a good European library was worth the whole native literature of India and Arabia'. Not only did Macaulay have, by his own admission, 'no knowledge of either Sanscrit or Arabic' when he said this, but apparently he had not read many translations from them either.

Though the official propagation of western knowledge through the use of English in India made the work of translating from the Indian languages into English considerably less urgent or useful, it also served to widen the field, and several other languages now began to contest the monopoly of Sanskrit. The attraction of Buddhism drew translators to Pali, though the rest of Europe led rather than followed English in this quest. Classical Tamil [II.l.3] came to be recognized as a Dravidian language comparable in its antiquity, its epic and lyrical poetry, and its treatises to Sanskrit itself. But the richest new area which now opened up was of literature in the modern Indian languages, well over a dozen of which had come into literary existence by c.1000 CE, and in which the literature of India continues to be written apart from the tiny fraction which has recently begun to be produced in 'Indian English'.

Literature in the modern Indian languages is seen to be divided into two broad and unequal phases: the medieval period from the beginning to *c*.1800 CE, and the modern period from that date on, i.e. roughly from the beginning of the western impact. The medieval period [II.l.4] has for its large theme *bhakti*, i.e. religious devotion to any of the manifestations of God—Vishnu, Shiva, Murugan, Rama, Krishna, the goddess Durga or Kali, or any of the countless other deities—while it also incorporates an alternative stream of writers who preached against traditional brahminism and all forms of worship, advocating instead good conduct or an approach to God through knowledge. As examples of the former, the *Ramayana* and the *Mahabharata* were translated or retold from Sanskrit into all the modern Indian languages in an act of protest against ritualistic priestly monopoly comparable with the Reformation in Europe. Again, as with the Bible in English, many of these new *Ramayanas* and *Mahabharatas* came to rank among the greatest literary works in their respective languages, and were in turn often translated into English, mostly by missionaries and civil servants.

In recent times, an Indian poet and Dravidian scholar, A. K. **Ramanujan**, achieved exceptional success in translating a selection of Kannada *bhakti* poetry, *Speaking of Siva* (1973), preferring to be so close and literal as even to lay down a new principle: 'In the act of translating, "the Spirit killeth and the Letter giveth Life".' Not that this fastidious procedure prevented another Indian theorist of translation, Tejaswini Niranjana, in her *Siting Translation* (1992), from somewhat airily accusing Ramanujan of using an English implicated in Christian protestantism and even colonialism. Perhaps to use the English language at all is to be complicit at some level in its whole cultural history! In any case, the later *bhakti* poetry often degenerated into virtuoso feats of prosody and rhetoric, and has for that reason proved virtually untranslatable.

Indeed, translation into English even of some of the commonest and simplest terms of Indian life brings out the fact that though English and the Indian languages may technically belong to the same family, they are poles apart in respect of culture and sensibility. *Dharma*, *karma*, *maya*, and *moksha* have always required complex glossing, but so have common items of food and dress, e.g. *roti*, *idli*, *kurta*, *veshti*. Numerous specific kinship terms have to be awkwardly expanded into English, e.g. 'maternal grandfather' or 'wife's brother's wife'. The word for both 'yesterday' and 'tomorrow' is

the same in Hindi, *kal*, while *se* (pronounced shay) in Bengali, which can mean either 'he' or 'she', so completely foxed a British translator recently that he mixed up two characters right through a short story. The use of particular dialects, especially for differentiating characters in terms of region or class, must, as R. E. **Asher** has confessed, be 'sacrificed entirely', though he does translate at least the title of such a work (in Tamil) so as to signal what has been lost: *Me Grandad 'ad an Elephant* (1980).

On the other hand, some Indian writers in the 20th c. have been so intimately conversant with the English language and with western literature that their own writings seem to be subtly intertextual. Some of them have in fact gone on to translate their works into English themselves. From this to Indians writing originally in English is but one small cultural step, and Indian writing in English in recent years, especially after the award of the Booker prize to Salman Rushdie (1981) and to Arundhati Roy (1997), has seriously threatened to eclipse Indian writing in English translation. In *The Vintage Book of Indian Writing* (1997), co-edited by Salman Rushdie, for example, all the pieces except one were written originally in English. Justifying his choice, Rushdie in his Introduction declares that in the half century of Indian independence, Indian writing in English 'is proving to be a stronger and more important body of writing than most of what has been produced in the eighteen "recognized" languages of India'. This postcolonial judgement seems uncannily to echo what Macaulay said of Indian literature at the beginning of colonial rule; it also seems based on a comparable ignorance of even the evidence available in translation.

Oddly enough, such denigration of Indian literature in English translation comes in the midst of a translation boom which has gone on for the last decade or more. A large part of the list of Penguin Books India comprises translations from both Sanskrit and the modern languages; Heinemann London, in a rare metropolitan initiative, published six novels in translation in their South Asian Writers series (which, however, failed to take off), and Macmillan India are in the process of publishing four novels from each of 12 languages in English translation at the behest of a private trust to propagate Indian literature and culture. Pioneering volumes of women's writing from India have been published within the last decade, most notably *The Inner Courtyard: Stories by Indian Women* (1990) edited by Lakshmi Holmström, *Women Writing in India: 600 BC to the Present* (2 vols., 1993) edited by Susie Tharu and K. Lalita, and *In Their Own*

Voice: The Penguin Anthology of Contemporary Indian Women Poets (1993) edited by Arlene Zide. At the same time, Indian languages are felt to be increasingly under threat from the spread of global, hegemonic English, and translations into it are sometimes viewed as postcolonial cooption if not a case of killing the golden goose. Though Indian literature in English translation occupies a disproportionately small place worldwide, it may in due course well become the literature with the widest reach within India, a literature in translation of, by, and largely for Indians themselves. HT

2. SANSKRIT

i. Historical Introduction Sanskrit, in its older form of Vedic Sanskrit (so termed from its use in the *Vedas*, the earliest sacred texts), was brought into the north-west of India by the Āryans some time in the second half of the 2nd millennium BCE and from there it spread to the rest of north India (and gradually to the whole of India), developing into the classical form of the language, which subsequently became fixed as the learned language of culture and religion, while the spoken language developed into the various Prākrits, although a variant form of Sanskrit was used for the two great Sanskrit epics, which grew to their present form between about the 5th c. BCE and the 4th c. CE. The older language was described with great precision around the 4th c. BCE by Pāṇini in his grammar; with the growth of classical Sanskrit literature (mainly in the 4th–10th c. CE) this description was regarded as prescriptive, and it is closely adhered to in the various forms of literature then produced: drama, narrative poetry, anthologies, fable, and story literature.

One work of Sanskrit literature has been circulating in Europe since the 11th c., the story collection relating to statecraft called the *Pañcatantra*. However, its various European adaptations derive through the Arabic *Kalilah wa Dimnah* from a Pahlavi translation; *The Morall Philosophie of Doni*, published in 1570, was translated by Sir Thomas **North** (?1535–?1601) from Doni's Italian version of a Latin version of that Arabic version, and thus its relationship to its ultimate source is somewhat distant. Individual stories have also entered the folk-tale tradition.

The history of direct translation from Sanskrit into English only begins in the early days of British rule in India, but even then competence in Sanskrit was initially so limited that Nathaniel Brassey **Halhed** (1751–1830), who as an undergraduate had collaborated with Richard Sheridan in several literary endeavours, translated *A Code of Gentoo Laws* from a Persian version of the *Vivādārṇavasetu* compiled in Sanskrit by pundits for the East India Company. This work, published in 1776, was primarily intended to facilitate the administration of civil justice, but proved to be of limited value as a legal document, owing largely to the defects of the way in which it was produced. However, it is a landmark in the process of acquainting Europeans with Indian culture; indeed, contemporary reviewers largely ignored its purpose and concentrated on its information about the nature of Indian civilization and Hinduism, contained especially in the translator's preface.

Although practical purposes were thus prominent, both religious and literary works were also translated. Indeed, the *Bhagavadgītā* (Kṛṣṇa's discourse to Arjuna on the nature of the self and on devotion to the *Bhagavat*, the Lord) was the first Sanskrit work directly translated into English and it has remained much the most popular, with over 300 translations into English having appeared to date. The first, by Sir Charles **Wilkins** (?1749–1836), appeared in 1785 and was published with the encouragement of the Governor-General of India, Warren Hastings. Wilkins's ultimate ambition was to translate the entire epic, the *Mahābhārata* (within which the *Bhagavadgītā* forms a small episode), but little more was published, apart from the Śakuntalā episode in 1794. His *Bhagavadgītā* translation was heavily dependent on the indigenous commentarial tradition and left many key terms untranslated; it attracted relatively little notice at the time in Britain, although it had rather more impact in America, especially on the 'New England Transcendentalists'. Two years later Wilkins published a translation of the *Hitopadeśa*, a later Sanskrit adaptation of the *Pañcatantra*.

Significantly, Sir William **Jones** (1746–94)—widely known for having publicized the fact that Sanskrit is related to Greek and Latin and for founding the Asiatick Society of Bengal—is remembered for his translation of the classic Sanskrit drama, Kālidāsa's *Śakuntalā*, published in 1789, which brought together his own considerable literary abilities and his newly acquired knowledge of Sanskrit; it proved an instant success in Europe, prompting a eulogy from Goethe (who also modelled the prologue to *Faust* on that to *Śakuntalā*) [II.h.5]. However, in line with his duties as a judge of the Bengal

Supreme Court, Jones first planned a translation of the *Laws of Manu* (a theoretical rather than a practical treatise on law), to replace Halhed's *Code*, and this was in due course completed and published by the government in 1794. In these first few translations, then, all three interests—practical, religious, and literary—are represented, and these particular texts have been translated repeatedly since.

By early in the 19th c., interests were broadening. William **Carey** (1761–1834) and Joshua **Marshman** (1768–1837) began a translation of the other great Sanskrit epic, the *Rāmāyaṇa*, as well as an edition of the text; the translation is far from elegant, since the translators' avowed aim was to be as literal as was practical, but the reason for its choice was its centrality to more popular Indian culture. Apart from the translation of one chapter of the *Kālikā Purāṇa*, published in 1797, the first translation of any of the Purāṇas, the great storehouses of Hindu mythology and traditional Hinduism, was published in 1840; this was the *Viṣṇu Purāṇa*, translated by H. H. **Wilson** (1786–1860), who had earlier translated Kālidāsa's *Meghadūta* (The Cloud Messenger) and *Select Specimens of the Theatre of the Hindus*. A major development subsequently was the inauguration in 1874 by Friedrich Max Müller of the Sacred Books of the East series, in which many of the principal religious and related texts of several Asian cultures were translated, including another version of the *Laws of Manu* by Georg **Bühler** (for long the standard translation, until the appearance of a livelier one by Wendy **Doniger**) and a translation of the major *Upaniṣads* by Max **Müller** himself.

ii. Vedic Literature The one major area which long lacked any substantial translation was that of the earliest sacred texts, the hymns of the Vedas, a lacuna which was eventually but inadequately filled by R. T. H. **Griffith**'s complete translation of the *Ṛgveda* in 1889. The Vedic hymns present particular problems of translation, since their language and vocabulary differ appreciably from classical Sanskrit, while their nature as hymns of praise to the gods mean that much of their material is allusive, elliptical, and at times deliberately obscure, leaving a number of passages unclear in meaning. These problems underlie the mixed reception from other scholars accorded to a substantial selection of hymns from the *Ṛgveda* translated by Wendy Doniger O'Flaherty, although another aspect is that the selection is not wholly representative, being heavily weighted to the latest book of the collection, the tenth, which contains the most speculative or 'philosophical' hymns. The translation is generally readable but has taken certain liberties

with the more obscure passages, as well as rendering the hymns in a lively, even colloquial style, which levels out the variety in the styles of the original poets; despite occasional minor errors of interpretation it does make the hymns more accessible to the ordinary reader than earlier selections intended for the student, but the choice of hymns translated conceals the extent to which the original is dominated by ritual concerns.

The last component of the Vedic literature, the speculations on the nature of the individual and of the world contained in the *Upaniṣads*, has been better served in the number of translations made. Of the two which have long been standard, each has its limitations: that by S. **Radhakrishnan**, though generally accurate, tends to impose on these varied texts the single interpretation adopted by the later Advaita Vedānta philosophical system, whereas that by Juan **Mascaró** is excessively free, reflecting his own romantic approach. They have now been superseded by the careful and idiomatic translation of Patrick **Olivelle**, which adopts a more informal style for the dialogues than for the discourses and in general captures the flavour of the texts better than any previous translation.

The brevity and religious character of the *Bhagavadgītā* partly account for its popularity with translators, many of whom have also tackled the *Upaniṣads* (e.g. both Radhakrishnan and Mascaró, whose translations of this text show the same features). There is space to mention only four more out of the hundreds produced. Two are significant for their accompanying scholarly commentary, those by Franklin **Edgerton** and by R. C. **Zaehner**, although in both cases the translation itself is too literal to be aesthetically pleasing; incidentally, Edgerton's includes also the metrical version by Sir Edwin **Arnold** (1832–1904), chiefly of interest now for its antiquated cadences, for example:

> Better to live on beggar's bread
>   With those we love alive,
> Than taste their blood in rich feasts spread,
>   And guiltily survive!

Two which are specifically aimed at the general reader are those by Barbara Stoler **Miller** and by W. J. **Johnson**. Miller gives a clear and elegant translation, whose directness conveys the message well. Johnson's is less showy, even at times pedestrian, but it is the more exact.

iii. Epics Translations of both the great Sanskrit epics, the *Mahābhārata* and the *Rāmāyaṇa*, which hold a central place in Indian culture (and provide the plots for much of classical Sanskrit literature), were commenced at an early date with the unfinished attempts by Charles Wilkins and by Carey and Marshman. Subsequently, various selections and abridgements were published, and Peter Brook produced a composite stage version, mainly based on French sources. However, the first and only complete translation of the *Mahābhārata* into English is that by K. M. **Ganguli**, published by P. C. Roy at the end of the 19th c., and this has perforce been the standard translation ever since, despite the extreme awkwardness of its Victorian English, which in no way does justice to the easy and direct style of the core of the epic; it illustrates only too well the limitations of sub-Shakespearean Indian English in capturing the spirit of the original. The translation begun by Hans **van Buitenen** but left incomplete by his early death (although there are now plans by one of his former students to continue it) gives much more of the flavour of the original, rendering the narrative epic verse in an easygoing prose which is generally contemporary in style, though slightly archaizing at times, and reserving a free versification for the verses in longer metres. The translator also adopted the convention—at times somewhat stilted—of using standard translations for key terms, such as 'Law' for *dharma* and 'baron' for the aristocratic warrior class.

The first complete translation of the *Rāmāyaṇa* was a fairly free metrical version made by Griffith, followed at the end of the 19th c. by a prose rendering by Manmatha Nath **Dutt**; neither is of any great literary merit, although they do give the reader access to the basic story. The translation in progress by a team of translators headed by Robert **Goldman** adopts the style in which normally each verse is translated as a separate prose paragraph, a layout which appears antiquated, wasteful of space, and distracting to read, as well as obscuring the fact that the *śloka* is essentially a narrative metre. Goldman's translation of the first book is generally accurate, but somewhat pedestrian; he does not even adopt the device of versification for stanzas in longer metres followed in van Buitenen's *Mahābhārata* translation. The translation of the second book by Sheldon **Pollock** is less stilted, while still remaining close to the original, despite an occasional tendency to over-interpretation; in the third book his tendency is more to a pedestrian, sometimes long-winded style even where something more elevated would be appropriate. Rosalind **Lefeber** has produced for the fourth book a translation that reads more easily than previous volumes, though still staying close to the original. The extensive annotations included are a feature of all the volumes but deal with its later interpretation rather than its original setting.

iv. Problems of Translation The cultural background of all Sanskrit literature is clearly an issue in all attempts at translation, but one that differs more between different periods than has perhaps been realized. The ritual background of the Vedic hymns is a far cry from the intellectual sophistication of most classical Sanskrit literature and the time-span may be up to two millennia; the Sanskrit epics have some analogies with Homer [II.i.2] or with *Beowulf* [II.0.1] but their scale is vastly greater and their impact on subsequent literature is more significant. Even in the epics, the symbolism of the lotus or the wealth of similes drawn from the flora and fauna of the subcontinent seem to an English readership exotic rather than natural and immediate. However, while these factors can be indicated with reasonable success in introductions or notes to works such as the epics, features inherent in the use of the classical language constitute more intractable problems.

Sanskrit metres have no equivalent in English poetry, their quantitative basis allying them with Greek and Latin verse, but the effects of their very varied forms being impossible to reproduce in modern European languages. While prose translations are preferable for primarily narrative works such as the epics, the loss involved in transposing classical Sanskrit verse into prose is considerable, linked as it is with the complex sound patterns involved. On the other hand, verse translations have not been notably successful, except for occasional renderings of epigrammatic verses, those called in Sanskrit *subhāṣita* (well uttered).

The extensive use of assonance and alliteration in all their forms is indeed usually lost in translation, and reference to it in notes is a poor substitute; this is allied to the freedom to choose from a large range of synonyms permitted by the fact that classical Sanskrit is a learned rather than a natural language. At its most extreme this is seen in poems that, for example, through constant word-play narrate simultaneously the stories of the *Mahābhārata* and the *Rāmāyaṇa*, a feat which not surprisingly has remained untranslated (although occasional verses employing the same techniques have been attempted in anthologies). Word-play is regarded as a positive embellishment, not treated with the disdain often accorded to puns in English. However, any attempt to retain such sound structure leads to severe penalties of non-equivalence in other respects. Again, the strongly hierarchical nature of Indian society is reflected in the convention of

Sanskrit drama that the main male characters speak Sanskrit but others speak one of the Prakrits (the more popular languages deriving from Sanskrit), reflecting their inferior education and status (this is broadly as though some spoke Ciceronian Latin and others Old French or Old Italian within the same play); this has never been reproduced in any translation but significant nuances of expression are thereby lost.

v. Drama Kālidāsa (probably 4th–5th c. CE), by common consent the outstanding poet and playwright in Sanskrit, is best known for his play *Śakuntalā* (so named from its heroine), which has been translated repeatedly since the first version by Sir William Jones. The next significant version by Sir Monier **Monier-Williams** (1819–99) showed some improvement in accuracy but a decline in literary quality. The standard translation for many years was that by Arthur W. **Ryder**, who, though using rhymed verse for the lyrics, stayed fairly close to the text and produced a version that was pleasant to read. Recently there have been three translations in succession, by Michael **Coulson** (in one volume with two other major plays, Viśākhadatta's *Mudrārākṣasa* and Bhavabhūti's *Mālatīmādhava*), by Barbara Stoler **Miller** (in a volume which includes translations of Kālidāsa's *Vikramorvaśīya* (Urvaśī Won by Valour) by David **Gitomer** and *Mālavikāgnimitra* (Mālavikā and Agnimitra) by Edwin **Gerow**), and by Chandra **Rajan** (together with two of his poems, the *Ṛtusaṃhāra* and the *Meghadūta*); the first two are in vigorous and generally idiomatic English, well suited to the task.

As an example of their styles, here is the verse in which her foster-father blesses Śakuntalā as she leaves his hermitage, invoking the sacred fires of Vedic ritual. Ryder's rhymed version is:

> The holy fires around the altar kindle,
>   And at their margins sacred grass is piled;
> Beneath their sacrificial odours dwindle
>   Misfortunes. May the fires protect you, child!

Coulson's somewhat stolid but accurate rendering is:

> Let those three fires of the sacrifice protect you,
> On their altars ranged around the principal altar,
> Heaped with firewood, banked with sacred grass,
> Repelling evil with the odours of the sacrifice.

Miller translates:

> Perfectly placed around the main altar,
> fed with fuel, strewn with holy grass,
> destroying sin by incense from oblations,
> may these sacred fires purify you!

Rajan expands to seven lines:

> May these Sacrificial Fires
> ranged round the Holy Altar
> that blaze fed with sacred wood
> within the circle of strewn darbhā grass,
> whose oblation-fragrant smoke
> billows out chasing away
> all evil, keep you good and pure.

This verse illustrates the problems of rendering its very different cultural assumptions into natural English, and none of the four translators is altogether successful (all manage better elsewhere). Coulson adopts a more natural word order for English at the expense of the build-up to the climax retained by the other three, while Miller's version is somewhat tauter.

Whereas *Śakuntalā* has been translated repeatedly, other Sanskrit plays, and even other works by Kālidāsa, have received less attention. Some have already been listed, and it is worth noting that Ryder translated all Kālidāsa's works, including the *Raghuvaṃśa* (The Dynasty of Raghu), which has also been translated—though rather stiffly—by R. **Antoine**. Kālidāsa's *Kumārasambhava* (The Birth of the Prince, i.e. Skanda) has been well translated by Hank **Heifetz**, who seeks to produce an equivalent effect in English rather than a literal translation, transposing phrases where necessary to achieve this, although the translation is closer to the original than this might suggest. However, his desire to improve intelligibility by occasionally inserting an explanatory remark into the translation tends to detract from the tautness of the original, while his free verse does not always rise above the prosaic.

Other significant translations of Kālidāsa's works include another version of the *Meghadūta* by Franklin and Eleanor **Edgerton**. The poem is in the form of a message that a lovelorn *yakṣa* or demigod, separated from his beloved, gives to a passing cloud to deliver, and the descriptions of the scenery over which the cloud will pass are strikingly handled by Kālidāsa; much of this comes over well in the translation, despite its rather old-fashioned style (including thees and thous). There is also a trendy free translation by L. **Nathan**.

Both the *Mudrārākṣasa* (Rākṣasa's Seal) of Viśākhadatta and the *Mṛcchakaṭikā* (Little Clay Cart) of Śūdraka have been translated, with a helpful introduction, by van Buitenen, and the latter has also been translated by A. L. **Basham** in a version specifically intended for production. An interesting lesser-known work is the play *Āścaryacūḍāmaṇi* by Śaktibhadra (9th–10th c. CE), based on part of the

Rāmāyaṇa narrative and still performed in the Kūṭiyāṭṭam theatre tradition of Kerala; this has been competently translated by V. **Raghavan**, who gives an accurate but unpretentious rendering of the text.

vi. Other Genres

The other major genre of Sanskrit literature beside the drama is the *mahākāvya*, the long connected poetic work (sometimes termed 'court epic', a designation which does not fit all examples), of which Kālidāsa's *Raghuvaṃśa* and *Kumārasambhava* are fine examples. The earliest specimens are in fact preclassical. Aśvaghoṣa's *Buddhacarita* (Life of the Buddha), and *Saundarananda* (Handsome Nanda, the Buddha's half-brother), rediscovered in 1906 and 1892 respectively, are definitely conceived as literary works, though translated mainly for their religious interest, for example by E. H. **Johnson**.

A development of the 7th c. CE was the writing of prose *mahākāvyas*, among which one of the most notable is the *Harṣacarita* (The Exploits of King Harṣa) by Bāṇa, translated by E. B. **Cowell** and F. W. **Thomas** at the end of the 19th c. Bāṇa's other poem, the *Kādambarī*, was translated at the same period by C. M. **Ridding**, but a better, modern translation has now been produced by Gwendolyn **Layne**. The translation of Subandhu's *Vāsavadattā* by Louis H. **Gray** makes extensive use of brackets in an attempt to render the frequent paronomasia, achieving accuracy at the expense of readability. Another prose narrative is Daṇḍin's *Daśakumāracarita* (Exploits of Ten Princes), a collection of exciting and ingenious stories originally held together by a framing narrative (in which it resembles the *Pañcatantra*, for example), which has been competently translated by Ryder.

Fable and story literature is well represented in Sanskrit literature. The *Pañcatantra* has been both studied and translated by Franklin Edgerton in a style that by now is slightly antiquated but clear. The best-known translation of the enormous collection of stories, based ultimately on the lost *Bṛhatkathā*, written in the 11th c. by Somadeva, the *Kathāsaritsāgara* (The Ocean of Rivers of Stories), was made by C. H. **Tawney** in the 19th c. (and subsequently edited by N. M. Penzer); its heavy-handed language robs the stories of much of their charm, but Penzer's wide-ranging notes were the most valuable part. A more readable translation of a selection of the stories has been made by van Buitenen.

The Sanskrit tradition developed a sophisticated theory of poetics, which has attracted more scholarly attention in some respects than the poetry itself, but the available translations are not particularly accessible to the ordinary reader (although there are, for example, several translations of Ānandavardhana's highly technical *Dhvanyāloka*).

vii. Anthologies

Another characteristic development was the emergence of a fashion for anthologies, often a *śataka* or 'century' of verses, either by a single author or a compilation. Among the earliest are the group of three 'centuries' on wise living, love, and renunciation, attributed to the grammarian and philosopher Bhartṛhari (?5th c.), torn according to tradition between his desire for renunciation and his longing for women; typical of this and of his resulting cynical approach is the following verse from a selection of such epigrams translated by John **Brough**:

> Her face is not the moon, nor are her eyes
> Twin lotuses, nor are her arms pure gold:
> She's flesh and blood. What lies the poets told!
> Ah, but we love her, we believe the lies.

The best translation of Bhartṛhari's poems alone is by the able American translator Barbara Stoler Miller, who has also translated both recensions of the lively *Caurapañcāśikā* (11th c., Fifty Verses by a Robber, on his secret intrigue with a princess) by Bilhaṇa. An ambivalence similar to Bhartṛhari's is seen in the 'century' attributed to Amaru, whose verses often have both an erotic and a philosophical interpretation (Brough's anthology contains examples).

One of the last anthologies was compiled by a Buddhist abbot, Vidyākara, late in the 11th c. and has been excellently translated by Daniel **Ingalls** (whose introduction on the nature of Sanskrit poetry is particularly valuable). The range of poets represented is wide and includes Yogeśvara (9th c.), noted for his descriptions of the apparently universal themes of nature and of village life; even so, his references can be highly culture-specific, as in

> The rain god has become a priest;
> he bathes the great linga of the Vindhya mountain
> with holy water poured upon it
> from a hundred sapphire cloud pots,

whereas the very next verse, as Ingalls deliberately translates it, will evoke echoes of T. S. Eliot for any English reader:

> Now the great cloud cat,
> darting out his lightning tongue,
> licks the creamy moonlight
> from the saucepan of the sky.

In fact, 'the great cloud cat' is as literal a translation as possible and the effect has been achieved by substituting 'licks' for 'drinks'. The coincidence on this occasion is just that, although Eliot did have some acquaintance with Sanskrit literature and, for example, quotes from the *Bṛhadāraṇyaka Upaniṣad* in *The Waste Land*. As Donne says, 'No man is an island.'   JLB

ANTHOLOGIES   Brough, John, *Poems from the Sanskrit*, Harmondsworth, 1968 [Penguin].

AŚVAGHOṢA   *Saundarananda*, tr. E. H. Johnston, Lahore, 1932; rep. Delhi, 1975 · *Buddhacarita*, tr. E. H. Johnston, Lahore, 1936; rep. Delhi, 1972.

BĀṆA   *The Kādambarī of Bāṇa*, tr. C. M. Ridding, London, 1896 · *The Harṣa-carita of Bāṇa*, tr. E. B. Cowell and F. W. Thomas, London, 1897; rep. Delhi, 1968 · *Kādambarī: A Classic Sanskrit Story of Magical Transformations*, tr. Gwendolyn Layne, New York, 1991.

BHAGAVADGĪTĀ   *The Bhăgvăt-Gēētā, or Dialogues of Krĕĕshnă and Ărjŏŏn*, tr. Sir Charles Wilkins, London, 1785 [rep. Khizurpoor (near Calcutta), 1809, and by the Theosophical Society at Bombay up to 1885; facsimile edn. published Gainesville, Fla., 1959] · *The Song Celestial or Bhagavad-Gîtâ*, tr. Sir Edwin Arnold, London, 1885 · *The Bhagavad Gītā*, ed. and tr. Franklin Edgerton, 2 vols., Cambridge, Mass., 1944 · *The Bhagavadgītā*, tr. Sarvepalli Radhakrishnan, London, 1948 [frequent reps.] · *The Bhagavad Gita*, tr. Juan Mascaró, Harmondsworth, 1962 [Penguin] · *The Bhagavad-Gītā*, ed. and tr. R. C. Zaehner, Oxford, 1969 · *The Bhagavad-Gita: Krishna's Counsel in Time of War*, tr. Barbara Stoler Miller, New York, 1986 · *The Bhagavad Gita*, tr. W. J. Johnson, Oxford, 1994 [World's Classics].

BHARTṚHARI   *Poems*, tr. Barbara Stoler Miller, New York, 1967.

BILHAṆA   *Phantasies of a Love-Thief: The Caurapañcāśikā Attributed to Bilhaṇa*, ed. and tr. Barbara Stoler Miller, New York, 1971.

DAṆḌIN   *Dandin's Dasha-kumara-charita: The Ten Princes*, tr. A. W. Ryder, Chicago, 1927; rep. 1974.

HITOPADEŚA   *The Hĕĕtopădĕs of Vĕĕshnŏŏ-Sărmă*, tr. Sir Charles Wilkins, Bath, 1787.

KĀLIDĀSA   *Sacontalá, or, The Fatal Ring: An Indian Drama*, tr. Sir William Jones, Calcutta, 1789 [4 reprints before 1800; further translated into French, German, and Italian] · *Megha Dūta or Cloud Messenger*, tr. H. H. Wilson, London, 1813 [rep. Varanasi, 1973] · *Śakuntalā*, tr. Sir Monier Monier-Williams, Oxford, 2nd edn., 1867; rep. Delhi, 1958, New York, 1966 · *Shakuntala and Other Writings by Kālidāsa*, tr. Arthur W. Ryder, c.1912 [Dutton Paperback, 1959] · *The Cloud Messenger, Translated from the Sanskrit Meghadūta*, tr. Franklin and Eleanor Edgerton, Ann Arbor, Mich., 1964 · *Raghuvaṃśa: the Dynasty of Raghu*, tr. R. Antoine, Calcutta, 1972 · *Meghadūta: the Transport of Love*, tr. L. Nathan, Berkeley, Calif., 1976 · *Three Sanskrit Plays*, tr. Michael Coulson, Harmondsworth, 1981 [Penguin] · *Theater of Memory: The Plays of Kālidāsa*, ed. Barbara Stoler Miller, New York, 1984 · *The Origin of the Young God: Kālidāsa's Kumārasambhava*, tr. Hank Heifetz, Berkeley, Calif., 1985 · *Kālidāsa, The Loom of Time: A Selection of his Plays and Poems*, tr. Chandra Rajan, New Delhi, 1990 [Penguin].

KĀLIKĀ PURĀṆA   'The Rudhira'dhya'yă, or Sanguinary Chapter, Translated from the Cálicá Puran', by W. C. Blacquiere, in *Asiatick Researches* 5 (1797), 371–91.

MAHĀBHĀRATA (see also *Bhagavadgītā*)   *The Story of Dooshwanta and Sakoontala Extracted from the Mahabharata*, tr. Sir Charles Wilkins, in *The Oriental Repertory*, ii, ed. A. Dalrymple, London, 1794 · *The Mahabharata of Krishna-Dwaipayana Vyasa*, 19 vols. (tr. Kisari Mohan Ganguli), published by P. C. Roy, Bharata Press, Calcutta, 1883–96; rep. New Delhi, 1981 · *The Mahābhārata*, i–iii, tr. J. A. B. van Buitenen, Chicago/London, 1973–8.

MĀNAVADHARMÁSĀSTRA/LAWS OF MANU   *The Institutes of Hindu Law: or, the Ordinances of Manu, According to the Gloss of Cullúca*, tr. Sir William Jones, Calcutta, 1794 · *The Laws of Manu*, tr. by G. Bühler, Oxford, 1886; rep. New York, 1969, Delhi, 1990 · *The Laws of Manu*, tr. Wendy Doniger with Brian K. Smith, London, 1991 [Penguin].

PAÑCATANTRA   *The Morall Philosophie of Doni*, tr. Sir Thomas North, London, 1570 [a version at many removes of the *Pañcatantra*] · *The Panchatantra Reconstructed*, ed. and tr. Franklin Edgerton, New Haven, Conn., 1924 [translation only rep. as *The Panchatantra*, London, 1965].

RĀMĀYAṆA   *The Ramayuna of Valmeeki in the Original Sungskrit, with a Prose Translation and Explanatory Notes*, ed. and tr. William Carey and Joshua Marshman, vols. i–iii, Serampore, 1806–10 · *The Rámáyan of Válmíki*, tr. Ralph T. H. Griffith, 5 vols., London/Benares, 1870–89; rep. Varanasi, 1963 · *Rāmāyaṇa*, tr. Manmatha Nath Dutt, 3 vols., London, 1889–94; rep. Varanasi, 1977 · *The Rāmāyaṇa of Vālmīki: An Epic of Ancient India*, tr. Robert P. Goldman et al., i–iv, Princeton, NJ, 1984– .

ṚGVEDA   *The Hymns of the Rig Veda*, tr. Ralph T. H. Griffith, London, 1889; rep. Delhi, 1973 · *The Rig Veda: An Anthology*, tr. Wendy Doniger O'Flaherty, London, 1982 [Penguin].

ŚAKTIBHADRA   *The Wondrous Crest-Jewel in Performance: Text and Translation of the Āścaryacūḍāmaṇi of Śaktibhadra*, ed. Clifford Reis Jones (tr. V. Raghavan), Delhi, 1984.

SOMADEVA   *The Ocean of Story*, being C. H. Tawney's translation of Somadeva's Kathā Sarit Sāgara, ed. N. M. Penzer, 10 vols., London, 1923–28; rep. Delhi, 1968 [1st edn., Calcutta, 1880–84] · *Tales of Ancient India*, tr. J. A. B. van Buitenen, Chicago, 1959; rep. 1965.

SUBANDHU   *Vāsavadattā: A Sanskrit Romance by Subandhu*, tr. Louis H. Gray, New York, 1913.

ŚŪDRAKA   *Two Plays of Ancient India*, tr. J. A. B. van Buitenen, New York, 1968 · *The Little Clay Cart: An English Translation of the Mṛcchakaṭikā of Śūdraka*, tr. A. L. Basham, Albany, NY, 1994.

UPANIṢADS   *The Upanishads*, tr. F. Max Müller, 2 vols., Oxford, 1879–84; rep. New York, 1962 · *Himalayas of the Soul: Translations of the Principal Upaniṣads*, tr. Juan Mascaró, London, 1938 [as *The Upanishads*, Penguin, 1965] · *The Principal Upaniṣads*, tr. S. Radhakrishnan, London, 1953 [frequent reprints] · *Upaniṣads*, tr. Patrick Olivelle, Oxford, 1996 [World's Classics].

VIDYĀKARA   *An Anthology of Sanskrit Court Poetry: Vidyākara's Subhāṣitaratnakośa*, tr. Daniel H. H. Ingalls, Cambridge, Mass., 1965 [simplified version rep. as *Sanskrit Poetry from Vidyākara's 'Treasury'*, Cambridge, Mass., 1968].

VIṢṆU PURĀṆA   *The Vishṅu Purāṅa: A System of Hindu Mythology and Tradition*, tr. H. H. Wilson, 6 vols., London, 1840; rep. Delhi, 1980, New York, 1981.

VIVĀDĀRṆAVASETU   *A Code of Gentoo Laws, or, Ordinations of the Pundits*, tr. Nathaniel Brassey Halhed, London, 1776.

3. CLASSICAL TAMIL

When applied to Tamil literature, the designation 'classical' refers to three categories of texts, dating from possibly as early as the 2nd c. BCE to as late as the 6th c. CE. This literature is termed *cankam* ('academy', 'assembly') in Tamil, in reference to the three great academies of scholars that are said to have composed this literature in and around the city of Madurai in present-day Tamilnadu. Legend has it that all the texts of the first *cankam* were lost in a terrible flood. The only text that remains from the second *cankam* is the *Tolkāppiyam* (the 'Old Work'). Arguably the most ancient of extant classical texts in Tamil, the *Tolkāppiyam* is divided into three large sections devoted (in order) to phonology and morphology, syntax and semantics, and poetic usage, and constitutes the first of the three categories of classical texts.

The second category is made up of the *Eṭṭu-t-tokai*, the 'Eight Anthologies', and the third of the *Pattu-p-pāṭṭu*, or the 'Ten Long Songs'. These two 'super-anthologies' are said to be the extant works of the third and final Tamil *cankam*. These last two categories consist of 2382 poems and represent the work of approximately 500 poets. The Eight Anthologies include the collections of love poetry titled *Naṟṟiṇai* ('The Good Landscape'), *Kuṟuntokai* ('The Anthology of Short Poems'), *Aiṅkuṟunūṟu* ('Five Hundred Short Poems'), *Kali-t-tokai* ('The Anthology in *Kali* Meter'), and *Akanāṉūṟu* ('Four Hundred Love Poems'). The anthologies with themes devoted to war and public life are *Patiṟṟu-p-pattu* ('The Ten Tens') and *Puṟanāṉūṟu* ('Four Hundred War Poems'). The *Paripāṭal* (the title of this anthology reflects the name of the metre in which the poems of the text are sung) contains poems composed on a mixture of erotic and devotional themes, as well as some devoted to water games. The Ten Long Songs consist of ten discrete poems ranging in length from 103 to 782 lines, and display mixed subject-matter concentrating on love, war, and religious devotion.

The history of the translation of classical Tamil literature into English is a short one. Out of all the texts listed above, only the *Tolkāppiyam*, *Kuṟuntokai*, *Aiṅkuṟunūṟu*, and *Pattu-p-pāṭṭu* have been wholly translated into English. There is a very fine complete translation of the *Paripāṭal* into French (made by François **Gros** in 1968), but to date no one has undertaken an English translation. Even though these texts are of great antiquity, they were not 'rediscovered' until the 19th c. In other words, they were unknown to most Tamils themselves, and those who did know about them were devout Hindu scholars who did not wish to concentrate on texts that were largely secular in nature, nor teach their students about them. What is more, many Tamil scholars of the time, devout or not, were not even aware that such ancient works existed. It was not until U. Vē. Cāminātaiyar (1855–1942) rescued them from obscurity that these classical texts came to light and into their own as world literature. The most brilliant and thoroughgoing Tamil scholar of his day, Cāminātaiyar had studied a medieval commentary on an old Jain epic which mentioned texts and authors unknown to him. He then set out on a mission to recover these old texts, make critical editions of them, and publish them in book form. In a corner of a Śaiva monastery, he came upon a bundle of palm-leaf manuscripts which had been stowed away in a basket. This bundle contained the Eight Anthologies.

The second great moment in this short history is the accidental discovery of Cāminātaiyar's printed editions in a dusty library basement in Chicago by A. K. **Ramanujan**, undoubtedly the foremost of the translators of these texts into English. In search of a grammar of Old Tamil in Harper Library's basement stacks at the University of Chicago in 1962, Ramanujan came upon an uncatalogued cache of books which the library had just acquired from a well-known South Indian historian. While looking for the grammar, Ramanujan picked up a volume of *cañkam* poems that had been edited in 1937 by Cāminātaiyar. Ramanujan read Cāminātaiyar's lucid prose commentary on a few of the verses, and found that it unlocked the meaning of the old poems for him. In Ramanujan's own words, he had 'gone looking for a donkey and had happened upon a kingdom'. Ramanujan then went on to make partial translations of the *cañkam* texts. *Kuruntokai* is represented in *The Interior Landscape*, and Ramanujan has also provided a luminous sampling of poems from all the anthologies in his 1985 *Poems of Love and War*. These translations have set an almost impossible standard for translating Tamil into English. Ramanujan was an award-winning poet in English and a gifted and sensitive linguist; his translations are accurate and of astonishing beauty, true to the originals in letter and in spirit. The following example is a short poem (No. 119) from *Kuruntokai*:

> As a little white snake
> with lovely stripes on its young body
> troubles the jungle elephant
>
> this slip of a girl
> her teeth like sprouts of new rice
> her wrists stacked with bangles
>
> troubles me.

Two complete and fairly reliable translations of the old work on grammar and poetics, the *Tolkāppiyam*, have been made, by P. S. Subrahmanya Sastri and S. Ilakkuvanār. These are useful to scholars of Tamil, but not to the general reader. Both works represent the contents of the text well, but Ilakkuvanār's translation is presented in a completely bare fashion without annotation or notes in spite of his title, though he provides a rather sketchy introduction. For the general reader in search of basic information on Tamil poetic convention, the best places to turn are to Ramanujan's brilliantly written afterwords to the two works cited above.

David **Ludden** and M. Shanmugam **Pillai** collaborated on a complete translation of *Kuruntokai*, published in 1976 by Koodal Publishers, Madurai. It is scholarly in its accuracy and useful, but not particularly sensitive as a poetic translation. The same can be said of P. **Jottimuttu**'s complete translation of *Aiñkurunūru* and of J. V. **Chelliah**'s *Pattu-p-pāṭṭu: Ten Tamil Idylls*. All these translations are excellent as sources for those who wish to conduct brief surveys of textual contents or to sample the characters and natures of these texts, but translations of high literary quality of any *cañkam* text in its entirety do not yet exist. Complete literary translations of *Narriṇai, Aiñkurunūru*, and *Kali-t-tokai* are at present under way, and should appear in print within the next 10 years. George Luzerne **Hart** has produced a book of selections from the *cañkam* anthologies in English which reads well, but pales when compared with Ramanujan's powerful and aesthetically pleasing work. For an excellent sampling of new translations from *cañkam*, medieval, and modern Tamil, interested readers should turn to *A Gift of Tamil*, edited by Norman Cutler and Paula Richman.   MAS

ANTHOLOGIES   Cutler, Norman, and Richman, Paula, eds., *A Gift of Tamil: Translations from Tamil Literature in Honor of K. Paramasivam*, New Delhi, 1992 · Hart, George L., *Poets of the Tamil Anthologies: Ancient Poems of Love and War*, Princeton, NJ, 1979 · Ramanujan, A. K., *Poems of Love and War: From the Eight Anthologies and Ten Long Poems of Classical Tamil*, New York, 1985.

AIÑKURUNŪRU   Jotimuttu, P., *Aiñkurunūru: The Short Five Hundred*, Madras, 1984 [complete].

KURUNTOKAI   Ludden, David E., and M. Shanmugam Pillai, *Kuruntokai: An Anthology of Classical Tamil Love Poetry*, Madurai, 1976 [complete] · Ramanujan, A. K., *Kuruntokai. The Interior Landscape: Love Poems from a Classical Tamil Anthology*, Bloomington, Ind., 1967; rep. 1975 [partial].

NARRIṆAI   Selby, Martha Ann, '*Narriṇai* or Good Landscape: Poems from the Old Tamil', *Comparative Criticism*, 16, (1994), 97–104 [partial].

PATTU-P-PĀṬṬU   Chelliah, J. V., *Pattu-p-pāṭṭu: Ten Tamil Idylls*, Thanjavur, 1975 [1st edn., 1946; complete] · Raghunathan, *Six Long Poems from Sangam Tamil*, Madras, 1978 [partial].

TOLKĀPPIYAM   Ilakkuvanār, S., *Tholkāppiyam (in English) with Critical Studies*, Madurai, 1963 [complete] · Subrahmanya Sastri, P. S., *Tolkāppiyam: The Earliest Extant Tamil Grammar; Text in Tamil and Roman Scripts with a Critical Commentary in English*, Madras, various dates intermittently [complete].

SEE ALSO   Rajam, V. S., *A Reference Grammar of Classical Tamil Poetry*. Philadelphia, 1992 · Takahashi, T., *Tamil Love Poetry and Poetics*, Leiden, 1995.

4. MEDIEVAL DEVOTIONAL WRITING

Medieval Indian literature is multilingual: the major works lie scattered in about 20 languages. The most important of these works are devotional in content and belong to the Bhakti or Sufi movement. Although the dates are not identical in the different literatures, the devotional poetry of medieval India manifests several common features. There are special concepts and terms which pose a challenge to translators in non-Indian languages. Translations from medieval Indian languages into English are of comparatively recent dates, and definitive translations are available only for a few works in each of the languages.

The Bhakti movement of the Vaishnavite school flourished in Assamese with Sankaradeva (1449–1569) as its founder. His *Kirttana Ghosha* has been translated into English by Chandrakanta **Mahanta**; it is considered faithful to the spirit of the original, although the lyrical and musical quality of these hymns cannot be easily transmitted into a non-Indian language.

The translations from Bengali are more numerous and more competently done. J. A. **Chapman**'s *Religious Lyrics of Bengal* (1926), Sukumar **Sen**'s *Vipradasa's Manasamangal* (1953), E. B. **Cowell**'s *Kavikankan's Candi* (1903), and N. R. **Majumdar**'s *Caitanyacaritamrita* (1925) are among those widely accepted and reputed. Deben **Bhattacharya**'s *The Mirror of the Sky* (1969) is an anthology of the folk-songs of the Bauls, the wandering mendicants. S. M. **Bandyopadhyay**'s renderings in *The Baul Songs of Bengal* (1976) and Alokeranjan and Mary Ann **Dasgupta**'s *Roots in the Void* (1977) are translations of the literary text of these songs, which are primarily musical texts. The oral-aural dimension cannot be fully captured in print or written form, and these folk-songs of the so-called illiterate people have a vitality and mystic aura which defy translation.

Sri Caitanyacaritamrita (1954), translated by Nagendra Kumar **Ray** and Sanjib Kumar **Choudhuri**, and Nihar Ranjan **Banarjee**'s *Shree Shree Caitanya Caritamrita* (1925) are both works of hagiography devoted to the great religious leader Caitanya. Repeated translations like these indicate the popularity of Caitanya among non-Bengalis. Extracts from Badu Chandidasa's *Shrikrishnakirtan* (15th c.) translated by Ajit Kumar **Ghosh** and from Krittivasa Ojha's *Ramayana* (15th c.) translated by Ujjwal Majumdar are published in Sahitya Akademi's anthology of *Medieval Indian Literature* (1997). One of the most widely translated of

medieval Bengali devotional poets is Chandidasa (15th c.). Dinesh Chandra **Datta** (1941), Samir Kanta **Gupta** (1957), and Deben Bhattacharya (1967) have brought out separate anthologies of translations of his poems. Edward C. **Dimock**'s translation of Bengali songs, *In Praise of Krishna* (1967), deserves special mention; the songs are about the relationship between Radha and Krishna.

The major figure of medieval Gujarati literature is Narasinha Mehta, whose *Prem Mala* (The Garland of Love), consisting of hymns, has been translated into English by Ardeshir M. **Modi**. Still more popular with translators has been the work of Mira Bai (1498–1547), who wrote in Gujarati, Hindi, and Rajasthani. Multiple translations are available for several of her beautiful hymns to Krishna: *The Poems of Mira Bai* by S. N. **Pandey** and Horman H. **Zide** (1964), *Mira Bai* by Usha S. **Nilsson** (1969), *The Devotional Songs of Mira Bai* by Shreeprakash **Kurl** (1973), *The Songs of Mira Bai* by Pritish **Nandy** (1975), *Songs of Meera: Lyrics in Ecstasy* by Baldoon **Dhingra** (1977), and the *Devotional Poems* of A. J. **Alston** (1980) are some of the best-known of these translations.

Among the chief medieval devotional poets in Hindi who are widely translated are Tulsi Das (16th–17th c.) and Kabir (1398–1518). S. P. **Bahadur**'s rendering of *The Complete Works of Gosvami Tulsi Das* (1978) in two volumes gives a fairly readable version of this medieval classic. *Ramacharitamanasa* has been translated by Douglas P. **Hill** under the title *The Holy Lake of the Acts of Rama* (1952, 1971). F. S. **Growse**'s version, *Ramayana of Tulasidasa*, was revised by R. C. **Prasad** and published in 1978. Tulsi Das's *The Petition to Rama* was translated by F. R. **Allchin** in 1966 for the Unesco collection. Allchin also rendered into English Tulsi Das's *Kavitavali* (1969).

Kabir's name appears chiefly in Hindi, but as a bilingual poet (writing in Urdu as well) he has attracted universal attention. The complete *Bijak* has been translated by Prem **Chand** (1911). Robert **Bly**'s translations of Kabir's poems are entitled *The Kabir Book* (1971) and *The Fish in the Sea Is Not Thirsty* (1972). S. M. **Jhabvala**'s translation, entitled *Kabir*, appeared in 1961. Perhaps the most famous of all Kabir translations is the one by Rabindranath **Tagore**, with the title *One Hundred Poems* (1915). Ahmad **Shah**'s translation of *The Bijak* came out in 1977.

Medieval Kannada literature is dominated by the Shaiva poets. Basaveswara (12th c.) popularized the *vachana* style. Among the translations of his works into English are: *Musings of Basava* (1941) by S. S. **Basavannal** and K. R. **Srinivasa Iyengar**; *Thus Spoke Basava* (1965) by A. S. **Theodore** and D. K. **Hakari**; *Vachanas of Basavanna* (1967) by A. **Menezes** and S. N. **Angadi**; *Sayings of Basavanna* (1935) by Masti V. **Iyengar**. The poems of Akkamahadevi, the chief woman poet of the group, have also attracted the attention of translators. Her *Fifty Vachanas* has been translated by B. A. **Patil** (1975).

Selected *vachanas* from the works of several of these poets have also been collected and translated: for example A. K. **Ramanujan**'s *Speaking of Siva* (1973) and Prabhu **Shankara**'s *101 Vachanas* (?1976). Ramanujan's translations, although some critics in Kannada have expressed reservations about them, have been widely accepted in the West; in fact, they have successfully projected medieval Kannada poetry to the outside world. His success depends on the idiom he has employed, which makes sense to western readers.

Two of the medieval devotional poets of Kashmir fairly well known outside the State are Lal Dyad (or Ded) and Nund Rishi or Ryosh. Jayalal **Kaul**'s 1973 monograph on Lal Dyad (16th c.) contains several of her poems in English translation. This work brings out the mystic vision of the poet as expressed in her *vakhs*. English translations of Nund Rishi have been published by the Kashmir Academy of Art, Culture, and Languages.

The best-known poet of medieval Maithili, who is widely translated, is no doubt Vidyapati (15th c.). Dinesh Chandra **Datta**'s *Renderings in English Verses* (1941), *The Songs of the Love of Radha and Krishna*, translated by Anand **Coomaraswamy** and Arun **Sen** (1915) from *Vidyapati Bangiya Padavali*, Deben Bhattacharya's *Love Songs of Vidyapati* (1963), *The Songs of Vidyapati* by Subhadra **Jha** (1954), and Sri **Aurobindo**'s rendering of *Songs of Vidyapati* (1956) bear witness to the tremendous popularity of the poet.

Very little of medieval Malayalam literature has been translated into English. This is in sharp contrast to the eagerness with which the language welcomes translations from other languages. A few passages from Tunchat Ezhutthacchan may be found in the Sahitya Akademi monograph on the author. Indifferent translations of Poontanam's *Jnanappana* (The Song of Wisdom, 16th-c.) have appeared in print. There are several poems or hymns extremely popular with the devout Malayalis, but these seem to defy translation.

The situation of Marathi is much better. Jnaneshwar, Eknath, Namdev, and Tukaram are well-known saints; their sacred poetry has been rendered successfully into English. Biographies of saint-poets have also been made available in English. Jnaneshwar's *Gita* has been translated by Swami **Kripanand**; *The Deeds of God in Rddhipur* by Ann **Feldhaus**; *Jnaneshwari: Bhavarthdipika* by V. G. **Pradhan** (1967, 1969); *Amritanubhav* by B. P. **Bahirat** (1963) and more recently by Dilip **Chitre**, the well-known bilingual poet. Justin E. **Abbott** translated Eknath's *Bhikshugita The Mendicant's Song* (1928); Prabhakar **Machwe** translated the poems of Namdev in his *Namdev: Life and Philosophy* (1968) as well as those of Tukaram (*Tukaram's Poems*, 1977); the latter also exist in an English version by Nelson **Fraser** and K. B. **Maratha** (1981). The autobiographical and poetical writings of Bahina Bai were translated by Abbott. The works of Jnaneshwar, Eknath, Namdev, Tukaram, and Bahina Bai constitute an impressive collection of devotional literature in Marathi, almost parallel in significance to the *Vachanas* of Kannada.

Medieval Oriya poetry is characterized by intense devotion, but there is an added human dimension to it. The works of Balarama Das, Sarala Das, and Jagannath Das have in a way humanized the divine. But it cannot be said that these works have been rendered into English in substantial quantity. In sharp contrast, medieval Punjabi literature has come into English in a big way. Two kinds of texts may be seen here: one represented by *Adi Grantha*, while the other is exemplified by the work of Sheikh Farid and Bulleh Shah in the Sufi tradition. *Adi Grantha* is perhaps the most widely translated work in Punjabi. There are translations by Ernest **Trumpp** (1877), M. L. **Peace** (1971), Gopal **Singh** (1978), and Duncan **Greenlees** (1975). Guru Nanak's *Japji* is also available in multiple translations. Translations of select poems by Sheikh Farid (13th–14th c.) may be found in *Baba Sheikh Farid* (1973) by Gurbachan Singh **Talib**. Specimens of Bulleh Shah's work are available in *Sai Bulleh Shah* (n.d.) by C. F. **Osborne** and *Punjabi Sufi Poets* (1973) by Lajwanti **Ramakrishna**.

Medieval Sanskrit [II.l.2] is the source of the largest number of translations into English. It is generally believed that the devotional movement started with works in Sanskrit like *Bhagavata*. Jayadeva's *Gita-Govinda* has attracted quite a few translators, including Barbara Stoller **Miller** (1971), Monika **Varma** (1968), S. Sen (1979), Durgadas **Mukhopadhyay** (1990), and George **Heyt** (1940, 1965). Narayana Bhattatiri's *Narayaniyam* (16th c.) is available in a prose translation done by Swami **Tapasyananda** (1976).

Shah Abdul Latif (1689–1752) is easily the greatest poet in Sindhi, and his works have been translated into English. H. T. Sorley's *Shah Abdul Latif of Bhil*

(1940) is among the more useful sources of information about him.

Medieval Tamil literature [see II.l.3], both prose and poetry, is predominantly devotional. *Avvaiyar: A Great Tamil Poetess* (1971) by C. **Rajagopalachari** gives some of her poems in English. The Tamil Writers' Association of New Delhi has brought out an anthology of Tamil works translated into English, *Gems from the Treasure House of Tamil Literature* (1976), which contains a section on devotional songs. Isaac **Tambyah** has translated *The Psalms of Tayumanavar* (1925). A. K. Ramanu-

jan's brilliant renderings of Vaishnavite hymns by Nammalvar may be found in *Hymns for the Drowning* (1981). B. **Natarajan** has produced an English version of Tirumular's *Tirumantiram* (1991). The works of Telugu composers like Annamacharya and Tyagaraja may be found in monographs on these authors. C. P. **Brown**'s *Verses of Vemana* appeared in 1957.

Medieval Urdu poets of the Sufi school had a pronounced spiritual bent; *Three Mughal Poets* (1969) by Khurshidul **Islam** and Ralph **Russell** is a good example.   KAP

The following brief bibliography lists only some of the more important of the translations mentioned above.

ANTHOLOGIES   Dimock, Edward C., *In Praise of Krishna*, n.p., 1967 · Paniker, K. Ayyappa, ed., *Medieval Indian Literature*, tr. various hands, New Delhi (Sahitya Akademi), 4 vols., 1997– [translations from 21 languages, covering the period 1100–1800] · Ramanujan, A. K., *Speaking of Siva*, Harmondsworth, 1973 [Penguin] · Trumpp, Ernest, *The Adi Granth, or The Holy Scriptures of the Sikhs*, n.p., 1877 [2nd edn., New Delhi, 1970].

BASAVA   Theodore, A. S., and Hakari, D. K., *Thus Spake Basava*, Bangalore, 1965.

DAS, SUR   Srivastava, S. N., ed., *Sur Das, Poetry and Personality*, tr. various hands, Agra, 1978.

DAS, TULSI   Hill, Douglas P., *The Holy Lake of the Acts of Rama*, Bombay/Calcutta/Delhi/Madras, 1952 [2nd edn., Calcutta, 1971].

JAYADEVA   Miller, Barbara Stoler, *Gita-Govinda: Love Songs of the Dark Lord*, Delhi, 1971.

JNANADEVA (JNANESHWAR)   Pradhan, V. G., *Jnaneshvari*, 2 vols., London, 1967–9.

KABIR   Tagore, Rabindranath, with Evelyn Underhill, *One Hundred Poems*, London, 1915 [new edn., 1948].

LAL DED   Kaul, Jayalal, *Lal Ded*, New Delhi, 1973.

MIRA BAI   Alston, A. J., *The Devotional Poems of Mira Bai*, Delhi, 1980.

SANKARADEVA   Mahanta, Chandrakanta, *The Kirttana*, Jorhat, 1990.

TUKARAM   Fraser, Nelson, and Maratha, K. B., *The Poems of Tukaram*, Delhi, 1981.

VIDYAPATI   Aurobindo, Sri, *Songs of Vidyapati*, Pondicherry, 1956.

5. MODERN INDIAN LANGUAGES

i. Introduction: Languages of Modern India

India has 18 major modern languages named in its Constitution, with Hindi as the official language of the country—besides the colonial language which persists postcolonially as the alternative official language, English. Of these, the four languages spoken in south India—Kannada, Malayalam, Tamil, and Telugu—belong to the Dravidian family of languages, while all the rest are Indo-Aryan: Assamese, Bengali, Gujarati, Hindi, Kashmiri, Konkani, Manipuri, Marathi, Nepali, Oriya, Punjabi, Sanskrit, Sindhi, and Urdu. At current census-based estimates, Hindi is spoken by about 390 million people, while four other languages are spoken by over 40 million people each: Bengali, Telugu, Marathi, and Tamil. All these languages arose and attained their present identity some time between 900 CE and 1300 CE (with the exception of modern Tamil, which descends directly from classical Tamil, and Urdu, which came into literary existence in the 17th c.), and have since then had a

distinct and continuous literary tradition. Annual prizes for the best book in each of these languages are awarded by the Sahitya Akademi (the National Academy of Literature), as well as in four other languages: Dogri, English, Maithili, and Rajasthani. Besides, in recognition not only of the remarkable variety of languages in India but also of the constant exchange between them, the Akademi awards an annual prize for the best work of translation into each of the 22 languages. (In 1997, five of the award-winning works were translated from Hindi, four from English, and three from Bengali.)

ii. Early Translations

Broadly speaking, the year 1800 can be taken to mark the beginning of the modern age in the literatures of most of the Indian languages. By this date, the pervasive influence of both the Sanskritic and the Perso-Arabic traditions was beginning to be complemented if not supplanted by the newer impact of the English language and western civilization (which incidentally was first felt in India not through translations of English works into the Indian languages but through some Indians reading western literature directly in English). Though translation into English of Sanskrit works had already begun in 1785, and though devotional or *Bhakti* literature from the early or 'medieval' phases of the modern Indian languages (i.e. up to 1800) had also begun to be translated in the 19th c., the modern literature of India was not translated into English in any considerable volume until well into the 20th c. Orientalism, it would appear, thrived best on the safely dead past; the problematic and politically resistant present was best left unmediated through translation.

One of the earliest translations into English of a work of modern Indian literature dramatically illustrates the colonial bind. *Nil-darpana* (1860), a Bengali play by Dinabandhu Mitra, depicting how cruelly white indigo planters oppressed and exploited the Indian peasantry and how courageously the latter resisted them, was anonymously translated into English the same year and published by the Revd James **Long**. But this caused such offence to the colonial British government that it fined and jailed Long, the white non-establishment accomplice! At about the same time, another remarkable and exceptional trend was inaugurated, of modern Indians translating their own works from an Indian language into English. Michael Madhusudan **Datta**, perhaps the most original and innovative Bengali writer of the 19th c., declared in the preface to his play, *Sharmishtha* (1858), that it was his 'intention to throw off the fetters' of the Sanskrit literary tradition, and that he wrote for such other Indians 'whose minds have been more or less imbued with western ideas and modes of thinking'. Given this agenda, it is not surprising that he promptly proceeded to translate his play into English.

The outstanding case of self-translation into English by an Indian writer is that of Rabindranath **Tagore**, whose poetic prose versions of a selection of his own Bengali songs, *Gitanjali*, won him the Nobel Prize in 1913. (However, no other writer from an Indian language has won the Nobel or achieved comparable international fame through English translation—a fact much lamented in India.) Though Tagore had been helped to revise the English of his translations by some British admirers, including W. B. Yeats (who contributed a gushing introduction to the book), his treatment of his own original text has come to be seen as problematic, for he cut, added, adapted, and diluted flagrantly so as to make his work acceptable and attractive to his intended western readers. When an

English translator and critic of his work, Edward **Thompson**, remonstrated with him in 1921, Tagore candidly admitted: 'In my translations I timidly avoid all difficulties, which has the effect of making them smooth and thin.... When I began this career of falsifying my own coins I did it in play. Now I am becoming frightened of its enormity and am willing to make a confession of my misdeeds.'

Tagore's acute self-reproach on having traduced himself for easy consumption by an alien readership does not detract from the fact that his watered-down *Gitanjali* remains possibly the most popular work of Indian literature ever published in English translation, and one of the best-known translations of a work from any non-European language, next only to the *Rubaiyat* [II.q.2.iv], as notoriously rendered by FitzGerald with a comparable lack of fidelity, and to Kahlil Gibran's *The Prophet*. Tagore's deviance from his own original work has been judged as criminally culpable (Sujit Mukherjee, 1981, has characterized *Gitanjali* as an example of 'translation as perjury'), but it is illustrative equally of how translators and writers alike in modern India have sought to internalize the literary expectations the West supposedly has of the East.

In modern Indian literature, the most popular literary form has been the novel, followed closely by the short story, which enjoys a popularity greater than in the West. Both these literary forms are often said to have been imported into India from the West (as distinct from the various older indigenous forms of narrative), and translation of Indian novels into English began almost as soon as they came to be written. The first major Indian novelist, Bankimchandra Chatterji, illustrates aptly the linguistic hybridity that lay behind the rise of the Indian variation of the novel. He was among the first graduates in 1858 of Calcutta, one of the three western-type universities set up in India, and was promptly appointed as a civil servant by the British administration. He wrote his first novel in English, *Rajmohan's Wife* (1864), but then returned to his mother tongue to write another dozen novels in it. Three of his novels were translated into English in the 1880s, and at least five have been translated at least three times each so far.

The first novel in Malayalam, *Indulekha* (1888) by O. Chandu Menon, was translated into English the year following publication by W. **Dumergue**, in an act probably meant to propagate further the anglophile author's didactic social purpose. As Menon explained in his Introduction, 'one of my objects in writing this book is to illustrate how a young Malayalee woman, possessing . . . a knowledge of the English language would conduct herself in matters of supreme interest to her, such as choosing a partner in life'. Indulekha marries a young man of her choice, rather than the one 'arranged' for her by her grandfather, because she knows the English language; she has thus translated herself culturally, in a novel which Menon intended, when he began to write it, to be an adaptation of Disraeli's *Henrietta Temple*. There are thus several layers and modes of translation simultaneously at work in a novel such as this and its immediate rendering into English; there could be few more apt examples of translation as a doubleness of enunciation, and as an in-between cultural space, in the sense theorized by Homi Bhabha.

iii. Modern Translation: The Novel These contemporary translations of some of the earliest novels written in the Indian languages were, however, quite exceptional. Not only fiction but modern writing in all other literary forms from the Indian languages which is now available in English was mostly translated not during the colonial period but far more recently, by and large after Independence in 1947, while what has been recognized as an ongoing translation boom in India began even later, in the 1980s. Most of these translations into English of Indian writing have been done by and for Indian readers, judging by their place of publication and area of sales. Beyond the rare enough phenomenon of self-translation into English by bilingual writers, which is perhaps more common in India than in any other country, here is an instance of what may be termed collective self-translation (by Indians of works from the Indian languages) which must be without parallel in the literary history of the world. The chief reason for this, of course, is that English has recently been adopted as an 'Indian' language for purposes of original writing (witness Salman Rushdie et al.) as well as translation into it, in what is perhaps the most significant fallout or 'after-life' (in Walter Benjamin's key phrase regarding translation) of British rule in India. Indeed, Sujit Mukherjee in his *Translation as Discovery* (1981) has suggested that translations into English from the various Indian languages could serve as 'a link literature for India', a common literary clearing-house, as it were, in a nation and literary culture which is as close to Babel as any in the world. He even suggests a name for it, 'Indo-English Literature', which may be the only literature anywhere consisting entirely of works in translation.

It is not possible here to examine in any textual detail particular translations of modern Indian literary works; all that can be attempted is to comment on a few individual works of translation which illustrate wider cultural issues, and to name some anthologies or other collective or institutional endeavours to produce and promote such translations. Of the 20th-c. Indian novels translated into English, *Pather Panchali* (1929) by Bibhutibhushan Bandhopadhyay attracted some extraliterary attention when Satyajit Ray's film of it (1955) won several awards at film festivals. Subsequently, a translation into English by T. W. **Clark** and Tarapada **Mukherjee**, both of whom taught Bengali in London, was published as *Pather Panchali: Song of the Road*. However, the translators followed not the original but the film in leaving out the third and final part of the novel, on the grounds, as they explained, that what follows after their own version stops is 'something of an anti-climax', except that the author, with his 'native genius', did not know it. This raises a large question: whether what one expects of a fictional climax or closure in India is the same as in the West. Edward Thompson had similarly stopped short of the original Bengali climax in his translation (titled *The Brothers*) of Taraknath Gangopadhyay's novel *Svarnalata* (1874).

More generally, western or westernized translators of Indian novels in both India and the West (and occasionally their publishers) have shown a tendency to prune and reshape the work so as to make it more acceptable. *Godan* (1936) by Premchand, generally acclaimed as the best of all Hindi novels, was apparently translated into English by S. H. **Vatsyayan**, a major Hindi novelist himself, in a version which retained only the strand of the plot set in a village while leaving out altogether the subplot set in a city—which constitutes nearly half of the novel. (Vatsyayan's unpublished version was eventually appropriated by Gordon C. **Roadarmel** in his rendering of the full text as *The Gift of a Cow*.) Similarly, about a quarter of the Malayalam novel *Chemmeen* (1956) by Thakazhi Sivasankara Pillai was cut in the English translation by V. K. Narayana **Menon**. And in the case of *Raag Darbari* (1968) by Shrilal Shukla, a postcolonial satire on grass-roots politics in independent India, it was apparently not the British translator, Gillian **Wright**, but the publisher, Penguin Books India, who cut passages amounting to about one-sixth of the novel for no other reason than to keep the price below a certain psychological barrier.

As will have been noticed, many of the Indian texts, from *Gitanjali* (An Offering of a Handful of Songs) to *Raag Darbari* (the name of a raga in Indian music, the Courtly Raga, here evoked ironically), have been translated into English under the original titles. This may be an initial acknowledgement of the sheer difficulty of translating the original text, for titles often encapsulate a variety of culture-specific connotations more tersely than the rest of the text might. For example, the title *The Gift of a Cow* does not even begin to indicate the reference to a traditional Hindu ritual in which a dying man gifts a cow to a priest to ensure that he will go to heaven; despairing of conveying all this, another translation of this novel, by Jai **Ratan** and P. **Lal**, sticks to the original title, *Godan*, which would be readily understood by all Indian readers. In a characteristic double-take, however, it adds for the benefit of foreign readers a subtitle, *A Novel of Peasant India*, which has been misprinted in some later reprints as *A Novel of Pleasant India*. (This is characteristic of the shoddy quality of production of the majority of English books published in India, including translations.) But the use of the original title often denotes also an urge on the part of the translator to lay claim to ethnic authenticity, and could even be seen as a tokenist manifestation of latter-day orientalism. (*Chemmeen*, for example, means nothing more ineffable than 'shrimps'.) The above sample is not quite representative in this regard, however; most translators do translate the title as well, sometimes with a vengeance. For example, Gillian Wright has translated another Hindi novel by Rahi Masoom Reza under the title *The Feuding Families of Village Gangauli* where the original Hindi title was *Adha Gaon* (1966, Half the Village or, a little more idiomatically, A Village Divided).

A translation which shares the above feature but is in the rest of its practice scrupulously different is that of the Kannada novel, *Samskara* (1965) by U. R. Anantha Murthy, rendered by A. K. **Ramanujan** as *Samskara: A Rite for a Dead Man*. This was probably the first case in India of a novel and an author being 'discovered' even by most Indian readers through translation into English, as distinct from the usual practice of novelists in the Indian languages who are already acclaimed in those languages being translated into English after an interval of many years. *Samskara* in English has since become heavily canonized, figuring in the English literature syllabuses of a large number of Indian and a few foreign universities. This is a rare example of a novel which is taught in English translation in many more classrooms in India than in its original language; part of the reason is that the translator had a reputation as a translator (largely of ancient and medieval works from Tamil and Kannada, however) and as a poet himself which was equal to that of the novelist. This translation, which keeps fastidiously close to the original even to the extent of employing numerous literalisms, has been seen as a benchmark for subsequent translations.

Another translation which promises to circulate substantially beyond the reach of the original in a different way is *Imaginary Maps*, three Bengali short stories by Mahasweta Devi, done into English by the eminent Indian feminist and postcolonial critic Gayatri Chakravarty **Spivak**. (It won her the Sahitya Akademi Prize for the best work of translation into English for 1997.) The intention behind this translation, at least in part, was to make available to students in North American universities and to other readers work by a radically committed woman writer from India. Interestingly, an Indian reviewer, Sujit Mukherjee, found the language of these translations to be 'too American' or international to sound right within India. This contrasts with the familiar charge against many Indian translators that their English is too heavily infected by their native language, is conventional and bookish to the point of being archaic, and is sometimes palpably unidiomatic and unacceptable even within India, to say nothing of Britain or the USA.

iv. Modern Translation: Short Stories A popular form of fiction quite as widely translated in India as the novel is the short story. Though some selections of short stories by a single author have been translated, the usual procedure is to translate one story each by several writers from the same language, or even a pan-Indian selection of writers from several Indian languages. David **Rubin** translated a collection of 30 Hindi short stories by Premchand under the title *The World of Premchand*, while 15 later Hindi writers are represented by one short story each in *A Death in Delhi: Modern Hindi Short Stories* translated by Gordon C. Roadarmel. A more recent collection of contemporary Hindi short stories is *The Golden Waist-Chain: A Selection of Hindi Short Stories* (1990), translated by Sara **Rai**. Nirmal Verma, the foremost contemporary writer of Hindi fiction, has half a dozen volumes of his short stories available in English translation, as well as all four novels, he may be the most comprehensively translated of all the modern Indian writers, with O. V. **Vijayan** of Malayalam, who, however, translates his work into English himself. From Urdu, Khalid **Hasan** has translated 24 short stories by Saadat Hasan Manto (one of the most acute writers on the Partition of India) in *Kingdom's End and Other Stories*, while M. U. **Memon**, in *The Colour of Nothingness: Modern Urdu Short Stories*, has 15 short stories by as many writers. *From Cauvery to Godavari: Modern Kannada Short Stories*, edited by Ramachandra Sharma, represents the work of 15 writers and eight translators, while the 18 *Classic Telugu Short Stories* have all been translated by Rango **Rao**, who himself writes fiction in English.

The misleadingly titled series *Katha Prize Stories* (for the stories as well as the authors and translators are hand-picked and not winners of any competition) has published seven annual volumes since 1990, carrying one story each from any 12 of the major languages. Edited with a strong reshaping hand by Geeta Dharmarajan, these anthologies highlight the translators in a way many similar publications do not. An anthology distinctive in some other ways is *Writing from India* (1994), in a series from the Cambridge University Press meant for British schoolchildren; edited by Lakshmi Holmström and Mike Hayhoe, it includes nine stories in translation alongside seven written originally in English.

Another common type of anthology of translation puts short stories and extracts from novels together with poetry and sometimes even a couple of essays. A pioneering selection, *New Writing in India*, was edited by Adil Jussawala, while two such recent volumes both came out of journals: *Another India: An Anthology of Contemporary Indian Fiction and Poetry*, selected by Nissim Ezekiel and Meenakshi Mukherjee from translations first published in the 25 issues of the journal *Vagartha* between 1973 and 1979, and *The Penguin New Writing in India*, which reprinted as a book a special issue of the *Chicago Review* (1992), edited by Aditya Behl and David Nicholls.

v. Modern Translation: Poetry Translations of poetry are generally acknowledged to be even more of a challenge and travel less well. In any case, no Indian poet of recent decades has achieved an international or even a pan-Indian reputation through English translation. The practice has been to publish anthologies of poetry in translation, either all from the same language or from several languages, done by a large number of translators. The one significant exception to this is volumes of poetry which have been awarded the Sahitya Akademi prize, in which the poets are sometimes translated singly, if only for the reason that the Akademi is committed to publishing translations of all the prize-winning books into all the other Indian languages.

Of the anthologies, several of the larger ones have been commissioned and sponsored by government-funded organizations. The Indian Council of Cultural Relations, which has the same promotional role to play as, for example, the British Council or the United States Information Service, published between 1974 and 1981 a massive collec-tion in English translation titled *Indian Poetry Today*, in four volumes, comprising work from 14 languages. A parallel enterprise by this organization was *Modern Indian Short Stories* in three volumes (1975–7). The Sahitya Akademi published in 1993 *Modern Indian Literature: An Anthology*, with K. M. George as its chief editor, which ran to three volumes of over 1000 pages each, the first comprising a survey of each language and translations of poems, the second translations of fiction, and the third plays and prose. All these are monumental publications likely to sit on library shelves awaiting the odd researcher; one is not supposed to ask if they could have been done differently or better, but to wonder that they have been done at all. These are not ordinary works of translation; they are gargantuan academic resources, with all the predictable dusty dryness.

Anthologies brought out by commercial publishers are necessarily less ambitious. *The Oxford Anthology of Modern Indian Poetry*, edited by Vinay Dharwadker and A. K. Ramanujan, ranges widely over languages, with 125 poets represented by just one poem each. *An Anthology of Modern Hindi Poetry*, edited by Kailash Vajpeyi, is the latest of several single-language anthologies in which each poet is represented by about half a dozen poems, often translated by a different translator or even by more than one. *The Return of Sarasvati: Four Hindi Poets*, translated by David Rubin is an exceptional single-handed attempt; it is notable that even in a title chosen by an American translator for a work whose target audience must be primarily international, the name of Sarasvati, the Indian muse of poetry and music, is invoked.

An interesting experiment in translating Indian poetry was undertaken in two different and unrelated collaborative efforts initiated by Indian editors and involving American poets who did not know the original language but worked on the basis of literal drafts provided to them. Vidyaniwas Mishra edited *Modern Hindi Poetry: An Anthology* (1967), comprising 81 poems by 41 poets which were translated by six American poets, and Aijaz Ahmad, in a more modest attempt, edited similar American 'versions' by seven collaborators of 37 poems by the greatest of Urdu poets, Ghalib, in his *Ghazals of Ghalib*. In an apologetic 'Note' to a reprint (1994), however, Ahmad confessed in hindsight to acute embarrassment at the fact that such a volume could convey no more than 'a rumour' of Ghalib's work. Both these anthologies were compiled in the USA and published by American university presses. The one Urdu poet most frequently and, in widely different ways, successfully translated into English has been Faiz Ahmad Faiz, for example, in miraculously faithful metre and rhyme by Victor **Kiernan** in *Poems by Faiz*, which provides for each poem the Urdu text, a transcription in the roman script, and a 'literal' translation besides the finished version, and in free verse in a recognizably contemporary Anglo-American poetic idiom by Agha Shahid **Ali** in *The Rebel's Silhouette*, a deliberately 'adapted' title which literally means 'the features of the petitioner'!

Another more recent instance of collaborative translation involved sustained live interaction between poets and translators in an exceptional experiment. In January 1990, the Sahitya Akademi got together in New Delhi for a workshop ten contemporary Hindi poets, as many Indian translators, and a foreign collaborator and catalyst, Daniel **Weissbort** (of the Iowa Translation Workshop), to work together on an anthology of English translations of about 15 poems by each of the poets. The experience was, according to Weissbort, intense and 'electrifying', even though the resulting anthology, *Survival: An Experience and an Experiment in Translating Modern Hindi Poetry*, edited by Daniel Weissbort and Girdhar Rathi, ultimately failed to achieve for Hindi poetry the much sought-after international break-through. Interestingly, the volume includes a detailed account of the unique procedure of the workshop as well as an extended debate on a number of issues between Weissbort and a participant.

In poetry as in fiction, most of the translations done by foreigners are by academics working in the Centres for South Asia in the USA and a few similar centres or departments in England and Australia. Clinton **Seely**, for example, translated over 100 poems of the Bengali poet Jibanananda Das as part of his doctoral dissertation for the University of Chicago, later published as *A Poet Apart*. Marjorie **Boulton**, a linguist and an expert in Esperanto at Oxford, translated, together with the Hindi-speaking Ram Swaroop **Vyas**, the phenomenally popular volume of Hindi romantic verse, *Madhushala* (1935), by Harivansh Rai Bachchan (itself inspired by the *Rubaiyat of Omar Khayyam*), as *The House of Wine*, without anything like the success of the original either in England or when reprinted under the original Hindi title in India. The Australian scholar Marian **Maddern** translated a selection of Bengali poems with each one immediately followed by a commentary on the poem and on the difficulties of translating it, in a volume with a title to which many translatorial bosoms would return a rueful echo: *Bengali Poetry into English: An Impossible Dream?*.

vi. Modern Translation: Drama Translations of modern Indian drama into English are few and far between, mainly because works of modern Indian drama have been thin on the ground but also because the often more realistic and colloquial language of dialogue presents a special challenge. Though drama in Sanskrit was a highly developed genre and at least as prominent as poetry, drama in the modern Indian languages remained almost non-existent (except for largely unscripted folk forms) until the arrival of the British and a consequent refashioning of dramatic form. The journal *Enact*, published in Delhi, was probably the richest resource in this regard; it published through the 1970s a translation into English of an Indian play in each issue. Some of the major plays to appear in this journal were Badal Sircar's *Sesh Nei* as *There's No End* and *Baki Itihas* as *That Other History*, translated from the Bengali respectively by Kironmoy **Raha** and Vinod **Doshi** (November 1971 and March/April 1977); Dharmavir Bharati's postcolonial Hindi allegory based on the *Mahabharata*, *Andha Yug*, translated by Paul **Jacob** as *The Blind Age* (May 1972); Mohan Rakesh's *Ashadh Ka Ek Din*, *Adhe Adhure*, and *Lehron Ke Rajhans*, all translated from the Hindi respectively by Sarat K. **Ensley** as *One Day in Ashadh* (August/September 1969), by Bindu **Batra** as *Half-way House* (May 1971), and by Paul Jacob and Meena **Williams** as *Royal Swans on the Waves* (January/February 1973). Several of the plays of the major Marathi playwrights Vijay Tendulkar and Mahesh Elkunchwar also appeared in the same journal.

Over the last decade and more, a publishing house from Calcutta, Seagull, has emerged as the chief publisher of Indian plays as well as film scripts in English translation, publishing for example *Three Plays* by Badal Sircar and *Five Plays* by Mahasweta Devi, all translated from the Bengali by one of the founders of the publishing house, Samik **Bandopadhyay**. Seagull has also published Vijay Tendulkar's *Ghashiram Kotwal*, translated under the same title (1984) from Marathi by Jayant **Karve** and Eleanor **Zelliot**, and *Uddhwasta Dharmashala* by G. P. Deshpande, translated again from the Marathi by Shanta **Gokhale** as *A Man in Dark Times*.

Another major contemporary playwright, Girish **Karnad**, is distinguished for having translated his plays into English himself, the only notable Indian dramatist to have done so. He writes in Kannada, which he has described as 'the language of my childhood', while English, he says, is the 'language of my adulthood', and he has been translating himself from the one to the other for the last quarter-century without so far being tempted to begin writing originally in English. All the English translations of his plays have been published by the Oxford University Press in India, for whom he himself once worked as an editor.

vii. Other Genres Other relatively minor forms of literature have not often been translated into English. M. K. Gandhi's autobiography, originally written in Gujarati, was translated into English by his secretary, Mahadev **Desai**, as *The Story of My Experiments with Truth*. The authorized Bengali biography of Rabindranath Tagore, *Rabindrajibani*, in four volumes by Prabhat Kumar Mukhopadhyay, was translated into English, in an abridged version by Sisir Kumar **Ghose**, as *Life of Tagore*; the four volumes of the autobiography (1969–91) of Harivansh Rai Bachchan were similarly abridged into a seamless narrative, *In the Afternoon of Time* by Rupert **Snell**. *Premchand: Qalam Ka Sipahi* (1962), the biography of the Hindi novelist by his son Amrit Rai, which itself won the Sahitya Akademi award for the best Hindi book of the year in any genre, was translated into English as *Premchand: His Life and Times* by Harish **Trivedi**. Of the few Indian diaries translated into English, the most remarkable is *The Private Diary of Anandaranga Pillai*, covering the period 1736 to 1761 and translated in 1904–24 from the Tamil in 12 volumes by J. Frederic **Price**

and K. **Rangachari**. (Pillai was interpreter to Joseph François Dupleix, the French governor and director-general in India in the mid-18th c. who eventually lost the battle for colonial supremacy in India to Robert Clive; he has been called 'the Pepys of French India'.) *Yuganta* by Irawati **Karve**, a socio-anthropological reinterpretation of some characters and episodes from the *Mahabharata*, was translated from the Marathi by the author herself as *Yuganta: The End of an Epoch*.

Two journals which have for long years been publishing translations of Indian literature are *Indian Literature*, now published six times a year by the Sahitya Akademi and completing in 1998 the 41st year of its publication with 190 issues, and *Mehfil*, renamed *Journal of South Asian Literature* (1963–), published in the USA. Of all the various resources of modern (and older) Indian literature in English translation, *Indian Literature* offers the widest range and variety. It has brought out numerous special issues devoted both to particular themes and individual languages, it carries creative writing as well as critical discussions, including book reviews, and though the quality of contributions has varied dramatically under different editors, this staid, stable, semi-governmental journal remains a treasure-house (or at worst a warehouse) unmatched in the field.   HT

ANTHOLOGIES   Behl, Aditya, and Nicholls, David, eds., *The Penguin New Writing in India*, New Delhi, 1994 · Dharmarajan, Geeta, ed., *Katha Prize Stories*, New Delhi, 1990– [annually] · Dharwadker, Vinay, and Ramanujan, A. K., eds., *The Oxford Anthology of Modern Indian Poetry*, Delhi, 1974 · Ezekiel, Nissim, and Mukherjee, Meenakshi, eds., *Another India: An Anthology of Contemporary Indian Fiction and Poetry*, New Delhi, 1990 [Penguin] · Indian Council for Cultural Relations, *Indian Poetry Today*, 3 vols., New Delhi, 1974–81 · Jussawalla, Adil, ed., *New Writing in India*, London, 1974 [Penguin] · Maddern, Marian, *Bengali Poetry into English: An Impossible Dream?*, Calcutta, 1977 · Memon, M. U., *The Colour of Nothingness: Urdu Short Stories*, New Delhi, 1991 [Penguin] · Ranga, Rao, *Classic Telegu Short Stories*, New Delhi, 1995 [Penguin] · Roadarmel, Gordon C., *A Death in Delhi: Modern Hindi Short Stories*, Berkeley, Calif., 1973; rep. Delhi, 1987 · Rubin, David, *The Return of Sarasvati: Four Modern Hindi Poets*, Delhi, 1998 · Sharma, Ramachandra, ed., *From Cauvery to Godavari: Kannada Short Stories*, New Delhi, 1992 [Penguin] · Vajpeyi, Kailash, ed., *An Anthology of Modern Hindi Poetry*, New Delhi, 1998 · Weissbort, Daniel, and Rathi, Girdhar, eds., *Survival: An Experience and an Experiment in Translating Modern Hindi Poetry*, New Delhi, 1994.
ANANTHA MURTHY, U. R.   Ramanujan, A. K., *Samskara: Rite for a Dead Man*, Delhi, 1976.
BACHCHAN, HARIVANSH RAI   Snell, Rupert, *In the Afternoon of Time*, New Delhi, 1998 [abr.].
BANDHOPADHYAY, BIBHUTIBHUSHAN   Clark, T. W., and Mukherjee, Tarapad, *Pather Panchali: Song of the Road*, London, 1968.
CHATTERJEE, BANKIM CHANDRA   Knight, Miriam S, *The Poison Tree*, London, 1884 · *Krishnakanta's Will*, London, 1885 · Maddern, Marian, and Mukherji, S. N., *The Poison Tree: Three Novellas*, New Delhi, 1996 [Penguin] · Sengupta, N. C., *The Abbey of Bliss*, Calcutta, 1914.
DAS, JIBANANANDA   Seely, Clinton, *A Poet Apart: A Literary Biography of the Bengali Poet Jibanananda Das*, Newark, NJ, 1990.
DATTA, MICHAEL MADHUSUDAN   Datta, Michael Madhusudan, *Shormishtha*, Calcutta, 1858.
DESHPANDE, G. P.   Gokhale, Shanta, *A Man in Dark Times*, Calcutta, 1990.
DEVI, MAHASWETA   Bandopadhyay, Samik, *Five Plays*, Calcutta, 1986 · Spivak, Gayatri Chakravarty, *Imaginary Maps: Three Stories*, New York, 1995.
FAIZ, AHMAD FAIZ   Ali, Agha Shahid, *The Rebel's Silhouette: Selected Poems*, Delhi, 1992 · Kiernan, Victor, *Poems by Faiz*, London, 1971; rep. Karachi.

GANDHI, M. K.   Desai, Mahadev, *An Autobiography, or The Story of my Experiments with Truth*, 2 vols., Ahmedabad, 1927–9.

GHALIB   Ahmad, Aijaz, ed., *Ghazals of Ghalib*, New York, 1971; rep. Delhi, 1994.

GANGOPADHYAY, TARAKNATH   Thompson, Edward, *The Brothers*, London, 1930.

KARNAD, GIRISH   Karnad, Girish, *Three Plays: Naga-Mandala, Hayavadana, Tughlaq*, Delhi, 1994 · *The Fire and the Rain*, Delhi, 1998.

KARVE, IRAWATI   Karve, Irawati, *Yuganta: The End of an Epoch*, New Delhi, 1969.

MANTO, SAADAT HASAN   Hasan, Khalid, *The Kingdom's End and Other Stories*, New Delhi, 1987 [Penguin].

MENON, O. CHANDU   Dumergue, W., *Indulekha*, Trivandrum, 1889.

MITRA, DINABANDHU   anon., *Nil-Darpana*, Calcutta, 1860.

MUKHOPADHYAY, PRABHAT KUMAR   Ghose, Sisir Kumar, *Life of Tagore*, Calcutta, 1975 [abr.].

PILLAI, ANANDARANGA   Price, J. Frederick, and Rangachari, K., *The Private Diary of Anandaranga Pillai*, Madras, 1904–24.

PILLAI, THAKAZHI S.   Menon, V. K. Narayan, *Chemmeen*, London, 1962.

PREMCHAND   Ratan, Jai, and Lal, P., *Godan*, Bombay, 1957 · Roadarmel, Gordon C., *The Gift of a Cow*, Berkeley, Calif., 1968 · Rubin, David, *The World of Premchand*, Berkeley, Calif., 1969; rep. Delhi, 1988.

RAI, AMRIT   Trivedi, Harish, *Premchand: His Life and Times*, Delhi, 1982; rep. 1991.

REZA, RAHI MASOOM   Wright, Gillian, *The Feuding Families of Village Gangauli*, New Delhi, 1994 [Penguin].

SHUKLA, SHRILAL   Wright, Gillian, *Raag Darbari*, New Delhi, 1992 [Penguin].

SIRCAR, BADAL   Bandopadhyay, Samik, *Three Plays*, Calcutta, 1983.

TAGORE, RABINDRANATH   Tagore, Rabindranath, *Gitanjali*, London, 1912 [many edns.].

TENDULKAR, VIJAY   Karve, Jayant, and Zelliot, Eleanor, *Ghashiram Kotwal*, Calcutta, 1984.

VERMA, NIRMAL   Singh, Kuldip, *A Rag Called Happiness*, New Delhi, 1993 [Penguin] · Singh, Kuldip, and Ratan, Jai, *Crows of Deliverance: Stories by Nirmal Verma*, London, 1991; rep. New Delhi, 1992 · Vaid, Krishna Baldev, *Days of Longing*, New Delhi, 1972 · various, *The World Elsewhere and Other Stories*, London/Delhi, 1986.

VIJAYAN, O. V.   Vijayan, O. V., *Selected Fiction*, New Delhi, 1998 [Penguin].

SEE ALSO   Bassnett, S., and Trivedi, H., eds., *Post-Colonial Translation: Theory and Practice*, London, 1999 · Mukherjee, S., *Translation as Discovery and Other Essays on Indian Writing in English Translation*, New Delhi, 1981.

m. Italian

1. INTRODUCTION

Italian literature has undoubtedly possessed an enduring fascination for English-language readers and writers. Yet the volume of translations has fluctuated greatly from period to period, probably reaching its height with Italian fiction since World War II. The choice of Italian texts for translation has always been extremely limited, focusing on relatively few major figures and establishing a canon of works which is generally recognized in Italy, but which hardly reproduces the native reception of Italian literature. And even though the language was known to English-language writers of every period, the influence of Italian on British and American literature has not been consistently strong. Nevertheless, Italian writing represents one of the richest strands in the history of English-language translating, one woven with the succession of trends and debates that have characterized Anglo-American cultures. On occasion this translating has also been decisive in the emergence of new literary styles and forms in English.

The most remarkable encounter occurred during the 16th and 17th c., when distinctions between authorship, adaptation, and translation were sufficiently blurred to produce a dazzling range of English writing in various genres. Early Tudor courtiers such as Sir Thomas **Wyatt** and Henry Howard, Earl of **Surrey**, wrote powerful versions of Petrarch's sonnets that have long achieved recognition as original compositions [see II.m.4.ii]. George **Gascoigne** (c.1534–77) wrote a witty translation of Ariosto's prose comedy, *I suppositi* (1509, The Substitutes), which was performed at Gray's Inn during 1566 and provided a plot for Shakespeare's

Taming of the Shrew. Shakespeare's plays were also inspired by the anthologist William **Painter** (c.1540–94), whose *Palace of Pleasure* (1566–7) gathered his translations of racy *novelle* by Boccaccio, Matteo Bandello, and Giraldi Cinthio. In 1561 Sir Thomas **Hoby** published his vigorous plain prose version of Castiglione's *Courtier* [II.m.8.iii], addressed to aristocratic readers but also accessible to the commoners who sought preferment at the Elizabethan court. Because Machiavelli's *Prince* [II.m.8.i] was read as a mirror of political corruption and a possible incitement to rebellion, translations circulated anonymously in manuscript until Edward **Dacres** (fl. 1636–40) published his version in 1640, the eve of the parliamentary revolution against Charles I. In 1647, the Royalist Sir Richard **Fanshawe** (1608–66) wrote a version of Giovanni Battista Guarini's pastoral drama *Il pastor fido* (1590, The Faithful Shepherd), in which he pioneered the free strategies that came to dominate English-language translating for the next two centuries.

Notwithstanding the myriad renderings of Carlo Collodi's *Adventures of Pinocchio* [II.m.11], Dante has been the most frequently translated Italian writer into English, and his *Divine Comedy* the most frequently translated Italian text [II.m.2]. It has been attempted in whole or part by many different translators, including major poets, from the Middle Ages to the present. In our own time it has reached a mass audience through inexpensive paperback editions. Although the translations have generally adopted a conservative treatment, reflecting the translators' high esteem for Dante's verse, they do represent a broad spectrum of approaches. Daniel Halpern's anthology offers a striking glimpse of contemporary strategies by collecting cantos of the *Inferno* rendered by a number of poets, including Seamus **Heaney**, Richard Howard, and Richard **Wilbur**. Dante's friend Guido Cavalcanti, in sharp contrast, has been translated rarely, mostly in anthology selections. Yet Cavalcanti's sonnets, ballatas, and canzones have prompted more innovative treatments. The versions of Dante Gabriel **Rossetti** and Ezra **Pound** are each representative of important poetic movements, Victorian Pre-Raphaelitism and modern experimentalism [see II.m.4.iv].

The translation of other Italian poetries has been sporadic. Of the Romantic poets, only Giacomo Leopardi has enjoyed a reputation in English comparable to his canonical status in Italy. Yet his prose attracted translators long before his poetry, which was not rendered in a substantial selection till after his death. Leopardi's contemporary, Ugo Foscolo, was deeply engaged in the political and military events of the Napoleonic era. He also lived in London during 1817. But his writing has been virtually neglected by English-language translators: only his long poem *I sepolcri* (1807, The Tombs) has appeared in a few versions. Italian poetry during the 20th c. has been more frequently translated, although the Nobel laureate Eugenio Montale has dominated the scene, rivalling Dante in the sheer number of versions [II.m.13.iii]. The main traditions of Italian poetry have been surveyed in several bilingual anthologies. William Jay Smith and Dana Gioia published the most comprehensive selection, over 63 poets from St Francis to Rocco Scotellaro, rendered into verse by numerous translators, past and present, British and American, poets and professionals.

20th-c. translators have made available a varied selection of Italian prose, philosophical and scientific as well as literary. Key works by Pico della Mirandola, Marsilio Ficino, Giordano Bruno, Galileo, and Tommaso Campanella can be found in annotated versions that are both reliable and readable. Because Cesare Beccaria's essay *Dei delitti e delle pena* (1764, On Crimes and Publishments) enunciated a concept of criminal law consistent with Enlightenment humanism, it was translated several times during the 18th c. and has since become a

classic of legal history, the object of multiple versions. Benedetto Croce's idealist philosophy also struck a responsive chord with British and American readers, so that more than 25 volumes of his dense, complicated prose were translated during his lifetime. For Giambattista Vico, one of the main influences on Croce, an English-language readership was much slower in forming. Vico was not translated until the 1940s, when Max H. **Fisch** and Thomas G. **Bergin** published fluent versions of the autobiography and *Scienza nuova* (3rd edn., 1744, The New Science) with illuminating expositions. In the 1970s and 1980s, when Anglo-American culture was strongly influenced by concurrent developments in Continental philosophy, translations of Antonio Gramsci and Galvano della Volpe responded to the burgeoning interest in cultural and political theory. The debates on postmodernism and ethics at the close of the 20th c. have been informed by resourceful English versions of such contemporary thinkers as Gianni Vattimo and Giorgio Agamben.

Many major Italian dramatists have appeared in translation, and the versions have often been staged. Torquato Tasso's [II.m.7] pastoral drama *Aminta* (1573) was translated repeatedly during the 17th and 18th c., although today it is of interest only to specialists. Renaissance comedies have been collected in several anthologies, and scholars have prepared translations of individual texts by such writers as Angelo Beolco il Ruzante, Pietro Aretino, and Giambattista della Porta. Descriptions of routines and scenarios from the *commedia dell'arte* have been culled from Italian collections and published in English for the use of directors and actors as well as scholars. English versions of 20th-c. Italian drama have been dominated by Pirandello's formally innovative plays [II.m.12], although representative work by Ugo Betti and by Edoardo De Filippo has been performed and published in translation. Long before Dario Fo [II.m.11] won the Nobel Prize for Literature, more than 15 of his political farces were rendered by accomplished translators like Stuart **Hood**, usually in the form of adaptations for performance. The anthology of Jane House and Antonio Attisani presents a comprehensive survey of modern dramatic traditions in Italy.   LV

ANTHOLOGIES   Bentley, Eric, ed., *The Classic Theatre*, i: *Six Italian Plays*, Garden City, NY, 1958 · Gordon, Mel, *Lazzi: The Comic Routines of the Commedia dell'arte*, New York, 1983 · Halpern, Daniel, ed., *Dante's Inferno: Translations by Twenty Contemporary Poets*, Hopewell, NJ, 1993 · House, Jane, and Attisani, Antonio, *Twentieth-Century Italian Drama*, New York, 1994 · Kay, George R., *The Penguin Book of Italian Verse*, Harmondsworth, 1958 · Penman, Bruce, *Five Italian Renaissance Comedies*, Harmondsworth, 1978 [Penguin] · Smith, William Jay, and Gioia, Dana, *Poems from Italy*, St Paul, Minn., 1985 · Tusiani, Joseph, *From Marino to Marinetti: An Anthology of Forty Italian Poets*, New York, 1974.

SEE ALSO   Healey, R., *Twentieth-Century Italian Literature in English Translation: An Annotated Bibliography, 1929–1997*, Toronto, 1998.

2. DANTE

i. The Divine Comedy: Introduction Dante Alighieri himself warned against the translation of poetry: 'Nothing', he said, 'that is harmonized by the laws of poetry can be changed from its own language to another without destroying all its sweetness and harmony.' Nevertheless, there are probably more translations of his *Divina commedia* (early 14th c., The Divine Comedy) than of any other postclassical literary work.

The first attempt in English, apart from a paraphrase by Chaucer of the story of Ugolino and of St Bernard's prayer to the Virgin, followed down the centuries by a few versions of isolated episodes, was Charles **Rogers**'s (1711–84) rendering of the *Inferno* into blank verse. The first translation of the whole work, by Henry **Boyd** (c.1755–1832) in rhymed six-line stanzas, was published in 1802. This was followed in 1814 by Henry Francis **Cary**'s (1772–1844) translation in blank verse. The best known of 19th-c. renderings, it still has its admirers. Cary is immortalized in Westminster Abbey as 'The Translator of Dante'.

The challenge of translating the *Commedia* poses in extreme form the fundamental questions which underlie the translation of all poetry. Should it be an aid to understanding the original or aimed at readers who read the work only in English? Should it be in prose or verse? If in verse, should it be a poem in its own right, a descant inspired by the original? Should the original rhyme scheme be retained? If blank verse is chosen, are occasional end-rhymes and internal rhymes desirable? As regards metre, should the Italian 11-syllable line (*endecasillabo*) be rendered by its near-equivalent, the pentameter, or are other metres and other stanzaic forms to be preferred? How important is it to adhere to Dante's paragraphing? If prose is chosen, should it be rhythmic, near-poetic, or plain narrative? There is no agreement on these matters, nor is there ever likely to be. Few translators have found much to admire in the attempts of their predecessors; few readers are entirely satisfied with any one version. It seems likely that new renderings will continue to appear, reflecting the changing literary tastes and prejudices of succeeding generations.

Some translators, holding the form and content of the *Commedia* to be indivisible, consider *terza rima* obligatory. Others reject it on the grounds that the difficulties are too costly, there being fewer rhymes in English than in Italian. This statement continues to be made, though it can easily be disproved. Geoffrey L. **Bickersteth** argues irrefutably in the Introduction to his *terza rima* translation that 'no-one, surely, can maintain that a language is deficient in [rhyme] which boasts of *The Faerie Queene* and *Don Juan*'. In her Introduction to her translation of *Inferno* Dorothy L. **Sayers** points out that though 'pure' rhymes, abundant in Italian, are comparatively scarce in English, 'impure' rhymes are frequent and legitimate and offer infinite variety.

Another problem, which arises whether the translation is in verse or prose, is the level of diction. Should it be traditional, formal, 'period', unvaryingly reverential, or idiomatic, informal, slangy, and up to date—or a mixture? Connected with this question is the 'thou'/'you' dilemma. Dante uses both the singular *tu* and the plural *voi* not only to distinguish number but also employing the latter as a respectful form of address to one person. The difficulty is that in English the difference between 'thou' and 'you' is not one of number; the plural of 'thou' is in fact 'ye'. Their use is now a matter of period and style. Furthermore, 'you', not 'thou', is the more intimate form. The effect of using 'thou', with the corresponding verb endings, the accusative 'thee' and the adjectives 'thy' and 'thine', is to produce a remoteness of style, Biblical in tone and echoing hymns or poetry of earlier centuries. In a translation designed to capture Dante's occasional colloquial, informal, even racy style, an irreconcilable contradiction is thus introduced. On the other hand, it must be said that the 'thou' forms give a truer impression of Dante's sublime moments than the flat up-to-dateness adopted by some present-day down-levelling translators.

ii. The Divine Comedy: Nineteenth and Twentieth Century Cary's decision to use blank verse met with the approval of the poet Ugo Foscolo, who said that if Dante had written in English that is the form he would have chosen! The stately, Miltonic, unvaried style set a pattern of acceptability. Here is his rendering of the inscription on the gateway to Hell (*Inferno*, iii. 1–9):

> Through me you pass into the city of woe:
> Through me you pass into eternal pain:
> Through me among the people lost for aye.
> Justice the founder of my fabric moved:
> To rear me was the task of power divine,
> Supremest wisdom, and primeval love.
> Before me things create were none, save things
> Eternal and eternal I endure.
> All hope abandon, ye who enter here.

The last line, frequently quoted, has become part of English literary tradition.

That was what Dante was assumed to be like. Nevertheless, during the 19th c. a few brave souls attempted *terza rima*. Others compromised with blank terzine, keeping closer than Cary did to Dante's paragraphing. The best-known example is by **Longfellow**. Prose was used, chiefly for exposition, notably by William Warren **Vernon** (1834–1919), accompanying his *Readings* on the poem in six volumes, by the American scholar Charles Eliot **Norton** (1827–1908), and by Henry Fanshawe **Tozer** (1829–1916), in a companion volume to his excellent line-by-line commentary. The Temple Classics rhythmic prose translation in three pocket-size volumes, published at the turn of the century (the *Inferno* by John Aitken **Carlyle** (1801–79), first published in 1849 and revised by Hermann **Oelsner**, the *Purgatorio* by Thomas **Okey** (1852–1935), the *Paradiso* by Philip **Wicksteed** (1844–1927)) provided the Italian text alongside the English. For over a century and a half this version and Cary's were the most influential conveyors of Dante's poem to British readers. A comparable work was published in 1921, also in three octavo volumes and also with a dual text, but with the translation in *terza rima*, by the American Melville B. **Anderson**. Between 1939 and 1946 John D. **Sinclair** brought out a very readable prose translation, facing the original, accompanied by excellent commentaries on every canto. This is one of the best aids in English to the understanding of Dante's text. The recent prose translation of the *Inferno* by the American Robert M. **Durling** is divided into paragraphs corresponding to the facing Italian text; it is a clinically accurate crib but pleasant to read, provided with introduction, notes, and illustrations.

Of 20th-c. translations in *terza rima*, the following three have been among the most admired: Laurence **Binyon**'s, Geoffrey L. **Bickersteth**'s, with dual text, and, containing the fullest commentary, the Penguin Classics version by Dorothy L. **Sayers**, the *Paradiso* being completed after her death by Barbara **Reynolds**. Though it has its detractors, the Sayers translation has met with deserved acclaim and is the most widely used.

Defective *terza rima* (i.e. leaving the middle line of each tercet unrhymed) has been used by an American translator, John **Ciardi**, who experimented, as others have since done, with an up-to-date and slangy style. Longfellow's choice—blank *terzine*—has been followed more recently by two other Americans, Mark **Musa** and Allen **Mandelbaum**. The freedom from the distortion which true *terza rima* is alleged to impose and the

greater fidelity to meaning which is claimed for these forms are not strikingly apparent in either Ciardi's or Musa's translation; while the loss of pattern is. Mandelbaum's diction is smoother and less prosaic than Musa's, as may be seen from a comparison between their versions of the first six lines of *Inferno*, canto 27:

> By now the flame was standing straight and still
> it said no more and had already turned
> from us, with sanction of the gentle poet,
>
> when another, coming right behind it,
> attracted our attention to its tip,
> where a roaring of confusing sounds had started.
>
> (Musa)

> The flame already was erect and silent—
> it had no more to say. Now it had left us
> with the permission of the gentle poet,
>
> when, just behind it, came another flame
> that drew our eyes to watch its tip because
> of the perplexing sound that it sent forth.
>
> (Mandelbaum)

Here is the same passage by Sayers, in *terza rima*:

> Erect and quiet now, its utterance done,
> The tall flame stood; and presently, dismissed
> By the sweet poet's licence, it passed on;
>
> When lo! our eyes were drawn towards the crest
> Of a new flame. coming behind its fellow,
> By the strange muffled roarings it expressed.

It is not plain what the two preceding versions have gained from the avoidance of rhyme and regularity of rhythm.

The flatness of C. H. **Sisson**'s recent translation—'plain Dante, plain as a board, and if flat, flat,' Donald Davie wrote of it (approvingly, it seems)—is apparently deliberate. Sisson says in his foreword that he chose to translate Dante in the language of his own day, as 'one does write'. He departs at random from the pentameter, using lines of varying length and beat. Here is his rendering of the first three lines of *Inferno*:

> Nel mezzo del cammin di nostra vita
> mi ritrovai in una selva oscura
> ché la diritta via era smarrita.
>
> Half way along the road we have to go,
> I found myself obscured in a great forest,
> Bewildered, and I knew I had lost the way.

There are some surprising departures from the original here. The adjective *oscura* (f.) applies to the wood, which is dark, not Dante. Nor does Dante call it a 'great' forest. It is not Dante who is 'bewildered', but the right road which is lost (*smarrita*). And *mi ritrovai* means, not 'I found myself', but 'I came to myself', 'I awoke'.

Here is another sample, from Sisson's version of the second canto of *Purgatorio* (ll. 19–21):

> Lo bel pianeta che d'amar conforta
> faceva tutto rider l'oriente,
> velando i Pesci, ch'erano in sua scorta.

> The lovely planet which gives comfort in love
> Was filling the whole eastern sky with laughter,
> Hiding the Fish which followed in her train.

Dante's word *conforta* does not mean 'gives comfort'. Venus empowers, urges, exhorts to love (much of Dante's vocabulary is nearer in meaning to Latin than to modern Italian, and this is an example). 'Filling the sky with laughter' suggests that souls or angels are singing—they are not: Venus is lighting up the east with joy. And the constellation mentioned is Pisces, the Fishes, not the Fish.

Here is Sayers' version:

> The lovely planet, love's own quickener,
> Now lit to laughter all the eastern sky,
> Veiling the Fishes that attended her.

This reproduces Dante's stress on *rider*, in the same strong position in the line, and leaves the 'eastern sky' at the end, where it should be. 'Quickener' is an excellent solution for Venus and her power, while 'lit to laughter' lifts the heart with joy. The rendering is accurate, lucid, simple, and the lines sing, which Sisson's fail to do.

His *Paradise*, also, is full of disconcerting jolts, as in the flat matter-of-factness, not to say misinterpretation, of Canto 28, lines 88–96. Dante, wishing to convey the sense of an infinite number of angels, says that they exceeded by thousands the figure arrived at by the progressive doubling of the number of squares on a chessboard. Sisson translates:

> And when her words had ceased, there was
>   such sparkling
> From the circles, as is seen in the sparks
> Which are thrown off by the iron when it boils.

> Every spark followed the fire it belonged to:
> There were so many that the number of them
> Was greater than all the combinations at chess.

The Sayers–Reynolds translation reads:

> Her words, when they had ceased, were greeted by
> A sparkling of scintillas in the spheres,
> As showers of sparks from molten metal fly.

> Tracing each fiery circle that was theirs,
> They numbered myriads more than the entire
> Progressive doubling of the chessboard squares.

The difficulties of writing *terza rima* in English have been much exaggerated. Of the twelve who contributed to the composite translation of *Inferno* broadcast by the BBC in 1966, nine chose *terza rima* and handled it with skill.

One of the best renderings in blank verse to have appeared in recent years is that by Tom **Phillips**, published in 1985 in a de luxe edition with Phillips's own illustrations. Here is his version of Dante's meeting with Brunetto Latini (*Inferno* xv. 16–30):

> We happened on a troop of souls who moved
> alongside the embankment, each of whom
> examined us, as, when the moon is new,
> men peer at one another in the dusk.
> They squinted at us, knitting up their brows
> like some old tailor at his needle's eye.
> I underwent this group's strange scrutiny
> till one of them discovered who I was;
> and, clutching at the corner of my cloak
> he cried aloud, 'Why, what a miracle!'
> Then, as he reached towards me with his arm,
> I tried to see beneath his facial burns
> for fear those roasted features might prevent
> my memory from knowing who he was,
> and, stretching down my hand towards his face
> said, 'Ser Brunetto is it you? Down here?'

If it must be blank verse, let it be of this quality.

Of two recent updated translations, Steve **Ellis**'s *Hell* aims at recapturing Dante's vigour by using 'primarily the language of the 1980s and 1990s'. Rejecting *terza rima* and the pentameter, he uses a racy four-foot line. Here is his beginning of Canto 22:

> I've seen troops get under way,
> whether to attack or to parade
> or sometimes to make a retreat;
> I've seen horsemen on your land,
> you Aretines, I've seen raiders,
> clashes at tournaments and jousts;
> I've witnessed clarions and bells,
> drum-rolls, signs from battlements
> or other signals, native or foreign;
> but I never heard a bugle like this
> get horses or infantry into action,
> or ships steering by land or stars.

The rapid pace is well suited to passages of this nature. But not even *Inferno* is as racy throughout, and there will be problems when he comes to *Purgatorio* and *Paradiso*.

Another recent verse translation of the *Inferno* is that by the American poet Robert **Pinsky**. His stated aim is to make the *Commedia* sound like a poem in English. He admits occasional rhymes, and varies the length of lines as the mood takes him. Here is his beginning of Canto 8:

> Continuing, I tell how for some time
> Before we reached the tower's base

Our eyes were following two points of flame
Visible at the top; and answering these
Another returned the signal, so far away
The eye could barely catch it. I turned to face
My sea of knowledge and said, 'O Master, say:
What does this beacon mean?
And the other fire—
What answer does it signal?
And who are they
Who set it there?' . . .

The jerkiness of this rendering may be compared with the controlled version in *terza rima* by Bickersteth:

I say, continuing, that long before
we reached its foot, our eyes had onward sped
up to the summit of the lofty tower,

because we saw two beacons it displayed
and—from so far, 'twas well nigh past discerning—
another, which gave back the sign they made.

And I, turned towards the deep sea of all learning,
said, 'What does this one say? And what replies
that other fire? And who have set it burning?'

iii. Other Works Translations of Dante's minor Italian writings are less numerous. Dante Gabriel **Rossetti**'s 1861 translation of *La vita nuova* (1290–4,

The New Life) does not always adhere to the original rhyme scheme. It was followed in 1867 by Charles Eliot Norton's, which does and is more accurate. The Penguin Classics translation by Barbara Reynolds follows the rhyme scheme and the length of lines of the original. That by Mark Musa, which in its earlier edition supplies the Italian original, avoids rhyme altogether.

The poems of *La vita nuova* and of *Il convivio* (1304–8, The Banquet), as well as others making up Dante's lyrical output, have been excellently translated into rhymed verse, in English equivalents of the original metres, by H. S. **Vere-Hodge**. This is a dual text, containing admirable notes and an Introduction in which Dante's poetic technique is knowledgeably discussed. *Dante's Lyric Poetry*, by Kenelm **Foster** and Patrick **Boyde** provides the original text and a prose translation. Dorothy L. Sayers's rhymed translation of the four 'Pietra' *canzoni*, previously circulated privately, was published posthumously in 1989.

Il convivio in its entirety was translated by Katharine **Hillard** in 1889; the poems are rendered in blank verse. She was followed by Philip Wicksteed in 1903 and by William Walrond **Jackson** in 1909, who both rendered the poems in prose. The best recent translation is by Christopher **Ryan**, who also renders the poems in prose.   BR

DIVINE COMEDY   *The Inferno of Dante Translated*, tr. Charles Rogers, London, 1785 · *The Divina Commedia*, tr. Henry Boyd, 3 vols., London, 1802 [*Inferno*, 1785] · *The Vision; or Hell, Purgatory, and Paradise of Dante Alighieri*, tr. Henry Francis Cary, 3 vols., London, 1814 [frequent reps.] · *The Divine Comedy*, tr. Henry Wadsworth Longfellow, 3 vols., Boston, 1867 [frequent reps.] · *Readings on the Purgatorio*, by William Warren Vernon, London, 1889 · *The Divine Comedy*, tr. Charles Eliot Norton, 3 vols., Boston / New York, 1891–2 · *Readings on the Inferno*, by William Warren Vernon, London, 1894 · *The Divina Commedia*, ed. Hermann Oelsner, 3 vols., London, 1899–1902 [Temple Classics; tr. John Aitken Carlyle, rev. H. Oelsner (*Inferno*); Thomas Okey (*Purgatorio*); Philip Henry Wicksteed (*Paradiso*)] · *Readings on the Paradiso*, by William Warren Vernon, London, 1900 · *Dante's Divine Comedy*, tr. Henry Fanshawe Tozer, Oxford, 1904 · *The Divine Comedy of Dante Alighieri*, tr. Melville Best Anderson, New York, 1921 · *Dante's Inferno*, tr. Laurence Binyon, London, 1933 · *Dante's Purgatorio*, tr. Laurence Binyon, London, 1938 · *The Divine Comedy*, tr. John D. Sinclair, 3 vols., London, 1939 · *Dante's Paradiso*, tr. Laurence Binyon, London, 1943 · *The Comedy of Dante Alighieri*, tr. Dorothy L. Sayers and Barbara Reynolds, 3 vols., Harmondsworth, 1949–62 [Penguin] · *The Divine Comedy*, tr. Geoffrey Langdale Bickersteth, 3 vols., Aberdeen, 1955 [*Paradiso* 1932] · *The Inferno*, tr. John Ciardi, New York, 1954 · *The Purgatorio*, tr. John Ciardi, New York, 1961 · *The Paradiso*, tr. John Ciardi, New York, 1970 · *Dante's Inferno*, tr. Mark Musa, Bloomington, Ind., 1971 [later Penguin] · *The Divine Comedy*, tr. Allen Mandelbaum, Berkeley, Calif., 1980 · *The Divine Comedy*, tr. C. H. Sisson, Manchester, 1980 [World's Classics] · *Dante's Purgatory*, tr. Mark Musa, Bloomington, Ind., 1981 [later Penguin] · *Dante's Paradise*, tr. Mark Musa, Bloomington, Ind., 1984 [later Penguin] · *Dante's Inferno*, tr. Tom Phillips, London, 1985 · *Hell*, tr. Steve Ellis, London, 1994 · *The 'Inferno' of Dante*, tr. Robert Pinsky, London, 1994 · *Inferno*, tr. Robert M. Durling, New York / Oxford, 1996.
CONVIVIO   *The Banquet*, tr. Katharine Hillard, London, 1889 · *The Convivio*, tr. Philip Wicksteed, London, 1903 · *Dante's Convivio*, tr. William Walrond Jackson, Oxford, 1909 · *The Banquet*, tr. Christopher Ryan, Stanford, Calif., 1989.
ODES   *The Odes of Dante*, tr. H. S. Vere-Hodge, Oxford, 1963 · *Dante's Lyric Poetry*, tr. Kenelm Foster and Patrick Boyde, vol. i, Cambridge, 1967 · *The Heart of Stone*, tr. Dorothy L. Sayers, in Barbara Reynolds, ed., *The Passionate Intellect*, Kent, OH, 1989.
VITA NUOVA   *The New Life*, tr. Dante Gabriel Rossetti, in his *The Early Italian Poets*, London, 1861 · *The New Life*, tr. Charles Eliot Norton, Boston, 1867 · *La Vita Nuova*, tr. Mark Musa, New Brunswick, NJ, 1957, 1992 [World's Classics] · *La Vita Nuova*, tr. Barbara Reynolds, Harmondsworth, 1969 [Penguin].

3. BOCCACCIO

The history of Giovanni Boccaccio's *Decamerone* (*c*.1350) in the English-speaking world is a curious one. Acclaimed from the 16th c. as a literary masterpiece, its canonical status reinforced by the imitations of Chaucer, Shakespeare, Dryden, Keats, and Tennyson, the *Decameron* nonetheless retained until relatively recently an aura of disreputability sufficient to dissuade all its translators prior to W. K. **Kelly** in 1885 from putting their names to their work. The first uncensored translation did not appear until 1886—even then only for book-club circulation—while the most popular version of the early 20th c., that of James Macmullan **Rigg**, still left untranslated the details of Alibech's devilish activities with the hermit Rustico (iii. 10).

Though many of Boccaccio's *novelle* had already been translated individually, the earliest complete (or near-complete) English *Decameron* did not appear until 1620, significantly later than the first translations into French, Spanish, Catalan, and German. Whether moral preoccupations had precluded an earlier translation is difficult to say; certainly, the 1620 translator shows a conspicuous alertness to the text's perceived breaches of sexual and religious decorum, replacing the Alibech story with a *novella* from Belleforest's *Histoires tragiques*, and following Boccaccio's Counter-Reformation censors in such details as having Frate Alberto disguise himself as Cupid rather than the angel Gabriel in his attempt to seduce the bird-brained Madonna Lisetta (iv. 1). Nor are opportunities ignored for local moral retouching through the interjection of admonitory comments: as the dedicatory letter promises, there is 'no spare made of reproofe in any degree whatsoever, where sin is embraced and grace neglected'. If this sounds ominous to the modern reader, moralizing intent is not here an index of drabness; on the contrary, the 1620 translation succeeds brilliantly in evoking the verve and immediacy of Boccaccio's narration. Immediacy, indeed, is a keynote of this version, narrative and visual detail often being supplied where the sparer Italian does without. The Priest of Varlungo (viii. 2) gains a name, 'sweet Sir Simon'; a casually mentioned pill becomes 'spotted with Gold, in verie formall and Physicall manner' (viii. 6); we even learn to which big toe (the left) Monna Sismonda ties the string by which her lover may alert her to his presence (vii. 8). Stylistically, the translation is distinguished from the original by its greater ornateness and linguistic exuberance, a marked feature, in particular, being a powerful commitment to alliter-ation that produces 'dark dungeons' for the original's 'prisons' and 'passionate pangs' for its '[love]throes'. The effect is very different from that of the Italian, but, in its calibrated richness and intricacy, the 1620 translator's prose offers a satisfying counterpart to Boccaccio's plainer, but still elaborate, style.

This translation was reprinted three times over the following century, and its traces are apparent in, for example, Dryden's Boccaccio adaptations in his *Fables* (1700). A new version of the *Decameron* was published in 1702, 'accommodated to the Gust of the present Age'—a 'gust', it appears from the preface, impatient of any 'multiplicity of words'. Much is correspondingly cut from this edition, including almost the entirety of the frame narrative; though the *novelle* remain, they have been subjected to cuts that radically alter their pacing and scope. Given the freedom of this and the 1620 version, there is justice in the claim of the next translator (1741) that his is the first translation of the *Decameron* deserving of the name. His version undoubtedly has the merit of fidelity, and, though serviceable rather than distinguished, it would long remain the standard translation, with revised editions appearing (often unacknowledged) at least until 1898.

The modern translation history of the *Decameron* begins with the much-admired version of John **Payne** (1842–1916). Payne's stately and rather lush neo-Tudor idiom dated rapidly, however, and it was the still archaizing but more accessible (and unprecedentedly accurate) rendering of J. M. Rigg that deservedly became the standard version for much of the 20th c. The main defect of Rigg's translation is its failure to do justice to the lower stylistic registers of the original, and particularly to Boccaccio's brilliant evocations of the rhythms of colloquial speech. Subsequent translators' attempts to remedy this lack have not been uniformly positive: not only do colloquialisms age notoriously badly (Richard **Aldington**'s 'Donna Windy-noddle'), but it might also be noted that certain modern renderings—particularly Aldington's and Guido **Waldman**'s but also, to a lesser extent, G. H. **McWilliam**'s—show a tendency to extend their use of a demotic register beyond the circumscribed use made of it by Boccaccio, with a resulting dilution of the stylistic variety of the original. In the case of McWilliam, however, this reservation must be balanced by a recognition of the translator's stylistic virtuosity, apparent, for example, in his fine translation of the glorious gibberish of Fra Cipolla's sermon (vi. 10), where a phrase like 'Verbum-caro fattialle-finestre' is memorably matched by 'word-made-flash-in-the-pan'. With the alternatives of McWilliam and the more sober and literal **Bondanella–Musa** (which reflects the textual

innovations of Vittore Branca's critical edition of 1974), the English-speaking reader of the *Decameron* is notably well served. Recent years have also seen new translations of a number of Boccaccio's other Latin and Italian works, including some previously unavailable in English.   VC

TRANSLATIONS   *The Decameron, Containing an Hundred Pleasant Novels*, London, 1620; rep. 1909 · *Il Decamerone. One Hundred Ingenious Novels*, London, 1702 · *The Decameron, or Ten Days Entertainment*, London, 1741 [many rev. edns., inc. W. K. Kelly, 1855] · *The Decameron of G. Boccacci* [sic], tr. John Payne, London, 1886 [rev. Charles S. Singleton, 1982] · *The Decameron*, tr. J. M. Rigg, London, 1903 [later Everyman] · *The Decameron*, tr. Frances Winwar, New York, 1930 · *The Decameron*, tr. Richard Aldington, London, 1930 · *Decameron*, tr. G. H. McWilliam, Harmondsworth, 1972 [Penguin] · *Decameron*, tr. Peter Bondanella and Mark Musa, London, 1982 · *Decameron*, tr. Guido Waldman, Oxford, 1993 [World's Classics].

SEE ALSO   Wright, H. G., *The First English Translation of the Decameron* (1620), Uppsala, 1953.

4. EARLY LYRIC POETRY

The love lyric occupied a central position in the early history of Italian as a literary language. Correspondingly (though, of course, to a lesser degree) translations of the Italian lyric made a decisive contribution at certain points to the development of English literary history. Sporadic instances of translations, almost always of Petrarch, can be discovered in almost every period of English literature, as for instance those by John **Nott** (1777) and more recently Thomas **Bergin** (1965), Marion **Shore** (1987), James Wyatt **Cook** (1995), and Mark **Musa** (1996). But sustained attention to the Italian model occurs in the 14th, 15th and 16th c., when **Chaucer**, **Wyatt**, **Sidney**, and **Spenser** turn to Petrarch and the Petrarchan tradition, and then again in the 19th and 20th c., when Dante Gabriel Rossetti and, later, Ezra Pound interested themselves in the poetry of Petrarch's predecessors, notably the *stil novisti*, Guido Guinizelli, Guido Cavalcanti, and Dante Alighieri.

i. The Early Italian Love Lyric The first known writings in literary Italian are the love lyrics of the Sicilian school, fostered at the court of the Emperor Frederick II (1194–1250), who was himself a poet and is included by Dante Gabriel Rossetti in his survey of 13th-c. Italian poetry. Sicilian poetry, drawing on Occitan traditions of courtly writing, is far more restricted in thematic and stylistic range than its models. This limitation, however, generates certain characteristic emphases which exerted an important influence over later Italian practice. The authors of these poems (often lawyers by training) manifest a keen interest in rhetoric (classical, vernacular, and even Arabic) and also at times proto-scientific propensities in their diction. The sonnet

seems to have been an invention of the Sicilian school, and was originally employed (as also by Dante and Cavalcanti) as a vehicle for epistolatory debate on love-questions between members of the coterie—as for instance in the *tenzone* between Pier delle Vigna, Lentini, and Mostacci, where, drawing analogies between love and effects of magnetism, the three poets consider whether love, being invisible, can really be said to exist at all.

Between the Sicilians and the *stil novo*, other schools of poetry develop. The most notable was dominated by Guittone d'Arezzo (*c.*1230–1294), whom Dante and Cavalcanti affected to despise for his strident over-complication of diction, for a lack of intellectual acumen, and for a concern with the political preoccupations of the nascent city-states. (Dante describes Guittone as a 'municipal' poet in the *De vulgari eloquentia*.) A single sonnet from Guittone's copious and varied output is translated by Rossetti, significantly a hymn to the Virgin Mary rather than one of Guittone's moral or political diatribes. The *stil novo*, distancing itself from Guittone's influence, looks back to the Sicilian school in its cultivation of an élite audience, and philosophical or scientific themes, while also advancing greatly in melodic finesse and refinement of diction. Chaucer seems to have known something of this school (reflecting the words of Guido Guinizelli's seminal *canzone* 'Al cor gentil rimpara sempre amore' in *The Knight's Tale* ii. 1761: 'pitee renneth soon in gentil hertes').

ii. Petrarch Within the Italian tradition, Petrarch (Francesco Petrarca, 1304–74), while attentive to many features of the *stil novo*, brought about a decisive change in the character of the love lyric,

eclipsing for centuries the achievements of his predecessors and introducing many of the tropes and
stylistic formulae which would characterize the literary language of Renaissance Italy, and equally stimulate a pan-European interest in the development of
vernacular verse. Where Dante accorded supremacy
among lyric forms to the *canzone*, Petrarch—experimenting in many of the lyric forms which were
ultimately to appeal as much to musicians as to
poets—established the sonnet as the principal vehicle for sentiments of love. The sonnet—once used
in correspondence between members of an intellectual coterie—becomes for Petrarch a medium in
which to trace prismatically the 'sighs' and 'weeping
discourses' of his inward self (*Rime* i. 2 and 5). But the
fluctuations of emotion and penitential conscience
recorded by Petrarch's *Rime sparse* (or 'scattered
rhymes') are accompanied by a conscious cultivation of an eloquent sonority which replaced the often
argumentative toughness underlying the 'sweetness' of Cavalcanti and Dante. A certain abstractness
of diction (evading descriptive reference), a high
degree of selectiveness in vocabulary, and a constant
attention to the musicality of rhythm and rhyme—
these are Petrarchan qualities which may not have
impressed the poets of the early 20th c. (unanimously
Dantean in their sympathies) but which certainly did
impress Petrarch's earliest readers.

The English engagement begins with the
isolated but brilliant instance of Chaucer, whose
interest in Petrarch (as also in Dante and Boccaccio)
is from the first particularly intelligent and critical.
In the Prologue to *The Clerk's Tale*, Chaucer recognizes the importance of Petrarch as a model of
vernacular eloquence, 'whose rhetorike sweete |
Enlumyned al Ytaille of poetrie' (ll. 32–3). Yet this
rhetorical view is pitched against the ribald argot of
the Host, insisting that the Clerk should avoid
'Heigh style': 'youre termes your colours and youre
figures' (ll. 15–18). Caution over Petrarchan rhetoric
is parralled in *Troilus and Criseyde* by creative freedom where in the first *canticus Troili* Chaucer offers
the first English translation of a Petrarchan sonnet,
selecting an instance strongly characterized by the
oxymoronic characteristics which became the hallmark of Petrarchism. Petrarch's sonnet 82 begins:

> S'Amore non è, che dunque è quel ch'io sento?
> ma s'egli è amore, per Dio, che cosa et quale?
> se bona, ond'è l'effetto aspro mortale?
> se ria, ond'è sì dolce ogni tormento?

Chaucer translates

> If no love is, O god, what fele I so?
> And if love is, what thing and which is he?
> If love be good from whennes cometh my woo?

> If it be wikke, a wonder thynketh me,
> Whenne every torment and adversite
> That cometh of hym, may to me savory thinke,
> for ay thurst I, the more that ich it drynke.

> (i. 404–10)

Chaucer's version is distinctly placed within a narrative setting as part of a diagnosis—conceivably even
a parody—of the Petrarchan love malady. Possibly
under French influence, the stanza form is changed
from sonnet to three seven-lined verses; the tensions and argumentative oppositions of the original
are dissipated but replaced by a character-voice,
dramatizing a self-indulgent melancholia. Substituting Petrarch's final 'e tremo a mezza state,
ardendo 'l verno', Chaucer offers an over-insistent,
even parodic, line—'for heet of cold for cold of hete
I dye'—where oxymoronic balances (meaning very
little) and a histrionic cadence replace the delicately
unbalanced grammar of *tremo* (an indicative)
against *ardendo* (a gerund) and the bleak, tragic
inclusiveness of 'burning in the winter'. Similar
effects of criticism and craft could be observed in the
lengthy translation of Boccaccio's original in the
canticus from *Troilus and Criseyde* v (ll. 638 ff.).

A hundred years after Chaucer, English poets
turned to Petrarch as much as to the classics in their
attempts to extend the linguistic competence of the
vernacular. The need was urgent, as will appear
from the following anonymous example from
Tottel's Miscellany of 1557, where the litheness of
rhythm, variation of stress, and skill in enjambement shown by Petrarch in the first sonnet of the
Rime sparse are coarsened into hefty alliterations
and poultering couplets:

> Voi ch'ascoltate in rime sparse il suono
> di quei sospiri ond'io nodriva 'l core
> in sul mio primo giovenile errore
> quand'era in parte altr'uomo da quel ch'io sono

> You that in play peruse my plaint, and reade in
>   rime the smart,
> Which in my youth with sighes full cold I harbourd
>   in my herte,
> Know ye that love in that frail age, drave me to that
>   distresse
> When I was halfe an other man, then I am now to gesse.

In the work of Sir Thomas **Wyatt** (1503–42) more
promising results ensue, but not without effort. Some
poems, such as 'My galley charged with forgetfulness', attempting fairly direct translation still betray a
need for technical instruction (though English critics
tend to applaud Wyatt's vigour of voice). Compare:

> My galley charged with forgetfulness
> Thorough sharp seas in winter nights doth pass

'Tween rock and rock; and eke mine enemy, alas,
That is my lord, steereth with cruelnesse.

with Petrarch's

> Passa la nave mia colma d'oblio
> per aspro mare a mezza notte il verno
> enfra Scilla e Caribdi et al governo
> siede 'l signore, anzi il nimico mio.

(*Rime* clxxxix)

Wyatt's rhyming is flaccid and undifferentiated; metrically, his lines require support from the ubiquitous 'eke'; an inattention to enjambement slackens the frenzy and disorientation which are Petrarch's moral theme in this poem; and 'forgetfulness'—for *oblio*—trivializes the issue which 'oblivion' would have come close to rendering. Yet in other poems Wyatt frees himself from the demands of translation and positively violates the Italian text, generating ambiguity and self-obsessions which can best be read in deliberate counterpoint with the original, nowhere more so than when, with subtle aggression, he renders Petrarch's delicately visionary 'Una candida cerva' (*Rime* cxc) as a poem wholly concerned with the dangers of sexual pursuit at the court of Henry VIII: 'Whoso list to hunt I know where is an hind' (ed. Rebholz, xi).

iii. Petrarchism Petrarch gave rise to Petrarchism. This movement in Italy took many forms, some of which emphasized the sober elegance which (in Bembo's eyes) made Petrarch a model for what the Italian language should be. Others—such as Serafino Aquilano—poet, singer, lutenist, composer, and favourite of Cesare Borgia—developed the latent vein of extravagance in Petrarch's conceits. Wyatt among others was capable of learning from these forms (as for example in Rebholz xxii, a *strambotto* based on an original by Serafino). Indeed, for a time in the 1560s and 1570s Petrarch's example was eclipsed by an interest in more contemporary Italian poetry such as Tasso's *Heroic Sonnets*. But a new and more complicated wave of Petrarchism began with Thomas **Watson**'s *Hecatompathia* of 1582. Here interest fell less upon the 'eloquence' which Petrarch's poetry exemplified—or upon exercises in direct translation—and more upon the architectonic of the *Rime sparse* and the ways in which ambitious sonnet-sequences might be constructed. Lodge, Constable, Daniel all followed suit. Finally, the morality inherent in Petrarch's writing could be either recorded (as in Spenser's *Visions of Petrarch* which are a version of Petrarch's *Rime*, xxx) or else rectified (as in Spenser's celebration of married rather than adulterous love in the

Amoretti). But in purely linguistic terms, the most interesting impact of Petrarch at this time was to raise, among the practitioners of an increasingly confident English tradition, a critical vein of anti-Petrarchism (which also had its equivalent in Italy). Daniel speaks of 'the muse of declined Italy'. But it is Sir Philip Sidney who provides the subtlest direct examples. Capable as he was of tackling in his double sestina of the *Arcadia* ('Ye Goatherde Gods') a virtuoso Italian form which had its origins in Petrarch, he was also to 'look in his heart', as he wrote, able to set himself apart from 'those that Petrarch's long deceased woes | with new-born sighs and denizened wit do sing'. The dangers of artificial eloquence are fruitfully revealed by inspection of the very Italy which gave birth to them.

iv. Cavalcanti and the *Stil Novo* Anti-Petrarchism of a later kind leads to a renewed interest in Petrarch's *stil novist* predecessors and above all in Dante, which was to run from the early 19th c. to the present day. Here Dante Gabriel **Rossetti** enters, giving a very full account of the 13th-c. Italian poetry. Rossetti's translations show marked attention to the original metre and a sensitivity both to the lightness and to the variety of diction which distinguishes early Italian poetry. However, he is unimpressed by the intellectual ambition and interest in technical terminology which is one of the most fertile characteristics of *stil novo* writing. He refuses to translate the most arduous of Cavalcanti's poems, 'Donna mi priega', recoiling from the 'scholastic pride' and the 'stiffness and cold conceits which prevail in this poetry'. Dante, Rossetti declares, displays a superior 'variety and personal directness'—which betrays Rossetti's own criteria while ignoring the extent to which Dante's mind, too, was in love with philosophy [for Dante's lyric poetry, see II.m.2.iii].

Ezra **Pound**, writing in 1910, acknowledges that 'in the matter of . . . Tuscan poetry, Rossetti is my father and mother', and purports to admire the qualities of Cavalcanti's verse which repel Rossetti: 'the perception of the intellect is given by the word, that of the emotions in the cadence. It is only, then, in perfect rhythm joined to the perfect word that the two-fold vision can be recorded' (*Translations*, pp. 20, 23). Pound proceeds to give intelligent comments on technical terminology: '*Gentile* is "noble"; "gentleness" in our current sense would be *soavitate*. *Valore* is "power". *Virtute*, "virtue", "potency", requires a separate treatise.' Finally, in his *Literary Essays* (pp. 153–4) Pound draws a polemical comparison between Petrarch and Cavalcanti, declaring that: 'in Guido the "figure", the strong metamorphic or "picturesque" expression is there with purpose to convey or interpret a definite meaning. In Petrarch it is ornament, the prettiest ornament that he could find, but not an irreplaceable ornament.'

In practice, Pound's translation of Cavalcanti seems incapable of freeing itself from conventions of rhythm and diction which he had inherited from Rossetti; and one would be hard put to justify these works as *personae*, as what Kenner calls 'interchanges of voice and personality with the dead' (Introduction to Pound, *Translations*, p. 14). Consider:

Chi è questa che vien che'ogni uom la mira,
che fa tremar di clarità l'aere.
E mena seco Amor, sì che parlare
Null'uom ne puote ma ciascun sospira.

Rossetti writes:

Who is she coming whom all gaze upon,
Who makes the air all tremulous with light
And at whose side is Love himself? that none
Dare speak, but each man's sighs are infinite.

In its fluency and command of unstressed syllables this is far preferable to Pound's version:

Who is she that comes, makying turn every man's eye
And makying the air to tremble with bright clearnesse
That leadeth with her Love in such nearness
No man may proffer of speech more than a sigh?

But later, Rossetti falters:

Cotanto d'umiltà donna mi pare,
Che ciascun d'altra in vêr di lei chiam'ira.

becomes

Lady she seems of such high benison
As makes all others graceless in men's sight.

Here the meaning of a term which is central to Cavalcanti's and Dante's moral scheme—*umiltà*—is lost, along with the contrasting violence and frustration of *ira* in a flurry of high-sounding archaisms. Equally, the bite of syntax (*Cotanto . . . che*) is smudged by a swooning emphasis on 'Lady' and by the alliterative tug which draws 'as' into association with 'benison' and 'graceless'. Pound is no better:

Such is her modesty, I would call
Every woman else but an useless uneasiness.

Here a lexical misogynism ensures that the great virtue of humility is replaced by its flirtatious little sister, 'modesty'; and a manly breadth of indignant generalization—relishing its own internal rhyme, 'useless uneasiness'—supplants the cold, even dispassionate articulation of the original.

Pound fares no better when he attempts to translate the philosophical *canzone* 'Donna mi priega' which he, unlike Rossetti, admired so greatly. Cavalcanti writes (following Pound's own Italian text):

In quella parte
        dove sta memoria
Prende suo state
        si formato
                chome
Diafan dal lume
        d'una schuritade
La qual da Marte
        viene e fa dimora
Elgli é creato
        e a sensato
                nome
D'alma chostume di chor volontade.

Pound translates:

In memory's locus taketh he his state
Formed there in manner as a mist of light
Upon a dusk that is come from Mars and stays,
Love is created, hath a sensate name,
His modus takes from soul, from heart his will.

It is not enough to sprinkle the text with words such as 'locus', 'modus', and 'sensate' to render the philosophical tenor of this passage, especially when the technical *diafan* or the hard conceptual quality stressed by rhyme in *volontade* is dissipated into impressionistic 'mist' and 'dusk' or lost in the lilt of 'from heart his will'.

Overall, the failure of Pound's translation arises from a mistrust of syntactical articulation (Cavalcanti's sentence is built around the comparative *sì come* and the rhythmically firm relative *la qual*. *Sì come* becomes the archaic and alliteratively melodic 'in manner'; *la qual* is lost—save again for an archaic and slightly arch cadence—in the centre of a line generating its own melodramatic atmosphere from emphases upon 'dusk', 'Mars', and 'stays'.) Likewise, Pound is inattentive to the philosophical weight attached throughout Cavalcanti's poems (and Dante's too) to modal verbs: the concluding emphasis on action, *viene a fa dimora*, is lost in the lingering of 'stays'. Among the many things that Dante learns from Cavalcanti is that 'seeing', 'moving', and 'being able' are the simple elements out of which the narrative action—of movement, surprise, and struggle—can be constructed, as in the *Commedia* [II.m.2]. If English poets have anything still to learn from early Italian poetry (and they do), it is that syntax can be as exciting, poetically, as any fine imagist phrase.   RK

CAVALCANTI AND THE STIL NOVO   Anderson, David, ed., *Pound's Cavalcanti*, Princeton, NJ, 1983 · Cirigliano, Marc A., *The Complete Poems of Guido Cavalcanti*, New York, 1992 · Lowry, Nelson, *The Poetry of Guido Cavalcanti*, New York, 1986 · Pound, Ezra, *The Translations of Ezra Pound*, ed. Hugh Kenner, London, 1963 · Rossetti, Dante Gabriel, *Poems and Translations 1850–1870*, Oxford, 1913; rep. 1959.

PETRARCH AND THE PETRARCHANS   Bergin, T., *The Sonnets of Petrarch*, Verona, 1965 · Chaucer, Geoffrey, *Troilus and Criseyde*, ed. F. Robinson, Oxford, 1957, pp. 394, 466 [trs. of Petrarch and Boccaccio] · *Troilus and Criseyde: 'The Book of Troilus' by Geoffrey Chaucer*, ed. B. Windeatt, London/New York, 1984 [with text of Boccaccio's *Filostrato*] · Cook, James Wyatt, *Petrarch's Song Book*, Binghamton, NY, 1995 · Mortimer, Anthony, ed., *Petrarch's Canzoniere in the English Renaissance*, Bergamo, 1975 · Musa, Mark, *Petrarch's Canzoniere*, Bloomington, Ind., 1996 [later World's Classics] · Nott, John, *Sonnets and Odes Translated from the Italian of Petrarch, with the Original Text and Some Account of his life*, London, 1777 [anon., rep., under Nott's name in 1808] · Shore, Marion, *For Love of Laura: Poetry of Petrarch*, Fayetville, Ark., 1987 · Spenser, Edmund, 'The Visions of Petrarch', in *Spenser's Minor Poems*, ed. Ernest de Selincourt, Oxford, 1910, pp. 282–5 · Tottel, Richard, ed., *Songs and Sonnets (Tottel's Miscellany)*, rev. edn. Hyder Edward Rollins, Cambridge, Mass., 1965 [1st edn., 1557] · Wyatt, Sir Thomas, *Sir Thomas Wyatt: The Complete Poems*, ed. R. A. Rebholz, London, 1978.

SEE ALSO   Watson, G., *The English Petrarchans: A Critical Bibliography of the Canzoniere*, London, 1967.

5. EPIC AND ROMANCE: PULCI AND BOIARDO

The two 15th-c. poets discussed here, Luigi Pulci and Matteo Boiardo, took as their subjects the Carolingian legends, to which Boiardo added an Arthurian content. Both Pulci's *Il Morgante* and Boiardo's *Orlando innamorato* (1495, Roland in Love) are not so much epics as chivalrous romances. A heroic and at times a solemn quality was added by Ludovico Ariosto [see II.m.6], whose completion of Boiardo's poem, the *Orlando furioso*, is more appropriately defined as a romantic epic. What all these poems and that of Tasso [II.m.7] have in common is that they are written in *ottava rima*, stanzas of eight lines rhyming *abababcc*.

The Carolingian cycle of legends had developed in Italy into popular entertainment, recitations in public squares by *cantastorie* who enthralled their audiences with rollicking accounts of battles, duels, treachery, and heroism. Linking the scattered stories was the unifying concept of Charlemagne and his Twelve Peers, divinely chosen to ensure the diffusion of the Christian faith. Such material, lodged in aural memories, was collected in written form by Andrea da Barberino, himself a *cantastorie*, in the form of a chronicle entitled *I reali di Francia* (The Royal House of France). The stories are still part of the repertoire of puppet shows in Sicily.

i. Pulci Luigi Pulci, a friend of Lorenzo de' Medici, was invited to write a poem to entertain Lucrezia Tornabuoni (Lorenzo's mother) and her court. He took up the story of Orlando (Roland) and combined with it fabulous stories of giants, enchantment, and buffoonery. The style is vigorous and racy, rich in Florentine idiom. *Il Morgante*, named after the giant character, was written in two forms,

the second, after an interval of several years and with an addition of five cantos relating the Battle of Roncesvalles, being entitled *Il Morgante maggiore* (1484, The Greater Morgante). The work is said to have been an important source for Rabelais [II.f.5.i].

Pulci, admired by Coleridge and Scott, also caught the fancy of **Byron**, who set himself to translate the poem. He did not get further than the first canto, which is perhaps just as well. His rhymes are forced and the rhythm bumpy, as, for example, in stanza 25, where the prior of a monastery tells Orlando that giants are throwing boulders at them from a mountain:

> Our ancient fathers living the desert in
> For just and holy works were duly fed;
> Think not they lived on locusts sole, 'tis certain
> That manna was rain'd down from heaven instead;
> But here 'tis fit we keep on the alert in
> Our bounds, or taste the stones shower'd down for
>   bread,
> From off yon mountain daily raining faster,
> And flung by Passamont and Alabaster.

It is evident that Byron is here not exerting himself to his best ability, for he used *ottava rima* more skilfully in his own mock-heroic poems, *Don Juan* and *Beppo*.

Leigh **Hunt** included a translation of four stanzas in his essay 'Pulci: His Life and Genius', and provided a brief prose paraphrase of the poem in 'Humours of Giants' and 'The Battle of Roncesvalles' in *Stories from the Italian Poets* (1846). Here is his skilful rendering of one of Pulci's playful and highly alliterative stanzas (xxiii. 47) describing conditions in a hermitage:

This holy hole was a vile thin-built thing,
Blown by the blast; the night nought else o'erhead
But staring stars the rude roof entering;
Their sup of supper was no splendid spread;
Poor pears their fare, and such-like libelling
Of quantum suff; their butt all but—bad bread;
A flash of fish instead of flush of flesh;
Their bed a frisk al-fresco, freezing fresh.

John Addington **Symonds** (1840–93) went further and did even better. His *Renaissance in Italy: Italian Literature*, part i (1906), contains excellent versions in rhymed octaves of 76 stanzas. Here, as an example, is part of his rendering of Margutte's defiant parody of the Creed (xviii. 115):

I believe in the tartlet and the tart;
One is the mother; t'other is her son:
The perfect paternoster is a part
Of liver, fried in slips, three two and one;
Which also from the primal liver start:
And since I'm dry, and fain would swill a tun,
If Mahomet forbids the juice of grape,
I reckon him a nightmare, phantom, ape.

It is a pity that Symonds did not persevere with the whole work. There has never been a complete English translation of *Il Morgante maggiore*.

ii. **Boiardo** Until recently this was true also of Boiardo's *Orlando innamorato*. In his *Renaissance in Italy* Symonds had provided renderings in rhymed octaves of 42 stanzas in his discussion of the art of Boiardo. John Cranfurd **Wordsworth** included over 175 stanzas, also in rhymed octaves, in his prose paraphrase of the poem, contained in *Adventures in Literature* (1929). Then in 1989 Charles Stanley **Ross** brought out his de luxe complete bilingual edition. Rejecting both the original rhyme scheme and the pentameter, Ross defended his choice as follows:

This translation seeks to . . . make [Boiardo] sound as noble as possible while still retaining the speed that makes reading him in the original such a pleasure. My choice of tetrameters allows a line-for-line translation without the need for padding. It also reproduces the feel of Boiardo's verse.

I have not adhered to the rhyme scheme of an ottava rima because I value Boiardo's text more than the external form he chose for his poetry. A poem written in stanzas inevitably calls attention to its own artificiality. Boiardo will seem strange enough without my forcing two sets of triple rhyme and a couplet into every eight lines.

These statements invite challenge. The unrhymed tetrameters chosen by Ross are without tradition in English prosody. On the other hand, the rhymed octave has gained an accepted place in English and has been used successfully for centuries. Harington used it for his rendering of *Orlando*

furioso [II.m.6], Fairfax for his translation of Tasso's *Gerusalemme liberata* [II.m.7]. Drayton used it for *The Barons' War* and *The Battle of Agincourt*, calling it 'the most complete and best proportioned' of all stanzas, especially suited for military subjects. William Browne used it for pastoral poetry. Keats used it for romantic narrative, in *Isabella*, Shelley used it for *The Witch of Atlas*, and Byron, as has been said, used it with skill in *Don Juan* and *Beppo*.

The Italian hendecasyllabic line has a near-equivalent in the English pentameter, the rhythm of which is related to English speech and bears a close resemblance to the stress pattern of the Italian. Both can be equally well modulated to admit of variation.

Ross speaks of the rhyme scheme of the *ottava rima* as 'external' to Boiardo's poetry. On the contrary, it is intrinsic to it. What Ross calls 'artificiality' is the form itself, a patterned structure of recurrence, giving pleasure as the anticipated rhyme falls on the ear with the effect of an echo, providing separateness and completeness to every stanza, yet linking them all in a continuous design.

The English four-foot line is traditionally associated with couplets or with the quatrain. The shape of the stanza on Ross's printed page arouses expectation of rhyme, which is left unfulfilled. Even more disconcerting are rhymes which Ross has introduced, at random, sometimes three in a stanza. The four-foot pulse provides speed certainly, but the lines are often ragged and broken-backed. The diction, too, is flat. Here is an example from the opening canto (stanza 18):

Ranaldo laughed, his face showed cheer;
'Report', he told the messenger,
'To Balugant, if he would like
To venerate the Christians, that
Whores in bed and, at dinner, gluttons
Most often get endearments from us,
But when our valour is on view,
Let each receive the honour due!'

Compare with this an unpublished version of the same stanza by Paul Ian Pritchard:

Ranaldo laughed, and smiling with good cheer
To the interpreter replied, 'Pray tell
King Balugante, since he's pleased to hear
How he should honour Christian people well,
That making merry, as he sees us here,
And making love, are things at which we excel;
But should we hear the noise of war's alarms,
We pay our debt of honour with our arms.'

This has a light, dancing quality. There is nothing forced about the rhymes; they make the stanza sing; and it captures the tone of the original.

Boiardo's style is sometimes rough and rollicking, but there are moments of delicacy and enchantment. One of these is the episode in Book I, Canto 18, where after a duel Orlando and the pagan king Agricane lie down to rest. Orlando looks up at the sky and remarks on its beauty (stanza 41). The renderings by Ross, Symonds, and Wordsworth may here be compared with the original:

E ragionando insieme tuttavia
Di cose degne e condecente a loro,
Guardava il conte il celo e poi dicia:
'Questo che or vediamo, è un bel lavoro,
Che fece la divina monarchia;
E la luna de argento, e stelle d'oro,
E la luce del giorno, e il sol lucente,
Dio tutto ha fatto per la umana gente.'

They talked together for a time
Of worthy and chivalric matters.
The Count, who watched the sky, then said,
'What we see is the lovely work
That was produced by heaven's monarch,
The silver moon, the golden stars,
The shining sun, the light of day,
God made them for the human race.'

(Ross)

Herewith the twain began to hold debate
Of fitting things and meet for noble knights.
The Count looked up to heaven and cried, 'How great
And fair is yonder frame of glittering lights,
Which God, the mighty monarch, did create:
The silvery moon, and stars that gem our nights,
The light of day, yea, and the lustrous sun,
For us poor men God made them every one!'

(Symonds)

And while they talked together, unafraid,
Of noble things becoming knights so bold,
The Count looked upward to the sky and said
''Tis a right glorious work that we behold,
This that the heavenly monarchy has made,
The moon all silver and the stars of gold,
The light of day, the sun's far-shining face;
All this has God made for the human race.'

(Wordsworth)

Of the three, the last is the most pleasing, as well as the most accurate. It may be noticed too how the rhymes enliven the meaning, especially in Wordsworth's version, where the word 'gold' is the more striking by being anticipated by the two previous rhymes, as in the original.   BR

BOIARDO, MATTEO   Ross, Charles Stanley, *Orlando innamorato*, Berkeley, Calif., 1989 · Symonds, John Addington, *Renaissance in Italy: Italian Literature*, pt. i, London, 1921, 411–27 · Wordsworth, J. C., 'Boiardo's *Orlando innamorato*', in his *Adventures in Literature*, London, 1929, 75–149.

PULCI, LUIGI   Byron, George Gordon, Lord, 'The Morgante Maggiore of Pulci', Canto I (tr. 1819–20), in *Complete Poetical Works*, ed. J. J. McGann, 5 vols., Oxford, 1980–6, vol. iv · Hunt, Leigh, 'Pulci, His Life and Genius', 'Humours of Giants', and 'The Battle of Roncesvalles', in his *Stories from the Italian Poets*, London, 1846 · Symonds, John Addington, 'Passages Translated from the *Morgante Maggiore* of Pulci', in his *Renaissance in Italy: Italian Literature*, pt. i, app. 5, London, 1906.

6. EPIC AND ROMANCE: ARIOSTO

i. Sixteenth to Eighteenth Century Following a pattern familiar from other early Italian texts, the first English translation of Ludovico Ariosto's *Orlando furioso* (1532) did not appear until relatively late (1591), although there is evidence of prior circulation of the poem in Tudor England, where it was an important source for Spenser's *Faerie Queen*, and in Scotland, where John **Stewart** of Baldyneiss reworked its central narrative in a poem of the 1580s [I.a.6.ii]. The first Englishman to take on the immense task of translating the *Furioso* was the Elizabethan courtier and wit Sir John **Harington** (1560–1612). (The legend that the translation was imposed on Harington by Elizabeth after he had first translated the lewd Canto 28 unfortunately has no historical basis.) Like most of Ariosto's subsequent English translators, Harington adopts the

metre of the original, *ottava rima*. His translation, however, is anything but literal, feeling itself at liberty to abbreviate 'matters impertinent to us' and 'tedious flatteries of persons we never heard of', as well as freely reworking the phrasing of the original ('it were simplicitie . . . to go word for word'). The result is a work quite distinct from the original, more robust and more directive of its readers, broader in its humour, less refined and allusive in its language, less airily speculative in its treatment of the 'marvellous'.

Harington's *Orlando* has been frequently derided (Ben Jonson flatly designated it 'under all translations the worst'). In recent criticism, however, it has tended to find a more sympathetic reception. Few would deny that the translation falls far short of the original in intellectual sophistication and stylistic refinement, or that Harington is uneven as a translator, and capable of moments of crassness. Nonetheless, certain of Harington's deviations from Ariosto now tend to be seen as determined by cultural difference rather than insensitivity, and he is given credit for the fluency and *élan* which make his version one of the most enduringly enjoyable translations of the *Furioso*, as well as one of its most historically interesting readings. At its best, moreover, Harington's translation is not merely dashing but precise, shadowing the inflections of the original with an attentiveness and intelligence few later translators have matched. An example is the fine opening stanza, in which Harington not only observes with great scruple the original's rhythms and emphases but flexibly recreates the alliterative patterning most modern translations have ignored.

> Of Dames, of Knights, of armes, of loves delights
> Of courtesies, of high attempts I speake,
> Then when the Moores transported all their might,
> On Africke seas, the force of France to breake:
> Incited by the youthfull heate and spight
> Of Agramant their king, that vowed to wreake
> The deathe of King Traiano (lately slaine)
> Upon the Romane Emperor Charlemaine.

Ariosto's fortunes suffered an eclipse in the later 17th c. and the first half of the 18th. From around 1750, however, interest in the *Furioso* revived, and the following 80 years saw three new complete translations of the work, as well as numerous partial ones. The first 18th-c. translator of the poem was William **Huggins** (1696–1761), a friend of the Italian critic Giuseppe Baretti and a sufficient enthusiast for Ariosto to have constructed a temple to the poet on his Hampshire estate. The interesting preface, by Temple Henry Croker, explains the work's aim of '[doing] honour to our language by naturalising the richest poetical book ever exhibited in the whole world', and expresses a fear that the translator's concern for fidelity may have resulted in a portrayal in the 'cold Dutch style', lacking the 'Italian fire' of the original. Croker's fears are not unfounded: doggedly literal, occasionally to the point of near-unintelligibility, and unfailingly pedestrian in its language, Huggins's translation conveys little of the grace of the *Furioso* and has no compensatory merits of its own.

The next translation, by John **Hoole** (1727–1803), also the translator of Tasso's *Gerusalemme liberata* [II.m.7], adopts an approach very different from that of Huggins, asserting the translator's right to take 'considerable liberties' in the interest of 'mak[ing] his author graceful to an English reader'.

Hoole's most striking liberty was, uniquely among English translators of Ariosto, to abandon the verse form of the original for a 'native' one, in this case the heroic couplet, whose appropriateness as a vehicle for a work of mixed register such as the *Furioso* the translator intelligently defends. Hoole's choice of metre has been much criticized, and it is true that his version of the *Furioso* differs radically from the original in pacing and emphasis. It is equally true, however, that Hoole's renunciation of the constraints of the octave, coupled with his breezy attitude to abridgement, allow him to move through the narrative with a debonair ease that at least distantly evokes the airiness of the original, avoiding the moments of overstuffing that afflict even the best of the octave translations. Hoole's *Orlando* is Ariosto 'lite', sacrificing much of the original's richness and tonal variety in its scamper through the plot, and dealing with linguistic difficulties by the simple expedient of omission. The popularity this translation enjoyed in its day is, however, a tribute to its zest and readability. Huggins's rendering of Rodomonte's invective against women (xxvii. 19) begins with the turgid quatrain:

> I think you were produc'd by Providence,
> O sex abominable, here below,
> For burden and a penalty immense,
> On man, who still without you joy would know …

In Hoole, the sentiment is condensed into a characteristically brisk couplet:

> O sex accurs'd—by God and Nature sent,
> A deadly bane to poison man's content!

ii. Nineteenth and Twentieth Century Hoole's reputation has suffered from Walter Scott's unpitying verdict: 'the noble transmuter of the gold of Ariosto into lead'. In reality, the epithet 'leaden' may more appropriately be reserved for the far more literal translation of Hoole's successor (and Scott's friend), William Stewart **Rose** (1775–1843). Rose's translation was a timely one, given the outdatedness, by this time, of Hoole's polite late Augustan idiom. It also represents an advance on previous translations where accuracy is concerned. This is all that may be said for it, however: fussy and laborious, larded with clumsy inversions, and frequently cloying in its straining after 'poetic' effects, Rose's translation represents at best a dogged crib of the original, and at worst an unintentionally comic travesty ('Of tears my ceaseless sorrow lacks supplies', Rose's Orlando cries in his incipient madness, 'They stopt when to mid-height scarce rose my pain').

Over a century separates Rose's from the next (equally lumpen and over-literal) English translation, that of Allan **Gilbert**. Two further prose versions have followed: the perfunctory crib of Richard **Hodgens**, and the more ambitious and successful translation of Guido **Waldman**, who justifies his choice of prose with a dismissive review of past attempts to lay the *Furioso* on the 'Procrustian bed of the "English'd octave" '. Waldman's scepticism must have seemed amply justified at the time of his writing. Soon afterwards, however, a new *ottava rima* translation of the poem was published, by Barbara **Reynolds**, prefaced by a committed defence of the English potentialities of this verseform [see II.m.5].

Reynolds's translation stands rather on the margins of later 20th-c. translation practice, as a verse translation of a 'classic' poem which nonetheless squarely presents itself as a translation, rather than an original work or a free adaptation. The result is an eminently readable work, reminiscent of Harington in its verve and relish, and displaying a familiarity with Italian idiom and a sensitivity to stylistic nuance which make it in certain respects more reliable than some of the more ostensibly faithful modern prose renderings. Whether it succeeds in its objective of redeeming the 'English'd octave' as a vehicle for Ariosto is a rather different matter. While it is certainly true that its use permits the retention, or evocation, of the characteristic rhythms of Ariostan narrative, the constraints of the verse form also appear to have motivated some of Reynolds's less happy and less Ariostan moments. In a stanza such as vi. 36, for example, describing Alcina drawing fish to the shore through her enchantments, Reynolds's spirited attempt to keep pace with Ariosto's dazzlingly exotic inventory of the enchantress's trawl is nevertheless impeded, in my view, by the inversion of the last line and the padding ('pleasurable to eat') of the fourth:

> The dolphins at her call come quickly leaping;
> The tunnys flounder, gasping, at her feet;
> Sperm whales and seals are started from their sleeping;
> Mullet and salmon, pleasurable to eat,
> Crowd in their hundreds, high and higher leaping;
> Pistrices, with the orcs, swim forth to meet
> The physiters, the grampuses and the whales
> In bulk gigantic and with thrashing tails.   VC

TRANSLATIONS   *Ane Abbregement of Roland Furious Translait out of Ariost*, in John Stewart of Baldynneis, *Poems*, ed. Thomas Crockett, Edinburgh, 1913 · *Orlando Furioso in English Heroical Verse*, tr. John Harington, London, 1591; rep. London, 1962, Oxford, 1972 · *Orlando Furioso*, tr. William Huggins, London, 1755 · *Orlando Furioso*, tr. John Hoole, London, 1783 · *Orlando Furioso*, tr. William Stewart Rose, London, 1823–31 · *Orlando Furioso*, tr. Allan Gilbert, New York, 1954 · *Orlando Furioso*, tr. Richard Hodgens, London, 1973– · *Orlando Furioso*, tr. Guido Waldman, Oxford, 1974 [World's Classics] · *Orlando Furioso*, tr. Barbara Reynolds, Harmondsworth, 1975 [Penguin].

SEE ALSO   Rich, T., *Harington and Ariosto: A Study in Elizabethan Verse Translation* (New Haven, Conn., 1940).

7. EPIC AND ROMANCE: TASSO

Torquato Tasso departed from Carolingian and Arthurian legends and chose instead the story of the First Crusade as the subject of his once immensely popular poem *Gerusalemme liberata* (1580–1, Jerusalem Delivered), in which his aim was to write a heroic, Christian epic. [For references to other works by Tasso, see II.m.1 and II.m.4.]

The *Gerusalemme* is much more difficult to translate than, say, Boiardo's *Orlando*. Tasso's style is elaborate, his diction latinized, his syntax complicated, his word order inverted, sometimes to the point of obscurity. The first attempt was made by Richard **Carew** in 1594. He completed only five cantos, about a quarter of the poem. He aimed at a strictly literal, line-for-line rendering, retaining the stanza form and an equivalent metre. When he allows himself some freedom, he attains a measure of beauty, but on the whole his version is considered a failure. It was eclipsed by the complete translation of Edward **Fairfax** (d. 1635). His aim was to english Tasso somewhat in the style of Spenser's *Faerie Queene* and in some passages he succeeded. Fairfax was not only a translator; he was a poet. His versification is smooth, controlled, and adorned with grace—a poem in its own right, recognized as a work of importance in Elizabethan literature. It is more florid in style than the original. There is a greater use of Biblical and classical allusions, and Fairfax takes it upon himself to stress the moral meaning of the poem more than Tasso himself does.

Despite the renown of Fairfax's version the *Gerusalemme* underwent several more translations. In the 18th c. a few translators of parts of the poem substituted heroic couplets for the octave. Philip **Doyne**'s complete version, *Delivery of Jerusalem*, is in blank verse, flat and not always faithful to the original. The most widely read of this period was

John **Hoole**'s version in couplets, shorter than the original and deliberately free [on Hoole's *Ariosto*, see II.m.6.i].

'My endeavour', Hoole wrote, 'has been to render the sense of my author as nearly as possible which could never be done merely by translating his words.' This is an excellent principle, especially for translation into verse. Hoole's translation was commended by Samuel Johnson, and indeed his use of couplets in the heroic metre captures much of the original. As C. P. Brand has pointed out, many of Tasso's octaves are constructed as four sections of two lines each. Here is Hoole's rendering of the first four lines of Canto 1 of Book III:

> Now from the golden east the zephyrs borne
> Proclaimed with balmy gales th'approach of morn,
> And fair Aurora deck'd her radiant head
> With roses cropt from Eden's flowery bed.

The technical difficulty with couplets is the proximity of the rhymes, resulting in long extracts in a monotony which the *ababababcc* pattern of the octave avoids. Hoole took the liberty of shortening several of the cantos, partly because the English language tends to be more compact than Italian and partly on moral grounds. His version, dominant for over 50 years, was read by Scott, Wordsworth, Southey, and De Quincey.

In the 19th c. eight more translations were published, one by J. H. **Hunt** in heroic couplets, and another by J. H. **Wiffen**, in the Spenserian nine-line stanza, a form requiring amplification of the original. J. R. **Broadhead**, using heroic couplets, aimed at a literal translation, reproducing the word order of the original, sometimes to strange effect. Two versions in unskilled octaves were produced by C. L. **Smith** and A. C. **Robertson**. A compromise stanza, rhyming *ababccdd*, was used by H. A. **Griffith** and the elegiac metre, rhyming *ababcdcd*, by J. K. **James**.

A recent translation in prose by Ralph **Nash** (1987), arranged in paragraphs numbered in relation to the stanzas, is a useful crib for students of the original. Nash aimed not only at accuracy but at enabling the reader to read smoothly and rapidly ('which I take to be one of the effects of the absence of rhyme'). The effect of the absence of stanzaic form and rhyme may be seen from the following. Here is Erminia lost in the forest in her pursuit of Tancredi (Canto 7, stanza 4):

She takes no food at all, for she feeds herself only on her misfortunes and is thirsty only for tears: but Sleep, who with his sweet oblivion is the repose and quiet of wretched mortals, lulled her sorrows along with her senses, and spread above her his wings, placid and still. Yet Love does not forbear with various shapes to trouble her peace while she lies sleeping.

This may be compared with Fairfax's:

> Her tears her drink, her food her sorrowings,
> This was her diet that unhappy night:
> But sleep, that sweet repose and quiet brings
> To ease the griefs of discontented wight,
> Spreads forth his tender, soft, and nimble wings,
> In his dull arms folding the virgin bright;
> And love, his mother, and the graces kept
> Strong watch and ward, while this fair lady slept.

The gap between J. K. James and Ralph Nash is a measure of the change in literary taste since the romantic era. The mixture of the heroic and the erotic appealed strongly to the sensibilities of early 19th-c. readers. The love stories especially made the *Gerusalemme*, as Leigh Hunt called it, 'a favourite epic of the young'. The tender and heroic love of Olindo and Sofronia, Erminia tremulous among the shepherds, the luxuriant description of Armida and her garden, the tragic death of Clorinda were favourite episodes not only among readers but also among painters. But there were critical voices too. Tasso was found contrived, artificial, and lacking in originality. Historical objections began to be raised, especially with a change in perspective concerning the Crusades. With a growing demand for realism, Tasso's romanticism was found excessive and his use of the supernatural no longer acceptable. The poem now has a hallowed place among classics which are studied by academics but left unread by others.   BR

TRANSLATIONS   *Tasso's Godfrey of Bulloigne* [5 cantos], tr. Richard Carew, Exeter, 1594; rep. Manchester, 1881 · *Godfrey of Bulloigne; or The Recoverie of Ierusalem*, tr. Edward Fairfax, London, 1600 [frequent reps.] · *The Delivery of Jerusalem. An Heroick Poem*, tr. Philip Doyne, 2 vols., Dublin, 1761 · *Jerusalem Delivered*, tr. John Hoole, London, 1763 [frequent reps.] · *Tasso's Jerusalem Delivered: An Heroic Poem*, tr. J. H. Hunt, London, 1818 · *Jerusalem Delivered*, tr. J. H. Wiffen, London, 1824 · *The Jerusalem Delivered of Torquato Tasso*, tr. J. R. Broadhead, London, 1837 · *The Jerusalem Delivered of Torquato Tasso*, tr. C. L. Smith, 2 vols., London, 1851 · *The Jerusalem Delivered of Torquato Tasso*, tr. A. C. Robertson, Edinburgh/London, 1853 · *Jerusalem Liberated*, tr. H. A. Griffith, Belfast, 1863 · *The Jerusalem Delivered of Torquato Tasso*, tr. J. K. James, Knt., 2 vols., London, 1865 · *Jerusalem Delivered*, tr. Ralph Nash, Detroit, 1987.

8. RENAISSANCE PROSE

i. Machiavelli The Italian Renaissance prose writer with the richest (if not the longest) translation history in English is Niccolò Machiavelli, whose *Il Principe* (1532, The Prince), in particular, must rate as one of the most frequently translated of all Italian works. The first writings of Machiavelli's to have been published in English were the relatively uncontroversial *Arte della guerra* (1521, Art of War) and *Istorie fiorentine* (1532, Florentine Histories). The *Prince* and *Discorsi* (1531, Discourses on Livy), by contrast, appear to have been banned from publication during the Elizabethan period, though translations of both circulated in manuscript (see Bibliography). The first published English translations of these works, both by the shadowy figure of Edward **Dacres**, date from 1636 and 1640. Collections of the principal works followed, by Henry **Nevile** (1620–94) and Ellis **Farneworth** (d. 1763).

Of these early translations, the most distinguished are by Dacres and Nevile. The former's are further remarkable for their rigorous fidelity to the letter of the text: not only does Dacres relegate his moral reservations to a set of marginal animadversions rather than allowing them to seep into the text, as do Nevile and Farneworth, but he also resists more than they do the temptation to improve on Machiavelli's style by rhetorical embellishments. Dacres's accuracy is not unfaltering (the centaur Chiron, for example, becomes a 'senator'), nor he does he always do justice to the more dramatic qualities of Machiavelli's prose. Overall, however, his translations of Machiavelli are deserving of their classic status, combining precision with an austere vigour of expression, and rising to the challenge of the more rhetorically heightened passages of the originals in a manner that has rarely been bettered.

The modern translation history of Machiavelli's works starts with Christian E. **Detmold** in 1882; recent translations are too numerous to discuss individually, especially those of *The Prince*. Of the general problems Machiavelli's political writings present to the modern English-speaking translator, two stand out: that of finding equivalents for a technical vocabulary whose ambiguities have been the focus of much recent scholarly analysis, and that of preserving the vividness and immediacy of Machiavelli's prose. The first of these problems has attracted a variety of solutions: some recent translations, for example (**Adams**, **Milner**), mark occurrences of the notoriously slippery term *virtù* in

parenthesis, while **Price** includes an appendix on Machiavelli's political vocabulary. The second problem appears to have engaged translators' attention rather less: few, with the exception of Adams and **Bull**, have attempted to convey the colloquiality of *The Prince*, while most tend to reduce Machiavelli's abrasive and energized style to something far more sedate, homogeneous, and conventional.

ii. Guicciardini Machiavelli's Florentine contemporary, the great historian and political thinker Francesco Guicciardini, enjoyed a reputation in Elizabethan and Jacobean England comparable to Machiavelli's own. A translation of Guicciardini's massive *Storia d'Italia* (1561, History of Italy), by Geoffrey **Fenton** (c.1539–1608), was published three times between 1579 and 1618; the same period also saw the publication of various abridgements and selections. Fenton's *Historie* derives from a French intermediary (Chomedy, 1568), which, however, is sufficiently faithful to have added no significant colouring of its own. The same cannot be said of Fenton's translation, which is notably free, and bears both the ideological and the stylistic imprint of Elizabethan culture, giving an anti-Catholic twist to Guicciardini's anti-clericalism, introducing patriotic and moralizing inflections at odds with the original's cool objectivity, and, most strikingly, transforming Guicciardini's soberly powerful architectonic prose with an injection of exuberant surface patterning.

Fenton must surely rank as the only reader of Guicciardini's *History* ever to have felt the work to be in need of expansion. The second English translator of the work, Austin Parkes **Goddard**, despite his stated intent to renounce elegance in the interests of fidelity, in fact abridges the text discreetly but consistently, massaging its weighty periods into a sleek and aphoristic sub-Gibbonian prose which entirely sacrifices the ruminative rhythms of the original. No translator since Goddard has attempted the massive task of translating the *History* in its entirety, though two partial modern translations exist: Cecil **Grayson**'s workmanlike translation of the first three books, and Sidney **Alexander**'s more stylistically ambitious and largely successful abridgement of the whole.

iii. Castiglione The third Italian writer of this period whose translation history is such as to deserve attention is Baldassare Castiglione, whose *Libro del cortegiano* (1528, Book of the Courtier) was the first major Italian prose work to receive an English translation (Thomas **Hoby**, 1561). Italian courtesy literature was a genre of compelling interest to Tudor readers, and this period also saw the translation of works such as Giovanni della Casa's *Galateo* (Robert **Paterson**, 1576) and Stefano Guazzo's *Civil conversazione* (Civil Conversation) (George **Pettie** and Bartholomew **Young**, 1581–6). Hoby's translation of Castiglione, however, deserves precedence on more than chronological grounds: though damned in the past with faint praises of its naïve charm and vigour, it has come to be regarded increasingly as a translation of remarkable quality, adhering to the translator's stated intent of 'folow[ing] the very meaning and woordes of the Author', but doing so with sufficient grace, energy, and idiomatic ease to stand up well as an autonomous work. Hoby's English is undoubtedly more colourful than Castiglione's Italian ('fools' become 'untowardely asseheads', the 'over-affectionate', 'too loving wormes'). To speak slightingly, however, of his 'crude Saxon idiom' (as one critic has done) is to misrepresent the complexity of the cultural operation involved in domesticating the original's profoundly foreign social and aesthetic ideals.

The *Courtier* received two further English translations in the early 18th c. The translations differ sharply in character: that of A. P. **Castiglione** has a solemn fidelity possibly attributable to family *pietas*, while the breezy and fluent version of Robert **Samber** shows fewer scruples about abridging and otherwise adapting the text to increase its attractions as a modern guide to manners. There are three 20th-c. English translations of *The Courtier*: Leonard **Opdycke**'s clean and accurate rendering; Charles **Singleton**'s version, heavily dependent on Opdycke; and George Bull's authoritative Penguin translation, which lives up well to its aim of putting *The Courtier* into 'fairly informal but still decorous English'. Bull's translation will supply the needs of most readers; some, however, may still prefer Hoby, whose translation has in some respects never been bettered. To take a deceptively simple phrase from the work's climactic hymn to divine love, 'tu le cose separate aduni', a glance through the dogged renderings of subsequent translators, from Samber's 'Thou bringest things separate into one Mass' to Bull's 'You join together the things that are separate', can only enhance by contrast the euphony and precision of Hoby's 'Thou bringest severed matters into one'.

iv. Cellini The works discussed so far enjoyed their greatest impact in England in the century or

so following their composition. A later discovery was Benvenuto Cellini's autobiography, first published in Italian in 1730, and an instant success throughout Europe for its picaresque brilliance and exceptional documentary interest. Translated into German by Goethe, Cellini received his first English translation from Thomas **Nugent** (1700–72). Thomas **Roscoe** (1791–1871) did little more than appropriate his predecessor's translation, correcting some of Nugent's numerous errors. The first genuinely new translation of Cellini to appear in the 19th c. was that of the Renaissance scholar and aesthete John Addington **Symonds** (1840–93), dashed off with a Cellini-like *sprezzatura* in four months. A vast improvement on the Nugent–Roscoe version in terms of accuracy, Symonds's lightly archaizing translation is also a work of stylistic distinction, effortlessly outclassing the two subsequent renderings of Anne **Macdonell** and Robert H. Hobart **Cust**. Cust aimed, unsuccessfully, to evoke in his version the original's demotic language and 'breathless and fiery incoherence' (Symonds). The more recent translation of George Bull—the most accurate to date and the first fully uncensored English version of the work—wisely settles instead for a colloquial but grammatically correct English.

v. Fiction Italian Renaissance fiction (if Cellini may be termed fact) has been less fortunate in its English translation history. This is not to say, of course, that it has been without influence: it is from Italian sources that the plots of *Romeo and Juliet, The Duchess of Malfi*, and *Othello* derive. However, although many Italian *novelle* were translated in Tudor and Jacobean England, this tended to take place in a piecemeal manner; moreover, such translations were often so free as to constitute independent works. The fortunes of the greatest Italian *novelliere* of the period, Matteo Bandello, are indicative. The closest Bandello came to an English translation in the 16th c. was Geoffrey Fenton's *Tragicall Discourses*, based on the French of Belleforest and Boaistuau (1558). Like his French predecessors' version, however, Fenton's contains only a selection of the *novelle*, stripped of the complex framing devices of the original, and so elaborated as to owe little to Bandello beyond the barest lines of their respective plots. More faithful translations of individual *novelle* were to follow, but for an integral translation Bandello had to wait until John **Payne**'s heavily archaizing version of 1890. The exercise has not been repeated, and Bandello remains one of the most important Italian writers unavailable in a modern translation.   VC

BANDELLO, MATTEO   *Certain Tragicall Discourses Written out of French and Latin*, tr. Geffraie Fenton, London, 1567 [rev. Hugh Harris, 1925] · *The Novels of Matteo Bandello*, tr. John Payne, London, 1890.

CASTIGLIONE, BALDASSARE   *The Courtyer*, tr. Thomas Hoby, London, 1561 [rep. in 20th c., e.g. Everyman] · *The Courtier*, tr. Robert Samber, London, 1724 · *Il Cortegiano, or The Courtier*, tr. A. P. Castiglione, London, 1727 [parallel text] · *The Book of the Courtier*, tr. Leonard Eckstein Opdycke, New York, 1901 · *The Book of the Courtier*, tr. Charles S. Singleton, New York, 1959 · *The Book of the Courtier*, tr. George Bull, Harmondsworth, 1967 [Penguin].

CELLINI, BENVENUTO   *The Life of Benvenuto Cellini*, tr. Thomas Nugent, London, 1771 · *Memoirs of Benvenuto Cellini*, tr. Thomas Roscoe, London, 1822 · *The Life of Benvenuto Cellini*, tr. John Addington Symonds, London, 1888 · *The Life of Benvenuto Cellini*, tr. Anne Macdonell, 2 vols., New York, 1903 · *The Life of Benvenuto Cellini*, tr. Robert H. Hobart Cust, London, 1910 · *The Autobiography of Benvenuto Cellini*, tr. George Bull, Harmondsworth, 1955 [Penguin].

GUICCIARDINI, FRANCESCO   *The Historie of Guicciardin*, tr. Geffray Fenton, London, 1579 · *The History of Italy from the Year 1490 to 1532*, tr. Chevalier Austin Parke Goddard, London, 1753–56 · *History of Italy and History of Florence*, tr. Cecil Grayson, ed. John R. Hale, New York, 1964 · *Maxims and Reflections of a Renaissance Statesman*, tr. Mario Domandi, New York/London, 1965 · *Selected Writings*, tr. Margaret Grayson, ed. Cecil Grayson, Oxford, 1965 · *The History of Italy*, tr. Sidney Alexander, Princeton, NJ, 1969 [abr.] · *The History of Florence*, tr. Mario Domandi, New York, 1970 · *Dialogue on the Government of Florence*, tr. Alison Brown, Cambridge, 1994.

MACHIAVELLI, NICCOLÒ   *The Arte of Warre*, tr. Peter Whitehorne, London, 1563; rep. 1905 · *The Florentine Historie*, tr. Thomas Bedingfield, London, 1595; rep. 1905 · *The Prince*, tr. William Fowler (1590s), in *The Works of William Fowler*, ed. Henry W. Meikle et al., 3 vols., Edinburgh, 1926–40 · *The Prince: An Elizabethan Translation* [anon.], ed. Hardin Craig, Chapel Hill, NC, 1944 · *Machiavel's Discourses upon the First Decade of T. Livius*, tr. Edward Dacres, London, 1636; rep. 1905 · *Nicholas Machiavel's Prince*, tr. Edward Dacres, London, 1640; rep. 1905 · *The Works of the Famous Nicholas Machiavel*, tr. Henry Nevile, London, 1675 · *The Works of Nicholas Machiavel*, tr. Ellis Farneworth, London, 1742 · *The Prince . . . to which is Prefixed an Introduction Shewing the Close Analogy between the Principles of Machiavelli and the Actions of Buonaparte*, tr. J. Scott Byerly, London, 1810 · *The Historical, Political, and Diplomatic Works*, tr. Christian E. Detmold, Boston, 1882 · *The Discourses of Niccolò Machiavelli*, tr. Leslie J. Walker, London, 1950 · *The Ruler*, tr. Peter Rodd, London, 1954 · *The Prince*, tr. George Bull, Harmondsworth, 1961 [Penguin] · *The Chief Works and Others*, tr. Allan H. Gilbert, Raleigh, NC, 1965 · *The History of Florence and Other Selections*, tr. Judith A. Rawson, ed. Myron P. Gilmore, New York, 1970 · *The Prince*, tr. Robert M. Adams, New York, 1977 · *The Portable Machiavelli*, tr. Peter Bondanella and Mark Musa, Harmondsworth, 1979 [Penguin; *The Prince* from this edn. subsequently rep. World's Classics] · *The Prince*, tr. Harvey C. Mansfield, Chicago, 1985 · *Florentine Histories*, tr. Laura F. Banfield and Harvey C. Mansfield, Princeton, NJ, 1988 · *The Prince*, tr. Russell Price, ed. Quentin Skinner, Cambridge, 1988 · *The Prince, and Other Political Writings*, tr. Stephen J. Milner, London, 1995 [Everyman] · *Discourses on Livy*, tr. Harvey C. Mansfield and Nathan Tarcov, Chicago, 1996.

SEE ALSO   Raab, F., *The English Face of Machiavelli: A Changing Interpretation 1500–1700*, London, 1964 · Scott, M. A., *Elizabethan Translations from the Italian*, Boston, 1916.

9. DRAMA SINCE GOLDONI

The translation of modern Italian drama raises interesting questions concerning both the choice of texts and the translation strategies employed. While some translation has aimed primarily to inform readers and students (e.g. Jane **House** and Antonio **Attisani**'s *Twentieth-Century Italian Drama*), more texts have been translated for performance reasons. Most recent translations aim to include performability within the text, at the expense of accuracy, and sometimes by means of double translation, a literal version from the Italian rendered into a stage text by a second translator. A number of English-speaking writers have acted as either direct or second translators (e.g. Henry **Reed** translated Ugo Betti's plays straight from the Italian while Willis **Hall** and Keith **Waterhouse** used an intermediary translation to provide a version of Eduardo De Filippo's *Filumena*).

The prolific dramatist and librettist Carlo Goldoni, 'father' of modern Italian drama, exponent of naturalism before its time, is known in English for a handful of his plays, the principal ones being *I servitori di due padroni* (1745, The Servant of Two Masters), *I gemelli veneziani* (1748, The Venetian Twins), *La locandiera* (1753, The Hostess), and *Il ventaglio* (1766, The Fan). Of these, *La locandiera* has attracted most attention. This play revolves around the innkeeper, Mirandolina, the focal attraction of the inn, whose charms ensure its success. Challenged by the presence of a mysogynist knight, she succeeds in conquering his aversion and his heart; she solves the problems her charms create by marrying an employee, Fabrizio, as her father had requested before he died. The play was written from a mysogynist perspective, Mirandolina being an example of women's wiles at the expense of gullible men, but some later interpreters provide a woman-centred perspective with Mirandolina as an example of mask-donning, game-playing behaviour. This interpretation is supported by the presence of two professional actresses as visitors to the inn, regrettably cut from Lady **Gregory**'s and Frederick **Davies**'s otherwise acceptable versions. Davies, like Ranjit **Bolt**, focuses attention by a translator's note on one of Mirandolina's speeches to the servant Fabrizio in Act I—'Son grata. Conosco il mio merito . . . Ma io non sono conosciuta' (literally 'I am grateful. I know my merit . . . But I am not known'), on which their interpretations of the play hinge. For Davies, Mirandolina is telling Fabrizio that 'she is not known sexually'; Davies sees the passage as an example of dramatic irony—Mirandolina does not know that she is in love with Fabrizio though Goldoni gives clues to the audience to convey that she is. Bolt thinks this speech highlights the ambiguity of the relationship between Mirandolina and Fabrizio, and suggests that if Mirandolina is sleeping with Fabrizio before the play begins she becomes a more interesting character for a modern audience—'an independent woman keeping her options open'. Bolt's lively, inventive, and economical version provides theatrical good fun; Clifford **Bax**'s earlier version provides the reader with a version closer to the Italian text.

The other two major 18th-c. dramatists have had less attention from translators into English. Vittorio Alfieri wrote several tragedies and one comedy; *Saul* is the most translated but there is nothing of note since 1870. Carlo Gozzi, Goldoni's Venetian rival, who was determined to vindicate the attractions of the masked *commedia dell'arte* criticized by Goldoni has fared better, especially in the late 20th c.

Italy's 19th-c. drama has received little attention, largely because much of it was influenced by the French, who provided better 'well-made plays'. Of 20th-c. dramatists Pirandello [II.m.12] is the best known and most translated. Translations by Henry Reed of some of Ugo Betti's stark plays, permeated with Christian symbolism, dramatizing the fallibility of human justice, were initially commissioned by the Third Programme of the BBC and later revised for stage production. Betti's austere, literary but deeply felt speech is well caught in Reed's and G. H. **McWilliam**'s versions.

Two later dramatists, Eduardo De Filippo and Dario Fo, offer the translator different problems. Harold Action has said that De Filippo's plays 'defy the translator's exertions'. This is because many of his compassionate and optimistic slices of Neapolitan life are presented in dialect or a mix of Italian (Tuscan) and Neapolitan. De Filippo stressed that his use of dialect had nothing to do with folklore (which he 'detested') and all to do with the reality of content, and his translators, Keith Waterhouse and Willis Hall, N. F. **Simpson**, Carlo **Ardito**, and Peter **Tinniswood**, have avoided dialect in their versions. Tinniswood shares De Filippo's attitude to dialect and in his adaptation of *Napoli Milionaria* (1945) aimed to create an impression of his native city Liverpool, which arguably best resembles the uniqueness of Naples, by catching the 'rhythms and rhymes and the lilt and swagger that reflect the verve and vigour' of his native city rather than transcribing the morphology of Liverpudlian dialect. All the plays in the De Filippo volume entitled *Four Plays* have withstood the test of radio or stage performance and read well.

Fo too offers the challenge of dialect, most notably in his subversive *Mistero buffo* (1969, Comic Mystery Play), based on medieval and later texts. Ed **Emery** provides a lively version in English. Fo's other most popular plays are hard-hitting satirical political farces written in a robust colloquial northen Italian. Initially conceived as radical comments on a contemporary political incident, they have become modern classics. These essentially Italian plays, full of references to Italian politics and customs, have been reshaped for the English stage by adapting the references to the English political scene. A challenge for the translator is to maintain the balance between biting satire and comic effect and not to succomb to solutions which are exclusively comic. Gavin **Richards**'s version of *Morte accidentale di un anarchico* (1970, Accidental Death of an Anarchist), popular in performance and influential on British political theatre, opted for comic and farcical choices in, for instance, the exaggerated disguise of the Maniac as Captain Piccinni in the second act. Of the four other versions, Emery is right in distinguishing his as 'close to Fo's original, maintaining the original references'. As Emery also notes, Fo's Italian gains its effect without the use of the many 'Very Rude Words' which English translators feel necessary to their versions. Fo himself has expressed the view that actors should themselves be 'authors'; Stuart **Hood**'s ideas on how to translate Fo reflect this view—'to provide a plain language text and to suggest that actors and directors should find their own solutions'; and Alan

Cumming's invitation to actor Tim Supple to co-translate *Morte accidentale di un anarchico* is another response to this notion. Some of the complexities of translating for the theatre can be most clearly seen when the playwright is also performer, as is the case with Dario Fo.   JL

ANTHOLOGIES   House, Jane, and Attisani, Antonio, *Twentieth-Century Italian Drama: An Anthology of the First Fifty Years*, New York, 1995.

BETTI, UGO   McWilliam, G. H., *Three Plays on Justice: Landslide; Struggle Till Dawn; The Fugitive*, San Francisco, 1964 · Reed, Henry, *Three Plays*, London, 1956; New York, 1958 [*The Queen and the Rebels, The Burnt Flower-Bed, Summertime*] · *Corruption in the Palace of Justice*, in *The New Theatre of Europe*, ed. Robert W. Corrigan, New York, 1962, and in *Classics of Modern Theatre*, ed. Alvin Kernan, New York, 1965 · *Crime on Goat Island* in *Masterpieces of the Modern Italian Theatre*, ed. Robert W. Corrigan, New York, 1967 · Rizzo, Gino, *Three Plays: The Inquiry; Crime on Goat Island; The Gambler*, New York, 1966.

DE FILIPPO, EDUARDO   Ardito, Carlo, *Four Plays*, London, 1992 [*The Local Authority, Grand Magic, Filumena Marturano*; and *Napoli Milionaria*, tr. Peter Tinniswood] · Bender, Robert G., 'Sik-Sik, The Masterful Magician', *Italian Quarterly*, 2 (1967) · Bentley, Eric, *Filumena Marturano* in his *Genius of the Italian Theatre*, New York, 1964 · Hall, Willis, with Keith Waterhouse, *Filumena*, London, 1978 · Simpson, N. F., *The Inner Voices*, Oxford, 1983 · Waterhouse, Keith, and Hall, Willis, *Saturday, Sunday, Monday*, London, 1974.

FO, DARIO   Cowan, Suzanne, *Accidental Death of an Anarchist*, *Theater*, 10, 2, 1979 · Cumming, Alan, and Supple, Tim, *Accidental Death of an Anarchist*, London, 1991 · Emery, Ed, *Accidental Death of an Anarchist* in *Plays: One*, ed. Stuart Hood, London, 1992 · Hood, Stuart, ed., *Plays: One*, London, 1992 [tr. Ed Emery, Joe Farrell, Stuart Hood, R. C. McAvoy, and A. M. Giugni] · *Plays: Two*, London, 1994 [tr. Joe Farrell, Gillian Hanna, Stuart Hood, and Lino Pertile, with Bill Colvill and Robert Walker] · Nelson, Richard, *Accidental Death of an Anarchist*, New York, 1987 · Richards, Gavin with Gillian Hanna, *Accidental Death of an Anarchist*, London, 1980.

GOLDONI, CARLO   Bax, Clifford, Farjeon, Eleanor, Farjeon, Herbert, and Rawson, I. M., *Three Comedies*, London, 1961 [*Mine Hostess, The Fan, The Boors*] · Bolt, Ranjit, *The Venetian Twins, Mirandolina*, Bath, 1993 · Davies, Frederick, *The Servant of Two Masters*, London, 1961 · *The Liar*, London, 1963 · *The Fan*, London, 1968 · *Four Comedies*, London, 1968 [*The Venetian Twins, The Artful Widow, Mirandolina, The Superior Residence*] · Dent, Edward J., *The Servant of Two Masters* in *The Classic Theatre I: Six Italian Plays*, ed. Eric Bentley, Garden City, NY, 1958 · Gregory, Lady Augusta, *Mirandolina* (1924) in *The Classic Theatre I: Six Italian Plays*, ed. Eric Bentley, Garden City, 1958 · Miller, John W., *The Comic Theatre: A Comedy in Three Acts*, Lincoln, Neb., 1969 · Zimmern, Helen, *The Comedies*, Westport, Conn., 1978 [rep. of 1892; *A Curious Mishap, The Beneficent Bear, The Fan, The Spendthrift Miser*].

GOZZI, CARLO   Bermel, Albert, and Emery, Ted, *Five Tales for the Theatre*, Chicago, 1989 [*The Raven, The King Stag, Turandot, The Serpent Woman*, and *The Green Bird*] · DiGaetani, John Louis, *The Love of Three Oranges, Turandot*, and *The Snake Lady*, New York, 1988 · Levy, Jonathan, *Turandot* in *The Genius of Italian Theatre*, ed. Eric Bentley, New York, 1964 · Wildman, Carl, 'The King Stag', in *The Classic Theatre I: Six Italian Plays*, ed. Eric Bentley, Garden City, NY, 1958.

10. LEOPARDI

Already in his lifetime Giacomo Leopardi was recognized by the discerning as a foremost Italian poet, and his ultimate renown as one of the great European poets of the early 19th c. remains unchallenged. The well-known difficulties of translating poetry are particularly acute in his case. He wrote at a time when the Italian language was undergoing a process of formation. An exceptionally learned scholar, deeply read in Greek and Latin, an admirer of Dante and especially of Petrarch, he strove to model his style on theirs. His aim was the achievement of two characteristics which he considered essential to poetry: simplicity and clarity. It took him many years to attain them. A legacy of rhetoric and formality is apparent in his early poems. In his striving for simplicity he has been compared with Wordsworth; and, as in the case of Wordsworth, what appears simple at a first reading is later revealed to be profound and complex.

What seems to be the earliest translation is found in an anonymous article of 1855 in *Blackwood's Magazine*. John Addington **Symonds** (1840–93) published versions of some of the *Canti* in *The Cliftonian* (1872), and Richard **Garnett** (1835–1906) in his *Italian Literature* (1895) included a translation of Leopardi's most famous lyric, 'L'infinito'.

The first complete English translation of Leopardi's *Canti*, by Geoffrey L. **Bickersteth**, appeared in 1923. Regrettably out of print, it offers the originals and verse translations on facing pages. They are preceded by three substantial introductory sections: 'The Poet's Life', 'The Poet's Art', and 'The Poet's Thought'. A section entitled 'Notes', consisting of 150 pages, two appendices, one on the structure of the *canzone*, and a bibliography complete this still unrivalled volume. A unique feature of Bickersteth's translation is that he perceives the *Canti* to be a single, coherent work of art. Written at different periods, they were arranged by the poet in a non-chronological order to which he attached importance. Bickersteth was also convinced of the indivisibility of form and meaning. For him, fidelity to the original entailed not only verbal accuracy but also, as near as possible, equivalence of form (metre, cadence, rhyme, sound, accent, rhythm, tone, and style).

Among later experiments are R. C. **Trevelyan**'s *Translations from Leopardi*, consisting of renderings of 14 out of a total of 34 *Canti*, plus a translation of a prose work, 'Dialogue between Torquato Tasso and his Familiar Spirit', and John **Heath-Stubbs**'s *Poems from Giacomo Leopardi*, consisting of translations of 17 poems, preceded by a brief introduction. Both these translators hold that strict adherence to the form of the original is a hindrance to the achievement of poetry and therefore better avoided.

J. H. **Whitfield**'s translation, *Leopardi's Canti*, advertised surprisingly in 1962 as the first complete version, is also in blank verse. It achieves a less poetic effect than Bickersteth and is for the most part somewhat pedestrian. The following two versions of the first seven lines of 'Il sabato del villaggio' show the effect of the disregard of rhyme.

> La donzelletta vien dalla campagna,
> In sul calar del sole,
> Col suo fascio dell'erba; e reca in mano
> Un mazzolin di rose e di viole,
> Onde, siccome suole,
> Ornare ella si appresta
> Dimani, al dí di festa, il petto e il crine.

> The village damsel coming from the fields
> At sunset homeward goes
> With her truss of hay, and bringing in her hand
> A nosegay of the violet and the rose,
> Wherewith she doth propose,
> As wonted, to adorn
> Upon the Sunday morn her breast and hair.
>
> (Bickersteth)

> The maiden from the countryside comes with
> The sunset, and she bears
> Her load of grass; and in her hand she brings
> A bunch of roses and of violets,
> With which, as she is wont,
> She means, tomorrow, for the festive day,
> To deck her bosom and her hair.   (Whitfield)

Jean-Pierre **Baricelli**, in *Giacomo Leopardi: Poems*, using what he calls 'poetic-prose translations', printed facing the original text, pays heed to struc-

ture and to some extent to rhyme and assonance. The effect is sensitive and pleasing. The introduction, though brief, is excellent.

An intriguing production, *Leopardi: A Scottis Quair*, was published in 1987 for the Italian Institute of Edinburgh. Beautifully printed, it contains two brief but excellent introductions, the first biographical, the second literary. The original texts of 12 poems follow, translated by various hands into English, Scots, and Gaelic, a creative experiment which only few can appreciate.

The most recent attempt at a translation of all the *Canti*, together with a selection of the prose, is by J. G. **Nichols**. In his view Leopardi is not only irreducibly foreign but also 'unlikeable'—a double challenge. Robert Cummings in his review in *Translation and Literature* (1997) finds it the most intelligent Leopardi in English and suggests that it will replace Bickersteth's version. It is early to pronounce but this could be shown only if Bickersteth's were brought back into print, as for many reasons it deserves to be. Two more attempts, in two successive years, by Eamon **Grennan** and Paul **Lawton**, both selections only, and with the original Italian *en face*, indicate that Leopardi, for all his difficulties, or perhaps because of them, acts like a magnet on present-day translators. Cummings considers that, of the three, Grennan is the most likely to draw the English reader to Leopardi.

In 1993 Alistair **Elliot** in *Italian Landscape Poems* offered a translation of three of Leopardi's poems: 'L'infinito', 'La sera del dì di festa' and 'La ginestra'. This delightful volume, containing translations of poems by 18 Italian poets (also with the originals *en face*), presents an impressive range of talent and skill. Elliot's masterly rendering of 'La ginestra' shows Leopardi as neither 'foreign' nor 'unlikeable'.

Leopardi's prose works, *Operette morali* and *Pensieri*, were first translated by James **Thomson**, the poet, author of *The City of Dreadful Night*. His *Essays, Dialogues and Thoughts of Giacomo Leopardi*, began to appear in the *National Reformer* in November 1867. The publication in volume form was prefixed by a biography. Thomson was much influenced by Leopardi and quoted from him in his own works. Next came the translation by Charles **Edwardes**, *Essays and Dialogues of Giacomo Leopardi*, also containing a biographical sketch. Patrick **Maxwell**'s *Essays, Dialogues and Thoughts of Count Giacomo Leopardi* followed in 1905, containing a biographical introduction and notes. The most recent, by Giovanni **Cecchetti** containing the *Operette morali* only, provides the original text facing the translation. BR

POEMS   Baricelli, Jean-Pierre, *Giacomo Leopardi: Poems Translated and with an Introduction*, New York, 1963 · Bicker-steth, Geoffrey L., *The Poems of Leopardi: Edited with Introduction and Notes and a Verse-Translation in the Metres of the Original*, Cambridge, 1923, New York, 1973 · Dunn, Douglas, et al., *Leopardi: A Scottis Quair*, Edinburgh, 1987 · Elliot, Alistair, *Italian Landscape Poems*, Newcastle upon Tyne, 1993 [bilingual] · Grennan, Eamon, *Giacomo Leopardi: Selected Poems*, Dublin, 1995 · Heath-Stubbs, John, *Poems from Leopardi*, London, 1946 · Lawton, Paul, *Canti*, ed. Franco Fortini, Dublin, 1996 · Nichols, J. G., *Leopardi: The Canti, with a Selection of His Prose*, Manchester, 1994 · Trevelyan, R. C., *Translations from Leopardi*, Cambridge, 1941 · Whitfield, J. H., *Leopardi's Canti Translated into English Verse*, Naples, 1962 [bilingual].

PROSE   Cecchetti, Giovanni, *Giacomo Leopardi. Operette Morali: Essays and Dialogues*, Berkeley, Calif., 1983 · Edwardes, Charles, *Essays and Dialogues of Giacomo Leopardi*, London, 1882 · Maxwell, Patrick, *Essays, Dialogues and Thoughts of Count Giacomo Leopardi*, Glasgow, 1905 · Thomson, James, *Essays, Dialogues and Thoughts of Giacomo Leopardi*, in *The National Reformer*, 1867 [in volume form, London, 1905].

11. NINETEENTH-CENTURY PROSE

Alessandro Manzoni and Giovanni Verga are the presiding figures of Italian fiction in the 19th c., a period which also includes some interesting lesser novelists—such as Nievo, De Roberto, Serao—much vivid autobiography, and the influential writings of Foscolo and the young d'Annunzio. The Risorgimento stimulated British interest in all things Italian, and the period has yielded much in the way of translation.

Verga's two great novels *I Malavoglia* (1881) and *Mastro-don Gesualdo* (1889) were quickly translated by Mary A. **Craig**. Both versions read easily enough and have some success in rendering the Sicilian colloquialisms which are characteristic of Verga's style; however, they are marred by some bizarre misunderstandings ('pizze' turning into 'little round cheeses'). It was not until the 1920s that Verga found his definitive translator in D. H. **Lawrence**, whose versions of *Master Don Gesualdo* and of the stories collected in *Little Novels of Sicily* (also known as *Short Sicilian Novels*) and *Cavalleria rusticana* (Rustic Chivalry) are among the masterpieces of English translation. Lawrence is precisely attentive to the fluidity of Verga's diction, as for instance when he turns 'dal confessionario rispondeva pacatamente una voce che insinuavasi come una carezza' into 'from the confession box came the placid reply of a voice that insinuates itself like a caress': 'placid' exactly catches the priest's ambiguous tranquillity, while 'insinuates' is one case where an Italian word rightly summons up its latinate sibling in English. Giovanni **Cecchetti**'s more recent rendering of the novel is, in comparison, gauche ('a calm voice that crept into her like a caress'); it is also spattered with errors. However Raymond **Rosenthal**'s translation of *I Malavoglia* (with the title *The House by the Medlar Tree*), in the same California series, is accurate and stylistically sensitive. Verga's early

works *Una peccatrice* (1866) and *Storia di una capinera* (1871) have recently been translated by, respectively, Iain **Halliday** (*A Mortal Sin*) and Christine **Donougher** (*Sparrow*).

Manzoni has yet to inspire a translator of Lawrence's distinction. *I promessi sposi* (1827) was foisted into English almost immediately; however, the Reverend Charles **Swan**'s *Betrothed Lovers* is a third shorter than the original and full of mistakes. Other versions soon followed, the best of which appeared anonymously in 1844 and was many times reprinted. Although sometimes literal to the point of awkwardness ('the man saw himself lost'), the 1844 translation reproduces something of the vigour and variety of Manzoni's prose; in this respect it is preferable to another anonymous version published the following year. The later translation was, however, the first to be based on the scrupulously 'tuscanized' second (1840–2) edition of the Italian text, and therefore included the new historical appendix, 'Storia della colonna infame' ('History of the Column of Infamy').

These early editions were reissued sporadically over the following century (an abridged *Betrothed* even appeared in 'The Amusing Library for Home and Railway' in 1867); however, there were no new versions until that of Archibald **Colquhoun** appeared in 1951. Colquhoun (especially in his later revisions) keeps very close to the original, is sensitive to register, and succeeds in bringing into English the contours of Manzoni's often involved syntax. In contrast, the other modern translation, by Bruce **Penman**, chops up Manzoni's sentences and reduces his various diction to a chatty level which soon becomes bland.

Of Manzoni's minor works, *Osservazioni sulla morale cattolica* (1819) was englished as *A Vindication of Catholic Morality* in 1836 because of its relevance to contemporary anxieties about the status of Catholics in Britain. *Del romanzo storico* (1831, On the Historical Novel) has been competently translated by Sandra **Berman**. 'Storia della colonna infame' exists in an elegant version by Kenelm **Foster** (1964), which has now been reprinted as an appendix to the latest edition of Colquhoun's *Betrothed* (1997).

The earliest piece of 19th-c. Italian prose to appear in English really belongs to the previous century: the *Vita* (1803, Life) of Vittorio Alfieri, a droll and energetic account of the eminent playwright's travels and amours. A serviceable, anonymous translation appeared in 1810: this has since been thoroughly revised by E. R. **Vincent**. The recollections of famous, usually political Italians continued to interest the English throughout the 19th c. Silvio Pellico's account of his 10 years' detention in Austrian prisons, *Le mie prigioni* (1832, My Prisons), was much read and talked about. Pellico's calm prose offers few challenges to the translator: of the 19th-c. versions, Thomas **Roscoe**'s is the best; there is also a faithful, plain rendering by I. G. **Capaldi**.

Another notable autobiography is that of the novelist, artist, and first prime minister of Italy Massimo d'Azeglio. His *I miei ricordi* (1867, My Recollections) was translated the following year, but has since appeared in a good scholarly version by E. R. Vincent. Giuseppe Mazzini's *Life and Writings* (1864–70) is an abridgement of the seven-volume Italian *Scritti* (1861–4) with added biographical material. Although long out of print, this book still offers the best English introduction to the life and works of the great revolutionary.

Ugo Foscolo's *Ultime lettere di Jacopo Ortis* (first edition 1799; definitive edition 1818, Last Letters of Jacopo Ortis), a cardinal text of European romanticism, gained its first, anonymous, rather stilted English version in 1814. No further translation appeared until Douglas **Radcliff-Umstead**'s in 1970. This, although it is based on the final Italian text, improves little on the 1814 rendering: Radcliff-Umstead tends always to moderate Foscolo's *élan*, diminishing *beatitudine*, for instance, into 'good-fortune'.

The minor novelists Francesco Guerrazzi, Antonio Bresciani, Giovanni Ruffini, and Salvatore Farina were all translated during the 19th c., but their books are now of little interest, at least for the English reader. Of more enduring value is *Le confessioni d'un italiano* (1867, The Confessions of an Italian Man) by Ippolito Nievo: this sprawling work,

which follows the life and one true love of a Venetian nobleman through 80-odd years of recent Italian history, was translated (and slightly abridged) for the first and only time by Lovett F. **Edwards** in 1954 as *The Castle of Fratta*. Likewise, Federico De Roberto's epic of 19th-c. Sicily, *I Viceré* (1894, The Viceroys), did not find a translator until 1962, when Archibald Colquhoun produced a readable version. Two novelists much translated at the turn of the century were Matilde Serao and Antonio Fogazzaro: the 1902 translation of Serao's *Conquista di Roma* (1885, The Conquest of Rome) has recently been reissued, while Fogazzaro's *Piccolo mondo antico* (1895, The Little World of the Past) exists in a competent version by W. J. **Strachan**. Perhaps the best introduction to many of these 'silver' novelists is the anthology *Italian Regional Tales of the Nineteenth Century*, edited by Archibald Colquhoun and Neville Rogers.

Italian literature at the end of the century was dominated by Gabriele d'Annunzio. He found an influential English admirer in Arthur **Symons** (1865–1945), who himself produced a version of *La città morta* (1895, The Dead City) for Heinemann, and watched over a series of d'Annunzio translations for the same publisher, including Georgina **Harding**'s rendering of *Il piacere* (1889, The Child of Pleasure). The recent surge of interest in decadence has prompted the reissue of this, as well as of Harding's version of *L'innocente* (1899, The Innocent). A volume of stories, *Nocturne and Five Tales of Love and Death*, has been well translated by Raymond Rosenthal. Two works by d'Annunzio's predecessor, I. U. Tarchetti, *Racconti fantastici* (1869) and *Fosca* (1869—the source of the Sondheim musical *Passion*) can now be read in interesting versions by Lawrence **Venuti**, as *Fantastic Tales* and *Passion* respectively.

The most translated piece of 19th-c. Italian prose, and not only translated but rewritten, continued, illustrated, Walt Disneyed and even turned into Basic English, is *Le avventure di Pinocchio* by Carlo Collodi (1883). M. A. **Murray**'s long-serving 1892 version is faithful and fluent, though to modern ears rather dated. The rendering by which it has largely been superseded, E. **Harden**'s, is quite accurate, though it tends always to mollify Collodi's often incisive diction. But it is the translation by Anne Lawson **Lucas** which, despite a few moments of awkwardness, brings the peccant marionette properly to life, as he tumbles unawares towards obedience and virtue, 'thinking great thoughts in his little head, and imagining all manner of castles in Spain'.

MR

ANTHOLOGIES   Colquhoun, Archibald, and Rogers, Neville, eds., *Italian Regional Tales of the Nineteenth Century*, London, 1961.

ALFIERI, VITTORIO   anon., *Memoirs*, London, 1810 [rev. edn., ed. E. R. Vincent, London, 1961].

COLLODI, CARLO   Harden, E., *Pinocchio*, London, 1944 [frequent reps.] · Lucas, Ann Lawson, *The Adventures of Pinocchio*, London, 1966 · Murray, M. A., *The Adventures of Pinocchio*, London, 1892.

D'ANNUNZIO, GABRIELE   Harding, Georgina, *The Child of Pleasure*, London, 1898; rep. London, 1991 · *L'Innocente: The Victim*, London, 1899; rep. London, 1991 · Rosenthal, Raymond, *Nocturne and Five Tales of Love*, London, 1988.

D'AZEGLIO, MASSIMO   Vincent, E. R., *Things I Remember*, London, 1966.

FOGAZZARO, ANTONIO   Strachan, W. J., *The Little World of the Past*, London, 1962.

FOSCOLO, UGO   anon., *The Letters of Ortis*, London, 1814 · Radcliff-Umstead, Douglas, *Ugo Foscolo's 'Ultime Lettere di Jacopo Ortis'*, Chapel Hill, NC, 1970.

MANZONI, ALESSANDRO   anon., *A Vindication of Catholic Morality*, London, 1836 · anon., *I Promessi Sposi The Betrothed*, London, 1844 · anon., *The Betrothed Lovers*, London, 1845 · Berman, Sandra, *On the Historical Novel*, London, 1984 · Colquhoun, Archibald, *The Betrothed*, London, 1951 [several further edns.] · Foster, Kenelm, *The Column of Infamy*, London, 1964 · Penman, Bruce, *The Betrothed*, London, 1972 · Swan, Revd Charles, *The Betrothed Lovers*, London, 1828.

MAZZINI, GIUSEPPE   anon., *Life and Writings*, London, 6 vols., 1864–70.

NIEVO, IPPOLITO   Edwards, Lovett F., *The Castle of Fratta*, London, 1957.

PELLICO, SILVIO   Capaldi, I. G., *My Prisons*, London, 1963 · Roscoe, Thomas, *My Imprisonments*, London, 1833 · Walker, Ann, *Le mie prigioni*, London, 1838.

ROBERTO, FEDERICO DE   Colquhoun, Archibald, *The Viceroys*, London, 1962; rep. London, 1989 · Symons, Arthur, *The Dead City*, London, 1900.

SERAO, MATILDE   Caesar, Anne, *The Conquest of Rome*, London, 1991.

TARCHETTI, IGINIO UGO   Venuti, Lawrence, *Fantastic Tales*, San Francisco, 1992 · *Passion*, San Francisco, 1994.

VERGA, GIOVANNI   Cecchetti, Giovanni, *Master-Don Gesualdo*, London, 1979 · Craig, Mary A., *I Malavoglia: The House by the Medlar Tree*, New York, 1890 · *Master Don Gesualdo*, New York, 1890 · Donougher, Christine, *Sparrow*, London, 1994 · Halliday, Iain, *A Mortal Sin*, London, 1995 · Lawrence, D. H., *Master Don Gesualdo*, London, 1923 [frequent reps.] · *Little Novels of Sicily*, London, 1925 [frequent reps.] · *Cavalleria Rusticana*, London, 1928 [frequent reps.] · Rosenthal, Raymond, *The House by the Medlar Tree*, London, 1964.

12. PIRANDELLO

Luigi Pirandello is best known in the English-speaking world as a playwright. All his plays have been translated, often for performance, though many are out of print and exist only in out-of-date versions. However, Pirandello first established his literary reputation in Italy as a novelist, short-story writer, and essayist; it was not until 1910 that he began to venture into the theatre, writing one-act plays in Sicilian dialect.

The novel that established Pirandello as a major writer was *Il fu Mattia Pascal*, first published in 1904. This was competently translated in 1923 by Arthur **Livingston**, who also translated several plays, as *The Late Mattia Pascal*. William **Weaver** published his translation in 1964 and Nicoletta **Simborowski** translated it for the third time in 1987. Other novels have been less successful: *L'esclusa* (1901, The Outcast) was translated by Leo **Ongley**, *Si gira* (1916, Shoot) by C. K. **Scott Moncrieff**, who also translated *I vecchi e i giovani* (1908, The Old and the Young), and *Uno, nessuno e centomila* (1925, One, No one, and a Hundred Thousand) was translated by Samuel **Putnam**. Putnam also brought out a trans-lation of 12 short stories by Pirandello in 1932 and was one of the leading Pirandello translators of his time.

With the exception of *The Late Mattia Pascal*, Pirandello's prose writing has largely disappeared without trace in English. This is not so much due to poor translations as to changes in the fortune of Pirandello himself. Most of the translations date from the period of the great Pirandello boom, the decade following the first production of *Sei personaggi in cerca d'autore* (Six Characters in Search of an Author) in 1921. By the early 1930s Pirandello was writing a different kind of play, mythical dramas with huge casts and magical realist plots, and international interest was beginning to wane.

The 1920s saw the translation of a great deal of Pirandello's output. In the United States, Elizabeth **Abbott**, Livingston, and Blanche Valentine **Mitchell** translated the one-act plays in 1928, and Livingston and Edward **Storer** had published their translations of *Six Characters . . .*, *Enrico IV* (1922, Henry IV), and *Così è (se vi pare)* (1917, Right You Are

(If You Think So)) in 1922. The following year, three more plays were translated by Livingston: *Ciascuno a suo modo* (1924, Each in His Own Way), *Il piacere dell' onestà* (1917, The Pleasure of Honesty), and *Vestire gl'ignudi* (1922, Naked), appearing in a single volume. After the high-water mark of the late 1920s translations began to decline, and very little was translated or performed in English for two decades. This may have been due to the change in taste that relegated Pirandello to the margins after a few years of intense international interest, or to the unpopularity of Mussolini's government, with which Pirandello had publicly aligned himself.

After World War II interest in Pirandello's theatre began to revive, due largely to the work of Frederick **May**, an Italianist at Leeds University, who single-handedly mounted a campaign to introduce Pirandello to English audiences. May not only translated plays, he also directed and performed in them, and endeavoured to promote Pirandello as a major 20th-c. writer. He brought out a translation of Pirandello's short stories in 1965, and his versions read far more fluently than the more stilted versions of earlier translators. In the 1950s May's campaign was joined by Robert **Rietti**, likewise a theatre practitioner, who is currently editing a definitive English translation of the complete works of Pirandello. In the United States, Eric **Bentley** has been a leading figure in the rehabilitation of Pirandello, translating and writing about Pirandello's theatre, following the lead set by Samuel Putnam.

One constant problem for translators of Pirandello is the difficulty presented by his titles. *Così è (se vi pare)* has been variously translated as *Right You Are (If You Think So), It is So (If You Think So)*, and as *And That's The Truth!*, the title of the first British production in 1925. In 1929 his play *Lazzaro* (1929) had its English première in Huddersfield, in a translation by Scott Moncrieff. A competition was held locally to decide on a title, and the one selected was *Though One Rose*, though Frederick May later published his own version entitled *Lazarus*. Some plays, such as *O di uno o di nessuno* (1929), which was translated (though never published) by May as *Either Somebody's or Nobody's*, have titles that sound awkward and confusing to English readers.

The copyright laws prevented a number of the plays being translated or performed until the late 1980s. Marta **Abba**, the actress for whom Pirandello had written several of his later works, held the translation rights, and had published her own translations of *I giganti della montagna* (1937, The Mountain Giants), *La nuova colonia* (1928, The New Colony), and *Quando si è qualcuno* (1933, When One Is Somebody) in 1958. These translations are almost unreadable, and certainly unperformable, but Abba refused for years to allow more talented translators to try their hand.

The history of translations of Pirandello's works into English is indeed Pirandellian in its intricacies. The pattern of translation activity is a random one, and very much dependent on individual personalities. Two plays have been translated and performed more frequently than all the others: *Six Characters . . . and Henry IV*, and both these plays are continually being retranslated by different writers; but most of his plays remain obscure and rarely performed or read. Pirandello himself had a low opinion of translators. In his famous essay *Illustrators, Actors and Translators* (1908) he accuses translators, along with actors and illustrators, of betraying the writer's text, and argues that the soul of a work can never be translated into any other language. SB

TRANSLATIONS Abbott, Elizabeth, Livingston A., and Mitchell, Blanche Valentine, *One-Act Plays*, New York, 1928 · Bentley, Eric, ed., *Naked Masks, Five Plays*, New York, 1952 · *Right You Are*, Columbia, NY, 1954 · *The Emperor* [Henry IV] in *The Genius of the Italian Theatre*, ed. Eric Bentley, New York, 1964 · *Pirandello's Major Plays*, Evanston, Ill., 1991 · Brown, E. Martin, ed., *The Rules of the Game*, tr. Robert Rietti, *The Life I Gave You; Lazarus*, tr. Frederick May, Harmondsworth, 1959 [Penguin] · Firth, Felicity, *The Mountain Giants*, in *The Yearbook of the British Pirandello Society*, 10, (1990) · Linstrum, John, *Six Characters in Search of an Author* [1925 text], London, 1979 · ed., *Three Plays*, London, 1985 · Livingston, Arthur, *Each in His Own Way and Two Other Plays*, London/New York, 1923 · *The Late Mattia Pascal*, London/New York, 1923 · May, Frederick, *Six Characters in Search of an Author*, London, 1954 · *A Dream (But Perhaps It Isn't), Stand*, 5, 3 (1959) · *The Man With the Flower in His Mouth*, Leeds, 1959 · *Luigi Pirandello: Short Stories*, London, 1965 · May, Frederick, and Reed, Henry, *Right You Are! (If You Think So); All For the Best; Henry IV*, Harmondsworth, 1962 [Penguin] · Mitchell, Julian, *Henry IV*, London, 1978 · Murray, William, *To Clothe the Naked and Two Other Plays*, New York, 1962 · *One-Act Plays*, New York, 1964 · Putnam, Samuel, *As You Desire Me*, New York, 1931 · *Tonight We Improvise*, New York, 1932 · Rietti, Robert, ed., *Collected Plays*, i, London, 1987 [tr. Robert Rietti and John Wardle, Gigi Gatti and Terry Doyle, Bruce Penman, Frederick May] · *Collected Plays*, ii, London, 1988 [tr. Felicity Firth, Henry Reed, Diane Cilento] · Storer, Edward, and Livingston, Arthur, *Three Plays of Pirandello*, London/New York, 1922.

13. TWENTIETH-CENTURY POETRY

i. General Tendencies 20th-c. Italian poetry appeared in English translation relatively late. It was not until the 1940s that brief selections surfaced with any frequency in British and American periodicals, typically accompanied by essays that surveyed current trends or offered appreciations of individual poets. Yet the 1952 *Oxford Book of Italian Verse* omitted the poets who were to become the major figures in English: Giuseppe Ungaretti, Salvatore Quasimodo, and Eugenio Montale. The first book-length translations of their work were not published until the late 1950s, long after they achieved canonical status in Italy and abroad. Quasimodo was awarded the Nobel Prize in 1959.

The time-lag meant that modern Italian poetry entered English when British and American literatures were enduring a mid-century reaction against modernism, a return to traditional poetic forms and a renewed interest in romantic expressivism. This fact of English literary history carried consequences for the translation of Italian poetry, shaping the selection of texts and the development of discursive strategies while forming a peculiar canon of poets—peculiar to the situation of English-language writing, not in complete conformity with Italian traditions and debates.

From the start, English translators tended to neglect modernist experimentation, the formal discontinuity, philosophical speculation, and political engagement characteristic of the avant-garde movements that dominated 20th-c. Italian poetry. Futurism, the great exemplar of modernist innovation in so many cultural traditions, seemed never to have existed for these translators. The first book-length versions of Filippo Tommaso Marinetti's radically disruptive poetry did not appear until the end of the century, and from academic publishers, presented as an object of scholarly research rather than the threat to Anglo-American poetic orthodoxies it might have been if issued earlier by a trade publisher.

The English-language reception of modern Italian poetry consistently favoured the personal, the autobiographical, cultivating a lyrical realism in translations that were immediately accessible and compellingly written for British and American readers. Italian poets like Ungaretti, Quasimodo, and Montale supported this tendency partly because in their long careers they gradually moved away from stylistic experiment toward a poetics of self-expression. In cases where romanticism was lacking, the translator's discursive strategies might supply it by making the verse more transparent, more evocative of an authorial presence.

ii. Ungaretti and Quasimodo Ungaretti entitled his collected poems *Vita d'un uomo* (1969, A Man's Life). Yet what made his earlier work seem so innovative in Italy was not a poet-centred theme, but the hard-edged language, a turn away from the ornate, rhetorical styles developed by decadent writers like Gabriele d'Annunzio. Ungaretti pioneered a modernist poetics of indirection, a combination of precise language, dense image, and abrupt line-break that was obscure enough to provoke the pejorative label 'hermetic' and powerful enough to be the most influential style in Italian poetry from the 1920s to the 1950s (*ermetismo*).

Allen **Mandelbaum**'s 1958 version adhered closely to the terse fragmentation of Ungaretti's Italian, but inflected it with a strain of late Victorian poeticism that heightened the emotion. Mandelbaum rendered *morire* as 'perish', *sonno* as 'slumber', *riposato* as 'reposed'. In his revised 1975 edition, an expanded selection with scholarly annotations, the academic format brought greater precision to the translating, and the poetical language was replaced by a plain register of current standard English: 'die', 'sleep', 'rested'.

Quasimodo, initially associated with the withdrawn lucubrations of hermeticism, later developed a more public poetry which dwelt, nonetheless, on the poet's personal experience. His writing attracted a variety of English versions, ranging from Edith **Farnsworth**'s uncertain treatment—at times literal, at others free, generally somewhat archaic—to Jack **Bevan**'s more adventurous approach in simple yet suggestive language. Quasimodo's surprising lines, 'il peso d'una vita | che sapeva di circo', became in Farnsworth 'the burden of a life | which seemed a carousel', but in Bevan 'the weight of a life | I knew circus-like', where the clipped syntax was very much akin to the hermetic experiment. Mandelbaum's Quasimodo was full of poetic resourcefulness in sound, lexicon, and linebreak:

> Come la schiuma s'avvinghia
> ai sassi, perdi il senso dello scorrere
> impassibile della destruzione.

> As the spume of the sea coils round the stones,
> you lose the sense of the impassive
> flow of the destruction.

iii. Montale and His Followers Montale's poetry has inspired not only the largest number of translations, but the full gamut of translation discourses in contemporary Anglo-American writing. Although Montale received the Nobel Prize in 1975, the watershed volume in his English canonization appeared a decade earlier: an ample selection from his first three books. This drew on the talents of 16 translators, leading poets as well as respected scholars, British, American, and Italian.

The versions have remained eminently readable, since the translators strove for poetic effects through pointed diction, interpolated phrases, even sheer rewriting. Maurice **English** rendered 'ha i segni della morte' ('has the signs of death') as 'bore death's stigmata', making the Italian more specific, more religious, and not a little sensational. Cid **Corman**, in contrast, sought to preserve Montale's elliptical style with an English that was remarkably precise, sonorous, and rhythmic: 'catene che s'allentano' ('chains that work loose') became 'chains easing off', while 'salti di tonni, sonno, lunghe strida | di sorci' ('leaps of tuna, sleep, long shrieks | of mice') became 'leaping tunny, sleep, squealings | of rats'.

The many translations of Montale make quite clear that English discourses for translating poetry were divided over the question of whether the translator should somehow reproduce the modernist differences of the Italian texts or assimilate them to the romantic expressivism prevailing in Anglo-American poetry. Robert **Lowell**'s solution was perhaps the most extreme. Because he translated foreign poems when his own inspiration flagged, he substantially revised Quasimodo and Montale ('I have dropped lines, moved lines, moved stanzas, changed images and altered meter and intent'), thereby transforming them into a contemporary American poet named Robert Lowell, fashioning, at least in theory, 'one voice running through many personalities, contrasts and repetitions' (Lowell 1961).

For translators of Montale like Corman and William **Arrowsmith**, the aim was not the domestication advocated by Lowell, but the preservation of foreign literary values that Ezra Pound sought in his experimental versions of various European and Chinese poetries [see e.g. II.f.2.iii, II.m.4.iv]. Arrowsmith's version of Montale's *The Occasions* 'resisted' any assimilation to Anglo-American poetic tastes by repressing 'the translator's temptation to fill in or otherwise modify Montale's constant ellipses, to accommodate *my* reader by providing smoother transitions'.

The literary authority that Montale acquired in English directed the attention of translators to the many poets he admired or influenced. Montale's own writing contained traces of *crepuscolarismo* (*crepuscolo* means 'twilight'), a *fin-de-siècle* trend that he found best exemplified in Guido Gozzano's ironic, introspective musings on mundane objects and events. During the 1980s Gozzano's poetry was rendered twice into English and in strikingly similar ways. The two translators, Michael **Palma** and J. G. **Nichols**, both recreated his private, conversational voice by resorting to rather free versions that imitated his rhymed stanzas.

Of course, English translators were not so much seeking Montalian echoes as the artful lyricism that he so well embodied. And the pursuit of this goal made available book-length translations of numerous lyric poets from different generations, including Attilio Bertolucci, Dino Campana, Margherita Guidacci, Mario Luzi, Valerio Magrelli, Sandro Penna, Lucio Piccolo, Umberto Saba, Vittorio Sereni, Leonardo Sinisgalli, Maria Luisa Spaziani, and Diego Valeri. These diverse poets were seen as modern, not modernist; some were recognized as more hermetic than others, but most were described as fashioning a poetry of personal expression. The translators explained their relationship to the Italian texts less in literary than in psychological terms, as an identification with a poetic sensibility, not an enthusiasm for a poetic form. A familiar Italian content or theme might also be attractive. The team of Ruth **Feldman** and Brian **Swann**, who rendered several poets of the southern Italian village and countryside (Vittorio Bodini, Bartolo Cattafi, Rocco Scotellaro), prefaced their version of Scotellaro's lyrics with the assertion that 'Ours was an emotional involvement' (Feldman and Swann 1979).

iv. Experiment and Innovation The romantic mainstream in Anglo-American translation most decisively affected the reception of Italian poetry by marginalizing the successive waves of post-World War II experimentalism. In the late 1950s an Italian 'neo-avant-garde' emerged to dominate the literary scene for the rest of the century. The many poets who comprised this broad trend returned to earlier modernist movements like Futurism and Surrealism, allied themselves to European intellectual traditions like marxism and psychoanalysis, and drew on such contemporary French developments as the *nouveau roman* and poststructuralism. The common thread was a highly discontinuous poetic discourse that explored the cultural and political conditions of human consciousness and action. Although the experiments took diverse forms and trajectories, the poets generally conceived of identity and representation as at once philosophical and social problems.

Thus not only were the experimental poetries difficult to translate because of their tampering with lexicon and syntax, but they also issued a radical challenge to the poet-centred aesthetic in Anglo-American poetry. In 1975, for example, Feldman and Swann daringly translated a selection of Andrea Zanzotto's polylingual montages, poems that force an attention upon the word as word while probing its mimetic and expressive functions. And they came upon inventive solutions, approximating Zanzotto's baby-talk evocations of preconscious thinking even at the level of sound:

E perché si è—il mondo pinoso il mondo nevoso—
perché si è fatto bambucci-ucci, odore di cristianucci,
perché si è fatto noi, roba per noi?

And why is it—the piney world the snowy world—
and why has the world become tiny totty-wotties, odor
    of human tots,
why has it become us, stuff for us?

Yet the translators found the poetry 'disturbing' because it 'ejects the reader forcibly from his habits'.

The experimentalism so frustrated the poetic expectations of most English-language readers that it received relatively little attention from translators and publishers. Two decades passed before another volume of Zanzotto's writing appeared in English. From the 1970s onward, translations of Italian experimentalists were issued by small publishers with limited distribution. Paul **Vangelisti** rendered several poets who had already achieved critical recognition in Italy, notably Adriano Spatola, Antonio Porta, and Giulia Niccolai. The crucial 1961 anthology *I novissimi* (The Newest), which aimed to consolidate a few experiments in poetry but wound up galvanizing Italian writers in every genre, was not translated into English until 1995.

The appearance of this anthology represented an important step in building a context in which English-language readers could understand and appreciate the postwar experimentalism. The inventive work of editor Alfredo Giuliani and his fellow contributors—Elio Pagliarani, Edoardo Sanguineti, Nanni Balestrini, and Porta—came across quite well in the careful English versions. The battery of translators—six altogether, including veterans like Vangelisti and the poet Luigi **Ballerini**—were determined to re-create the heterogeneity of the Italian texts, their sampling of different languages, discourses, and genres.

The prevailing romanticism in Anglo-American translation also played some part in delaying the appearance of two other innovative poets in English: Cesare Pavese and Pier Paolo Pasolini. In the decade following Pavese's death in 1950, his novels and stories were translated to critical acclaim, but almost 20 years passed before his poems were made available. The fact that he chose to write narrative poems, filled with details that were at once prosaic and enigmatic, ensured that they would not be immediately appealing to English-language readers with a preference for lyricism. It was precisely these unusual qualities, however, that William Arrowsmith managed to capture in the plain, colloquial language of his versions.

Pasolini's poetry presented its own difficulties, but it was similarly overlooked at first. Any readership that emphasizes the poet's personality would quickly look askance at his socially committed project, the creation of ambitiously imagined texts that combine neorealism with marxist theory, traditional poetic forms with cinematic techniques. Although by the 1960s Pasolini had achieved international renown for his novels and films, the first English-language selection of his poetry was not issued until 1982. Norman **MacAfee** and Luciano **Martinengo**'s translation avoids Pasolini's prosodic experiments, as well as his delicate poems in Friulian dialect. But the translators do offer a poetic version in a lively English that shifts easily among the varying tones and registers of Pasolini's rich Italian.

v. Anthologies Anthologies of translations have been extremely useful in introducing British and American readers to 20th-c. Italian poetry. In several instances, editorial agendas have helped to correct the partial image that was inevitably projected by books featuring the work of a single, canonized poet. Stanley **Burnshaw**'s anthology, *The Poem Itself*, took the novel approach of printing the Italian texts of various poets (Gozzano, Campana, Ungaretti, Montale, Saba, and Quasimodo) along with close translations and brief analytical essays. Carlo **Golino**'s anthology assembled 24 poets to trace the various movements in modern Italian poetry. In the late 1970s Feldman and Swann presented a broad survey of current trends that lacked a comprehensive introductory essay but included versions of emerging younger poets, such as Milo De Angelis. And Lawrence **Smith** published a bilingual selection of post-World War II poets organized according to earlier traditions (hermeticism, neorealism) and experimental departures (neo-avant-garde).

The Italian experimentalism has been particularly well served by anthologies, even though published by literary and academic presses and not readily available. Thomas **Harrison** documented post-*Novissimi* trends by gathering essays, lectures, and poems from a late 1970s conference that situated contemporary Italian poetry in the broader context of Continental philosophical literature, specifically Nietzsche and Heidegger. Justin **Vitiello** offered a unique glimpse into Italian poetry publishing by focusing his anthology on the list of a small Milanese press, Corpo 10.

The 1990s saw the publication of translation anthologies that mapped the latest developments. The selections were widely divergent yet complementary. Dana **Gioia** and Michael **Palma** gathered poets who in most cases could be assimilated to the prevailing romanticism in English-language poetry, whereas Luigi Ballerini emphasized recent experimental tendencies.

English-language readers approaching modern Italian poetry for the first time can learn much from Alessandro **Gentili** and Catherine **O'Brien**'s excellent anthology. The editors collected 44 poets from throughout this century, introduced them with a historical essay, and provided detailed biographical sketches. Best of all, the anthology was edited in a bilingual format, allowing the accurate translations to serve as effective guides to the Italian texts.

LV

ANTHOLOGIES   Ballerini, Luigi, ed., *Shearsmen of Sorts: Italian Poetry 1975–1993*, Stony Brook, New York, 1992 · Burnshaw, Stanley, ed., *The Poem Itself: 45 Modern Poets in a New Perspective*, New York, 1960 · Feldman, Ruth, and Brian Swann, eds., *Italian Poetry Today: Currents and Trends*, St Paul, 1979 · Gentili, Alessandro, and Catherine O'Brien, *The Green Flame: Contemporary Italian Poetry with English Translations*, Dublin, 1987 · Gioia, Dana, and Michael Palma, eds., *New Italian Poets*, Brownsville, Oreg., 1991 · Giuliani, Alfredo, ed., *I novissimi: Poetry for the Sixties*, Los Angeles, 1995 · Golino, Carlo, ed., *Contemporary Italian Poetry*, Berkeley/Los Angeles, 1962 · Harrison, Thomas J., *The Favorite Malice: Ontology and Reference in Contemporary Italian Poetry*, New York/Norristown/Milan, 1983 · Lowell, Robert, *Imitations*, New York, 1961 · O'Brien, Catherine, *Italian Women Poets of the Twentieth Century*, Dublin, 1996 · Smith, Lawrence R., *The New Italian Poetry, 1945 to the Present*, Berkeley/Los Angeles, 1981 · Vitiello, Justin, *Italy's Ultramodern Experimental Lyrics: Corpo 10*, New York, 1992.

BERTOLUCCI, ATTILIO   Tomlinson, Charles, *Selected Poems*, Newcastle upon Tyne, 1993.

BODINI, VITTORIO   Feldman, Ruth, and Swann, Brian, *The Hands of the South*, Washington, DC, 1980.

CAMPANA, DINO   Bonaffini, Luigi, *Orphic Songs and Other Poems*, New York, 1991 · Salomon, I. L., *Orphic Songs*, New York, 1968 · Wright, Charles, *Orphic Songs*, Oberlin, OH, 1984.

CATTAFI, BARTOLO   Feldman, Ruth, and Swann, Brian, *The Dry Air of the Fire*, Ann Arbor, Mich., 1981.

DE ANGELIS, MILO   Venuti, Lawrence, *Finite Intuition*, Los Angeles, 1995.

GOZZANO, GUIDO   Nichols, J. G., *The Colloquies and Selected Letters*, Manchester, 1987 · Palma, Michael, *The Man I Pretend to Be*, Princeton, NJ, 1981.

GUIDACCI, MARGHERITA   Feldman, Ruth, *Landscape with Ruins*, Detroit, 1993 · O'Brien, Catherine, *In the Eastern Sky*, Dublin, 1993.

LUZI, MARIO   Bonaffini, Luigi, *For the Baptism of Our Fragments*, Montreal, 1992 · O'Brien, Catherine, *After Many Years*, Dublin, 1990 · Salomon, I. L., *In the Dark Body of Metamorphosis*, New York, 1975.

MAGRELLI, VALERIO   Molino, Anthony, *Nearsights*, St Paul, Minn., 1991.

MARINETTI, FILIPPO TOMMASO   Napier, Elizabeth R., and Studholme, Barbara R., *Selected Poems and Related Prose*, New Haven, Conn., 1997 · Pioli, Richard J., *Stung by Salt and War*, New York, 1987.

MONTALE, EUGENIO   Arrowsmith, William, *The Storm and Other Things*, New York, 1986 · *The Occasions*, New York, 1987 · *Cuttlefish Bones*, New York, 1990 · Cambon, Glauco, ed., *Selected Poems*, New York, 1966 · Farnsworth, Edith, *Provisional Conclusions*, Chicago, 1970 · Galassi, Jonathan, *Otherwise*, New York, 1984 · *Collected Poems 1920–1954*, New York, 1998 · Kay, George, *Selected Poems*, Edinburgh, 1959 · Singh, G., *New Poems*, New York, 1976 · *It Depends*, New York, 1980 · Wright, Charles, *The Storm and Other Poems*, Oberlin, OH, 1978.

NICCOLAI, GIULIA   Vangelisti, Paul, *Substitution*, Los Angeles, 1975.

PASOLINI, PIER PAOLO   Ferlinghetti, Lawrence, and Valente, Francesca, *Roman Poems*, San Francisco, 1986 · MacAfee, Norman, with Luciano Martinengo, *Poems*, New York, 1982.

PAVESE, CESARE   Arrowsmith, William, *Hard Labor*, New York, 1976 · Crosland, Margaret, *A Mania for Solitude*, London, 1969.

PENNA, SANDRO   Di Piero, W. S., *This Strange Joy*, Columbus, OH, 1982 · Robinson, Blake, *Remember Me, God of Love*, Manchester, 1993 · Scrivani, George, *Confused Dream*, Madras/New York, 1988.

PICCOLO, LUCIO   Feldman, Ruth, and Swann, Brian, *Collected Poems*, Princeton, NJ, 1972.

PORTA ANTONIO   Molino, Anthony, *Kisses from Another Dream*, San Francisco, 1987 · *Melusine*, Montreal, 1992 · Vangelisti, Paul, *As If It Were a Rhythm*, Los Angeles, 1978 · ed., *Invasions*, Los Angeles, 1986 · Verdicchio, Pasquale, *Passenger*, Toronto, 1995.

QUASIMODO, SALVATORE   Bevan, Jack, *Complete Poems*, London, 1983 · Farnsworth, Edith, *To Give and To Have*, Chicago, 1969 · Mandelbaum, Allen, *Selected Writings*, New York, 1960.

SABA, UMBERTO   Millis, Christopher, *The Dark of the Sun*, Lanham, Md., 1994 · Sartarelli, Stephen, *Songbook: Selected Poems*, New York, 1998 · Stefanile, Felix, *Thirty-One Poems*, New Rochelle, NY, 1978.

SCOTELLARO, ROCCO   Feldman, Ruth, and Swann, Brian, *The Dawn Is Always New*, Princeton, NJ, 1980.

SERENI, VITTORIO   Perryman, Marcus, and Robinson, Peter, *Selected Poems*, London, 1989 · Vangelisti, Paul, *Sixteen Poems*, Los Angeles, 1971.

SINISGALLI, LEONARDO   Di Piero, W. S., *The Ellipse*, Princeton, NJ, 1982.

SPATOLA, ADRIANO   Vangelisti, Paul, *Majakovskiiiiiiij*, Los Angeles, 1975 · *Various Devices*, Los Angeles, 1978.

SPAZIANI, MARIA LUISA   Lettieri, Carol, and Jones, Irene Marchegiani, *Star of Free Will*, Toronto, 1996.

UNGARETTI, GIUSEPPE   Creagh, Patrick, *Selected Poems*, Harmondsworth, 1971 [Penguin] · Mandelbaum, Allen, *Life of a Man*, London/New York/Milan, 1958 · *Selected Poems*, Ithaca, NY, 1975.

VALERI, DIEGO   Palma, Michael, *My Name on the Wind*, Princeton, NJ, 1989.

ZANZOTTO, ANDREA   Feldman, Ruth, and Swann, Brian, *Selected Poems*, Princeton, NJ, 1975 · Welle, John P., and Feldman, Ruth, *Peasant's Wake for Fellini's Casanova and Other Poems*, Urbana, Ill., 1997.

SEE ALSO   Molinaro, J. A., 'American Studies and Translations of Contemporary Italian Poetry, 1945–1965: An Historical Survey and a Bibliography', *Bulletin of the New York Public Library*, 72 (1968), 522–58 · Venuti, L., *The Translator's Invisibility: A History of Translation*, London/New York, 1995.

14. TWENTIETH-CENTURY PROSE

English translations of 20th-c. Italian prose were often motivated by the critical acclaim that individual writers achieved at home and abroad. Yet the works chosen for translation also satisfied the distinctive tastes and curiosities of English-language readers, reflecting in various ways the trends that prevailed in contemporary Anglo-American culture. The Italian prose that appeared in English did in fact sample most of the key literary developments in Italy. But it was inevitably a partial representation, far from comprehensive and decisively shaped by domestic interests that were formal as well as thematic, commercial as well as cultural and political. These interests were served at the level of the sentence, in the use of translation strategies that made Italian writing not just intelligible, but familiar to different linguistic and cultural constituencies by adhering to the most common dialect of English.

i. 1900–1946 Between 1900 and 1946 approximately 80 Italian novels and story collections were published in translation, offering a broad cross-section of the current scene. The most frequently translated writers at the turn of the century included the immensely prolific Matilde Serao, whose tales of Neapolitan life treated sensational themes like lottery winners and chorus girls, frustrated political ambitions and marital infidelity; Gabriele d'Annunzio, whose decadent fiction proved to be as notorious as his unconventional sexuality and his daring military exploits; and Grazia Deledda, whose simple yet moving narratives portrayed strong female characters in her native Sardinia. English-language readers gravitated toward melodrama, but they also nurtured a veritable ethnographic fascination with Italy. Reviewers praised Deledda's debut in English, the novel *Dopo il divorzio* (1902, After the Divorce), as a perfect example of regional realism. In 1926 she won the Nobel Prize for Literature, although by that point her work had stopped appearing in translation.

In the 1930s, as Italian politics took a repressive turn, translators and publishers favoured varieties of fiction that were more socially engaged and, in some cases, more formally innovative. The most frequently translated writers now included Ignazio Silone, whose scathing left-wing critiques of the Fascist regime focused on the hard lives of southern Italian peasants, and Alberto Moravia, whose scandalous accounts of bourgeois sexual morality were regarded as bold challenges to Mussolini's censors. The same decade saw increased attention paid to Luigi Pirandello's novels and short stories, previously eclipsed by the experimental plays that earned him the Nobel Prize in 1934 [II.m.12], and to Italo Svevo's wryly sophisticated narratives, whose combination of modernist techniques and psychoanalytic themes had been championed by James Joyce.

During this early period, English versions were fairly representative of the Italian texts while sometimes shifting between different translating strategies. Kassandra **Vivaria**'s translation of d'Annunzio's novel *Il fuoco* (1900, The Flame) typically resorts to various freedoms to enhance readability. She simplifies his elaborate syntax by breaking suspended periods into smaller units, makes additions for clarification (as in her title, *The Flame of Life*), and occasionally inserts a colourful expression, rendering *l'ultimo supplizio* ('the ultimate punishment') as 'the scaffold'. Yet at points she takes the opposite tack and adheres quite closely to the Italian, producing an English equivalent that seems foreign compared to the fluent domestication she pursues for great expanses of the text.

The translating was definitely more free than literal, and it succeeded in communicating the overall sense of the Italian. Gwenda **David** and Eric **Mosbacher**'s version of Silone's novel *Fontamara* (1933) contains some freedoms that were apparently designed to make Silone's political ironies immediately comprehensible in English. They maintain a lively plain register of current usage, smooth out the syntax, and insert phrases that are clarifying or even colloquializing. The narrator's abrupt denunciation of Piedmontese novelties—'Le sigarette? Si possa soffocare chi le ha fumate una sola volta' ('The cigarettes? Anyone who's ever smoked them can suffocate himself')—is made more continuous and intensified: 'and as for the cigarettes, those who've smoked them may choke for all we care'. The drive for accessibility sometimes results in English cliché. David and Mosbacher transform Silone's simple declaration, 'Egli era molto prudente' ('He was very prudent'), into a Shakespearean allusion: 'The man certainly thought discretion the better part of valour.'

Even a stylistically rich work like Svevo's *La conscienza di Zeno* (1923, Confessions of Zeno) might be rendered with sufficient latitude to bring it closer to Anglo-American culture. As a result, Beryl **de Zoete**'s version, still the only one in English, has remained highly readable for many decades. Her freedoms are not always so consequential, as when she turns 'il mio stomaco si contorcesse' ('my stomach was twisted') into 'I felt horribly bad inside'. And she does add some evocative details, expanding Svevo's curt 'Si volse e uscí' ('He turned and left') into 'He turned on his heel and went out'. Yet the scientific themes of the novel are less pronounced in English because de Zoete occasionally deletes technical terms in favour of more commonly used expressions. A particularly suggestive passage like Zeno's address to himself as an infant—'inconscio, vai investigando il tuo organismo alla ricerca del piacere' ('unconscious, you go on investigating your organism in search of pleasure')—is given a homely familiarity: 'poor innocent, you continue to explore your tiny body in search of pleasure'.

ii. 1947–1969 After World War II, the volume of Italian prose translated into English increased rapidly. Between 1947 and 1969 British and American publishers issued approximately 250 Italian novels, short-story collections, and works of literary non-fiction. The most frequently translated writers included Alberto Moravia, who continued to explore the sexual dimensions of Italian social and political life; Cesare Pavese, whose unsettling narratives depicted class and regional divisions by fusing realistic techniques with mythopoeic motifs; and Giovanni Guareschi, whose humorous sketches about a village priest's triumphs over a Communist mayor became immediate bestsellers. English-language readers were especially drawn to nuanced representations of Italian society that invited emotional involvement. Yet Guareschi's success demonstrated that they also delighted in simplistic writing that confirmed their political values as the ideological differences between the West and the Soviet Union hardened into the Cold War.

During this period, a canon of modern Italian prose emerged in English, and at its centre stood realism. To be sure, the Anglo-American interest in this literary form corresponded to a dominant trend in Italy, notably the so-called neorealism that revived late 19th-c. models like Giovanni Verga's impersonal *verismo* to examine social conflicts. And although generally realistic, the prose chosen for translation was extremely diverse. It included novels of the anti-Fascist resistance by Italo Calvino, Carlo Cassola, and Vasco Pratolini; Carlo Levi's mixture of autobiography and social commentary, *Cristo si è fermato a Eboli* (1945, Christ Stopped at Eboli); tales of strained marital relations by Alba de Céspedes and by Natalia Ginzburg; Giuseppe Tomasi di Lampedusa's bestselling historical novel about the demise of the Sicilian aristocracy, *Il gattopardo* (1958, The Leopard); Pier Paolo Pasolini's documentary-like narratives of the Roman working-class poor; and Giorgio Bassani's elegiac portrait of Italian Jews under Mussolini's racial laws, *Il giardino dei Finzi-Contini* (1962, The Garden of the Finzi-Continis).

Nonetheless, in emphasizing realism, translators and publishers selected Italian works cast in the form that has long dominated British and American fiction, finding their own tastes matched in Italy. When Ernest Hemingway introduced Elio Vittorini's novel *Conversazione in Sicilia* (1941, In Sicily), he explicitly set aside the Italian writer's political commitment to praise his skill in communicating the 'knowledge' and 'experience' that Hemingway considered the source of his own fiction.

The realistic canon of Italian prose in English led to the neglect of more innovative writing. Although Dino Buzzati's Kafkaesque parable, *Il deserto dei Tartari* (1940, The Tartar Steppe), and Calvino's amusing chivalric fables were translated, they were not yet greeted by English-language readers with the same enthusiasm they enjoyed in Italy. Other Italian writers who abandoned realism fared worse. Tommaso Landolfi's challenging work, at once wildly fantastic and philosophically speculative, earned the admiration of Italian critics in the 1930s, but the first book-length selection of his stories did not appear in English until some 30 years later. Anna Maria Ortese's novel *L'iguana* (1965, The Iguana), a grotesque exploration of class and gender relations that echoes Shakespeare and Kafka, waited 20 years to be published in translation by a small press. Little of the radical experimentalism that characterized Italian prose in the 1960s has been made available in English.

Still, the emphasis on realistic fiction did coincide with greater precision and consistency in the translating. Leading Italian writers such as Moravia were reissued in more accurate versions indicative of their canonical status. And fluent translation became the standard because it produced an illusory effect of transparency that reinforced the verisimilitude of the texts. Thus, whereas Aida **Mastrangelo**'s 1932 version of Moravia's novel *Gli indifferenti* (1929, The Indifferent Ones), resorted to literalisms, rendering the opening line, 'Entrò Carla', simply as 'Carla entered', Angus **Davidson**'s 1953 version was more free, adding concrete details that supported the realism of the narrative: 'Carla came into the room.' Throughout, Davidson's writing was not only seamlessly idiomatic, but briskly conversational.

A fluent translation discourse undoubtedly contributed to the commercial success of Guareschi's anti-Communist satires. Yet translators and publishers also assimilated his prose to Anglo-American codes and ideologies. The English version by Una Vincenzo **Troubridge** of Guareschi's first book, *Mondo piccolo: Don Camillo* (1948, The Little World of Don Camillo), offered comic relief from the postwar fear of Soviet subversion by using a lexicon that was both topical and exaggerated. His routine references to *frazioni* of Italian Communists became more ominous 'cells', suggesting a clandestine group involved in espionage. And the mayor and his associates were further stigmatized through the recurrent use of pejoratives like 'henchmen' and 'gang' to translate Italian words that were neutral or in fact positive: *banda* ('group') and *fedelissimi* ('most loyal').

With innovative writing, fluent translation yielded mixed results. When confronted with the multiple dialects and the dense literary and historical allusions that distinguish Carlo Emilio Gadda's novel *Quer pasticciaccio brutto de Via Merulana* (1957, That Awful Mess on Via Merulana), William **Weaver** relied on 'straightforward spoken English' and inserted explanatory footnotes. These strategies made his version engaging yet limited in reproducing Gadda's virtuoso effects. Fluency better suited Calvino's lucid fiction, so that Weaver's translations played an indispensable role in the canonization that it subsequently attained in Anglo-American culture. He turned the Italian writer's playful fantasies into English that was exceedingly felicitous. His version of *Le cosmicomiche* (1965, Cosmicomics), wherein Calvino aimed to humanize the most abstract scientific concepts, emulated the witty experiment by developing a slangy lexicon. Common Italian expressions—'Vedrà che ci si trova bene' ('You'll see how well you'll get along'), 'Mica storie' ('[It is] not a lie'), 'Se ci stai, stella' ('If you stay with us, beautiful')—were replaced by charming English colloquialisms: 'You'll be nice and snug', 'No fooling', 'If you're game, sweetie'. Weaver's translation won the National Book Award in 1968.

iii. Since 1970 Between 1970 and the closing years of the century, the volume of Italian prose translated into English decreased slightly as British and American publishers issued approximately 250 works. Their choices continued to be dominated by diverse forms of realism. The most frequently translated writers now included Primo Levi, whose powerful tales recounted his own and others' experiences as prisoners in Nazi extermination camps; Dacia Maraini, who scrutinized the sometimes brutal constraints under which contemporary women lived; Leonardo Sciascia, who represented various aspects of Sicilian culture while deploying genres like the mystery and the historical novel to question the nature of representation; and Antonio Tabucchi, whose subtle narratives exploited points of view to probe the vagaries of human subjectivity. At the same time, translators inspired by the feminist agenda of restoring forgotten women writers rediscovered the work of Sibilla Aleramo, Anna Banti, and Grazia Deledda. The favourable reception accorded to William Weaver's translation of Elsa Morante's *La storia* (1974, History), a novel about Rome during the 1940s, indicated the sustained vitality of domestic interests that had motivated many postwar translations of Italian prose.

All the same, more recent fascinations deepened and led to new and unexpected developments. Calvino's success guaranteed that virtually all his books—fiction, literary criticism, and autobiographical essays—would appear in English. It also signalled an increasing sophistication among English-language readers which encouraged translators and publishers to relaunch neglected fantasists like Buzzati and to introduce younger innovators like Paola Capriolo. And the Italian novels that became bestsellers in English, although very different in form and theme, appealed to a mass audience because they made use of popular genres. The romance informed Oriana Fallaci's *Un uomo* (1979, A Man), a fictional account of her affair with a hero of the Greek resistance, while Umberto Eco framed his meditation on intellectual freedom, *Il nome della rosa* (1981, The Name of the Rose), as a murder mystery set in a medieval monastery.

During this period, translation reached a high level of accomplishment. Translators generally cultivated fluent discourses in current usage, seeking simultaneously to communicate the literary values of the Italian texts and to solicit the English-language reader's vicarious participation. With Eco's learned novels, the translating process involved significant rewriting. Weaver's version of *The Name of the Rose* omitted more than 12 pages of the Italian, including lengthy catalogues of medieval terms and Latin passages. The deletions improved the intelligibility and continuity of the narrative and thereby strengthened the realist illusion, no doubt helping the translation to reach the bestseller list.

Other translators, while relying mostly on standard English to ensure easy readability, experimented with different dialects and styles. Patrick **Creagh**'s version of Tabucchi's *Sostiene Pereira* (1994, Declares Pereira) mimicked the conversational tone of the Italian by using slang, turning 'un personaggio del regime' ('a figure in the regime') into 'bigwig' and 'sono nei guai' ('I'm in trouble') into 'I'm in a pickle'. Similarly, Liz **Heron**'s version of Capriolo's *Vissi d'amore* (1992, I Lived by Love, or Floria Tosca) (1992, Floria Tosca), a retelling of Puccini's opera from the villainous baron's point of view, imitated the Italian writer's 19th-c. style by using archaisms, turning 'ti autorizzo' ('I authorize you') into 'I give you leave' and 'giudicato' ('judged') into 'deemed'. Heron's enhancements of the period flavour invited reflection on the similarities and differences between Capriolo's baron and the diabolical heroes of the English gothic tradition. The resourcefulness of such translating promises to make readers more open to innovative prose and more aware of the translator's crucial intervention.

Although anthologies devoted to modern Italian fiction did not begin appearing until mid-century, they have consistently provided illuminating surveys of the main trends. In the 1950s Marc Slonim edited what long remained the most comprehensive selection, including 34 writers accompanied by incisive critical prefaces. Several decades later Kathrine Jason presented a wide-ranging selection of 26 writers that included major contemporary figures as well as others who were once welcomed in English but subsequently fell into neglect, such as Vitaliano Brancati and Luigi Malerba. The latest developments were admirably represented by Ann and Michael Caesar's selection of 22 younger writers, some of whom were appearing in English for the first time.   LV

Anthologies   Caesar, Ann, and Caesar, Michael, eds., *The Quality of Light*, London, 1993 · Jason, Kathrine, ed., *Name and Tears and Other Stories*, St Paul, Minn., 1990 · Johnson, Ben, ed., *Stories of Modern Italy from Verga, Svevo, and Pirandello to the Present*, New York, 1960 · King, Martha, ed., *New Italian Women*, New York, 1989 · Slonim, Marc, ed., *Modern Italian Short Stories*, New York, 1954 · Trevelyan, Raleigh, *Italian Short Stories*, Harmondsworth, 1965 [Penguin].

Aleramo, Sibilla   Delmar, Rosalind, *A Woman*, London, 1979.

Banti, Anna   Caracciolo, Shirley D'Ardia, *Artemisia*, Lincoln, Neb., 1988.

Bassani, Giorgio   Quigley, Isabel, *The Garden of the Finzi-Continis*, London, 1965.

Brancati, Vitaliano   Kean, Vladimir, *Antonio the Great Lover*, London, 1952.

Buzzati, Dino   Hood, Stuart, *The Tartar Steppe*, London, 1952 · Venuti, Lawrence, *Restless Nights*, San Francisco, 1983.

Calvino, Italo   Colquhoun, Archibald, *The Path to the Nest of the Spiders*, London, 1956 · *Baron in the Trees*, London, 1959 · Creagh, Patrick, *The Uses of Literature: Essays*, San Diego, Calif., 1986 · Parks, Tim, *The Road to San Giovanni*, New York, 1993 · Weaver, William, *Cosmicomics*, New York, 1968 · *If On a Winter's Night a Traveller*, New York, 1979.

Capriolo, Paola   Heron, Liz, *Floria Tosca*, London, 1997.

Cassola, Carlo   Quigley, Isabel, *Fausto and Anna*, London, 1960.

Céspedes, Alba de   Frenaye, Frances, *The Best of Husbands*, New York, 1952.

d'Annunzio, Gabriele   Bassnett, Susan, *The Flame*, London, 1991 · Vivaria, Kassandra, *The Flame of Life*, London, 1900.

DELEDDA, GRAZIA   King, Martha, *Cosima*, New York, 1988 · Lansdale, Maria Hornor, *After the Divorce*, New York, 1905 · Steegman, Mary G., *The Woman and the Priest*, London, 1922.

ECO, UMBERTO   Weaver, William, *The Name of the Rose*, San Diego, Calif., 1983 · *Foucault's Pendulum*, San Diego, Calif., 1989 · *The Island of the Day Before*, New York, 1995.

FALLACI, ORIANA   Weaver, William, *A Man*, New York, 1980.

GADDA, CARLO EMILIO   Weaver, William, *That Awful Mess on Via Merulana*, New York, 1965.

GINZBURG, NATALIA   Frenaye, Frances, *The Road to the City*, London, 1952 · Low, D. M., *Voices in the Evening*, London, 1963 · *Family Sayings*, London, 1967.

GUARESCHI, GIOVANNI   Frenaye, Frances, *Don Camillo and His Flock*, New York, 1952 · Troubridge, Una Vincenzo, *The Little World of Don Camillo*, New York, 1950.

LAMPEDUSA, GIUSEPPE TOMASI DE   Colquhoun, Archibald, *The Leopard*, London, 1960.

LANDOLFI, TOMMASO   Rosenthal, Raymond, Longrigg, John, and Young, Wayland, *Gogol's Wife and Other Stories*, Norfolk, Conn., 1963.

LEVI, CARLO   Frenaye, Frances, *Christ Stopped at Eboli*, New York, 1947.

LEVI, PRIMO   Rosenthal, Raymond, *The Periodic Table*, New York, 1984 · Woolf, Stuart, *If This Is a Man*, London, 1966.

MALERBA, LUIGI   Weaver, William, *The Serpent*, New York, 1968.

MARAINI, DACIA   Kitto, Dick, and Elspeth Spottiswood, *Voices*, London, 1997 · Williams, Siân, *Isolina*, London, 1993.

MORANTE, ELSA   Weaver, William, *History: A Novel*, New York, 1977.

MORAVIA, ALBERTO   Davidson, Angus, *The Time of Indifference*, London/New York, 1953 · Mastrangelo, Aida, *The Indifferent Ones*, New York, 1932.

ORTESE, ANNA MARIA   Martin, Henry, *The Iguana*, New York, 1987.

PASOLINI, PIER PAOLO   Capouya, Emile, *The Ragazzi*, New York, 1968 · Weaver, William, *A Violent Life*, London, 1968.

PAVESE, CESARE   Flint, R. W., *Selected Works*, New York, 1968 · Sinclair, Louise, *The Moon and the Bonfire*, London, 1952.

PIRANDELLO, LUIGI   Mayne, Arthur, and Henrie Mayne, *Better Think Twice About It*, London, 1933 · Putnam, Samuel, *The Horse in the Moon*, New York, 1932 · *One, None, and a Hundred Thousand*, New York, 1933.

PRATOLINI, VASCO   anon., *A Tale of Poor Lovers*, London, 1949.

SCIASCIA, LEONARDO   Bardoni, Avril, *The Wine-Dark Sea*, Manchester, 1985 · Foulke, Adrienne, *Candido: or, A Dream Dreamed in Sicily*, New York, 1979.

SERAO, MATILDE   anon., *The Ballet Dancer and On Guard*, London, 1901 · Ranous, Dora Knowlton, *The Conquest of Rome*, London, 1902.

SILONE, IGNAZIO   David, Gwenda, and Mosbacher, Eric, *Fontamara*, London, 1934 · *Bread and Wine*, London, 1936 · Mosbacher, Eric, *Fontamara*, rev. edn., London, 1985.

SVEVO, ITALO   De Zoete, Beryl, *Confessions of Zeno*, New York, 1930.

TABUCCHI, ANTONIO   Creagh, Patrick, *Declares Pereira*, London, 1995 · Parks, Tim, *Indian Nocturne*, London, 1988 · Thresher, Janice, *Letter from Casablanca*, New York, 1986.

VITTORINI, ELIO   David, Wilfrid, *In Sicily*, New York, 1949.

SEE ALSO   Keenoy, R., and Conte, F., *The Babel Guide to Italian Fiction in English Translation*, London, 1995 · Luciani, V., 'Modern Italian Fiction in America, 1929–1954: An Annotated Bibliography of Translations', *Bulletin of the New York Public Library*, 60 (1956), 12–34 · Shields, N. C., *Italian Translations in America*, New York, 1931 · Venuti, L., 'The Art of Literary Translation: An Interview with William Weaver', *Denver Quarterly*, 17 (1982), 16–26 · Weaver, W., 'Pendulum Diary', *Southwest Review*, 75 (1990), 150–78.

n. Latin

1. INTRODUCTION

The English literary tradition of translation from the Latin classics is as old as English literature itself, and many of the greatest English writers have been contributors to it. But a much larger number of translations from the Latin has been published in the 20th c. than in any previous era, partly because of the rapid decline in knowledge of the Latin language soon after the Victorian period. It is important to understand one fundamental difference between modern and earlier translations: most pre-20th-c. Latin translators take for granted at least a working knowledge of the source text on their reader's part, whereas ignorance is now assumed. There are exceptions to this rule, but much English translation from Latin literature could be historically described in terms of a long tradition of 'dialogue' between Latin and English writers, in which a Latin work forms a starting-point known to both writer and reader from which a new English work is (when things go well) creatively developed, followed by a period in which the typical translation is a practical guide to a text for those who cannot read it in the Latin.

But the latter condition is not irremediable, and the modern parallel-text edition is often designed for students of Latin. The most significant modern series of such editions has been the Loeb Classical Library, founded by James Loeb in 1912, now published by Heinemann and Harvard University Press, covering practically all extant Latin literature, and still issuing new and revised volumes. The translations, invariably in prose and by classical scholars, are unpretentious but reliable 'cribs', devoid of inspiration but serviceable as representing what is normally accepted as the meaning of the

Latin. The Loeb translations cannot, however, be described as readable. They have never been written in the English of their day, adopting instead an esoteric but distinctive dialect: 'Or shall we bear these hardships with such resolve as befitteth stalwart men?' (Horace's Epode I, translated by C. E. **Bennett** in 1914, but reprinted for many decades).

Significant works of translation in other series are referred to in the sections which follow; the remainder of this introduction covers individual assemblages of translations (almost exclusively of poetry—there are few collections of miscellaneous Latin prose or drama in translation). Several are organized by period. No anthology is available of medieval translation from classical Latin writing, in part no doubt because a rather incoherent volume would result; for one thing, much of the work involved is done at second hand, through an intermediate (often French) version of a Latin text.

It is not until the 16th c. that major direct translations begin to appear with any frequency, and two older collections specialize in translations from this period, taking in Greek as well as Latin. A. F. Clements's *Tudor Translations: An Anthology* and O. L. Jiriczek's *Specimens of Tudor Translations from the Classics* will only be found in larger academic libraries. Jiriczek displays some of the riches and some of the idiosyncrasies of the work of major English translators from Gavin **Douglas** [II.n.3.i] to George **Chapman** [II.i.2.i], including Arthur **Golding** [II.n.6.iii] and several lesser figures along the way in selections of English renderings from Virgil, Horace, and Ovid, printing some rare texts, adding the source texts for reference, and providing a helpful glossary. Clements, a judge with literary leanings, includes a dozen classical writers in an anthology extending also to Tudor translations from French and Italian. All the classics sampled are prose writers—Cicero (Sir John **Harington**), Tacitus (Richard **Greneway**), and so on—and the historians and moralists predominate strongly.

For poetry up to the late 17th c., which is probably the golden age of English translation from Latin literature, there is Robin Sowerby's *The Classical Legacy in Renaissance Poetry*. This is not a collection of texts as such, but an introduction to English writers' responses to classical poetry and drama in the period. Sowerby prints so many translations in the course of his discussion, however, that the volume constitutes virtually an anthology of, as well as a guide to, Renaissance English treatments of classical Latin and Greek poetry and drama, divided into generic sections (epic, lyric, etc).

Three further collections are organized generically or thematically. Helen **Waddell**'s *More Latin Lyrics: From Virgil to Milton* is an accomplished single-translator volume. Peter **Hadley**'s *Epic to Epigram* is a short collection of translations from a small range of Latin (and some Greek) poets. Hadley 're-verses' (as he puts it) selections from Lucretius, Catullus, Horace, Ovid, and Martial. These are accessible renderings, scarcely rising to the intensity of Lucretius, happiest in lighter and shorter poems such as Martial's, which are treated in rhymed verse. Charles Tomlinson's *Eros English'd* anthologizes historical translations from 'erotic' Latin and Greek verse, and is explicitly determined to admit only those which 'stand up as poems'. Tomlinson includes renderings of Lucretius, Ovid, Catullus, Horace, Virgil, Juvenal, Tibullus, and Martial, and the anthology, which deserves to be better known, contains work by many of the great translators among the English poets.

The more general collections of Latin literature in translation, of which there are many, tend to be large in scale. Historical English renderings of classical Greek and Latin poetry can be found gathered together in the multi-volume English poetry collections published during the 19th c., in particular Alexander Chalmers's revision of Samuel Johnson's *Works of the English Poets*. This includes 'the most approved translations' in its three final volumes—**Pope**'s Homer and **Dryden**'s Virgil getting pride of place. This collection, then, is a showcase for some of the major achievements of the English literary translating tradition.

The bulky 20th-c. anthologies of Latin literature

in translation for student use have different aims. Guinagh and Dorjahn's *Latin Literature in Translation* (1942) gives 28 authors in translations sometimes historical but more often, alas, by modern academic classicists. The 20th-c. verse translation in this volume is particularly poor. Howe and Harrer's *Roman Literature in Translation* (1924) is on similar lines, with similar drawbacks. These are both American productions; a smaller British cousin is G. R. Hamilton's *The Latin Portrait* (1929). Hamilton presents translations exclusively of Latin verse, from Lucretius to Claudian; the source-texts accompany them. The editor aims to select only translations which have 'the vigour and freshness of creation', and ranges fairly widely to this end among historical texts from the early 17th c. onwards. But there is a surfeit of Victorian and Edwardian translators, whose shortcomings are more apparent now than they would have been in 1929.

In more recent times, Michael Grant's *Latin Literature: An Anthology* has had a deservedly long shelf-life as a popular paperback compilation of English translations from Latin prose as well as verse. Grant allocates a section to each of 25 Latin authors, and provides wherever possible a range of translators (often major English writers, usually over a wide chronological range but with some emphasis on the 20th c.) for each. Even at a length of 464 pages, drastic selection is necessary, and many works are represented only by excerpts. But this is still a useful introduction, and Grant's crisp headnotes for each Latin author give helpful pointers on the Latin texts as well as on English and European responses to them. Another anthology first published in the 1950s, L. R. Lind's *Latin Poetry in Verse Translation from the Beginnings to the Renaissance*, offers mainly 20th-c. and mainly American translations; but their overall quality is not high.

The two most recent general compilations are Richard Stoneman's *Daphne into Laurel* and *The Oxford Book of Classical Verse in English Translation*, edited by Adrian Poole and Jeremy Maule. Stoneman presents historical versions of both Latin and Greek poetry in a simple chronological structure, hence giving some sense of the type of translation going on in different periods. His long introduction is also chronologically arranged. One noteworthy feature of this anthology is a generous interpretation of the term 'translation' so as to include 'imitations' such as Samuel **Johnson**'s *The Vanity of Human Wishes* (based on Juvenal's Tenth Satire). The *Oxford Book* is a more generous selection still, running to over 600 pages and again providing

English incarnations of Greek as well as Latin poets; it runs from Homer to the 5th c. CE. 'Translation' covers imitations and more distant connections too. Organization is by classical author, so that the range of translators of a given writer or work stands out—over 50 different versions of Martial appear, for example, including six poems translated by two different writers for comparison. One of the strongest impressions to emerge is the importance of the period 1660–1800 in English translation from the classics: over a third of the inclusions date from this era.

Finally, a reminder that Latin literature does not end with the Middle Ages, or even the Renaissance [see II.n.12]. No more than a quarter of the *Penguin Book of Latin Verse* is given over to the classical period, and the latest author included is Allan Ramsay (d. 1955). The Latin texts are accompanied by 'plain prose translations' by the editor, Frederick **Brittain**.   SG

ANTHOLOGIES   Brittain, Frederick, *The Penguin Book of Latin Verse*, Harmondsworth, 1962 · Chalmers, Alexander, ed., *The Works of the English Poets from Chaucer to Cowper*, 21 vols., London, 1810 · Clements, A. F., ed., *Tudor Translations: An Anthology*, Oxford, 1940 · Grant, Michael, ed., *Latin Literature—An Anthology: Translations from Latin Prose and Poetry*, 1958 (as *Roman Readings*); rev. edn., Harmondsworth, 1978 [Penguin] · Guinagh, Kevin, and Dorjahn, Alfred P., eds., *Latin Literature in Translation*, New York, 1942; 2nd edn., 1952 · Hadley, Peter, *Epic to Epigram: An Anthology of Classical Verse*, London, 1991 · Hamilton, G. Rostrevor, ed., *The Latin Portrait: An Anthology*, London, 1929 · Howe, George, and Harrer, Gustave Adolphus, eds., *Roman Literature in Translation*, New York, 1944 · Jiriczek, O. L., ed., *Specimens of Tudor Translations from the Classics: with a Glossary*, Heidelberg, 1923 · Lind, L. R., ed., *Latin Poetry in Verse Translation from the Beginnings to the Renaissance*, Boston, 1957 · Poole, Adrian, and Maule, Jeremy, eds., *The Oxford Book of Classical Verse in English Translation*, Oxford, 1995 · Sowerby, Robin, *The Classical Legacy in Renaissance Poetry*, London, 1994 · Stoneman, Richard, ed., *Daphne into Laurel: Translations of Classical Poetry from Chaucer to the Present*, London, 1982 · Tomlinson, Charles, ed., *Eros English'd: Classical Erotic Poetry in Translation from Golding to Hardy*, London, 1992 · Waddell, Helen, *More Latin Lyrics: From Virgil to Milton*, London, 1976.

2. LUCRETIUS

Lucretius (Titus Lucretius Carus) made the Montaigne of the *Apology of Raimond de Sebond* reflect on the relationship between words and thoughts: 'When I see these brave forms of expression, so lively, so profound,' he tells us, 'I do not say that 'tis well said, but well thought.' But English translators of Lucretius have been too concerned with what Lucretius 'thought', with Lucretius as philosopher or sage, and too little with the unique power of what he 'says'—with Lucretius as poet. The *De Rerum Natura* (*c*.60–50 BCE, Of the Nature of Things) has been called not only 'the most passionate didactic poem ever written' but 'the greatest poem in Latin'. Yet a large number of English translations have been in prose, a disproportionately large number compared with translations of other major Latin poems. As poetry, only one English version, and that only partial, can stand comparison with the Latin: John **Dryden**'s translation is poetically the showpiece of English Lucretianism. Other versions are useful at least by virtue of providing complete texts, and some have other merits.

John **Evelyn** (1620–1706) is responsible for the first published English translation. Though he translated the whole, only Book I was printed; Evelyn was discouraged, he complained, by his troubles with proofreaders and printers. The trans-

lation is of only historical interest. Evelyn's response reflects a traditional humanistic acceptance of the poetry and rejection of the Epicurean metaphysics: he admires Lucretius as a poet but rejects his 'irreligion', hoping that his notes will 'totally acquit [him] either of glory or impiety'. This kind of unease becomes outright horror in the work of Lucy **Hutchinson** (b. 1620), whose complete verse translation made in the 1650s has only recently been published as a whole. Hutchinson's dedicatory letter displays a classic Puritan response to Lucretius, charging him with 'impietie' and labelling his system 'pernitious' and 'execrable'. She is not a reliable translator, though some of her version's apparent errors arise from the incorrect Latin editions she used. The verse of her translation has usually been considered awkward and uneven, though a recent attempt has been made to defend its 'irregular kind of ease and flow' as a virtue (de Quehen, 1996).

Thomas **Creech** (1659–1700), an Oxford scholar and translator of several classical poets, next produced a complete English version in rhymed couplets; this remained standard for over a century, at least partly on account of its useful notes, elaborated by successive editors. Creech's translation itself is in parts surprisingly readable. It suffers from a laboured, sometimes wooden manner and a generally homespun quality, but it has some claim to be one of the more successful complete verse translations as well as the first. This sample from Book IV, on dreams, shows Creech at his best:

Besides, what raise Heroick thoughts in Men?
E'en such are often rais'd in Dreams: For then
They fight, are taken Captive, and rebell,
They shout, and groan, as if the Victor fell:
Some strive, some weep, some sigh, and oft afraid,
Pursu'd or torn by Beasts, cry out for aid:
Some talk of State-affairs, and some betray
Those Plots, their treacherous minds had fram'd by day.

On the other hand, Creech has a cavalier attitude to his task, adding sections of his own invention and freely cutting more technical passages at will: he is sometimes more concerned to produce an effect than to render the Latin.

The partial translation by John Dryden owes something to Creech, who was a protégé of Dryden's, but it is on a very different poetic level. Dryden's work runs to some 750 lines (in English) and includes from the *De Rerum Natura* the *proem*, 250 lines from the conclusion of Book III, the section on sexual love in Book IV, and shorter excerpts. As Emrys Jones has written, Dryden responded profoundly to Lucretius: 'his translation was not a matter of merely turning Latin hexameters into heroic couplets but of ingesting as completely as possible his philosophical outlook, his personal temperament, his artistic sensibility, and his more narrowly poetic way of handling words' (Jones 1985).

Dryden's poetry has commanding assurance and enormous power. For one thing, he sees Lucretius as master of a full range of verse textures and tones where other translators seem to see only unvaried regularity. In Dryden there are passages of turbulent, boldly unconventional ruggedness, as in the description of sexual intercourse in Book IV:

When hands in hands they lock, and thighs in thighs they
    twine;
Just in the raging foam of full desire,
When both press on, both murmur, both expire,
They gripe, they squeeze, their humid tongues they dart,
As each wou'd force their way to t'other's heart:
In vain; they only cruze about the coast,
For bodies cannot pierce, not be in bodies lost:
As sure they strive to be, when both engage,
In that tumultuous momentary rage . . .

Elsewhere Dryden's grave eloquence answers to what George Saintsbury found in Lucretius: 'the majesty of his manner is in no way theatrical, but it *is* majestic,' Saintsbury wrote. In the exhortation

to accept nature's laws of life and death in Book III, for example, Dryden's pronounced antithetical balancing of words, phrases, and metrical units evokes a mood of serene contemplation reinforced by the echoes from *Ecclesiastes*:

One Being worn, another Being makes;
Chang'd but not lost; for Nature gives and takes:
New Matter must be found for things to come,
And these must waste like those, and follow
    Natures doom.
All things, like thee, have time to rise and rot;
And from each others ruin are begot;
For life is not confin'd to him or thee;
'Tis giv'n to all for use; to none for Property.

Dryden has the greatest respect for what he calls the 'sublime and daring genius' of Lucretius but owns that he 'takes liberty' in translating him because his aim is to make him 'as pleasing as I could'. Yet, where he departs from literal sense, Dryden is constantly able to suggest implications which appear to be somewhere present in, or deducible from, his original. This is a translation which seems more than a translation: it is a re-imagining of the *De Rerum Natura* not necessarily exactly reflecting the paraphrasable meaning of the Latin but boldly suggesting how Lucretius might have written had he been a 17th-c. English poet.

There are numerous 19th-c. versions, from a selective rendering by W. H. **Drummond** in 1808 to W. H. **Mallock**'s translations into FitzGerald's *Omar Khayyám* metre of 1900. Among these the influential prose version of 1864 by Tennyson's friend H. A. J. **Munro** (1819–85) can be singled out. It was seen in its day as authoritative, and it is certainly full of striking phrases: 'vitai claustra' becomes 'fastnesses of life', 'alte terminus haerens' 'the deepset boundary-mark'. But Munro's notion of poetical language now seems often risible, with expressions such as 'methinks', 'forsooth', and 'in no wise'. There is also much mere prose, and especially in the more technical sections the language becomes that of a scientific textbook. Munro's work is avowedly the basis for Cyril **Bailey**'s 1910 version, which aims to improve on its predecessor in such respects, so as to 'leave the impression that the De Rerum Natura, even in its most scientific discussions, is still poetry'. Bailey probably succeeds in this aim as well as can be expected, given that he is committed to prose himself:

So then we must suppose that out of the infinite all things are supplied to the whole heaven and earth in number enough that on a sudden the earth might be shaken and moved, and a tearing hurricane course over sea and land, the fire of Etna well forth, and the heaven be aflame.

Bailey's translation was later included in his three-volume edition of Lucretius, still a standard scholarly text.

Lucretius translations were something of an industry in the 19th c., which produced at least a dozen different English versions. The 20th c. continues and even accelerates this rate of output. The principal reasons for this are suggested by the introduction to Ronald **Latham**'s Penguin version of 1951, which appeals to those who 'believe that civilization with all its conventional values has been debunked', to the 'puzzled seeker after the Unknown God', and to anyone 'ready to welcome the assurance that modern science has disposed, once and for all, of the fairy-tales that pleased our grandparents'. Lucretius is emphatically modern, as Matthew Arnold observed. Revealingly, Latham sees Lucretius as 'trying to convey a . . . message in direct and forcible language'; the message is primary and the language only a medium for communication of it. Latham's language is direct, sometimes forcible, and for the most part modern, but his Lucretius is

clearly a thinker who makes expository points rather than a poet whose power resides in words and rhythms.

Most other 20th-c. translations have similar starting-points and similar deficiencies. Two are worth mentioning, the first because it is by an accomplished writer and displays a lively appreciation of Lucretius as a poet—but only in its introduction. C. H. **Sisson**'s translation is, in practice, disappointingly prosy, sometimes clumsy, and even unclear:

> For as children are afraid in the dark of everything
> So even in the light we have our fears
> Although there is nothing more to be afraid of
> Than what, in the dark, makes children fear
>   what is coming.

A second modern version, in W. H. D. **Rouse**'s Loeb parallel-text edition, has long been a standard resource. Its accuracy is usually unimpeachable and is its principal merit; its English prose style has been brought more up to date in a revision by M. F. Smith.   SG

TRANSLATIONS   *An Essay on the First Book of T. Lucretius Carus de Rerum Natura*, tr. John Evelyn, London, 1656 · *Titus Lucretius Carus the Epicurean Philosopher: His Six Books De Natura Rerum*, tr. Thomas Creech, London, 1682 · *Sylvae; or, the Second Part of Poetical Miscellanies*, by John Dryden et al., London, 1685 [the first edn. of Dryden's Lucretius; his translations can also be found in most larger collected editions of Dryden's poems] · *T. Lucreti Cari De Rerum Natura Libri Sex*, ed. and tr. H. A. J. Munro, 3 vols., London, 1864 · *Lucretius on the Nature of Things*, tr. Cyril Bailey, Oxford, 1910 · *Titi Lucreti Cari De Rerum Natura Libri Sex*, ed. and tr. Cyril Bailey, 3 vols., Oxford, 1947 [subsequent reps.] · *Lucretius: On the Nature of the Universe*, tr. Ronald Latham, Harmondsworth, 1951 [Penguin] · *Lucretius: De Rerum Natura*, tr. W. H. D. Rouse, rev. M. F. Smith, Cambridge, Mass./London, 1975 [Loeb] · *Lucretius: De Rerum Natura*, tr. C. H. Sisson, Manchester, 1976 · *Lucy Hutchinson's Translation of Lucretius: 'De Rerum Natura'*, ed. Hugh de Quehen, London, 1996.

SEE ALSO   Fleischmann, W. B., *Lucretius and English Literature 1680–1740*, Paris, 1964 · Hadzits, G. D., *Lucretius and His Influence*, Boston, Mass., 1927 · Hammond, P., 'The Integrity of Dryden's Lucretius', *Modern Language Review*, 78 (1983), 1–23 · Jones, E., 'A "Perpetual Torrent": Dryden's Lucretian Style', in D. K. Patey and T. Keegan, eds., *Augustan Studies: Essays in Honour of Ervin Ehrenpreis*, London, 1985, 47–63 · de Quehen, H., 'Ease and Flow in Lucy Hutchinson's Lucretius', *Studies in Philology*, 93 (1996), 288–303.

3. VIRGIL

Virgil (Publius Vergilius Maro) has been regarded as the great representative touchstone of Roman culture and the supreme model of elegant Latinity in verse. It is not surprising, therefore, that he has been much translated; indeed, the whole history of English poetry can be charted with reference to translations of Virgil. Some Roman authors, such as Ovid, went out of fashion with what may be described as the demise of neoclassicism. This did not happen to the same extent with Virgil, whose position at the centre of the school curriculum in Britain until as late as the 1960s

ensured a continuing interest in his poetry and its translation.

i. *Aeneid*: Douglas to Dryden The first formal translation of Virgil's epic the *Aeneid* (30–19 BCE) is by Gavin **Douglas** (?1474–1522) made (in rhyming couplets) between 1512 and 1517 and first published in 1553 [see I.a.6.ii]. Written in Scots, it looks forbidding to the modern reader, but if an effort is made with the spelling the linguistic difficulties are not as great as may be first thought; in fact, Douglas is a good storyteller and his version is surprisingly readable. He incorporates material of his own in the form of extensive poetic prologues to the various books. He follows humanistic principles in being faithful to Virgil's text, not necessarily to its letter, but to its essential matter. His primary aim as translator is to render faithfully what he calls Virgil's 'sentence'. Aware that he had not the resources in Scots to match the 'eloquence' of the original, he writes in a direct and vivid vernacular style that recalls Chaucer and the medieval tradition of alliterative verse. The horror of the cave and lake of Avernus, for example, is vividly conveyed in this style:

> Thar stude a dirk and profound cave fast by,
> A hidduus hoill, deip gapand and grisly,
> All ful of cragis and of thir scharp flynt stanys,
> Quilk was weil dekkit and closit for the nanys
> With a fowle layk, als blak as any craw,
> And skuggis dym of ful dern wod schaw,
> Abuse the quilk na fowle may fle but skath

(vi. 237–40)

His natural scenes are rooted in particulars (the black crow above is an importation) and his battles are vigorous. When Aeneas casts his lance at Turnus in the final combat, we can feel the physical effort involved and hear it in the sound of the words:

> And with the hail fors of hys body soyn
> Furth from hys hand weil far the lance gan thraw.
> Never sa swyftly quhidderand the stane flaw
> Swakkit from the engyne onto the wall.
> Ne fulderis dynt, that causis towris fall,
> With sik a rummyll com bratland on sa fast.

(xii. 920–4)

He is not at his best when responding to the Roman theme, but, sensitive to 'reuthe', he often finds a sympathetic equivalent for the pathos that underlies much Virgilian narrative.

The version of Douglas was used by Henry Howard, Earl of **Surrey** (?1517–1547), in his translation of *Aeneid* ii and iv. This is a landmark version as it represents the first use in English of blank verse. Many of Surrey's lines are end-stopped and often the lack of rhyme seems a defect; on the other hand, there are many passages where he uses enjambement and varied caesurae to render successfully, if a little stiffly, the rhythm and movement of Virgil's periodic style in which, as Milton pointed out in rejecting the 'barbarity' of rhyme in *Paradise Lost*, 'the sense [is] variously drawn out from one verse into another', for example:

> As wrestling winds, out of dispers'd whirl
> Befight themselves, the west with southern blast,

And gladsome east proud of Aurora's horse;
The woods do whiz; and foamy Nereus
Raging in fury, with three fork'd mace
From bottom's depth doth welter up the seas;
So came the Greekes.   (ii. 531–7)

There are Latinisms in the translation in both diction and word order but Surrey avoids aureation, the use of polysyllabic words new-coined from the Latin that was a feature of the contemporary high style.

Early translation of Virgil is intimately bound up with debates about English metre. A curiosity is the experimental version of *Aeneid* i–iv by Richard **Stanyhurst** (1547–1618) in English hexameters, published in 1582, proof, if any were needed, of the inappropriateness of this metre in English. It begins: 'Now manhood and garboils I chant and martial horror'. Its hobbling metre and execrable diction were much mocked from the beginning. The first complete *Aeneid* in English (1573) is the version by Thomas **Phaer** (?1510–60) and Thomas **Twyne** (1543–1613). They use the fourteener, the metre that George Chapman was later to use in translating Homer's *Iliad* [II.1.2.i]. They do not have the metrical variety of the mature Chapman and their version is rhythmically predictable, undignified, and flat. The influence of the Italian tradition is apparent in the choice of *ottava rima* by Sir John **Harington** (1560–1612) for his version of the Book VI. Sir Richard **Fanshawe** (1608–66) used the Spenserian stanza for his version of Book IV, an odd choice, for, plain and prosaic in its language, the translation is not in the least Spenserian in style, with no archaisms or ornate diction.

Otherwise the most popular metre for nearly all versions in the 17th c. was the heroic couplet. The earliest complete couplet version of the *Aeneid* is by John **Vicars** (1580–1652). More popular was John **Ogilby** (1600–76), the first translator of the complete works. He produced two quite different versions, the first in 1649 and the second, a magnificent folio volume, in 1654, both volumes with notes and plates. But the first couplet versions of quality were composed by Sidney **Godolphin** (1610–43) in his translation of most of *Aeneid* iv, entitled 'The Passion of Dido for Aeneas' published in 1658, completed with additional lines by Edmund **Waller** (1606–87) and by John **Denham** (1615–69). Denham translated *Aeneid* ii–iv relatively crudely in the 1630s and published a much more polished version, *The Destruction of Troy*, in 1656; this was followed by part of Book IV in 1668. The death of Priam (doubtless recalling the death of Charles I) is translated with particular vigour and moral point:

He, whom such Titles swell'd, such Power made proud
To whom the Sceptres of all Asia bow'd,
On the cold earth lies th'abandoned King,
A headless Carkass, and a nameless Thing.   (546–9)

Denham was a pioneer in advocating a freer mode
of translation wherein the translator, having due
regard for his native idiom, aims to convert poetry
into poetry [see I.b.3.i]. He therefore does not scruple to omit intractable details and is not tied to the
requirement for verbal accuracy. These early
Augustans translate Virgil with new freedom, clarity, and confidence and, in the case of Denham,
with a new modishness.

John **Dryden** first published versions of Virgil
in 1684; his complete translation of the works
appeared in 1697. His is the best translation of Virgil
into English and is one of the few great creative
translations of any poet in the language. Written in
heroic couplets, it may in part be regarded as the
grand summation of the 17th-c. couplet tradition:
he took phrases, rhyme-words, and sometimes
whole lines from published predecessors. Dryden
borrowed from good and bad alike; the dross he
converted to gold and the good he integrated seamlessly into his own poetic style, as in the following
instance:

Thus Priam fell: and shar'd one common Fate
With Troy in Ashes, and his ruin'd State:
He, who the Scepter of all Asia sway'd,
Whom Monarchs like Domestick Slaves obey'd,
On the bleak Shoar now lies th'abandon'd king,
A headless Carcass, and a nameless thing.

(ii. 758–63)

In his notes, Dryden drew attention to the debt to
Denham here. He also acknowledged a debt to the
couplet version of the Earl of **Lauderdale** (1633–95),
which he had seen in manuscript and which was
first printed after his death in 1709. Lauderdale is
uneven; there are strong lines (sometimes taken
over by Dryden) amidst quite feeble writing.

Dryden encountered difficulties with Virgil. He
found his concentrated brevity, 'the sober retrench-
ments of his sense', impossible to emulate: he chose
instead to aim for an expansive clarity, sometimes
adding to the sense what he felt could reasonably be
deduced from it. At the same time he rarely
curtailed the Latin in the manner of Denham. He
also felt taxed by Virgil's almost inexhaustible stock
of 'figurative, elegant and sounding words'. In a
postscript after completion, Dryden specifically
recommended his version to posterity for its choice
of words. Dr Johnson remarked that he had given
the world many happy combinations of heroic

diction; at the same time, like Denham, Dryden
wished to make Virgil speak in a proper native
idiom. What Gerard Manley Hopkins said of Dryden's poetry, that it represents 'the native thew and
sinew of the English language', is essentially true of
his Virgil; elevated diction and Latinisms are har-
moniously integrated in a living style, as evidenced
in the quotations here, in a way that is not always
true of the poetry of his 18th-c. successors.

Within the discipline of the couplet form Dryden
not only perpetuated the refinement and harmony
of the early Augustans but was able to achieve a new
metrical variety, suppleness and strength which put
him in a class beyond the best of his predecessors.
He commended Virgil for being everywhere elegant, sweet, and flowing in his hexameters. This
may be illustrated by the following simile in which
the souls of the dead are likened to bees:

About the Boughs an Airy Nation flew,
Thick as the humming Bees, that hunt the golden Dew;
In Summer's heat, on tops of Lillies feed,
And creep within their Bells, to suck the balmy Seed.

(vi. 958–63)

But he also remarked upon his great metrical
variety and the propriety with which Virgil can
adapt his numbers to the differing requirements of
his subject matter. The movement of Dryden's
couplets and the sound of his verse are quite different when the subject matter calls for energetic
treatment:

Salmoneus, suff'ring cruel Pains, I found,
For emulating Jove; the rattling Sound
Of Mimick Thunder, and the glitt'ring Blaze
Of pointed Lightnings, and their forky Rays....
But he, the King of Heav'n, obscure on high,
Bar'd his red Arm, and launching from the Sky
His writhen Bolt, not shaking empty Smoak,
Down to the deep Abyss the flaming Felon strook.

(vi. 788–91, 800–3)

No other translator has been able to represent so
successfully the range of the original from the quiet
beauty of natural description to the noise and clamour of battles and sieges.

In the end, Dryden's hope was that he had
captured 'the clearness, the purity, the easiness and
the magnificence of his [Virgil's] style'. The verdict
of his most illustrious editor Walter Scott has as
much force now as it had when he delivered it in the
early 19th c.: 'It is in this art of communicating the
ancient poet's ideas with force and energy equal to
his own that Dryden has so completely exceeded all
who have gone before, and all who have succeeded
him.'

ii. *Aeneid*: Since Dryden What to do after Dryden? One answer was to adopt blank verse. Joseph **Addison** published in 1704 'Milton's Style Imitated, in a Translation of a Story out of the Third Aeneid'. This episode, featuring the horrific story of Achaemenides, a companion of Ulysses left behind in the cave of the Cyclops, well supports the Miltonic treatment given to it, and the translation suggests the possibility of a fruitful alternative to the couplet tradition for the 18th c. But neither Nicolas **Brady** (1659–1726), in his version begun in 1716, nor Joseph **Trapp** (1679–1747), in his often stilted translation of 1718–20, had the poetic talent to succeed. The successful alternative to Dryden, which to some extent replaced him in popularity in the second half of the century, was another couplet version of 1740, that of Christopher **Pitt** (1699–1748), a protégé of Pope and very accomplished versifier who translated Virgil in the manner of his master but without his rhythmical and metrical variety, so that his smooth and harmonious couplets are soon felt to be bland and enervated.

The 19th c. was not generally speaking a propitious time for the translation of the classics. In the case of Virgil, the fact that English poetry in the romantic era and beyond no longer ran so obviously parallel with the Roman classics meant that poets were often uncertain about the language and style to adopt. The century's demand for accuracy was a further hindrance. Nor did the frequent desire for exact metrical equivalence produce any good translations. William **Wordsworth** strangely used the rhyming couplet, with some triplets and the occasional alexandrine, in his versions of Virgil published in 1832. His often end-stopped couplets are sometimes awkwardly reminiscent of Dryden, while at times his enjambements and inversions recall Milton, as when his Venus worries for the welcome being provided for Aeneas, her son:

> Him now the generous Dido by soft chains
> Of bland entreaty at her court detains;
> Junonian hospitalities prepare
> Such apt occasion that I dread a snare.

> (i. 919–22)

John **Conington** (1825–69), a classical scholar who edited Virgil's works with an extensive commentary and wrote intelligently about translation, produced in 1867 a translation much praised at the time for its simplicity (despite its obvious lack of anything approaching a grand note) in the jaunty ballad metre used by Walter Scott in *Marmion*. His Dido, deserted by Aeneas, curses thus (translating iv. 620–1):

> But let him fall in manhood's strength
> And welter tombless on the strand
> Such malison to heaven I pore
> A last libation with my gore.

William **Morris** chose the fourteener for his rendering of the poem in 1876. Its archaizing style gives it a fey, folksy poeticality (even worse than Conington's) and its heavy dragging rhythms make it impossible to read over a long stretch. His poetic idiom is often hideously remote from the classical poet, as when the Fury Allecto announces herself to Turnus:

> Lo, I am she, the mouldy-dull, whom Eld, the void of sooth,
> Bemocks amid the arms of kings with empty lies of fear!
> Look, look! For from the Sisters' House, the Dread Ones, come I here;
> And war and death I have in hand.   (vii. 452–5)

Equally archaizing and quaint is the hexameter version of parts of *Aeneid* vi published under the title *Ibant Obscuri* in 1916 by Robert **Bridges**. Aeneas and the Sibyl commence their descent into Hades as follows (translating vi. 227–8):

> They wer' amid the shadows by night in loneliness obscure
> Walking forth i' the void and vasty dominyon of Ades;

Most 20th-c. translators, however, turn their back upon archaic diction, poetic inversions, and metrical experiment, setting their sights more modestly on producing something that will render the sense unpretentiously for a modern audience suspicious of the high style and unfamiliar with classic niceties. C. Day **Lewis** translated the entire works of Virgil; he was least happy with the epic, lamenting the absence in the 20th c. of anything corresponding to the tradition of narrative verse in which Dryden worked. His *Aeneid* of 1952 veers awkwardly between colloquialism and the formal patterns of speech he deemed necessary to render Virgilian seriousness (he composed the poem for recitation on the radio): the goddess Venus hails the companions of Aeneas with the matey address: 'Hullo there, young men!' Much more even and unexceptionable in their style are the simple and clear versions of Rolfe **Humphries**, in duodecasyllabic lines without rhyme, of Allen **Mandelbaum**, and of Robert **Fitzgerald**, both in blank verse. In prose, David **West** improves upon the dull version of W. F. Jackson **Knight**.

iii. Eclogues However humble the pastoral might be in the generic hierarchy, for the translator it presents a virtually insuperable challenge. Virgil's ten Eclogues (43–37 BCE, often referred to as his Bucolics by earlier writers) are among the prettiest poems in world literature; they cannot be read as the *Aeneid* and the Georgics might possibly be read for their content alone; they have no great story to tell or instruction to offer, but a poetic vision to impart. Without their art they are nothing. Even in the hands of a good poet the English hexameter will scarcely do; the versions of William **Webbe** (*fl.* 1568–91) certainly will not. The drearily diffuse fourteeners of Abraham **Fleming** (?1522–1607) in his Eclogues of 1589 are also artistically crude. On the other hand, the versions in couplets by several hands published in *Miscellany Poems* in 1684 do capture some of the charm and polish of their originals. Even minor poetical talents like John **Caryll** (1625–1711), Thomas **Creech** (1659–1700), Richard **Duke** (?1659–1711), Wentworth Dillon, Earl of **Roscommon** (?1635–1685), and Sir William **Temple** (1628–99) manage to convey some of the poetic pleasure of the Latin. Dryden also contributed to this miscellany and translated all the pastorals for his version of the works in 1697. For the eclogue, the obvious artistry of the Augustan couplet form, with its neat rhetorical patterning, its mellifluous rhythms, its regularity of cadence, and its careful choice of decorous diction, is the best medium in English. Joseph **Warton** (1722–1800) also produced a good couplet version in 1753. Pure pastoral is not a mode that survives happily in the 20th c. With any trace of slang or prosaic diction the mood evaporates, as in the case of 'Shepherds, let Codrus burst his guts with envy' (vii. 26) in the version of Paul **Alpers**, or 'Cynthius pulled | My ear in admonition' (vi. 3–4) in the version of Guy **Lee**.

iv. Georgics The Georgics (37–30 BCE) treat the cultivation of crops, trees, animals and bees. In Book IV, the treatment of the bees is interlaced with humour and this part of the work is a *locus classicus* for the mock heroic. This book also contains an extended mythological episode, the story of Orpheus and Eurydice.

There are fewer early versions of the Georgics than of the other poems, and once again the best translations are in the neoclassical period, when the georgic form itself was in vogue. Worth looking at is the version in rhyming couplets (frequently enjambed) by Thomas **May** (1595–1650); what it lacks in polish it supplies in freshness and vigour. Virgil's praise of retirement and the county life and rejection of the life of ambition in the second Georgic is stylishly rendered paraphrastically in elegant closed couplets by Abraham **Cowley** (1618–67); this version (published in 1663) is a royalist's stoic response to lack of preferment by an ungrate-

ful monarch after the Restoration. James **Thomson** (1700–48) translated famous lines in the *Georgics* (ii. 475–86), in which Virgil as priest of the Muses celebrates rural retirement and declares his intention to disclose the secrets of nature; he then incorporated a paraphrase of the larger section from which it is taken into *Autumn* (1235–end) and echoes georgic themes and expression throughout *The Seasons* (1730).

Of the poem in general Addison remarked in his 'Essay on Virgil's *Georgics*': 'He delivers the meanest of his precepts with a kind of grandeur, he breaks the clods and tosses the dung about with an air of gracefulness.' The version of Dryden illustrates his point:

But sweet Vicissitudes of Rest and Toyl
Make easy Labour, and renew the Soil.
Yet sprinkle sordid Ashes all around,
And load with fat'ning Dung thy fallow Ground.
Thus change of Seeds for meagre Soils is best;
And Earth manur'd, not idle, though at rest.

(i. 116–21)

Dryden's mastery of the couplet here and his excellent sense of the diction required enable him to maintain majesty in the midst of plainness and to rise to the challenge presented by the Georgics in finding a poetic style that can cope with prosaic particularities without sinking into banality or evading them by the inappropriate importation of pompous and elevated diction. When Virgil represents the forces of elemental or animal nature, no translator has rendered him as dynamically as Dryden:

Oft Have I seen a sudden Storm arise,
From all the warring Winds that sweep the Skies:
The heavy Harvest from the Root is torn,
And whirl'd aloft the lighter Stubble born;

(i. 431–4)

Of modern versions, that of C. Day Lewis written at the outbreak of World War II is a serviceable reminder, despite its metrical slackness, of the appeal of the original in times of national and personal stress:

Evil has so many faces, the plough so little
Honour, the labourers are taken, the fields untended,
And the curving sickle is beaten into the sword that yields not.
There the East is in arms, here Germany marches:
Neighbour cities, breaking their treaties, attack each other.
The wicked War-god runs amok through all the world.

(i. 507–12)

Most Renaissance editions printed a series of short

poems thought wrongly to be juvenile works of Virgil. Edmund **Spenser** (?1552–99) produced in 1591 an expanded version of the *Culex*, under the title *Virgil's Gnat*. Thomas **Stanley** (1625–78) produced a couplet version of the Epicurean *Copa* with the title *The Hostesse* in 1651. William **Cowper** (1731–1800) in the year before he died composed a

couplet version of the *Moretum* under the title *The Sallad*.

Samples of most of the versions mentioned here can be found in: Adrian Poole and Jeremy Maule, eds., *The Oxford Book of Classical Verse in Translation*, Oxford, 1995, and K. W. Gransden, ed., *Virgil in English*, Harmondsworth, 1996 [Penguin Classics].　　　　　　RS

WORKS　*The Works of Publius Virgilius Maro*, tr. John Ogilby, London, 1649; 2nd edn., 1654 · *The Works of Virgil*, tr. John Dryden, London, 1697 [rep. in some but not all edns. of Dryden's works, and as a separate vol.] · *The Works of Virgil*, tr. Richard Maitland, Earl of Lauderdale, London, ?1709 · *The Works of Virgil [Aeneis*, 1718–20], tr. Joseph Trapp, London, 1731 · *The Works of Virgil in Latin and English*, 4 vols. [vols. ii–iv, *The Aeneid*, tr. Christopher Pitt, 1740], London, 1753 · *The Eclogues* [1963], *The Georgics* [1940], *The Aeneid of Virgil* [1952], tr. C. Day Lewis, Oxford, 1966.

AENEID　*The Legend of Good Women*, by Geoffrey Chaucer, in *The Works of Geoffrey Chaucer*, ed. F. N. Robinson, 2nd edn., Oxford, 1974 · *The xiii Bukes of Eneados . . . Translated into Scottish Metir*, tr. Gavin Douglas, 1553 [rep. in *Virgil's 'Aeneid' Translated into Scottish Verse by Gavin Douglas*, ed. David F. C. Coldwell, 4 vols., Edinburgh / London, 1964] · *Certain bokes* [ii and iv] *of Virgil's Aeneis*, tr. Henry Howard, Earl of Surrey, London, 1557 [rep. in *The Aeneid of Henry Howard, Earl of Surrey*, ed. Florence H. Ridley, Berkeley / Los Angeles, 1963] · *The Whole xii Bookes of the Aeneidos of Virgill*, tr. Thomas Phaer and Thomas Twyne, London, 1573 [rep. in *The 'Aeneid' of Thomas Phaer and Thomas Twyne (1584)*, ed. Stephen Lally, New York, 1987] · *The First Foure Bookes of Virgil his Aeneis*, tr. Richard Stanyhurst, London, 1582 [rep. in *Richard Stanyhurst's Aeneis*, ed. Dirk van der Haar, Amsterdam, 1933] · *The Sixth Book of Virgil's 'Aeneid'*, tr. Sir John Harington (in MS 1604), ed. Simon Cauchi, Oxford, 1991 · *The XII Aeneids of Virgil*, tr. John Vicars, London, 1632 · 'The Loves of Dido and Aeneas', tr. Sir Richard Fanshawe, in *Il Pastor Fido*, London, 1648 [rep. in *The Fourth Book of Virgil's Aeneid . . . Done into English . . . by Sir Richard Fanshawe*, ed. A. L. Irvine, Oxford, 1924] · 'The Passion of Dido for Aeneas', tr. Sir John Denham in *Poems and Translations*, London, 1668; *The Destruction of Troy*, London, 1656 [rep. in *The Poetical Works of John Denham*, ed. Theodore Howard Banks, Jr., New Haven, Conn. / London, 1928] · *The Passion of Dido for Aeneas as It Is Incomparably Expressed in the Fourth Book of Virgil*, tr. S. Godolphin and E. Waller, London, 1658 [for Godolphin, see *The Poems of Sidney Godolphin*, ed. William Dighton, Oxford, 1931, and for Waller, *The Poems of Edmund Waller*, ed. G. Thorn Drury, New York, 1905] · 'Milton's Style Imitated, in a Translation of a Story out of the Third Aeneid', tr. Joseph Addison, in *Poetical Miscellanies: The Fifth Part*, London, 1704 · *Virgil's Aeneis*, tr. Nicolas Brady, 4 vols., London, 1716–26 · 'Translation of Part of the First Book of the Aeneid', tr. William Wordsworth, in *The Philological Museum*, i, London, 1832 [with books ii and iii and a short passage from book viii in *William Wordsworth: The Poems*, vol. ii, ed. John O. Hayden, Harmondsworth, 1977, Penguin] · *The Aeneid of Virgil*, tr. John Conington, London, 1866 · *The Aeneids of Virgil*, tr. William Morris, London, 1876 · *Ibant Obscuri*, tr. Robert Seymor Bridges, Oxford, 1916 · *The Aeneid of Virgil*, tr. Rolfe Humphries, New York, 1951 · *Virgil: The Aeneid*, tr. W. F. Jackson Knight, Harmondsworth, 1956 [Penguin] · *The Aeneid of Virgil*, tr. Allen Mandelbaum, Berkeley, Calif. / London, 1971 · *The Aeneid*, tr. Robert Fitzgerald, London, 1983 · *Virgil: The Aeneid*, tr. David West, Harmondsworth, 1991 [Penguin].

ECLOGUES　*Discourse of English Poetrie*, by William Webbe, London, 1586 [includes his translations of Eclogues I and II] · *The Bucolics of Publius Virgilius Maro, Together with His Georgiks, Newly Translated*, tr. A[braham] F[leming], London, 1589 · 'Virgil's Eclogues, Translated by Several Hands' [Caryll, Creech, Dryden, Duke, Roscommon, Temple], in *Miscellany Poems*, London, 1684 · *The Works of Virgil in Latin and English*, 4 vols. [vol. i, *The Eclogues and Georgics*, tr. Joseph Warton], London 1753 · *The Singer of the Eclogues: A Study of Virgilian Pastoral with a New Translation of the Eclogues*, by Paul Alpers, Berkeley, Calif., 1979 · *Virgil. The Eclogues*, tr. Guy Lee, Harmondsworth, 1984 [Penguin].

GEORGICS　*Virgil's Georgicks*, tr. Thomas May, London, 1628 · 'A Translation out of Virgil, Georgics, Book II', tr. Abraham Cowley, in *Verses Lately Written upon Several Occasions*, London, 1663 [rep. in most edns. of Cowley's works] · *The Seasons*, by James Thomson, London, 1730 [incorporates translations and paraphrases].

VIRGILIAN APPENDIX　'Virgil's Gnat', tr. Edmund Spencer, in his *Complaints*, London, 1591 [rep. in modern editions of Spencer] · 'The Hostesse', tr. Thomas Stanley, in his *Poems*, London, 1651 [rep. in *The Oxford Book of Classical Verse in Translation*, ed. Adrian Poole and Jeremy Maule, Oxford, 1995] · 'The Sallad—by Virgil', tr. William Cowper, in *The Poems of William Cowper*, ed. John D. Baird and Charles Ryskamp, vol. iii, Oxford, 1995 [first pub. 1803].

SEE ALSO　Austin, R. G., *Some English Translations of Virgil*, Liverpool, 1955 · Burrow, C., 'Virgil in English Translation', in C. Martindale, ed., *The Cambridge Companion to Virgil*, Cambridge, 1997 · Conington, J., 'The English Translators of Virgil', in *Miscellaneous Writings of John Conington*, ed. A. J. Symonds, i, London, 1872 · Frost, W., 'Translating Virgil: Douglas to Dryden', in M. Mack and G. de F. Lord, eds., *Poetic Traditions of the English Renaissance*, New Haven, Conn., 1982 · Harrison, T. W., 'English Virgil: The *Aeneid* in the XVIII Century' *Philologica Pragensia*, 10 (1967), 1–11, 80–90 · Havelock, E. A., 'The *Aeneid* and Its Translators', *Hudson Review*, 27 (1974), 338–70 · Proudfoot, L., *Dryden's Aeneid and Its Seventeenth-Century Predecessors*, Manchester, 1960 · Ziolkowski, T., *Virgil and the Moderns*, Princeton, NJ, 1993.

4. LYRIC POETRY

i. Introduction The term 'lyric' was applied by Alexandrian scholars to those Greek poems that were performed to musical accompaniment (traditionally to that of the lyre). Dr Johnson defined the word as 'pertaining to an harp, or to odes or poetry sung to an harp; singing to an harp'. In modern English the term probably suggests a poem that combines brevity with powerful personal emotion, and is, therefore, not entirely appropriate for Latin poetry—which was not sung, and was written by those who did not associate personal passion with concision. It is by pure convention that certain poems by Catullus, Propertius, Tibullus, Horace, and Ovid are sometimes classed under the title 'lyric'. Of these 'lyric' or 'elegiac' poets Horace and Ovid are discussed elsewhere [II.n.5] and [II.n.6].

The linking of the names Catullus, Propertius, and Tibullus, poets of the IST c. BCE, is ancient and appears to have affected the way each has been read and translated. All three poets, it seems, have presented similar attractions and difficulties to readers and translators. All three came in obviously corrupt texts—but offered the enticements of apparently passionate love poetry, apparently arising from real life, interspersed with comments upon, or restatements of, the great commonplaces of human existence. The 'real life' represented, however, has forced recognition that the 'love' depicted in these poems implied very different customs and feelings in the IST c. BCE from those of the translators' times. Accordingly, some poems have proved much more amenable than others. Many translators have attempted to incorporate selected works of Catullus, Tibullus, and Propertius into the vocabulary of the love poetry of their own day. However, those who have attempted complete collections have tended, despite themselves, to represent the Latin poets in the language of English love poetry of the generation previous to that of the translator, employ the literary idiom of their grandparents, and in effect to impersonate Latin poetry with English poeticism. Translations of all three poets are therefore intermittent and variable. Catullus has been the best served of the three Latin poets, but even in his case a non-Latinate reader is forced to more desperate expedients than in the case of Virgil, Horace, or Ovid.

The association between the three Latin poets was strengthened by the fact that they often appeared in the same volume—both in English and in Latin. Sir Aston Cokayne (1608–84) explained the association in his epigram 'Of Catullus, Tibullus, and Propertius':

> The ancient Epigrammatist Catullus,
> Propertius, and the amorous Tibullus,
> Are often bound together: whats the reason?
> They all were merry Blades at every season;
> Whilst they did live they often were together:
> And now th'are dead th'are bound up so in Leather.

ii. Catullus It is very much to the point that Cokayne calls Gaius Valerius Catullus an 'Epigrammatist' and a 'merry Blade'; until the 19th c. Catullus appears to have been valued more for the wry, the playful, and the pithy in his writings than for the soft or the tender. Among the most frequently translated of his poems was that (usually numbered 70) which, in the version by Thomas **Gilbert** (d. 1747), ends with the observation that 'The fleeting passion of the fickle fair | Should be describ'd in sand, or writ in air' or, as Sir Philip **Sidney** has it, that 'woman's words to a love that is eager, | In wind or water streame do require to be writ' (many of the one-off translations are included in Duckett's 1925 anthology).

Cockayne implies that Catullus was a 'merry Blade' both in literature and in life (others called him 'Waggish Catullus'). He seems to have been for many years a poet whose most striking quality was his licentiousness. From that point of view, the version of Carmina 5, 'Vivamus, mea Lesbia', by Ben **Jonson**, as the song 'Come my Celia' (sung by the would-be-adulterous Volpone), which culminates in the suggestion that '"Tis no sinne, loves fruit to steale, | But the sweet theft to reveale', is more representative of the prevailing view than the version of the same poem by Thomas **Campion** (1567–1620), which emphasizes the pathos implied by the discrepancy between the momentary joys of the lover and the 'ever-during night' of insensibility in death.

The potential pathos of this poem, however, attracted innumerable translators and imitators (for Renaissance ones, see Braden 1979). There are interesting versions by Richard **Crashaw**, John **Langhorne** (1735–1779), **Wordsworth**, Walter Savage **Landor**, and **Byron**. Other parts of Catullus' work proved more troublesome. One difficulty facing the translator was that form and content were thought to be peculiarly indivisible in the case of Catullus' poems—so that the delicate versification was felt to be both an expression and an embodiment of his wit. For many readers in the 17th c. the nearest English equivalent to Catullus was Edmund Waller. So one writer claimed that 'Waller in Verse as Tender as his Love, | Like soft Catullus, does our passions move'. The comparison here seems to be dependent upon the 'softness' of Catullus' versification and 'spirit'—an emotional playfulness, an extreme delicacy of subject expressed in a verse that was itself light, playful, and delicate. In this vein, and for these reasons, the charming 'Ode: Acme and Septimus, out of Catullus' from Carmina 45 by Abraham **Cowley** (1618–67) appears to have been as popular with readers as Catullus' poem on Lesbia's sparrow (Carmina 2) was with translators.

John **Nott** (1751–1825), in 1795 the first translator of the complete surviving collection of Catullus' poems, called the dialogue between Acme and Septimus 'one of the loveliest little poems that ever graced the Roman language'. His own version of this and the other poems reflected an attempt to reproduce the 'strength and simplicity, elegance and perspicuity' of Catullus' style. While none of Nott's versions could stand on its own as an English poem, 'perspicuity' rather than expressiveness being their leading quality, the two volumes of his translations are extremely serviceable. Nott claims to 'have given the whole of Catullus without reserve', and, while all his versions tend towards the bland, there is little that is excluded on grounds of impropriety.

In the 19th c. Catullus became, in Tennyson's words, the 'tenderest of Roman poets' who was believed to have suffered 'hopeless woe' (and who, on these and other grounds, rose in critical esteem far above Tibullus and Propertius). The so-called 'Lesbia poems' became the most cherished of Catullus' works. Lesbia herself became an object of fascination, and the poems were read as if they were fragments of a novel in which Catullus experienced by turns deep passion, absolute devotion, corrosive self-pity, hatred, and scorn for a beautiful but unscrupulous woman. The 19th-c. Catullus, that is, resembled one that first emerged in 1701 in the anonymous *Adventures Of Catullus And History Of His Amours With Lesbia, Intermixt With Translations Of His Choicest Poems By Several Hands, Done From The French* [of Jean de la Chapelle]. Theodore **Martin**, for example, in 1861 rearranged the 'Lesbia poems' to form a narrative which told the story of a 'devilish witchery' in Lesbia's 'smile' from which Catullus 'cannot break away'. Lesbia's fascination was even stronger for J. H. **Tremenheere** ('of the Indian Civil Service'), who made Catullus' poems tell an extraordinarily sentimental tale.

From the mid-19th c., every few years has produced a new translation of Catullus. Some have been radical and experimental, such as the 'homophonic' versions by the Americans Louis and Celia Zukofsky [see I.a.2.i], while others have aimed at little more than utility. A beginner would probably do best with Walter K. **Kelly**'s *Poems of Catullus and Tibullus*. This volume consists of a literal prose translation accompanied with notes, and followed by metrical versions by various writers. Occasionally, and most usefully, several versions of the same original are included. On a similar plan, but without the literal version, is Eleanor Shipley Duckett's collection of English translations. Until the appearance of Julia Haig Gaisser's Penguin *Catullus in English*, forthcoming at the time of writing, these are the only collections of historical translations available; Gaisser's will almost certainly supersede them entirely.

A familiar difficulty for many modern translators is that a great love of Latin verse does not automatically confer technical mastery on the English admirer. Many writers who could compose no other verses have thought they could write like Catullus. J. F. **Symons-Jeune**, for example, published lush but amateurish versions of some of Catullus' poems despite observing that 'none but a gifted poet can hope to reproduce the felicitous simplicity of his lyrics, his passionate directness of apprehension expressed with a fastidious instinct for the music of his words, and with a refinement of polish perfect enough to hide all labour and carry the conviction of unpremeditated outburst'.

Symons-Jeune congratulates himself as much for what he has not as for what he has done. His versions are bowdlerized (indeed, he offers a spirited defence of Bowdler). Along with many other translators, he found it difficult to account for the fact that among Catullus' poems, interspersed with those to or about Lesbia, are epigrammatic verses attacking literary rivals and personal enemies, and (worse) that many of these verses (and, indeed, some of the poems about Lesbia) were unacceptably obscene. But where 19th-c. translators expurgated, or toned down the implications of the Latin, translators of the later 20th c. have been proud of their ability to match Catullus at his most lewd. It is, however, apparent that no area of language belongs more completely to its period than the colloquially obscene. Not much of the flavour of the Roman world is evoked by reading of a lover 'rogering his bird' or 'wanking'. Another difficulty is that Catullus' obscenities often imply a sexual world very different from any that a modern scholar might inhabit.

These problems become acute, for example, in poem 56 (a poem that was left partially untranslated in many complete translations—including F. W. **Cornish**'s Loeb), where Catullus assumes that it is enormously amusing to tell his reader that, coming across a copulating couple, 'I caught the young shit in the grass | Screwing his girl, and ran my prick, | Just like a spear, right up his ass'. That version, by Reney **Myers** and Robert J. **Ormbsy**, was first published in 1972 but is not much more brutal than most of its rivals—of which there have been many since 1945, Peter **Whigham**'s being among the most free, that by Frederic **Raphael** and Kenneth **McLeish** one of the most libertine, and that by George **Goold** the most literal (for Guy **Lee**'s, see under Tibullus below). Neither modern English nor American idiom seems to provide a vocabulary that is capable of combining obscenity, verse and wit:

> I surprised a lad bent on shafting his girl
> And promptly rammed home my advantage.
> Grateful thanks to the mother of Venus,
> I found myself tailor-made for the job.

> (Raphael and McLeish)

When these versions are amusing they are often so for reasons not always intended by the translators—who leave much for both Venus and the Muse to forgive.

iii. Tibullus Before the 19th c., it appears to have been Albius Tibullus rather than Catullus whose love elegies were considered to be gentle, wistful, tender, and 'natural'. John Armstrong in 1753 expressed the common opinion:

> Ah! who but feels the sweet contagious smart
> While soft Tibullus pours his tender heart?
> With him the Loves and Muses melt in tears.

One problem for English translators was that it was not only the female fair who caused Tibullus' heart to melt. In Elegy 4, for example, the poet, apparently unsuccessful in an attempt to seduce a boy, consults the god Priapus, who delivers so animated a lecture on the art of homosexual love (interspersed with general laments on the passage of time and the corruptions of modernity) that his pupil at once proclaims himself advanced to the rank of a professor. Walter Kelly, the translator of Catullus, commented in 1861 that in the case of this poem he had been 'compelled to be unfaithful to the original with regard to gender', observing that the change has 'occasioned some awkwardness in a few places'.

Nevertheless, Kelly's collection of his own prose translations plus verse ones by several hands is again, as a whole, very useful. His chosen verse versions are sufficiently accomplished and uniform to convey some notion of Tibullus' verse, but sufficiently different to save the collection from monotony (the besetting defect of all complete translations by a single hand). Some of the versions he includes—those of Thomas **Otway**, for example—contain some good lines. The inclusion of Otway is a reminder, however, that Kelly's collection is not the best that could be assembled. An interesting volume might be made up of other earlier versions such as those by Charles **Hopkins** (1664–1700), who translated Elegies iii.2, iv.4, and iv.13.

Before Kelly's, the most serious attempt to render the complete poems in English was one in accomplished pentameter couplets by John **Dart** (d. 1730); it deserves to be more widely known. James **Grainger** (?1721–66) uses the same verse form some 30 years later in 1759, but is more conventional for his period; the epithets are predictable and the impassioned exclamations monotonous.

Of 20th-c. versions, Philip **Dunlop**'s are often lucid, and Guy Lee's, while not quite free-standing English poems, provide (as in the case of his Catullus) an interesting and often surprising gloss on the Latin with which (in the case of Tibullus) they are printed *en face*.

iv. Propertius The third in the triumvirate of poetical lovers, Sextus Propertius, was for many years as closely linked to the source of his inspiration, the mistress whom he called Cynthia, as Catullus had been to Lesbia and Tibullus to his Delia. As is the case with his companion poets, Propertius provided the occasional source for poems by many writers—sometimes calling distinguished work from otherwise forgotten authors. Deserving particular mention are a version of Elegy ii.28 by Thomas Campion; 'Reflections on the Picture of Cupid' by John **Hopkins** (*fl.* 1698); the imitation of Propertius' 'Dream' (iii.3) by Elijah **Fenton** (1683–1730); the imitation of Elegy ii.12 by John **Smith** (*fl.* 1713); Richardson **Pack**'s (1682–1728) version of ii.12, John **Glanvill**'s (?1664–1735) of i.4, and Thomas **Gray**'s of iii.5. The best version of Elegy ii.15, *O me felicam* (and among the most vigorous of all translations of Propertius), is that published in 1693 by Benjamin **Hawkshaw** (d. 1738).

John Nott had preceded his version of Catullus with a translation of Propertius in 1782. Interestingly, his versions of Propertius are more obviously 'poetical' than those of Catullus—a tendency which is also marked in the versions by Sir Charles

Elton (1778–1853). C. R. **Moore**'s attempt to render the Elegies in 1870 also relies almost entirely on conventional (and prissy) poeticisms. S. G. **Tremenheere**'s octosyllabic version of 1899 mingles the poetic with the chatty, but falls into frequent bathos ('Anon she made me sober down'). Jack **Lindsay**'s version of 1927 was an interesting departure which attempted to forge a genuinely poetic use of colloquial English. E. H. W. **Meyerstein**'s version of 1935 is again excessively 'poetic' ('O happiness! O night of splendour mine! | O bed beatified by my sweet fay!'). A. S. **Way**'s of 1937 is rendered difficult by an unwieldy line. Of recent versions, W. G. **Shepherd**'s means well but is hard going; Ronald **Musker**'s is more lively, but verse only in intention. *The Monobiblos of Propertius*, an account of the first book of Propertius' poems (consisting of a text, translation, and critical essays on each poem) by R. I. V. **Hodge** and R. A. **Buttimore**, provides an

intelligent introduction, the extensive commentary making good the inevitable deficiencies of the translations.

Many 20th-c. versions were responding to or reacting against *Homage to Sextus Propertius* by Ezra **Pound**, a version of selections from Propertius' poems which has perhaps been the most influential translation of any poet in the 20th c., raising both Propertius and poetic translation to high critical esteem. Pound's extraordinary poem varies continually between strict transliteration and very free paraphrase. It has, however, proved to be a mistake to assume that Pound was providing a *method*. Before and after Pound, most versions of Catullus, Tibullus, and Propertius suggest that, while translators *can* rise above themselves in the act of translation, they cannot rise very high. Pound's Propertius, it appears, is strictly *sui generis*.

TM

ANTHOLOGIES   *Erotica: The Poems of Catullus and Tibullus and the Vigil of Venus*, tr. Walter K. Kelly et al., London, 1854 [Bohn] · *Catullus, Tibullus, and Pervigilium Veneris*, tr. (respectively) F. W. Cornish, J. P. Postgate, and J. W. Mackail, London, 1912 [Loeb] · *Catullus and Tibullus in English Verse*, tr. Arthur S. Way, London, 1936.

CATULLUS   *The Poems of Gaius Valerius Catullus in English Verse*, tr. J. Nott, 2 vols., London, 1795 · *The Poems of Catullus*, tr. Theodore Martin, London, 1861 · *The Lesbia of Catullus*, tr. J. H. A. Tremenheere, London, 1897 · *Some Poems of Catullus*, tr. J. F. Symons-Jeune, London, 1923 · *Catullus in English Poetry*, ed. Eleanor Shipley Duckett, Northampton, Mass., 1925 [selected English trs. with facing Latin text] · *The Poems of Catullus*, tr. Peter Whigham, Harmondsworth, 1966 [Penguin] · *Catullus*, tr. Celia Zukovsky and Louis Zukofsky, London, 1969 · *Catullus: The Complete Poems for Modern Readers*, tr. Reney Myers and Robert J. Ormsby, London, 1972 · *The Poems of Catullus*, tr. Frederic Raphael and Kenneth McLeish, London, 1978 · *Catullus*, tr. G. P. Goold, Bristol, 1983 · *The Poems of Catullus*, tr. Guy Lee, Oxford, 1990.

PROPERTIUS   *Propertii Monobiblos*, tr. [John Nott], London, 1782 [*Elegies*, bk. i] · *Specimens of the Classic Poets*, tr. Sir Charles Elton, 3 vols., London, 1814 · *The Elegies of Propertius*, tr. C. R. Moore, London, 1870 · *The Cynthia of Propertius*, tr. S. G. Tremenheere, London, 1899 · *Homage to Sextus Propertius*, tr. Ezra Pound, New York, 1921, London, 1934 [J. P. Sullivan's *Ezra Pound and Sextus Propertius*, London, 1964, includes the text of Pound's poem] · *Propertius in Love*, tr. J. Lindsay, London, 1927 · *Four Elegies of Propertius*, tr. E. H. W. Meyerstein, London, 1932 · *Propertius*, tr. Arthur S. Way, London, 1937 · *The Poems of Propertius*, tr. Ronald Musker, London, 1972 [Everyman] · *The 'Monobiblos' of Propertius*, tr. R. I. V. Hodge and R. A. Buttimore, Cambridge, 1977 · *The Poems of Propertius*, tr. W. G. Shepherd, Harmondsworth, 1985 [Penguin].

TIBULLUS   *Epistolary Poems on Several Occasions*, by Charles Hopkins, London, 1694 [includes trs. of Elegies III.2, IV.4, IV.13] · *The Works of Tibullus*, tr. J. Dart, London, 1720 · *A Poetical Translation of the Elegies*, J. Grainger, 2 vols., London, 1759 · *The Poems of Tibullus*, tr. Philip Dunlop, Harmondsworth, 1972 [Penguin] · *Tibullus: Elegies*, tr. Guy Lee, Cambridge, 1975 [expanded 1982].

SEE ALSO   Braden, G., ' "Vivamus, Mea Lesbia" in the English Renaissance', *ELR*, 9 (1979), 199–224 · McPeek, J. A. S., *Catullus in Strange and Distant Britain*, Cambridge, Mass., 1939 · Smith, K. F., 'Notes on Tibullus', *American Journal of Philology*, 37 (1916), 131–55 [on Tibullus' imitators] · Townend, G., 'Propertius among the Poets', *Greece and Rome*, 2nd ser., 8 (1961), 36–49 · Wiseman, T. P., *Catullus and His World*, Cambridge, 1985 [ch. 8 on 19–20 c. views/versions].

5. HORACE

After Ovid and Virgil, Quintus Horatius Flaccus, who wrote in the 1st c. BCE, is the most quoted, most passionately admired, most frequently and most successfully translated of all Roman poets. He has been found profoundly witty, profoundly moving,

and profoundly wise. A great many English poets have known large portions of Horace's works by heart, and, especially from the time of Ben Jonson to that of Tennyson, have looked upon the Latin poet as a poetic mentor, constant companion, or chosen friend, whose thoughts and phrases mingled with theirs almost as if he were a contemporary who spoke their language. While no poet seems to have found Horace's poetry easy to translate, so many writers who combined a love of the original with considerable poetic skill in English have made the attempt that the Latinless reader can afford to be extremely selective, to concentrate on those versions that are at once self-explaining English poems and intelligent commentaries on their Latin originals, and to disregard innumerable worthy but dull translations, old and new. Like precious stones, the best versions of Horace were produced in small clusters and in unpredictable places, but, when collected, have a strong claim to constitute a more convincing 'English Horace' than any of the many complete translations.

Some poets were drawn to Horace's Satires and Epistles, discussed elsewhere [II.n.7.ii]. A special case, however, is presented by the epistle to the Pisones (*Ad Pisones*), known as the *Ars Poetica* or *Art of Poetry* (probably unfinished at Horace's death), which offers advice to an aspiring writer. Almost every poet read, and many translated or imitated, this work, which was admired as much for its manner as for its critical precepts. Alexander Pope, for example, writes in his own heavily indebted *Essay on Criticism* that Horace 'charms with graceful negligence | And without method *talks* us into sense', thus teaching the 'truest notions in the easiest way'. The *Ars Poetica* is translated with close attention to the Latin by Thomas **Drant** (*fl.* 1570) and Ben **Jonson**, with greater freedom and in blank verse by Wentworth Dillon, Earl of **Roscommon** (1637–85), in elegant couplets by Thomas **Creech** (1659–1700) and Philip **Francis** (1708–73), in more chatty couplets by Francis **Howes** (1776–1844) and John **Conington** (1825–69), and with application to modern times by John **Oldham** (1653–83), **Byron**, and, in the 20th c., C. H. **Sisson**.

Other poets have been attracted by the 17 Epodes. The Second Epode (often known from its first line as *Beatus ille*), a poem spoken by a businessman contemplating the potential happiness of a country life, was in the 17th and 18th c. one of the most influential of all Latin poems. The history of English verse may be traced in the succession of renderings by Ben Jonson, John **Beaumont** (1583–1627), Richard **Fanshawe** (1608–66), Abraham **Cowley** (1618–67), John **Dryden**, and again most recently, C. H. Sisson (all these versions except Cowley's are included in Carne-Ross and Haynes 1996).

Most alluring of all the works of Horace have been the four books of *Carmina* or Odes, containing 103 short poems. But though the sentiments and general manner of the Odes have been found peculiarly familiar, their essential effects seem to be achieved by means very different from anything available in the English language or English versification. While the topics of the Odes look familiar enough—love, wine, friends, the benefits of moderation, praise of the patron or the monarch—few confine themselves to a single subject or maintain a single stance. Their art has always been felt to reside in their allusiveness and delicacy, as manifested in Horace's perfectly executed and yet surprising transitions, the complicated motions of his mind being reflected in the subtle movement of his syntax through a metrically complicated stanza. Dryden wrote that Horace's style was distinguished by its 'noble and bold Purity' and the 'secret happiness' (*curiosa felicitas*) of his choice of words, while Johnson claimed categorically that the Odes 'never can be properly translated' for 'so much of the excellence is in the numbers and the expression'. And yet few poets could resist the challenge.

The desire to translate Horace—which in some periods seems to have been almost a collective endeavour—has therefore involved a debate between sharply conflicting notions of poetic translation. At one extreme are those who have attempted to write as Horace might have written were he an Englishman living in the English present. At the other are the 'foreignizers' bent on reproducing their sense of the strangeness and difficulty of the experience of reading Horace in Latin. Both camps have been attracted by the 'bold purity' and the *curiosa felicitas* of the original, which has been seen as a *poetic* challenge: 'in a prose translation' of the Odes, writes J. B. **Leishman** (himself a powerful defender of those who attempt to represent the 'latinity' of the Latin), 'the meaningfulness of their meaning very largely disappears, and what remains appears in varying degrees as commonplace, flat, trivial, tediously elaborate and artificial' (Leishman 1956). To this day, those translators who, like James **Michie**, present themselves first of all as serviceable guides to the Latin make considerable efforts to rise to the *poetic* challenge, and versions of Horace's Odes offering themselves as modern poems continue to appear.

One of the best single-handed translations of Horace, which steers elegantly between the conflicting demands, is that produced by Philip **Francis**. Francis is sufficiently accomplished as a versifier to maintain a balance between metrical elegance and solid sense, and his book (particularly if his versions are read with his notes) is always useful. Although he drew on the versions of Dryden and others, his own versifications tend towards 'a punctual, regular Translation'. 'Francis', claims Carne-Ross, 'can write like a poet but, not being a poet himself, does not have to clear the ground of his own poetry to make way for Horace's', so that 'his achievement is to have made himself at home in the *Odes* more completely than any other translator had done' (Carne-Ross and Haynes 1996). Francis's knowledge of his own limitations in comparison with the English poets he draws on and his admiration for the superior sense of the Latin poet make his translation an excellent introduction to Horace. It reached a ninth edition in 1791 and might be usefully reprinted today.

One of the marks of Francis's modesty is his acknowledgement that 'it is hardly to be expected that any one Translator shall ever be capable of following this great poet with equal Spirit through all his Odes'. The plethora of interesting and distinguished partial translations, of a single ode or of a handful, makes it easiest to approach the English life of the *Carmina* through a composite volume representing a number of translators' work, and there have been several of these over the centuries. Three of them merit special attention, and between them present a full picture. The earliest was edited in 1666 by Alexander Brome (or Broome): *The Poems of Horace, Consisting of Odes, Satyres, and Epistles, Rendered in English Verse by Several Persons*. This includes translations by William **Cartwright** (1611–43), Charles **Cotton** (1630–87), Abraham Cowley, Richard Fanshawe, Sir John **Hawkins** (d. 1640), and Ben Jonson. Of these Fanshawe's, which dominate the volume, are the most metrically various, but Cowley's the most innovative. The *Art of Poetry* appears in Jonson's accurate rather than elegant version. The quality of the collection is uneven, and Brome himself is apologetic, trusting that future translators will take forward the venture he has pioneered.

Brome's hopes were partly fulfilled by *The Odes, Satyrs and Epistles of Horace . . . by the Most Eminent Hands*, issued by the publisher Jacob Tonson in 1715. These 'eminent hands' include many of the most admired poets of the preceding half-century, which is to say of one of the most important periods of translation from the classics by English literary figures: **Milton**, Dryden, Abraham Cowley, Thomas **Otway**, Matthew **Prior**, and William **Congreve**. The *Art of Poetry* is given in the blank verse translation by the Earl of Roscommon. Not all Horace's poems are represented, but the standard of this little volume is high.

Tonson's collection, like Brome's, includes where it was possible several versions of the same

ode. The fifth Ode of the first Book, for example, is represented in Brome's collection by versions by Fanshawe and Cowley, and in Tonson's by Cowley, Horneck, and Milton—Cowley and Milton representing opposite extremes of translation method (for a full collection of English versions of this poem see Storrs 1959). Milton's version is, as his title has it, *Rendered almost Word for Word without Rhyme according to the Latin Measure, as near as the Language will permit*. It begins:

> What slender Youth bedew'd with liquid odors
> Courts thee on Roses in some pleasant Cave,
> Pyrrha? For whom bind'st thou
> In wreaths thy golden Hair,
> Plain in thy neatness?

Cowley's version is described as an 'imitation'. Only the principal metaphors have been retained, and the verse form makes no concession to the 'Latin measure':

> To whom now, Pyrrha, art thou kind?
> To what Heart-ravish'd Lover
> Dost thou thy golden Locks unbind,
> Thy hidden Sweets discover,
> And with large Bounty open set
> All the bright Stores of thy rich Cabinet?

Readers have always been divided over the merits of these two approaches. Johnson thought parts of Cowley's poem were beneath the dignity of Horace. Some readers have felt Milton's version (the stanza form of which was adopted by Thomas **Warton** (1728–90) in his two translations of Horatian odes) hardly to count as English writing at all.

The most innovative and influential translations in Tonson's collection are the four odes by John Dryden, who extended the freedoms opened to him by Fanshawe and Cowley. Dryden claimed to have 'taken some pains' to make his version of Ode iii.29, in particular, his 'Master-Piece in English'. This translation was widely read, imitated, and anthologized—particularly the lines spoken by the Happy Man:

> Happy the Man, and happy he alone,
> He, who can call to day his own:
> He, who secure within, can say
> To morrow do thy worst, for I have liv'd to day.
> Be fair, or foul, or rain, or shine,
> The joys I have possest, in spight of fate are mine.
> Not Heav'n it self upon the past has pow'r;
> But what has been, has been, and I have had my hour.

And yet there is a paradox. This version of Horace bears, in many of its parts, only a loose relation to the Latin. Dryden, to be sure, called it a 'paraphrase' rather than a translation; but J. B. Leishman (1956) rightly goes further in commenting upon this 'superb stanza' in particular: it is 'not so much a translation of Horace as a magnificent expansion of, and variation upon, a familiar thought which Dryden might have found in almost any ancient author'.

The third and last collection of English Horatian translations to be discussed here provides a near-perfect introduction to the subject and takes it down to the present day. *Horace in English*, edited by D. S. Carne-Ross and Kenneth Haynes (with an informative introduction by Carne-Ross), is an anthology of versions and imitations by poets from the Earl of **Surrey** (?1517–1547) to Charles **Tomlinson** (whose versions of two Odes are here published for the first time), together with a selection of 'original' poems inspired by Horace. Taken together with Martindale and Hopkins (1993), this volume provides a comprehensive guide to the major English translations. (Antony Lentin's anthology, *Horace: The Odes*, published the following year, has many similar qualities but is less discriminating in its selections of translations, and disappointingly allows only one for each poem.)

Many of Carne-Ross and Haynes's inclusions can be described as interesting curiosities: those by Henry Howard, Earl of Surrey, Sir Philip **Sidney**, Sir John Hawkins, Thomas Creech, Thomas Warton, William **Wordsworth**, and Arthur Hugh **Clough**. In some cases they represent the only examples of Horace translation by the poet in question. In others, such as those of Creech and of the Victorians John Conington and Charles Stuart **Calverley** (1831–84), Carne-Ross and Haynes select the most intelligent efforts from a writer who translated a considerable number of Horace's poems. Included also are renderings by Tom **Brown** (1663–1704), Samuel **Johnson**, Christopher **Smart**, Thomas **Moore**, Gerard Manley **Hopkins**, and Rudyard **Kipling**, which are all idiosyncratic and in their way delightful. The versions by Jonson, Herrick, Milton, Cowley, Dryden, Pope, and Cowper are at once translations of Horace and English poems in their own right. Finally, and ingeniously, the *Ars Poetica* is represented by a composite version assembled from samples of translations and imitations by ten poets over four centuries.

TM

TRANSLATIONS   *Horace His Arte of Poetrie, Pistles, and Satyrs Englished*, tr. Thomas Drant, London, 1567 · *Horace His Art of Poetrie*, tr. Ben Jonson, in *The Workes of Benjamin Jonson*, London, 1640 · *The Poems of Horace, Consisting of Odes, Satyres, and Epistles, rendered in English Verse by Several Persons*, ed. Alexander Brome, London, 1666 · *Horace His Art of Poetry*, tr. John Oldham, in *Some New Pieces*, London, 1681 [rep. in Oldham's *Poems*, ed. Harold F. Brooks, Oxford, 1987] · *Horace of the Art of Poetry*, tr. Wentworth Dillon, Earl of Roscommon, London, 1684 [rep. in *Poems by the Earl of Roscommon*, 1717, with Latin text and extensive commentary by Charles Gildon, and subsequently] · *The Odes, Satyrs and Epistles of Horace*, tr. Thomas Creech, London, 1684 [regularly rep. through the 18th c.] · *The Odes, Satyrs and Epistles of Horace That Have Been Done into English by the Most Eminent Hands*, London, 1715 [rev. 1717, etc., under modified titles] · *A Poetical Translation of the Works of Horace*, tr. Philip Francis, London, 1749 [many reprints] · *Hints from Horace*, tr. George Gordon, Lord Byron, London, 1811 [*Ars Poetica*; rep. in edns. of Byron's works] · *Epodes, Satires and Epistles of Horace*, tr. Francis Howes, London, 1845 · *Translating Horace: Thirty Odes Translated into the Original Metres*, by J. B. Leishman, Oxford, 1956 · *Ad Pyrrham: A Polyglot Collection of Translations of Horace's Ode to Pyrrha*, ed. Ronald Storrs, Oxford, 1959 · *The Odes of Horace*, tr. James Michie, London, 1963 [Penguin, 1976] · *The Poetic Art*, tr. C. H. Sisson, Manchester, 1974 · *Horace in English*, ed. D. S. Carne-Ross and Kenneth Haynes, Harmondsworth, 1996 [Penguin] · *Horace: The Odes in English Verse*, ed. Antony Lentin, Ware, 1997 [anthology of historical trs.].

SEE ALSO   Benham, A. R., 'Horace and His "Ars Poetica" in English: A Bibliography', *Classical World*, 49 (1956), 1–5 · Edden V., 'The Best of Lyric Poets', in C. D. N. Costa, ed., *Horace*, London, 1973, 135–60 [on 17th-c. trs.] · Martindale, C., and Hopkins, D., eds., *Horace Made New: Horatian Influences on British Writing from the Renaissance to the Twentieth Century*, Cambridge, 1993 · Røstvig, M.-S., *The Happy Man: Studies in the Metamorphosis of a Classical Ideal*, 2 vols., Oxford, 1954–8 · Sherbo, A., ed., *Christopher Smart's Verse Translation of Horace's 'Odes'*, Victoria, BC, 1979 [full introd. on Horace in the 18th c.] · Wilkinson, L. P., *Horace and His Lyric Poetry*, 2nd edn., Cambridge, 1951 [ch. 6 on trs.].

6. OVID

i. Introduction   The extant work of Ovid (Publius Ovidius Naso), written between *c.*20 BCE and 17 CE, comprises a collection of love elegies (*Amores*), two mock-didactic poems for lovers (*Ars Amatoria* and *Remedia Amoris*), a collection of the fictional correspondence of mythological heroines (*Heroides*), a poem on Roman festivals (*Fasti*), two collections of personal poems written during the poet's exile by the Black Sea (*Tristia* and *Ex Ponto*), a short personal invective (*Ibis*), and, most famously, a mythological poem in 15 books on transformation and change (*Metamorphoses*).

From Ovid's own day, critical responses to the poet's work have been marked by a curious schizophrenia. He has been perhaps the most frequently imitated and widely influential writer in the whole European tradition—until romantic demands for 'sincerity' and 'originality' caused his highly literary and self-conscious artistry to fall out of favour. His love poetry—outspoken, shrewd, witty, knowing, self-mocking—offered later poets an alternative to the ardent solemnities of the Petrarchan tradition. *Heroides* engendered a literature of 'female complaint' (of which perhaps the most celebrated English example is Pope's 'Eloisa to Abelard'), and was an important influence on the epistolary novel. *Metamorphoses* impressed readers with its psychological acuteness, pictorial precision, and imaginative vision of nature's continuity and flux. It was regularly translated, adapted, echoed, and alluded to by poets in all the major European vernaculars, and drawn upon as a major source of mythological data by dramatists, musicians, and visual artists. However, despite Ovid's popularity, commentators regularly expressed their disapproval of his salacious or taboo subject-matter, his prolixity, and his deployment of obtrusive word-play and near-comedy in inappropriate situations. Consequently, his work was frequently proscribed, bowdlerized, recast, or sanitized by various kinds of moralizing or allegorizing commentary.

Ovid has been best translated in periods when the resources of English poetry have allowed a high degree of formal clarity, tonal sophistication, and rhetorical polish. He is not susceptible to flat, slangy, verbose, or rhythmically flaccid renderings, and while prose translations can be invaluable aids to basic understanding, they can convey little of his artful patternings and playful strategies. (The elaborately annotated prose translation of *Fasti* by Sir J. G. **Frazer** (1854–1941) was, however, influential earlier this century in stimulating an anthropological interest in Ovid's Roman lore.) It is no surprise, therefore, that many of the most valuable versions of Ovid are to be found among the verse translations made before 1800.

ii. Works other than *Metamorphoses* Though not a translation as such, *The Legend of Good Women* by Geoffrey **Chaucer** is clearly indebted to Ovid's portrayals of celebrated women in love in *Heroides*. Among versions of *Amores*, pride of place goes to the first complete rendering, that of Christopher **Marlowe**. Marlowe's translations, probably written during the 1580s, were the first rendering of Ovid's erotic elegies in any vernacular. Marlowe uses iambic pentameter couplets and follows his original closely, expanding only to clarify meaning, and to elucidate mythological references. The translation contains occasional mistakes and awkwardnesses—though some apparent errors are, in fact, accurate renderings of the texts then available. But the version as a whole offers an extremely spirited, energetic, and plausible re-creation of Ovid's sophisticated amatory style, in couplets of great dexterity, and Marlowe is particularly resourceful in finding neat English equivalents for Ovid's verbal figures.

Lively versions of individual *Amores* by John **Dryden**, Sir Charles **Sedley** (?1639–1701), and others appeared during the later 17th c., a substantial collection being included in the publisher Jacob Tonson's *Miscellany Poems* (1684). Many of these versions—where Ovid is sometimes given something of the tone and manner of a Restoration rake—were included in later editions of *Ovid's Epistles*, the translation of *Heroides* by Dryden and others, first published in 1680. This collection, largely the work of dramatists and court wits (including Thomas **Otway** (1652–85), Nahum **Tate** (1652–1715), and Aphra **Behn** (1640–89)), renders Ovid's poems in heroic couplets, and combines declamatory pathos with deft imitation of the chiasmic and antithetical structures of Ovid's elegiacs. Contemporary parodists pounced on the knowing and prurient note which is sometimes evident in the volume. The collection nevertheless achieves a fluency and elegance which had been conspicuously lacking in the lumbering version of *Heroides* in 'fourteeners' (rhymed iambic heptameters) by the Tudor poet George **Turbervile** (*c*.1544–*c*.1597).

Dryden was also, along with Thomas **Yalden** (1671–1736) and William **Congreve**, one of the translators of *Ovid's Art of Love* (1709), the standard version of *Ars Amatoria* during the 18th and early 19th c. This translation, in masterfully deft and subtly modulated couplets, combines a confident, rakish swagger with notes of rueful self-mockery and witty self-exposure which suggest that *Ars* is a more sophisticated, and less straightforwardly complacent, chauvinistic, or cynical poem than has often been assumed.

No translation of similar stature exists for the poems of Ovid's exile. The early 17th-c. versions of *Tristia* and *Ex Ponto* by Zachary **Catlin** (*fl.* 1630–40) and Wye **Saltonstall** (*fl.* 1625–40) are lucid, and achieve a consistent decorum, but their couplets seem rather staid and wooden in comparison with later achievements in the form. Perhaps the most successful English versions from this part of Ovid's *œuvre* are the translations, in freely enjambed couplets, of *Tristia* iii.3, v.3, and *Ex Ponto* iii.7, iv.3 by Henry **Vaughan** (1621–95), which convey the poems' personal pathos, while simultaneously doing justice to their formal control and elegiac conventions. The modern version of *Ovid's Poetry of Exile* by David R. **Slavitt** is freely imitative, its loosely discursive manner giving an impression of rambling conversation rather than the self-consciously 'literary' self-presentation to be found in Ovid's original. The only version of *Ibis* to have achieved any fame is the translation by the Tudor writer Thomas **Underdowne** (*fl.* 1566–87), whose 'fourteeners' give Ovid's allusive elegiacs an intense, incantatory vigour—rougher than the original, but convincing on their own terms.

iii. *Metamorphoses* *Metamorphoses* was widely influential in the Middle Ages, particularly on such works as Chaucer's *Book of the Duchess* (which incorporates a retelling of the story of Ceyx and Alcyone from *Met.* xi) and *Confessio Amantis* by John **Gower** (?1330–1408) (which contains reworkings of several Ovidian narratives). The complete prose *Metamorphoses* by William **Caxton** (*c.*1422–91) was made from a French adaptation rather than from Ovid's original. The first major English translation of *Metamorphoses*, by Arthur **Golding** (?1536–?1605), was the version used by Shakespeare and famously described by Ezra Pound as 'the most beautiful book in the language'. Despite Golding's own Calvinism, and a prefatory 'Epistle' in which *Metamorphoses* is systematically allegorized in the medieval manner, the translation itself is substantially free of moralistic intrusion, and follows the Latin closely, except for the incorporation of explanatory glosses within the text and some rather wordy local 'padding'. Golding 'naturalizes' Ovid, giving English equivalents for some mythological names ('Orphey' for 'Orpheus', 'Penthey' for 'Pentheus' etc.), and incorporating homely English diction and folklore ('queach', 'flacker', 'whewl', 'foolish noddie', 'elves'). His fourteeners have inbuilt disadvantages: the lines tend to break down into ballad-like subdivisions (tetrameter + trimeter) or to move with 'a kind of lickety-spit lightness that will not support any very grave style of utterance' (Braden 1978). The translation can thus sometimes seem quaint, and its comedy unintentional or uncontrolled. But Golding gives a clear, vigorous sense of Ovid's narrative, and can at times convey a note of detached wonder—one of the features which have often been thought to characterize Ovid's original.

The version in iambic pentameter couplets by George **Sandys** (1578–1644), first published in 1626, revised (with substantial commentary) in 1632, and regularly reprinted until the 1690s, replaced Golding as the standard English *Metamorphoses* for much of the 17th c. [see I.b.2.ii]. Sandys restricts allegorizing to his commentary, and follows Ovid's original line by line, seeking English equivalents not only for the Latin poet's sense but also for his numerous rhetorical figures. This produces a version of great verbal density and compression which, though it contains numerous local ingenuities and some passages of genuinely limpid narrative, generally has less clarity and forward momentum than Golding's. This effect is heightened by Sandys's numerous marginal glosses on points of mythology, geography, or ancient custom, which constantly interrupt the reader's concentration on the narrative flow and make the translation 'a thing more to be studied than to be read' (Braden).

Sandys's couplets often anticipate later developments in the form, and his local felicities are often best appreciated from the vantage-point of later translators who drew on, and improved, his phrases and cadences. Chief among these was John Dryden, whose versions from *Metamorphoses* long enjoyed a unique status as the only substantial translations from Ovid's masterpiece by an English poet of the first rank at the height of his powers. Dryden's plans for a complete new English *Metamorphoses* in the 1690s (in which he would have acted as coordinator and principal contributor) came to posthumous fruition in the version of 1717, edited by Samuel **Garth** (1661–1719), and frequently reprinted during the 18th and early 19th c. This collection incorporates all Dryden's versions, interspersed with renderings by younger poets of his school, including Joseph **Addison**, Alexander **Pope**, John **Gay**, Nahum Tate, and Garth himself.

Though in his prose criticism Dryden often repeated the stock criticisms of Ovid's 'wit out of season', his versions show him to have responded, in the act of translation, to the Latin poet's verbal figures as a set of 'distancing' or 'controlling' devices which allow simultaneous play to perspectives which would otherwise have seemed irreconcilable. Ovid's fantastic narratives, in Dryden's renderings, seem to be written from a stance which is both sympathetic and impassive, witty and intimate, cool and compassionate, playful and grave. Dryden's Ovid is simultaneously alert to the comedy and pathos and to the cruelty and tenderness of the human condition, and is able to encompass all four in a single, extraordinarily inclusive, vision. Dryden's versions from the *Metamorphoses* maintain a consistent level of excellence, but some episodes are rendered with particular distinction: the story of Myrrha (*Met.* x), in which the heroine's incestuous passion for her father is portrayed in all its turbulent paradoxicality; the tale of Baucis and Philemon (*Met.* viii), which combines domestic comedy and homely detail with a tender depiction of marital devotion and divine mercy; the episode of Ceyx and Alcyone (*Met.* xi), in which a wife's bereavement is treated with the characteristically Ovidian fusion of tenderness and humour, fancy and psychological precision; the discourse of Pythagoras (*Met.* xv), whose exposition of the principles of metempsychosis and flux was clearly regarded by Dryden as lying near the heart of Ovid's poetic vision of nature's continuity in change, and which achieves an extra poignancy in Dryden's rendering, by being imbued with the 68-year-old English poet's own reflections on death and immortality.

For reasons already given, few romantic or Victorian poets attempted to translate *Metamorphoses*. More recently, educational demand, together with shifts in aesthetic fashion which ensure that Ovid is no longer routinely dismissed as 'artificial' and 'insincere', have encouraged a number of new versions. None of the translations produced in the USA in the 1950s (by A. E. **Watts**, Rolfe **Humphries**, and Horace **Gregory**) proved sufficiently distinctive to establish itself as a 'standard' modern version. David Slavitt, in his free rendering of 1994, attempts to mimic Latin hexameters in English, thereby producing a verse too shapeless and wordy to be a suitable vehicle for a lengthy narrative. The version by Charles **Boer** rejects regular metre for free verse, and continuous syntax for a broken, breathless, note-form style, designed to convey the violent power of Ovid's mythic material.

After Ovid: New Metamorphoses, edited by Michael Hofmann and James Lasdun, is a collection of newly commissioned poems inspired by *Metamorphoses*. These range from close translations to 'original' poems loosely based on Ovidian themes. The volume as a whole offers a fascinating cross-section of responses to Ovid by some of the best-known poets of the later 20th c. The writers represented include Amy **Clampitt**, Thom **Gunn**, Seamus **Heaney**, Michael **Longley**, Derek **Mahon**, and Charles **Tomlinson**. The most distinctive contributions to the volume are the four episodes translated by Ted **Hughes**. These are collected, in revised versions, together with renderings of 20 other passages, in *Tales from Ovid*. Hughes's stabbing, short-breathed free verse might at first sight seem an inappropriate medium in which to render Ovid's suavely flowing hexameters, and some of Hughes's own pronouncements might encourage one to see his intention as being not so much to render Ovid as to reach 'behind' and 'beyond' the Roman poet's sophisticated retellings to the raw 'physical life' of the original myths. Hughes can, however, command an attractive laconic wit as well as an earthy vividness, and can sometimes even create his own deadpan equivalent of Ovid's verbal 'turns'. Moreover, the sheer energy, pace, and liveliness of his renderings at the local level makes them by far the most poetically compelling versions of *Metamorphoses* to have been written this century.

Among recent complete translations probably the most widely used, at least in the UK, is that of the retired solicitor A. D. **Melville** first published in 1986. This version, in blank verse with occasional rhymes, is close, fluent, and workmanlike, and maintains a decent linguistic decorum. Its introduction and notes by E. J. Kenney clearly enhance its usefulness to teachers of 'classics in translation' courses. Only a major poet, however, could be expected to command the rhythmic control, subtlety of movement, flexibility of diction, and fluency of verse-music required to produce a sustainedly plausible recreation of Ovid's consummately crafted Latin. The most distinguished and satisfying complete English rendering of *Metamorphoses* thus remains the Dryden–Garth version of 1717.   DH

TRANSLATIONS *The Metamorphoses of Ovid*, tr. William Caxton [in MS, 1480; facsimile rep., New York, 1968] · *The xv Bookes of P. Ovidius Naso, entytuled Metamorphosis*, tr. Arthur Golding, London, 1567 [modern edns., London 1904, 1961, New York, 1965; extracts in *Ovid: Selected Works* (Everyman, 1939), which also contains selections from other 16th- and 17th-c. versions of Ovid's work] · *The Heroycall Epistles of the Learned Poet Publius Ovidius Naso, in English Verse*, tr. George Turbervile, London, 1567 [modern edn., London, 1928; extracts in Everyman *Ovid*] · *Ovid his Invective against Ibis. Translated into English Meter*, tr. Thomas Underdowne, 1569 [extracts in Everyman *Ovid*] · *All Ovid's Elegies: 3 Bookes*, tr. Christopher Marlowe, 'Middleburgh', *c.*1597 [rep. in modern edns. of Marlowe's works; extracts in Everyman *Ovid*] · *Ovid's Metamorphosis Englished*, tr. George Sandys, London, 1626; rev. edn. with commentary, Oxford, 1632 [facsimile rep. New York, 1976; modern edn., Lincoln, Neb., 1970] · *Ovids Tristia: Containinge Five Bookes of Mournfull Elegies*, tr. W[ye] S[altonstall], London, 1633 [extracts in Everyman *Ovid*] · *Ovid de Ponto: Containing Foure Books of Elegies*, tr. W[ye] S[altonstall], London, 1639 [extracts in Everyman *Ovid*] · *Publ. Ovid. De Tristibus: or Mournfull Elegies, in Five Bookes*, tr. Zachary Catlin, London, 1639 [extracts in Everyman *Ovid*] · Vaughan, Henry, *Olor*

Iscanus, London, 1651 [versions of *Ex Ponto* iii. 7; iv. 3 and *Tristia* iii. 3; v. 3] · *Ovid's Epistles*, tr. John Dryden et al., London, 1680 [many reprints in 18th-c. version of *Amores* added in 1725 edn.] · *Ovid's Art of Love*, tr. John Dryden et al., London, 1709 [many reprints in 18th and early 19th c.] · *Ovid's Metamorphoses in Fifteen Books: Translated by the Most Eminent Hands*, tr. John Dryden et al., ed. Sir Samuel Garth, London, 1717 [frequent reprints in 18th c.; facsimile rep. New York, 1982; see also edns. of Dryden's works] · *Ovid's Fasti*, ed. J. G. Frazer, London, 1929 · *The Metamorphoses of Ovid: An English Version . . . with the Etchings of Pablo Picasso*, tr. A. E. Watts, Los Angeles, 1954 · *Ovid's Metamorphoses*, tr. Rolfe Humphries, Bloomington, Ind., 1955 · *The Metamorphoses: A Complete New Version*, tr. Horace Gregory, New York, 1958 · *Ovid: Metamorphoses*, tr. A. D. Melville, Oxford, 1986 · *Ovid's Metamorphoses*, tr. Charles Boer, Dallas, Tex., 1989 · *Ovid's Poetry of Exile*, tr. David R. Slavitt, Baltimore, 1990 · *The Metamorphoses of Ovid: Translated Freely into Verse*, tr. David R. Slavitt, Baltimore, 1994 · *After Ovid: New Metamorphoses*, ed. Michael Hofmann and James Lasdun, London, 1994 · *Tales from Ovid: 24 Passages from the 'Metamorphoses'*, tr. Ted Hughes, London, 1997.

SEE ALSO   Braden, G., 'Golding's Ovid', in his *The Classics and English Renaissance Poetry: Three Case Studies*, New Haven, Conn./London, 1978 · Martindale, C., ed., *Ovid Renewed: Ovidian Influences on Literature and Art from the Middle Ages to the Twentieth Century*, Cambridge, 1988 · Sowerby, R., 'Ovidian Genres', ch. 5 in his *The Classical Legacy in Renaissance Poetry*, London, 1994 · Tomlinson, C., *Poetry and Metamorphosis*, Cambridge, 1983.

7. SATIRE AND EPIGRAM

i. Introduction The *Satires* of Horace (Quintus Horatius Flaccus), Persius (Aulus Persius Flaccus), and Juvenal (Decimus Junius Juvenalis), and the *Epigrams* of Martial (Marcus Valerius Martialis), all written in the 1st and 2nd c. CE, were widely read in England from the Renaissance onwards, with particular attention being focused on all four during the 17th and 18th c. Translators' activity was not evenly distributed: some poems (e.g. Horace, *Sat.* ii. 6; Juvenal, *Sat.* x; Martial, *Ep.* x. 47) were returned to repeatedly, while others were generally only included in complete renderings of their author. The English absorption of Roman satire and epigram extended far beyond the bounds of translation as normally understood, and passages, motifs, and stylistic features from all four poets were regularly incorporated and adapted at the local level in a wide range of dramatic, satiric, lyric, and conversational verse.

The obscenity in all four poets (particularly Juvenal and Martial) ensured that many earlier translations were bowdlerized. Furthermore, the Latin writers' density of reference to (real and imagined) Roman personalities, mores, and situations faced translators with a choice: either to provide extensive annotation, or to 'imitate' their originals, transposing and updating their settings, and applying their insights and judgements to the modern world. In practice, however, the decision was seldom absolute: many close translations contained local patches of 'imitation'. And among imitations some genuinely attempted to convey the tone or 'spirit' of their originals, while others merely used their framework for acts of independent creation. Others, again, invited readers to follow a complex 'intertextual' interplay between imitation and original.

ii. Horace [see also II.n.5] Satire has been traditionally portrayed as an agent of moral, political, or social reform. A major challenge for English translators has thus been to define each Roman satirist's claim to moral authority, and its relation to his chosen form and manner and to the distinctive aesthetic pleasures which his work provides.

In the case of Horace, a major problem was to determine the connections between Horace's self-proclaimed role as a moral teacher and the urbane ambiguities, witty paradoxes, deft transitions, delicate ironies, and philosophical eclecticism which were felt to characterize his work. On the stylistic level, the challenge was to find an English equivalent for Horace's *sermo pedestris* ('low style') which was not merely flat, banal, or prosaic, and which conveyed something of the subtlety, variety, and flexibility of Horace's conversational manner in Latin.

The first complete English version of Horace's *Satires*, that of Thomas **Drant** (*fl.* 1570), uses cumbersome 'fourteeners' (rhymed iambic heptameters). In keeping with his puritanism, Drant concentrates on portraying Horace as 'a muche zelous controller of sinne'. His version is generally close to Horace's literal meaning, but includes some drastic bowdlerizing and moralizing interventions. Drant substitutes, for example, a passage on extravagant apparel for the section of *Sat.* i. 2 dealing with sexual mores, replaces *Sat.* i. 5 altogether by a satire on the evils of recusancy, and modifies *Sat.* ii. 8 with a vehement attack on drunkenness and gluttony.

A clearer impression of Horace's urbanity and ease is conveyed by the accomplished couplet versions by Sir John **Beaumont** (?1583–1627) and

Sir Richard **Fanshawe** (1608–66). Beaumont's close rendering of *Sat.* ii. 6 forms a companion piece to his renderings of Persius, *Sat.* ii and Juvenal, *Sat.* x: all three poems touch on the pleasures of retirement, and on the need to cultivate happiness in virtue, and Beaumont discreetly identifies Horace's sentiments with his own recusancy. Fanshawe recreates Horace's relaxed, conversational mode in well-controlled couplets, incorporating the occasional modern detail without substantially altering the original setting. The couplets of Alexander **Brome** (1620–66) are less decorous and shapely, but the composite *Poems of Horace* edited by Brome in 1666 includes one of the finest achievements of English Horatian imitation: the version of the fable of 'The Country Mouse' (from *Sat.* ii. 6) by Abraham **Cowley** (1618–67). In Brome's collection, the first half of Horace's poem is imitated by Cowley's friend Thomas **Sprat** (1635–1713), who humorously identifies Cowley with the garrulous narrator of Horace's fable, thereby reinforcing the note of delicate self-irony already apparent in Cowley's imitation, where the Horatian/Cowleian ideal of Epicurean rural content is both celebrated and mocked by being identified with the fortunes of two mice.

Later in the Restoration period, Horatian satire was imitated by John Wilmot, Earl of **Rochester** (1647–80), whose 'An Allusion to Horace' (based on *Sat.* i. 10) includes an attack on John Dryden (identified with Horace's Lucilius). The vigorously colloquial version of *Sat.* i. 9 by John **Oldham** (1653–83) transforms Horace's bore on the Via Sacra into a 'fop' encountered in 'The Mall' at the time of the Popish Plot. The standard complete translation of Horace in this period was that of Thomas **Creech** (1659–1700). Though its couplets are more pedestrian and less rhythmically and tonally adroit than the best verse of Creech's contemporaries (or of his own *Lucretius*, 1682), this version was frequently reprinted until the mid-18th c. and is still worth consulting as an intelligent response—seldom sparkling, but always thoughtful and workmanlike—to the full corpus of Horatian satire.

The *Imitations of Horace* by Alexander **Pope**—that of *Sat.* ii. 6 written in collaboration with Jonathan **Swift**—are the prime English examples of the 'intertextual' style of imitation: Pope engages in a complex, dynamic dialogue with Horace (whose text is printed opposite) for purposes of self-presentation, self-defence, and self-discovery, in the course of which paradoxes and contradictions in both poets are revealed and explored, and simultaneous light is shed on both. A more straightforward response is contained in the translation by

Philip **Francis** (?1708–73), which replaced Creech as the standard complete English Horace until the mid-19th c. In this version, the *Satires* are translated in a mixture of heroic couplets and octosyllabics (the latter reminiscent of Swift), and three versions are by Francis's friend William **Dunkin** (?1709–65). Francis provides a facing Latin text and detailed notes, many of them elegantly translated from the best Continental commentators, and his version achieves a dependable standard of elegance and tonal flexibility that makes it to this day one of the most satisfying complete versions.

Notable among later 18th-c. versions are the renderings of two satires (i. 5; i. 9) by William **Cowper**, the latter neatly 'adapted to the present times', and the complete translation by Christopher **Smart**. Both use octosyllabics, a form which is well suited to suggesting Horace's conversational ease, but which can make him seem rather lightweight. Considerably less well known but in some ways more impressive is the accomplished version in heroic couplets by Francis **Howes** (1776–1844), written early in the 19th c. but not published until 1848, and justly praised by John **Conington** (1825–69) as 'unforced, idiomatic, and felicitous'. Conington's own version of 1870 replaced Francis, to become the standard English Horace during the Victorian period. Conington deliberately avoids a contemporary idiom, opting for rhyming couplets which are competent and dexterous and which follow Horace's literal sense with remarkable fidelity, but which seem to exist in a stylistic limbo, neither authentically Augustan nor distinctively modern.

Of later versions that of Smith Palmer **Bovie**, in stress-based verse, renders Horace in a 1950s American idiom that now seems rather dated. More generally admired today is the Penguin translation by Niall **Rudd**. Rudd opts for a plain contemporary diction, avoiding excessive slang, and uses an unrhymed verse of six variable beats 'with a sufficient number of dactyls or anapaests to recall the movement of the original'. In this medium Horace appears as a decent, rather prosaic, man of sense, rather than a subtly nuanced wit. But the version is extremely successful at clarifying Horace's obscurities, and Rudd's excellent notes offer invaluable illumination of the poems' allusions and context.

iii. Persius If Horatian satire has been admired for its urbane poise, Persius, a committed Stoic writing in the reign of Nero, has been regularly praised for his philosophical consistency and moral sincerity. Persius' exhortations to Stoic virtue are, however, expressed in poetry of notorious allusiveness, compression, and obscurity—a fact which has constituted the major problem for English translators of his work in all periods. The first English Persius, that of Barten **Holyday** (1593–1661) was published in 1616 and reissued (revised) with the same translator's Juvenal (discussed below) in 1673. Both translations are accompanied by extensive and learned 'Illustrations'. Holyday uses heavily enjambed couplets in which he attempts a looser, more colloquial effect than in his Juvenal. John **Dryden** judged Holyday's versions to be more obscure, and more in need of commentary, than their originals. Others have argued, however, that Holyday's version gives the English reader a good impression of what it is like to read Persius' strangely contorted Latin. Dryden's own version was immediately praised by William Congreve for having made Persius' 'dark Poesie' intelligible in English for the first time. He translates more freely than Holyday, clarifying the Roman poet's obscurities in couplets of masterful vigour and pace, discovering personal resonances in some of Persius' sentiments, and devising resourceful means for giving the English reader a sense of the parodic and allusive strands in the text. The lively couplet version of Sir William **Drummond** (d. 1828) is freer than Dryden's, boldly interpolating sentiments which have no immediate equivalent in Persius' text. The translation by William **Gifford** (1756–1826), in couplets and accompanied by an extensive and intelligent commentary, combines fidelity to Persius' literal meaning with an elegance and readability which make it one of the most permanently valuable renderings. Another admirable late Augustan rendering is that of Francis Howes, which has similar virtues to the same translator's Horace (see above), and is similarly neglected.

Of the modern versions, three deserve special mention. The lively translation by the American poet W. S. **Merwin** (with an extensive introduction and notes by W. S. Anderson) employs unrhymed lines of five or six beats, and expands and elucidates Persius' obscurities, making free use of slang, and sudden shifts of tone and diction, to invest the poems with a frenetic, sardonic energy. Niall Rudd employs a similar style of language and versification to that of his Horace, keeping to the same number of lines as his original, and steering a middle course between literal fidelity and paraphrase. Useful endnotes provide further clarification of allusions and references which cannot be elucidated within the translation itself. The version in alexandrines by Guy **Lee**, with facing text and an introduction and substantial commentary by William Barr, offers itself unashamedly as a 'metaphrase' which attempts 'to represent every

metaphor and every peculiarity of diction and to reproduce the Latin syntax, as far as that is possible in English', and which is 'meant to read like a translation and does not pretend to be a factitious original'.

iv. Juvenal Juvenal has traditionally been portrayed as a high-minded scourge of Roman vice whose lofty style is matched by a caustic vehemence and hysterical bitterness caused by personal frustration and disappointment. Some, however, have seen Juvenal's satirical tirades as extravagantly hyperbolic, outrageously scurrilous, and indiscriminately opportunistic. An alternative conception of the poet has thus emerged, in which Juvenal is seen as a witty declaimer who deploys even the sublime epic register to remorselessly belittling effect, and whose art is more (or more immediately) concerned with vivid caricature and fanciful scene-painting than with exhortations to moral reform. A central problem for translators, therefore, has been to determine the connection (if any) between Juvenal's obscenity, extravagance, and opportunism and any reformist intention which his work might be thought to contain.

Several translations of individual Juvenal satires were published in the early 17th c., of which the most satisfying is probably the elegant, quietistic version of *Sat. x* by Sir John Beaumont (see above). Substantial portions of *Sat. x* are also translated in Act V of the tragedy *Sejanus His Fall* (performed 1603, published 1605) by Ben **Jonson**, a rendering which stresses Juvenal's vivid scene-painting rather than his wit. The first complete translation, however, did not appear until 1647, when Robert **Stapleton** (d. 1669) published *Juvenal's Sixteen Satyrs* (further revised as *Mores Hominum* in 1660). Stapleton's version, in freely enjambed couplets, contains some felicitous local touches, but is flat, solemn, and sometimes clumsy, conveying little sense of Juvenal's rhetorical dynamism. The inventory of Juvenalian *sententiae* included in the 1660 edition reveals Stapleton's interest in Juvenal as a provider of portable moral wisdom. The version of Barten Holyday became a byword for crabbed obscurity soon after its very belated posthumous publication in 1673. Holyday translates line for line, almost word for word, producing a contorted syntax that is consistently clumsy and at times almost unintelligible. The main value of the version lies in its encyclopedic commentary (see above). The Royalist poet Henry **Vaughan** (1621–95), writing in the 1640s, saw an urgent contemporary relevance in Juvenal's denunciation (in *Sat. x*) of the destruction caused by excessive political ambition.

Vaughan translates in an expansive, loosely para-phrastic way (his couplets have been thought to resemble rhymed blank verse) and Christianizes Juvenal's conclusion.

Notable among Restoration 'imitations' of Juvenal are the versions of *Sat*. iii and xii by John Oldham, which provide dramatically vivid realizations of Juvenal's satiric *vignettes*, applying them resourcefully to contemporary life, in verse which combines pointed wit with a flexibility and rhythmic verve not previously apparent in any English Juvenal. The 'modern essays' on *Sat*. x and xiii by Henry **Higden** have been criticized for trivializing Juvenal in the burlesque medium of *Hudibras*. But Higden's versions at times achieve a moving lapidary dignity, and his light, irreverent touch with Juvenal's more fanciful imaginings proved a fruitful stimulus for his most illustrious successor, John Dryden. The best passages in the 'Dryden' Juvenal of 1693, a collaborative project (in which Dryden rendered *Sat*. i, iii, vi, x, and xvi), raised English Juvenalian translation to unsurpassed heights. Dryden, writing with a virtuosic command of tone, rhythm, imagery, and rhetorical flow, combines a responsiveness to the hyperbolic and pictorially vivid aspects of Juvenalian satire ('Juvenal . . . gives me', he wrote, 'as much Pleasure as I can bear') with a sense of its power 'to purge the Passions'. In Dryden's rendering, Juvenal effects his moral re-formation not by delivering earnest jeremiads or portable platitudes but by scoffing at the delusions and disasters of life in a spirit of headily scornful and insouciant delight.

In sharp contrast to the exuberant *élan* of Dryden, the two early imitations of Juvenal by Samuel **Johnson** imbue Juvenal with their author's own sober preoccupations and anxieties. *London* (1738), a version of *Sat*. iii, includes idealistic jibes at Walpole's government and poignantly personal depictions of the lot of the impoverished Grub Street writer. *The Vanity of Human Wishes* (1749) converts *Sat*. x into a sombre Christian vision of human delusion which culminates in a near-despairing plea for divine grace. The last of the 'Augustan' couplet renderings, the complete version by William Gifford, lacks the breakneck impetus and vivid point of the best passages in the 'Dryden' version, but achieves a remarkably high overall level of elegance, clarity, and rhetorical pace. Though slightly bowdlerized, and (like all the earlier versions) based on Latin texts which lack the refinements of modern scholarship, Gifford's translation is accompanied by excellent notes, and provides perhaps the best overall entrée in English to the full range of Juvenalian satire.

Of more recent versions, the blank-verse rendering of *Sat*. x by Robert **Lowell** deserves special mention as the only translation of Juvenal by a major 20th-c. poet. The version's muted decorum produces a coherent English poem which, however, conveys little of Juvenal's verbal exuberance. Of recent translations by classicists, the most widely read are probably those by Peter **Green** and Niall Rudd. Both adopt an unrhymed, six-stress line. Green allows himself more latitude in stresses, incorporates explanatory glosses within his text, and makes free use of slang and obscenity. The result is comprehensible and racy but vulgar, giving little sense of Juvenal's 'declamatory grandeur'. Rudd allows himself less rhythmic and verbal latitude and produces a version of greater plainness and sobriety. Both versions provide valuable insight into Juvenal's meaning, but neither replaces the best of the earlier versions, whose formal resources allow a more powerful re-creation of the declamatory flow and pictorial vividness for which Juvenal was renowned.

v. Martial The *Epigrams* of Martial (over 1500 in number) vary greatly in subject-matter, metrical form, and degree of seriousness, and include flattering addresses to patrons, tender elegies, poems of Epicurean retirement, and various kinds of satiric jibe and social comment. Most of the poems treat a single theme, and turn upon, or culminate in, a graceful, ingenious, or witty thought, encapsulated in an elegant or pointed verbal formulation. The obscenity of many of the *Epigrams* formerly caused embarrassment, but has proved a positive attraction for more recent translators, who have revelled in the poems' 'explicitness'—though often at the expense of the polished artistry of which Martial was so proud.

Readers seeking basic elucidation of Martial's meaning are well served by the Loeb translation (in prose) by D. R. Shackleton **Bailey**. Of the many collections of verse translations and imitations of Martial (for a full list, see Sullivan and Boyle 1996), each has its own distinctive characteristics and emphasis. Sir John **Harington** (*c*.1560–1612), for example, pays particular attention to Martial's word-play. William **Hay** (1695–1755) concentrates on the 'moral' epigrams at the expense of more risqué items, while George Augustus **Sala** (1828–96) does precisely the opposite. Nathaniel Brassey **Halhed** (1751–1830) adapts Martial to contemporary politics. The '**Eton Master**' (*fl*. 1900) stresses Martial's usefulness as a guide to Roman manners and customs. Tony **Harrison** renders Martial in coarse US slang. Many of these collections achieve various kinds and levels of success with individual poems, but none of them is adequate to the full range of Martial's art. None of the earlier collections, moreover, has been reprinted in its entirety. Readers seeking 'the best of Martial' in English need therefore to combine the most successful versions from the collections with renderings of individual epigrams or groups of epigrams culled from a variety of English poets.

Notable among these is Ben Jonson, who translated only two of Martial's poems (x. 47 and viii. 77) directly, but whose 'original' verse abounds with numerous creative adaptations of Martial's work. In Jonson's recreations, Martial's verbal wit becomes a vehicle for acute moral perception and a means of holding conflicting emotions in a complex equipoise. The *Hesperides* of Robert **Herrick** contains many renderings of Martial, including versions of the more satiric and offensive poems avoided by other translators. For Abraham Cowley, Martial's most congenial poems were those treating the Horatian themes of friendship, happiness, rural retirement, and the good life. Sir John **Denham** (1615–69) and John Oldham both produced outstanding 'imitations' of individual epigrams (xi. 104 and i. 117), in which Martial is applied vigorously to the 17th-c. world. The versions of Sir Charles **Sedley** (?1639–1701) blend refined wit with sexual suggestiveness, and reground Martial in the mores of Restoration London. The dignified renderings by Robert Louis **Stevenson**, made with help of a French 'crib', concentrate on Martial's tender elegies, and on his poems of contentment and friendship. The American poet J. V. **Cunningham** included eight versions from Martial among his own collection of spare, pithy *Poems and Epigrams*. The imitations of Martial by the Australian poet Peter **Porter** have been called 'the most successful versions . . . this century' (Sullivan and Boyle). Porter is alert to the intellectual subtleties of Martial, and creates a complex intertextual effect by offering his versions as allusive dialogues with a historically distant original, rather than as 'naturalizations' or 'accommodations' of Martial in modern English.

Many of the best English versions of Martial are conveniently reprinted in two collections listed below: Henry G. Bohn, 1860, and J. P. Sullivan and A. J. Boyle, 1996.   DH

HORACE   *A Medicinable Morall, that is the Two Bookes of Horace his Satyres, Englyshed Accordyng to the Prescription of Saint Hierome*, tr. Thomas Drant, London, 1566 [incorporated in *Horace his Arte of Poetrie, Pistles, and Satyrs Englished*, London, 1567; facsimile rep. New York, 1972] · 'The Sixth Satire of the Second Book', tr. Sir John Beaumont in *Bosworthfield*, London, 1629 [also contains versions of Persius *Sat*. ii and Juvenal *Sat*. x] · *The Poems of Horace*, ed. Alexander Brome, London, 1666 [facsimile rep., New York, 1978; contains translations by Fanshawe, Brome, Cowley, etc.] · 'An Allusion to Horace. The 10th Satyr of the 1st Book', by John Wilmot, Earl of Rochester, in *Poems*, 'Antwerp' [i.e. London], 1680 · 'An Imitation of Horace: Book I, Satyr IX', by John Oldham, in *Some New Pieces*, London, 1681 [modern edn. in *The Poems of John Oldham*, ed. Harold F. Brooks with Raman Selden, Oxford, 1987] · *The Odes, Satyrs, and Epistles of Horace*, tr. Thomas Creech, London, 1684 [frequent reprints into the 18th c.] · *Imitations of Horace*, by Alexander Pope, originally published piecemeal, London, 1733–51 [standard modern edn. in *The Twickenham Edition of the Poems of Alexander Pope*, iv: *Imitations of Horace*, ed. John Butt, London, 1939] · *The Satires of Horace*, tr. Philip Francis, London 1746 [vol. iii of Francis's complete translation of Horace, 1743–6; frequent reps. in the 18th and 19th c.] · 'The Fifth Satire of the First Book of Horace: A Humorous Description of the Author's Journey from Rome to Brundisium' and 'The Ninth Satire of the First Book of Horace: Adapted to the Present Times: The Description of an Impertinent', tr. William Cowper, in vol. ii of *The Works of Horace in English Verse, by Several Hands* [ed. William Duncombe,] London 1759 [frequent reps. in edns. of Cowper's poems] · *The Works of Horace*, tr. Christopher Smart, London, 1767 [modern edn. in *The Poetical Works of Christopher Smart*, v: *The Works of Horace, Translated into Verse*, ed. Karina Williamson, Oxford, 1996] · *Epodes, Satires, and Epistles of Horace*, tr. Francis Howes, London, 1845 · *Horace: Satires, Epistles and Art of Poetry*, tr. John Conington, London, 1870 · *The Satires and Epistles of Horace*, tr. Smith Palmer Bovie, Chicago, 1959 · *Horace: Satires and Epistles; Persius: Satires*, tr. Niall Rudd, rev. edn., London, 1979 [Penguin] · *Horace in English*, ed. D. S. Carne-Ross and Kenneth Haynes, London, 1996 [Penguin].

JUVENAL   *Sejanus His Fall*, by Ben Jonson, London, 1605 [Act v contains substantial translated extracts from Juvenal, *Sat*. x] · 'The Tenth Satyre of Juvenal Englished', tr. Henry Vaughan, in his *Poems*, London, 1646 · *Juvenal's Sixteen Satyrs: or, A Survey of the Manners and Actions of Mankind*, tr. Sir Robert Stapleton, London, 1647 [rev. as *Mores Hominum: The Manners of Men, Described in Sixteen Satyrs, by Juvenal*, London, 1660] · *Decimus Junius Juvenalis, and Aulus Persius Flaccus Translated and Illustrated, As Well with Sculpture as Notes*, tr. Barten Holyday, Oxford, 1673 · 'The Thirteenth Satyr of Juvenal, Imitated' and 'A Satyr, In Imitation of the Third of Juvenal', by John Oldham, in *Poems and Translations*, London, 1683 [modern edn. in *The Poems of John Oldham*, ed. Harold F. Brooks with Raman Selden, Oxford, 1987] · *A Modern Essay on the Thirteenth Satyr of Juvenal*, tr. Henry Higden, London, 1686 · *A Modern Essay on the Tenth Satyr of Juvenal*, tr. Henry Higden, London, 1687 · *The Satires of Decimus Junius Juvenalis*, tr. John Dryden and others,

London, 1693 [frequent reprints during the 18th c.; Dryden's contributions reprinted in edns. of his poems] · *London: A Poem, In Imitation of the Third Satire of Juvenal*, by Samuel Johnson, London, 1738 · *The Vanity of Human Wishes. The Tenth Satire of Juvenal, Imitated*, by Samuel Johnson, London, 1749 · *The Satires of Decimus Junius Juvenalis*, tr. William Gifford, London, 1802 [rev. version, expanded by John Warrington, Everyman, 1954; rep. 1992] · 'The Vanity of Human Wishes: A Version of Juvenal's Tenth Satire', by Robert Lowell, in his *Near the Ocean*, London, 1967 · *Juvenal: The Sixteen Satires*, tr. Peter Green, London, 1967 [rev. 1974, Penguin] · *Juvenal: The Satires*, tr. Niall Rudd, Oxford, 1991.

MARTIAL   *The Most Elegant and Witty Epigrams of Sir John Harington, Knight, Digested into Foure Bookes*, London, 1615 · *Epigrams of Martial Englished*, tr. Henry Killigrew, London, 1689 (anonymously), 1695 (enlarged) · *Select Epigrams of Martial Translated and Imitated. With an Appendix of Some by Cowley and Other Hands*, tr. William Hay, London, 1755 · *Imitations of Some of the Epigrams of Martial, Parts 1 and 2*, tr. Nathaniel Brassey Halhed, London, 1793 · *The Epigrams of Martial, Translated into English Prose, Each Accompanied by One or More Verse Translations from the Works of English Poets, and Various Other Sources*, ed. Henry George Bohn, London, 1860 · *The Index Expurgatorius of Martial, Literally Translated, Comprising All the Epigrams Hitherto Omitted by English Translators, to Which is Added an Original Metrical Version and Copious Explanatory Notes*, tr. George Augustus Sala, London, 1868 · *Fifty Epigrams from the First Book of Martial, Translated into English Verse*, tr. 'An Eton Master', London, 1900 · *Martial, The Twelve Books of Epigrams*, tr. J. A. Pott and F. A. Wright, London, 1925 · *After Martial*, by Peter Porter, London, 1972 · *US Martial*, by Tony Harrison, Newcastle upon Tyne, 1981 · *Epigrams of Martial, Englished by Various Hands*, ed. J. P. Sullivan and Peter Whigham, Berkeley / Los Angeles / London, 1987 · *Martial*, tr. D. R. Shackleton Bailey, London, 1993 [Loeb] · *Martial in English*, ed. J. P. Sullivan and A. J. Boyle, London, 1996 [Penguin].

PERSIUS   *Aulus Persius Flaccus his Satyres*, tr. Barten Holyday, London, 1616 [rev. in Holyday's *Juvenal*, 1673] · *The Satires of Decimus Junius Juvenalis . . . Together with the Satires of Aulus Persius Flaccus*, tr. John Dryden, London, 1693 [frequent reps.] · *The Satires of Aulus Persius Flaccus*, tr. Sir William Drummond, London, 1797 · *The Satires of Aulus Persius Flaccus*, tr. Francis Howes, London, 1809 · *The Satires of Aulus Persius Flaccus*, tr. William Gifford, London, 1821 [frequent reps.] · *The Satires of Persius*, tr. W. S. Merwin, Bloomington, Ind., 1961 · *Horace: Satires and Epistles; Persius: Satires*, tr. Niall Rudd, rev. edn., London, 1979 [Penguin] · *The Satires of Persius*, tr. Guy Lee, Liverpool, 1987.

SEE ALSO   Frost, W., 'English Persius: The Golden Age', *Eighteenth-Century Studies*, 2 (1968), 77–101 · Hopkins, D., 'Dryden and the Tenth Satire of Juvenal', *Translation and Literature*, 4 (1995), 31–60 · Kupersmith, W., *Roman Satirists in Seventeenth-Century England*, Lincoln, Neb. / London, 1985 · Martindale, C., and Hopkins, D., eds., *Horace Made New: Horatian Influences on British Writing from the Renaissance to the Twentieth Century*, Cambridge, 1993 · Stack, F., *Pope and Horace: Studies in Imitation*, Cambridge, 1985.

8. SILVER EPIC

Two major poems are included under this heading: Statius' *Thebaid* (or *Thebais*, 92 CE) and Lucan's *Bellum Civile* or *De Bello Civili* (*c*.62–5 CE, The Civil War, in late Renaissance Britain known as the *Pharsalia* after the battle at its climax). Two other works of less account, and rarely translated into English, are dealt with more summarily: Statius' *Achilleid* (*c*.92–6 CE) and the *Punica* of Silius Italicus (88–98 CE).

i. **Lucan** The grand and flawed poem of Lucan (Marcus Annaeus Lucanus), historically always seen as a foil to the *Aeneid* [II.n.3], has fitfully captured the imagination of translators ever since the Renaissance, but there is no accepted classic English version. Indeed, the history of English Lucan translations, with a couple of 17th-c. exceptions, is one of failure, sometimes disastrous. Most of the earliest attempts are of no particular merit. Sir Arthur **Gorges** (d. 1625) published the first complete English Lucan in 1614; it is in clumsy octo-

syllabic couplets. Thomas **May** (1595–1650), later to become a Cromwellian parliamentary secretary, also used rhyming couplets. May's version [I.b.2.vi] adheres closely to the sense of the Latin; this tends to lead to syntactical difficulties everywhere, and it is not an accomplished piece of writing. A line-for-line translation by the poet and dramatist Christopher **Marlowe** was published in 1600. His blank verse has real power, as Ben Jonson recognized in commending the work's 'admirable height', and Lucan's extravagance and hyperbole finds an echoing taste in Marlowe, but the rendering extends only to the first of Lucan's ten books. Other incomplete versions from the 17th and 18th c. are by the minor writers John **Beaumont**, Jabez **Hughes**, and William **Duncombe**.

The first version of the complete *Bellum Civile* which is likely to interest readers today is by Nicholas **Rowe** (1674–1718). Rowe's Whig politics encouraged his sympathies with Lucan, the upholder of freedom from tyranny; his translation is also a fairly free one, in conformity with the tastes of his era—over 12,000 lines for Lucan's 8,060. This version was standard for two centuries. The following sample is from the celebrated account of the witch Erictho from Book VI, her search of the battle-field for a suitable corpse for use in her divination:

> While yet she spoke, a double darkness spread,
> Black clouds and murky fogs involve her head,
> While o'er th'unbury'd heaps her footsteps tread.
> Wolves howl'd, and fled where'er she took her way,
> And hungry vultures left the mangled prey:
> The savage race, abash'd, before her yield,
> And while she culls her prophet, quit the field.
> To various carcasses by turns she flies,
> And, griping with her gory fingers, tries;
> Till one of perfect organs can be found,
> And fibrous lungs uninjur'd by a wound.

This shows Rowe's workmanlike skill in turning melodious and varied couplets, but it also displays a certain predictability—there are too many formulas here. Rowe's version is nevertheless consistently competent.

The next significant translations come in the 19th c. H. T. **Ridley**'s Bohn translation of 1853 is the first prose version. It has an extensive and very helpful commentary in footnotes and margins, but is unreadable as a translation—as a mere portion of the first sentence indicates:

Wars more than civil upon the Emathian plains, and license conceded to lawlessness, I sing; and a powerful people turning with victorious right-hand against its own vitals . . .

This Victorian prose version can be paired not unfairly with the Victorian verse rendering by Edward **Riley**; both were reprinted into the 20th c. Riley's syntax is parody schoolboy Latin translationese, the diction not much better:

> But in the distant regions of the earth
> Fierce Caesar warring, though in fight he dealt
> No baneful slaughter, hastened on the doom
> To swift fulfilment.

Two 20th-c. prose versions are less dated, but are intended to be no more than reference material. J. D. **Duff**'s Loeb text is consciously pedestrian but reliable. Robert **Graves** tends to see Lucan merely as a 'phenomenon'—a 'prodigiously vital writer with hysterical tendencies'. As a translator Graves is, indeed, conspicuous for his dislike of Lucan, and takes all kinds of liberties with his text. His prose is readable, but again conveys little sense that Lucan is a poet.

The most recent English Lucans are those by S. H. **Braund**, P. F. **Widdows**, and Jane Wilson **Joyce**. Braund's is supposedly in 'free verse' with an

'underlying iambic rhythm'; it is avowedly literalist, and occupies the same number of lines in English as the original in Latin. The lineation is of no aesthetic significance, however, since in practice the rhythms of Braund's writing are usually indistinguishable from those of prose, and the literalism clogs the writing to the point of coagulation. Had this version been printed en face with the Latin it would have served quite well as a line-by-line crib. The detailed notes giving historical information and literary parallels are helpful. P. F. Widdows elaborates a metrical scheme of 'anglicized hexameter' in his introduction, but even if his translation is in a kind of verse it is not poetry. The recommendation of this translation must be that it conveys Lucan's sense—laboriously so.

Jane Wilson Joyce's translation can be more generally recommended, as the most readable of the recent renderings. Joyce herself would like 'the paramount importance to Lucan of the spoken word' to be reflected in her work: 'ideally, I want mine to be a translation that can be read aloud.' A number of devices help suggest changes in tempo or voice to this end, but overall it is the translator's ear that is most important in achieving verse that 'follows natural English rhythms'. Something of Lucan's keyed-up intensity certainly comes over in these dense, adjective-laden lines, and Joyce's work reflects sound scholarly knowledge too. The only real oddities are the Americanisms—'feisty Domitius' occurs more than once (but is fortunately uncharacteristic).

ii. Statius Statius (Publius Papinius Statius) enjoyed a high reputation for many centuries and was influential for English and other European poets; his work is now little known. His historical importance ought to have led to translations of greater quality and quantity: though many a good version of an episode can be found, especially in the work of 17th- and 18th-c. English poets, the more extensive renderings are usually disappointing.

An obscure schoolmaster, Thomas **Stephens**, is credited with the first English Thebaid, but his Essay upon Statius of 1648 is a translation of Books I–V only. Stephens tells his readers his work was 'intended for a help to my Scholars', and that if it proved 'satisfactory' to his 'friends' he would continue it. He did not, perhaps because his friends' judgement was sound: the translation is in often hilariously bad doggerel. Sir Robert **Howard** (1626–89), the playwright, was responsible for a version of the Achilleid which is now entirely unread but which achieves a respectable standard within its self-imposed constraints. These consist principally of the decision to work roughly line-for-line when Statius' lines are hexameters and Howard's only pentameters. Hence this heroic couplet version often simply does not have space to convey the full meaning of the Latin. There are occasional mistranslations too. Yet the translation is remarkable, given these limitations, for what it manages to retain of Statius' meaning and tone. Howard is also skilful at managing narrative, and can achieve genuine pathos too—both features uncharacteristic of the *Achilleid* itself.

More writers of minor literary repute—Christopher **Pitt**, Jabez Hughes—translate occasional episodes from the *Thebaid* in the 18th c. But the most major English literary figure to have englished Statius at any length in this period is Alexander **Pope**. His Book I of the *Thebaid* was done at a very early age; the published version of 1709 is, Pope tells us, 'corrected' with the help of others at a later date. Joseph Spence, Pope's memorialist, wrote that the poet 'used to call him the best of all the Latin epic poets after Virgil'. The translation is experimental, but its versification is polished and its high style anticipates Pope's Homer, particularly in descriptive passages. The 18th c. also saw the first and for long the standard complete translation of this poem. The 1767 heroic couplet *Thebaid* by William Lillington **Lewis** is now unknown even to specialists, but is a competent product of its time, matching Pope in elegance and in some sense maintaining what Lewis thought of as the 'loftiness' of his original. The translation was published with extensive critical notes.

There are three 20th-c. translations of the *Thebaid*. J. H. **Mozley**'s prose Loeb version employs the Loeb series's characteristically arcane English, and is not especially accurate. J. B. **Poynton**'s version of Books I–III is, eccentrically, in Spenserian stanzas; the choice of verse form multiplies the translator's difficulties most unnecessarily, though Poynton's scholarship, when it comes to

interpretation of the Latin, commands respect. A. D. **Melville**'s is the most recent and the best modern translation. Using the blank verse form (with variations) previously employed in his well-received translation of Ovid's *Metamorphoses* [II.n.6.iii], Melville tries to match what he sees as the 'swift and vivid narrative' and the 'apt and moving rhetoric' of the speeches in a poem tending to the 'baroque' and 'mannerist'. The result is an admirable range of textures which draws on English poetic styles from Shakespeare onwards as in these three examples:

> Obscure you died and saw great count of dead;
> Unseen, unpraised, that stream of blood was shed!

> those dark jaws that guard the first-found sea

> To hear the pale-cheeked virgin promulgate
> Her ghastly riddles.

Melville composes an elaborate amalgam (or hotchpotch) equating in some sense to Statius' own allusive, recondite style, and in particular the irretrievably overdone diction—such expressions as 'sable gore' and 'peerless chief' are in abundant supply.

iii. Silius Italicus Silius Italicus' *Punica*, the longest and, according to some, the dullest of extant Latin poems, has attracted only three English translators. As it happens, the historical translations are by two Scots. The 17th-c. version by Thomas **Ross** (d. 1675), dedicated to Charles II, is in competent heroic couplets and adds a 'continuation' of the story. A version by Henry William **Tytler** (1752–1808), a literary hack and scientific dabbler, was issued posthumously in 1828 in Calcutta; it is full of typographical errors but seems not to have been reprinted and remains rare. For reasons of availability, J. D. **Duff**'s Loeb version of Silius Italicus, with many of the same limitations as his Lucan (above), will probably have to serve most readers' needs.   SG

LUCAN   *Lucans First Booke Translated Line for Line*, tr. Christopher Marlowe, London, 1600 · *Lucan's Pharsalia*, tr. Sir Arthur Gorges, London, 1614 · *Lucan's Pharsalia*, tr. Thomas May, London, 1626–7 · *Lucan's Pharsalia*, tr. Nicholas Rowe, London, 1718 · *Lucan's Pharsalia*, tr. H. T. Riley, London, 1853 · *The Pharsalia of Lucan*, tr. Edward Ridley, London, 1896 [Bohn] · *Lucan: The Civil War*, tr. J. D. Duff, London, 1928 · *Pharsalia: Dramatic Episodes of the Civil Wars*, tr. Robert Graves, Harmondsworth, 1957 [Penguin] · *Lucan's Civil War*, tr. P. F. Widdows, Bloomington, Ind., 1988 · *Lucan: Civil War*, tr. S. H. Braund, Oxford, 1992 [World's Classics] · *Lucan: Pharsalia*, tr. Jane Wilson Joyce, Ithaca, NY, 1993.

SILIUS ITALICUS   *The Second Punick War between Hannibal and the Romanes*, tr. Thomas Ross, London, 1661 · *The Punics of Silius Italicus*, tr. H. W. Tytler, 2 vols., Calcutta, 1828 · *Silius Italicus: Punica*, tr. J. D. Duff, 2 vols., London, 1927 [Loeb].

STATIUS   *An Essay upon Statius; or, the First Five Books of Publ: Papinius Statius his Thebais*, tr. T[homas] S[tephens], London, 1648 · *P. Papinius Statius His Achilleis with Annotations*, tr. Sir Robert Howard, London, 1660 · *The First Book of Statius His Thebais*, tr. Alexander Pope, in *Miscellaneous Poems and Translations*, London, 1712 [and in later edns. of Pope] · *The Thebaid of Statius*, tr. William Lillington Lewis, 2 vols., Oxford, 1767 · *Statius*, tr. J. H. Mozley, 2 vols.,

London, 1928 · *Thebais I–III*, tr. J. B. Poynton, Oxford, 1971 · *Statius: Thebaid*, tr. A. D. Melville, Oxford, 1992 [World's Classics].

SEE ALSO   Bassett, E. L., 'Silius Italicus in England', *Classical Philology*, 48 (1953), 155–68 · Hesse, A. W., *Nicholas Rowe's Translation of Lucan's Pharsalia, 1703–1718: A Study in Literary History*, Philadelphia, 1950 · Norbrook, D., 'Lucan, Thomas May, and the Creation of a Republican Literary Culture', in K. Sharpe and P. Lake, eds., *Culture and Politics in Early Stuart England*, Basingstoke, 1994, 45–66.

9. DRAMA

Among the earliest published renderings in English of the works of Roman drama are some *florilegia* (collections of prized passages) from Terence translated into English in the late 15th c. Such a collection was published in Oxford in 1483, and again in 1486 and 1529. Another was that produced in 1533 (reprinted 1575) by Nicholas **Udall** (1505–56), the author of *Ralph Roister Doister* (c.1541), which might reasonably be called the first English comedy and which is in large part derived from Plautus' *Miles Gloriosus* and Terence's *Eunuchus*. An early *Terens in Englysh: The Translacyon of the Furst Comedy, called Andria* was written c.1500 and printed c.1520. After these beginnings, it was the Elizabethan era which saw the first real flourishing of English translations of Plautus, Terence, and Seneca, alongside the birth of the early modern English theatre, massively influenced as it was by these three classical authors.

i. Seneca The most important Elizabethan work is the *Tenne Tragedies* of Lucius Annaeus Seneca (?4 BCE–65 CE) (including the *Octavia*, and the *Hercules Oetaeus*, which may be spurious), collected by Thomas **Newton** (?1542–1607) and published in 1581. Most of the translations date from the 1560s and were first published then; in some cases they underwent significant modification for the collected volume. The *Tenne Tragedies* includes the work of various translators, the most famous of whom is the Jesuit Jasper **Heywood** (1535–98): he is responsible for *Hercules Furens*, *Thyestes*, and *Troas*. Alexander **Neville** (1544–1614) translated the *Oedipus*; John **Studley** (?1545–?1590) the *Hippolytus* (sometimes called *Phaedra*), *Medea*, *Agamemnon*, and *Hercules Oetaeus*; Thomas **Nuce** (d. 1617) the *Octavia*; Newton himself the *Thebais*. There is considerable uniformity of style among the translations, all of which, except Nuce's *Octavia* in heroic couplets, are written primarily in the 'fourteener', and all of which take liberties with the content of the original, elaborating on and explaining Seneca's rhetoric, and adding and adapting both episodes and choric interludes. It is unlikely that the translations had a major impact on the great outpouring of dramatic literature which occurred in the late 16th and early 17th c.; their existence and popularity

should rather be seen as part of that same cultural movement which also produced the 'Senecals' (Latin plays written in the style of Seneca) and which constituted the high point of Seneca's fame as a dramatist.

The translations have lived on through various editions, including one with an introduction by T. S. Eliot, whose appreciation of them is astute if somewhat generous: 'they do not yield their charm easily' (Eliot 1932). The fourteener has an archaic flavour which can be effective but which is rigid and quickly palls, while at times the diction sounds faintly ridiculous to modern ears. There are undoubtedly successes, however. Here is Heywood's *Thyestes* [I.i], on the horrific perversion of eating, hunger, and fertility which afflicts Tantalus and his descendants in the child-eating house of Atreus:

> ... behold this day we have to thee releast,
> And hunger starved wombe of thyne we send to
>   such a feast.
> With fowlest foode thy famyne fyll, let bloud in
>   wyne be drownd,
> And dronke in sight of thee ...

The alliteration that just succeeds in avoiding bathos, the deathly image of blood drowning in wine, the allusion to Tantalus' punishment (seeing untouchable food and drink while afflicted with raging hunger and thirst) contrasted with the horrible feast he tries to avoid seeing in the play (Thyestes eating his children)—all these are appropriate evocations of Seneca.

Translations of Seneca's tragedies wane with his popularity: through the 17th c. various individual plays are newly translated, including a group by Sir Edward **Sherburne** (1618–1702), who believed that the only surviving authentic plays were *Medea*, *Phaedra and Hippolytus* (as he calls it), and *Troades*, but the next two centuries see the rate slow to a dribble.

The verse translations of Ella **Harris**, between 1898 and 1904, together with the prose versions of W. **Bradshaw**, mark a resurgence of interest. The Loeb edition, always a landmark in the history of classics in English translation, is by Frank Justus

Miller, and is a rather stiff prose translation. It follows Miller's earlier metrical version, an edition which was steeped in both classical and renaissance dramatic learning. The Penguin version, by E. F. **Watling**, contains only five plays (including *Octavia*). Like many Penguins, it is pleasant and readable but unexciting.

The grim violence and despairing horror of Senecan tragedy and of the Neronian age resonate forcibly with the anxieties of the modern world. Seneca is generally well served in the *magnum opus* edited by David R. **Slavitt** and Palmer **Bovie**, the *Complete Roman Drama in Translation*, in which the most successful translations reflect the way in which Seneca's great power is generally more in language than in what might loosely be called 'theatre', although a number of them have also been adapted for the modern stage. Volume I, where the translations are by Slavitt himself, is perhaps the more successful. In his version of the *Thyestes* passage discussed above, Slavitt employs an epigrammatic style reminiscent of Seneca's silver Latin to bring out the mystical force which evil has in ancient thought: 'Men will respect this place as a shrine, | the holy of unholies'. Slavitt's Fury taunts Tantalus with the horrors of eating:

> You say you are hungry? Feast
> on the gory banquet we have prepared, and drink
> deep of the bloodied wine till your belly is full!

Contrast Ella Harris's version, which of the three considered here has the closest verbal correspondence with Seneca, but which lacks both force and point:

> satisfy
> Thy hunger at those tables, end thy fast.
> Blood mixed with wine shall in thy sight be drunk,
> Food have I found that even thou wouldst shun.

Seneca's plays pose many challenges for producers. In 1968, Peter Brook produced Seneca's *Oedipus* at the Old Vic theatre, London, in a new translation by the poet Ted **Hughes**. The original plan had been to use the version of David **Turner**, which has its own strengths but which did not suit Brook's ideas for the production. Something of the range of Senecan translation can be seen if we look at a few versions of the moment of realization in this play, when Oedipus discovers that he has killed his father and married his mother. The Elizabethan version by Neville offers us a fleeting vision of damned souls in a medieval Hell, and a sense of innocent loss in the plague victims 'consumed . . . to dust' (IV. iii). Turner's prose version brings to modern life Oedipus' pollution of the community's intimate relationships:

> Earth! Gape open! And you, emperor of darkness, snatch this monstrous soiler of birth and bed down to the farthest pit of Tartarus! Countrymen, together now. Piles stones on my head—bury me! Take weapons—butcher me! Fathers, sons, make me the target for your swords. Wives, brothers, take up arms, sick people, drag brands from your funeral fires, hurl them at me . . . ! My life infects the air like a pox fouling the universe, scourging the hallowed laws of marriage, tainting even the gods. The day I drew my first struggling breath, *then* I should have died.

Hughes's disjointed prose-verse rises slowly from its first words, alliteratively confounding bed, birth, and blood, then gains momentum as Oedipus tries to give voice to the full horror of his unspeakable deeds.

> birth   birthbed blood   take this   open
> the earth bury it   bottom of the darkness
> under everything I am not fit for the light
> Thebans your stones   now put a mountain on
> me   hack me to pieces   pile the plague fires
> on me   make me ashes   finish me   put me
> where I know nothing   I am the plague   I am
> the monster Creon saw in hell   I am the cancer
> at the roots of this city   and in your blood and in
> the air   I should have died in the womb
> suffocated   inside there   drowned in my
> mother's blood   come out dead . . .

By contrast, Rachel **Hadas**'s version (in the Slavitt and Bovie series), which certainly has its virtues, tries too hard: 'I'm a miasma, harm for civilisation' (l. 919).

The most accessible way in which readers may now experience the flavour of English translations of Seneca is through the Penguin anthology, *Seneca in Translation*, edited by Don Share. Excerpts from almost all the great English versions of Senecan tragedy are included, in passages ranging from a few lines to several pages. As reflects Seneca's fortunes, the collection is concentrated in the Renaissance period, and includes examples that might be called 'imitations' rather than 'translations', such as two passages of stichomythia from Shakespeare's *Richard III*.

ii. Plautus Given the undoubted importance and popularity of Plautus (Titus Maccius Plautus, *fl.* 205–184 BCE) in the early modern period, there is remarkably little evidence of translation of his plays in the 16th and 17th c., presumably because so many people would have understood them in Latin, in which language they were regularly performed at universities and Inns of Court. Best known is the

Menaechmi translated by William **Warner** (?1558–1609) and printed in 1595, just too late to contribute authoritatively to the question of how far Shakespeare used the original Latin in preparation for *The Comedy of Errors* (c.1591). Warner's translation is loose, in the Elizabethan manner, and the diction is not unlike Shakespeare's, but there is no clear evidence of straightforward influence. Warner probably translated other plays of Plautus, but they were not published. After this time, there are many versions of Plautine plays, whether 'translations', 'adaptations', or plays variously influenced by Plautus. The relationship of these plays with the Plautine 'originals' is as playful and intertextual as Plautus' plays' own relationship with the works of Greek New Comedy, almost entirely unknown, of course, in the early modern period.

In the late 17th and 18th c., the brilliant scholar Laurence **Echard** (1670–1730) and the dramatist George **Colman** (1732–94) translated Plautus (as did many others), but it is in the 19th and 20th c. that translation of Plautus becomes big business, with the appearance of a number of collections, and very many versions of individual plays, significant numbers of which were produced for particular performances. After the 17th c., Plautus is the most known, read, and performed of Roman playwrights, and has had the most influence on the modern media, in television and films, and particularly in that masterful mishmash of Plautine plots, the musical *A Funny Thing Happened on the Way to the Forum*. This work, originally a stage play by Harold S. Prince, was produced in 1966 by Melvin Frank.

Plautus is fairly well catered for in modern translations, although neither the Penguin nor the World's Classics is complete. E. F. Watling's two volumes (nine plays) in the Penguin series make a useful standby, but he is rather coy with the suggestive bawdiness of the plays, and in some places strives for a tonal topicality which dates, still more of a problem in the Loeb editions. Slavitt and Bovie's *Complete Roman Drama*, which *is* complete, contains some translations which are particularly effective in evoking the Plautine spirit. Modern readers who want to experience Plautus at his best, through reading (rather than viewing), without struggling with Latin, might try Richard **Beacham**'s translation of the *Pseudolus* (in vol. iv of the Slavitt and Bovie series). With a bit of help from stage directions, but mostly through the power of words, Beacham brings Plautus to life. He makes a sustained attempt to reproduce Plautine word- and sound-play, with some fine results:

PSEUDOLUS: Why are you moping around so many days so

moribund, moaning and moistening this message with tears, and never sharing your suffering with a single soul? Speak! *Speak!* Show Pseudolus your little secret sorrow.

Only a year later (1996) comes Erich **Segal**'s World's Classics volume, containing *Miles Gloriosus* (The Braggart Soldier), *Menaechmi* (The Brothers Menaechmus), *Mostellaria* (The Haunted House), and *Aulularia* (The Pot of Gold), all but the last of which had been published previously. Like many in the World's Classics series, the volume is as scholarly as a cheap translation could be. The translation generally seeks line-by-line correspondence, with Plautine metres reflected in similar modern rhythms. Like Beacham, Segal seeks to recreate Plautine alliterative word-play, which is enjoying a renaissance of interest after years of scholarly disapproval. If one is not seeking simplicity and realism, it's hard not to laugh at lines like Segal's rendition of the end of *The Braggart Soldier* (*Miles Gloriosus*):

[*Philosophically*] There would be less lechery if lechers
   were to learn from this;
Lots would be more leery and less lustful.

Older translations tend to strive for a more natural, simpler style, which is less Plautine but more polite. An example is Frank O. **Copley**'s 1965 versions of *Menaechmi*, *Mostellaria*, and *Rudens*, which use American colloquialisms like 'downtown' and 'honey' as a term of endearment.

iii. Terence Terence (Publius Terentius Afer, c.185–c.158 BCE) has had a fairly steady translation history. After the early works mentioned above, there continues a regular if moderate supply of new and revised versions from the 16th to the 19th c., popular ones like those of Echard, Samuel **Patrick** (1684–1748), and Colman being reprinted, revised, and generally tidied up many times. Terence's elegant Latin engenders some elegant English, although also some instances of insipidity. Some of the older editions have 'aged' particularly well: Colman's 1765 version sounds in some ways more modern than some later translations, and is comfortable and easy for the modern reader. Just one example: in the scene in *Adelphoi* (The Brothers), in which Micio makes clear to Aeschinus that he is aware of his son's affair, and will approve the marriage, Colman's speed and gentle wit effectively evoke those qualities in Terence.

AES: The Gods desert me, Sir, but I do love you, More
        than my eyes!
MIC: Than her?
AES: As well.
MIC: That's much.

AES: But where is that Milesian?
MIC: Gone. Vanish'd on board the ship.

Colman effectively reproduces various Terentian features: economy of words; ironic teasing of Aeschinus (desperate but now happy lover and grateful son) by his adoptive father; playfulness with the narrative line, when the 'Milesian visitor' who was invented by Micio (with the threat that Aeschinus' girl was to marry him) is dismissed back to his ship and out of the play. Echard's version is quite serviceable, but rather heavier:

AESCHINUS.   Let me never see daylight, Sir, if I don't love
             ye better than my very eyes.
MICIO.   Or than your mistress too?
AESCHINUS.   Full as well.
MICIO.   That's much indeed.
AESCHINUS.   But what's become of that Milesian
             kinsman?
MICIO.   He's vanished, been shipped off, and
             already wrecked by this time.

The translation history of Latin works in England is always complicated by their relationship with that language's dominant role in English education. It is interesting, in this regard, to see what Colman says in his preface about earlier translators of Terence:

that they 'seem to have confined their labours to the humble endeavour of assisting learners of Latin in the construction of the original text'. Colman may be reacting particularly to the Patrick version (20 years earlier than his), which is avowedly as literal as possible. Colman explicitly distances his own aim. By contrast, Echard's 1694 translation, made when he was a 19-year-old Cambridge student and which Colman castigated, is a work both of considerable dramatic learning and also of some licence, particularly in the introduction of a Restoration-type humour into some scenes. Of the modern versions, the Loeb and the Penguin are products of their days and the purpose of their series. The Loeb, originally a 1912 translation by John **Sargeaunt**, although perfectly readable and helpful, has the stiffness of the (post-)Edwardian and, apart from some odd changes which perhaps have not worn well, the literalness of Colman's 'humble endeavour'. The Penguin, by Betty **Radice**, a 1976 revision of two volumes from 1965 and 1967, is neat and, in an appropriately understated way, bordering on the colloquial, without being too quickly dated. Many people respond to Terence with the feeling that his comedies are 'timeless' and 'universal'; such translations contribute to that impression.   ARS

ANTHOLOGIES   Copley, F. O., and Hadas, Moses, *Roman Drama: The Plays of Plautus and Terence* [tr. Copley]; *The Plays of Seneca* [tr. Hadas], 2 vols., New York, 1942 · Duckworth, George E., ed., *The Complete Roman Drama: All the Extant Comedies of Plautus and Terence, and the Tragedies of Seneca, in a Variety of Translations*, 2 vols., New York, 1942 · Slavitt, David R., and Bovie, Palmer, eds., *The Complete Roman Drama in Translation*, 7 vols., Baltimore / London, 1992–5.

PLAUTUS   *Menaechmi*, tr. William Warner(?), London, 1595 [rep. ed. W. H. Rouse, *The Menaechmi: The Original of Shakespeare's 'Comedy of Errors': The Latin Text together with the Elizabethan Translation*, London, 1912] · *Plautus's Comedies, Amphitryon, Epidicus, and Rudens*, tr. Laurence Echard, London, 1694 · *Comedies of Plautus*, tr. Bonnell Thornton, London, 1767 [7 plays] · *The Comedies*, tr. Richard Warner, 5 vols., London, 1769–74 · *The Comedies of Plautus*, tr. H. T. Riley, 2 vols., London, 1852 · *Plautus*, tr. Paul Nixon, 5 vols., London, 1916–38 [Loeb] · *Plautus: The Rope and Other Plays*, tr. E. F. Watling, Harmondsworth, 1964 [Penguin] · *Plautus: The Pot of Gold and Other Plays*, tr. E. F. Watling, Harmondsworth, 1965 [Penguin].

SENECA   *Seneca, His Tenne Tragedies: Translated into Englysh*, ed. Thomas Newton, London, 1581 [frequent reps., including one with introd. by T. S. Eliot, London, 1927] · *The Tragedies of L. Annaeus Seneca, the Philosopher*, tr. E. Sherburne, London, 1701 [the translations date from 1648–79] · *The Ten Tragedies of Seneca*, tr. Watson Bradshaw, London, 1902 · *The Tragedies of Seneca*, tr. Ella Isabel Harris, London, 1904 · *The Tragedies of Seneca*, tr. Frank Justus Miller, Chicago / London, 1907 · *Seneca's Tragedies*, tr. Frank Justus Miller, 2 vols., London, 1917 [Loeb] · *Seneca: Four Tragedies and Octavia*, tr. E. F. Watling, Harmondsworth, 1966 [Penguin] · *Seneca in English*, ed. Don Share, Harmondsworth, 1998 [Penguin].

TERENCE   *Floures for Latin Spekynge Selected and Gathered oute of Terence*, tr. Nicholas Udall, London, 1533 · *Terence in English (fabulae Anglicae factae opera R. Bernard)*, tr. R. Bernard, Cambridge, 1598 [five edns. to 1629] · *The Comedies of Terence*, tr. Laurence Echard (or Eachard), London, 1694 [ed. Robert Graves, Chicago, 1962] · *Terence's Comedies*, tr. Samuel Patrick, 2 vols., London, 1745 · *The Comedies of Terence*, tr. George Colman, London, 1765 · *The Comedies of Terence and the Fables of Phaedrus*, tr. H. T. Riley, London, 1853 · *Terence*, tr. John Sargeaunt, London, 1912 [Loeb] · *Terence: The Comedies*, tr. Betty Radice, Harmondsworth, 1976 [Penguin].

SEE ALSO   Braden, G., *Renaissance Tragedy and the Senecan Tradition: Anger's Privilege*, New Haven, Conn. / London, 1985 · Duckworth, G. E., *The Nature of Roman Comedy*, Princeton, NJ, 1952 · Eliot, T. S., *Selected Essays*, London, 1932 · Miola, R. S., *Shakespeare and Classical Tragedy: The Influence of Seneca*, Oxford, 1992 · Simpson (Spearing), E. M., *The Elizabethan Translations of Seneca's Tragedies*, Cambridge, 1912.

10. HISTORY

The earliest English translators of Latin historians spread their nets widely but paid relatively little attention to those whom we should now regard as major authors. There were early translations of the late epitomators and summarizers such as Eutropius (4th c. CE) and Justin (2nd or 3rd c. CE) and a translation of Quintus Curtius Rufus' Latin history of Alexander the Great; but before the reign of Elizabeth the major Roman historians are represented only by the loose and paraphrastical version of Sallust's *Jugurtha* by the Scottish poet Alexander **Barclay** (?1475–1552), a translation of such parts of Caesar's *Gallic War* 'as concernyth thys realm of England', and some excerpts from Livy. A complete translation of Caesar's *Gallic War* appeared in 1565; then in the 20 years between 1591 and 1610 there were major translations of the four other authors (Sallust, Livy, Tacitus, and Suetonius) whose works are discussed in the following pages.

Of the five authors in question, two—Livy and Suetonius—received such definitive translations in the 17th c. that no further translations are discussed here before the 20th c.; for Caesar, Sallust, and Tacitus a small number of 18th- and 19th-c. translations are discussed. The 19th c. saw a marked increase in the number of pedestrian translations as study aids (which are largely ignored here), but in the 20th c. the Penguin Classics gave new popular currency to all five historians.

i. Caesar The earliest Latin historical works to survive other than in fragments are the *Bellum Gallicum* (58–52 BCE, Gallic War) and *Bellum Civile* (49–48 BCE, Civil War) of C. Iulius Caesar. For English readers the former work had the additional interest that it contained Caesar's own account of his two invasions of their country. The first complete translation, in 1565, of the *Gallic War* was by Arthur **Golding** (?1536–?1605), better known as the translator of Ovid's *Metamorphoses* [II.n.6.iii]. Despite some inaccuracies (not all of them corrected by his immediate successors) and an occasional tendency to resort to colourful language that departs from the classical reserve of Caesar's Latin, Golding successfully conveys the sense of the original and its changes in pace and emphasis. A dramatic incident as the Romans seek to force a landing on the shores of Britain illustrates those qualities:

But when our men staied and semed to make curtsy [Caesar has only 'as our soldiers hesitated'] the chief standerdbearer of the tenth legion making earnest protestacion to the Goddes, that the thing whych he purposed to doe might happen luckely to the legion, sayd, leap downe my fellowes onles you wyll betray our standerd to the enemy: surely I wyll do my dutye to thuttermost for my common wealth and for my groundcapteine. When he had spoke this with a loud voice, he threw hymself out of the shyppe and began to carry the standerd against the enemies. (*Gallic War* iv. 25)

One translation of Caesar dominated the 17th c., that of Clement **Edmondes** (Edmunds) (?1564–1622), Remembrancer of the City of London. The translation has little merit, and its continuing success in folio editions to 1695 is due to its extensive 'Observations . . . setting forth the Practise of ye Art militarie in the time of the Romaine Empire for the better direction of our moderne Warrs'. The work is dedicated to Henry Frederick, Prince of Wales, and the cultured readership for which it was intended can be seen from a series of commendatory epigrams from such notable figures as William Camden and Ben Jonson.

In 1704 a new translation of the complete works of Caesar appeared. Unlike his predecessors, its author, Martin **Bladen** (1680–1746), had seen active service in the Low Countries and Spain; he does not draw on his experience to elucidate military matters, but seeks only to offer 'Caesar in a Modern Stile . . . to such as either do not understand, or are not willing to give themselves the Trouble of reading the Latin'. His modest octavo edition seems to have met a contemporary need, for it reached an eighth edition in 1770.

Jane **Gardner**'s Penguin translation of Caesar (the *Gallic War* a revision of S. A. **Handford**'s version) is among the best translations in the series of a Latin prose author. In a style well attuned to the contemporary ear, it has much of the directness and lucidity of the Latin original.

ii. Sallust The historian C. Sallustius Crispus had supported Caesar both in the Senate and in the civil war, and it was only after Caesar's assassination in 44 BCE that he turned to writing. For his subject-matter he chose events from within that century of political and social turmoil that followed the tribunate of Tiberius Gracchus in 133 BCE. Rapid narrative and descriptive brevity, which are distinguishing features of an innovative style, enhance the dramatic nature of the events he describes but make translation into English difficult.

The first writer to translate both *Catiline*

(*De coniuratione Catilinae*) and *Jugurtha* (*De bello Iugurthino*) was Thomas **Heywood** (*c.*1573–1641), author of *A Woman Killed with Kindness*. Although his translation has an undeniable vigour, it is inaccurate and has a diffuseness quite alien to Sallust's style. Nor are translations during the next 100 years more successful; they are either literal and dull or lively and unreliable.

In 1744 Thomas **Gordon** (?1691–1750), political journalist and former editor of the *Independent Whig*, published *The Works of Sallust Translated into English. With Political Discourses upon that Author.* Gordon had already translated Tacitus (see below), and the political sympathies proclaimed in that work are now reaffirmed in the Dedication to the Duke of Cumberland (son of George II): 'it is incumbent upon all Men, especially the Greatest, to support the best Government . . . That Ours is the best, I not only sincerely believe, but think demonstrable.'

In his translation Gordon claims to revert to his 'usual Style', abandoning what, in his *Tacitus*, he had called his 'Variations', and which had incurred some criticism. So, for the most part, his translation both keeps close to the Latin and is written in agreeable English. Occasionally, though, he cannot resist the fine phrase. So, at *Catiline* x. 2 'iis otium divitiae, optanda alias, oneri miseriaeque fuere' ('for them leisure and riches, things otherwise desirable, proved a burden and source of woe') becomes 'The same People . . . were baned by a life of Ease: The Romans became depressed by Riches, which are the great Idol and pursuit of other Nations.' The use of 'bane' as a transitive verb was already archaic by Gordon's day, while the embellishment of 'the great Idol and pursuit' (for *optanda*, 'things to be desired') is palpable.

It was not until 1807 that a Sallust to challenge Gordon's appeared. Arthur **Murphy** (1727–1805), former actor and author of mediocre plays, had, like Gordon, already translated Tacitus. That work, though well received, was commonly judged to be too paraphrastical, and the same criticism applies to his Sallust. At *Catiline* xxv Murphy translates: 'in the number of Catiline's profligate women, Sempronia, a celebrated courtezan, claims particular notice', where Sallust has only 'in iis erat Sempronia' ('among them was Sempronia'); and in the very last sentence of the *Catiline* the simple adverb *varie* ('variously') leads Murphy to write: 'The impressions made by this melancholy scene were various.'

S. A. Handford's Penguin translation has useful introductions to both *Jugurtha* and *Catiline*, and conveys the sense admirably. Though the translation lacks the bite of the original, the last paragraph

of the Introduction gives an excellent summary of the main features of Sallust's style.

iii. Livy Though T. Livius began writing barely a decade after Sallust, the difference between their works both in scale and style is immense. When complete, Livy's *Ab urbe condita* (From the Foundation of the City) comprised 142 books covering seven-and-a-half centuries of Roman history. Throughout the work Livy's fervent patriotism is repeatedly conveyed in dramatic episodes that embody those moral virtues that he, and his fellow-countrymen, regarded as essentially Roman.

By good fortune the first complete translation of the 35 surviving books (bringing the narrative down to 167 BCE) was by an able Latinist with a fine ear for the telling English phrase. Philemon **Holland** (1552–1637), described in Thomas Fuller's *The History of the Worthies of England* (1662) as 'the Translator General in his Age', dedicated his translation to Queen Elizabeth. In his Preface to the Reader he writes, 'I framed my pen, not to any affected phrase, but to a meane and popular stile'; and, shortly after, 'if the sentence be not so concise, couched and knit togither, as the originall, loth I was to be obscure and darke.' Both these qualities add colour to his translation, as does a mannerism he shares with other Elizabethans, the doubling of verbs, nouns, and adjectives where the Latin has only one. Paradoxically, his failure to match the conciseness of Livy's Latin touches on one of Holland's most effective features. Latin is indeed more concise than English, but among Latin writers Livy is rather characterized by his flowing style, and for that Holland's expansions are an appropriate equivalent.

Two well-known incidents in Roman history may illustrate Holland's style. Lucretia, after being raped by Tarquin, is resolved to die:

How now my deere (quoth her husband) is all well? No God wot sir (quoth she againe:) For how can ought be well with a woman that is despoiled of her honour and her womanhood? . . . Howbeit, my bodie only is distained: my mind and heart remaineth yet unspotted: and that my death shall make good and justifie.　(i. 58.7)

This is superb; but note how Holland varies the degree of closeness to Livy's Latin. 'Howbeit, my bodie only is distained' corresponds exactly to 'ceterum corpus est tantum violatum', whereas the English for Livy's final 'animus insons; mors testis erit' (two staccato phrases, 'My mind is guiltless, death shall be my witness') gains its emphasis by expansion to 16 words. The genius of the two languages produces different solutions.

Holland's ability to reproduce what he calls the

'patheticall spirit' of the original is illustrated by his description of the Roman troops after their humiliating surrender at the Caudine Forks in 321 BCE:

They set before their eies, the gallows prepared by the enemie for them to pass under, the skornes and reprochfull taunts of the Victor, his proud and disdainefull lookes . . . then afterwards, the piteous spectacle of the way which they must go, & the shamefull dismarch of their disgraced armie.   (ix. 5.8)

Here the expansion of the English is unmistakable (*ludibria victoris* becomes 'the skornes and reprochfull taunts of the Victor' and *voltus superbos* 'his proud and disdainefull lookes'); it is different from Livy, but no less effective.

iv. Tacitus 'Tacitus . . . hath written the most matter with best conceite in fewest words of any Historiographer ancient or modern. But he is harde. *Difficilia quae pulchra.*' So the anonymous Preface to the Reader in the translation of Tacitus' (P. or C. Cornelius Tacitus) *Historiae* (c.115 CE, Histories) and *Agricola* (c.97) in 1591 by (Sir) Henry **Savile** (1549–1622). Savile was a remarkable man and scholar: Warden of Merton, Provost of Eton, Tutor in Greek and Secretary in Latin to Queen Elizabeth, to whom the translation is dedicated. There are copious notes drawn from Greek and Latin sources, Savile's own account of events covering 'The Ende of Nero and the Beginning of Galba', and an appendix on 'Certaine Militar matters'.

The surviving books (i–v) of the *Histories* dealt with civil wars and the violent deaths of emperors (Nero and Otho by suicide, Galba and Vitellius by murder); those events provided Savile's readers with a theme that was of riveting interest but required delicate handling—witness the ill-fated Earl of Essex, who may have been the author of the anonymous Preface to the Reader. The political relevance of Tacitus became even more apparent when his last work, the *Annales* (Annals), came to be translated (cf. Ben Jonson's *Sejanus* in 1603). For all his scholarship, Savile's translation is disappointing. It mostly seeks to follow Tacitus' order of words and phrases; too often the result is a version that is difficult to understand without recourse to the original Latin.

Galba's bodie long neglected, and in the darke despitefully intreated, Argius his stewarde, one of his principall bondmen, buried with small ceremonie in his private gardens. His heade by the followers and rascalles of the camps, mangled and stabbed was found the day after this Patrobius toombe, a freed-man of Nero, whom Galba had executed, and so was put with his body burned before.

(*Histories* i. 19.1)

Nevertheless the translation enjoyed considerable success. In 1598 a second edition was published with an undistinguished translation of the *Annals* and *Germania* by Richard **Greneway**. Further joint editions followed, reaching a sixth edition in 1640.

In 1698 a new translation by various hands appeared, most contributors translating a single book of *Annals* or *Histories*. *Annals* I–VI are accompanied by 'Political Reflections and Historical Notes' from the French of Amelot de la Houssay(e), while for *Histories* and *Agricola* Savile's notes and additional material are reprinted. The named contributors (several are indicated only by initials) include John **Dryden** (*Annals* I) and Sir Roger **L'Estrange**, both known for their Jacobite sympathies and opposition to the settlement of 1688. Dryden's contribution is in essence a translation from Amelot's French, and shares both its merits and defects; most notably the tautness of Tacitus' sentence structure is relaxed into a more flowing style. Occasionally Dryden comes closer to Tacitus' Latin than Amelot; somewhat more often he expands the French version to produce greater emphasis or effect. Such expansion is particularly noticeable in emotional and dramatic scenes, such as Germanicus' handling of the mutinous German legions or his visit to the scene of Varus' disaster in the Teutoberg Forest.

The translation of the Whig Thomas Gordon was better suited to the political climate of the new century. Volume I (*Annals*, 1728) was dedicated to Robert Walpole, Volume II (*Histories*, etc., 1731) to Frederick, Prince of Wales, while the extensive 'Political Discourses' prefixed to each volume championed liberty and denounced tyranny. Of his translation Gordon writes: 'I have sometimes ventured upon a new phrase, and a way of my own . . . dropping particles, transposing words, and sometimes beginning a sentence where it is usual to end it.' Thus *stuprum* is translated by 'constupration', a word virtually obsolete by 1700, and syntactical inversion becomes a deliberate mannerism: 'Terrifying to him proved the dismal solitude' (*Histories* iii. 33.1) and 'vehement had been his ambition to see them declared Princes of the Roman Youth' (*Annals* i. 3.2). Such singularities were an easy target for ridicule: The *Critical Review* for 1793 opined that Gordon's version 'has become almost proverbial for the vicious and affected style in which it is composed'. Yet much of his translation is in clear, straightforward English, and it continued to be read in North America as well as in Britain for the next half-century.

In 1793 the actor-playwright Arthur **Murphy** published his translation, deliberately aimed at replacing Gordon's version. His work was immensely popular and continued to be reprinted till the beginning of the 20th c. *The Critical Review* in that year found Murphy's translation 'extremely correct and generally animated and agreeable': other contemporaries rightly judged it too paraphrastical, and one can never be sure whether one is reading Tacitus or paraphrase—or, indeed, Murphy's own invention. To find out what Tacitus actually says the Latin-less reader will do better to consult the unpretentious translation of A. J. **Church** and W. J. **Brodribb**.

In the 20th c. the Penguin translations by Michael **Grant** (*Annals*) and Kenneth **Wellesley** (*Histories*) are strikingly different. Grant hurries the narrative along by breaking up Tacitus' sentence-structure into smaller units—and converting legions, centurions etc. into their British army equivalents; Wellesley's version is much more solid and scholarly. Neither gives the reader much idea of the magic of Tacitus' style; but that is true of all earlier translations also.

v. Suetonius For the Romans biography was a different and less elevated genre than history. The Elizabethans made no such distinction, and welcomed in Suetonius (C. Suetonius Tranquillus) his wealth of anecdote and physical description. So, in Philemon Holland's translation of *De vita Caesarum* (2nd c. CE, The Lives of the Caesars), the emperor Claudius is described:

many things disgraced him: to wit, undecent laughter and unseemly anger, by reason, that hee would froth and slaver at the mouth, and had evermore his nose dropping: besides, his tongue stutted and stammered: his head likewise at all times, but especially if he did

anything were it never so little used to shake and tremble very much.   (*Claudius* 30)

The whole of the passage describing Nero's final moments (Tacitus' version is unfortunately lost) is especially memorable. It begins:

He commaunded a grave to be made before his face, and ... weeping at every word he spake, and inserting ever and anone this pittifull speech, *Qualis artifex pereo!* What an excellent Artisane am I! and yet nowe must I die.

                                 (*Nero* 49)

The modern reader has a choice between J. C. **Rolfe**'s Loeb edition and the Penguin translation by Robert **Graves**. Rolfe commends Holland's translation for its style and spirit, and seeks to 'compete with it in the only possible way, namely in greater fidelity to a better text than was available in his day'. Those who have enjoyed Graves's Claudius novels may find his Suetonius disappointing; there is an unevenness in the register of his language in describing Claudius' physical characteristics (Holland's version is given above):

he had several disagreeable traits. These included an uncontrolled laugh, a horrible habit, under the stress of anger, of slobbering at the mouth and running at the nose, and a persistent nervous tic—which grew so bad under emotional stress that his head would toss from side to side.

For this Rolfe's version is both closer to Suetonius and more of one piece:

he had many disagreeable traits . . . his laughter was unseemly and his anger still more disgusting, for he would foam at the mouth and trickle at the nose; he stammered besides and his head was very shaky at all times, but especially when he made the least exertion.   RHM

CAESAR   *The Eyght Bookes of Caius Julius Caesar Conteyning his Martiall Exploytes in Gallia*, tr. Arthur Golding, London, 1565 · *Observations upon Caesars Commentaries*, tr. C. Edmondes, London, 1604 (*Gallic War*) and 1609 (*Civil War*) · *C. Julius Caesar's Commentaries of his War in Gaul and Civil War with Pompey*, tr. M. Bladen, London, 1705 · *The Conquest of Gaul*, tr. S. A. Handford, London, 1951; rev. Jane F. Gardner, 1982 [Penguin] · *The Civil War*, tr. Jane F. Gardner, London, 1967 [Penguin].

LIVY   *The Romane Historie Written by T. Livius of Padua*, tr. Philemon Holland, London, 1600 · *The Early History of Rome* (bks. i–v), tr. Aubrey de Selincourt, London, 1960 [Penguin] · *The War with Hannibal* (bks. xxi–xxx), tr. Aubrey de Selincourt, London, 1965 [Penguin] · *Rome and the Mediterranean* (bks. xxxi–xlv), tr. Henry Bettenson, London, 1976 [Penguin] · *Rome and Italy* (bks. vi–x), tr. Betty Radice, London, 1982 [Penguin].

SALLUST   *The Conspiracy of Catiline and the War of Jugurtha*, tr. Thomas Heywood, London, 1608; rep. London, 1924 · *The Works of Sallust Translated into English, with Political Discourses upon that Author, To which is Added, a Translation of Cicero's Four Orations against Catiline*, tr. Thomas Gordon, London, 1744 · *The Works of Sallust*, tr. Arthur Murphy, London, 1807 · *Sallust: The Jugurthine War and the Conspiracy of Catiline*, tr. S. A. Handford, London, 1963 [Penguin].

SUETONIUS   *Historie of Twelve Caesars*, tr. Philemon Holland, London, 1606; rep. London, 1899 · *The Lives of the Caesars*, tr. J. C. Rolfe, London / Cambridge, Mass., 1913–4 [Loeb] · *The Twelve Caesars*, tr. Robert Graves, London, 1957 [Penguin].

TACITUS   *The Ende of Nero and Beginning of Galba; Fower Bookes of the Histories of Cornelius Tacitus; The Life of Agricola*, tr. Henry Savile, Oxford, 1591 · *The Annales of Cornelius Tacitus; The Description of Germanie*, tr. R. Grenewey, London, 1598 [printed jointly with Savile's translation] · *The Annals and History of Cornelius Tacitus ... with the Political and*

Historical notes of Amelot de la Houssay, tr. by various hands (incl. John Dryden), London, 1698 [Dryden's tr. of *Annals* i is in vol. xx (1989) of the California edn. of Dryden's works] · *The Works of Tacitus, with Political Discourses on the Author*, tr. Thomas Gordon, London, 1728 (*Annals*) and 1731 (*Histories*, etc.) · *The Works of Cornelius Tacitus*, tr. Arthur Murphy, London, 1793 · *The Works of Tacitus*, tr. A. J. Church and W. J. Brodribb, London, 1864 (*Histories*) and 1869 (*Annals*) [both works often rep. into the 20th c.] · *Tacitus on Britain and Germany*, tr. H. Mattingly, London, 1948 [Penguin] · *Annals*, tr. Michael Grant, London, 1956 [Penguin] · *Histories*, tr. Kenneth Wellesley, London, 1964 [Penguin].

SEE ALSO   Lathrop, H. B., *Translations from the Classics into English from Caxton to Chapman 1477–1620*, New York, 1932; rep. 1967, pp. 80–91, 168–93, 235–55 · Matthiessen, F. O., *Translation: an Elizabethan Art*, Cambridge, Mass., 1931, pp. 169–227 · Mellor, R., *Tacitus*, New York/London, 1993, ch. 8.

11. PROSE AUTHORS

i. Pliny the Elder   The enormous *Naturalis Historia* (77 CE, *Natural History*) of Pliny the Elder (Gaius Plinius Secundus) would be a daunting project for any translator purely on account of its size, and attempts to english it have been unsurprisingly few. The 'poetical–philosophical Pliny', as Italo Calvino calls him, can be distinguished from the 'neurotic collector of data', but it is likely that the latter was the main attraction for earlier readers. The first English version, by '**I.A.**' (perhaps John Alday) from an intermediate French translation, is no more than a sampler, a few dozen stylistically clumsy pages. But its successor, the complete rendering by Philemon **Holland** (1552–1637), is one of the most characteristic products of its period. Holland successfully evokes Pliny's quizzical wonderment in the early parts of the *History*:

The wealth is such of mettals and mines, in such varietie, so rich, so fruitfull, rising still one under another for so many ages, notwithstanding daily there is so much wasted and consumed ... yet see how many sorts of jemmes there be still, so painted and set out with colours?

Later on, the crowded pages of this large folio have the effect almost of a Renaissance phantasmagoria when read at a stretch, with Holland vainly struggling to gloss and correct the hotchpotch of Pliny's information in interpolations and marginal notes. This, the most popular of Holland's numerous translations, lies behind many an image in 17th-c. English literature and the other arts.

Nor was it quickly replaced: nearly three centuries elapse before the next version, mainly by John **Bostock** (1773–1846). This 1855 Bohn edition, with copious notes, is rather flat and ponderous, a practical guide to Pliny but with no aesthetic appeal. Nevertheless it remained, like Holland's, for long the sole offering. Apart from specialized selections such as Katherine **Jex-Blake**'s of sections relating to art history and Kenneth **Bailey**'s of those on chemistry, the next and for the time being final

point in the English translation history is H. **Rackham**'s 1938 Loeb. This is a reliable modern rendering, but still much stronger on data than poetry.

ii. Pliny the Younger   Pliny the Younger (Gaius Plinius Caecilius Secundus, who was adopted by his uncle, and took his name) is known as a voluminous letter-writer in a mode mixing common sense with calculated sensibility. So it is perhaps natural that while his earlier English translators, such as Abraham **Fleming** (?1552–1607), attended to only limited selections or even single letters, English writers of the age of politeness felt themselves on much closer terms with him. There are small-scale 18th-c. versions of various works by, for example, George **Smith**, Tom **Brown**, and John **Toland**; but the best-known English translation also belongs to this period. William **Melmoth**'s (1710–99) *Letters of Pliny* was received with universal acclaim and described by Thomas Warton as superior to its original. Mannered and periphrastic ('he has often recruited his health under my roof'), this complete 1746 version is much reprinted, and used in revised form as the Loeb translation until as late as 1969. It has, eventually, come to seem too florid and loose, so that Betty **Radice**'s more economical (yet not inelegant) version, first published in 1963, is now judged more suitable for that series as a working guide to the Latin.

Alexander Pope's friend John Boyle, Earl of **Orrery** (1706–62), brought out another version of the complete letters five years later, after a long-term labour of love. It is an urbane and elegant rendering, full of intelligent 'observations', carrying an extensive 'Life of Pliny', and showing many signs of affectionate admiration for his original. Its style has lasted arguably somewhat better than that of its immediate predecessor.

The appeal of the *Epistles* having declined over the last century and more, few successors to Melmoth and Orrery have presented themselves.

539

J. B. **Firth**'s rendering of 1900 is easily surpassed by Radice; that of J. D. **Lewis**'s (1828–84) is a literal version only; others are short selections, often cribs for examination work. The Younger Pliny is conspicuous by his absence from the various modern paperback 'classics' series.

iii. Seneca Lucius Annaeus Seneca, Seneca the Younger, appears in this entry primarily as the writer of his 15 treatises (of which most are dialogues) on ethical subjects, secondarily as author of 124 letters (*Epistles*, or *Epistulae Morales*) and his *Naturales Quaestiones*. Notwithstanding T. S. Eliot's strictures on the non-dramatic works—'that extraordinarily dull and uninteresting body of Seneca's prose' (Eliot 1951)—they have ranked second only to Plutarch's as practical guides to morality in the western world. They have an extensive English translation history and some have been importantly influential on English writers such as Bacon, Milton, and Dryden.

The very early translators, beginning with Robert **Whittington** (*fl.* 1520) in 1547, occupied themselves with single dialogues. One was Arthur **Golding** (*c.*1536–*c.*1605), the Elizabethan translator of Ovid [II.n.6]. His version of *De Beneficiis* is compared linguistically by Sørensen with that made as part of Thomas **Lodge**'s (*c.*1558–1625) complete English translation of Seneca's non-dramatic works. Golding's version is meticulous and thorough, though not a classic of English prose; together with French translations, it was drawn upon by Lodge. Lodge's Latin is competent but there are occasional aberrations. Overall, this first large-scale English Seneca is heterogeneous and a little haphazard, something of a digest instead of a translation in its tendency to free rearrangements of passages. But Lodge's ambitious enterprise is a success to the extent that his own English is expressive and flavoursome:

Why hide I a public Ulcer, under milder words? We are all of us noughts. Whatsoever therefore is reprehended in another, that shall every man find within his owne bosome. Why observest thou his bleaknesse of colour, his leanenesse of body? It is a common plague.   (*Of Anger*, iii)

Lodge ushers in what has been called the 'Senecan century'. Though no translator chooses to compete with him on the complete works, there is a rash of activity on single items. A study could be made of the phenomenon of translating Senecan treatises into verse in the mid-17th c.: some examples, notably by Ralph **Freeman** (*fl.* 1610–55) and Sir Edward **Sherburne** (1618–1702), repay attention. But much the best-known of Lodge's successors

was Sir Roger **L'Estrange** (1616–1704), whose *Seneca's Morals by Way of Abstract*, first published in 1678 and reissued in many forms until the late 19th c., is advertised as reducing to order Seneca's 'scattered Ethics' so that 'any man, upon occasion, may know where to find them'. As such, L'Estrange's work is not really a translation. Though he adds nothing of his own (he omits much), he is stitching together a patchwork, or to use his own simile: 'it would be as hard to refer each sentence, text, and precept, to the very place whence it was drawn, as to bring every distinct drop in a cask of wine to the particular grape from whence it was pressed.' This sentence is a fair sample of L'Estrange's vigorous and still readable English. He appends to the main part of his volume an equally reworked version of Seneca's *Epistles*.

A few of L'Estrange's comments are quoted by Thomas **Morell** (1703–84), but Morell's translation of the *Epistles* is an altogether more sophisticated affair. He was a classical scholar of some repute. His version presents the text in two expensive quartos as a guide for a gentleman's conduct. Today his prose, particularly in his copious commentary but also in his translation, seems with its leisurely syntax and orotund periods over-elaborate, even affected.

The 19th and 20th c. produce regular translations, and the earlier renderings have mainly been improved upon by their more modern replacements. E. Phillips **Barker**'s 1932 *Epistles* is already showing signs of age and Aubrey **Stewart**'s Victorian one still more so; Robin **Campbell**'s has succeeded them. Thomas H. **Corcoran** and M. **Winterbottom**'s Loebs have the usual Loeb virtues, while C. D. N. **Costa**'s two more recent parallel-text selections, of *Letters* and *Dialogues* respectively, are more manageable in size, offer fuller notes, and are in more up-to-date English.

iv. Cicero The treatises (dialogues), speeches, and letters of Marcus Tullius Cicero are from the early Renaissance extraordinarily influential in all western countries. They are also voluminous; this account of their English translations must necessarily be highly selective.

The earliest published translation is found in an extremely rare volume edited by William Caxton in 1481 from work by John **Tiptoft**, Earl of Worcester (1427–79). It is a curiosity, a version of *De Amicitia* (44 BCE, Of Friendship) from an intermediate French translation. In the 16th c., some of the translators of letters by Seneca or the Younger Pliny englished Cicero too: Robert **Whittington** (*fl.* 1520) and Abraham **Fleming** (?1552–1607) are examples.

The former's literal rendering of *De Officiis* (44 BCE, Of Duties) as *Tullyes Offyces* suggests Cicero's prestige by being dedicated to Henry VIII and beautifully printed as a parallel text in black letter. And in Fleming's *Panoplie of Epistles*, Cicero is the first and easily the best-represented of the letter-writers on whom readers of this practical compilation are meant to model their own efforts. The humanists' promotion of Cicero as a stylistic model helped to ensure that by 1600, thanks to further work by figures such as Nicholas **Grimalde** (1519–62), John **Harington** (1561–1612), and Thomas **Newton** (?1542–1607), the bulk of his writings were easily accessible in English, the most popular sometimes in a choice of translations.

The orators, preachers, and prose stylists of the next two centuries consciously emulated Cicero; the thinking of humanists and deists of the Enlightenment—Bolingbroke, Locke, Hume—is also indebted to him. Of most importance is the high style of the oratorical works and the appeal of the treatises' ideal of *humanitas*—the qualities of the truly civilized individual. But this period does not throw up many translations that would readily be used today. A large number owe their existence to Cicero's status as a school and university text. Such are the versions of the orations by **Guthrie**, 1741, and his followers **Rutherford** and **Duncan** (the latter a professor of philosophy at Aberdeen University). These aspire to a rhetorical manner apt to seem pompous nowadays, when we no longer, for instance, find ourselves unable 'sufficiently to applaud' our friends' 'fortitude' (Duncan). The most durable versions of this era were those by William Melmoth, produced in the second half of the 18th c. but still used in 20th-c. series such as Everyman.

In the 20th c., a monopoly on translation of Cicero appears to have been held by classical scholars; *littérateurs* may have shared the opinion of Kingsley Amis's schoolmaster that 'for a man so long and so thoroughly dead it was remarkable how much boredom . . . Cicero could generate'. Evelyn S. **Shuckburgh**'s 1899–1900 translation of the *Letters* adds some material unknown to his predecessors Melmoth and William **Heberden**. Its serpentine syntax is a challenge but it has worn fairly well so far. L. P. **Wilkinson**'s selected *Letters* of 1947 is an intelligent and still readable version by a classicist with literary skills. Of the 28 volumes of the Loeb Cicero, H. Rackham's, of a large number of the treatises, are often considered among the best, with both accuracy and a measure of elegance. The rest are uneven, sometimes misrepresenting their originals. H. C. P. **McGregor**'s and Michael **Grant**'s

Penguin translations are freer, with a more relaxed and modern attitude to syntax, but not misleadingly so. A translator such as John **Higginbotham** claims to go further, by rigorously pruning what is purely rhetorical or pleonastic in his version of *De Officiis*; yet the more recent rendering of this work by M. T. **Griffin** and E. M. **Atkins** reads no less naturally. Among the latest translations at the time of writing, P. G. **Walsh**'s version of *The Nature of the Gods* is stiff as prose but authoritative for sense; and a fully satisfactory *Philippics* is at last available in the form of D. R. **Shackleton Bailey**'s masterly rendering.

v. Petronius The *Satyricon* of Petronius Arbiter (written 60–70 CE), properly the *Satyricōn libri* or the *Satyrica*, is a collection of stylistically various fragments, the remains of a long satirical novel. The fragments are sometimes independently transmitted, and sometimes come with additions. The most famous single episode (*Satyricon* 27–78, the 'Cena Trimalchionis', Trimalchio's Feast) was not translated into English until 1694. If we leave aside Ben Jonson's version of Fragment 54 (*Brevis in coitu voluptas*, 'Doing a filthy pleasure is, and short', almost certainly not part of the *Satyricon* and probably not by Petronius), then Sir Richard **Fanshawe**'s (1608–66) too energetically brilliant version of the mock heroic 'Civil War' (*Satyricon* 119–24) is the first attempt to render any part of the *Satyricon*. The 'Cena Trimalchionis' in particular has in modern times attracted independent translation. The story of the 'Widow of Ephesus' (*Satyricon* 111–12) was given in an amplified version by Walter **Charleton** (1619–1707) in the 17th c., and more than once in the 18th c. From George Chapman's *Widow's Tears* (1605) to Christopher Fry's *A Phoenix Too Frequent* (1948) it has been staged surprisingly often.

Fragmentary though it is, the *Satyricon* is more like the modern realist novel than any other classical fiction. But far from simplifying the translator's problem, this compounds it. This is for two reasons. First because its milieu and language are so specific to its time and place that they are reproducible only obliquely. Secondly, because its excursions into verse challenge not only the translator's virtuosity but, since modern novels are uniformly in prose, the tolerance of novel readers.

The first attempt to render the work as a whole is that of William **Burnaby** (1673–1706). 'Enlarging' his author, Burnaby naturalizes the *Satyricon* as a work of picaresque fiction, written in easy late Restoration prose and more than competent verse. From 1708, it was frequently reprinted. Its reprintings this century sometimes include a startlingly camp introduction by C. K. Scott Moncrieff [see II.g.13], who (rather against the tendency of Burnaby's version) prizes the *Satyricon* for its modernist fragmentariness. Another 18th-c. version is by a Mr [John] **Addison** (the translator of Anacreon and Sappho), sometimes mentioned with embarrassment by editors of the 'chaste' Joseph Addison.

The mid-19th-c. Bohn Classical Library includes, in a volume with other supposedly adult material, a literal version by Walter **Kelly**. The Edwardian *Satiricon* of 1902, falsely attributed to Oscar Wilde, is still well regarded, especially for its treatment of the verse. Michael **Heseltine** introduces his Loeb version by confessing that 'the translator dulls his brilliance'; it has been revised by E. H. **Warmington**. Others flee dullness. John **Mitchell**'s period attempts to catch off-standard speech have not been well received, and those by Jack **Lindsay** and Paul **Dinnage**, still described as 'lively', have been overtaken. But William **Arrowsmith**'s up-market and therefore flexible American idiom has great staying power. J. P. **Sullivan**, who values 'fidelity and poise', goes for the sense of dialect, but not the dialect of anywhere in particular. At least in Britain, his translation was standard until recently. The recent Everyman by Robert Bracht **Brahnam** and Daniel **Kinney** will probably replace Arrowsmith as standard for the American market. Erich Segal suggests that P. G. Walsh's idiom in the new Oxford edition is too 'insularly English' for his ear, and it may be too sober even for an English ear. Both versions are in quite different ways rather splendid; and both (though Walsh is weightier here) come with abundant commentary and introductory material.

vi. Apuleius Lucius Apuleius (born in North Africa *c*.123 CE) enjoys the reputation of a Platonist philosopher who, as Keats thought, invented the soul, as well as that of a teller of scurrilous tales. The paradox of the combination is crudely evident already in the early variant title of the *Metamorphoses*: *Asinus Aureus* or the *Golden Ass*. Since no translator attempts to reproduce the oddities of Apuleius' African style—learned and luscious, a cross between Amanda Ros and John Lyly (says Robert Graves)—the English sense of Apuleius is bewilderingly at the mercy of the divisions in his subject-matter. It is for this reason that the story of 'Cupid and Psyche' is so often rescued from the 'merry tales' with which Apuleius makes it keep company. It has enjoyed a vigorous independent life, often in adaptation, often in verse. It has even been 'retold for boys'.

The title of William **Adlington**'s (*fl.* 1566) version, which distinguishes the 'sundry pleasant' tales of the book from the 'excellent narration' of the central books, already establishes the pattern of interest. His prose registers the difficulty he has with the novel's 'plenty of mirth' being communicated in 'dark and high' terms, 'strange and absurd words', 'new invented phrases'. Adlington's version was revived in the Tudor Translation series and, partly because it formed the basis of Stephen **Gaselee**'s 1915 Loeb version, has survived amazingly well since.

In the later 18th c. Thomas **Taylor**'s (1758–1835) separate version of 'Cupid and Psyche' was well received; his learning and the chastity of his intentions earned him an influence in the reception of Apuleius beyond the success of his translation of the whole, apparently literal but heavily pruned and designed frankly as a vehicle for Platonist allegories. Sir George **Head**'s (1782–1855) ineptly bowdlerized version initiated the habit of breaking up the book divisions into episodes. The anonymous Bohn version succeeds Taylor's as a collection of Apuleian material: its bias is evident in the inclusion of Hudson Gurney's verse rendering of 'Cupid and Psyche' and Mary Tighe's 'Psyche' (a poem admired by Keats until he saw though it). The best-known of the 19th-c. translations is Walter **Pater**'s (1839–94) of 'Cupid and Psyche', done into an other-worldly English which owes a lot to Adlington, but which conspicuously lacks Elizabethan (or Apuleian) robustness and variety.

In the 20th c. Walsh calls H. E. **Butler**'s translation 'squeamish'. Less so is the energetic but unreliable version of Jack Lindsay, or that of Francis D. **Byrne** designed 'for the man of the world *par excellence*'. The ill-tempered and amusing introduction accords well with the uneven temper of the translation, which has an appropriate kind of wobble. It is less than frank with the obscenity, but makes its compromises by contriving a sexy macaronic ('for a moment she places one rosy palm upon *glabellum feminale*').

Robert **Graves** makes no attempt to reproduce the Apuleian manner: 'The effect of oddness is best achieved in convulsed times like the present [1950] by writing in as easy and sedate and English as possible.' The revision by Michael Grant changes only detail, and for a fiction riddled (he says) with *aporia*—the figure which by confronting us with unresolvable paradox makes reading impossible—he holds to a style with ambitions to be natural, easy, readable. It is indeed incomparably the most readable version. Subsequent versions, while genuinely faithful to their original, do not escape the lure of readability. J. A. **Hanson** admits that at his hands the Latin 'suffers metamorphosis into standard English'. P. G. Walsh's fidelity is combined with an unsympathetic want of gusto and extravagance, which can make the translation actually distasteful.

SG and RC

APULEIUS   *The Eleven Books of the Golden Asse, containing the Metamorphosie of Lucius Apuleius*, by William Adlington, London, 1566; rep. London, 1893 [adapted for Loeb, 1915] · *The Fable of Cupid and Psyche*, tr. Thomas Taylor, London, 1795 · *Cupid and Psyche*, tr. Hudson Gurney, London, 1799 [verse; frequent reps.] · *Apuleius' Golden Ass, or, The Metamorphosis*, by Thomas Taylor, London, 1822 · *The Metamorphoses*, tr. Sir George Head, London, 1851 · *The Works of Apuleius*, tr. anon., London, 1853 [Bohn] · 'The Golden Book: The Story of Cupid and Psyche' in *Marius the Epicurean*, by Walter Pater, London, 1885 [often issued independently] · *The Golden Ass*, tr. Francis D. Byrne, London, 1904 · *The Metamorphoses, or Golden Ass of Apuleius of Madaura*, tr. H. E. Butler, 2 vols., Oxford, 1910 · *The Golden Ass*, tr. Jack Lindsay, New York, 1932 · *The Transformations of Lucius, otherwise known as The Golden Ass*, tr. Robert Graves, Harmondsworth, 1950 [Penguin; rev. Michael Grant, 1990] · *Metamorphoses*, tr. J. A. Hanson, 2 vols., London 1989 [Loeb] · *The Golden Ass*, tr. P. G. Walsh, Oxford, 1994.

CICERO   ... *The Boke of Tulle of Olde Age ... and Boke of Freendship*, etc., tr. John Tiptoft, Earl of Worcester, ed. William Caxton, London, 1481 [there is no title-page. The tr. of *De Senectute* is not by Worcester] · *The Thre Bookes of Tullyes Offyces, bothe in Latynge Tonge and in Englysshe*, tr. Robert Whyttington, London, 1533 · *Marcus Tullius Ciceroes Three Bookes of Dueties*, tr. Nicholas Grimalde, London, 1555 · *The Booke of Freendship of Marcus Tullius Cicero*, tr. John Harington, London, 1562 · *The Booke of Marcus Tullius Cicero entitled Paradoxa Stoicorum*, tr. Thomas Newton, London, 1569 · *A Panoplie of Epistles, Or, a Looking Glasse for the Unlearned*, tr. Abraham Fleming, London, 1576 · *Four Severall Treatises of M. Tullius Cicero*, tr. Thomas Newton, London, 1577 · *The Orations of Marcus Tullius Cicero*, tr. William Guthrie, 2 vols., London, 1741 · *Marcus Tullius Cicero to Several of His Friends*, tr. William Melmoth, London, 1753 · *Cato Major*, tr. William Melmoth, London, 1773 [see below] · *Cato and Laelius; or, Essays on Old-Age and Friendship*, tr. William Melmoth, 2 vols., London, 1777 [Everyman, *Cicero's Offices*, 1909] · *The Principal Orations of Cicero*, tr. John Rutherford, London, 1797 · *Select Orations*, tr. William Duncan, Edinburgh, 1801 [parallel text] · *The Letters of Marcus Tullius Cicero to Titus Pomponius Atticus*, tr. William Heberden, 2 vols., London, 1825 · *The Letters of Cicero*, tr. Evelyn S. Shuckburgh, 4 vols., London, 1888–1900 [Bohn] · *Cicero*, tr. several hands, 28 vols., London, 1912–77 [Loeb] · *The Letters of Cicero: A Selection in Translation*, tr. L. P. Wilkinson, London, 1949 · *Cicero: On Moral Obligation*, tr. John Higginbotham, London, 1967 · *The Nature of the Gods*, tr. Horace C. P. McGregor, Harmondsworth, 1972 [Penguin] · *Cicero: Philippics*, tr. D. R. Shackleton Bailey, Chapel Hill, NC, 1986 · *Cicero: On Duties*, tr. M. T. Griffin and E. M. Atkins, Cambridge, 1991 · *On Government*, tr. Michael Grant, Harmondsworth, 1993 [Penguin; a substantial selection from various works] · *Cicero: The Nature of the Gods*, tr. P. G. Walsh, Oxford, 1997.

PETRONIUS   'Petronius His Rapture', tr. Sir Richard Fanshawe in *Lusiads*, London, 1655 · 'The Ephesian Matron', tr. Walter Charleton, London, 1659 · *The Satyr of Titus Petronius Arbiter*, tr. William Burnaby and 'another hand', London, 1694 (two edns.) [Many reprints, from 1708 with additional material as *The Satyrical Works in Prose and Verse*, and notably 1910 with the Latin *en face*, 1923 with an intro, by C. K. Scott Moncrieff] · *The Works of Petronius Arbiter, in Prose and Verse*, tr. John Addison, London, 1736; rep. New York, 1975 · *The Satyricon of Petronius Arbiter*, tr. Walter K. Kelly, London, 1854 [Bohn] · *Trimalchio's Dinner*, tr. Harry Thurston Peck, New York, 1898 · *The Satiricon of Petronius Arbiter*, tr. 'Sebastian Melmoth', Paris, 1902 [frequent reprints; see *The Satiricon of Petronius Arbiter in the Translation Attributed to Oscar Wilde*, ed, Allen Lewis, Chicago, 1927] · *Petronius*, tr. Michael Heseltine, London, 1913; rev. 1930 [Loeb; rev. E. H. Warmington, 1969] · *Petronius, Leader of Fashion*, tr. J. M. Mitchell, London, 1922 · *The Satyricon of Petronius Arbiter*, tr. W. C. Firebaugh, New York, 1922 · *The Complete Works of Gaius Petronius*, tr. Jack Lindsay, London, 1927 · *Dinner at Trimalchio's*, tr. G. J. Acheson, Johannesburg, 1950; rev. 1962 · *The Satyricon of Petronius*, tr. Paul Dinnage, London, 1953 · *The Satyricon*, tr. William Arrowsmith, New York, 1959 · *The Satyricon, and the Fragments*, tr. J. P. Sullivan, Harmondsworth, 1965 [Penguin] · *Satyrica*, tr. Robert Bracht Branham and Daniel Kinney, Berkeley, Calif., 1996 [Everyman] · *The Satyricon*, tr. P. G. Walsh, Oxford, 1996 [World's Classics, 1997].

PLINY THE ELDER   *A Summarie of the antiquities and wonders of the worlds, abstracted out of the sixteene first bookes of Plinie*, translated oute of French by I. A., London [1565] [rep. as *The Secrets and Wonders of the World*, 1585, 1587] · *The Historie of the World: Commonly called, the Naturall Historie of C. Plinius Secundus*, tr. Philemon Holland, 2 vols., London, 1601 [abr. P. Turner, Carbondale, Ill., 1962; J. Newsome, Oxford, 1964] · *The Natural History of Pliny*, tr. John Bostock and H. T. Riley, 6 vols., London, 1855–7 [Bohn] · *The Elder Pliny's Chapters on the History of Art*, tr. Katherine Jex-Blake, London, 1896 · *The Elder Pliny's Chapters on Chemical Subjects*, tr. Kenneth C. Bailey, London, 1929 · *Pliny: Natural History*, tr. H. Rackham, 10 vols., London, 1938 [Loeb].

PLINY THE YOUNGER   *A Panoplie of Epistles, Or, a Looking Glasse for the unlearned*, tr. Abraham Fleming, London, 1576 · *Pliny's Panegyrick upon the Emperor Trajan*, tr. George Smith, London, 1702 · *The Works of Mr. Thomas Brown*, 3 vols., London, 1707–8 [vol. i contains nine of Pliny's epistles] · *The Description of Epsom*, by Britto-Batavus (i.e. John Toland), London, 1726 [contains translations of four letters] · *The Letters of Pliny*, tr. William Melmoth, London, 1746 [subsequently Bohn and Loeb] · *The Letters of Pliny the Younger*, tr. John Earl of Orrery, 2 vols., London, 1751 · *The Letters of the Younger Pliny*, tr. J. D. Lewis, London, 1879 · *The Letters of the Younger Pliny*, tr. J. B. Firth, 2 vols., London, 1892 · *The Letters of Pliny*, tr. Betty Radice, Harmondsworth, 1963 [Penguin; reissued with corrections as *Pliny: Letters and Panegyrics*, 2 vols., Loeb, London, 1969].

Seneca   *A Frutefull Worke of Lucius Annaeus Seneca named the forme and Rule of Honest lyvynge*, tr. Robert Whittington, London, 1546 · *The remedyes agaynst all casuall chaunces*, tr. Robert Whittington, London, 1547 · *The Woorke of . . . Lucius Annaeus Seneca Concerning Benefyting*, tr. Arthur Golding, London, 1578 · *The Workes*, tr. Thomas Lodge, London, 1614 [excludes plays] · *L. A. Seneca, the Philosopher . . . His Book of Consolation to Marcia*, tr. [Ralph Freeman], London, 1635 · *Seneca's Answer to Lucilius*, tr. Edward Sherburne, London, 1648 [verse] · *Lucius Annaeus Seneca, his First Book of Clemency*, tr. anon., London, 1653 [verse] · *Lucius Annaeus Seneca, the Philosopher: His Book of the Shortness of Life*, tr. Ralph Freeman, 2nd edn., London, 1663 [in verse; the 1st edn. is not extant] · *Seneca's Morals by Way of Abstract*, tr. Sir Roger L'Estrange, London, 1678 [over 20 further edns. and adaptations up to 1888] · *The Epistles*, tr. Thomas Morell, London, 1786 · *Select Orations*, tr. William Duncan, Edinburgh, 1814 · *L. Annaeus Seneca on Benefits*, tr. Aubrey Stewart, London, 1848 [Bohn] · *Minor Dialogues*, tr. Aubrey Stewart, London, 1884 [Bohn] · *Physical Science in the Time of Nero. Being a Translation of the Quaestiones Naturales of Seneca*, by John Clarke, London, 1910 · *Letters of Seneca*, tr. E. Phillips Barker, Oxford, 1932 · *Letters from a Stoic: Epistulae Morales*, tr. Robin Campbell, Harmondsworth, 1969 [Penguin] · *Naturales Quaestiones*, tr. Thomas H. Corcoran, London, 1971 [Loeb] · *Declamations*, tr. M. Winterbottom, London, 1974 [Loeb] · *Seneca: Epistulae Morales: English and Latin Selections*, tr. C. D. N. Costa, Warminster, 1988 · *Seneca: Four Dialogues*, tr. C. D. N. Costa, Warminster, 1994 [parallel texts].

See also   Haight, E. H., *Apuleius and His Influence*, New York, 1927 · MacKendrick, P., *The Philosophical Books of Cicero*, London, 1989 [includes recommendations of modern translations for individual texts] · *The Speeches of Cicero: Context, Law, Rhetoric*, London, 1995 [a companion volume to the above covering 20 selected speeches] · Palmer, R. G., *Seneca's De Remediis Fortuitorum and the Elizabethans*, Chicago, 1953 · Schmeling, G. L., and Stuckey, J. H., *A Bibliography of Petronius*, Leiden, 1977 · Sørensen, K., *Thomas Lodge's Translation of Seneca's De Beneficiis Compared with Arthur Golding's Version: A Textual Analysis with Special Reference to Latinisms*, Copenhagen, 1960 · Sullivan, J. P., 'Appropriating Petronius', in W. Radice et al., eds., *The Translator's Art: Essays in Honour of Betty Radice*, Harmondsworth, 1987 · Tobin, J. J. M., *Shakespeare's Favorite Novel*, New York, 1984 [on Apuleius].

12. LATE LATIN AND POSTCLASSICAL LATIN

The amount of Latin literature that was written after the classical period—whether we define the period narrowly as extending only until 200 CE or more generously as stretching through late antiquity until 500 CE—dwarfs that produced during antiquity itself. Furthermore, the quantity of Latin texts extant from the Middle Ages far exceeds that recorded in medieval vernacular literatures, such as Old English, Middle English, Old French, and Italian. This postclassical Latin literature—here designated Late Latin for the stretch between 200 and 500, Medieval Latin for the expanse between 500 and 1300, and Neo-Latin for everything thereafter—has special qualities stylistically. Late Latin, which will be considered solely in the writings of St Augustine (354–430) and Boethius (c.480–524), saw the development of a new aesthetics that is as evident in literature as it is in mosaics. Less complexly but no less portentously, it witnessed a lexical shift caused by the advent of Christianity, with many new words from Greek and Hebrew and innovative meanings attached to words taken from Latin itself. Medieval Latin has even more distinctive qualities, since it was composed by authors for whom Latin was not a fully living mother-tongue

but rather what has been aptly called a 'father-tongue'—a language used mainly by boys and men and especially within male-dominated institutions such as churches, courts, schools, and universities.

Drawing general conclusions about which post-classical Latin texts have been translated by whom is a difficult proposition, because so many texts are involved and such a long span of time must be taken into account. In addition to all the texts that were originally composed in Latin we should also attend to those which were originally in Greek, Hebrew, Arabic, or other languages but which were brought into English through the intermediary of Latin. To focus only on the most important such text, the Catholic Bible used for centuries in English—the Douay–Rheims version [see II.c.1.vi]—was translated from the Latin Vulgate, rather than from the Biblical Hebrew or Greek.

In numerous fields of culture and scholarship even extremely significant Latin texts have languished untranslated down to recent decades or even to the present day. Petrarch may have thought that his fame rested not on his Italian sonnets but on his Latin epic entitled *Africa* (c.1338), and yet the latter was first put into English only 20 years ago, whereas the former have been translated repeatedly [see II.m.4]. In other branches of learning, translations into English were made relatively early; for instance, a good number of Latin medical works were translated during the 14th and 15th c. Sometimes translations into the spoken languages, especially from postmedieval Latin, have become so entrenched that few people realize that the texts were originally in Latin at all. Such would be the case with the philosophical writings of René Descartes [II.g.8.i], the astronomical texts of Kepler, and so forth.

Despite the many reasons why thousands upon thousands of Medieval Latin and Neo-Latin texts have never been translated, there have been powerful incentives since the Middle Ages to render many texts into modern spoken languages such as English. Only translation could have made the texts accessible to those non-clerics and women who would not have had the opportunity or the leisure to learn Latin. Even within the clergy in the epoch often known as the Latin Middle Ages, many ecclesiastics who had a non-Romance language as their native tongue lacked the proficiency in Latin to read it comfortably. It was for churchmen of the lower ranks, not for peasants, that the Venerable **Bede** (673–735) on his deathbed spent his last hours rendering the Gospel of St John from the Vulgate Latin into Old English, just as he had earlier translated from Latin hymns, the Creed, and part of Isidore [see I.b.1.ii]. The same holds true of **Alfred** the Great (849–901), King of England, who translated Pope Gregory the Great's 6th-c. *Pastoral Care*, Orosius' 5th-c. *History against the Pagans*, Boethius' *Consolation of Philosophy*, and Augustine's *Soliloquies* [see I.b.1.ii].

After the Norman Conquest much of the energy that would have been invested in translation or adaptation in English became diverted to performing the same tasks in Norman French: Latin remained the dominant tongue of Church and record-keeping as it had been, but French usurped the position of English as the most prestigious vernacular language in England, since it became the mother-tongue of the ruling class. During this same period the vernaculars were poised to become entrenched as literary languages in their own right in many areas of western Europe, but doubts about the advisability of translation out of Latin into the spoken languages remained acute. Adam of Perseigne, a canon regular who flourished from *c.*1188 to *c.*1221, refused to translate any of his works into the vulgar tongue, out of the conviction that in the process they would lose their tastefulness and artistry.

As far as English is concerned, although occasional adaptations from postclassical Latin occur in Early Middle English, only later do we encounter the extent of translation and adaptation that had become routine earlier in French. An example would be **Chaucer**'s 'Tale of Melibeus' (in the *Canterbury Tales*), a free rendering in English prose of the Latin prose *Liber de consolatione et consilio* composed by Albertano of Brescia in 1246 and vailable to Chaucer in a French prose version completed in 1336 by Renaud de Louens. Also in the late 14th and early 15th c. appeared English translations of parts of Jacobus de Voragine's (*c.*1230–98) *Golden Legend*. And a real heyday of translation from Latin to English, at least in terms of quantity, comes first with John **Lydgate** (*c.*1370–*c.*1450), who translated such works as the *Troy Book*, and slightly later with the publisher William **Caxton** (*c.*1422–91), who was responsible for the englishing and/or printing of works such as (to name only a few) the *Golden Legend* (1483, with one of its sources being an English translation of 1438, another being a Latin text, and a third being a French version), the *Vitae patrum*, and **John of Trevisa**'s translation (produced in 1387 and printed in 1482) of Ranulf Higden's *Polychronicon* [see I.b.1].

In early modernity Latin continued not only to be studied but also to be used in the composition of new literature: Neo-Latin literature emanated in abundance from the New World as well as the Old. Some of these Latin texts generated enough interest and appreciation to be translated into vernacular languages such as English; and some postclassical texts from the Middle Ages and especially earlier Neo-Latin were also rendered into English. Among texts that are still widely known, Erasmus's *Encomium Moriae* (1510, Praise of Folly) and Thomas More's *Utopia* (1515), both originally written in Latin, were first translated into English in the mid-16th c. by Sir Thomas **Chaloner** and Ralph **Robinson** respectively. But it should not be forgotten that other Neo-Latin texts which have become much less familiar were also put into English: for example, Alexander **Barclay** (*c.*1475–1552) translated a Latin poem on the four cardinal virtues by Dominicus Mancinus (who flourished in the fourth quarter of the 15th c.) under the English title *The Mirror of Good Manners*. Some early translations of these Neo-Latin compositions wore extraordinarily well. For instance, Ralph Robinson's translation of *Utopia* was reprinted at least twice in the 17th c. and three times in the 19th, even in the face of strong competition from that of Bishop Gilbert **Burnet** (1643–1715), which was reprinted at least five times in the 18th c. and four in the 19th. Chaloner's *Praise* *of Folly* was not supplanted definitively until Paul **Turner**'s Penguin Classics volume appeared in 1965.

Because Latin had been ensconced for more than a millennium as the language of theology in western Europe, many religious materials cried out to be translated into English. To give an idea of the spectrum, the texts that Sir Thomas **Elyot** (1490–1546) translated from Latin ranged chronologically from a sermon of St Cyprian (4th c. CE) all the way to the *Rules of a Christian Life* by the Italian Renaissance writer Giovanni Pico della Mirandola. An anonymous author known by the initials **I.T.** (1609) produced an English translation of Boethius' *The Consolation of Philosophy* that was appropriated almost unchanged as the basis for the Loeb Classical Library edition of 1918, with the observation: 'the rendering is most exact. This in a translation of that date is not a little remarkable. We look for fine English and poetry in an Elizabethan; but we do not often get from him such loyalty to the original as is here displayed.' Only in 1973 was this translation replaced by a fresh one, evidently because I.T.'s version was no longer deemed adequately faithful for the standards of the series.

During the Reformation and Counter-Reformation controversial documents often achieved their initial international circulation in Latin, after which they passed into the vernaculars. Thus John **Bale** (1495–1563) translated in 1538 the anti-papal *Pammachius* of Thomas Naogeorgus (*c.*1508–63, real name Kirchmair), while Barnabe **Googe** (1540–94) englished the *Regnum Papisticum* of the same author under the title *The Popish Kingdom, or Reign of Antichrist*. Nor were theological treatises the only religious texts to be translated: Thomas **Cranmer** (1489–1556) brought into English much of the liturgy that had previously been in Latin, most notably in prayer-books.

During this same period, even when authors translated texts that we associate with a modern European language, they may have used a Latin translation rather than—or alongside—the vernacular. Thus Alexander Barclay in translating Sebastian Brant's *Ship of Fools* [see II.h.2.i] relied most heavily upon a translation of it by Jacob Locher in Latin elegiacs. By the same token translators may have resorted to vernacular translations in other modern languages, with French being the likeliest culprit, as auxiliaries to the Latin texts of works that had been composed originally in Latin. It was probably over the course of the 17th and 18th c. that the position of Latin as a lingua franca for the learned and cultural élite slipped to the point where authors and publishers who hoped to disseminate texts internationally would prefer a vernacular language over Latin rather than vice versa. In these centuries the postclassical texts that stood the greatest likelihood of being brought into English were the most classicizing in style; thus the *Basia* of Johannes Secundus (1511–36) enjoyed a spell of popularity first when a translation by Thomas **Stanley** appeared in the mid-17th c. and especially when another (by John **Nott**) was reprinted repeatedly in the late 18th and early 19th c. Canons of taste affected not just what was translated from Latin into English but also how it was translated. In reference to translations of Boethius in the 18th c. it has been observed that the temperament of 'the Age of Reason' prevailed: 'the eighteenth-century versions are collectively more sober, in a plainer, unadorned style, even bare in places, and the verse translations are correspondingly restrained' (Donaghey 1996).

In the 19th and 20th c. Medieval Latin tended to fall between two stools: when the pendulum moved toward classicism, medieval uses of the language were judged too distant from Ciceronian or Virgilian measures to merit a place in the canon; and yet when it swung toward the rosy view of the Middle Ages held by romantics and Pre-Raphaelites among others, Latin even in its medieval forms must have come across as not having the fresh qualities and personal immediacy of the vernacular. Whatever the reasons, Medieval Latin and Neo-Latin texts never became sufficiently canonical to warrant the sorts of interlinear and literal school translations that were published routinely for major Greek and Latin classics: what induced William Cowper to translate Milton's Latin poems into English verse was presumably the fame of Milton as an English poet rather than any burgeoning appetite for postclassical Latinity.

Just as Medieval Latin texts tended to be excluded or at least marginalized in Latin- and Greek-only collections such as the Oxford Classics, so too they failed to gain a niche in the premier original-language-and-translation series of Greek and Latin classics. The Loeb Classical Library contains authors and texts from the second half of the 4th c., such as Ammianus Marcellinus, Augustine's *Confessions*, Ausonius, Avian, Claudian, and Jerome's *Letters*, and from the 5th and early 6th c., such as Rutilius Namatianus, Sidonius Apollinaris, and Boethius. But the only truly Medieval Latin author featured in the Library is Bede, even though its initiator had envisaged a series encompassing texts down to the fall of Constantinople in 1453. Yet Medieval Latin works were incorporated, though without the Latin texts, into other translation series. Thus Bohn's Antiquarian Library made available prose translations of many texts that interested historians of the Middle Ages.

The 20th c. has seen a proliferation of scholarship that has facilitated translations and translation series of postclassical Latin texts into English. The lexicographic tools—dictionaries, word lists, lexica, and so forth—that had been wanting in previous centuries have become available, although often only in partially completed form. Great collaborative enterprises have been undertaken internationally to produce reference works of a kind taken for granted in many more established fields of study.

One burst of energy came in the 1920s and early 1930s—when medieval studies was being institutionalized in the New World with the foundation of the Medieval Academy of America and when Medieval Latin was brought to the attention of scholars through the publication of two great anthologies of Latin texts (without accompanying translations) by Charles H. Beeson and Karl Pomeroy Harrington. Less than a decade saw the publication of Gregory of Tours's 6th-c. *The History of the Franks* translated by O. M. **Dalton**, Hrotsvitha of Gandersheim's 10th-c. plays by Christopher Marie **St John**, Liudprand of Cremona's 10th-c. historical writings by Frederick Adam **Wright**, Caesarius of Heisterbach's early 13th-c. *Dialogue on Miracles* by Henry von Essen **Scott** and Charles Cooke Swinton **Bland**, Roger Bacon's 13th-c. *Opus majus* by Robert Belle **Burke**, and Johannes Secundus' lyric poetry by Frederick Adam Wright. G. C. **Richards**'s 1923 translation of Thomas More's *Utopia*, although less in the limelight now because of competition from the version in Penguin Classics and the Norton Critical Edition, is exemplary of the high quality attained by translators during these years: it is idiomatic without slipping into colloquialisms that could otherwise have dated it swiftly, and it ranges smoothly from the elegantly formal through the calmly expository to the bluntly emotional.

The second half of the century has witnessed an even greater explosion of translations. Among translation series associated with this growth, the most securely entrenched would probably be the Oxford Medieval Texts, which absorbed and greatly extended the earlier Nelson's Medieval Texts. All volumes in this series print the Latin text facing the English translation. Offering only the English is the Records of Civilization: Sources and Studies, which has covered the gamut from Macrobius's 5th-c. *Commentary on the Dream of Scipio* to Marsilius of Padua's 14th-c. *Defensor pacis*. An extensive newer series that promulgates English translations of Greek and Latin source materials for late

antiquity and the early Middle Ages is Translated Texts for Historians. Most of the texts have been prose, a few—such as the poems of Venantius Fortunatus (second half of the 6th c.)—verse. Specialized series have brought into print translations of the writings of particular religious figures (e.g. Saints Augustine, Francis, and Bonaventure, to say nothing of Erasmus) or orders (Cistercian Fathers Series). Series devoted to Medieval Latin secular literature have not fared well, although the positive reception that has been accorded to a recent verse translation of Walter of Châtillon's *Alexandreis* in 'The Middle Ages Series' of the University of Pennsylvania Press may mark the start of a new trend. Only a handful of volumes in the Garland Library of Medieval Literature offered translations from the Latin. The Cambridge Medieval Classics, in a format with Latin text and facing English translation, has been limited to not even a dozen volumes. The main reason for the failure of Medieval Latin literature, excepting texts important to historians, to win a foothold is no fault of any of the series but rather probably the fact that in the English-speaking world the literature of the Middle Ages has entered the curricula of schools and universities mainly through the teaching of English literary history. As a result, much more weight has been assigned to works such as *Beowulf* and authors such as Chaucer than to any of the Latin literature that constituted the bedrock of medieval intellectual training and life.

In the penumbra between mass marketing and scholarship would fall the Penguin Classics, which include a few Medieval Latin works in translation; most of them are historical works, but additionally the series has purveyed to a large readership, in translations that have sometimes been revised since their initial publication in the Classics, Augustine's *Confessions* and *City of God*, Boethius' *Consolation of Philosophy*, the letters of Abelard and Heloise, a selection from the *Carmina burana*, and Erasmus' *Praise of Folly*. The only translation of a verse text among these is D. S. **Parlett**'s handling of the *Carmina burana*, which is not very accurate. V. E. **Watts** achieved greater success in translating Boethius' metres, which he put into deliberately old-fashioned language so as to convey solemnity. The transition from the simple colloquiality of its prose to the more ornate tone of the verse can be very forceful, as when the dreamer and Lady Philosophy exchange a few last words before she breaks into the famous 'O qui perpetua' hymn:

'We ought to pray to the Father of all things. To omit to do so would not be laying a proper foundation.'

'Right,' she said, and immediately began the following hymn.

> 'O Thou who dost by everlasting reason rule,
> Creator of the planets and sky, who time
> From timelessness didst bring, unchanging Mover,
> No cause drove Thee to mould unstable matter, but
> The form benign of highest good within Thee set.

Other translators dispense with such attempts to render the meters poetic in translation. Compare, for instance, Richard **Green**'s handling of the same passage:

'We must invoke the Father of all things without whose aid no beginning can be properly made.'

'You are right,' said Philosophy, and she began to sing this song:

'Oh God, Maker of heaven and earth, Who govern the world with eternal reason, at your command time passes from the beginning. You place all things in motion, though You are yourself without change. No external causes impelled You to make this work from chaotic matter. Rather it was the form of the highest good . . .'

Augustine's *Confessions* pose similar problems. Although without the alternation between prose and verse that forms an essential framework of the *Consolation*, the *Confessions* express deeply personal reflections in a style dense with allusions and references. Compare how two translators, first R. S. **Pine-Coffin** and then Henry **Chadwick**, handle the first few lines in Augustine's account of the famous pear-tree episode:

There was a pear-tree near our vineyard, loaded with fruit that was attractive neither to look at nor to taste. Late one night a band of ruffians, myself included, went off to shake down the fruit and carry it away, for we had continued our games out of doors until well after dark, as was our pernicious habit.

There was a pear tree near our vineyard laden with fruit, though attractive in neither colour nor taste. To shake the fruit off the tree and carry off the pears, I and a gang of naughty adolescents set off late at night after (in our usual pestilential way) we had continued our game in the streets.

The Penguin translation by Pine-Coffin is very readable, although not as punctilious and scholarly as the Oxford World's Classics translation by Chadwick.

Apart from scholarly translations—which have been devoted mainly to prose texts—the first major translator of Medieval Latin verse was John Addington **Symonds** (1840–93). His *Wine, Women, and Song* of 1884 brought poems of the sort found in the *Carmina burana* for the first time to the attention of a broader public in the English-speaking world.

Symonds's little volume is remembered these days as a minor classic because of the vogue that it enjoyed. The first stanza of the first poem gives a typical taste of Symonds's style:

> At the mandate, Go ye forth,
>   Through the whole world hurry!
> Priests tramp out toward south and north,
>   Monks and hermits skurry,
> Levites smooth the gospel leave,
>   Bent on ambulation;
> Each and all to our sect cleave,
>   Which is life's salvation.

As the pronoun in 'Go ye forth' suggests, Symonds belonged to a school that believed in peppering its translations of medieval literature with archaisms. Just within his translation of this poem he offers forms such as "tis', 'doth', and 'hath'. Similarly old-fashioned vocabulary is salient in phrases such as 'in sooth' and 'as I ken'. A willingness to incorporate latinate vocabulary shows in the word 'ambulation'; the final stanza ends with a string of *figurae etymologicae* that would have passed muster with any medieval rhetorician: 'To reprove the reprobate, | Probity approving, | Improbate from approbate | To remove, I'm moving'.

If Symonds was a pioneer, the first lasting settlers came more than a generation later. Philip Schuyler **Allen** spread awareness of Medieval Latin lyric poetry in overviews that included frequent snatches of translation, *The Romanesque Lyric* (1928) and *Medieval Latin Lyrics* (1931). Since then the two bestselling anthologies of Medieval Latin lyric in paperback with the Latin facing English translations have been the oft-reprinted *Mediaeval Latin Lyrics* of Helen **Waddell**, which led to a sequel by her entitled *More Latin Lyrics*, and *The Goliard Poets* of George F. **Whicher**. Directly inspired by Symonds, Allen, and Waddell was Jack **Lindsay**'s *Medieval Latin Poets*, of which the first stanza of the Archpoet's 'Confession' conveys the flavour:

> Seething deep within with rage
> that does not pass away,
> my consuming bitterness
> to my heart I'll say.
> Light's the stuff that met in me
> on my begetting-day.
> I am nothing but a leaf
> with which the breezes play.

Compare Waddell's treatment of the same stanza:

> Seething over inwardly
> With fierce indignation,
> In my bitterness of soul,
> Hear my declaration.

I am of one element,
Levity my matter,
Like enough a withered leaf
For the winds to scatter.

Whicher's translations rely less on outdated forms and vocabulary than do Symonds's, but a shared difficulty in finding a tone in English to capture the special qualities of much Medieval Latin rhythmic verse is apparent in his rendering of the same Latin stanza quoted from Symonds above:

When through all the realms of earth
'Go ye out' resounded,
Priests began to gad about,
Monks with rapture bounded,
Deacons from the Evangels rose,
Weary of redundance—
One and all our order join,
Seeking life's abundance.

Though the Latin that Whicher translates is not especially difficult in syntax or vocabulary, it combines a simplicity of metrical form with a density of Biblical allusion and Christian terminology that is hard to replicate naturally in English.

Whicher's *The Goliard Poets* was dedicated to Robert Frost, a few of whose lines on Medieval Latin verse are even cited in the introduction:

singing but Dione in the wood
And *ver aspergit terram floribus*
They slowly led old Latin verse to rhyme
And to forget the ancient lengths of time,
And so began the modern world for us.

Such attentiveness to the nature of Medieval Latin verse—whether or not Frost was correct in his characterization of its prosody—has been exceedingly rare among the most influential of modern English poets. T. S. Eliot may have relied in *The Waste Land* upon the theories of the medieval literary anthropologist Jessie Weston, and Ezra Pound may have given ample proof of his credentials as a student of medieval Romance vernaculars, but their predilections for the Middle Ages seem to have stopped considerably short of its Latin literature. Thus Medieval Latin secular lyric poetry has not had as pervasive an impact in English literature as in German, where the *Carmina burana* have made themselves felt forcefully since the 19th c., but especially since the oratorio of Carl Orff. Whereas the entire anthology has been printed in

paperback by a major publisher with the Latin and Middle High German *en face* to a modern German verse translation, and another version has appeared in hardback in the same format in a standard series of German classics, in English we have had only in the past two decades translations of all the love poems, and a full translation has yet to be published. The marvellous *Carmina cantabrigiensia*, assembled in the second half of the 11th c., have all been translated into English, but in an edition for advanced students and scholars rather than for general readers. In contrast to the limited reception of the secular verse, Medieval Latin religious songs—especially hymns—continue to be widely sung in English translation.

Anthologies of Latin texts, especially verse, with English translations are frequently used by scholars and aficionados of the Latin Middle Ages and the Renaissance. Whereas none of the general anthologies of Medieval Latin verse has become established, those that focus on a specific genre or period (such as Peter **Dronke**'s translations of Medieval Latin love lyric included in his books or Peter **Godman**'s *Poetry of the Carolingian Renaissance*) have admirably served the needs of experts while still meriting the name of poetry in their own right. Not too many professional poets have ventured to translate Medieval Latin verse, Fleur **Adcock** being the most prominent and prolific example. Among anthologies of Neo-Latin literature, I. D. **McFarlane**'s *Renaissance Latin Poetry* deserves particular notice since its parallel text-and-translation format is still rarer than collections with Latin alone.

Probably the most powerful effect of postclassical Latin on English has not come through any specific text or group of texts that, upon being translated, has altered the course of English literary history, but rather through a general stylistic influence that was exercised in the 15th c. and that contributed to the shaping of English literary style. Though by around 1500 translations from vernacular languages, especially French, had come to outnumber those from postclassical Latin, and though centuries passed before translators of Latin showed much desire to venture beyond the pale of Silver Latin, the Medieval Latin texts that had been translated before then had already left their mark, and the Neo-Latin texts that continued to be translated would prevent that mark from being obliterated altogether.   JZ

ANTHOLOGIES   Beeson, Charles H., ed., *A Primer of Medieval Latin: An Anthology of Prose and Poetry*, Chicago, 1925 · Godman, Peter, *Poetry of the Carolingian Renaissance*, London, 1985 · Harrington, Karl Pomeroy, ed., *Mediaeval Latin*, Boston, 1925 · Lindsay, Jack, *Medieval Latin Poets*, London, 1934 · McFarlane, I. D., *Renaissance Latin Poetry*, Manchester, 1980 · Symonds, John Addington, *Wine, Women, and Song: Mediaeval Latin Students' Songs Now First*

Translated into English Verse with an Essay, London, 1884 · Waddell, Helen, *Mediaeval Latin Lyrics*, London, 1929 · *More Latin lyrics, from Virgil to Milton*, London, 1976 · Whicher, George F., *The Goliard Poets*, Norfolk, Conn., 1949.

ABELARD, PETER   Radice, Betty, *Letters of Abelard and Heloise*, Harmondsworth, 1974 [Penguin].

ALBERTANUS OF BRESCIA   Sundby, Thor, ed., *Liber consolationis et consilii*, London, 1873.

AUGUSTINE, SAINT   Bettenson, Henry, *City of God against the Pagans*, Harmondsworth, 1972 [Penguin] · Chadwick, Henry, *Confessions*, Oxford, 1991 [World's Classics] · Pine-Coffin, R. S., *Confessions*, Harmondsworth, 1961 [Penguin].

BACON, ROGER   Burke, Robert Belle, *Opus majus*, 2 vols., Philadelphia, 1928.

BOETHIUS   Green, Richard, *The Consolation of Philosophy*, New York, 1962 · I.T., *The Consolation of Philosophy*, rev. H. F. Stewart, London, 1918 [Loeb; 1st edn. 1609] · Tester, S. J., *The Consolation of Philosophy, with an English Translation*, London, 1978 [Loeb] · Watts, V. E., *The Consolation of Philosophy*, Harmondsworth, 1969 [Penguin].

BRAND, SEBASTIAN   Barclay, Alexander, *The Shyp of fooles*, tr. from the Latin version of Jacob Locher, London, 1509 · Zeydel, Edwin Hermann, *The Ship of Fools*, New York, 1944.

CAESARIUS OF HEISTERBACH   Scott, Henry von Essen, and Bland, Charles Cooke Swinton, *Dialogue on Miracles*, London/New York, 1929.

CARMINA BURANA   Blodgett, E. D., and Swanson, Roy Arthur, *The Love Songs of the Carmina Burana*, New York/London, 1987 · Parlett, David Sidney, *Carmina Burana*, Harmondsworth, 1986 [Penguin].

CARMINA CANTABRIGIENSIA   Ziolkowski, Jan M., *Carmina Cantabrigiensia (The Cambridge Songs)*, New York, 1994.

CYPRIAN   Elyot, Sir Thomas, *A Swete and Devoute Ssermon of Holy Saynt Ciprian of Mortalitie of Man. The Rules of a Christian Lyfe Made by Picus Erle of Mirandula*, London, 1534.

ERASMUS, DESIDERIUS   Chaloner, Sir Thomas, *The Praise of Folie*, London, 1549 · Radice, Betty, *Praise of Folly; and Letter to Maarten Van Dorp, 1515*, London, 1993 [Penguin].

GREGORY OF TOURS   Dalton, O. M., *The History of the Franks*, Oxford, 1927 · Thorpe, Lewis, *The History of the Franks*, Harmondsworth, 1974 [Penguin].

HIGDEN, RANULF   Babington, Churchill, and Rawson, Joseph, eds., *Polychronicon Ranulphi Higden monachi Cestrensis: Together with the English Translations of John Trevisa and of an Unknown Writer of the Fifteenth Century*, 9 vols., London, 1865–86 · Taylor, John, *The 'Universal Chronicle'*, Oxford, 1966.

HROTSWITHA OF GANDERSHEIM   St John, Christopher Marie, *The Plays*, London, 1923.

JACOBUS DE VORAGINE   Caxton, William, *The Golden Legend: or, Lives of the Saints*, London, 1483; rep. New York, 1973.

JOHANNES SECUNDUS   Nott, John, *Kisses: Being a Poetical Translation of the Basia of Joannes Secundus Nicolaius, accompanied by the Latin Text*, London, 1778 · Stanley, Thomas, *Kisses, being the Basia of Iohannes Secundus*, London, 1923 [first pub. 17th c.] · Wright, Frederick Adam, *Love Poems*, London/New York, 1930.

LIUDPRAND OF CREMONA   Wright, Frederick Adam, *The Works*, London/New York, 1930.

MACROBIUS, AMBROSIUS AURELIUS THEODOSIUS   Stahl, William Harris, *Commentary on the Dream of Scipio*, New York, 1952.

MANCINUS, DOMINICUS   Barclay, Alexander, *The Mirrour of Good Manners*, Manchester, 1885 [first pub. early 16th c.].

MARSILIUS OF PADUA   Gewirth, Alan, *The Defensor pacis*, New York, 1956.

MILTON, JOHN   Cowper, William, *Latin and Italian Poems*, ed. William Hayley, London, 1808.

MORE, THOMAS   Adams, Robert Martin, *Utopia*, New York, 1975 [2nd edn., New York, 1991] · Richards, George Chatterton, *Utopia*, Oxford, 1923 · Robinson, Ralph, *A Fruteful and Pleasaunt Worke of the Beste State of a Publyque Weale, and of the Newe Yle Called Vtopia*, London, 1551 · Turner, Paul, *Utopia*, Harmondsworth, 1965 [Penguin].

NAOGEORGUS, THOMAS   Bale, John, *Tragoedia nova Pammachius*, Wittenberg, 1538 · Googe, Barnabe, *The Popish Kingdom; or, Reign of Antichrist, Written in Latin Verse*, London, 1570.

PETRARCA, FRANCESCO   Bergin, Thomas Godard, and Wilson, Alice S., *Africa*, New Haven, Conn., 1977.

PICO DELLA MIRANDOLA, GIOVANNI, see CYPRIAN.

VITAE PATRUM   Caxton, William, *Vitae patrum*, Westminster, 1495 · Waddell, Helen, *The Desert Fathers*, London, 1936.

WALTHER OF CHÂTILLON   Townsend, David, *Alexandreis*, Philadelphia, 1996.

SEE ALSO   Allen, P. S., *The Romanesque Lyric: Studies in Its Background and Development from Petronius to the Cambridge Songs*, Chapel Hill, NC, 1928 · *Medieval Latin Lyrics*, with trs. by Howard Mumford Jones, Chicago, 1931 · Donaghey, B., 'The Post-Medieval English Translations of the *De Consolatione Philosophiae* of Boethius, 1500–1800', in R. Ellis and R. Tixier, eds., *The Medieval Translator/Traduire au Moyen Âge*, v, Turnhout, 1996, 302–21 · Goldschmidt, E. P., *Medieval Texts and Their First Appearance in Print*, Supplement to the Bibliographical Society's Transactions, 16; 1943; rep. New York, 1969 · Workman, S. K., *Fifteenth Century Translation as an Influence on English Prose*, Princeton, NJ, 1940.

o. Northern European Languages

1. OLD ENGLISH

After the Norman Conquest, Old English was not known in Britain as a literary language until its study was revived during the Reformation. Interest in Old English was then primarily political and theological: its religious prose was used to support Protestant doctrine. Archbishop Matthew **Parker** (1504–75) and his secretary, John **Joscelyn**, were responsible for the first ever printing of Old English, and include English translations of Ælfric and Wulfstan in *A Testimonie of Antiquitie*. John Foxe reprinted a large part of that work in the second edition of his *Book of Martyrs* (1570), and went on to publish the Gospels in Old English with an English translation by Parker or Joscelyn.

Antiquarian and patriotic interest in Old English gradually outstripped the theological (Hakluyt's *Voyages*, 1599, includes a translation of part of King Alfred's *Orosius*, for instance, and William Camden's *Remaines of a Greater Worke, Concerning Britaine, the Inhabitants thereof, their Language . . .*, 1605, has comparative versions of the Lord's Prayer in Old and later English). Old English began to be presented with Latin translations and apparatus, and apart from the pioneering translations of Old English prose published by Elizabeth **Elstob** (1683–1756) and her brother William (1673–1715), it was not until the 19th c. that translation into English resumed, focusing now on Old English poetry, which comprises the great epic *Beowulf*, and a number of heroic and elegiac shorter poems as well as a large corpus of Biblical and religious verse.

Once the Icelander Grímur Jónsson Thorkelín published in 1815 the first transcription of *Beowulf* with a Latin translation, English translations of the whole poem began to appear; in 1837 John Mitchell **Kemble** (1807–57) followed his edition of *Beowulf* with a literal, prose translation of the whole poem—the first in English.

The choice between faithfulness and readability is acute with poems so distant in time and different in culture. Verse translators must additionally decide how far to imitate Old English poetic form— a four-stress, alliterating line with a marked caesura, and a rich poetic diction which was probably arcane even in its own time.

Literal translations, such as that of Benjamin **Thorpe** (1782–1870), which begins:

> Ay, we the Gar-Danes'
> in days of yore,
> [the] great kings'
> renown have heard of . . .

have been dismissed as simply unreadable except by those who already know some Old English. Similarly, William **Morris** produced a translation from a prose rendering by the Anglo-Saxon scholar A. J. Wyatt which echoes Old English metre, retains the original word order, and makes full use of archaic diction. Morris despised non-imitative translations, but his work has been attacked as more obscure than the original, and even ridiculous. Compare Kemble's 'Beowulf was famous; widely spread the glory of Scyld's offspring' with Morris's 'Brim Beowulf waxed, and wide the weal upsprang | of the offspring of Scyld'. Charles **Kennedy**'s more recent imitative translation is more intelligible.

Throughout the 19th c. and into the 20th c., a passion for the medieval, the epic, and the

Germanic fuelled a steady stream of *Beowulf* translations, variously literal, imitative, or paraphrastic. Chauncey B. Tinker's *The Translations of Beowulf: A Critical Bibliography* offers pithy accounts of their very different qualities and reception.

Early *Beowulf* translators had regularly included other Old English poems, but the rise of English Literature as a discipline led to the emergence of 'textbook' anthologies for either specialists in Old English, or students wanting an overview of English literature. Notable amongst the widely available 'textbook' translations are those by R. K. **Gordon**, S. A. J. **Bradley**, Michael **Alexander**, and Michael **Swanton**. Richard **Hamer**'s parallel text edition of a selection of Old English poems is especially good, as is E. Talbot **Donaldson**'s prose translation of *Beowulf*. Burton **Raffel** has produced free versions of *Beowulf* and other short poems, and has also published on the theory of translation, especially from Old English. Kevin **Crossley-Holland**'s work is a happy combination of faithful translating by an established poet. The very first word of *Beowulf*—'Hwæt!'—a (possibly onomatopoeic) call for attention, immediately presents difficulties for translators of the poem; as well as Thorpe's 'Ay', it has been rendered by 'Lo!' (dignified, but inappropriately religious) and 'What Ho!' (imitative, but undignified). Crossley-Holland achieves both solemnity and an uninflated register with his simple 'Listen!', continuing:

> The fame of Danish kings
> In days gone by, the daring feats
> worked by those heroes are well known to us.

Here we have the echo of Old English alliteration and the line's caesura, but with no loss of syntactic clarity, and no distracting archaisms.

Other poets who have been inspired to translate Old English verse include **Tennyson**, who produced a powerful imitative and archaizing translation of 'The Battle of Brunanburh', and **Longfellow**, who translated part of *Beowulf* and two short poems on mortality. Tennyson's short lines but very long sentences convey surprisingly well the chains of appositive half-lines so characteristic of Old English poetic style:

> Never had huger
> Slaughter of heroes
> Slain by the sword-edge—
> Such as old writers
> Have writ of in histories—
> Hapt in this isle, since
> Up from the East hither
> Saxon and Angle from
> Over the broad billow

> Broke into Britain with
> Haughty war-workers who
> Harried the Welshman, when
> Earls that were lured by the
> Hunger of glory gat
> Hold of the land.

Ezra **Pound**'s version of 'The Seafarer' is very celebrated, although its freedom initially excited controversy. In fact, a comparison of Pound's translation of the seafarer's hardships—

> Hung with hard ice-flakes, where hail-scur flew,
> There I heard naught save the harsh sea
> And the ice-cold wave, at whiles the swan cries,
> Did for my games the gannet's clamour,
> Sea-fowls' loudness was for me laughter . . .—

with Hamer's much less knotty and archaic

> . . . hung round by icicles
> While hail flew past in showers. There I heard nothing
> But the resounding sea, the ice-cold waves.
> Sometimes I made the song of the wild swan
> My pleasure, or the gannet's call, the cries
> Of curlews for the missing mirth of men

shows Pound to be the more imitative archaizer.

W. H. **Auden**'s 'The Wanderer' is certainly very free, but it transmits the elegiac mode of the original with remarkable force and precision. Its celebrated opening line: 'Doom is dark and deeper than any sea-dingle' forms a remarkable contrast to Bradley's literal prose: 'Often the man on his own experiences grace, the mercy of the ordaining Lord'.

Amongst contemporary poets, Edwin **Morgan**'s translations—especially his *Beowulf*—have been admired. Because the backgrounds of the speakers of the Old English elegies remain shadowy and unexplained in the originals, translations into contemporary idiom can seem to transpose a whole poem into the 20th c.—as is the case with Craig **Raine**'s 'Wulf and Eadwacer', or Bernard **O'Donoghue**'s version of the same poem, which begins: 'You'd think they were doing us a favour | with their custody'. Somewhat similarly, the physical hardships and social dislocation of the elegies have inspired some notable Scots translations, for example Alexander **Scott**'s 'Seaman's Sang', whose seafarer is 'hung about wi ice and the hard hail's onding', or Bruce **Gorrie**'s version of 'The Wanderer', whose vividly colloquial speaker is a Glaswegian down-and-out.

No doubt the challenge of Old English verse will continue to attract poets; the Nobel Laureate Seamus **Heaney** is working on a translation of *Beowulf*, of which only extracts have so far been published.

HO'D

ANTHOLOGIES   Alexander, Michael, *The Earliest English Poems*, London, 1966 [3rd edn., 1991; Penguin] · Bradley, S. A. J., *Anglo-Saxon Poetry*, London, 1982 · Crossley-Holland, Kevin, *The Anglo-Saxon World*, Oxford, 1982 · Gordon, R. K., *Anglo-Saxon Poetry Selected and Translated*, London, 1926 [rev. edn. 1954] · Hamer, Richard, *A Choice of Anglo-Saxon Verse*, London, 1970 · Parker, Matthew, and Joscelyn, John, *A Testament of Antiquitie*, London, 1556–7 · Raffel, Burton, *Poems from the Old English*, Lincoln, Neb., 1964 · Swanton, Michael, *Anglo-Saxon Prose*, London, 1975 [enlarged edn. 1993].

BEOWULF   Crossley-Holland, Kevin, *Beowulf*, London, 1968 [rev. edn. Oxford, 1998] · Donaldson, E. Talbot, *Beowulf*, New York, 1966 [rep. in M. H. Abrams, ed., *The Norton Anthology of English Literature*, 6th edn., New York, 1993] · Kemble, J. M., *A Translation of the Anglo-Saxon Poem of 'Beowulf'*, London, 1837 · Morgan, Edwin, *Beowulf*, Aldington, UK, 1952 · Morris, William, and Wyatt, A. J., *The Tale of Beowulf, Sometime King of the Weder-Geats*, London, 1895 · Raffel, Burton, *Beowulf*, New York, 1963 · Thorpe, Benjamin, *The Anglo-Saxon Poems of Beowulf, the Scop or Gleeman's Tale, and the Fight at Finnsburg*, Oxford, 1855.

OTHER TEXTS   Auden, W. H., 'The Wanderer', in his *Collected Shorter Poems*, London, 1966 · Crossley-Holland, Kevin, *The Exeter Book Riddles*, Harmondsworth, 1979; rev. edn. 1996 [Penguin] · Elstob, Elizabeth, *An Anglo-Saxon Homily on the Birth-Day of St Gregory*, London, 1709 · Gorrie, Bruce, 'The Glasgow Wanderer', *Agenda*, 34 (May 1997) · Longfellow, Henry W., 'Translations from the Anglo-Saxon', in his *Poetical Works*, London, 1877 · O'Donoghue, Bernard, 'Wulf and Eadwacer', in his *The Weakness*, London, 1991 · Pound, Ezra, 'The Seafarer', in his *Ripostes*, London, 1912 · Raine, Craig, 'Wulf and Eadwacer', in his *Rich*, London, 1983 · Scott, Alexander, 'Seaman's Sang', in *European Poetry in Scotland*, ed. P. France and D. Glen, Edinburgh, 1989 · Tennyson, Alfred, Lord, 'The Battle of Brunanburh', in his *Ballads and Other Poems*, London, 1880.

SEE ALSO   Greenfield, S. B., and Robinson, F. C., *A Bibliography of Publications on Old English Literature*, Toronto, 1980 · Raffel, B., 'Translating Old English Elegies', in M. Green, ed., *The Old English Elegies*, Rutherford, NJ, 1983 · Tinker, C. B., *The Translations of Beowulf: A Critical Bibliography*, rev. edn., Hamden, Conn., 1974.

2. OLD NORSE / ICELANDIC

Most Old Norse / Icelandic literature was written in medieval Iceland in the language at that time common to Iceland and Norway, Old Norse. For readers of English, the best-known texts from this extensive and wide-ranging literature are the family sagas (*Íslendingasögur*), semi-fictional naturalistic prose narratives with a deceptive resemblance to historical novels. They are set in the period following the settlement of Iceland in the 9th c., but were written down 300 or 400 years later. Other kinds of saga include historical works (*konungasögur*), lively accounts of the early rulers of Norway; legendary sagas (*fornaldarsögur*); and chivalric romances (*riddarasögur*).

The *Poetic Edda* is a 13th-c. anthology of mythological and heroic poems, some of considerable antiquity. These Eddaic poems (including a handful of similar works not in the main manuscript) are stanzaic in form, written in alliterative metres. Perhaps the least familiar branch of Old Norse / Icelandic literature is the poetry of Icelandic court poets, or skalds, even though most skaldic stanzas have survived embedded in saga narrative. But with their cryptic diction, extraordinarily intricate metres, and often oblique relation to the prose context, they have proved a stumbling-block to saga translators and readers alike, and have often been very loosely translated. Some skaldic verse—

especially mythological poems and praise poems dedicated to Norwegian rulers—dates from the 9th and 10th c. Other stanzas may have been composed later, perhaps even at the same time as their saga prose.

In the 13th c., the Icelander Snorri Sturluson wrote a handbook of Old Norse poetry, Eddaic and skaldic, known now as the *Prose Edda* or Snorri's *Edda*. This work cites a good deal of verse to illustrate its difficult diction and metres, and is especially valued for its prose narratives which explain poetic allusions to myth and legend.

In Britain, interest in Old Norse literature first flourished in the 17th c., following the Latin work of Scandinavian scholars such as Ole Worm (*Antiquitates Danicae, Literatura Runica* 1636), Olaus Magnus (whose *Historia de Gentibus Septentrionalibus* was translated into English in 1658), and Thomas Bartholin (*Antiquitatum Danicarum*, 1689). Peder Hansen Resen's editions of Snorri's *Edda* and the mythological poems *Völuspá* and *Hávamál*, and Olaus Verelius's *fornaldarsaga* editions also appeared during this period.

The first piece of Old Norse writing translated into a modern language was the *Hervararkviða*, entitled *The Waking of Angantýr* in the remarkable *Thesaurus Linguarum Septentrionalium* (1705) of George **Hickes** (1642–1715), which also included an

Old Icelandic grammar and a list of Old Norse books and manuscripts. Hickes's *Angantýr* was reprinted in Dryden's *Miscellany* in 1716. In 1763, Bishop **Percy** (1729–1811) produced his pioneering *Five Pieces of Runic Poetry*. The five poems in question had previously appeared in Latin or Swedish translations, but a colleague, Edward Lye, helped Percy with the Icelandic, and 'islandic originals' are appended. The 18th-c. passion for Old Norse literature was fuelled by such works, but versions of the poetry, including, for instance, Thomas Gray's celebrated 'The Fatal Sisters' and 'The Descent of Odin', were still loosely based on second- or even third-hand knowledge of the originals through the Latin or Scandinavian of earlier scholars. In 1770, Percy translated Mallet's influential *Introduction à l'Histoire de Dannemarc*; later editions contained much Icelandic material, including an abstract of *Eyrbyggja saga* by Sir Walter Scott.

In 1804, the first scholarly and accurate translations of Old Norse poetry directly into English appeared: *Select Icelandic Poetry*, by William **Herbert** (1778–1847). Herbert is scathing about previous translators: introducing his own 'Vegtam's Song' (*Baldrs draumar*, Gray's 'Descent of Odin') he remarks that if Amos **Cottle** had published his 'translation' of the poem (in *The Elder Edda*, 1797) as his own work, 'he could scarcely have been accused of plagiarism'. Even Percy did not escape criticism. Herbert justifiably complains that translation made 'by a person unacquainted with the Icelandic language, through the medium of a Latin prose version, cannot be expected to represent the style and spirit of the originals'. In addition, the contemporary reading public's 'predilection for wild or romantic incident', as J. A. W. Bennett puts it, determined the rather unrepresentative and very limited selection of poems offered: what captured the imagination in the 18th c. was the weird and the warlike. Herbert himself began by translating the usual martial fragments, but moved on to include a remarkably various selection of Eddaic poems. There was as yet in England no experience of the 'cool, clear prose' of the Icelandic sagas.

The translation of saga prose began in Scotland, with James **Johnstone** (d. 1798). Helped by the Icelandic scholar Grímur **Thorkelín** (1752–1829), between 1780 and 1786 he published a series of close translations, mostly extracts from *Heimskringla*. These pieces all relate to British, and especially Scottish, history. Thorkelín himself translated part of *Laxdoela saga* into English, presenting it as history.

The first complete saga to be published in an English translation was *Fridthiofs saga* by George **Stephens** (1813–95). *Friðþjófs saga*, a romantic *fornaldarsaga*, was universally acclaimed by readers of its many English translations throughout the 19th c., but tastes have changed, and as Andrew Wawn puts it, 'current scholarly silence on the saga is well-nigh deafening'. Stephens believed that Britain's cultural and linguistic roots were Anglo-Scandinavian rather than Germanic; his literal translation, with its lexical and syntactic archaism, reinforces his vision of a 'mighty and noble and thoroly Scandinavian NORTH ENGLISH . . . the birth-tung of England'.

George Webbe **Dasent** (1817–96) was the first of the great Victorian saga translators who made available to English readers those sagas which are today recognized as the masterpieces of Old Norse / Icelandic prose, and he may be said to have formed the modern taste for saga literature. His first translation, of Snorri's *Edda*, was attacked for archaism and inaccuracy; celebrated as classics are his translations of *Njáls saga* and *Gísla saga*. Unlike Stephens, he aimed at a contemporary style, but only 'as literal as the idiom of the two languages would permit'. Dasent's sense of the dignity and grandeur of the Norse further lends his prose an archaic ring which is intensified by the distance between his work and our day.

Other major and influential Victorian saga translations include Samuel **Laing**'s *The Heimskringla*, Sir Edmund **Head**'s *Viga Glum's saga*, Muriel **Press**'s *Laxdaela Saga* and John **Sephton**'s *The Saga of Olaf Tryggwason*; following a little later in the same tradition, G. A. **Hight** translated *Grettis saga*.

In 1868, William **Morris** met the Icelander Eiríkur **Magnússon** (1833–1913), and together they embarked on a large number of saga translations, most famously the Saga Library series, 15 projected volumes of Icelandic sagas, of which only six were completed. Morris's translations have always divided saga enthusiasts. He attempted to retain the word order of the original, to echo its syntax, and to use archaisms—wherever possible Icelandic/English cognates, like Stephens. He deplored what he termed the 'Frenchification' of English. Naturally, readability suffers—but not the accuracy which was one of Morris's prime concerns and indeed, achievements. Poetic works such as *The Lovers of Gudrun* (1870) and *Sigurd the Volsung* (1876) illustrate the extent of Old Icelandic influence on Morris's own work.

The Icelandic scholar Guðbrandur **Vigfússon** and his collaborator Frederick **York Powell** mocked Morris's 'affectation of archaism'. Together they produced two monumental collections of edited texts with parallel translations, the *Corpus*

Poeticum Boreale and *Origines Islandicae* (revised by York Powell after Vigfússon's death). These two collections of Icelandic verse and prose teem with ideas and insights, but also with inaccuracies and eccentric editing; they were fiercely criticized when they appeared, and mark the end of the major translation projects, although they stimulated a surge of late Victorian translations. Work done in the 19th c. continued to provide the popular translations of sagas for decades to come.

Largely due to the work of Icelandic scholars, a shift in the perception of saga literature occurred: sagas came to be seen as fictional constructs, the products of individual authors. Modern saga translations have reflected this, emphasizing the novelistic naturalism of saga prose with their easy and colloquial modern English. Notable are the translations of *Njáls saga, Laxdaela saga, the Vinland Sagas* (concerning the Norse discovery of America), and *King Harald's Saga* by Magnus **Magnusson** and Hermann **Pálsson**. Pálsson also translated *Hrafnkels saga* and a number of other sagas in collaboration with both Paul **Edwards** and Denton **Fox**. Margaret **Arent** produced a distinguished version of *Laxdoela saga*, and *Sturlunga saga*, set, unlike the family sagas, in 12th- and 13th-c. Iceland, has been translated by Julia **McGrew** and R. George **Thomas**.

Few challenged the new colloquial orthodoxy, but there is now a growing feeling that such translations do not properly convey the alterity of sagas. As George **Johnston** puts it, 'the events and sentiments of the saga world are not . . . ours, and they sound out of place in our idiom'. Johnston's version of *Gísla saga* is faithful to saga style, but with no 'whiff of quaintness'; he aims for the 'narrow way between archaism and anachronism'.

The Complete Sagas of Icelanders, published in Iceland in 1997 with the express purpose of making the full range of family sagas (the title means all family sagas, not all Icelandic sagas) more widely available to English-speaking readers, contains translations of all 40 family sagas, plus 49 shorter tales, or *þættir*. The translations have been done by a number of scholars (whose drafts have been edited by native Icelandic speakers), but all follow the same editorial criteria: they have been required

to aim precisely for Johnston's 'narrow way', avoiding archaism but still reflecting characteristic features of saga style such as parataxis, limited use of adjectives, understatement and economical phrasing. It is now possible to read all the family sagas in uniform style and register (perhaps even more uniform than the originals). Translators have also avoided 'improving' their originals. The compromise between readability and faithfulness to original features of style is easier to bring off with saga prose than with the skaldic verses quoted in it (and the editors aim in addition to 'achieve some poetic validity in English' for the verses) but there is no doubt that this ambitious project has both set a standard and established a norm for saga translation for some time to come.

The translations of *Egils saga* (by Christine **Fell**, the poetry translated by John **Lucas**) and *Víga-Glúms saga* (by John **McKinnell**) offer especially good versions of the skaldic stanzas in the prose. Although Old Norse translation history began with poetry, saga translators have dominated this century. A major exception is L. M. **Hollander**, whose translation of *The Poetic Edda* and a collection of skaldic verse (amongst a number of saga translations) reproduces the elaborate metres and poetic diction of Old Norse poetry; literalness and readability are (probably inevitably) sacrificed. Perhaps the only really successful way of presenting skaldic verse is to offer parallel translation in a scholarly edition, as E. O. G. **Turville-Petre** has done.

Only W. H. **Auden** has approached *The Poetic Edda* as a poet; his versions have their own literary worth, but are very free. Ursula **Dronke**'s scholarly edition of *The Poetic Edda* has a remarkably successful parallel translation. Carolyne **Larrington**'s translation is both faithful and readable. The standard modern translation of Snorri's *Edda* is by Anthony **Faulkes**.

Apart from the ground-breaking work of Margaret **Schlauch**, and in spite of their prominence in the early history of Norse scholarship, the *fornaldarsögur* and *riddarasögur* were neglected until relatively recently. They have generally been the last of the sagas to be translated in the idiomatic tradition, and constitute the majority of those sagas which still await translation. HO'D

EARLY COLLECTIONS Herbert, William, *Select Icelandic Poetry Translated from the Originals, with Notes*, 2 vols., London, 1804–6 · Hickes, George, *Thesaurus Linguarum Septentrionalium*, Oxford, 1705 · Johnstone, James, *Anecdotes of Olaf the Black*, Copenhagen, 1780 · *Krákumál (Lodbrokar-quida)*, Copenhagen, 1782 · *The Norwegian Account of Haco's Expedition against Scotland*, Edinburgh, 1782 · *Antiquitates Celto-Scandicae*, Copenhagen, 1786 · Percy, Bishop Thomas, *Five Pieces of Runic Poetry Translated from the Islandic Language*, London, 1763 · Thorkelin, Grímur, *Fragments of English and Irish History of the Ninth and Tenth Century*, London, 1788.

SAGAS Arent, Margaret, *The Laxdoela Saga*, Seattle, 1964 · Dasent, George Webbe, *The Story of Burnt Njal*, Edinburgh,

1861 · *The Story of Gisli the Outlaw*, Edinburgh, 1866 · *Icelandic Sagas and Other Documents* (Rolls Series 88), London, 1887–94 · Fell, Christine, and Lucas, John, *Egil's Saga*, London/Toronto, 1975; rep. 1993 · Fox, Denton, and Pálsson, Hermann, *Grettir's Saga*, Toronto, 1974 · Head, Sir Edmund, *Viga Glum's Saga*, Edinburgh/London, 1866 · Hight, G. A., *The Saga of Grettir the Strong*, London, 1914 [rev. 1965, rep. 1972] · Hreinsson, Viðar, ed., *The Complete Sagas of Icelanders including 49 Tales*, 5 vols., Reykjavik, 1997 [over 30 translators] · Johnston, George, *The Saga of Gisli*, London/Toronto, 1973 · Laing, Samuel, *The Heimskringla*, London, 1844 [rev. edn. 1984] · McGrew, Julia, and Thomas, R. George, *Sturlunga Saga*, 2 vols., New York, 1970–4 · McKinnell, John, *Viga-Glums Saga*, Edinburgh, 1987 · Magnússon, Eirkur, and Morris, William, *The Story of Grettir the Strong*, London, 1869; rep. 1980 · *The Story of the Volsungs and the Niblungs, with Certain Songs from the Elder Edda*, London, 1870; rep. New York, 1962 · *Three Northern Love Stories and Tales*, London, 1875 · *The Story of Howard the Halt; The Banded Men; Hen-Thorir*, London, 1891 · *The Eredwellers; The Heath Slayings*, London, 1892 · *Heimskringla*, London, 1893–5 · Magnússon, Magnus, and Pálsson, Hermann, *Njal's Saga*, Harmondsworth, 1960 [Penguin] · *The Vinland Sagas*, Harmondsworth, 1965 [Penguin] · *Laxdoela Saga*, Harmondsworth, 1969 [Penguin] · Pálsson, Hermann, *Hrafnkel's Saga and Other Icelandic Stories*, Harmondsworth, 1971 [Penguin] · Pálsson, Hermann, and Edwards, Paul, *Eyrbyggja Saga*, Toronto, 1973 · *Göngu-Hrolf's Saga: A Viking Romance*, Edinburgh, 1980 · *Seven Viking Romances*, Harmondsworth, 1985 [Penguin] · Press, Muriel, *Laxdaela Saga*, London, 1899 · Schlauch, Margaret, *Medieval Narratives*, New York, 1928; rep. 1970 · *The Saga of the Volsungs*, New York, 1930; rep. 1976 · Sephton, John, *The Saga of Olaf Tryggwason*, London, 1895 · Stephens, George, *Fridthiofs Saga*, Stockholm/London, 1842.

EDDAIC AND SKALDIC VERSE, AND SNORRI'S EDDA   Auden, W. H., with Paul B. Taylor, *The Elder Edda: A Selection*, London, 1969; rep. 1973 · *Norse Poems*, London, 1981; rep. 1983 · Dasent, George Webbe, *The Prose or Younger Edda*, Stockholm, 1842 · Dronke, Ursula, *The Poetic Edda*, i: *Heroic Poems*, Oxford, 1969; ii: *The Mythological Poems*, Oxford, 1997 · Faulkes, Anthony, Snorri Sturluson: Edda, London, 1987; rep. 1992 · Hollander, Lee M., *The Poetic Edda*, Austin, Tex., 1928 · *The Skalds*, Princeton, NJ, 1945 · Larrington, Carolyne, *The Poetic Edda*, Oxford, 1996 [World's Classics] · Turville-Petre, E. O. G., *Scaldic Poetry*, Oxford, 1976.

SEE ALSO   Bennett, J. A. W., 'The History of Old English and Old Norse Studies in England from the Time of Junius till the End of the Eighteenth Century', D.Phil. thesis, Oxford, 1937 · Fry, D. K., *Norse Sagas Translated into English*, New York, 1980, supplemented by Paul Acker, *Scandinavian Studies*, 65 (1993) · Wawn, A., *Northern Antiquity: The Post-Medieval Reception of Edda and Saga*, Enfield Lock, UK, 1994.

3. THE *KALEVALA*

The epic narrative folk poetry from Karelia and eastern Finland which Elias Lönnrot (1802–84) compiled into what is commonly referred to as 'the national epic of Finland' was published under the title *Kalevala* in two versions, first with 32 poems and some 12,000 lines in 1835, later, in 1849, expanded to 50 poems and 22,795 lines. The original title of the Old Kalevala (1835) was *Kalewala taikka Karjalan Runoja Suomen kansan muinaisista ajoista* (Kalevala or Karelian Poems about the Ancient Times of the Finnish People'), while the 1849 version, which quickly became the standard Kalevala, was simply titled *Kalevala*.

The *Kalevala* is an epic about the rivalry between two districts, Kalevala, with heroes such as the old Väinämöinen, the eternal smith Ilmarinen, and the wanton, reckless Lemminkäinen, and Pohjola, the northern district, with its powerful Mistress Louhi and her beautiful daughter. Rich in old myths, the epic structure revolves around a prosperity machine called the Sampo, which is magically forged, later stolen, and finally the object of an all-out struggle at sea. An epic of a largely shamanistic world view, the *Kalevala* is exceedingly rich in

magic charms. Courtship adventures and other ritualized human behaviour abound. To Finns the *Kalevala* soon became an almost sacred text.

The *Kalevala* became an international success even before its unique qualities were fully understood by Finland's intellectuals of the time. This fact is to be understood in the context of the preponderance in Europe at the time of national romantic sentiment inspired by J. G. von Herder, which, during the early decades of the 19th c., had created a receptive atmosphere for the publication of folkloric collections. In Finland, the *Kalevala* soon became the catalyst for the construction of Finnish nationalism and a Finnish identity in the Finnish language, an agenda adopted in response to Finland's specific historical-political situation—the abrupt severance in 1809 of a 650-year alliance with Sweden and subsequent annexation of Finland by its arch-enemy, Russia. The *Kalevala* brought about two major consequences: contrary to claims often presented at the time, it proved the Finnish language capable of poetic and aesthetic grandeur; and it gave direction for standard literary Finnish by incorporating previously excluded eastern Finnish dialects.

The story of the genesis of Longfellow's *The Song of Hiawatha* (1856) indicates significant influence of the *Kalevala* upon English literature. During Longfellow's stay in Stockholm in 1852, he so much wanted to read the *Kalevala* in Finnish that he tried to learn the Finnish language, actually with Elias Lönnrot's brother-in-law as his teacher. When Anton Schiefner's German translation appeared in 1852, Longfellow tried to read the Finnish and German versions side by side but gave up, reading the *Kalevala* only in German. This prompted him to write *Hiawatha*, which he invented on the Kalevala model, not just the trochaic tetrametre but the idea of writing an American national epic. Although not a case of direct translation, *The Song of Hiawatha* illustrates the most powerful impact any Finnish work ever had on American literature.

The first full-length English-language translation of the *Kalevala* was undertaken by John Martin **Crawford** and published in 1888. The book *Selections from the Kalevala*, published in 1868 in the United States and translated by J. A. **Porter**, contained only segments of two poems. Crawford's *The Kalevala [into English]*, as it was called, was based on Anton Schiefner's German translation of 1852, which both J. A. Porter in *Selections* and Crawford's teacher, T. C. **Porter**, used in their attempts to translate the *Kalevala*.

Unable to read Finnish, Crawford did not, however, develop a sensitivity to the full aesthetic qualities of the Finnish original, and as a result produced a rather monotonous rendition in trochaic tetrametre, the so-called Kalevala metre. Even so, his rendition was enthusiastically received and reprinted several times. Soon after the publication of William Forsell **Kirby**'s translation in 1907, however, Crawford's version fell into oblivion. Based on the original Finnish, which Kirby had taken great pains to learn, *Kalevala: The Land of Heroes* instantly became a classic, with numerous reprintings. Kirby used the unique four-footed 'Kalevala metre', which by this time was familiar in English from *Hiawatha*. The Finnish metre is well suited to the characteristics of the Finnish language, particularly its syllabic structure and consistent stress on the first syllable, but becomes exceedingly bouncy in English, whose syllabic structure is quite different.

For 50 years, the definitive English *Kalevala* was Kirby's translation. In the early 1960s, however, employing the scholarly perspective of a medievalist, the Harvard professor Francis Peabody **Magoun** published a new translation in which he attempted to capture the rich, rustic peasant culture of the original by creating a prose translation, *The Kalevala: Poems of the Kalevala District*. Well

researched and annotated, it succeeded in its ambition of enabling scholars working in English to come closer to the original meanings than those translations which also needed to meet the requirements of the metre. In the interest of *Kalevala* research, Magoun also translated *Old Kalevala* of 1835, published in 1969.

The internationally celebrated 150th Anniversary of the *Kalevala* in 1985 provided impetus for publishers to sponsor two new translations. In the 1970s, the British translator Keith **Bosley** had used transcriptions in the Finnish Literature Society archives in Helsinki to translate authentic Finnish epic poems for the ambitious *Finnish Folk Poetry: Epic*. Now he translated the (standard) *Kalevala* for Oxford University Press World Classics, using metre reminiscent of the medieval Welsh *cywydd*. He has also translated about 100 of the 650 poems of *Kalevala*'s lyrical companion piece, the *Kanteletar*, '(female) Spirit of the *kantele*' (the Finish national instrument). Bosley's translations have been well received, particularly in Europe where British English is the norm.

In 1989, the year after Bosley's, yet another translation of the *Kalevala* was published, this one by Finnish-born Eino **Friberg**, who came to the USA at the age of 3 and fell blind following an accident at the age of 7. Friberg's special strength was his ability to render in English the acoustic properties of the *Kalevala*; his translation reads and sounds right, especially when recited or sung, though it follows the Kalevala metre only selectively.

At present then, four very different translations of the *Kalevala* are available in English; the following extract will give an idea of the different styles:

> Now the isles were formed already,
> In the sea the rocks were planted;
> Pillars of the sky established,
> Land and continents created (Kirby)

> Now the islands were arranged,
> little islands created in the sea;
> the pillars of the sky erected,
> lands and continents sung into being (Magoun)

> Now the islands were in order
> And the small isles of the sea;
> Pillars for the sky were planted,
> Lands and continents created (Fribert)

> Now the islands were arranged
> and the crags formed in the sea
> the sky's pillars set upright
> the lands and mainlands called up (Bosley)

Translated into some 45 languages, the *Kalevala* appears, for the time being, to be well served with English renditions. BV

557

TRANSLATIONS   Bosley, Keith, *The Kalevala: An Epic Poem after Oral Tradition by Elias Lönnrot*, Oxford, 1988 [World's Classics] · Crawford, J. M., *The Kalevala into English*, New York, 1888 · Friberg, Eino, *The Kalevala, Epic of the Finnish People*, Helsinki, 1989 · Kirby, W. F., *Kalevala: The Land of the Heroes*, London, 1907 · Magoun, F. P., *The Kalevala, or Poems of the Kalevala District*, Cambridge, Mass./London, 1963.

SEE ALSO   Branch, M., Kuusi, M., and Bosley, K., *Finnish Folk Poetry: Epic*, Helsinki, 1977 · Lönnrot, E., *The Kanteletar*, tr. Keith Bosley, Oxford, 1988 · Puranen, Rauni, *The Kalevala Abroad: Translations and Foreign Language Adaptations of the Kalevala*, Helsinki, 1985.

4. DANISH

The different anthologies listed in the bibliography testify to the very considerable amount of Danish literature which has been translated into English; a visit to a good bookshop or local library testifies to the very limited amount which is widely available. The criterion guiding selection for mention here has been availability; this entry is confined to a small number of important prose writers.

i. Steen Steensen Blicher The Danish tradition of 'novelle' composition was founded by Thomasine Gyllembourg and Steen Steensen Blicher. Blicher's *Brudstykker af en Landsbydegns Dagbog* (1824, Fragments of a Parish Clerk's Diary) also marks the breakthrough of realism in Danish prose. It charts the life of Morten Vinge as he observes the fall of the woman he loves, introducing Blicher's basic theme of tragic change. A translation by Hanna Astrup **Larsen** of this and 11 further stories was published in English in 1945. A second translation, by Paula **Hostrup-Jessen**, followed in 1968, and a third version, included in *The Diary of a Parish Clerk and Other Stories*, also translated by Paula Hostrup-Jessen, came out in 1996. A certain degree of modernization has taken place in the later of the two Hostrup-Jessen translations. Generally, all three translations reflect the source well, though Hostrup-Jessen makes some minor omissions.

Another recurrent theme in Blicher's writing is madness. *Hosekræmmeren* (1829, The Hosier) combines this theme, and the theme of tragic change, with a third: the fateful contribution of coincidence to personal tragedies: the father of the beautiful Cecilia tries to force her to marry a rich farmer instead of Esben, the poor neighbour's son whom she loves. Esben goes to Holstein and Cecilia goes mad. Believing herself to be dead, she kills Esben when he returns, enriched, from Holstein, so that he can marry her in heaven. Cecilia regains her sanity, but loses it again when, upon her repeated rejection of a rich suitor, he tells her what she has done. The story frame is two visits paid by the narrator, six years apart, to Cecilia's home, and the text challenges the translator in contrasting the narrator's erudite style with the representation of rural dialect in character speech. Astrup Larsen reproduces as far as possible local idioms and conveys the rural flavour well. For example, her 'may happen you won't come back at all' (p. 225) is arguably more successful in this respect than Hostrup-Jessen's 'you may never come back at all' (p. 86).

ii. Hans Christian Andersen Andersen's output includes plays, poetry, travel writing, diaries, autobiography, and novels, in addition to the well-known fairy tales and stories. It was the novels which initially established his fame both at home and abroad, but none has been retranslated into English since their first appearance in translations by Mary **Howitt** (from German), Charles Beckwith **Lohmeyer**, and Anne S. **Bushby** in the 1840s and 1850s.

The autobiographical *Mit eget Eventyr uden Digtning (en Skizze)* (1846, My Life's Fairy Tale Without Invention) was not published in Danish until 1942. It appeared initially in a German translation by Julius Reuscher as the introduction to an 1847 German collection of Andersen's works. Howitt used this German version as the basis for her own translation, *The True Story of My Life* (1847). It covers Andersen's childhood and youth, and was followed by an updated version, *Mit Livs Eventyr*, which was published as the last two volumes of Andersen's collected works in Danish in 1855. Andersen updated the life-story for the publication of his collected works in the United States in 1871 where it appeared in a translation by Horace **Scudder**, *The Story of My Life*. This adds new material on the later life, and revises the earlier version. Other translations include those by W. Glyn **Jones** and Maurice **Michael**. Jones does not include the extension of the memoirs up to 1867, but the account of the first 50 years of Andersen's life is complete. Michael uses the subtitle 'A New and Abridged Translation' and leaves out a great deal of interesting material.

Three of Andersen's travelogues exist in 20th-c. translations. First published in English in a complete translation by Lohmeyer (1846), *En Digter's*

Bazar (1842) was translated by Grace **Thornton** as *A Poet's Bazaar*. Thornton's translation begins at Chapter 4 and omits large sections throughout. *I Spanien* (1863) appeared in Bushby's translation in 1864, and as *A Visit to Spain and North Africa* (1975) in a reduced version, without any of the poetry included, translated by Thornton. Finally, *Et Besøg i Portugal* (1868) exists in English only as Thornton's *A Visit to Portugal 1866*; this translation is unabridged and extremely well annotated.

In the 20th c., Andersen's fame in English rests on his stories, collections of which have appeared regularly since 1846 and which remain immensely popular. Bredsdorff (1948) lists and discusses translations produced up to that date. The only early translations still relatively freely available are the collections of Henry William **Dulcken**, which have been reprinted regularly and which appear in *The Complete Illustrated Works of Hans Christian Andersen*. The most scholarly complete edition is Jean **Hersholt**'s, also available on CD-ROM. The most widely available is Erik Christian **Haugaard**'s. For further discussion see the entry on children's literature [I.c.4.iii].

iii. Søren Aabye Kierkegaard Kierkegaard made an essential contribution to existentialist philosophy, through which he expressed opposition to the philosophy of Hegel. The stress here is on works in which he presents his philosophy in a more literary mode.

In *Enten-Eller* (1843, Either-Or), Kierkegaard discusses the two basic forms of existence: the aesthetic and the ethical; the contrast between the two is visible also in the style of the work's two parts. *Either-Or* is available in its entirety in two translations: David and Lillian **Swenson** (vol. i) and Walter **Lowrie** (vol. ii) (1944; revised by Howard A. Johnson in 1959); and Howard and Edna **Hong**. An abridged version by Alastair **Hannay** is also available, and the final section of Part I has been separately translated by Gerd **Gillhoff** as *Diary of a Seducer*.

Frygt og Bæven, Dialektisk Lyrik af Johannes de Silentio (1843, Fear and Trembling, Dialectical Lyric by Johannes de Silentio) addresses questions raised by the Biblical account of Abraham who sets off to sacrifice his only son, believing he must sacrifice him, but believing also, absurdly, that he will regain him, not in an afterlife, but in this life. There are four translations, by **Payne**, Lowrie, Hong and Hong, and Hannay. The last of these contains a particularly helpful exposition of the philosophical content of the book, and provides philosophical justifications for some of his choices of translation equivalents.

Lowrie and Hong and Hong have also translated two further works. The question of loss and regaining the lost through faith is again prominent in *Gjentagelsen* (1843, The Repetition), in which Kierkegaard's talent for hilarity is more evident than in any of his other works. *Stadier paa Livets Vej: Studier af Forskjellige, befordrede til Trykken og udgivne af Hilarius Bogbinder* (1845, Stages on Life's Way: Studies by Various People, Brought Together, Conveyed to the Press and Published by Hilarious Bookbinder) adds to the aesthetic and ethical modes of existence discussed in *Either-Or* the religious mode of life discussed in *Fear and Trembling*.

It is difficult to translate an author like Kierkegaard, who in these works couches his discussion of complex philosophical issues in the most literary, whimsical, and witty narratives. Of the two most widely available translations, Hannay and Hong, Hannay would probably strike readers with no access to the Danish source as the most natural English text. Unsurprisingly, this impression is achieved at the price of loss of conformity to the precise detail of the original. However, both translations are very good, Hannay never straying damagingly far from the source in the quest for naturalness and Hong never straying damagingly far from naturalness in the quest for accuracy.

iv. Modern fiction Only six writers will be considered here. The first, Herman Bang, wrote three novels which have been translated into English. Of these *Tine* (1889) was described by Walter Allen in his preface to the translation as 'the first truly modern war novel', and by Claude Monet as the only impressionist novel he knew. It tells the story of the effect of the Danish defeat in Schleswig in 1864 on the people of a small town on the island of Als, and, in parallel, the story of Tine's love for a man of a higher social class than her own. The translation by Paul **Christopherson** is without significant omissions, but does not fully convey the nuances of speech style in the original.

The mid-20th-c. author Tove Ditlevsen wrote poetry and prose, and distinguished herself from most Danish writers of her generation in preferring direct, though sensitive, lyrical description and narration to more abstract reflection on ideas. Her themes are childhood, dread (*angst*) and alienation, her setting the modern city, and her characters the urban poor and (lower) middle classes. Two prose works exist in English translation: a collection of short stories translated by Jack **Brøndum**, and the autobiographical novels, *Barndom: Erindringer* (Childhood: Memories) and *Ungdom: Erindringer* (Youth: Memories), both published in 1967 and reissued in one volume under the title *Det tidlige forar* (Early Spring) in 1976, translated, with helpful notes on characters, events and places, by Tiina **Nunnally**, under the title *Early Spring*.

Early Spring documents Ditlevsen's childhood and youth, culminating in the publication of her first collection of poetry. The translation is accurate and is a fine representation of Ditlevsen's prose. However, the development of her poetic talent forms a strand of the narrative, and the text contains several poems. This is challenging for a translator, because poems from different times represent different stages of the writer's development as a poet. Nunnally generally presents Ditlevsen as a worse poet than she was at any stage, and her rendering of the first poem Ditlevsen published is near unforgivable. In altering the meaning of the final line, and the relationship between the first two and the second two lines from one of contrast to one of complementarity, Nunnally prevents the reader from grasping why this poem was considered publishable by the editor of the small magazine which accepted it: namely the impression it gives of the intimacy which the mother of the stillborn child had felt with the child while it lived inside her and which she will always remember. Translated literally, the stanza would read: 'Never did I hear your infant voice. | Never did your pale lips smile at me. | But the tiny, tiny feet's kicking | I will never forget' (*Youth*, Ch. 16). The published translation, however, is: 'I never heard your little voice. | Your pale lips never smiled at me. | And the kick of your tiny feet | is something I will never see.'

The contemporary writer Henrik Stangerup writes in a variety of literary and critical genres, and is also a film-maker. Most of his prose works are characterized by a highly visual style, strongly suggestive of film, with flashbacks and with the main part of the narration in the present tense. His first novel, *Slangen i brystet* (1969, The Snake in the Breast), was published in Anne **Born**'s translation in 1996. Part I is prefaced with a quotation from a student essay by Karl Marx which, strangely, is provided on the dust-jacket in a different translation from that given in the text. Born's translation captures well the variety of voices which people the book, but there are some inexplicable slips, and there is a whole paragraph of text missing on p. 210 of the translation. Born has also translated *Broder Jacob* (1991, Brother Jacob), a novel about the effect of the Reformation in Europe.

Manden der ville være skyldig (1973, The Man Who Wanted to Be Guilty) adds a futuristic, dystopic dimension to the theme of mental breakdown

which figures in the first novel, and has been very well translated by David **Gress-Wright**. There is also an excellent translation by Barbara **Bluestone** of *Vejen til Lagoa Santa* (1981, The Road to Lagoa Santa), a fictional version of the life of the Danish naturalist P. W. Lund (1801–80); the poems here are translated by John **Muckle**.

Stangerup's *Det er svært at do i Dieppe* (1985), translated by Sean **Martin** as *The Seducer: It Is Hard to Die in Dieppe*, focuses on the life of Peder Ludvig Møller (1814–65), a fellow theology student of Kierkegaard's, literary critic, poet, and notorious womanizer, widely believed to be the model for Kierkegaard's seducer from *Either-Or*. Stangerup's novel is 'a "fantasy" of Kierkegaard's sadistic seducer seen from beneath the skin, when the wolves are howling at three o'clock in the morning' (Introduction to the English edition), and the narrative is a brilliant blend of highly visual, third-person, present-tense narrative and documentation of a life. The translation is excellent, and includes notes by Stangerup on historical characters and places.

Sales of English translations of Peter Høeg's novels have exceeded those of any other Danish writer, including Andersen. His writing has been compared to the magical realist work of Allende and García Márquez, to Karen Blixen's storytelling and to the ironical social criticism of the novelist Hans Scherfig (1905–79). His novel *Frøken Smillas fornemmelse for sne* (1990, Miss Smilla's Feeling for Snow) has been made into a major film.

Apart from *Smilla*, all of his novels (listed in the bibliography) have been translated by Barbara **Haveland**. *Smilla*, which initially made Høeg's name in English, was published in the United States in a translation by Tiina Nunnally, in 1993. Høeg wanted alterations made in the translation before publication in Britain, but Nunnally refused to let the altered translation go out under her name and the name 'F. David' was invented for the version published in Britain. The translations published in Britain are excellent, and include useful extra material to make them more approachable for the English reader. For example, the English edition of *Smilla* includes a map of Copenhagen, and *The History of Danish Dreams* (a translation of *Forestilling om det tyvende arhundrede*, 1988), includes a list of historical characters.

Finally, we should mention two young writers, Michael Larsen and Solvej Balle. Like Anders Bodelsen, who enjoyed great popularity in English translation in the 1970s, Larsen uses a popular genre, in the case of his second novel, *Uden Sikker Viden* (1994, translated as *Uncertainty*) a futuristic crime and love story, to criticize contemporary values and society; he focuses on industrial theft and the exploitation of computer graphics. The translation is excellent.

Solvej Balle's *If følge Loven: Fire beretninger om mennesket* (1993) was published in English in 1996, translated by Barbara Haveland as *According to the Law: Four Accounts of Mankind.* The original and the translation differ in structure in that the four stories which in the original are presented as paragraphs are presented in the translation as four separate stories, listed on a contents page and each given as a title the name of its main character. This may obscure the connection between the first and the final story (the suicide whose brain is the subject of investigation in the first story is the main character in the last). This is an interesting work in an excellent translation.   KM

ANTHOLOGIES   Allwood, Martin S., ed., *Twentieth-Century Scandinavian Poetry*, Reykjavik, 1950 · *Modern Scandinavian Poetry*, Mullsjö, Sweden, 1982 · Fries, Erik, ed., *Modern Nordic Plays: Denmark*, New York, 1974 · Heitmann, Annegret, ed., *No Man's Land: An Anthology of Modern Danish Women's Literature*, Norwich, 1987 · Ingwersen, Niels, ed., *Seventeen Danish Poets*, Lincoln, Neb., 1981.

ANDERSEN, HANS CHRISTIAN   Bushby, Anne S., *To Be, or Not to Be*, London, 1857 · *In Spain*, London, 1864 · Dulcken, Henry William, *Stories and Tales*, London, 1864 · *What the Moon Saw, and Other Tales*, London, 1865 · *Hans Christian Andersen's Stories for the Household*, London, 1866 [reissued as *The Complete Illustrated Works of Hans Christian Andersen*, London, 1983; 2nd edn. 1994] · Haugaard, Erik Christian, *The Complete Fairy Tales and Stories*, London/New York, 1974; rep. 1994 · Hersholt, Jean, *The Complete Andersen: All of the 168 Stories by Hans Christian Andersen*, New York, 1942–7 [available on CD-ROM] · Howitt, Mary, *The Improvisatore, or, Life in Italy*, London, 1845 · *Only a Fiddler; and O.T., or Life in Denmark*, London, 1845 · *The True Story of My Life*, London, 1847 · Jones, W. Glyn, *The Fairy-Tale of My Life*, Copenhagen, 1954 · Lohmeyer, Charles Beckwith, *A Poet's Bazaar*, London, 1846 · [Lohmeyer, Charles Beckwith,] *The Two Baronesses*, London, 1848 · Michael, Maurice, *The Mermaid Man: The Autobiography of Hans Christian Andersen*, London, 1955 · Scudder, Horace, *The Story of My Life*, Boston/New York, 1971 · Thornton, Grace, *A Visit to Portugal 1866*, London, 1972 · *A Visit to Spain and North Africa*, London, 1975 · *A Poet's Bazaar*, New York, 1988.

BALLE, SOLVEJ   Haveland, Barbara, *According to the Law: Four Accounts of Mankind*, London/Dover, NH, 1996.

BANG, HERMAN   Christophersen, Paul, *Tina*, London/Dover, NH, 1984.

BLICHER, STEEN STEENSEN   Astrup Larsen, Hanna, *Twelve Stories*, Princeton, NJ, 1945 · Hostrup-Jessen, Paula, *The Diary of a Parish Clerk*, Copenhagen, 1968 · *The Diary of a Parish Clerk and Other Stories*, London, 1996.

DITLEVSEN, TOVE   Nunnally, Tiina, *Early Spring*, Washington, DC/London, 1985.

HØEG, PETER   David, F., *Miss Smilla's Feeling for Snow*, London, 1996 · Haveland, Barbara, *Borderliners*, London, 1994 · *The History of Danish Dreams*, London, 1995 · *The Woman and the Ape*, London, 1996 · Nunnally, Tiina, *Smilla's Sense of Snow*, New York, 1993.

KIERKEGAARD, SØREN   Gillhoff, Gerd, *Diary of a Seducer*, New York, 1966; London, 1969 · Hannay, Alastair, *Fear and Trembling: Dialectical Lyric by Johannes de Silentio*, Harmondsworth, 1985 [Penguin] · *Either/Or: A Fragment of Life Edited by Victor Eremita*, London, 1992 [Penguin] · Hong, Howard V., and Hong, Edna, H., *Fear and Trembling* and *Repetition*, Princeton, NJ, 1983 · *Either/Or*, Princeton, NJ, 1987 · *Stages on Life's Way: Studies by Various Persons*, Princeton, NJ, 1988 · Lowrie, Walter, *Stages on Life's Way*, Princeton, NJ, 1940; rep. New York, 1967 · *Fear and Trembling: A Dialectical Lyric*, and *The Book on Adler*, Princeton, NJ, 1941 [new edns., 1952, 1964; London, 1994, Everyman] · *Repetition: An Essay in Experimental Psychology*, New York, 1941 [new edn., 1964] · *Either/Or, ii*, New York, 1959; rep. Princeton, NJ, 1971 · Payne, Robert, *Fear and Trembling: A Dialectical Lyric by Johannes de Silentio*, London, 1939 · Swenson, David F., and Swenson, Lillian M., *Either/Or, i*, New York, 1959; rep. Princeton, NJ, 1971.

LARSEN, MICHAEL   Blecher, Lone Thygesen, and Blecher, George, *Uncertainty*, New York/London, 1996.

STANGERUP, HENRIK   Bluestone, Barbara, *The Road to Lagoa Santa*, London/New York, 1984 · Born, Anne, *Brother Jacob*, New York/London, 1993 · *Snake in the Heart*, London/New York, 1996 · Gress-Wright, David, *The Man Who Wanted to Be Guilty*, London/New York, 1984 · Martin, Sean, *The Seducer: It is Hard to Die in Dieppe*, London/New York, 1990.

SEE ALSO   Bredsdorff, E., *Danish Literature in English Translation*, Copenhagen, 1948 · Rossel, S. H., ed., *A History of Danish Literature*, Lincoln, Neb./London, 1992 · Schroeder, C. L., *A Bibliography of Danish Literature in English Translation 1950–1980. With a Selection of Books about Denmark*, Copenhagen, 1982.

5. DUTCH

The term 'Dutch literature' means literature written in Dutch, the language used both in the Netherlands and in Flanders, the Dutch-speaking part of Belgium. The whole of the Dutch-language area is also referred to as the Low Countries. The Dutch written tradition begins roughly in the 10th c. CE.

Despite the geographical proximity of Britain to the Dutch-speaking area, close economic ties and numerous social, political, and cultural contacts through the ages, Dutch literature translated into English has never been more than a very minor presence, a trickle at best. Moreover, since the 18th c. most of the cultural traffic has been in one direction, from the English-speaking world to the Low Countries. The impact of *The Spectator* and similar writings in the 18th c., the influence of Sir Walter Scott's novels in the 19th, and the hegemony of Anglo-American popular culture in the latter half of the 20th, can serve to illustrate the point. It should be borne in mind, however, that the contemporary perspective, which casts Dutch as a minor language compared with the global importance of English, can be misleading. In the 16th and 17th c., for example, English was relatively unknown in Europe, while Dutch, especially in the 17th c., was spoken and read more widely than it is today.

i. **Middle Ages** During the Middle Ages, Latin literary and learned writings originating in the Low Countries did not need to be translated to be read abroad, since Latin was the international language of intellectual discourse throughout Europe. The earliest sample of a western form of Old Dutch, a single sentence in Dutch with an interlinear Latin translation (or vice versa) probably dating from the latter part of the 11th c., was almost certainly written in England (it was found in an Oxford manuscript in 1932). If there were other written contacts involving translation, they have not come down to us.

Of the vernacular literary writings in Middle Dutch virtually nothing was translated into English at the time. Most translations from Middle Dutch were made by philologists in the 19th and especially the 20th c. The few exceptions date from the very end of the medieval period. However, they include the best-known work of medieval Dutch literature, the 13th-c. Flemish animal epic *Reynart the Fox*, by the otherwise unknown 'William who made Madoc'. It was translated and printed in 1481 by William **Caxton** (c.1422–1491), who himself had

learnt the art of printing in Cologne and subsequently in Bruges, where he lived for several years as a 'merchant adventurer'.

Although the relation between the English *Everyman* (printed c.1509–19) and the 15th-c. *Elckerlijc* (printed c.1496) attributed to Petrus Dorlandus of Diest (near Louvain) was the subject of protracted scholarly debate in the first part of the 20th c., it is now accepted that *Everyman* is a translation of *Elckerlijc* rather than the other way round. The argument was finally settled in favour of *Elckerlijc* as the source on the basis of a detailed analysis of paired rhyming words; it showed a significantly greater occurrence of padding in the English version. The anonymous play *Mariken van Nieumeghen* (c.1500; first printed c.1515), written in verse and prose, appeared in English as *Mary of Nemmegen*, printed in Antwerp by Jan van Doesborch in 1518. More than a third of van Doesborch's output was in English, including a number of translations from Dutch, among them the popular *Tyll Howleglass* (printed c.1520–30), the Dutch source of which goes back to a German original (*Till Eulenspiegel*) [II.h.2.i]. Van Doesborch himself was in London in 1523–4. Several of the English books he published were translated by Lawrence **Andrewe** (1510–37), who afterwards also settled in London as a printer. Towards the middle of the century a series of protectionist measures eliminated the foreign presence in English book production.

ii. **Sixteenth to Eighteenth Century** In the later 16th c. the Antwerp Renaissance poet Jan van der Noot published *Het theatre* in London (1568). The collection, a cycle of visionary sonnets followed by a lengthy and virulently anti-Catholic prose commentary, was translated in 1569 as *The Theatre of Voluptuous Worldlings* and printed by Henry Bynneman, who himself hailed from the Low Countries. The verse was almost certainly translated by the then 17-year-old Edmund **Spenser**, who may have worked from Van der Noot's own French version of the poems; Spenser later incorporated some of the renderings into his *Complaints* of 1591. The prose was translated by one Theodore **Roest**, from either 'the Brabants speech' or the French. The *Biencorf der H. Roomsche Kercke* (1569), the major anti-Catholic satire of the period, written in Rabelaisian prose by the staunchly Calvinist Philips van Marnix van Sint-Aldegonde, a leading figure in the revolt of the Netherlands against Spain, was translated as *The Beehive of the Romish*

Churche (1578) by George **Gilpin** the Elder (?1514–1602), dedicated to Philip Sidney, and reprinted several times. Among Catholic translators who entered the religious controversies of the day were Thomas **Stapleton** (1535–98) and Richard **Shacklock** (*fl.* 1575); both spent time in Flanders, and their translations, done from Latin rather than from Dutch into English, included work by Cardinal Stanislaus Hosius, one of the presidents of the Council of Trent. Nevertheless, despite the presence of substantial numbers of English exiles in the Low Countries and of Dutch and Flemish exiles in England for a good part of the 16th c., no sustained translation effort from Dutch into English or vice versa came into being.

In the 17th c. the southern part of the Low Countries (roughly, contemporary Belgium) had been regained by Catholic Spain. In the north, however, the Calvinist-dominated Dutch Republic had struggled free and quickly evolved into a world power, if only for a relatively short time. Its 'Golden Age' culture produced the likes of Rembrandt, Vermeer, and Spinoza. Although the first English–Dutch / Dutch–English dictionary was produced in this period (by Henry Hexham, 1658), very little vernacular writing was being translated into English. This is in contrast with the Neo-Latin writings from the Low Countries. Here the tradition begun with translations of Erasmus of Rotterdam [II.n.12] in the 16th c. was continued in the 17th; for example, several of the political, legal, and theological works of Hugo Grotius were translated into English (mostly from Latin, occasionally from Dutch), as were two of his three Latin tragedies: *Christus patiens*, (1608), rendered as *Christ's Passion* by G. **Sandys** (1578–1644) in 1640; and *Sophompaneas* (1635), translated by F. **Goldsmith** (1613–55) in 1652. The Latin treatise on the right of women to advanced study, by the polyglot Anna Maria van Schurman, *Dissertatio de ingenii muliebris* (1641, Dissertation on the Feminine Mind), appeared in English as *The Learned Maid, or Whether a Maid May Be a Scholar* (1659), translated by the clergyman Clement **Barksdale** (1609–87).

Among the few translated works by literary authors writing in Dutch was the poetry of Jacob Cats. The 'Emblematicall Dialogue' in Thomas **Heywood**'s (*c.*1573–1641) *Pleasant Dialogues* of 1637 was given as 'interpreted from . . . I. Catzius', and Cats himself had brought out a trilingual edition of some of his emblems at the end of the 1620s, with the English versions probably by Josuah **Sylvester** (1563–1618). But despite the fact that both Cats and Constantijn Huygens were knighted by Charles I, and that Huygens became the first foreign translator of John Donne, Dutch literature remained largely untranslated and hence unread in the Anglophone world. The first English translations of the leading Golden Age dramatist and 'prince of poets' Joost van den Vondel did not appear until the early 19th c. (beginning with some poems and dramatic extracts in John **Bowring**'s *Batavian Anthology* of 1824), and the first complete play by Vondel, *Lucifer*, translated by Charles **van Noppen** (1868–1935), had to wait until 1898. The claim that Milton read Vondel's *Lucifer* (1654) in Dutch and drew inspiration from it for his *Paradise Lost* was hotly debated in the 19th c. but could not be substantiated.

Dutch prose accounts of sea voyages and explorations found English translators and readers more readily. This tradition begins in the last decade of the 16th c., as the travel journals of Jan Huighen van Linschoten, Cornelis de Houtman, and Cornelis Gerrits, all of them dealing with journeys to the East Indies, were published in English within a few years of their appearance in Dutch. Gerrit de Veer's harrowing story of the Dutch expedition under Willem Barentsz that wintered in Nova Zembla, first published in Dutch in 1598 (*Waerachtighe Beschryvinghe Van drie seylagien . . .*), was issued in English translation in 1609 (*The True and Perfect Description of Three Voyages*), following translations into French, Latin, German, and Italian. Willem Schouten's *Oost-Indische Voyage* of 1618 appeared in an English translation by W. **Phillip** a year later (*Relation of a Wonderfull Voyage . . . round about the World*). The most popular of the Dutch travel accounts, however, Willem IJsbrantsz Bontekoe's 1646 *Journael* describing his East India voyage, was not translated until the 20th c.

Other Anglo-Dutch contacts involving translation in one form or another during this period include the large numbers of English and Scottish students attending Leiden University, and regular exchanges and translations of Puritan, Pietist, and Quaker writings. The best-known figure here is the bilingual William **Sewell** (1654–1720), author of a Quaker history but also of a Dutch–English dictionary (1691) and of a Dutch grammar in English which appeared in the early 18th c. Generally however, knowledge of English was spreading more rapidly among the Dutch at this time than knowledge of Dutch among the English. With English mercantile supremacy beginning to assert itself through a series of Anglo-Dutch wars, the pattern of one-directional translation became established in the 18th c. with the massive influence of English spectatorial writings in the Netherlands. Although it has been argued that Daniel Defoe derived the material for his *Robinson Crusoe* in part from Hendrik Smeeks's *Krinke Kesmes* (1708), an imaginary travel account, the evidence has remained inconclusive. The *Poetry for Children* by the popular Hieronymus van Alphen, first published in 1778–82, was translated by F. J. **Millard** as late as 1856.

iii. Nineteenth Century In the early 19th c. the opening words of the introduction to the *Batavian Anthology, or Specimens of the Dutch Poets* (1824), edited by John Bowring and Harry van Dyk, summed up the state of English literary translation from Dutch: 'There is a country almost within sight of the shores of our island whose literature is less known to us than that of Persia or Hindostan . . . it is indeed most strange, that while the poets of Germany have found hundreds of admirers and thousands of critics, those of a land nearer to us in position—more allied by habit and by history with our thoughts and recollections—should have been passed by unnoticed.' The translator and later Member of Parliament and diplomat Sir John Bowring (1792–1872) translated poetry from eastern Europe and Spain as well as the Netherlands, and produced also a *Sketch of the Language and Literature of Holland* (1829), the first more or less systematic presentation of Dutch literature in English (it was translated into Dutch in the same year). Bowring's example as a poetry translator would be followed later in the 19th and in the early 20th c. by Edmund **Gosse** and Jethro **Bithell**, then by Herbert **Grierson**, James **Russell**, Adriaan **Barnouw**, and Theodoor **Weevers**, and in recent decades by James **Holmes** and James **Brockway**.

Although the 19th c. saw rather more translations from Dutch into English than the preceding centuries, they were still appearing piecemeal. Bowring had identified Hendrik Tollens as Holland's most popular living poet. Tollens's patriotic poem on the Barentsz expedition of the 1590s was translated twice, first by one **'Anglo-Saxon'** in 1860 (*The Wintering of the Hollanders on Nova Zembla*, published in the Netherlands with a Dutch preface), then in New York in 1884 (*The Hollanders in Nova Zembla*, first published in the *New Amsterdam Gazette*), translated by Daniel **van Pelt** in an effort to counter the 'barbarously literal' version of 1860. The work now generally regarded as the most innovative and important Dutch novel of the century, *Max Havelaar* (1860) by Multatuli (pseudonym of Eduard Douwes Dekker), was rendered into English by Alphonse **Nahuijs** in 1868; Nahuijs emphasized the book's documentary quality as a critique of Dutch colonial rule in the East Indies. Two further translations would follow in the 20th c., one

by William **Siebenhaar** with an introduction by D. H. Lawrence in 1927, the other by Roy **Edwards** in 1967.

The genre attracting most attention was the historical novel which fitted the mould created by Walter Scott. Thus E. W. **Hoskin** translated Jacob van Lennep's *De Pieegzoon* (1833, The Adopted Son) and F. **Woodley** Van Lennep's *De roos van Dekama* (1836, The Rose of Dekama). A. L. G. Bosboom-Toussaint's *Majoor Frans* (1874), however, translated by James **Akeroyd** as *Major Frank*, is a sketch of contemporary life. The most widely translated 19th c. author was the Flemish Hendrik Conscience, who wrote numerous historical novels and romances. Individual works were brought out in translation in Britain and the USA from the 1840s onwards (beginning with *Sketches from Flemish Life*, three novellas translated by Napoleon **Trübner**, 1848), and multi-volume editions appeared throughout the latter half of the 19th c., culminating in the 10-volume compilation *Conscience's Tales* (1888–95). Very soon however Conscience came to be seen as a writer of popular rather than serious literature, a fate which also befell his work in other countries and in his native Flanders.

iv. Twentieth Century The number of English translations of Dutch literary work began to increase significantly in the latter half of the 19th c.. At the end of the 19th and in the first few decades of the 20th c. Louis Couperus became the best-known Dutch novelist in English translation, thanks largely to the efforts of his translator, Alexander **Teixeira de Mattos**. His translations include the four *Books of the Small Souls* (*De boeken der kleine zielen*, 1901–3) and *Old People and the Things That Pass* (*Van oude menschen, de dingen die voorbijgaan*, 1906). On a visit to London in 1921 Couperus was hailed as a writer on a par with Thomas Mann, Conrad, and Tolstoy. His popularity ended rather abruptly in the 1930s; the reasons for the sudden decline remain unclear. The most frequently translated authors in the first half of the century were popular writers like Jo van Ammers-Küller and Johan Fabricius, followed by a second league made up of more canonical literary figures including, apart from Couperus, the novelists Arthur van Schendel, Frederik van Eeden and Madelon Lulofs, the playwright Herman Heijermans, and the essayist and historian Johan Huizinga. Even so, literary translations from Dutch into English in the first half of the century numbered less than 250 titles, including reprints. E. S. Bates was obviously right when, in his *Modern Translation* (1936), he listed Dutch together with Portuguese, Modern Greek, and Modern Hebrew as the most neglected literatures as regards translation into English.

After World War II this situation seemed set to continue, despite the phenomenal success worldwide of Anne Frank's *Diary of a Young Girl* (translated by B. M. **Mooyaart-Doubleday**). The *Guardian* newspaper appeared to have good reasons for echoing John Bowring's *Batavian Anthology* when it opened a book review in 1980 with the observation that 'Dutch literature is about as familiar to English readers as that of Georgia or Korea'. Nevertheless, thanks at least in part to the efforts of the Dutch government-sponsored Foundation for the Production and Translation of Dutch Literature and its predecessor (originally set up in 1954), the last decade or so has witnessed a rapid and sizeable increase in the number of English translations especially of modern and contemporary Dutch literature. Seen from the perspective of current English-language writing, where translations from other languages count for little anyway, the impact of translations from Dutch is negligible. From the Dutch-language point of view, however, the active role of the Foundation has meant that works which are regarded as canonical or as having literary merit are brought to the attention of Anglophone publishers, and their translation receives financial support. Some ventures initiated in this way have been largely academic (e.g. the Library of Netherlandic Literature in the 1960s, and the Library of the Indies directed by E. M. Beekman in the 1980s); the lack of commercial success may be offset by the knowledge that a representative sample of modern Dutch classics is at least available in English, if only in major libraries. Increasingly, however, both established and younger contemporary Dutch and Flemish writers are now being translated into English and marketed by prominent literary publishers in Britain and the USA. Among the most frequently translated literary authors of the postwar generation are the novelists J. Bernlef, Hugo Claus, Marga Minco, Harry Mulisch, and Cees Nooteboom. The leading prose translators of the moment include Richard **Huijing**, Stacey **Knecht**, Susan **Massotty**, Claire **Nicholas White**, Arnold **Pomerans**, and Paul **Vincent**. TH

ANTHOLOGIES   Aercke, Kristiaan, ed., *Women Writing in Dutch*, New York/London, 1994 · Barnouw, Adriaan, *Coming After: An Anthology of Poetry from the Low Countries*, New Brunswick, NJ, 1948 · Bithell, Jethro, *Contemporary Flemish Poetry*, London, 1917 · Bowring, John, and Van Dyk, Harry, *Batavian Anthology, or Specimens of the Dutch Poets*, London, 1824 · Brockway, James, *Singers Behind Glass: Eight Modern Dutch Poets*, Lincoln, Neb., 1995 · Hermans, Theo, ed., 'Dutch and Flemish Poetry', *Modern Poetry in Translation*, 12 (1997) · Holmes, James S, and Smith, William Jay, eds., *Dutch Interior: Postwar Poetry from the Netherlands and Flanders*, New York, 1984 · Van de Kamp, Peter, ed., *Turning Tides: Modern Dutch and Flemish Verse in English Versions by Irish Poets*, Brownsville, Tex., 1994 · Weevers, Theodoor, *Poetry of the Netherlands in its European Context*, London, 1960.

ALPHEN, HIERONYMUS VAN   Millard, F. J., *Poetry for Children*, London, 1856.

BERNLEF, J.   Dixon, Adrienne, *Out of Mind*, London, 1988 · *Public Secret*, London, 1992.

BOON, L. P.   Dixon, Adrienne, *Chapel Road*, New York, 1972 · *Minuet*, New York, 1979.

BOSBOOM-TOUSSAINT, A. L. G.   Akeroyd, James, *Major Frank*, London, 1885.

CATS, JACOB   Heywood, Thomas, 'Emblematicall Dialogue', in his *Pleasant Dialogues*, London, 1637 · Pigot, Richard, *Moral Emblems*, London, 1860; rep. 1862, 1865.

CLAUS, HUGO   Levitt, Ruth, *The Swordfish*, London, 1996 · Pomerans, Arnold, *The Sorrow of Belgium*, London, 1990.

COUPERUS, LOUIS   Bell, Clara, *Footsteps of Fate*, London, 1891; New York, 1892 · Teixeira de Mattos, Alexander, *The Books of the Small Souls*, London/New York, 1914–18 · *Old People and the Things That Pass*, New York, 1918, London, 1919; rep. Leiden, 1963 · *The Hidden Force*, New York, 1921, London, 1922; rep. Amherst, Mass., 1985; London, 1992.

DORLANDUS, PETRUS   anon., *Everyman*, London, c.1509–19.

ELSSCHOT, WILLEM   Brotherton, Alex, *Three Novels*, Leiden, 1965 · Vincent, Paul, *Villa des Roses*, London, 1992.

FRANK, ANNE   Manheim, Ralph, and Mok, Michel, *Tales from the Secret Annex*, London, 1982, 1986 · Mooyaart-Doubleday, B. M., *Diary of a Young Girl*, New York, 1947 · Pomerans, Arnold, and Mooyaart-Doubleday, B. M., *The Diary of Anne Frank: The Critical Edition*, London, 1989.

GROTIUS, HUGO   Goldsmith, F., *Sophompaneas*, London, 1652 · Sandys, G., *Christ's Passion*, London, 1640.

HAASSE, HELLA   Kaplan, Lewis, *In a Dark Wood Wandering*, London, 1990 · Miller, Anita, *The Scarlet City*, Chicago, 1990 · Miller, Anita, and Blinstrub, Nini, *Threshold of Fire*, Chicago, 1993.

LENNEP, JACOB VAN   Hoskin, E. W., *The Adopted Son*, London, 1847 · Woodley, F., *The Rose of Dekama*, London, 1846.

MARIKEN VAN NIEUMEGEN   anon., *Mary of Nemmegen*, Antwerp, 1518.

MARNIX VAN SINT-ALDEGONDE, PHILIPS VAN   Gilpin the Elder, George, *The Beehive of the Romish Churche*, London, 1578 [4 reps.].

MINCO, MARGA   Clegg, Margaret, *An Empty House*, London, 1990 · Edwards, Roy, *Bitter Herbs*, Oxford, 1960, London, 1990 · Knecht, Stacey, *The Glass Bridge*, London, 1988.

MULISCH, HARRY   Vincent, Paul, *The Discovery of Heaven*, New York/London, 1997 · White, Claire Nicholas, *The Assault*, London, 1986.

MULTATULI   Edwards, Roy, *Max Havelaar*, Leiden/London/New York, 1967; Harmondsworth, 1982 [Penguin] · Nahuijs, Alphonse, *Max Havelaar*, Edinburgh, 1868 · Siebenhaar, William, *Max Havelaar*, New York, 1927.

NOOT, JAN VAN DER   Spenser, Edmund and Roest, Theodore, *The Theatre of Voluptuous Worldlings*, London, 1569.

NOOTEBOOM, CEES   Dixon, Adrienne, *Rituals*, Baton Rouge, La., 1983 · Rilke, Ina, *The Following Story*, London, 1993 · *Roads to Santiago*, London/New York, 1997.

REINAERT DE VOS   Caxton, William, *Reynard the Foxe*, London, 1481.

SCHOUTEN, WILLEM   Phillip, W., *Relation of a Wonderfull Voyage . . . round about the World*, London, 1619.

SCHURMAN, ANNA MARIA VAN   Barksdale, Clement, *The Learned Maid, or Whether a Maid May Be a Scholar*, London, 1659.

TOLLENS, HENDRIK   'Anglo-Saxon', *The Wintering of the Hollanders on Nova Zembla*, Leeuwarden, 1860 · Pelt, Daniel van, *The Hollanders in Nova Zembla*, New York, 1884.

VEER, GERRIT DE   Phillip, W., *The True and Perfect Description of Three Voyages . . .*, London, 1609.

VESTDIJK, SIMON   Brotherton, Alex, *The Garden Where the Brass Band Played*, Leiden, 1965.

VONDEL, JOOST VAN DEN   Noppen, Charles van, *Lucifer*, New York, 1989.

SEE ALSO   Arents, P., *De Vlaamse schrijvers in het Engels vertaald, 1481–1949*, Ghent, 1949 · Beekman, E. M., *Troubled Pleasures: Dutch Colonial Literature from the East Indies 1600–1950*, New York, 1996 · Haley, K. H. D., *The British and the Dutch. Political and Cultural Relations Through the Ages*, London, 1988 · Kooper, Erik, ed., *Middle Dutch Literature in Its European Context*, Cambridge, 1994 · Schenkeveld-van der Dussen, M., *Dutch Literature in the Age of Rembrandt*, tr. A. F. Harms, Amsterdam, 1991 · Vanderauwera, R., *Dutch Novels Translated into English: The Transformation of a 'Minority' Literature*, Amsterdam, 1985.

6. FINNISH AND FINLAND-SWEDISH

i. The Birth of a National Literature Until the 1960s, Finnish-language literature was intimately connected with Finland's emerging national identity. Following more than six centuries of Swedish rule (1157–1809), Finland was suddenly annexed in 1809 to Russia as a Grand Duchy. With national romantic sentiment blossoming in Europe, the new situation engendered an identity crisis: no longer Swedes, unwilling to become Russians, the Finns decided: 'Let us be Finns.' The task of making Finland Finnish required a versatile agenda for the development of social, judicial, educational, economic, and cultural activities in the Finnish language, which, save for religious life, had been neglected. This linguistic and literary agenda, conceptualized largely by the philosopher and literary critic Johan Vilhelm Snellman, prescribed that Finnish literature be the prime tool of Finnish nationalism and Finnish identity-building, which continued in varying manifestations until the 1950s.

Johan Ludvig Runeberg (1802–77), Finland's national poet, built a solid foundation for the ensuing nation-building work with historical dramas in hexametre and, most significantly, with *Fältskärns Berättelser I–II* (1848–60 The Songs of Ensign Stål), translated in the original metres by Clement Burbank **Shaw**, but not until 1925. This collection of patriotic poems about the war of 1808–9 was designed to instil admiration for 'Finnish character traits' and a sense of national pride; it includes

Finland's national anthem, 'Vårt land' (Our Land). Using the Swedish language, the lingua franca of Finland until the 1860s, Runeberg wrote about Finns for Finns, establishing a canon for literary national characters, such as the simpleton Sven Dufva, the unyielding, tenacious Munter, the veteran Ensign Stål, and the Cloud's Brother, a Finn of anonymous lineage. Shaw says of Runeberg's poems: 'Runeberg is mighty in his charming simplicity. Always the simplest words prevail.' 'Proud humility', the famed Finnish characteristic, may count its origins from Runeberg. Zacharias Topelius (1818–98) continued, also in Swedish, the national character-building agenda with historical novels, poetry, and hymns as well as didactic tales for children.

ii. Literature in Finnish The Swedish-speaking intellectuals of the young Grand Duchy, first the Turku Romantics, later, after the university was moved to Helsinki in 1827, the Saturday Society, stressed the need for literature in the Finnish language. The Finnish Literature Society was established in 1831 for the express purpose of encouraging, supporting and publishing a literature in the Finnish language as well as collecting and publishing Finnish folk poetry. The society's role was as central in the publication of the folk epic the *Kalevala* [II.o.3] as it was for the work of Aleksis Kivi, Finland's first Finnish-language author of international calibre.

Kivi (the pseudonym of Alexis Stenvall) was the son of a poor tailor, but has rightly earned the epithet 'father of Finnish literature'. Not only did he create a Finnish literary language by drawing on the Bible and on peasant dialects, but his novel *Seitsemän veljestä* (1870, Seven Brothers), his comedy *Nummisuutarit* (1864, Heath Cobblers), and the *Kalevala*-inspired five-act tragedy *Kullervo* (1864, both plays translated by Douglas **Robinson** in 1993), all became classics of Finnish literature despite being the first serious works in their respective genres. Kivi's poetry, too, published in his *Kanervala* (1866, Heatherland) or integrated into his novels and plays, is still considered to be of exceptional quality. A selection of his poems was published in English translation by Keith **Bosley** under the title *Odes*.

Seven Brothers, the best-known Finnish work of literature after *The Kalevala*, has been translated into English twice, by Alex **Matson** and Richard **Impola**. The novel represents the social and educational development of 19th-c. Finns from a rural and illiterate to a literate and educationally diverse people. In fact, much of Kivi's work is structured around dual worlds: the peaceful, rural village-type world on the one hand and the strange and sophisticated world of the cultural élite on the other. The Finnish-language majority, over 80 per cent in 1809, not having been given an opportunity to participate in public cultural, administrative, or judicial society, were slated to adopt the leadership role that was rightfully theirs but that they found intimidating. Literacy came to symbolize this dichotomy; it facilitated the integration of Finns into western civilization and underlined the importance of literature to a culture.

This dichotomy, in fact, was to define Finnish prose literature for almost a century in what is called the 'Great tradition in Finnish prose': the protagonists of Juhani Aho, Ilmari Kianto, Joel Lehtonen, and F. E. Sillanpää are frequently illiterate and therefore resent, even reject, civilized society. The 'great tradition' describes the transition of Finns from forest creatures to city-dwellers and is reasonably represented in English translation.

F. E. Sillanpää, the only Finn to be so honoured, won the Nobel Prize for Literature in 1939. The work cited by the Nobel committee, *Nuorena nukkunut* (1931), appeared in English translation by Alex Matson under the title *Fallen Asleep while Young*, also as *The Maid Silja*. This story of 'the last off-shoot of a family tree' illustrates well Sillanpää's biological and Bergsonian view of human existence. Two other Sillanpää novels in English translation, *Hurskas kurjuus* (1919, Meek Heritage),

translated by Alex Matson, and *Ihmiset suviyössä* (1934, People in the Summer Night), translated by Alan **Blair**, have survived changing times and literary tastes better than *The Maid Silja*. *Meek Heritage* offers a portrait of a simple-minded, lonely, left-leaning crofter who in the aftermath of Finland's civil war of 1918 was executed without real cause. *People in the Summer Night* in Blair's excellent translation and with its 'symphonic qualities', stands as Sillanpää's formally highest accomplishment.

It has been argued that this nationalist agenda has served to render Finnish literature uninteresting to non-Finns. One also not infrequently encounters the claim that Finnish, a non-Indo-European language, is all but impossible to translate, especially into English. Consequently, some notable masterpieces of Finnish literature have been deemed 'untranslatable'. Alex Matson's translation of Kivi's *Seven Brothers* and of Sillanpää have been severely criticized, mostly due to Matson's less than adequate work, but both authors are notoriously difficult to translate. Both translations of Väinö Linna's *Tuntematon sotilas* (1954, The Unknown Soldier) have been fraught with problems: Linna actually sued the publisher of the American translation and got the translation taken off the market, but the British version has also been subject to criticism. Two of Finnish literature's most towering works, Joel Lehtonen's *Putkinotko* (1919–20) and Volter Kilpi's *Alastalon salissa* (1933, In the Alastalo Parlour) have not even appeared in English. These, the argument goes, defy translation because they are burdened by 'obstacles of Finnishness': their character development and cultural values are expressed through fine nuances of regional culture and dialect, which, although perhaps exceptionally enjoyable to Finnish readers, often lack an equivalent in other languages.

Interestingly, the most widely read work of Finnish literature in English, Mika Waltari's *Sinuhe* (1945, also published under the title *The Egyptian*), translated by Naomi **Walford**, is remarkably free of such 'obstacles of Finnishness'. No other novel by a Finnish author has come close to the popularity of *Sinuhe*. Waltari's is the only Finnish novel turned into a major Hollywood movie, in 1951. Set in ancient Egypt, *Sinuhe the Egyptian* derives its success from its universal appeal and its particular relevance to the post-World War II generation: it is the story of how the individual loses faith in old ideals, searches for a new foundation for existence, yet ends up lonely, disillusioned, and marginalized.

After the unparalleled success of Walford's translation, she was commissioned to translate further works by Waltari, mostly his historical novels, including *Mikael Karvajalka* (1948, The Adventurer, also Michael the Finn), *Mikael Hakim* (1949, The Sultan's Renegade, also The Wanderer), *Johannes Angelos* (1952, The Dark Angel), and *Valtakunnan salaisuus* (1959, The Secret of the Kingdom). Waltari's success enticed other publishers and translators to undertake translations of his work as well, e.g. *Turms kuolematon* (1995, The Etruscan), translated by Lily **Leino** and again by Evelyn **Ramsden**, and *Ihmiskunnan viholliset* (1964, The Roman), translated by Joan **Tate**. By virtue of his many books in English, Mika Waltari gained international celebrity. In an interview in the *New York Herald Tribune* he commented that his main themes were individual freedom, humanity, and tolerance.

Väinö Linna epitomizes the dilemma of English translations of Finnish literature. His two masterpieces, *The Unknown Soldier* and *Täällä Pohjantähden alla I–III* (1958–62, Here Under the North Star), were chosen in 1997 by a representative group of Finland's cultural élite as well as by the general public as the two most significant works of art created during Finland's 80 years of independence, yet only *The Unknown Soldier* has appeared in English. It tells the grass-roots story of a Finnish artillery platoon during Finland's war (1941–4) against the Soviet Union. Buoyed by its domestic success, the English translation has been reprinted several times in Finland by Linna's Finnish publisher, although burdened by its 'excessive Finnishness': the characters all speak different dialects and display concomitant regional characteristics.

Other Finnish prose writers who have made inroads into English-language literature include the feminist Eeva Kilpi with *Tamara* (1972), translated by Philip **Binham**, the prose modernist Veijo Meri with *Manillaköysi* (1957, The Manila Rope), translated by John **McGahern** and Annikki **Laaksi**, and Toivo Pekkanen with *Lapsuuteni* (1953, My Childhood), translated by Alan Blair. Recently the great tradition has been continued with two novels by Finnish best-selling author Kalle Päätalo, translated by Richard Impola.

Remarkably, no monograph has yet appeared in English translation of Finland's early feminist genius Minna Canth, yet many of her plays have been translated for occasional English theatre productions. In 1996 Canth's play *Annaliisa* (1895) finally appeared in translation by Aili and Austin **Flint** in Steve Wilmer's anthology *Portraits of Courage: Plays by Finnish Women*, a volume which also includes Maria Jotuni's *Kultainen vasikka* (1918, The Golden Calf), translated by Ritva **Poom**, and Hella Wuolijoki's *Laki ja järjestys* (1933, Law and

Order), translated by Marja and Steve **Wilmer**. Other remarkable women writers include Aino Kallas with several novels on Baltic themes, and Eeva Joenpelto with two novels. Contemporary women authors who have been translated into English include Annika Idström, Leena Krohn, Leena Lander, and Eeva-Liisa Manner. Rosa Liksom's *Yhden yön pysäkki* (1985, One-Night Stands), translated by Anselm **Hollo** has been received with exceptionally great interest, particularly among young readers.

Finnish poets who have left a mark on English poetry include J. L. Runeberg, Eino Leino, Paavo Haavikko, Pentti Saarikoski, and of course, the Finland-Swedish modernists of the early 20th c. Haavikko was championed in North America by the long-standing editor of *World Literature Today* (formerly *Books Abroad*), Dr Ivar Ivask. He was awarded the Neustadt Prize for Literature in 1982, and his *Selected Poems*, translated by Anselm **Hollo**, established Haavikko's reputation as a modernist and brilliantly intellectual poet with a penetrating analysis of power, (ir)responsibility, and the darker forces in the human psyche. Some other modern poets who have been translated into English include Tuomas Anhava, Eeva-Liisa Manner, Aila Meriluoto, Pentti Saaritsa, Sirkka Turkka, and Eira Stenberg. Douglas Robinson has published electronically a collection of translations of contemporary Finnish lyric poetry, about 100 poems by a dozen poets, under the title *Turnings*.

iii. Literature in Finland-Swedish In literary terms, the recognition of Finland-Swedish literature, as distinct from Finnish-language literature, becomes meaningful after the Finnish language gained its rightful status in Finland, being officially recognized in 1863. Runeberg and Topelius wrote for and about Finns, albeit in Swedish, but when pushed off centre stage, Finland-Swedish authors set an agenda of their own and began to reflect a minority experience. Historians of Swedish literature (of Sweden) have occasionally appropriated authors from Finland, particularly Runeberg and Edith Södergran, but Finland-Swedish authors are not Swedish. Their historical experiences are Finnish and their national loyalties are to Finland. The Swedish-speaking minority of Finland lives in geographical and linguistic isolation along the west coast, the south-west archipelago, and the southern coast of Finland, but in interaction also with Sweden's literary tradition. Finland-Swedish culture is distinct and has strong roots in Finland's soil.

Finland-Swedish authors have enjoyed proportionately greater success in English than their

Finnish-language counterparts. Finland-Swedish authors also seem to excel in poetry; Edith Södergran and Bo Carpelan, in particular, have captivated audiences in the English-speaking world. Several extensive translations of Södergran's poetry have appeared in English. Best-received are the ones by David **McDuff** and Stina **Katchadourian**. The leading Finland-Swedish modernist and the first to use free verse, Södergran became the leading force in the Finland-Swedish school of modernist poetry which included Elmer Diktonius and Gunnar Björling. Bo Carpelan is widely acclaimed in English for several collections of poetry and the successful novels *Axel* (1986) and *Urwind* (1995), both translated by David McDuff. Other Finland-Swedish poets of considerable success in English include Finland's Minister of Culture 1995–8, Claes Andersson, and Märta Tikkanen with a gripping cycle about her marriage to author-artist Henrik Tikkanen, *Århundradets kärlekshistoria* (1978, Love Story of the Century), translated by Stina Katchadourian. Other excellent translated poets include Tua Forsström, Gösta Ågren, Lars Huldén, and Solveigh von Schoultz.

Tove Jansson is a renowed example of the successful prose writer [see also I.c.4.iv]. Her Moomin books, most of which were translated by Thomas **Warburton** in the 1970s and 1980s, are loved around the world by children and adults alike. Other successful prose writers include Christer Kihlman with four novels translated by Joan Tate, and Henrik Tikkanen with two novels, *30-åriga kriget* (1977, The Thirty Years War), translated by George **Schoolfield**, and *Brändövägen 8* (1976, A Winter's Day, also as Snob's Island) translated by Mary **Sandbach**. Märta Tikkanen and Solveigh von Schoultz are also noted prose writers.

iv. Anthologies and the Circulation in English of Literature from Finland

Small literatures such as Finnish and Finland-Swedish literature must often rely upon anthologies for exposure in translation. A classic anthology is George Schoolfield's *Swedo-Finnish Short Story*. Such anthologies contain a number of writers not otherwise represented; they include Aili Jarvenpa's *Salt of Pleasure*, Herbert **Lomas**'s *Territorial Song* and *Contemporary Finnish Poetry*, Kirsti **Simonsuuri**'s *Enchanting Beasts: An Anthology of Modern Women Poets in Finland*, Börje **Vähämäki**'s *A Treasury of Finnish Love Poems*, Keith Bosley's *Skating on the Sea: Poetry from Finland*, Richard **Dauenhauer** and Philip Binham's *Snow in May*, Anne **Fried**'s *Thank You for These Illusions: Poems by Finnish Women Writers*, and Philip Landon's *The Review of Contemporary Fiction: New Finnish Fiction*.

The impact of Finnish and Finland-Swedish literature on English literature has been minimal. Small editions do not make an impact and are seldom reprinted. Exceptions are Mika Waltari's *Sinuhe the Egyptian*, Edith Södergran's early modernist poetry, and Tove Jansson's Moomin children's books, and perhaps Kivi's *Seven Brothers*, which have clearly made an impression and so continue to be available in print. Overall, however, translation of the literature of Finland is a story of scattered single undertakings. The initiative is normally taken by enthusiastic bilingual reader-translators who wish to see a favourite work in English translation and who might interest a small publisher to apply for financial assistance to be able to publish the work. Finnish literature in English is rarely commercially viable but is a labour of love. Unfavourable reviews have occasionally discouraged publishers from taking on more than one Finnish project.

In this context the Finnish Literature Information Centre, a government-funded agency in Finland, does the field an indispensable service by promoting and supporting translations. A valuable English-language quarterly, *Books from Finland*, publishes information about Finnish literature and introduces authors, excerpts, and literary trends. Highly accomplished and prolific translators of Finnish literature include, in the UK: Keith Bosley, Hildi Hawkins, and Herbert Lomas; in the USA: Anselm Hollo (from both Finnish and Swedish), Aili and Austin Flint, Richard Impola, Ritva Koivu, Ritva Poom, and Douglas Robinson; in Canada: Seija Paddon and Börje Vähämäki; from the Swedish: David McDuff, Stina Katchadourian, George Schoolfield, Joan Tate, and Thomas Warburton.   BV

ANTHOLOGIES   Bosley, Keith, *Skating on the Sea: Poetry from Finland*, Newcastle upon Tyne, 1997 · Carpelan, Bo, Meri, Veijo, and Suurp, Matti, eds., *A Way to Measure Time*, Helsinki, 1992 · Dauenhauer, Richard, and Binham, Philip, *Snow in May: An Anthology of Finnish Writing 1945–1972*, London, 1978 · Fried, Anne, *Thank You for These Illusions: Poems by Finnish Women Writers*, Helsinki, 1981 · Jarvenpa, Aili, *Salt of Pleasure: Twentieth-Century Finnish Poetry*, St Paul, Minn., 1983 · Landon, Philip, ed., *The Review of Contemporary Fiction: New Finnish Writing*, Normal, Ill., 1996 · Lomas, Herbert, *Territorial Song: New Writing in Finland*, London, 1981 · *Contemporary Finnish Poetry*, Newcastle upon Tyne, 1991 · Robinson, Douglas, *Turnings: Translations of Contemporary Finnish Lyric Poetry*, Internet:

http://home.olemiss.edu/—djr/turn-tc.html · Schoolfield, George C., *Swedo-Finnish Short Stories*, New York, 1974 · Simonsuuri, Kirsti, *Enchanting Beasts: An Anthology of Modern Women Poets in Finland*, London/Boston, Mass., 1990 · Tompuri, Elli, ed., *Voices from Finland*, Helsinki, 1947 · Väänänen-Jensen, Ingrid, and Vähämäki, Börje, *Finnish Short Stories*, Iowa City, 1991 · Vähämäki, Börje, *A Treasury of Finnish Love Poems, Proverbs and Quotations*, New York, 1996 · Wilmer, Steve, ed., *Portraits of Courage: Plays by Finnish Women*, Helsinki, 1996.

ÅGREN, GÖSTA McDuff, David, *A Valley in the Midst of Violence*, Newcastle upon Tyne, 1992.

AHO, JUHANI Larson, Ralph V., *Juhani Aho's Shavings*, New Brighton, Minn., 1997 · Väänänen-Jensen, Ingrid, *Forbidden Fruit and Other Tales*, Iowa City, 1994.

ANDERSSON, CLAES Bruce, Lennart, and Bruce, Sonja, *Poems in Our Absence*, Cleveland, OH, 1994 · Lesser, Rika, *What Became Words*, Los Angeles, 1996.

ANHAVA, TUOMAS Hollo, Anselm, *In the Dark Move Slowly*, London, 1969.

CARPELAN, BO McDuff, David, *Axel*, Manchester, 1989 · *Urwind*, London, 1996.

HAAVIKKO, PAAVO Hollo, Anselm, *Selected Poems*, London, 1991.

IDSTRÖM, ANNIKA Tate, Joan, *My Brother Sebastian* (tr. from the Swedish), London, 1991.

JOENPELTO, EEVA Koivu, Ritva, *The Bride of Life*, Ann Arbor, Mich., 1995.

KIHLMAN, CHRISTER Tate, Joan, *Sweet Prince*, London, 1983 · *All My Sons*, London, 1984 · *The Blue Mother*, Lincoln, Neb., 1990.

KILPI, EEVA Binham, Philip, *Tamara*, New York, 1978.

KIVI, ALEKSIS Bosley, Keith, *Odes*, Helsinki, 1996 · Impola, Richard, *Seven Brothers*, New York, 1991 · Matson, Alex, *Seven Brothers*, London/New York, 1929., repr. Helsinki, 1959, 1973, etc. · Robinson, Douglas, *Heath Cobblers* and *Kullervo*, St Cloud, Minn., 1993.

KROHN, LEENA Hawkins, Hildi, *Dona Quixote and Gold of Ophir*, London, 1995.

LANDER, LEENA Paddon, Seija, *Cast a Long Shadow*, Toronto, 1995.

LEINO, EINO Bosley, Keith, *Whitsun Songs*, London, 1978.

LIKSON, ROSA Hollo, Anselm, *One Night Stands*, London, 1993.

LINNA, VÄINÖ anon., *The Unknown Soldier*, London, 1957.

MANNER, EEVA-LIISA Binham, Philip, *Snow in May*, in Dauenhaur and Binham (1978) · Poom, Ritva, *Fog Horses*, New York, 1986.

MERI, VEIJO McGahern, John, and Laaksi, Annikki, *The Manila Rope*, New York, 1956.

MERILUOTO, AILA Vuosalo, Leo, and Stone, Steve, *Statue of Fire*, New York, 1993.

PEKKANEN, TOIVO Blair, Alan, *My Childhood*, Madison, Wis., 1966.

RUNEBERG, JOHAN LUDVIG Shaw, Clement Burbank, *The Songs of Ensign Stål*, New York, 1925.

SAARIKISKI, PENTTI Cole, Michael, and Kimball, Karen, *Hämärän tanssit/Dances of the Obscure*, Durango, Colo., 1987 · Hollo, Anselm, *Helsinki: Selected Poems*, London, 1967 · *Poems 1958–1980*, West Branch, Io., 1983.

SAARITSA, PERTTI Paddon, Seija, *Gathering Fragments*, Waterloo, Canada, 1991.

SILLANPÄÄ, F. E. Blair, Alan, *People in the Summer Night*, Madison, Wis., 1966 · Matson, Alex, *Fallen Asleep while Young*, London, 1933; also as *The Maid Silja*, New York, 1933; rep. 1939 · *Meek Heritage*, London/New York, 1938.

SÖDERGRAN, EDITH Katchadourian, Stina, *Love and Solitude*, Seattle, 1992 · McDuff, David, *Complete Poems*, Newcastle upon Tyne, 1984.

STENBERG, EIRA Lomas, Herbert, *Wings of Hope and Daring*, Newcastle upon Tyne, 1992.

TIKKANEN, HENRIK Sandbach, Mary, *A Winter's Day*, New York, 1980 [also as *Snob's Island*, London, 1980] · Schoolfield, George, *The 30 Years War*, Lincoln, Neb., 1987.

TIKKANEN, MÄRTA Katchaduorian, Stina, *The Love Story of the Century*, Santa Barbara, Calif., 1984.

TURKKA, SIRKKA Paddon, Seija, *Not You, Not the Rain*, Waterloo, Canada, 1991.

WALTARI, MIKA Leino, Lily, *The Etruscan*, New York/Toronto, 1956 · Ramsden, Evelyn, *The Etruscan*, London, 1957 · Tate, Joan, *The Roman*, London, 1966 · Walford, Naomi, *Sinuhe the Egyptian*, London, 1949 [as *The Egyptian*, New York, 1949] · *The Adventurer*, also as *Michael the Finn*, New York/Toronto, 1950 · *The Sultan's Renegade* also as *The Wanderer*, London/Sydney, 1951 · *The Dark Angel*, London, 1953 · *The Secret of the Kingdom*, New York, 1960.

SEE ALSO Kiiskinen, J., ed., *Books from Finland*, quarterly, Helsinki · Schoolfield, G. C., ed., *A History of Finland's Literature*, Lincoln, Neb./London, 1998 · Zuck, V., ed., *Dictionary of Scandinavian Literature*, New York/London, 1990.

7. ICELANDIC

Definitions of 'modern' Icelandic literature may make varying claims as to when it begins, but for the translation of modern literature the question is much clearer: it begins with the founding of the Icelandic Republic in 1944. The occupation of Iceland during World War II, first by the British and subsequently by the USA, marked the beginning of a period of rapid modernization and of ever-closer relations with neighbouring countries: Iceland became a member of NATO in 1949, the Nordic Council in 1952, and the European Economic Area in 1993. As a result, the country was effectively 'rediscovered' for the second time since its settlement in the 9th c., and curious foreigners provided a new market for literary products from the 'land of the Sagas' [II.o.2].

The first modern writer to be translated extensively into English was Halldór Kiljan Laxness, whose work *Sjálfstætt fólk* (1934–5, Independent People), published in the UK in 1945 and in the USA a year later, was the first to make a name for its author abroad. In this tale of the sturdy farmer, determined to be dependent upon no one, Laxness was considering the lot of a newly independent microstate coping with a superpower in its backyard, a theme he would subsequently treat from a variety of different approaches. Yet his uniquely Icelandic characters had universal echoes that made the translation by the American J. A. **Thompson** extremely popular and earned Laxness a Nobel Prize in 1955. The work has been reissued, and the translation is still a pleasure to read, its flashes of local colour and tensely humorous renderings conveying well the uniqueness of the author.

Several other major works by Laxness have appeared in English translations by Magnús **Magnússon**, notably *Heimsljós* (1937–40, World Light), a four-volume *Bildungsroman* telling the story of a victimized and misunderstood poet. The 1936 English version of *Salka Valka* (1931), a story of a simple girl from a fishing village caught up in the social transformation of the early decades of the century, was made from a Danish translation by another Icelandic writer, Gunnar Gunnarsson. Another superb work by Laxness, the three-volume historical novel *Íslandsklukkan* (1943–6, The Bell of Iceland), intertwines the lives and fates of three classes in 17th-c. colonial Iceland and has never been published in English translation, although dozens of versions in other foreign languages are available.

Gunnar Gunnarsson was a novelist, poet, and playwright who spent most of his adult life in Denmark and wrote somewhat nostalgically of the rural Iceland of his youth. His play *Svartfugl* (1929, The Black Cliffs), translated from the Danish by Cecil **Wood**, was published by the American Scandinavian Society, who also published an English translation of *Íslenskur aðall* (1938, In Search of My Beloved) by Þórbergur Þórðarson.

Icelanders are even more prolific writers of poetry than of prose, and three sizeable collections of Icelandic poetry have been published in English. The most recent anthology, with by far the best translations, *Brushstrokes of Blue*, includes the works of nine young poets who could be considered fairly representative of postmodernist Icelandic poetry. The translations are by Bernard **Scudder**, a journalist and the most prolific translator of recent Icelandic literature. A parallel-text poetry anthology, *Treasures of Iceland*, uses nature photographs to expand on the images of poets from the late 19th c. to the present, with English versions by several translators.

In the past two decades a whole new generation of narrative writers has also dominated the Icelandic literary scene following the turbulence of modernist insurgents in the 1960s and 1970s. A number of their works have been translated into Nordic languages, but fewer into English. Since the establishment of the Nordic Literary Prize some 25 years ago, Icelandic prose writers have been regular winners; their titles include Thor Vilhjálmsson's *Grámosinn Glóir* (1986, Justice Undone), translated by Bernard Scudder, which focuses on a 19th-c. trial of siblings accused of incest and infanticide, Fríða Sigurðardóttir's *Meðan nóttin líður* (1990, The Night Watch) translated by Katjanka **Edwardsen**, which follows a family through three generations of women, and *Englar Alheimsins* (1993, Angels of the Universe) by Einar Már Guðmundsson, translated by Bernard Scudder, which describes the life of a young schizophrenic. An earlier work by Guðmundsson, *Eftirmáli regndropanna* (1986, Epilogue of the Raindrops), is also available in an English translation by Scudder, and his translation of a work by the writer, translator, and critic Guðbergur Bergsson, *Svanurinn* (1991, The Swan), won high praise from such reviewers as Milan Kundera.

Halldór Laxness himself claimed that writers from small language communities (when the Republic was founded in 1944 Icelanders numbered only 125,000; today the population is *c.*270,000) were absolutely dependent upon translators to reach a larger reading public, and thus had to accept, gratefully and unknowingly, practically any offer to transmogrify their texts into some incomprehensible foreign tongue. Obviously, few capable English wordsmiths develop the necessary expertise in such an exotic language as Icelandic and most of the translations have been done, in fact, by Icelanders. And as in most small language communities, translation tends to be mainly in one direction: for every work translated into English in recent decades, some ten were translated from English.

Many of the difficulties inherent in translating into English from a small and in this instance homogeneous language community are caused by the lack of a comparable universality in English-speaking culture. Isolated for centuries geographically and linguistically, practically all Icelanders share a common culture. Quotations from or references to other literary works, religious texts or hymns, popular songs, or even well-known public figures, past and present, evoke a response from Icelanders that is impossible to duplicate in today's English language, where even the two great standard texts, the King James Bible and Shakespeare, can no longer be assumed to be part of the common heritage.   KK

ANTHOLOGIES   Benedikz, Eiríkur, ed., *An Anthology of Icelandic Poetry*, Reykjavik, 1969 · Magnússon, Sigurður A., *The Postwar Poetry of Iceland*, Iowa City, 1982 · Scudder, B., *Brushstrokes of Blue: The Young Poets of Iceland*, London, 1994 · various, *Treasures of Iceland*, Reykjavik (1996).

BERGSSON, GUÐBERGUR   Scudder, B., *The Swan*, London, 1997.

GUÐMUNDSSON, EINAR MÁR   Scudder, B., *Epilogue of the Raindrops*, London, 1994 · *Angels of the Universe*, London, 1995.

GUNNARSSON, GUNNAR   Magnússon, Magnús, *The Black Cliffs*, Madison, Wis., 1967.

LAXNESS, HALLDÓR KILJAN   Lyon, F. H., *Salka Valka* (via Danish), London, 1936 · Magnússon, Magnús, *The Atom Station*, London, 1961 · *Paradise Regained*, London/New York, 1962 · *The Fish Can Sing*, London, 1966 · *World Light*, Madison, Wis., 1969 · *Christianity at Glacier*, Reykjavik, 1972 · Thompson, J. A., *Independent People*, London, 1945.

ÞÓRÐARSON, ÞÓRBERGUR   Chapman, K., *In Search of My Beloved*, New York, 1967.

SIGURÐARDÓTTIR, FRÍÐA   Edwardsen, K., *The Night Watch*, London, 1995.

VILHJÁLMSSON, THOR   Scudder, B., *Justice Undone*, London, 1995

8. NORWEGIAN

In the late 19th c. there was quite a vogue in Britain for translating the literature of Scandinavia; the Romantic interest in folk literature, legend, and saga [II.o.2] had fostered the image of the northern lands as mysterious, exotic regions. Translators emphasized the alien nature of the country, sometimes in archaic renderings, such as R. Nisbet **Bain**'s book of short stories by Jonas Lie from the early 1890s, *Weird Tales from the Northern Seas* (a title invented by Bain). Yet at the same time, other more modern writing by socially conscious writers such as Henrik Ibsen [II.o.9] and his equally famous contemporary Bjørnstjerne Bjørnson was beginning to make its way abroad; quite a number of Bjørnson's novels and plays were translated around the turn of the century.

i. Hamsun The most important writer to come out of Norway at the end of the 19th c. after Ibsen was Knut Hamsun, whose novels from the 1890s, with their fey, quixotic heroes and evocation of 'the unconscious life of the soul' were among the early masterpieces of modernism. Although his importance was early recognized in Germany, Hamsun did not fare well in English translation; only one of his major novels, *Sult* (1890, Hunger), appeared in English before World War I. It was only after the award of a Nobel Prize in 1920 that he was really introduced in English—unfortunately through the medium of his most recent novel, *Markens Grøde* (1917, Growth of the Soil), his most read and least characteristic work, a misguided attempt to provide a template for his ideal of Natural Man. The history of Hamsun translation since then has been uneven. Many of his novels were translated in the 1930s, but some of the best, like *Mysterier* (1892, Mysteries), are still waiting for an adequate translation. Other more modern versions, however, do give a flavour of the true Hamsun; translations by Oliver and Gunnvor **Stallybrass**, kept in print by Souvenir Press, of novels like *Victoria* (1898), *Under høststjærnen* (1906, Under the Autumn Star), and *Konerne ved vandposten* (1920, The Women at the Pump) are carefully crafted, accurate renderings. James **McFarlane**'s inspired translation of *Pan* (1894) captures the haunting poetry of the novel, the wildness and sweetness of its tone, in a version as near perfection as one can hope to come.

Hunger provides an instructive example of the fate of Hamsun in English. It has been translated three times, by George **Egerton** in 1899, by Robert **Bly** in 1967, and by Sverre **Lyngstad** in 1996. George Egerton is a pseudonym for the Irish writer Mary Chavelita Dunne (1859–1954), whose enthusiasm was for Hamsun the man as much as for Hamsun the writer—she seems literally to have fallen in love with him. Her version is fairly correct as far as it goes, but is unfaithful to the original because she, in common with many other Victorian translators of Scandinavian literature, felt it incumbent on her to censor the sexual content. She has taken out all scenes which contain anything more erotic than a kiss, and thus the central scene of the hero's pathetic failure as a seducer of his dream-lover Ylajali is gone. Robert Bly is unfaithful to the original in a different way, producing a text full of gross mistranslations and distortions of tone and style. Sverre Lyngstad's new American translation is the first one which can be called both complete and accurate; and in an entertaining introduction he examines the shortcomings of the other two and takes Robert Bly's translation apart. This is an example of a part of the seduction scene passed over in silence by Egerton, where the hero is baffled by the mixture of resistance and teasing he encounters, and also afraid that he might be impotent:

'Oh, you little fox!' I burst out. *'All right, you'll see then.'* And I threw my arms firmly around her shoulders. *Girl at a distance, beware!* So she took me for an inexperienced boy. By the Lord, she would change her tune . . . No one should say about me that I couldn't keep up in *this* game. *By the living Jesus*, if all I had to do was to stay with it . . . *As though there were anything in this world I couldn't do!*

(Bly)

'Well, I never!' I blurted out. 'Just you wait and see!' And I flung my arms lustily around her shoulders. Was the girl out of her mind? Did she take me for a complete greenhorn? Haw-haw, wouldn't I, though, by the living . . . No one should say about me that I was backward on that score. What a little devil! If it was just a matter of pushing on, then . . . As though I was good for much of anything!

(Lyngstad)

The italicized sentences of Bly's translation are simply wrong; the last one contrives to mean the exact opposite of Hamsun's text. With such translations, it is little wonder Hamsun has had such a hard time of it in English.

ii. Nineteenth- and Twentieth-Century Fiction

19th-c. women writers have had to wait even longer for translation. It is only in recent years, with the modern women's movement, that their works have received belated recognition in English. Camilla Collett wrote the first major Norwegian novel, *Amtmandens døtre* (1854–5, The District Governor's Daughters), a study of rural society reminiscent of Jane Austen, but more despairing; it was not translated into English until 1992. Amalie Skram had to wait nearly as long; it was the 1980s before translations of her novels, based on her own anguished experiences of the double standard of sexual morality which sold inexperienced young girls into marriage, were published in English. *Constance Ring* (1885) and *Forrådt* (1892, Betrayal) appeared in English in the 1980s, followed by Skram's study of a woman artist driven to the brink of madness by the conflicting demands of art and family life, and then incarcerated in an asylum, *Professor Hieronymus | På St. Jørgen* (1895, Under Observation). When they did finally appear, at least, the translations did justice to the merits of the original, thanks largely to the efforts of two talented American translators, Katherine **Hanson** and Judith **Messick**.

Early 20th-c. Norwegian writers are not well represented in English; it must be admitted that it was not a rich literary period. Sigrid Undset is one exception. She became well known abroad partly as a result of being awarded the Nobel Prize in 1928, and many of her books were translated during the 1930s. Arthur G. **Chater** was responsible for the translations of ten of her novels, and her major trilogy, *Kristin Lavransdatter* (1920–2), was translated in 1930 by Charles **Archer** and J. S. **Scott**. The trilogy is an immensely popular historical epic about a young girl in medieval Norway torn between human and divine love, between pagan sensuality and Christian renunciation. The translation is competent and has been frequently reprinted, but with its deliberate archaisms it sounds a little quaint to the modern ear; the text would be better served by a new modern translation.

Elizabeth **Rokkan** is a translator who has done much for 20th-c. Norwegian writers, in particular Cora Sandel and Tarjei Vesaas. Cora Sandel, a novelist and short-story writer, had particular success with her trilogy about a young girl from the frozen north who joins the colony of Scandinavian artists in Paris, and her slow struggle towards becoming a writer: *Alberte og Jakob* (1926, Alberta and Jacob), *Alberte og friheten* (1931, Alberta and Freedom), *Bare Alberte* (1939, Alberta Alone). Elizabeth Rokkan's translations from the 1960s convey the intense impressions of cold and hunger, light and warmth with a sure touch which captures the immediacy of the original. Tarjei Vesaas, a challenge to any translator with his deceptively simple stories of everyday life, written in a hauntingly poetic language which subtly evokes psychological complexities, also found a sensitive mediator in Rokkan's translations of novels like *Det store spelet* (1934, The Great Cycle), *Huset i mørkret* (1945, The House in the Dark), *Isslottet* (1963, The Ice Palace), *Bruene* (1966, The Bridges), and his dreamlike, partly autobiographical last work, *Båten om kvelden* (1972, The Boat in the Evening).

In recent years there have been more translations of Norwegian writers, both classical and contemporary, due largely to the efforts of small presses such as Peter Owen and Norvik Press in England and Seal Press, Fjord Press, and Dufour Editions in the USA. The iconoclast and humanist Jens Bjørneboe's tortured studies of man's inhumanity and obstinate defiance have awoken an answering chord particularly in the USA, with works like *Frihetens øyeblikk* (1966, Moment of Freedom) and *Haiene* (1974, The Sharks). Several of Knut Faldbakken's novels about the complications of sexuality, and especially the problems of men in a postfeminist age, have been translated, achieving at times a *succès de scandale* with their explicit erotic content (e.g. *Maude danser* (1971, The Sleeping Prince), *Insektsommer* (1972, Insect Summer), *Adams dagbok* (1978, Adam's Diary), *Bryllupsreisen* (1981, The Honeymoon)). Bjørg Vik's short stories of women's lives of quiet desperation or awakening protest have been well received (e.g. *Kvinneakvariet*, 1972, The Aquarium of Women). Gerd Brantenberg's hilarious parody *Egalias døtre* (1977, The Daughters of Egalia), set in a matriarchal society where men wear skirts, and written in a 'female tongue' which reinvents the language, found in Louis **Mackay** a translator equal (with the author's help) to the linguistic challenge and became a bestseller in English. Even more successful was an unlikely introduction to philosophy in fictionalized form, Jostein Gaarder's *Sofies verden* (1995, Sophie's World). Generally speaking, these translations are faithful to the tone and the spirit of these widely differing authors; taken together, they present an illuminating cross-section of the range of modern Norwegian writing.

iii. Poetry and Drama

Poetry and plays, as might be expected, have had more difficulty than novels in crossing the linguistic boundaries into English.

Ibsen still dominates the English-speaking world as far as Norwegian drama is concerned (as he does the Norwegian stage). More modern dramatists have been very sporadically translated, often in small-stage versions which have not been published in book form. A sample of contemporary dramatic writing is provided in *New Norwegian Plays* (1989), with experimental writing like Edvard Hoem's *God natt, Europa* (1982, Good Night, Europe), a Brechtian exploration of a politician's coming to terms with past evasions, and Cecilie Løveid's *Måkespisere* (1983, Seagull Eaters). The latter translation uses a lively, sometimes racy American idiom to capture the rapid exchanges and shifts of mood in Løveid's story of a young girl's aspirations to be a great actress and her exploitation by a greedy profiteer, against a tapestry of quotations from Norway's Mrs Beeton on how to truss and cook a goose.

Two translations of modern Norwegian poets are worthy of note: those of the two recently deceased 'grand old men' of Norwegian poetry, Rolf Jacobsen and Olav H. Hauge. A selection of Jacobsen's poetry has been translated by Roger **Greenwald** as *The Silence Afterwards*; a poet translating another poet, Greenwald has provided a creative rendering which at times eschews literal accuracy for a version which, by being slightly freer, brings the experience closer to the foreign reader. Hauge, himself a fine translator of poetry into Norwegian, has also had the benefit of another poet's talent in English, when Robin **Fulton**, together with James **Greene**, translated a selection of his poetry called *Don't Give Me the Whole Truth*. The anthology takes its title from a typical Hauge poem:

Don't give me the whole truth,
don't give me the sea for my thirst,
don't give me the sky when I ask for light,
but give me a glint, a dewy wisp, a mote
as the birds bear water-drops from their bathing
and the wind a grain of salt.

Hauge's poems are written in his native western Norwegian dialect, conveying by their very word forms both an earthiness and a down-to-earth acceptance of the cycle of life which standard English cannot transmit in the same way; yet this translation, with its simple, concrete vocabulary, repetition, and straightforward syntax, is as close as one can hope to get to the deceptive simplicity of the original.   JMG

ANTHOLOGIES   Allwood, Martin, ed., *Modern Scandinavian Poetry 1900–1975*, Mullsjö, Sweden, 1982 · Hanson, Katherine, ed., *An Everyday Story: Norwegian Women's Fiction*, Seattle, 1984 · Garton, Janet, ed., *Contemporary Norwegian Women's Writing*, Norwich, 1995 · Garton, Janet, and Sehmsdorf, Henning, *New Norwegian Plays*,

Norwich, 1989 · McFarlane, James, and Garton, Janet, *Slaves of Love and Other Norwegian Short Stories*, Oxford, 1982.

BJØRNEBOE, JENS   Murer, Esther Greenleaf, *Moment of Freedom*, New York, 1975 · *The Sharks*, Norwich, 1992.

BRANTENBERG, GERD   Mackay, Louis, and Brantenberg, Gerd, *The Daughters of Egalia*, London/New York, 1985.

COLLETT, CAMILLA   Seaver, Kirsten, *The District Governor's Daughters*, Norwich, 1992.

FALDBAKKEN, KNUT   Garton, Janet, *The Sleeping Prince*, London, 1988 · Lyngstad, Sverre, *Adam's Diary*, London, 1989 · Myhre, Liv, *The Honeymoon*, New York, 1987 · Sutcliffe, Hal and Støverud, Torbjørn, *Insect Summer*, London, 1991.

GAARDER, JOSTEIN   Møller, Paulette, *Sophie's World*, London, 1995.

HAMSUN, KNUT   Bly, Robert, *Hunger*, New York, 1967 · Bothmer, Gerry, *Mysteries*, New York, 1971 · Egerton, George, *Hunger*, London, 1899 · Lyngstad, Sverre, *Hunger*, Edinburgh, 1996 · McFarlane, James, *Pan*, London, 1955 · Stallybrass, Oliver, *Victoria*, New York, 1969 · Stallybrass, Oliver, and Stallybrass, Gunnvor, *The Wanderer (Under the Autumn Star* and *On Muted Strings)*, New York, 1975 · *The Women at the Pump*, New York, 1978 · Worster, W. W., *Growth of the Soil*, London, 1920.

HAUGE, OLAV H.   Fulton, Robin, and Greene, James, with Siv Hennum, *Don't Give Me the Whole Truth*, London, 1985.

JACOBSEN, ROLF   Greenwald, Roger, *The Silence Afterwards*, Princeton, NJ, 1981.

LIE, JONAS   Morton, Brian, and Trevor, Richard, *The Seer and Other Stories*, London, 1990 · Nisbet Bain, R., *Weird Tales from the Northern Seas*, New York, 1893, 1969.

SANDEL, CORA   Rokkan, Elizabeth, *Alberta and Jacob*, London, 1962; rep. 1980 · *Alberta and Freedom*, London, 1963; rep. 1980 · *Alberta Alone*, London, 1965; rep. 1980 · Wilson, Barbara, *Selected Short Stories*, Seattle, 1985.

SKRAM, AMALIE   Hanson, Katherine, and Messick, Judith, *Constance Ring*, Seattle, 1988 · *Under Observation*, Seattle, 1992 · Hennes, Aileen, *Betrayal*, London, 1986.

UNDSET, SIGRID   Archer, Charles, and Scott, J. S., *Kristin Lavransdatter*, London, 1930; rep. 1969, 1977 · Chater, Arthur G., *The Master of Hestviken*, New York, 1928–30; rep. 1962 · *The Wild Orchid*, London, 1931 · *The Burning Bush*, New York, 1932 · *Ida Elisabeth*, New York, 1933 · *The Longest Years*, New York, 1935; rep. 1971 · *Gunnar's Daughter*, London, 1936 · *The Faithful Wife*, London, 1937 · *Images in a Mirror*, New York, 1938 · *Madam Dorothea*, London, 1941 · Emme, William, *Jenny*, New York, 1920; rep. 1974.

VESAAS, TARJEI   · Rokkan, Elizabeth, *The Ice Palace*, London, 1966 · *The Great Cycle*, Madison, Wis., 1967 · *The Bridges*, London, 1969 · *The Boat in the Evening*, London, 1972 · *The House in the Dark*, London, 1976 · Støverud, Torbjørn, and Barnes, Michael, *The Birds*, London, 1968.

VIK, BJØRG   Garton, Janet, *An Aquarium of Women*, Norwich, 1987 · McDuff, David, and Browne, Patrick, *Out of Season and Other Stories*, London, 1983.

SEE ALSO   Garton, J., *Norwegian Women's Writing 1850–1990*, Norwich, 1993 · McFarlane, J. W., *Ibsen and the Temper of Norwegian Literature*, London, 1960 · Naess, H., *A History of Norwegian Literature*, Lincoln, Neb., 1993.

9. IBSEN

The impact of Henrik Ibsen on the English theatre was explosive. After a few unremarkable bowdlerized productions in the 1880s, the first unabridged translation of an Ibsen play, *Et dukkehjem* (1879, A Doll's House), was staged at the Novelty Theatre in 1889 in William **Archer**'s translation. Audiences approved; critics, in the main, dismissed the play as dreary, morbid, immoral. Things were to get worse two years later, when Archer's translation of *Gengangere* (1881, Ghosts) was performed at the Royalty, provoking an outpouring of critical venom ('absolutely loathsome and fetid') which has scarcely been surpassed. It was not many years, however, before Ibsen became respectable, and critics and audiences alike were positive, if sometimes puzzled, in their reaction. Since that time his supremacy as a dramatist in both Britain and America has been so assured that he is often regarded as an English-language author; there can be no week

in which an Ibsen play is not being staged somewhere in English.

The drama critic William Archer (1856–1924) was the pioneer of English translations and performances of Ibsen; his grandparents had settled in Norway and he had grown up bilingual. He discovered Ibsen's work in 1873 and soon began to translate it, at first with more enthusiasm than success. But he persevered, contacted and visited Ibsen on several occasions to discuss his work, and it was mainly his translations which were staged in London around the turn of the century. They were accurate and painstaking. They were also the first published translations; in 1888 he published a volume of three plays translated by himself and Eleanor Marx-**Aveling** [I.a.5.i], and in 1890–1 an authorized English edition in five volumes. Edmund Gosse, another early champion, published the first review of Ibsen's work in

English—an article on the poems—as early as 1872. Gosse edited an overlapping three-volume edition of translations of the plays in 1890, which was followed by Archer's authoritative copyright edition in 1906–12, in 12 volumes. These workmanlike translations of the complete plays (with the exception of some minor early dramas) were the most frequently performed during the first half of the 20th c. From 1910 onwards the Everyman editions began to appear, largely the painstaking work of R. Farquharson **Sharp**. Penguin began to publish new translations in the 1950s by Peter **Watts** and Una **Ellis-Fermor**, the former somewhat stilted, the latter more readable if rather cautious renditions.

In more recent years, there have been two major new retranslations of Ibsen's plays. Michael **Meyer** began publishing the major plays in English in 1960. His versions are lively and colloquial, popular with actors because the lines lend themselves to being spoken on stage; they have been the most frequently used in British productions since. In 1960–77 James **McFarlane** edited and largely translated *The Oxford Ibsen*, the most comprehensive version of Ibsen's works available, which provides an annotated scholarly translation of all Ibsen's plays, including the little-known early ones, and in addition translations of the early drafts of the plays and many of Ibsen's sources, as well as a wealth of background material. In American English, the most successful versions from the same period have been those by Rolf **Fjelde**, published from 1965 onwards.

The translation history of a couple of the plays will provide more specific examples. *A Doll's House* is probably Ibsen's most frequently performed play. Adaptations of it were performed in England and America in the 1880s, but the first printed translation was assayed by a Dane, T. **Weber**, and published in Copenhagen in 1880. It remains today a delightful example of the English which can be produced by a non-native with a dictionary:

You have loved me like a wife ought to love her husband. You wanted but thorough knowledge to form a judgement of the expedients . . . I was no man if this feminine helplessness did not just make you much more attractive in my eyes. You must not take to heart the angry words I told you in the first consternation as I thought that all would fall over me.

Archer's translation, however, has scarcely been bettered:

You loved me as a wife should love her husband. It was only the means that, in your experience, you misjudged

. . . I should be no true man if this very womanly helplessness did not make you doubly dear in my eyes. You mustn't dwell upon the hard things I said in my first moment of terror, when the world seemed to be tumbling about my ears.

The Meyer and McFarlane translations provide only slight modifications to Archer's, McFarlane's being at times more explanatory: 'It was simply that you didn't have the experience to judge what was the best way of going about things . . .' Fjelde's Americanized version, on the other hand, produces a more concise, snappier dialogue:

You loved me the way a wife ought to love her husband. It's simply the means that you couldn't judge . . . I wouldn't be a man if this feminine helplessness didn't make you twice as attractive to me. You mustn't mind those sharp words I said—that was all in the first confusion of thinking my world had collapsed.

Ibsen wrote his poetic drama *Peer Gynt* in 1867, some time before *A Doll's House*, but it took longer for the former to be either published or performed in English. The first English translation was by Charles and William Archer, published in 1892, and the first performances in English were in New York in 1906 and Edinburgh in 1908. Difficult as Ibsen's deceptively simple prose dialogue could be for a translator, this play seems to pose insuperable problems, being composed in a tightly knit, intricately rhymed verse which speeds along at breakneck pace. Peer's description of his ride on the buck's back, for example, is a *tour de force* of verve and dash at which most translators have stumbled.

Charles and William Archer have again produced a convincing translation, which amply conveys the meaning and retains much of the speed and rhythm, though sacrificing the rhyme:

> Have you ever
> chanced to see the Gendin-Edge?
> Nigh on four miles long it stretches
> sharp before you like a scythe.

Michael Meyer's version, though it moves at quite a pace, is a prose rather than a poetic rendering:

> Have you seen the Gjendin edge?
> Three miles long and sharp as a scythe.
> Down over glacier, slide and cliff,
> Straight down over sheer grey scree . . .

The version in *The Oxford Ibsen*, which is a collaboration between Johan **Fillinger**, who provided a literal translation, and Christopher **Fry**, who dressed it in poetic garb, is a lyrical rendering, but tends to sacrifice both speed and completeness:

Have you seen
That Gjendin ridge? It cuts along
With an edge like a scythe for miles and miles.

Rolf Fjelde's American translation is rhythmic and quite fast-moving, at the price of a certain awkwardness of expression and occasional distortions of language:

Have you
Seen the Gendin edge? So lightly
Like a scythe, straight on it stretches,
Stretches on for nigh four miles.

The only English translation to make a determined attempt to reproduce not only the sense and the movement but also the complicated internal and end-rhyme scheme of the original is a recent one by John **Northam**, who has also produced a fine version of Ibsen's poetry:

Have you seen or
been on Gjendin ridge before?
Two miles long, perhaps, or more,
stretching like a scythe's sharp blade.
Down past glacier, slope and slide
you could see where grey screes made
mirrors of the tarns that cower
black and heavy, some thirteen or
fourteen hundred metres lower.

Northam's translation is the one in English which best conveys the whole, though even he has on occasion made slight adaptations to accommodate the demands of the verse form. The English language does not lend itself so readily to rattling along; the reader must turn to a translation into a more cognate language such as German, and read Christian Morgenstern's version, published in the *Sämtliche Werke in deutscher Sprache* edited by Georg Brandes, Julius Elias, and Paul Schlenther in 1898–1903, to get the fullest impression of the richness and bounding exuberance of the verse.

On the whole, however, Ibsen has been well served by his English translators, who have made him at home on the stages of the English-speaking world to the extent that British dramatists from George Bernard Shaw onwards have regarded him as one of their own; and he came very early to seem a part of the native repertoire. So many translations now exist that new versions are not infrequently produced by 'translators' who know not a word of Norwegian, but have cut and pasted the efforts of those who do. Yet it is at the time of writing a generation since the 'definitive' McFarlane and Meyer translations were published. With each new generation, theatres feel the need for a new, contemporary version; McFarlane now seems not colloquial enough, Meyer not modern enough in his references. Ibsen's plays, like Shakespeare's, seem impervious to the passing of time, but the translations of them do not.   JMG

TRANSLATIONS   Archer, William, ed., *Ibsen's Prose Dramas*, 5 vols. London, 1890–91 [translation by William Archer, Charles Archer, and Mrs. F. E. Archer] · *The Collected Works of Henrik Ibsen*, 12 vols. London, 1906–12 [translations by William Archer and others] · Archer, William, and Marx-Aveling, Eleanor, *The Pillars of Society, and Other Plays* [*The Pillars of Society; Ghosts; An Enemy of Society*], London, 1888 · Ellis-Fermor, Una, *Hedda Gabler, and Other Plays* [*The Pillars of the Community; The Wild Duck*], Harmondsworth, 1950, 1961 [Penguin] · *The Master Builder, and Other Plays* [*Rosmersholm; Little Eyolf; John Gabriel Borkman*], Harmondsworth, 1958 [Penguin] · Farquharson Sharp, R., and Marx-Aveling, E., *A Doll's House; The Wild Duck; The Lady from the Sea*, London, 1910, 1958 [Everyman] · *Ghosts; The Warriors at Helgeland; An Enemy of the People*, London, 1911, 1969 [Everyman] · *The Pretenders; Pillars of Society; Rosmersholm*, London, 1913, 1960 [Everyman] · *Peer Gynt*, London, 1921 [Everyman] · Fjelde, Rolf, *Peer Gynt*, New York, 1965. [Signet] · *Four Major Plays, i* [*A Doll House; The Wild Duck; Hedda Gabler; The Master Builder*], New York, 1965 [Signet] · *Four Major Plays, ii* [*Ghosts; An Enemy of the People; The Lady from the Sea; John Gabriel Borkman*], New York, 1970 [Signet] · Le Gallienne, Eva, *Six Plays by Ibsen* [*A Doll's House; Ghosts; An Enemy of the People; Rosmersholm; Hedda Gabler; The Master Builder*], New York, 1957 · Le Gallienne, Eva, and Ginsbury, Norman, *Hedda Gabler; The Master Builder; John Gabriel Borkman*, London, 1966 · Gosse, Edmund, ed., *The Prose Dramas of Henrik Ibsen*, 3 vols. New York/London, 1890 · McFarlane, James, ed., *The Oxford Ibsen*, 8 vols., Oxford/London/New York, 1960–77 [many of the trs. are by McFarlane; several vols. in World's Classics] · Meyer, Michael, *The Plays of Ibsen*, London, 1960– · Northam, John, *Ibsen's Poems*, Oslo, 1986 · *Peer Gynt*, Oslo, 1993, Oxford, 1995 · Orbeck, Anders, *Early Plays* [*Cataline; The Warrior's Barrow; Olaf Liljekrans*], New York, 1921 · Sprinchorn, Evert, ed., *Ibsen: Letters and Speeches*, New York, 1964 · Watts, Peter, *Ghosts, and Other Plays* [*A Public Enemy; When We Dead Wake*], Harmondsworth, 1964 [Penguin] · *A Doll's House, and Other Plays* [*The League of Youth; The Lady from the Sea*], Harmondsworth, 1965 [Penguin] · Watts, Peter, *Peer Gynt*, Harmondsworth, 1966 [Penguin].

SEE ALSO   Egan, M., *Ibsen: The Critical Heritage*, London, 1972 · McFarlane, J., *The Cambridge Companion to Ibsen*, Cambridge, 1994.

10. SWEDISH

i. Eighteenth and Nineteenth Century The 18th c. witnessed the appearance of the work of two eminent Swedish writers in English translation. Emanuel Swedenborg was a scientist turned mystic, whose writing was to influence William Blake as well as W. B. Yeats, and Carl von Linné or Linnaeus, originator of the classificatory system of plants, was also a travel writer of repute. Their writing, however, was to a large extent in Latin.

Translation of literary works originating in Swedish, on the other hand, seems to have started in earnest with the poems of Esaias Tegnér, the towering figure of the next generation of writers. In 1835 Henry Wadsworth **Longfellow** spent the summer in Sweden, which resulted, two years later, in an enthusiastic essay in the *North American Review* (July 1837) on Tegnér's heroic poem *Frithiof's Saga* (1825), the first public notice of Swedish literature in the English-speaking world. Longfellow's translation of selected passages in the original metres included in the essay met with the unreserved approval of the author—'the only attempts', Longfellow wrote in a letter to a friend, 'that have fully satisfied him'. Longfellow also translated *Nattvardsbarnen* (1820, The Children of the Lord's Supper), Tegnér's portrayal of Swedish peasant life which is included in *Ballads and Other Poems* (1842). Applying his customary word-for-word approach, Longfellow's translation is, in his own words, 'literal, perhaps to a fault'. *Axel* (1821), a Byronic love poem, also attracted considerable attention and is found in more than a dozen English translations. One of the best, a version dated 1866 by A. **Dobree**, British consul in Gothenburg, is faithful in reproduction not only of the metre but also of the rhymes of the original. Other attempts, however, appear to have been less successful. 'So far as I can see', Tegnér wrote to a friend about an unsigned translation that appeared in *Blackwood's Edinburgh Magazine* (February 1826), 'it is only a paraphrase and leaves little of the original except the fable—which, by the way, is not the strongest part of the piece.'

By the mid-19th c., however, the most widely read Swedish writer in English translation was Fredrika Bremer, often referred to as Sweden's Charlotte Brontë. Her translator, Mary **Howitt**, translated in all 14 of Bremer's books including *Hemmen i den nya verlden*, (1853, Homes of the New World), which when it first appeared, simultaneously in Sweden, the United States, and England,

did not meet with critical acclaim. At the time, Bremer laid the blame for the mixed reception of the work on the quality of the translation.

More recently, however, voices have been raised in defence of Howitt, who, it now emerges, had been expected to act not only as a translator but also as the author's 'criticizing friend', editing her often forthright observations of her visit to the American continent. More modern English renderings of Bremer's work includes *Familjen* ✳✳✳ (1830–1), in Sara **Death**'s fluent and accurate translation, *The Colonel's Family*.

Interest in Fredrika Bremer seems to have attracted attention in the English-speaking world to another Swedish woman writer. The daughter of a sea captain, Emilie Flygare-Carlén wrote gripping yarns of the sea-faring inhabitants of the Swedish west coast, enjoying a following throughout the 20th c. Amongst translated works is an unsigned but excellent, at times shortened and edited version of *Rosen på tistelön* (1842, The Rose of Tistelön) with a translator's preface commenting on the Swedish geographical setting. In literary standing, however, the writing of Flygare-Carlén could not be compared to that of C. J. L. Almquist, initiator of a new Swedish literary genre of social realism, whose work has only sparingly been translated into English, evidence that selection for translation does not necessarily reflect literary merit.

ii. Twentieth Century The works of Selma Lagerlöf, a storyteller par excellence and the 1909 recipient of the Nobel Prize for Literature, were early contenders for translation into English, a large number of her books being translated by Velma S. **Howard**. Most translations at the time, however, failed to capture her narrative talent. With *Gösta Berlings saga* (1891), her first novel, she revolutionized Swedish narrative fiction. Pauline Bancroft **Flack**'s translation, *The Story of Gösta Berling*, however, turns Lagerlöf's gripping story into a somewhat flat-footed, melodramatic tale. Other, more recent English versions of Lagerlöf's Värmland tales have been more successful, such as *The Löwensköld Ring*, Linda **Schenck**'s translation of *Löwensköldska ringen* (1925).

Another Swedish writer of the early 20th c., equally rooted in his local milieu, is Hjalmar Söderberg, the atmospheric verbal portrayer of Stockholm. His astute observations on the human condition are, however, universal and the failure of his writing to attract greater attention amongst

English readers may well be due to reasons related to translation. Although the masterly craftmanship of *Historietter* (1898) is still evident, *Short Stories*, Carl **Lofmark**'s translation fails to capture much of the gentle irony and the lightness of touch of the original.

One of the new voices to emerge in Sweden in the 1940s was that of Stig Dagerman, who, following his premature death in 1954 at the age of 31, rapidly became something of a legend. Interest in Dagerman's writing has more recently been revived. His first, hotly debated novel, *Ormen* (1945), giving voice to the angst of a war-weary generation, has been translated into English by Laurie **Thompson**, editor of the *Swedish Book Review*, the main forum for Swedish literature in English translation. Thompson's translation, *The Snake*, is precise yet keenly interpretative of the source text, and the result is an engaging prose style closely, if not completely, reflecting Dagerman's linguistic brilliance.

The first half of the 20th c. saw the emergence of some key literary figures including Pär Lagerkvist, Harry Martinson, and Eyvind Johnson, all recipients of the Nobel Prize for Literature, and poets such as Nils Ferlin and Hjalmar Gullberg. Much of their work, however, may be too deeply rooted in Swedish language and culture to allow easy transfer into English and, although some of it is available in translation, the spirit of the original has not always proved easy to capture.

Swedish writers of the period who have succeeded in reaching a greater number of readers in English translation have often been proponents of the historic, epic tradition. One of the most popular is Vilhelm Moberg, an agricultural worker turned writer. His account of the life of the Swedish settlers in North America, starting with *Utvandrarna* (1951, The Emigrants), has been rendered into English in a close translation by Gustaf **Lannestock**. Another epic, often quoted as a contributing factor to the revival of international interest in the Viking Age, is *Röde Orm* (1941–5) by Frans G. Bengtsson. 'The author can invent behaviour which fits in with the great Sagas', proclaimed the *Times Literary Supplement*, joining in the praise of the translation, *The Long Ships*, by Michael **Meyer**.

Amongst 20th-c. poets, the work of Gunnar Ekelöf, often compared to that of T. S. Eliot and a major influence on later Swedish poets, has been rendered into English by a number of translators. Poems from the first two parts of the trilogy written in 1965–6 just before his death, have been translated by Leif **Sjöberg** and W. H. **Auden** as *Selected Poems: Gunnar Ekelöf*, while Rika **Lesser** has translated the

concluding part (1967) as *Guide to the Underworld*. Both translations do justice to the spirit of the original, as does *Modus Vivendi*, selected prose by Ekelöf, edited and translated by Erik **Thygesen**.

The most frequently translated contemporary Swedish poet, however, is Tomas Tranströmer, whose keen observation of nature places him in a Swedish tradition reaching back to Strindberg [II.o.11] and Linnaeus. Robin **Fulton**, translator of Tranströmer's *New Collected Poems*, takes pains to capture accurately the local imagery in this poetry, which he describes as 'sparing with words, yet generous in spirit'.

In August 1976 *Om sju flickor* (1971) by Carl-Johan Seth was staged as *Seven Girls* at the Open Space Theatre in London, the first contemporary Swedish play to be given a professional English-language production. Marginally adapted while retaining Swedish references and local milieu, it was translated by Gunilla **Anderman**, also the translator of several plays by Lars Norén, including *München-Aten* (1983), staged in English translation as *Munich-Athens* at London's Soho-Poly Theatre in 1987. Another contemporary Swedish playwright whose often documentary-based writing regularly appears in English translation following publication in Sweden is P.-O. Enquist, whose *I lodjurets timma* (1988) has been given a close, source-language-oriented translation, *The Hour of the Lynx*, by Ross **Shideler**.

By far the most frequently encountered genre of Swedish literature in English translation is children's literature [I.c.4]. With the appearance of *Pippi Långstrump* (Pippi Longstocking) in 1945, Astrid Lindgren broke away from previous, moralistic traditions of children's stories. In Edna **Hurup**'s translation (1954), however, although it is both idiomatic and accurate, Pippi's puns and neologisms are not infrequently lost. But it is not only Pippi's use of innovative language that seems to lose its edge in translation. Her anti-authoritarian behaviour is also frequently toned down through the use of euphemisms, often replacing matter-of-factness, an overall characteristic not only of the work of Astrid Lindgren but also of books for children by other Swedish writers.

While interest in Astrid Lindgren has drawn attention to more recent Swedish literature for children, books by other contemporary writers of Swedish fiction in English translation appear to attract considerably less interest. As a rule, translations are uncompromisingly source-language-oriented, which, given the lack of familiarity with Swedish culture and traditions, may account for the often less than enthusiastic reception awarded the work of many present-day Swedish writers. Those who have fared better than most include Torgny Lindgren, whose *Till sanningens lov* (1991, In Praise of Truth) was awarded the *Independent*'s prize for best foreign work of the year in Tom **Geddes**'s translation. As in the case of children's literature, the less understated, more direct form of narrative frequently employed by Swedish writers compounds the translator's difficulty, as does their inclination to act as the 'conscience of the world'. The critical reception of *Händelser vid vatten* (1993, Events by the Waterside), a novel by Kerstin Ekman, firmly established as one of Sweden's leading writers in a translation by Joan **Tate**, *Blackwater* (1995), illustrates both factors at work. Reviews expressed astonishment at 'the town people's toxic hatred', noted 'the painstaking philosophizing' and found the environmental concern 'preachy', observations which would suggest that a higher degree of target-language adaptation might go some way towards fuller acceptance. The impression is easily created that for the work of a Swedish writer to attract attention some identifiable characteristic of its country of origin is required, as illustrated by Kerstin Ekman's most recent novel in English translation. First published in Swedish as *De tre små mästarna* (1961, The Three Little Masters), it appeared in English translation by Joan Tate as *Under the Snow* (1977).

It can only be hoped that as cultural divides diminish, interest among English readers in Swedish literature will become sufficiently wide-ranging to include other matters not immediately related to snow and a cold climate.   GA

ANTHOLOGIES   Anderman, Gunilla, ed., *New Swedish Plays*, Norwich, 1992 · Fulton, Robin, *Five Swedish Poets*, Norwich, 1997 · Wästberg, Per, ed., *An Anthology of Modern Swedish Literature*, New York, 1979 · Smith, William Jay, and Sjöberg, Leif, *The Forests of Childhood*, Minneapolis, 1996 · Thompson, Laurie, ed., *Swedish Book Review*, Lampeter, Wales, 1983– .
BENGTSSON, FRANS G.   Meyer, Michael, *The Long Ships*, New York, 1957.
BREMER, FREDRIKA   Death, Sara, *The Colonel's Family*, Norwich, 1997 · Friedländer, E. A. et al., *The Novels of Fredrika Bremer*, 11 vols., London, 1844–9 · Howitt, Mary, *The Homes of the New World*, 3 vols., New York, 1853.
DAGERMAN, STIG   Thompson, Laurie, *The Snake*, London, 1995.
EKELÖF, GUNNAR   Auden, W. H., and Sjöberg, Leif, *Selected Poems*, Harmondsworth, 1971 [Penguin] · Lesser, Rika, *Guide to the Underworld*, Amherst, 1980 · Thygesen, Erik, *Modus Vivendi*, Norwich, 1996.
EKMAN, KERSTIN   Tate, Joan, *Blackwater*, London, 1995 · *Under the Snow*, London, 1997.
ENQUIST, P.-O.   Shideler, Ross, *The Hour of the Lynx*, London, 1992.
LAGERLÖF, SELMA   Flack, P. B., *Gösta Berling's Saga*, London/Cambridge, Mass., 1898 · Howard, Velma S., *The Wonderful Adventures of Nils*, London, 1910 · Schenk, Linda, *The Löwensköld Ring*, Norwich, 1991.
LINDGREN, ASTRID   Harup, Edna, *Pippi Longstocking*, Oxford, 1954.
LINDGREN, TORGNY   Geddes, Tom, *In Praise of Truth*, London, 1994.
MOBERG, VILHELM   Lannestock, Gustaf, *The Emigrants*, New York, 1951.
NORÉN, LARS   Anderman, Gunilla, *Munich–Athens*, in her *New Swedish Plays*, Norwich, 1992.
SÖDERBERG, HJALMAR   Lofmark, Carl, *Short Stories*, Norwich, 1987.
TEGNÉR, ESAIAS   Dobree, A., *Axel*, Gothenburg, 1866 · Longfellow, Henry Wadsworth, *Children of the Lord's Supper*, Cambridge, Mass., 1842.
TRANSTRÖMER, TOMAS   Fulton, Robin, *New Collected Poems*, Newcastle upon Tyne, 1998.

11. STRINDBERG

August Strindberg was first introduced to English readers through the preface to *Fröken Julie* (1888, Miss Julie) in translation by Justin Huntley **McCarthy**, published in the *Gentleman's Magazine* in August 1892. A year later Strindberg, together with his second wife, Frida Uhl, paid a visit to England in an attempt to interest publishers and theatres in his work. It was to take another six years, however, before *Fadern* (1887, The Father) was published in a translation by Nelly **Erichsen**. Staged in London in July 1911, the play attracted notices referring to Strindberg as 'the most pessimistic of all living pes-

simists', a reaction that was to be echoed throughout the English-speaking world in years to come.

In the United States, on the other hand, the reception given to Strindberg was initially more favourable, partly due to the presence of the large number of Scandinavian immigrants who were also among the first to provide translations of his writing. Best-known among early American translators is perhaps Edwin **Björkman**, who between 1912 and 1916 translated 24 of Strindberg's plays, published in a series of five volumes.

Another early American translator whose translations included *Påsk* (1900) and *Sagor* (1903), published together as *Easter and Stories* (1912), was Velma S. **Howard**. Although she was praised for her 'light, tender touch', an examination of her translation of *Ett halvt ark papper, Half a Sheet of Paper*, reveals an almost word-for-word rendering of Strindberg's short story, conveying little of the original verbal mastery.

Following Strindberg's death in 1912, the English market was flooded with translations of his works. Many of these translations, however, were based not on the Swedish original but on translations into other languages. It is known, for instance, that Claud **Field**'s translation of Strindberg's prose works, including the four-volume autobiographical *Tjänstekvinnans son* (1886–1909, Son of a Servant), was based on German versions, as were Ellie **Schleussner**'s translations of some of the novels such as *Röda rummet* (1879, The Red Room), Strindberg's observations of Stockholm life in the 1870s. Unfortunately, the translations by Emil Schering, Strindberg's devoted German translator, were often less than perfect in their interpretation of the source text and their frequent failure to recreate Strindberg's highly personal use of style and syntax.

Around the time of the centenary of Strindberg's birth in 1949, however, many of the early translations were out of print and updated versions began to appear. In America, the Swedish-born actor Arvid **Paulson** turned his attention to Strindberg and, between 1959 and 1978, translated a large number of his works, adding and rearranging stage directions to conform to American stage custom. Other translations were often the work of scholars, such as Elizabeth **Sprigge**, who completed her biographical work on Strindberg by translating many of his dramas into fluent and accurate English. Several American scholars also combined studies of Strindberg's *œuvre* with translations of his works. A major contribution was made by Walter **Johnson**. From 1955 until his death in 1983, Johnson translated a large body of Strindberg's work, including his historical plays such as *Mäster Olof* (prose edition 1872), *Gustav Vasa* (1899), and *Erik XIV* (1899). Together the three plays in translation, rendered in perhaps more aca-

demic than 'performable' American English, form the Vasa Trilogy. Strindberg's undisputed importance in the development of modern drama also attracted the attention of American scholars with an interest in theatre such as Harry G. **Carlson**, whose *Strindberg and the Poetry of Myth* (1982) was accompanied by *Strindberg: Five Plays*. This was followed in 1986 by a selection of plays from the pre- and post-*Inferno* periods translated by Evert **Sprinchorn**, author of *Strindberg as Dramatist* (1982).

In England, interest in Strindberg as a playwright has been shared by Michael **Meyer**, whose highly 'actable' translations of some of Strindberg's major plays appeared in two volumes, preceding his voluminous *Strindberg: A Biography* (1985).

The problems facing the translator of Strindberg are linguistic as well as socio-cultural. Strindberg is an acknowledged innovator in his use of the Swedish language, and the price of a fluent English translation is often a watered-down version of his sometimes quirky mode of expression. A further linguistic obstacle for present-day translators is the familiarity required with the language usage of the day. In a comparative study of different translations of *Spöksonaten* (1907, The Ghost Sonata), Egil Törnqvist has pointed to source-text misinterpretations in all existing English translations resulting from insufficient familiarity with Swedish language usage or prevailing customs at the time. More recent translations by Eivor **Martinus** (e.g. *The Chamber Plays*) have helped to redress the situation on both counts, as have Mary **Sandbach**'s terse, precise English translations of some of Strindberg's prose works such as *Giftas* (1884–6, Getting Married) and *Inferno* (1897) and *Ur en ockult dagbok* (1977, From an Occult Diary). Also available now in English translation, providing detailed information about Strindberg's life and the world in which he lived, is a collection of his letters translated and edited by Michael **Robinson**. These more recent efforts may go some way towards vindicating the view that what the English-speaking world tends to see as flaws in Strindberg, widely acknowledged to be Sweden's greatest writer, may in fact be problems in translation. GA

TRANSLATIONS Björkman, Edwin, *Plays by August Strindberg*, 5 vols., New York, 1912–16 · Carlson, Harry G., *Five Plays*, Berkeley, Calif., 1981 · Erichsen, N., *The Father*, London, 1899 · Field, Claud, *The Son of a Servant*, London, 1913 · Howard, Velma S., *Easter and Stories*, Cincinnati, 1912 · Johnson, Walter, *The Vasa Trilogy*, Seattle, 1959 · Martinus, Eivor, *The Chamber Plays*, Bath, 1991 · Meyer, Michael, *The Plays*, 2 vols., London, 1964, 1975 · Paulson, Arvid, *Seven Plays by August Strindberg*, New York, 1960 · *Eight Expressionist Plays*, Toronto, 1965 · Robinson, Michael, *Strindberg's Letters*, 2 vols., London, 1992 · Sandbach, Mary, *Getting Married*, London, 1972 · *Inferno* and *From an Occult Diary*, Harmondsworth, 1979 [Penguin] · Sprigge, Elizabeth, *Six Plays of Strindberg*, Garden City, NY, 1955 · *Five Plays of Strindberg*, Garden City, NY, 1960 · Sprinchorn, Evert, *Selected Plays*, 2 vols., Minneapolis, 1986.

SEE ALSO Törnqvist, E., *Strindbergian Drama: Themes and Structures*, Atlantic Highlands, NJ, 1982.

p. Russian

1. INTRODUCTION

Donald Davie described the 'awakening of the Anglo-Saxon people to Russian literature' as 'a turning point no less momentous than the discovery of Italian literature by the generations of the English Renaissance'. This awakening took place between 1880 and 1920; the new craze for Russian literature was fed by translations of the great prose writers, first Turgenev, then Tolstoy, Dostoevsky, and Chekhov, all of them translated by Constance **Garnett** (1861–1946), who virtually single-handed, in some 80 well-written volumes, established both the essential Russian canon for English-speakers and what remained for much of the century the accepted manner of conveying it to readers who mostly know no Russian.

Another major moment in the discovery of Russian literature was the publication in 1902–3 of Leo **Wiener**'s two-volume *Anthology of Russian Literature*, with prose translations by the editor and verse by various hands. The first of these volumes is devoted to writing produced before 1800, with 200 pages on medieval literature. Nearly a century before, however, John **Bowring** (1792–1872) [see II.e.3.ii] had stated in his pioneering *Specimens of the Russian Poets* that Russia had recently 'emerged, as it were instantaneously, from a night of ignorance'. This ignorance was in the eye of the beholder, since the history of Russian literature stretches back over most of a millennium. Even so, for most foreign readers it is still confined to what has been written since 1800.

Some of the early literature has in fact been translated. For versions of the heroic *Tale of Igor's* [*Ihor's*] *Campaign*, the great *Primary Chronicle*, and other works of the Kievan period, see the entry on Ukrainian literature [II.e.11]. There is a wide-ranging anthology of medieval Russian literature edited by

Serge A. **Zenkovsky**; many of the translations are his own, but he also gives much of the classic translation by Jane **Harrison** and Hope **Mirrlees** (London, 1924) of the fascinating autobiographical *Zhitie* (Life) of Archpriest Avvakum, leader of the Old Believers in the great schism of the 17th c.

Russia's rich oral tradition has had some impact in the English-speaking world. Selections of the heroic ballads known as *byliny* have been published by L. A. **Magnus** and Nora K. **Chadwick**. Folksongs figure in a number of anthologies and in collections such as Roberta **Reeder**'s *Down Along the Mother Volga*. More importantly, Russian folktales have been much translated. As early as 1873 W. R. S. **Ralston** published a scholarly *Russian Folk-Tales*; more modern versions include the *Russian Fairy Tales* of Norbert **Guterman** and the appealing retelling for children by Arthur **Ransome**, *Old Peter's Russian Tales*.

In modern Russian literature there are fields which have attracted relatively few translations and are therefore not covered in the following entries. Russia's 18th-c. literature is little known abroad, but there are many texts in Harold B. **Segel**'s *The Literature of Eighteenth-Century Russia*, including a sizeable selection of the eloquent poetry of Gavrila Derzhavin, who has not been widely translated.

Translations of Russia's rich 19th-c. poetry are neither numerous nor particularly good in general. Konstantin Batyushkov, Yevgeny Baratynsky, and Vasily Zhukovsky exist only in anthologies. The translations of Mikhail Lermontov, one of Russia's outstanding poets, are generally disappointing. There are, however, three translations of 19th c. poets worth mentioning: *Versions from Fyodor*

Tyutchev (London, 1960), containing attractive free translations by Charles **Tomlinson** and Henry **Gifford**; James **Greene**'s renderings of the fragile lyrics of Afanasy Fet, *I Have Come to Greet You* (London, 1982); and the spirited translation by Juliet M. **Soskice** of Nikolay Nekrasov's long satirical poem *Komu na Rusi zhit' khorosho* (1878), *Who Can Be Happy and Free in Russia* (London, 1917).

There are, however, general anthologies of Russian poetry in translation, in which the 19th c. is prominent, for instance the volumes edited by Maurice Bowra and the selection translated by Babette **Deutsch** and Avrahm **Yarmolinsky**. These approach verse translation in a premodern way and will seem outdated to most western poetry readers. A more interesting, more recent small collection of 11 major 19th-c. poets, retaining original metres and rhymes, is Alan **Myers**'s *An Age Ago*, with an introduction and notes by Joseph Brodsky. There is also a small selection of poems from Pushkin to Blok in quietly elegant translations by Frances **Cornford** and Esther **Polianowsky** Salaman, while Vladimir **Nabokov** has a slim and attractive volume of Pushkin, Lermontov, and Tyutchev. And for those with some Russian, Dimitri **Obolensky**'s bilingual *Heritage of Russian Verse* (with prose translations) extends alluringly from the *Lay of Igor's Campaign* to poetry of the 1950s.

Another little-known area is Russian drama, with the great exception of Chekhov. There have of course been translations of such masterpieces as Nikolay Gogol's *Revizor* (1836, The Inspector-General), and there are a number of anthologies, the most sizeable being those of George Rapall **Noyes** and Franklin D. **Reeve**, and, for the 20th c., a Moscow-produced volume edited by Alla **Mikhailova**. Given the male predominance in most anthologies, Catriona **Kelly**'s *An Anthology of Russian Women's Writing, 1777–1992* is a particularly important contribution.

In the Soviet period, the translation of Russian literature, like that of many Communist countries, was much affected by propaganda aims. Many translations of approved texts (including the Russian classics) came from the state-controlled presses of Moscow, using the services of Russian-based English-speakers as well as native Russian translators. The results were variable, and with some exceptions cannot be said to have greatly enriched the canon of Russian literature in translation. By the same token, western publishers often chose to issue translations from Russian for political reasons, and as a consequence certain reputations became unduly inflated. Whether a return to the market economy has changed things for the better remains to be seen. PF

ANTHOLOGIES   Bowra, Maurice, ed., *A Book of Russian Verse*, London, 1943 · *A Second Book of Russian Verse*, London, 1948 · Bowring, John, *Specimens of the Russian Poets*, 2 vols., London, 1821–3 · Chadwick, Nora K., *Russian Heroic Poetry*, Cambridge, 1932 · Cooper, Joshua, *Four Russian Plays*, Harmondsworth, 1972 [Penguin] · Cornford, Frances, and Salaman, Esther Polianowsky, *Poems from the Russian*, London, 1943 · Deutsch, Babette, and Yarmolinsky, Avrahm, *Russian Poetry*, 2 vols., New York, 1929 · Guterman, Norbert, *Russian Fairy Tales*, London, 1946 [introd. by Roman Jakobson] · Kelly, Catriona, ed., *An Anthology of Russian Women's Writing, 1777–1992*, Oxford, 1994 · Magarshack, David, *The Storm and Other Russian Plays*, New York, 1960 · Magnus, L. A., *The Heroic Ballads of Russia*, London, 1932 · Mikhailova, Alla, ed., *Classic Soviet Plays*, Moscow, 1980 · Myers, Alan, *An Age Ago: A Selection of Nineteenth-Century Russian Poetry*, New York, 1988 · Nabokov, Vladimir, *Pushkin, Lermontov, Tyutchev. Poems*, London 1947 · Noyes, George Rapall, ed., *Masterpieces of the Russian Drama*, 2 vols., New York, 1960–1 · Obolensky, Dimitri, *The Heritage of Russian Verse*, Bloomington, Ind., 1976 [previously as the *Penguin Book of Russian Verse*] · Ralston, W. R. S., *Russian Folk-Tales*, London, 1873 · Ransome, Arthur, *Old Peter's Russian Tales*, London, 1916 · Reeder, Roberta, *Down Along the Mother Volga*, Philadelphia, 1975 · Reeve, Franklin D., ed., *An Anthology of Russian Plays*, 2 vols., New York, 1961–3 · Segel, Harold B., ed., *The Literature of Eighteenth-Century Russia*, 2 vols., New York, 1967 · Wiener, Leo, ed., *An Anthology of Russian Literature from the Earliest Period to the Present Time*, 2 vols., New York/London, 1902–3 · Zenkovsky, Serge A., ed., *Medieval Russia's Epics, Chronicles and Tales*, New York, 1963; 2nd edn., 1974.

SEE ALSO   Davie, D., *Russian Literature and Modern English Fiction*, London/Chicago, 1965 · May, R., *The Translator in the Text: On Reading Russian Literature in English*, Evanston, Ill., 1994.

2. PUSHKIN

Despite his early death, Aleksandr Pushkin left a prolific literary legacy: over 800 lyric poems, a dozen narrative poems (culminating in *Medny Vsadnik* (1833, The Bronze Horseman)), a full-length play (the Shakespearean *Boris Godunov*, 1825) and several miniature dramas, a novel in verse, *Yevgeny Onegin* (1823–31, Eugene Onegin), several short stories and novellas (including *Pikovaya Dama*

(1833, The Queen of Spades), and *Kapitanskaya Dochka* (1833–5, The Captain's Daughter)), as well as historical studies, many articles of literary criticism, and a voluminous correspondence. Most of these texts, though by no means all of the lyrics, have been translated into English, as well as numerous other languages. The translation of Pushkin, which increased steadily throughout the 20th c., seems set to continue apace in the new millennium. More than 200 different works have been translated, and the total continues to rise. Some of his works have been rendered many times over, the crown going to a lyric of 1826, 'Prorok' (The Prophet), which has appeared in at least 30 different versions.

i. Nineteenth Century Translation of Pushkin's poetry began early, at least a decade before he died; in 1827 the journal *Foreign Review* published *A. S. Pushkin: a Notice, with Specimens of His Verse.* Although born too late to appear in John **Bowring**'s (1792–1872) celebrated *Specimens of the Russian Poets* [II.p.1], Pushkin did catch the eye of George **Borrow**, who published *The Talisman with Other Pieces* in St Petersburg as early as 1835. From then on translations appeared sporadically and arbitrarily in various English-language journals, their existence not necessarily guaranteeing literary quality either in the original Russian or in English. Works not now regarded as flawless masterpieces were among the first to be translated, such as 'Chernaya Shal'' (1820, The Black Shawl) (with other lyrics in *Blackwood's Edinburgh Magazine*, 1845) and 'Bakhchisaraysky Fontan' (1822, The Fountain of Bakhchisaray), which appeared as the title-poem in a small volume, *The Bakchesarian Fountain and Other Poems by Various [Russian] Authors*, translated by W. D. **Lewis** (1792–1881) and published in Philadelphia in 1849. W. R. **Morfill** (1834–1909) emerged as a notable translator of Pushkin in mid-century, publishing, for instance, 'Klevetnikam Rossii' (1831) as 'On the Calumniators of Russia' in *Literary Gazette* and also *Several Poems* (London Constitutional Press), both in 1860.

Translations of his prose works were not long in coming. One of the *Povesti Belkina* (1830, Tales of Belkin), 'Metel'' (The Snowstorm), appeared in *Living Age* in 1856; others trickled out sporadically before the whole collection was published in English in Mrs J. **Telfer**'s *Russian Romance* (1875), but the collection does not seem to have been published under Belkin's name until well into the 20th c. *The Queen of Spades* gained rapid and enduring popularity. English versions of this story appeared twice in 1850 (in *Living Age* and in *Chambers' Papers for the People*), followed by a pla-

giarized one in 1853, *A Russian Legend* in *The Gift of Friendship for 1854* (Philadelphia, Anters). Further translations appeared in 1857, 1876, 1884, and 1892 (Mrs Sutherland **Edwards**, *The Queen of Spades and Other Stories* (including *The Gypsies*)). *The Captain's Daughter* proved as popular as *The Queen of Spades*. Its first English rendition, by G. **Hebbe** (1804–93) bearing the subtitle *The Generosity of the Russian Usurper Pugatscheff*, was published in New York as early as 1846; further versions followed, under curiously differing titles, in 1859, 1875, 1883, 1890 and 1891, in places as far apart as New York and Calcutta. The first more or less complete collection of Pushkin's prose was issued by T. **Keane** in 1896, containing the three works already referred to plus *Dubrovsky* (1832–3), *Kirdjali* (1834), *Yegipetskie Nochi* (1824, Egyptian Nights), and *Arap Petra Velikogo* (1827, Peter the Great's Negro).

Apart from Keane's volume, the two most significant publications of Pushkin in translation before 1900 were undoubtedly Spalding's 1881 version of *Eugene Onegin* (see below) and a collection of 1888 by I. **Panin** published in Boston, entitled *Poems* and including in its 179 pages an introduction along with translations of 67 poems under five generic headings, several with new titles imposed by the translator. By the turn of the century, although Pushkin's name was vaguely known in the West, he was represented more by prose than poetry and in translations varying considerably in their accuracy and style. Although numerous operas (especially three by Tchaikovsky, and including Mussorgsky's *Boris Godunov*) had adapted Pushkin's texts for their libretti, none of his plays had been translated and there were no serious versions of his narrative poetry.

ii. Twentieth Century The new century opened with a major landmark in the translation of Russian literature into English, two volumes, almost 1,000 pages, of materials from 'The Oldest Period' through to living writers such as Chekhov and Gorky; the editor was Leo Wiener, and Pushkin was well represented, with 11 works translated, some of them in excerpts. From then on, as russophilia infected the English-speaking intelligentsia, Pushkin's name spread slowly, but steadily. Translations now become too common to be enumerated. Several of the translators were women. Many of the translations were included in anthologies of Russian literature or poetry, some of them anonymously presented. Significantly, we are now witnessing a steady stream of verse translations. In 1925 the first translation of *Boris Godunov* was published, by Alfred **Hayes** (1857–1936);

accurate and poetically sensitive, this remained the only available version for several decades.

The 1930s proved to be a decisive decade for Pushkin translations. Oliver **Elton** issued a book of Russian poetry in English translation (1935), most of it Pushkin, and, marking the centenary of the poet's death, he followed this with his translation of *Yevgeny Onegin* (1937), only to find it competing (successfully) with two others published at the same time (see below). A great tribute to Russia's first poet was paid at this time by Avrahm **Yarmolinsky**, who published a huge collection, *The Works of Alexander Pushkin*, in New York (1936). It is worth noting that at this time learned journals as distinguished as the *Slavonic and East European Review* were willing to publish verse (and other) translations. This practice has long been discontinued in England, where the art of literary translation is seriously undervalued, but some American journals have continued to publish them in recent times.

The 1940s saw several collections of verse translations, the most successful by **Baring**, **Coxwell**, **Cornford**, **Nabokov**, and **Bowra**. Forty-five Pushkin poems appeared in *A Treasury of Russian Verse* (1949), edited by Max **Eastman** and others, he having defied convention by publishing a translation of the very naughty *Gavriiliada* as early as 1927. Smaller collections continued to appear.

In more recent years translations have flowed regularly from many pens in the USA, UK, and Russia; among the prominent translators, some of them still active, are Walter **Arndt** (probably the most prolific), Irina **Zheleznova**, Robert **Daglish**, Charles **Johnston**, D. M. **Thomas**, and Paul **Debreczeny** (a comprehensive edition of the prose with a detailed accompanying study). The year 1997 saw a new paperback edition of Pushkin's prose (World Classics, **Myers**) and a popular edition of his poetry (Everyman, **Briggs**), containing 60 poems, including three narratives. By the end of the century Pushkin was thus reaching an ever-broadening readership, and at low cost.

iii. *Eugene Onegin* The most interesting aspect of Pushkin's work in translation concerns the many attempts which have been made to produce a satisfactory English version of his finest work, the novel in verse, *Yevgeny Onegin*. This masterpiece, which consists of 366 sonnet-like stanzas, depends for its effectiveness less on story or character than on the quality of its poetry. By common acknowledgement it represents Russian at its finest. No translation has come near to capturing the acoustic opulence and skill of this novel; the two languages, despite some similarities, are simply too far apart.

The most remarkable of all the translations is the first, published as early as 1881, the work of Lt-Col. H. **Spalding**. It stands out like a lonely landmark half-way through the century separating Pushkin's death from the centenary of that death in 1937, when *Onegin* suddenly gained currency in the west. Tasteful and largely accurate in detail, it is still readable with much satisfaction, despite the archaisms which have now grown over it. Its easy assimilation is due to a bold decision taken by the translator, to use only masculine rhymes (rhymes of one syllable). All of the others use feminine rhymes (of two syllables, e.g. 'sickened / quickened') as well as masculine ones, on a regular basis. This alone, although considered essential by each translator in order to preserve the rhythmic flow of Pushkin's stanza, cannot fail to weary the reader, since such rhymes are hard to find in English, so that hackneyed rhymes and the jingling use of participles become indispensable.

This is not to say that the translations are of low value. There are now 11 of them, by Spalding (1881), **Deutsch** (1936), **Prall**, **Radin**, and **Patrick** (1937), Elton (1937), **Simmons** (1950), Arndt (1963), **Kayden** (1964), Nabokov (1964), Johnston (1977), **Clough** (1988), and **Falen** (1995). They render the story well enough, and all of them read fluently and manage to rise at times to a flow of verse which can be convincing and beautiful. The ones which preceded Nabokov by no means deserved the withering scorn which he poured upon them as pernicious, paraphrastic nonsense. His own translation is unlike the others, being a literal version, its deadly accuracy vitiated by quirky English prose with a vague iambic plod. On the other hand, this definitive version is so dependable for pedantic accuracy that modern translators never make mistakes; the accompanying commentary provides two volumes of succulent detail. Conversely, the Johnston version scarcely deserved its extravagant acclaim in the 1970s, nor was his anachronistic decision to use lower-case letters at the beginnings of lines acceptable.

None of these laudable versions has outclassed all the others by consensus; they remain, unfortunately, closer to each other in effect than they are to Alexander Pushkin. Some flavour of the various translations may be gained by comparing three different versions of the preparations made for the fateful duel in Chapter 6 (stanza 29). Spalding's early version (1881):

> The shining pistols are uncased,
> The mallet loud the ramrod strikes,
> Bullets are down the barrels pressed,

> For the first time the hammer clicks.
> Lo! poured in a thin gray cascade,
> The powder in the pan is laid . . .

compares not unfavourably with Nabokov's literal translation (1964):

> The pistols have already gleamed.
> The mallet clanks against the ramrod.
> Into the polyhedral barrel go the balls,
> and the first time the cock has clicked.
> Now powder in a grayish streamlet
> is poured into the pan . . .

or with Johnston's (1977):

> Pistols are out, they gleam, the hammer
> thumps as the balls are pressed inside
> faceted muzzles by the rammer;
> with a first click the catch is tried.
> Now powder's greyish stream is slipping
> into the pan . . .

An attempt to issue a multi-volume Pushkin-in-English set for the bicentenary (1999) brought many offerings (most still unpublished) from all over the globe, which suggests both that verse translation is alive and well in the modern world and that Pushkin will continue to exert his appeal on many translators to come.   ADPB

POETRY AND PROSE   Arndt, Walter, *Alexander Pushkin: Collected Narrative and Lyrical Poetry*, Ann Arbor, Mich., 1984 · Bowra, C. M., et al., *A Book of Russian Verse*, London, 1943 · *A Second Book of Russian Verse*, London, 1948 · Briggs, A. D. P., *Alexander Pushkin*, London, 1997 [Everyman] · Cornford, F., and Salaman, E., *Poems from the Russian*, London, 1943 · Coxwell, C. F., *Russian Poems*, London, 1929 · Debreczeny, Paul, *Alexander Pushkin: Complete Prose Fiction*, Stanford, Calif., 1983 · Eastman, Max, *A Treasury of Russian Verse*, New York, 1949 · Elton, Oliver, *Verse from Pushkin and Others*, New York/London, 1935 · Keane, T., *The Prose Tales*, London, 1896; rep. 1914, 1916 · Kisch, C. H., *The Wagon of Life and Other Lyrics by Russian Poets of the Nineteenth Century*, London, 1947 · Morison, Walter, *Pushkin's Poems*, London, 1945 · Nabokov, Vladimir, *Three Russian Poets*, Norfolk, Conn., 1944 · Newmarch, Rosa, *Poetry and Progress in Russia*, London, 1927 · Pancheff, T., *The Fairy Tales*, London, 1947 · Panin, I., *Poems*, Boston, 1888 · Telfer, Mrs J., *Russian Romance*, London, 1875 · Turner, C., *Translations from Pushkin in Memory of the Hundredth Anniversary of the Poet's Birth*, London/St Petersburg, 1899 · Wiener, Leo, ed., *Anthology of Russian Literature*, 2 vols., London, 1902 · Yarmolinsky, Avrahm, *The Works of Alexander Pushkin: Lyrics, Narrative Poems, Folk Tales, Prose*, New York, 1936.

EUGENE ONEGIN   Arndt, Walter, New York, 1963 · Elton, Oliver, London, 1937 (rev. A. D. P. Briggs, 1995) · Falen, James, Oxford, 1995 [World's Classics] · Johnston, Charles, Harmondsworth, 1979 [Penguin] · Nabokov, Vladimir, with commentary, 4 vols., New York, 1964 · Spalding, H., London, 1881.

SEE ALSO   Simmons, E. J., 'English Translations of *Eugene Onegin*', *Slavonic and East European Review*, 17 (1938), 208–14.

3. NINETEENTH-CENTURY FICTION

The reception of 19th-c. Russian fiction in Britain forms a distinct part of the history of fiction as such. Among other commentators, Gilbert Phelps remarks that in 1912, when Constance **Garnett** published her translation of Dostoevsky's *Brothers Karamazov* [see II.p.5], she started a vogue for Russian writing which swept up, along with Dostoevsky, the other great novelists whose publishing history in Britain was substantial in some cases (Turgenev) and patchy in others (Gogol, Lermontov). It was the modern spirit, represented by Lawrence, the Bloomsbury group, Eliot, Huxley, and others, which called out across the decades to Russia, finding in the writing of a dispossessed and oppressed 'intelligentsia' an analogy for their sense of stylistic and emotional crisis, of a comprehensive loss of identity (Joyce compared his own writing to Lermontov's in 1905).

Many of the classic translations are so impressive that later ones have little to add by way of accuracy, insight, or felicity (though there are, of course, some laughably bad ones).

i. Turgenev With some writers the process of assimilation had already gone far by the turn of the century. The most striking example is Ivan Turgenev. Even though the first translation, 'edited' by J. D. **Meiklejohn**, of *Zapiski okhotnika* (1852, A Sportsman's Sketches) is described by Phelps as a clumsy piracy, it made a considerable impression. The title it was given, *Russian Life in the Interior, or the Experiences of a Sportsman*, betrays an emphasis, reiterated in the case of other novelists, on the documentary or truth value of the writing, a simple sales strategy perhaps, but also a revelation of the sense that Russia was very far away, and documentary accounts very necessary. Translators like Eugene **Schuyler** (1840–90), with his version of *Ottsy i deti* (1862, Fathers and Sons), and W. R. S. **Ralston** (1828–89), who translated *Dvoryanskoe*

Gnezdo (1859, A Nest of Gentlefolk), had already turned Turgenev into an English-speaking author before Henry James came along to complete the assimilation. Huda Jabboury notes that it was writers, rather than readers, who especially welcomed Turgenev in the 'complete' (*sic*!) version by Garnett (Jabboury 1992). As for James, his admiration literally speaks for itself, in the classic essay of 1897, 'Ivan Turgenieff 1818–1883'.

James strikes the authentic Anglo-American note at once: 'There is perhaps no novelist of alien race who more naturally than Ivan Turgenev inherits a niche in a library for English readers.' Turgenev had been translated from French into English as early as 1858 (a bad practice that continued for many years, in the case of many novelists). Somehow the 'alienness' of the Russian, mediated through a French version in which the author had himself had a hand, was dissipated to some degree and rendered 'naturally' English. What James most admired was Turgenev's 'firm, deliberate hand'. Where Tolstoy is 'a reflector as vast as a natural lake', or 'an elephant . . . harnessed . . . to a coach-house', Turgenev is always concise, and has a tender and ironic hand for 'the individual figure'. Turgenev could thus be assimilated to a fictional tradition in which Flaubert occupied a crucial position. If there is no place here for Tolstoy, or only on sufferance, still less is there any for Dostoevsky.

But the other side of Turgenev (the man who coined the term 'superfluous man' and wrote with passion about the marginal figures of his society) could be rediscovered, or assimilated into the English tradition, only with the help of Dostoevsky, whose world is of course packed with such problematic individuals. *Dnevnik lishnego cheloveka* (1850, The Diary of a Superfluous Man) was not translated (by H. **Gersoni** (1844–97)) until 1884; *Rudin* (1856) came earlier in English (anon. 1873), but made much less impression than other works. Both contain too much of what Donald Davie called 'strenuous washing of dirty linen in public'— a practice too common with the Russians, in the view of many English reviewers, even though they *did* eschew the common dirt of Zola and the French. This tells us a lot about what English readers expected from their Russians (apart from the documentary functions referred to above).

Although Turgenev did not catch the fancy of the modernists as other Russians did, his special status as 'almost a westerner' guaranteed him decades of respectful attention and numerous translations. Among the many translators, Richard **Freeborn**'s vigorous work for Penguin and Oxford means that he stakes a special claim to this writer. The novel

where the generational conflict is sharpest, *Fathers and Sons*, has clocked up a remarkable list of versions (see Bibliography), being almost certainly his most popular book in English (it has also been translated more accurately under the title *Fathers and Children*). Interestingly, a new version of *Rudin* (the 'other' Turgenev) is announced by Oxford for 1999, so perhaps we shall see a new cult of the 'outsider'.

The charm of Turgenev's descriptive writing accounts for much of his appeal. Freeborn's translation of Chapter 20 of *Home of the Gentry* evokes Turgenev's characteristic *stillness*, a sort of timeless hush that was increasingly scarce in modern Europe:

At that very time, in other places on the earth, life was seething, hurrying, roaring on its way; here the same life flowed by inaudibly, like water through marshy grass; and until evening Lavretsky could not tear himself away from contemplation of this receding outflowing life; anguish for the past was melting in his soul like spring snow . . .

Jessie **Coulson** brings this to a more lilting, personal, individual, perhaps more old-fashioned emotional climax; it is the kind of nature mysticism that many English readers still like in Russian fiction, and that English writers imitated:

Meanwhile, in other places on the earth's suface, life seethed and bustled and made thunderous noises; here, the same life flowed silently, like water among marsh grasses; until the evening, Lavretsky could not drag himself away from the contemplation of this life flowing past, slipping past; in his heart sorrow for what was gone melted away like the spring snows . . .

ii. Lermontov The implications for translators of such criteria as those discussed above has undoubtedly exerted a considerable influence on the reception of Russian fiction in English. Robert Reid's study of translations of Mikhail Lermontov's remarkable *Geroy nashego vremeni* (1837–40, A Hero of Our Time) raises precisely the issue of the 'superflous man', and the extent to which such a stereotype, and the narrative disruptions corresponding to the originality of the vision, were comprehensible in the English cultural context (Reid 1986). Reid would have us think of the different versions of a text as what he calls a 'corporate text', a sort of intertext formed of the available versions engaging in a kind of dialogue. What he calls the 'complex and highly visible' structure of *A Hero of Our Time* may have something to do with the fact that the five 19th-c. translations culminate in a dual-language version, as if to tell the reader that there is a dimension of style here that may be for ever puzzling (a dual-language text, which has been described as an admission of failure, is in fact always an invitation to dialogue). This is a suggestion which Vladimir **Nabokov** picks up on in the introduction to his classic 1958 translation.

Reid notes that the novel is already a sort of 'corporate text', even before it is translated. The image of Pechorin, the protagonist, is refracted through a number of interleaved narratives, including travelogue (the 1853 translation, a free version which omits the story *Taman'*, carries the subtitle *Sketches of Russian Life in the Caucasus, by a Russe, Many Years Resident amongst the Various Mountain Tribes*). The formal freedom and innovation are linked existentially to the personality, life-style, values, and relations to others of the 'superfluous' hero, who may be no hero at all, and his 'time', which may be a specific historical moment (after the suppression of the Decembrist Uprising) or may be a much more 'metaphysical' time that is out of joint. The ambivalence of the work means that the translator must feel his or her way through complex sets of possibilities at every stage.

Take, for instance, that Russian element which Dostoevsky foregrounded, but which was lurking, an enticement to westerners, long before him: the Russian soul. Reid's analysis of a part of *Maxim Maximych*, a free-floating section like all the rest, speaks of hard-heartedness and of hiding one's feelings. Reid comments on the expression *dusha zakroetsya*:

'Dusha' is a word of so many psychic connotations that only the full corporate text is capable of restoring them in English: 'soul', 'mind', 'spirit', 'heart' . . . The verb 'zakroetsya' is also divergent, though five translations use some directional variant of 'close' ('close up' in three cases). The most normative conflation would therefore be 'the soul closes up', an unfamiliar combination which does little to elucidate the experience it refers to. It is noticeable that the two translations (1899 and 1940) which use 'mind' as their translation are able in so doing to provide it with a conventionally familiar predicate ('suspicious' and 'narrow') and thus effectively offer an interpretation or 'smuggled commentary' on this enigmatic utterance.

Vladimir Nabokov's comments on Lermontov's style, which preface his superb translation of *A Hero of Our Time*, raise fundamental questions about the translator's 'fidelity'. Lermontov, he says provocatively, is 'dry and drab', and 'his Russian is, at times, almost as crude as Stendhal's French', lacking the 'prodigiously elaborate and magically artistic style of Tolstoy'. While, as Davie says, this is not really about Tolstoy at all, but is actually a kind of footnote to a defence of *Lolita*, nevertheless the reader

cannot but pay attention to Nabokov's careful listing of Lermontov's 'key' terms, and his bold assertion that, for a translation to be good, it must sound like a translation. The 'beautiful timing of all parts and particles of the novel' is the secret of Lermontov's classic status and perennial appeal, not his characterization or his language (though there are memorable uses of sterotypes in both cases).

iii. Gogol What might be very loosely called a postmodern emphasis in Nabokov's critique of Lermontov, while deliberately coat-trailing, certainly throws a different, and very important, light upon the whole history of the reception of Russian literature in English. If Turgenev was assimilable, almost (indeed) a friend, this intimacy was bought at the cost of a refusal to accept or assimilate other writers. Even if we allow that Lermontov was, as far as the novel went, some kind of a sport, and that Goncharov, Leskov, Saltykov-Schedrin, and Aksakov (to name but four) could not, in the nature of things, make a very considerable impact, there is still the case of Nabokov's beloved Nikolay Gogol, one of the greatest writers of any time in any language. Even more than Lermontov, he was dragged screaming by his translators into the realist fold, and made to yield up 'descriptions' of Russian life which surely (if taken literally) warped people's imaginings of Russia and Russians for generations. It seemed as if very few of his (English) readers could see him for what he was: a fantasist, a satirist, a master of the grotesque, maybe a surrealist before the event, an inspired 'folk' entertainer (like Dickens but more so).

The first English translation of *Myortvye dushi* (1842–52, Dead Souls), by Krystyn **Lach-Szyrma** (?1791–1866), was called *Home Life in Old Russia, by a Russian Noble, Revised by the Author of 'Revelations of Siberia'*. This version started the fashion for only publishing Part I, or altering the ending. Even the redoubtable Isabel F. **Hapgood** translated Gogol's great novel as *Tchitchikoff's Journeys, or Dead Souls*, appending to it the spurious conclusion by A. E. Zakharchenko, which had actually been translated from French. In 1888 *Taras Bulba* (1835) was described by one of its first translators, Jeremiah **Curtin** (1835–1906), very misleadingly, as 'a historical novel of Russia and Poland'.

Donald Davie's 1950 thesis contains a particularly fine chapter on the reception of Gogol. From it, we learn (amazingly) that the *Westminster Review* in 1841 noticed Gogol's *Mirgorod* (1835), giving a very hostile account of this fiction in which a dull couple— 'merely animated digesting-machines'—live an 'intolerably stupid' life. This triumph of English good sense marks the tone for Gogol's reception, and makes one all the more incredulous that enough had changed, in English cultural life, for Dostoevsky to get something like the beginnings of a proper appraisal of his genius when Constance Garnett had done her perennially wonderful translations.

It gets worse: in 1843, T. B. Shaw accurately predicted that Gogol's language would defeat his translators and his readers, though in Ireland an anonymous critic was invoking Sterne and Swift, most apt comparisons. But as far as England was concerned, reviewers fell over themselves to congratulate Gogol on his authentic portrayal of a truly brutal nation. By 1873 a reviewer could at least see Gogol as an 'unmerciful accuser' of the old order, while another saw Gogol as an enemy of Russia's 'metaphysical dreaming' and 'foolish romantic affectation', which was certainly a step forward. Meanwhile Turgenev, forging ahead in the esteem of professional *literati*, and gradually accumulating a mass readership as well, was trotted out as the kind of writer Gogol would have liked to be if only he had had the talent.

In France, de Vogüé's classic *Le Roman russe* (1886) saw things steadily and whole: Gogol, he said, excelled all English humorists except Swift. Other critics, worried already by naturalism's obscenity, and the marked tendency of some English writers to follow in its footsteps, used Gogol in the same way as Russian fiction as a whole had been used: as a stick to beat the obscene French. But the consequence of this was that Brandes (for instance) could see nothing of any interest in *Nos* (1836, The Nose). Since Freud, the phallic interpretation of noseness has perhaps gone too much the other way; but in the end this is better than describing this mad story (as Brandes does) as 'an ingenious and humorous story for children of an older growth'.

By the 1890s Gogol's lack of plot, combined with his pathos, are attracting positive comment, instead of disparagement. With R. G. Burton, in the *Westminster Review* in 1895, we discover another of those set phrases which bedevil critical commentary on the Russians: 'if his humour arouses laughter it is laughter through tears.' This phrase, more often used of Chekhov than of Gogol, smoothes away the knotty surface of Gogol's prose, as well as all the sharp contradictions of his moral and aesthetic world; maybe it was somehow truer to him to find (as the *Athenaeum* did) 'crudity' in his work, since at least this hostile observation may be a way of registering the abrasive stylizations that are crucial to his effects.

It was certainly the Dostoevsky cult during World War I that revived the flagging interest in Gogol. Stephen Graham, introducing the reissue of

the Isabel Hapgood translation of *Dead Souls* in 1915, was at pains to point out that the terrifying title, when understood, lost all its terror (just as Dostoevsky took very harsh topics and spiritualized them, Russian fiction so often being credited, for all its extremism, with great wisdom and compassion). Janko Lavrin's 1925 study of Gogol, despite its defects (roundly denounced by Davie), made a considerable impact, and coincided with the redoubtable Constance Garnett's 'complete' translation. The *TLS* was struck by Gogol's 'grinning ferocity', but in general reviewers altogether failed to see what kind of a thing they had in front of them. It was only with the publication of Nabokov's *Gogol* in 1947, that Anglo-Saxon readers were given an overview of the author that did him justice. Within the limits of translated texts, this original study communicated brilliantly a sense of Gogol's astonishing verbal inventiveness.

One short passage from *Shinel'* (1833, The Overcoat) will have to serve to indicate what I mean, and I hope it may stand in for the countless other instances, in translations of Russian fiction, where the English language is very hard pressed indeed to keep up with an imagination working under extraordinary pressure. When Boris Eikhenbaum wrote his classic *How Gogol's Overcoat Was Made* (1919, not translated into English until 1963), he highlighted the element of *skaz*: folk-based narrative with a very high degree of mimicry and of expressive 'sonic' gesturing. *The Overcoat* is an extreme case of Gogol's practice of 'miming' the world of his grotesque personages, like some overwrought puppeteer. The passage shows the protagonist, Akaky, leaving the tailor who tells him he must have a new coat. The Garnett translation, revised by Leonard **Kent**, reads as follows:

When he got into the street, Akaky Akakievich felt as if he was in a dream. 'So that is how it is', he said to himself. 'I really did not think it would be this way . . .' and then after a pause he added, 'So that's it! So that's how it is at last! and I really could never have supposed it would be this way. And there . . .' There followed another long silence, after which he said: 'So that's it! well, it really is so unexpected . . . who would have thought . . . what a circumstance . . .'

David **Magarshack** in 1949 is quite close to this; Ronald **Wilks**, on the other hand, makes some sort of attempt in 1972 to come to terms with Gogol's own description and imitation of Akaky's peculiar idiolect. In Magarshack's translation, the passage in which the author comments on this 'little language' runs as follows:

Akaky mostly talked in prepositions, adverbs, and, lastly, such parts of speech as have no meaning whatsoever. . . .

often, having begun his speech with, 'This is—er—you know . . . a bit of that, you know . . .'

(Garnett's version of this quite misses the 'sonic gesturing'.) Wilks imposes an English colloquial manner which nevertheless still misses the coughs and sneezes that compose Akaky's 'syntax':

Out on the street Akaky felt as if he were in a dream. 'What a to-do now', he said to himself. 'I never thought it would turn out like this, for the life of me . . .' And then, after a brief silence, he added: 'Well now then! So that's how it's turned out and I would never have guessed it would end . . .' Whereupon followed a long silence, after which he murmured: 'So that's it!'

The point here is that Akaky's name (an odd reduplication, Akaky Akakievich) acquires a 'gestural' power by virtue of the fact that *kak* is Russian for 'how' or (in some contexts) 'what', and *tak* is 'so' or 'in this way', so that when Akaky mutters something like 'Tak vot kak!' or 'Etakovo-to delo etakoe', he is running a set of grotesque variations upon the sounds of his own name, and thus his marionette-like identity.

It is hard to say how popular Gogol is with present-day English readers. His acid, violent humour demands a translator with a true sense of the grotesque, like Nabokov's beloved Bernard Guilbert **Guerney** (real name Bronstein), translator of *Dead Souls*. More recent translations by Christopher **English** and by Richard **Pevear** and Larissa **Volokhonsky** may persuade British and American readers respectively that we too have a writer called Gogol who is equal to the absurdities of internet consumerism. But not all translators have been equal to the terminal paranoid vision that shapes Gogol's world.

iv. Goncharov With the greatest writers, it has taken the Anglo-Saxon world a very long time to catch up with Russian criticism and form something like a true perception of what the real issues are. With lesser authors, who naturally get discussed less, one would therefore expect there to be huge blind spots on the retina of English criticism. However, the facts of the matter (as usual) turn out to be more complex, as in the case of Ivan Goncharov's *Oblomov* (1859). This outrageously funny and deeply melancholy novel has had its eccentric admirers and imitators (Spike Milligan is surely the most prominent), but little proper criticism or exegesis. Davie, again, is helpful: by 1920 or thereabouts, as he tells us, Russian commentary on the novel *was* known in the Anglo-Saxon world, and influenced (excessively, one might add) the way the novel was perceived. Dobrolyubov's powerful,

deeply biased essay (*What Is Oblomovitis?*), and Belinksy's contributions, seemed to many people to have provided all the answers: a kind of condition-of-Russia argument that put the whole of Goncharov's imaginative and moral world behind the bars of a relentless social thesis (Oblomov as symptom of Russia's backwardness). There was no translation of *Oblomov* into English before C. J. **Hogarth**'s abridged version of 1915 (which was followed in 1929 by Natalie **Duddington**'s and in 1954 by David Magarshack's). By this time, the social-committed reading of the novel had swept the board, almost certainly because the Russian Revolution reinforced social-realist readings of Russian classic fiction generally.

However, Phelps notes that Goncharov *did* have some kind of influence on Anglo-Saxon writing (e.g. Waldo Franks's *The Unwelcome Man*, 1917); and it may well be the case that some writers saw in him something different from the victim / denouncer of Russia's social ills. As Davie puts it, there was a 'turning-point' when the character of Oblomov became some sort of a mirror held up to an English reader 'robbed of his Victorian or Edwardian assurance', an image of the shared existential crisis of Modernism. By 1946, V. S. Pritchett was writing that 'under that passivity lies a possible madness, a frantic, abysmal, screaming despair', and supporting this contention with new-found knowledge of Goncharov's own paranoid depression. But no Anglo-Saxon critic at this stage was equipped to address the *nature* of that symbolism: the terrifying Oedipal subtext with its overwhelming dream-images of abysses and ravines and hunger for the irreponsible wonder of childhood.

Prince Mirsky noted the flatness of Goncharov's Russian prose style, and it may be significant that Magarshack was often content to stay close to Duddington, apparently not feeling that anything important had been overlooked (an utterly different case from that of Gogol!), and underlining the ordinariness of Goncharov's vocabulary and syntax:

It was a glorious morning—the air was cool, the sun was still low. Long shadows fell from the house, the trees, the dovecote, and the balcony. Cool recesses, inviting sleep and dreaminess, appeared in the yard and the garden.

(Duddington)

It was a glorious morning; the air was cool; the sun was still low. Long shadows fell from the house, the trees, the dovecote, and the gallery. The garden and the yard were full of cool places, inviting sleep and day-dreaming.

(Magarshack)

Goncharov, one might say, writes a *diagnostic* kind of prose: but its objectivity is a strange way of mastering an extremely turbulent inner life.

v. Conclusion The impact of Russian fiction on Anglo-Saxon fiction has been so large that even to deal with one or two major cases would take (indeed, has taken) whole books. Conrad and Dostoevsky, Lawrence, Dostoevsky and Tolstoy, Katherine Mansfield and Chekhov: these are some of the more striking instances of writers whose reading of Russian classics went right to the roots of their art. Bloomsbury 'Russianitis', recorded in more than one essay by Virginia Woolf, was sustained very largely by the amazing achievements of Constance Garnett as a translator. Even with the writers she did not translate, like Saltykov-Shchedrin (whom the English have never taken to), somehow her thumbprint appeared on the volume (when Everyman reissued Natalie Duddington's rather good version of Shchedrin's *Gospoda Golov-lyovy* (1872–6, The Golovlyovs), Edward Garnett, Constance's admirable husband, wrote an introduction). A translator of the same 'type' as Constance Garnett, J. D. **Duff**, gave us Aksakov in the 1920s; and D. H. Lawrence's friend the redoubtable S. S. **Koteliansky** offered Shestov, Bunin, Rozanov, and other very significant representatives of Silver Age [see II.p.8.i] and émigré writing who indubitably contributed (via France, mainly) to existential tendencies in fiction (Camus and Sartre, for example, both greatly admired Shestov). The Russian tradition in fiction, short enough, yet infinitely rich, continues to fascinate translators, and new (and very interesting) versions of the classics continue to appear, especially in America.

I would like to express my gratitude to Mrs Doreen Davie for allowing me to make use of her husband's unpublished thesis on the English reception of Russian literature.   GH

GOGOL, NIKOLAY   Curtin, Jeremiah, *Taras Bulba*, New York, 1888 · English, Christopher, *Village Evenings near Dikanka; Mirgorod*, Oxford, 1994 [World's Classics] · *Plays and Petersburg Tales*, Oxford, 1995 [World's Classics] · *Dead Souls*, Oxford, 1997 [World's Classics] · Garnett, Constance, *The Works of Nikolay Gogol*, 6 vols., London, 1922–8 · *The Complete Tales*, rev. Leonard Kent, 2 vols., Chicago, 1954 · Guerney, Bernard Gilbert, *Dead Souls*, New York, 1942; rep. 1996 · Hapgood, Isabel F., *Tchitchikoff's Journeys, or Dead Souls*, 2 vols., New York, 1886; rep. 1915 · Lach-Szyrma, Krystyn, *Home Life in Old Russia*, London, 1854 · Magarshack, David, *Tales of Good and Evil*, London, 1949 · *Dead Souls*, Harmondsworth, 1961 [Penguin] · Pevear, Richard, and Volokhonsky, Larissa, *Collected Tales*, New York, 1998 · Wilks, Ronald, *Diary of a Madman and Other Stories*, Harmondsworth, 1972 [Penguin].

GONCHAROV, IVAN   Duddington, Natalie, *Oblomov*, London, 1929 [later Everyman] · Hogarth, C. J., *Oblomov*, London, 1915 · Magarshack, David, *Oblomov*, Harmondsworth, 1954 [Penguin].

LERMONTOV, MIKHAIL   anon., *Sketches of Russian Life in the Caucasus*, London, 1953 · Foote, Paul, *A Hero of Our Time*, Harmondsworth, 1966 [Penguin] · Lipman, R. I., *A Hero of Our Time*, London, 1887 · Longworth, Philip, *A Hero of Our Time*, London, 1962 · Nabokov, Vladimir, and Nabokov, Dmitri, *A Hero of Our Time*, New York, 1958 [later World's Classics] · Merton, Reginald, *A Hero of Our Time*, London, 1928 · Paul, Eden, and Paul, Cedar, *A Hero of Our Times*, London, 1940 · Pulszky, Thereza, *The Hero of Our Days*, London, 1854 [rev. version by Ivan Nestor Schnurmann as *Lermontov's Modern Hero*, Cambridge, 1899 (bilingual)] · Swinnerton-Phillimore, John, *A Hero of Nowadays*, London, 1903 · Wisdom, J. H., and Murray, Marr, *A Hero of Our Own Time*, London, 1854 [rep. as *The Heart of a Russian*, London, 1912].

TURGENEV, IVAN   Berlin, Isaiah, and Schapiro, Leonard, *First Love and Other Stories*, London, 1994 [Everyman; Berlin's *First Love*, pub. 1950] · Coulson, Jessie, *A Nest of Gentlefolk and Other Stories*, Oxford, 1959 [World's Classics] · Duddington, Natalie, *Smoke*, London, 1949 [Everyman] · Edmonds, Rosemary, *Fathers and Sons*, Harmondsworth, 1965 [Penguin] · Freeborn, Richard, *Home of the Gentry*, Harmondsworth, 1970 [Penguin] · *Rudin*, Harmondsworth, 1975 [Penguin] · *First Love and Other Stories*, Oxford, 1982 [World's Classics] · *Sketches from a Hunter's Album*, London, 1990 [Penguin] · *Fathers and Sons*, Oxford, 1991 [World's Classics] · Gardiner, Gilbert, *On the Eve*, Harmondsworth, 1950 [Penguin] · Garnett, Constance, *The Novels of Ivan Turgenev*, 15 vols., London, 1894–9 [Several reprints of individual titles] · Gersoni, H., *Diary of a Superfluous Man*, London, 1884 · Guerney, Bernard Gilbert, *Fathers and Sons*, New York, 1961 · Hapgood, Isabel F., *The Novels and Stories of Ivan Turgenieff*, 16 vols., New York, 1903–4 · Hepburn, Charles, and Hepburn, Natasha, *Sketches from a Hunter's Album*, London, 1992 [Everyman] · Hogarth, C. J., *Fathers and Sons*, London, 1921 [Everyman] · Katz, Michael R., *Fathers and Sons*, New York, 1994 · McDuff, David, *Rudin*, Oxford, 1999 [World's Classics] · Meiklejohn, J. D., ed., *Russian Life in the Interior, or The Experiences of a Sportsman*, Edinburgh, 1855 [from the French] · Patterson, David, *Diary of a Superfluous Man*, New York/London, 1984 · Pyman, Avril, *Fathers and Children*, London, 1961 [Everyman] · Ralston, W. R. S., *Liza, or A Nest of Nobles*, London, 1873 [later Everyman] · Schapiro, Leonard, *Spring Torrents*, London, 1972 [Penguin, 1980] · Schuyler, Eugene, *Fathers and Sons*, New York, 1867.

SEE ALSO   Davie, D., 'The English Idea of Russian Fiction', Ph.D. thesis, Cambridge University, 1950 · *Russian*

Literature and Modern English Fiction. Chicago/London, 1965 · Jabboury, H. A., 'Constance Garnett, Aylmer Maude, S. S. Koteliansky: Russian Literature in England', Ph.D. thesis, University of Sheffield, 1992 [useful bibliography] · Line, M. B., et al., *Bibliography of Russian Literature in English Translation* (to 1945), London, 1972 · Phelps, G., *The Russian Novel in English Fiction*, London, 1956 · Reid, R., 'The Critical Uses of Translation: Lermontov's *A Hero of Our Time*', *Essays in Poetics*, II.2 (1986), 55–90.

4. TOLSTOY

A recurrent theme in Anglophone criticism of Lev Tolstoy during the late 19th and early 20th c. was the paradoxical lack of artistry of this artist whose massive importance was recognized by everyone. It was Tolstoy who roused Henry James to his famous puzzlement at the poor construction of Russian novels, 'those large loose baggy monsters, with their queer elements of the accidental and the arbitrary'. Matthew Arnold thought that 'we are not to take *Anna Karénine* as a work of art; we are to take it as a piece of life', while Edmund Gosse complained: 'his style seems so negligent and even confused'.

For his British contemporaries, then, Tolstoy seemed a quintessential realist, whose style was at best unnoticeable, at worst an obstacle to the process of total identification with his characters that was assumed to have been his ambition as a writer. Yet Tolstoy's multifarious writings on art never suggested that the writer's aim should be to hold a mirror up to nature, and as author he was often concerned to alienate readers, to shock their perceptions by 'defamiliarizing' apparently ordinary experiences and objects, rather than to stimulate the joy of recognition. And, as many 20th-c. critics have shown, he was also a highly conscious stylist, in whose work such rhetorical features as repetition and parallelism play an important role, and who was meticulous in his choice of words.

The early critical reception of Tolstoy is directly relevant to the canonical translations of his major novels. Constance **Garnett**'s versions of *Voyna i mir* (1865–9, War and Peace) and of *Anna Karenina* (1875–7) date from the early 1900s, Louise (1855–1939) and Aylmer (1858–1953) **Maude**'s *Anna Karenina* and *War and Peace* (the most frequently reprinted versions) from 1918 and 1922–3 respectively. The most recent translations commissioned by a major Anglo-American publisher, Rosemary **Edmonds**'s *War and Peace* and *Anna Karenin*, done for the Penguin Classics series, date from the 1950s, though a version of *Anna Karenina* by Margaret **Wettlin**, an American *émigrée*, did appear in Moscow during the 1970s.

All the 20th-c. translators were thorough and conscientious compared with their predecessors, whose treatment of Tolstoy was often cavalier (the grossest example being the publication in 1889 of extracts from *War and Peace*, translated via French by Huntington **Smith** (1857–1926), as *The Physiology of War*). None made elementary errors like those made by Nathan **Dole** (1852–1935), who was capable of rendering *bakenbardy*, 'sideburns' as 'beard', and *ryaboe*, 'pockmarked' as 'pimply', and all wrote more fluently than Leo **Wiener** (1862–1939), who translated Tolstoy into a sort of Baltic English, Germano-Russian in lexis, syntax, and even punctuation ('It was on this account that Rostov was angry, when they joked him about Princess Bolkonski'). However, they were in some ways just as insensitive as their critical contemporaries to the specificities of Tolstoy's style. Though all of them score quite highly on what one might call the 'negative index' (the absence of versions clearly impossible in terms of elementary grammar and syntax), all are disappointingly insensitive to the aspects of style that readers of the Russian text would identify as characteristically 'Tolstoyan', whether admiring or abominating these.

For example, Tolstoy's bizarre sense of humour, one characteristic element in his 'defamiliarization' of the world, is seriously impaired. Take, for example, the superb passage in *War and Peace* that shows Napoleon preparing for the battle of Borodino. In this key piece of 'defamiliarization', the charger-mounted hero of David's paintings is turned into a fat gelding, wriggling with pleasure as his grooms give him the body-brush. The image is suggested, among other things, by the equine connotations of the verb *fyrkat'*, 'to snort', and by the pleonastic insistency with which Tolstoy refers to Napoleon's fatness: he is *zhirny*, 'greasily fat' and *obrosshy [zhirom]* 'overgrown with fat'. An adequate English version needs to observe these nuances; since 'to snort' does not immediately suggest horses, one must compensate elsewhere. A reasonably accurate translation might read:

The Emperor Napoleon had not yet emerged from his bedroom, and was completing his toilet. Giving little whinnies and snorts of delight, he turned now his stout back, now his lardy, fat-covered chest under the body-brush that his valet was using to rub him down. . . . Napoleon's short forelock was wet and tangled, but his puffy, yellow face expressed physical satisfaction.

In their nearly identical versions of the passage, however, the Maudes, Garnett, and Edmonds strip out all Tolstoy's humour. The repellent *zhirny* becomes the genteel 'plump'; *obrosshy* is generally mistranslated as 'hairy' or 'hirsute' (Maude has 'plump' *and* 'hairy'), and the curious term 'flesh-brush' is preferred by Garnett and Edmonds to 'body-brush', with its nice sense of a device used on both humans and horses (the Maudes just have 'brush'). The Maudes' version can stand for the rest in its unimpeachable banality:

The Emperor Napoleon had not yet left his bedroom and was finishing his toilette. Slightly snorting and grunting, he presented now his back and now his plump, hairy chest to the brush with which his valet was rubbing him down. . . . Napoleon's short hair was wet and tangled on his forehead, but his face, though puffy and yellow, expressed physical satisfaction.

One might perhaps see a correlation between Donald Davie's impatient dismissal of 'defamiliar-ization' as 'the kind of thing that all readers may have attempted in their bungling attempts to write' (Gifford 1971), and the bungling of the device by translators. But passages in which Tolstoy aims for fusion with, rather than alienation from, his charac-ters have not always fared much better. Take, for instance, the heart-rending scene where Vronsky remembers his first sight of Anna's dead body. In Tolstoy's original (of which my own clumsily lit-eral version can give only a faint sense), the distinc-tion between Vronsky's involuntarily recollection of Anna's corpse and his willed remembrance of her the first time that they met is made in several ways. Anna's appearance in death is conveyed through a chain of past participles, her appearance in life suggested by present participles. Dactylic rhythms in the unwanted recollection contrast with anapaestic rhythms in the willed memory. Tolstoy also uses a passive construction for the first instance of memory ('she remembered herself to him') and an active construction for the second ('he tried to remember').

As [Vronsky] looked at the tender and the rails, under the effects of the conversation with an acquaintance whom he had not seen since his tragedy, *she* suddenly came into his memory, that is, what had been left of her when he, like a madman, rushed into the barracks at the railway station: on the table at the barracks the bloodied body shamelessly stretched out among the living, still full of life not long [gone]; the head flung back and untouched with its heavy plaits and the curling hairs at the temples, and on the mar-vellous face with its half-open rosy mouth a frozen, strange expression, pathetic on the lips and frightful in the petrified and still unclosed eyes, which appeared to be uttering in words that terrible word—that he would regret this—which she had said to him during their quarrel.

Granted, the rhythmical variation may be beyond capturing, but none of the four translators repro-duces the passive construction used by Tolstoy, or his chain of past participles; what is worse, all blur some vital details in the text. Anna's 'rosy mouth' (*rumyany rot*) has become the more familiar 'red mouth' (Wettlin, Garnett) or even 'red lips' (Maude, Edmonds). Only Garnett has the courage to write as Tolstoy did, baldly conveying the obscenity of death, 'the bloodied body shamelessly stretched out among the living'. In all the other ver-sions, the prurience of the penny dreadful has inter-vened: 'stretched out shamelessly before the eyes of strangers, lay the mangled body still warm with recent life' (Maude); 'her mangled body . . . shame-lessly exposed to the gaze of all' (Edmonds), and even 'her blood-drenched body . . . shamefully exposed to numerous strange staring eyes' (Wettlin: the substitution of 'shameful' for 'shame-less' is a characteristic piece of carelessness on this translator's part).

In her percipient appraisal of Tolstoy, Virginia Woolf argued that the disturbing effect of his work was above all traceable to an uneasy tension between philosophical pessimism and linguistic vitality (Gifford 1971). However, many aspects of Tolstoy's vitality are sadly muted in translation. In the wonderful passage in which Stiva Oblonsky is observed by Levin eating oysters, for example, Tolstoy employs the dialectism *shlyupayushchie* to evoke the sound of the fish as they emerge from their mother-of-pearl shells. The onomatopoeic qualities of the participle are hard to render in Eng-lish: 'slurpaceous' would sound too Wodehousian and facetious. Even Nabokov could only manage the uncharacteristically pallid 'softly plopping'. However, this is considerably better than the ver-sions available in the classic translations: both Edmonds and Maude offer 'quivering', Wettlin has 'juicy molluscs', while Garnett leaves the participle out altogether.

Tolstoy's late fiction has raised problems of rather a different order, not simply because didacti-cism is more explicit here, but because texts such as *Khozyain i rabotnik* (1895, Master and Man) represent a patchwork of diverse linguistic materials, from the Biblical to the sermonistic to the folkloric, with stretches of dialogue and interior monologue in lightly stylized dialect. No one version of this story has successfully rendered all the different levels.

593

The Maudes, for example, disastrously flatten the ending, a rhetorical *memento mori* in which Tolstoy yet slyly suggests that Nikita is not only a moral exemplum but a living person whom a reader might expect to encounter after his or her own inevitable death: 'Whether he is better or worse off there where he awoke after his death, whether he was disappointed or found there what he expected, we shall all soon learn.' Here, our voyage into the hereafter sounds about as interesting as the arrival of an income tax demand. Paul **Foote**'s rendering is not only more accurate (leaving in Tolstoy's rhetorical questions, and the important detail 'his *actual* death'), but also much closer to the sonorous rhythm of the original: 'Is he better or worse off in the place where he awoke after this, his actual death? Was he disappointed, or did he there find what he expected? That we shall all soon know.'

In rendering another layer of the text, the interior monologues of Brekhunov, whose rapacious entrepreneurial instincts unravel as he is left facing death, the Maudes are sometimes more convincing. Dialogue, however, is denaturalized in both versions. While neither Foote nor the Maudes go as far as one early translator, R. Nisbet **Bain** (1854–1909), who had his Russian peasants address each other in phrases such as 'Mischief take you, accursed one!', and described the dead Brekhunov as 'stiff as a cured and salted porpoise' (the original has 'deep-frozen ox-carcass', a rather less exotic sight in the Russian countryside), both employ almost equally unlikely locutions such as 'dear fellow' or 'it seems I must humour the old woman' (Maude), or 'old chap' and 'back in a jiffy' (Foote).

In his comparison of the various translations of Tolstoy's major novels, Henry Gifford suggested that the Maudes' versions were the most accurate, but also commended Edmonds for her rendition of dialogue, and Garnett for her 'modest harmonies' (1978). My consideration of the same material has led me to rather different conclusions. Garnett omits more than the Maudes or Edmonds (which may be the reason why she appears more 'harmonious'), but otherwise the similarities of the various versions are a good deal more striking than their differences (with the possible exception of Wettlin's *Anna Karenina*, where occasional felicities, such as the rendering of Sappho Stolz's *eshafodazh pricheski* as 'gazebo of a coiffure', appear at the price of much carelessness). In all the classic versions, and to some extent also in Foote's and the Maudes' versions of *Master and Man*, Tolstoy emerges as what many British readers have wished that he was: a more intellectually demanding, if less pleasing, version of Turgenev. In versions of his work, the Anglophone conviction that translation of Russian literature is the more or less effortless recovery of a 'message' (May 1994) appears to have interacted with conventional views that realism is a transparent reflection of reality to produce dull and uninspired work. One can only regret that Nabokov never achieved his aim of retranslating *Anna Karenina*, controversial as the result would have been, and wonder whether it might not be time, 40 years after the last serious versions of *Anna Karenina* and *War and Peace*, for a more adventurous rendering, treating the English language as recklessly as Tolstoy did his own mother-tongue. CK

TRANSLATIONS   Bain, R. Nisbet, *Tales from Tolstoi*, London, 1901 · Dole, N. H., *Anna Karenina*, New York, 1887 · *War and Peace*, New York, 1889 · Edmonds, Rosemary, *Anna Karenina*, Harmondsworth, 1954 [Penguin] · *War and Peace*, Harmondsworth, 1957 [Penguin] · Foote, I. P., *Master and Man and Other Stories*, Harmondsworth, 1977 [Penguin] · Garnett, Constance, *The Library Edition of the Works of Count L. N. Tolstoy*, 6 vols., London, 1901–4 [many rep. in Everyman] · Maude, Louise, and Maude, Aylmer, *The Works of L. Tolstoy; Centenary Edition*, 21 vols., Oxford, 1928–37 [many reps. in World's Classics] · Smith, H., *The Physiology of War* [extracts from *War and Peace*], London, 1889 · Wettlin, M., *Anna Karenina*, Moscow, 1978 · Wiener, L., *The Complete* [sic] *works of Count Lev N. Tolstoy*, 24 vols., Boston, 1904–5.

SEE ALSO   Gifford, H., *Leo Tolstoy: a Critical Anthology*, Harmondsworth, 1971 [Penguin] · 'On Translating Tolstoy', in M. V. Jones, ed., *New Essays on Tolstoy*, Cambridge, 1978, pp. 17–38 · May, R., *The Translator in the Text: On Reading Russian Literature in English*, Evanston, Ill., 1994.

5. DOSTOEVSKY

i. **Introduction**   The novels of Fedor Dostoevsky, first published between 1846 and 1880, have been immensely influential throughout the English-speaking world in the 20th c.. To a large extent this is due to a single translator, Constance **Garnett**, but

the second half of the century has seen a flood of new translations of all the major novels. With this has come a heightened awareness of the problems Dostoevsky poses for the translator.

Vladimir Nabokov famously described the

author of *Crime and Punishment* as 'not a great writer, but a rather mediocre one' (Nabokov 1982). Other critics before him had expressed similar reservations, though less provocatively, suggesting that Dostoevsky's powerful emotional and ideological impact was achieved *in spite of* his style. This, compared with that of masters such as Turgenev, was seen as marred by clumsy construction, excessive emotionalism, banality and vulgarity. Translators might thus be expected to smooth out the rough edges in order to make their author more acceptable to western good taste.

This view has not gone unchallenged. Since Mikhail Bakhtin's *Problems of Dostoevsky's Poetics* (1929) became available in English, many of Dostoevsky's so-called faults have become virtues. Bakhtin stressed the polyphony in his novels, the weave and clash of voices. This is clearly seen in the highly individual speech of the characters; the odd voices of Dostoevsky's narrators also play an essential part in the stylistic composition. In a monologue such as *Zapiski iz podpol'ia* (1864, Notes from Underground), the 'bad writing' expresses the violent dialogical pressure within the narrator's language.

An important recent tendency has therefore been to 'unsmooth' Dostoevsky. In France the jagged, vulgar versions produced since 1990 by André Markowicz have created a furore. The English-speaking world has not seen such violent polemics, but both translators and critics have spoken of the need to render the 'vitality and physical strength' of Dostoevsky's writing, the awkwardness or even ungrammaticality of his narrators, the grotesque clash of different voices.

ii. Constance Garnett The first translations came in the 1880s; several authors were involved, the most prolific being Frederick **Whishaw** (1854–1934), several of whose translations were first published in Vizetelly's Russian Novels series before being taken over by Everyman's Library. The real vogue for Dostoevsky, however, came only with the translations produced by Constance Garnett. Garnett began to study Russian in 1892, and only made two visits to the country. Nevertheless, for half a century her versions of Tolstoy, Dostoevsky, Chekhov, Turgenev, Gogol, and others played an inestimable part in introducing Russian fiction to the English-speaking world. Her Dostoevsky in particular made an enormous impact on Virginia Woolf and many others. For Middleton Murry her translation of *Brat'ya Karamazovy* (1880, The Brothers Karamazov) was 'the most successful translation in the history of English literature'.

The Brothers Karamazov, previously untranslated, came out in 1912 and was followed by 11 further volumes in a mere eight years, including the major novels *Idiot* (1868), *Besy* (1872, The Possessed), *Prestuplenie i nakazanie* (1866, Crime and Punishment), *Podrostok* (1875, A Raw Youth), many other shorter novels and stories, and the account of Dostoevsky's years in Siberia, *Zapiski iz mertvogo doma* (1860–2, The House of the Dead). Thereafter, Garnett's translations dominated the scene for 40 years or more; frequently reprinted, notably by Everyman (in some cases replacing earlier versions), they were variously revised, updated, abridged, and adapted for the stage. By the late 20th c. they have been largely ousted from the popular market by their numerous competitors, but they still retain their value.

Garnett's translations read easily (though the relative formality of the style may strike later readers as old-fashioned), and the basic meaning of the Russian text is accurately rendered on the whole. It is true, as critics such as Nikoliukin have demonstrated, that she shortens and simplifies, muting Dostoevsky's jarring contrasts, sacrificing his insistent rhythms and repetitions, toning down the Russian colouring, explaining and normalizing in all kinds of ways. To take one example, in the climactic passage in *Crime and Punishment* where Raskolnikoff kisses Sonya's foot, Garnett simplifies Sonya's breathless reaction (*Chto vy, chto vy eto? Peredo mnoy?*, 'What are you, what are you doing? In front of me?') to 'What are you doing to me?' and her 'a sudden anguish clutched her heart' tones down the perhaps embarrassing emotionalism of Dostoevsky's narrator. Nevertheless, her fluent renderings allow Dostoevsky's current to pass over into English. Take, for instance, this passage from the penultimate chapter of *The Brothers Karamazov*, which may be compared with other translations quoted below:

Grushenka walked suddenly and noiselessly into the room. No one had expected her. Katya moved swiftly to the door, but when she reached Grushenka she stopped suddenly, turned as white as chalk and moaned softly, almost in a whisper:
'Forgive me!'
Grushenka stared at her and, pausing for an instant, in a vindictive, venomous voice, answered:
'We are full of hatred, my girl, you and I! We are both full of hatred! As though we could forgive one another! Save him, and I'll worship you all my life!'

Garnett sacrificed some of Dostoevsky's idiosyncrasy in order to produce an acceptable English text, but her versions were in many cases pioneering versions; decorous they may be, but they allowed this strange new voice to invade English literature and thus made it possible for later translators to go further in the search for a more authentic voice.

iii. After Garnett 1949 saw the publication of a translation of Dostoevsky's *Dnevnik pisatelya* (The Diary of a Writer) by Boris **Brasol**, an important event not so much for the quality of the translation (which is adequate) as for the importance of the text. Shortly afterwards began a long series of new translations produced by David **Magarshack** in the 1950s and 1960s for Penguin Classics. It is not as complete as Garnett's, but it includes what are generally regarded as the 'great four novels' (*The Possessed* being now given the more literal translation of *The Devils*) and many shorter works. In the second edition of his *Tolstoy or Dostoevsky* (1967), George Steiner wrote that these translations 'supersede those that have gone before', but it is not certain that Magarshack has worn as well as Garnett. He certainly corrects some of her errors; he also aims for a more up-to-date style which flows easily in English. A small example from the first page of *Crime and Punishment* will illustrate this: where David McDuff's more literal version (see below) follows Dostoevsky's word order: ' "I plan to attempt a thing like this, yet I allow that kind of rubbish to scare me!" he thought with a strange smile', Magarshack's free rendering reads more naturally: ' "Good Lord!" he thought to himself with a strange smile, "here I am thinking of such a thing and at the same time I am in a jitter over such a trivial matter." ' Being even more thoroughly englished than Garnett's, Magarshack's translations lack some of the excitement of the foreign.

A similar domestication is at work in the unsatisfactory translations, including *The Possessed* and *The Brothers Karamazov*, published in America in the 1960s and 1970s by Andrew **MacAndrew**. This translator, comparing his work to that of a conductor performing a classic on an orchestra of outlandish instruments, speaks of the need to adapt the music to the instruments. He therefore translates fairly freely, altering details, rearranging, shortening and explaining the Russian to produce texts which lack a distinctive voice. Like Magarshack, he tends to anglicize proper names ('Mr Karamazov' rather than 'Dmitry Fyodorovich').

Over the same period as Magarshack and MacAndrew, Jessie **Coulson** translated a number of important works for Penguin or Oxford, in particular *Crime and Punishment* and *Notes from Underground*, both of which have enjoyed lasting success. Like Garnett's, these versions are fluent

but tend to flatten and abbreviate the text. The passage from Book IV of *Crime and Punishment* mentioned above is rather more accurately done than in the Garnett translation. Sonia's words are better rendered ('Why, why do you do that? To me!'), but then Coulson reduces the narrator's emotionalism even further ('her heart contracted painfully'). In her *Notes from Underground*, likewise, the abrasive tone of the narrator is noticeably toned down; Coulson's correct English syntax and her sense of stylistic decorum contrast with the vivid bad writing of Markowicz's French version—but no other English-language translator of this text matches the explosive jaggedness of the original (the best is perhaps that of Michael **Katz**).

The late 1980s and the 1990s saw the beginning of two major new series of Dostoevsky translations, by David **McDuff** in Britain and by Richard **Pevear** and Larissa **Volokhonsky** in America. Both of these, in prefaces and publicity material, proclaim the need to restore what McDuff calls the 'sound, tone and timbre' of Dostoevsky's voice and Pevear and Volokhonsky his 'idiosyncratic prose' and the 'distinctive voicing of his novel'. In both cases this leads to literal rendering, including an attempt to echo in English the syntax and word order of the Russian—and since Dostoevsky, both in his narrative and his dialogue, exploits the freedom of Russian word order to the full, the resulting English translation sometimes seems distinctly odd—deliberately so, of course.

McDuff carries this literalism the furthest of any of the translators. In his *Brothers Karamazov* the odd, fussy tone of the narrator is well rendered in the preface (entirely omitted by Garnett) and in the body of the text. Compare for instance the presentation of Father Paisy in Book II, Chapter 2, 'a man ill though not old, but very—as was said of him—learned', with the much more normal-sounding version in Garnett: 'a very learned man, so they said, in delicate health, though not old'. At times, indeed, the convoluted style might make the reader unfamiliar with Dostoevsky's Russian question the translator's command of English. More seriously, this literalism means that the dialogue is sometimes impossibly odd—and as a result rather dead. McDuff's carefully literal version of the passage from *The Brothers Karamazov* quoted earlier reads as follows:

Into the room, suddenly, though very quietly, Grushenka had come. No one had expected her. Katya took an impetuous step towards the door, but, on drawing even with Grushenka suddenly stopped, turned white as chalk all over and quietly, almost in a whisper, moaned to her:

'Forgive me!'

The other stared at her and then, after a moment's wait, in a venomous, malice-poisoned voice replied:

'It's wicked we are, mother, you and I! Wicked, both of us! How can it be for us to forgive, you and I? Now if you'll rescue him, all the rest of my life I will pray for you.'

Garnett's 'worship you' is more accurate here than McDuff's 'pray for you', and her 'full of hatred' is arguably a better translation than 'wicked' of the difficult Russian adjective *zloy*. Otherwise, the differences between the two versions are mainly due to McDuff's decision to stick closely to the original: such things as the word order of the first sentence, the odd 'drawing even with', the indication 'to her' after 'moaned', the foreign-sounding 'the other', the compound adjective 'malice-poisoned', and the literal translation of the Russian term of address 'mother'. Such 'foreignizing' fidelity makes for difficult reading.

Pevear and Volokhonsky, while they too stress the need to exhume the real, rough-edged Dostoevsky from the normalization practised by earlier translators, generally offer a rather more satisfactory compromise between the literal and the readable. In particular, their rendering of dialogue is often livelier and more colloquial than McDuff's, though they are not more successful than other translators in rendering the narrator's tone in *Notes from Underground*. Here is their translation of the same passage from *The Brothers Karamazov*:

All at once, though very quietly, Grushenka came into the room. No one was expecting her. Katya stepped swiftly towards the door, but, coming up with Grushenka, she suddenly stopped, turned white as chalk, and softly, almost in a whisper, moaned to her:

'Forgive me!!

The other woman stared her in the face and, pausing for a moment, answered in a venomous voice, poisoned with wickedness:

'We are wicked, sister, you and I! We're both wicked! It's not for us to forgive! Save him, and I'll pray to you all my life.'

One could argue about the 'wicked' here, but generally this rendering is accurate even in small details (with the exception that the penultimate sentence is changed from a rhetorical question to an exclamation), yet preserves much of the life of Dostoevsky's text. Elsewhere, it has to be said, the desire to replicate the vocabulary or the syntax of the Russian results sometimes in unnecessary awkwardness and obscurity. Take this little sentence from *Demons*: 'The old woman brings her something from the wing every once in a while for the love of Christ.' With greater freedom, this is much better rendered by Michael Katz in his *Devils*: 'The old woman who lives in the annexe sometimes gives her something to eat out of charity.'

Katz is one of several translators who have translated just one or two of Dostoevsky's texts. His *Devils* is lively and readable, bringing across effectively something of the humour of this strange work. It belongs to a series of new translations by various hands published in the Oxford World's Classics. The same collection includes what is at least the tenth version of *Notes from Underground*, the work of Jane **Kentish**; this translates Dostoevsky's meaning and shifting tone scrupulously if a little flatly. Unlike *Notes*, the novel translated by Garnett as *A Raw Youth* has not attracted many translators; Richard **Freeborn**'s World's Classics version of *Podrostok, An Accidental Family*, while it is not noticeably more accurate than Garnett, transmits more strongly than she does the frantic tone of its incompetent narrator.

This series also offers a new translation of *The Karamazov Brothers* by Ignat **Avsey**, who claims quite rightly that the usual order of words in the title is an unjustified calque of the normal Russian word order. His not entirely unprecedented choice of a more natural-sounding English formulation is symptomatic of his general desire to make his text English. Warning against the danger of 'being mesmerized by the original, and in the process violating the norms of [the] target language', he is quite willing to be free in order to be readable— thus, in the passage already quoted above, his Katya is not 'white as chalk', but 'white as a sheet'. His is an enjoyable version in the domesticating tradition.

Finally, also in World's Classics, there are two fine translations by Alan **Myers**. These are *The Idiot*, the best version currently available, and a remarkable small volume including the short novels *A Gentle Creature* and *White Nights*. Both of these, like *Notes from Underground*, are presented in the distraught voice of a tragic narrator, and Myers manages to convey this type of frantic orality better than any other translator.

There can be few, if any, examples of a modern novelist who has been so copiously retranslated as Dostoevsky. The special features of his writing offer an unusual challenge. While one may criticize the normalizing tendency so well illustrated by Constance Garnett, it does not seem that the literal echoing of the syntactical and stylistic peculiarities of the Russian is enough to convey the life of the text. Above all, translating Dostoevsky calls for daring.   PF

TRANSLATIONS   Avsey, Ignat, *The Village of Stepanchikovo and Its Inhabitants*, London, 1983 · *The Karamazov Brothers*, Oxford, 1994 [World's Classics] · Bird, George, *The Double*, London, 1957 · Brasol, Boris, *The Diary of a Writer*, New York, 1949 · Coulson, Jessie, *Crime and Punishment*, Oxford, 1953 [World's Classics] · *Memoirs from the House of the Dead*, Oxford, 1956 [World's Classics] · *The Gambler and Other Stories*, Harmondsworth, 1966 [Penguin] · *Notes from Underground; The Double*, Harmondsworth; 1972 [Penguin] · Freeborn, Richard, *An Accidental Family*, Oxford, 1994 [World's Classics] · Garnett, Constance, *The Novels of Fyodor Dostoevsky*, 12 vols., London, 1912–20 [frequent reprints, including Everyman] · Katz, Michael, *Notes from Underground*, New York, 1989 · *Devils*, Oxford, 1992 [World's Classics] · Kentish, Jane, *Netochka Nezvanova*, London, 1985 [Penguin] · *Notes from Underground; The Gambler*, Oxford, 1991 [World's Classics] · MacAndrew, Andrew R., *Notes from Underground and Selected Stories*, New York, 1961 · *The Possessed*, New York, 1962 · *The Gambler*, New York, 1964 · *Three Short Novels*, New York, 1966 · *The Brothers Karamazov*, Toronto, 1970 [all Signet] · McDuff, David, *The Brothers Karamazov*, London, 1974 · *The House of the Dead*, London, 1985 · *Poor Folk and Other Stories*, London, 1988 · *Uncle's Dream and Other Stories*, London, 1989 · *Crime and Punishment*, London, 1991 [all Penguin] · Magarshack, David, *Crime and Punishment*, London, 1951 · *The Devils*, London, 1953 · *The Idiot*, London, 1955 · *The Brothers Karamazov*, London, 1958 [all Penguin] · Monas, Sidney, *Crime and Punishment*, New York, 1968 · Myers, Alan, *The Idiot*, Oxford, 1992 [World's Classics] · *A Gentle Creature and Other Stories*, Oxford, 1995 [World's Classics] · Pevear, Richard, and Volokhonsky, Larissa, *The Brothers Karamazov*, New York, 1990 · *Crime and Punishment*, New York, 1992 [Everyman, 1993] · *Notes from Underground*, New York, 1993 · *Demons*, New York, 1994 · Whishaw, Frederick, *Crime and Punishment*, London, 1885 · *The Idiot*, London, 1887 [both subsequently Everyman].

SEE ALSO   Bakhtin, M., *Problems of Dostoevsky's Poetics*, tr. Caryl Emerson, Manchester, 1973 · France, P., 'Dostoevskii Rough and Smooth', *Forum in Modern Language Studies*, 32 (1996), 1–9 · Nabokov, V., *Lectures on Russian Literature*, ed. F. Bowers, London, 1982 · Nikoliukin, A. N., 'Dostoevskii in Constance Garnett's Translation', in W. J. Leatherbarrow, ed., *Dostoevskii and Britain*, Oxford/Providence, RI, 1985.

6. CHEKHOV

i. Fiction, Prose, and Letters English was one of the last major languages into which Anton Chekhov's stories and plays were translated—a fact partially explained by the relative indifference of English, as opposed to German or central European critics, writers and theatres, to Russian literature, and partly by Chekhov's own reluctance to encourage translators—he told Olga Vasilieva, who undertook a series of translations (which never saw print), that being translated was a matter of complete indifference to him, since the English could have nothing in common with the life of his characters. As Russia was not party to international copyright agreements, Chekhov had no financial inducements for encouraging translation: he was never offered a penny by those translating him into English. In his lifetime, in the United States a couple of minor stories were published in periodicals. Before World War I the only significant story of Chekhov's to be published in America was 'Khudozhestvo' (1886, A Work of Art), translated in 1908 by Archibald J. **Wolfe**.

The first British publication of Chekhov came in 1903, only a year before the author's death: 'Cherny monakh' (1894, The Black Monk) was the title-story of R. C. E. **Long**'s anthology. English-language writers, such as James Joyce and Katherine Mansfield, first read Chekhov, as they did other Russian writers, in German, although in 1908 Long pro-

duced one more selection in which 'Potseluy' (1887, The Kiss) was the title story.

The reputation, even notoriety of Russian opera and ballet in France, reports of the innovations in the Russian Arts Theatre and a new attitude to Russia generated by political entente led to the first wave of translations and productions of Chekhov's plays in Scotland, England, and then the United States. The primitive quality of the translations, in which knowledge of Russian was inadequate and that of the theatre amateurish, evoked dismay. World War I, however, gave public and official support to projects that would show Russian culture worth fighting for. From 1916 a comprehensive, 13-volume set of Chekhov's stories began to appear in a translation by Constance **Garnett** (1861–1946) which, despite elementary linguistic mistakes and an unfamiliarity with Russian everyday life, were sufficiently distinguished in style and presentation to secure Chekhov's reputation as a major writer.

Garnett, writing in a 'timeless' 19th-c. language, was close enough to the original to make further translation redundant. When 1918 brought an influx of Russian refugees into Britain, and Russian literature became a force in modernism, new translators filled the gaps, rather than displacing Garnett. Her multi-volume collection, despite including most mature work, included an unrepresentative selection of Chekhov's stories before 1888, and lacked those mature stories, such as 'Ogni' (1890, Lights), or 'U znakomykh' (1898, A Visit to Friends), which Chekhov had excluded from the collected works published in his lifetime. S. S. **Koteliansky**, in the 1920s and 1930s, was the most effective of supplementary translators, for he sought help from writers in the same Bloomsbury circle as Garnett— D. H. Lawrence, John Middleton Murry, Leonard Woolf—to polish his English. Some major stories, such as 'Moya zhizn'' (1896, My Life), were retranslated by Koteliansky, and his version of this story (with Gilbert Canaan, 1920) is finer than Garnett's.

Nevertheless some Chekhov stories remained untranslated, notably the curious novel, unique in Chekhov's œuvre, *Drama na okhote* (1884–5, A Shooting Party). This was translated by A. **Chamot** in 1926, as well as other forgotten pieces, in versions which despite their imperfections were reprinted in 1945 and 1986.

In America, comprehensive selections of Chekhov's stories by Marian **Fell**, of appalling incompetence, began to appear in 1914. (Adeline Lister **Kaye** in 1915 was no better.) They were superseded by Garnett, although reluctance to pay copyright still leads publishers to reprint them.

The spirit of the wartime Alliance from 1941 to 1945 led to the reissue of many Chekhov stories and to further translations, although there was no advance in the quality of the versions. In the last 30 years, however, Constance Garnett has herself been superseded by translators with a more profound knowledge of Russian, first by David **Magarshack** and Jessie **Coulson** in the 1960s and then by Ronald **Hingley**, whose Oxford Chekhov (1966–75) embraces all the mature work, almost faultlessly translated and admirably annotated. Hingley's approach to translation is radical: not just sentence order, but sometimes paragraph order is reversed, and even Christian names are translated. His colloquial language is sometimes reminiscent of P. G. Wodehouse, a quality that has prevented his versions of Chekhov's plays reaching the stage. Revisions of Constance Garnett are still justified, not merely because they are now out of copyright, but because once her lexical errors are put right, a subtle version, stylistically compatible with the original, emerges. Following Hingley, a new force, Ronald **Wilks** (an equally accurate but blander translator) has produced a substantial number of the mature stories, in four Penguin volumes, carefully arranged so that the purchaser has to buy all four to obtain a representative collection.

A very few stories exist in versions far superior to those done by translators of selected or collected works: David **Tutaev**'s 1959 version of 'Zhivoy tovar' (1882, Wife for Sale) is unsurpassed, as is Charles **Dowsett**'s 'Kashtanka' (1887, Kashtanka).

Readers in search of early (1880–8) or obscure Chekhov stories have had to search the catalogues and shelves of major libraries for those that have escaped Garnett, Chamot, Koteliansky, Coulson, Hingley, and Wilks. Some were collected, in often poor translation, by Avrahm **Yarmolinsky** in 1959, a collection expanded to *The Portable Chekhov* in 1977. Raduga and Progress publishers in Moscow produced versions which were faithful to the Russian but whose translators' English was often insecure. These volumes were not systematically marketed outside Russia. Nevertheless, the five-volume collection of 1987 is a well-produced and readable collection.

Nora **Gottlieb** skilfully retranslated a number of early stories in 1960. Only in the 1970s and 1980s did Harvey **Pitcher**, first with James **Forsyth** and then with Patrick **Miles**, produce a representative and beautifully translated selection of Chekhov's early work, misleadingly treated as juvenilia by the major translators. In 1998 Peter **Constantine** published over 30 early comic tales in thoughtful, if over-hyped, translations. Nevertheless at least a dozen important early stories, as well as *A Shooting Party*, await professional translation.

Of Chekhov's non-fictional prose, his satirical journalism of the 1880s has barely been touched by translators. Chekhov's most intriguing heritage, the only writing he did not intend for others' eyes, four *Zapisnye knizhki* (1891–1904, Notebooks), are a bibliographical rarity in English, published in Koteliansky's version by Virginia and Leonard Woolf at the Hogarth Press in 1921. *Ostrov Sakhalin* (1895, The Island of Sakhalin) has, however, been translated three times since 1977, each version an improvement, the last by Brian **Reeves** in 1993.

Chekhov's letters have appeared in several collections over the last 70 years. Constance Garnett produced two selections, to friends and family and then to Olga Knipper, in 1920 and 1926. Letters on literary matters were translated by Louis S. **Friedland** and published in 1924. Koteliansky produced a varied selection a year later. Comprehensive selections appeared only in the 1970s: Avrahm Yarmolinsky's the larger, Michael **Heim**'s the better translated, while Lillian Hellman's edition, translated by Sidonie **Lederer**, followed in 1985. Both sides of Chekhov's correspondence with Olga Knipper have been translated, but with gross errors introduced and all Soviet editorial cuts preserved, in a deplorable version by Jean **Benedetti** in 1997. Previous versions of Chekhov's letters are superseded by the beautifully translated, annotated, and produced *Anton Chekhov: A Life in Letters* by Gordon **McVay**, where a greater number of letters has been presented in extract to give a biographical portrait. The only lacunae are the bawdy passages bowdlerized in Soviet editions; major deletions can be restored from the present author's article in *Comparative Criticism*, 16 (1994).

ii. Drama Proliferation and confusion of translation reign in the plays. Throughout the history of Chekhov on the British and American stage we see a version translated, adapted, cobbled together for each new major production, very often by a theatre director with no knowledge of the original, working from a crib prepared by a Russian with no knowledge of the stage. Translations—Garnett, Koteliansky, Hingley—which were more than adequate to the short story have proved unusable for actors, although good reading versions have been produced. Some widely distributed versions, by Elizaveta **Fen** and Marian Fell, have nothing to be said in their favour. Nevertheless, they have been used as a basis by actors wary of literally unspeakable texts. Stark Young, John Gielgud, Trevor Griffiths, Pam Gems, and David Mamet (as well as anonymous tamperers) are all examples of critics, actors, or directors who have produced stageable versions which ignore Chekhov's original text.

In Britain, the Armed Forces Joint Service Courses of the 1950s produced Russian translators of a standard previously unknown. One of them, himself an important dramatist, is Michael **Frayn** and his versions of Chekhov's major plays (up to 1988) are the first to be fully actable and true renderings of the original. Only the impecuniousness or egotism of directors prevents them monopolizing the British and American stage. Nevertheless, Frayn has left some of Chekhov's heritage untranslated; here Ronald Hingley's versions must stand. A few experiments, more adaptation than translation, deserve mention: Basil **Ashmore**'s *Platonov* (1883) as *Don Juan in the Russian Manner* is one. Finally, there have been adaptations of both plays and early stories to make virtually new works. Michael Frayn's *The Sneeze* is one such actor's vehicle, compiled from farces both dramatic and prosaic, like Neil Simon's *The Good Doctor* in 1973. 'Pari' (1889, The Bet) was anonymously transformed to a farce in 1957. Plays—particularly *Dyadya Vanya* (1897, Uncle Vanya), and *Vishnevy sad* (1904, The Cherry Orchard)—have been reset in Ireland, Australia, and the American Appalachians. Sporadically, Chekhov's works have been adapted for opera—e.g. William Walton's version of *Medved'* (1888, The Bear), based on a libretto by Paul Dehn (published 1967), or Sharon Gans and Jordan Chaung's *A Chekhov Concert* of arias and duets (1993). Other adaptations, such as John Fletcher's radio play *The Apple Orchard* (1992), are more parody than translation.   PDR

Fiction, Prose, and Letters   Chamot, A., *The Shooting Party*, London, 1986 · Constantine, Peter, *The Undiscovered Chekhov*, London, 1998 · Coulson, Jessie, *Selected Stories*, London, 1963 · Dowsett, Charles, *Kashtanka*, London, 1959 · Friedland, Louis S., *Letters on the Short Story, the Drama and Other Literary Topics*, London, 1924 · Garnett, Constance, *The Tales of Anton Tchechov*, 13 vols., London, 1916–22 · *Letters of Anton Tchechov to His Family and Friends*, London, 1920 · *The Letters of Anton Tchechov to O. L. Knipper*, London, 1926 · rev. D. Rayfield, *The Chekhov Omnibus*, London, 1994 [Everyman] · Heim, Michael, and Karlinsky, Simon, *Letters of Anton Chekhov*, London, 1973 · Helman, Lillian, and Lederer, Sidonie, *Selected Letters*, London, 1984 · Hingley, Ronald, *The Oxford Chekhov*, 9 vols., 1972– · Kaye, Adeline Lister, *The Steppe*, London, 1915 · Koteliansky, S. S., *The Notebooks of Anton Tchechov*, Richmond, UK, 1921 · *Literary and Theatrical Writings, and Other Unpublished Work*, London, 1927 · *The Lady with the Toy Dog*, London, 1943 · Koteliansky, S. S., and Cameron, Gilbert, *My Life*, London, 1920 · Koteliansky, S. S., and Murry, John Middleton, *The Bet*, London, 1915 · Litvinov, Ivy, et al., *Collected Works*, 5 vols., Moscow, 1987 · Long, R. C. E., *The Black Monk and Other Stories*, London, 1903 · McVay, Gordon, *Anton Chekhov: A Life in Letters*, London, 1994 · Magarshack, David, *Lady with Lapdog*, London, 1964 [Penguin] · Miles, Patrick, and Pitcher, Harvey, *Early Stories*, London, 1994 · Reeves, Brian, *The Island of Sakhalin*, London, 1993 · Schimanskaya, E. R., *My Life*, London, 1943 · Tutaev, David, *A Wife for Sale*, London, 1959 · Wilks, Ronald, *The Kiss and Other Stories*, London, 1982 [Penguin] · *The Duel and Other Stories*, London, 1984 [Penguin] · *The Party and Other Stories*, London, 1985 [Penguin] · *The Fiancée and Other Stories*, London, 1986 [Penguin] · Yarmolinsky, Avrahm, *Letters of Anton Chekhov*, London, 1974.

Drama   Ashmore, Basil, *Don Juan in the Russian Manner* [*Platonov*], London, 1952 · Calderon, George, *Two Plays of Tchekhof* [*The Seagull; The Cherry Orchard*], London, 1912 · Fell, Marian, *Plays. First Series* [*Uncle Vanya; Ivanov; The Seagull*], New York, 1912 · Fen, Elisaveta, *Three Plays* [*Ivanov; Three Sisters; The Cherry Orchard*], London, 1951 · Frayn, Michael, *Wild Honey* [*Platonov*], London, 1984 · *Plays* [excluding *The Wood Demon*], London, 1993 · Gielgud, John, *The Cherry Orchard*, London, 1963 · Gielgud, John, and Nicolaeff, Ariadne, *Ivanov*, London, 1966 · Griffiths, Trevor, and Rappaport, Helen, *The Cherry Orchard*, London, 1989 · Harwood, Ronald, *Ivanov*, Charlbury, UK, 1989 · Hingley, Ronald, *Twelve Plays*, Oxford, 1992 · Koteliansky, S. S., *The Wood Demon*, London, 1926 · *Three Plays*

[*The Wood Demon*; *The Seagull*; *The Cherry Orchard*], New York, 1940 · Magarshack, David, *The Seagull* [as produced by Stanislavsky], London, 1952 · *Platonov*, London, 1964 · Mamet, David, and Chernomordov, Vlada, *Three Sisters*, New York, 1993 · Mitchell, Julian, and Alexander, Tania, *August* [*Uncle Vanya*], London, 1994 · West, Julius, *Plays: Second Series* [*The Cherry Orchard*; *Three Sisters*; *On the Highway*; *The Proposal*; *The Marriage*; *The Bear*; *The Tragedy Actor*], New York, 1916.

SEE ALSO   Heifetz, A., *Chekhov in English*, *Bulletin of New York Public Library*, 1949 · Rayfield, D., 'Sanitizing the Classics', *Comparative Criticism*, 16 (1994), 19–32 · Senelick, L., *The Chekhov Theatre*, Cambridge, 1997 · Terras, V., 'Bibliography' and other articles, in T. Clyman, ed., *A Chekhov Companion*, Westport, Conn., 1985 · Worrall, N., *File on Chekhov*, London, 1986 · Yachnin, R., *Chekhov in English 1949–1960*, New York, 1960.

7. TWENTIETH-CENTURY POETRY

i. Introduction It was in the second half of the 20th c. that the English-speaking public really became aware of the greatness of some of the Russian poetry written since 1900. There had been many earlier translations of individual poems in anthologies and elsewhere (including a fine rendering of Blok's 'Neznakomka' (1906, The Stranger) into Scots in Hugh **MacDiarmid**'s *A Drunk Man Looks at the Thistle* (1926)), but for the most part separate volumes devoted to individual poets came later. The translation and reception of Russian poetry was affected, moreover, by developments within the Soviet Union; the appeal of poets was sometimes that of heroes or martyrs.

For a long period the officially approved poetry of Mayakovsky was the most visible. The 'Thaw' around 1960 saw the appearance of a new generation of poets who achieved great popularity. Thereafter the English-speaking public began to discover the poets who had inspired these new young stars, a canonic group including Blok, Pasternak, Akhmatova, Mandelstam, and Tsvetaeva. Other important poets, even when translated, tended to be relegated to a second division. From the 1970s, however, Brodsky rose to a lonely eminence which was consecrated by his Nobel Prize in 1987.

The case of Brodsky highlights a particular dilemma which has affected the translation of 20th-c. Russian poetry. Not only are there major differences between the Russian and English languages, but the two poetic cultures are markedly divergent. Free verse was until recently rare in Russia, and even today traditional prosody, though used in a flexible and inventive manner, retains a central position. In addition, Russian is not known to many of the English-language poets who have felt drawn to translate the Russian poets from 'literals', but have no first-hand experience of the formal qualities of the original.

Rather than run the risk of doggerel by matching form with form, many have preferred to translate into the normal free verse of 20th-c. poetic translation, where image dominates at the expense of sound and shape. This practice was attacked by Brodsky [see I.c.1.iv], who believed that 'metres in verse are kinds of spiritual magnitudes for which nothing can be substituted'; his defence of rhyming translation is in line with Russian practice, but few translators have been willing to go as far as he would have wished down this road.

ii. The Symbolists The symbolist movement was at the cutting edge of Russian modernism from the 1890s to about 1910, but many of the great poets of this period, such as Valery Bryusov, Vyacheslav Ivanov, and Innokenty Annensky, have apparently never achieved separate book publication in English. Andrey Bely is a partial exception; while his poetry has not had the appeal of his novel *Petersburg* [II.p.8.ii], there is a good bilingual edition of his coruscating *Pervoe svidanie* (1921, First Encounter) by Gerald **Janecek**, and a sensitive rendering by Roger and Angela **Keys** of his innovative prose poem *Dramaticheskaya simfonia* (1901, Dramatic Symphony).

But the symbolist who stands out in translation is Aleksandr Blok. In particular, a dozen or more translators have risen to the challenge of his 12-poem cycle of the Revolution, *Dvenadtsat'* (1918, The Twelve), with its whirling rhythms and virtuoso mix of slang, popular song, political slogan, parody romance, and high poetry. The first translation, a plain version by C. E. **Bechofer**, appeared almost immediately. There is a fine Scots version by Sydney Goodsir **Smith**, whose Red Guard says: 'Flee awa, bourgeois, like wee speugs!', and among other translations one should at least mention those of Robin **Fulton** and Alex **Miller**. Fulton's version is vividly phrased but rather lacking in rhythmic force: Miller's was unaccountably criticized for vulgarity on its first appearance in *Stand* (8, 1954), but was later included in Miller's *Selected Poems*, published in Moscow, which gives an extensive view of Blok's varied *œuvre*. Like Miller's, the smaller collection translated by Jon **Stallworthy** and Peter **France** aims to reflect something of Blok's verse forms, but pulls Blok further in the direction of English poetry; it includes a fine attempt at *The Twelve* done by Stallworthy with Max **Hayward**.

iii. The Generation of 1910 A remarkable group of poets began writing or publishing around 1910. The least translated of them is the 'futurian' Velimir Khlebnikov, described by Roman Jakobson as 'perhaps the most important modern poet in the world'. His great and disorderly poetic *œuvre*, delving among the roots of the Russian language to create modern myths, is often considered untranslatable. However, 1976 brought an interesting volume of excerpts, *Snake Train*, translated by various hands, and this was followed in 1985 by a selection entirely translated by Paul **Schmidt**, a sampler for his translation of the complete writings, which began to appear in 1987. The verse is rendered here with inventiveness and vigour, as in the famous 'Incantation by Laughter': 'Hlahla! Uthlofan, lauflings!'

The other great futurist poet, Vladimir Mayakovsky, was to become after his suicide in 1930 the official Soviet bard; he has not fared particularly well in translation. The three-volume Moscow edition is translated in a quite lively manner by Dorian **Rottenberg**, although his insistence on full rhyming forces quite a few infelicities and shifts of meaning. The full and well-illustrated selection by Herbert **Marshall**, also rhyming, but less obtrusively so, stays closer to Mayakovsky's meaning and often reads quite well, though it has its wooden passages, as do the poems translated by George **Reavey** in the bilingual volume edited by Patricia Blake. A few early poems are rendered with some vigour in Maria **Enzensberger**'s *Listen!* However, the translation which best reflects Mayakovsky's energy and verbal inventiveness is Edwin **Morgan**'s version of 25 poems in Scots; here is the opening of the poem about Brooklyn Bridge:

> Coolidge ahoy!
> Can ye shout wi joy?
> This makar'll no be blate
>   at namin
> what's guid.
>   Blush rid
>   at my praises, you s-
> uperunited states-man—
>   rid
>   as the flamin
> flag o Sovetsky Soyuz.

Mayakovsky's one-time friend and rival, Boris Pasternak, a great lyric poet over nearly 50 years,

was relatively little translated until the award of the Nobel Prize for *Doctor Zhivago* in 1958 made him the target of persecution at home and intense interest abroad. Volumes appeared in quick succession. These include a selection by his sister, Lydia Pasternak **Slater**, which quite successfully catches something of his rhythm and voice, especially in the early poems, a longer, less interesting collection by George Reavey, and a later volume by Jon Stallworthy and Peter France, a fairly close translation attempting to convey something of the formal qualities of the original.

There has been no 'complete works' of Pasternak in English, and his lyrical masterpiece, *Sestra moya—zhizn'* (1922, My Sister Life) was only recently translated complete, by Mark **Rudman** and Bohdan **Boychuk**. These versions are bold, free, and unrhymed, and the success rate is uneven. An exciting recent volume is the selection of early poems by Andrei **Navrozov**, an unrepentant 'foreignizer', who stresses rhyme and the roots of words, and sometimes achieves shockingly Pasternakian moments:

> The buds burnt to butts their unctuous essence
> To lighten and lessen the burden of kindling
> April. The parks grew redolent of adolescence
> And forest replies redounded, dwindling.

Anna Akhmatova, the other member of this Pleiade to outlive Stalin, has also been much praised and translated, for the most part since 1960, though there is an early volume by Natalie **Duddington**. Two selections in particular make some attempt to echo Akhmatova's forms and sounds, the bilingual volume of Stanley **Kunitz** and Max Hayward and the Penguin of D. M. **Thomas**. The latter rhymes lightly and departs from the original meaning at times, but at his best is surprisingly successful at conjuring up Akhmatova's voice, notably in the haunting poem of memory, *Poema bez geroya* (1940–62, Poem Without a Hero).

Richard **McKane**'s translations, which have grown to include a very large selection of Akhmatova's verse, concentrate on meaning and image at the expense of rhyme and prosody; they are very exact and sometimes impressive, as in the bleak lament for the purges, *Rekviem* (1963, Requiem), and generally have more force than the more recent *Complete Poems* of Judith **Hemschemeyer**. The attempt at a complete translation is perhaps unwise, since there is an inevitable tendency to iron out the differences in a long and varied *œuvre*. Hemschemeyer's versions are careful and accurate, sacrificing sound to sense; the early poems in particular often come over rather flatly.

Osip Mandelstam became known later than Pasternak or Akhmatova, largely through the publication in 1971 of his widow Nadezhda's memoirs. His rich and difficult work has attracted many translations, of varying quality. There was an early *Complete Poetry* from Burton **Raffel** and Alla **Burago**, whose translations are rather cavalier and do not convey a great deal of Mandelstam. There is also a complete bilingual version of the early *Kamen'* (1913, Stone) by Robert **Tracy**; this imitates the highly crafted form of the original, and does so with more success than Bernard **Meares**, in whose selection rhyme and metre lead to some padding and awkwardness.

Most translators, however, aim to convey Mandelstam's matter rather than imitating his manner; such are the selections of David **McDuff** and R. H. **Morrison**. The early translations by Clarence **Brown** and W. S. **Merwin** have their virtues, but have been much criticized, and are now replaced in the Penguin collection by a remarkable short volume from James **Greene**. Greene does not attempt to mimic the powerful sound and shape of the originals and in some cases he translates only parts of poems, but his Mandelstam is an arresting poet:

Oh if some day—sidestepping sleep and death—
A goad of air or summer's sting
Could pierce me into hearing
The buzz of earth, buzz of the earth.

This is from the cryptic, inspired *Voronezhskie Tetradi* (written 1935–8, Voronezh Notebooks), recently, like the *Moscow Notebooks*, translated in full by Richard and Elizabeth McKane. Avoiding poeticization, the McKanes represent the sense of the often difficult original scrupulously and with a striking sharpness of word and image, giving support to the view that the *Notebooks* are among the great works of 20th-c. poetry.

The last great poet of the generation of 1910, Marina Tsvetaeva, has fared less well, though she has become very popular in English. This is largely thanks to Elaine **Feinstein**, author of a life of the poet, whose 1971 translations have been frequently reprinted. These read impressively as poems, even though they give little idea of Tsvetaeva's extraordinary way with syntax and prosody and contain many significant misreadings. David McDuff's selection comes rather closer to Tsvetaeva's form and is quite an exact translation, as is the bilingual version of *Posle Rossii* (1928, After Russia) done by Michael M. **Nayden** and Slava **Yastremski**. There is, however, one translation, Angela **Livingstone**'s version of excerpts from Tsvetaeva's Pied Piper poem, *Krysolov* (1926, The Ratcatcher), which in

its inventive strangeness suggests to an English reader the sheer originality that marks the original. Livingstone also published in 1992 a fine translation of the essay *Art in the Light of Conscience*.

Such is the established pantheon of poets. It excludes some major writers. There is only one satisfying English selection, by Geoffrey **Thurley**, of Mayakovsky's contemporary, the very popular peasant poet and 'hooligan' Sergey Yesenin. Of a somewhat later generation, the essential figure is Nikolay Zabolotsky, whose poems, at first grotesque, later more classical, convey a unique vision of humanity's place in the world. A small and attractive volume translated by Daniel **Weissbort** in 1971, has been superseded by his much larger selection in 1999, and there are also some fine translations by various hands in Robin **Milner-Gulland**'s translation of the *Life of Zabolotsky* by his son.

iv. The Thaw and After Several new poets came to prominence in the late 1950s. They included much-praised writers such as Bella Akhmadulina and the singer-poet Bulat Okudzhava, but the two figures who stood out in translation were Yevgeny Yevtushenko and Andrey Voznesensky, both accomplished performers who travelled widely in the West.

Yevtushenko was fortunate in the early publication of his *Selected Poems* translated by Robin Milner-Gulland and Peter **Levi**. This slim volume, containing fine, vigorous versions of poems such as the famous 'Babiy Yar' (about the massacre of Jews in wartime Ukraine), probably sold better than any other translation mentioned in this entry. It has not been bettered by the quite numerous subsequent translations of Yevtushenko; the most comprehensive collection, edited by Albert **Todd**, makes less of an impact, since the size of the volume reveals the thinness of much of the poetry, and the quality of the translations is distinctly uneven.

Voznesensky has also found many translators, most of whom have tried their hand at his remarkable youthful tour de force on the horrors of war, 'Goya'. The best of the early translations, among them some by W. H. **Auden**, can be found in *An Arrow in the Wall*, together with rather dull versions of more recent work done by the editors William Jay **Smith** and F. D. **Reeve**. Richard McKane's 1991 volume is devoted to newer poems, clearly and strongly translated.

A number of volumes have been devoted to individual living poets, often the result of a translator's enthusiasm. One could cite, among others: *The War is Over* (Cheadle, 1976) by the influential older poet Yevgeny Vinokurov, translated by Daniel Weissbort and Anthony **Rudolf**; *Apollo in the Snow* (New York, 1988), poems by Aleksandr Kushner, stylishly translated by Paul **Graves** and Carol **Ueland**; the bilingual *Selected Poems, 1954–1994* (London, 1997) of the metaphysical Chuvash poet Gennady Aygi, translated by Peter France; a bilingual volume of the deep, quiet poems of Olga Sedakova, *The Wild Rose* (London, 1997), translated by Richard McKane; and *Paradise* (Newcastle upon Tyne, 1993), a bilingual collection by the powerful Petersburg poet Yelena Shvarts in versions by Michael **Molnar** and Catriona **Kelly**. But since the 1970s the scene has been dominated by Joseph (Iosif) Brodsky, who lived in exile in the West from 1972 until his death in 1996.

From the beginning, Brodsky worked with his English-language translators, pressing them, in line with his theory of poetic translation, to respect the prosody of the original. In the early volumes, the *Selected Poems* of George L. **Kline** and *A Part of Speech*, on which Brodsky collaborated with some major poets and translators, a fine balance is often struck between faithfulness and beauty. Increasingly, however, in volumes such *To Urania* and the posthumous *So Forth*, he preferred self-translation 'rather than get into a relationship with any human being, simply because if I have to hate somebody I'd rather it be myself'. The results have been criticized, but at times Brodsky makes the English language do things most translators would not dare.

v. Anthologies It is through anthologies that English-speaking readers must encounter many important Russian poets. Some of the general volumes mentioned in the Introduction [II.p.1] include 20th-c. poets, but several important collections devoted entirely to the 20th c. have been published since the 1960s.

A pioneering publication was the bilingual *Modern Russian Poetry* produced by the scholar Vladimir **Markov** and the poet Merrill **Sparks**. It includes a great number of poets, paying particular attention to poetry of the emigration and playing down the Thaw generation. The drawback is that Sparks's style is too present across the whole range of varied work. For this reason, most anthologies have grouped work by several hands, an exception being the volume in which Richard McKane, who has worked tirelessly in this field, brings together his deliberately plain versions of a wide range of poets.

The most important anthologizer is Daniel Weissbort, himself a notable translator of poetry. His first anthology (1974) is devoted to postwar poetry translated by many good translators. A second volume, produced with John **Glad** in 1978 and updated in 1991, goes back as far as Blok; quite a few of the translations were specially commissioned and generally attempt 'to reproduce metered rhymed poetry in rhythmic but unrhymed verse'. A third selection, published as a number of *Modern Poetry in Translation*, concentrates on recent or less translated poets. Weissbort also took part in the early stages of the mammoth *Twentieth-Century Russian Poetry*, masterminded by Yevtushenko. This collection is perhaps too big, giving shortish selections from too many poets; it includes some classic translations, but many of those done specially for the volume, especially in its later stages, are uninspiring.

Four more volumes should be briefly mentioned. Gerald S. **Smith**'s bilingual collection is aimed at those who know some Russian; the translations are avowedly aids to reading the originals. And there are three recent collections which are devoted to new developments: *The Third Wave: The New Russian Poetry, The Poetry of Perestroika*, and *In the Grip of Strange Thoughts: Russian Poetry in a New Era*. Russian poets may have lost their heroic aura, but their work continues to attract translators and readers.   PF

ANTHOLOGIES   Glad, John, and Weissbort, Daniel, eds., *Russian Poetry: The Modern Period*, Iowa City, 1978 [rev. edn., 1991] · Johnston, Kent, and Ashby, Stephen M., eds., *The Third Wave: The New Russian Poetry*, Ann Arbor, Mich., 1992 · Kates, Jim, ed., *In the Grip of Strange Thoughts: Russian Poetry in a New Era*, Somerville, Mass., 1999 · McKane, Richard, *Twentieth-Century Russian Poetry*, Newcastle upon Tyne, 1990 · Markov, Vladimir, and Sparks, Merrill, *Modern Russian Poetry*, London, 1966; Indianapolis, 1967 · Mortimer, Peter, and Litherland, S. J., eds., *The Poetry of Perestroika*, North Shields, UK, 1991 · Smith, Gerald S., ed., *Contemporary Russian Poetry: A Bilingual Anthology*, Bloomington, Ind., 1993 · Todd, Albert C., Hayward, Max, and Weissbort, Daniel, eds., *Twentieth-Century Russian Poetry, Selected with Annotations by Yevgeny Yevtushenko*, New York/London, 1993 · Weissbort, Daniel, ed., *Post-War Russian Poetry*, Harmondsworth, 1974 [Penguin] · *Modern Poetry in Translation*, n.s. 10, 1997.

AKHMATOVA, ANNA   Hemschemeyer, Judith, *Complete Poems*, Somerville, Mass., 1990 [2nd edn., Somerville, Mass./Edinburgh, 1992] · Kunitz, Stanley, and Hayward, Max, *Poems of Akhmatova*, Boston, 1973, London, 1974 · McKane, Richard, *Selected Poems*, London/New York/Toronto, 1969 [subsequently Penguin; enlarged edn. Newcastle upon Tyne, 1989] · Thomas, D. M., *Selected Poems*, London, 1985 [Penguin, 1988].

BELY, ANDREY   Janecek, Gerald, *The First Encounter*, Princeton, NJ, 1979 · Keys, Roger, and Keys, Angela, *The Dramatic Symphony*, Edinburgh, 1986.

BLOK, ALEKSANDR   Bechofer, C. E., *The Twelve*, London, 1920 · Fulton, Robin, *Blok's Twelve*, Preston, UK, 1968 · Miller, Alex, *Selected Poems*, Moscow, 1981 · Smith, Sydney Goodsir, 'The Twal', in his *Collected Poems 1941–75*, London, 1975 · Stallworthy, Jon, and France, Peter, *The Twelve and Other Poems*, London, 1970 [subsequently *Selected Poems*, Penguin].

BRODSKY, IOSIF   Brodsky, Joseph, et al., *A Part of Speech*, New York/Oxford, 1980 · *To Urania*, New York/London, 1988 [Penguin] · *So Forth*, New York/London, 1996 · Kline, George L., *Selected Poems*, New York/Harmondsworth, 1973 [Penguin].

KHLEBNIKOV, VELIMIR   Kern, Gary, et al., *Snake Train: Poetry and Prose*, Ann Arbor, Mich., 1976 · Schmidt, Paul, *The King of Time*, Cambridge, Mass., 1985 · *Collected Writings*, 3 vols., Cambridge, Mass., 1987–97.

MANDELSTAM, OSIP   Greene, James, *The Eyesight of Wasps*, London, 1989 [subsequently *Selected Poems*, Penguin] · McKane, Richard, and McKane, Elizabeth, *The Moscow Notebooks*, Newcastle upon Tyne, 1991 · *The Voronezh Notebooks*, 1996 · Meares, Bernard, *Fifty Poems*, New York, 1977 · Merwin, W. S., and Brown, Clarence, *Selected Poems*, London/Melbourne/Toronto, 1973 [subsequently Penguin] · Morrison, R. H., *Poems from Mandelstam*, London/Toronto, 1990 · Raffel, Burton, and Burago, Alla, *The Complete Poetry of Osip Emilevich Mandelstam*, New York, 1973 · Tracy, Robert, *Stone*, New York, 1981, London, 1991.

MAYAKOVSKY, VLADIMIR   Enzensberger, Maria, *Listen!; Early Poems 1913–1918*, London, 1987 · Hayward, Max, and Reavey, George, *The Bedbug and Selected Poetry*, ed. Patricia Blake, New York, 1960, London, 1961 · Marshall, Herbert, *Mayakovsky*, London, 1965 · Morgan, Edwin, *Wi the Haill Voice*, South Hinksey, UK, 1972.

PASTERNAK, BORIS   Navrozov, Andrei, *Second Nature: Forty-Six Poems by Boris Pasternak*, London, 1990 · Reavey, George, *The Poetry of Boris Pasternak*, New York, 1959 · Rudman, Mark, and Boychuk, Bohdan, *My Sister Life*, Evanston, Ill., 1983 [new edn., 1992] · Slater, Lydia Pasternak, *Poems of Boris Pasternak*, London, 1984 [first as *Fifty Poems*, 1963] · Stallworthy, Jon, and France, Peter, *Selected Poems*, London/New York, 1983 [Penguin, 1984].

TSVETAEVA, MARINA   Feinstein, Elaine, *Selected Poems*, London, 1971 [several new edns.] · Livingstone, Angela, 'The Ratcatcher' (extracts), *Modern Poetry in Translation*, n.s., 10, 1997 · McDuff, David, *Selected Poems*, Newcastle upon Tyne, 1987 · Naydan, Michael M., and Yastremski, Slava, *After Russia*, Ann Arbor, Mich., 1992.

VOZNESENSKY, ANDREY   McKane, Richard, *On the Edge*, London, 1991 · Smith, William Jay, and Reeve, F. D., eds., *An Arrow in the Wall*, London/New York, 1987.

YESENIN, SERGEY   Thurley, Geoffrey, *Confessions of a Hooligan*, Cheadle Hulme, UK, 1973.

YEVTUSHENKO, YEVGENY   Milner-Gulland, Robin, and Levi, Peter, *Selected Poems*, 1962 [Penguin] · Todd, Albert C., ed., *The Collected Poems 1952–1990*, New York, 1990, Edinburgh, 1991.

ZABOLOTSKY, NIKOLAY   Weissbort, Daniel, *Scrolls: Selected Poems*, London, 1971 · *Selected Poems*, Manchester, 1999 · Zabolotsky, Nikita, *The Life of Zabolotsky*, tr. R. Milner-Gulland and C. G. Bearne, Cardiff, 1994 [poems in Appendix B].

8. TWENTIETH-CENTURY FICTION

i. Introduction 'I don't know what he stands for or reveals, but I do know he is too Russian for me'. Thus the anglicized Pole Joseph Conrad characterized the first English versions of Dostoevsky's novels [II.p.5]. Often arriving through a fog of garbled misconception (e.g. *Home Life in Old Russia* as a travesty of *Dead Souls*), Russian literature may at first have seemed exotic and impenetrable to the British reader. But by the early 20th c., the 'anglification' of Turgenev in the 1870s and the subsequent pioneering efforts of devotees such as Constance **Garnett** and Aylmer **Maude** [see II.p.4] had put Russian prose into the mainstream, while the rapid acceptance of Chekhov as a household name in the British theatre [see II.p.6] and the excitement aroused by the visits of the Russian Ballet further boosted the status of Russian culture. The 1917 Revolution and subsequent civil war resulted in a temporary cultural hiatus, but for a long time thereafter reader and critic alike had to contend with the competing claims of the new Soviet literature and the 'old' literature of the emigration.

Indeed, the picture is more complicated still, since for perhaps 70 of the 75 years of its existence, the Soviet Union contained within itself both an official culture and a counterculture. The starting-point for all this is European modernism, which in its multifarious forms spread throughout most of the world around the beginning of the 20th c. For Russia, the remnants of indigenous modernism continued after 1917, both within the boundaries of the USSR and in the diaspora. Within Russia, the move to party-minded socialist realism was officially completed by the time of the first Soviet Writers' Congress in 1934, but works belonging to a different, non-conforming tradition continued to emerge, often against all expectations. This article will be mainly concerned with works which belong in this latter category.

Russian fiction of the 20th c., therefore, does not present itself to the historian, translator, or reader as a monolithic, indisputable literary canon. Thus, for example, the post-1917 emigration produced only one prose writer of world stature in the already established Ivan Bunin (though one could add the unusual case of Nabokov, whose fame rests largely in his adoptive language). Bunin's powerful short story 'Gospodin iz San-Frantsisko' (1915, The Gentleman from San Francisco) first appeared in English in 1922 in a volume co-translated by S. S. **Koteliansky**, D. H. **Lawrence**, and Leonard **Woolf**, and a number of his other works have appeared in translation in subsequent years. The so-called dissident emigration of the 1970s included a rather larger number of writers with an established reputation in the West, most notably Aleksandr Solzhenitsyn, but much of what emerged from it was firmly rooted in the Soviet Union, however nonconformist in character.

Until perhaps ten years ago, there were thus conflicting political agendas. Many western publishers, translators, and indeed sometimes the writers themselves sought to engage their public with works which could be described as 'banned', 'dissident', or 'taking the lid off Soviet society'. Many of these were works which by any standards were important and worthwhile, but the political subtext was unavoidable, just as, on the other side of the divide, the Soviet authorities sought, through bodies like the Foreign Languages Publishing House, to disseminate examples of 'progressive' literature. For example, Maxim Gorky and Mikhail Sholokhov have enjoyed a high profile as ambassadors for Soviet literature. In the case of Gorky, the artistically inept *Mat'* (1906, Mother) has appeared in translation many times for political reasons in preference to the more interesting earlier works, though the various versions of the autobiographical trilogy *Detstvo* (1913, Childhood), *V liudiakh* (1916, In the World), and *Moi universitety* (1922, My Universities) have been deservedly popular in the West. As for Sholokhov, though his powers as a writer declined with his rise as a public figure, he produced one weighty masterpiece in *Tikhii Don* (1928–40, The Quiet Don), known to the English-speaking world since Stephen **Garry**'s 1934 translation as *And Quiet Flows the Don*. Thus it should be emphasized that over the 75 years of the Soviet Union there have been many writers of merit who are neither openly dissident nor slavishly conformist; one of the most important gains of the *glasnost'* of the 1980s has been the fusion of these conflicting trends and the depoliticization of the arts in Russia.

ii. Andrey Bely The starting-point, then, is Russian modernism. The most striking example of this genre in prose is Andrey Bely's *Petersburg* (1913–22, Petersburg). An extraordinary mixture of urban myth, literary allusion, and linguistic play, underpinned by the plot of a political thriller, *Petersburg* is set in the autumn of 1905—the time of the first Russian Revolution. The novel first appeared in 1913, was substantially revised in 1922, and was not republished in Russia between 1935 and 1978. It remained unknown to English-speaking readers, however, until John **Cournos**'s translation of 1959. Almost 20 years later, two American Slavists, Robert **Maguire** and John **Malmstad**, produced what remains the definitive English version of the 1922 ('Berlin') text. Accompanied by extensive notes (very necessary, in view of the novel's complex literary and historical references), theirs is a meticulous piece of work with remarkably few errors, which captures very well the multi-textured quality of Bely's style and its sudden, unsettling shifts from the melodramatic to the comic-grotesque. In their introduction, these translators make short shrift of Cournos's earlier effort. Certainly, he perpetrates many errors—some of them comic (e.g. *gospoda*, 'gentlemen' is translated as 'girls')—but a more serious criticism concerns the many passages that he 'abridges' or simply omits altogether, especially those where the narrator addresses the reader directly. Still, in dismissing Cournos's translation as bearing 'only incidental resemblance to the original', they are being less than fair—there are even places where his version might be preferred.

Maguire and Malmstad's translation coincided with the first Soviet republication of *Petersburg* since 1935. In 1981, the earlier 'Sirin' text of 1913 was reissued in Moscow, thus raising the question of which is the 'authentic' *Petersburg*. In 1995, there appeared a translation by David **McDuff** of this earlier version, so that the reader now has essentially the choice of two translations of two differing originals. The earlier *Petersburg* is longer and the later version removes some of the more impenetrable passages, and though the 1913 version is sometimes cited as more true to Bely's original vision, this writer prefers the 1922 text. As far as the two translations go, McDuff is as meticulous and as erudite as Maguire and Malmstad, but in passages where direct comparison is possible, Maguire and Malmstad handle the often inconsequential dialogue rather better and deal more adroitly with Bely's (sometimes rather tiresome) verbal wit, e.g. wordplay on *grafinia*/*grafin* (Russian for 'countess'/'decanter') becomes 'countess'/'counter', whereas

McDuff tends to leave the Russian, as he does with words like *droshky* and *raznochinets*, or invents hybrids like 'coursiste' or 'gimnasiast'. McDuff's introduction is very good on the genesis of the novel, whereas Maguire and Malmstad offer rather more in the way of critical appraisal with more extensive notes.

iii. Translations of the 1950s and 1960s

The period from the 1920s to the end of the 1950s saw sporadic and somewhat random ventures at translating contemporary Russian literature. As we have seen, Bely's masterpiece took almost 40 years to reach the English-language reader, but a few translations of some of the younger Soviet prose writers (e.g. Isaak Babel, Boris Pilnyak, Valentin Kataev, and Yevgeny Zamyatin) exist from the interwar period. However, the post-Stalin Thaw, coupled with the expansion of Slavonic studies in the West, led to a much broader output of translated texts and greater professionalism. In this context, the period 1958–60 seems to be a turning-point. Apart from *Petersburg*, two highly significant works appeared at this point—Boris Pasternak's *Doctor Zhivago* (1958) and Zamyatin's *My* (1920–1, We).

Zamyatin's dystopian fable was, admittedly, not entirely unknown at this point. It remained unpublished in Russia for political reasons, but an American translation by the Kiev-born Gregory **Zilboorg** had appeared in 1924. There are questions, however, surrounding the authenticity of Zilboorg's Russian source, and it was the 1929 French edition, *Nous autres*, on which George Orwell drew for *1984*. However, in 1952, a definitive Russian edition of *We* appeared in New York, and this resulted in both a revision of the earlier Zilboorg version and a new translation by Bernard Gilbert **Guerney**. There have been further versions, by Mirra **Ginsburg** and, most recently, by Clarence **Brown**. The Guerney version is the one most frequently encountered by British readers. It is certainly accurate, though at times a little lifeless. Brown is better at capturing the jagged, jocular style of the narrator, D-503, when he departs from his 'officialese' and attempts flights of fancy. Again, there are few errors of note, though one might query Brown's use of 'Record', rather than the more usual 'Entry' to head the diary extracts. His introduction is also highly entertaining and informative, and is particularly shrewd in relating *We* to its author's experiences in England. The new versions of *We* were followed by several translations during the 1970s and 1980s of other Zamyatin works, none of which stayed in print for very long, and it seems that his fame will continue to rest on this one work.

During the same period under discussion, however, the most momentous event in the literary dialogue between Russia and the West must surely be the publication, in all the major European languages, of Pasternak's *Doctor Zhivago*. The work's significance was obviously heightened by the dramatic circumstances surrounding its appearance—a first novel, many years in the writing, by a 68-year-old poet, the hasty publication in Italy of a work deemed unpublishable in Russia, the high politics of the Nobel Prize, the rush for translation and then film rights, all contrasted poignantly with the author's personal situation. This has affected the long-term view of the novel. There are those who regard it as an important event, but the book itself as second-rate. This writer's view is that, though flawed in some respects, *Doctor Zhivago* is none the less remarkable for its breadth of vision and its sensitivity to atmosphere.

Notwithstanding continuing interest in Pasternak, the Anglophone reader is still able to view this novel solely through the Max **Hayward**–Manya **Harari** translation. There have been many republications of the original 1958 Collins edition, but no alternative version. It has been much criticized, but on balance it has worn well. Despite its occasional ellipses, it remains true to the spirit of the original, conveying memorably both the novel's historical sweep and its gift for capturing the vivid details of everyday life. Especially given the speed with which it was completed, this work stands as one of the great monuments to the art of translation. Following the success of *Doctor Zhivago* there have over the years been a number of translations of other prose works of Pasternak, particularly *Detstvo Lyuvers* (1922, Zhenia Luvers' Childhood) and the autobiographical *Okhrannaya gramota* (1931, Safe Conduct), but notwithstanding their individual merits, it is clear that they remain, by comparison, of minority interest.

In the wake of *We* and *Doctor Zhivago*, during the 1960s, translations of several younger Soviet writers, such as Vasily Aksenov, Yury Kazakov, Viktor Nekrasov, and Vladimir Voynovich, enjoyed modest success amongst British readers. However, the next major literary phenomenon, Solzhenitsyn, though certainly widely translated over the years, has always enjoyed something of a problematic relationship with his translators. The novels *Odin den' Ivana Denisovicha* (1962, One Day in the Life of Ivan Denisovich), *V kruge pervom* (1968, First Circle), and *Rakovy korpus* (1969, Cancer Ward) all appeared rapidly in rival English translations, but the general consensus is that no version was wholly successful and some were extremely sketchy.

iv. Bulgakov For many Russian readers, the supreme achievement of the 1960s was the publication, in 1966, after a quarter of a century in a manuscript known to only a few people, of Mikhail Bulgakov's *Master i Margarita* (The Master and Margarita). This remarkable work clearly continues to influence the course of Russian literature to this day and perhaps a little surprisingly, given its esoteric subject-matter and treatment, it has retained its popularity amongst British readers, the most widely available version, that of Michael **Glenny** having been reissued under different imprints at least five times. Glenny's version, first issued in 1967, has stood the test of time better than Mirra Ginsburg's of the same year, not least because Ginsburg was using the expurgated Russian text from the journal *Moskva*, whereas Glenny was fortunate enough to be given a more complete text by Bulgakov's widow. Even so, subsequent Russian reprintings indicate a slightly fuller text still.

The success of *The Master and Margarita* sparked off a series of translations of Bulgakov's prose. These included two very different works of the 1920s—*Sobach'e serdtse* (written 1925, Heart of a Dog) and *Belaya gvardiya* (1924, The White Guard)—and a short novel dating from the period when Bulgakov was working on *The Master and Margarita*—*Teatral'ny roman* (1967, Black Snow). Western readers have come to Bulgakov in quite a different way from Russians. *The White Guard* would have been known to older Russians, particularly in its stage version, *Dni Turbinikh* (Days of the Turbins). It was rapidly reprinted after the appearance of *The Master and Margarita*, but *Black Snow* (written 30 years previously) had its first ever Russian printing in 1965, followed in 1967 by Glenny's translation, whilst *Heart of a Dog*, though dating from 1925, had never been published in Russia when Mirra Ginsburg's English version of 1968 appeared, thus predating the work's first publication in Russia by 19 years. Ginsburg is a careful translator, remaining true to the spirit of the original, though sometimes striking an uncertain note in the passages of dialogue. Her occasional misreading of idioms (such as rendering *zarubi na nosu* as 'keep your nose out', instead of 'you bear that in mind') seems a little surprising for someone with a Russian background.

The late Michael Glenny was a prolific translator from the 1960s until his death. He was responsible for bringing much of Bulgakov's work (including *Black Snow* and *The White Guard*) to the British reader, as was Mirra Ginsburg, correspondingly, in America. Glenny also had a hand in one of the early translations of Solzhenitsyn's *The First Circle* and later his 1983 translation of Yury Trifonov's *Dom na naberezhnoy* (1983, The House on the Embankment) had a considerable impact. Glenny's translations are never less than highly readable. He has a great feel for language and is not afraid to take idiomatic risks. But he is prone to the occasional blunder. Thus, for example, his *Black Snow* is extremely readable, bringing out very well Bulgakov's sardonic humour, but includes one extraordinary blunder, when he renders *Osenilo! osenilo!* ('It suddenly struck me') as 'The autumn drew on'. He also misreads *'gostinaya'*, 'drawing-room' as *gostinitsa*, 'hotel', thus spoiling the point of an anecdote. But no translator is perfect, and Glenny deserves the highest praise for his efforts to bring Russian literature to the British public.

v. Platonov Beginning in the mid-1980s, the period of *glasnost'* saw the different strands of Russian literature reunited. A major part of this healing process, of course, was the rediscovery of Russia's lost writers. One such figure is Andrey Platonov. A rarity amongst Soviet writers in that he came from a genuine working-class background, Platonov's first literary ventures in the 1920s were influenced by the tail-end of modernism. He died in great hardship in 1951, virtually unpublished for the last 20 years of his life. From the 1970s his works trickled back into publication in Russia and translations began to appear. Now that almost the whole of Platonov's work is available once more, we can begin to see that he looks both forward to the 'village prose' of the late Soviet period and back to the satirical dissonance of the 1920s. Two major novels, *Kotlovan* (The Foundation Pit) and *Chevengur*, written at the end of the 1920s, when collectivization, industrialization, and urbanization were changing the Soviet Union even more profoundly than in 1917, remained unpublished in the author's lifetime. Both present an almost unremittingly pessimistic picture of a society in upheaval, all the more poignant in that Platonov began as a true believer in the possibility of a better world.

In the 1970s two American translations of *Kotlovan* appeared, by Thomas P. **Whitney** and Mirra Ginsburg respectively. Whitney's is a conscientious effort, but carries a fair number of minor errors and sometimes strikes an uncertain note. The 1996 Harvill translation by Robert **Chandler** and Geoffrey **Smith** is the first British edition. It has a useful introduction and a dedication by Platonov's daughter. The translators have on the whole done an excellent job in conveying Platonov's strange mixture of mournful lyricism, parodied officialese, and vivid colloquial speech. Very occasionally, their ear lets them down, as in 'living without mind' (rather than 'act foolishly') for *zhit' bez uma*, or, again, where the exclamation 'you Capitalism, you bastard!' should obviously be 'You capitalist bastard!' It will be interesting to see whether this fine effort sparks off a major wave of interest in Platonov. Indeed, amidst the plethora of new work coming out of Russia, as the 20th c. comes to an end, the challenge for translator, critic, and reader alike will be to discern those works which in years to come will stand out from the rest as true monuments to an extraordinary era in human and cultural history.   MF

BELY, ANDREY   Cournos, John, *Petersburg*, New York, 1961, London, 1962 · McDuff, David, *Petersburg*, London, 1995 · Maguire, Robert A., and Malmstad, John E., *Petersburg*, Bloomington, Ind., 1978 [Penguin, 1983].

BULGAKOV, MIKHAIL   Burgin, Dianne, and Treanor, Catherine, *The Master and Margarita*, London, 1996 · Ginsburg, Mirra, *The Master and Margarita*, New York, 1967; rep. 1980 · *Heart of a Dog*, New York, 1968; rep. 1987 · Glenny, Michael, *Black Snow*, London, 1967 [Penguin, 1971] · *The Master and Margarita*, London, 1967 [five subsequent edns., incl. Everyman, 1992] · *The White Guard*, London, 1971; rep. 1973, 1984.

PASTERNAK, BORIS   Hayward, Max, and Harari, Manya, *Doctor Zhivago*, London, 1958 [frequent reps.].

PLATONOV, ANDREY   Chandler, Robert, and Smith, Geoffrey, *The Foundation Pit*, London, 1996 · Ginsburg, Mirra, *The Foundation Pit*, New York, 1975 · Olcott, Anthony, *Chevengur*, Ann Arbor, Mich., 1978 · Whitney, Thomas P., *The Foundation Pit*, Ann Arbor, Mich., 1973.

ZAMYATIN, YEVGENY   Brown, Clarence, *We*, New York/London, 1993 [Penguin] · Guerney, Bernard Gilbert, *We*, New York, 1960 [later Penguin] · Zilboorg, Gregory, *We*, New York, 1924; rev. edn. 1959.

q. West Asian Languages

1. ANCIENT MESOPOTAMIAN LITERATURE

In the middle of the 19th c. British and French archaeologists began to uncover the literature of ancient Mesopotamia. Written in Sumerian and Akkadian languages, in cuneiform script, mainly on unbaked clay, it had vanished from human knowledge since around the time of Christ. To recover the world's oldest myths and epics, hymns and prayers, was made even more exciting by the recognition that the Flood story and the account of Sennacherib's attack on Jerusalem were recorded not only in the Bible but also in cuneiform.

At first it was impossible to appreciate how complex the script was. 'Very shortly I feel perfectly certain they [the inscriptions] will be completely intelligible,' wrote Henry Rawlinson in 1849. 150 years later, well-provided with dictionaries and grammars, Assyriologists still struggle with fragmentary clay tablets, damaged signforms, and a patchy historical framework. The writing system uses hundreds of signs in a variety of ways, logographic, syllabic, and determinative, from which the reader must select. The semantic range of words is very different from that of English, and is sometimes linked to vanished customs. Pronunciation of words is almost impossible to establish, and would not have remained constant over the 2,000 years in which the literature flourished, which makes it difficult to establish metrical rules. Assyriologists know that by comparison with alphabetic writing, cuneiform contains a greater complexity, rather like the wealth of meaning found in Chinese and Japanese, because each sign embodies much more than one simple sound. This gives particular problems to the translator.

Translation styles have varied from a literal word-for-word correspondence following the word order of the original, to a poetic paraphrase flowing through lacunae. The two main works which were sufficiently preserved to be translatable from the early days were the *Epic of Creation* and the *Epic of Gilgamesh*. In fact the former is written in an archaic style, whereas the latter is more colloquial, but this is seldom apparent in translation. Stephen **Langdon**'s 1923 translation of the *Epic of Creation* was fluent, but he included such archaic usages as 'verily not shall we sleep', feeling, as many translators did, that such ancient literature should be translated in a manner that alluded to its great antiquity. Because Biblical parallels were evident from the start of decipherment, early translations into English tended to adopt the style of the King James Bible [see II.c.2]. William **Fox Talbot** (1800–77), translating an extract from the Flood story in 1875, 'Who, when thou wast enraged, a great storm didst make', selected the King James Bible and current hymn-writing as his models. This style, however, was soon modified as scholars, grappling with minutiae, tended towards a more literal translation.

In translating the *Epic of Gilgamesh*, for which comparisons with Homeric epic were made early, some tended to imitate the current style of Homeric translation [II.i.2]. In 1928 Reginald **Campbell Thompson** rendered the work 'literally into English hexameters' even though he did not claim that the epic was written in hexameters, and he included archaic English such as 'holpen' and 'like unto'. Occasionally the modern reader is left with the impression that the epic in Akkadian used a wider range of vocabulary than is in fact the case. The standard epithets for heroes and cities are reproduced in Homeric style, giving almost recognizable expressions but combining them with, for example, the Biblical name Erech for the city Uruk, in 'Erech, the high-walled'. As with Homeric epic, each work has a standard line-length, which most translators observe.

Alexander **Heidel**'s translations observe line-lengths, and are fairly literal, not always observing the word order of current English:

After Tiamat had made str[ong] preparations,
She made ready to join battle with the gods her offspring.
[To avenge] Apsu, Tiamat did (this) evil.

Since the vocabulary is quite restricted, and the richness of semantic association and alliteration could not be reproduced, such a translation seems quite flat and monotonous. The translations made for James **Pritchard**'s corpus of texts (unchanged in subsequent 'revised' versions) follow the same strategy. Samuel **Kramer**, in the same volume and in his popular translations of Sumerian myths, took a similar course.

Quite different are the translations of Nancy **Sandars**. Her *Epic of Gilgamesh* puts together and reworks existing translations to form a fluent patchwork, inserting text from other compositions, and inventing linking passages such as: 'At his coming the house-snake fled from her hole in the building. Humbaba sucked in his breath, it sounded like the slap of a kiss, and his teeth were shaking.' She ignores the fact that different versions might be 1,500 years apart in time, and has to abandon the original arrangement by lines, a decision made inevitable by the incorporation of different compositions. Her translations brought Mesopotamian literature to a much wider public.

Thorkild **Jacobsen**'s translations are poetic and imaginative, reflecting his view of early society as a Golden Age of primitive democracy:

At the stepping onto heaven
by Utu
did from Izin's shore's
standing bollards,
from Nanna's radiant
[temple up high,]
from the mouth of the waters
running underground,
sweet waters run out
of the ground for her.

His translations are widely enjoyed, whereas scholarly translations of hymns and laments, given alongside careful editions, are more literal and pedantic.

Stephanie **Dalley**'s translations of Akkadian myths attempt to bridge the gap between pedantic-scholarly and poetic-inaccurate, and use current English. They bring consistency of translation to the major Akkadian myths, and combine textual accuracy with attention to rhythm and alliteration, noting instances of play on words.

Each translation has eliminated some of the mistakes of its predecessors. An epithet for the god Ea, once analysed to mean 'Lord of the Bright Eye', is now more prosaically 'prince' or 'sheikh', according to taste. The anachronistic 'zodiac' in the *Epic of Creation* has been discarded, and Marduk's miracle concerns a constellation, not a garment. The ferryman who transported Gilgamesh was found cutting pines for poles, not involved with snakes or mint. Above all, each new translation is able to use more fragments of text as they come to light in museums and from excavations. These advances mean that older translations are less reliable and less complete than recent translations. Writers of stories and plays based on the *Epic of Gilgamesh* usually do not avoid the pitfalls.   SMD

TRANSLATIONS Campbell Thompson, R. C., *The Epic of Gilgamesh*, Oxford, 1928 · Dalley, Stephanie, *Myths from Mesopotamia*, Oxford, 1989 [World's Classics] · Foster, B., *Before the Muses*, Bethesda, Md., 1993 · Fox Talbot, W. H., 'Commentary on the Deluge Tablet', *Transactions of the Society of Biblical Archaeology*, 4 (1875), 49 · Jacobsen, Thorkild, *The Harps That Once . . .* New Haven, Conn., London, 1987 · Heidel, Alexander, *The Babylonian Genesis*, Chicago, 1942 · Kramer, Samuel, *Sumerian Mythology*, Philadelphia, 1944 · Langdon, Stephen, *The Babylonian Epic of Creation*, Oxford, 1923 · Pritchard, James, *Ancient Near Eastern Texts Relating to the Old Testament*, Princeton, NJ, 1950 · Sandars, Nancy, *The Epic of Gilgamesh*, Harmondsworth, 1960 [Penguin].

2. CLASSICAL PERSIAN

The classical literature of Persia (modern Iran and Afghanistan) has left behind a rich 1,000-year legacy of prose and particularly of poetry. This entry concentrates on five Persian poets, in the chronological order in which they came to the attention of English-speaking readers: the humorous ethicist

Sa'di, the lyric genius Hâfez, the national epic poet Ferdowsi, the epicurean Omar Khayyâm, and the great mystic Rumi.

i. Sa'di (also Saadi) Though Persian literature began to appear in Latin, German, and French translations in the 16th and 17th c., the first Persian work 'made English' did not appear until 1699, and then via a French adaptation. The moralizing oriental tale proved a popular genre with Enlightenment thinkers, and the 13th-c. humanist Sa'di was one of its most charming and witty practitioners. The anecdotes and maxims of his didactic poem *Bustân* and the mixed prose and verse *Golestân* were championed, imitated, or exploited by writers from Voltaire to Emerson. Many officials in British India, where Persian was an official language, acquired their Persian through Sa'di, and this created a thriving industry of English translations, beginning in 1774 with Stephen **Sulivan**'s selections from the *Golestân*, followed by Francis **Gladwin**, James **Ross** in prose, and many others. For the *Bustân*, W. C. **MacKinnon** produced delightful rhyming couplets, followed by G. S. **Davie**'s somewhat less facile verse. Sa'di was still exercising an influence over original works as recently as 1888, when Sir Edwin **Arnold** (1832–1904) embedded part of the *Bustân* in a play.

Modern readers seeking an acquaintance with Sa'di will probably prefer the copiously annotated linear prose version of the *Bustân* by G. M. **Wickens** and the *Golestân* translation by Edward **Rehatsek** (1819–91), once thought to be the work of Richard Burton.

ii. Hâfez (also Hâfiz) If Persian literature initially came to English second-hand, Sir William 'Oriental' **Jones** [see II.l.2.i] reversed the course of translation history. In 1771 he rendered one *ghazal* (a form akin to the sonnet) of Hâfez in stanzaic verse, complete with interpolated commentary on the nature of eastern poetry ('Orient pearls at random strung'). As part of his programme to reinvigorate European verse with foreign forms and ideas, Jones begged in the closing lines that his 'simple lay' might 'go boldly forth', and indeed it did, inspiring a virtual cottage industry of Hâfez translations and grammars of Persian; by 1801 there were at least five different collections, most quite faithful and most with parallel Persian text. This enthusiasm then passed to Goethe [see II.h.5.i] and German romanticism, which in turn inspired Emerson, who introduced Hâfez to America.

Hâfez is a poet of well-sculpted language and a range of vibrant emotions, revered in some circles as a libertine and apotheosized in others as a thoroughgoing mystic, in which guise Colonel H. Wilberforce **Clarke** and Paul **Smith** have rendered his entire *œuvre* into cumbersome, parenthetical, explanatory prose. An equally grandiose failure, but for formal rather than interpretive reasons, is John **Payne**'s (1842–1916) effort to replicate the entire Hâfez corpus, mimicking the rhythms, monorhymes, and refrains.

The 43 *ghazals* interpolatively rendered by Gertrude **Bell** (1868–1926) are generally praised as the best verse translation, though contemporary readers will take greater delight in the verse of Richard **Le Gallienne** (1866–1947), who though knowing no Persian ironically offers a clearer glimpse into the wit, and jaunty charm of Hâfez. English poets have also fallen under the spell of Hâfez: Elizabeth **Bridges** (**Daryush**) exploited the reputation of Hâfez to launch her own career; Basil **Bunting** brought out the libertine Hâfez in Poundian form; and John **Heath-Stubbs** joined with Persian scholar Peter **Avery** in a version both accurate and readable, though marred by its submission to the medieval critical dictum that the *ghazal* form lacks organic unity.

Recent Hâfez versions include English-to-English free verse by David **Cloutier**, Michael **Boylan**, the latter in a beautifully made book with gorgeous illustrations, and Elizabeth **Gray**, who looks to the poetic model of Robert Lowell and Elizabeth Bishop, the latter a poet uniquely unsuited to the timbre and temperament of Hâfez. In 1947 A. J. **Arberry** published a selection of 50 Hâfez poems by 15 translators; his judgement that English translators had not yet completely succeeded with Hâfez still holds.

iii. Ferdowsi (also Firdawsi) Ferdowsi's *Shâh-nâmeh* (980–1000, The Book of Kings), the epic history of the Iranian people, has often been compared to Homer. In view of its inordinate length, translators have generally confined themselves to single episodes or abridgements. In 1785 Joseph **Champion** produced an abridged selection in the style of Pope's *Iliad*. James **Atkinson**'s (1780–1852) attractive 1814 version of the Sohrab and Rostam story in heroic couplets led to a later abridgement of the entire work in prose and verse; his felicitous phrasing comes from copious searching for parallel themes and expressions in English poetry of the 16th and 17th c. Matthew **Arnold** produced his 'Sohrab and Rustum' on the basis of a review of the French translation by J. Mohl; though more under the stylistic influence of Arnold's Hellenism than Ferdowsi's Persian, it has won for itself a place in English literary history.

Early translators felt free to interpolate commentary into the body of their text, whereas 20th-c. versions have restricted themselves to Ferdowsi's text and adopted blank verse instead of heroic couplets. A. G. and E. **Warner** devoted 20 years to rendering the entire poem in blank verse, attempting to imitate the style of Ferdowsi with archaic diction, but few readers will possess the stamina to plough through all nine volumes. Jerome **Clinton** revisits the *Sohráb and Rostám* tale with Persian on facing pages and Dick **Davis** renders another episode, *The Legend of Seyavash*. Both recent translators opt for a clear and modern idiom, using blank verse to suggest something of the form of Ferdowsi; however accessible, the language strikes a rather incongruous note for the dialogue of heroic epic.

Prose paraphrases of the poem can be found in the archaizing and deliberately Biblical diction of Helen **Zimmern**, done from the French version of Mohl, and in the plain exposition by Reuben **Levy**, done from the Persian. The latter has been the Ferdowsi of choice for most readers, though it bleaches out the literary qualities of the poem. The recent prose summary by Ehsan **Yarshater** interspersed with the verse of Dick Davis promises to replace Levy, as it successfully gives a flavour of the best poetry passages and still provides an epitome of the entire poem.

iv. Omar Khayyâm (also 'Umar Khayyâm)

Edward **FitzGerald** (1809–93) created what is arguably the most successful verse translation, both artistically and commercially, in the history of the English language. Finding a kindred spirit in the the quatrains (*robâ'iyât*) ascribed to Khayyâm (better known in his lifetime as mathematician and astronomer), FitzGerald 'ingeniously tessellated' from them his *The Rubáiyát of Omar Khayyám*. He drew upon a solid grasp of Persian as well as the scholarly advice of his friend Edward Cowell; that he chose to organize the disparate poems of Khayyâm into a quasi-narrative stanzaic poem and to render some of the quatrains quite freely, illustrates FitzGerald's deliberate programme of creative translation, also apparent in his adaptation of Calderón [see II.k.4.ii] and to a lesser extent in his renderings of Jâmi's *Salámán and Absál* (1856) and 'Attâr's *Bird Parliament* (1899).

Published anonymously in 1859 (FitzGerald was not revealed as translator until 1875), the *Rubáiyát* was ignored until after a price reduction, at which point Dante Gabriel Rossetti discovered it and bought copies for Swinburne, Browning, and Ruskin, all of whom received it enthusiastically. FitzGerald's penchant for extensive revision led to five separate editions of the poem and several comparative editions, though the first and fifth editions are most frequently reprinted and read.

The Omar Khayyâm craze led to dozens of other translations in many languages; in addition to over 1500 books about Khayyâm, there have been satires (including one by Mark Twain), musical settings (including one by Hovhaness), and Omar Khayyâm clubs throughout the parlours of major cities in the British Isles, India, and North America.

FitzGerald's Omar inspired E. H. **Whinfield**'s (1836–1922) scholarly and more accurate verse rendering (though it includes many poems spuriously attributed to Khayyâm); the prose version of Justin **McCarthy** (1860–1936), founder of the Omar Khayyam Club of London; several literal versions (based on various Persian manuscripts) by the scholar Edward **Heron-Allen** (1861–1943), two of them accompanied by verse renditions, the one by Arthur **Talbot** being of high quality. In the 1960s J. C. E. **Bowen** added a new but rather old-fashioned verse translation together in one volume with a literal rendering by A. J. Arberry; this was followed by the collaborative version of poet Robert **Graves** and Omar Ali **Shah**, which shrilly and in manifest error insists on a Sufi reading. Both of these versions are based upon newly discovered manuscripts now thought to be forgeries. Peter Avery and John Heath-Stubbs provide a modern if somewhat fastidious reading, beautifully illustrated in the Penguin edition by Persian miniatures. None of these can, however, replace FitzGerald.

v. Rumi

Jalâl al-Din Rumi, the 13th-c. founder of the whirling dervishes and author of a huge volume of mystical *ghazals*, the *Divân-e Shams-e Tabrizi*, also penned what is arguably the most influential poem in the Islamic world, a mystical narrative known as the *Masnavi*. Rumi appeals strongly to New Age spirituality, and is said to be the best-selling poet in America today, available in versions by almost a dozen different translators. E. H. Whinfield produced the first English selections of the *Masnavi*, wisely chosen and well translated. James **Redhouse** (1811–92) and C. E. **Wilson** (1858–1938) provided unabridged translations of Books I and II respectively, the former in rhythmically clunky verse, the latter in prose. Reynold **Nicholson**, who devoted his scholarly career to Rumi, provided an extensively annotated literal but non-literary rendering of all six books of the *Masnavi*, along with a critical edition of the Persian. In hopes of reaching a wider audience, Nicholson also provided two small volumes of excerpts. He had earlier produced a selection of Rumi's *ghazals*, again rather literal, aiming to convey the content more than the poetry. Nicholson's student, A. J. Arberry, followed this approach for 400 further poems, after an earlier and unsuccessful attempt to render the quatrains in verse. Annemarie **Schimmel**, a German Islamicist, has also done an English selection of Rumi under the influence of Rückert's immensely popular 19th-c. German adaptations.

The literal scholarly versions proved unsuited to a general audience, but American free verse poets Robert **Bly** and Coleman **Barks**, though ignorant of Persian (Barks has sometimes collaborated with a Persian linguistics professor, John Moyne), have 'released these poems from their cages' in ameri-canizing English-to-English versions which have proved immensely popular. Working directly from the Persian, architect Nader **Khalili** provides a more ecstatic Rumi that depicts the longing and pain of his mysticism, in contrast to the calm guru that the new age audience tends to find. Nevit **Ergin** offers versions from a Turkish translation by Gölpinarli and Andrew **Harvey** relies upon a variety of the scholarly cribs for his devotional translations. But the small collections by Kabir **Helminski**, head of the Mevlevi Order of whirling dervishes in America, and by Daniel **Liebert** provide the most authentic taste of Rumi's mystical experience in free verse.   FL

ANTHOLOGIES AND MISCELLANEA   *The Fables of Pilpay, a Famous Indian Phylosopher, Containing Many Useful Rules for the Conduct of Humane Life*, tr. Joseph Harris, London, 1699 · *The Rose Garden of Persia*, tr. Louisa Stuart Costello, London, 1845 · Translations by Ralph Waldo Emerson in *Poems*, Boston, 1847; 'Persian Poetry', *Atlantic Monthly*, 1858; *May Day and Other Pieces*, Boston, 1867; and in various versions of his collected works · *Song of the Reed and Other Pieces*, by E. H. Palmer, London, 1877 [includes trs. from Persian] · *Persian Poetry for English Readers*, tr. Samuel Robinson, Glasgow, 1883; rep. Tehran, 1976 · *Poems from the Persian*, tr. J. C. E. Bowen, Oxford, 1948 [frequent reprints] · *Persian Poems: An Anthology of Verse Translations*, ed. A. J. Arberry, London/New York, 1954 [frequent reps.] · *Arabic and Persian Poems*, tr. Omar Pound, New York, 1970 · *The Drunken Universe: An Anthology of Persian Sufi Poetry*, tr. P. L. Wilson and N. Pourjavady, Grand Rapids, Miss., 1987 · Translations by Basil Bunting in his *Collected Poems*, Oxford, 1968, and in *Uncollected Poems*, Oxford, 1991 [rep. in *Complete Poems*, Oxford, 1994].

FERDOWSI   *The Poems of Ferdosi*, tr. Joseph Champion, Calcutta, 1785 · *Soohrab: A Poem, Freely Translated from the Original Persian of Firdousee*, tr. James Atkinson, Calcutta, 1814; rep. 1972 · *The Shah Nameh of the Persian Poet Firdausi*, tr. James Atkinson, London, 1832; rep. 1898 · 'Sohrab and Rustum', tr. Matthew Arnold, in *Poems*, London, 1853 [subsequently in edns. of Arnold's poems] · *Epic of Kings: Stories Retold from Firdusi*, by Helen Zimmern, London, 1882 [available gratis on the Internet as electronic text] · *The Shah-namah of Fardusi*, tr. Alexander Rogers, London, 1907 · *The Shahnama of Firdausi Done into English*, tr. Arthur George Warner and Edmond Warner, 9 vols., London, 1905–25 · *The Epic of the Kings*, tr. Reuben Levy, London, 1967 · *The Tragedy of Sohráb and Rostám*, tr. Jerome Clinton, Seattle, 1987 · *The Legend of Seyavash*, tr. Dick Davis, Harmondsworth, 1992 [Penguin] · *The Lion and the Throne: Stories from the Shahnameh of Ferdowsi*, prose rendition by Ehsan Yarshater, verse passages by Dick Davis, Washington, DC, 1998 [a further volume is expected].

HÂFEZ   *Grammar of the Persian Language*, by Sir William Jones, Oxford, 1771 [contains his translation from Hâfez, also rep. in *Poems Consisting Chiefly of Translations from the Asiatick Languages*, Oxford, 1772, and in his collected works] · *Hafiz of Shiraz, Selections from His Poems*, tr. Herman Bicknell, London, 1875; rep. Tehran, 1976 · *The Divan, Written in the Fourteenth Century*, by Khwaja Shamsu-d-Din Muhammad-i-Hafiz-i Shirazi, tr. H. Wilberforce Clarke, 2 vols., Calcutta, 1891 [several reps.] · *Poems from the Divan of Hafiz*, tr. Gertrude Bell, London, 1897 [several reprints] · *Versions from Hafiz: An Essay in Persian metre*, tr. Walter Leaf, London, 1898 · *The Poems of Shemseddin Mohammad Hafiz of Shiraz*, tr. John Payne, 3 vols., London, 1901 · *Odes from the Divan of Hafiz, Freely Rendered from Literal Translations*, tr. Richard Le Gallienne, New York, 1903; London, 1905 · *Sonnets from Hafez and Other Verses*, tr. Elizabeth Bridges (Daryush), London, 1921 · *Hâfiz: Fifty Poems*, ed. A. J. Arberry, Cambridge, 1947 [several reprints] · *Hafiz of Shiraz: Thirty Poems*, tr. Peter Avery and John Heath-Stubbs, London, 1952 · *Divan of Hafiz*, tr. Paul Smith, 2 vols., Melbourne, 1983; rep. 1986 · *News of Love: Poems of Separation and Union*, tr. David Cloutier, Greensboro, NC, 1984 · *Hafiz: Dance of Life*, tr. Michael Boylan, Washington, DC, 1988 · *The Green Sea of Heaven*, tr. Elizabeth Gray, Ashland, Or., 1995.

OMAR KHAYYÂM   *The Rubáiyát of Omar Khayyám*, tr. Edward FitzGerald, London, 1859 [2nd edn., 1868; 3rd edn., 1872; 4th edn., 1879; 5th edn., 1896; centennial edn., 1959; scores of reprints] · *The Quatrains of Omar Khayyam*, tr. E. H. Whinfield, London, 1882 [1st edn. has 253 poems; 2nd edn. of 1901 has 476 poems; 1st edn. frequently rep.] · *Rubaiyat of Omar Khayyam*, tr. Justin Huntly McCarthy, London, 1889 · *Edward FitzGerald's Ruba'iyat of Omar Khayyam with their Original Persian Sources Collated from his own Mss., and Literally Translated*, tr. Edward Heron-Allen, London, 1899 · *Quatrains of Omar Khayyam from a Literal Prose Translation*, by Edward Heron-Allen, of the Earliest Known Manuscript, Done into Verse, tr. Arthur B. Talbot, London, 1908 · *The Rub'aiyat of Omar Khayyam, the Literal Translation of the Ousely Ms. at Oxford*, by Edward Heron-Allen, with a Rendering into English Verse, tr. C. S. Tute, Exeter, 1926 · *The Rubaiyat of Omar Khayyam, Edited from a Newly Discovered Ms.*, ed. A. J. Arberry, London, 1949 · *Omar Khayyam: A New Version*

Based upon Recent Discoveries, tr. A. J. Arberry, New Haven, Conn., 1952 · *A New Selection from the Rubaiyat of Omar Khayyam*, tr. John Charles Edward Bowen, London, 1961 · *The Rubaiyyat of Omar Khayyam*, tr. Robert Graves and Omar Ali Shah, London, 1967 · *The Ruba'iyat of Omar Khayyam*, tr. Peter Avery and John Heath-Stubbs, London, 1979 [Penguin, 1981].

RUMI *Masnavi i Manavi, the Spiritual Couplets of Maulana Jalalu-d'-Din Muhammad i Rumi*, tr. E. H. Whinfield, London, 1887 · *The Mesnevi*, i, tr. James Redhouse, London, 1881 · *Selected Poems from the Divani Shamsi Tabriz*, tr. Reynold Nicholson, Cambridge, 1898 · *The Masnavi*, tr. C. E. Wilson, London, 1910; rep. 1976 · *The Mathnawi of Jalaluddin Rumi*, tr. R. Nicholson, London, 1925–40; rep. 1989, 1996 [selections in *Tales of Mystic Meaning*, London / New York, 1931 and *Rumi: Poet and Mystic*, London, 1950, both frequently reprinted] · *The Ruba'iyat of Jalal al-Din Rumi*, tr. A. J. Arberry, London, 1949 · *The Mystical Poems of Rumi*, tr. A. J. Arberry, Chicago, 1968 [followed by posthumous vol. ii, *The Mystical Poems of Rumi*, ii, Chicago, 1979] · *Rumi: Fragments, Ecstasies*, tr. Daniel Liebert, Cedar Hill, Mo., 1981 · *Night and Sleep*, tr. Robert Bly and Coleman Barks, Cambridge, Mass., 1981 · *Open Secret*, tr. Coleman Barks and John Moyne, Brattleboro, Vt., 1984 · *Look! This Is Love*, tr. Annemarie Schimmel, Boston, 1991; rep. 1996 · *Magnificent One*, tr. Nevit O. Ergin, Burdett, NY, 1993 [Ergin has gone on to work on an English version of the Turkish tr. of Rumi's *Divân-i Kebir*, 1995–] · *Love Is a Stranger*, tr. Kabir (Edmund) Helminksi, Brattleboro, Vt., 1993 · *The Way of Passion*, Andrew Harvey, Berkeley, Calif., 1994 · *Rumi Fountain of Fire*, tr. Nader Khalili, Hesperia, Calif., 1994 · *The Essential Rumi*, tr. Coleman Barks and John Moyne, San Francisco, 1995 [selected from smaller books by Barks and by Barks and Moyne published 1984–95].

SA'DI *Select Tales from Gulistan, or, the Bed of Roses*, tr. Stephen Sulivan, London, 1774 · *The Gulistan, or Rose Garden*, tr. Francis Gladwin, London, 1822 [rep. 1834 and Boston, 1865, with preface by Ralph W. Emerson] · *The Gulistan, or Flower-Garden of Shaikh Sadi of Shiraz*, tr. James Ross, London, 1823 [rep. in cheap Iranian edn. for tourists in the 1970s] · *The Golistan, or, Rose-Garden of Shekh Muslihu'd-din Sadi of Shiraz*, tr. Edward Eastwick, Hertford, 1852; rep. London, 1974, 1979 · *A Few Flowers from the Garden of Saadi Shirazi, being Translations into English Verse of Portions of the Bustan*, tr. W. C. MacKinnon, Calcutta, 1877 · *The Garden of Fragrance [Bostân]*, tr. G. S. Davie, London, 1882. *The Gulistan, Being the Rose-Garden of Shaikh Sa'di*, tr. Edward Rehatsek, Benares, 1888; rep. New York, 1966 · *With Sa'di in the Garden: or, The Book of Love*, tr. Sir Edwin Arnold, London, 1893 · *The Gulistan; Being the Rose-garden of Shaikh Sa'di; the First Four Babs, or 'Gateways'*, tr. Sir Edwin Arnold, London, 1899 · *The Bustan of Sadi*, tr. A. H. Edwards, London, 1911 · *Morals Pointed and Tales Adorned: The Bustan of Sa'di*, tr. G. M. Wickens, Toronto, 1974.

SEE ALSO Arberry, A. J., *The Romance of the Rubaiyat*, London, 1959 · Yohannan, J. D., *Persian Poetry in England and America: A 200-Year History*, Delmar, NY, 1977 · *The Poet Sadi: A Persian Humanist*, Lanham, Md., 1987.

3. MODERN PERSIAN

Before the 1978 Iranian revolution, western 'specialists' on Iran generally agreed Iran was on 'the road to modernity'. 'Modernity' entailed, necessarily, not only the 'withering away' of such specific phenomena as religion but, more generally, the adoption of all things western. The limits of such analyses were laid all too bare by 1978.

Initially, western discussions of Persian literature reproduced this analysis and selected for consideration and translation literature with themes familiar to western audiences, extolling these as examples or forerunners of the 'modern' Persian literature which was overshadowing 'traditional' literary expression. Iranian analyses, following the pattern of reverse orientalism or 'nativism' recently described so well by Boroujerdi, too often only adopted this paradigm. Only since the later 1970s has this paradigm been challenged.

i. Before the Late 1970s Traditional discussions of modern Persian literature extol Sadiq Hidayat as the foremost innovator of Persian literature in this century. Although Hidayat cut an interesting figure, it was his 'renaissance' character, the themes of his work, and his style of expression, coupled with his fascination with the West and especially the tragedy of his suicide, which facilitated this fixation. His aristocratic background allowed him access to the foremost western-style opportunities available to his class at that time. Selected in 1925–6 to be sent abroad to study, once in Europe Hidayat abandoned, in turn, the study of engineering, architecture, and dentistry to focus finally on literature. After an attempted suicide in 1927 Hidayat returned to Iran in 1930, where he published his first collection of stories, *Zendeh be-gur* (Buried Alive). He fell in with other students returning from abroad and suffering under the censorship and repression that marked what is too often styled as the 'battle' of Reza Shah to 'modernize' the country which also aimed, not incidentally, to maintain himself in power. Many of these students shared Hidayat's own growing antipathy for the monarchy.

Hidayat's politics found only literary expression, however, especially between 1930 and 1937, during which he published two later collections of short stories, and continued his study of Omar Khayyâm and Buddhism, in a 'nativist' effort—as Boroujerdi suggests—to celebrate the eastern roots of Iranian civilization. His study of Iran's past took him to India in 1938–9, where he published *Buf-e Kur* (The Blind Owl) in mimeo form. He returned to Iran, took up a bank job, and then moved to Tehran University.

Reza Shah's overthrow by the Allies during World War II resulted in a lull in censorship, allowing the appearance of the Tudeh Party, a nationalist Marxist-oriented party formed by progressive intellectuals. Hidayat stayed on the fringe of this political activity, however. Captivated instead by despair, he turned to drugs and alcohol. In 1942 he published his fourth and last collection of stories, *Sag-e Velgard* (The Stray Dog). In 1945 appeared the novella *Hajji Agha* (Mr Pilgrim), wherein he portrayed Reza Shah as a confidence man selling off the country's resources. In his last years he translated Kafka and other European writers. In 1950 he returned to Paris where, after four months, he committed suicide.

The Kafkaesque style of such works as *The Blind Owl* proved interesting to western circles. (D. P. **Costello**'s 1957 translation is of historical interest, as Grove Press was the US-based publishing house which litigated the Henry Miller and D. H. Lawrence cases.) Thereafter 'Hidayat studies' became something of an industry. A number of his short stories were translated in the 1960s and early 1970s. Ehsan **Yarshater**'s 1979 anthology of short stories, some translated for the first time and others excellently retranslated, heralded a new interest in Hidayat's legacy.

The forerunner of Hidayat's 'modernism' is generally acknowledged to have been Mohammed Ali Jamalzadah. His 1921 collection of short stories *Yeki Bud Yeki Nabud* (Once Upon a Time) is seen as the clarion call for literary reform which such writers as Hidayat took up. Jamalzadah occupied a social stratum as privileged as Hidayat's. His father was a *sayyid* (descendant of the prophet Mohammed) who took a role in Iran's constitutional revolution. The son studied at a Catholic school in Beirut and then travelled to Egypt, France, and Switzerland, though he lived largely in poverty. During World War I he joined a Persian nationalist movement in Berlin and helped establish a Persian newspaper in Baghdad. In 1917 he attended the World Congress of Socialists in Stockholm, where he attacked Anglo-Russian policies in Iran. After *Yeki Bud* he

worked at the International Labour Organization for 25 years. Following Reza Shah's forced abdication, Jamalzadah resumed publishing with *Dar al-Majanin* (1943, The Lunatic Asylum), a work featuring characters modelled on Hidayat's *The Blind Owl*, the 1947 *Sahra-ye Mahshar* (Plain of Resurrection), in which the religious classes are shut out from heaven but other false claimants are admitted, and the 1948 *Ra-ab Nama* (The Drainage Controversy), about a European-educated Iranian spending a summer at home. He also published further short-story collections and, like Hidayat, translated Ibsen, Schiller, and Molière. There have been relatively few western studies of his life and legacy: *Yeki Bud* was not translated until recently, so preoccupied was the field with Hidayat.

Buzurg Alavi came from a similar socio-political stratum. Born of an old merchant family, Alavi received his secondary and university education in Germany and returned to Iran to join an illegal Marxist group. With many others he was arrested in 1937, remaining in jail until the Allies occupied Iran in August 1941, and then helped found the Tudeh Party. At the 1953 CIA coup Alavi was in Europe, and took up a post at Humboldt University in East Germany.

If Alavi's political activities were more extensive, his output was considerably less than that of his contemporaries. He produced three collections of short stories and the 1952 novel *Cheshmahayash* (Her Eyes). As with the work of Hidayat, Alavi's writings are often psychological studies: the smothering atmosphere of *Her Eyes* replicates the stifling of Reza Shah's dictatorship. Alavi translated works by Chekhov, Bernard Shaw, Schiller, and J. B. Priestley. As with Jamalzadeh, 'Hidayat studies' have contributed to unfamiliarity with Alavi in the English-speaking world.

Sadiq Chubak led a similarly privileged existence. Born in Bushehr to a cloth merchant, he later studied in Shiraz and graduated from the exclusive American College in Tehran in 1937. He worked for the Ministry of Education, as a translator for the British embassy, and from 1949 worked for the oil industry. In 1975 he retired to devote more time to writing and travel abroad. In 1955 he participated in a seminar at Harvard, and in 1970–1 taught at the University of Utah, and finally settled in the USA.

Chubak was close to Hidayat and felt his death deeply. Like others of this generation, he is interested in Persian literary history and the work of Chekhov, Dostoevsky, Ibsen, Joyce, Mann, Faulkner, and Hemingway. Also overshadowed by Hidayat, an anthology of his work has only recently appeared in translation.

ii Persian Literature in the 1970s If Western analyses initially placed Hidayat's 'fictional legacy' on a western pedestal, and if that process has served nationalist nativism, more recent Iranian writers have not always received the same treatment. Ironically, the US Peace Corps—John Kennedy's effort to save the third world from communism 'on the cheap' by sending potentially wayward American youth to shore up the Shah's precarious position—is partly to be thanked for this process. Without the Peace Corps in Iran there would have been no Michael **Hillmann**, Thomas **Ricks**, or Eric and Mary **Hoogland** (now Mary Hegland), for example, to take an interest in and translate the work of other Iranian writers.

These and others learnt their Persian 'on the ground' and as scholars revitalized Iranian studies in the USA. They engaged modern Persian literature on its own historical rather than on western terms and, most importantly, brought to western attention important works of previously lesser-known authors of considerably different social strata. The establishment of Three Continents Press in Washington, DC advanced that agenda. The legacy of '3CP' was inexpensive, sensitive translations of Arab and Persian literature with well-crafted introductions, notes, and commentary. In 1996 Donald Herdeck sold 3CP's rights to Lynne Rienner Publications, and many of 3CP's works thereby remain in print. Especially following the Revolution, the prospects and potential market for Persian translation were transformed. Yarshater's Modern Persian Literature series dated from 1978. Several publishing houses appeared in the USA soon thereafter, notably Iranbooks (1979), Jahan Book Company (1980), and Mage (1985), all based in the Washington DC area. Late in the 1980s Mazda Publishers (1980) moved from Kentucky to California and gained a new lease on life.

3CP is especially to be thanked for assisting these scholars in bringing to outside attention the life and works of Jalal Al-e Ahmad and Samad Bihrangi. Moreover, each 3CP volume introduces Iranian history and literature and discusses the career and contributions of the author in question in relation to both.

Al-e Ahmad bridged the older and newer generations. The son of a Tehran religious leader, with a brother active in ministering to the Shii community, Jalal was active in his youth with the pro-nationalization faction over the issue of oil. After the 1953 coup he entered a self-imposed quiet period during which he taught at a teachers' training college in Tehran. Like some of the older generation, he was a translator, producing Persian translations

of works by Sartre, Camus, and Dostoevsky. He also travelled to the USA.

Al-e Ahmad is best known as the author of belles-lettres, short stories, novellas, and essays in social criticism. He also wrote about older Iranian literary figures whom he felt were under-appreciated, and produced some anthropological material. His famous *Gharbzadegi* (1961, Weststruckness, and other titles) critiqued Iranians' fascination with things western. This reproach figured prominently in Ayatollah Khomeini's polemic. The work has been translated twice, and Hillmann's excellent 1982 anthology of his works is a seminal contribution to the study of modern Persian literature.

Bihrangi studied English at Tabriz University, and taught in Azerbaijan's local schools and at a teacher's training college in Tabriz. His face-to-face encounters with rural life and poverty and Azeri folk culture are the stuff of his work. He composed folk-tales, essays on the Iranian educational system, Azeri history, the Azeri Turkish language, village life, grammar, and problems in education. He also translated material from his native Azeri Turkish into Persian, though the Shah's dislike of local languages prevented their publication. Less self-absorbed, despairing, or mystical about the causes of the Iranian malaise than Hidayat and Jamalzadeh, Bihrangi's best-known material, though directed to adults, appeared in the form of Azeri children's tales to avoid censorship. His famous 1960s story *Mah-e Siyah-hi Kuchelu* (The Little Black Fish) is just such a children's tale, focusing on the acquisition of knowledge and its use to help solve social problems and self-sacrifice. The work became popular after his mysterious death, at which Bihrangi became a hero of the Iranian left. The Hooglands' introduction to and translation of *The Little Black Fish* and other stories, with Ricks's historical essay, is another key work, bringing to western audiences the life and works of an author whose social origins would not otherwise have marked him out for western attention.

Like Bihrangi, Ghulam Housayn Sa'idi was born in Azerbaijan. He trained as a doctor and psychiatrist. Swept up by the oil nationalization movement in the 1950s after the CIA coup he was imprisoned for the first of 16 times, the last of which lasted a year and ended in 1975. His first collection of stories appeared in 1960. He also published articles in literary magazines and wrote plays and film scripts. His 1968 collection *Dandil* has been translated, and Minoo **Southgate**'s excellent translation of Sa'idi's near-anthropological story of life among the peoples of the Persian Gulf coast, the six-part *Traz va Larz* (1968, Fear and Trembling), places the author and his work in the broader context of modern Iranian literature, in the best 3CP tradition.

If the major male prose writers had all been introduced to English-language audience, women's literature—in which poetry figured prominently—provided a new focus for both markets and academic study. The poetry of Furugh Farroukhzad provided an early focus for attention. Following Nima Yusij, himself dubbed the 'founder of modern Persian poetry', Farroukhzad created an unprecedented expression of feeling about love, sex, society, and self. Her five volumes of poetry display a growing maturity, from a focus on self to a broader social vision and universalist approach to issues of life and death, paralleling her own experience of personal, social and spiritual disillusion. Michael Hillmann's 1987 translation enhanced her, and his own reputation at the same time. Like others of these prose writers and poets, beginning with Hidayat himself, however, it is precisely this universalist dimension which facilitates their acceptance abroad.

iii. Persian Literature in the Later 1980s Interest in women's writing in turn sparked long-overdue consideration of the prose contributions of Simin

Daneshvar, overshadowed in Iran and abroad by the work of her husband, Al-e Ahmad. Sadly, Roxanne **Zand**'s very good translation of Daneshvar's *Savushun* (1978, A Persian Requiem) lacks any introduction, bibliography, or biographical sketch of its author. The **Ghanoonparvar** translation includes such introductory notes. The poetry of such women as Parvin E'tisami (1907–41) and Sohrab Sephery (1928–80) also attracted some attention and translation.

As the newly established publishing houses gained experience and markets, they also began to publish anthologies of prose and poetry and to republish some out-of-print material. These specialist houses are also beginning to promote Persian literature to date little known in the West. This attention has further encouraged the interest of larger academic publishers.

The Hidayat 'industry' continues apace. But, just as US- and UK-based Iranian Studies entered a period of decline, the appearance of so much additional, newly translated material is significantly advancing the cause of Persian language and literature, both for westerners and for the many second-generation émigrés coming of age outside Iran.

AN

ANTHOLOGIES   Ghanoonparvar, M. R., and Green, John, *Iranian Drama: An Anthology*, Costa Mesa, Calif., 1989 · Green, John, and Yazdanfar, Farzin, *A Walnut Sapling on Masih's Grave and Other Stories*, Portsmouth, NH, 1993 · Kapuscinski, G., *Modern Persian Drama*, Lanham, Md., 1987 · Karimi-Hakkak, Ahmad, *An Anthology of Modern Persian Poetry*, Boulder, Colo., 1978 · Kianush, M., *Modern Persian Poetry*, Ware, UK, 1996 · Lewis, Franklin, and Yazdanfar, Farzin, *In a Voice of Their Own: A Collection of Stories by Iranian Women Written since the Revolution of 1979*, Costa Mesa, Calif., 1996 · Moayyad, H., ed., *Stories from Iran: A Chicago Anthology*, Washington, DC, 1991 · Southgate, Minoo, *Modern Persian Short Stories*, Washington, DC, 1980 · Sullivan, S. Paknazar, *Stories by Iranian Women since the Revolution*, Austin, Tex., 1991.

ALAVI, BUZURG   O'Kane, John, *Chasmahayash [Her Eyes / Bozorg Alavi]*, Lanham, Md., 1989.

AL-E AHMAD, JALAL   Campbell, R., *Occidentosis [Gharbzadegi]*, Berkeley, Calif., 1983, 1984 · Ghanoonparvar, M. R., *By the Pen*, with an introduction by Michael C. Hillmann, Austin, Tex., 1988 · Green, John, et al., *Lost in the Crowd*, Washington, DC, 1985 · Green, John, and Alizadeh, A., *Weststruckness [Gharbzadegi]*, Costa Mesa, Calif., 1982, 1997 · Hillmann, Michael C., ed., *Iranian Society: An Anthology of Writings by Jalal Al-e Ahmad*, Lexington, Ky., 1982 · Newton, John K., *The School Principal*, with an introduction by Michael C. Hillmann, Minneapolis, 1974 · Sprachman, Paul, *Plagued by the West [Gharbzadegi]*, Delmar, NY, 1982.

BIHRANGI, SAMAD   Amuzegar, H., *The Little Black Fish* [English and Persian text], Bethesda, Md., 1997 · Hoogland, Eric, and Hoogland (Hegland), Mary, *The Little Black Fish and Other Modern Persian Short Stories*, Washington, DC, 1976, 1987.

CHUBAK, SADIQ   Bagley, F. R. C., ed., *Sadeq Chubak: An Anthology*, New York, 1981 · Ghanoonparvar, M. R., *The Patient Stone*, Costa Mesa, Calif., 1989.

DANESHVAR, SIMIN   Ghanoonparvar, M. R., *A Persian Requiem*, with introd. by Brian Spooner, Washington, DC, 1990 · Javadi, Hasan, and Neshati, Amin, *Sutra and Other Stories*, Washington, DC, 1994 · Mafi, Maryam, *Daneshvar's Playhouse: A Collection of Short Stories*, Washington, DC, 1989 · Zand, Roxanne, *A Persian Requiem: A Novel*, New York, 1992.

FARROUKHZAD, FURUGH   Hillmann, Michael C., *A Lonely Woman: Forough Farrokhzad and Her Poetry*, Washington, DC, 1987 · Javadi, Hasan, and Sallee, Susan, *Another Birth: Selected Poems of Forugh Farrokhzad*, Emeryville, Calif., 1981, 1985 · Kessler, J., and Banani, Amin, *Bride of the Acacias: Selected Poems*, New York, 1982.

E'TESAMI, PARVIN   Moayyad, H., and Madelung, A. Margaret, *A Nightingale's Lament: Selections from the Fables and Poems of Parvin E'tesami*, Lexington, Ky., 1985.

HIDAYAT, SADIQ   Bashiri, I., 'The Blind Owl' [literal translation], in Bashiri, ed., *Hidayat's Ivory Tower*, Minneapolis, 1974, pp. 53–135 · Christensen, Russell P., *The Blind Owl and Other Hidayat Stories*, Minneapolis, 1984 · Costello, D. P., *The Blind Owl*, New York/London, 1957 · Wickens, G. M., *Haji Agha: Portrait of an Iranian Confidence Man*, Austin, Tex., 1979 · Yarshater, Ehsan, ed., *Sadiq Hidayat: An Anthology*, Boulder, Colo., 1979.

JAMALZADAH, MUHAMMAD ALI   Moayyad, Heshmet, and Sprachman, Paul, *Once Upon a Time* [*Yeki Bud, yeki nabud*], New York, 1985.

SA'IDI, GHULAM HUSAYN   Campbell, Robert, Javad, Hasan, and Scott-Meisami, Julie, *Dandil: Stories from an Iranian Life*, New York, 1981 · Southgate, Minoo, *Fear and Trembling*, Washington, DC, 1984.

SEPEHRY, SOHRAB   Martin, David L., *The Expanse of Green* [*Hajam-i Sabz*], Los Angeles, 1987.

SEE ALSO   Bashiri, I., *The Fiction of Sadiq-e Hidayat*, Lexington, Ky., 1984 [contains a full bibliography of Hidayat's works, English translations, and a bibliography of works on modern Persian literature and society] · Boroujerdi, M., *Iranian Intellectuals and the West: The Tormented Triumph of Nativism*, Syracuse, NY, 1996 · Ghanoonparvar, M. R., *Prophets of Doom: Literature as a Socio-political Phenomenon in Modern Iran*, Lanham, Md., 1984 · Javadi, H., *Satire in Persian Literature*, London/Toronto, 1988 · Kamshad, H., *Modern Persian Prose Literature*, Cambridge, 1966 · Milani, Farzaneh, *Veils and Words: The Emerging Voices of Iranian Women Writers*, Syracuse, NY, 1992 · Ricks, Thomas R., ed., *Critical Perspectives on Modern Persian Literature*, Washington, DC, 1984.

There are a plethora of transliteration schemes in use for Persian (and Arabic). Despite the names as they may appear in actual titles of books, the transliteration system used herein is that of the RLIN browser available at most university libraries. Using the RLIN scheme will produce the most 'hits' when searching for these authors.

4. TURKISH

i. Introduction The vast literary output of Ottoman and modern Turkish cultures is represented only in a limited number of translations in English. One is, therefore, prompted to look into the relationships between questions such as the following:

what was translated (selection);

why (motivation, i.e. the dynamics in Anglophone and/or Turkish culture, or the interaction between Anglophone and other target cultures such as French and German, that prompted the translation/s; the central or marginal position of the original work/s in the source culture); and

when (whether the translation was more or less contemporaneous with the original work or produced much later).

The framework for the following brief survey is set in the light of these considerations.

Until the emergence of a 'national' literature and its gradual recognition from the time of the Turkish Republic (1923), Europeans identified Ottoman-Turkish literature primarily as Islamic poetry, i.e. an offshoot of the Perso-Arabic literary tradition [see II.b and II.q.2] which lay outside western literature and was 'foreign' to it. They became more receptive to translations as western genres and literary modes, introduced into Ottoman culture in the second half of the 19th c., gained ground in modern Turkish literature in the 20th c. Translating mainstream works or those that had won recognition in the source culture seems to have been the general trend, though there were some notable exceptions.

ii. Anthologies Literary contact limited to specialist, often Orientalist interest gave rise to academic translations in the late 19th c. The now obscure readers like Charles **Wells**'s *The Literature of the Turks* and Epiphanius **Wilson**'s *Turkish Literature* are such examples with telling titles. E. J. W. **Gibb**'s prestigious translations in *Ottoman Poems* and the *History of Ottoman Poetry* aimed at the 'non-Orientalist reader' but were shaped by the literary norms of a Cambridge scholar. In his introduction to the former, Gibb wrote: 'My object in reproducing, as closely as possible, the metres and rhyme-movements of the originals has been to give . . . a distinct idea of the construction and sound which prevail in Turkish verse.' The dramatic shift in norms of poetic translation over the last 100 years is to be seen in the 1997 *Ottoman Lyric Poetry*, the product of a collaboration between two scholars, Walter G. **Andrews** and Mehmet **Kalpaklı**, and the poet Najaat **Black**. In his introduction, Andrews offers a powerful critique of Gibb's translation strategies based on the concept of the 'difficulty' of Ottoman poetry, and argues for the principle of accessibility, for translations to be enjoyed as poetry, by scholars and lay readers alike.

A similar shift in emphasis on readability as well as on scholarly norms in the translational approach to Ottoman court poetry can also be seen in John R. **Walsh**'s much admired versions in the 1978

Penguin Book of Turkish Verse edited by Nermin Menemencioğlu with Fahir İz. This volume, the earliest comprehensive anthology, was successful in targeting a lay readership and promoted a general interest not only in Ottoman poetry but in the continuity of the Turkish poetic tradition up to the 1970s. It was also the first to anthologize canonical examples from the 13th-c. oral poetry of Yunus Emre, whose poems were radically different in outlook, diction, and prosody from the courtly tradition. The first and largest individual collection of this highly influential mystic 'folk' poet appeared in 1981 in Talat S. **Halman**'s distinguished translation, followed by other collections.

A selection of Halman's versions was also published in 1996 in Kemal Silay's *An Anthology of Turkish Literature*, along with examples from Ottoman court poets and the popular minstrel tradition. Silay's 648-page volume, which covers material from the 8th-c. Old Turkic Orkhon inscriptions (tr. Kurtuluş **Öztopçu** and Sherry **Smith-Williams**) to the postmodern fiction of Orhan Pamuk (tr. Victoria **Holbrook**), aims to be the most comprehensive anthology of translations to date. It seems to have been compiled mostly in response to the need for an academic reader (similar in intention to those published at the turn of the century) for the growing number of university courses in Turkish literature and culture that are largely dependent on 'good' translations. As well as representing well-known names up to the 1990s, it aims to draw attention to the wide range of written and oral genres belonging to the Turkish literary/cultural tradition: e.g. Turkic Manichean poetry of the 8th c. (tr. Larry **Clark**); the heroic narratives collected in the *Book of Dede Korkut* (tr. Faruk **Sümer**, Ahmet E. **Uysal** and Warren S. **Walker**); 'The Romance of Aşık Garip and Shah Sanem', a popular romance recorded in the 19th c. in a version by the minstrel Müdami (tr. İlhan **Başgöz**); folk riddles (tr. İlhan Başgöz and Andreas **Tietze**); Nasreddin Hoca stories (tr. İlhan Başgöz); 'The Tale of Me 'ali' from Aşık Çelebi's 16th-c. collection of poets' biographies (tr. Walter G. **Andrews**); 'The Girl Who Gave Birth to an Elephant' from Evliya Çelebi's *Book of Travels* (17th c., tr. Robert **Dankoff**); İbrahim Şinasi's *Şair Evlenmesi* (1859, The Wedding of a Poet), a pioneering play in the European dramatic tradition, translated for the first time (by Edward **Allworth**). The volume also includes 12 useful critical essays on Turkish literature.

Like earlier anthologies by Talat S. Halman, *Contemporary Turkish Literature: Fiction and Poetry*, and by Feyyaz Kayacan **Fergar**, *Modern Turkish Poetry*, Silay's *Anthology* (approximately two-thirds of which is devoted to translations of modern Turkish poetry and fiction) also serves to introduce modern work previously unavailable: e.g. excerpts from Ahmet Hamdi Tanpınar's *Saatleri Ayarlama Enstitüsü* (1961, The Clock-Setting Institute, tr. Walter **Feldman**), and Yusuf Atılgan's *Anayurt Oteli* (1973, Motherland Hotel, tr. Nebile **Direkçigil**), two modern classics awaiting publication in versions by Ender **Gürol** and Fred **Stark** respectively; Memet Fuat's 'Düşüncenin Sınırları' (1986, Limits of Freedom, tr. Yurdanur **Salman**), an essay by one of Turkey's leading contemporary literary critics; and Enis Batur's *Ağlayan Kadınlar Lahdi* (1993, Elegies: The Sarcophagus of Mourning Women, tr. Saliha **Paker** and Clifford **Endres**). There have also been some 'accidental' omissions. For example, Enis Batur, an outstanding poet who has been writing for over 20 years was not included in Fergar's selection of 1992, and Silay's *Anthology* has somehow overlooked one of Turkey's most eminent living poets: Melih Cevdet Anday, a founder of the 'Garip' movement (see below).

iii. Modern Poetry Over the years, an increasing number of modern Turkish poets have found their way into distinguished magazines and compilations in the English-speaking world, a fact of some importance, indicative of the extent of international reception: e.g. *Greek and Turkish Poets of Today*, a special issue of the New Zealand *Pacific Quarterly Moana* (1980), edited by Yannis Goumas and Talat S. Halman, which covered 43 Turkish poets. More recent publications have featured Oktay Rifat, in *Anvil New Poets* (1990), edited by Graham Fawcett, and the *PN Review* (1996, 1998), edited by Michael Schmidt, in translations by Ruth **Christie** and Richard **McKane** and by Christopher **Middleton** respectively; Özdemir İnce in *Talisman* (1991, 1993, 1994–5), in translations by Simon **Pettit** and Ülker **İnce**, and by Saliha Paker, edited by Edward Foster, and eight poets (Cemal Süreya, Ece Ayhan, İlhan Berk, Behçet Necatigil, Özdemir İnce, Nilgün Marmara, Mustafa Ziyalan, and Melisa Gürpınar, representing the 'Second New' movement in the 1950s–1970s and its aftermath) in the same journal (1995), with a penetrating introduction by the translator Murat **Nemet-Nejat** (see Silay 1996 for earlier periodicals).

A focus on Turkish poetry from an informed, external perspective has brought about a fresh, uninhibited evaluation of certain works to be introduced or reintroduced into British and American literature. The outstanding example is the translation of Nazım Hikmet's poetry. With the publication of most of his major works in Turkish before he was imprisoned in 1938 on grounds of propagating communism, Hikmet was already established both as a revolutionary poet and poet-revolutionary. His poetry was banned in Turkey till 1965, but available in English soon after the poet fled to Moscow in 1951. The first selection appeared, interestingly, in Calcutta in 1952, followed by a second one in 1954 in the translation by Ali **Yunus** (pseudonym of Nilüfer M. **Reddy** and Rosette A. **Coryell**). However, it was the three subsequent collections 'done into English' by the Turkish Cypriot poet Taner **Baybars** between 1967 and 1972, which served the English-speaking world as a substantial introduction to Hikmet's work. These and the six translations by Randy **Blasing** and Mutlu **Konuk** cover the full range of Hikmet's poetry, epic and lyric, in free verse and traditional forms. To these must be added eight translations (by Ruth Christie, Richard McKane, and Feyyaz K. Fergar) in Fergar's anthology, and 12 hitherto unpublished versions (by Larry Clark), including *The Epic of Sheik Bedreddin* and *Poems for Piraye*, in Silay's anthology. Blasing and Konuk, who worked on Hikmet for over two decades, thus contributing greatly to his reputation as one of the leading international poets of the 20th c., have rightly received great critical acclaim for their translations. Their latest collection, *Poems of Nazım Hikmet*, consists of what they 'consider his best in Turkish and in translation', reflecting an additional critical sensitivity on their part. As it is useless on the reader's part to entertain the illusion of 'sameness' in translation, a comparison of the multiple versions allows for a fuller appreciation of Hikmet in English, and for an awareness of each translator's way of interpreting 'the original' and giving it a poetic form.

No other Turkish poet has been as widely translated as Hikmet. It was only in the 1970s that the translation of other eminent poets in individual collections began to gain momentum, largely due to the initiative taken by their translator, Talat Sait Halman. His first collection, from Fazıl Hüsnü Dağlarca, winner of the Turkish Award of the International Poetry Forum in 1968, was followed by one from Orhan Veli and two from Melih Cevdet Anday (with N. **Menemencioğlu** and B. **Swann** respectively). Orhan Veli and Melih Cevdet, along with Oktay Rifat, were the leaders of the 'Garip' (Strange), a radical movement for a colloquial, transparent poetic idiom that flourished in the 1940s while Hikmet was writing in prison. Derek **Patmore**'s *The Star and the Crescent: an Anthology of Modern Turkish Poetry* had included the 'Garip' poets in 1946, but an individual selection from Oktay Rifat was not published till 1992, translated

by Ruth Christie and Richard McKane. It was the Christie–McKane collaboration that was instrumental in introducing the poetry of Oktay Rifat to the English speaking world, and further collaboration with Feyyaz Kayacan Fergar that drew more attention to another unique poet, Can Yücel. Except for a recent selection by Murat **Nemet-Nejat**, of the poetry of Ece Ayhan, who revolutionized modern Turkish poetic syntax, the 'Second New' movement (1950–75) is hardly represented in individual collections.

iv. Fiction Gaps are more conspicuous in the field of translated Turkish fiction, which, from the 1960s to the 1990s, was almost entirely dominated by Yashar Kemal's corpus of novels. It was the first of his works, *İnce Memed* (1955, Memed, My Hawk), translated by Edouard **Roditi** in 1961, that brought him success in English, but without the accumulation of powerful translations (in remarkably quick succession) by Thilda **Kemal**, his wife, it would have been difficult to sustain success for over 30 years. One of Thilda Kemal's main accomplishments is that her 12 translations (the latest of which, *Salman the Solitary*, appeared in 1997) have consistently built up an English 'universe of discourse' for Yashar Kemal's vision of Anatolia and Istanbul as reflected in the diversity of his characters, their natural and social environment, their myths, their dialects. Yashar Kemal may be regarded as Nazım Hikmet's counterpart in fiction, in terms of popularity in translation.

The earliest Turkish novel to appear in English was Halide **Edib**'s self-translated version of *Ateşten Gömlek* (1922, Shirt of Flame, later retranslated in India), a tragic romance set in the Turkish war of independence. The author's later works, such as *Mor Salkımlı Ev* (1963, Memoirs), *Türkün Ateşle İmtihanı* (1962, The Turkish Ordeal), a first-hand account of the war of independence, and her classic novel, *Sinekli Bakkal* (1936, The Clown and His Daughter), were in fact first written and published in English, during a period of exile in London, before she produced their respective Turkish versions. No doubt it was the English works of Edib, the earliest Turkish woman writer of international reputation, that first attracted attention to the literary, social, and political changes involving Turkish source culture in the transition from the Ottoman to the Republican.

Apart from the two novels of Edib, early Republican mainstream fiction was represented in English by Reşat Nuri Güntekin's *Çalıkuşu* (1922, The Autobiography of a Turkish Girl) and *Akşam Güneşi* (1926, Afternoon Sun), translated by Sir Wyndham

Deedes in 1949 and 1951 respectively. In the preface to the latter, Deedes explained the reasons for his choice: '*Çalıkuşu* . . . revolutionised the novel in Turkey' because it was 'the first Turkish novel about ordinary and real people, written in straightforward spoken Turkish, without any claim to literary effect', while *Afternoon Sun*, in the same genre, was associated with his own fond memories of Turkey. In 1954, Deedes translated Mahmut Makal's *Bizim Köy* (1950, A Village in Anatolia,) only four years after the original publication. This book was a disturbing first-hand account of the conditions of village life which, as indicated in the foreword, created a considerable political stir because its publication in 1950 coincided with a turning-point in Turkish democracy: the end of the single-party era. According to the sociologist Paul Stirling, who edited the translation, Makal was 'the first genuine villager from the inarticulate millions of peasants all over the world, to describe the village from within'. Deedes's translation highlighted a sociological event which also marked a turning-point in Turkish fiction. It was Makal's nonfictional account which really sparked the movement for rural fiction that was to become mainstream in the 1960s. The work of Yashar Kemal reflects not only his mastery of the Turkish narrative tradition but also the importance of the rural novel in Turkey and the social involvement of the novelist. It is this corpus in translation that has served till the 1990s as the principal representative of modern Turkish fiction abroad, having produced a growing interest in Turkish society and the narratives generated by it. The 1976 translation by Esin B. **Rey** and Marianna **Fitzpatrick** of Kemal Bilbaşar's *Cemo* (1966, Gemmo), an award-winning rural novel about the south-east, becomes more significant in this context.

The shift to urban fiction which gained ground in the 1970s and 1980s is represented in translation chiefly by Orhan Pamuk who stands second to Yashar Kemal in the international market as the most widely translated Turkish novelist. His three novels, *Beyaz Kale* (1979, The White Castle), *Kara Kitap* (1990, The Black Book), and *Yeni Hayat* (1994, The New Life), all translated in the 1990s, are concerned specifically with the historical or modern psyche of the Turkish intellectual, with the literary heritage of the East and the West, and with textuality. They have been served remarkably well in a rapid succession of excellent translations by Victoria Holbrook and Güneli **Gün**, a Turkish-American novelist. Gün's art in rendering the complexities of Pamuk's more recent fiction is a major

contribution to the success of *The Black Book* and *The New Life*.

The social/historical backdrop to Orhan Pamuk's works becomes clearer when viewed in the light of fiction by other award-winning authors who focused on the dark, city-centred politics of social division in the 1970s and early 1980s: Aysel Özakın's *Genç Kız ve Ölüm* (1980, The Prizegiving), Bilge Karasu's *Gece* (1985, Night), and Adalet Ağaoğlu's *Üç Beş Kişi* (1984, Curfew), translated by Celia **Kerslake**, Güneli Gün and Bilge **Karasu**, and John **Goulden** respectively. Latife Tekin's *Berci Kristin Çöp Masalları* (1984, Berji Kristin Tales from the Garbage Hills), translated by Ruth Christie and Saliha Paker, is different from the works grouped above because it focuses exclusively on the shanty-town communities of migrant villagers and their dramatic and often colourful ways of coping with poverty. As each of these works is stylistically unlike the other, it is very much to the credit of the translators cited above that they have so effectively reflected the distinctive features of each author's narrative.

The thematic and stylistic concerns of the vast range of writers from the 1920s to the late 1990s, both in the novel and in the short story, are best represented in collections such as Ali Alpaslan's *An Anthology of Turkish Short Stories*, Fahir İz's *An Anthology of Modern Turkish Short Stories*, Talat S. Halman's *Contemporary Turkish Literature: Fiction and Poetry*, Nilufer Mizanoglu Reddy's *Twenty Stories by Turkish Women Writers*, *The Turkish PEN Reader*, edited by Suat Karantay, and *nar'96*, edited by Saliha Paker and Senay Haznedaroğlu. However, among the many masters (both male and female) of short fiction, which has been a major genre in the modern Turkish literary tradition, only three (male) authors, Sait Faik, Haldun Taner, and Aziz Nesin, are represented by individual collections: *Sait Faik: A Dot on the Map, Selected Stories and Poems*, by Talat S. Halman, *Thickhead and other Turkish stories by Haldun Taner*, by Geoffrey **Lewis**, and *Turkish Stories from Four Decades by Aziz Nesin*, by Louis **Mitler**.

v. Conclusion Observable gaps in the short history of translations from Turkish literature might be taken to indicate a haphazard selection of authors and texts, but closer investigation shows that selections were not made on a random basis. For instance, the internationally renowned and highly prolific satirical writer Aziz Nesin has only one collection to his name in English (though several in German and Russian), but his life-story published in two parts, *Böyle Gelmiş Böyle Gitmez* (1966–76, Istanbul Boy), which is a modern social history in itself, has been patiently and lovingly translated by Joseph S. **Jacobsen**. Similarly Haldun Taner, whose satirical humour is celebrated in Geoffrey Lewis's admirable translation of short stories, is also represented in Talat S. Halman's *Modern Turkish Drama: An Anthology of Plays in Translation* with his masterpiece for the theatre: *Keşanlı Ali Destanı* (1964, The Ballad of Ali of Keshan), translated by Nüvit **Özdoğru**. What has been selected for translation in fiction and poetry are works that achieved a certain distinction (e.g. as prize-winners or bestsellers) in modern Turkish literature. But due to shifts in the norms that govern literary taste in Turkey, as well as those (like judging a novel 'not Turkish enough') that govern the academic or more general expectations of British and American readers and publishers, numerous writers of great literary merit, like Yakup Kadri Karaosmanoğlu, Sabahattin Ali, Ahmet Hamdi Tanpınar, Oğuz Atay, Yusuf Atılgan, not to mention the remarkable representatives of the boom in women's writing, have failed to attract the individual attention they deserve.

Another important constraint affecting translation has been the continuous change in spoken and literary Turkish since the 1930s. This has no doubt played a very important part in deterring many non-native speakers of Turkish from undertaking translations of novels and plays. Linguistic competence justifiably carries a particular importance (also because English versions often serve as source-texts for translations into other, especially non-European, languages), but translators from Turkish have also functioned as mediators between cultures. Not only translations but critical/biographical introductions, explanatory notes, glossaries, pronunciation guides, not to mention anthologies, individual collections, contributions to literary magazines, critical reviews, bibliographies, public readings, and last but not least the business of finding publishers, have all been part of the mediating role of some of the most distinguished translators resident in the UK and the USA, such as Nermin Menemencioğlu, Talat S. Halman, Feyyaz K. Fergar, and many others cited above. It is impossible to overestimate the role of the translators as agents of linguistic, literary, and cultural transfer, and their contribution to the recognition of Turkish literature in English. However few compared to the original output, works of poetry and fiction translated so far have effectively challenged so-called 'cultural barriers'. The current attitude of readers and publishers in Britain and America is very different from what it was 10 years ago. Translations from Orhan Pamuk have been particularly influential in effecting the breakthrough. At the end of the 20th c., greater receptiveness towards international writing in English and an expanding interest in all cultures are encouraging signs for translators interested in earlier masterpieces as well as in works that represent new Turkish writing.   SP

ANTHOLOGIES Alpaslan, Ali, *An Anthology of Turkish Short Stories*, Istanbul, 1973 · Andrews, Walter G., Black, Najaat, and Kalpaklı, Mehmet, *Ottoman Lyric Poetry: An Anthology*, Austin, Tex., 1997 · Fawcett, Graham, ed., *Anvil New Poets*, London, 1990 · Fergar, Feyyaz Kayacan, *Modern Turkish Poetry*, Ware, UK, 1992 · Gibb, E. J. W., *Ottoman Poems, Translated into English Verse, In the Original Forms, with Introduction, Biographical Notices, and Notes*, London, 1882 · *A History of Ottoman Poetry*, 6 vols., London, 1900–7 · Goumas, Yannis, and Halman, Talat Sait, *Greek and Turkish Poets of Today*, special issue of *Pacific Quarterly Moana*, Hamilton, 1980 · Halman, Talat Sait, *Modern Turkish Drama: An Anthology of Plays in Translation*, Chicago/Minneapolis, 1976 · *Contemporary Turkish Literature: Fiction and Poetry*, East Brunswick, NJ/London/Toronto, 1982 · *Living Poets of Turkey*, Istanbul, 1989 · *Turkish Legends and Folk Poems*, Istanbul, 1992 · İz, Fahir, *An Anthology of Modern Turkish Short Stories*, Minneapolis, 1978 · Karantay, Suat, *Short Dramas from Contemporary Turkish Literature*, Istanbul, 1993 · Lewis, Geoffrey, *The Book of Dede Korkut*, Harmondsworth, 1974 [Penguin] · Menemencioğlu, Nermin, with İz, Fahir, *The Penguin Book of Turkish Verse*, Harmondsworth, 1978 · Paker, Saliha, and Haznedaroğlu, Senay, *nar:' 96: A Selection* (bilingual), Istanbul, 1996 · Patmore, Derek, *The Star and the Crescent: An Anthology of Modern Turkish Poetry*, Bungay, UK, 1946 · Reddy, Nilufer Mizanoğlu, *Twenty Stories by Turkish Women Writers*, Bloomington, Ind., 1988 · Silay, Kemal, *An Anthology of Turkish Literature*, Bloomington, Ind., 1996 · Wells, Charles, *The Literature of the Turks: A Turkish Chrestomathy Consisting of Extracts in Turkish from the Best Turkish Authors (Historians, Novelists, Dramatists, etc.) with Interlinear and Free Translations in English, Biographical and Grammatical Notes, and Facsimiles of Ms., Letters and Documents*, London, 1891 · Wilson, Epiphanius, *Turkish Literature, Comprising Fables, Belles-Lettres and Sacred Tradition*, New York, 1901.

(ABASIYANIK) SAİT FAİK Halman, Talat Sait, ed., *Sait Faik, A Dot on the Map: Selected Stories and Poems*, Bloomington, Ind., 1983.

(ADIVAR) HALİDE EDİB (Adıvar) Halide Edib, *The Shirt of Flame*, New York, 1924 · Muhammed Yakub Khan, *The Daughter of Smyrna*, Lahore, 1941.

AĞAOĞLU, ADALET Goulden, John, *Curfew*, Austin, Tex., 1997.

ANDAY, MELİH CEVDET Halman, Talat Sait, and Menemencioğlu, Nermin, *On the Nomad Sea: Poems by Melih Cevdet*

Anday, New York, 1974 · Halman, Talat Sait, and Swann, Brian, *Rain One Step Away: Poems by Melih Cevdet Anday*, Washington, DC, 1980.

AYHAN, ECE Nemet-Nejat, Murat, *A Blind Cat Black and Orthodoxies*, New York, 1997.

BİLBAŞAR, KEMAL Rey, Esin B., with Fitzpatrick, Marina, *Gemmo*, London, 1976.

DAĞLARCA, FAZIL HÜSNÜ Halman, Talat Sait, *F. H. Dağlarca: Selected Poems* [bilingual], Pittsburgh, 1969 · *Quatrains of Holland* [bilingual], Istanbul, 1977 · *The Bird and I* [bilingual], New York, 1968.

(GÖĞCELİ) YASHAR KEMAL Kemal, Thilda, *The Wind from the Plain*, London, 1962 · *Anatolian Tales*, London/New York, 1968 · *Iron Earth, Copper Sky*, London, 1974 · *The Legend of Ararat*, London, 1975 · *The Legend of the Thousand Bulls*, London, 1976 · *The Undying Grass*, London, 1977 · *The Lords of Akchasaz: Murder in the Ironsmiths' Market*, London, 1979 · *The Saga of a Seagull*, New York, 1981 · *The Sea-Crossed Fisherman*, London, 1985 · *The Birds Have Also Gone*, London, 1987 · *To Crush the Serpent*, London, 1991 · *Salman the Solitary*, London, 1997 · Platon, Margaret E., *They Burn the Thistles*, London, 1973 · Roditi, Edouard, *Memed, My Hawk*, London, 1961.

GÜNTEKİN, REŞAT NURİ Deedes, Sir Wyndham, *The Autobiography of a Turkish Girl*, London, 1949 · *Afternoon Sun*, London, 1951.

(KANIK) ORHAN VELİ Halman, Talat Sait, *I am Listening to Istanbul: Selected Poems of Orhan Veli Kanık*, New York, 1971 · Nemet-Nejat, Murat, *I, Orhan Veli: Poems by Orhan Veli*, New York, 1989.

KARASU, BİLGE Gün, Güneli, with the author, *Night*, Baton Rouge, La./London, 1994.

MAKAL, MAHMUT Deedes, Sir Wyndham, *A Village in Anatolia*, London, 1954.

NESİN, AZİZ Jacobson, Joseph S., *Istanbul Boy: Böyle Gelmis, Böyle Gitmez: The Autobiography of Aziz Nesin*, i, Austin, Tex., 1977 · *Istanbul Boy: Yol (The Path): The Autobiography of Aziz Nesin*, ii, Austin, Tex., 1979 · *Istanbul Boy: The Autobiography of Aziz Nesin*, iii, Austin, Tex., 1990 · Mitler, Louis, *Turkish Stories from Four Decades by Aziz Nesin (Mehmet Nusret Nesin)*, Washington, DC, 1991.

ÖZAKIN, AYSEL Kerslake, Celia, *The Prizegiving*, London, 1988.

PAMUK, ORHAN Gün, Güneli, *The Black Book*, New York, 1994, London, 1995 · *The New Life*, New York, 1997 · Holbrook, Victoria, *The White Castle*, Manchester, 1990.

(RAN) NAZIM HİKMET Baybars, Taner, *Selected Poems of Nazım Hikmet*, London, 1967 · *The Moscow Symphony and Other Poems by Nazım Hikmet*, London, 1970 · *The Day Before Tomorrow*, Oxford, 1972 · Blasing, Randy, and Konuk, Mutlu, *Things I Didn't Know I Loved*, New York, 1975 · *The Epic of Sheikh Bedreddin and Other Poems*, New York, 1977 · *Human Landscapes*, New York, 1982 · *Rubaiyat*, Providence, RI, 1985 · *Nazım Hikmet: Selected Poetry*, New York, 1986 · *Poems of Nazım Hikmet*, New York, 1994 · Ghosh, Asoke, *Selected Poems by Nazım Hikmet*, Calcutta, 1952 · Goksu, Saime, and Timms, Edward, *Romantic Communist: The Life and Work of Nazım Hikmet*, London, 1998 [contains translations] · Yunus, Ali, *Poems by Nazım Hikmet*, New York, 1954.

RIFAT, OKTAY Christie, Ruth, and McKane, Richard, *Voices of Memory: Selected Poems of Oktay Rifat*, Ware, UK/Istanbul, 1993.

TANER, HALDUN Lewis, Geoffrey, *Thickhead and Other Turkish Stories by Haldun Taner*, London/Boston, 1988.

TEKİN, LATİFE Christie, Ruth, and Paker, Saliha, *Berji Kristin Tales from the Garbage Hills*, London/New York, 1993 (rep.).

YUNUS EMRE Halman, Talat, ed., *Yunus Emre and His Mystical Poetry*, Bloomington, Ind., 1981, 1989 · Helminski, Kabir, and Algan, Refik, *The Drop That Became the Sea: Lyric Poems of Yunus Emre*, Putney, Vt., 1989 · Faiz, Süha, *The City of the Heart: Yunus Emre's Verses of Wisdom and Love*, UK, Mass., 1992 · Smith, Grace Martin, *The Poetry of Yunus Emre, a Turkish Sufi Poet*, University of California Publications in Modern Philology, 127, Berkeley/Los Angeles/London, 1993.

YÜCEL, CAN Fergar, Feyyaz Kayacan, ed., *The Poetry of Can Yücel: A Selection*, Istanbul, 1993.

SEE ALSO Kut, G., and Chambers, R. L., 'A Bibliography of Modern Turkish Literature in English Translation', *Journal of Turkish Studies*, 2 (1978), 47–54.

Index

The index includes the following: *a*) translated authors (surnames printed in capitals); *b*) translators into English; *c*) other significant authors, critics, and theorists; *d*) titles of anonymous or collective works. It does not include names figuring only in the bibliographies.

651